THE ENCYCLOPEDIA OF HISTORIC PLACES

THE ENCYCLOPEDIA OF HISTORIC PLACES

Volume II

By Courtlandt Canby
Advisory Editor: Gorton Carruth

A HUDSON GROUP BOOK

Picture Editor: Judith Linn
Picture Research Assistant: Anita Jacobson
Photographic Reproduction: Bill Lichtman, Universal Photo

Facts On File Publications
New York, New York • Bicester, England

Every effort has been made to locate the copyright owners of all maps and photographs reproduced in this book. Omissions brought to our attention will be corrected in subsequent editions.

All photographs, unless otherwise noted, are from the New York Public Library, Picture Collection, and The Astor, Lenox and Tilden Foundations.

THE ENCYCLOPEDIA OF HISTORIC PLACES

By Courtlandt Canby
Advisory Editor: Gorton Carruth

Published by Facts On File, Inc.
460 Park Avenue South, New York, N.Y. 10016

Library of Congress Cataloging in Publication Data
Canby, Courtlandt.
   Encyclopedia of historic places.
   Includes index.
   1. History—Dictionaries.   2. Gazetteers.   I. Carruth, Gorton.
   II. Title.
D9.C29   1983   903′.21   80-25121
ISBN 0-87196-126-1 (set)
ISBN 0-87196-397-3 (v. 1)
ISBN 0-87196-125-3 (v. 2)

Printed in the United States of America
10 9 8 7 6 5 4 3 2 1

PREFACE

Until now there has been no comprehensive encyclopedia or dictionary in English covering places of historical importance throughout the world. *The Encyclopedia of Historic Places*, unlike other standard short-entry alphabetical reference books, such as *Webster's New Geographical Dictionary*, the *Columbia-Lippincott Gazetteer of the World*, or the one-volume *New Columbia Encyclopedia*, provides detailed coverage on all geographic locations of historical significance—towns, cities, countries, provinces, regions, empires, deserts, forts, battle sites, lakes, mountains, rivers, shrines, and archaeological sites—including many places not found in standard reference books. The scope is broad, ranging from the remains of human beginnings to the present. The reader will also find many place names, such as Acadia, Bessarabia, or Gaul, that are no longer current in English, as well as many other places, now unimportant, that once played a role in history.

While not exhaustive, the brief histories provided for each entry—whether of a village, a country, or a battle site—are designed to pinpoint the importance of that place in history. Special care has been taken to locate each site in terms of a modern country and to position it, if appropriate, at or close to a modern town or city. While major rivers, and many minor ones, as well as mountain ranges, deserts, and seas have been covered, places of purely geographic interest, with little or no history of significance, have been omitted.

Each entry follows a formal pattern, beginning with the name of the place, listed alphabetically under its most common English name. This is followed by its alternate names printed in bold type within square brackets, its variant spellings, native name or spelling, and ancient and former names. These alternate names and spellings are again listed alphabetically in the book and cross-referenced back to the original entry, so that any place can be located under any one of its names. Next, the modern country within which the entry lies (in parentheses) and its geographical location are given, followed by its history: the important events that took place there, the historical significance of the place, or if a longer entry, a précis of its history.

An extensive cross-referencing system is at the heart of the work. Numerous cross-references to related entries (in capitals and small capitals) appear within each entry. Other cross-references occur from time to time at the ends of articles, or as separate entries. However, to avoid a clutter of useless cross-references, these are restricted to only those names that may lead the reader to additional information on the subject. There is also no cross-referencing of places mentioned for purposes of geographical location only, unless considered pertinent, nor usually of the modern country within which the entry is placed.

While any alphabetical listing of historical places necessarily gives a fragmented view of history, this comprehensive system of cross-references will enable the reader to fill in for himself the broad historical background that lies behind any specific entry.

In the spelling of Chinese names we have used the older Wade-Giles system of transliteration throughout rather than the modern Pinyin system, because most of these names are more familiar to our readers in the old spellings than in the new.

I wish to express my particular appreciation to Gorton Carruth, Advisory Editor, whose long experience in reference publishing proved invaluable in organizing and compiling the encyclopedia; to Edward W. Knappman, Executive Vice President of Facts On File, who conceived the project and proved to be an exemplary editor as well as publisher; and to Fon W. Boardman, Jr., who wrote a disproportionate number of the entries with admirable speed and accuracy.

In addition, the following editors and writers all contributed their share to the completion of the work:

Elsa van Bergen, Gene Brown, Louise D. Brown, Douglass Brownstone, Christopher Carruth, Gérard Cochepin, David D'Arcy, Mary Ann McCollester, Dorcas H. Malott, Edward O. Malott, Jr., David Merrill, Ronald D. Musto, Martha Ramsey, Dr. E.M. Reilly, Joseph Reilly, Charles Rickett, Ellen Russell, Nicola Sissons, Celia Smith and Mary Varchaver.

Courtlandt Canby

August 1983
Ossining, New York

CONTENTS

Volume I
Preface v
Historic Places 1-542

Volume II
Historic Places 543-1051
Credits 1052

M

MAALEH-ACRABBIM (Israel?) Pass S of the DEAD SEA. It was also called "the ascent of Akrabbim" in Joshua 15:3 and Num. 34:4, and newly translated as the Scorpion Pass, it was a boundary of CANAAN as dictated to Moses from God, and later of JUDAH.

MA'AN (Jordan) Town in the SW, 60 mi SSE of the Dead Sea, located at the terminus of the main railroad line to Damascus, Syria. A leading trade and governmental center since biblical times, Maan was on an early caravan route from AMMAN to AQABA and on the road taken by pilgrims going to MECCA.

MAARIANHAMINA [*Swedish:* **Mariehamn**] (Finland) Seaport on Ahvenanmaa Island (ÅLAND ISLANDS) in the Gulf of Bothnia. Founded in 1861 by Czar Alexander II as part of his general modernization and expansion program and ceded to Finland in 1922, it has developed into a major commercial center as well as a summer resort.

MAAS. See MEUSE RIVER.

MAASSLUIS (The Netherlands) River port in SOUTH HOLLAND, 10 mi W of Rotterdam. A fort erected here in 1572 by the Flemish leader Philip van Marnix, lord of Sainte-Aldegonde, was captured by the Spanish in 1573.

MAASTRICHT [**Maestricht**] [*Latin:* **Mosae Trajectum**] (Netherlands) Capital city of Limburg province on the Maas, or Meuse, River near the Belgian frontier and on the Albert Canal system. It was founded on the site of a Roman town and as a strategic border fortress. An episcopal see from 382 to 721 AD, it has the oldest church in the Netherlands, the sixth-century cathedral of St. Servatius. In 1284 the city came under the joint rule of the dukes of BRABANT and the prince-bishop of LIÈGE. In 1579 the Spanish captured it from Dutch rebels, who withstood a siege for four months during the revolt of the Netherlands. They massacred 8,000 of its inhabitants in retaliation for 4,000 Spanish casualties. In 1632 Prince Frederick Henry took it for the Dutch, who subsequently lost it to the French on several occasions, notably in 1673 and 1794. It withstood a siege in 1830. In World War II it was captured by the Germans on the first day of their Low Country invasion in 1940 and was retaken by U.S. forces on Sept. 15, 1944. Of additional historic interest in Maastricht and its suburb, Wijk, are the Romanesque church of Our Lady from the 11th century, a 13th-century bridge across the Maas, and the 17th-century town hall.

MACAO [*Portuguese:* **Macau**] (Portugal) An overseas province which includes the Macao peninsula on the SE coast of CHINA and the islands of Taipa and Colôane, approx. 40 mi W of HONG KONG. Its name was derived from the Ma Kwok temple built there in the 14th century. First visited by Vasco da Gama in 1497 and settled by Portugal in 1557, it is the oldest permanent European settlement in the Far East. From 1717 until the 19th century Macao and CANTON were the only Chinese ports open to European trade. Portugal declared the independence of Macao in 1849, but it was not recognized by China until 1887 in the Protocol of Lisbon. The burial place of Robert Morrison and of St. Francis Xavier, it was also the residence *c.*1560 of the Portuguese poet, Camõens, who wrote part of *The Lusiads* here. Separated from China by a barrier gate, Macao had been a haven for mainland refugees after 1949 until the Portuguese administration faced considerable opposition from the Chinese in 1967. Notable buildings include St. Paul's Basilica, built in 1635 by Roman Catholic Japanese artisans; St. Domingo's church and convent, founded in 1670; the fort and chapel of Guia from 1626; and the fort of São Paolo de Monte of the 16th century.

MACAPÁ (Brazil) City, on the AMAZON RIVER, N of the Amazon delta. Founded in 1688, it grew around a fort, now a museum, and became the capital of the federal territory of Amapá created in 1944.

MACARTHUR. See ORMOC.

MACASSAR. See MAKASAR.

MACAU. See MACAO.

MACCLESFIELD (England) Town of CHESHIRE, on the Bollin River, 17 mi S of Manchester. Chartered in 1220, the ancient town was largely destroyed during the Civil War. Also a principal center of silk manufacture after 1756, it has the Church of St. Michael, which dates from 1278, and a grammar school from the early 16th century. Nearby is the Jodrell Bank Experimental Station, which in 1957 tracked the first Russian Sputnik under the direction of Prof. Bernard Lovell.

McDOWELL (United States) Town in Highland County, WEST VIRGINIA. On May 8, 1862, it was the scene of a Confederate victory led by Gens. Stonewall Jackson and Edward Johnson.

MACEDON, EMPIRE OF (Greece) Ancient empire that first rose to power in that part of MACEDONIA, NW, N, and NE of the Chalcidice peninsula in N Greece. Macedon's capital was PELLA. A political unit developed here in the seventh century BC that at the start of the fifth century was a tributary of PERSIA. Alexander I (d. 450 BC) became involved in Greek politics and adopted features of Greek culture. By the time of Philip II (ruled 359–336 BC), Macedon annexed more of Macedonia, CHALCIDICE, and THRACE. Philip's defeat of a confederation of Greek city-states at CHAERONEA in 338 made him the ruler of Greece.

Macao, a Portuguese enclave in China since 1557, the oldest European foothold in China and one of the last to survive.

Philip's son, Alexander the Great (356–323 BC), built the kingdom of Macedon into the most extensive empire the world had yet seen. In 334 BC he invaded ASIA MINOR and in 333 BC entered SYRIA and defeated the forces of the Persian Empire at the battle of ISSUS. By the next year he held all of Syria and advanced on EGYPT where he met no resistance. Returning to Syria and marching on to MESOPOTAMIA, he again defeated the Persians in the battle of GUAGAMELA. Proceeding south to BABYLON, then SUSA, PERSEPOLIS, ECBATANA, and BACTRIA, Alexander completed the conquest of the Persian Empire. Once in Central Asia his troops became restless, but Alexander pressed them onward from AFGHANISTAN into northern INDIA, where he overran the PUNJAB. Here his men refused to go further east. Alexander led them down the INDUS RIVER and on a long desert march that ended at Susa in present Iran in 324 BC. A mutiny was then put down. The next year Alexander caught a fever and died in Babylon at the age of 33.

The empire began to fall apart almost as soon as he died. His commanders, the Diadochi (Greek meaning "successors"), fell to quarreling and attempted to seize parts of the empire, although Antipater tried to hold it together. Antigonus, Ptolemy I of Egypt, and Craterus supported him; but they were opposed by Eumenes, who held CAPPADOCIA and PAPHLAGONIA, and Perdiccas, who ruled in Babylon. Antipater and his allies defeated the others in 321 BC, but when Antipater died in 319 BC the struggle resumed. The chief figure now was Antigonus I, who had control of Asia Minor, Syria, and Mesopotamia; but he and his son Demetrius were defeated at the battle of IPSUS in 301 BC. Among the victors this time were Cassander, son of Antipater and king of Macedon, and Lysimachus, who controlled Thrace.

The struggle is usually said to have ended when Seleucus I, king of Syria, conquered Lysimachus, who had taken over Asia Minor, at the battle of CORUPEDION in Lydia in 281 BC. By this time the survivors in power included the Ptolemies in Egypt, and Seleucus in Asia Minor and Syria. In Greece and Macedon Cassander had held sway until he died in 297 BC. After fighting off rivals, Antigonus II established control there and in a long reign, from 277 to 239 BC, revived Macedon's economy. Antigonus III (reigned 229 to 221 BC), regained power over the Greek city-states.

The Romans entered the picture in the second century BC. The First Macedonian War lasted from 215 to 205 BC; and Philip V was able to hold off the enemy. In the Second Macedonian War he was badly defeated in 197 BC, and thereafter collaborated with the Romans. Philip's son and successor, Perseus, fought the Third Macedonian War from 171 to 168 BC, which ended when the Romans won decisively at PYDNA on the Gulf of Thessaloniki. Rome divided the defeated country into four republics, but when a pretender tried to revive the kingdom, Macedonia became the first Roman province in 146 BC.

Although Alexander the Great caused much bloodshed and turmoil, he did carry Hellenism over much of Asia and the Near East and into India. And the influence of this Hellenistic civilization continued to spread out, especially in the Mediterranean world and into the heritage of Rome. One of its great centers of influence was the city of ALEXANDRIA, Egypt, which Alexander founded. See also SELEUCID EMPIRE.

MACEDONIA [*Bulgarian and Macedonian:* **Makedoniya;** *Greek:* **Makedhonia, Makedonia;** *Serbo-Croatian:* **Makedonija, Makedoniya**] (Bulgaria, Greece, Yugoslavia) Region of SE Europe, occupying part of the BALKAN PENINSULA and extending northward from the Aegean Sea. In general it corresponds with the ancient country of Macedon, which formed the nucleus of the MACEDONIAN EMPIRE. Today part of it is in NE Greece, part in SW Bulgaria, and the rest in SE Yugoslavia. The original inhabitants were introduced to Greek culture as early as the eighth century BC when colonies were founded on the coast. PERSIA occupied the region from 490 to 480 BC, and after 146 BC it was a Roman province. After the ROMAN EMPIRE was divided between east and west in 395 AD, Macedonia came under the BYZANTINE EMPIRE but suffered invasion by the Goths and the Huns. Slavs began penetrating the Byzantine Empire in 576, and they made most of Macedonia a Slavic region.

Macedonia changed hands many times in the following centuries. In the ninth century Bulgaria took it, but between 1014 and 1018 the Byzantines won it back. After the Byzantine Empire was broken up temporarily in 1204 by Crusaders, Macedonia was fought over by the Latin Empire of CONSTANTINOPLE, Ivan II of Bulgaria, the despots of EPIRUS, and the empire of NICAEA. In 1261 it became part of a restored Byzantine Empire, but in the 14th century Stephen Dushan, king of SERBIA, conquered almost all of the region. Next came the OTTOMAN EMPIRE, which controlled it from the late 14th until the 19th century. The Ottoman Turks fell into decline by the late 19th century; and the Treaty of SAN STEFANO, which ended a war between RUSSIA and the Turks, gave most of Macedonia to Bulgaria. Later in the same year, however, the major powers of Europe reversed this decision at the Congress of Berlin and left Macedonia to the Turks. A strong independence movement arose, but the treaty ending the Second Balkan War in 1913 divided Macedonia mostly along present lines, leaving a small part to Bulgaria.

In World War I Greece allowed the Allies to operate the Salonika, now THESSALONÍKI, campaigns aimed at Bulgaria from Macedonian territory. The post-World War I period was one of much agitation and upheaval among the ethnic groups in the region. Greece invaded Bulgaria in 1925, charging that Greeks in Bulgarian Macedonia were being mistreated, but the League of Nations ended the fighting. In Yugoslavia, Macedonian hatred of Serbian rule resulted in 1934 in the assassination of Yugoslav King Alexander. Macedonia was occu-

pied from 1941 to 1944 in World War II by Bulgaria, which was a German ally. After the war, prewar boundaries were restored, and Yugoslavian Macedonia became an autonomous region. During the civil war in Greece from 1946 to 1949 there was conflict between Greece and Yugoslavia over the area. Tensions between Greece, Bulgaria, and Yugoslavia over the Macedonian issue have finally eased.

MACEDONIAN EMPIRE. See MACEDON, EMPIRE OF.

MACEIÓ (Brazil) City in Alagoas state, 130 mi SSW of Recife. Dutch occupation and the establishment of a sugar mill in the 17th century stimulated the growth of the city. It came under Portuguese control in 1654. An important sugar-exporting center in the early 19th century, it became a provincial capital in 1839. At present, it is an important cultural center with a state university, historical institute, and academy of letters. The most important landmark is a lighthouse in the center of the city.

MACERATA (Italy) Town between the Chienti and Potenza rivers in the MARCHE region, Macerata Province, 110 mi NNE of ROME. Founded with Recanati by inhabitants of Ricuna after the destruction of their city by the Visigoth Alaric in 408 AD, it was a thriving town during the Lombard period. Ruled by the papacy from the mid-15th century until 1797, it gained significance when it became the seat of the governors of the Marches under Nicholas IV. The town retains its 13th-century walls and has a university founded in 1290.

MACHAERUS. See MUKĀWIR.

McHENRY, FORT. See FORT McHENRY.

MACHILIPATNAM [**Bandar, Masulipatnam**] (India) Port city of NE Andhra Pradesh, on the Bay of Bengal, at one of the mouths of the Krishna River, 215 mi NNE of Madras. The English agency established here in 1611 was the earliest British settlement on the COROMANDEL COAST. Taken by the French, the city was retaken by the British in 1759 during the wars of the CARNATIC. It was partly destroyed in 1864 by cyclone and flood that took 30,000 lives.

MACHPELAH, CAVE OF (Jordan) Located in a region occupied by ISRAEL in 1967, the cave is enclosed by a mosque in HEBRON, 20 mi SSW of Jerusalem. According to the Bible, Abraham bought it from Ephron, a son of Zohar the Hittite, for a family burial. Abraham and Sarah are believed to have been buried there. It was taken by Joshua, for a time it was the home of David, and was captured by Judas Maccabaeus. The cave figured in the wars of the Romans, Muslims, and Crusaders. The mosque of Hebron now on the site may be the successor to the structure built there by the Herods.

MACHRAMION. See ASSOS.

MACHU PICCHU (Peru) Ruins of an Inca fortress-city, located approx. 50 mi NW of Cuzco, between two high peaks overlooking the URUBAMBA RIVER, approx. 9,000 ft high. This pre-Columbian stone city was discovered almost intact in 1911 by Hiram Bingham and includes temples and a citadel surrounded by houses and terraced fields. These spread over an area of five square miles and are linked by at least 3,000 steps. Legend relates that the city was the home of the Incas prior to their migration to CUZCO. It was their last stronghold after the Spanish conquest. The Spanish never came across the site.

MACIEJOWICE (Poland) Town near the E bank of the VISTULA RIVER, 43 mi SE of Warsaw. Here on Oct. 10, 1794 Polish troops under Thaddeus Kosciusko, hero of the American Revolution and leader of a national rebellion against Russian control, were defeated, leading to the division of Poland among AUSTRIA, PRUSSIA, and RUSSIA; Kosciusko himself was wounded and captured.

McKEESPORT (United States) City in Allegheny county, SW PENNSYLVANIA, at the confluence of the Youghiogheny and MONONGAHELA rivers, 10 mi ESE of Pittsburgh. Settled in 1755 by Scotch and Irish groups, it was a center of conflict in 1794 during the Whiskey Rebellion against Federal enforcement of a tax on liquor. See also CANONSBURG.

MACKENZIE ISLAND. See ULITHI.

MACKINAC [*former:* **Michilimackinac**] (United States) Region of the SE MICHIGAN peninsula, including the Straits of Mackinac, Mackinac Island, St. Ignace, also called Ancient Michilimackinac, and Mackinaw City on the southern shore, the site of a fort called Old Mackinac. The region served for many years as an important Indian gathering place. In 1634 the first European passed through the straits. Father Jacques Marquette established a mission at St. Ignace in 1671. A fort built there became the center of French trading in New France until DETROIT was founded. In 1761 the area passed to the British during the French and Indian War. Two years later the British garrison at Old Mackinac was massacred by the Ottawa Indians during Pontiac's Rebellion. The fort was moved during the American Revolution to Mackinac Island, which was awarded to the United States in 1783 by the Treaty of Paris, but remained in British hands until 1794. During the War of 1812, the British captured Mackinac, but it was returned to the United States by the Treaty of Ghent in 1814. For the next two decades Mackinac Island was the headquarters for John Jacob Astor's American Fur Company. The U.S. Army post on the island was abandoned in 1894, and it is now a state park and scenic summer resort.

MACOMER (Italy) Village of SARDINIA, in Cagliari province, 95 mi NNW of Cagliari. It dates back to Roman times, as evidenced by three milestones in front of the old parish church of San Pantaleone. It was on the Roman high road from Carales to Turris Libisonis, which is identical with the route of the modern road.

MÂCON [*ancient:* **Matisco Aeduorum**] (France) City of the Saône-et-Loire department, located on the Saône River, 42 mi N of Lyons. An important town of the Aedui in the first century BC, it was again prominent as an episcopal see from the sixth century AD until the Revolution. It suffered successively at the hands of the Germans, Burgundians, Vandals, Hungarians, and Carolingian kings. It was sold in 1238 to the king of France; from 1435 to 1477 it was Burgundian. A Huguenot stronghold in the 16th century, it fell into the hands of the Catholic League and did not yield to Henry IV until 1594. The birthplace of Alphonse Lamartine, it has the remains of a 12th-century cathedral.

MACON [*former:* **Newtown**] (United States) City on the OCMULGEE RIVER, in GEORGIA, 78 mi SE of Atlanta. Named for the political leader Nathaniel Macon, it was settled in 1821 and chartered in 1832. A Confederate gold depository and ammunition source during the Civil War, it was captured by Union forces on April 20, 1865. Of additional historic interest are the birthplace of Sidney Lanier, a restored grand opera house from 1884 and Fort Hawkins, now partially restored. Nearby is Ocmulgee National Monument, which contains prehistoric Indian mounds.

MACORABA. See MECCA.

MACQUARIE ISLAND (Australia) Island in the S Pacific Ocean, 850 mi SE of Tasmania. Discovered in 1810, it served as the base for the Mawson polar expedition of 1911 to 1914. An Australian research station was established here in 1948, and it is now a nature reserve.

MACROOM (Irish Republic) Town, approx. 25 mi E of Cork. Besieged several times during the 17th century, it is presumably the birthplace of Admiral Sir William Penn, naval officer in the Civil Wars and the Dutch Wars, whose son founded PENNSYLVANIA. Of historic interest is a castle said to have been founded by King John, but possibly built by Norman invaders. In 1798 it was the scene of the execution of several rebels against British domination.

MACTAN (Philippines) An island off the E coast of Cebu Island. On April 27, 1521 Ferdinand Magellan was killed by Mactan natives in an expedition launched on behalf of a Cebuan sovereign. The spot is marked by a monument.

MACTARIS. See MAKTAR.

MA'DABĀ. See MADEBA.

MADAGASCAR [**Malagasy Republic, Malgache Republic**] [*French:* **République Malgache**] The world's fourth-largest island, which together with the isles of Sainte Marie, Nossi-Bé, Juan de Nova, Europa, and Bassas de India form the republic. Reached 2,000 years ago by black Africans and Indonesians, it was settled in the ninth century AD by Muslim traders, including some Arabs. It was probably first seen by Europeans under Diego Dias, the Portuguese navigator who reached it in 1500. From 1600 to 1619 Portuguese missionaries tried unsuccessfully to convert the native Malagasy.

By the beginning of the 17th century there were several small kingdoms on the island. From 1642 until the late 18th century the French maintained strongholds, and the British controlled it from 1810 to 1811. A native ruling group, the Hovas, had virtually expelled Westerners when a Christian ruler took control in 1861. A treaty with FRANCE was concluded in 1868, and the island became a French protectorate in 1882. There was heavy fighting between 1894 and 1896 when the French were victorious and abolished the monarchy. In a major rebellion in 1947/48 possibly as many as 80,000 natives were killed. Ties with France continued through to 1958, when the republic joined the French Community. It was granted its independence in 1960. Its capital is TANANARIVE.

MADANG [*former:* **Friedrich Wilhelmshafen**] (Papua New Guinea) Port town on Astrolabe Bay, E NEW GUINEA ISLAND. In World War II Australian troops battered this leading Japanese air base from September 1943 until February 1944 and captured it with the help of U.S. forces on April 24, 1944.

MADAUROS (Algeria) City of ancient NUMIDIA, near Mdaourouch, approx. 50 mi NNW of Tebessa. Known for its schools, in the second century BC it was the birthplace of the writer Apuleius, author of the influential novel, *The Golden Ass.* Of additional historic interest are the ruins of a Roman mausoleum and baths and a Byzantine basilica and fortress.

MADEBA [**Ma'daba**] [*ancient:* **Medeba**] (Jordan) Town in the N central region, SSW of Amman. An ancient Moabite town, it was the scene of fighting during the long wars of the Maccabees, beginning *c.*170 BC.

MADEIRA ISLANDS [*Roman:* **Purpuriarae (Purple Islands)**] (Portugal) Island group in the E Atlantic Ocean, 350 mi off the coast of Morocco, N of the CANARY ISLANDS and SE of the AZORES, comprised of Madeira and Porto Santo, plus two groups of barren islets: the Desertas and the Selvagens. The islands were known to the Romans as the Purpuriarae or Purple Islands, and possibly to the Phoenicians. Porto Santo was sighted by João Gonalves Zarco and Tristão Vox Teixeria in 1418. Madeira was discovered in 1420 by Zarco, who founded the capital city of FUNCHAL in 1421. The islands were settled immediately after that. They were occupied by the British for a short time in 1801 and again from 1807 to 1814. An English proclamation in 1663 allowed the local wine to be carried to all English possessions, hence initiating trade in the famed wine.

MADHYA PRADESH [*former:* **Central Provinces and Berar**] (India) The country's largest state, located between the DECCAN and the GANGES plain. It was originally inhabited by primitive ancestors of its modern tribal groups. Part of the GUPTA EMPIRE, the area was invaded by Muslims in the 13th century. During the reign of Akbar the region became nominally part of the MOGUL EMPIRE. Ruled in the 16th and 17th centuries by the aboriginal Gonds, who still dwell in forests here, the territory was conquered by the MARATHAS, or Mahrattas, in the 18th century. The British occupied it in 1820 and began conquest. On June 14, 1857 the first rebellion of the Indian Mutiny was staged at MORAR by Gwalior troops; by 1859 all regional mutinies had been put down. BERAR, one of the five kingdoms of the Deccan and later ruled by the Nizam of HYDERABAD, was incorporated in 1903. The area became part of independent India in 1949. In 1956 it was expanded

with the addition of Madhya Bahrat, Vindhya Pradesh, Bhopal, and part of Rajasthan.

MADINAT ASH SHAB [*former:* **Al-Ittahad, Al-Ittihad**] (South Yemen) Town in the SW, approx. 10 mi W of ADEN. Created in the 1960's to be capital of the Federation of SOUTH ARABIA, from 1967 to 1970 it was, along with Aden, the capital of Southern Yemen.

MADINAT RASUL ALLAH. See MEDINA.

MADIOEN. See MADIUN.

MADISON [*former:* **Bottle Hill**] (United States) Town of N NEW JERSEY, 4 mi SE of Morristown. Sayre House, built here in 1745, served as headquarters for Gen. Anthony Wayne during the American Revolution. The town is the site of Drew University and part of Fairleigh Dickinson University.

MADISON (United States) State capital of WISCONSIN, on an isthmus between Lake Monona and Lake Mendota. On a site chosen for the capital of Wisconsin Territory in 1836, before it was settled, it was incorporated as a city in 1856. An elaborate capitol building houses the legislative library, the first such in the United States, organized by political scientist Charles McCarthy. The University of Wisconsin was located here in 1836. A Unitarian Church designed by Frank Lloyd Wright is also here.

MADISON ISLAND. See NUKU HIVA.

MADIUN [*Dutch:* **Madioen**] (Indonesia) City and provincial subdivision of East JAVA province, in the central plain, 90 mi WSW of Surabaja. Located in the former Netherlands Indies, the city was the scene of heavy fighting in 1948 during the Indonesian revolution. Notable is the Taman Pahlawan, burial place of soldiers killed then.

MADJAPAHIT EMPIRE (Indonesia) Former kingdom, centered in JAVA. It was founded in 1292 by Prince Vijaya, who overthrew the SINGOSARI kingdom of eastern Java. The last Hindu empire of Java, Madjapahit expanded its rule between 1335 and 1380 so that it controlled most of the Malay archipelago and some of the MALAY PENINSULA, overthrowing the SIRIVIJAYA Empire of SUMATRA in the process. The kingdom began to decline after the death of its ruler, Gajah Mada, in 1364. The spread of Islam and the growth of Muslim states resulted in Madjapahit's destruction in 1518. BANTAM and MATARAM became the leading Javanese states.

MADOERA. See MADURA.

MADRAS [*former:* **Madraspatam, Madraspatnam**] (India) Capital of Tamil Nadu state, in the SE, on the COROMANDEL COAST of the Bay of Bengal. The main port on India's southeast coast, it was founded in 1639 by Francis Day of the English East India Company and became an important British trading center that grew around the original outpost, Fort St. George. It received the East's first charter in 1687. In 1702 it was blockaded by Daud Khan, in 1741 it was unsuccessfully attacked by the MARATHAS, and in 1746 it was captured by the French under Joseph Dupleix but was returned to Britain by the Treaty of AIX-LA-CHAPELLE in 1748.

Besieged by the French in 1758, it was relieved by the British fleet and was again successfully defended against Haidar Ali in 1769 and 1780. St. Thomé, the traditional burial place of the Apostle Thomas and now part of the city, was founded by the Portuguese in 1504, held by the French from 1672 to 1674, and ceded to the British in 1749. Outside the city is Mt St. Thomas, the traditional site of the martyrdom of the Apostle Thomas. In 1782 the French, allied with the American colonies, blockaded the port in a vain attempt to keep British troops from landing.

MADRASPATAM. See MADRAS.

MADRASPATNAM. See MADRAS.

MADRID (Spain) The nation's capital, located in New Castile on the Manzanares River, 40 mi NNE of Toledo. Originally a Moorish fortress, it was captured in 932 AD by Ramiro II of LEÓN. It was again taken from the Moors by Alfonso VI of CASTILE in 1083. The cortes of Castile met in Madrid several times, and Ferdinand and Isabella as well as Charles V resided there. It was made the capital by Philip II in 1561. The city expanded rapidly in the 18th century under the Bourbon kings, especially Charles III, and the huge royal palace and the Prado date from this time. It sided with the Bourbons in the War of the Spanish Succession. From 1808 until 1812 it was occupied by the French during the Peninsular campaign. On May 2, 1808 there was severe fighting against Napoleon's troops at the Puerta del Sol in the center of the city. That popular uprising is immortalized in two paintings by Goya. During the Spanish civil war it was besieged for two-and-one-half years until Nationalist troops entered it on March 28, 1939. The Buen Retiro Park dates from 1631, and the National Library is from 1712.

MADURA, India. See MADURAI.

MADURA [*Dutch:* **Madoera**] (Indonesia) Island of E Java province, off the NE coast of JAVA. From the 11th to the 18th centuries Madura was controlled by the Javanese. It was under Mataram from 1624 to 1674, and the Dutch became paramount at the end of the 17th century. In 1885 it was attached to Java as a residency by the Dutch, ending three separate regencies that had been created to stem the power of an aggressive prince. Madura Strait, south of the island, was the site of a battle on Feb. 4, 1942 during World War II, involving the U.S.S. *Marblehead*.

MADURAI [**Madura**] (India) City in Tamil Nadu state, on the Vaigai River. Known as the "city of festivals and temples," it is particularly noted for the Meenakshi temple with its 1,000 carved pillars and nine massive gate-towers or *gopuras*, adorned with elaborate carving and enclosing a quadrangle known as the Tank of the Golden Lilies. Madurai was the capital of the old Pandya dynasty from the fifth century BC to the end of the 11th century AD. In the early 14th century it was invaded by Muslims who held it until 1378, when it came under the Hindu VIJAYANAGARA kingdom. It served as capital under the Nayak dynasty from the mid-16th century until c.1735, when it was taken by the Nawab of CARNATIC who ceded it to the British East

India Co. in 1801. The Nayak palace from the 17th century is another notable building.

MAEANDER. See MENDERES.

MAEBASHI [**Mayebashi**] (Japan) Capital city of the Gumma prefecture, in central HONSHŪ, on the Tone River. It was formerly the castle town of the Matsudaira clan.

MAEIDESSTANA. See MAIDSTONE.

MAE NAM KHONG. See SALWEEN.

MAEONIA. See LYDIA.

MAES HOWE (Scotland) Neolithic tomb-mound on MAINLAND, ORKNEY ISLANDS, off the N coast, near STENNESS. It is a Megalithic passage grave with chambers inside a mound approx. 300 ft. in circumference. There are runic inscriptions on the walls left by later Viking marauders. Maes Howe is one of the finest passage graves in the British Isles.

MAESTRICHT. See MAASTRICHT.

MAFEKING (South Africa) Town in N CAPE PROVINCE, 160 mi W of Pretoria, near the W TRANSVAAL border. Founded in 1885, it was the starting point for the unsuccessful raid in 1895 by Sir Leander Jameson, going to the aid of settlers rebelling against the Boers in the Transvaal and hoping to further a South African Union. During the Boer War the British garrison here under Lord Baden-Powell withstood a Boer siege for 217 days from Oct. 12, 1899 until May 17, 1900 when the British cavalry relieved them. Mafeking was the extraterritorial capital of Bechuanaland Protectorate until it became independent as BOTSWANA in 1965.

MAGADAN. See MAGDALA, Israel.

MAGADHA (India) Ancient kingdom situated within the modern state of BIHAR, S of the GANGES RIVER. Strategically located, it was used by various dynasties as a base for their evolving domination. Becoming prominent in the seventh century BC, it was especially powerful under the MAURYA dynasty (c.320–185 BC) founded by Chandragupta and extended by Asoka (273–232 BC) and by the later GUPTA dynasty of the fourth century AD. It declined in the fifth century. Buddhism and Jainism first developed here, and the Buddha used the Magadhi dialect of Sanskrit. Several incidents in his life occurred here. Its capital, Pataliputra, is the modern PATNA.

MAGALLANES. See PUNTA ARENAS.

MAGAMA. See TISSAMAHARAMA.

MAGDALA (Ethiopia) Village in the N, in Welo province. In the mid-19th century Emperor Theodore II used this natural stronghold as a base for his conquest of the surrounding Galla territory. In 1867 he made it his capital and threw some British diplomats living here into prison as a reaction to a presumed snub by Queen Victoria. Sir Robert Napier led a British expedition to rescue the prisoners and destroyed Magdala, causing Theodore, who had become mentally unstable, to commit suicide. Napier was later named Baron Napier of Magdala.

MAGDALA [**Magadan**] [*Arab:* **Al-Majdal, Mejdel;**

Hebrew: **Migdal]** (Israel) Ancient town on the W shore of the SEA OF GALILEE, now an archaeological site just N of TIBERIAS. A modern settlement called Migdal is nearby. The supposed home of St. Mary Magdalene, it is probably to be identified with Majdol, a hamlet in approximately the same place. Matthew 15:39 gives its names as *Magdala*, other books give Magadan, otherwise unidentifiable, and one reads Dalmanutha. See also MIGDAL-EL.

MAGDALENA RIVER (Colombia) River rising in the Cordillera Central in the SW and flowing approx. 1,000 mi N to the CARIBBEAN SEA near BARRANQUILLA. Discovered in 1501 by the Spanish explorer Rodrigode Bastidas, it was explored in 1536 by the Spanish conquistador Gonzalo Jiménez de Quesada. Since the colonial era, it has been an important avenue of communication and trade between the interior and the Caribbean.

MAGDEBURG (East Germany) Most important inland port of the country, located on the ELBE RIVER, 82 mi WSW of Berlin. First mentioned as a trading settlement in 805 AD, under Emperor Otto I it became a base for the Germanization of the Wendish territories. It was made an archiepiscopal see in the 960's, with the archbishops of Magdeburg ruling a large territory as princes of the HOLY ROMAN EMPIRE. It burned down in 1188 but was an important commercial center by the 13th century and received a charter that was a model for hundreds of towns in Germany, Austria, Bohemia, and Poland. These charters provided for an elected council, local courts of justice, and other local freedoms. It was a member of the HANSEATIC LEAGUE for nearly 200 years. The city accepted the Reformation in 1524 and in 1531 joined the Schmalkalden League and continued its resistance to Emperor Charles V until its fall in 1551 to Maurice of Saxony. On May 20/21, 1631 it was sacked and burned during the Thirty Years War. Its destruction led to stronger alliances among Protestant rulers. It was rebuilt after the Peace of WESTPHALIA in 1648, which also transferred both city and archbishopric to the electorate of BRANDENBURG. An important Prussian fortress from the late 17th century, it was taken by the French in 1806 and returned to PRUSSIA in 1814. Heavily bombed in World War II, it was taken by the Allies on April 18/19, 1945. Notable buildings include an 11th-century Romanesque church and a 13th-century cathedral. It was the birthplace of Otto von Guericke (1602–86), the physicist and inventor of the Magdeburg hemispheres which demonstrated air pressure; of the composer G.P. Telemann (1681–1767); and of Baron von Steuben, the Prussian general who fought in the American Revolution.

MAGELLAN, STRAIT OF [*Spanish:* **Estrecho de Magallanes]** (Argentina, Chile) Body of water, approx.

The forbidding Strait of Magellan, a dangerous passage around southern South America into the Pacific. It has been superseded by the Panama Canal.

350 mi long and 3 to 15 mi wide, off the S coast of South America, separating the TIERRA DEL FUEGO archipelago from the mainland and joining the Atlantic and Pacific oceans. Although previously believed to exist, it was actually discovered in October/November 1520 by Ferdinand Magellan, seeking a route to the MOLUCCAS that could be controlled by SPAIN. It was important in the days of sailing ships, especially before the building of the PANAMA CANAL, as it afforded an inland passage around the tip of South America and protection from the exceptionally heavy storms of the CAPE HORN area. Magellan's smooth crossing of the "Sea of the South" by his three remaining ships after leaving the strait led him to rename the sea the Pacific Ocean.

MAGENTA (Italy) Town, in Milano province, LOMBARDY region, 14 mi W of Milan. In the fourth century AD the Roman emperor Marcus Maxentius had his headquarters here, hence the name. At the nearby TICINO RIVER the French and Sardinians, allies of Italians fighting for independence, won a decisive victory over the Austrians on June 4, 1859, thereby opening the way to MILAN. The victory was an important step toward Italian nationhood. For his leadership, Gen. MacMahon was made duke of Magenta by Napoleon III.

MAGERSFONTEIN (South Africa) Battlefield in W ORANGE FREE STATE. Afrikaner commander Piet Cronje here halted the British under Gen. Lord Methuen in their advance toward besieged KIMBERLEY in December 1899 during the Boer War; he was soon after surrounded and defeated at PAARDEBERG.

MAGGIORE, LAGO [Verbano] [*ancient:* **Verbanus Lacus**] (Italy) Lake formed by the TICINO RIVER, in the Alpine foothills of PIEDMONT, LOMBARDY, and SWITZERLAND, the second-largest lake in Italy. The SIMPLON PASS road built by Napoleon between 1800 and 1806 runs along part of its west shore. Among the resorts along its shores are ISOLA BÈLLA, LOCARNO, and STRESA.

MAGHREB [Maghrib, Magrib] Region in NW Africa, generally including MOROCCO, ALGERIA and TUNISIA, and sometimes LIBYA. It is the Arabic name for northwest Africa and also for SPAIN during the Moorish occupation. Only in the eighth century, in the early years of Arab rule, and in the late 12th and early 13th centuries under the ALMOHADS, was it a political entity.

MAGHRIB. See MAGHREB.

MAGINOT LINE (France) System of fortifications, mostly trenches and underground forts, along the eastern frontier of France, extending 200 mi from the Swiss to the Belgian border. Built between 1930 and 1934, it was named after André Maginot (1877–1932), a French minister of war who oversaw its construction. Although not completely covering the Belgian frontier at the outbreak of World War II, it was the position of a major part of the French army during the first months of the war. This traditional fixed line was easily flanked by tactics of rapid movement of the Germans after their invasion of the Low Countries, thus bringing about the collapse of the French army in May 1940. The belief in

its impregnability created a fatally unfounded sense of security. The line has become a symbol of such attitudes.

MAGLEMOSE (Denmark) Archeological site, on the W coast of Sjaelland, NW of SLAGELSE. Here bone and stone implements have been found. The site gives its name to a Danish division of the Mesolithic period in Europe of *c.*10,000 to 3000 BC.

MAGNA GRAECIA (Italy) Collective name for the ancient Greek seaport colonies in S Italy, part of the Greek overseas expansion of the eighth and seventh centuries BC. Its chief cities were Tarentum (modern: TARANTO), SYBARIS, Crotona (modern: CROTONE), HERACLEA, and CUMAE. Others included ELEA and Neapolis (modern: NAPLES). These cities nurtured two philosophical groups in the sixth century BC: those of Parmenides at Elea and of Pythagoras at Crotona. The Etruscans of CAPUA and the Romans came to know Greek civilization first through the settlers of Cumae. Magna Graecia began to decline by 500 BC. Malaria and attacks by Lucanians and Bruttians, the native mountain people who controlled the interior, were significant causes.

MAGNESIA [Magnesia ad Maeandrum] (Turkey) Ancient city of LYDIA, W Asia Minor, on the MENDERES RIVER, near its mouth, NE of Söke, one of two cities that were colonies of the Magnetes, a tribe from Magnesia in Thessaly, Greece. Destroyed *c.*650 BC by the Cimmerians, it was later colonized by the Ionians and given by Artaxerxes I to Themistocles, then exiled from ATHENS, who died here. It was later moved to a less isolated location near Mt Thorax, where it flourished through the first century AD. Important ruins on this site include the celebrated temple to Artemis Leucophryene, built in the second century BC.

MAGNESIA [Magnesia ad Sipylum] (Turkey) Ancient city on the Hermes River, at the foot of Mt Sipylus, NE of Smyrna, now Izmir. Founded along with MAGNESIA AD MAEANDRUM by the Magretes, a tribe from Magnesia in Thessaly, it is chiefly of historical interest as the scene of the defeat of Antiochus the Great by the Romans in 190 BC. The Romans stampeded the Syrian ruler's elephants as part of their impressive victory over an army of 80,000. MANISA later rose near this spot.

MAGNESIA AD MAEANDRUM. See MAGNESIA.

MAGNESIA AD SIPYLUM. See MAGNESIA.

MAGNITNAYA. See MAGNITOGORSK.

MAGNITOGORSK [*former:* **Magnitnaya**] (USSR) City of SW Chelyabinsk oblast, on the left bank of the Ural River, 160 mi SSW of Chelyabinsk. For centuries a village of Bashkirs and Kirghiz cattle breeders, it was named Magnitnaya in the early 18th century with the discovery that two small mountains nearby consisted of magnetized iron. Built between 1929 and 1931 under the First Five-Year Plan, it grew rapidly to represent Soviet industrial might. From World War II on it has been a major producer of military equipment. See URAL INDUSTRIAL REGION.

MAGOG (Canada) City in S QUEBEC, on the N end of Lake Memphremagog, 17 mi SW of Sherbrooke. It was founded in 1776 by Tory refugees from the American Revolution.

MAGRIB. See MAGHREB.

MAGUNTIACUM. See MAINZ.

MAGUSA. See FAMAGUSTA.

MAGYAR NÉBKÖZTÁRSASÁG. See HUNGARY.

MAHABALIPURAM [Mamallapuram] (India) Village of Tamil Nadu state in the SE, on the COROMANDEL COAST. Archaeological remains here include some examples of early Dravidian architecture of the seventh century AD. Later the PALLAVA dynasty undertook their preservation and had a number of temples carved from granite hills. The site is also known as Seven Pagodas because of the high pinnacles of seven of its temples.

MAHAGAMA. See TISSAMAHARAMA.

MAHARAJPUR (India) Village of GWALIOR state in the central region. On Dec. 29, 1843 it was the scene of a battle in which Sir Hugh Gough and the British governor general, Lord Ellenborough, defeated the insurgent army of Gwalior state.

MAHARASHTRA (India) Region in W central India, marking the original land of the MARATHAS, S of the Narmada and extending from E of Nagpur westward to the coast between Daman and Goa. Its chief cities were POONA and Salara. It was ruled in the sixth century AD by the CHALUKYA dynasty. The region was controlled by Muslims from the early 14th to the mid-17th century, when the great Maratha leader, Savaji, formed a Maharashtran confederacy, representing Hindu autonomy under the MOGULS. Although Portugal exercised influence in the region in the 16th century, the presence of Great Britain was increasingly felt. By the 19th century the Maharashtran area was part of the Bombay presidency, which later became a province of British India. Since the division of the state of BOMBAY in 1960 it has become the name of a modern state.

MAHDIA [Mehdia] [*ancient:* **Gummi, Turris Hannibalis**] (Tunisia) Town on the coast, between the gulfs of Hammamet and Gabes, 47 mi SSE of Sousse. In a strategic location jutting into the sea, it is on the site of the Phoenician settlement of Gummi, later called Turris Hannibalis by the Romans. Hannibal is said to have embarked here on his exile from CARTHAGE. It declined rapidly after the Arab conquest of North Africa but was refounded in 912 AD by Caliph Obaidallah-al-Mahdi, after whom it was named. It was occupied by the Normans of SICILY in the 12th century, who were in turn driven out in 1159 by the ALMOHADS. In 1390 it was besieged vainly for 61 days by a French and English Crusading force. In the early 16th century the corsair Dragut seized the town and made it his capital but lost it to the Spaniards in 1550. They occupied it until 1574, when it was taken by the Turks and the beys of TUNIS. From 1881 until Tunisian independence it was part of the French colonial empire.

MAHÉ [*former:* **Mayyali**] (India) Town in the SW, on the MALABAR COAST, approx. 40 mi N of Calicut. The only French settlement on the west coast of India, it was occupied by them under La Bourdonnais, comte de Mahé, in 1726. It fell to the British in 1761 and several times thereafter in the French and British wars and was restored to France in 1817. Its administration was reorganized in 1947. Given over to the Republic of India in 1954, it was made part of PONDICHERRY.

MAHEDIA. See AL-MAHDIYAH.

MAHESHWAR (India) Town of Indore state, in the central region on the N bank of the Narbada River. It is of great sanctity and antiquity, dating back at least to 2000 BC. It is chiefly known as the residence of Ahalya Bai, the queen of the Holkar dynasty during the last half of the 18th century, whose benevolence is famous throughout India. Here is the family temple of the Holkars. On the south bank traces of a very early settlement at Navdatoli have been excavated.

MAHIDPUR. See MEHIDPUR.

MAHISHAPURA. See MYSORE.

MAHISHMATI. See MYSORE.

MAHOBA (India) Ancient town in the Hamipur district, United Provinces. It served as capital of the Chandel dynasty, who ruled over the BUNDELKHAND from the ninth to the 13th centuries AD. The area is rich in antiquities, including many artificial lakes created by masonry dams.

MAHÓN [Port Mahon] [*ancient:* **Portus Magonis**] (Spain) Port of Baleares province, on MINORCA ISLAND, 89 mi ENE of Palma. Probably founded c.205 BC by the Carthaginian general Mago, youngest brother of Hannibal, and named for him, it was held by the Moors from the eighth to the 13th centuries and was sacked by the Corsair Barbarossa in 1535. Controlled by the British from 1708 to 1756, until taken by the French, it was recaptured in 1763 and held until 1782. During this period it replaced Ciudadela as the capital of Minorca. In 1756 Admiral John Byng, who had been sent to relieve the besieged town, was executed for retreating. Charges that he was used as a scapegoat are alluded to in Voltaire's *Candide*. The port was captured by Spain in 1782 and 1798 and was eventually restored to Spain by the Treaty of AMIENS in 1802. It has a fine harbor, once defended by the forts of San Felipe and Marlborough, and is the site of an important air and naval base.

MAHRATTA. See MARATHA CONFEDERACY.

MÄHREN. See MORAVIA.

MAIDA (Italy) Town of Cantanzaro province, CALABRIA region, 12 mi NNE of Pizzo. During the Napoleonic Wars, on July 4, 1806 British troops under Sir John Stuart defeated the French under Reynier on the plain of Maida. The names Maida Hill and Maida Vale in London derive from this battle, which frustrated French preparations to invade SICILY. Stuart had, with Admiral Smith's forces, 4,000 troops to oppose Reynier's command; military historians see the battle of Maida as an excellent example of the element of surprise made possible through seapower.

MAIDEN CASTLE [*ancient:* **Durnovaria**] (England) Impressive prehistoric hill fort in Dorset, near Dorchester. Some 115 acres in extent, it is probably the largest ancient earthwork in Great Britain. Excavations in the 1930's established the presence of a Neolithic village from c.2000 BC, as well as of later Iron Age fortified villages, the latest lying within massive ramparts of four concentric circles. The Belgae later took it over early in the first century BC. It was finally subdued in 44 or 45 AD by the Romans under Vespasian in a fierce siege. Later, about 70 AD, the inhabitants were moved by the Romans down to the site of DORCHESTER, then called Durnovaria.

MAIDENHEAD (England) Town in BERKSHIRE, on the THAMES RIVER, 27 mi W of London. Chartered in 1582, it contains traces of both a prehistoric settlement and a Roman camp. Its history is bound up with that of an ancient bridge, rebuilt between 1772 and 1777, which carries the London Road over the Thames River. The crossing has been maintained, with the support of the Crown, beginning with Edward I in 1297.

MAIDSTONE [*Anglo-Saxon:* **Maeidesstana**] (England) Admin. hq. of KENT, on the MEDWAY RIVER, 30 mi ESE of London. There is evidence of a Roman settlement and road here. It was a residence of the archbishops of Canterbury from before the Domesday Book account until the Reformation. In 1260 Archbishop Boniface founded Newark hospital here for poor wayfarers; its chapel is now St. Peter's Church. Historic buildings include Chillington Manor from Elizabethan times, a grammar school dating from 1549, where the poet Christopher Smart, astronomer John Pond, and others were educated; the 14th-century church of All Saints; and the palace of the archbishops. There is also historic Penenden Heath—the scene of executions, fairs, and county meetings until the 19th century— Cobtree Manor, the birthplace of William Hazlitt, and Dingley Dell of Dickens's *Pickwick Papers*.

MAIHAR (India) Town and former native state of the BAGHELKHAND agency, 97 mi N of Udbalpur. Its raja claimed descent from the Rajput clan. Extensive ruins of shrines and other buildings indicate its former glory. See also RAJPUTANA.

MAIKOP (USSR) City and battle site in Krasnodar Kraj, ADYGEI AUTONOMOUS OBLAST, at the foot of the CAUCASUS MTS, on the Belaya River. Founded in 1857/58, it was a fortress for RUSSIA, which in 1783 began annexing parts of the oblast. In World War II it was captured by the Germans in August 1942 and retaken by Soviet forces in February 1943.

MAIMANA [**Mymana**] (Afghanistan) Town and former khanate in Afghan TURKISTAN, 100 mi SW of Balkh, and 25 mi from the old frontier of Russian Turkistan. Long a subject of dispute between BUKHARA and KABUL, in 1868 it was besieged and taken by Abdur Rahman; its status as an Afghan province was confirmed by a Russo-Afghan boundary commission in 1885.

MAINE [**Le Maine**] (France) Historic region in the NW, bounded on the N by NORMANDY, on the E by ORLÉANAIS, on the S by TOURAINE and ANJOU, and on the W by BRITTANY. Important during Roman times, it was inhabited by the Aulerci Cenomani, who were Christianized between the fourth and sixth centuries AD. A countship since the 10th century, it was united with Anjou in 1126. It became English in 1154 when Henry Plantagenet became King Henry II of England. Taken from King John's territories by Philip II in 1204, it passed back to the house of Anjou. In 1481 it was made a duchy under Louis XII. It was finally united with the French crown upon the death of the duke of Alençon in 1584.

MAINE (United States) In the far NE coastal region, Maine is bordered mostly by Canada on the N and E and touches only one state, New Hampshire, to the W. It was admitted to the Union in 1820 as the 23rd state, as part of the Missouri Compromise.

Burial mounds of the Red Paint people, dating back to the Indian Archaic period (8000–1000 BC), are found in the south-central part of the state, while great heaps of shells indicate that later Indians lived here anywhere from 1,000 to 5,000 years ago. When Europeans arrived the local inhabitants were Abnaki Indians. Norsemen may have visited the coast in the early 11th century and in the 16th century it was known to British, French, and Spanish mariners. Pierre de Monts and Samuel de Champlain of FRANCE established a colony at the mouth of the ST. CROIX RIVER in 1604, but it did not last long. A grant by King James I of ENGLAND to the Plymouth Company included the region, and a colonizing attempt was made in 1607 under George Popham at the present location of Phippsburg, but the colonists returned to England the next year. The French then attempted a colony in 1613 on MOUNT DESERT ISLAND, but the English expelled them.

In 1620 the Council for NEW ENGLAND, which had succeeded the Plymouth Company, granted part of the territory to Ferdinando Gorges and John Mason. The area became known as Maine, and most likely the word was simply meant to refer to the mainland as contrasted with the islands. In 1639 Charles I issued a charter to Gorges for "the Province and Countie of Maine." In the meantime, the first permanent settlements were made at MONHEGAN, SACO, and YORK. After Gorges died in 1647 the colony was neglected until MASSACHUSETTS took it over in 1652.

Maine suffered during King Philip's War of 1675/76 and afterwards as the French and British, with Indian allies, struggled for control of CANADA. Maine colonists participated in the capture of the French stronghold of LOUISBOURG on CAPE BRETON ISLAND in 1745. Patriotic sentiment was strong in the revolutionary period, and in 1765 there was violent opposition to the Stamp Act. A British fleet destroyed Falmouth in 1775, and that same year Maine soldiers fought at BUNKER HILL, while Benedict Arnold led his expedition against QUEBEC through the Maine wilderness. After the American Revolution Maine prospered, particularly with its shipping industry, but it suffered from the Embargo Act of 1807 and the War of 1812. Out of this experience came dissatisfaction with Massachusetts's rule and finally Maine's separation from it.

Maine again prospered and was noted for the quality

of the wooden sailing ships built in its ports. The only major disturbance came when a boundary dispute with the Canadian province of NEW BRUNSWICK set off the Aroostook War in 1839. However, the Webster-Ashburton Treaty of 1842 settled matters without violence. Maine gave loyal support to the Union in the Civil War and for many years afterwards voted Republican. It was the first state to adopt prohibition laws, one in 1846 and another in 1851.

Lumbering and its products have always been a mainstay of the Maine economy, and even today 90 percent of the state is forested. The coast line is very rocky. Soil and climate are not ideal, but Maine grows more potatoes than any other state except Idaho. PORTLAND was the first capital, and AUGUSTA is the capital today. Other cities are BANGOR and LEWISTON. The Appalachian Trail begins at Mt Katahdin, running south to GEORGIA. Old YORK Gaol from 1635 is one of the oldest public buildings in New England.

MAINISTIR BHUITHE. See MONASTERBOICE.

MAINLAND (Scotland) Isle of the SHETLAND ISLANDS, NE of N Scotland, with LERWICK as the admin. hq. There are the remains of a prehistoric village at JARLSHOF.

MAINLAND [Pomona] (Scotland) Main isle of the ORKNEY ISLANDS, off Scotland's N coast; KIRKWALL is the admin. hq. Burial mounds, underground dwellings, the Standing Stones of STENNESS and MAES HOWE are among the prehistoric remains here. SKARA BRAE is an excavated prehistoric village. Traces of Norse tradition are carried on through various local customs.

MAINZ [*French:* **Mayence;** *Roman:* **Maguntiacum, Mogontiacum**] (West Germany) City of Rhineland-Palatinate on the RHINE RIVER, at the mouth of the Main River, 20 mi WSW of Frankfurt-am-Main. One of the oldest of German cities, it grew on the site of a Roman camp founded by Drusus in the first century BC and was destroyed several times by barbarians until Frankish rule was established. In 747 it was made the seat of the first German archbishop, St. Boniface. Later archbishops added considerable territory, which they ruled as princes of the HOLY ROMAN EMPIRE. They had precedence over other electors and crowned the German kings. Under them, "Golden Mainz" flourished as a commercial and cultural center of the Rhenish League. Mainz had one of the oldest Jewish settlements in Germany. It was the home of Johann Gutenberg (1397–1468), who made it the first printing center of Europe. It was occupied by French and Swedes during the Thirty Years War and by France, which took it in 1793 after a long siege. It was ceded to France by the treaties of CAMPO FORMIO of 1797 and LUNÉVILLE of 1801. The Congress of Vienna in 1815 made Mainz a federal fortress of the GERMAN CONFEDERATION and awarded it with Rhenish HESSE to the grand duchy of Hesse-Darmstadt. In 1816 it was made the provincial capital of Rhenish Hesse and from 1873 to 1918 was a fortress of the German Confederation and after that of the Reich. Severely damaged in World War II, it has been rebuilt. Notable buildings include a six-towered Romanesque cathedral consecrated in 1069 and restored in the 19th century; a Renaissance-style electoral palace of the 17th and 18th centuries, now an art gallery and museum; the church of St. Peter of the 18th century; and the University of Mainz, founded in 1477, discontinued in 1816 when the French left, and reestablished in 1946 as the Johannes Gutenburg University. From 1918 to 1930, the university was the headquarters of the French army of the occupation following World War I.

MAIPO [Maipú] (Chile) River in Santiago province in the central region. On the river south of SANTIAGO San Martín defeated the Spanish royalist army on April 5, 1818. The Spanish were attempting to regain Chile after its independence had been proclaimed on Feb. 12, 1818. The victory secured Chilean independence and led to San Martín's conquest of PERU.

MAIPÚ. See MAIPO.

MAISUR. See MYSORE.

MAJĀZ-AL-BĀB [Medjez-el-Bab] (Tunisia) Town in the N, approx. 40 mi WSW of Tunis. During World War II, it was important in the Tunisian campaign from November 1942 until April 1943. See also MASSICAULT.

MAJDANEK (Poland) Village in the SE, a suburb of LUBLIN. This was the location of a German concentration camp in World War II, where 1.5 million Jews, Russians, Poles, and people of 20 other nationalities were killed in gas chambers.

MAJDOL. See MAGDALA.

MAJORCA [*ancient:* **Balearis Major;** *Spanish:* **Mallorca**] (Spain) Largest of the BALEARIC ISLANDS, located in the W Mediterranean, 145 mi E of the Spanish coast. Its capital is PALMA. The kingdom of Mallorca, created by James I of ARAGON (1213–76) after its conquest from the Moors, included MINORCA, IBIZA, ROUSSILLON, and CERDAÑA, or Cerdagne. Reunited to Aragon under Peter IV in the mid-14th century, it prospered until civil disorders and the rise of the Italian cities ruined its trade by the 15th century. From 1521 to 1523 it was the scene of peasant revolts against both the Aragonese nobles and the Italian merchants. During the Spanish civil war of 1936 to 1939 it joined the insurgents and was a base for Italian aid against the Loyalists. The island is known, among other things, for its prehistoric monuments. The abandoned monastery where Chopin and George Sand lived is an island landmark.

MAJUBA HILL (South Africa) Battle site in NW NATAL, in the Drakensberg Range, approx. 75 mi N of Ladysmith. On February 27, 1881 it was the scene of a decisive victory over the British by Boer troops commanded by P.J. Joubert, who had successfully engaged them twice before. The British force was driven from this strategically important location, and their commander, Sir George Colley, was killed.

MAJUNGA (Madagascar) Port town on Bombetoka Bay, in the Mozambique Channel, on the NW coast of Madagascar. Capital of the 18th-century Sakalava kingdom, it was occupied by France from 1883 to 1885.

Retaken by France in 1894, it was the base in 1895 for a French expeditionary force that went on to TANANARIVE and established a protectorate over the country.

MAJURO (United States) Island of the Ratak Chain in the W Pacific. Among the islands seized by Japan in 1914, it was occupied in World War II by the Allies on January 31, 1944. See also MARSHALL ISLANDS.

MAKARSKA [*Latin:* **Mocrum**] (Yugoslavia) Town on the coast of DALMATIA, approx. 35 mi SE of Split. Flourishing under the Romans, it was destroyed in 639 AD by the Avars, who had pushed west from the Steppes to dominate the Balkan area until being defeated by the Franks under Charlemagne in 796 AD.

MAKASAR [**Macassar, Makassar**] [*Dutch:* **Rotterdam; Vlaardingen;** *modern:* **Ujung Pandang**] (Indonesia) Port city in SW SULAWESI. A fort was built here in 1512 by Portuguese travelers to the already active port. Dutch settlers who came in 1607 were massacred in 1618. The fort which they called Rotterdam, and the trading settlement of Vlaardingen were taken in 1667 by the Dutch during the Makasar War of 1666 to 1669. They made Vlaardingen the chief town of their government of the Celebes, or Sulawesi, during the colonial era. It was made a free port in 1848. Occupied during World War II by Japanese forces from 1942 to 1945, it was the site of a five-day battle between Japanese and U.S. and Dutch sea and air forces in January 1942, when the Allies unsuccessfully tried to prevent the Japanese from reaching Borneo.

MAKASAR STRAIT. See BALIKPAPAN.

MAKASSAR. See MAKASAR.

MAKEDHONIA. See MACEDONIA.

MAKEDONIA. See MACEDONIA.

MAKEDONIJA. See MACEDONIA.

MAKEDONIYA. See MACEDONIA.

MAKHACHKALA [*former:* **Petrovsk**] (USSR) City in the Dagestan Autonomous Soviet Socialist Republic of SE European USSR. It is a port on the Caspian Sea, 90 mi ESE of Grozny. Makhachkala was founded in 1844 on the site of an 18th-century armed camp of Czar Peter I. Fought over in the Russian civil war, it was renamed in 1921 for Makhach, a Dagestan revolutionary.

MAKIN [**Butaritari**] [*former:* **Pitt Island**] (Kiribati) Island in what was formerly the Gilbert and Ellice Islands Colony, located at the N end of the former Gilbert Islands, approx. 100 mi N of Tarawa in the W Pacific Ocean. During World War II it was occupied by the Japanese in 1942 and taken by the U.S. Army as part of their attack on Tarawa from November 20 to 24, 1943. This was the first island in the central Pacific to be regained by the Allies.

MAKKAH. See MECCA.

MAKKEDAH (Israel) Ancient Canaanite royal city located in SW PALESTINE. At present not indentifiable. Joshua 10:10ff relates that it was taken by Joshua. Five kings of the enemy nations of Jerusalem, Hebron, Jarmuth, Lachish, and Eglon hid in a cave in which Joshua later had their bodies sealed after he had hanged them.

MAKNASSY (Tunisia) Town, approx. 65 mi WSW of Sfax. During World War II it was the scene of battles in March and April 1943 following the German push through the FAÏD and KASSERINE passes and just prior to the surrender of 200,000 Axis troops in North Africa on May 12.

MAKO. See P'ENG-HU.

MAKTAR [*ancient:* **Mactaris**] (Tunisia) Town in the N, W of Ousseltia. A former Roman town, made a colony in 200 AD, it is notable for the triumphal arch of Trajan, a temple, and the remains of an aqueduct.

MAKUN. See P'ENG-HU.

MAKUNG. See P'ENG-HU.

MAKURIA An ancient kingdom of northern NUBIA that rose into prominence after the fall of MEROË in the fourth century AD. Christianity was adopted by the middle of the sixth century. The capital city, DUNGULAH, located on the NILE RIVER, boasted many churches and major buildings. Christianity's influence here was weakened after EGYPT became a powerful Muslim center. In 1317 it was lost to Christianity when Islam became the official religion of Makuria's rulers.

MALABAR COAST (India) Region comprising the SW coast, stretching approx. 525 mi from GOA to the S tip of the peninsula at Cape Comorin. Coextensive with the old kingdom of Chera or KERALA, it was the scene of commercial struggles in the 16th and early 17th centuries between the Portuguese and their European and Indian rivals. It had had strong ties with the Middle East since mass immigrations of Syrian Christians, especially in 315 and 880 AD, and was largely Christian before Portuguese missionaries arrived early in the 16th century. In 1653 most swore never to submit to Portuguese domination. Various Malabar Christian groups, totalling five million, pursued independent practices until the Second Vatican Council fostered ecumenism in the 1970's. See also CALICUT.

MALABO [*former:* **Clarencetown, Port Clarence, Santa Isabel**] (Equatorial Guinea) Capital city, on FERNANDO PO ISLAND, now Bioko, in the Gulf of Guinea. It was founded in 1827 by the British who leased Port Clarence as a base for the suppression of the slave trade. Many slaves freed by their patrols settled in the area.

MALACA. See MÁLAGA.

MALACCA [**Melaka**] (Malaysia) City and state of the S MALAY PENINSULA, on the Strait of Malacca. Until the 17th century one of the leading commercial centers of the Far East, it was founded c.1400 by a Malay prince who had been driven from SINGAPORE after a brief reign there. The city quickly became a trading link between China, Indonesia, India, and the Middle East; it was an early center of the East Indian spice trade established by Chinese, Arabs, and Indians. Its sultans were in the process of developing a Muslim empire and using Malacca as an avenue for the introduction of their religion to the area when it was taken by the Portuguese under Afonso de Albuquerque in 1511. The last sultan fled to establish his rule in JOHOR. Malacca was captured in 1641 by the Dutch who secured their predominance in the Indies. They used Albuquerque's fort there to guard the Strait of Malacca, then, as now, one of the world's most important sea passages. During the French Revolution and the Napoleonic period, the Dutch retained nominal control, but the government in exile requested that the British occupy the area. Held by the British from 1795 to 1802 and from 1811 to 1817, it was ceded to Great Britain in exchange for BENGKULU in 1824. It was occupied by Japan between 1942 and 1945.

MÁLAGA [ancient: **Malaca**] (Spain) Port city of Málaga province, on the Bay of Málaga on the Mediterranean Sea, 66 mi NE of Gibraltar. Founded in the 12th century BC by the Phoenicians, it was taken by the Romans, Visigoths, and finally the Moors in 711 AD. From the 13th century it flourished as a seaport of the Moorish kingdom of GRANADA and was an independent kingdom after the disintegration of CÓRDOBA. After repeated attempts, Christians took it for Ferdinand and Isabella in August 1487. It was occupied by the French from 1810 until 1812. An important battle of the Spanish civil war was fought here on Feb. 6, 1937, in which Nationalist troops defeated the Loyalists. Historic buildings include a 13th-century citadel, the Gibralfaro. It is the birthplace of Pablo Picasso.

MALAGASY REPUBLIC. See MADAGASCAR.

MALAKAND PASS (Pakistan) Mountain pass of the old NORTH WEST FRONTIER PROVINCE between the former British district of PESHAWAR and the Swat Valley. Important in 1895 during the CHITRAL campaign, it was the origin of the Malakand Expedition of 1897 against the Pathans.

MALAKHOV [**Malakoff**] (USSR) Strategic hill in the CRIMEA, in the UKRAINE, just east of the city of the same name. A major fortification in the Crimean War, it was taken by the French, ending an 11-month siege, on September 18, 1855, shortly before the fall of the besieged fortress of SEVASTOPOL. During World War II it was captured by the Germans in July 1942.

MALAKOFF. See MALAKHOV.

MALANG (Indonesia) City in the Malang regency, 50 mi S of SURABAJA. Traces of its ancient history can be seen nearby in the ruins of the palaces of several kings of JAVA. Developed primarily after 1914 when it became a Dutch garrison town, it was the scene of a Dutch military headquarters during World War II and of the first session of the Indonesian parliament in February 1947. The parliamentary building was burned during the Indonesian revolution.

MÄLAR. See MÄLAREN.

MÄLAREN [**Mälar**] (Sweden) Lake in the SE, extending from the Baltic Sea inland for 70 mi. The site of numerous historic castles and ruins, notably Skokloster and Gripsholm, it was from this general area that the original Swedes, or Svear, developed. BIRKA, on an island here, was the commercial center of Sweden in the ninth and 10th centuries until it was destroyed by Danish invaders. See also UPPSALA, SIGTUNA.

MALASKIRT. See MANZIKERT.

MALATIA. See MALATYA.

MALATYA [**Malatia**] [ancient: **Melitene, Milid, Milidia**] (Turkey) Provincial capital city situated at a strategic crossroads W of the Euphrates, 150 mi SE of Sivas. In an area where known settlement dates back to 4000 BC, it was the capital of a small Hittite kingdom c.1200 BC and was then known as Milidia and was an independent city-state following the collapse of the HITTITE EMPIRE. It was a Roman city much later under Trajan (98–117 AD). Then slightly relocated and known as Melitene, it became a military headquarters, later enlarged and improved under Justinian (527–65). An important city of CAPPADOCIA, it became a metropolitan see in early Christian times. As a frontier town, it has suffered many attacks and has changed hands many times. It became Turkish in 1102 and was annexed by the OTTOMAN EMPIRE in 1516. The modern city is on the site of the headquarters of Hafiz Pasha before his advance to fight the disastrous battle of NIZIP against Mehmet Ali of Egypt in 1838. Melitene includes baths and a 13th-century mosque; four miles farther north is a mound containing traces of the Hittite city.

MALAWI [former: **Nyasaland**; from 1893–1907: **British Central Africa Protectorate**] Republic in SE Africa, bounded on the N and NE by Tanzania, on the E, S, and SW by Mozambique; and on the W by Zambia. The original inhabitants of the area were probably a Pygmy-like people, but in the 15th century Bantu-speaking tribes migrated from the west and north and merged with the Malawi kingdom centered in the Shire River valley. In the 18th century the kingdom conquered much of modern ZIMBABWE and MOZAMBIQUE before its decline due to civil strife and invasion by Yao slave traders. In the 1840's there was further turmoil in the area with the arrival of the Ngoni from SOUTH AFRICA.

The region was visited by Livingstone in 1859. It became a British protectorate in 1891. In 1915 the area was the scene of a rebellion led by a Yao Christian missionary, John Chilembwe, primarily as a protest against British taxation policies. More recently, and before its independence, Nyasaland was part of the Federation of RHODESIA and Nyasaland from 1953 to 1963; this was protested by Nyasaland's black leadership. The nation achieved independence in 1964 and became a republic in 1966. In 1971 its leader, Dr. Hastings Banda, who had led the anti-British movement in the 1950's and 1960's, became the first head of an independent black African nation to visit South Africa. He has alienated many because of his autocracy and by his allowing Europeans to hold considerable influence in the country.

MALAYA. See MALAY PENINSULA.

MALAYA, FEDERATION OF. See MALAYSIA.

MALAY PENINSULA [**Malaya**] [ancient: **Chersonesus Aurea**; *English:* **Golden Chersonese**] Region consisting of the S extremity of Asia. The peninsula lies between the Andaman Sea and the Strait of Malacca on the W and the Gulf of Siam and the South China Sea on the E. It is approx. 700 mi long from its narrowest point at the Isthmus of Kra to SINGAPORE; it is occupied by THAILAND and part of the Federation of MALAYSIA. Over the centuries the peninsula and its inhabitants have been influenced by many cultures: Buddhist, Brahman, Hindu, Malay, Javanese, Siamese, and European. The Malays historically have been the dominant cultural group, and they probably arrived from southern CHINA c.2000 BC. The early Hindu kingdom of Langkasuka in KEDAH state flourished between the sixth and eighth centuries AD. In the second half of the eighth century the peninsula was dominated by the Sailendra dynasty of the SRIVIJAYA, centered in SUMATRA. In the 11th century the Sailendras were replaced by the CHOLA dynasty from the COROMANDEL COAST of India. Beginning in the late 13th century there were other rulers of the region: the Javanese, the Thai king of SUKHOTHAI, the Sumatran kingdom of Melayu, and in the late 14th century the last Hindu holding of JAVA, the state of MADJAPAHIT, and the Thai king of Ayutthaya.

In the 15th century a Malay state, MALACCA, in the southern part of the peninsula, became the most powerful. In this century, too, the Malays were converted to Islam. Europeans then appeared on the scene, PORTUGAL seizing Malacca in 1511. They were followed by the Dutch, who took over Malacca in 1641. Meanwhile, in the 15th and 16th centuries a Malay group from Sumatra, the Minangkabaus, founded settlements inland from Malacca that became the state of NEGERI. In the late 17th century a Malay people, the Bugis, migrated to SELANGOR from CELEBES ISLAND and in 1721 captured JOHOR.

The British appeared in 1786 when they obtained the island of PINANG, and in 1824 acquired Malacca from the Dutch. In 1826 they put Pinang, Malacca, and Singapore under joint administration as the STRAITS SETTLEMENTS. In this same period, SIAM controlled Kedah and PERAK. A new state, PERLIS, taken from Kedah, was also under Siamese control. Following a period of conflict between Chinese and Malays, civil war among the Malays, and piracy in certain areas, in 1896 the British organized PERAK, PAHANG, SELANGOR, and Negeri Sembilan as the Federated Malay States. By 1909 the British also controlled KEDAH, KELANTAN, PERLIS, and TERENGGANU; these states, together with JOHOR, were called the Unfederated Malay States. The peninsula's natural resources and its strategic location made it an inviting target for aggression by JAPAN in World War II. It was invaded and occupied early in 1942 and retaken by the Allies in 1945.

MALAYSIA. See MALAYSIA, FEDERATION OF.

MALAYSIA, FEDERATION OF [Malaysia] Nation in SE Asia, consisting of two parts. West Malaysia takes in all the MALAY PENINSULA not part of THAILAND and is divided into 11 states: JOHOR, KEDAH, KELANTAN, MALACCA, NEGERI, PAHANG, PERAK, PERLIS, PINANG, SELANGOR, and TERENGGANU. East Malaysia consists of SABAH and SARAWAK, the former in N BORNEO and the latter in NW Borneo. KUALA LUMPUR is the capital. After the Japanese were defeated in 1945, the British returned to those areas that they had controlled before World War II. They centralized the peninsular colony as the Malayan Union, but influential Malayans were opposed on the grounds that this brought in so many Chinese and Indians resident in Pinang and Malacca that they would be able to control political affairs. The British gave in and in 1948 established the Federation of Malaya, in which there was no common citizenship. At this time an insurrection by communists broke out, and guerrilla warfare and terrorist acts followed. The revolt was not put down until 1960.

Meanwhile agitation for independence grew and in 1957 was granted. The federation became a member of the COMMONWEALTH OF NATIONS. The first prime minister was Tunku Abdul Rahman, a prince and son of a sultan. Sabah, Sarawak, and SINGAPORE were added to the federation in 1963, and its name was changed to the Federation of Malaysia. Two years later Singapore withdrew from the union. INDONESIA, believing that the British had put Sabah and Sarawak into the federation to keep them out of its hands, opened hostilities on Borneo that lasted until 1965. The government is a federal constitutional monarchy.

MALAZGIRT. See MANZIKERT.

MALBORGETH. See MALBORGHETTO.

MALBORGHETTO [Malborgeth] (Italy) Battle site in Udine province, Friuli-Venezia Giulia region, W of Tarvisio in the Carnic Alps. On March 23, 1797, during the French Revolutionary Wars, French troops pushed back Austrians defending this village and thus opened the way to AUSTRIA through the ALPS. See also LEOBEN.

MALBORK [German: Marienburg, Marienburg in Westpreussen] (Poland) City of Gdańsk province, on the Nogat River, 25 mi SE of GDAŃSK. Originally a castle founded in 1274 by the Teutonic Knights, which withstood Polish sieges in both 1410 and 1454, it was sold to Poland in 1457 by mercenaries. In 1772 it passed to PRUSSIA. The castle, restored in the 14th and 19th centuries, is an outstanding example of German secular medieval architecture.

MALDEN [former: Mauldon, Mystic Side] (United States) City, 5 mi N of BOSTON, in the Mystic River Valley, in E MASSACHUSETTS. Founded in 1640 and originally part of Charlestown, it is the site of several old historic churches. Puritan writer and clergyman Michael Wigglesworth (1631–1705) was minister here for many years. It is the birthplace of Adoniram Judson, Baptist missionary to Burma who has had a church in GREENWICH VILLAGE, New York City named after him. Bell Rock Memorial Park here commemorates the existence of an alarm bell used by the colonists.

MALDEN ISLAND. See KIRIBATI.

MALDIVE ISLANDS. See MALDIVES, REPUBLIC OF.

MALDIVES, REPUBLIC OF [former: Maldive Islands] Republic composed of 19 clusters of coral islands located in the INDIAN OCEAN, approx. 400 mi SW of Sri

Lanka. Originally settled by people from South Asia, the islands were introduced to Islam in the 12th century. The 16th century saw the arrival of the Portuguese, and European domination during the next 300 years. In 1887 the islands became a British protectorate and military base but retained internal self-government. The Maldives gained independence as a sultanate in 1965, and in 1968 the ad-Din dynasty, which had ruled since the 14th century, was ended and a republic declared.

MALDON (England) Town in ESSEX, on Blackwater Estuary, 38 mi ENE of London. It was the scene of a battle in 991 AD between East Saxons and Viking Danes, recounted in one of the last Anglo-Saxon heroic poems, *The Battle of Maldon*, of unknown authorship. The leader of the East Saxons, Byrhtnoth or Brihtnoth, was killed in the battle, after which the Vikings freely raided England. The area has traces of a prehistoric and of an Anglo-Saxon settlement. The 13th-century church of All Saints here has an unusual triangular tower. The town hall dates from the 15th century.

MALEGAON (India) Town and battlefield, in Maharashtra state, 160 mi NE of Bombay, at the confluence of the Girna and Masam rivers. Formerly a military post, it was captured by the British in 1818 during a war with the plundering Pindaris, casteless wanderers who often served as mercenaries for MARATHA leaders. See also MAHARASHTRA.

MÁLEME (Greece) Village and important airport in the CANEA region, on the NW coast of CRETE. In World War II German airborne troops succeeded in taking it from the British after a battle lasting from May 20 to 25, 1941.

MALEVENTUM. See BENEVENTO.

MALGACHE REPUBLIC. See MADAGASCAR.

MALHON. See HOMONHON.

MALI EMPIRE [Melle] Medieval trading empire of West Africa that dominated the Niger bend region and at its height controlled an area as large as Western Europe.

Mali developed from the state of Kangabu on the upper NIGER RIVER and was originally peopled before 1000 AD. Kangabu was a subject state of the GHANA EMPIRE and served as an important link in the lucrative gold trade. As Ghana's control over its empire declined, the Mandingo people of Kangabu regained their independence and strengthened their position. In 1240 their ruler, Sundiata, incorporated the remnants of Ghana into his growing new empire of Mali.

Mali's succeeding rulers continued the pattern of territorial expansion set by Sundiata, capturing gold-producing Bondu and Bambuk in the south; claiming the Niger lands to Lake Deba; and controlling the southern SAHARA DESERT. Under Emperor Kankan Musa (1307–32) Mali reached the peak of its power. Successful diplomacy and military conquest extended Mali's dominion from Taghaza on the northern rim of the Sahara to the southern edges of the savannah and the approaches to the gold-producing countries. The eastern edge of the empire reached the caravan outpost of Takedda, and on the west it bordered on the Atlantic Ocean.

Kankan Musa spread Mali's fame in 1324 when he made a legendary pilgrimage to MECCA at the head of a tremendous, gold-bedecked company. He established embassies in EGYPT and MOROCCO as he went and on his return in 1325 visited the Saharan cities of TIMBUKTU and Gao, which had just been added to Mali through conquest. Kankan Musa set up seats of Muslim scholarship in both places that became famous throughout the Arab world.

Mali's trading empire was active across West Africa and imported great quantitites of fine goods from Egypt and the Mediterranean. Local industry and commerce also flourished, and the city of DJENNE became a great center of learning and wealth. Mali's rapid rise to power outpaced its ability to maintain tightly centralized control over its dominions, leading to its downfall. In the early 15th century, Gao, Walata, and Timbuktu were lost; and the empire was shattered by a multitude of successful rebellions by subject peoples along its fringes. By 1550 Mali had fallen into total and irrevocable ruin.

MALI FEDERATION (Mali) A federation of SENEGAL and the French Sudan, now MALI, from 1959 to 1960. The capital was at DAKAR.

MALINDI (Kenya) Port town in the SE, on the INDIAN OCEAN. Probably founded in the 10th century by Arab traders, it became an important city-state. In 1498 it was reached by Vasco da Gama, who erected a monument that still stands here. It was the early capital of Portuguese East Africa. Nearby, the ruins of the ancient Persian town of Gedi include a mosque, tombs, palace, and encircling wall.

MALINES. See MECHELEN.

MALI, REPUBLIC OF [*former:* **French Sudan**] Landlocked sub-Saharan nation of West Africa bordered by Algeria to the NE, Mauritania and Senegal to the W, Guinea and Upper Volta to the S, and Niger to the E.

Mali's history is linked with the great trans-Saharan trade route of slaves, salt, and gold that passed through its borders. The immensely lucrative trade gave rise to a succession of important medieval powers that dominated West Africa. The empires of GHANA, MALI, and SONGHAI wielded great power from the eighth to the 16th centuries, and the fabled Saharan cities of TIMBUKTU, Gao, and DJENNE flourished as seats of learning and commerce.

Songhai was destroyed by invaders from MOROCCO in the late 16th century, and the country was fragmented into minor power centers led by local chieftains. During the 19th century FRANCE began to expand its colonial dominion into Mali and encountered fierce resistance. In 1898 French dominion became complete over the area, which was renamed the French Sudan. The colony languished as an impoverished agricultural territory under French rule until 1959, when French Sudan and SENEGAL joined together to form the Federation of Mali. This union collapsed in 1960, and French Sudan

The trading town of Timbuktu in the Sahara, now in Mali. The fabled seat of Prester John, it was once a wealthy center of Islamic learning.

became the independent Republic of Mali.

The new nation closely allied itself with CHINA and attempted to develop a Maoist-influenced socialist state. In 1968 a military coup took power and immediately had to contend with the ravages of the devastating sub-Saharan drought, which caused widespread starvation and death. The nation is currently trying to establish a healthy free-enterprise economy.

MALLI. See MULTAN.

MALLORCA. See MAJORCA.

MALMÉDY (Belgium) Town in Liège province. The town and surrounding district belonged to the abbey of Stavelot until they passed to PRUSSIA in 1815. The town, with EUPEN, became Belgian through the Treaty of VERSAILLES in 1919. In World War II it was the scene on Dec. 17, 1944 of the "Malmédy Massacre." Here about 100 U.S. prisoners were shot by the Germans who had just broken through the U.S. front in the ARDENNES, marking the beginning of the Battle of the Bulge.

MALMESBURY (England) Town in WILTSHIRE, ap-

prox. 23 mi ENE of Bristol. It is known for its seventh to 12th-century Benedictine abbey, of which only the nave survives. Aldhelm was its first abbot c.675. William of Malmesbury (c.1095–1143), author of *Deeds of the Kings of the English,* was a monk at the abbey. The town is the burial place of King Athelstan of WESSEX and the birthplace of the philosopher Thomas Hobbes. The tombs of George Washington's ancestors are at nearby Garsdon.

MALMÖ (Sweden) Fortified port in Malmöhus county, opposite COPENHAGEN, DENMARK. Dating back to the 12th century, it was an important commercial center during the period of the HANSEATIC LEAGUE. It played a significant role in the Reformation. On Sept. 1, 1524 Sweden signed a treaty here called the Malmö Recess, which relinquished GOTLAND and Blekinge to Denmark. Under Danish rule until 1658, it was conquered and included in Sweden by Charles X. When the harbor was developed in 1775 it regained importance. Now Sweden's third-largest city, its historic buildings include Malmöhus Castle, begun in 1434 and now a museum, the town hall dating from

1546, and St. Peter's, a Baltic Gothic church from the 14th century.

MALMSEY. See MONEMVASIA.

MALMSTROM AIR FORCE BASE (United States) Military installation in W central MONTANA, E of Great Falls. Developed in 1942, it was the base from which war supplies were sent to Russia under the 1941 Lend Lease Act and later was used to prepare crews for the BERLIN Airlift. Taken over by SAC (Strategic Air Command) in 1954, it was home for the first Minuteman missile wing in 1961.

MALOLOS (Philippines) City of Bulacan province, SW LUZON N of Manila. Settled by the Spanish in 1580, it was the capital of the Philippine republic proclaimed in June 1898 by the insurrectionary leader Emilio Aguinaldo. It was also the meeting place of the revolutionary congress. The republic's constitution was framed here in September and November 1898 and was proclaimed on January 23, 1899, after the transfer by the Treaty of Paris of the Philippines to the United States at the end of the Spanish-American War. The town was captured by U.S. forces in March 1899.

MALONE (United States) Village in Franklin county, NE NEW YORK State, 45 mi WNW of Plattsburg. It was selected as a base for an invasion of Canada in 1866 by the Irish-American secret revolutionary group called Fenians, named after a third-century military corps. Formed in the United States in 1848, it assumed the thrust of the international organization after the Civil War. Eight hundred men, mostly war veterans, crossed the Niagara River in June 1866, captured FORT ERIE, but had to retreat. Most were arrested.

MALOYAROSLAVETS (USSR) City in the KALUGA oblast, E central European USSR, on the Luzh River. Founded in the 14th century, it was a fort for several centuries. In October 1812 a retreating French force found itself confronted by Russians holding a bridge here. After a fierce fight in which control of the battle changed several times, the French drove the Russians from the bridge. This encounter led Napoleon to make a detour, however, so that his troops had to march through the devastated MOZHAISK region. An outer defense of Moscow during World War II, it was held briefly by the Germans. See also FRANCE, RUSSIA.

MALPLAQUET (France) Hamlet in Nord department. In what the duke of Marlborough called a "very bloody battle," in the War of the Spanish Succession, the combined forces of GREAT BRITAIN and the Holy Roman emperor, led by the duke of Marlborough and Prince Eugene of Savoy here met the French army under Marshal Villars on Sept. 11, 1709. Although the French were ultimately forced to retreat after a bitter attack through the forest north of the village, the Allied army suffered more than 20,000 casualties compared to the French 11,000 and were prevented from advancing on Paris. See also FRANCE, MONS.

MALTA, SOVEREIGN STATE OF [Maltese Islands] [*Greek:* Melita] Independent nation in the Mediterranean Sea, S of Sicily, consisting of the main island of Malta and two smaller ones, Gozo and Comino. Malta has been fought over for centuries because of its strategic location in relation to some of the most vital sealanes in the world. The earliest archaeological remains found on Malta date from before 3000 BC to c.1500 BC and include a number of enormous Neolithic, stone temple-tombs. The Phoenicians were the first of the early civilizations to occupy Malta, followed by the Greeks, and, in the sixth century BC, the Carthaginians. ROME, in its deadly war with CARTHAGE, captured the island in 218 BC. Saint Paul was shipwrecked on Malta in 60 AD on his way to Rome as a prisoner. The Saracens conquered Malta in 870 and the Norman kingdom of SICILY followed in 1090.

After the Knights Hospitalers-of St. John of JERUSALEM were driven from RHODES in 1522 by the OTTOMAN EMPIRE, the Holy Roman Emperor Charles V gave them sovereignty over Malta. They founded the capital, VALLETTA and successfully defended it against the Turks in 1565. The Knights of Malta were forced to leave when Napoleon I of FRANCE captured the island in 1798. He was driven out by the British in 1800, and their ownership was confirmed by the Congress of VIENNA in 1815.

The opening of the SUEZ CANAL in 1869 further increased Malta's strategic importance, which was confirmed in World War II when the Axis powers bombed it some 1,200 times without entirely depriving the Allies of its use. George VI of Great Britain conferred the George Cross on the entire population in 1942 to honor their bravery. On Sept. 21, 1964 Malta became independent but remained in the Commonwealth of Nations. The government, however, wished to be nonaligned in world affairs and insisted on the closing of the British naval base when an agreement concerning its use expired in 1979. The base had been maintained for 179 years and, until recently, had been a valuable asset in the Maltese economy.

MALTESE ISLANDS. See MALTA, SOVEREIGN STATE OF.

MAŁUJOWICE [*German:* Mollwitz] (Poland) Village in SE Wrocław province, just W of Brzeg. On April 10, 1741, early in the War of the Austrian Succession, Frederick the Great defeated the Austrians in this town, which was formerly part of SILESIA, PRUSSIA. His victory won him the alliance of France, Spain, Bavaria, and Saxony. See also AUSTRIA.

MALUKU. See MOLUCCAS.

MALVASIA. See MONEMVASIA.

MALVERN (England) Resort town in Hereford and Worcester, 7 mi SW of Worcester, on the eastern slopes of the scenic Malvern Hills. It occupies the site of an ancient British camp and of the medieval Chase of Malvern, a royal forest of 7,000 acres, and was earlier an important ecclesiastical settlement. The Benedictine church, dating from 1083 to 1085, originated in a hermitage endowed by Edward the Confessor. The priory church of Saints Mary and Michael is a fine cruciform Perpendicular building.

MALVERN HILL (United States) Plateau in VIRGINIA, on the JAMES RIVER, 14 mi SE of Richmond. On

July 1, 1862 the last of the Seven Days Battles in the Peninsular campaign was fought here. After extremely severe fighting, the Confederate attack was repulsed, but the Union troops under George McClellan withdrew and did not attack RICHMOND, the object of the campaign. See also FRAYSER'S FARM.

MALVESIE. See MONEMVASIA.

MALVOISIE. See MONEMVASIA.

MALWA (India) Province and plateau region, lying mostly N of the Vindhya Mts but extending S to include part of the Narmada Valley. The seat of an ancient kingdom first ruled by the Avanti, then the GUPTA EMPIRE, it was invaded by Muslims in 1235 AD. An independent kingdom from 1401 to 1531, it was annexed to the MOGUL EMPIRE in 1561. In the 18th and 19th centuries it was a battleground of rival MARATHA powers until British troops took the entire area in 1817. See also MEHIDPUR, UJJAIN.

MALYKOVKA. See VOLSK.

MAMAI KURGAN. See HILL 102.

MAMALLAPURAM. See MAHABALIPURAM.

MAMARONECK (United States) Town in WESTCHESTER COUNTY, NEW YORK State, on LONG ISLAND SOUND, 20 mi NE of New York City. Although in an area acquired by the Dutch West India Company, it was purchased by an Englishman, John Richbell, from the Indians in 1660 and settled in 1676. During the American Revolution it was the scene of skirmishes between Loyalists and militia men and was the home of Loyalist soldier Peter DeLancey. It is the birthplace of the well-known Episcopal clergyman, William Heathcote DeLancey. It was also the home of novelist James Fenimore Cooper, who married a daughter of John Peter DeLancey.

MAMECASTER. See MANCHESTER.

MAMLUK EMPIRE The Mamluks ruled EGYPT from 1250 to 1517, during which time they pursued an aggressive foreign policy, creating an empire that included at one time PALESTINE, SYRIA, and CYPRUS. Originally slaves from the CAUCASUS, the Mamluks were palace guards, and eventually came to be a powerful force within Egyptian society until the early 19th century.

The Mamluks came to power in 1250 when they killed the last Ayyubid sultan and placed Aybak on the Egyptian throne. Under Baybars the Mamluks won an important victory over the Mongols at AIN JALUT in 1260, thus checking the Mongol advance in the Middle East. The Bahrite dynasty, which had ruled since 1250, finally drove the Crusaders from the Holy Land in 1291, with their capture of ACRE, but were succeeded by the Burjite dynasty in 1382.

The rule of the Burjites represents a bloody period in Egyptian history. The Mamluks fought Tamerlane and by 1426 had conquered Cyprus from the Christians. In 1517 the Mamluks were overthrown when the OTTOMAN EMPIRE conquered Egypt and garrisoned CAIRO. However the power of the Mamluks was not completely destroyed, and they were allowed to remain as provincial governors and to join the Ottoman army. As the Ottoman Empire declined in the 18th century they won back much power, but in 1811 their leaders were massacred by the usurper Mehmet Ali, after which they were no longer important as a class.

MAMMOTH CAVE (United States) Cave in SW central KENTUCKY, approx. 28 mi ENE of Bowling Green. Discovered by settlers in 1799, it previously had been an Indian dwelling place. It was significant in the War of 1812 when saltpeter for gunpowder was mined here. It is now a national park.

MANADO [Menado] (Indonesia) Port of N SULAWESI. Established by the Dutch in 1657, it has long been important in the sea routes from Hong Kong to Manila and Australia. In World War II it was held by the Japanese from 1942 to 1945.

MANAGUA (Nicaragua) The nation's capital, on the S shore of Lake Managua. Of minor importance during the Spanish era, it was made the compromise permanent capital in 1857 to end the bitter feuds between GRANADA and LÉON. It was occupied by the U.S. Marines between 1912 and 1925 and 1926 to 1933. It was nearly destroyed by earthquakes in 1931 and 1972. The Palacio Nacional, a government building in the Corinthian style, and the National Library, an ornate Renaissance structure, still stand.

MANAMA. See BAHRAIN.

MANÁOS. See MANAUS.

MANASSAS [*former:* Manassas Junction] (United States) Town in Prince William County, NE VIRGINIA 25 mi W of Alexandria. It was a key railroad junction between the Shenandoah Valley, Washington, and Richmond during the Civil War. The first and second battles of Bull Run, called Manassas by the Confederates, were fought here on July 21, 1861 and August 29/30, 1862.

MANASSAS JUNCTION. See MANASSAS.

MANAUS [Manáos] [*former:* **São José do Rio Negro**] (Brazil) City of Amazonas state, on the left bank of the Rio Negro River, 12 mi above its junction with the AMAZON RIVER. Founded in 1660, when Europeans erected a fort called São José do Rio Negro here, it was then a mission and made provincial capital in 1850. It was renamed after the Indian tribes originally living here.

MANCENION. See MANCHESTER.

MANCHESTER [*former:* **Mancenion, Mamecaster, Memcestre;** *Latin:* **Mancunium**] (England) City and admin. hq. of the metropolitan county of Greater Manchester, on the Irwell River, 32 mi E of Liverpool. The city is on the site of a Celtic settlement. Remains of the Roman occupation are in evidence to the present day. The city was destroyed by Danes in 870 and rebuilt in 920. It has been industrial since the 14th century when wool and linen manufacturing were introduced, followed by the opening of the first cotton mill in 1781. A center of Puritanism in the 17th century and strongly Jacobite in the 18th century, the city became prominent in the liberal reform movements of the 19th century as

The Amazonas Theater in the flourishing city of Manaus in Brazil, surrounded by the Amazon jungles. It was founded in the 17th century.

the center of the Manchester school of economics and the Anti-Corn Law League, led by Richard Cobden and John Bright. It was the site of the PETERLOO Massacre in 1819, when several of those protesting the lack of representation in Parliament were killed by cavalrymen on St. Peter's fields. It was heavily bombed in World War II. The city is the birthplace of David Lloyd George, Robert Peel, and Thomas de Quincey.

MANCHESTER [*former:* **Derryfield, Old Harrystown, Tyngstown**] (United States) City in NEW HAMPSHIRE, on the MERRIMACK RIVER, 57 mi NNW of Boston. John Eliot, Apostle to the Indians, preached here in 1651. Settled by Scotch Irish *c.*1720, it was early significant for its fisheries. For a century prior to the Depression it was a major textile center. It is also the site of the residence of Gen. John Stark, a famous figure

of the American Revolution, who distinguished himself at BUNKER HILL and BENNINGTON.

MAN-CHOU-LI [**Manchouli**] [*1913–1949:* **Lupin**] (China) City in Heilungkiang province on the Soviet-Chinese border. In 1917 and later it became a haven and home for many Russian émigrés fleeing the Russian Revolution.

MANCHOW. See MANCHURIA.

MANCHUKUO. See MANCHURIA.

MANCHURIA [*Chinese:* **Manchow;** *from 1932 to 1945:* **Manchukuo**] (China) Region in the NE comprising the three provinces of Liaoning, Kirin, and Heilungkiang, bordering on the NW, N, and E with the USSR; on the S with Hopeh province and North KOREA; and on the W with MONGOLIA. A center in early history of various Mongol tribes who invaded North China, it was the original home of the Manchus, who rose to power under Nurhachu (d. 1627), conquered China, and founded the ruling Chinese dynasty that lasted from 1644 until 1912. Manchuria, under loose Chinese control from the 17th century, was coveted by both RUSSIA and JAPAN whose rivalry over it was one cause of the Russo-Japanese War of 1904/05. Chinese administration of the area was established in 1907. After the MUKDEN incident of 1931 and the League of Nations' action, it was set up by Japan as the independent Republic of Manchukuo, alternately Manchoukuo, in February 1932 and was made a puppet state ruled by Manchu emperor K'ang Te in 1934. JEHOL was added to the "empire" in 1933, but the entire entity was dissolved at the end of World War II. From 1946 to 1948 it was the scene of fighting between Chinese Nationalist and communist troops, and it became the first important region of China to come under communist control when they occupied Mukden on November 1, 1948. It was a major supply facility, then a base for Chinese troops participating in the Korean War after October 1950. See also DAIREN.

MANCUNIUM. See MANCHESTER.

MANDALAY [*former:* **Fort Dufferin**] (Burma) City and district in the central region, on the IRRAWADDY RIVER, approx. 365 mi N of Rangoon. The second largest city in Burma, it is a religious center for Burmese Buddhists and is noted for the Arakan Pagoda, over an ancient shrine, and the 730 pagodas of the Kuthodaw. It originated as a moated citadel, known as Fort Dufferin, built between 1857 and 1859 by King Thebaw to replace AMARAPURA as the capital of the kingdom of Burma. It was annexed to British Burma in 1885. Heavily damaged in World War II, it was occupied by the Japanese from May 1942 until March 1945, when it was captured by the British after a 12-day siege.

MANDALI [**Mendali, Mendeli**] (Iraq) Town in Diyala province, 75 mi NE of Baghdad. The oldest known canal was built here *c.*4000 BC.

MANDAN (United States) City and county seat of Morton county, in the SW central region of NORTH DAKOTA, across the MISSOURI RIVER from BISMARCK.

Lewis and Clark spent the winter of 1804/05 here, in the course of their expedition to the Pacific, staying in the stockaded Mandan Indian villages.

MANDASOR (India) Town in the former native state of GWALIOR 31 mi S of Neemuch. The Mandasor treaty with Holkar after his defeat at MEHIDPUR concluded the Maratha-Pindari War in 1818. This region has much of archaeological interest. An inscription discovered nearby reveals that a temple of the sun was built here in 437 AD. At Sondani are two great pillars recording a victory of Yasodharma, king of MALWA, in 528. A fort dates from the 14th and 15th centuries, and Hindu and Jain remains are numerous, although the town is now Muslim.

MANDHATA (India) Village in the Nimar district of the old Central Provinces, on the S bank of the Narmada River. It has many temples and is a sacred place to Hindus since it contains one of the 12 great *lingas*, a religious symbol, of Siva. As late as 1824 pilgrims threw themselves from the cliffs above the town into the river. See also KHANDWA.

MANDI (India) Former native state and town within the PUNJAB, on the Beas River, 45 mi NW of Simla. Founded in 1527, it was the most important of the hill states to which British influence extended in 1846 after the First Sikh War. It contains a 17th-century palace.

MANDOGARH. See MANDU.

MANDOR. See JODHPUR.

MANDU [**Mandogarh**] (India) Ruined city in the old DHAR state of central India, the ancient capital of the Mohammedan kingdom of MALWA. Its pinnacle of splendor was reached under Hoshang Shah (1405–34), who is buried here in a marble-domed tomb. A 23-mile wall encloses numerous palaces and mosques, the oldest mosque dating from 1405. Jama Masjid, or great mosque, was founded by Hoshang Shah and is an outstanding example of Pathan architecture.

MANDURIA (Italy) Town in Taranto province, APULIA region, ESE of Taranto. In ancient times it was an important stronghold of the Messapii against Greek Tarentum. Archidamus III, king of SPARTA, fell beneath its walls in 338 BC. The town allied itself with Hannibal, but was stormed by the Romans in 209 BC a few years after his loss of CAPUA. There are ruins of pre-Roman walls here.

MANEHAFD. See MINEHEAD.

MANFREDONIA (Italy) Port town in Foggia province, APULIA region, on the Gulf of Manfredonia, 22 mi NE of Foggia. Nearby is a 12th-century Romanesque cathedral on the site of ancient Sipontum, conquered by the Romans in the second century BC. This was the center of habitation here until stagnant lagoons forced a move to the new town, founded in 1263 by King Manfred, the last Hohenstaufen on the throne of the kingdom of the TWO SICILIES. It was largely destroyed by the Turks in 1620. Of historic interest are a 13th-century church and castle.

MANGALIA (Rumania) Town on the Black Sea coast, 10 mi N of the Bulgarian frontier. Identified with the Thracian Kallatis or Acervitis, it was a colony of MILETUS that flourished until the close of the Roman period. In the 14th century it had 30,000 people and a flourishing trade with GENOA.

MANGALORE (India) Ancient city in SW Mysore state, on the MALABAR COAST, 190 mi W of Bangalore. In the 13th century it was capital of the Alupa kingdom. In 1596 the Portuguese built a trading factory here. The city was seized by Haidar Ali of MYSORE in 1763, then was captured by the British in 1783, only to fall to Tipu Sahib a year later. The British regained it in 1799. Today it is a large and flourishing commercial port.

MANHATTAN ISLAND (United States) Island in SE NEW YORK State, part of NEW YORK CITY, between the HUDSON RIVER on the W, New York Bay to the S, and the East River on the E and the BRONX to the N. With a few small nearby islands, it makes up one of the five boroughs of the City of New York. Giovanni da Verrazano, the Italian explorer, saw the island from New York Bay in 1524, and Henry Hudson, exploring for ENGLAND, sailed past it up the Hudson River in 1609. The Dutch West India Company bought the island from the Manhattan Indians, a small tribe belonging to the Wappinger Confederacy, in 1626. Peter Minuit, the first director general of the Dutch colony of NEW NETHERLAND, paid them approx. $24 worth of assorted merchandise. The town of NEW AMSTERDAM was built at the lower end of the island and was the capital of the colony. The English captured the colony in 1664 and renamed it New York.

Manhattan is the commercial, financial, cultural, and entertainment heart of the city, just as the city fulfills those functions for the country. Manhattan's skyline of towers of commerce symbolizes the city.

MANIKIALA (India) Village in the Rawalpindi district of the PUNJAB. The site of one of the largest *stupas*, or Buddhist memorial shrines, in northern India, and the one first known to Europeans, it was excavated by Gen. Court in 1834. It is noted for its early Greek-influenced sculptural elements, transmitted through the Hellenistic kingdom of BACTRIA.

MANILA [*former:* **Intramuros**] (Philippines) Former capital, replaced in 1948 by QUEZON CITY as the official capital and still the principal commercial and cultural center of the Philippines, located on SW LUZON island, on Manila Bay. Founded by López de Legaspi, the first governor-general, in 1571, the original Spanish fortified settlement of Intramuros, or Walled City, was surrounded by a thick stone wall 25 feet high and 2.5 miles in circumference until World War II. It was developed mainly by Spanish missionaries. During the 18th century, Manila withstood attacks from the Dutch and the British, but on Oct. 5, 1762 a British naval and land force from India forced the city's surrender. In February 1763 Manila was returned to Spain. In the Spanish-American War it was captured by U.S. forces on August 13, 1898 after Admiral Dewey's defeat of the Spanish fleet in Manila Bay. It became the capital under the new Philippine government in 1901. In World War II it was taken by the Japanese on Jan. 2, 1942 and retaken by U.S. forces in February 1945 after lengthy bombardment. Much of the Intramuros was destroyed in the intense fighting, but is somewhat restored now. The church of the San Agustin, built in 1606, remained intact. The 17th-century university complex was used as a prisoner-of-war camp by the Japanese in World War II. There is a monument to nationalist hero José Rizal y Mercado, whose execution on Dec. 30, 1896 led to the Revolution. See also CAVITE.

MANILA BAY (Philippines) Nearly land-locked inlet in the South China Sea, SW LUZON. During the Spanish-American War, on May 1, 1898, U.S. Admiral Dewey's fleet swiftly destroyed the Spanish fleet off CAVITE here with no U.S. losses. In World War II the bay was captured by the Japanese on Jan. 2, 1942 and retaken by U.S. forces in February 1945 after the sinking of numerous Japanese ships. See also BATAAN PENINSULA, CORREGIDOR.

MANIPUR (India) State on the BURMA border, inhabited chiefly by Manipuris and Meitheis. Manipur first came into contact with the British in 1762 when the raja of Manipur signed a treaty whereby the British would protect it against invading Burmese. After a serious uprising took place in 1890, the government was reorganized and again in 1907 and 1917, and remained stable until World War II when the area was invaded by the Japanese from March to June of 1944. They had been repulsed by August 1944.

MANISA [Manissa] [*ancient:* Magnesia] (Turkey) City and province in the W, 20 mi NE of Izmir. Made the seat of the Byzantine government in 1204 under the Nicaean emperors and in 1313 capital of a Turkoman emirate, it was conquered by the Ottoman Bazajet I in 1398. There are many notable buildings from the Seljuk and early Osmanli periods, among them the Muradye mosque. The city was the residence of the Ottoman sultans Murad II and Murad III. Nearby are the ruins of MAGNESIA AD SIPYLUM.

MAN, ISLE OF [*ancient:* **Mona, Monapia**] (United Kingdom) Island in the Irish Sea, off the NW coast of England. Inhabited since prehistoric times, it was under the Vikings from the ninth century until 1266, when it passed to SCOTLAND. All the kings of Man were English after Edward III defeated Scotland in the mid-14th century. In 1765 the island was purchased by the British from the duke of Atholl and became a crown dependency, ending the growth of contraband trade to England. It has its own laws, and its legislature, the Tynwald, is one of the oldest such bodies in the world. There are megalithic monuments, Bronze Age graves, hilltop forts from the Iron Age, and many Celtic and Norse mounds.

MANISSA. See MANISA.

MANITOBA (Canada) One of the Prairie Provinces in the W central region. French and English explorers and fur traders were the first Europeans in the area, at HUDSON BAY, part of which forms its northeastern boundary. Henry Hudson reached the bay in 1610 for ENGLAND, and in 1612 Sir Thomas Button discovered the mouth of the NELSON RIVER. In 1670 Charles II of England granted a large region, including Manitoba, to the Hudson's Bay Company. The area was then inhabited by Assiniboin, Ojibwa, and Cree Indians.

In 1670, the company established its first post, PORT

Churchill, once Fort Churchill, now a major northern port on Hudson Bay in Manitoba, Canada. Its modern docks now ship wheat directly to Europe.

NELSON, at the mouth of the Nelson River, and from 1682 until 1957 it maintained a trading post at YORK FACTORY at the mouth of the HAYES RIVER. In 1717 Fort Prince of Wales was set up at the mouth of the CHURCHILL RIVER. FRANCE was active too, and Pierre de la Vérendrye built a post on the site of present WINNIPEG in 1738. There was off-and-on warfare between the French and the British until 1763 when the former were forced to cede Canada to GREAT BRITAIN. In 1812 the Scottish earl of Selkirk started the RED RIVER SETTLEMENT, but the village was destroyed in 1816 by the North West Company in the massacre of Seven Oaks. Conflict ended in 1821.

The takeover of the Hudson's Bay Company's land by the Dominion led to the Red River Rebellion of 1869. Half-breeds, or métis, in the area feared they would lose their land and their seminomadic life-style. Manitoba became a province in 1870. Its area was enlarged in 1881 and again in 1912. Canada's fame as a wheat-growing nation originated here.

MANJU-PATAN. See KATMANDU.

MANKATO (United States) City in S MINNESOTA, at the confluence of the Blue Earth and Minnesota rivers. In 1862 the Sioux under Little Crow massacred approx. 800 settlers and soldiers. Three hundred Indians were subsequently imprisoned here at Camp Lincoln; 38 were hanged.

MANNERHEIM LINE (USSR) Fortified line across the Isthmus of KARELIA, extending from the Gulf of Finland to LAKE LADOGA, approx. 80 mi long and with deep defenses reaching back nearly to VYBORG. It was planned by Baron Carl Gustav Emil Mannerheim, a Finnish field marshal during the Finnish-Russian War of 1939/1940 and later president of Finland from 1944 to 1946. It was begun in 1939, but Soviet forces penetrated it in February 1940 before it could be completed. It was retaken in 1941 by the Finns and the Germans and retaken a second time by the Soviets on June 18, 1944. The area is now entirely within the Soviet Union.

MANNHEIM (West Germany) City with one of Europe's largest inland harbors, located on the RHINE RIVER, across from LUDWIGSHAFEN AM RHEIN, at the confluence of the Neckar River, 44 mi S of Frankfurt am Main. First mentioned in 766 AD, it was fortified and chartered in 1606/07. By the nature of its geographical location it was involved in many European wars; in 1622 it was taken by Gen. Johannes Tilly in the Thirty Years War; it was completely destroyed by the French in 1689. Rebuilt in 1697, from 1719 to 1777 it served as the seat of the RHINELAND PALATINATE. Captured by the French in 1795 and by the Austrians in 1799, it was awarded to BADEN in 1802. Heavily damaged in World War II, the city's palace and 18th-century buildings, including a Jesuit church built between 1733 and 1760 and the city hall of 1700 to 1723, have been restored. Carl Benz built the first internal combustion motor-driven vehicle here in 1885. Mozart, who lived here in 1777–78, was much influenced by the style of the famous Mannheim orchestra, and Schiller began his career at the Mannheim theater in 1782.

MANNHEVE. See MINEHEAD.

MANRESA (Spain) City in CATALONIA, on the Cardoner River. Probably Munorisa in ancient times, it was important during the Middle Ages. Below a Jesuit convent is the grotto where St. Ignatius Loyola stayed and wrote the *Spiritual Exercises* of 1522/23 on his way back from MONTSERRAT. From here he left for the Holy Land. It has a Roman bridge and a Gothic collegiate church.

MANSFIELD (England) Town in NOTTINGHAM-SHIRE, on the W border of SHERWOOD FOREST, 14 mi NNW of Nottingham. Prehistoric cave dwellings are in the area; and a church here dates back to Anglo-Saxon days. Hardwick Hall, an Elizabethan great house, and Newstead Abbey, home of Lord Byron, are in the vicinity.

MANSFIELD, Louisiana. See SABINE CROSS-ROADS.

MANSFIELD (United States) City in N central OHIO, approx. 55 mi SW of Akron. The site was laid out in 1808 and named for Jared Mansfield, the surveyor general of the United States. It was incorporated in 1828 and is now a manufacturing and commercial center. John Chapman, better known as Johnny Appleseed, the man who traveled from Pennsylvania to this region and into Indiana c.1800 sowing apple seeds as he went, lived here for nearly 20 years. During the War of 1812 he made a trip of 30 miles to bring American troops to Mansfield to prevent an Indian attack. In 1939 the author Louis Bromfield began scientific farming experiments at Malabar Farm, approx. 12 miles south of the city. This ecological center has been continued since his death in 1956. A reconstructed blockhouse of the War of 1812 is in South Park.

MANSURA (Egypt) Capital of the province of Dakahlia, Lower Egypt, near the west side of Lake Menzala. Dating from 1221, it is famous as the scene of the Battle of Mansura of February 8, 1250 between Crusaders commanded by the King of France, Louis IX, and the Egyptians. The indecisive battle led to the Crusaders' retreat and the surrender of King (later St.) Louis.

MANTES-GASSICOURT. See MANTES-LA-JOLIE.

MANTES-LA-JOLIE [Mantes-sur-Seine] [*former:* Mantes-Gassicourt; *Latin:* Medunta] (France) Town of Yvelines department, on the left bank of the SEINE RIVER, 34 mi WNW of Paris. This is the site of the celebrated church of Notre Dame, dating from the end of the 12th century. The previous edifice was burnt down by William the Conqueror, together with the rest of the town. In 1087 in the capture of the town he suffered a riding accident that cost him his life. He bequeathed a large sum for rebuilding the church.

MANTES-SUR-SEINE. See MANTES-LA-JOLIE.

MANTINEA [Mantineia] [*207 BC–125 AD:* Antigonia] (Greece) Ancient village of E ARCADIA, near the Argolis border in the E PELOPONNESUS. Three battles were waged here: in 418 BC, in the Peloponnesian Wars, when Agis, King of SPARTA, defeated a coalition

The 11th-century church of San Lorenzo in Mantua, northern Italy, once a leading cultural center of the Italian Renaissance.

of the Argives and Mantineans urged on by ATHENS; in 362 BC in which Epaminondas was killed in a victory of THEBES over Sparta; and in 207 BC in which the Spartans were defeated by Philopoemen. The victorious Achaean League renamed it Antigonia, but in 125 AD the original name was restored.

MANTINEIA. See MANTINEA.

MANTOVA. See MANTUA.

MANTUA [*Italian:* **Mantova**] (Italy) Capital city of Mantova province, in N LOMBARDY region, on the Mincio River, 80 mi WSW of Venice. Originally an Etruscan settlement and later a Roman municipium where Virgil was born, it was taken by the Lombards in the sixth century AD. The possession of the margrave of Canossa in the 11th century, it became independent in 1115 and was a free commune in the 12th and 13th centuries and a member of the Lombard League. From 1328 to 1708 it was ruled by the Gonzaga family who were magnificent patrons of the arts. It became a duchy in the 16th century. In the War of the Mantuan Succession of 1627 to 1631, France and the German emperor backed different branches of the Gonzagan family. Ceded to AUSTRIA in 1714, it was besieged and taken by Napoleon in 1797. It belonged to the CISALPINE REPUBLIC he created and was restored to Austria in 1814. It was one of the forts of the famous Quadrilateral by which Austria controlled northern Italy and was finally ceded to the Italian kingdom in 1866. The Gonzaga palace has frescoes by Mantegna and Giulio da Romano among other works of art. Other notable build-

ings are the Palazzo del Te built by Palladio between 1525 and 1535, the church of Sant'Andrea designed by Alberti in the 15th century, Mantegna's burial place, and the 13th-century law courts.

MANUS (Papua New Guinea) Administrative district of Papua New Guinea in the S Pacific Ocean, including the ADMIRALTY ISLANDS and adjacent islands; also Great Admiralty Island, largest of the group, with the district capital at Lorengau. The island was the scene of several battles during World War II. Seized by the Japanese in April 1942, it was occupied by the Allies after Lorengau, a large harbor at its eastern tip, was captured on March 18, 1944. It was taken over by Australia in 1947 and became part of independent Papua New Guinea in 1975.

MANZANARES (Spain) Town in the S central region, in Ciudad Real province, on the Manzanares River, 30 mi E of Ciudad Real. The site of a medieval castle, it is one of the chief towns of LA MANCHA. Here is also a Christian citadel founded after the defeat of the Moors in 1212.

MANZANILLO (Cuba) Port city in ORIENTE province, on Guacanayabo Bay. Founded in 1784, it was long a smuggling center for British merchants from JAMAICA. A British attack in 1792 destroyed several Spanish ships in the harbor; this resulted in the fortification of the city.

MANZIKERT [Malaskirt, Malazgirt] (Turkey) Village, approx. 25 mi W of Lake Van. Manzikert was an important town of ancient ARMENIA. A council held here in 726 AD reaffirmed the independence of the Armenian Church from the Orthodox Eastern Church. In 1071 it was the scene of the defeat and capture of Byzantine Emperor Romanus IV by the invading Seljuk Turks under Alp Arslan. This crucial battle crushed the power of the BYZANTINE EMPIRE in Asia Minor, opened the Turks' way to much of the Middle East, and helped lead to the Crusades.

MANZINI [*former:* **Bremersdorp**] (Swaziland) Town in the central region, SE Africa. Founded in 1890, it served as the capital of Swaziland protectorate from 1894 to 1902.

MAON (Israel) Town, approx. 10 mi S of Hebron. Located in the wilderness, it was the home of the biblical figure Nabal, a wealthy man whose insolence angered David in Joshua 15:55 and I Sam 23:24-25; 25:2. The Maonites were apparently a Canaanite tribe of southern Palestine.

MAPUTO [**Lourenço Marques**] (Mozambique) City, port, and capital of Mozambique, on the Indian Ocean, 300 mi E of Johannesburg. Founded in the late 18th century, it became capital of Portuguese East Africa in 1907 and one of its most important ports. In 1975 Mozambique became independent, and the city was renamed in 1976.

MARACAIBO [*former:* **Nueva Zamora**] (Venezuela) Capital city of Zulia state at the outlet of Lake Maracaibo. The country's second largest city, it was founded in 1571 and after 1668 was a center for inland trade. In the 17th century it was sacked five times, in 1669 by the privateer Sir Henry Morgan. Again in the 1820's it was attacked several times during the war for independence; it was captured by the revolutionists in 1823. Since the discovery of oil in 1917, it has become the oil capital of South America.

MARACANDA. See SAMARKAND.

MARACAY (Venezuela) Capital city of Aragua state, 50 mi WSW of Caracas. Under the dictatorship of Juan Vicente Gómez (1908–35) it was the effective capital of Venezuela. It has, from that period, an opera house, a bull ring, which is a replica of one in Seville, and a triumphal arch.

MARAGHA. See MARAGHEH.

MARAGHEH [**Maragha**] (Iran) City in E AZERBAIJAN province, approx. 18 mi E of Lake Urmia, on the S slopes of Mt Sahand. After the Arab conquest in the seventh century AD, it developed rapidly. It was seized by Turks in 1029 but a Kurdish chief soon took control. Significant in the later Middle Ages, the city was destroyed by the Mongols in 1221, but Hulagu Khan held court there from 1256 to 1265 until the establishment of a fixed capital at TABRIZ. Russia controlled it briefly in 1828. A tower built in 1147 is an outstanding example of Iranian brickwork; four other tomb towers and the ruins of a 13th-century observatory are here.

MARAH (Egypt) Locality on the E coast of the Gulf of Suez, the SINAI PENINSULA, in a region occupied by ISRAEL in 1967. According to the Bible, the Israelites first rested here after passing through the RED SEA and entering the wilderness. The waters were bitter, which is the meaning of its Hebrew name in Exodus 15:23. Moses sweetened them.

MARAIS (France) Old quarter in PARIS, on the right bank of the SEINE RIVER. Until the 18th century it was the most aristocratic section of Paris. The Hôtel des Tournelles, once located here, was long the residence of the kings of France; Henry II was killed in its court during a joust. It was replaced by the Place des Vosges, a charming square surrounded by 17th-century houses of pink brick and gray slate.

Maracaibo, Venezuela, a 16th-century town between Lake Maracaibo and the Caribbean. Once a prey for pirates, it is now a major oil center.

MARAJÓ (Brazil) Island in the Amazon delta, between the AMAZON and PARÁ rivers. Pottery has been excavated from prehistoric mounds in the northeast that seems to link the island with pre-Columbian, Andean civilizations.

MARAKESH. See MARRAKECH.

MARAMBA. See LIVINGSTONE.

MARANHAM. See MARANHÃO.

MARANHÃO [Maranham] [*Spanish:* **Maranon**] (Brazil) A state bounded on the N by the Atlantic, E and SE by Pihauy, SW and W by Goyaz and Pará. Discovered by Vicente Pinzón in 1500, it was included in a group of Portuguese captaincies in 1534, but the first European settlement was made on the chief island of São Luís, often called Maranhão, in 1594 by a French expedition under Jacques Riffault. Daniel de la Rivardière was sent to found a colony (now the state capital, São Luís) on the island in 1612 that lasted until the Portuguese took it in 1615. The Dutch held the island from 1641 to 1644, but in 1621 three districts had united to form the state of Maranhão, which remained independent until 1774 when it again became subject to the colonial administration of Brazil. In 1823 Admiral Lord Cochrane drove out the Portuguese, and the state became part of the new empire of Brazil under Pedro I.

MARANON. See MARANHÃO.

MARAŞ [Marash] [*ancient:* **Germaníkeia-Caesara, Germanikeîa-Marasíon, Margasi, Markasi**] (Turkey) Province and city in Anatolia in the TAURUS MOUNTAINS. Inscriptions found here indicate that it was a Hittite city-state c.1000 BC. Captured by Arabs in 638 AD, it was under Muslim control to 1097 when it was captured by Crusaders marching towards ANTIOCH. In 1147 it was taken by the Seljuk Turks. Annexed by the OTTOMAN EMPIRE in the early 16th century, it was held for a short time by the Egyptians in 1832.

MARASH. See MARAŞ.

MARATHA CONFEDERACY [Mahratta] (India) Loosely organized empire of W central India that in the mid-18th century AD was the leading power in India. The Marathas were known for their devotion to Hinduism and their skill as warriors. Their rule began in MAHARASHTRA, a state on the Arabian Sea that was controlled by the MOGUL EMPIRE until the mid-17th century. Sivaji, the greatest leader of the Maratha confederacy, fought the Moguls in 1657 and was defeated, but by 1674 he was victorious enough to crown himself king. Marathan power expanded to include the DECCAN and a good deal of southern India. Marathan princes soon fell to fighting among themselves, however, and by the late 18th century there were a number of separate states. One was in BARODA, now part of Gujarat state, while two others were in INDORE and GWALIOR, both now part of Madhya Pradesh state. Later still, the Marathas fought several wars with the British and were finally defeated in 1818. POONA in Maharashtra was the Marathan capital.

MARATHON [*modern:* **Marathón**] (Greece) Village and plain, approx. 26 mi NE of ATHENS. It was the scene of a battle in September 490 BC in which the Athenians and Plataeans under Miltiades defeated a larger Persian army under Datis and Artaphernes in the Persian Wars. A runner was sent to convey news of the victory to Athens and collapsed after the run. Historians see the Battle of Marathon as one of the first to have long-range influence. The distance of the battle site from Athens, traditionally set at 26 miles and 385 yards, has become the length of the standard Marathon footrace.

MARATHUS. See AMRIT.

MARAZION (England) Small port in CORNWALL, on the shore of Mount's Bay, 2 mi E of Penzance. There are remains of unusual archaeological interest in the churchyard of St. Hilary: inscribed stones date from the fourth century AD—one honoring Constantine the Great, another with Cornish lettering no longer decipherable. There are also numerous British and Roman crosses here. The town is also the site of ST. MICHAEL'S MOUNT where fishermen saw a vision of Christ in 495.

MARBLEHEAD (United States) Town in NE MASSACHUSETTS on Massachusetts Bay, approx. 15 mi NE of Boston. Settled in 1629 by fisherfolk from England, it was important in the early history of the American Navy as an embarkation point; it declined after the War of 1812. It has numerous 18th-century buildings, among them Abbot Hall, which contains Archibald Willard's painting *Spirit of '76*. The birthplace of statesman Elbridge Gerry (1744–1814), the town is also the site of Fort Sewall and Burial Hill cemetery, which contains the graves of hundreds of American Revolutionary soldiers.

MARBURG [Marburg an der Lahn] (West Germany) City of HESSE, on the LAHN RIVER, 46 mi N of Frankfurt am Main. The site of Europe's first Protestant university, founded in 1527 by Philip of Hesse, the town grew in the 12th century around a castle which was the residence of the landgraves of Hesse during the 13th to 17th centuries and which still dominates the city. In 1529 this castle was the scene of the famous Marburg Colloquy, which was significant in its failure to bring about an agreement between Protestants Luther and Melanchthon on one side and Zwingli on the other. A Gothic church dating from the 13th and 14th centuries is the burial place of St. Elizabeth of Hungary, who came here in 1228 to dedicate herself to good works, and also contains the remains of Field Marshal Hindenburg and of Frederick William I and Frederick II of Prussia.

MARBURG, Yugoslavia. See MARIBOR.

MARBURG AN DER LAHN. See MARBURG, West Germany.

MARCHE (Belgium) Town in Luxembourg province, 33 mi SW of Liège. Dating from the seventh century, it was a fairly important fortified town in the Middle Ages and was the site of a treaty signed in 1577 between Philip II and the UNITED PROVINCES. In 1792 Lafayette was taken prisoner by the Austrians in a skirmish nearby.

MARCHE [La Marche] [*Latin:* **Marchia**] (France) Region in the NW margin of the Massif central, bounded on the N by Touraine, on the NE by Berry and Bourbonnais, on the SE by Auvergne, on the S by Limousin, and on the W by Poitou. A countship in the 10th century, it was a border district between the duchy of AQUITAINE and the domains of the Frankish kings in central France. The possession of the Lusignan family in the 13th century, it was seized in the early 14th century by Philip IV of France. From this time it has been known for tapestries and carpets, particularly those made at AUBUSSON. Later acquired by the house of Bourbon, it became French in 1531, following the royal confiscation of the lands of the duke of Bourbon.

MARCHENA (Spain) Town in Seville province, 31 mi E of Seville, near the Corbones River. It is the site of the palace of the dukes of Arcos within whose ruined walls is an ancient Moorish building, now the church of Santa Maria de la Mota, which was taken from the Moors by King Ferdinand III of LEÓN and CASTILE in 1240.

MARCHES, THE [The March of Ancona] [*Italian:* **Le Marche**] (Italy) Region extending from the eastern slopes of the Appenines to the Adriatic Sea, bounded by Emilia Romagna on the N, Umbria on the W, and Abruzzi on the S. Inhabited by the native Umbri and Picentes, Greek colonists for whom part of the region was called PICENUM, it was colonized by ROME in the third century BC. After the fall of Rome in the fifth century, it was invaded by the Goths. In the sixth century the northern section came under Byzantine rule, and the south went to the Lombard duchy of SPOLETO. In the eighth century, Pepin the Short in 754 and Charlemagne in 774, defending Rome against the Lombardian threat, ceded parts of this region to the Pope, thus laying ground for the PAPAL STATES. The name *Le Marche* originated in the 10th century when the fiefs of ANCONA, FERMO, and CAMERINO were established at the border of the HOLY ROMAN EMPIRE. From the 13th to the 16th centuries the popes gradually reestablished their rule and ended local autonomy. The region was occupied by the French from 1797 to 1815, when it was restored to the papacy. United with the kingdom of SARDINIA, it became part of Italy in 1860.

MARCHFELD (Austria) Plain and battlefield NE of Vienna, between the DANUBE and Morava Rivers, on the Czechoslovak border. In 1260 Ottokar II of BOHEMIA defeated Bela IV of HUNGARY here; and in a battle between Ottokar II and Rudolf of Hapsburg in August 1278, Ottokar was killed and the long rule of the Hapsburgs in this region established. In the Napoleonic Wars it was the scene of the battles of ASPERN, ESSLING, and WAGRAM.

MARCHIA. See MARCHE.

MARCH OF ANCONA, THE. See MARCHES, THE.

MARCODURUM. See DÜREN.

MARCOING (France) Town in the Nord department, on the SCHELDE canal near CAMBRAI. In World War I it suffered from fighting around Cambrai from Nov. 20 to Dec. 7, 1917.

MARCO POLO BRIDGE (China) Bridge across the Yungting at Lu-Kou-ch'iao, 9 mi SW of PEKING. Constructed of marble with many arches, pillars, and sculptured lions, and 900 ft long, it is named after the famous Venetian traveler who described it in the travel account that he wrote at the end of the 13th century. See also LU-KOU-CH'IAO.

MARCUS ISLAND [*Japanese:* **Minami-Tori-Shima**] (Japan) Island NE of the MARIANA ISLANDS, approx. 725 mi NW of Wake Island. A Japanese air base during World War II, it was repeatedly bombed by U.S. forces. Administered by the United States after 1945, it was returned to Japan in 1968.

MAREA NEAGRĂ. See BLACK SEA.

MARE CANTABRICUM. See BISCAY, BAY OF.

MAREE, LOCH (Scotland) Lake in the HIGHLAND region. Isle Marse near the N shore is the site of an ancient burial ground and the ruins of the seventh-century chapel founded by St. Maelrubha, or Maree.

MARE GERMANICUM. See NORTH SEA.

MAREMMA (Italy) Coastal area in SW TUSCANY region, chiefly in Grosseto province, along the Tyrrhenian Sea and extending E to the Apennines. A flourishing farming region in Etruscan and early Roman times, it had been drained by underground canals. It was allowed to revert to marshland and was largely abandoned in the Middle Ages because of malaria. It has now been largely reclaimed again through government projects begun in the 19th century by the grand dukes of Tuscany.

MARENGO (Italy) Village in Alessandria province, of SE PIEDMONT Region. During the Napoleonic wars it was the site of a famous battle on June 14, 1800 between the French and the Austrians under Gen. Baron von Melas. With a surprise attack, Melas had almost won when Gen. Desaix de Veygoux arrived with fresh troops to bolster Napoleon's army. Desaix was killed, but the Austrians were defeated and retired to the Mincio. Approximately 15,000 lives were lost in this engagement that did much to further Napoleon's reputation.

MARE RUBRUM. See RED SEA.

MARE SUEVICUM. See BALTIC SEA.

MARETH LINE (Tunisia) Battle site and line of fortification in SE Tunisia, starting at the village of Mareth, near the Libyan border. German Field Marshall Rommel's Panzer Corps, which had made a long retreat across Libya, stopped behind this defensive line and struck out at the Allied armies. From this position on March 6, 1943 Rommel mounted his last raids, directed at the British supply dumps at Médinine. On March 20 the Allies attacked the line and had virtually demolished it by early April.

MARGARITA [Isle of Pearls] [*Spanish:* **Isla de Margarita**] (Venezuela) Island in Nueva Esparta state, in the CARIBBEAN SEA off the coast of Venezuela. Discovered by Columbus in 1498, it became a pearl-fishing center during the colonial era as it is today. In

1561 it was seized and ravaged by the infamous Spanish adventurer Lope de Aguirre, who then sailed to the mainland to attempt the taking of PANAMA. British pirates began to raid the island, and its leading port was destroyed by the Dutch in 1662. Because the people supported Simón Bolívar, who used it as his base in 1816 during the wars of independence, Margarita and neighboring islands were made a state of Venezuela called Nueva Esparta after the country's independence from Spain.

MARGASI. See MARAŞ.

MARGATE [*former:* **Mergate, St. John's, Thanet**] (England) Town in KENT, on the coast of the ISLE OF THANET, 65 mi E of London. Long an important port on the SE end of the THAMES estuary, it sent 15 ships to the siege of CALAIS in 1346/47 during the Hundred Years War. On March 24, 1387 a French fleet was decisively defeated here by English vessels commanded by the earls of Arundel and Nottingham. A popular seaside resort since the early 18th century, it was severely damaged by bombings in World War II. Its church of St. John the Baptist is partly Norman. Just south of Margate the foundation of a Roman villa has been discovered.

MARGELAN. See MARGILAN.

MARGIANA. See MERV.

MARGILAN [**Margelan**] [*former:* **Old Margilan, Stary**] (USSR) Town in the Fergana oblast, E UZBEK SSR, E of Kokand and adjoining Fergana. It is in an area that was important in trade as early as 3000 BC. Situated on the SILK ROAD, since the 10th century it has been a leading silk-weaving center; this ancient city has numerous mosques and bazaars. It is surrounded by high earthen walls with 12 gates and is commanded by a fort. From 1876 to 1907 it was called Stary or Old Margilan to distinguish it from New Margelan, now Fergana.

MARGU. See MERV.

MARGUM [**Margus**] Town in the ancient Roman province of MOESIA Superior, at the mouth of the Margus, modern Morava, River on the Danube. It was the scene of a battle in 285 AD in which Carinus, who had become Roman emperor two years before, defeated Diocletian, who in 284 had been elected emperor of the eastern lands by his soldiers. Immediately after the battle, however, Carinus was killed by one of his men, thus ending the dispute in favor of Diocletian.

MARGUS. See MARGUM.

MARI (Syria) Ancient city of MESOPOTAMIA on the middle EUPHRATES RIVER, S of its junction with the Kahbur River. Excavations by the French revealed temples and other remains of a metropolis of the Jemdet Nasr period in the 3rd millennium BC. Flourishing throughout the Early Dynastic period, it was a sophisticated artistic center. By 1800 BC it was the commercial and political focus of western Asia. The archives of the great king, Zimri-lim, a contemporary of Hammurabi of BABYLON, have been uncovered, as well as his five-acre palace complex of more than 200 rooms. The tablets of diplomatic exchanges allow scholars to fix dates in Mesopotamia in the second millennium BC and provide vivid pictures of life within and outside the city. Hammurabi conquered Mari c.1700 BC, after which it was eclipsed by BABLYON.

MARIANA ISLANDS [**Marianas**] [*former:* **Ladrone Islands;** *Spanish:* **Islas de los Ladrones, Las Marianas**] (United States) Island group, part of the U.S. Trust Territory of the Pacific Islands, including GUAM, located in the W Pacific Ocean, approx. 1,500 mi E of the Philippines. A group of 15 islands discovered by Magellan in 1521, they were named Islas de los Ladrones (Thieves) because of the natives' propensity for pilfering from the Spanish. In 1668 they were renamed Las Marianas by Spanish Jesuits in honor of Mariana of Austria, widow of Philip IV of SPAIN. They were sold by Spain to Germany in 1899, except for Guam, which was ceded to the United States after the Spanish-American War, and were assigned by the League of Nations as a Japanese mandate in 1919 after World War I. During World War II they became strategically important in 1941 and were fortified by the Japanese as powerful bases. From June 15 to Aug. 9, 1944 SAIPAN and TINIAN were attacked and seized by U.S. forces. The Marianas became part of the Trust Territory of the Pacific Islands assigned to the United States in 1947. They now form an important strategic link in the U.S. military network in the Pacific. All but Guam are on the way to becoming a commonwealth within the United States.

MARIANAO [**Quemados de Marianao**] (Cuba) City of Habana province and a suburb of HAVANA. Founded in 1719 by Dominican and Augustinian monks, it was destroyed by fire and rebuilt in 1765 as Quemados de Marianao, developing rapidly with the sugar boom of the 19th century. A military headquarters, Camp Columbia, is located here.

MARIANAS. See MARIANA ISLANDS.

MARIÁNSKÉ LÁZNĚ [*German:* **Marienbad**] (Czechoslovakia) Town in BOHEMIA, approx. 20 mi SSW of Karlovy Vary. It contains a famous spa, the springs of which are located nearby at the 12th-century Tepl abbey. At the end of the 18th century the abbey physician demonstrated the waters' curative powers, and toward the end of the Austrian Empire visitors came from all parts of the world to take the waters. The city has been the site of numerous international congresses.

MARI AUTONOMOUS SOVIET SOCIALIST REPUBLIC (USSR) Autonomous republic in the E central European USSR, in the middle of the VOLGA RIVER valley, N of the Volga. Ruled by the Eastern Bulgars from the ninth to the 12th centuries, it was conquered by the Empire of the GOLDEN HORDE in 1236. The Russians under Ivan IV assumed control in 1552. The region was created an autonomous area in 1920 and made a republic in 1936. The Maris, who are one of the leading ethnic groups here, speak a Finno-Ugric dialect and are akin to Mordvinians and Peremiaks. They are called Cheremiss by the Russians. See also RUSSIA.

MARIA WÖRTH (Austria) Village of CARINTHIA

province, on the S shore of the Wörther See. An early Christian center, it attracts pilgrims to its two 12th-century churches, one with the oldest fresco of the apostles in the country.

MARIAZELL (Austria) Town in STYRIA province in the E central region. Widely noted as a place of pilgrimage, it is famous for its 12th-century woodcarving of the Virgin and child and for the story of a monk carrying it, whose path was blocked by a huge rock, which then miraculously parted. There is also a church erected in 1644 as an expansion of a smaller church built by Louis I, king of Hungary, after a victory over the Turks in 1363.

MARIB (Yemen) Ancient city of the Sabaeans in the Yemen Arab Republic and one of the chief cities, perhaps the capital, of ancient SHEBA, located on the ARABIAN PENINSULA, 60 mi ENE of San'a. Ancient ruins include a great dam, built in the sixth or seventh century BC, which collapsed in the sixth century AD and flooded the countryside, a significant event in early Arab chronicles.

MARIBOR [*German:* **Marburg**] (Yugoslavia) City of SLOVENIA, on the Drava River, near the Austrian border, approx. 65 mi NE of Ljubljana. On the site of a Roman settlement, the present city was known from the 10th century and was important as a Hapsburg trading center in STYRIA until its transfer in 1919 to Yugoslavia. It has a 12th-century Gothic cathedral, a 15th-century castle, and a fine Renaissance town hall.

MARIDUNUM. See CARMARTHEN.

MARIEHAMN. See MAARIANHAMINA.

MARIENBAD. See MARIANSKE LAZNE.

MARIENBURG. See MALBORK.

MARIENBURG IN WESTPREUSSEN. See MALBORK.

MARIENWERDER. See KWIDZYŃ.

MARIETTA (United States) City in Cobb County, NW GEORGIA, approx. 20 mi NW of Atlanta, at the foot of Kennesaw Mountain. In the Civil War it was held for a time by Confederates against Sherman's advance on ATLANTA and was the site of the Battle of KENNESAW MOUNTAIN. There is a large national cemetery where many Civil War dead are buried.

MARIETTA [*former:* **Campus Martius**] (United States) City in SE OHIO, on the OHIO RIVER, 45 mi SE of Zanesville. A pioneer city in the NORTHWEST TERRITORY and the oldest permanent settlement in Ohio, it was founded in 1788 by Gen. Rufus Putnam and the Ohio Company of Associates. In an area then abundant in Indian mounds, the first houses were in a stockaded enclosure called Campus Martius. Gen. Putnam's house is preserved as a local museum, and Mound Cemetery, named for a large Indian mound within its enclosure, is the burial place of numerous American Revolutionary officers.

MARIGNANO [*modern:* **Melegnano**] (Italy) Battle site in Milano province, LOMBARDY region, 10 mi SE of Milan. Marignano was destroyed by Frederick II in 1239. In 1515 in one of the major battles of the Italian Wars, Francis I and his Venetian allies here won MILAN for France. Soldiers for the Swiss Confederates which controlled the duchy retreated, and Milan was then surrendered by Massimiliano Sforza. The battle checked the Swiss military drive and led to the negotiation in 1516 of a "perpetual alliance" between the French and the Swiss. Considered a "battle of giants," it demonstrated the superiority of artillery combined with cavalry, over Swiss infantry. It was also the scene of a French victory over the Austrians on June 8, 1859.

MARIGOT. See ST. MARTIN, West Indies.

MARIINSK WATERWAY. See VOLGA-BALTIC WATERWAY.

MARINA DI CARDO. See BASTIA.

MARINETTE (United States) City and county in WISCONSIN, located on Green Bay, 44 mi NNE of Green Bay city. Named for a Menominee Indian queen who established a trading post and built the frame house here, it was a center for fur trading from 1795 and then of lumbering well into the 20th century.

MARINO [*ancient:* **Castrimoenium**] (Italy) Town in Roma province, LATIUM region, 15 mi SE of Rome. In 1378 it was the scene of a battle between the partisans of Pope Urban VI and those of anti-pope Clement VII of Geneva, supported by the Orsini, who were defeated. Nevertheless Clement retained his power, which led to the Great Schism. In 1399 Marino passed to the papacy, but in 1408 it went to the Colonna family, to whom it still belongs. There are remains of medieval fortifications here.

MARION [*former:* **Jacob's Well**] (United States) City in central OHIO, 43 mi N of Columbus. Named for American Revolutionary Gen. Francis Marion, it was the home of Warren G. Harding, the 29th president of the United States. His house is preserved as a museum, and his burial place is marked by a circular marble monument.

MÄRISCH-OSTRAU. See OSTRAVA.

MARITSA RIVER [**Maritza**] [*Greek:* **Evros, Hebros, Hevros**; *Turkish:* **Meriç**] (Bulgaria) Battle site and river flowing from Stalin Peak to the Aegean Sea. On Sept. 26, 1371 a Turkish army under Murad I decisively defeated a force under three Christian princes of SERBIA who were trying to halt the spread of the OTTOMAN EMPIRE over the Balkans.

MARITZA. See MARITSA RIVER.

MARITZBURG. See PIETERMARITZBURG.

MARIUPOL [*ancient:* **Adamakha**; *modern:* **Zhdanov**] (USSR) Port on the N shore of the Sea of Azov, at the mouth of the Kalmius River, 60 mi W of Taganrog. The present town was built on the site of an old Slavic town in 1779 by Greek emigrants from the CRIMEA and has become a leading industrial center. During World War II the Germans held Mariupol from October 1941 to the end of August 1943. The town was renamed after the war.

MARIVELES (Philippines) Town of LUZON, at the S

end of BATAAN, WNW of Corregidor Island, on Mariveles Bay. In World War II it was the scene of severe fighting in the Bataan campaign in April 1942. It was retaken by U.S. forces on February 15, 1945.

MARKASI. See MARAŞ.

MARKET BOSWORTH (England) Village in Leicestershire, 11 mi E of Leicester. Nearby is the scene of the battle of BOSWORTH FIELD, where, in 1485, Richard III fell before Henry Tudor, earl of Richmond, who then assumed the crown as Henry VII. Circa 1730 Dr. Samuel Johnson was a master at the local grammar school founded here in 1558. The town's church of St. Peter is in Perpendicular Gothic style.

MARKET DRAYTON [Drayton-in-Hales, Drayton Magna] (England) Market town in Salop, on the Tern River and the Shropshire Union Canal, 178 mi NW of London. This ancient town was held successively by the abbots of St. Ebrulph in NORMANDY and Combermere in CHESHIRE. On nearby BLORE HEATH stands Audley Cross, which marks the site of a great battle in the Wars of the Roses in 1459.

MARKET HARBOROUGH (England) Market town in Leicestershire, 14 mi SE of Leicester, on the Welland River and the Grand Union Canal. Of historic interest are the Decorated and Perpendicular Gothic church of St. Dionysius and the grammar school, founded in 1614, a half-timbered building elevated on pillars of wood. There are both ancient British and Roman remains in the vicinity.

MARKHAM (Papua New Guinea) River on E NEW GUINEA ISLAND, which flows S and SE to the Huon Gulf at Lae. In World War II its valley was the scene of fighting during the campaign for LAE in 1943.

MARKIRCH. See SAINTE-MARIE-AUX-MINES.

MARKS [former: Ekaterinenstadt, Katherinenstadt, Yekaterinenshtadt; German: Marxstadt] (USSR) Town in the Saratov oblast, on the left bank of the VOLGA RIVER, 35 mi NNE of Saratov. Founded in 1795, it was named after Empress Catherine II but was renamed in 1922 in honor of Karl Marx.

MARLBORO [Marlborough] (United States) City in MASSACHUSETTS, 28 mi W of Boston. In 1665 settlers from SUDBURY took possession of a hill called Whipsuffenicke by the Indians and gradually hemmed in the Indian village of Ockoocangansett. The town was abandoned for a year after it was destroyed by the Indians in March 1676 during King Philip's War.

MARLBOROUGH (England) Market town in Wiltshire, 76 mi W of London. The Perpendicular Gothic St. Peter's church is said to have been the scene of the ordination of Cardinal Wolsey in 1498. The church of Preshute is where King John is said to have been baptized, and Castle Mound, a prehistoric earthwork, is by tradition the grave of Merlin. The nearby site of a Roman *castrum* called Cunetio was later a Norman fortress in which William I established a mint. A castle built under Henry I was the favorite residence of Henry II and in 1267 was the scene of the last parliament of Henry III. It ceased to be an important strong-

hold after the Wars of the Roses but was garrisoned by the Seymour family for Charles I. The town was besieged and captured in 1642 during the Civil War. Much of it was destroyed by fires, notably in 1653. Seven miles west is AVEBURY.

MARLBOROUGH, United States. See MARLBORO.

MARLOW [Great Marlow] (England) Market town in Buckinghamshire, 32 mi W of London. It is the site of Marlow Place, built for George II, and of a house occupied by the poet Shelley in 1817. Nearby at Little Marlow are the foundations of a Benedictine nunnery from the time of Henry III. Bisham Abbey, mentioned in the Domesday Book, is one mile north.

MARLY-LE-ROI (France) Suburb of VERSAILLES, in Yvelines department, on the SEINE RIVER. In the town are the ruins of a castle and a church built in 1689 by J.H. Mansart, whose work included parts of Versailles. Nearby a huge hydraulic machine, known as the *machine de Marly*, was built in 1682 to supply water to the fountains of Versailles. Judged as one of the marvels of its age, it remained in use until 1804.

MARMANDA. See MARMANDE.

MARMANDE [ancient: Marmanda] (France) Town in Lot-et-Garonne department, 35 mi NW of Agen, on the Garonne River. Founded in 1195 by Richard Coeur de Lion, it passed to the counts of TOULOUSE. It was three times besieged and taken during the Albigensian Crusade; its capture by Amaury de Montfort in 1219 was followed by a massacre of its inhabitants. It was united to the French crown under Louis IX. The notable church of Notre Dame dates from the 13th, 14th, and 15th centuries.

MARMARA DENIZI. See MARMARA, SEA OF.

MARMARA, SEA OF [Marmora] [ancient: Propontis; Turkish: Marmara Denizi] (Turkey) Sea between Europe and Asia, connected with the BLACK SEA through the BOSPORUS and with the AEGEAN SEA through the DARDANELLES. Strategically important throughout history, in modern times it has gained a name derived from the island of Marmara, or Marmora, the ancient Proconnesus, famous for its extensive marble quarries.

MARMARICA (Africa) Desert plateau region in North Africa, along the Mediterranean Sea, between ancient CYRENAICA and EGYPT. In ancient times the scene of conflict in many wars involving Romans, Egyptians, Libyans, and Arabs, it was given its modern name by Italians referring to the northeastern section of Cyrenaica. In World War II it was the scene of fighting in 1942 and 1943.

MARMORA. See MARMARA, SEA OF.

MARNE RIVER [ancient: Matrona] (France) River, 326 mi long, rising in central France and flowing NW and W into the SEINE RIVER at Charenton-le-Pont. It was the scene of major World War I battles, two of them named after it. From September 6 to 9, 1914 the Allies under Joffre, Galliani, and Sir John French forced a German retreat that signalled the abandonment of the

Schlieffen Plan. From July 15 to August 4, 1918, after German successes around RHEIMS, French and U.S. troops under Foch made a successful counterattack at CHÂTEAU-THIERRY, resulting in a defeat of the Germans under Ludendorff and ending the last great German offensive of World War I. In World War II the river was reached by U.S. forces on August 27/28, 1944.

MAROS VÁSÁRHELY. See TÎRGU-MUREȘ.

MARQUESAS ISLANDS [Marquezas] [*French:* Îles Marquises] (France) Island group of FRENCH POLYNE-SIA, in the S Pacific Ocean, N of the Tuamotu Archipelago, 2,000 mi SSE of Honolulu. The southern islands of the group, first discovered by Alvaro de Mendaña de Neira in 1595, were rediscovered by Capt. Cook in 1774. The northern islands, sometimes called the Washington Islands, were discovered by the American navigator Joseph Ingraham in 1791. Commodore David Porter claimed the largest island, NUKU HIVA, for the United States and renamed it Madison Island. The group as a whole was taken by France in 1842, with their administration established by 1870. The islands were the setting for Herman Melville's novel *Typee*.

MARQUEZAS. See MARQUESAS ISLANDS.

The towering minaret of the Koutoubya Mosque in the picturesque inland Moroccan city of Marrakech, built by the Almohad dynasty in the 12th century AD.

MARRAKECH [Marakesh, Marrakesh] [*former:* Morocco] (Morocco) City in the W central region, in the N foothills of the W end of the Grand Atlas Mts. The site of many mosques, fountains, and a 14th-century palace, it was founded in 1062 by Yusuf ibn-Tashfin as the African capital of the ALMORAVID dynasty. In 1147 it fell to the ALMOHADS and passed under the control of the Marinids, whose main city was FÈS. Marrakech was capital of Morocco for a second time from 1550 to 1660. It was taken by the French on September 7, 1912. The former palace of the sultan is now a museum of Moroccan art. Completed in 1195, the 220-ft minaret of the Koutoubya mosque dominates the city.

MARRAKESH. See MARRAKECH.

MARSAH AL ALLAH. See MARSALA.

MARSALA [*ancient:* **Lilybaeum;** *Arabic:* **Marsah al Allah**] (Italy) Port of Trapani province, SICILY, on the Mediterranean Sea, 18 mi S of Trapani. The ancient Lilybaeum was the principal Sicilian stronghold of CARTHAGE in the third century BC. In the late 18th century the town became the center of a rich export trade in its famous wine to Great Britain. Garibaldi landed here with 1,000 volunteers called the Red Shirts at the start of his successful campaign to conquer the kingdom of the TWO SICILIES in May 1860. Its cathedral is dedicated to St. Thomas à Becket of CANTERBURY.

MARSEILLE. See MARSEILLES.

MARSEILLES [*ancient:* **Massalia, Massilia;** *French:* **Marseille**] (France) Port and capital city of Bouches-du-Rhône department, on the NE shore of the Gulf of Lion, 98 mi WSW of Nice. Its settlement by Phocaean Greeks from Asia Minor *c.*600 BC makes it the oldest town in France. It became an independent colonizer, spreading its settlements from Spain to Monaco and was significant in trade as far as Africa. In the Punic Wars it sided with ROME against its commercial rival, CARTHAGE. Rome annexed it in 49 BC after it pitted itself against Caesar in the Roman civil war. Falling into decline in the early Middle Ages, it again emerged as a commercial center during the Crusades and was a main transit port for the Holy Land. Taken by Charles I of ANJOU in the 13th century, it was sacked by Alfonso V of ARAGON in 1423. In the 15th century it was a flourishing center of art and trade. Several times besieged, it was invaded by Louis XIV to put down uprisings during the Fronde. Half the population died of plague in 1720. The scene of conflict in the French Revolution, it gave its name to the French national anthem, supposedly composed here. The opening of the SUEZ CANAL led to development of the port, which was a military embarkation point during and after World War I. In World War II it was occupied by the Germans from November 1942 until August 1944. The landmark of its harbor is the Château d'If, a castle on a small rocky isle.

MARSHALL (United States) City in Harrison county, NE TEXAS, 38 miles W of Shreveport, Louisiana. Settled in 1841, during the Civil War it served as the temporary capital of MISSOURI for the Confederacy.

MARSHALL ISLANDS (United States) Island group in Micronesia in the central Pacific Ocean, E of the Carolines and NW of the Gilberts. Possibly first sighted by a Spanish navigator in 1529, in 1788 they were explored by the British captains Gilbert and Marshall and mapped by 19th-century Russian expeditions. Germany claimed the islands in 1885 and purchased rights to them from Spain in 1899. In 1914 they were invaded and seized by Japan. Made a Japanese mandate in 1920, they were held by Japan from 1935 until January/February 1944 when they were captured by U.S.

forces. In 1947 they became part of the U.S. Trust Territory of the Pacific Islands. See also BIKINI, ENIWETOK.

MARSHFIELD (United States) Town in Plymouth county, SE MASSACHUSETTS, 15 mi E of Brockton. The residence of Daniel Webster during the latter part of his life and his burial place, it is also the site of several colonial buildings, including Winslow House, home of the colonial leader Edward Winslow.

MARS-LA-TOUR (France) Village in Meurthe-et-Moselle department, SW of Metz. With nearby Vionville, it was the scene of a battle on Aug. 16, 1870 during the Franco-Prussian War. Following the Battle of COLOMBEY, the retreating French under newly-appointed Supreme Commander Achille François Bazaine were surrounded and defeated here by the army led by Prince Frederick Charles of PRUSSIA.

MARSTON MOOR (England) Battlefield in North Yorkshire, 7 mi W of York. In the English Civil War it was the scene of a battle on July 2, 1644. Here the Parliamentarians under Lord Fairfax of Cameron, Oliver Cromwell, and Leslie, earl of Leven, defeated the Royalists under Prince Rupert and Goring, duke of Newcastle after Prince Rupert had rescued York from siege. This first major victory for the Parliamentarians was the largest and bloodiest battle of the war.

MARTABAN (Burma) Town in the Thaton district of Lower Burma, on the right bank of the SALWEEN, opposite MOULMEIN. Founded in 573 AD by the first king of PEGU, it was once the capital of a powerful Talaing (Mon) kingdom. It was twice captured by the British, in 1824 and 1852. It is now known primarily for its pottery vessels, called Pegu jars in India.

MARTHASVILLE. See ATLANTA.

MARTHA'S VINEYARD (United States) Island in the Atlantic Ocean, off the SW coast of CAPE COD, SE MASSACHUSETTS. Discovered in 1602 by Capt. Bartholomew Gosnold, it was first settled by the English in 1642 and became an important commercial center. Whaling and fishing became the main occupations in the 18th and 19th centuries. These industries were seriously crippled by the American Revolution and the War of 1812. At present it is a popular summer resort.

MARTINIQUE [La Martinique] (France) Island of the Caribbean Windward Islands, in the E WEST INDIES. Discovered by Columbus in 1502, in 1635 it was settled by the French who promised the Caribs half the island, but instead killed them off to bring in slaves. It passed to the French crown in 1674 and was attacked by both the Dutch and the English in the 17th century. Captured by Baron George Rodney in 1762, but restored to France, it was occupied by Great Britain from 1794 to 1802 and 1809 to 1814. Slavery was abolished in 1848 but sugar remained a major industry. The island supported the Vichy government at the outset of World War II, but in 1943 a U.S. naval blockade forced it to transfer its allegiance to the Free French. The French constitution of 1946 made it an overseas department of France. It was the birthplace of the Empress Joséphine, Napoleon's consort.

MARTINPUICH (France) Village in the Pas-de-Calais department 6 mi NE of Albert. In World War I it was the site of a battle on September 15, 1916. See also SOMME.

MARTINSBURG (United States) Industrial city in the E panhandle of NE WEST VIRGINIA. Strategically placed on a railroad, it was an important base and objective in the SHENANDOAH VALLEY campaigns of 1861 to 1863 during the Civil War. The Confederate spy, Belle Boyd, lived here and was imprisoned in the old courthouse.

MARTINS FERRY (United States) Industrial city on the OHIO RIVER, in E Ohio, 19 mi S of Steubenville. The birthplace of William Dean Howells, the novelist, it is also the burial place of Elizabeth and Ebenezer Zane. These were siblings in the family noted for its pioneering and heroic combat during the American Revolution and for the settlement at WHEELING, West Virginia.

MARWAR. See JODHPUR.

MARXSTADT. See MARKS.

MARY. See MERV.

MARY ISLAND. See CANTON ATOLL.

MARYLAND (United States) Seaboard state in the country's Middle Atlantic region, it was the seventh of the original 13 colonies to ratify the Constitution, in April 1788. It is bounded by Pennsylvania to the N, Delaware to the E, Virginia to the S, and West Virginia to the W.

In 1498 John Cabot sailed along its coast and was probably the first European to see Maryland. In 1524 Giovanni da Verrazano, an Italian sailing for FRANCE, probably visited the CHESAPEAKE BAY area. Later explorers included Pedro Menéndez Marqués in 1574, Bartholomew Gilbert in 1603, and Captain John Smith in 1608. William Claiborne of Virginia set up a fur-trading post in 1631 on KENT ISLAND. The next year Charles I of ENGLAND granted a vaguely defined area that included Maryland to George Calvert, first Lord Baltimore. The grant was named in honor of Henrietta Maria, the queen consort. Lord Baltimore's son undertook to develop the colony, partly to provide a haven for his persecuted fellow Catholics, partly to make money; and in 1634 two ships brought a party that established ST. MARY'S CITY.

As early as 1650 the colony had a legislature that was empowered to make laws. The year before that a toleration law to protect Catholics against Puritan bigotry went into effect, but it was repealed in 1654 following a civil war in which the Protestant small farmers defeated the Catholic large landholders. After the Glorious Revolution of 1688 in England, the crown took control, and in 1691 Maryland became a royal province. During the American Revolution, Maryland supplied troops to the Continental Army and added a bill of rights to a new constitution. BALTIMORE, founded in 1729, boomed and by 1800 had a population of 30,000. In the 1830's Baltimore was famous for the speedy clipper ships built in its shipyards.

During the War of 1812, the British attack in 1814 on FORT McHENRY, which protected Baltimore, inspired

Francis Scott Key to write *The Star-Spangled Banner* on the spot. The war was followed by bustling expansion, aided by the NATIONAL ROAD, started in 1815, the eastern end of which was in Maryland; by the Chesapeake and Delaware Canal in 1829; and by the United States' first railroad, the Baltimore and Ohio, in 1830. Despite some strong Confederate sentiment, the state remained in the Union in the Civil War, although in April, 1861 a mob attacked MASSACHUSETTS troops as they passed through Baltimore. Marylanders fought on both sides in the conflict. In September 1862 Gen. Robert E. Lee was repulsed at the Battle of ANTIETAM, and in 1863 his army crossed the state going to and from the Battle of GETTYSBURG. Maryland abolished slavery in 1864.

Industry revived after the war until the Panic of 1873, which caused serious labor trouble. In 1877 a railroad strike over wages resulted in rioting with bloodshed in CUMBERLAND and Baltimore. The 20th century, however, has seen Maryland a leader in labor and social-reform legislation. Large numbers of people moved into Maryland during both world wars for jobs in shipbuilding and the aircraft industry. In more recent years, many Marylanders found jobs with the growing Federal bureaucracy in WASHINGTON D.C., and the government now has many facilities in the state.

ANNAPOLIS has been the capital since 1694 and is the site of the United States Naval Academy. Baltimore is the largest city.

MARYPORT (England) Market town and seaport in Cumbria, 25 mi WSW of Carlisle. It is the site of many remains of the Roman period. Of particular interest is the Roman fort called Uxellodunum, which guarded the coast from a hill north of the town.

MARYVILLE (United States) City in Blount county, E TENNESEE, near the Great Smoky Mountains National Park, 15 mi S of Knoxville. Sam Houston of TEXAS (1793–1863) and his family arrived here in 1807. He spent much of his youth with the local Cherokee Indians and taught in the nearby log schoolhouse, which still stands.

MARZABOTTO (Italy) Village in Bologna province, Emilia-Romagna region, 17 mi SSW of Bologna. At nearby Villa Aria are the excavated ruins of an Etruscan town with tombs and temples from the fifth century BC.

MASADA (Israel) Ancient fortified citadel and palace in the desert of JUDAEA, on the W shore of the DEAD SEA. It is situated atop a flat rock that towers some 1300 feet above desert and sea. It was built in the first or second century BC and substantially expanded between 37 and 31 BC by Herod the Great, king of Judaea. In 66 AD at the beginning of the great Jewish revolt against Rome, an extremist Jewish sect, the Zealots, surprised and masssacred the Roman garrison. The fortress remained under Zealot control until 73 AD when 15,000 Roman soldiers finally subdued it. Most of the 1,000 men, women, and children holding the fortress chose to commit suicide rather than surrender. Only two women and five children survived to tell of the Zealots' last action. Excavated between 1963 and 1965,

it is now a prized Israeli historic shrine. Roman military campsites at its foot are also preserved, as well as the huge ramp up its side built in the siege. Masada is today a ceremonial center for the Israeli army.

MASCARA (Algeria) Town in the Mostaganem department, 60 mi SE of Oran. Located on the site of a Roman settlement, from the 16th to the 18th centuries it served as the capital of the Turkish province in Western Algeria. Its importance increased in 1832 when it became the headquarters of the Algerian emir, Abd-el-Kader, or Kadir, who preached a holy war against the French at a mosque here. Captured by the French in 1835, it changed hands several times in the next six years and suffered considerable damage.

MASCARENE ISLANDS Island group in the Indian Ocean approx. 450 mi E of Madagascar. Probably known much earlier to the Arabs, the islands were rediscovered by Pedro Mascarenhas of PORTUGAL c.1510. See MAURITIUS, RÉUNION, RODRIGUEZ.

MAS D'AZIL, LE. See LE MAS D'AZIL.

MASERFIELD Town in NW Salop, 17 mi NW of Shrewsbury. As a village in medieval MERCIA, it was the site of a battle in 642 AD in which King Oswald of NORTHUMBRIA was defeated and slain in battle against King Penda's Mercian soldiers. The town was fortified in the 12th century and was involved in the wars with WALES.

MASERU (Lesotho) Capital town in S Africa on the Caledon River, near the border with ORANGE FREE STATE, Republic of SOUTH AFRICA. Established in 1869 as capital of the Basuto people by Moshesh I, their paramount chief, it served as capital of the British Basutoland protectorate from 1869 to 1871 and from 1884 to 1966, when Lesotho achieved independence. It is one of the first capitals in all of southern Africa. Many of the original buildings were destroyed during conflicts in 1880.

MASHHAD [Meshed] [*former:* **Sanabadh**] (Iran) City, shrine, and provincial capital, in the valley of a tributary of the Hari Rud. For centuries it was an important trading center and junction point on caravan routes and highways from India to TEHERAN and from north to south between TURKISTAN and the Gulf of OMAN. The city was attacked by Oghuz Turks in the 12th century and by Mongols in the 13th century. It was revived in the 14th century and renamed. It enjoyed its greatest significance in the 18th century when Nadir Shah made it the capital of PERSIA. In the 19th and 20th centuries it has become strategically important because of its location on the Russian and Afghan borders. Its name is Arabic for "place of martyrdom," and it is the site of the beautiful shrine of Imam Ali Riza, the goal of extensive Shiite pilgrimages. Nearby are the ruins of Tus, the birthplace of the poet Firdausi and the philosopher al-Ghazali.

MASHONALAND (Zimbabwe) Former province, now divided into Northern and Southern Mashonaland and inhabited by the Mashonas, a Bantu tribe. Acquired by the British South Africa Company in 1890, it became part of the colony of Southern Rhodesia in 1923. See also MATABELALAND, RHODESIA, SALISBURY.

MASIS. See ARARAT, MOUNT.

MASKAT. See MASQAT.

MASON AND DIXON'S LINE [Mason-Dixon Line] (United States) The S boundary line of PENNSYLVANIA, except for its westernmost 36 mi. It was established between 1763 and 1767 by two English astronomers, Charles Mason and Jeremiah Dixon, to settle an old boundary dispute between the Penn and Calvert families, the proprietors of Pennsylvania and MARYLAND, submitted to a British court in 1735. Later the western part was accepted as the boundary between VIRGINIA and Pennsylvania. By 1820, with the Missouri Compromise, the line was used to mark the boundary between free and slave states. The name was later generally applied as the dividing line between the states of the North and of the South.

MASON-DIXON LINE. See MASON AND DIXON'S LINE.

MASOVIA [*Polish:* Mazowsze] (Poland) Region almost coextensive with Warsaw province, in central Poland. Part of Poland since the 10th century, Masovia became an independent duchy when Boleslaus III died in 1138. In 1351 it became a fief of Great Poland and was finally united with it in 1526. Passed to PRUSSIA during the 18th-century partitions of Poland, it became part of the Russian Empire from 1807 to 1814, and reverted to Poland in 1918.

MASQAT [Maskat, Muscat] (Oman) Capital city of Oman in the SE ARABIAN PENINSULA, on the S coast of the Gulf of Oman. Under the Persians from the sixth century BC, it embraced the Muslim faith in 630 AD. Seized by the Portuguese navigator Alfonso de Albuquerque in 1508, it was a minor Portuguese port until made their Arabian headquarters from 1622 to 1648 after the loss of HORMUZ. Held by the Persians from 1650 to 1741, it became an independent sultanate with its capital at ZANZIBAR from 1832 to 1856. Its greatest influence was in the 19th century. See also PERSIA.

MASQAT AND OMAN. See OMAN.

MASSA (Italy) Capital city of Massa-Carrara province, TUSCANY region. From the 15th century until 1829 it was the capital of the independent principality, later duchy, of Massa-Carrara. It then passed through marriage to the house of Austria-Este, dukes of MODENA, and in 1859 was united with the kingdom of SARDINIA. The old town centers around the 15th-century Malaspina family castle. See also CARRARA.

MASSACHUSETTS (United States) State in the NE, in the NEW ENGLAND region, it was the sixth of the original 13 colonies to ratify the Constitution, in February 1788. The state takes its name from an Algonquian word, originally the name of a village, meaning "large-hill-place." It borders New York on the W and every state in New England but Maine; it includes the Cape Cod peninsula and the islands of Martha's Vineyard and Nantucket. The Connecticut, Concord and Merrimack, and Charles are its major rivers.

Norsemen probably sailed along the Massachusetts coast in the 11th century, and in the late 16th and early 17th centuries various navigators, mostly English, reached the area. In November 1620 the ship *Mayflower*, from PLYMOUTH, ENGLAND, landed the Pilgrims, who established PLYMOUTH Colony. The Pilgrims celebrated the first American Thanksgiving in October 1621. Life was hard, but other settlements were soon made: Weymouth in 1622, QUINCY in 1625, and SALEM in 1626. BOSTON was founded in 1630. Beginning in 1629, the Massachusetts Bay Company ruled this colony from Boston for approx. 50 years. The colony was also a Puritan theocracy, and dissenters such as Roger Williams were suppressed or exiled. Nevertheless, Massachusetts town meetings were the beginnings of American democracy. The Puritans believed strongly in education, and founded the Boston Latin School in 1635 and Harvard College in 1636.

The colony engaged in a long struggle with neighboring Indians, scattering one tribe in 1638 in the Pequot War and breaking the power of the Wampanoags in King Philip's War of 1675/76. During the French and Indian War the frontier was often attacked, and pioneers suffered such horrors as the massacre at DEERFIELD in 1704. In 1688 a royal colony was formed out of Massachusetts Bay, Plymouth, and MAINE. As enemies outside disappeared, the colonists found them within; in Salem in 1692 twenty persons were put to death on a charge of witchcraft.

From 1763 on Massachusetts struggled against restrictions placed on it by the Navigation Acts, the Stamp Act of 1765, and other British laws. The first violence occurred in March 1770 in the Boston Massacre, when British soldiers fired on a rioting crowd, killing five. Three years later, in December 1773 Bostonians protested against the tax on tea by holding the Boston Tea Party and dumping imported tea into Boston harbor. The first battles of the American Revolution occurred in April 1775 when at LEXINGTON and CONCORD "embattled farmers" confronted British troops and harried them back to Boston after losses on both sides. In June came the Battle of BUNKER HILL, which the British won after heavy casualties. After the Americans set up artillery on the surrounding hills, however, the British evacuated Boston in March 1776. During the ensuing American Revolution, Massachusetts, with VIRGINIA, was a mainstay of the cause, providing wise leadership.

After the Revolution, economic conditions were poor, especially for the debt-ridden farmers. The result was Shays's Rebellion of 1786/87, led by Daniel Shays against the commercial interests which controlled the state. Troops routed the rebels. The importance of shipping, including the growing CHINA trade, caused Massachusetts to resent the Embargo Act of 1807 and the War of 1812. On the other hand, these circumstances helped American industry, and Massachusetts soon became the first center of textile manufacturing, focused on the MERRIMACK and other rivers. Massachusetts whalers from NEWBURYPORT, NANTUCKET, MARTHA'S VINEYARD, and NEW BEDFORD continued its sea life, while fishing fleets from CAPE COD and Cape Ann, especially GLOUCESTER, remained important.

For a number of years during the mid-19th century, Massachusetts was the intellectual and cultural center of the nation. It was the home of religious movements such as Unitarianism; of philosophical movements such as Ralph Waldo Emerson's Transcendentalism; of reforms in education and the treatment of the mentally ill; of experiments in utopianism such as Brook Farm; and the writers Nathaniel Hawthorne, Henry Wadsworth Longfellow, and Henry David Thoreau. The state was also a hotbed of abolitionism, and when the Civil War came it sent more than 130,000 men to the Union armies. Industry grew after the war as bankers financed western expansion and many new immigrants provided labor. Shipping declined as steamboats replaced clipper ships and petroleum replaced whale oil. There were violent labor disputes such as the LOWELL textile strike of 1912, but World War II later spurred more industrial growth.

The state is the home of several of the nation's most prestigious colleges and universities, including Harvard, MIT, Amherst, and Smith. From the 1960's on the Boston suburbs of Route 128 have been a national center of high technology, computer, and electronics industries.

Boston is the capital and largest city; others include CAMBRIDGE, FALL RIVER, LOWELL, NEW BEDFORD, SPRINGFIELD, and WORCESTER.

MASSACRE BAY (United States) Inlet on the SE coast of Attu Island in the ALEUTIAN ISLANDS, ALASKA. In World War II, the landing of U.S. troops here resulted in a defeat of the Japanese in May and June 1943.

MASSACRE HILL (United States) Battlefield in WYOMING, approx. 5 mi from site of Fort Phil Kearny. Here on Dec. 21, 1866 during the Sioux Wars, a force of some 80 men under Capt. William Fetterman from Fort Phil Kearney were massacred by the Sioux Indians under Chief High Backbone when they attempted to rescue a besieged baggage train. They were trapped by a vastly larger Sioux force. The battle called "The Fetterman Massacre," was followed by a siege of the fort.

MASSACRE ISLAND. See DAUPHIN ISLAND.

MASSAH [Massah and Meribah, Meribah] (Israel) Symbolic place near HOREB where Moses brought forth water from the rock, as narrated in Exodus 17:7.

MASSAH AND MERIBAH. See MASSAH.

MASSALIA. See MARSEILLES.

MASSAUA. See MASSAWA.

MASSAWA [Massaua, Massowa, Mesewa, Mitsiwa] (Ethiopia) Port city of Eritrea province, on the RED SEA. It was part of the kingdom of AXUM from the first to the eighth centuries AD. It was invaded in 1541 by the son of Vasco da Gama, who arrived to help push back the Muslim takeover of Ethiopia. In 1557 the city was captured by the OTTOMAN EMPIRE, which finally transferred it to Egyptian control in 1865. Taken by ITALY in 1885, from 1889 to 1900 it was the capital of the Italian colony of ERITREA. It was the base from which Italy invaded Ethiopia in 1935/36 and was captured by the British on April 8, 1941. At present it is the main base of the Ethiopian navy.

MASSÉNYA. See BAGUIRMI.

MASSICAULT (Tunisia) Town, 12 mi SW of TUNIS, on the road between Tunis and MAJĀZ-AL-BĀB. In World War II it was taken by the British on May 6, 1943.

MASSILIA. See MARSEILLES.

MASSILLON (United States) City in NE OHIO, 8 mi W of Canton. Founded by James Duncan in 1826 with the opening of the OHIO AND ERIE CANAL and named for a French bishop, it was the home of Jacob S. Coxey, the social reformer who advocated public works for the jobless. With more than a hundred in his "Army," he left the city on Easter 1894 to reach Washington, D. C. for a May Day protest against unemployment. Few joined along the way, and its leaders were arrested in front of the Capitol. Coxey, who also served as Massillon's mayor in the early 1930's, unsuccessfully ran for the U.S. presidency in 1932 and 1936.

MASSOWA. See MASSAWA.

MASUREN. See MASURIA.

MASURIA [Mazuria] [German: **Masuren**; Polish: **Mazury**] (Poland) Region in the NE, including the 2,700 Masurian Lakes. In the 14th century the Teutonic Knights pushed out the native Prussians and Polish settlers and moved in. Later the region became part of EAST PRUSSIA and was largely under German influence by the early 20th century. It was the scene of three battles in World War I resulting in severe defeats for the Russian armies. In August 1914 Samsonov was defeated by Hindenburg at TANNENBERG; in September 1914 Rennenkampf was defeated by Mackensen; a third defeat occurred at SUWALKI between February 7 and 14, 1915 in the Winter Battle of Masuria. Under Soviet control at the end of World War II, it was assigned to Poland by the Potsdam Conference of 1945; the German population was replaced by Poles once again. See also MAZOVIA.

MASYĀF (Syria) Mountain stronghold in E LATAKIA, at the S end of Djebel Ansariya. In the 12th century it became the chief seat of the Syrian branch of the Assassins, a secret order encountered by Marco Polo and the Crusaders; the English word "assassin" derives from this Ismaili sect, reportedly spurred on to their killing by the taking of hashish, hence their name. It was taken in 1272 by the MAMLUK sultan of Egypt, Baybars.

MATABELELAND (Zimbabwe) Former province in the SW in the region between the Limpopo and Zambezi rivers. Now divided into Northern and Southern Matabeleland, it is inhabited by the Matabele, a Zulu tribe of the Bantu nation. Under the leadership of Mzilikazi in 1823, they became a warring, raiding group. Driven from NATAL in 1827 and from the TRANSVAAL by Boers and Zulus in 1837, they submitted to the British South Africa Company in 1889. Lobengula, the successor to Mzilikazi, was later tricked by Cecil

Rhodes into granting mineral concessions to the British for all Matabeleland. In 1896, they abandoned war and became herdsmen and farmers. The region became part of Southern Rhodesia, now Zimbabwe, in 1923. See also MASHONALAND.

MATAGORDA BAY (United States) An inlet of the Gulf of Mexico, in SE TEXAS, approx. 100 mi SW of Houston, that receives the Texas COLORADO RIVER. Probably first visited by the French explorer Robert La Salle in 1685 on his last expedition, it served as a port for Stephen F. Austin's colony in Texas begun in 1822.

MATAMOROS [*former:* **San Juan de los Esteros**] (Mexico) Town of Tamaulipas state on the RIO GRANDE RIVER, 25 mi from its mouth, opposite BROWNSVILLE, Texas. Founded c.1700 and renamed in 1851 in honor of Mariano Matamoros, a leader of Mexican independence, it defended itself against numerous U.S. adventurers in the 19th century. In the Mexican War it fell to the forces of Zachary Taylor on May 18, 1846, following his victories at PALO ALTO and RESACA DE LA PALMA. It was occupied by the Mexican imperialists under Mejia in 1864 and by the French in 1866.

MATANZAS (Cuba) City in the NW, approx. 60 mi E of Havana. Founded in 1693, it was once a small buccaneer haven, but in the 19th century grew with the sugar industry. It was the birthplace of the mulatto poet, Gabriel de la Concepción Valdés, known as Plácido. It is famous in Cuban history for Plácido's execution here in 1844 for his role in a black conspiracy.

MATAPAN, CAPE [**Cape Tainaron**] [*ancient:* **Taenarum**] (Greece) Battle site at the S extremity of the PELOPONNESUS, and the Taygetus Mts., projecting into the Ionian Sea. In World War II it was the site of an important naval battle on Mar. 28, 1941, in which the British defeated the Italians.

MATARA (Sri Lanka) Town on the Indian Ocean, 24 mi E of Galle. Once a leading commercial center under Portuguese and Dutch influence, it is the site of the old Dutch Star fort.

MATARAM (Indonesia and Malaysia) Former sultanate in the Malay archipelago that included most of JAVA and SE BORNEO. Founded in 1582, it reached the height of its power in the 17th century. Taken by the Dutch by 1755, it was divided between the principalities of SURAKARTA and JOGJAKARTA.

MATARÓ (Spain) Port and city in Barcelona province, 15 mi NE of BARCELONA. It was a terminus for the first Spanish rail line, which ran from Barcelona and was completed in 1848. Its notable baroque church of Santa Maria has good paintings and wood carvings, and the old part of town preserves its ancient character.

MATERA (Italy) City of Basilicata region, and capital of Matera province approx. 32 mi SW of Bari. In the Middle Ages it was occupied by the Norman and Aragonese rulers of NAPLES and by the Roman Orsini family. It is the site of a 13th-century Romanesque cathedral and a castle; it also has a museum of antiquities. Matera was an important Neolithic site in the prehistoric period, giving its name to a Middle Neolithic ware widespread in Italy.

MATEUR (Tunisia) Town, approx. 10 mi SSW of Menzel Bourguiba. In World War II it was occupied by the Germans in December 1942 and was taken by the Americans May 3, 1943 during the battle for BIZERTE. See also HILL 609.

MATHURA [**Muttra**] (India) City in W UTTAR PRADESH State, on the right bank of the Yamuna River, 30 mi NW of Agra. An ancient city in a region with numerous archaeological remains, it may date from the seventh century BC and was one of the most important centers of Indian art. The local school, with its red sandstone sculpture, dates from the third century BC to the sixth century AD. Sacred to Hindus as the birthplace of Krishna, in the early Christian era it was a center of Buddhism and Jainism. It has been attacked and partially destroyed on various occasions: by Mahmud of GHAZNI c.1020, and by the Lodi Sultan Sikandar II c.1500. In 1667 the great temple was destroyed by the Mogul Aurangzeb. The city was sacked by Ahmad Shah in 1756. It came under British sovereignty in 1803.

MATISCO AEDUORUM. See MÂCON.

MATLOCK (England) Admin. hq. of Derbyshire, on the Derwent River, 19 mi S of Sheffield. Nearby in Rutland cavern are the remains of Roman lead-mining activities from the first and second centuries AD. The town was once famous for therapeutic treatment, using the river water that also powered the first water-driven spinning mill, invented by Richard Arkwright in 1771.

MATMATA (Tunisia) Town, approx. 27 mi S of Gabès. Nearby are the Matmata Hills, long inhabited by cave dwellers. The caves formed part of the German North African defense line in World War II and were taken by the Allies in March 1943.

MATO GROSSO [**Matto Grosso**] (Brazil) State in the W bounded on the N by Amazonas and Pará; on the E by Goyaz, Minas Geraes, São Paulo, and Paraná; on the S by Paraguay; and on the SW and W by Bolivia. Archaeologists think that this poorly explored region may contain relics of ancient civilizations. Settled in 1709 by pioneers retreating from nearby conflicts over gold rights, it was the site of a Paraguayan invasion in the war of 1860 to 1865.

MATOPO HILLS [**Matoppo Hills**] (Zimbabwe) Mountain group S of BULAWAYO. It is the site of World's View, the tomb of Cecil Rhodes.

MATOPPO HILLS. See MATOPO HILLS.

MATRONA. See MARNE RIVER.

MATRŪH [**Mersa Matrūh**] [*ancient:* **Paraetonium**] (Egypt) Town on the coastal road, 150 mi W of Alexandria. Built on the site of an ancient Roman town, in World War II it was the site of a number of battles; it changed hands several times between the British and Germans in 1942 and 1943.

MA-TSU (Taiwan) Island of SE CHINA, off the coast ENE of Foochow. Remaining Nationalist after the communist takeover of the mainland in 1949, it is heavily defended. Since 1958 it had been the object of sporadic heavy artillery and propaganda bombardment from the mainland. Its defense was a major campaign issue of the 1960 U.S. presidential election. See also QUEMOY ISLAND.

MATSUE [Matsuye] (Japan) City and capital of Shimane prefecture, on the N coast of W HONSHU. In addition to its castle, also noteworthy is a museum housing the manuscripts and letters of American author Lafcadio Hearn, who lived in Matsue from 1890 to 1891, thereafter taking a Japanese wife, name, and identity.

MATSUMAE [*former:* **Fukuyama**] (Japan) Town at the SW tip of HOKKAIDO, on Tsugaru Strait. The oldest town on Hokkaido, its importance in feudal times is shown by its large citadel.

MATSUYAMA (Japan) Port city of Ehime prefecture, on W SHIKOKU ISLAND, on the Inland Sea. Situated in a magnificent park, a feudal castle here dates from 1603 and is one of the best preserved in Japan.

MATSUYE. See MATSUE.

MATTANCHERI (India) Town in the S, in central KERALA STATE, on the MALABAR COAST, just S of CALICUT. It has a 16th-century palace dating from the Portuguese settlement after Vasco da Gama's arrival in COCHIN in 1502. It is also the site of a community of Jews, descendants of those expelled from Portugal in the same century; their first synagogue survives.

MATTO GROSSO. See MATO GROSSO.

MATTOON (United States) City in E central ILLINOIS, 40 mi SE of Decatur. Southeast of the city are the farm and graves of Abraham Lincoln's father and stepmother. With the outbreak of the Civil War, Ulysses S. Grant, who had been working in the family business in Illinois, was commissioned colonel of the 21st Illinois Volunteers, and took command of his first troops here.

MAUBAN (Philippines) Municipality on LUZON Island near the E coast of Lamon Bay, 19 mi NNE of Lucena. When hostilities broke out in the Pacific during World War II, this leading port was the site of the Japanese landing on December 23, 1941.

MAUBEUGE (France) Industrial city on the SAMBRE RIVER, near the Belgian border, 49 mi SE of Lille. It was built around a double monastery for men and women founded in the seventh century by St. Aldegonde. It fell to France in 1678. In World War I the city was besieged, damaged, and captured by the Germans in 1914. In World War II the city's position on the MAGINOT LINE also resulted in heavy destruction. Nearby are parts of the fortifications dating from 1685, built on the orders of Louis XIV by Sebastien Vauban.

MAUCHLINE (Scotland) Town in Strathclyde region, 8 mi SSE of Kilmarnock. One mile to the north is Mossgiel, the farm where Robert Burns lived with his brother, Gilbert, from 1784 to 1788. The town was the setting for several of his poems and is the site of the Burns National Memorial. Another monument is dedicated to Covenanters who were killed here in 1685.

MAUER (West Germany) Village in Baden-Württemberg, SE of HEIDELBERG. It was the site of the discovery in 1907 of the Heidelberg jaw, an example of the extinct species, Homo erectus, which immediately preceded Homo sapiens.

MAULDON. See MALDEN.

MAULE (Chile) Coastal province between the Maule and Itata rivers. It takes its name from the river that is said to have marked the southern limits of the INCA EMPIRE.

MAULMAIN. See MOULMEIN.

MAUMBURY RINGS. See DORCHESTER, DORSET.

MAUMEE (United States) Town in NW OHIO, 8 mi SW of Toledo. It was settled in 1817 on the site of Fort Miami dating from 1764, where Gen. Anthony Wayne defeated the Indians on August 20, 1794 in the battle of FALLEN TIMBERS. The Treaty of GREENVILLE followed. During the War of 1812 Fort Miami was used by the British, who then surrendered it to the U.S. forces.

MAUPERTIUS. See POITIERS, POITOU.

MAURETANIA Roman name of an ancient region in North Africa, now in Morocco and Algeria. As part of the Carthaginian Empire until CARTHAGE fell to ROME in 146 BC, it was inhabited by various wandering Berber tribes. After the fall of Jugurtha in 106 BC, the Mauretanian kingdom under Bocchus received the western part of NUMIDIA as reward for siding with Rome. Rebellions began c.25 BC when Augustus made Juba II, a Numidian king, ruler of Mauretania. The tribesmen were useful in Roman cavalries, and one Mauretanian chief was one of Trajan's most outstanding generals. By the fifth century AD the Roman influence was dead, and the region was overrun by the Vandals. It fell to the Arabs in the seventh century.

MAURETANIA TINGITANA. See MOROCCO.

MAURITANIA [Islamic Republic of Mauritania] [*French:* **Mauritanie**] Nation of West Africa bordered by Morocco and Algeria to the N, Mali to the E and SE, Senegal to the SW, and the Atlantic Ocean to the W.

Mauritania has long been a contested border country between black Africa and the Berber-Islamic culture of North Africa. Berbers moved south as early as 200 BC, forcing the local black population to pay tribute. In the 10th century AD the Berbers clashed with the great empire of GHANA over control of the caravan trade, and in 1076 a Berber confederation captured Ghana's capital Kumbi and asserted supremacy. The Berbers were in their turn dominated by the Arab Beni-Hassan from the 15th to the 17th centuries, and Islam became the dominant cultural force of the region.

Mauritania's coast was first explored by Portuguese traders in the 15th century, and for the next 300 years ENGLAND, the NETHERLANDS and FRANCE vied for control of the region's trade. French commercial interests prevailed, and by the early 19th century merchants based in the French colony of SENEGAL tried to wrest control of the lucrative trade in gum arabic from the Arab rulers of Mauritania. In the mid-19th century military expeditions from Senegal extended French control over the country, and in 1903 it was made a

French protectorate. Mauritania was incorporated into FRENCH WEST AFRICA in 1920 and remained a colony until 1958, when it joined the French Community.

In 1960 full independence was achieved, and under the leadership of President Moktar Ould Daddah the country built a stable economy with financial assistance from France and other foreign countries. In 1976 Mauritania and MOROCCO agreed on the partition of the former Spanish colony of SPANISH SAHARA, but guerrilla warfare by the Polisario front of Saharan liberation made this acquisition a costly one. Fighting continued until 1978 when a military coup ended Daddah's long elected tenure, and a cease-fire with Polisario was signed. The dispute, however, continues.

MAURITIUS [*1722–1810: Île de France*] Island and independent state in the SW Indian Ocean, part of the MASCARENE group, approx. 475 mi E of Madagascar. Probably visited by Arabs and Malays in the Middle Ages and definitely by the Portuguese in the 16th century, it was occupied by the Dutch from 1598 to 1710. First named for Prince Maurice of Nassau, it was renamed Île de France in 1722 when the French settled the island and began huge sugar plantations. The British captured it in 1810, restored the Dutch name, and gained formal control in 1814. After the end of slavery here in 1833, the British brought indentured laborers from India, whose descendants constitute a majority of the population today. It gained its independence in 1968.

MAURITZSTAD. See RECIFE.

MAURYA EMPIRE (India) Ancient kingdom that held power from *c.*325 BC to *c.*185 BC. It was founded by Chandragupta Maurya when he conquered the kingdom of MAGADHA, and it reached its greatest extent *c.*250 BC when it became the first dynasty to rule all of India—except for the southern tip—AFGHANISTAN, and BALUCHISTAN. Chandragupta made Pataliputra, now PATNA, his capital and *c.*305 BC defeated an invasion led by Seleucus I Nicator, Macedonian king of SYRIA, who had been one of Alexander the Great's generals. The empire was expanded to the Narmada River in the south, and the DECCAN was added in the late third century BC.

The Maurya's greatest ruler was Asoka, who reigned from *c.*275 BC to *c.*230 BC. He completed the dynasty's conquests, although after a particularly bloody victory over the KALINGA kingdom he suffered such remorse that he disavowed violence, converted to Buddhism, made it the state religion, and erected many monuments and stupas. The remains of a tall memorial pillar to Asoka may be seen at SARNATH. Within 50 years of Asoka's death the Mauryan Empire was much reduced, and its last ruler was assassinated in 185 BC. During the Mauryan period India enjoyed the full flowering of the first native Indian culture. The level it reached was not equalled until the time of the GUPTA EMPIRE.

MAUTHAUSEN (Austria) Village on the DANUBE RIVER, opposite the mouth of the Enns River. It was the site of a Nazi concentration camp during World War II.

MA WARA AN NAHR. See TRANSOXIANA.

MAXEN (East Germany) Village in Saxony, 10 mi SE of Dresden. In 1759, during the Seven Years War, Austrian troops under Field Marshall van Daun surrounded Gen. Friedrich von Finck's Prussian troops, which had been sent to cut off the Austrians in DRESDEN. The Austrians had surprised the Prussians by pulling back to Maxen, where, after refusing to allow the Prussians to break out, they accepted their surrender on November 20. See also PRUSSIA.

MAYA EMPIRE Ancient New World civilization, chiefly in GUATEMALA and the YUCATÁN PENINSULA, but also in Chiapas state, MEXICO, and in W HONDURAS. Not a centralized nation, it consisted of ceremonial and governmental city-states, from which nobles and priests ruled the agricultural countryside. With the INCA and AZTEC EMPIRES, the Mayan was one of three advanced Indian civilizations of the New World and stands comparison with the ancient civilizations of the Old World. Mayan achievements were remarkable, especially in fields of abstract knowledge.

The early history of the Maya is obscure. Their culture may have grown out of that of the Olmec, which flourished in Mexico from *c.*1000 BC to 1150 AD. Another theory is that the unique Mayan culture developed among nomadic tribes in the PETÉN region of N Guatemala, beginning *c.*1000 BC. This area became the center of the Old Empire of the Maya, and the ruins of TIKAL and UAXACTÚN indicate the presence of a prospering culture.

The so-called Caracol at Chichen-Itza, a Post-Classic ruin of the Maya Empire, which had fused here with Mexican Toltecs.

Mayan civilization can be divided into three periods: Pre-Classic, from *c.*1500 BC to 300 AD; Classic, from 300 to 900; and Post-Classic, from 900 to the 16th century, when Spain invaded and conquered CENTRAL AMERICA. By the latter part of the Pre-Classic era the

Maya had invented a calendar, a system of chronology, and hieroglyphic writing. The earliest major works of architecture date from this time. In the early Classic period the culture spread widely and became fairly uniform. The finest developments in the arts and sciences took place in the late Classic period. As engineers and architects, the Maya built large stone structures, many of which were temples on top of pyramids. Sculpture was an adjunct of architecture and appeared on the buildings and temples. The Maya kept careful records of their studies and their history, using their hieroglyphic system of approx. 850 characters. Unfortunately, the Spanish destroyed all but three of these records, and the hieroglyphics remain mostly undeciphered. Mayan calendars—one a 365-day year, the other a 260-day ceremonial year—were very accurate, while their mathematical system, vigesimal (base 20), rather than decimal, was a stupendous intellectual achievement. The priesthood, which supplied scholars and scientists, presided over a religion in which the chief gods were Hunab Ku and his son Itzamna. There seems to have been little human sacrifice until late in the Post-Classic period.

The skill of the Maya can be seen in the ruins of such cities as COPÁN, PALENQUE, PIEDRAS NEGRAS, QUIRIGUA, and UXMAL. These cities were all abandoned for reasons still not clear. Perhaps the peasants revolted against their rulers, or perhaps the soil, long used, could not sustain the population. The Mayan center moved further north and west into Yucatán in the Post-Classic period, while the Toltecs moved south from the Valley of Mexico, beginning c.1000 and dominated the Yucatán Maya from the 11th to the 13th centuries. The Itza, Mayan Indians of Yucatán and Petén, together with the Toltecs, made the city of CHICHEN ITZA their capital; MAYAPAN and reoccupied Uxmal also became centers of power. The three cities formed a league, but in 1194 Uxmal defeated Chichen Itza and became dominant. In 1441 the Xiu, an Indian group that had taken over Uxmal, revolted against the tyrannical Cocom rulers of Mayapan and destroyed the city. Such civil strife continued to weaken the Mayan culture. The Spanish appeared in 1527, and although the Maya were in decline, the Europeans failed in 1528 and from 1531 to 1535 to conquer them. Western Yucatán yielded in 1542 and the eastern part in 1546, but the Itza held out in Tayasal until 1697.

MAYAPAN (Mexico) Ruined city of the MAYA EMPIRE, 35 mi SE of Mérida, Yucatán. From c.900 AD to 1441 it was one of the most important cities of the region. It was a walled city, constructed around a large well. Approximately 3,600 buildings have been discovered, including a large pyramid, a circular temple, and another temple with serpent columns. For a time Mayapan, UXMAL, and CHICHEN ITZA formed a league of cities, but in a civil war in 1194 Mayapan defeated Chichen Itza, which was abandoned. Mayapan then dominated YUCATÁN politically and religiously; but in 1441 its despotic Cocom rulers were overthrown in a revolt, and it too was abandoned.

MAYBOLE (Scotland) Town in Strathclyde region, 8 mi S of Ayr, approx. 40 mi SW of Glasgow. It is an ancient place chartered by Duncan II in 1193 and is the site of Culzean Castle dating from 1777 and the castle of the earls of Cassillis. To the south are the ruins of Turnberry Castle where Robert Bruce is said to have been born. Nearby to the north are the ruins of Dunure Castle, an ancient stronghold of the Kennedys.

MAYEBASHI. See MAEBASHI.

MAYEN (West Germany) Town, 16 mi W of Koblenz. Founded in 1291, the town is on the site of a Roman settlement. The ruins of a castle rise above the town, still partly surrounded by its medieval walls.

MAYENCE. See MAINZ.

MAYENNE (France) Town in N Mayenne department. It was the scene of battles in campaigns of William the Conqueror in the 11th century. It played a part in the Wars of Religion of the 16th century and in the 18th-century wars of the VENDÉE. During the 16th century it belonged to the Guise family, led by Charles of Lorraine, duke of Mayenne. After the murder of his brothers in 1588 he became head of the Holy League, which was determined to put down all Protestant influence. He conducted himself as virtual king over the League's regions. In 1596 he made peace with Henry IV.

MAYERLING (Austria) Village on the Schwechat River, in the WIENERWALD, or Vienna Woods. Crown Prince Rudolf (1858–89) of Austria-Hungary and his mistress Baroness Maria Vetsera, died in a hunting lodge here in January 1889, in what was called a double suicide. Since Rudolf had no siblings, following the death of his father Franz Joseph the emperor's grand-nephew, Charles I, succeeded to the throne.

MAY, ISLE OF (Scotland) Island in Fife region at the entrance to the Firth of FORTH, 28 mi NE of Edinburgh. It is the site of the martyrdom of the Hungarian missionary St. Adrian by the Danes in the mid-ninth century. Pilgrims' Haven, on the coast, refers to the attraction, especially during the 16th century, of a 12th-century Benedictine monastery, now in ruins, which was erected over his grave.

MAYNOOTH (Irish Republic) Town in NE County Kildare. Nearby are the ruins of Maynooth Castle, also called Geraldine Castle, founded c.1175 and besieged in the reign of Henry VIII, who had himself proclaimed king of Ireland in 1542 and under whose reign attacks on Irish and Catholic places began. They continued in the reign of Edward VI. It was demolished during the Cromwellian Wars of the 17th century.

MAYO, COUNTY [*Gaelic:* **Mhuigheo**] (Irish Republic) County in the NW. In 1198 the last high king of Ireland, Roderic O'Connor, died here. The region was granted to the de Burghs at the end of the 12th century after the Anglo-Norman invasion of Ireland; the county only gradually came under English control. There were many confiscations of property by Englishmen, notably in 1586, 1641, and 1666. During the French Revolutionary Wars a French squadron captured part of the county before being defeated at Ballinamuck and driven out in 1798. See also CASTLEBAR.

MAYOTTE. See COMOROS.

MAYU POINT (Burma) Neck of land extending S between the Mayu River and the Bay of Bengal. During World War II it was the scene of fighting in 1943/44 during the Japanese attack on India.

MAYYALI. See MAHÉ.

MAZACA. See KAYSERI.

MAZAGAN [*modern:* **Al-Jadida**] (Morocco) Town in Casablanca region, SW of Casablanca. Founded by the Portuguese in 1502, it became their headquarters in Morocco. After 1541 it was their only stronghold in Morocco, and it was finally evacuated by them in 1769. In the late 19th century a new city began to grow around the ramparts of the old Portuguese settlement.

MÁZANDARAN. See MAZANDERAN.

MAZANDERAN [**Mazandaran**] [*former:* **Tabaristan**] (Iran) Province in the N bordering on the Caspian Sea. It was the scene of conflict with the Arabs and of frequent changes of authority in its early history. It became part of the Persian empire under Shah Abbas I in 1596. From 1723 to 1732 it was under Russian control. See also PERSIA.

MAZARA DEL VALLO [**Mazzara del Vallo**] (Italy) Port of Trapani province, NW SICILY, 32 mi S of Trapani. It was the site of a Carthaginian fortress from the first Punic War, and has a cathedral founded in 1093 AD and rebuilt in the 17th century, and a castle dating from 1073.

MAZAR-I-SHARIF (Afghanistan) Capital of Balkh province, near the Soviet border, 190 mi NW of Kabul, and just E of ancient BALKH. It is the site of the noted mosque of Ali, built by Sultan Mirza *c.*1450 AD and venerated by Shiite Muslims as the alleged burial place of Ali, a son-in-law and cousin of Muhammed. Najaf, Iraq also claims to have Caliph Ali's burial place, however. In 1869 Mazar-I-Sharif became the main political center of Afghan-Turkistan. See AN NAJAF.

MAZOVIA [*Polish:* **Mazowsze**] (Poland) Ancient principality E of the VISTULA RIVER. Although the name first appears in the 11th century, it was already incorporated into the Polish state in the early 10th century. From the 14th to 16th centuries Prussian inhabitants were forced out by the Teutonic Knights, and left here to colonize MASURIA. With the partitions of Poland in the 18th century it was taken over by PRUSSIA and during the Napoleonic Wars made part of the duchy of WARSAW. It remained in Russian Poland until 1918. After 1945 the original Mazovia was divided between Warsaw and BIAŁYSTOK provinces.

MAZOWSZE. See MAZOVIA.

MAZURIA. See MASURIA.

MAZURY. See MASURIA.

MAZZARA DEL VALLO. See MAZARA DEL VALLO.

MBABANE. See SWAZILAND.

MBALA [*former:* **Abercorn**] (Zambia) Town in the

NE, 15 mi SE of the S end of LAKE TANGANYIKA. In World War I the last German African forces surrendered here on November 14, 1918.

MBANDAKA [*former:* **Coquilhatville, Equator**] (Zaire) Town of Équateur province, on the CONGO RIVER where it is joined by the Ruki. It was founded in 1883 by the explorer, Henry M. Stanley, who called it Equator.

MBUJI-MAYI [*former:* **Bakwanga**] (Zaire) City in the S central region on the Sankuru River. Following the independence of Zaire in 1960 it grew rapidly and from 1960 to 1963 served as capital of the secessionist mining state of Katanga, now SHABA.

MDINA [*former:* **Città Notabile, Città Vecchia, Notabile**] (Malta) City in W Malta, 7 mi W of Valletta. Possibly dating back to the Neolithic Period, it is an ancient fortified strongpoint atop a rocky hill, the capital of Malta until VALLETTA succeeded it in 1570. It played a key role in the successful defense of Malta by the vastly outnumbered Knights of St. John, besieged by the huge forces of the Turkish OTTOMAN EMPIRE, in 1565. It is known for its extensive Punic, Roman, and medieval fortifications and other buildings. The apostle Paul is said to have visited here; there remain catacombs, some pre-Christian, in Mdina and nearby Rabat.

MEATH [*Gaelic:* **Contae na Midhe**] (Irish Republic) County in Leinster province. Comprised mostly of an ancient kingdom dating from the second century BC, it was first made an English earldom in 1172 AD and finally organized as a county in the 17th century. At Oldbridge, on the northern boundary west of DROGHEDA, William III defeated James II on July 1, 1690 in the Battle of the BOYNE. Of archaeological interest are the large Bronze Age burial mounds at NEW GRANGE, and KNOWTH. See also KELLS, NAVAN, TARA.

MEAUX (France) Town, in the Seine-et-Marne department in Brie, 28 mi E of Paris. First recorded in 58 BC, it was taken by Clovis in the fifth century AD. An episcopal see since 375 AD, it has a cathedral dating from the 13th and 14th centuries that contains the tomb of Bossuet, the city's most famous bishop. It also has an episcopal palace. In 1358 it was the scene of the massacre of thousands of peasants who had participated in the Jacquerie revolt during the Hundred Years War. After a siege it was taken in 1422 by Henry V of England and remained English until 1439. In the 16th century it was prominent in the Wars of Religion. Prussians and Russians took it in 1814 and 1815 in the Napoleonic Wars. On Sept. 5, 1914 retreating French troops took a stand here and pushed back the Germans. During World War II it was occupied by the Germans.

MECCA [**Mekka**] [*ancient:* **Macoraba**; *Arabic:* **Makkah**] (Saudi Arabia) Holy city of Islam and the birthplace *c.*570 of Muhammed the prophet, located in the HEJAZ, approx. 45 mi from the port of JIDDA. It was an ancient commercial center linking the Far East and Mediterranean. The site of the Kaaba and its sacred Black Stone, it was sacred to idol-worshipping Arabs even before Muhammed's flight from Mecca to MEDINA in 622, which marked the beginning of the Muslim era. It was sacked by the Karmathians in the early 10th century, came under the OTTOMAN EMPIRE in 1517, and was seized in the early 19th century by Wahabis whom Mehmet Ali of EGYPT defeated. It was the seat of the grand sherif of Mecca, Husein ibn-Ali, who declared his independence from Turkey in 1916; Mecca then became the capital of the kingdom of Hejaz. In 1924 it was occupied by Wahabis under ibn-Saud, who later created the Kingdom of Saudi Arabia. It is the site of the Great Mosque.

Inner court of the Great Mosque at Mecca, with the Kaaba at its center containing the sacred Black Stone, actually a pre-Islamic idol.

MECHANICSVILLE (United States) Village and Civil War battle site in VIRGINIA, approx. 7 mi NE of RICHMOND. On June 26, 1862 the Confederates under Gens. Ambrose Hill and James Longstreet were pushed back by the Union forces after heavy casualties in what is also referred to as the Battle of Beaver Dam Creek.

MECHELEN [Mechlin] [*French:* **Malines;** *Latin:* **Mechlinia**] (Belgium) Ancient city on the Dyle River midway between Brussels and Antwerp. By the 11th century Mechelen was a fiefdom, which in 1356 passed to Louis de Mâle and the Burgundian dukes. Since 1559 it has been the seat of the only archbishopric in Belgium and is, in a sense, the religious capital of Belgium. It suffered many attacks from the 16th to the 18th centuries during wars in the Low Countries. It retains a number of richly historic buildings, including the cathedral of St. Rombaut, dating from the 12th to the 14th centuries and modified in the 15th century after a fire, an outstanding example of Gothic architecture. Philip the Good of BURGUNDY made Mechelen the seat of the supreme court of the Low Countries. The palace of Margaret of Austria, who as regent of Charles V ruled the SPANISH NETHERLANDS from this flourishing capital between 1507 and 1530, is now a court of justice. The church of Notre Dame from the 16th century contains Rubens's masterpiece, *The Miraculous Draught of Fishes*. The city was severely damaged during World War II.

MECHERFE. See QATNA.

MECHLIN. See MECHELEN.

MECHLINIA. See MECHELEN.

MECKLENBURG (East Germany) Former state bordering the Baltic Sea. Originally held by Germans, it was occupied *c.*600 AD by a Slavic people, the Wends, whose power was weakened in the 12th century by the inroads of the duke of Saxony, Henry the Lion. Ruled briefly by Waldemar II of Denmark in the 13th century, it became a duchy in 1348. Divisions of the region were made throughout the 16th and early 17th centuries. Because of its participation on the Danish side in the first part of the Thirty Years War, it lost lands to Wallenstein in 1629. These were restored by Gustavus II, the Swedish king, who conquered the entire duchy in 1631. Both parts of Mecklenburg became grand duchies in 1815 and joined the GERMAN CONFEDERATION and the GERMAN EMPIRE. They became republics in 1918 and were reunited in 1934, again losing their former sovereign rights between 1933 and 1935. They were divided into the districts of ROSTOCK, SCHWERIN, and NEUBRANDENBURG in 1952.

MECKLENBURG COUNTY (United States) County of S NORTH CAROLINA. On May 20, 1775, after news of the battles of CONCORD and LEXINGTON reached the county, a meeting was held by residents of the area at which a series of resolutions was passed that called for dissolving their ties to Great Britain. These resolutions, of which only a disputed version exists, are called the Mecklenburg Declaration of Independence and as such may constitute the first such declaration in the American colonies. See CHARLOTTE, N.C.

MEDEBA. See MADEBA.

MEDELLÍN (Colombia) The nation's second largest city and chief commercial center, located at 5,000 ft in Antioquia department, 150 mi NW of Bogotá. Founded in 1675, it has three universities and other cultural institutions and is the site of several notable 17th-century churches.

MEDEMBLICK (Netherlands) Port in West FRIESLAND on what was once the ZUIDER ZEE, 10 mi S of Hoorn. The West Church, formerly named after St. Boniface, the apostle of Germany, contains the tomb of Lord George Murray, who sought refuge here following his defeat at CULLODEN MOOR. The castle, built by Florens V in 1285, is now the court of justice.

MÉDENINE (Tunisia) Town in the Southern Territories, 40 mi SE of Gabès. During World War II, on Mar. 6, 1943, the 10th, 15th, and 21st German Panzer divisions burst out of the MARETH LINE in an attack on the British supply dumps here. The British 8th Army drove them back. It was Rommel's last attack.

MEDESHAMSTEDE. See PETERBOROUGH, England.

MEDFIELD (United States) Town in E MASSACHUSETTS, 17 mi SW of Boston. It was burned, along with nearly 40 other towns damaged or destroyed, in King Philip's War of 1675/76 in which the Wampanoag Indians turned on the New England colonists who had encroached on their lands and privileges.

MEDFORD (United States) City in E MASSACHUSETTS, 5 mi N of BOSTON, situated on the course of Paul Revere's ride. Settled in 1630, it was a shipping and a shipbuilding center until the early 20th century. It is also the site of Tufts University, founded in 1852 as a Universalist institution by Hosea Ballou. He moved the denomination away from Calvinist doctrine and closer to Unitarianism.

MEDFORD (United States) City in SW OREGON, 60 mi W of Klamath Falls. From 1836 to 1856, pioneers and the Rogue River Indians repeatedly battled each other here. Nearby is the restored town of Jacksonville, founded following the discovery of gold in 1851.

MEDIA (Iran) Ancient country in W Asia comprising what is now W Iran and S Azerbaijan. It extended from the Caspian Sea to the Zagros Mountains. The history of the Indo-European people called the Medes can be traced back to 836 BC when the Assyrians under King Shalmaneser III invaded Media—the first of many Assyrian invasions. The Medes extended their rule over PERSIA during the reign of Sargon (d. 705 BC) and reached their height under Cyaxares, who was perhaps the first to establish a kingdom and who reigned from 625 to 585 BC, capturing NINEVEH in 612 BC and aiding BABYLON in bringing about the downfall of ASSYRIA. The Medes were thus the first people to free themselves from Assyrian rule. The Median dynasty was overthrown c.550 BC by Cyrus the Great of Persia and, retaining its prestige, was united with the Persian Empire. Alexander the Great invaded Media in 330 BC. In the second century BC Media became part of the Parthian Kingdom, and under the Romans it was divided into Media Atropatene in the north, which once again came under the influence of PARTHIA, and Media Magna in the south, which eventually became a sacred place to Zoroastrianism, especially in the city of Rhagae, now RAI.

MEDILIKE. See MELK.

MEDINA [*Arabic:* **Al-Madinah, Madinat Rasul Allah, Medinat an-Nabi;** *former:* **Yathrib**] (Saudi Arabia) The second most important city of Islam, located in the HEJAZ, 210 mi N of MECCA and 120 mi from the Red Sea coast. Founded by Jewish settlers more than 2,000 years ago, it is noted for its mosque enclosing the tomb of Muhammed. It served as a refuge for Muhammed after his flight from Mecca and as his base for the conversion of Arabia. The date of his arrival, Sept. 20, 622, was later adopted as the beginning of the Muslim calendar. The capital of a caliphate from 622 to 661, it declined after 683 when it was sacked by the Omayyad caliphs of DAMASCUS. In later periods, it fell to the Turks, the Egyptians, and the Wahabis. It was under Turkish control from 1812 to 1912, when the reformist Wahabi sect again wielded power. Husayn ibn Ali, who revolted against Turkey during World War I, captured Medina in 1916. It was a city of the new kingdom of HEJAZ from 1919 until 1924 when, after a long siege, it fell to Ibn-Saud, founder of Saudi Arabia.

MEDINA-ARKOSH. See ARCOS DE LA FRONTERA.

MEDINA-SIDONIA [**Medinasidonia**] (Spain) Town in Cádiz province, 19 mi ESE of Cádiz. It is the site of the ancestral palace of the dukes of Medina-Sidonia, one of whom led the Spanish Armada in 1588. It attained some importance under the Visigoths who made it a bishopric. The town was taken c.710 AD by Tariq in the Moorish invasion, which led to Moorish dominance of Spain.

MEDINAT AN-NABI. See MEDINA.

MEDIOLANUM. See ÉVREUX, MILAN.

MEDIOLANUM SANTORUM. See SAINTES.

MEDIOMATRICA. See METZ.

MEDITERRANEAN SEA Body of water bordered by Africa, Asia, and Europe, the largest inland sea, approx. 2,400 mi from east to west. Its name is Latin for "in the middle of the earth." Its chief arms east to west are the Aegean, Ionian, Adriatic, and Tyrrhenian seas, and it is connected to the Atlantic Ocean to the W, the Black Sea to the NE, and the Red Sea to the SE. It is watered by the Nile, Tiber, Rhône, Ebro and other historic rivers. The Mediterranean is, perhaps, the most historic body of water in the world, because on it and in the lands around it have arisen, prospered, and declined the first powerful empires, while the high culture and religions that developed here created the basic elements of Western and Middle Eastern civilizations.

One of the world's oldest cultures, the Aegean, developed in the Mediterranean after the third millennium BC, especially on the island of CRETE, while about the same time the Mycenaean civilization came into being in GREECE. Both were the first to use the Mediterranean as a trade route, followed by the sailors of PHOENICIA by 1250 BC. In the eighth, seventh, and sixth centuries BC, the Greeks dominated the Sea and founded colonies in SYRIA, SICILY, ITALY, FRANCE, SPAIN, and North Africa.

Greek art, drama, philosophy, literature, and political theory were disseminated both eastward and westward. The MACEDONIAN EMPIRE in the third century BC carried Hellenic culture to the Middle East, while Greek colonies had spread this culture earlier to the western Mediterranean. Next to extend its sway over the sea and found colonies was CARTHAGE, in North Africa, in the sixth and fifth centuries BC. ROME, however, destroyed Carthage's power; and by the early second century AD the ROMAN EMPIRE ruled all the lands around the Mediterranean, making it *Mare Nostrum* (Our Sea). The Romans adopted and adapted Greek culture, and their military conquests and political organization carried it to all of Western Europe, whence, eventually, it crossed the Atlantic to the New World. In addition, two of the world's most influential religions, Judaism and Christianity, were born in PALESTINE, while a third, Islam, originated in the ARABIAN PENINSULA and between the seventh and 11th centuries controlled much of the Mediterranean area.

After the Roman Empire was divided in 395 AD, the BYZANTINE EMPIRE in Asia ruled the eastern Mediterranean for centuries until its capital, CONSTANTINOPLE, finally fell to the OTTOMAN EMPIRE in 1453. In the meantime, in the west, the Arabs, carrying the creed of Islam with them, gained control of North Africa and Spain in the sixth to eighth centuries AD. From the 10th century on the city-states of Italy regained the initiative on the sea, making the Crusades possible between the 11th and the 14th centuries and founding numerous trading colonies in the Levant. AMALFI, PISA, and GENOA were among the most important Italian ports. The Republic of VENICE reached its peak in the 15th century, at which time it was the most powerful state in the region and the primary link between Europe and Asia. Its decline, however, began with the rise of the Ottoman Empire, which in turn began a long descent in the 17th century. National states were established around the sea, but it was not until the mid-20th century that all the present nations came into being.

The Mediterranean has been a vital trade route ever since humans first learned to navigate, and for centuries it was the main route between Europe and Asia. It finally lost importance in the late 17th century after the New World was discovered and the route around Africa was pioneered in the 15th century, and the nation-states of the Atlantic seaboard rose to power. However, the opening of the SUEZ CANAL in 1869 connected it with the Red Sea and restored its value to shipping. The sea has been the scene of decisive naval battles. In 480 BC a Greek fleet crushed a Persian fleet off the Greek island of SALAMIS, at ACTIUM in 31 BC Octavius defeated Antony and Cleopatra to become the first Roman emperor, and on Oct. 7, 1571 a Christian fleet defeated that of the Ottoman Empire off LEPANTO, Greece, thus keeping the Turks from dominating the Mediterranean. It was the site of naval engagements in both world wars and today powerful U.S., NATO, and Soviet fleets cruise the sea at all times, in part because of its strategic importance in relation to the defense of Europe and the vital oil fields of North Africa and the Middle East.

MEDJERDA RIVER. See BAGRADAS RIVER.

MEDJEZ-EL-BAB. See MAJĀZ-AL-BĀB.

MEDŪM (Egypt) Archaeological site between Memphis and Al-Faiyum, approx. 40 mi S of Cairo. It is the site of a pyramid built by Snefru, the first king of the Fourth dynasty (c.2650–2500 BC), who greatly advanced Egyptian commerce and control of the Sinai peninsula. The pyramid, one of the first true pyramids, apparently collapsed because of faulty design; but it was the immediate predecessor of the Great Pyramids of GIZA.

MEDUNTA. See MANTES-LA-JOLIE.

MEDWAY RIVER (England) Tributary of the THAMES RIVER that rises in Sussex, flows through Kent, the site of several battles. In 43 AD, during the Roman invasion of England under Claudius I, the Roman legions under the command of Aulus Plautius met a British force here under Caractacus. With the assistance of troops under Vespasian the Romans defeated them in a battle that opened the way for the Roman conquest of the island. During the Second Dutch War the Dutch naval forces entered the Medway, burned SHEERNESS, and destroyed the ships of the English navy in June 1667.

MEEANEE. See MIANI.

MEENEN. See MENEN.

MEERSEN [Mersen] (Netherlands) Town in Limburg province, just NNE of Maastricht. A treaty signed here on Aug. 8, 870 AD, between Charlemagne's heirs, Charles the Bald and Louis the German, king of Germany, divided the kingdom of their nephew, Lothair II of LORRAINE (*d.* 869). The treaty's lasting effect was to set the German-Frankish frontier.

MEERUT (India) City in Uttar Pradesh state, on a tributary of the Ganges River, 40 mi NE of Delhi. The settlement dates back at least to 250 BC. Conquered by the Muslims in 1192, it was largely destroyed by Tamerlane in 1399 and became part of the MOGUL EMPIRE. In 1775 Walter Reinhardt, a Walloon who had originally been in the service of the French but by then headed a gang of European deserters and Sepoys, gained control of the region. His wife, the Begum Samru, took Reinhardt's place after his death in 1778. Meerut was ceded to the British in 1803 and taken over by the East India Company in 1836. It was the scene of the first outbreak of the Indian Mutiny in May 1857. The British held the city, however.

MEGALOPOLIS (Greece) Ancient city of ARCADIA on a plain of the central PELOPONNESUS, just N of the modern Megalopolis, 20 mi SW of Tegea. Founded in 370 BC by the Theban general Epaminondas after the Battle of LEUCTRA, it was, true to its name, a big city. It was the seat of the "10,000" in the federal assembly and was headquarters for the anti-Spartan Arcadian League. It withstood several sieges, the longest in 331 and 318 BC. Usually an ally of THEBES and MACEDON, it joined the Achaean League in 234 BC but was destroyed by Cleomenes III of SPARTA in 222 BC and thereafter declined. The home of Philopoemen and Polybius, it is currently the site of much archaeological excavation.

MÉGARA [*ancient*: Megara] (Greece) Port city of Attica department, located on the N coast of the Saronic Gulf, W of ATHENS, on the road from Attica to CORINTH. The capital of ancient Megaris, it flourished under the Dorians who in the eighth century BC built it into a center of commerce with Sicily and the Black Sea. They founded colonies at Propontis and Euxine (the SEA OF MARMARA), as well as at CHALCEDON and Byzantium. Megara's commercial importance was diminished by the rise of MILETUS and Athens. After the Persian Wars its citizens summoned the aid of Athens against Corinth in 459 BC, but soon after they expelled the Athenians, who placed an embargo on Megarian trade. In the Peloponnesian Wars blockades and invasions ruined Megara. It was incorporated into the Achaean League in 243 BC. In the late Middle Ages the city was controlled by VENICE but finally abandoned in 1500 AD. It was the birthplace of Euclid, founder of the Megarian school of philosophy. See also CONSTANTINOPLE, MEGARA HYBLAEA.

MEGARA HYBLAEA (Italy) Ancient city of SICILY, on the E coast near Augusta, 12 mi NNW of SYRACUSE. It was founded in 728 BC by Dorians from MÉGARA in Greece, who had previously established settlements at Trotilon, LEONTINI, and Thapsus. Destroyed by Gelon in 481 BC, it was fortified by Syracuse against the Athenians in 412 BC and was captured by Marcellus for the Romans in 214 BC. Excavations were begun in 1891 and have uncovered Archaic Greek as well as important Neolithic remains.

MEGIDDO [Tel Megiddo] (Israel) City of ancient PALESTINE, on the S side of the PLAIN OF ESDRAELON, approx. 15 mi S of Haifa. Modern excavations have shown that it was settled by 3500 BC and was inhabited until c.450 BC. Strategically placed on the commercial and military routes between Egypt and Mesopotamia, it has been the scene of many battles. The word Armageddon, referring to a great battle of the biblical last days, is derived from the Hebrew for "hill of Megiddo." In 1468 BC Thutmose III of EGYPT defeated a Syrian army here. Judges 4 relates how in the 13th century BC Deborah and Barak overcame Sisera near this site. King Josiah was killed here by Necho II of Egypt c.610 BC. More recently during World War I Gen. Allenby, later Viscount Allenby of Megiddo, began his major offensive against the Turks here on Sept. 18, 1918. Excavations in recent years have unearthed 20 strata of settlements. In those from the Canaanite period to c.500 BC were the exquisite Megiddo ivories, along with the "Stables of Solomon," who rebuilt Megiddo as a horse-trading and chariot center.

MEHÁDIA [ancient: **Ad Mediam**] (Hungary) Market town of Krassó-Szörény province, 287 mi SE of Budapest. It was the site of an ancient Roman colony, near the road from the DANUBE RIVER to DACIA. Nearby are the Hercules Baths, mineral hot springs famous in the Roman period, as attested to by numerous inscriptions. After the fall of the ROMAN EMPIRE, they fell into disuse until 1735. Roman remains are still visible here.

MEHDIA. See MAHDIA.

MEHDIYA. See KENITRA, Morocco.

MEHIDPUR [Mahidpur] (India) Town of Indore state, on the right bank of the Sipra River, 24 mi N of Ujjain. It was the scene of a battle on Dec. 20, 1817, in which Sir John Malcolm defeated the army of Holkar,

resulting in the Treaty of MANDASOR and the British takeover of MALWA. It was again the scene of severe fighting during the Indian Mutiny in 1857.

MEHSANA (India) City and district in Gujarat state. The state is in W India on the Arabian Sea; the city is approx. 40 mi NNW of Ahmadabad and is the administrative headquarters of the district. The city was founded sometime between the 12th and 14th centuries by settlers from RAJPUTANA. The MARATHA ruler of BARODA, now also part of Gujarat, built a royal residence here in the 18th century. PATAN is the largest town in the district and is known for its handwoven cloth.

MEHUN-SUR-YÈVRE (France) Town of Cher department, in the central region, NW of Bourges. It is the site of the ruins of the 14th-century castle where Charles VII ascended the throne in 1422 and died in 1461.

MEIGS, FORT. See FORT MEIGS.

MEIKTILA (Burma) Town and district of Upper Burma bordering the Shan states on the E. A Buddhist center, it is the site of an artificial lake which, according to Burmese legend, was begun 2,400 years ago by the grandfather of Gautama Buddha. In World War II it was a key site in the battle of Burma between the Japanese and Allies.

MEININGEN (East Germany) City in the Suhl district, near the Werra River, 40 mi SW of Erfurt. First described in 982 AD, it became a city in 1344. Passed to the dukes of SAXONY in 1583, from 1680 to 1918 it served as capital for the dukes of SAXE-MEININGEN. In the second half of the 19th century, the theater and orchestra of Meiningen acquired an international reputation, setting the style for German performance.

MEIRINGEN (Switzerland) Town in the Hasle Valley of BERN canton, on the right bank of the Aar River. In 1234 it passed from the emperor to the Knights of Lazarus, who sold it in 1272 to the Austin Canons of INTERLAKEN. They retained it until their suppression in 1528. There is an ancient parish church in the town, and above it are the ruins of the medieval church of Resti.

MEISSEN [former: **Misnia**] (East Germany) Manufacturing city in the Dresden district on the ELBE RIVER, 14 mi NW of Dresden. It was founded in 929 by Henry of SAXONY, later the German king Henry I, as a defense against the Slavs. In 965 it became the seat of the margraviate of Meissen when Otto I divided the East Saxon region. The diocese of Meissen, founded in 968, came under the Wettin dynasty in 1123. Suppressed during the Reformation, it was restored in 1921 with its see at Bautzen. The Albrechtsburg, a large 15th-century castle, dominates the city. From 1710 to 1864 it housed the royal porcelain manufacture, the first such in Europe, begun by J.F. Bottger, under the patronage of Elector Frederick Augustus I, later Augustus II of Poland. Other notable buildings are the cathedral and the church of St. Afra, both from the 13th to the 15th centuries.

MEJDEL. See MAGDALA.

MEJERDA RIVER. See BAGRADAS RIVER.

MÉJICO. See MEXICO.

MEKKA. See MECCA.

MEKNES [*Arabic:* **Miknasa**; *French:* **Meknès**; *Spanish:* **Mequinez**] (Morocco) City 36 mi WSW of Fès. Founded in the 10th century, in the Middle Ages it was a citadel of the ALMOHADS. It became Morocco's capital and the residence of the Moroccan sultan in 1672. Because of Sultan Ismail's ambitious construction projects, the city came to be known as the Versailles of Morocco. The huge palace, a few mosques, and a gateway have survived.

MEKONE. See SICYON.

MEKONG RIVER [*Chinese:* **Lan-Ts'ang**; *Tibetan:* **Dzāchu**] (Southeast Asia) River, 2,600 mi long, rising in E TIBET and flowing SE through Yunnan Province, S CHINA, through LAOS, BURMA, THAILAND, KAMPUCHEA, and SOUTH VIETNAM, where it empties into the South China Sea through several mouths forming the Mekong Delta. The subject of various international agreements and arrangements in modern history, it was most recently the scene of heavy fighting during the Vietnam War. It has also been known as the Saigon River in Vietnam. See also PHNOM PENH.

MELAKA. See MALACCA.

MELANESIA (Pacific Ocean) Islands forming one of the three main groupings of Oceania in the Pacific Ocean. The other groups are MICRONESIA and POLYNESIA. Melanesia consists of those islands NE of AUSTRALIA and S of the equator. European explorers began to discover them in the early 16th century, but it was the late 18th century before all the important ones were located and explored. The islands of Melanesia include: the ADMIRALTY ISLANDS, the BISMARCK ARCHIPELAGO, the D'ENTRECASTEAUX ISLANDS, the FIJI ISLANDS, the LOUISIADE ARCHIPELAGO, NEW CALEDONIA, the NEW HEBRIDES, and the SOLOMON ISLANDS. NEW GUINEA is sometimes included. The Melanesians are mainly of Australoid stock.

MELBOURNE (Australia) Capital city of Victoria, at the mouth of the Yarra River, on the N end of Port Philip Bay. Founded in 1835 by settlers from TASMANIA, in 1837 it was named for Lord Melbourne, the British prime minister. It was at the center of the gold rush of the 1850's. From 1901 to 1927 it was the temporary capital of Australia and the seat of the federal government.

MELEDA [*Latin:* **Melita**; *Serbo-Croatian:* **Mljet**] (Yugoslavia) One of the larger islands in the SE Adriatic Sea, off the coast of DALMATIA. It has been regarded by some, including Constantine Porphyrogenitus in the 10th century, as the Melita on which St. Paul was shipwrecked. As at Malta, there is a St. Paul's Bay.

MELEGNANO. See MARIGNANO.

MELFI (Italy) Town in Potenza province, Basilicata region, 26 mi NNW of Potenza. The site of Roman remains, in 1041 AD it was made the first capital of the Norman county of APULIA. Emperor Frederick II assembled his parliament here in 1231 to pass the Consti-

Melbourne at its founding in the 1830's. Later a crude gold-rush town, Melbourne is now heavily industrialized and is Australia's second-largest city.

tutions of Melfi, or *Liber Augustalis*. In 1528 the town was sacked by the French under the vicomte de Lautrec, who as marshal led the forces that reconquered MILAN. Thereafter declining as a commercial center, Melfi passed to Italy in 1861. Of historic interest are its 12th-century cathedral and campanile and a 13th-century castle.

MELILLA [*ancient:* **Rusaddir**] (Spain) Spanish possession on the N coast of MOROCCO, on the SE coast of Cape Tres Forcas in the Er Rif region. In antiquity it was settled by Phoenicians, then by their successors from CARTHAGE. Conquered by ROME, it became a Berber town after the end of the ROMAN EMPIRE. In the seventh century AD it was overrun by the Arabs. Spain took it in 1496–97 and held on to it despite repeated attacks by Morocco. It was the center of the Riffian revolt in 1921 under Abd-al-Krim. Recovered by Spain in 1926, in 1936 it was the site of the revolt of army chiefs that led to the Spanish civil war. See also RIF MOUNTAINS, PHOENICIA.

MELITA. See MALTA, SOVEREIGN STATE OF, MELEDA.

MELITENE. See MALATYA.

MELITOPOL [*former:* **Novo-Aleksandrovka**] (USSR) City in the UKRAINE, on the Molochnoy River, near the NW shore of the Sea of Azov, 70 mi S of Zaporozhye. Settled in the late 18th century by Cossacks, Mennonites, and others, it gained its present name in 1841. An important agricultural center on the route between Moscow and the CRIMEA, during World War II it was occupied by the Germans from 1941 to 1943.

MELK [*former:* **Medilike; Namare**] (Austria) Town in Lower Austria province on the DANUBE RIVER, 50 mi W of Vienna. One of the earliest residences of Austrian rulers, it was the Austrian capital during the 11th century. A famous Benedictine abbey, founded in the castle built in 1089, has a large library with some 2,000 manuscripts. It was plundered by the Turks in 1683 but was rebuilt between 1702 and 1749. It is an outstanding example of the baroque style.

MELLE, Africa. See MALI EMPIRE.

MELLE [*ancient:* **Metallum**] (France) Town in the Deux-Sèvres department, on the left bank of the Béronne River, 21 mi ESE of Niort. A lead mine first worked here by the Romans gave the town its original name. There are two Romanesque churches in the style of POITOU and the 11th-century church of St. Savinien, now a prison. Between the Middle Ages and the 16th century the town was a possession of the counts of MAINE.

MELLEOIKI. See MILWAUKEE.

MELODUNUM. See MELUN.

MELORIA (Italy) Small island, 4 mi off LEGHORN in the Mediterranean Sea. It was the scene of two naval battles. On May 3, 1241 the Sicilian King and Holy Roman Emperor Frederick II Hohenstaufen defeated the Genoese and captured foreign prelates en route to meet with Pope Gregory IX, who had just excommunicated Frederick. In August 1284, during a long conflict over CORSICA, the Genoese here destroyed the Pisan fleet, which never recovered. See GENOA, PISA.

MELOS [*Greek:* **Mílos**; *Italian:* **Milo**] (Greece) Island in the AEGEAN SEA, a member of the CYCLADES group. Deposits of obsidian and its strategic location between CRETE and the mainland made it an early center of civilization, as attested by the rich lower levels of the excavated settlement of Phylakopi, which later became a Minoan and Mycenaean town. Later it was occupied by the Dorians, but it lost its major importance when bronze replaced obsidian for tools and weapons. During the Peloponnesian Wars it was attacked by ATHENS and its inhabitants brutally wiped out. The famous Venus de Milo, a Hellenistic statue now in the Louvre, was discovered here in 1820.

MELPUM. See MILAN.

MELROSE (Scotland) Town in Borders region, on the Tweed River, 31 mi SE of Edinburgh. It is the site of one of the finest ruins in Scotland, Melrose Abbey, founded for the Cistercians by David I in 1136. Attacked and rebuilt several times, it was finally destroyed by the earl of Hertford in 1545. It is the "Kennaquhair" of Scott's *Abbot and Monastery*, and his *Lay of the Last Minstrel* describes the finely carved east window. Its high altar contains the heart of Robert Bruce. Two miles to the east is the site of a seventh-century monastery burned in the ninth century during conflicts between Scots and Anglo-Saxons, rebuilt, and finally destroyed by English invaders. Nearby was Trimontium, a large Roman fortification.

MELTON MOWBRAY (England) Market town of Leicestershire, in a fertile valley at the confluence of the Wreake and the Eye rivers, 15 mi NE of Leicester. In February 1644, during the Civil War, it was the scene of a defeat of the Parliamentary forces by the Royalists. It is the birthplace of John Henley, the orator, and is the site of the early Gothic church of St. Mary.

MELUN [*ancient:* **Melodunum**] (France) Ancient town and capital of Seine-et-Marne department, on the SEINE RIVER, 27 mi SSE of Paris. Founded on an island in the Seine, it was conquered by the Romans in 53 BC. It expanded to both banks in Gallo-Roman times and contains vestiges of a Roman fortress. Often attacked by the Normans, it was later taken after heavy fighting by the English in 1420 and retaken by Joan of Arc in 1430. The city was briefly controlled by the Catholic League in 1589. There is an 11th- and 12th-century Romanesque church and a castle that was an early residence of the Capetian kings.

MEMCESTRE. See MANCHESTER.

MEMDE. See MENDE.

MEMEL. See KLAIPEDA, NEMAN RIVER.

MEMELBURG. See KLAIPEDA.

MEMMINGEN (West Germany) City in BAVARIA, 42 mi SW of Augsburg. First mentioned in 1010 AD, this Swabian town became a free imperial city in 1286. It took part in the Tetrapolitan Confession. During the Peasants' War the Twelve Articles of the Peasantry, demanding an end to serfdom and certain freedoms from ecclesiatical control, were drawn up here in 1525. Nearby in 1800 the Austrians were defeated by Gen. Moreau during the Napoleonic Wars. Parts of the city's 15th-century walls and gates remain.

MEMPHIS [*Assyrian:* **Mempi**; *Biblical:* **Noph**] (Egypt) Ancient city on a site now partly covered by the village of Mit Rahina, approx. 13 mi S of Cairo at the apex of the NILE RIVER Delta. Probably founded by Menes, the first known king of Egypt, it might have been the site of royal palaces and tombs earlier than that. It served as capital for most rulers of the Old Kingdom (*c.*3100–2258 BC) and of the Middle Kingdom (*c.*2000–1786 BC) up to the XVIII dynasty of the New Kingdom (1570–*c.*1342 BC). Its temple of Ptah was never surpassed. The palace of Apries and two huge statues of Ramses II are some of the other notable monuments found here. The Memphite school of art and craftsmanship was important, especially for relief work. The necropolis of SAKKARA is nearby. Across the Nile are the great pyramids, extending 20 miles to GIZA.

Superseded by HERACLEOPOLIS during the IX and X dynasties and later by THEBES at the beginning of the New Kingdom, it was taken by Nubians in 730 BC and later besieged by Assyrians, Persians, and others. It became the seat of Persian satraps *c.*525 BC and lost its importance after the conquest of Egypt by Alexander the Great *c.*330. Important again and second only to Alexandria under the Ptolemies and under Rome, it finally declined when many of its ancient buildings were used in the construction of the new Arabic city of Fustat, which became CAIRO.

MEMPHIS (United States) River city in SW TENNESSEE, on the MISSISSIPPI RIVER, 10 mi N of the Mississippi border, at the mouth of the Wolf River. Strategically important river port for British, French, and Spanish rivalries of the 18th century, it was the site of several forts. The United States erected a fort in 1797, and in 1819 the area was settled by a colony mission sent by Andrew Jackson, John Overton, and James Winchester. Quickly becoming a cotton market second only to NEW ORLEANS, it became a Confederate military center at the beginning of the Civil War and in 1862 was made the temporary state capital. Captured by Union forces under the elder Charles Henry Davis after the battle of Memphis in 1862, it remained an important Union base. It was swept by yellow fever epidemics in 1867, 1873, and 1878. From 1909 to 1948 the city was ruled by the politician E.H. "Boss" Crump and was long known for its high levels of vice and crime. It is the site of Beale Street, made famous by W.C. Handy, the black blues composer.

MEMPI. See MEMPHIS.

MENADO. See MANADO.

MENAI STRAIT (Wales) Channel, 14 mi long, between ANGLESEY ISLAND and mainland GWYNEDD, off the N coast of Wales. It is the site of two historic bridges. Thomas Telford's suspension bridge dating from 1826 and rebuilt between 1938 and 1941 carries the road from BANGOR on the mainland to Anglesey; and Robert Stephenson's tubular bridge of 1850 carries a railroad line.

MENASHA (United States) City in E WISCONSIN on Lake Winnebago and the Fox River, 5 mi S of Appleton, adjacent to its twin city of NEENAH. It was settled in 1843 in a region visited by Jean Nicolet c.1635 as part of an expedition directed by Champlain to find a NORTHWEST PASSAGE. The area is described by Jonathan Carver in his *Travels* of 1778.

MENDALI. See MANDALI.

MENDE [Memde] [*ancient:* **Mimatum**] (France) Town in Lozère department, 76 mi NW of Avignon. A settlement in Roman times, it became an episcopal see in the fifth century AD. The town was ruled by bishops until 1306 when they were forced to cede a portion of it to Philip the Handsome. During the Wars of Religion, from 1562 to 1598, it was often sacked. Notable buildings include a cathedral begun by Urban V in 1369, destroyed in 1580 during the Huguenots' sacking of the town, and rebuilt in the 17th century. The 13th-century bridge Pont Notre-Dame spans the Lot River here.

MENDELI. See MANDALI.

MENDERES [*ancient:* **Maeander;** *Turkish:* **Büyük Menderes Nehri**] (Turkey) River, flowing SW and W into the AEGEAN SEA S of the island of SAMOS. It was notable in ancient legends for its wanderings, i.e.: meanderings. Along or near its banks were the ancient cities of LAODICEA, MAGNESIA, and MILETUS.

MENDES (Egypt) Archaeological site, E of the Damietta branch of the NILE RIVER and just SE of Al-Mansūra. Worship of Osiris, god of the earth's abundance, originated in this area and spread throughout the Mediterranean. Near here the Egyptians under Nectanebo I defeated the Persians c.380 BC.

MENDIP HILLS (England) Range of hills, in NE Somerset, extending approx. 18 mi from the vicinity of Hutton to the Frome Valley. They are the site of caves with traces of prehistoric usage and of ruins of Roman lead mines, an amphitheater, and a Roman road.

MENDOZA (Argentina) City and provincial capital approx. 60 mi SE of Alconcagua. It was settled by Spanish colonists from CHILE c.1560 and belonged to Chile until 1776. It was the headquarters of San Martín for training troops to march across the ANDES in 1817 in the liberation of Chile from Spain. It is the site of a Franciscan monastery that serves as the burial place of Argentine national heroes. The present city is located near the ruins of the original, which was almost totally destroyed by earthquake in 1861.

MENEN [Meenen] [*French:* **Menin**] (Belgium) Town in West Flanders province, on the Lys River, at the French border. Founded in 1578, it was, like YPRES, strongly fortified by Vauban in the 17th century; but these fortifications were removed in 1748 under the terms of the Treaty of Aix-la-Chapelle (see AACHEN). During World War I it was taken and retaken by German and British forces in the severe fighting that took place all through this area.

MENESK. See MINSK.

MENEVIA. See SAINT DAVID'S.

MÊNG CHIANG (China) Former Japanese buffer state between Manchukuo and Outer Mongolia, comprising approximately the provinces of Chahar and Suiyuan of INNER MONGOLIA. The capital was HU-HO-HAO-T'E. Established in 1937, it ceased to exist after World War II. See also MANCHURIA, MONGOLIA.

MENG-TSEU. See MENG-TZU.

MENGTSZ. See MENG-TZU.

MENG-TZE. See MENG-TZU.

MENG-TZU [Meng-Tseu, Mengtsz, Meng-Tze] [*French:* **Mong-Tseu**] (China) City in SE Yunnan province, near the border of VIETNAM, SSE of K'un-Ming. The French convention of 1886 established its prominence on an overland trade route between Tongking and YUNNAN. It is now the commercial center of a mining region. Evidence of its prosperity before the Taiping Rebellion can be seen in the remains of several impressive temples.

MENIN. See MENEN.

MENLO PARK (United States) Unincorporated community in Middlesex county, central NEW JERSEY, approx. 6 mi SE of Plainfield. Established after the founding of the East Jersey colony in 1674, it is the site of the laboratory where Thomas Edison invented the incandescent light bulb in 1879.

MENNIX. See JERBA.

MENOMINEE (United States) City in MICHIGAN, located on Green Bay, at the mouth of the Menominee River, opposite Marinette, Wisconsin. It is named after the Menominee Indians, an Algonquin tribe. Their first European visitor seems to have been the French explorer, Jean Nicolet, in 1634. A trading post was established here by 1796, and it was long famous as a shipping point for lumber throughout the world.

MENORCA. See MINORCA.

MENSK. See MINSK.

MENTANA (Italy) Town in Roma province, W LATIUM, NE of Rome. It was the scene of a battle on Nov. 3, 1867 in which Garibaldi was defeated by combined papal and French troops during his second unsuccessful attempt to take ROME and incorporate it into the newly formed kingdom of Italy under Victor Emmanuel. See also PAPAL STATES.

MENTEITH [Monteith] (Scotland) Lake in Central region, 14 mi WNW of Stirling. When just five years of age, Mary, Queen of Scots, was hidden at Inchmahome priory on the largest of the lake's three islands for a few months. This was prior to her departure for France in 1548 to live with her mother's family and prepare for her marriage to the dauphin. It was an Augustinian priory founded in 1238 by Walter Comyn. On Inch Talla stands the ruined tower of the earls of Menteith, dating from 1428.

MENTON [*Italian:* **Mentone**] (France) Town on the Mediterranean, in Alpes-Maritimes department, 12 mi ENE of Nice, on the RIVIERA. Probably the site of an earlier Roman settlement, it was founded in the 10th century. It was owned by the Grimaldis of MONACO from the 14th century until 1848, when it became a free city of SARDINIA. A plebiscite in 1860 gave it to France. During World War II Menton was occupied by Italians and Germans and liberated, but it was subsequently bombarded and greatly damaged. A 16th-century fort overlooks the harbor, and there is a notable baroque church here. Nearby are caves where the remains of the prehistoric Grimaldi man—a Negroid type from the late Paleolithic period—have been discovered. See GRIMALDI.

MENTONE. See MENTON.

MENTOR (United States) Residential village in OHIO, near LAKE ERIE, 22 mi NE of Cleveland. Founded in 1799, it was the home of James Garfield when he was elected president. His home, Lawnfield, is preserved here.

MENZEL-BOURGUIBA [*former:* **Ferryville**] (Tunisia) Town on the S shore of Lake Bizerte. Founded around a naval base during French rule, in World War II it was occupied by U.S. troops on May 7, 1943. When Tunisian independence was declared in 1956, it was renamed for Habib Bourguiba, Tunisia's first president. See also BIZERTE.

MEQUINEZ. See MEKNES.

MERAN. See MERANO.

MERANO [*German:* **Meran**] (Italy) City in Bolzano Province, Trentino-Alto Adige region, on the S slope of the Alps, 17 mi NW of Bolzano. It is located near the site of the Roman settlement of Castrum Maiense of the first century AD. First mentioned in 857, it served as the capital of TYROL from the 12th century until *c.*1420 when the capital was moved to INNSBRUCK. Merano remained under Austrian rule until ceded to Italy by the Treaty of St. Germain in 1919. To the northwest on the Kuchelberg is a half-ruined castle.

MERCER (New Zealand) Village in N North Island, on the Waikato River, 32 mi SSE of Auckland. An outpost during the period of colonization, it was the scene of many skirmishes between Maori and British troops in 1863/64.

MERCIA (England) Anglo-Saxon kingdom consisting generally of the region of the Midlands. It was one of a group of seven Anglo-Saxon kingdoms sometimes known as the Heptarchy. Settled by Angles *c.*500 AD, its growth stems from Penda's domination over WESSEX in 645 and over EAST ANGLIA in 650. Following his death and a three-year lapse when Mercia was converted to Christianity, Penda's son Wulfhere assumed a vigorous leadership, reestablishing a greater Mercia, which under his brother Aethelbald included all of southern England. Offa (757–96) controlled East Anglia, KENT, and SUSSEX and maintained superiority over all of England, except NORTHUMBRIA. He built the great OFFA'S DYKE to protect western Mercia from the Welsh and strengthened ties with continental Europe. After his death Mercia's power waned in the face of the growing power of Egbert of Wessex whose victories established him briefly as overlord. The establishment of a kingdom of Kent and several military defeats added to Mercia's decline. In 874 Mercia fell before an invading Danish army, and its eastern part became a part of the DANELAW while the west came under Alfred the Great of Wessex. See also MONTGOMERY (Wales).

MEREDITH BRIDGE. See LACONIA.

MERGATE. See MARGATE.

MERGENTHEIM (West Germany) Town of WÜRTTEMBERG, in the valley of the Tauber River, 7 mi S of Lauda. It is the site of a splendid castle that from 1058 until the early 13th century was the residence of the counts of Hohenlohe. The counts then turned over much of their property to the Teutonic Knights when they moved their base from the Middle East, where the order originated during the Crusades. On the secularization of the order in 1525, Mergentheim became the residence of the grand master and remained so until the order was finally dissolved in 1809.

MERIBAH. See MASSAH.

MERIÇ. See MARITSA RIVER.

MÉRIDA (Mexico) City of YUCATÁN state in the SE. Founded in 1542 by Francisco de Montejo the Younger, it is located on the site of a ruined Mayan city that was called Tihoo or Thó. Mérida's Spanish colonial architecture includes a 16th-century cathedral and a Franciscan convent. Nearby are the remains of a great Mayan city at UXMAL.

MÉRIDA [*ancient:* **Augusta Emerita**] (Spain) Town in Badajoz province, on the Guadiana River, 33 mi ENE of Badajoz, ancient Pax Augusta. It began as the Roman colony of Augusta Emerita, founded in 25 BC and is a town still rich in Roman antiquities. These include a splendid granite bridge constructed under Trajan, a triumphal arch, an amphitheater, a temple, an aqueduct, and an impressive circus. Later the capital of Visigothic LUSITANIA, it was taken by the Moors in 713 AD but still prospered. Alfonso IX of LEÓN captured it in 1228 and presented it to the Knights of Santiago, who brought about its hasty decline.

MÉRIDA (Venezuela) Town of MÉRIDA State, in the Cordillera Mérida, approx. 30 mi S of Lake Maracaibo on the highway to Colombia. Founded in 1558 and twice destroyed by earthquakes, it has a university dating from 1785 and a cathedral.

MERIDIAN (United States) City in Lauderdale county, MISSISSIPPI, 16 mi W of the Alabama border. Named the capital of Mississippi in 1863 during the Civil War, it was destroyed by Union Gen. William Sherman in 1864. In 1871, during the Reconstruction period, it was the site of the Meridian Riot when a black man being tried for urging mob violence shot the white judge, prompting a retaliation by whites that left a number of blacks dead and a black school burned.

MERIONETH (Wales) Former county on Cardigan Bay, now incorporated in the new county of GWYNEDD. With HARLECH as its capital in the Middle Ages, it was long a center of resistance to the English, largely because it is completely surrounded by hills. With little influence from Saxons, Normans, or Scandinavians, many of its inhabitants still speak Welsh. The Normans were repulsed in 1096, and several other attempts at conquest came to nought during the 11th to 14th centuries. Near Dolgellau is Cymmer Abbey, a Cistercian establishment founded c.1200 and dissolved by Henry VIII. Its architecture ranges from Norman to Perpendicular styles. Towen Y Bala, east of Bala, is a former Roman encampment. Here has been unearthed evidence of Bronze Age and earlier settlement as well as of commerce with Ireland.

MERITI STATION. See DUQUE DE CAXIAS.

MERKUS, CAPE (Papua New Guinea) Cape on the SW coast of NEW BRITAIN ISLAND, in the BISMARCK ARCHIPELAGO. In World War II U.S. forces landed here in December 1943 in their push to capture Japanese air and naval bases throughout the region.

MEROË [Merowe] [*Meroitic:* **Bedewe**] (Sudan) Ancient city on the E bank of the NILE RIVER, N of KHARTOUM, near modern Kabū Shī Yah. It served as capital for the Ethiopian kings from c.750 BC, of NUBIA from 500 to 300 BC, and of the later kingdom of Meroë, which lasted until c.350 AD and included the Isle of Meroë, the ancient Meroe Insula region between the Nile, the Blue Nile, and the Atbara rivers. The site has extensive ruins that include temples, palaces, a necropolis, a temple of Amon and three groups of pyramids. It was notable as a center of commerce and caravan trade, and by the first century BC, of iron smelting. It would appear that knowledge of iron-casting was carried into Africa from Meroë. See also KUSH.

MEROVINGIAN KINGDOM. See FRANKISH EMPIRE.

MEROWE. See MEROË.

MERRIMACK RIVER (United States) River, approx. 110 mi long, rising in S central NEW HAMPSHIRE. It flows S into NE MASSACHUSETTS and then NE into the Atlantic Ocean. The water power of the Merrimack played an early and major role in the development of American industry. Among the cities and towns on the river that became pioneer industrial centers are CONCORD and MANCHESTER, New Hampshire and LAWRENCE, LOWELL, and HAVERHILL, Massachusetts. At Manchester, in 1805, the Amoskeag Falls, dropping 85 ft, powered one of the first textile mills. At Lowell, named for Francis Cabot Lowell, a pioneer in cotton manufacturing, the Pawtucket Falls, 32 ft high, provided power. Use of the Merrimack here was stimulated by the building of the Middlesex Canal, which joined BOSTON Harbor with the river. Lawrence, renamed for Abbott Lawrence after Boston industrialists built a dam here, became one of the world's largest woolen textile-manufacturing centers. For about a century until the 1920's when textile plants began moving south, the Merrimack River powered most of New England's factories, producing textiles, hosiery, shoes, and other products. NEWBURYPORT, at the mouth of the river, was an early shipbuilding and whaling center. In 1849 Henry David Thoreau published his first book, *A Week on the Concord and Merrimack Rivers,* based on a voyage made here in 1839.

MERS-AL-KABIR. See MERS-EL-KEBIR.

MERSA MATRŪH. See MATRŪH.

MERSEBURG (East Germany) City in the Halle district, on the Saale River, 18 mi W of Leipzig. An important frontier fortification in Carolingian times, it was a favorite residence of Henry I the Fowler and of Emperor Otto I. It was an episcopal see from 968 until its suppression in 1561 during the Reformation, when the bishopric passed to Saxony. The city was severely damaged in both the Peasants War of 1524 to 1526 and the Thirty Years War, during which it was taken by Swedish forces. It passed to PRUSSIA with the Congress of Vienna in 1815. Heavily bombed in World War II, it was taken by the Allies in April 1945. Notable buildings include a Gothic cathedral with a great 17th-century organ and a Gothic palace, formerly the residence of the bishops of Merseburg.

MERS-EL-KEBIR [Mers-al-Kabir] (Algeria) Town on the Gulf of Oran on the NW coast, approx. 10 mi NW of Oran. As a center of pirate activity in the 15th century, it was twice occupied by the Portuguese. Held by the Spanish from 1505 to 1792, it became a naval base under the French in the 19th century. After the German defeat of France in 1940, the French fleet sought refuge here, but the British navy destroyed most of its ships. The base was finally seized by the Allies on Nov. 10, 1942. By 1962, when the Evian Agreement gave Algeria independence, the base had underground atomic testing sites.

MERSEN. See MEERSEN.

MERSIN [Mersina] [*former:* **Içel**] (Turkey) Port city,

Cliff House at Mesa Verde in Colorado, largest of the astonishing 13th-century cliff dwellings built here by the enterprising pre-Pueblo Anasazi Indians.

40 mi WSW of Adana on the Mediterranean Sea. Excavations carried out in the 1930's showed that the site was occupied in the early Neolithic period, c.3600 BC. It was also a fortress during the HITTITE EMPIRE. To the west are ruins of a Roman port named Soli-Pompeiopolis. See SOLI.

MERSINA. See MERSIN.

MERTHYR TUDFUL. See MERTHYR TYDFIL.

MERTHYR TYDFIL [Merthyr Tudful] (Wales) Town in Mid-Glamorgan, on the Taff River, 21 mi NNW of Cardiff. The source of its name lies in the tale of the martyrdom of St. Tydfil, a Welsh princess killed by Pict warriors in the fifth century AD. In 1804 Richard Trevithick's steam locomotive, the first on rails, pulled a train of ten tons of iron and seventy men on the Merthyr Tydfil-Pontypridd tramway. At Penydarren are traces of a Roman fort.

MERTON (England) Outer LONDON borough, in the SW, that includes Wimbledon, England's tennis headquarters since 1877, and Mitcham, which has a fair dating from Elizabeth I's visit in 1598. In 1236 a meeting of barons here passed the Statute of Merton amending the law concerning the conflicting rights of lords and their tenants to profit from surrounding lands, pastures, and woods. Merton Priory provided early education to Walter de Merton, lord high chancellor to Henry III and founder of Merton College, Oxford, and to Thomas à Becket. It is the site of the ruins of an Augustinian priory founded in 1115 and destroyed by Oliver Cromwell.

MERV [ancient: **Antiochia Margiana, Margiana, Margu, Mouru;** modern: **Mary**] (USSR) Ancient city of Turkmen SSR, 19 mi E of the modern town of Mary, called Merv until 1937, in a large oasis of the Kara-Kum desert on the Murghab River. Founded in the third century BC on the site of an earlier settlement, it is looked upon in Hindu, Parsi, and Arab tradition as the ancient paradise or cradle (Mouru) of the Aryan race. It enjoyed two periods of greatness: as Margiana from 651 to 821 AD, when it was the capital of the Arab rulers of KHORASAN and TRANSOXIANA and an Islamic cultural center; and from 1118 to 1157, when it was the capital of the Seljuk Turks under Sandzhar. Destroyed by Mongols in the early 13th century, it was rebuilt, then destroyed by BUKHARA in 1793. In 1884 it was conquered by RUSSIA. Its 11th- and 12th- century mausoleums, castles, and mosques are exceptional examples of Islamic architecture and art.

MESA VERDE NATIONAL PARK (United States) National park covering 52,074 acres in SW COLORADO. It contains the most outstanding and best-preserved Indian cliff dwellings in the United States, showing Anasazi-Pueblo culture from the 7th through 13th centuries AD. Cliff Palace has 223 rooms, with many kivas, or sacred pits. The area was explored by the Spanish, but these dwellings were first discovered during the Hayden survey of the 1870's.

MESEN. See MESSINES.

MESEWA. See MASSAWA.

MESHCHERSKI GORODETS. See KASIMOV.

MESHED. See MASSHAD.

MESILLA (United States) Unincorporated town in S NEW MEXICO, on the RIO GRANDE RIVER, near Las Cruces. Founded after the Mexican War, it was in Mexican territory until it became part of the United Sates with the GADSDEN PURCHASE of 1853. During the Civil War, from July 1861 until August 1862, it served as headquarters for Col. John R. Baylor who named it the capital of the new Confederate territory. A museum is devoted to the exploits of the outlaw Billy the Kid, who moved to the area as a child and who was tried for murder here.

MESOLÓNGION [Missolonghi] [*ancient:* Elaeus] (Greece) Town in W central Greece on the N shore of the Gulf of Patras. During the Greek war for independence, which began in 1821, Mesolóngion was one of the major strong points of the insurgents. The OTTOMAN EMPIRE besieged it unsuccessfully in 1822/23, and the town held out again with great tenacity in 1825/26 before finally surrendering. Lord Byron, the English poet and a strong supporter of the Greek independence movement, died here of a fever in 1824. There is a statue to his memory. The leader of the successful defense was Marco Bozzaris, a friend of Byron, who was killed in August 1823 in the course of his defeat of the Turks at KARPENISION. He is buried here.

MESOPOTAMIA (Iraq, Syria, Turkey) Ancient historic region of SW Asia, extending from the Persian Gulf in the S to the mountains of Asia Minor in the N, and from the Zagros and Kurdish mountains on the E to the Syrian Desert on the W. More specifically, in historical terms, the name is applied to the heartland of the region, the area between the TIGRIS and EUPHRATES rivers. The name derives from the Greek for "between the rivers." This small region is often called the cradle of civilization because of the remains of cultures found here, some of which date back to c.5000 BC. For example, fifth-millennium BC remains have been found at TEPE GAWRA in northern Iraq and pottery at SAMARRA on the Tigris; while MARI in Syria reveals habitation in the third millennium BC, and NIPPUR on the Euphrates has temples of the same period.

The earliest organized state was that of SUMER, which by 3000 BC had a flourishing urban culture in the south and later controlled a large area. Among its

ANCIENT MESOPOTAMIA, 3100 B.C.–1600 B.C.

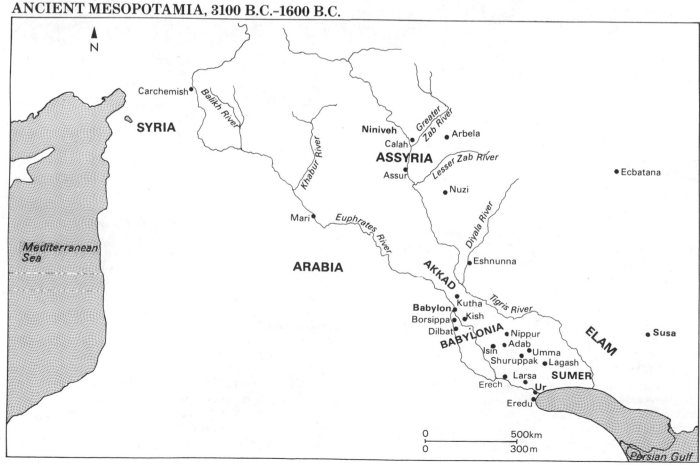

Babylon   Important cities

Mari   Cities

important cities were ERECH, ERIDU, KISH, LAGASH, and UR. The Sumerians are thought to have invented cuneiform writing. Circa 2340 BC Sargon, king of AKKAD to the north, conquered Sumer; but Akkad's rule of Mesopotamia collapsed c.2180 BC, throwing the region into chaos. A MITANNI kingdom was founded in northwestern Mesopotamia in the second millennium BC, but c.1335 BC it fell to Hittites and Assyrians. CARCHEMISH was an important Mitanni city.

A first kingdom of Babylonia was established c.1750 BC by Hammurabi. ELAM was a rival. ASSYRIA developed as a state around ASHUR on the upper Tigris as early as the third millennium BC and expanded. Under Assurbanipal, ruler from 669 to 633 BC, it was at the height of its power. NINEVEH was an Assyrian capital. The Neo-Babylonian, or Chaldaean, Empire came into existence in 625 BC after the fall of Assyria, and the city of BABYLON became the greatest in the world. However, PERSIA under Cyrus the Great conquered Babylonia in 538 BC, but this empire in turn was defeated in 331 BC by Alexander the Great of MACEDON.

The newly risen power of Islam under the ABBASID CALIPHATE, which ruled from 749 to 1258 AD, took Mesopotamia from the BYZANTINE EMPIRE. In 1258 Hulagu Khan, the Mongol conqueror, ravaged the region. He destroyed one of the vital reasons for Mesopotamia's long preeminence: the intricate system of irrigation canals that had made the fertile valleys of the two rivers able to sustain powerful empires and proud cities. The OTTOMAN EMPIRE included Mesopotamia until World War I, when the British occupied it. After the war it became a British mandate until 1921, when most of Mesopotamia became part of the kingdom of Iraq.

MESSANA. See MESSINA.

MESSAPIA (Italy) Region which in ancient times referred to that part of SE Italy, including the "heel," inhabited by the Messapii, who came across the Adriatic c.1000 BC. Later the term also included CALABRIA. See also APULIA.

MESSENE. See MESSINA.

MESSENIA (Greece) Ancient region corresponding to modern Messinías in the PELOPONNESUS. Excavations at PYLOS have uncovered a palace and other traces of a highly developed Mycenaean civilization of the 13th century BC. From the 12th century BC Dorian Greek invaders united with the local inhabitans to form the Messenians. Incapable of resisting SPARTA, they became involved in a series of revolts. Following the First Messenian War of c.735 to 716 BC, Sparta occupied the eastern part of Messenia and enslaved its people. In the Second Messenian War of 650 to 630 BC, they were again subjugated after an attempted revolt under Aristomenes. With the third war in 465/64 BC, which included years of siege of the citadel of Ithome, many were forced to leave their homeland c.460. It was in this period that they colonized SICILY, giving their name to MESSINA. Following the battle of LEUCTRA in 371 BC the freed Messenians founded the city of Mes-

sene in 369 BC and later joined the Achaean League. From 146 BC they were under Roman authority. In the early Middle Ages Slavs conquered the region, which was the scene of battles between Byzantines, Franks, Turks, and Venetians striving for control of Peloponnesus. At Pylos there were major conflicts in 425 BC and in the Battle of NAVARINO in 1827 AD. The acropolis of Messene was the peak Ithome on which a temple of Zeus was erected. Ruins of the city walls, dating from the fourth century BC, are well-preserved, as are a stadium, theater, and governmental buildings.

MESSINA [Messana, Messene] [*ancient:* **Zancle**] (Italy) Port in NE SICILY, on the Straits of Messina, across from Peggiodi, CALABRIA on the mainland. Founded c.730 BC, it might have been settled previously by Sicilian tribes. It was named ZANCLE by Greek colonists from CHALCIS. It was later called Messene in the fifth century BC after colonists from MESSENIA. It was captured by Anaxilas of Rhegium, now REGGIO DI CALABRIA, in the fifth century BC. Destroyed by the Carthaginians in 397 BC, it then became involved in wars between CARTHAGE and SYRACUSE and was eventually taken in 282 BC by mercenaries called Mamertines. ROME came to the aid of the mercenaries and its presence in Sicily triggered the first of the Punic Wars. Messina became the Roman free city Messana in 241 BC and was a military center during the Roman civil wars. Captured by the Byzantines in 535 AD, it was taken by the Saracens in 831 and liberated by the Normans in 1061. Next pillaged by Crusaders under Richard I of England in 1190, it was later under the Angevin, the Aragonese and, from 1735, Spanish Bourbon kings of NAPLES and Sicily. From 1774 to 1778 it was the scene of insurrections against the Bourbons. Garibaldi took Messina in July 1860, but the Bourbon garrison held the fortress until March 1861. The Sicilian campaign in World War II ended with the fall of Messina to the Allies on Aug. 17, 1943. Despite almost total destruction by earthquakes in 1783 and 1908, it is the site of a rebuilt Norman-Romanesque cathedral, a university founded in 1548, and several palaces. See also MILAZZO.

MESSINES [Mesen] (Belgium) Town in West Flanders province, near YPRES. During World War I Messines Ridge was the scene of two major battles: one on Nov. 1, 1914, in which the Germans seized the ridge; and another from June 7 to 14, 1917, in which it passed back to the British.

METALLUM. See MELLE, France.

METAPONA (Solomon Islands) Stream E of Koli Point, on the N coast of GUADALCANAL ISLAND. During World War II it was the scene of fighting from Nov. 8 to 10, 1942 in the Battle of Guadalcanal.

METAPONTION. See METAPONTUM.

METAPONTUM [Greek: Metapontion] (Italy) Ancient city of MAGNA GRAECIA on the Gulf of Taranto, in present Matera province, Basilicata region, approx. 23 mi WSW of Taranto. It was settled by Greek colonists from CROTONE and SYBARIS c.700 BC. Pythagoras taught and died here in 497 BC. It later gave refuge to

Pythagoreans expelled from Crotone. Hannibal made the city his headquarters after the Battle of CANNAE in 216 BC. Two temples—one a Doric building called Tavole Paladine—and some walls remain.

METAURO [ancient: **Metaurus**] (Italy) River rising from the Meta and the Aura in the Etruscan Appenines and flowing E into the Adriatic Sea N of Ancona near Fano. In a major Roman victory on its banks during the Second Punic War in 207 BC, the Romans defeated the Carthaginians under Hasdrubal, who had come into Italy to aid his brother Hannibal. The defeat ended Hannibal's drive to conquer ROME. See CARTHAGE.

METAURUS. See METAURO.

METEORA (Greece) Site of old monasteries in THESSALY in N central Greece, approx. 32 mi NW of the town of Trikkala. They are built on the top of natural stone pillars that have been eroded into isolated columns. The earliest structure, atop the pillar of Doupiani, with a chapel at the base, is possibly of 12th-century construction. Circa 1350 Athanasius, a Hesychast monk from MT ATHOS, built a chapel on another of the pillars. This became the nucleus of the monastery of the Great Meteoron. A hermit named Neilos built four churches in 1367, and in 1381 a Serbian prince, John Urosh, retired and became a monk here.

There were as many as 23 monasteries at one time, and in the 15th and 16th centuries they had special privileges under the Ottoman Turks, who then ruled Greece. The monasteries were accessible only by ropes and nets. Only four are now inhabited, and they can be reached by steps cut in the rock. Much damage was done to the monasteries in World War II and in the following Greek civil war, but they have been restored, and their impressive art and valuable manuscripts are on display. The four remaining are Great Meteoron, St. Stephen from 1312, All Saints of c.1350, and Holy Trinity of 1458.

METHONE [Methoni] [former: Modon] (Greece) Town in the PELOPONNESUS 30 mi SW of Kalamata. Venetians founded a town here that they called Modon on the site of an older settlement. Later an important Venetian stronghold, it was taken by the Turks in 1500 and reoccupied by the Venetians from 1699 to 1718. See also VENICE.

METHONI. See METHONE.

METHVEN (Scotland) Village in Tayside region, 7 mi WNW of Perth. The English defeated Robert Bruce in a battle here on June 19, 1306 after which he was forced into exile. Methven castle is one mile to the east. In September 1644 at nearby TIPPERMUIR Gen. James Montrose defeated the Covenanters in the first of six battles.

METIS. See METZ.

METUCHEN (United States) Town in NE NEW JERSEY, 5 mi WNW of Perth Amboy. In June 1777 during the American Revolution, it was the scene of an encounter between British troops under Gen. William Howe, and a small force of Americans led by Gen. William

Alexander, Lord Stirling; both had met the year before at the Battle of LONG ISLAND.

METZ [ancient: **Divodurum, Divodurum Mediomatricum, Mediomatrica, Metis**] (France) Capital of Moselle department, on the MOSELLE RIVER, 178 mi ENE of Paris. A commercial and cultural center of LORRAINE, it dates from pre-Roman times and was the capital city of a Gallic people called the Mediomatrici. Strategically located, it was an important city of Roman GAUL. It was plundered by the Vandals in 406 AD and by the Huns in 451. An early episcopal see, it became the capital of the eastern portion of the Merovingian Frankish Kingdom of AUSTRASIA in the sixth century. In the eighth century, following the decline of the Frankish Merovingians, the bishops of Metz expanded their powers under the jurisdiction of the HOLY ROMAN EMPIRE. Metz flourished during the Carolingian Renaissance. A prosperous commercial center in the 10th century, with a large Jewish community, it became a free imperial city in the 12th and 13th centuries. Initially embracing Protestantism in the Reformation, it eventually accepted the protection of the French crown. When Henry II annexed three bishoprics of Lorraine, however, Metz endured a long siege in 1552/53 by Emperor Charles V. The Peace of Westphalia in 1648 confirmed the bishoprics as French. An important base in the Franco-Prussian War, Metz was under German attack for two months in 1870 before Marshall Achille Bazaine and his 179,000 French soldiers surrendered. Under German authority from 1871 to 1918, it became a center of strong French patriotic sentiment. Occupied by the Nazis in World War II, the city suffered greatly before being taken by the Allies on Nov. 20, 1944. Gallo-Roman ruins include part of an amphitheater, an aqueduct, and thermal baths. Other architectural treasures include the fourth-century church of St. Pierre-aux-Nonnains, the oldest church in France, the 13th- to 16th-century cathedral of St. Etienne, and the Place St. Croix—a square surrounded by medieval houses from the 13th to the 15th centuries.

MEUDON (France) A suburb SW of PARIS, on the SEINE RIVER. Part of a 17th-century château designed by Jules Mansart for Louis XIV now houses the astrophysics department of the Paris Observatory. The original castle was largely burned in the siege of Paris in 1871. The area was at one time home for artists and musicians, including Renoir, Manet, Wagner, and Rodin, whose estate, with his tomb, is now a museum of his work.

MEUSE RIVER [ancient: **Mosa**; Dutch and Flemish: **Maas**] (Belgium, France, Netherlands) River rising in the Haute Marne department and flowing NE across France, Belgium, and the Netherlands, eventually flowing W into the North Sea. Its valley, especially in France, where it forms a natural protection for Paris, was the scene of heavy fighting in World War I and was held by the Germans until 1918. In World War II it was again taken by the Germans in May/June 1940 and was held by them until the end of the war, figuring importantly in the Battle of the Bulge in January 1945. Its main towns include VERDUN, SEDAN, and

CHARLEVILLE-MÉZIÈRES in France, NAMUR and LIÈGE in Belgium, and MAASTRICHT in the Netherlands.

MEWAR. See UDAIPUR.

MEXICAN EMPIRE. See MEXICO.

MEXICO [Estados Unidos Mexicanos] [*Spanish: Méjico*] Republic in S North America, bordered on the north by the United States, with the Rio Grande the NE boundary, on the S by Belize and Guatemala, on the E by the Gulf of Mexico, and on the W by the Pacific Ocean.

Before Europeans arrived, Mexico harbored the most highly developed Indian cultures in the New World, except for the Incas of PERU. They were the Olmec, whose power was at its height from 1200 to 400 BC; the Zapotec, with a religious center at MITLA and an imposing city at MONTE ALBÁN; the Mixtec, who by the 14th century overshadowed the Zapotec; the Toltec, the most powerful culture in the Valley of Mexico c.900 AD, whose main centers were TULA and CHOLULA; the post-classic Maya in YUCATAN, whose era of greatest development was from c.600 to 900 AD and whose noted city, CHICHEN ITZA, was founded c.515 AD; and the Aztecs, who dominated central Mexico at the time of the Spanish conquest, and whose capital city, TENOCHTITLAN, was founded c.1325 on the site of present MEXICO CITY.

The first Europeans in Mexico were two Spanish voyagers, shipwrecked in 1511. Francisco Hernández de Córdoba from SPAIN discovered Yucatan in 1517, and the next year Juan de Grijalva explored the coast at least as far as Veracruz. Hernando Cortés, the conqueror, reached Mexico in early 1519, founded VERACRUZ, and marched to the Aztec capital. He took the ruler Montezuma captive, but a revolt forced him to flee in 1520. Returning in August 1521, he destroyed Aztec power. Francisco de Coronado started north in 1540 in search of the mythical kingdom of QUIVIRA and opened up what became the southwestern United States. In 1598, Juan de Oñate led an expedition that gave Spain possession of modern NEW MEXICO.

Spanish towns were established by the conquistadors, including Culiacan in 1531, PUEBLA in 1535; CAMPECHE in 1540, Valladolid, later MORELIA, in 1541, and GUADALAJARA and MÉRIDA in 1542. In 1535 the region as far south as PANAMA became the Viceroyalty of NEW SPAIN, which six years later put down an Indian revolt in the Mixton War. During the colonial period Mexico was a source of vast wealth for Spain from Central America and from the Spanish Pacific. Every year vast treasure fleets would land at ACAPULCO on the west coast; their cargo would be carried overland for shipment from Veracruz to Spain. The Spanish pushed north to found SAN FRANCISCO in 1776, and to claim the land as far north as the present United States-Canada border.

The first movement for independence began in 1810 but ended on Jan. 17, 1811 with a defeat at CALDERON BRIDGE. On Feb. 24, 1821 Augustín de Iturbide and Vicente Guerrero agreed on the Plan of IGUALA, which called for independence but would protect the ruling classes. Spain reluctantly acquiesced, and Iturbide became the Emperor Augustin I. The emperor reigned only until February 1823, when he was forced to abdicate; Guadalupe Victoria then became president. For more than 30 years politics was a series of revolts and changes in government, dominated by the eccentric Antonio López de Santa Anna.

In 1836 TEXAS, to which large numbers of Americans had moved, won independence from Mexico by defeating Santa Anna. The annexation of Texas by the UNITED STATES in 1845 brought on the Mexican War. In March 1846 U.S. troops invaded Mexico, won several battles, and captured Mexico City. By the Treaty of GUADALUPE HIDALGO on Feb. 2, 1848 Mexico gave up any claim to Texas and ceded a large region north of the present border. The United States paid Mexico $15 million and assumed claims of American citizens. By the GADSDEN PURCHASE in 1853, Mexico sold the United States land now making up parts of Arizona and New Mexico.

In 1854 leaders opposed to Santa Anna drew up the Plan of AYUTLA, calling for a liberal government. This led to the War of Reform and the overthrow of Santa Anna in 1855. British, French, and Spanish forces landed at Veracruz in 1862, ostensibly to collect debts. GREAT BRITAIN and Spain withdrew, but FRANCE remained and in June 1864 took Mexico City. The French set up an Austrian archduke as Emperor Maximilian I. When French forces withdrew in 1867 and the United States threatened action, a revolt ended Maximilian's brief rule, and he was executed.

In 1876 Porfirio Díaz led a successful revolt against the existing government and thereafter was the effective ruler of Mexico for 34 years. He brought prosperity but governed in the interests of the wealthy. A period of revolts began in 1910 and ended, temporarily, in 1913 when Aldolfo de la Huerta seized power. President Woodrow Wilson of the United States refused to recognize his regime and, using the excuse of an incident at TAMPICO involving American sailors, landed troops in Veracruz in 1914. ARGENTINA, BRAZIL, and CHILE interceded to prevent war. He followed this with an invasion of Northern Mexico in 1917 in pursuit of the revolutionary Pancho Villa. In the 1920's and 1930's, Presidents Álvaro Obregón and Plutarco Elías Calles, socialists, put through labor and agrarian reforms and took control of natural resources from foreign owners.

This trend continued after World War II as the nation emphasized industrialization. Today the government is stable; the candidate of the official party always wins the presidency. Mexico is the fourth-largest oil-producing nation, but its rapid population growth has created a need for increased food production. In late 1982 a drop in oil prices caused severe balance of payments problems and a capital outflow that threatened the nation's stability.

Mexico City is the capital and largest city; the next largest are Guadalajara and MONTERREY.

MEXICO CITY [Ciudad de México, Mexico] (Mexico) Capital city and the country's political, cultural, and

The cathedral in Mexico City's Plaza Mayor in the 1830's. The principal temple of the ancient Aztec city has recently been excavated nearby.

financial center, located at the S end of the great central plateau, approx. 200 mi WNW of Veracruz. Before the Spanish invasion it was the location of the Aztec capital TENOCHTITLÁN, which stood on an island in Lake Texcoco, now the heart of the city. Captured by Cortés after a siege in November 1521, it was rebuilt as Mexico City and for 300 years was the seat of the viceroyalty of NEW SPAIN. Taken by Mexican revolutionaries under Gen. Iturbide in 1821, it was next captured in 1847 by U.S. Gen. Winfield Scott during the Mexican War. Taken by a French army in 1863, it was the scene of Emperor Maximilian's coronation in 1864 and was much improved by him until it was recaptured by Mexican forces under Benito Juarez in 1867. The presidency of Porfirio Díaz (1876–80, 1884–1911) brought many additional improvements. From 1910, during the years of revolution, it was a center for diverse revolutionary forces, led most notably by Francisco Villa and Emiliano Zapata. An extremely colorful city, it has numerous churches and buildings from the Spanish colonial era. The National University was founded in 1551 by the Spanish King Charles I, the Holy Roman Emperor Charles V. There is also an outstanding anthropological museum. The Plaza Mayor is the site of a cathedral, a municipal building, and a national palace. A palace built by Cortés is in COYOACÁN, the city's oldest suburb. See also CHAPULTEPEC, TEOTIHUACÁN.

MÉZIÈRES. See CHARLEVILLE-MÉZIÈRES.

MFUMBIRO. See VIRUNGA MOUNTAINS.

MHUIGHEO. See MAYO, COUNTY.

MIAMI (United States) Second largest city in FLORIDA, on Biscayne Bay, at the mouth of the Miami River. In 1567 the Spanish founded a mission here to pacify the hostile Tequesta Indians who had inhabited the area for at least 2,000 years prior to this time. Briefly under British control c.1770, the land was again occupied by the Spanish from 1784 to 1821. The American Richard Fitzpatrick bought these lands and began a cotton plantation on the site. Fort Dallas was established here in 1836 during the Seminole War. After removal of the Indians, Mrs. Julia Tuttle acquired the land, and settlers began arriving in the 1880's. Its boom as a tourist resort began in the 1920's. Since then Miami has acquired a substantial population of refugees from CUBA and HAITI and has developed dangerous racial tensions.

MIAMI, FORT. See MAUMEE.

MIANI [Meeanee] (Pakistan) Village in central SIND, 6 mi N of Hyderabad. On Feb. 17, 1843 it was the scene of a victory of a small British force led by Sir Charles Napier over the mirs of Sind, an event that led to the eventual British conquest and annexation of this region.

MICHIGAN (United States) State in the N central Great Lakes region; it was the 26th state admitted to the Union, in 1837. It is in two parts, the Upper and Lower peninsulas, separated by the Straits of Mackinac. Michigan was the name of an Indian tribe, so called because it lived near the "big lake."

The Ojibwa, Ottawa, Potawatomi and other Indian tribes inhabited the area when it was first visited by a European, Etienne Brulé, who reached the site of SAULT SAINTE MARIE in 1618. Other Frenchmen came, seeking the NORTHWEST PASSAGE; among them were Jean Nicolet, Jacques Marquette, and Robert de La Salle. Marquette established a mission, and La Salle was aboard the first ship to sail the Great Lakes. The French established trading posts, and MACKINAC Island became a fur-trading center. DETROIT was founded in 1701 as Fort Pontchartrain by Antoine de la Mothe Cadillac. Robert Rogers of VIRGINIA and his rangers captured Detroit from the French in 1760 and in 1763; after the French and Indian War GREAT BRITAIN gained possession of the region.

The area's Indians disliked the British because the fierce Iroquois were their allies. Accordingly, the British were faced with Pontiac's Rebellion of 1763 to 1766, which they subdued after a struggle. Nevertheless, the Indians supported the British in the American Revolution. After the war, the British were supposed to give up the region to the United States, but they held on to Detroit and Mackinac until 1796. In the meantime, Michigan became part of the NORTHWEST TERRITORY under the Ordinance of 1787, and in 1805 Michigan Territory was established.

The Indians were still under British influence and fought beside them in the War of 1812. Early in the war Detroit and Mackinac fell to the British because of incompetent American leadership, but later battles elsewhere restored American control. Lewis Cass, governor from 1813 to 1831, prevailed on the Indians to cede much of their land and move west. This brought in settlers as the movement was stimulated by the coming of steamboats to the Great Lakes and by the opening of the ERIE CANAL in 1825.

After statehood was achieved, railroads, roads, and canals were built, the canal at Sault Sainte Marie in 1855 being especially important. In the late 1840's the discovery of iron ore caused a rush much like the California gold rush. The Republican Party was founded at JACKSON in 1854, and the state was firmly Union and Republican in the Civil War. In the late 19th century, Michigan's farmers were active in reform movements led by the Grangers, and the Greenback and the Populist parties.

The development that industrialized Michigan began in 1903 when Henry Ford opened his automobile-manufacturing plant in Detroit. In the ensuing years he was joined by General Motors and Chrysler, and Detroit became a synonym for automotive mass production and the assembly line. The automotive industry's unions have exemplified the American working ideal, although labor trouble in the auto industry erupted in the 1940's. In World War II most of Michigan's auto plants were adapted to the production of tanks and other weapons. The return of peace brought spectacular prosperity, which continued despite a growth lag in the early 1960's. Growth was helped by the opening of the St. Lawrence Seaway in 1959. Despite its wealth Michigan has had racial troubles; growing unemployment, disparities of income, and inner city neglect erupted into a riot in Detroit in 1967. In 1971 tensions over school integration broke into violence in PONTIAC. In the early 1980's a slump in the U.S. auto market severely hurt Michigan's economy.

LANSING has been the capital since 1847, Detroit is the largest city, others include DEARBORN, FLINT, and GRAND RAPIDS.

MICHIGAN, LAKE (United States) Third largest of the Great Lakes and the only one entirely within the United States, bounded chiefly by Wisconsin on the W, and Michigan on the N and E, and Indiana and Illinois on the S. For centuries the lake has been an important transportation route for Indians and for French and British traders and conquerors, and it is once more today a part of the Great Lakes-ST. LAWRENCE Seaway. The first European here was the French explorer Jean Nicolet in 1634. In 1673 Père Marquette and Louis Jolliet, another French explorer, voyaged on the lake to GREEN BAY, an inlet on the northwest side of the lake, before setting off cross-country to seek the MISSISSIPPI RIVER. Green Bay itself became the well-used head of a portage route between the Great Lakes and the Mississippi River. On his return trip, Jolliet took to the lake again at the site of present CHICAGO. In 1679 Robert de La Salle headed an expedition that used the first recorded sailing vessel on the Great Lakes to voyage as far as Green Bay. As an outcome of the French and Indian War, a large region that included Lake Michigan became British in 1763; in 1783, after the American Revolution, the lake area became part of the new United States. The British, however, did not evacuate it until 1796.

MICHILIMACKINAC. See MACKINAC.

MICHMAS. See MICHMASH.

MICHMASH [Michmas] [*Arabic:* Mukhmas] (Jordan) Locality, 8 mi NE of Jerusalem in the region occupied by ISRAEL in 1967. On the north of a strategically located pass, it was the Philistine headquarters in their attempt to put down uprisings led by the first Hebrew king, Saul. Later it was the scene of his son Jonathan's victory in the Philistine Wars as related in 1 Sam. 13–14; Ezra 2:27; Nehemiah 7:31 and 1 Macc. 9:73.

MICHOACÁN (Mexico) State in the SW, with its capital at MORELIA. Isolated by forested mountains, the native Tarascan Indians have succeeded in keeping their freedom from Aztec, Spanish, and modern civilizations. The region played an important role in Mexico's revolution against Spain. See also PÁTZCUARO.

MICHURINSK [*former:* Kozlov] (USSR) City in W Tambov oblast, 35 mi WNW of Tambov, approx. 115 mi S of Ryazan. Beginning as a small forest monastery founded in 1627, it later became a frontier fortress against the Tatars. It was renamed in 1932 to honor the Russian scientist, Michurin, who had established an experimental horticultural institute in the city.

MICRONESIA Island group and one of the three main divisions of Oceania in the W Pacific Ocean, N of the equator. It includes the CAROLINE ISLANDS, the MARSHALLS, the MARIANAS, the GILBERT ISLANDS, and NAURU. All were put under Japanese mandate in 1919 except GUAM, WAKE, Nauru, and the Gilberts, which were taken by Japan at the outset of World War II in 1941/42. Most were retaken by U.S. forces between 1943 and 1945. See also KIRIBATI.

MIDDELBURG (Netherlands) Ancient capital city of ZEELAND province, on the island of WALCHEREN. Dating from 1217, it became an important medieval center of trade and a city in the HANSEATIC LEAGUE. In 1505 it was the scene of a meeting of the Knights of the Golden Fleece, and it was frequently visited by royalty, including Maximilian, Philip the Fair, and Charles V. It later prospered in trade with the East and West Indies. The last Spanish fortress in Zeeland, it was captured in 1574 by Dutch privateers called the Beggars of the Sea. It was heavily damaged in World War II, but several buildings survive, including a 16th-century town hall and the 12th-century abbey of St. Nicholas.

MIDDELBURG (South Africa) Town of the TRANSVAAL, 80 mi E of Pretoria. In February and March 1901 it was the scene of an unproductive conference between Lord Kitchener and Gen. Botha to negotiate an end to the Boer War; the war continued until 1902.

MIDDLEBORO [**Middleborough**] (United States) Town in SE MASSACHUSETTS, 14 mi S of Brockton. Destroyed by Indians in King Philip's War of 1675/76, it was later rebuilt. Of historic interest is an Indian site thought to date from *c*.2500 BC.

MIDDLEBOROUGH. See MIDDLEBORO.

MIDDLEBROOKS. See MIDWAY.

MIDDLEBURY (United States) Village in W VERMONT, 30 mi NNW of Rutland. The area was chartered in 1761 by a grant from the governor of NEW HAMPSHIRE at a time when New Hampshire and New York State both claimed title to the present state of Vermont. Middlebury was settled three years later, but it was abandoned from 1778 to 1783 during the American Revolution for fear of attacks by Indians and Tories. It was settled permanently in 1783. The quarrying of Vermont marble, a major product of the state, began here in 1803. Middlebury College, which opened in 1800, is known for its summer language courses and its writers' conferences.

MIDDLE CONGO, THE. See CONGO, PEOPLE'S REPUBLIC OF.

MIDDLE COUNTRY. See MIDDLE KINGDOM.

MIDDLE KINGDOM [**Middle Country**] [*modern:* **Chung Hua Jen Min Kung Ho Kuo, People's Republic of China**] (China) Former Chinese name for China dating from 1000 BC and designating the Chou empire and the North China Plain. It reflects the belief that this empire occupied the middle of the earth and was surrounded by barbarians. The Chinese word for middle has been part of the nation's official name since the Communist takeover in 1949.

MIDDLESEX (England) Ancient county, now part of Greater LONDON. The area along the THAMES RIVER was settled from the Stone Age as shown by excavations of tools from many different eras. The first permanent settlements date from 500 BC at BRENTFORD and Heathrow. Middlesex was important in Roman times when the road known as WATLING STREET crossed the district. Danish invasions and civil strife affected much of its subsequent history. See also HARINGEY, HARROW, HILLINGDON, and RICHMOND UPON THAMES.

MIDDLETOWN (United States) City in S CONNECTICUT, on the Connecticut River, 14 mi S of Hartford. Established on the site of the principal village of the Mattabesec Indians, an Algonquin tribe, it was settled in 1650/51 and became Connecticut's leading cultural, commercial, and shipping center during the colonial era. It is the site of well-known Wesleyan University.

MIDDLETOWN (United States) Town in SE RHODE ISLAND, on NARRANGANSETT BAY, 5 mi N of Newport. Its name derives from its location between PORTSMOUTH and NEWPORT. It was pillaged by the British fleet in 1776. Here preserved is "Whitehall," the home of Irish Bishop George Berkeley, the philosopher, from 1729 to 1731. He waited here in vain for funds promised to build a missionary school in Bermuda.

MID-GLAMORGAN (Wales) County in the S, on the Bristol Channel. Created from parts of the former counties of Glamorganshire and MONMOUTHSHIRE, it is an important coal-mining area. Its admin. hq. is CARDIFF, in SOUTH GLAMORGAN.

MIDIAN (Israel) Ancient biblical region E of the Gulf of Aqaba, between EDOM and PARAN. According to Gen. 25:2; 37:28, 36; Exodus 3:1; and Num. 31:1-9, it was inhabited by a nomadic Bedouin people who frequently met the Israelites in battle. Moses, however, married the daughter of their priest, Jethro, who befriended him. According to Judges 6-8 the Midianites invaded PALESTINE and were eventually defeated by Gideon.

MIDLAND (Canada) Town in SE ONTARIO, on Georgian Bay, 27 mi NNW of Barrie. It is known particularly for the Martyrs' Shrine commemorating the deaths during the colonial era of five Jesuit priests, who were among eight North American martyrs canonized in 1930.

MIDLOTHIAN [*former:* **Edinburgh, Edinburghshire**] (Scotland) Former county now incorporated in the Lothian region, whose county town was EDINBURGH. It was the site of numerous mounds, traces of ancient fortifications, and Roman remains, notably at INVERESK, as well as vestiges of secular and ecclesiastical medieval life. In the countryside were the sites of the battles of PINKIE, CARBERRY HILL, and Rullion Green in 1666. The "Heart of Midlothian" was a popular name for Tolbooth prison in Edinburgh and became the title of one of Sir Walter Scott's novels.

MIDNAPORE [**Midnapur**] (India) Town and district of BENGAL, 68 mi W of Calcutta. Its history begins with the ancient town of TAMLUK, an important Buddhist settlement in the fifth century BC and now in ruins. As payment for his elevation to the throne of Bengal, Mir Kasim ceded both town and district to the British East India Company in 1760.

MIDNAPUR. See MIDNAPORE.

MIDWAY [*former:* **Brooks, Middlebrooks**] (United States) Administrative district comprised of Eastern Island and Sand Island, located in the central Pacific Ocean, 1,304 mi WNW of Honolulu. Claimed by the United States in 1859, it was formally occupied in 1867. In 1903 it was put under the control of the U.S. Navy, which started construction of a major submarine base here in 1940. During World War II it was attacked unsuccessfully by the Japanese in December 1941 and in January 1942. Finally, from June 3 to 6, 1942 in what is considered a turning point in World War II, U.S. naval aircraft in the Battle of Midway destroyed three Japanese aircraft carriers, severely damaging the Japanese navy.

MIE [**Miye**]. See ISE (Japan).

MIFRAZ SCHLOMO. See SHARM EL-SHEIKH.

MIGDAL. See MAGDALA.

MIGDAL-EL (Israel) Fortified town in ancient N PALESTINE, thought to be identical with the biblical MAGDALA of Joshua 19:38.

MIGDOL (Israel) The Israelites' crossing of the RED SEA took place near here according to Exodus 14:2 and Numbers 33:7.

MIKNASA. See MEKNES.

MIKULOV [*German:* **Nikolsburg**] (Czechoslovakia) Town, 30 mi S of Brno, which was the site of several important treaties. In 1621 Emperor Ferdinand II and Gabriel Bethlen, prince of TRANSYLVANIA signed an agreement whereby Bethlen renounced his kingship of HUNGARY. In 1805 armistice agreements ending the Franco-Austrian War were signed here; and the treaty ending the Austro-Prussian War was put into effect here on July 26, 1866.

MILAN [*ancient:* **Mediolanium, Mediolanum;** *Italian:* **Milano**] (Italy) Provincial capital and important city of LOMBARDY region and of the nation, between the Adda and Ticino rivers. The ancient name is Celtic, and the city is thought to have been founded by the Galli Insubres after they destroyed the existing Etruscan city of Melpum nearby in 396 BC. The Romans captured the Celtic city in 222 BC. By the third century AD Milan was the chief city of AEMILIA and LIGURIA and in the next century the residence of the emperors of the western ROMAN EMPIRE and an important center of the early Christian Church. Constantine issued his Edict of Milan here in 313. It retained much of its Celtic heritage as it grew in both secular and ecclesiastical significance, particularly under St. Ambrose, bishop of Milan from 374 to 397. The city was invaded by Huns under Attila in 452, by the Heruli under Odoacer in 476, and by Goths under Theodoric in 493. Led by Uraia, the Goths totally destroyed Mediolanum in 539. By the 12th century the new city had developed sufficient political influence to lead the Lombard League in its opposition to Emperor Frederick I. Rebuilt in 1162 after its de-

struction by Frederick, under the Visconti family it eventually contested control of northern Italy with VENICE and rivaled FLORENCE for domination of central Italy. Under the Sforza family from 1447 to 1535, it became a pawn in the Hapsburg-French rivalries during the Italian wars of the 16th century. Under Spanish control from 1535, it was next ceded to AUSTRIA at the end of the War of the Spanish Succession in 1713. As part of Napoleon's empire from 1796 to 1814, it became capital of his CISALPINE REPUBLIC and kingdom of Italy in 1805. Again part of Austria from 1815 to 1859, it was a leading center of the Risorgimento, the Italian independence movement, and was the scene of the insurrection of the Cinque Giornate on March 17 to 22, 1848, when the Milanese drove the Austrians from their city after bitter fighting. The Lombard campaign, with the battles of SOLFERINO and MAGENTA, made it a part of the kingdom of SARDINIA and eventually of a united Italy in 1860/61. Heavily damaged by bombing in World War II, it was reached by the Allies on April 29, 1945. Its white marble Gothic cathedral, the third largest in Europe, dates from 1387 to 1858. The city's Ambrosian library is the oldest public library in Europe and houses an outstanding collection of paintings and manuscripts. Its Ospedale Maggiore, dating from 1456, is Europe's first municipal hospital. The church of Santa Maria della Grazie built between 1465 and 1490 houses Leonardo da Vinci's masterpiece *The Last Supper*. The world-famous La Scala opera house dates from 1778. Today the fast-paced city is the center of Italy's industrial north and is a major capital of corporate activity, finance, design, and fashion.

MILANO. See MILAN.

MILAZZO [*ancient:* **Mylae**] (Italy) Port of NE SICILY, on the Tyrrhenian Sea, 17 mi W of Messina. As ancient Mylae it served as an outpost of Zancle, now MESSINA, and was occupied before 648 BC. During the First Punic War in 260 BC the Romans under Gaius Duilius defeated the Carthaginians off this coast. In 36 BC Marcus Vipsanius Agrippa was victorious over Sextus Pompeius in a naval battle at the end of the Roman civil war. In modern times, during the campaign for the unification of Italy, Garibaldi won a decisive victory over the Bourbon garrison here in 1860. A Spanish castle dating from the 13th century is now a prison, and there is a cathedral dating from the 16th and 17th centuries.

MILDENHALL (England) Town of Suffolk, 19 mi ENE of Cambridge. Of historic interest are the remains of a small Roman settlement, a 15th-century market cross, a gabled 17th-century manor house, and the early English to Perpendicular Gothic church of St. Andrew with a splendidly carved oak roof. In 1942 a farmer plowing fields nearby unearthed 34 pieces of silver from a fourth-century Roman dwelling. Now in the British Museum, the find is called the Mildenhall Treasure.

MILETUS [*Byzantine:* **Palation;** *Turkish:* **Balat**] (Turkey) Ancient seaport near the mouth of the MENDERES River, on the coast of CARIA in modern Aydin, near the island of SAMOS. Located on a site inhabited from the latest Minoan age, it was occupied by the early Greeks c.1000 BC and became one of the principal cities of IONIA. From the eighth century BC it was significant in the colonization movement, particularly in the Black Sea area but also in Egypt and Italy, and became the most important of the 12 Ionian cities and a rival of LYDIA. As leader of an Ionian revolt in 500 BC, it was subdued by PERSIA after the battle of Lade in 494 BC. Darius sacked the city and massacred most of its inhabitants. With the expulsion of the Persians in 479 BC, Miletus became a member of the Delian League under the domination of ATHENS but revolted, joining SPARTA in 412 BC. It fell to Alexander the Great in 334 BC. Distinguished as a literary center, it was the home of early Greek philosophers, including Thales and Anaximander. It was twice visited by St. Paul.

MILFORD (United States) City in S CONNECTICUT, 10 mi SW of New Haven. Settled in 1639 on land purchased from the Paugusset Indians, it was repeatedly attacked in the following years, causing the inhabitants to construct defensive palisades. It served as the temporary home and burial place of Robert Treat (1622–1710), commander of the Connecticut troops in King Philip's War and governor of Connecticut from 1683 to 1689, and of Jonathan Law, governor of Connecticut from 1742 to 1751. During the American Revolution the people of Milford repulsed the British attempt to land from LONG ISLAND SOUND.

MILFORD HAVEN (Wales) Port in Dyfed, 47 mi E of Swansea. In 1172 Henry II set sail from here for the invasion of IRELAND. Richard II landed at the haven from Ireland in 1399 and soon after surrendered to Henry of Bolingbroke, later Henry IV. In 1485 Henry Tudor, earl of Richmond, later Henry VII, landed here from France to wage his successful campaign for the English throne. In 1588 its citizens petitioned Queen Elizabeth I to fortify the haven in the face of the expected Spanish invasion; the result was the construction of a blockhouse at either side of the mouth of the harbor.

MILHAU. See MILLAU.

MILID. See MALATYA.

MILIDIA. See MALATYA.

MILLAU [Milhau] [*ancient:* **Aemilianum**] (France) Town in Aveyron department approx. 30 mi SE of Rodez, on the right bank of the TARN RIVER. A Huguenot stronghold in the 16th century, in 1620 it revolted against Louis XIII, with the result that Cardinal Richelieu, his chief minister, ordered its fortifications dismantled. The site of Gallo-Roman ruins, it also has the Romanesque church of Notre Dame, restored in the 16th century.

MILLEDGEVILLE (United States) City of central GEORGIA, 30 mi NE of Macon, on the Oconee River. Laid out in 1803, it served as the seat of state government from 1807 to 1868. In the Civil War it was seized by Union Gen. William T. Sherman on Nov. 23, 1864. Many antebellum homes survive, including the former executive mansion and the state capitol, both now part of Georgia Military College.

MILLE LACS LAKE (United States) Lake in E central MINNESOTA, N of MINNEAPOLIS. In 1679 the French explorer Sieur Duluth visited the Ojibwa Indians living along its shores. In 1680 the French friar and explorer of North America, Louis Hennepin, was held captive nearby with his companions for several weeks following their exploration of the upper MISSISSIPPI RIVER Valley. During his detention by the Sioux he discovered the Falls of St. Anthony, which later was the site of Minneapolis.

MILLER'S HOLLOW. See COUNCIL BLUFFS.

MILLOM (England) Market town in Cumbria, 21 mi NW of Lancaster. Millom Castle, dating from the Norman Conquest and fortified by Sir John Huddlestone in the 14th century, was held for centuries by a family that exercised absolute power over the surrounding area until the castle's siege by Parliamentary forces in 1648. The church of the Holy Trinity dates from early Norman to the Decorated Gothic periods.

MILL SPRINGS (United States) Village in SE KENTUCKY, on the Cumberland River, S of Frankfort. In the first battle of the Kentucky-Tennessee campaign in the Civil War, Union forces under Gen. George Thomas pushed back Confederate troops led by Gen. George Crittenden on Jan. 19, 1862 at Logan's Crossroads, 10 miles north of the river, thereby opening a Union advance through eastern TENNESSEE.

MILLTOWN. See PLAINFIELD.

MILNE BAY (Papua New Guinea) Bay at the SE extremity of NEW GUINEA ISLAND. Occupied by the Japanese in August 1942, during World War II, it was liberated by Australian troops in September and October 1942.

MILO. See MELOS.

MÍLOS. See MELOS.

MILVIAN BRIDGE [Mulvian Bridge] [*Latin:* **Pons Milvius, Pons Mulvius**] (Italy) Bridge N of ROME over the TIBER, built by Marcus Aemilius Scaurus in 109 BC as part of the FLAMINIAN WAY. Roman Emperor Constantine I defeated Maxentius here in 312 AD, thereby establishing his supremacy in the West. According to Eusebius, during the battle Constantine saw a cross in the sky with the words "By this conquer." His victory led to his conversion to Christianity and a tolerance of the faith throughout the empire.

MILWAUKEE [*Indian:* **Melleoiki**] (United States) City in SE WISCONSIN, where the Milwaukee, Menomonee, and Kinnickinnic rivers enter LAKE MICHIGAN. Starting as an Indian gathering and trading center, it was first visited by the European explorers Father Jacques Marquette and Louis Jolliet in 1673. In 1795 the North West Company established a fur-trading post here, and in 1818 Solomon Juneau, the fur trader, became the first permanent settler. Founded in 1839 out of a merger of several towns, it was a major center of German immigration from 1840 to 1900. Following the Civil War the city was also a leader in the labor movement. In the 1960's Father Groppi mobilized the city's blacks in the civil rights movement.

MIMATUM. See MENDE.

MIMS, FORT. See FORT MIMS.

MINCHINHAMPTON (England) Town in Gloucestershire, 12 mi SSE of Gloucester. Many traces of prehistoric settlements and earthworks are found here. Nearby is a valley called Woeful Dane Bottom, possibly named after a defeat of the Danes in c.920.

MINDANAO (Philippines) Largest island in the S part of the group, NE of Borneo. The island was introduced to Islam in the mid-14th century as it spread from MALAYA and BORNEO to the SULU ARCHIPELAGO. In the late 16th century native Muslim groups launched a holy war against the Spanish invaders that continued into the 20th century, when the same groups resisted U.S. domination. Suffering little damage in World War II, the island was a center of terrorist activities in the 1960's as a result of rapid change and its accompanying problems. In 1971 a Stone Age people, the Tasaday, were discovered living in one of the areas being developed. They are now protected.

MINDEN [*ancient:* **Minthun**] (West Germany) Town of North Rhine-Westphalia, 44 mi WSW of Hanover, on the Weser River, 58 mi ENE of Münster. A trading center of some importance in the time of Charlemagne, it was made the seat of a bishopric in the eighth century. It was later a member of the HANSEATIC LEAGUE. Punished with military occupation for its reception of the Reformation, it endured similar trials in the Thirty Years War and passed to BRANDENBURG by the Peace of Westphalia in 1648. On Aug. 1, 1759 during the Seven Years War, the Battle of Minden was fought between Anglo-Allied forces under Duke Ferdinand of Brunswick and the French under Marshal Coutades. The French, who had held the town, were decisively defeated. In World War II the city was entered by Allied troops on April 6, 1945. Historic buildings include two 12th-century churches, a town hall with a 13th-century facade, and a 13th-century Gothic cathedral.

MINDORO (Philippines) Island SW of LUZON. Visited by the Chinese before the arrival of the Spaniards in 1570, it was subject to Moro Muslim raids in the 17th and 18th centuries. Taken under U.S. control in 1901, it was held by the Japanese in World War II and invaded by U.S. forces on Dec. 15, 1944.

MINEHEAD [*ancient:* **Manehafd, Mannheve, Mynneheved**] (England) Town on the Bristol Channel, 21 mi NW of Taunton, in Somerset. It is the supposed birth and burial place, marked by a 13th-century monument, of the famous lawyer and writer, Henry de Bracton, who died in 1268. St. Michael's, the parish church, has a striking Perpendicular Gothic tower.

MINEO [*ancient:* **Menaeum**] (Italy) Town in Catania province, SICILY, 27 mi SW of Catania. Ancient Menaeum was the possible birthplace of Ducetius before he founded the actual town in 459 BC. The remains of ancient Greek fortifications attest to its age. Nearby was the temple of the Palici, the twin gods of the native Sicilian Sicels, once the most holy place in Sicily. It is also the site of medieval crypts.

MING EMPIRE. See CHINA.

MINGRELIA [*ancient:* **Colchis**] (USSR) Former principality on the Black Sea coast in Transcaucasia, now included in NW GEORGIAN SSR, once part of ancient COLCHIS. It is also identified with ancient Dioscurias, now SUKHUMI, a colony of MILETUS. Declaring its independence as a principality in the 15th century AD, it remained more or less subject to PERSIA and TURKEY. In 1803/04 it became part of RUSSIA and was permanently incorporated in 1867, with POTI as its main port.

MINHOW. See FOOCHOW.

MINNEAPOLIS [*former:* **Fort Saint Anthony, Saint Anthony**] (United States) Largest city in MINNESOTA, on the banks of the MISSISSIPPI RIVER, at the Falls of ST. ANTHONY, twin city with ST. PAUL. The French Jesuit missionary Father Louis Hennepin made the first recorded visit to the area, discovering and naming the Falls of St. Anthony in 1680. This became the site of the area's first settlement in 1837; Fort Saint Anthony and a gristmill had been constructed here a few years earlier. The city was under different sovereignties for many years, its east side becoming U.S. territory after the American Revolution, but its west side remaining under Spanish and then French rule until the LOUISIANA PURCHASE of 1803. It now includes the former city of St. Anthony. Known as "the flour city of the United States," it lost half its mills and many workers in an explosion in 1878, which led to research and protective measures against industrial dust. See also MILLE LACS LAKE, MINNEHAHA.

MINNEHAHA (United States) Falls and creek in SE MINNESOTA at the outlet of Lake Minnetonka. The creek flows through the southern part of MINNEAPOLIS to the MISSISSIPPI RIVER. The falls are famous from Longfellow's use of them in his poem, *The Song of Hiawatha*. Minnehaha was the Indian maiden who married Hiawatha.

MINNESOTA (United States) State in the N central Great Lakes region; it was admitted to the Union in 1858 as the 32nd state. Its name derives from a Sioux Indian word meaning "water-cloudy," referring to the Minnesota River.

A human skeleton discovered in 1931 indicates that this region was inhabited as far back as the Pleistocene epoch, approx. 20,000 years ago, long before the Mound Builders. Although its authenticity is very much in doubt, the Kensington Rune Stone, found in 1898, would place Norsemen here in 1362. In any event, French fur traders were active in the mid-17th century; the Sieur Daniel Duluth reached here, and Father Hennepin and Michel Aco discovered the St. Anthony Falls in 1683. At the time there were Ojibwa Indians in the east and Sioux in the west; both were friendly to the French.

A number of American explorers visited the region between 1766 and 1829, including Zebulon M. Pike and Henry Schoolcraft. The area was good fur country, and after the War of 1812 the American Fur Company dominated the trade. At that time, too, more settlers came. Fort Snelling was established in 1819 in the area of the present twin cities of MINNEAPOLIS and ST. PAUL, the village of St. Anthony c.1840, and Minneapolis c.1845. By four treaties negotiated between 1837 and 1855, the Indians gave up much of their land, and this further stimulated settlement. When Minnesota was made a territory in 1849, its eastern part came from a piece of the old NORTHWEST TERRITORY and its western section from the LOUISIANA PURCHASE.

A land boom followed, railroads and roads were built, and the University of Minnesota was founded seven years before statehood. The Panic of 1857 hit the state hard, however, because of land speculation. Even so, people continued to move in, mostly small farmers. Minnesota supported the Union in the Civil War, and its wheat helped feed the armies. At this same time, the Sioux, disturbed by broken promises and infringements on their land, raided and killed settlers. In 1862, under Little Crow's leadership, more than 800 settlers died; the end of the trouble did not come until 1867.

The Federal Homestead Act of 1862, however, encouraged immigration, and many Scandinavians arrived during the late 19th century. With settlement Minnesota became a center of agrarian discontent, partly owing to natural causes, such as insect plagues, and partly due to economic problems of debt and low prices. An 1874 law attempted to control railroad rates in the farmers' favor. Large-scale lumbering was carried on, creating the legend of the giant woodsman, Paul Bunyan, and Babe the Blue Ox. The discovery of the greatest iron ore deposits in the world, in the Mesabi Range in 1890, helped economic conditions and made Minnesota the nation's largest producer of iron ore.

There was more discontent on the farms in the 20th century, leading to the founding of the Nonpartisan League in 1915. Later, farmers and workers joined in forming the Farmer-Labor party, which dominated politics in the 1930's. This movement merged with the Democratic Party in 1944. Minnesota has been the scene of experiments with cooperative organizations, stemming in part at least from its Scandinavian heritage.

St. Paul is the capital, and with Minneapolis across the Mississippi River, makes up its largest urban area. DULUTH became a major port after the opening of the St. Lawrence Seaway in 1959.

MINNI. See ARMENIA.

MINOA. See MONEMVASIA.

MINORCA [*Spanish:* **Menorca**] (Spain) One of the BALEARIC ISLANDS in the W Mediterranean Sea, approx. 25 mi NE of MAJORCA. The site of numerous megalithic monuments, it gained importance apart from the other islands in 1708 when it was occupied by the British during the War of the Spanish Succession. During the Seven Years War it was taken by the French in 1756, restored to Great Britain by the Treaty of Paris in 1763, and seized again by the French and Spanish in 1782. In 1798, during the French Revolutionary Wars, Great Britain regained control but relinquished it and much else it had wrested from France in the Peace of Amiens of 1802, which restored Minorca to Spain. Dur-

ing the Spanish civil war of 1936 to 1939 Minorca was in Loyalist hands until February 1939, when it was forced to surrender.

MINSK [*former:* **Menesk, Mensk**] (USSR) City and capital of Belorussian SSR, located on a tributary of the BEREZINA RIVER, near the Polish border. Known from 1067 AD, it was an outpost in the POLOTSK principality. The city became capital of the Minsk principality in 1101 and was made part of LITHUANIA in 1326. At the time it was attacked by the Tatars in 1505 it was a commercial center of considerable importance. For its status in the 16th to the 18th centuries, see MINSK historic region. It was partly destroyed in 1812 during the Napoleonic Wars. It was a key point in the Russian Revolution of 1917. The city was occupied by the Germans in 1918 and by the Poles in 1919. It was taken by the Germans in July 1941 and retaken by the Soviets on July 3, 1944. A Jewish center from the Middle Ages on, during World War II it was a German concentration center for Jews before their extermination. Historic buildings include the 17th-century Bernardine convent and the Ekaterin Cathedral, formerly Petropavlovsk Church.

MINSK (USSR) Region and political unit of old W RUSSIA, originally peopled by Slavs. One part, inhabited by the Krivichi, became part of White Russia; the other part, settled by Dregovichi and Drevlyans, became part of so called Black Russia. Its southwestern part was occupied by LITHUANIA from the 12th to the 14th centuries. The entire region was successively incorporated into Lithuania, annexed to POLAND in 1569, and taken by Russia in 1793. Significant archaeological finds dating from the Neolithic and subsequent ages were made in the early 20th century. See also BELORUSSIA, city of MINSK.

MINSTER-IN-SHEPPEY (England) Town on ISLE OF SHEPPEY, KENT, 40 mi E of London. The church dedicated to St. Mary and St. Sexburga was originally part of a seventh-century convent founded by Sexburga, the widow of Erconberht, king of Kent. It is now incorporated into a 12th-century church founded by William de Corbeuil, archbishop of Canterbury.

MINTURNAE (Italy) Ancient town of Latina province, LATIUM region, on the Appian Way, 7 mi E of Formia. Founded by the Aurunci, in 295 BC it became a Roman colony important both commercially and strategically, since it controlled the bridge on the APPIAN WAY over the LIRI RIVER. Ruins include an aqueduct, two theaters, forums, and other buildings north of modern MINTURNO.

MINTURNO (Italy) Town in Latina province, Latium region, on the Appian Way, 47 mi ESE of Latina, near the ruins of ancient MINTURNAE. In May 1944, during World War II, it served as a base for the Allied advance from the coast.

MIQUELON. See SAINT PIERRE AND MIQUELON.

MIRANDOLA (Italy) Town in Modena province, EMILIA-ROMAGNA region, 19 mi NNE of Modena. The few remains of a castle recall the period from the 14th century, when the Pico family first held the town, until

1710, when its last member was deprived of his dominions by Holy Roman Emperor Joseph I (1678–1711) as part of his plan for internal reforms. The Gothic Palazzo del Commune dates from the 15th century, and a restored cathedral dates from the 16th century. San Francesco is a fine Gothic church.

MIRZAPUR (India) City in SE Uttar Pradesh state, on the right bank of the GANGES RIVER, 45 mi ESE of Allahabad. Founded c.1650, it now includes the town of Bindhachal, which has the shrine of Vindhyeshwari and is a center of pilgrimage. On its river front are mosques and Hindu temples.

MIRZOYAN. See DZHAMBUL.

MISANTLA (Mexico) City in Veracruz state, 70 mi NW of Veracruz. Here in 1817 the Spanish won a battle during the Mexican War of Independence of 1810 to 1821.

MISENUM [*modern:* **Porto di Miseno**] (Italy) Ancient town on the promontory at the NW end of the Bay of Naples, Napoli province, Campania region, S of the ruins of CUMAE, approx. 12 mi W of Naples. A naval station under Augustus, it had been constructed by Agrippa in 31 BC. It was destroyed by the Arabs in the ninth century AD. Emperor Tiberius died in his villa here.

MISHRIFEH. See QATNA.

MISITHRA. See MISTRA.

MISKITO COAST. See MOSQUITO COAST.

MISKOLC [Miskolcz] (Hungary) Major industrial city, 85 mi NE of Budapest. The settlement was nearly destroyed by the Mongols between 1241 and 1243 during their conflicts with the Magyars. Made a free city in the 15th century, it was invaded by the Turks in the 16th and 17th centuries and by German forces in the 17th and 18th centuries. Parts of a 13th-century castle survive; the Avas Reformed Church dates from the 15th century; and there is a museum of Scythian art. To the south is the heath of Mohi on the banks of the Sajó River, renowned as the scene of a great defeat of the Hungarians by the Mongols in 1241.

MISKOLCZ. See MISKOLC.

MISNIA. See MEISSEN.

MISORE ISLANDS. See SCHOUTEN ISLANDS.

MISQUAMICUT. See WESTERLY.

MISR. See EGYPT.

MISRATAH [Misurata] [*ancient:* **Tubartis**] (Libya) Port city in an oasis in the NW, on the Mediterranean Sea, 125 mi E of Tripoli. Known to the Romans as Tubartis, in recent history it was an important Italian garrison town captured by the British in January 1943 during World War II.

MISSIONARY RIDGE (United States) Ridge extending NE to SW in Hamilton county, TENNESSEE and Dade county, Georgia. A section of this ridge near CHATTANOOGA, Tennessee was the site of a Union victory on Nov. 25, 1863 during the Chattanooga campaign in the Civil War. Confederate Gen. Braxton Bragg had two months earlier established his troops along the ridge from which he besieged Chattanooga. Union Gens. Joseph Hooker and George Thomas led their men in a courageous attack up the ridge. Within the day Bragg was retreating, leaving Chattanooga in Union control.

MISSISSIPPI (United States) State in the S central region, most of whose W boundary is formed by the MISSISSIPPI RIVER; to the S are Louisiana and the Gulf of Mexico, to the N Tennessee, to the E Alabama, and to the W Arkansas and Louisiana. It was admitted to the Union in 1817 as the 20th state. Mississippi is a form of an Algonquian word for "big river."

Choctaw, Chickasaw, and Natchez Indians inhabited the region when the first Europeans, led by Hernando de Soto, explored it from 1540 to 1542. The Frenchman Pierre le Moyne, the Sieur d'Iberville, made the first settlement on Biloxi Bay in 1699. Settlement was speeded up in 1718 by the Mississippi Scheme of John Law, a Scottish resident in FRANCE, even though the plan went bankrupt in the "Mississippi Bubble," which caused financial disasters all over France. Mississippi was part of LOUISIANA until 1763, when the British, by the treaty ending the French and Indian War, received almost all the land east of the Mississippi. During the American Revolution, SPAIN, which sided with the colonists, captured NATCHEZ, which had been founded in 1719, but refused to turn it over to the United States until U.S. troops arrived in 1798.

Mississippi Territory was then created. After GEORGIA ceded its claim to some of this region in 1802 and after the LOUISIANA PURCHASE in 1803, there was a land boom. The NATCHEZ TRACE, which grew from Indian trails and ran from NASHVILLE, Tennessee, to Natchez, provided the main route to Mississippi from the 1780's to the 1830's. Large plantations became dominant, but as Jacksonian democracy spread the small farmers gained power, and this was reflected in a liberal constitution of 1832. Treaties of 1820, 1830, and 1832 pushed all Indians west of the Mississippi, while black slaves were brought in until they outnumbered the whites.

In January 1861 Mississippi became the second state to secede from the Union. During the Civil War, in April 1862, CORINTH was abandoned to Union forces, and the next year VICKSBURG fell on July 4, after 14 months of attack and siege. The state suffered much damage in 1864 when Gen. W.T. Sherman marched his army from Vicksburg to MERIDIAN, destroying the latter on his way to ATLANTA, Georgia. After the war, when Mississippi refused to ratify the 13th and 14th Amendments, it was made part of a Federal military district in 1867 along with ARKANSAS. It was readmitted to the Union in 1870, with the state's Republicans in power. Within five years they were defeated, however, partly because of violent opposition from the Ku Klux Klan, and by 1890 a new constitution assured white supremacy. The sharecropping system, which succeeded the plantation system, kept black and white farmers poor, and "Jim Crow" laws in 1904 further eroded black civil rights.

Beginning in the mid-1950's there was great resistance to school integration, marked in 1961 by mass violence against the "freedom riders" from the North. Federal troops were sent in in 1962 when an attempt was made to block the admittance of a black to the University of Mississippi law school. There were other disorders and deaths in 1963, 1964, and 1970 but the course of integration and civil rights continued. Since 1965, as a result of the Federal Voting Rights Act, many more blacks vote, and some have been elected to public office. The state is attempting to raise the literacy rate, long the lowest in the country. In politics, Mississippi was for many years overwhelmingly Democratic, but in three of the presidential elections since 1948 it has given its vote to right-wing, third party candidates.

Mississippi is one of the few states still basically agricultural; it leads in cotton production. JACKSON is the capital and largest city; others include Greenville, Gulfport, and Hattiesburg.

MISSISSIPPI RIVER (United States) Legendary "old man" of North American rivers and the world's third-longest river system, after the NILE and the AMAZON Rivers. It rises from two sources—at Itasca Lake in N Minnesota and at the fountainhead of the MISSOURI RIVER in the ROCKY MTS of SW Montana—and flows 3,740 mi (6,020 km) to the Gulf of Mexico. Its major tributaries, more than 250, include the Missouri, the Ohio, the Illinois, and the Arkansas rivers.

It was discovered by Hernando De Soto in 1541. The late 17th century brought middle-river exploration by Jacques Marquette and Louis Jolliet, upper river penetration by Louis Hennepin and lower river exploration by Robert de La Salle, who claimed the territory from the Illinois River to the Gulf of Mexico in 1682 for Louis XIV and FRANCE, naming it "Louisiana."

Following the founding of NEW ORLEANS in 1718 and the establishment of upper river settlements, the Mississippi became both ploy and prize in 18th-century power politics. With the Treaty of PARIS, which ended the Seven Years War in Europe and the French and Indian War in America in 1763, France ceded the territory east of mid-river to GREAT BRITAIN. In the same period, however, France secretly ceded the remainder of the Mississippi basin to SPAIN, regaining it only in 1800, shortly before the LOUISIANA PURCHASE of 1803.

During the American Revolution rights of river navigation became an increasingly bothersome question. Attempts by John Jay to negotiate a treaty with Spain assuring free navigation failed in both 1779 and 1785, and until 1795 Spain imposed heavy taxes on U.S. commerce down the river. Ultimately, James Monroe, then U.S. minister to France, convinced the French government to intercede, opening the way to successful negotiations with Spain.

The introduction of steam navigation in 1811 brought a revolution to river trade and traffic. The steamboat *New Orleans*, financed by Nicholas Roosevelt, made the first trip from PITTSBURGH to New Orleans. By 1817 a steamboat of improved power made a trip upriver to ST. LOUIS, and by 1838 transport time had been cut from several months to a few days, with some 230 steamboats active in river trade. By 1842 an extensive canal system through OHIO linked the Mississippi with the Great Lakes, which were in turn connected via the ERIE CANAL, opened in 1825, with the HUDSON RIVER and the Atlantic Ocean. The population of the Mississippi Valley increased from under 2 million in 1811 to more than 14 million in 1860.

During the Civil War, the lower Mississippi and the Ohio River with its two main tributaries were still the most important avenues of communications west of the Appalachian Mts, and Kentucky's adherence to the Union was crucial in excluding the Confederacy from the use of the Ohio. The capture of New Orleans in 1862 by the Union's Adm. David Farragut and the Union victories at VICKSBURG in 1863 and PORT HUDSON succeeded in cutting the Confederacy in two by giving the Union effective control of the river. It was closed to commerce, and the prosperity of the South was crushed. Revived river traffic following the war is well described in Mark Twain's *Life on the Mississippi*, published in 1883.

In the early 20th century, the building of the PANAMA CANAL and its prospects for communication with the west coasts of North and South America stimulated river improvements. Since the mid-1950's improvements in the river channels have brought an enormous increase in river traffic, despite recurring disastrous floods. The river itself flows through or forms the boundary of MINNESOTA, WISCONSIN, IOWA, ILLINOIS, MISSOURI, TENNESSEE, ARKANSAS, MISSISSIPPI, and LOUISIANA. Major cities along its course include MINNEAPOLIS and ST. PAUL, St. Louis, CAIRO, MEMPHIS, BATON ROUGE, and New Orleans. Its delta is a huge complex of swamps, called bayous, small streams, and coastal inlets, the traditional home of Louisiana's Cajun people.

MISSOLONGHI. See MESOLÓNGION.

MISSOULA (United States) City and county seat in W MONTANA, on the Clark fork of the Columbia River near Hellgate. In a region first settled in 1841 by French missionaries, it is near the site in Hellgate Valley of the signing of a treaty that in 1855 ended the war between the Salish Flathead and the Blackfoot Indian nations. The town of Hellgate was founded in 1860 and moved to the Missoula site in 1866.

MISSOURI (United States) State in the S central region; it was admitted to the Union in 1821 as the 24th state. Its E border is the MISSISSIPPI RIVER, which separates it from Illinois and Kentucky; Iowa is on the N, Kansas and Nebraska on the W, and Arkansas on the S. One source says Missouri was the Algonquian name of a tribe living at the mouth of the MISSOURI RIVER; another that it means "muddy water."

Osage and Missouri Indians lived here in the latter part of the 17th century when French explorers Père Jacques Marquette and Louis Jolliet came down the Mississippi River. A little later Robert de La Salle claimed a large region for FRANCE and called it Louisiana. By the early 18th century the French were working lead mines here—the state is still a leading producer—and trading for furs. Traffic on the Mississippi resulted in the founding of St. Geneviève c.1735 and ST. LOUIS in 1764. The founders of the latter were fur traders Pierre Laclède and René Auguste Chouteau.

France ceded the Louisiana region to SPAIN in 1762, received it back in 1800, and sold it to the United States in the LOUISIANA PURCHASE of 1803. Missouri was made a territory in 1812, but settlement was slow, and the Indians were a danger until 1816. By the Missouri Compromise of 1820, Missouri was to be admitted as a slave state, but no others were to be allowed in the Louisiana Purchase north of the 36°, 30′ line.

In the 1830's Mormons arrived here in sizable numbers, but their rapid growth and opposition to slavery led to their being driven out in 1839. In the 1840's and 1850's many Germans arrived, settling largely around St. Louis. The Kansas-Nebraska Act of 1854 left it up to the settlers of neighboring KANSAS to decide for or against slavery, and the slave interests of Missouri contributed to the ensuing violence that created "Bleeding Kansas." In March 1861, however, Missouri voted not to secede. During the Civil War there was some minor fighting and much guerrilla activity, which perhaps contributed to postwar lawlessness, such as that of Jesse James and his gang of bank robbers.

Much of Missouri's history is tied to its proximity to the Mississippi River. The Missouri River flows across the state, emptying into the Mississippi above St. Louis. The Mississippi, especially after the coming of the steamboat, tied the state to both the North and the South by the traffic on it and on the OHIO RIVER and the Missouri. In the early 19th century southern slave owners moved up to Missouri. At the same time, the state was becoming the gateway to the West. The Missouri River was the main route in that direction and most of the pioneers who were headed for the OREGON TRAIL started from INDEPENDENCE or Westport, later KANSAS CITY. Traders also went southwest over the SANTA FE TRAIL, starting from Independence and ending up in SANTA FE.

The spirit of steamboating on the Mississippi expressed in the writings of Mark Twain lived on to some extent, but gradually Missouri became more industrialized and urban. The state experienced very hard times in the 1930's Great Depression. During and since World War II St. Louis and Kansas City became busy mid-continent transportation centers, but Chicago's bid for the major railroads earlier in the century has since diminished Missouri's potential in this regard. Missouri was also the home of one of the most powerful big city political machines, that of Thomas J. Pendergast, later helpful in the career of President Harry S. Truman. In the 1950's and 1960's, school integration was achieved without much difficulty throughout the state.

JEFFERSON CITY is the capital; ST. JOSEPH and Springfield are also important.

MISSOURI RIVER (United States) River in the central and NW central region, the principal tributary of the MISSISSIPPI RIVER, which it joins approx. 10 mi above ST. LOUIS. It flows approx. 2,500 miles from its source in southern MONTANA through NORTH and SOUTH DAKOTA, forming in part the boundaries between South Dakota/NEBRASKA, Nebraska/IOWA, Nebraska/MISSOURI, and KANSAS/Missouri. The principal cities on its banks include BISMARCK, N.D.; SIOUX CITY and COUNCIL BLUFFS, Iowa; OMAHA, Neb.; ST. JOSEPH, Mo.; and KANSAS CITY, Kan. and Mo. It was an important artery of commerce for the Indians of the plains before its discovery and exploration by Marquette and Jolliet, and by the Lewis and Clark expedition of 1803 to 1806. It was also explored by the Canadians Vérendrye in 1738 and Thompson in 1797.

MISTRA [Misithra, Mistras] (Greece) Ruined fortress-city on a peak in old LACONIA, in the SE PELOPONNESUS, approx. 5 mi W of Sparta. It was founded in 1248 as a Frankish stronghold. In 1262 under the treaty of Constantinople it was made the capital of the principality of Michael VIII Paleologus, emperor of the Byzantines, who had taken the fortress in 1259. Until the 15th century it was a center of late Byzantine culture. Occupied by Turks and then Venetians, it had lost its significance by the time Greece was independent. When it was designated an archaeological area in the 1950's, it was virtually deserted. The town is dominated by a Crusader castle and the palace of the Paleologi and has many churches, some restored, with fine late Byzantine wall paintings. See BYZANTINE EMPIRE.

MISTRAS. See MISTRA.

MISURATA. See MISRATAH.

MITANNI EMPIRE (Syria) Ancient kingdom that flourished from c.1500 to 1350 BC in Syria and ancient MESOPOTAMIA, extending from the bend of the EUPHRATES RIVER to the TIGRIS RIVER. It was founded by an Indo-European warrior aristocracy from the northeast who spoke the Hurrian language. Its capital city, not yet found or excavated, was called Washshukkanni; other major cities were CARCHEMISH and ALEPPO. Circa 1450 BC the armies of Thutmose III of EGYPT reached the Euphrates and entered into friendly relations with Mitanni, as is known from an exchange of letters between King Tushratta of Mitanni and Amenhotep III of Egypt discovered in the TELL AL-AMARNA letters. Struggles with the HITTITE EMPIRE began in the early 14th century BC, and by the mid or late 14th century the kingdom had fallen to the Hittites and to resurgent forces of ASSYRIA. A remnant in the northwest survived as URARTU. See also ARMENIA.

MITAU. See JELGAVA.

MITAVA. See JELGAVA.

MITCHAM. See MERTON.

MITCHELSTOWN [*Gaelic:* **Baile an Mhistealaigh**] (Irish Republic) Market town in County Cork between the Kilworth and Galty Mts. A castle built in 1823 was the scene on Sept. 9, 1887 of a riot by Irish Nationalists, two of whom were killed by the police. The event fed the fires of Irish nationalist sentiment. The Mitchelstown limestone caves are famous geologically, and historically as the hiding place in 1601 of the earl of Desmond, an Irish nobleman contesting English domination.

MITHILA (India and Nepal) Ancient city and kingdom that corresponded to the part of BIHAR N of the GANGES RIVER, with an extension into Nepal, where the capital was Janakpur. Built on swampland reclaimed by Aryans, it has an obscure history, but it reached a peak of influence in the eighth century BC and was later synonymous with the kingdom of Videha or Tirabhukti, modern Tirhut, known for the conservatism and the learning of its Brahmans. The heroine of the *Ramayana*, a Sanskrit epic written circa the third century BC, was a Mithilan princess.

MITILÍNI. See LESBOS.

MITLA (Mexico) Village in the SE, in OAXACA state. A religious center of the Zapotec Indians, it is the site of many Zapotec ruins, especially long stone buildings with columns, unusual for this part of the world. Probably built in the 13th century, they include mosaic wall panels in many different designs. These may have been made by the Mixtec, who conquered Mitla.

MITO (Japan) Industrial and commercial city of Ibaraki prefecture, in SE HONSHŪ, 60 mi NE of Tokyo. It was important especially under the Tokugawa shogun, who administered a type of federal feudalism from 1603 to 1867. The capital was at Edo, modern TOKYO, but Mito was headquarters for one branch of the Tokugawa family.

MITROVICA. See SIRMIUM.

MITSIWA. See MASSAWA.

MITTERBURG. See PAZIN.

MIYA-JIMA. See ITSUKU-SHIMA.

MIYAKO. See KYŌTO.

MIYAZAKI (Japan) City and seaport of Miyazaki prefecture, in SE KYŪSHŪ, on the Hyuga Sea. It is the seat of a great Shinto shrine and archaeological museum dedicated to Jimmu Tennō, the traditional first emperor of Japan, believed to be a descendant of the goddess of the sun. He reportedly began his travels through the empire he founded c.660 BC by setting out from this place.

MIYAZU (Japan) Town in KYOTO prefecture, S HONSHŪ, on Miyazu Bay. A legend says that Miyazu was the site where the creators Izanagi and Izanami stood while they fashioned the islands of Japan. Nearby is the Amano-hashidate, or "heaven's bridge," a promontory and geographical phenomenon.

MIZORAM (India) Union territory in the Mizo Hills, bordered on the E by Burma. In an area taken over at the end of the 18th century by the Lushai tribes from Burma, it was for a time a part of ASSAM State. Before the creation of BANGLADESH, India accused PAKISTAN of aiding and abetting the secessionists who are active in this area.

MLJET. See MELEDA.

MOAB (Jordan) Ancient kingdom E of the DEAD SEA, bounded on the S by EDOM and on the N separated by the Arnon River from the territory of the Amorites. It is now in the SW part of Jordan. The Moabites developed their civilization in the 14th century BC on highlands where a successful agricultural society had emerged almost 1,000 years earlier. They were closely related to the Hebrews, who were often their allies as well as their enemies. They spoke a very similar language and are mentioned many times in the Old Testament.

In 1868 the famous Moabite Stone was discovered at DHIBAN. It has a long text inscribed by Mesha, king of Moab, in 850 BC, which tells of his triumph over the northern Hebrew kingdom of ISRAEL and of an earlier victory by the Israelite King Omri. Moab's power seems to have ended c.735 BC after an invasion by the Assyrian King Tiglath-pileser II, although one source places the conquest of Moab by the Babylonians in 582 BC. The Moabites were later absorbed into NABATAEA. See also CANAAN, PALESTINE.

MOBILE (United States) City and port in ALABAMA, at the mouth of the Mobile River, on the N shore of Mobile Bay. Explored by the Spanish beginning with de Piñeda in 1519 and founded by Jean Baptiste le Moyne, Sieur de Bienville, in 1710, it served as the capital of French LOUISIANA from 1710 to 1719. It was next held by the British from 1763 until 1780, when Spain took control. Taken by the U.S. forces under Gen. James Wilkinson in 1813, it became important in the Civil War as a port for ships running the Union blockade. From Aug. 5 to 23, 1864 Mobile Bay was the scene of a major battle in which Adm. David Farragut established a blockade of mines, pushing by the strong harbor fortifications and uttering the famous line "Damn the torpedoes." The Confederate fleet sailed off, and forts Morgan and Gaines surrendered. The city itself was captured by Union troops under Gen. E.R.S. Canby in April 1865. Mobile has many antebellum homes and gardens.

MOBILE BAY. See MOBILE.

MOÇAMBIQUE. See MOZAMBIQUE.

MOCHA [Mokha] [*Arabic:* **Mukhā**] (Yemen) Port, in the SW, on the RED SEA, Yemen Arab Republic. It was noted for its export of the coffee to which it gave its name, but declined in importance in the late 19th century.

MOCHICA (Peru) Ancient Indian civilization on the N coast. Formerly called the Early CHIMU, the Mochica were warriors with a highly-developed social and political organization. Building pyramids, temples, and aqueducts of adobe, they were also skilled in irrigation and produced unusual ceramics depicting everyday life, people, humor, and fantasy. Begun c.100 BC, the civilization is thought to have lasted about 1,000 years.

MOCHLOS (Greece) Ancient ruins in E CRETE, on the N coast on Mirabella Bay, site of an excavated town settlement dating from the Bronze Age Late Minoan I period. The town boasted many large houses with living quarters and storage rooms. In 1906 rich stone-built tombs containing jewelry and pottery were discovered in the cliffs of Mochlos. See also GOURNIA.

MOCRUM. See MAKARSKA, Yugoslavia.

MODDER (South Africa) River in ORANGE FREE

STATE, a tributary of the Riet, approx. 180 mi long. On Nov. 28, 1899, during the Boer War, British forces under Gen. Lord Paul Methuen defeated the Boers under Gen. Piet Cronje, who soon met final defeat at PAARDEBERG, also on the river.

MODENA [*ancient:* **Mutina**] (Italy) City and manufacturing center, in Reggio nell'Emilia province, Emilia-Romagna region on the Panaro River approx. 22 mi NW of Bologna. Originally an Etruscan city, Mutina became a Roman colony in 183 BC. Reconstructed by Constantine in the fourth century AD, in 1288 it passed to the Este family of FERRARA. With the duchy of Modena, established in 1452, it became the seat of the Este family after they lost Ferrara in 1598. During the Napoleonic Wars it was taken by the French in 1796, was made part of the CISALPINE REPUBLIC of 1797, and became part of the Napoleonic Kingdom of Italy in 1805. In 1815 it passed to an Este descendant, Francis IV and became part of the kingdom of Italy in 1860. Historic buildings include an 11th- and 12th-century Romanesque cathedral, the Palazzo dei Musei of 1753 to 1767, and a ducal palace dating from the 17th century. Nearby is Nonantola Abbey founded in 752 and long a center of learning.

MODICA [*ancient:* **Motyca**] (Italy) City of Ragusa province, SE SICILY, 5 mi SSE of Ragusa. One of Sicily's first cities, Modica may have been a fortified settlement as early as the Stone Age. Nearby grottoes, the Cava d'Ispica, include cave dwellings and tombs from the 14th century BC to early Christian times. There are the remains of a castle destroyed by an earthquake in 1693, an Arab-Norman chapel, and a 15th-century convent, now a prison. Independent and prosperous for many centuries, especially from the 14th to the 18th, it has several other noteworthy churches.

MODJOKERTO [**Mojokerto**] (Indonesia) Town in East Java province on the Brantas River, 20 mi SW of Surabaja. Near the town the remains of an early hominid were discovered in 1934 and named Homo modjokertensis. The bones seem to predate the earlier discovery of Pithecanthropus erectus, or Java Man.

MODLIN [*Russian:* **Novogeorgievsk**] (Poland) Fortified town in Warszawa department, 20 mi NW of Warsaw. This fort built by Napoleon in 1807 became a Russian military post in World War I. It was taken by the Germans on Aug. 12, 1915.

MODON. See METHONE.

MOEHNE. See MÖHNE.

MOERIS, LAKE [**Lake Karun**] [*Arabic:* **Birkat Qarun**] (Egypt) Ancient name of Lake Karun, in the NE in Al FAIYUM. Now much reduced from its former size as reported by travelers such as Herodotus in 450 BC, it was first dug by King Moeris c.1000 BC and was the object of early irrigation work during the Middle Kingdom, as shown by excavations in the 1920's. Its chief town was Crocodilopolis, later ARSINOË, a residence of the Ptolemies.

MOESIA Ancient region in SE Europe, located S of the Danube and extending from the Drinus River to the lower Euxine, now the Black Sea. Inhabited by a Thracian people, it was conquered by the Romans in the first century BC, made part of MACEDONIA, and was organized as a Roman province c.15 BC. It comprised roughly what is now SERBIA and BULGARIA. Extended under Trajan, it included several Greek cities and prospered until invaded by the Goths in the fourth century AD. It was overrun by Slavs and Bulgarians in the seventh century.

MOGADISHU [**Mogadisho, Mukdishu**] [*Arabic:* **Maqdishu;** *Italian:* **Mogadiscio**] (Somalia) Capital city and the country's largest port, located in eastern Africa on the Indian Ocean. Settled by Arabs c.900 AD, it quickly emerged as a leading commercial center that impressed Marco Polo. It was controlled by PORTUGAL in the 16th century and declined during this period. For a time under the rule of MASQAT, it became practically independent in the 18th century but was occupied in 1871 by the sultan of ZANZIBAR, who leased it in 1892 to the Italians. The Italians later purchased the city for their colony of Somaliland. In World War II it was captured and occupied by British forces. Historic buildings include the mosque of Fakr ad-Din from 1269, the Garesa Palace of the 19th century, and a massive tower to the north built by the Portuguese in the 16th century.

MOGILEV [**Mogilev on the Dnieper; Mohilev**] (USSR) Capital city of Mogilev oblast, BELORUSSIAN SSR, on both banks of the DNIEPER RIVER, 112 mi E of MINSK. It was founded on territory of SMOLENSK principality, at the site of a castle dating from 1267, and became a noted commercial center from the 14th century. As part of the grand duchy of LITHUANIA it was united with POLAND in 1569 and was later held by SWEDEN. It suffered from religious persecution and was partly destroyed by Peter the Great in 1708, but in 1772 it passed to RUSSIA in the first partition of Poland. Nearby in 1812, a Russian army under Prince Piotr Bagration was defeated by the French. From 1917 to 1920 it was the scene of much civil disorder during the Russian Revolution. Although it was occupied and heavily damaged by the Axis powers in World War II between 1941 and 1944, several old churches and an ancient tower built by the Tatars survive.

MOGILEV ON THE DNIEPER. See MOGILEV.

MOGILEV ON THE DNIESTER. See MOGILEV-PODOLSKI.

MOGILEV-PODOLSKI [**Mogilev on the Dniester**] (USSR) City in SW Vinnitsa oblast, W Ukrainian SSR, on the DNIESTER RIVER, 60 mi S of Vinnitsa. Important as a trading center located at a much-used crossing of the river on a route from MOLDAVIA to the UKRAINE, the city was founded in the late 16th century and grew up around a fortress. In the 17th century it was controlled by Cossacks, Poles, and Turks. It passed to RUSSIA in 1795. Suffering severely in both World War I and the Russian Revolution, in World War II it was held by the Axis from 1941 until March 1944. Around the city are archaeological remains dating from the third century BC.

MOGONTIACUM. See MAINZ.

MOGUL EMPIRE [Mughal] (India) Muslim empire from 1526 to 1857. It was the most powerful and extensive empire in India before the British conquest in the 19th century. Its rulers tried to achieve a united state of Hindus and Muslims; they were serious patrons of art and architecture, their style developing out of that of PERSIA. Although the name Mogul is derived from Mongol, the founders of the empire were mainly Turks. The chief founder was Babur, who invaded India in 1526 and defeated the DELHI SULTANATE at the battle of PANIPAT. Babur had earlier established a kingdom in AFGHANISTAN. He succeeded in overrunning nearly all of northern India. Babur's son and successor, Humayun (1530 to 1556), was less successful. Although he defeated the rule of GUJARAT, he was beaten in battle in 1539 and 1540 by Sher Khan, an Afghan, who took over the empire. Humayun was forced to flee to SIND, but in 1555, with Persian aid, he returned and restored Mogul authority. Akbar, son of Humayun and his successor from 1556 to 1605, was unusually successful and is generally considered to have been the greatest of the Mogul rulers. He enlarged the empire so that it included Afghanistan, BALUCHISTAN, and practically all of the Indian subcontinent north of the Godavari River, defeating the Rajputs in the process. Akbar fostered religious toleration and the arts and established AGRA as the Mogul capital for many years. He also founded FATEHPUR SIKRI in 1569 to honor a Muslim saint.

Akbar's son Jahangir, emperor from 1605 to 1627, continued to expand the empire, taking areas in the DECCAN. He granted trading privileges to the Portuguese and later to the British. Shah Jahan, son of Jahangir and ruler from 1628 to 1658, was able but ruthless, conquering more territory in the Deccan and recovering KANDAHAR from the Persians. His rule marked the high point of Mogul art and architecture. Shah Jahan erected the Taj Mahal at Agra and the Red Fort at DELHI. Aurangzeb, son of Shah Jahan and emperor from 1658 to 1707, brought the empire to its greatest extent, but his persecution of Hindus caused revolts, and the empire started to fall to pieces after he died. The Sikhs, Rajputs, Jats, and MARATHAS all took part in the dismemberment. After the British conquered India they used the Mogul emperors as puppet rulers until they exiled the last one, Banadur Shah II, to Rangoon, Burma because of his involvement in the Indian Mutiny of 1857.

MOHÁCS (Hungary) City on the DANUBE RIVER, near the Yugoslav border. It was the scene of a famous battle and overwhelming defeat of Louis II of Hungary and BOHEMIA by Sulayman I of Turkey. Louis had tried, with little success, to rally all Christendom and was not prepared for the attack. With 28,000 Hungarian troops pitted against 200,000 Turks, the rout on Aug. 29/30, 1526 left the king and 25,000 soldiers dead. The event began Hungary's 150-year domination by the Turks. This was weakened after the so-called Second Battle of Mohács on Aug. 12, 1687, when Charles V of Lorraine defeated the Turks at nearby HARKÁNY. See OTTOMAN EMPIRE.

MOHAMMERAH. See KHORRAMSHAHR.

MOHAWK (United States) Village in NE central NEW YORK State, 12 mi ESE of Utica; also an important river and its valley, named for the native Iroquois Indian tribe. Settled by Palatines, emigrants from the PALATINATE in Germany, the village and region were the scene of many battles during the French and Indian Wars, and the American Revolution. The 148-mile-long river, the largest tributary to the HUDSON RIVER, was significant as the route for westward movement and for the ERIE CANAL. See also MOHAWK TRAIL.

MOHAWK TRAIL (United States) Old road in central NEW YORK State following the MOHAWK River for approx. 100 mi through the Appalachians. Settlers heading to the Midwest followed the route from SCHENECTADY until the ERIE CANAL was opened in 1825. The term also refers to a highway across northern Massachusetts from Greenfield to North Adams, following a trail originally blazed by the Mohawk Indians.

MOHENJO-DARO (Pakistan) Archaeological site in S Sind. This was one of the twin capitals of the INDUS RIVER valley civilization of c.2500 to 1750 BC, one of the world's earliest civilizations, which may have been influenced by SUMER in MESOPOTAMIA. The city, built of baked brick and laid out in the earliest recorded grid plan, covered approx. one square mile and had a massive citadel, a great bath, a granary, and broad streets with an elaborate drainage system. Often subjected to floods, the great city may have become flooded out, or perhaps destroyed by the incoming Aryan tribes, as huddles of unburied skeletons on the highest level suggest. See also HARAPPA.

MOHILEV. See MOGILEV.

MÖHNE [Moehne] (West Germany) River of North Rhine-Westphalia, flowing W to the Ruhr at Neheim. In its lower reaches it is the site of an enormous reservoir that was bombed and broken during World War II by the Royal Air Force on May 16, 1943 in a daring raid. It was restored in 1946.

MOISSAC (France) Town of Tarn-et-Garonne department, approx. 35 mi NW of Toulouse, on the TARN RIVER. It grew up around an abbey founded in the seventh century, destroyed in the next by the Saracens, and restored by Louis d'Aquitaine, the Pious, a son of Charlemagne. The town was taken by Richard the Lion Hearted (1157–99) and Simon de Montfort. The portal and cloister of the 15th-century church of St. Pierre date back to the 12th century and preserve excellent examples of Romanesque sculpture.

MOJOKERTO. See MODJOKERTO.

MOKHA. See MOCHA.

MOLD (Wales) Admin. hq. of Clwyd, 11 mi NW of Wrexham. In 430 AD St. Germain led Christian inhabitants to victory here over pagan Picts and Scots.

MOLDAU. See VLTAVA RIVER.

MOLDAVIA [German: Moldau; Rumanian: Moldova] (Rumania) Province E of TRANSYLVANIA, separated by the Carpathian Mts, N and E of WALACHIA.

Part of SCYTHIA during the first millennium BC, it was included in DACIA under the ROMAN EMPIRE and was overrun by various barbaric groups until it was controlled by KIEV from the ninth to the 12th centuries AD. In 1359 it became an independent principality and included BESSARABIA and BUKOVINA. At its most powerful under Stephen the Great (1457–1504), it fell to the OTTOMAN EMPIRE after his death. It was united briefly to Walachia by Michael the Bold (d. 1601) and in the early 18th century was governed for the Turks by Greek Phanariots. Bukovina was annexed to AUSTRIA in 1774, Bessarabia to RUSSIA in 1812, and Moldavia and Walachia became known as the Danubian Principalities. In 1822 a period of corrupt rule ended after an insurrection led by Alexander Ypsilanti. Following the Russo-Turkish War of 1828/29, Moldavia and Walachia were made protectorates of Russia, though they continued to pay tribute to the Sultan of Turkey. In the Crimean War of 1854 to 1856 Moldavia was again occupied by Russia. After Alexander John Cuza became prince of Moldavia and Walachia in 1859, the principalities became united as Rumania in 1861. See also MOLDAVIAN SSR.

MOLDAVIAN FEDERAL SOVIET REPUBLIC. See MOLDAVIAN SOVIET SOCIALIST REPUBLIC.

MOLDAVIAN SOVIET SOCIALIST REPUBLIC [*former:* **Moldavian Federal Soviet Republic**] (USSR) Constituent republic bounded on the SE by the Black Sea, on the N and NE by the Ukrainian SSR and on the S and W by Rumania. In 1924 several districts of the former Podolsk region were organized into the Moldavian Autonomous Soviet Socialist Republic. In 1940 this merged with most of BESSARABIA to form the Moldavian SSR. During World War II it was taken by Rumania in 1941 and retaken by the Soviet Union in 1944. See also MOLDAVIA.

MOLDOVA. See MOLDAVIA.

MÔLE SAINT NICHOLAS (Haiti) Town in the NW, near the tip of a peninsula just N of Cap à Foux. Christopher Columbus landed here on his first voyage to the WEST INDIES in 1492.

MOLINO DEL REY [*English:* **King's Mill**] (Mexico) Town SW of Mexico City. On Sept. 8, 1847, during the Mexican War, it was the scene of a battle in which Gen. Winfield Scott, in part of his push toward Mexico City, defeated the forces under Santa Ana. See also CHAPULTEPEC.

MOLISE (Italy) S central region on the Adriatic Sea bordered by Campania to the W, Abruzzi to the N, and Puglia (Apulia) to the S. Conquered by the Romans in the fourth century BC, after the fall of the ROMAN EMPIRE it came under the southern Lombard Duchy from the sixth to the 11th centuries. From the 12th century its history is that of ABRUZZI. And from 1948 to 1965 it was included in the region of ABRUZZI E MOLISE. Its capital is CAMPOBASSO.

MOLLWITZ. See MAŁUJOWICE.

MOLOKAI (United States) Island in the state of HAWAII, between Oahu and Maui. On the N coast is the well-known Kalaupapa leper settlement run by the government. Father Damian, the legendary Belgian missionary, worked here, serving the lepers from 1873 until his death from leprosy in 1889.

MOLOSSIA. See MOLOSSIS.

MOLOSSIS [**Molossia**] (Greece) District of ancient EPIRUS in the NW, extending along the W bank of the Arachthus River. It eventually grew to dominate the whole country of Epirus.

MOLOTOV. See PERM.

MOLUCCAS [**Maluku, Spice Islands**] [*Dutch:* **Molukken**] (Indonesia) Island group in the W Pacific Ocean between SULAWESI, or Celebes, and NEW GUINEA. Long the object of European fantasy and exploration for their spices and wealth, they were discovered by Magellan in 1512 and occupied by PORTUGAL later. They were captured between 1605 and 1621 by the Dutch, who thereby gained a monopoly of the valuable spice trade. Ambon, AMBOINA, was the early seat of Dutch control and served as the residency of the former Netherlands Indies, including the Moluccas and Netherlands New Guinea (see IRIAN BARAT). Administered by the British from 1810 to 1814, the islands then passed finally to the Dutch in the 19th century until Indonesian independence. See also HALMAHERA.

MOLUKKEN. See MOLUCCAS.

MOMBASA (Kenya) The country's chief port city, located on Mombasa Island in the Indian Ocean, 150 mi N of Zanzibar. An Arab trading center from the eighth century, it was visited by Vasco da Gama in 1498 on his first voyage to India. His belief that the local ruler was trying to imprison him led to a series of conflicts between Arabs and the Portuguese. The Portuguese eventually controlled the city from 1529 to 1698, when a three-year siege of Fort Jesus by Arabs ended with their expulsion. In the 18th century Mombasa was again briefly held by the Portuguese but then became subject to OMAN, whose local representative eventually became the independent ruler of ZANZIBAR. In 1887 it passed to the British and became capital of the British East Africa Protectorate of Kenya until 1907.

MONA, United Kingdom. See MAN, ISLE OF.

MONA, Wales. See ANGLESEY.

MONACO [*ancient:* **Monoecus**] Independent principality in SE FRANCE, on the Mediterranean Sea, near the French-Italian border. Probably Phoenician in origin, it was annexed by MARSEILLES in the first century AD. Part of the Lombard kingdom in the seventh century and of ARLES in the eighth century, it came under the Grimaldi family in 1070. An independent principality in the 13th century, it was subsequently under Spanish protection between 1542 and 1641, under French protection from 1641 to 1793, and annexed to France in 1793. The Treaty of Paris of 1814 restored the family's domination, but the next year it fell under Sardinian protection. After 1861 it again came under French protection. The princes ruled as absolute monarchs until 1911, when Prince Albert I granted a new constitution. In 1962 Prince Rainier established the present liberal constitution. Notable buildings include the 16th-century palace, the 19th-century Byzantine-style cathedral, and the famous casino of MONTE CARLO.

MONA ISLAND (Puerto Rico) Island in the CARIBBEAN SEA near the main island of Puerto Rico. Discovered by Columbus in 1493, it was also visited by Ponce de León in 1508, and in 1511 the island was ceded to Columbus's younger brother, Bartholomew. It soon gained renown as a haven for corsairs and pirates.

MONAPIA. See MAN, ISLE OF.

MONASTERBOICE [*Gaelic:* **Mainistir Bhuithe**] (Irish Republic) In county Louth, near Drogheda, it is among the very first monastic sites to be established in IRELAND. It was founded by Buite, who died in 521 AD. Historic remains include a round tower, two churches, and various elaborately carved Celtic crosses.

MONASTIR. See BITOLA (Yugoslavia).

MÖNCHENGLADBACH [*former:* **München-Gladbach**] (West Germany) City in North Rhine-Westphalia. Chartered in 1336, it had developed around a Benedictine abbey that was founded *c.*970 and was rebuilt several times, beginning in the 14th century until its suppression in 1802. There is also an interesting church from the 11th to the 13th centuries. It is now a NATO headquarters.

MONCHY-LE-PREUX (France) Village in Pas-de-Calais department, 5 mi E of Arras. During World War I it was held by the Germans from 1914 until April 11, 1917 and from March until August 1918.

MONCONTOUR (France) Village in Vienne department, in the W central region, 27 mi NW of Poitiers. In the Wars of Religion, on Oct. 3, 1569, it was the scene of a battle in which the Huguenots were defeated by forces under Henry of Lorraine, the third duke of Guise, who in 1572 planned the St. Bartholomew's Day Massacre of French Protestants.

MONDOÑEDO (Spain) Town in Lugo province, in ASTURIAS, approx. 55 mi E of La Coruña. In the hands of the Moors for 150 years after the Moorish conquest, it was recaptured by Ordoño I in 858. It was held briefly by the French in 1809, during the Napoleonic Wars.

MONDOVI (Italy) Town in Cuneo province, PIEDMONT region, 13 mi ESE of Cuneo. The French under the young Napoleon defeated the Austrians in a battle here in 1796. This forced the Piedmontese, Austrian allies, to make a separate peace with FRANCE.

MONEMBASIA. See MONEMVASIA.

MONEMVASIA [**Malvasia, Malvesie, Monembasia**] [*ancient:* **Minoa;** *English:* **Malmsey;** *French:* **Malvoisie;** *Italian:* **Napoli de Malvasia**] (Greece) Village on a rocky promontory off the coast of the SE PELOPONNESUS. Earlier a refuge for Greeks from LACONIA, it was a leading commercial port and a fortress under the BYZANTINE EMPIRE in the Middle Ages. It was held by VENICE from 1463 to 1540 and by the Turks from 1540 until 1690, when it became Venetian again. Turkish again from 1715 to 1821, it was the first town of the Morea, or Peloponnesus, to be taken by the Greeks in

their war of independence and was made the seat of the first Greek national assembly in 1821. Since the Middle Ages it has been noted for the export of malmsey or Malvasian wine to England in particular. The ruins of the Byzantine town and the cathedral survive. The town is rapidly becoming restored as a resort.

MONFALCONE (Italy) Town in Gorizia province, Friuli-Venezia Giulia region, near the mouth of the ISONZO RIVER, 17 mi NW of Trieste. It was the scene of severe fighting in 1917 in World War I, during which it was nearly destroyed. See also KOBARID.

MONFERRATO. See MONTFERRAT.

MONGHYR [*former:* **Mudgagiri**] (India) City of Bihar state on the right bank of the GANGES RIVER, 235 mi NNW of Calcutta. Tradition says it was founded during the Gupta dynasty (*c.*320–535 AD). By 1195 AD it had become a strong fortress and was taken by the first Muslim conqueror of BENGAL, Muhammed Bakhiyar Khilji. After 1590 when Akbar of the MOGUL EMPIRE achieved supremacy over the Afghan chiefs of Bengal, Monghyr was a military headquarters for one of his generals. In 1761 it served as a residence and base for the Muslim leader, Mir Kasim Ali, during his war against the British. Part of the old Muslim fort still stands.

MONGIBELLO. See ETNA, MOUNT.

MONGOL EMPIRES Several empires and khanates, conquered and ruled over by the Mongols, a nomadic people of the Asian steppes whose power relied on massive numbers and lightning mobility. They spread from their homeland in what is now the MONGOLIAN PEOPLE'S REPUBLIC. After subjugating many tribes, their first and greatest leader Genghis Khan, was proclaimed great khan in 1206 and established his capital at KARAKORUM in MONGOLIA. In 1213 he attacked the Chin Empire of northern CHINA and captured PEKING in 1215. Moving west with his barbaric, hard-riding soldiers, Genghis Khan conquered TURKISTAN, TRANSOXIANA, and AFGHANISTAN between 1218 and 1224 and carried out raids in PERSIA and eastern Europe as far as the DNIEPER RIVER. Among his conquests were the ancient cities of SAMARKAND and BUKHARA in central Asia. By destroying entire cities and massacreing their populations the khan spread terror before him. A brilliant military leader and merciless to his enemies, at his death in 1227 Genghis Khan left one of the largest land empires known. It has been estimated that the rise of the Mongol Empire cost as many lives as the total military and civilian casualties in World War II. This empire was divided among his sons and grandsons, the four parts consisting of China and KOREA, two khanates, in Persia and Turkistan, and the Kipchak khanate, or GOLDEN HORDE, so called because of the splended tents its army erected. With succeeding generations Mongol barbarity subsided as artisans and merchants were spared and the soldiers began to intermarry with their subjects. A grandson, Batu Khan, who ruled the empire of the Golden Horde, held most of RUSSIA by 1240 and in the next two years conquered HUNGARY and POLAND and invaded GERMANY, reach-

MONGOL EMPIRES OF EURASIA, 1227–1405

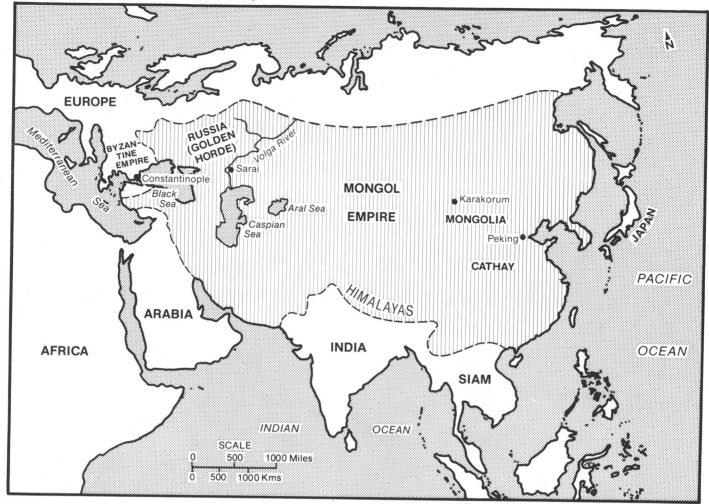

● Capitals

ing the Adriatic in 1242. Another grandson, Hulagu Khan, sacked BAGHDAD in 1258, bringing to an end the ABBASID CALIPHATE. Kublai Khan, also a grandson, became the chief Mongol emperor in 1259, his power concentrated in the Far East. Here he brought the realm to its greatest extent when he defeated the Chinese Sung dynasty in 1279 and founded the Yüan dynasty, which ruled China until 1368. His campaigns against JAPAN, INDONESIA, and Southeast Asia, however, were unsuccessful.

Another Mongol conqueror arose in the 14th century who claimed descent from Genghis Khan. By 1369 Tamerlane had gained control of what is now Soviet Turkistan and by 1387 possessed a large area east of the EUPHRATES RIVER. Moving west in 1392, he overcame the rulers of the lands between the Caspian and Black seas and invaded Russia. Turning toward INDIA in 1398, Tamerlane captured Delhi and put an end to the DELHI SULTANATE. In 1400 he invaded GEORGIA and also captured ALEPPO in present SYRIA and Baghdad in present Iraq. His last great triumph was the defeat of the Ottoman Turks in 1402, when he took prisoner their sultan, Beyazid I. Tamerlane was a savage conqueror whose reputation for cruelty and conquest filled the West with mixed awe and horror.

Another remote descendant of Genghis Khan, Babur,

established a kingdom in Afghanistan in 1504. In 1525 he invaded India, won a decisive battle in 1526, and eventually conquered all of northern India, establishing the MOGUL EMPIRE, which lasted until 1857.

The Mongols, mingled in some places with large numbers of Turkic peoples, came to be known in Europe as Tatars. Their conquests, except in China and India, were mostly matters of pillage and left behind little of value or consequence, for example, such ephemeral dynasties as the 14th-century Il-Khans in Persia, under whom, nevertheless, Persian culture and architecture reached great heights.

In the West the Mongols were seen both as possible converts to Christianity, because of their religious tolerance, and as allies to balance off the power of the Muslim Arabs and Turks. Their control of Asia in the late Middle Ages favored a reopening of overland trade with the East, disrupted since the fall of Rome, and allowed missionary journeys and such famed voyages as that of Marco Polo between 1271 and 1295.

MONGOLIA Region in E central Asia, now divided into the MONGOLIAN PEOPLE'S REPUBLIC, INNER MONGOLIA, and TUVA ASSR. The area lies between CHINA and the USSR. Inhabited by nomadic peoples from at least the second millennium BC, it was successively dominated by the Huns in the first to the fifth centuries AD, the UIGUR Turks from the eighth to the ninth centuries, and the Liao dynasty from the 10th to the 12th centuries. It emerged into history *c.*1205 when Genghis Khan, the leader of the nomadic Mongols, began his wars of expansion that eventually created the MONGOL EMPIRE stretching from China to the DANUBE RIVER. Kublai Khan, a grandson of Genghis, completed the conquest of China after overcoming the Sung dynasty and founding the Yüan dynasty, which lasted from 1279 to 1368. He was visited by Marco Polo of VENICE. The vast empire began to break up on the death of Kublai Khan and was succeeded by such entities as the Empire of the GOLDEN HORDE in RUSSIA, the Il-Khans (Hulagid) in PERSIA, and the continuing Yüan dynasty in China. Tamerlane, a descendant of Genghis Khan, later established a short-lived empire in western Asia. Its northern border was delimited in 1727 in a treaty between Russia and China. Mongolia was loosely dependent on China until Tannu Tuva (Tuva ASSR) became a republic in 1911 and Outer Mongolia, now the Mongolian People's Republic, declared its independence. Inner Mongolia came under Chinese control until 1937, when the two eastern provinces of Chahar and Suiyuan were overrun by the Japanese, who formed MÊNG CHIANG, renamed in 1939 the Mongolian Federated Autonomous Government. Following World War II Inner Mongolia was made an autonomous region of China, and Tannu Tuva was incorporated within the USSR.

MONGOLIAN FEDERATED AUTONOMOUS GOVERNMENT. See MONGOLIA.

MONGOLIAN PEOPLE'S REPUBLIC [Mongolia; Outer Mongolia] Country of E central Asia between CHINA and the USSR. Its capital is ULAN BATOR. It was part of China from 1691 until the end of the Manchu dynasty in China and the formation of an independent Mongolian kingdom in 1911. The treaties of 1913 and 1915 established it as an autonomous state under Chinese sovereignty. China's attempt to reassert its sovereignty from 1919 to 1921 resulted in its forces being driven out with Soviet help. Mongolia was proclaimed a republic in 1924, Soviet forces withdrew in 1925, and a mutual assistance pact with the Soviet Union was signed in 1936. Admitted to the United Nations in 1961, Mongolia has sided with the Soviets in the Soviet-Chinese ideological disputes.

MONG-TSEU. See MENG-TZU.

MONHEGAN (United States) Island in the Atlantic Ocean 10 mi off the S coast of MAINE, SE of Boothbay Harbor. It was settled *c.*1620. During the War of 1812 the waters to the southeast of the island were the scene of the defeat of the British ship *Boxer* by the U.S. ship *Enterprise.*

MONKWEARMOUTH (England) Suburb of SUNDERLAND, Tyne and Wear, 10 mi ESE of Newcastle upon Tyne. Wearmouth, an early Benedictine monastery founded here in 674, was the place where the historian the Venerable Bede studied and lived until he moved to YARROW. The church of St. Peter here contains what was left of the monastery after its destruction by Danish Vikings.

An early 19th-century temple in Ulan Bator, Outer Mongolia. This part of ancient Mongolia, homeland of the Mongol conquerors, lies in the Soviet sphere.

MONMOUTH (Wales) Town in Gwent, near the junction of the Monnow, Wye, and Trothy rivers, 26 mi N of Bristol. The town grew around a Norman castle that was taken by Simon de Montfort in 1264, by Owen Glendower in 1404, and by the Parliamentarians in 1646. Of historic interest are the ruins of a Norman church, a bridge built in 1272, and the ruins of the castle in which Henry V was born.

MONMOUTH COURTHOUSE. See FREEHOLD.

MONMOUTHSHIRE (Wales) Former county, most of which is now incorporated in Gwent. It was legally an English county from 1536 to 1830. The area was settled at least by the Iron Age, as attested by the remains of several large hill forts. After the Roman conquest in 75 AD a fortress was established at Isca, modern CAERLEON. Attacked by Vikings from the ninth to the 11th centuries, it formed the Welsh kingdom of GWENT, in the time of the Heptarchy, which was conquered by the English king, Harold, about 1065—just before the Battle of HASTINGS, in which he died. The lordship of MONMOUTH lent its name to the region in the early 16th century. Notable architectural remains include those of TINTERN ABBEY, made famous by the poet William Wordsworth. See also CAERWENT, NEWPORT.

MONOCACY (United States) Battle site and river that joins the POTOMAC RIVER near Frederick, MARYLAND. In July 1864, during the Civil War, Union forces under Gen. Lew Wallace were defeated in an encounter on the river banks. But he managed to delay the Confederates under Gen. J.A. Early sufficiently to give Grant time to send troops for the defense of WASHINGTON and force Gen. Early back into Virginia.

MONOECUS. See MONACO.

MONOMOTAPA. See MWANAMUTAPA.

MONONGAHELA [former: **Parkinson's Ferry, Williamsport**] City in PENNSYLVANIA, on the MONONGAHELA RIVER, 17 mi S of Pittsburgh. First known as Williamsport, then as Parkinson's Ferry until 1833, it was renamed Monongahela in 1837. The Whiskey Rebellion convention met here on Aug. 14, 1794.

MONONGAHELA RIVER (United States) River, 128 mi long, formed by the junction of the West Fork and Tygart rivers at Fairmont, West Virginia. It flows north into southwestern Pennsylvania and at PITTSBURGH joins the ALLEGHENY RIVER to form the OHIO RIVER. The river was the first in the United States to be improved for navigation. On the river are MORGANTOWN, West Virginia, settled in 1772; McKEESPORT, Pennsylvania, a center of the Whiskey Rebellion of 1794; and BRADDOCK, Pennsylvania, scene of the defeat of British Gen. Edward Braddock by the French and Indians on July 9, 1755. Monongahela is an Indian word probably meaning "high-banks-falling-down," referring to some particular place along its course.

MONOTICUT. See BRAINTREE.

MONREALE (Italy) Town of Palermo province, SICILY, 5 mi SW of Palermo. Its name derives from *monte reale* (Mount Royal), a palace built here by the Norman King Roger I. It is the site of an impressive cathedral that is unusual in its combination of Norman, Moorish, Sicilian, and Byzantine styles. Begun in 1174 by the Norman King William II of Sicily, it has outstanding copper doors designed by Bonanno Pisano, and an interior of exceptional Byzantine mosaics. Nearby are some remains of the Benedictine monastery that was one of the most important centers of the 12th-century Renaissance.

MONROE [*former:* **Fort Miró, Ouachita Post**] (United States) Town in LOUISIANA, on the Ouachita River, 96 mi E of Shreveport. Here in 1785, during the Spanish occupation of Louisiana, Don Juan Filhiol, commandant of the district of Ouachita, founded a settlement called Ouachita Post. It was renamed Fort Miró in 1790 in honor of the governor-general. It was renamed Monroe in 1819 in honor of the *James Monroe*, first steamboat to arrive at the port. During the Civil War it was damaged by heavy artillery bombardment, but it still contains several fine antebellum homes.

MONROE [*until 1817:* **Frenchtown**] (United States) City on LAKE ERIE, at the mouth of the Raisin River, 35 mi SW of Detroit, MICHIGAN. During the War of 1812 an encounter between the British and their Indian allies and U.S. forces under Gen. James Winchester forced the British from the town. A few days later the Americans were surprised by a British-Indian force that captured Gen. Winchester and forced him to order the surrender of the entire U.S. force. In 1813 Monroe was the scene of the RAISIN RIVER Massacre following the defeat of the Americans by a British-Indian force under Col. H. Proctor. The home of Gen. George A. Custer, Monroe has a local museum with a large collection of Custer memorabilia.

MONROE, FORT. See FORT MONROE.

MONROVIA (Liberia) Capital, city, and port located near the mouth of the St. Paul River, in West Africa. Founded in 1822 by the American Colonization Society as a haven for freed slaves from the United States and the British West Indies, it was named for James Monroe, then the president of the UNITED STATES. Until recently the city was still controlled by descendants of the early settlers who arrived between 1830 and 1870. Since it broke ties with the United States after 1871, it long remained an interesting cultural combination of pre-Civil War Southern American and West African influences.

MONS [*Flemish:* **Bergen**] (Belgium) City and provincial capital, near the French border, in the SW at the junction of the Canal du Centre and the Condé-Mons canal. Built on the site of a Roman camp, the present town dates from the seventh century AD. It became the capital of HAINAUT in 804. In various wars from the 16th to the 18th centuries it was frequently contested by Dutch, Spanish, and French forces. In 1572 it was surrendered by Louis of NASSAU during the Wars of Religion. In World War I the first engagement of the British Expeditionary Force took place here on Aug. 23, 1914. It was also the scene of several other battles in both world wars. Historic buildings include the Gothic church of St. Waltrude dating from the mid-15th and

16th centuries, and a 15th-century town hall. Nearby are MALPLAQUET and JEMAPPES, both sites of important 18th-century battles.

MONSALVAT. See MONTSERRAT.

MONS AUREUS. See SMEDEREVO.

MONS BADONICUS [Mount Badon] (England) Battle site of disputed locality, possibly near Swindon, N central England. The site was said to have been the scene of the greatest battle fought by the British knights of the semi-legendary King Arthur against invading Anglo-Saxon tribes c.500 AD. The battle temporarily stemmed the tide that would later overrun Britain. By another, earlier tradition, related by Gildas, the battle here was fought by Ambrosius Aurelianus, "the last of the Romans." Historians have speculated that Ambrosius's real exploits may have given rise to the earliest Arthurian legend.

MONS BRISIACUS. See BREISACH.

MONS CAPITOLINUS. See CAPITOLINE HILL.

MONSCHAU [*former:* **Montjoie**] (West Germany) Town of North Rhine-Westphalia, SE of Aachen, on the French border. It was the scene of severe fighting in World War II from December 1944 until January 1945.

MONSERRAT. See MONTSERRAT.

MONS GRAUPIUS. See GRAUPIUS, MOUNT.

MONS SERRATUS. See MONTSERRAT.

MONTAGNE PELÉE. See PELÉE, MOUNT.

MONTALTO UFFUGO (Italy) Town in Cosenza province, CALABRIA region, 10 mi NNW of Cosenza. The town was settled in the 14th century by the Waldensians, a medieval reform sect who from 1211 on were judged heretics and persecuted. See also DAUPHINÉ, PIEDMONT.

MONTANA (United States) State, in the NW part of the country, in the region of the Rocky Mts Montana has Canada as its northern boundary, North and South Dakota on the E, Wyoming on the S, and Idaho on the W. It was admitted as the 41st state in 1889, and its name is the Spanish word for mountain.

Montana was a land of many Indian tribes—Blackfoot, Sioux, Shoshone, Arapaho, Cheyenne, Flathead, and others—when the first Europeans, who were French fur traders from CANADA, arrived. The very first may have been the brothers François and Louis Vérendrye in 1742. The land was barely known to Europeans until after the Lewis and Clark expedition of 1803 to 1806, which crossed this area in 1805. Manuel Lisa of ST. LOUIS, Missouri set up the first trading post in 1807 at the mouth of the BIGHORN RIVER. Men of the North West Fur Company of Canada were also here and dominated the fur trade for a time, establishing posts between 1807 and 1812. Furs also attracted mountain men, and later the American Fur Company became active; but by the 1840's the region had been overtrapped.

The United States did not get title to all the area until 1846, when a treaty with GREAT BRITAIN settled the boundary of the far northwest region known as the OREGON COUNTRY. Most of Montana was already part of the LOUISIANA PURCHASE of 1803, but few settlers came here; and there was little growth until the discovery of gold in 1852. Miners settled BANNACK in 1862 and VIRGINIA CITY in 1864. During this period FORT BENTON at the head of navigation of the MISSOURI RIVER was important; and Capt. John Mullan later built a wagon road over the Rockies to WALLA WALLA, Washington. Montana became a separate territory in 1864.

Ranching began after the Civil War, and the first cattle brought from TEXAS arrived in 1866 through the BOZEMAN PASS. As the number of settlers grew, the Sioux Indians took up arms. After prospectors entered their sacred Black Hills in search of gold over government prohibitions, the Indians killed Gen. George Custer and all of his men at the Battle of LITTLE BIGHORN in 1876. The last Indian resistance ended in 1877 when Chief Joseph of the Nez Percé surrendered as they wearily sought to reach sanctuary in Canada. Ranches grew; and as the railroads arrived, beginning in the 1880's, cow towns sprang up.

The great impetus to Montana's economy came with the discovery of silver at BUTTE in 1875 and copper in 1880, in "the richest hill in the world." The men who gained control of valuable mining properties warred with each other and battled for political power. They also engaged in violent disputes with miners seeking to organize unions.

Montana suffered during the Great Depression of the 1930's, but irrigation projects later improved agricultural prospects. Copper was much in demand during World War II, and ever since the 1950's oil production has played a prominent role here. Even as it becomes more industrialized, Montana appeals to urban vacationers as "the land of the big sky." The state usually votes Republican. HELENA is the capital; Billings and GREAT FALLS are the largest cities; MISSOULA and Butte are also important centers.

MONTARGIS (France) Town of Loiret department, 38 mi E of Orléans, near the Montargis forest. Ceded to the French crown in 1188 by the house of Courtenay, in the 14th and 15th centuries it was a royal residence. The town is known for its statue of the Dog of Montargis, a pet of Aubry de Montdidier, courtier to King Charles V. According to legend the dog tracked down his master's murderer and vanquished him in a duel ordered by the king in 1371. The nearby castle of Bignon was the birthplace of the French revolutionary leader Honoré de Mirabeau.

MONTAUBAN (France) Village of Somme department in the N, 6 mi E of Albert. It was the scene of a stage of the Battle of the SOMME on July 1, 1916 during World War I.

MONTAUBAN (France) City, ancient capital of QUERCY, in Tarn-et-Garonne department, on the TARN RIVER, 31 mi N of Toulouse. Founded in 1144, it is one of the oldest fortified towns in France. From 1360 to 1369 it was in English hands. Often attacked, it was a stronghold of the heretic Albigensians in the 13th century and of the Huguenots after 1560, when its bishops adopted Protestantism. Prosperous until the period of religious persecution in the 17th century, it was the center of the Huguenot rebellion in 1621 and was only taken by Richelieu, Louis XIII's chief minister, in 1629. Notable structures include a 14th-century brick bridge over the Tarn, an episcopal palace, and a town hall.

MONTAUK (United States) Village and point at the eastern tip of LONG ISLAND in NEW YORK State, approx. 115 mi E of NEW YORK CITY. From the 17th century Montauk was used as grazing land for cattle, horses, and sheep; and the first three houses of the settlement were built in the 18th century to house the keepers of the cattle. A witness to many wrecks, a lighthouse that still stands was built on the point in 1796. In the late 19th century the small settlement began to grow, and the area was developed with a number of summer cottages. After the Spanish American War of 1898 almost 30,000 veterans of the war, including Theodore Roosevelt and his Rough Riders, were brought to Montauk to recuperate from the effects of yellow fever, typhoid, and bad food. Several attempts to develop Montauk as a resort area were made in the 1920's and later; but the community, now a popular seaside vacation area, has grown slowly.

MONTBÉLIARD (France) Town of Doubs department, 43 mi ENE of Besançon. By the Treaty of Verdun in 843 it became part of LORRAINE after having earlier belonged to the Burgundians and the Franks. Following the 12th century, the town and environs formed a county of the HOLY ROMAN EMPIRE. In 1397 the county passed to the counts of WÜRTTEMBERG who held it, except for French occupations from 1674 to 1697 and 1723 to 1748, until it became part of France by the Treaty of Lunéville in 1801. Roman remains and parts of the 15th- and 16th-century castle are visible.

MONT BEUVRAY. See BRIBRACTE.

MONT BLANC. See ALPS, CHAMONIX.

MONTBRISON (France) Town of Loire department, 21 mi NW of St. Étienne. It was the property of the counts of FOREZ in the Middle Ages. Notable buildings include the 13th to 15th-century church of Notre Dame d'Esperance and a 14th-century building known as the Salle de la Diana, restored by Viollet-le-Duc in the 19th century.

MONT CHEVALIER. See CANNES.

MONTCLAIR (United States) City in NE NEW JERSEY, 6 mi NNW of Newark. Settled in 1666 and originally a part of Newark, it became a separate town in 1812. It served as Washington's headquarters in 1780 and more recently was the home of George Inness, the 19th-century American landscape painter. The local art museum has several of his paintings.

MONT-DE-MARSAN (France) Town of Landes department, 66 mi S of Bordeaux. Founded in 1141 as the capital of the viscounts of Marsan, and the first of the bastides, or market-garrison colonies of the Middle Ages, it became part of BÉARN in 1256. The scene of conflicts during the Wars of Religion, it was taken by the Calvinists, besieged in 1569, and captured in 1580 by the Catholics. It passed to the French crown in 1589

on the accession of Henry IV. Of historical note are traces of 12th-century walls and other fortifications.

MONTDIDIER (France) Town in PICARDY, in Somme department, approx. 55 mi NNE of Paris. Dating from the Merovingian period of the FRANKISH EMPIRE, it owes its name to the imprisonment here of the Lombard King Didier in the eighth century. The town suffered devastation in several battles in 1918 during World War I.

MONTE ALBÁN (Mexico) Ancient capital city of the Zapotec Indians, in the SW, 7 mi from Oaxaca. Sprawling, low buildings surround an enormous plaza here, where excavations of the tombs, begun by the Mexican archaeologist Alfonso Caso in 1931, have yielded significant finds. The Zapotec civilization flourished here c.200 BC, with some borrowings from the Mayan culture. Its final epoch from 1300 to 1521 AD covers the ascendancy of the Mixtec, when the Zapotec were driven from Monte Albán and MITLA until all was terminated by the Spanish conquest.

MONTEBOURG. See COTENTIN PENINSULA.

MONTE CARLO (Monaco) Town on the Mediterranean coast, a part of Monaco. It is the site of the world-famous gambling casino built in 1858. In 1954 the casino concession came under the control of Aristotle Onassis, but has since been returned to the Monaco government. It is also the site of the Monaco Grand Prix auto race. Sergei Diaghilev's ballets were first performed here.

MONTE CASSINO. See CASSINO.

MONTECATINI (Italy) Town in Pisa province, TUSCANY region, 5 mi W of Volterra. It was the site of a Florentine defeat by Uguccione della Faggiuola of PISA in 1315 during the wars between the Black and the White Guelph factions. It gained wide recognition in the 14th century for the mineral baths constructed here and still in use today.

MONTE CRISTO (Italy) Small island in the Tyrrhenian Sea, S of Elba. Its fame is due to its role in the novel by Alexandre Dumas, Sr., *The Count of Monte Cristo*. On the island, now a hunting preserve, are the ruins of a Camaldulensian monastery founded in the 13th century and destroyed in the 16th century.

MONTE CROCE. See PLÖCKEN.

MONTEFIASCONE (Italy) Town of Viterbo province, Latium region, in the volcanic region E of Lake Bolsena, 10 mi NNW of Viterbo. The town may occupy the site of Fanum Voltumnae, where representatives of the 12 city-states of ETRURIA met during the period of Etruscan independence, at its peak c.500 BC. It is the site of a 16th-century cathedral and castle and a Romanesque church.

MONTEFRIO (Spain) Town on the Bilano River, in the province of Granada, approx. 27 mi NW of Granada. Largely Moorish in character and dominated by a Moorish castle, it was one of the chief frontier fortresses of the Moors in the 15th century.

MONTEGO BAY (Jamaica) Port and famous CARIBBEAN SEA resort in the NW part of the island. Originally occupied by a large Arawak Indian village, it was discovered by Columbus in 1494.

MONTE GRAPPA. See GRAPPA, MOUNT.

MONTEITH. See MENTEITH.

MONTELEONE DI CALABRIA. See VIBO VALENTIA.

MONTÉLIMAR [*ancient:* **Acunum Acusio**; *former:* **Montilium Adhemari**] (France) Town in Drôme department, on the RHÔNE RIVER, 27 mi SSW of Valence. After this Roman settlement was plundered by the Visigoths in the fifth century, it belonged next to the Adhémar family, who sold it to the dauphins of Viennois and the pope. In 1198 it became a commune, served as the capital of the state of Valdaine, and with DAUPHINÉ came to the French crown. It was besieged by the Huguenots in 1562, 1585, and 1587. In modern times it was seized by the Allies on Aug. 25, 1944 during World War II.

MONTELLO (Italy) Plateau SW of the Piave River, NE of Montebelluna, Treviso province, VENETO region, approx. 27 mi NW of Venice. It was the scene of several battles in World War I, especially one in June 1918, which was won by the Italians. It also played a part in the fighting here in World War II.

MONTENEGRO [*Serbo-Croatian:* **Crna Gora, Tsernagora**] (Yugoslavia) Former kingdom in SE Europe that originated after the Battle of KOSOVO in 1389, when the Serbs were forced to retreat into the Black Mountain area. Sporadic warfare with the Turks lasted, however, until the 19th century. Ruled by prince-bishops after 1515, Montenegro never accepted Turkish authority. Danilo I (1696–1735) made the episcopal succession hereditary in the Niegosh family and began alliances with RUSSIA. Under Peter I (1782–1830) Montenegro fought beside Russia in its wars against Turkey and in 1799 gained recognition from Sultan Selim III as an independent kingdom. Peter also began reforms that were continued by Peter II (1830–1851). Under Nicholas I (1910–1918) Montenegro gained both formal recognition as an independent state by the Congress of Berlin in 1878, and territory that included a small outlet on the Adriatic Sea. Proclaiming himself king in 1910, Nicholas was involved in the Balkan Wars and declared war on AUSTRIA-HUNGARY in 1914 in displeasure over its annexation of BOSNIA AND HERZAGOVINA. The country was overrun by Austro-German forces in 1915 as World War I progressed. A national assembly in 1918 deposed Nicholas and joined with SERBIA, thus creating a kingdom of Serbs, Croats, and Slovenes. In 1946 Montenegro became one of the six republics of Yugoslavia, with its capital at TITOGRAD. See also KOTOR, OTTOMAN EMPIRE.

MONTEPULCIANO (Italy) Town, in Siena province, TUSCANY region, 29 mi SE of Siena. Dating from *c.*715 AD, it was alternately controlled by FLORENCE and SIENA, finally passing to Florence. It is the birthplace of the scholar and poet Angelo Anbrogini (1454–1494) and of the theologian, later canonized, Cardinal Bellarmine (1542–1621). Historic buildings include a 16th-century cathedral, a 13th-century church, the 14th-

A village street in mountainous Montenegro, now part of Yugoslavia. Unlike the other peoples of Yugoslavia, the proud natives of this former kingdom never submitted to Turkish rule.

century Palazzo Publico and several fine Renaissance houses from the 15th and 16th centuries.

MONTEREAU [**Montereau faut Yonne**] [*ancient:* **Condate**] (France) Town of Seine-et-Marne department, at the confluence of the Seine and Yonne rivers, 21 mi SE of Melun. In 1419 the dauphin, later Charles VII, here witnessed the assassination of Jean Sans-Peur, the duke of BURGUNDY. The town was captured toward the end of the Hundred Years War by Charles in 1438. In 1814 it was the scene of Napoleon's victory over the troops of WÜRTTEMBERG under Gen. Karl Schwarzenberg. Of note here is a 13th-century church with a Renaissance facade.

MONTEREY (United States) City in CALIFORNIA at the S end of Monterey Bay. Discovered by Juan Cabrillo and named by Sebastian Vizcaíno in 1602, it was visited in 1770 by Gaspar de Portola, who established a presidio, and by Father Junipero Serra, who founded a Franciscan mission here now located in CARMEL. The missions of the type set up by Serra helped Spain retain control of Alta, or Upper, California until 1822 after the wars of independence. Under Mexican control Monte-

An 1865 view of Montevideo, capital of Uruguay. It was founded in the 18th century. The Portuguese, Spanish, Brazilians, Argentinians, French, and British have contested the city.

rey became the social, political, and military center for the vast Empire of the Pacific. Passed to the United States in 1846, after the Mexican War, it was the site of the first California constitutional convention in 1849. Historic buildings include California's first theater from 1844, its first newspaper plant, built in 1846, and the presidio.

MONTERREY (Mexico) Capital city of Nuevo León state, c.150 mi S of Laredo, Texas. Founded in 1579, it was captured by Zachary Taylor during the Mexican War after a valiant defense by the Mexicans from Sept. 19 to 24, 1846. Its Obispado chapel and cathedral are in the colonial style.

MONTE SAN GIULIANO. See Eryx.

MONTE SANT'ANGELO (Italy) Commune of Foggia province, Apulia region, 27 mi NE of Foggia. It is a center of pilgrimage to the sanctuary of San Michele, founded in 491 AD over a cave in which the archangel Michael is said to have appeared to St. Laurentius, archbishop of Sipontum. The church's bronze door was made in Constantinople in 1076. Other historic structures include a Norman castle and a 13th-century campanile.

MONTE TOMBE. See Mont-Saint-Michel.

MONTEVIDEO (Uruguay) Seaport and capital city on the N shore of the Rio de La Plata estuary, 135 mi E of Buenos Aires, Argentina. A fort was established here by the Portuguese in 1717 and captured by the Spanish in 1724. The city grew from a Spanish settlement founded in 1726 by the governor of Buenos Aires to stem Portuguese influence in the area. From 1807 to 1830 it was variously occupied by British, Spanish, Argentine, Portuguese, and Brazilian forces, being named in 1830 the capital of an independent Uruguay. During political turmoil in Uruguay, it endured a siege by Argentine and Uruguayan forces from 1843 to 1851. British and French naval forces aided the inhabitants during the country's 19th-century civil wars. On Dec. 13, 1939, during World War II, the German pocket battleship *Graf Spee* was trapped in Montevideo harbor by British cruisers. It was scuttled outside the harbor by its crew.

MONTEZUMA CASTLE NATIONAL MONUMENT (United States) A five-story 20-room Anasazi pueblo apartment house atop cliffs in central Arizona. Built c.1250, it was named by early pioneers who believed that the Aztecs had built it.

MONTFAUCON (France) Village of Meuse department, 13 mi NW of Verdun. In German hands during World War I, it was taken by U.S. forces in the Meuse-Argonne offensive of Oct. 4, 1918.

MONTFERRAND. See Clermont-Ferrand.

MONTFERRAT [*Italian:* **Monferrato**] (Italy) Region of Piedmont, S of the Po River, now mostly in Alessandria province. Under Emperor Otto I (912–73) it was given to the Aleramo family who played an important role in the Crusades. Passing to the Byzantine Paleologus family in 1310, Casale Monferrato was made the capital in 1435. During the 16th century its control was in dispute, and in 1613 Savoy invaded the region. Spain and France intervened, and Montferrat became a major battleground in the War of the Mantuan Succession of 1628 to 1631. The issue was eventually resolved by the Treaty of Cherasco, which assigned parts to Savoy and the rest, including Casale, to the duchy of Mantua. It passed eventually to the French Nevers branch of the Gonzaga family. The Peace of Utrecht in 1713 assigned the entire region to the house of Savoy.

MONTGOMERY [*former:* **Fort Toulouse**] (United States) City and state capital in SE central Alabama, on the Alabama River, 85 mi SSE of Birmingham. Its site was originally inhabited by mound builders and later by two Indian villages. It was visited by Hernando De Soto in 1540, and in 1715 it became the site of the French Fort Toulouse. During the American Revolution this was a center for Tories. The city was founded in 1819, was named the state capital in 1847, and boomed as a river port and cotton market. Often called "the Cradle of the Confederacy," it was the scene in

February 1861 of a convention that met in the capitol building to form the CONFEDERATE STATES OF AMERICA. Jefferson Davis was inaugurated president here, and the city served as the capital of the Confederacy until May 1861, when the seat was moved to RICHMOND, Va. It was occupied by Union troops in the spring of 1865. In addition to the historic state capitol building, the "first White House of the Confederacy" is preserved as a Confederate museum. Many antebellum homes and buildings survive. The Rev. Martin Luther King, Jr. of Montgomery organized several civil rights demonstrations here, notably the 1965 march on Montgomery after racial violence in SELMA.

MONTGOMERY [*Welsh:* **Trefaldwyn**] (Wales) Town in Powys, 20 mi SW of Shrewsbury. OFFA'S DYKE, a fortification built against the Welsh, is particularly well preserved here, where it forms the border with England. Evidence of a Neolithic settlement and an Early Iron Age camp is just above the town. One mile away is Hendomen, where Roger de Montgomery, a relative of William the Conqueror, first erected a castle. Henry III's castle, now in ruins, was built in 1223 on the site of present Montgomery. It was taken in 1644 by the Parliamentarians, who destroyed most of it.

MONTIEL (Spain) Town, in CIUDAD REAL province, in the La Mancha region of New Castile. Nearby is the site of a battle in which Peter the Cruel, king of LEÓN and CASTILE, was defeated in 1369 by Bertrand Du Guesclin, later marshal of France, leader of the French mercenaries who invaded Castile in 1366. With him was Henry of Trastamara, later Henry II, who had led several rebellions against King Peter, whose ally was John of Gaunt of ENGLAND. The victory allowed Henry to ascend the throne of Castile.

MONTIGNAC. See LASCAUX.

MONTIJO (Spain) Town in Badajoz province, approx. 18 mi ENE of Badajoz. Here on May 26, 1644 the Portuguese under Alburquerque defeated the Spanish, who opposed the reign of John IV. He became king of an independent PORTUGAL following a revolution to free the country from the control of Philip IV of Spain. In 1668 Spain officially recognized the Portuguese throne.

MONTILIUM ADHEMARI. See MONTÉLIMAR.

MONTILLA (Spain) Town of Córdoba province, ANDALUSIA, 22 mi SSE of Córdoba. It was the birthplace of "The Great Captain" Gonsalvo or Gonzalo of Córdoba (1453–1515), a general whose achievements included the conquest of GRANADA and whose father's ruined castle still stands here. The town's notable buildings include a ducal palace and Moorish mosque that now serves as a Christian church.

MONTJOIE. See MONSCHAU.

MONT LIBAN. See LEBANON MOUNTAINS.

MONTLUÇON (France) City of Allier department, on the Cher River, 38 mi WSW of Moulins. Founded in the 11th century, it was part of the duchy of BOURBON and was held from 1171 to 1181 by the English. It became part of the royal domain in 1527. The castle of

the dukes of Bourbon, dating from the 15th and 16th centuries, was taken by Henry IV during the Wars of Religion of 1562 to 1598. Other historic buildings include the 12th-century church of St. Pierre, the Gothic church of Notre Dame, and many houses from the 15th and 16th centuries. Nearby is the ancient city of Néris-les-Bains.

MONTMARTRE (France) Part of PARIS, in the N section on a hill above the SEINE RIVER. A former independent town, now within the city limits, it was annexed to Paris in 1860. The highest point in Paris, crowned by the church of Sacré Coeur, its hill was of military importance, especially during the Paris Commune formed in 1871 by workers angered by the conservative government's dealings after the Franco-Prussian War. Following a terrible siege, it fell in May to government troops from Versailles. Many thousands were then executed. The district's famous cemetery is the burial place of Stendhal, Renan, Heine, Berlioz, and Alfred de Vigny. The area has traditionally been a center of Paris bohemian life.

MONTMÉDY (France) Town of Meuse department, near the Belgian frontier, 25 mi N of Verdun. An old town dominated by a castle built in 1235, it was joined to France in 1659 and was fortified under Louis XIV as a frontier post.

MONTMORENCY [*former:* **Enghien**] (France) Suburb of PARIS, located 9 mi N in Val d'Oise department. It was formerly the seat of the Montmorency family, whose many services to France date back to the 10th century. From 1689 it was under the Condé family, into which the last of the Montmorencys married, and was also the home of Jean-Jacques Rousseau, who from 1756 to 1762 resided here and completed *Julie, ou la Nouvelle Héloïse*, *Émile*, and *Du contrat social*. *Émile* led to such controversy that Rousseau had to flee the town and the country.

MONTORO [*Latin:* **Epora**] (Spain) Town of Córdoba province, 27 mi NE of Córdoba. Now largely modernized, it was an important Moorish stronghold in the Middle Ages. Its fine four-arch bridge dates from the 16th century.

MONTPELIER (United States) State capital located in N central VERMONT, at the junction of the Winooski and North Branch rivers. Founded in 1780 and named after the French city, it became the state capital in 1805. It was the birthplace of Admiral George Dewey.

MONTPELLIER (France) Old city, now an industrial and commercial center, in Hérault department, near the Mediterranean, 77 mi WNW of Marseilles. Founded in the eighth century AD around a Benedictine abbey, it was ruled by the counts of TOULOUSE until the 13th century, when it passed to the king of MAJORCA, from whom Philip VI of France purchased it in 1349. An important Jewish center, it was also a center of religious dissent and a Huguenot stronghold during the Wars of Religion. It was captured in 1622 by Louis XIII. Its famous university, founded in 1289, has a medical faculty that dates from the 11th century, and possibly earlier. Rabelais was a student here. Notable buildings include a château, a citadel, a 14th-century cathedral, the palace of justice, and a Doric triumphal arch. The oldest botanical garden in France is here, dating from 1593.

A street in 19th-century Montreal, now Canada's largest city and still a center of French culture, although it has belonged to British Canada since 1760.

MONTREAL [*former:* **Ville-Marie de Montréal;** *French:* **Montréal**] (Canada) Canada's largest city, in S QUEBEC, on Montreal Island in the ST. LAWRENCE RIVER, at the foot of Mt Royal. When discovered and named by Jacques Cartier in 1535 it was the site of the Indian town of HOCHELAGA. In 1642, Paul de Chomedey, Sieur de Maisonneuve, established the first permanent French settlement, which became an important fur-trading center and the starting point for the expeditions of La Salle, Jolliet, Vérendrye, and Duluth. Constant skirmishes with the Iroquois marked Montreal's early days. Fortified in 1725, it remained a French possession until 1760 after the fall of Quebec in the French and Indian War, when Vaudreuil de Cavagnal surrendered it to British forces under Lord Jeffrey Amherst. During the American Revolution it was occupied for a short time in 1775/76 by Americans under Richard Montgomery. Benjamin Franklin and others came here in an unproductive attempt to gain Canadian support for the revolution. The opening of the Lachine Canal link with the Great Lakes in 1825 helped its growth enormously, and from 1844 to 1849 it served as the capital of United Canada. The center of French-English conflicts, it was involved in open rebellion in 1837 and 1838 as civil riots led to the burning of the parliament building. Old Montreal, extensively restored, is the site of the Gothic church of Notre Dame from *c.*1820, St. Sulpice Seminary of 1685 and the Château de Ramezay, dating from 1705.

MONTREUIL [**Montreuil-sous-Bois**] (France) A suburb of PARIS, in Seine-Saint-Denis department. Founded before 1000 AD, it is the site of the church of Saints Peter and Paul from the 12th century where Charles V (1337–1380) was baptized. A museum in a nearby park is dedicated to the socialist and workers' movements.

MONTREUIL-SOUS-BOIS. See MONTREUIL.

MONTREUX (Switzerland) Resort area composed of several villages at the E end of LAKE GENEVA. In June 1936 it was the site of a conference of European nations that met to revise the Straits, or LAUSANNE, Convention with TURKEY. The revision, known as the Montreux Convention, dealt with the DARDANELLES. Still in effect, it returned control of the straits to Turkey and stipulated the rights of foreign ships in the area both in times of peace and in times of war. See also the BLACK SEA.

MONTROSE (Scotland) Port and popular resort town of Tayside region, 25 mi NE of Dundee, at the mouth of the Esk River. Here in 1296 John de Baliol lost the Scottish throne he had accepted in 1292 with the understanding he would pay homage to King Edward I of England. After Scotland allied itself with France in 1295 and invaded England early in 1296, Edward advanced toward BERWICK-ON-TWEED and at Dunbar quickly defeated John who thereafter surrendered the crown here to Edward.

MONT-SAINT-JEAN (Belgium) Village of central Brabant province, on a height S of WATERLOO. Toward the end of the Waterloo campaign of the Napoleonic Wars in 1815, the British under Wellington dug in between this village and La Belle-Alliance on June 18 and held the French attack until Prussian relief forces arrived and routed the forces of Napoleon. Four days later Napoleon abdicated for the second and last time.

MONT-SAINT-MICHEL [**Monte Tombe**] (France) Rocky islet and famous sanctuary in Manche department, NORMANDY, in a bay of the ENGLISH CHANNEL, 8 mi SW of AVRANCHES. In 708 St. Aubert, bishop of Avranches, built an oratory here that became a pilgrimage center. A Benedictine abbey succeeded it in 966 and was partly burned in 1203 when Philip II of France tried to take it. Heavily fortified, it resisted sieges during the Hundred Years War and the Wars of Religion but declined during the 18th century and was made into a prison by Napoleon. The islet is cut off from the mainland at high tide. It is now one of the greatest tourist attractions in France. Henry Adams's *Mont-Saint-Michel and Chartres* gives the classic description in the English language.

MONTSERRAT (Great Britain) One of the Leeward Islands of the WEST INDIES, 27 mi SW of Antigua in the CARIBBEAN Sea. Discovered by Columbus in 1493, it was settled by the English in 1632 and was occupied by the French from 1664 to 1668 and from 1782 to 1784. Part of the Colony of the Leeward Islands from 1871 to 1956 and of the West Indies Federation from 1958 to 1962, the island rejected self-government in 1966.

MONTSERRAT [**Monsalvat, Monserrat**] [*Latin:*

The impressive abbey of Mont-St.-Michel in Normandy, once a true off shore fortress and now a major tourist center.

Mons Serratus] (Spain) Mountain in Barcelona province. More than halfway up the craggy slope is a renowned Benedictine monastery, built in the 18th century near the ruins of an earlier monastery dating from the ninth to the 11th centuries and restored after its destruction by French troops in 1812. Its Renaissance church contains a black wooden image of the Virgin that tradition says was carved by St. Luke, brought to Spain by St. Peter, and hidden from the Moors in a nearby cave. Inhabited since the beginning of history, Montserrat was purportedly the site of the castle of the Holy Grail. St. Ignatius Loyola (1491–1556) resided here before traveling to MANRESA.

MONT VALÉRIEN. See VALÉRIEN, MONT.

MONYWA (Burma) Town of Sagaing division, located on the left bank of the lower Chindwin River, 55 mi W of Mandalay. A Japanese communications center in World War II, it was taken by the British on Jan. 22, 1945.

MONZA (Italy) Medieval capital of LOMBARDY in Milan province, Lombardy region, 10 mi NE of MILAN. Its history is intermingled with that of Milan. Its cathedral, founded in 595 AD by the Lombard Queen Theodolinda and remodeled in the 14th century, contains the iron crown of Lombardy, so named since it is believed to be made from a nail used in the Crucifixion. It has been used in the coronations of Charlemagne, Charles

V, Napoleon I and other emperors as kings of Lombardy or of Italy. The town was attacked by Charles V and was besieged on several other occasions. King Humbert I was assassinated here on July 29, 1900 after evading two previous attempts on his life. Historic buildings include the 13th-century town hall and the palace of the Lombard kings.

MOODKEE. See MUDKI.

MOOLTAN. See MULTAN.

MOORE'S BLUFF. See SELMA.

MOORES CREEK BRIDGE (United States) Battle site in Pender county, SE NORTH CAROLINA. American Loyalists were defeated here during the American Revolution by a band of patriots on Feb. 27, 1776. This prevented the planned British invasion of North Carolina and helped to make the colony the first to vote for independence. The site of the battle, considered the "Lexington and Concord of the South," is now a 50-acre national military park established in 1926.

MOORE'S LANDING. See SELMA.

MOORESTOWN (United States) Township in S central NEW JERSEY, 9 mi E of Camden. Settled by Quakers in the late 17th century, in 1776 it served as headquarters for the Hessians, German mercenaries employed by the British during the American Revolution. The town has several interesting 18th-century houses.

MOOSBURG (West Germany) Town in BAVARIA, on the Isar River, approx. 10 mi WSW of Landshut. On April 29, 1945 during World War II U.S. forces liberated over 100,000 prisoners from the German prisoner-of-war camp here.

MOOSE FACTORY (Canada) Trading post in NE ONTARIO, on the Moose River, approx. 15 mi from where it empties into James Bay. It was built in 1672/73 by the Hudson's Bay Company and captured by the French in 1686. It changed hands several times in the wars between the French and the British, and the French abandoned it in 1710. Reestablished in 1730 by the Hudson's Bay Company, it is still in operation.

MORADABAD (India) City of Uttar Pradesh state, approx. 100 mi E of Delhi on the right bank of the Ramaganga River. It was founded in 1625 by Rustum Khan, who built a fort over the river bank and constructed the great mosque or Jama Masjid in 1631. The city passed to the British in 1801.

MORAR (India) Town of Gwalior state, 3 mi E of GWALIOR. A former British military post in central India, during the Indian Mutiny of 1857 it was the scene of the most serious uprising in that area.

MORAT [*German:* **Murten**] (Switzerland) Town of Fribourg canton, on the E shore of Lake Morat, 14 mi N of Fribourg. Founded by the dukes of ZÄHRINGEN in the 12th century, here Charles the Bold of BURGUNDY was defeated by the Swiss on June 22, 1476. The battle was a landmark in the ascendancy of massed Swiss infantry formations. Its historic structures include a 13th-century castle, a 15th-century French Gothic church, and the surrounding town walls from the 14th and 15th centuries.

MORAVA. See MORAVIA.

MORAVIA [*Czech:* **Morava;** *German:* **Mähren**] (Czechoslovakia) Region bounded by Bohemia to the W, Silesia to the NE, Slovakia to the E, and Austria to the S. First occupied by Celtic Bori and Cotini peoples and taken by Germanic tribes from the first to fifth centuries AD, it was settled from the late sixth century by a Slavic people, the Moravians, who under Samo (627–660) established the first state of Western Slavs. This in turn became a tributary to the empire of Charlemagne (*d.*814). The ruler, Svatopluk (870–894), expanded it to become an independent kingdom, Great Moravia, which included BOHEMIA and other central European territories. After his death, however, Moravia was defeated by the Magyars in 906 who had settled in the Tisza Valley in 893. Later in the 10th century it became part of the Bohemian and, for a short time, the Polish kingdoms. In this same period the missionaries Cyril and Methodius converted the region to Christianity. From the early 11th century a crownland of the kingdom of Bohemia, in 1526 it passed to Austrian rule. Generally more tolerant of the Hapsburg authority, Moravia suffered less than other areas in the religious and civil strife of the 16th century. From the 13th century on, Moravian towns had undergone a thorough Germanization. From 1849 Moravia was a separate crownland of AUSTRIA with its capital at BRNO. In 1918, when Hapsburg rule was overthrown, it was organized as a province of Czechoslovakia and in 1927 was united with SILESIA to form Moravia and Silesia. With the Munich Pact of 1938, all of Silesia and parts of northern and southern Moravia became part of German SUDETENLAND. They were restored to Czechoslovakia in 1945 following World War II.

MORAVIA, Scotland. See MORAY.

MORAVIAN GAP [**Moravian Gate**] (Czechoslovakia, Poland) A mountain pass along the upper ODER and VISTULA RIVERS, where former German SILESIA, Poland, and Czechoslovakia meet. An ancient trade route in central Europe, it also has been of military importance as a communications line between north and south.

MORAVIAN GATE. See MORAVIAN GAP.

MORAVSKÁ. See OSTRAVA.

MORAY [**Elgin, Elginshire, Morayshire**] [*Latin:* **Moravia**] (Scotland) Former county, now incorporated in the Highland and Grampian regions, on the Firth of Moray. A region associated with the legends of Macbeth, it was originally colonized by Northern Picts who formed the kingdom of Pictavia, which then became Moravia, the eastern part of the modern province of Moray; it also comprises NAIRNSHIRE, Ross, Cromarty, and INVERNESS-SHIRE. It came under royal control in the reign of Malcolm III of Scotland in the late 11th century. The area suffered in the Civil War and from natural calamities. There are traces of prehistoric settlement at Innesmill.

MORAYSHIRE. See MORAY.

MORDOVIAN AUTONOMOUS SOVIET SOCIALIST REPUBLIC [**Mordvinian**] (USSR) Soviet East European autonomous republic formed in 1934 and consisting of the Volga upland in the E and the Oka-Don lowland in the W. Taken by the Empire of the GOLDEN HORDE in the mid-13th century, it was next part of the KAZAN Khanate and was annexed by RUSSIA in 1552. The Mordovians, who speak a Finno-Ugric language and are orthodox Christians, were first mentioned by the Gothic historian Jordanes in the sixth century AD. With the Russians, they make up the bulk of the republic's population.

MORDVINIAN. See MORDOVIAN AUTONOMOUS SOVIET SOCIALIST REPUBLIC.

MOREA. See PELOPONNESUS.

MORELIA [*former:* **Valladolid**] (Mexico) City and capital of MICHOACÁN state in the SW. Predominantly populated by the original Indian group, the Tarascans, and founded in 1541 by Antonio de Mendoza, it was the birthplace of Augustín de Iturbide, emperor of Mexico in 1822/23, and of the revolutionary leader, Morelos y Pavón, for whom it was renamed in 1828. Another leader, Miguel Hidalgo y Costilla, used the place as his headquarters during the Mexican revolution. Of historic interest are its 17th-century baroque cathedral, an 18th-century aqueduct, and other vestiges of the colonial era. The Colegio de San Nicolás, founded in 1540, is the oldest institution of higher learning in Mexico.

MORELOS (Mexico) A state of the Mexican plateau with its capital at CUERNAVACA. In the war against Spain in 1812 its other principal town, Cuautla Morelos, was heroically defended by José María Morelos y Pavón, for whom the state, created in 1869, was named. The revolt led by Zapata in the early 20th century destroyed much property in the state. See also MORELIA.

MORENO (Argentina) City of BUENOS AIRES province, in the E. Several battles were fought here during the Argentine War of Independence between 1810 and 1816 and during the federalist-unitarian conflicts that followed.

MORESNET (Belgium) Former neutral territory between GERMANY and Belgium near AACHEN, since 1919 a part of LIÈGE province. It was under joint Prussian and Dutch administration from 1816; Belgium assumed Holland's role after 1830. Formerly an important lead- and zinc-mining center, the territory was awarded to Belgium by the Treaty of Versailles in 1919. See also EUPEN and MALMÉDY.

MORGANTOWN (United States) City in N WEST VIRGINIA, near the Pennsylvania border and on the MONONGAHELA RIVER. It was founded in 1767 by Zackquill Morgan, son of Morgan ap Morgan, the first European settler in what is now West Virginia. Iron was discovered in 1789, and its processing was the city's major industry until the Civil War. The city is the seat of West Virginia University, chartered in 1867.

MORGARTEN (Switzerland) Mountain slope of ZUG

canton, on the border of Schwyz canton, just SE of the Lake of Aegeri. Here on Nov. 15, 1315 the Hapsburg Austrians were defeated by a small Swiss force in a bloody, decisive battle that hastened Swiss independence and did much to give the Swiss their reputation for military prowess.

MORIAH (Israel) Region in the S part of ancient PALESTINE. Here is located the mountain where Abraham came to sacrifice Isaac as related in Gen. 22:2. Elsewhere the Bible says it is where God appeared to David and Solomon, who later built the temple of JERUSALEM, central to Jewish spiritual life. Mt Moriah is by some identified with Mt ZION, by others with Mt GERIZIM.

MORLAIX (France) Town of Finistère department, 37 mi ENE of Brest. Probably occupied in Roman times, it was held in the 12th century by the counts of Leon whose authority was disputed by the dukes of BRITTANY. In 1187 Henry II of England, as guardian of Arthur of Brittany, held the town briefly. In the War of the Breton Succession of 1341 to 1365 during the Hundred Years War, it was held alternately by the French and the English. The English wreaked much damage on Morlaix in 1522. A member of the Catholic League, the town was taken in the name of Henry IV in 1594.

MORLEY (England) Town in South Yorkshire, 4 mi SSW of Leeds. Nearby are the ruins of Howley Hall, a mansion dating from 1590 that housed a garrison of Parliamentarians and underwent a heavy siege by the Royalists in the English Civil War.

MORMON STATION. See NEVADA.

MORMON TRAIL. See OVERLAND TRAIL.

MOROCCO. See MARRAKECH.

MOROCCO [*Arabic:* **Al-Mamlakah, al-Maghribīyah;** *French:* **Maroc;** *Spanish:* **Marruecos**] Coastal nation of NW Africa, bordered by Algeria on the E, Mauritania on the S, the Atlantic Ocean on the W, and the Mediterranean Sea on the N.

Morocco's early inhabitants were Berber farmers living in small tribal units. Circa 1000 BC Phoenicians from TYRE established a coastal trading presence here. CARTHAGE, founded by the Phoenicians, succeeded them and settled several trading posts along the Mediterranean coastline. Present Morocco was part of the old kingdom of MAURETANIA and was within the sphere of influence of ROME. Though the capital appears to have been at Opar, the city of Tingis, now TANGIER, was of major importance. The country became the Roman province of Mauretania Tingitana in 40 AD and remained under Roman rule until the Vandal invasion of 429.

Morocco was brought under the control of the BYZANTINE EMPIRE during the sixth century AD but fell to the irresistible wave of Arab Muslim conquest that began in 682. In 788 Idris I founded a small Arab kingdom around the former Roman capital of VOLUBILIS. After his death in 793 his successor, Idris II, shifted the seat of government to the city of FÈS. From the 11th through the 14th centuries Morocco was ruled by Berber dynasties. Under the ALMORAVID and ALMOHAD Caliphates, a Moroccan empire spread across all of North Africa and included Muslim SPAIN. By 1268, however, when the Beni Merin took power, all imperial ambitions ended, and Spain was escaping Muslim control. However, the influx of Spanish Muslim art and architecture enriched Morocco during this time. Magnificent mosques, gateways, and minarets were built in Fès, MARRAKECH, and RABAT.

In the late 15th century PORTUGAL and Spain captured Morocco's port cities and held the coast. But by the late 16th century a resurgent Morocco had regained most of the coast and had extended its rule to the bend of the NIGER RIVER, destroying the great SONGHAI EMPIRE and capturing control of the West African gold trade. However, by the 19th century Morocco's once powerful armies found themselves hopelessly antiquated and powerless as FRANCE, GREAT BRITAIN, and Spain pressed their colonial ambitions on the country.

In 1912 Morocco was made a protectorate entirely under French administration except for a small Spanish territory in the north. Rebellion flared in the 1920's, but a strong independence movement did not emerge until the 1950's. In 1956 Morocco became an independent monarchy led by Mohammed V. His successor, Hassan II, consolidated his absolute monarchical power. In 1976 the oil-rich territory of the SPANISH SAHARA in the southwest was taken over jointly with MAURITANIA. In 1979 Mauritania renounced its interest in the face of bitter guerrilla fighting for Saharan liberation, and Morocco assumed full control of the region.

MOROTAI (Indonesia) Island in the N MOLUCCAS, N of Halmahera. Occupied by the Japanese in January 1942, it was captured by troops under Gen. Douglas MacArthur on Sept. 14, 1944.

MORRISTOWN [*former:* **West Hanover**] (United States) Town of N NEW JERSEY, 17 mi WNW of Newark. Settled in 1710, it was a center of activity in the American Revolution, particularly in the winters of 1776/77 and 1779/80, when it served as Washington's headquarters. Fort Nonsense was built here at his orders, largely to keep his troops occupied. From December 1779 to January 1780 Dickerson Tavern was the site of a military courtmartial presided over by Gen. Robert Howe to try Gen. Benedict Arnold who had turned traitor. In 1837 Samuel F.B. Morse and Alfred Vail carried out their electric telegraph experiments at the iron works here. The Schuyler-Hamilton House, where Alexander Hamilton courted Elizabeth Schuyler, is now the headquarters for the Daughters of the American Revolution.

MORRISTOWN, North Carolina. See ASHEVILLE.

MORRISVILLE (United States) Town of SE PENNSYLVANIA, in Bucks County, on the DELAWARE RIVER, opposite TRENTON, New Jersey. Settled c.1625 by the Dutch East India Company, it was Washington's headquarters from Dec. 8 to 14, 1776. Nearby is William Penn's manor, Pennsbury.

MORRO CASTLE (Cuba, Puerto Rico) Name for

three different fortifications. One, at the entrance to HAVANA harbor, was erected by the Spanish in 1589 to protect the city from buccaneers. It was captured by the British under Sir George Pocock in 1762. Another Morro Castle, named after the Havana structure, is located at the entrance to the harbor of SANTIAGO DE CUBA and was taken by U.S. forces in 1898, after a blockade and heavy fighting during the Spanish-American War. A third Morro Castle is the picturesque fort located on the harbor of SAN JUAN, Puerto Rico.

MORTAGNE [Mortagne-au-Perchey] (France) Town of Orne department, 24 mi ENE of Alençon. Dating from the 10th century, it was capital of the PERCHE before its absorption by the French crown. Its church of Notre Dame dates from the 15th and 16th centuries, and a vaulted entrance of an old stronghold dates from the 15th century.

MORTAGNE-AU-PERCHEY. See MORTAGNE.

MORTAIN (France) Town of Manche department, E of AVRANCHES. In the Middle Ages it was an important county belonging to the ruling house of NORMANDY. During World War II U.S. troops accomplished a significant advance here on Aug. 3, 1944; the battle with the Germans for control took place between Aug. 7 and 11, 1944. Its parish church of St. Évroult dates from the 13th century.

MORTARA (Italy) Commune of Pavia province, LOMBARDY region, 22 mi WNW of Pavia. It was the scene of an Austrian victory over the Piedmontese in 1849 during a period of widespread rebellions against Hapsburg rule. There is an 11th-century convent and a 14th-century Gothic church.

MORTIMER'S CROSS (England) Village and battlefield of Hereford and Worcester, 15 mi NNW of Hereford, on the Lugg River. On Feb. 2, 1461 during the Wars of the Roses Edward, duke of York, and his Yorkist forces won a major victory here over the Lancastrians. It was followed by Edward's march to London where he proclaimed himself Edward IV. His conflicts with the Lancastrians did not end until Henry VI's death and Edward's victory at TEWKESBURY, both in May 1471. See also WAKEFIELD.

MORZE BALTYCKIE. See BALTIC SEA.

MOSA. See MEUSE RIVER.

MOSAE TRAJECTUM. See MAASTRICHT.

MOSCOW [*Russian:* **Moskva**] (USSR) Capital city and the nation's political, economic, cultural, and transportation center, in the W central European Soviet Union on both sides of the Moskva River. On a site inhabited since Neolithic times, it is first mentioned as a village in 1147 AD. The prince of SUZDAL built a wooden *kremlin*, or fort, here in 1156. Strategically placed at a crossroads of medieval trade routes, it was burned in 1237 by the Tatars who then plundered the restored settlement in 1293. The principality of VLADIMIR joined it, and later the Metropolitan of the Russian Orthodox Church moved to Moscow. The present Kremlin was started in 1367 during the reign of Dmitri Donskoi. Although again stormed by Tatars in 1382,

Moscow was now strong enough to resist. Grand Duke Ivan III assumed leadership over the rival NOVGOROD and was able to throw over the Tatar domination, at the same time building up what had now become the Grand Duchy of Moscow.

By the 15th century Moscow had become capital of RUSSIA, and in 1547 Grand Duke Ivan IV first assumed the title of czar. Conquered by the Poles during the "Time of Troubles," in 1611 Muscovites, led by the butcher Kuzman Minin and Prince Dmitri Pozharski, attacked the Polish garrison and received its surrender in 1612. Commercial development in the 17th century stimulated the need for a maritime outlet and led Czar Peter the Great to build St. Petersburg on the Baltic. Peter transferred the capital there in 1712, but Moscow's leadership in Russian life continued uninterrupted.

Built largely of wood until the 19th century, the city was victim to fires throughout its early history. By the 16th century the czars were patronizing Italian artists and architects to transform the city to the latest Renaissance styles. The most notable fire was in 1812, following Napoleon I's occupation of the city, when it was almost totally burned. The conflagration, which was thought to have been set by the French, sparked patriotic sentiment among the peasants who helped to force Napoleon's retreat from Moscow. In the late 19th and early 20th centuries Moscow became a center for labor and social democratic movements. Following the revolution, begun in 1917, the capital was returned to Moscow in 1918 by the Bolshevik government. During World War II a massive German advance was stopped approx. 23 miles from the city. The Kremlin's present walls represent the city limits in the 15th century. Red Square joins the Kremlin on the east. On the south the multi-spired cathedral of St. Basil the Beatified, built in the 16th century to commemorate the conquest of KAZAN, is now a museum. On the west side are the tombs of Lenin and other political leaders. Around the Kremlin are the Bely Gorod, the aristocratic white city, and the Zenlyanoy Gorod, the earth city, named for the earthen and wooden ramparts that once surrounded it. Inside the Kremlin, the Palace of Congresses, built in 1961, houses meetings of the Supreme Soviet. See also Empire of the GOLDEN HORDE, KIEV, LENINGRAD.

MOSCOW, GRAND DUCHY OF [Muscovy] (USSR) Former principality of W central RUSSIA founded c.1280 by Daniel, son of Alexander Nevski, on a site inhabited since the Stone Age. The fortified village of MOSCOW was at its center. Daniel's son Yuri (1303–25) began the struggle to establish Moscow's predominance in Russia and was temporarily appointed grand duke of VLADIMIR by the Khan of the GOLDEN HORDE. His younger brother, Ivan I, or Ivan Kalita (1328–41) was again granted the title of grand duke and was given the right to collect Tatar tributes. He established Moscow as the seat of the Russian Church. Dmitri Donskoi, Ivan I's grandson (1359–89), was the first to bear the title of Grand Duke of Moscow. Dmitri's heirs, particularly Ivan III (1462–1505) increased the power of the Muscovite state. By the mid-16th century, with the Tatars overthrown, the unity and independence of the Great Russian lands was complete and the Grand Duchy was at the same time extended to and absorbed by Russia as a whole.

MOSELLE (France) Department of NE France, in Lorraine, between Luxembourg on the N, the Saarland of West Germany to the E, and Bas-Rhin and Marche-et-Moselle departments to the S. Its chief city is METZ; its capital is Thionville. It was made part of Germany in 1871 after the Franco-Prussian War until the end of World War I, and again in World War II between 1940 and 1944.

MOSELLE RIVER [*ancient:* **Mosella;** *German:* **Mosel**] (France, Luxembourg, West Germany) River that rises in NE France, flows N to form part of the border between Luxembourg and West Germany, and enters West Germany reaching the Rhine at KOBLENZ. Its banks are dotted with numerous historic castles and many famous vineyards.

MOSHI (Tanzania) Capital city of Kilimanjaro province, on the S slope of Mt Kilimanjaro, near Kenya. The original town, called Old Moshi, is nearby and was the capital of a kingdom of the Chagga people in the 19th century. It became a governmental center of German East Africa (1891–1916). The British moved Moshi to its present site following World War I.

MOSI-OA-TUNYA. See VICTORIA FALLS.

MOSKVA. See MOSCOW.

MOSQUITIA. See MOSQUITO COAST.

MOSQUITO COAST [**Miskito Coast, Mosquitia**] [*Spanish:* **Costa de Mosquitos**] (Honduras and Nicaragua) Region extending in a 40-mi-wide belt from the N San Juan River into NE Honduras. Its name is derived from the Mosquito, or Miskitto, Indians. It was discovered by Columbus in 1502. In the early colonial era English and Dutch pirates preyed on Spanish shipping from here, while English loggers exploited the region's forest products. In 1678 the English established a protective kingdom at Bluefields, and in 1848 expanded their holdings to include SAN JUAN DEL NORTE in order to stave off U.S. interest in the area for a short cut across the isthmus to California. The Clayton-Bulwer Treaty of 1850 between the United States and Great Britain stopped British expansion, but the coast was not relinquished until 1860, when a separate treaty with Nicaragua established an autonomous Mosquito kingdom. In 1894 the dictator José Santos Zelaya forcibly incorporated it into Nicaragua. This issue was finally settled in 1960 when the International Court of Justice awarded the northern part of the coast to Honduras. In the early 1980's the region became the focus of international debate over alleged Nicaraguan massacres of the Indian population in the region on both sides of its border with Honduras.

MOSS (Norway) County seat and port of Østfold county in the SE, on the Oslofjord. Here on Aug. 14, 1814 an armistice was concluded ending SWEDEN's invasion of Norway and uniting the two countries.

MOSSELBAAI. See MOSSEL BAY.

MOSSEL BAY [*Afrikaans:* **Mosselbaai**] (South Africa) Port of CAPE PROVINCE, on Mossel Bay, an inlet of the Indian Ocean, 230 mi E of Cape Town. First visited by Bartholomew Dias in 1488, it was the site of a hermitage founded in 1501, the first Christian place of worship in South Africa.

MOSSI EMPIRE. See UPPER VOLTA.

MOSSLEY (England) Town in Greater Manchester, 9 mi ENE of Manchester. Across the Tame River from the town are the ancient earthworks known as Bucton Castle, as well as the remains of a Roman road.

MOSTAGANEM (Algeria) Port city and departmental capital on the Mediterranean Sea, 44 mi ENE of Oran. Founded in the 11th century on the site of a Roman town, it flourished as part of the OTTOMAN EMPIRE in the 16th century and fell to the French in 1833. It is the site of an 11th-century citadel.

MOSTAR (Yugoslavia) Former capital and now chief city of Herzogovina, on the Neretva River, 50 mi SW of Sarajevo. Known from 1442, in the later 15th century it became the military, administrative, and commercial center for an area that gradually declined under Turkish rule. A rebellion occurred here in 1875, and AUSTRIA took it over three years later. A growing center of Serbian sentiment, literature and political activism, it passed to Yugoslavia in 1918. Vestiges of its Turkish period include a stone bridge built in 1566 and many mosques. See BOSNIA AND HERZOGOVINA.

MOSUL [*Arabic:* **Al-Mawsil**] (Iraq) Old Arabic town on the W bank of the TIGRIS, opposite the ruins of NINEVEH, and near the site of TEPE GAWRA, 220 mi NNW of Baghdad. Formerly an important town on the caravan route from PERSIA across northern MESOPOTAMIA, it was taken by Muslims in 636 AD. From the eighth to 13th centuries it was the leading city of the area and capital of an independent principality until devastated by the Mongols. It never recovered during occupations by the Persians in 1508 and by the Turks between 1534 and 1918. Under British mandate between 1918 and 1932, it regained its former stature. Its possession by Iraq was disputed by TURKEY from 1923 to 1925 but confirmed by the League of Nations in 1926. A center of Nestorian Christianity, it is also the seat of Mosul University. The Great and the Red mosques are among the notable shrines; of historical interest are the remains of Qara Saray, a palace.

MOTYA [*modern:* **San Pantaleo**] (Italy) Ruins of an ancient Phoenician town on the island of San Pantaleo, or San Pantaleone, off the W coast of SICILY, just N of MARSALA. Settled by Phoenicians from Syria in the eighth century BC, it was a leading commercial center until it was destroyed in 397 BC by Dionysius the Elder of SYRACUSE after a long siege. Excavations have revealed numerous monuments and a sanctuary from the sixth century BC.

MOTYCA. See MODICA.

MOUKDEN. See MUKDEN.

MOULINS (France) Manufacturing city and capital of Allier department, 58 mi SE of Bourges. The capital of the duchy of BOURBONNAIS in the 14th century, in 1412 it was besieged by Burgundians. It was confiscated by the French crown in 1527 and besieged by Protestants in 1562. In 1566 Charles IX held a great assembly here at which sweeping legal and administrative reforms, including religious toleration, were adopted. The city's outstanding artistic and historic treasures include a 14th-century tower remaining from the Bourbon castle, a 15th-century Gothic cathedral with an outstanding triptych, a 15th-century campanile, and the town hall. The tomb of Henri de Montmorency, designed by François Anguier, is also located here. See also MONTLUÇON.

MOULMEIN [Maulmain] (Burma) Commercial city of the Tenasserim division of Lower Burma, at the mouth of the SALWEEN RIVER, on the E shore of the Gulf of Martaban. An important port, from 1826 to 1852 it was the chief town of British Burma. A pagoda here is celebrated in Kipling's poem *Mandalay.*

MOULTRIE, FORT. See FORT MOULTRIE.

MOUNDSVILLE (United States) City in the N panhandle of WEST VIRGINIA, on the OHIO RIVER, 12 mi S of Wheeling. It is named after the Grave Creek Indian Burial Mound, a prehistoric conical mound 320 ft in diameter at its base and 70 ft high, located in the center of the city, one of many that formerly existed here. It is the largest of the mounds made by the Woodland Adena Indian people, who disappeared near the beginning of the Christian era.

MOUNTAIN ALTAI. See GORNO-ALTAI AUTONOMOUS OBLAST.

MOUNTAIN BADAKHSHAN. See GORNO-BADAKHSHAN AUTONOMOUS OBLAST.

MOUNTAIN MEADOWS (United States) Valley in Iron and Washington counties, SW UTAH. In 1857 it was the scene of the massacre of 140 people from Arkansas, Missouri, and Illinois who had camped on the Spanish Trail en route to California. In an incident apparently growing out of the Mormons' anger at the arrival of Federal troops in Utah, the settlers were attacked by a large band of Paiute Indians and some white men, led by John Doyle Lee, a Mormon fanatic. After three days of siege between Sept. 8 and 11, the emigrants were tricked into proceeding unarmed and on foot to allay the Indians' suspicions. The entire party except for a few children were then murdered. Subsequent anti-Mormon feeling ran high, but it was not until 1874 that Lee was arrested. Convicted of murder, he was executed March 23, 1877 on the site of the massacre.

MOUNTAIN PROVINCE (Philippines) Province of N central LUZON, with its capital at Bontoc. It is in a region inhabited by isolated tribes and little known in the 17th and 18th centuries. It was the scene of various Spanish expeditions between 1829 and 1850 and was later divided into several politico-military units. Benguet, a part of the region, was organized in 1900 under U.S. rule, with Baguio as its capital, now La Trinidad. The region evolved administratively from 1908 to 1968, so that the present province is much smaller than it originally was. The area is known for rice terraces, which have been cultivated for at least 3,000 years.

MOUNT ATHOS. See ATHOS, MOUNT.

MOUNT BADON. See MONS BADONICUS.

MOUNT CARMEL. See CARMEL, MOUNT.

MOUNT DESERT ISLAND (United States) Island, 14 mi long and 8 mi wide, off the SE coast of MAINE. A chain of rounded granite peaks that dominate the island were named *Monts Deserts* (Wilderness Mountains) by the French explorer Samuel Champlain, who first visited it in 1604. In 1613 the first French Jesuit mission and colony in America were established here, but the French gave up their claim to the island in 1713. British settlers arrived in 1762; by the late 19th century it had become a well-known resort area. Its main towns are Bar Harbor, Mt. Desert, Tremont, and Southwest Harbor.

MOUNT HOLLY (United States) Township of Burlington county, NEW JERSEY, 16 mi S of Trenton, on land bought by Quakers in 1676. In 1779, as the temporary capital of New Jersey, it was occupied by British troops during the American Revolution.

MOUNT LEBANON. See LEBANON MOUNTAINS.

MOUNT LYDIA. See MYCALE.

MOUNT MARIE. See PINE BLUFF.

MOUNT OLYMPUS. See OLYMPUS.

MOUNT VERNON (United States) City of Westchester County, in SE NEW YORK State, on the Bronx River, adjacent to New York City. It was first settled in 1664 by colonists from Connecticut on a site near where the controversial religious leader Anne Hutchinson and her family were killed by Indians in 1643. John Peter Zenger was arrested on a newspaper libel charge here in 1733. St. Paul's Church from 1761 was a British hospital during the American Revolution. In October 1776 a small American force here held off a British attack on Washington's forces as they retreated to WHITE PLAINS.

MOURU. See MERV.

MOUSTIER, LE. See LE MOUSTIER.

MOYALE (Kenya) Town of E Africa, near the Ethiopian border. It served as a British base in their attack on Italian East Africa in 1941 during World War II.

MOZAMBIQUE [Moçambique] (Mozambique) Port city on a small coral island off the NE coast of Mozambique, SE Africa. It was the site of a flourishing Arab port when visited by Vasco da Gama in 1498, but no traces of that town remain. Occupied by the Portuguese in 1505, it was capital of their holdings in Mozambique until 1907. Three old forts and the governor's palace still stand.

MOZAMBIQUE [*former:* Portuguese East Africa; *Portuguese:* Moçambique] Nation on the E coast of Africa, bordered by Tanzania to the N, South Africa to the S, and Zimbabwe, Malawi, and Zambia to the W. The LIMPOPO and ZAMBEZI rivers run through it.

Bantu migrations peopled Mozambique after 1000 AD, while the seacoast was worked by Arab traders. In

1498 PORTUGAL became involved with the country after Vasco da Gama visited a small coastal island and Arab town with this name on his way to India. The town was already an active trade center for the INDIAN OCEAN. Portugal soon established trading posts on the coast and attempted to control all trade in the region. By the end of the 16th century Dutch and English competition had grown, and their traders competed for the lucrative East African commerce in gold, ivory, pearls, amber and wax. The Portuguese valued Mozambique mainly as part of their plan to dominate the Indian Ocean trade on the east coast, considering it a minor territory compared to Portuguese INDIA. The lure of gold was strong enough to spur inland exploration, however, and by the 17th century Portugal dominated the interior as well as the coast of Mozambique.

Modern architecture in Maputo c.1950. Once Portuguese Lourenço Marques, the town is now the capital of the struggling young country of Mozambique in East Africa.

Portugal's power waned in the 18th century, and the colony began to be used as a dumping ground for convicts. Slave trading became very important from the late 18th through the 19th centuries, owing to a tremendous demand for labor from BRAZIL. Native and renegade settler revolts wrested actual control of much of the colony from Portugal during the 19th century, and interior Mozambique was not entirely reclaimed until 1920. Portugal successfully developed the colony's economy, but it was at the expense of the harshly exploited native African population. In 1907 the town of MOZAMBIQUE was replaced as capital by Lourenço Marques, since 1976 called MAPUTO.

Portugal grudgingly initiated token reforms in 1961, after guerrilla warfare had erupted in their colony of ANGOLA. In 1964 the Mozambique Liberation Front, FRELIMO, opened warfare against the colonial government, and Portugal became mired in a rapidly escalating and costly war. In 1974 the Lisbon regime was overthrown, and Portugal's new government swiftly moved to negotiate with the rebels. Mozambique became independent in 1975, led by Samora Machel, FRE-LIMO's leader, and began to implement a socialist program. In 1976 war was declared with RHODESIA and border clashes were common. ZIMBABWE guerrillas operated out of Mozambique until Rhodesia attained independence in 1979 as the nation of Zimbabwe.

MOZDOK (USSR) Town of old Terek province, in the Caucasus, on the Terek River, 50 mi N of Vladikavkaz. Built in 1763 by a Kabardian prince, it became a stronghold in the Russian conquest of the CAUCASUS MOUNTAINS. In 1840 it was attacked by a large group of Muslims from CIRCASSIA.

MOZHAISK (USSR) Town in the W central European Soviet Union on the Moskva River. First mentioned in 1231, it was joined with MOSCOW in 1303 and became an important fort and trading center. During World War II it was the easternmost conquest of the Germans on Oct. 15, 1941 and was won back by the Soviets in the winter of 1941/42.

MOZYR (USSR) Town of Belorussian SSR in the Gomel oblast on the Pripyat River, 75 mi SW of Gomel. Held by the Germans during World War II from 1941 until 1944, it was retaken by the Soviets on Jan. 12, 1944.

MSUS (Libya) Village in the desert of the NE, 68 mi SE of Benghazi. During World War II German forces defeated the British here on Dec. 28, 1941 and Jan. 23, 1942.

MTSENSK (USSR) Town of old Orel, on the Zusha River, 32 mi NE of the city of Orel. Under the rule of LITHUANIA from 1320 until taken by RUSSIA in 1530, it became a stronghold against raids by the Tatars.

MTSKHET. See MTSKHETA.

MTSKHETA [Mtskhet] (USSR) Town of GEORGIAN SSR, on the Kura River and the Georgian Military Road, 13 mi NNW of TBILISI. The capital of ancient IBERIA until the sixth century AD when this was moved to Tbilisi, Mtskhet retained its ecclesiastical importance since its Sveti-Tskhoveli cathedral—founded in the fourth century, destroyed by Tamerlane, and rebuilt in the 15th century—contained the burial vaults of the Georgian kings. Armaz-Tsikhe castle opposite the town is a more ancient seat of the Georgian kings, and the ruins of the Dzhvari temple of the late sixth or early seventh century are nearby. See also TRANSCAUCASIAN SFSR.

MUCH WENLOCK. See WENLOCK.

MUCKROSS (Ireland) Peninsula in County KERRY, between the upper and lower lakes of KILLARNEY. It is the site of the ruins of a Franciscan abbey founded in 1440 on the shore of Muckross Lake.

MUCROSS. See SAINT ANDREWS.

MUDDE KALAPUWA. See BATTICALOA.

MUDGAGIRI. See MONGHYR.

MUDHOL (India) Former native state in the S division of BOMBAY. It was a MARATHA principality dating from Muslim rule before the rise of Sivaji (1627–80). See also MAHARASHTRA, MARATHA CONFEDERACY.

MUDKI [Moodkee] (India) Village of PUNJAB state,

near the Sutlej River, 18 mi SE of Firozpur. Here in December 1845 the British under Sir Hugh Gough won a victory over the Sikhs in the very first battle of the Sikh Wars of 1845/46 and 1848/49.

MUFUMBIRO. See VIRUNGA MOUNTAINS.

MUGHĀL. See MOGUL EMPIRE.

MUGHEIR. See UR.

MUHAMMAD, RA'S (Egypt) Cape at the S end of the SINAI peninsula, extending into the RED SEA. It was occupied by ISRAEL in the 1967 war.

MÜHLBERG (East Germany) Town on the ELBE RIVER, approx. 37 mi E of Leipzig. On April 24, 1547 Elector John Frederick I of SAXONY and the Schmalkaldic League of Protestant princes were defeated in battle here by Emperor Charles V; and the elector was captured. Charles's victory appeared to pave the way for his planned suppression of the entire Protestant revolt. His victory was annulled, however, by later Protestant successes and by the Treaty of PASSAU in 1552. During World War II the town was taken by Russian troops on April 23, 1945.

MÜHLBERG, BATTLE OF. See SCHMALKALDEN.

MÜHLDORF (West Germany) Town of BAVARIA, on the Inn River, 45 mi E of Munich. During World War II it was the site of a subterranean jet plane factory built in 1944 by 5,000 slave laborers.

MÜHLHAUSEN. See MÜHLHAUSEN IN THÜRINGEN.

MÜHLHAUSEN IN THÜRINGEN [Mühlhausen] (East Germany) Industrial city in the Erfurt district, 29 mi NW of Erfurt. An ancient Germanic village first mentioned in 775 AD, it was fortified by Henry I in the 10th century and became a free imperial city in the 13th century and joined the HANSEATIC LEAGUE. In the 16th century it became an Anabaptist center and during the Peasants War was dominated by Thomas Münzer and Heinrich Pfeiffer, who were beheaded here in 1525. Subsequently denied its rights, it regained its independence in 1548. It passed definitively to PRUSSIA in 1815. Notable buildings include several Gothic churches, a 17th-century town hall, medieval fortifications, and numerous houses from the 16th, 17th, and 18th centuries.

MU'IZZIYAH. See TAORMINA.

MUKAČEVO. See MUKACHEVO.

MUKACHEVO [Czech: Mukačevo; Hungarian: Munkács] (USSR) Town in the Transcarpathian oblast of the Ukrainian SSR, on the Latorcza River, 220 mi ENE of Budapest. According to Hungarian legend, it was near Munkács that the Magyars first entered HUNGARY toward the end of the ninth century. Then part of the Kievan state, it was taken in 1018 by the Hungarians. By the 15th century, it was a commercial and governmental center, and from the 16th century it was part of the duchy of TRANSYLVANIA. Under Austrian control, it became a key fortress of the AUSTRO-HUNGARIAN empire. Passed to CZECHOSLOVAKIA in 1919, it was under German-Hungarian occupation from 1938 to 1945 following the MUNICH Agreement of 1938.

Historic buildings include a 14th-century castle and monastery, as well as an 18th-century wooden church. Nearby is the old fort of Munkács, famous in Hungarian history for its defense under Helene Zrinyi against the Austrians from 1685 to 1688.

MUKĀWIR [former: Machaerus] (Jordan) Town E of the DEAD SEA. It once was the fortified village of Machaerus of ancient MOAB, the place where John the Baptist was beheaded.

MUKAYYAR. See UR.

MUKDEN [Moukden] [Chinese: Shen-Yang; former: Feng-tien, Shengking] (China) Provincial capital of Liao-ning province in the NE, on the Hun River, controlling N-S routes in the S Manchurian plain. The 12th-century capital of the Kin Tatars and the 17th-century base for the Manchu conquest of China, it was the seat of the royal treasury during the Manchu dynasty (1644–1912). It was a stronghold in the conflicts between RUSSIA and JAPAN over MANCHURIA, and was won by the Russians and then taken by the Japanese after the Battle of Mukden on Feb. 19 to Mar. 10, 1905. The warlord Chang Tso-Lin made it his headquarters from 1924 to 1928 during the Chinese civil war; he was assassinated here in 1928. On Sept. 18, 1931 the Japanese used the blowing up of a railroad, the Mukden or Manchurian Incident, as a justification for invading Manchuria and setting up the puppet government of Manchukuo. Occupied by the Japanese from 1931 to 1945, it was the scene of a major battle from Feb. 19 to Mar. 10, 1945 when the Soviets were defeated by the Japanese. Again the scene of heavy fighting in 1947/48 during the Chinese civil war, it was occupied by communist forces Nov. 1, 1948 after a 10-month siege when thousands starved, and again was the base for further conquests. Historic structures include the old walled city, approx. 4 miles in circumference, several notable palaces, and the royal tombs of the Manchu rulers. See also FU-SHUN, PEN-CH'I, AN-SHAN, LIAO-YANG, all parts of the Greater Mukden area.

MUKHĀ. See MOCHA.

MUKHMAS. See MICHMASH.

MULASTHAY. See MULTAN.

MÜLHAUSEN. See MULHOUSE.

MÜLHEIM. See MÜLHEIM AN DER RUHR.

MÜLHEIM AN DER RUHR [Mülheim] (West Germany) City of North Rhine-Westphalia, on the RUHR RIVER near its mouth, 7 mi WSW of Essen. First mentioned in 1093, it was formerly a part of the duchy of BERG and passed to PRUSSIA in 1815. Bombed by the Allies from 1943 to 1945, it was taken by them in 1945 in the surrender of the Ruhr at the end of World War II. Notable buildings include a restored 11th-century church and a castle, Schloss Broich, containing parts dating from 1000 AD.

MULHOUSE [German: Mülhausen] (France) Industrial and commercial town of Haut-Rhin department, on the Ill River, 22 mi S of Colmar. First mentioned in 803 AD, it became a free imperial city in 1308 and in 1515 became an allied member of the Swiss Confederation.

Although it did not join France with the other areas of ALSACE, as outlined by the Treaty of WESTPHALIA in 1648, it was united by vote with France in 1798. Following the Franco-Prussian War in 1871 it was made a part of GERMANY until 1918, when it reverted to France. Occupied by the Germans in 1940, it was liberated by the Allies in late 1944. Of charm and historic interest are its 13th-century towers, 16th-century town hall, and its narrow, winding streets and old houses. See also SWITZERLAND.

MULL (Scotland) One of the Inner HEBRIDES islands, Strathclyde region. Its only town, Tobermory, is 88 mi NW of Glasgow. The site of several medieval castles, in 1588 it was the scene of the sinking of a galleon from the Spanish Armada in the bay of Tobermory.

MULLAN TRAIL (United States) Wagon trail in the NW, extending from FORT BENTON, MONTANA across the Bitterroot Range of the Rocky Mts to WALLA WALLA, WASHINGTON. Built c.1860 by the U.S. Army, it helped to open a rich mining region in the Northwest.

MULLINGAR [*Gaelic:* **Muileann Cearr**] (Irish Republic) Market and county town of County Westmeath, 50 mi NW of Dublin. An ancient palatinate town, it had both an Augustinian convent from 1227 and a Dominican convent from 1239. Both were dissolved by Elizabeth I. It served as headquarters for William III before the siege of ATHLONE.

MULTAN [**Mooltan**] [*former:* **Bagpur, Hanspur, Kastpur, Mulasthay, Sanabpur**] (Pakistan) Ancient city of the PUNJAB, near the Punjab River, 200 mi WSW of Lahore. One of India's oldest settlements, it was in the kingdom of SIND and derives its name from pre-Muslim gods. A desirable prize for numerous conquerors, it was probably taken by Alexander the Great c.325 BC and is identified with ancient Malli. Visited by the Chinese Buddhist scholar Hsüan-tsang in 641 AD, it was conquered by the Arabs in the eighth century and by Mahmud of GHAZNI, a Muslim Turkish conqueror, in 1005/06. Captured by Tamerlane in 1398, the city was again taken by the Sikhs under Ranjit Singh in 1818. It came under British control from 1849 until the country gained independence in 1947. Of historic interest are the fort and walls, tombs of Muslim saints, and an ancient Hindu temple.

MULVIAN BRIDGE. See MILIVIAN BRIDGE.

MÜNCHEN. See MUNICH.

MÜNCHEN-GLADBACH. See MÜNCHENGLADBACH.

MUNCIE [*former:* **Munseytown**] (United States) Industrial city in INDIANA, 50 mi ENE of Indianapolis, on the West Fork of the White River. A town established by the Delaware Indians and named for one of their tribes, the Munsee, it passed by treaty to the U.S. government in 1818. Here Robert and Helen Lynd conducted the pioneering sociological research that was published as *Middletown* in 1929.

MUNDA (Solomon Islands) Former air base located at the NW end of NEW GEORGIA Island, in the central Solomons, W Pacific Ocean. During World War II there was a Japanese air base here from 1942. It was taken by U.S. forces on Aug. 5, 1943.

MUNDA (Spain) Town in ancient BAETICA in the S of the Iberian peninsula, probably S of Osuna. Caesar's victory during the Roman civil war, over Pompey's sons, his last over the Pompeians, occurred here in 45 BC. When Caesar could not bring the Pompeians to battle at CÓRDOBA, he lured them into combat down the sloping plain here, which they mistakenly believed would benefit their tactical position.

MÜNDEN [**Hannoversch-Münden**] (West Germany) City of Lower SAXONY, at the confluence of the Werra and Fulda rivers, 10 mi NE of Kassel. Founded in the 12th century on the site of a Carolingian palace, its municipal rights were granted in 1247 by the landgraves of THURINGIA. Still preserved here are the palace, built by Duke Eric III and renovated in the 16th century, a 14th-century stone bridge, a 17th-century town hall, and numerous half-timbered houses.

MUNICH [*former:* **Munichen;** *German:* **München**] (West Germany) Industrial city and capital of BAVARIA, on the Isar River. It was founded near an old settlement by Duke Henry the Lion, who established a mint here in 1158; but the Emperor Frederick Barbarossa deposed Henry in 1181 and gave the city to a prince of the house of Wittelsbach. Duke Louis of Wittelsbach made it his capital in 1255, building walls and a moat and establishing a dynasty that ruled here until the end of World War I. It was occupied by Gustavus Adolphus of Sweden in 1632 and by the Austrians in 1705 and 1742. Its fortifications were razed in 1791. From 1919 until the end of World War II the history of Munich is interwoven with that of the Nazi party. November 8/9, 1923 was the date of Adolf Hitler's Beer Hall Putsch, a mass meeting in a beer hall following which he tried to seize power from the Bavarian government. In September 1938 the Munich Pact was signed, by which Great Britain and France allowed Hitler to take over the SUDETENLAND of Czechoslovakia. Its appeasement of Hitler's ambitions led directly to the outbreak of World War II. Severely bombed by the Allies in World War II and since extensively rebuilt, it still has historic buildings including the Frauenkirche, dating from 1468 to 1488, the Renaissance-style St. Michael's church of 1583 to 1597, and the Nymphenburg castle of 1664 to 1728.

MUNICHEN. See MUNICH.

MUNICIPIUM BRUGENSE. See BRUGES.

MUNI RIVER SETTLEMENTS. See EQUATORIAL GUINEA.

MUNKÁCS. See MUKACHEVO.

MUNSEYTOWN. See MUNCIE.

MUNSTER (Irish Republic) Largest of the Irish provinces, located in the SW and including counties CLARE, CORK, KERRY, LIMERICK, TIPPERARY, and WATERFORD. In this, one of the ancient kingdoms of Ireland, the Érainn dominated the south, the Leinstermen the north. After the Anglo-Norman invasion, control of the region passed to the Fitzgerald earls of Desmond and the Butler earls of Ormonde.

The famous German city of Munich, ruled for over 730 years by one family, the Wittelsbachs, and also closely identified with the rise of Hitler.

MÜNSTER [Münster in Westfalen] (West Germany) Town in North Rhine-Westphalia, near the Dortmund-Ems canal, 78 mi NNE of Cologne. Founded *c*.800 as a Carolingian episcopal see, it developed in the 12th century around a monastery, its bishops eventually ruling a large part of WESTPHALIA. It was important in the HANSEATIC LEAGUE from the 14th century. From 1532 to 1535 it fell to the Anabaptists and was the seat of an Anabaptist experimental government under John of Leiden. The Treaty of Münster, better known as the Treaty or Peace of Westphalia, was signed here Oct. 24, 1648, ending the Thirty Years War. Passed to PRUSSIA in 1816, it became the capital of the province of Westphalia. Despite severe damage in World War II, it retains a 13th-century cathedral, a 14th-century Gothic town hall and the Liebfrauenkirche, an 18th-century baroque church. It was taken by the Allies on April 3, 1945 toward the end of World War II.

MÜNSTER AM STEIN (West Germany) Town and watering place on the Nahe River, approx 3 mi S of Kreuznach. Above the village are the ruins of the 12th-century castle of Rheingrafenstein, residence of the count of the RHINELAND PALATINATE, which was destroyed by the French in 1689. Nearby are the ruins of the castle of Ebernburg, the birthplace of Franz von Sickingen, a 15th-century knight who led the Knights' War against ecclesiastical princes, and with whose death at LANDSTUHL the traditional power of German knighthood ended.

MÜNSTERBURG (East Germany) Town and former principality of SILESIA, on the Oblau River, 36 mi S of Breslau. It is the former capital of the Münsterburg principality that existed from the 14th century until 1791, when it was purchased by the Prussian crown. It retains some of its medieval walls. See also PRUSSIA.

MUNTENIA [Greater Walachia] (Rumania) Historic region and former province, now making up the E part of WALACHIA.

MUONG SWA. See LUANG PRABANG.

MUQAIYIR. See UR.

MUQAYYAR. See UR.

MURANO (Italy) Town and suburb of VENICE, located on five small islands in the Lagoon of Venice. Although founded perhaps as early as the fifth century AD, it became important as the center of the Venetian glass industry from the late 13th century until the 16th century. After a period of decline, the town and its industry were revived in the 19th century. Of historic interest are its Venetian-Byzantine basilica dating from the seventh to the 12th centuries and many old houses, bridges, and canals.

MURBITER. See SAGUNTO.

MURCIA (Spain) A city and province, as well as a former Moorish kingdom included in the modern Albacete and Murcia province in the SE. An early center of Carthaginian colonization in Spain, possibly identified with Vergilia, it was conquered by the Moors in the eighth century AD and was made a province of the caliphate of CÓRDOBA. After the fall of the caliphate in the 11th century, it emerged as an independent kingdom that also included parts of the modern provinces of ALICANTE and ALMERIA. Later occupied by the ALMORAVIDS and the ALMOHADS, in 1243 it became a vassal state of CASTILE and in 1266 was annexed by Castile. In modern times, the city of Murcia, on the Segura River, was the scene of heavy fighting and much suffering in the Spanish civil war of 1936 to 1939. Notable buildings here include a 14th- and 15th-century Gothic-Romanesque cathedral and episcopal palace, a Moorish granary, and the old city walls. See also CARTAGENA.

MURET (France) Town of Haute-Garonne department, approx. 11 mi SW of Toulouse. Here in September 1213 Simon de Montfort, leader of the Albigensian Crusade, defeated the nobles of southern France, thus ending their independence and destroying the culture of LANGUEDOC. King Peter II of Aragon died in the battle. Simon's victory here led to the submission of TOULOUSE. Notable buildings include a 12th-century church and several houses from the 15th and 16th centuries.

MURFREESBORO (United States) City of central TENNESSEE, located on the West Fork of the Stones River, 33 mi SE of Nashville. The capital of Tennessee from 1819 to 1826, it was the scene of the Civil War Battle of Stones River, or Murfreesboro, fought from Dec. 31, 1862 until Jan. 2, 1863. The Union Gen. Rosecrans won a strategic victory over the Confederate Gen. Braxton Bragg, who retreated to TULLAHOMA.

Earlier, Oakland Mansion here was the scene of the surrender in July 1862 of the Union garrison to Gen. N.B. Forrest. Stones River Battlefield Park commemorates the battle. Many Civil War dead are buried in Stones River National Cemetery.

MURI (Nigeria) Former province in the N, divided by the Benue River. It included the ancient Jukon Empire and was the home of hostile pagans who interfered with the Hausa traders. Its position between German territory and HAUSALAND made it a favorite route for smuggling slaves in the early days of British administration.

MURMANSK (USSR) Capital city of Murmansk oblast on the N KOLA Peninsula, in the Barents Sea. An ice-free port warmed by the Gulf Stream, it was only a village before World War I. It was built, along with an inland railroad from Petrograd, now LENINGRAD, in 1915/16, when the Central Powers cut off Russian Black and Baltic Sea supply routes. From 1918 to 1920 during the Russian civil war, Allied forces occupied the Murmansk area, which they used as a base for their advance on the Bolsheviks. A major supply base and port for Anglo-American convoys during World War II, it was bombed by the Germans. It is now the largest city north of the Arctic Circle.

MUROM (USSR) City of the E central European Soviet Union, on the Oka River 90 mi SW of Gorki. Long a leading trading center and one of the oldest of Russian cities, it was first mentioned in the chronicles of 862 AD and became capital of Murom principality in the 12th century. Sacked by the Mongols in the 13th century, it passed to the GRAND DUCHY OF MOSCOW in 1393. A cathedral and several monasteries here date from the 16th and 17th centuries.

MURRAY BAY. See LA MALBAIE.

MURSA. See OSIJEK.

MURSHIDABAD (India) Town of West BENGAL, on the left bank of the Bhagirathi River. Founded in 1704 by Murshid Kuli Khan as the Muslim capital of Bengal, it quickly flourished and was the headquarters of Siraj-ud-daula at the time of the Battle of PLASSEY in 1757. It is the site of the fine palace of the Nawab of Bengal.

MURTANA. See PERGA.

MURTEN. See MORAT.

MURUA. See WOODLARK.

MURVIEDRO. See SAGUNTO.

MUŞ [*ancient:* **Mush;** *Arabic:* **Tarun**] (Turkey) Capital city of Muş province, 45 mi W of Lake Van. Founded *c.*400 BC, it was an important town of ARMENIA. Called Tarun by the Arabs, it was captured by the Seljuk Turks, the Mongols, and Tamerlane before being annexed by the OTTOMAN EMPIRE in 1515.

MUSA DAGH. See MUSA DAĞI.

MUSA DAĞI [**Musa Dagh**] (Turkey) Mountain peak in the S, rising from the Mediterranean Sea W of Antakya. During World War I it was the scene of the Armenians' heroic resistance against the Turks and was the subject of Franz Werfel's novel *The Forty Days of Musa Dagh.*

MUSA, GEBEL (Egypt) Mountain group of the S SINAI peninsula, its highest peak being Gebel Katherina at 8,652 ft. The northern slope is the site of St. Catherine's monastery of MT SINAI, known for its fine library. In it in 1844/45 the scholar H. von Tischendorf found one of the oldest Greek Biblical manuscripts known, the Codex Sinaiticus, now in the British Museum.

MUSCAT. See MASQAT.

MUSCAT AND OMAN. See OMAN.

MUSCOVY. See MOSCOW, GRAND DUCHY OF.

MUSGROVE MILL. See CLINTON.

MUSH. See MUŞ.

MUSHRIFE. See QATNA.

MUSIC PASS (United States) Mountain pass and trail in Huerfono and Saguache counties of S COLORADO, in the Sangre de Cristo Range of the ROCKY MOUNTAINS. It was a main trail used by travelers along the Arkansas River route to California and New Mexico in the late 19th century.

MUSKEGON (United States) City in W MICHIGAN, on LAKE MICHIGAN, 35 mi WNW of Grand Rapids. It has a landlocked harbor and is the largest port on the eastern shore of the lake. A fur-trading post was established here *c.*1810. After a sawmill was built in 1837, Muskegon became a thriving lumber center until 1890, when fire swept the city. There is an Indian burial ground here.

MUSKETAQUID. See CONCORD.

MUSKOGEE (United States) City and county seat in OKLAHOMA, 130 mi ENE of Oklahoma City. Founded *c.*1870, it became the chief town of the Creek Indian Nation, whose language was called Muskogee, and was the administrative center for the Union Indian Agency to the Five Civilized Tribes. There is a Five Civilized Tribes Museum and the restored Fort Gibson built in 1824.

MUSSELBURGH (Scotland) Town of Lothian region, 5 mi E of Edinburgh, on the S shore of the Firth of FORTH. The town dates from Roman times and has a Roman bridge across the Esk River and Roman remains in the vicinity. It is the site of a chapel built in 1534 and destroyed 10 years later by the earl of Hertford, rebuilt and again destroyed by Reformers. One mile to the southeast is the site of the Battle of PINKIE and, nearby, of CARBERRY HILL where Mary, Queen of Scots, surrendered. See also INVERESK and PRESTONPANS.

MUSTAFAABAD. See JUNAGADH.

MUTINA. See MODENA.

MUTTRA. See MATHURA.

MUZAFFARNAGAR (India) Town in NW Uttar Pradesh, in the plain between the Ganges and Jumna rivers. It was founded in 1633 by the son of Muzaffar Khan, Khan-i-Jahan. Hindu tradition says it was part of the Pandava kingdom of the *Mahabharata*, but its real

The Lion Gate at Mycenae in the ruins of the one-time citadel of Agamemnon, leader of the hosts that besieged Troy, as told in Homer's *Iliad*.

history begins with the Muslim conquests in the 13th century. Ruled from DELHI until the downfall of the MOGUL EMPIRE in the mid-18th century, it then passed to the MARATHAS.

MWANAMUTAPA [Monomotapa, Mwene Mutapa] (Zimbabwe) An empire of the Rhodesian plateau formed during the 15th century by the Rozwi King Mutota and his son Mutope. At its height, Mwanamutapa stretched from the Indian Ocean westward 600 miles and had a north-south axis of another 700 miles from the ZAMBEZI RIVER to the LIMPOPO RIVER. The shrine of GREAT ZIMBABWE was included in its territory.

After Mutope's death in 1480, the empire split into two sections, with the kingdom of Changamire in the south controlling eastern RHODESIA and part of MOZAMBIQUE. An important source of gold and ivory, it attracted Swahili traders from what is now TANZANIA. Mwanamutapa's power slowly eroded in the face of a growing Portuguese presence and the rising power of Changamire. By the end of the 17th century the once formidable empire had been reduced to a small territory surrounding the Portuguese strongholds of Tete and SENA.

MWENE MUTAPA. See MWANAMUTAPA.

MYCALE [Mount Lydia] [*modern:* **Samsun Daği**] (Turkey) Promontory in W Asia Minor opposite Samós

Island. An ancient religious site, its temple of Poseidon was also a center of the Ionian League. The Greek naval victory here over the Persians in 479 BC assured an end to the Persian threat to Greece. See IONIA.

MYCENAE (Greece) Archaeological site, ancient city of ARGOLIS, in the NE PELOPONNESUS, approx. 7 mi N of Argos. In ancient times it was the center of the Bronze Age Mycenaean civilization and capital of Agamemnon of Homer's *Iliad*. The excavated remains from the Mycenaean period include the magnificent Lion Gate entrance to the city, the palace, and the Treasury of Atreus, the largest of the beehive tombs outside the city walls.

Mycenaeans, or early Greeks, entered Greece from the north or northeast *c.*2000 BC, displacing a Neolithic culture dating from *c.*4000 BC. These Indo-European, Greek-speaking invaders brought techniques in pottery, architecture, and metallurgy not previously known. Commerce with the Minoan civilization of CRETE built a distinctive art and culture termed Mycenaean or Late Helladic, lasting from *c.*1600 to 1100 BC and corresponding to the Late Minoan. It reached its height *c.*1400 BC after the violent destruction of KNOSSOS and declined *c.*1100 in the face of new Greek invaders, the Dorians from the N. Mycenae was besieged and destroyed by the Persians in 468 BC and rebuilt in the Hellenistic period; by the second century AD it was

again in ruins. TIRYNS, PYLOS, THEBES, and ORCHO-
MENOS were other major cities of the period. Mycenae
at its height was characterized by massive fortifications
of fitted polygonal stonework.

MYITKYINA (Burma) Town, on the left bank of the
IRRAWADDY RIVER, near the border with China, 260 mi
NNE of Mandalay. Formerly an important town on the
LEDO Road, during World War II it was taken by the
Japanese in 1942 and after a 78-day siege was retaken
by the Allies in August 1944. Control of this terminus of
the RANGOON railroad was key to the liberation of
Burma.

MYKONOS [*Greek:* **Mýkonos**] (Greece) Island in the
CYCLADES, in the AEGEAN SEA, close to DELOS. Its
chief settlement, a favorite of tourists today, is the
picturesque town of Mykonos.

MYLAE. See MILAZZO.

MYLAI (Vietnam) Hamlet in the south. It was the
scene of the infamous Mylai Incident in March 1968
when U.S. soldiers under Lt. William Calley massacred
347 Vietnamese civilians in the course of raiding a
supposed Viet Cong stronghold during the Vietnam
War. Several soldiers were charged with murder, and
five were court-martialed. Calley was convicted, arous-
ing much controversy and affecting public opinion of the
entire war.

MYMANA. See MAIMANA.

MYNNEHEVED. See MINEHEAD.

MYRA (Turkey) Important city of ancient LYCIA in S
Asia Minor, it was visited by St. Paul. According to
Acts 27:5 it was later the see of St. Nicholas. While the
Byzantine capital of Lycia, it was attacked and captured by Harun al-Rashid in 808, after which it declined
in importance. The ruins of a theater are atop the
acropolis here, and the remains of the port area are
visible.

MYSIA (Turkey) Ancient country of NW Asia Minor
N of LYDIA. Its coast faced LESBOS, and its chief cities
were PERGAMUM and CYZICUS. Not a political entity, it
was subject to Croesus of Lydia, then successively to
PERSIA, MACEDON, SYRIA, and Pergamum. In 129 BC

it became part of the Roman province of ASIA. It was
visited by St. Paul on his second journey as recorded in
Acts 16:7, 8.

MYSORE [*former:* **Mahishapura, Mahishmati,
Purigere**] (India) City of S MYSORE state, S of the
Cauvery River, 85 mi SW of Bangalore. Located on a
site occupied before the third century BC and known
then as Purigere, it was one of the capitals of a Muslim
state in the late 16th century. It was occupied by the
British in 1831 and lost its importance to BANGALORE
in 1881. Historic buildings include the former maharaja's palace located inside the fort.

MYSORE [**Maisur**] (India) State on the plateau region of the
southern Deccan, including the KRISHNA
RIVER, renamed Karnataka in 1973. Ruled mostly by
Hindu dynasties of the Cholas, Cheras and others from
c.1400, it was under the control of VIJAYANAGARA and
was then overrun by Muslims from the north in 1565.
Mysore seized SERINGAPATAM in 1610 and entered a
prosperous period that lasted until Haidar Ali usurped
the throne in 1761. With his son Tipu Sultan, he ruled
until 1799 during the period of the Mysore Wars. Under
British administration from 1831, Mysore was returned
to native rule in 1881 and in 1947 became part of India.
Its capital is BANGALORE. See also CARNATIC.

MYSTIC. See STONINGTON, Connecticut.

MYSTIC SIDE. See MALDEN.

MY THO (Vietnam) Former naval base on the ME-
KONG RIVER delta, 45 mi SSW of Saigon. It was an
important naval fortification on the South China Sea
during French colonial rule.

MYTILENE. See LESBOS..

MZAB (Algeria) Valley and region in the N SAHARA
Desert, with GHARDAIA as its principal town. It was
settled c.1000 AD by a strict Muslim sect called the
Kharijites, who created seven oases. These were joined
into a confederation that became an important caravan
junction for northern Africa. The community is still
thriving. The French occupied the region in 1853 and
formally annexed it in 1882.

N

NAAS [*Gaelic:* **Nás na Riogh**] (Irish Republic) County town of Kildare, in E central Ireland, 19 mi WSW of Dublin. The former stronghold of the kings of LEINSTER, it was controlled by ENGLAND after 1171, when Henry II occupied IRELAND. In 1597 it was pillaged and burned by Owen McRory O'More during an insurrection against Queen Elizabeth I that led to England's temporary defeat at the Battle of Yellow Ford in 1598. See also DROGHEDA.

NABADWIP [*former:* **Nadia**] (India) Town in West Bengal, on the Bhagirathi River, approx. 60 mi N of Calcutta. Founded in the 11th century AD, it was a holy town to Hindu pilgrims and a center of Sanskrit studies. In the 12th century it became capital of the Sen Kingdom after being relinquished by the old city of GAUR.

NABATAEA (Jordan) Ancient kingdom of the ARABIAN PENINSULA S of EDOM. It flourished as an east-west commercial route and trading center from the fourth century BC through the first century AD. It was taken by ROME in 106 AD and became the province of Arabia Petraea. Its capital, PETRA, was captured from the Edomites c.300 BC. With its Hellenistic temples carved out of the red sandstone cliffs, it is now a significant archaeological and tourist site.

NABEUL [*ancient:* **Neapolis;** *Arabic:* **Nabul**] (Tunisia) Town at the base of Cape Bon peninsula, 38 mi SE of Tunis. Early Phoenician ruins have been discovered here. In 146 BC, near the end of the Third Punic War, Rome laid waste the Phoenician town, which later became a Roman colony. See also CARTHAGE, PHOENICIA.

NABLUS [*Arabic:* **Nabulus;** *biblical:* **Shechem;** *Greek:* **Neapolis**] (Jordan) Town, 30 mi N of Jerusalem. An ancient Canaanite town, it was under Egyptian rule c.2000 BC. Jeroboam I led an unsuccessful revolt here against Solomon, but as the first king of northern ISRAEL later returned to make it his capital. Joshua held his farewell convention in Shechem; and Jacob's tomb and well and Joseph's tomb are here. It was sacked and destroyed in 129 BC by John Hyrcanus I of the Maccabees. It was an ancient religious center of the Samaritans; Jesus asked the Samaritan woman for water in this town. It was damaged during the Crusades in the Middle Ages. The town was occupied by the Israelis after 1967. See also JUDAEA, SAMARIA.

NABRISSA. See LEBRIJA.

NABUL. See NABEUL.

NABULUS. See NABLUS.

NÁCHOD (Czechoslovakia) Old town in Czech SR, approx. 75 mi NE of Prague, on the border of Poland. PRUSSIA was victorious in a battle fought here in June

1866 against AUSTRIA, during the Austro-Prussian War. The war ended on Aug. 23, 1866 with the signing of the Treaty of Prague. See also GERMAN CONFEDERATION, SCHLESWIG-HOLSTEIN.

NACOGDOCHES (United States) Industrial and resort city, 135 mi NE of Houston, E TEXAS. Explored in the 16th century, it was the site in 1716 of a Spanish Franciscan mission from which the town developed. It was permanently settled in 1779 as a Spanish stronghold against the French presence in LOUISIANA. The Fredonian Rebellion occurred here in 1826/27, when Anglo-American families tried to settle the Mexican area with U.S. land grants. It was involved in the resulting Texas Revolution against MEXICO in 1835/36. The 18th-century Old Stone Fort is in the city, as are the remains of the city university, established in 1845, and the graves of four signers of the Texas Declaration of Independence.

NADIA. See NABADWIP.

NADVORNAYA [*Polish:* **Nadwórna**] (USSR) Town in the UKRAINE, 22 mi SSW of Ivano-Frankovsk. AUSTRIA took it from POLAND in 1772. The Austrians and Russians fought here for a week in mid-February 1915 during World War I. In 1919 it was returned to Poland and was ceded to the USSR in 1945 after the POTSDAM Conference.

NADWÓRNA. See NADVORNAYA.

NADZAB (Papua New Guinea) Village on NEW GUINEA, 19 mi NW of Lae. A Japanese air base established here in 1942 was taken by U.S. paratroopers in a daring aerial attack in September 1943 during World War II.

NAFA. See NAHA.

NÄFELS (Switzerland) Town and battle site in Glarus canton. A defensive league of local towns—the Everlasting League, formed, according to legend, by William Tell in 1291 against Austrian Hapsburg encroachments—won an important victory here in 1388 against the imperial army. With MORGARTEN and SEMPACH the victory marked an important step on the way to Swiss independence.

NAGA [*former:* **Nueva Caceres**] (Philippines) City and capital of Camarines Sur, on the Bicol River, LUZON. The Spanish city was founded here in 1573. Naga was the capital of Camarines province until 1919, when it continued as the capital of the subdivision of Camarines Sur of that province.

NAGA HILLS (Burma, India) Hill region, which includes Naga and Patkai hills, N Arakan Yoma Mts. Once dominated by head-hunting Nagas, a Tibeto-

Burman tribe, it was occupied by GREAT BRITAIN in 1880 after 15 years of fighting. See also NAGALAND.

NAGALAND (India) A state of India since 1961, Nagaland has been the scene of missionary activity since 1840. British posts here were raided during World War II by JAPAN, which failed in an attempt to take KOHIMA, the capital. The animistic Nagas have fiercely opposed incorporation into India since the 1940's and fought against government troops in 1956/57. They remain in favor of independence today. See also NAGA HILLS.

NAGANO (Japan) Commercial and religious center, approx. 100 mi NW of Tokyo, HONSHŪ. It has been a major Buddhist center, influenced since the sixth century AD by the Korean deity Amita and his related deities, including Kwannon. The famous seventh-century temple of Zenkoji is still a major shrine.

NAGAOKA (Japan) Industrial city approx. 227 mi NW of Tokyo, HONSHŪ. It flourished in the period of the late shogunate and was once a major government seat, but declined after the fall of the Tokugawa shogunate in the mid-19th century. It regained importance with the discovery of oil fields in the area in the late 19th century.

NAGAPATTINAM [Negapatam, Negapattinam] (India) Town and port in SE Tamil Nadu, 160 mi S of Madras. The Portuguese established a factory here early in the 16th century. It was occupied by the Dutch from 1660 to 1671 and taken by GREAT BRITAIN in 1799.

NAGARA PATHOM. See NAKHON PATHOM.

NAGARKET. See KANGRA.

NAGASAKI (Japan) City, port, and capital of Nagasaki prefecture, approx. 590 mi SW of Tokyo, KYŪSHŪ. Its port was the first opened to Western trade, in the 16th century, and became a Christian cultural and religious center for relations with PORTUGAL, SPAIN, and the NETHERLANDS. Although foreign trade was again restricted from 1637 to 1859, it was continued by the Dutch at DESHIMA, an island in Nagasaki's harbor, then Japan's only free port. Nagasaki was largely destroyed on Aug. 9, 1945 when it was the second city devastated by the new atomic bomb, dropped by the UNITED STATES near the end of World War II.

NAGB AL-HALFAYAH. See HALFAYA PASS.

NAGOD (India) Town and district in Madhya Pradesh, 16 mi W of Satna. It was the capital of the former princely state of Nagod. This region was ruled during the 16th and 17th centuries by the Gonds, a mostly Hindu ethnic group. In the 18th century the MARATHA CONFEDERACY conquered the area. GREAT BRITAIN occupied the territory in 1820. In 1857, during the Indian Mutiny, there were uprisings in Nagod. In 1956 the town and district were merged into Madhya Pradesh State.

NAGORNO-KARABAKH AUTONOMOUS OBLAST [former: Karabakh Mountain Area] (USSR) Region of Azerbaijan, SE European USSR. Controlled in the first century AD by ARMENIA, it was taken by the Arabs in the seventh century and by PERSIA in the 17th century. It became a khanate in the mid-18th century, a province of RUSSIA in 1822, and a Soviet oblast in 1923.

NAGOYA (Japan) City and capital of Aichi prefecture, between Kyoto and Tokyo, S HONSHŪ. An old castle town, its most significant castle was built in 1610 by Tokugawa Iyeasu of the Minamoto shogunate. This famous fortified structure has been rebuilt since it was destroyed, along with much of the city, in World War II. A famous Shinto shrine, the Atsuta Jingu of the second century AD houses the imperial sword.

NAGPUR (India) City and capital of the district of the same name, approx. 440 mi NE of Bombay. Part of the Gond Kingdom in the early 18th century, it passed to the MARATHA CONFEDERACY in 1740 and became the capital of Maratha Bhonsla soon after. Taken by the British in 1853, it became part of Madhya Pradesh State in 1947 and was briefly its capital. See also BHOPAL.

NAGYKANIZSA [Kanizsa] (Hungary) City, approx. 65 mi NW of Pécs. An early 14th-century fortress, it was ruled by the Turks through most of the 17th century. The remains of the medieval fortress are here, as is an 18th-century Franciscan church. There are now oil fields in the area.

NAGYKÖRÖS (Hungary) Market center and city, 47 mi SE of Budapest. János Arany (1817–82), considered one of the founders of modern Hungarian poetry, was born in this town.

NAGYSZEBEN. See SIBIU.

NAGYVÁRAD. See ORADEA.

NAHA [Nafa, Nawa] (Japan) Port and capital of Okinawa prefecture, RYUKYU ISLANDS, on the East China Sea. It dates back to at least the sixth century AD; its possession was disputed between CHINA and Japan in the 17th century. It was Comm. Perry's initial base in Japan in 1853 and became the capital of OKINAWA in 1879. It developed into an important military center and was heavily damaged by U.S. forces in fighting in May and early June 1945, during World War II.

NAHĀVAND [Nehavend, Nihavand] (Iran) Town, 42 mi S of Hamadān. The Arabs won a decisive victory over the Persians here in 642 AD. The Sassanid dynasty was overthrown, and Islam replaced Zoroastrianism in the area. In 1602 Shah Abbas the Great defeated the Turks here. See PERSIA.

NAHR AL-'ĀṢĪ. See ORONTES RIVER.

NAIN [Nein] (Israel) Village in GALILEE, ancient PALESTINE, 5 mi SSE of Nazareth. Its modern name is Nein. It was here that Jesus resurrected a widow's son from his deathbed. It is mentioned in the New Testament in Luke 7:11–17.

NAIRNSHIRE (Scotland) Agricultural region, former county, now part of Highland region, partly on the Moray Firth. Situated at the border between the Highlands and the Lowlands, it was settled by Northern Picts and became part of MORAY prior to its passing to the Scottish crown. The 15th-century Cawdor Castle, located in the county, provided the Shakespearean scene for Macbeth's murder of Duncan. Nairn is its chief town.

NAIROBI (Kenya) City and capital of Kenya, East Africa. It was only a waterhole in 1899 when it was founded as a depot on the Mombasa-Lake Victoria-Uganda railroad line. It became the seat of the British administration in 1907 and was the capital from 1920 to 1963 of Kenya Colony; it then continued as the capital of the independent state. It was incorporated as a city in 1950 and shortly after was the scene of Mau Mau struggles for independence. It is now a city of some 900,000 people and the commercial and cultural center of Kenya.

NAISSUS. See Niš.

NAJAF. See An Najaf, Mazar-i-Sharif.

NÁJERA (Spain) Town in Logroño province, W of Logroño. Edward the Black Prince of England defeated Henry II of Trastamara in an important battle fought here in 1367. The victory, during the Hundred Years War, temporarily restored Peter the Cruel of Castile to his throne.

NAJIBABAD (India) Trading town in NW Uttar Pradesh, 98 mi NE of Delhi. It was founded in the mid-18th century by a Rohilla chief, Najib-ud-daula, whose tomb and the remains of a fort built by him are here. There are several fine examples of Rohilla architecture in the town.

NAKAGUSUKU BAY [Buckner Bay] (Japan) Inlet of the Pacific Ocean, in SE Okinawa Island, part of the Ryuku Islands. A U.S. fleet moored here during the U.S. campaign against Okinawa from April to June 1945. The fleet suffered heavy damage from Japanese kamikaze air attacks.

NAKA IWO. See Iwo Jima.

NAKATSU (Japan) Commercial town and port on the Suō Sea, NE Kyūshū. It was the birthplace and home of Yukichi Fukuzawa (1835–1901), the Japanese author and educator who was a proponent of modernization for Japan.

NAKHICHEVAN [ancient: Naxuana] (USSR) Capital city of Nakhichevan ASSR, 85 mi SE of Yerevan, on the Araks River, Azerbaijan. It was founded by Noah, according to Armenian tradition. Known since antiquity, it was ruled by Persians, Mongols, and Arabs and flourished as a 15th-century trading center in Armenia. Following the Russo-Persian War of 1825 to 1828 it was ceded to Russia and developed as a significant trading post between the two countries. There are Greek and Roman remains in the city, as well as two 12th-century mausoleums.

NAKHON PATHOM [Nagara Pathom] (Thailand) Transportation center and town, approx. 38 mi NW of Bangkok, on the Mekong River. The Phra Pathom, Thailand's largest Buddhist temple, or stupa, is located in the town. It was built in the mid-19th century on the site of the original structure. The town held a U.S. air base during the Vietnam War.

NAKHON RATCHASIMA [Khorat, Korat] (Thailand) Town and capital of Nakhon Ratchasima province, on the Mun River. It was an ancient walled town, formerly under Cambodian rule. Established in the 17th century, it developed with the advent of the railway from Bangkok in 1890.

NALCHIK (USSR) Resort town and capital of Kabardino-Balkarian ASSR, 63 mi NW of Ordzhonikidze. Founded as a Russian military outpost in 1817, it was occupied in late 1942 by Germany during World War II but was recaptured in 1943.

NAMANGAN (USSR) Industrial town and capital of Namangan oblast, in the Fergana Valley, 130 mi E of Tashkent, NE Uzbek SSR. Founded in 1610 as a nomadic trading center, it was seized by Russian troops in 1875. It became the capital of its newly created oblast in 1941.

NAMARE. See Melk.

NAMEN. See Namur.

NAMHKAM (Burma) Border town, in the NE, on the Shweli River, approx. 100 mi S of Myitkyina. Occupied by Japan from 1942 to 1945, it was liberated on Jan. 15, 1945 by China near the end of the Sino-Japanese War of 1937 to 1945, which largely coincided with World War II in the Far East. See also Burma Road.

NAMHOI. See Fo-Shan.

NAMNETES. See Nantes.

NAM PHAN. See Cochin China.

NAMSOS (Norway) Town and port in the N, at the head of Namsen Fjord. British and German forces engaged in heavy fighting here in 1940 during World War II. British troops occupied it from April 14 to May 3, while on a mission to assist Norway after its occupation by Germany on April 9, 1940.

NAMUR [Flemish: Namen] (Belgium) Industrial town on the Meuse River, and capital of Namur province in the S. A Merovingian fortress, it was mentioned in the seventh century AD and has been the provincial capital since the 10th century. Ruled by Flanders and Burgundy in the Middle Ages, it was taken by William of Orange in 1695 during the War of the Grand Alliance. Strategically located on the Meuse, it was fortified against attacks by Germany but was captured in World War I on Aug. 25, 1914 and on May 16, 1940 during World War II after heavy fighting. There is a Roman-Flemish archaeological museum here, as well as a medieval citadel. See also Netherlands.

NAM VIET. See Vietnam.

NAMYUNG. See Nan-Hsiung.

NANAIMO (Canada) Mining and lumbering center on SE Vancouver Island, 34 mi W of Vancouver, in British Columbia. A blockhouse was built here in 1833 by the Hudson's Bay Company, and the town took shape as a coal-mining village in 1854. The bastion of its old fort of 1852 is still preserved here.

NAN-CH'ANG [Nanchang] [ancient: Yuchang] (China) City and capital of Kiangsi province, on the Kan River in the SE. It dates back to c.205 BC under the Han dynasty when it was called Yuchang. The modern walled city was founded in the 12th century AD under

The citadel of Belgian Namur, in a 19th-century print. Heavily fortified since early Frankish times, Namur was often besieged and fell to the Germans in both world wars.

the Sung dynasty. The People's Liberation Army was created here in 1927 when communist forces rebelled against the Kuomintang Nationalists, who eventually regained control of the city in 1933 and made it their headquarters. It was occupied by JAPAN from 1939 to 1945 during World War II and became communist in 1949 at the end of the civil war.

NANCHAO. See LAOS.

NANCY (France) City and capital of Meurthe-et-Moselle department, 178 mi E of Paris, on the Meurthe River. A ninth-century fortress, it became the capital of LORRAINE in the 12th century and was the scene of the defeat and death, in 1477, of Charles the Bold of BURGUNDY. The former king of Poland, Stanislaus I, ruled Lorraine from 1738 to 1766 from his lavish ducal court at Nancy. Occupied from 1870 to 1873 by PRUSSIA during the Franco-Prussian War, it was an important rail center during World War I, when it was heavily damaged. During World War II it was liberated by U.S. forces on Sept. 15, 1944 after heavy bombing. Among its many churches are the 15th-century church of Cordeliers, where the tombs of the princes of Lorraine are located. Its university was established in 1768.

NANDED. See NANDER.

NANDER [Nanded] (India) Market town in SE Ma-

harashtra state, on the Godavari River, 140 mi NW of Hyderabad. It is a Sikh place of pilgrimage. The remains of a MOGUL fort are in the vicinity.

NANDIDROOG. See NANDI DRUG.

NANDI DRUG [Nandidroog] (India) Hill in E Mysore, 31 mi N of Bangalore. A fort established here by Haidar Ali and his son Tipu Sahib was captured in 1791 by British forces led by Lord Cornwallis during the MYSORE wars. See also SERINGATAPAM.

NAN-HSIUNG [Namyung] (China) Town in N Kwangtung province, approx. 150 mi NE of Canton. A U.S. air base in World War II, it was seized by JAPAN in February 1945 but was regained by Chinese forces in July.

NANIWA. See OSAKA.

NANKING [*ancient:*** Tanyang; ***former:*** Chian-ning, Kiang-ning]** (China) City and modern capital of Kiangsu province, on the YANGTZE RIVER, 150 mi NW of Shanghai. Known as Tanyang as early as 206 BC, during the Han dynasty, it became the capital of China from the third to the sixth century AD and again, in the Ming dynasty, from 1368 to 1403. It was captured in 1842 by GREAT BRITAIN during the Opium War, and China was opened to the West by the Treaty of Nanking in the same year, which also ceded HONGKONG to Britain. It was a rebel Taiping stronghold and headquarters from 1853 to 1864 and became the capital of China's first National president, Sun Yat-sen, in 1912. It fell to the communists in 1927 but became the Nationalist Kuomintang capital under Chiang Kai-shek the next year. The Japanese Rape of Nanking in 1937 began the foreign occupation that lasted until the end of World War II. It was taken by the communists in 1949. Most of the Ming city wall is intact today, and the tomb of the founder of the Ming dynasty and the mausoleum of Sun Yat-sen are in the city.

NAN-K'OU [Nankow] (China) Town in the present area of Peking, approx. 25 mi NW of the capital. The grand tombs of 13 of the 16 rulers of the Ming dynasty (1368–1644) are located to the east of the city. They are approached by an avenue, the Holy Way, lined with stone animal statues. Northwest, through a gate in the GREAT WALL, is the Nan-k'ou Pass.

NANKOW. See NAN-K'OU.

NANNING [Nan-Ning] [*former:* **Yung-ning**] (China) City and capital of Kwangsi Chuang, approx. 360 mi W of Wuchow. A former treaty port, opened to the West in 1907, it was taken by the communists in 1949 and was their supply base in their war against FRANCE in INDOCHINA from 1946 to 1954. See also VIETNAM.

NANSEI. See RYUKYU ISLANDS.

NANTES [*ancient:* **Condivincum;** *Breton:* **Naoned;** *Gallic:* **Namnetes**] (France) City on the LOIRE RIVER, capital of Loire-Atlantique department, 107 mi W of Tours. The capital of the ancient Namnetes of GAUL, it was later a major trading center under ROME. The Huns failed to take it in 445 AD, but the Norsemen succeeded and held it from 843 to 936. It was the residence of the dukes of BRITTANY from the 10th century to 1498, when it was joined to France through the marriage of Anne of Brittany to Louis XII. In 1598 Henry IV issued the Edict of Nantes permitting some religious tolerance to Huguenots; but it was revoked by Louis XIV in 1685. Royalists made it the scene of *noyades*, or mass drownings, during the French Revolution. In World War II it was heavily damaged as a center of French resistance to occupation by GERMANY. A 10th-century castle and a 15th-century church and the university, founded in 1460, are here.

NANTICOKE (United States) Mining city on the SUSQUEHANNA RIVER, 8 mi W of Wilkes-Barre, E PENNSYLVANIA. A former Indian village, it was founded in 1793 and became a major coal-mining center in the 19th century. It was incorporated in 1874.

NANTUCKET (United States) Island, approx. 14 mi long and 3 to 6 mi wide, S of CAPE COD, MASSACHUSETTS, on Nantucket Sound, in the Atlantic Ocean. Part of the original grant to Plymouth Colony in 1621, it was

Ancient city of Nanking, often China's capital, in an 1850 view. Eight years earlier the British took it in the Opium War. The Ming walls can be seen at the left.

settled by Quakers in 1659. Its main town, also Nantucket, was a major whaling center from the 17th to mid-19th centuries. It then became a trading center and a major resort, due to its good beaches. Approximately 50 miles offshore is the first U.S. lightship, first used in 1856. SIASCONSET, or Sconset, another resort town, is on the Atlantic coast. There are many fine colonial houses in the town, as well as an old Friends Meeting house. See also MARTHA'S VINEYARD.

NANUMEA (Tuvalu) Island and atoll in the W Pacific Ocean, now part of Tuvalu. It was captured in September 1943 by U.S. forces and used by them as a military base in World War II.

NAONED. See NANTES.

NAPATA (Egypt) Town in ancient Egypt, just below the Fourth Cataract of the NILE RIVER, near modern Marawī. It was the capital of the kingdom of KUSH in NUBIA, which was much influenced by Egyptian culture from c.1500 BC. In the sixth century BC the Egyptians drove back the Kushites, who then established a new capital at MEROË, while Napata remained as a religious center. The ruins include several imposing pyramids and temples.

NAPLES [ancient: **Neapolis, Parthenope;** *Italian:* **Napoli**] (Italy) Former kingdom and city, Napoli province, Campania region, on the Bay of Naples, 117 mi SE of Rome. The city was first founded in the seventh century BC by colonists from Rhodes, who called it Parthenope. It was taken by Chalcidians from nearby CUMAE c.600 BC, and a new city, *Neapolis* in Greek, was built next to the old one. More Greek colonists arrived c.450 BC, and c.400 BC the Samnites from south-central Italy took the city and the region of Campania. In 326 BC ROME seized it from the Samnites and allowed the Greek population great autonomy. The city soon became a center of learning for southern Italy and attracted many students from Rome itself. Vergil composed the *Georgics* and the *Aeneid* here, and Roman emperors and patricians built villas near the city on the bay.

Naples declined somewhat in the fourth century AD under Constantine, but its harbor and wealth continued to make it important. From 568 to 1130 it was ruled by a series of dukes, nominally under the BYZANTINE EMPIRE. In the 11th and 12th centuries the Normans under Robert Guiscard and his successors gradually conquered a realm in southern Italy consisting of the present regions of Abruzzi, Apulia, Basilicata, Calabria, Campania, and Molise, as well as Naples and SICILY. The popes, however, legitimized the Normans' claims in return for their feudal homage. In 1139 Pope Innocent II invested Guiscard's nephew, Roger II, with the kingdom of Sicily, including these lands. In 1194 the German Hohenstaufens inherited the kingdom and made Naples a center of learning and international culture, combining German, Norman, Muslim, and Byzantine influences with the native Italian. In 1224 Emperor Frederick II founded the University of Naples.

The Hohenstaufen conflict with the papacy, however, soon resulted in a papal alliance with FRANCE; and in 1266 Charles of Anjou, the French king's brother, invaded the kingdom and defeated and killed King Manfred at BENEVENTO. Charles was made a king of Naples and Sicily by the pope. In 1282, however, a revolt of the Sicilians, known as the Sicilian Vespers, overthrew Angevin rule there and invited in ARAGON, while the Angevins retained the kingdom of Naples. Under the Angevins the city became a center of French and northern European culture, while under King Robert the Wise (1275–1343) and Queen Sancia (1286–1345) it attracted Greek and Latin scholars, scientists, painters like Giotto and Simone Martini, and poets like Petrarch and Boccaccio. The kingdom at this time also became a refuge for reformers, heretics, and unorthodox thinkers of all types.

Naples under the Angevins in 1381. Held by a succession of rulers for over 2,500 years, Naples has always been the lively, brawling, civilized city it is today.

Between 1343 and 1442 the Italian and Hungarian branches of the Angevins fought over the royal succession in Naples, until Alfonso V of Aragon invaded the kingdom, defeated King René, and became king of the TWO SICILIES. As Alfonso I, the Magnanimous, he was a great patron of the Renaissance. On his death in 1458 his illegitimate son Ferrante (1458–94) took the kingdom, while his legitimate son, John II, retained Aragon and Sicily. In 1495 Charles VIII of France, claiming Naples through the Angevin line, invaded Italy and seized Naples. His invasion started the Italian Wars.

In 1504, Hapsburg SPAIN ousted the French and reunited Naples with Sicily, and for two centuries Spain ruled Naples in a heavy-handed manner, interrupted only by the creation of the Parthenopean Republic for a few months in 1647. AUSTRIA occupied the kingdom in 1707, but the Spanish Bourbons reconquered it between 1733 and 1735 and in 1744 founded the Bourbon dynasty. Under the Bourbons Naples entered a new period of cultural brilliance. In 1799 the French Revolutionary Army established the short-lived second Parthenopean Republic. The French returned in 1806 and made Joseph Bonaparte, brother of Napoleon I, king of Naples. He was replaced two years later by Joachim Murat, a French marshal. When French rule ended in 1816 after the defeat of Napoleon, Ferdinand of Bourbon took the Neapolitan throne as Ferdinand I, king of the Two Sicilies. A series of reactionary and oppressive kings held the throne until 1860, when the forces of Giuseppe Garibaldi, the Italian patriot, took both Sicily and Naples. The next year the region and the city became part of the unified kingdom of Italy.

Since 1860 the Italian government has tried, with only limited success, to restore both the crumbling city structure and efficient government. After a severe cholera epidemic in 1884 a new urban plan was adopted that plowed wide boulevards and piazzas through the ancient and medieval city. Naples was badly damaged in World World II. It was bombed by the Allies on Aug. 4, 1943 and seized by Germany after the Italian surrender on September 8. After the Neapolitan uprising of September 28 the Germans destroyed many buildings and facilities and retreated north. The Allies liberated Naples on Oct. 7, 1943. A typhus epidemic soon ravaged the city. It was badly shaken by an earthquake in 1980 that left 100,000 homeless.

Naples is noted for its natural setting, which has given rise to the expression, "See Naples and Die." It is also known for its generous people, its raucous gaiety, its corruption, and its great poverty. The last two sent thousands of emigrants to the United States and other countries in the Western Hemisphere in the late 19th and 20th centuries. Their food and culture came to symbolize Italy abroad for decades. Naples today remains a major seaport and an important industrial and commercial center. Its many interesting buildings include the Norman Castel dell'Ovo, the Angevin Castel Nuovo of 1282, the Carthusian monastery of St. Martin, and many churches, including the 14th-century Gothic church of Santa Chiara, destroyed in World War II and restored, and the 13th- and 14th-century Duomo. The National Archaeological Museum has an unmatched collection of objects excavated at POMPEII and HERCULANEUM. The Capodimonte Palace Museum also houses a major collection of art. The city was a brilliant musical center in the 17th and 18th centuries and was the home of Carlo Gesualdo (1560–1613) and Alessandro (1660–1725) and Domenico (1685–1757) Scarlatti. The Roman poet Vergil is buried here. The Renaissance poet Sannazaro (1458–1530), the scientist G.B. Vico (1668–1744), and the singer Enrico Caruso were also born here.

The city's environs include the Bay of Naples, with the Gulf of POZZUOLI to the west, including Pozzuoli and Posillipo and the ancient sites of Cumae, BAIA, and Lake AVERNUS. Just south and east of the city lies Mt VESUVIUS with the ruins of Herculaneum and Pompeii; and across the bay are SORRENTO and the AMALFI peninsula. The islands of Procida and ISCHIA lie to the northwest of the bay, and CAPRI is on the southwest.

NAPOLÉON VENDÉE. See LA ROCHE-SUR-YON.

NAPOLI. See NAPLES.

NAPOLI DE MALVASIA. See MONEMVASIA.

NAQADA (Egypt) Village, just N of KARNAK, on the NILE RIVER. Excavations made at its archaeological site, on the left bank of the Nile, by Sir William Petrie in 1895 uncovered important pre-dynastic remains of the early Naqada culture. In 1897 a large Early Dynastic mastaba tomb was excavated nearby.

NARA (Japan) City and capital of Nara prefecture, 26 mi E of Ōsaka, W central HONSHŪ. The first permanent capital of Japan, from 710 to 784 AD, it was the center of early Japanese art, culture, and religion until its decline in the ninth century. In historic Nara Park is a tremendous bronze statue of Buddha, housed in the world's largest wooden edifice, the Daibutsu-den. The Imperial Museum, with art and relics from Nara's classical period, is also here.

NARAINGANJ. See NARAYANGANJ.

NARAYANGANJ [**Narainganj, Narayungunj**] (Bangladesh) City and port on the Meghna River, 12 mi SE of Dacca. Opposite the town is the famous mosque of the Muslim saint Kadam Rasul. Several 17th-century Mogul forts nearby were used to repel attacks by the Arakanese from BURMA.

NARAYUNGUNJ. See NARAYANGANJ.

NARBADA [**Narmada, Nerbudda**] (India) River, approx. 800 mi long, rising in the Maikala Range in Madhya Pradesh State and flowing W into the Gulf of Cambay. It forms the old boundary between HINDUSTAN and the DECCAN. Its valley has long been a famous trade route. Its waters are next to those of the GANGES RIVER in their importance to Hindus, who believe the river sprang from the body of the god Shiva. There are holy baths and a 12th-century temple along its banks, which also mark the course of a traditionally significant pilgrimage route.

NARBO MARTIUS. See NARBONNE.

NARBONENSIS [**Gallia Narbonensis**] (France) Region in the SE of ancient GAUL. The emperors Augustus and Tiberius made it one of Gaul's five administrative districts. NARBONNE, the chief city, had been settled by Greeks, who asked for help from ROME in 118 BC against possible invaders. The region was taken over by Rome. The region's later history is that of SEPTIMANIA and of LANGUEDOC.

NARBONNE [*ancient:* **Narbo Martius;** *Arabic:* **Arbūnah**] (France) City in Aude department, 31 mi E of Carcassonne, and near the Mediterranean Sea. Taken in 118 BC, it was the first Roman colony in GAUL and later became the capital of NARBONENSIS. After the fall of the ROMAN EMPIRE it was ruled by Visigoths, Saracens, and Franks until its prosperous port silted up in 1320. The 13th-century expulsion of a significant group of Jewish residents c.1310 and the Black Death in 1348 also contributed to its decline. The city was a center of heresy and religious controversy in the later Middle Ages. Roman ruins, the fortified medieval palace of its archiepiscopal see, established in the fourth century, and the 13th-century cathedral of St. Just are all located in the town. See also MARSEILLES.

NARDA. See ÁRTA.

NAREV. See NAREW.

NAREW [*Russian:* **Narev**] (Poland) River, 296 mi long, rising in the Białowieza Forest, flowing W and SW into the VISTULA RIVER. Heavy fighting took place along its banks in both world wars. The Germans occupied the area during World War I after severe fighting that lasted from March to August 1915.

NARMADA. See NARBADA.

NARNI [*ancient:* **Narnia**] (Italy) Town on the Nera River, 8 mi SW of Terni, Terni province, Umbria region. An important city in ancient UMBRIA, it was later conquered by ROME. In 1527 it was destroyed by forces sent by Charles V, Holy Roman emperor. Roman ruins and medieval churches and palaces have survived here. Emperor Nerva was born here in 32 AD, as was Pope John XIII (965–72).

NARNIA. See NARNI.

NAROCH [*Polish:* **Narocz**] (USSR) Lake in N Belorussian SSR. RUSSIA was badly defeated in a battle fought on its shores from March 18 to April 30, 1916 in World War I.

NAROCZ. See NAROCH.

NARODNA REPUBLIKA BULGARIYA. See BULGARIA.

NARRAGANSETT (United States) Resort town on NARRAGANSETT BAY, 9 mi SW of Newport, S RHODE ISLAND. It was settled in 1675, the year that a battle was fought here between the new colonists and the local Indians after whom it was named. It was incorporated in 1901.

NARRAGANSETT BAY (United States) Inlet of the Atlantic Ocean in SE RHODE ISLAND, extending N 28 mi to the city of PROVIDENCE and containing several islands. Named after the Narragansett Indians, its many harbors were important colonial trading ports and centers of anti-British activity during the American Revolution. Among its islands are Rhode Island, from which the state takes it name; on it are the city of NEWPORT, and a major U.S. naval installation.

NARVA (USSR) City in NE ESTONIAN SSR, on the Narva River, 86 mi SW of Leningrad. Founded by Danes in 1223, it flourished from 1336 to 1558 as a commercial center under the Livonian Knights and as a member of the HANSEATIC LEAGUE. It passed to RUSSIA in 1558, then to SWEDEN in 1581, and was contested by the two for many years following. Charles XII of Sweden defeated Russia's Peter the Great here on Nov. 30, 1700, but Peter regained the city in 1704. It was part of independent Estonia from 1919 to 1940 before it was occupied by GERMANY in World War II. Two fortresses stand here facing each other, one built in 1492 by Ivan III of Russia and the other a century earlier by the knights.

NARVIK (Norway) Port and city on a peninsula in the Ofoten Fjord, in the N. Founded in 1887, it was taken on April 9, 1940 by GERMANY during World War II. In the next week heavy naval fighting took place off its coast between British and German vessels. The British held the port from May 28 to June 9, 1940. See also NAMSOS.

NASCA. See NAZCA.

NASEBY (England) Village in Northamptonshire, 12 mi NNW of Northampton. It was the scene of an important English Civil War victory for Sir Thomas Fairfax and Oliver Cromwell on June 14, 1645. Their Parliamentarian army not only defeated the Royalist troops led by Prince Rupert but also seized documents of Charles I that crippled his cause and led to a speedy end to the war.

NASHOBA (United States) Former community on the Wolf River, near Memphis, SW TENNESSEE. Inspired by Robert Owen's NEW HARMONY colony, Frances Wright purchased some slaves and this plot of land in 1825 to educate a nucleus of slaves, so that they might stand as examples of freedom among their brethren. Mismanaged and unpopular, the community was abandoned by 1829. The slaves were sent to HAITI.

NASHUA [*former:* **Dunstable**] (United States) Industrial city on the MERRIMACK RIVER, 15 mi S of Manchester, S NEW HAMPSHIRE. Founded as Dunstable in 1673, it was incorporated under its present name in 1853. It was a prosperous textile mill center in the early 19th century due to the development of hydroelectric power in NEW ENGLAND.

NASHVILLE [*former:* **Fort Nashborough**] (United States) Industrial and commercial city on the Cumberland River, capital of TENNESSEE, 200 mi NE of Memphis. Founded in 1779 as Fort Nashborough, it was incorporated five years later as Nashville. It became the permanent capital of the state in 1843, and seven years later it was host to the Southern Convention in which nine southern states declared their right to secede from the Union. It developed as a cotton center and river port before being captured in February 1862 by Union troops, who held it as an important base for the remainder of the Civil War. Gen. Hood's Confederate troops were unable to recapture the town in the Battle of Nashville, fought here against Union forces led by Gen. Thomas on December 15 and 16, 1864. The old state capitol is located here, as is the Grand Ole Opry, which has made the city the American country-music center.

NASIK [*ancient:* **Panchavati**] (India) Town on the Godavari River, Maharashtra, 100 mi NE of Bombay. A sacred pilgrimage city of the Hindus, it is believed to have been the place of exile for the deities Rama and Sita. It was founded on the site of the ancient town of Panchavati and has been a Jain, Buddhist, and Hindu center since at least the first century BC. Ancient Buddhist and Jain holy caves and rock temples are nearby.

NÁS NA RIOGH. See NAAS.

NASRATABAD. See SEISTAN.

NASSAU (Great Britain) Commercial city, port, and capital of the BAHAMA ISLANDS, NE New Providence Island. Granted in 1629 to Sir Robert Heath by Charles I of ENGLAND, it became a popular 17th-century pirate haunt. The British regained it in 1718 and heavily fortified it. It was attacked and occupied several times by SPAIN and once, during the American Revolution, by the American navy. Great Britain finally recaptured it in 1783 and has held it ever since. Confederate blockade runners used it as their base from 1861 to 1865 during the U.S. Civil War.

NASSAU (West Germany) German duchy and region, now part of W Hesse and NE Rhineland-Palatinate. Inhabited since Roman times, it was ruled by the Franks beginning in the fifth century AD. The castle of the counts of Nassau was built in the ancestral small town of Nassau in the 12th century. The region became a duchy in 1806, and in 1816 it was enlarged by Duke William to include contiguous family lands. One branch of the family gave rise to the house of Orange in the NETHERLANDS. The duchy's capital was WIESBADEN.

NASSER, LAKE (Egypt, Sudan) Lake in S Egypt and N Sudan, formed by the construction of ASWAN High Dam in the 1960's to produce hydroelectric power. It has flooded several important archaeological sites, including that of ABU-SIMBEL whose temple was moved farther inland. Close to 90,000 people, mostly from Sudan, had to be relocated when the lake was formed.

NASUGBU (Philippines) Town on the South China Sea, LUZON, 45 mi SW of Manila. On Jan. 31, 1945 a U.S. force landed on its beach as part of an offensive to retake the islands from JAPAN during World War II.

NATAL (Brazil) Port and capital of Rio Grande do Norte state, 135 mi N of Recife. Founded in 1597, it was held by the Dutch from 1633 to 1654. It was important as an air base, used by the UNITED STATES as a stopover on missions to Africa and the Near and Far East in World War II.

NATAL (South Africa) Province in the E, with its coast on the Indian Ocean. Vasco da Gama of PORTUGAL saw it on Christmas Day 1497 and named it *Terra Natalis*. The English visited here in 1684 but did not settle it until they founded Port Natal in 1824, renamed DURBAN in 1835. Natal was reached by Boers in 1837 during the Great Trek of 1836 to 1838. After warring with local Zulus and British colonists, they ceded it in 1843 to GREAT BRITAIN, when it became part of CAPE COLONY. Many Boers then left the area, but it became a separate province again in 1856. In 1910 it was incorporated into the Union of South Africa shortly after the Boer War of 1899 to 1902, which was in part fought in Natal.

NATANYA. See NETANYA.

NATCHEZ (United States) Trading center and city on the MISSISSIPPI RIVER, 86 mi SW of Jackson, SW MISSISSIPPI. Once inhabited by the Natchez Indians, it was first settled in 1716 and was owned by FRANCE, GREAT BRITAIN, and SPAIN successively before becoming the capital of Mississippi Territory from 1798 to 1802. Aaron Burr made it his headquarters while planning for a new republic in the Southwest, for which he was arrested in 1807 but acquitted in a trial for treason. Incorporated in 1803, it became a famous haven for river traders and was dominated by cotton-plantation owners before the Civil War. Union forces held the city from 1863 to 1865. Many magnificent antebellum plantation estates are in the area.

NATCHEZ TRACE (United States) Old road from NASHVILLE, Tennessee to NATCHEZ, Mississippi. Originally an Indian trail, it became a popular route for traders going to and from the MISSISSIPPI RIVER port of Natchez, particularly from 1780 to 1830. It was used by Andrew Jackson during the War of 1812 as he marched on NEW ORLEANS. It was important also as a post road and for settlers and frontiersmen.

NATCHITOCHES (United States) City, 52 mi NW of Alexandria, NW central LOUISIANA. Founded c.1715 as a French military and trading post, it was the first lasting settlement in the area of the LOUISIANA PURCHASE of 1803. It was early connected by road with MEXICO CITY, and was an important port until the RED RIVER changed its course in 1800. The town figured prominently in the Mexican War of 1846 to 1848. It is the oldest town in Louisiana.

NATHANIA. See NETANYA.

NATICK (United States) Manufacturing town in NE MASSACHUSETTS, 15 mi WSW of Boston. It was founded in 1651 as the first of John Eliot's Praying Towns. The missionary ran it as a self-governing Indian village until European settlers took it over in 1718, incorporating it in 1781. The old Indian burial plot is located here. The town has become a producer of electronic and machine parts.

NATIONAL ROAD (United States) Highway, beginning in CUMBERLAND, MARYLAND and ending in ST. LOUIS, MISSOURI. It was first opened in 1818 as the CUMBERLAND ROAD and stretched then as far as WHEELING, WEST VIRGINIA. In the mid-18th century a part of it had been known as Braddock's Road. It was an important overland route and the most heavily used pathway for westward-bound emigrants. It declined later in the century as canals and railroads were constructed.

NATURAL BRIDGE (United States) Village, 16 mi S of Lexington, W central VIRGINIA. The famous stone arch of the same name is located over Cedar Creek, nearby. Thomas Jefferson once owned the bridge and operated a small traveling station here. Now the Lee Highway runs across the bridge.

NAUCRATIS [Naukratis] (Egypt) Ancient city on the Canopic branch of the NILE RIVER, 45 mi SE of Alexandria. The site was probably given to Greek colonists from MILETUS in W Asia Minor by Psamtik, king of Egypt, who died in 609 BC. Naucratis was the first Greek settlement in Egypt. Amasis II, who ruled Egypt from 569 to 525 BC, further encouraged Greek artisans and merchants to settle here, and the city became important in the economic life of the country. However, the founding of ALEXANDRIA in 332 BC by Alexander the Great and its rise, together with a shifting of the Nile, caused Naucratis to decline in importance. The site was discovered by an English archaeologist Sir W. M. Flinders Petrie in 1884. Excavations then and later brought finds that shed light on the commercial activities of some Greek states as well as on the early development of the alphabet. See also GREECE, MACEDONIAN EMPIRE.

NAUGATUCK (United States) Town on the NAUGATUCK River, 15 mi NW of New Haven, S central CONNECTICUT. It was settled in 1704 in Algonquin Indian territory. It was the locus of Henry Goodyear's rubber factory of 1843. The town was incorporated in 1844 and has several buildings designed by the famous architectural team of McKim, Mead & White.

NAUGATUCK RIVER (United States) River, 65 mi long, rising in Litchfield county, NW CONNECTICUT and flowing south into the HOUSATONIC RIVER at Derby. Its banks are dotted with old towns whose factories date from the early Industrial Revolution in NEW ENGLAND. See also NAUGATUCK, WATERBURY.

NAULOCHUS (Italy) Ancient port in Messina province, on the N coast of SICILY, E of Milazzo (Mylae). A Roman naval base during the Roman civil wars, it was the scene of a naval victory in 36 BC by Octavian Augustus's fleet commanded by Marcus Agrippa over Sextus Pompeius, son of Pompey, who fled to Asia Minor, where he was captured and killed.

NAUMBURG [Naumburg an der Saale] (East Germany) Industrial city on the Saale River, 25 mi SW of Halle. Founded in the 10th century, it became the seat of the bishopric of Zeitz in 1028 and received city rights in 1142. It passed to SAXONY in 1564 and was the scene of a treaty with PRUSSIA in 1815, by which it was ceded to that country. Medieval ruins and later churches, one with important Gothic sculptures, are located in the city.

NAUMBURG AN DER SAALE. See NAUMBURG.

NAUPACTUS. See LEPANTO.

NAUPLIA [Greek: Návplion] (Greece) City and port, capital of Argolis department, NE PELOPONNESUS, on the Gulf of Argolis. An ancient city on Mycenaean foundations, it is associated with Homeric legends. It fell to ARGOS in c.625 BC, and by the second century AD was deserted. A Venetian port in the 11th century, it came under Crusader rule and then Turkish. It was taken by Greek revolutionaries during the country's struggle for independence, and it became the first capital of independent Greece from 1830 to 1834. During World War II the British evacuated nearly 7,000 hard-pressed troops from Nauplia on April 26, 1941. An old Venetian fortress survives here.

NAURU [former: Pleasant Island] Independent state and island, W Pacific Ocean, W of KIRIBATI. Discovered in 1798, it was taken by GERMANY in 1888 and became a League of Nations Australian mandate after World War I. It was occupied by JAPAN from August 1942 through World War II. It became a trust territory of AUSTRALIA, GREAT BRITAIN, and NEW ZEALAND in 1947 and gained independence in 1968.

NAUVOO (United States) City on the MISSISSIPPI RIVER, 45 mi N of Quincy, W ILLINOIS. A thriving city while populated by Mormons under their leader Joseph Smith in the early 1840's, it was abandoned by the Mormons after Smith was killed in 1844, when he declared himself to be a presidential candidate. In 1849 it was the haven of a group of French Utopians led by Étienne Cabet. Their community was dissolved in 1856 because of internal dissension. The settlement still exists as a small town.

NAVAN [Gaelic: An Uaimh] (Irish Republic) Agricultural town on the BOYNE RIVER, 16 mi S of Drogheda. Navan Mote, a notable prehistoric earthwork, is located here, as are some medieval and city-wall remains.

NAVANAGAR. See JĀMNAGAR.

NAVARINO. See PYLOS.

NAVARRA. See NAVARRE.

NAVARRE [Spanish: Navarra] (France, Spain) Historic kingdom of N Spain and NW France, now in Spanish Navarra province and part of Pyrénées-Atlantiques department in France. Inhabited in early times by the Basques, it has always been open to France through the pass of RONCESVALLES. It was conquered by ROME, then by the Visigoths in 470 AD and by Charlemagne in 778. It flourished as the kingdom of Navarre in the 10th and 11th centuries. Following the death of Sancho III in 1035, it was united with LEÓN and CASTILE, which was then divided into the kingdoms of Navarre, ARAGON and Castile. It was reunified with Aragon for a while, passed to the lords of CHAMPAGNE in 1234, and to the French crown in 1305. It was important in the Hundred Years War of 1337 to 1453 and was restructured many times through royal marriages and local military conquests. Jean d'Albret of Gascony received the kingdom through his marriage with Catherine de Foix in 1484, who inherited it from Francois Phoebus. The southern part was taken by Ferdinand II and annexed to Aragon in 1511. The northern part passed to the French house of Bourbon through the marriage of Charles of Bourbon, duke of Vendôme, to Jeanne d'Albret in 1548. It then passed to Henry IV of Bourbon, often called Henry of Navarre, king of France, in 1589.

NAVAS DE TOLOSA, LAS (Spain) Village in the NE part of the region of ANDALUSIA. Here, on July 16, 1212 Alfonso VIII, the Spanish king of CASTILE, leading an army consisting of troops of Castile, LEÓN, and NAVARRE, all former kingdoms in present Spain, defeated a Moorish army of the ALMOHADS, a Berber Muslim dynasty that ruled Spain and MOROCCO in the 12th and 13th centuries. This battle destroyed the Almohads' power and marked a major turning point in Spanish history.

NAVASOTA (United States) Trading city, 69 mi NW of Houston, E central TEXAS. One of the great explorers of New France, Robert Cavalier de La Salle (1643–87) was murdered near here by his mutinous crew as they sought an overland route to the MISSISSIPPI RIVER. The city was founded by railroad workers in 1854 and was incorporated in 1866.

NÁVPAKTOS. See LEPANTO.

NÁVPLION. See NAUPLIA.

NAVY ISLAND (Canada) Island in the Niagara River, N of NIAGARA FALLS, S ONTARIO. William Lyon Mackenzie led a Reform Party group of insurgents into the Upper Canadian Rebellion of 1837/38, in which he attempted a takeover of TORONTO. Navy Island was the scene of his last stand before escaping to the UNITED STATES.

NAWA. See NAHA.

NAWABGANJ (India) Market town in E Uttar Pradesh, 17 mi E of Lucknow. Sir Hope Grant won a victory here on June 12, 1858 for the British over insurgents during the Indian Mutiny. See also DELHI, KANPUR.

NAXOS [Greek: **Náxos**] (Greece) Island in the CYCLADES, in the AEGEAN SEA. It was here, according to Greek mythology, that Theseus left Ariadne before Dionysus found her; his worship was centered on this island, which was also famous for its marble. Colonized by the Ionians and sacked by PERSIA in 490 BC, it was taken by ATHENS in 471 BC when it tried to secede from the Delian League. It was the residence from 1207 to 1566 AD of the dukes under VENICE before being captured by the OTTOMAN EMPIRE. It became Greek in 1829. See also DELOS.

NAXOS (Italy) Ruins of an ancient Greek colony, the first in SICILY, close to Taormina, on the E coast in Messina province, approx. 28 mi SSW of Messina. Founded c.735 BC, it was sacked and leveled in 403 BC by Dionysius the Elder of SYRACUSE and was supplanted by TAORMINA. It is now an archaeological site.

NAXUANA. See NAKHICHEVAN.

NAYARIT (Mexico) State in the W, on the Pacific Ocean, established in 1917. The Spanish knew of the region in the 16th century but did not settle permanently here until the 17th century. Part of the province of NUEVA GALICIA, its town of Compostela, dating from 1535, became the first capital. Pre-Columbian clay figures of naturalistic style have been discovered in the state.

NAZARETH [Arabic: **En Nasira**; Hebrew: **Nazerat**] (Israel) Town and capital of Northern district, approx. 18 mi SE of Haifa. The biblical home of Joseph, Mary, and Jesus, it is a Christian pilgrimage center. It changed hands often during the Crusades and was taken in 1263 by the Muslim Baybars of the MAMLUK EMPIRE, who massacred its Christian populace. It became part of the OTTOMAN EMPIRE in 1517. Near the end of World War I it was retaken by the British and became part of modern Israel in 1948.

NAZCA [**Nasca**] (Peru) Town in Ica department, on the SW coast. The Nazca culture throve here in the river valleys from the second century BC until the seventh century AD, when it was replaced by the Huari, and eventually, the INCA EMPIRE. Archaeological excavations have been carried out here. Aerial observations have discovered outlines of huge animals traced on the arid tablelands, meant probably for sky gods to see. Other lines may have had an astronomical use.

NAZERAT. See NAZARETH.

N'DJAMENA [former: **Fort-Lamy**] (Chad) City in the SW, on the border with Cameroon, at the confluence of the Chari and Logone rivers. Founded by the French in 1900 as a base for conquest of the central SUDAN region, it was named after a French explorer. Fort-Lamy was a Free French base in World War II. Territorial capital since 1920 and national capital since independence in 1960, the city was renamed N'Djamena in 1973.

NEAGH, LOUGH (Northern Ireland) Largest lake in the British Isles, 153 sq. mi. Excavations at the northwest corner of the lake have established that Mesolithic man first settled in Ireland at this spot between 8000 and 7000 BC. According to legend, the lake contains a former town, now submerged beneath its waters and occasionally glimpsed. See also IRELAND.

NEAH BAY (United States) Village on an inlet of the Juan de Fuca Strait, NW WASHINGTON. The earliest European settlement in present Washington state was established here by SPAIN in 1791; but it lasted only briefly. It is now the chief town of an Indian reservation.

NEANDERTHAL (West Germany) Valley E of Düsseldorf, in North Rhine-Westphalia. Skeletal remains of the prehistoric Neanderthal Man were first discovered here in 1856. He lived in Europe during the last glacial age, and other examples of his fossil bones have since been found in many localities in the Middle East, North Africa, and Siberia.

NEAPOLIS, Greece. See KAVALLA.

NEAPOLIS, Italy. See NAPLES.

NEAPOLIS, Jordan. See NABLUS.

NEAPOLIS, Tunisia. See NABEUL.

NEAPOLIS, USSR. See SIMFEROPOL.

NEÁ PSARÁ. See ERETRIA.

NEAR ISLANDS. See ALEUTIAN ISLANDS.

NEBO, MOUNT [**Pisgah**] (Jordan) Mountain, E of the N end of the DEAD SEA, in ancient PALESTINE, in modern N Jordan. According to the Bible Moses viewed the Promised Land from this location just before he died. It is mentioned in the Old Testament books of Numbers 21:20 and 23:14 and Deuteronomy 3:27.

NEBRASKA (United States) State in the central Great Plains. It was admitted to the Union as the 37th state in 1867. Nebraska is a Sioux word meaning both "water" and "flat," and refers to the PLATTE RIVER. South Dakota is to the N, Wyoming and Colorado to the W, Kansas to the S, and Iowa and Missouri to the E.

People have farmed Nebraska's plains since prehistoric times, but after they acquired horses through the Spanish the Indians, chiefly Pawnees, relied more on hunting buffalo for food. The first European in the area was probably Francisco Vásquez de Coronado in 1541. In the 18th century French fur traders were here, but there was no further development until after the United States acquired the region from France by the LOUISIANA PURCHASE of 1803. Meriwether Lewis and William Clark, exploring that vast purchase, were in Nebraska in 1804; the explorer Zebulon M. Pike came through in 1806; and Stephen H. Long headed a scientific expedition in 1820. The first trading post was apparently established by Manuel Lisa, a fur trader, in 1813; and the first permanent settlement was at Bellevue, near present Omaha, c.1825.

When steamboats began appearing on the MISSOURI RIVER, activity increased, and Fort Atkinson of 1819 and other forts were built to protect settlers from the Indians. By the 1840's and 1850's deep wagon wheel ruts along the Platte River valley traced the routes of pioneers headed for the OREGON TRAIL and for CALIFORNIA and of Mormons bound for UTAH. Nebraskans sold them food and pack animals. By the controversial Kansas-Nebraska Act of 1854 Nebraska Territory was established, extending at that time north to the border with CANADA. The territory was strongly pro-Union in the Civil War. A large-scale land boom took place after 1867 when the Union Pacific Railroad began laying its tracks across the state to join in 1869 with the Central Pacific and create the first transcontinental railroad. Settlement was also encouraged by the Homestead Act of 1862. The railroads brought into being cow towns, such as Ogallala and Schuyler, shipping points on the overland trails.

In the meantime, in 1859, the Pawnee Indians had been subdued, but it was 1880 before warfare with the Sioux and other tribes was over. As settlement increased the ranchers and the farmers fought over the use of the land, and the farmers won. Both suffered often from natural disasters: the bitter winter of 1880/81, insect plagues from 1856 to 1875, prairie fires, and a severe drought in 1890. The farmers' discontent led to their participation in the Granger Movement, and the first national convention of the Populist Party gathered in OMAHA in 1882. The party held the governorship from 1895 to 1901.

Prosperity returned in the early 20th century; and the state passed progressive laws, built roads, and inaugurated conservation measures. World War I created a great demand for food, but the resulting overexpansion of credit made the Great Depression of the 1930's even more painful. Added to this was a drought. The New Deal, World War II, and its aftermath again helped agriculture, which is still primary in Nebraska. The Missouri Basin Project, authorized by Congress in 1944, has brought benefits in flood control, irrigation, and hydroelectric power. Nebraska is unique among the states in having a one-house legislature. The state has voted Democratic in presidential elections only once since 1940. LINCOLN became the capital in 1867.

NEBRASKA CITY (United States) City on the MISSOURI RIVER, 55 mi S of Omaha, SE NEBRASKA. Founded in 1850 and incorporated in 1854, it became a thriving shipping center on the OREGON TRAIL. John Brown's Cave, a haven for runaway slaves before the Civil War, is located in the area, as is the former residence of J. Sterling Morton, founder of Arbor Day in 1872.

NEBRASKA TERRITORY. See NEBRASKA.

NEBRIJA. See LEBRIJA.

NEBRISSA. See LEBRIJA.

NEBRITZA. See LEBRIJA.

NEBRIXA. See LEBRIJA.

NECESSITY, FORT. See FORT NECESSITY.

NEENAH (United States) City on Lake Winnebago, 38 mi SW of Green Bay, E WISCONSIN. Its name, derived from that of an Indian village, meant "water." Founded in 1843 and incorporated in 1873, it became a flour- and paper-milling center in the mid-19th century. James Duane Doty, second governor of Wisconsin Territory, resided here at Doty Cabin, now restored.

NEERWINDEN (Belgium) Village in Liège province, 22 mi NW of Liège. The French, led by the duke of Luxembourg, suffered heavy losses but defeated William III of ENGLAND here on July 19, 1693 during the War of the Grand Alliance. On March 18, 1793, during the French Revolution, Gen. Charles Dumouriez of FRANCE was defeated by the Austrians and defected to them.

NEGAPATAM. See NAGAPATTINAM.

NEGAPATTINAM. See NAGAPATTINAM.

NEGAUNEE (United States) Industrial city, 10 mi SW of Marquette, NW MICHIGAN. Iron ore was discovered here in 1844, and the city was founded the following year. It grew rapidly as an iron-production center, was incorporated in 1873, and is now a leader in iron-ore research.

NEGEB. See NEGEV.

NEGERI [Negri Sembilan] (Malaysia) State in the S MALAY PENINSULA, on the Strait of Malacca. It was separated in 1777 from the sultanate of Riau and Johor to form a confederation, which eventually included nine states. It was under British control from 1874 to 1889 and became one of the Federated Malay States in 1896. It was occupied by JAPAN from 1942 to 1945 during World War II.

NEGEV [Negeb] (Israel) Desert region in S Israel, extending S to EILAT on the Red Sea. Much severe fighting took place here in 1948/49 as Egyptian and Israeli forces clashed after the partition of PALESTINE. It was assigned to Israel in 1948.

NEGOMBO (Sri Lanka) Old colonial town and port at the mouth of the Negombo Lagoon, 19 mi N of Colombo. Colonized by Portugal, it was taken by the Dutch in 1644 and finally seized by the British in 1796. The long Dutch tenure is reflected in many fine examples of 17th-century architecture. Sri Lanka's international airport is nearby.

NEGRI SEMBILAN. See NEGERI.

NEGROPONT. See CHALCIS, EUBOEA.

NEGROPONTE. See EUBOEA.

NEHAVEND. See NAHÁVAND.

NEI MENG KU TZU-CHIH CH-'Ü. See INNER MONGOLIA.

NEIN. See NAIN.

NEISSE. See NYSA.

NEISSE RIVER [Lausitzer Neisse, Lusatian Neisse] (Czechoslovakia) River, 159 mi long, rising in the Sudetic Mts, in the NW, and flowing N to the ODER RIVER in East Germany. It has formed part of the German-Polish border, from the Czech border to the Oder junction, since the POTSDAM Conference in 1945 following World War II. See also ODER-NEISSE LINE.

NEJD (Saudi Arabia) Central region of Saudi Arabia, known formerly as the Turkish sultanate of Nejd. It was the stronghold from 1889 to 1912 of ibn-Saud, leader of the Wahabi movement. From here, ibn-Saud obtained independence for Nejd, which he used as a base for future conquests of the HEJAZ and AL HASA, all of which were incorporated into his new kingdom of Saudi Arabia in 1932.

NELSON RIVER (Canada) River, 400 mi long, flowing NE from N Lake Winnipeg, through central MANITOBA, to HUDSON BAY at Port Nelson. Discovered by Sir Thomas Button in 1612, it was used for many years as a fur-trading, inland water route. Hudson's Bay Company established its first trading post, PORT NELSON, on the river in 1670, and it operated nearby YORK FACTORY, also a trading post, from 1682 to 1957. The river has been developed for hydroelectric power, and its Kettle Rapids dam is among the largest in Canada.

NEMACOLIN'S PATH (United States) Old Indian road connecting the Potomac and Monongahela rivers, from modern Cumberland in MARYLAND to Brownsville in PENNSYLVANIA. Cleared c.1750 by Delaware Indian Chief Nemacolin, it was an important military route in the colonial era. George Washington and Gen. Braddock used it during the French and Indian War in the mid-18th century, and it was then known as Braddock's Road until the construction, c.1800, of the NATIONAL ROAD on the same route. See also CUMBERLAND ROAD.

NEMAN RIVER [Nyeman] [German: **Memel**; Lithuanian: **Nemanus**; Polish: **Niemen**] (USSR) River, 582 mi long, rising S of Minsk in Belorussian SSR, and flowing N and NW into the SE BALTIC SEA. Its lower basin has been the scene of German-Lithuanian conflict for centuries, especially from 1919 to 1924. Napoleon and Alexander I of Russia met on a raft in the middle of the river before signing the Treaty of Tilsit (SOVETSK) in 1807. The Germans, led by Gen. Hindenburg, were defeated in September 1914 by the Russians in a World War I battle fought in a region between GRODNO and KAUNAS during World War I. See BELORUSSIA, LITHUANIA.

NEMANUS. See NEMAN RIVER.

NEMAUSUS. See NÎMES.

NEMEA (Greece) Ancient valley in N Argolis. The modern town of Nemea is in the valley, 15 mi SW of Corinth, NE PELOPONNESUS. It was the mythological site of the slaying of the Nemean lion by Hercules. At the temple of Zeus in the valley the Nemean Games were held every second and fourth year of each Olympiad, beginning in 573 BC. The prizes were crowns of wild celery. Excavations of the temple and of the games area have been carried on here. In 394 BC SPARTA won a battle against CORINTH in this region. See also ARGOS, DELPHI, OLYMPIA.

NEMETACUM. See ARRAS.

NEMETOCENNA. See ARRAS.

NEMI, LAKE [ancient: **Nemorensis Lacus**, Italian: **Lago di Nemi**] (Italy) Crater lake in the Alban Hills, SE of Rome. The ruins of a temple of Diana are located on the lakeshores below the town of Nemi, where there was also a sacred forest. Two huge Roman pleasure barges of the Roman Emperor Caligula (37–41 AD) were raised from the depths of the lake in 1930 and 1931. The remains of the ships, in their museum, were destroyed by the retreating Germans in World War II. The lake was a favorite subject of classical revival and Romantic landscape painters.

NEMI-NESU. See HERACLEOPOLIS.

NEMORENSIS LACUS. See NEMI, LAKE.

NEMOURS (France) Town near Melun, Seine-et-Marne department, a favorite resort of Parisians. Held by several members of royal families, it was a medieval holding of the dukes of Nemours, notably from 1489 to 1512 of Gaston de Foix, a nephew of Louis XII and brilliant general in the Italian Wars, where he was killed. It had been held by the counts of ARMAGNAC and from 1528 to 1659 by a branch of the house of SAVOY. At Nemours in 1585 Henry III took back his concessions to the Protestants during the Wars of Religion. There is a restored 12th-century castle here.

NENAGH (Irish Republic) Urban district in TIPPERARY. It contains the ruins of Nenagh Castle, built c.1200 by King John of ENGLAND, and those of a 13th-century monastery, destroyed in 1650 by a Parliamentarian army in the English Civil War. It was burned by Jacobite rebels in 1688.

NEO PAPHOS. See PAPHOS.

NEPAL Independent kingdom in central Asia, landlocked and isolated by the HIMALAYAS, on the NE border of India, bordered on the N by Tibet and China. A cultural and religious center since the fourth century AD, it developed from the eighth through the 11th century as a haven for Buddhist and Hindu Rajputs from INDIA, the latter establishing the kingdom of GURKHA. In the second half of the 18th century Gurkha King Prithvi Narayan Shah conquered the KATMANDU valley from the long-established ruling Mallas, ethnically belonging to the native Newar majority. In 1815 GREAT BRITAIN turned back the Gurkha expansion into northern India, and it finally recognized Nepal's independence in 1923. As prime ministers, the Rana family held power from 1846 to 1950. Nepal exacted tribute from TIBET until 1956. A constitutional form of government replaced autocratic rule following a successful democratic revolt in 1950, but this was modified in the 1960's, during the regime of King Mahendra. Upon

Mahendra's death in 1972, his son, Prince Birendra, took the throne. In May 1980 Nepal's first election ratified Birendra's monarchy and a parliament. The king has promised full-scale democracy in the future. Basically isolationist over the years, Nepal aided the British during the Indian Mutiny of 1857/58 and in World War I. It has accepted financial aid from the USSR, the UNITED STATES, and CHINA. See also PATAN (Nepal).

NEPHI (United States) City in W UTAH, 38 mi S of Provo. Settled in 1851, it became a primary target of Indian raids, before the Mormon leader Brigham Young negotiated a peace treaty nearby with Chief Walker in 1854.

NÉRAC (France) Small town on the Baîse River, Lot-et-Garonne department. Once the capital city of the dukes of Albret and a Protestant stronghold during the Reformation, it was taken by the Catholic League in 1562. Seventeen years later the Catholics signed a peace agreement with the Protestant Huguenots here. In 1580 the town became the military base of Henry of Navarre, before he became king of France as Henry IV. It took part in a Protestant uprising in 1621 but was taken by Louis XIII and its fortifications dismantled. Thereafter, as a Protestant town in Catholic France, it was neglected and ruined. Part of the castle in which Henry of Navarre lived survives.

NERBUDDA. See NARBADA.

NERCHINSK (USSR) Town in S central Chita oblast, approx. 135 mi E of Chita, Russian SFSR. A Russian Far Eastern outpost from the 17th to 19th centuries, it was founded in 1654. The Treaty of Nerchinsk signed here in 1689 was the first treaty that CHINA entered into with a European nation. Until 1858 it established the Russo-Chinese border, and Nerchinsk became an important center of the caravan trade that resulted between the two countries.

NÉRIS LES BAINS. See MONTLUCON.

NERIUM PROMONTORIUM. See FINISTERRE, CAPE.

NESVIZH [*Polish:* **Niewież**] (USSR) Town in W Belorussian SSR, 44 mi SE of Novogrudok. Chartered in 1586 as capital of an independent duchy, it was contested for centuries by SWEDEN and RUSSIA, passing to the latter in 1945. Its 16th-century castle was a stronghold of the Polish-Lithuanian princes of Radziwill.

NETANYA [**Natanya, Nathania**] (Israel) City on the Israeli coast, on the Mediterranean Sea, approx. 35 mi SW of Haifa. Founded in 1929, it was named for Nathan Straus, American philanthropist, who had contributed to educational and social causes in PALESTINE. One of the earliest Jewish settlements, Zichron Ya'akov, was established nearby in 1882. Baron Edmond de Rothschild is now buried there.

NETHERLANDS ANTILLES [*former:* **Curaçao**] (Netherlands) Overseas Territory in the WEST INDIES, in the CARIBBEAN SEA. It contains the islands of CURAÇAO, Bonaire, and ARUBA, off the South American coast, and several of the northern Leeward Islands. A colony until 1954, when it attained territorial status, it was the scene of civil disorders on Curaçao in 1969. The capital is WILLEMSTAD, on Curaçao. See also SABA, SAINT EUSTATIUS, SAINT MARTIN.

NETHERLANDS EAST INDIES. See INDONESIA, REPUBLIC OF.

NETHERLANDS GUIANA. See SURINAME.

NETHERLANDS INDIES. See INDONESIA, REPUBLIC OF.

NETHERLANDS NEW GUINEA. See IRIAN BARAT.

NETHERLANDS, THE Kingdom of NW Europe, on the NORTH SEA, N of Belgium and W of West Germany. Originally one of the Low Countries, the Netherlands began to emerge as an independent national unit in the late 16th century and quickly became an important maritime power, with many overseas possessions. With much of its land below sea level, it is today one of Europe's smallest nations, although additional land has been gained from the sea by remarkable land reclamation programs. The capital, AMSTERDAM, is an important European city and port with many fine art museums.

At the time of the ROMAN EMPIRE only the southern part of the country, below the RHINE RIVER, was occupied by the Romans; and the northern part was inhabited by Teutonic Frisian tribes. Between the fourth and eighth centuries AD the whole region passed to the FRANKISH EMPIRE; and after the death of Charlemagne in 814 it became part of the eastern Frankish kingdom, which was later incorporated into the HOLY ROMAN EMPIRE. In the medieval period the counts of HOLLAND were powerful in the area, and in the 14th century the country passed to the dukes of BURGUNDY. In the 15th century many Dutch cities enjoyed great prosperity and autonomy as members of the HANSEATIC LEAGUE, but this independence was threatened in 1555 when the Low Countries passed to Philip II of SPAIN.

Spanish rule was made all the more intolerable when the Inquisition was introduced to stamp out Calvinism, and in 1562 the Dutch revolted. In the ensuing struggle, led by William of Orange, the seven provinces north and immediately south of the Rhine united as the UNITED PROVINCES at the Union of UTRECHT of 1579 and declared their independence in 1581, thus laying the foundations of the modern Dutch state. The Dutch were again at war with Spain in the Thirty Years War from 1618 to 1648, which ended with Spain's recognition of Dutch independence at the Peace of WESTPHALIA in 1648. In the meantime the Dutch had won territories overseas, in the WEST INDIES, the East Indies, INDIA, and the Americas. At home Jews and Huguenots were encouraged to settle, and their business talents helped to lay the foundations for the great wealth of the United Provinces in the 17th century.

The 17th century was also the golden age of Dutch art with such painters as Rembrandt, Vermeer, and Frans Hals working in Amsterdam, DELFT, and HAARLEM respectively. Inevitably the worldwide commercial activities of the Dutch led to conflict with FRANCE and ENGLAND, rival colonial powers, so that by the end of the 17th century the country was exhausted by repeated wars. In the 18th century the importance of the United Provinces was diminished further by the growing might of her colonial rivals. In the French Revolutionary Wars the French overran the country in 1794/95, setting up the BATAVIAN REPUBLIC which, in 1806 was given by Napoleon to his brother Louis Bonaparte as the Kingdom of Holland.

The neat Dutch buildings of Middleburg Abbey on Walcheren Island, the Netherlands, near Vlissingen (Flushing). Middleburg was one of the ports of the medieval Hanseatic League.

After the Napoleonic Wars the Congress of VIENNA in 1815 joined the United Provinces to the Austrian Netherlands under a single monarch. After BELGIUM revolted in 1830 this arrangement was amended by the LONDON Conference of 1839, which established the separate states of Belgium and the Netherlands in their present form. During the latter half of the 19th century the Netherlands experienced rapid growth due to widespread industrialization. The country remained neutral during World War I, but at the start of World War II was overrun by GERMANY without formal declaration of war in May 1940. Under the Nazi occupation 104,000 Dutch Jews were deported and exterminated, but numbers were sheltered by the populace. In the postwar years the Netherlands, despite the loss of its major colonies, INDONESIA, NEW GUINEA, and SURINAME,

has enjoyed commercial expansion and has played an active role in the European Economic Community and in NATO. See also BRABANT, FLANDERS, FRIESLAND, LUXEMBOURG, SPANISH NETHERLANDS.

NETHER STOWEY (England) Small village in Somerset, 7 mi WNW of Bridgwater, with a 15th-century manor house. It is distinguished by the fact that the English Romantic poet Samuel Taylor Coleridge (1772–1834) spent several years here during which he wrote his famous poem *The Rime of the Ancient Mariner*.

NETTUNO (Italy) Resort town on the Tyrrhenian Sea, 31 mi SSE of Rome, Roma province, LATIUM region. The Treaty of Nettuno was signed here in 1925 by Italy and YUGOSLAVIA. On Jan. 22, 1944 the town was taken, along with neighboring ANZIO, as Allied troops began their campaign aimed at ROME in World War II.

NEUBRANDENBURG [New Brandenburg] (East Germany) City and capital of its district, on the Tollense Lake, 74 mi E of Schwerin. Fortified in 1248 by the margraves of BRANDENBURG, it became part of MECKLENBURG in 1292. From 1359 to 1471 it was the capital of a duchy. During World War II it suffered heavy bombing.

NEUBREISACH. See NEUF-BRISACH.

NEUBURG [Neuburg an der Donau] (West Germany) Town on the DANUBE RIVER, approx. 10 mi W of Ingolstadt in BAVARIA. Held by Bavaria, it became part of the PALATINATE in the 16th century and again in the 18th century, until it was returned to Bavaria in 1777. In between it was the capital of the small independent principality of Neuburg.

NEUBURG AN DER DONAU. See NEUBURG.

NEUCHÂTEL (Switzerland) Town and capital of NEUCHÂTEL Canton, on LAKE OF NEUCHÂTEL, 25 mi W of Bern. It has been the cultural, administrative, and aristocratic center of the canton since the 12th century, when its castle was begun. A Gothic church from the same era is also here, as is a renowned university established in 1838.

NEUCHÂTEL [*German:*** Neuenburg]** (Switzerland) Canton in the JURA MOUNTAINS, in the NW. It was part of BURGUNDY in the 10th century, was ruled later by counts of the HOLY ROMAN EMPIRE, and in 1504 was taken by a French family, the Longuevilles. In 1648 it became independent, but in 1707 it chose as its prince Frederick I of PRUSSIA. Joining the Swiss Confederation in 1815 as the only monarchical canton, it abolished the monarchical connection within the canton after the 1848 revolutions, replacing it with a local republican form of government.

NEUCHÂTEL, LAKE OF [*ancient:*** Eburodunensis; ***German:*** Neuenburgersee]** (Switzerland) Large lake in S NEUCHÂTEL canton, bordering on the JURA MOUNTAINS, with its chief cities NEUCHÂTEL and YVERDON. The prehistoric site of LA TÈNE, at the east of the lake, excavated between 1907 and 1917, has given its name to the late second period of the European Iron

Age, ending at the Roman period in Europe. Rome conquered this region in 58 BC, giving the lake its ancient name.

NEUENBURG. See NEUCHATEL.

NEUENBURGERSEE. See NEUCHATEL, LAKE OF.

NEUF-BRISACH [*German:* **Neubreisach**] (France) Town near Colmar, NE Haut-Rhin department. Established as a military outpost by Louis XIV in 1699, it was incorporated in 1870 into a newly unified GERMANY until after World War I, when it was returned to France.

NEUF-CHÂTEAU (France) Town in Vosges department, on the MEUSE RIVER, 35 mi NW of Épinal, NE France. Its castle, now in ruins, was the medieval residence of the dukes of LORRAINE. There are also several medieval churches here.

NEUHÄUSEL. See NOVÉ ZÁMKY.

NEUILLY-PLAISANCE (France) Industrial town, a suburb E of PARIS. During the Franco-Prussian War German and French troops disputed the town in several battles in 1870 and 1871.

NEUILLY-SUR-SEINE (France) Wealthy suburb of PARIS, in Hauts-de-Seine department. The Treaty of Neuilly was signed here on Nov. 27, 1919 by BULGARIA and the Allies at the end of World War I. Its terms also affected GREECE, RUMANIA, and YUGOSLAVIA.

NEU LAUENBURG. See DUKE OF YORK ISLANDS.

NEUMARKT. See TÎRGU-MUREȘ.

NEU-MECKLENBURG. See NEW IRELAND.

NEUNKIRCHEN (West Germany) City in SAARLAND, on the Blies River, 12 mi NE of Saarbrücken. First mentioned in 1281, it was incorporated in 1922. The center of an important coal-mining region since the 19th century, it was a chief target of Allied bombing in World War II and was severely damaged.

NEU-POMMERN. See NEW BRITAIN.

NEURUPPIN (East Germany) Industrial city in BRANDENBURG, 40 mi NW of West Berlin. A city by 1256, it was capital of Ruppin county until 1524. It was almost wiped out by fire in 1787. As crown prince, Frederick the Great lived here from 1732 to 1736.

NEUSALZ AN DER ODER. See NOWA SÓL.

NEUSANDEZ. See NOWY SĄCZ.

NEUSATZ. See NOVI SAD.

NEUSIEDLER, LAKE [*German:* **Neusiedlersee**; *Hungarian:* **Fertö tó**] (Austria, Hungary) Lake on the border of AUSTRIA and HUNGARY, 23 mi long. Prehistoric remains of lake dwellers have been discovered in the area. It was formerly in Hungary, but most of the lake was ceded to Austria in 1922 with BURGENLAND.

NEUSIEDLERSEE. See NEUSIEDLER LAKE.

NEUSOHL. See BANSKA BYSTRICA.

NEUSS, Switzerland. See NYON.

NEUSS [*ancient:* **Novaesium**] (West Germany) City and port, connected by canal to the RHINE RIVER, 5 mi W of Düsseldorf, in North Rhine-Westphalia. Once a Roman fortress, it was chartered as a town in the 12th century. It withstood an 11-month siege in 1474 by Charles the Bold of BURGUNDY and was leveled by the duke of Parma in 1586 during the Dutch wars of independence. It passed to PRUSSIA in 1815, after the Napoleonic Wars. In World War II it was heavily damaged before the Allies occupied it on March 2, 1945.

NEUSTADT. See PRUDNIK.

NEUSTADT AN DER HAARDT. See NEUSTADT AN DER WEINSTRASSE.

NEUSTADT AN DER WEINSTRASSE [*ancient:* **Nova Civitas**; *former:* **Neustadt an der Haardt**; *medieval:* **Niewenstat**] (West Germany) City in Rhineland-Palatinate, 18 mi SW of Mannheim. It was first mentioned in 1235 and was chartered in 1275. It was often a battle site during the Thirty Years War of 1618 to 1648 and was captured many times. It was occupied by FRANCE during the War of the Grand Alliance between 1688 and 1697 and again during the French Revolutionary Wars from 1793 to 1795. On March 22, 1945 it was taken by the Allies at the end of World War II.

NEUSTETTIN. See SZCZECINEK.

NEUSTRELITZ (East Germany) Transportation center and city in Neubrandenburg district, 61 mi NW of West Berlin. It was founded in 1733 as the capital of former Mecklenburg-Strelitz to replace Strelitz, the state's previous capital, which burned down in 1712 and is now a suburb of Neustrelitz. An 18th-century palace, the former ducal residence, is located in the city. See also MECKLENBURG.

NEUSTRIA (France) Former western kingdom of the Franks during the Merovingian period, now in northern France, centering around PARIS and SOISSONS. Created after the death of Clovis in 511 AD, it was constantly at war with the eastern portion of the kingdom, AUSTRASIA. Following many brief unifications, the two kingdoms were finally brought together under Pepin of Heristal from Austrasia, after he subdued Neustria in 687. His descendants, the Carolingians, subsequently ruled the united FRANKISH EMPIRE.

NEUTRA. See NITRA.

NEUVE-CHAPELLE (France) Town in Pas-de-Calais department, 7 mi N of Béthune. The British occupied the town after a bloody battle near the start of World War I, from March 10 to 13, 1915. During the battle they lost 13,000 soldiers and failed to take the ridge above the town due to a heavy artillery barrage, the first of the war. See also NEUVILLE-ST.-VAAST.

NEUVE-ÉGLISE [*Flemish:* **Nieuwkerke**] (Belgium) Village in West Flanders province, near Ypres. It was the scene of fierce World War I combat on April 12 and 13, 1918 after the third battle of YPRES.

NEUVILLE-SAINT-VAAST (France) Town in Pas-de-Calais department, near VIMY RIDGE, 4 mi N of ARRAS. It was the scene of heavy fighting between the British and Germans in the early stages of World War I, especially in May 1915. The town was completely destroyed and then rebuilt after the war.

NEUWIED (West Germany) Port on the RHINE RIVER, Rhineland-Palatinate, 7 mi NW of Koblenz. Once a Roman military post, it was founded in 1653 where the palace of Frederick III, count of Wied, had been established in 1648. Roman ruins have been excavated nearby.

NEVADA (United States) State in the W, mostly in the Great Basin, with California on the S and W Oregon and Idaho to the N, and Utah and Arizona on the E. It was admitted to the Union in 1864 as the 36th state. Nevada is a Spanish word for "snowed upon," a term used to describe mountains covered with snow.

Several Spanish explorers were near the area in the 1770's, but Father Silvestre Vélez de Escalante gave a discouraging report on this arid, and in places very mountainous, country. Indians in the region, mostly Paiutes, were barely able to gain a living from the land. In the 1820's traders seeking furs were here; and in 1827 Jedediah S. Smith, one of the Mountain Men, crossed Nevada on his way to California. The next year Peter Skene Ogden of the Hudson's Bay Company discovered the HUMBOLDT RIVER, and in 1833 and 1834 Joseph Walker traveled along the Humboldt and over the Sierra Nevada to California. The first useful information about the region resulted from John C. Frémont's explorations of 1843 to 1845.

The United States acquired title to the area in 1848 as a result of the Mexican War. A group of Mormon pioneers founded Mormon Station c.1850, which was renamed Genoa in 1855, in the extreme western part. The next year, when Utah Territory was established, it included most of Nevada. The discovery of the COMSTOCK LODE in 1857, the richest silver deposit in the United States, and of gold in 1859 resulted in a rush of miners. Cities were founded that in a few years became ghost towns, such as VIRGINIA CITY. Large fortunes were made in silver by a few outside capitalists, but the state gained very little. Most of the men who sought riches became mine workers. By 1898 the lode was nearly abandoned. Nevada was made a separate territory in 1861, but not until 1866 were the present boundaries settled. The first transcontinental railroad came through in 1869.

The Ghost Dance originated here c.1870 among the Paiute Indians. The dance, invented by a leader named Wovoka, was part of the ritual of a religion that prophesied the end of the settlers' expansion, the return of the buffalo, and of Indian life as it had been in the past. The Ghost Dance inspired war against settlers all over the West. In the meantime, more silver was discovered in 1873, and in 1900 copper and gold were found as well. Through the 1870's to the 1890's the state citizens rabidly supported "cheap money," i.e., government purchase and coinage of silver in a favorable ratio to the value of gold. This movement linked up with that of the discontented farmers of the Midwest to support the Populist Party.

The first Federal irrigation project was undertaken in Nevada in 1907, and the mammoth HOOVER DAM was completed in 1936. In the 1950's the government began using Nevada's desert spaces for testing nuclear explosive devices. The state has voted Republican in the last four presidential elections ending in 1980. CARSON CITY is the capital; LAS VEGAS, where gambling was legalized in 1931, is the largest city; RENO claims to be "the divorce capital of the world."

NEVERS [*ancient:* **Noviodunum**] (France) Town and capital of Nièvre department, on the LOIRE RIVER, 38 mi ESE of Bourges. A former Roman military station, it was made the seat of a bishopric in 506 AD and became the medieval capital of the duchy of Nevers, or NIVERNAIS. It passed to the Gonzaga family in 1538 and was given by Cardinal Mazarin to his relatives, the Mancini family, in 1659. The convent where St. Bernadette-du-Banlay lived from 1860 to 1879 is here.

NEVILLE'S CROSS (England) Historic site near DURHAM, in Durham administrative county. In a battle fought here against invading Scots, the English king, Edward III, directed an army that on Oct. 17, 1346 defeated the forces of King David Bruce, who was captured at this time and later ransomed. See also HALIDON HILL.

NEVIS. See SAINT KITTS-NEVIS.

NEW ALBANY (United States) City on the OHIO RIVER, opposite LOUISVILLE, Kentucky, in S INDIANA. Founded in 1813 and incorporated in 1839, it developed into a major shipbuilding center in the 19th century. The famous riverboats *Robert E. Lee* and *Eclipse* were constructed at its shipyards.

NEW AMSTERDAM. See NEW YORK CITY.

NEW ARCHANGEL. See SITKA.

NEWARK (England) Town in Nottinghamshire, 16 mi NE of Nottingham. Located on the ancient FOSSE WAY, built by the Romans, it is the locus of a 12th- to 15th-century castle that was besieged several times during the English Civil War in the 17th century. King John died in the castle in 1216.

NEWARK (United States) City and port on the PASSAIC RIVER, 9 mi W of New York City, NE NEW JERSEY. Settled in 1666 by Puritans from the NEW HAVEN colony, it was originally intended to operate as a theocracy. In 1776 it served as a supply base for George Washington during the American Revolution. With the advent of the Morris Canal in 1832 and railroads in 1834/35, it became the region's foremost industrial center and was incorporated in 1836. There is an 18th- and 19th-century cathedral and an 18th-century church in the city. Stephen Crane, the writer, and Aaron Burr, who in 1806 killed Alexander Hamilton in a duel, were born here.

NEWARK (United States) Industrial city on the Licking River, 30 mi E of Columbus, central OHIO. Settled in 1802 and incorporated in 1826, it has important prehistoric Indian earthworks, called the Newark Earthworks, which include massive Indian mounds of the Mound Builders, and ancient weapon quarries.

NEW BARBADOS. See HACKENSACK.

NEW BEDFORD (United States) Port and city on Buzzard's Bay, 50 mi S of Boston, SE MASSACHUSETTS. Settled in 1640, it was set off from DARTMOUTH in 1787, when it was incorporated as a town. It became a major shipping and whaling port in the 18th and 19th centuries and was one of the world's greatest whaling centers in the late 1850's. It was attacked during the American Revolution by the British, who burned the town in 1778. The Seamen's Bethel, the scene of part of Herman Melville's novel *Moby Dick*, is in the city, along with the Bourne Whaling Museum.

NEW BERN (United States) City and port at the confluence of the Neuse and Trent rivers 100 miles SE of Raleigh, SE NORTH CAROLINA. Settled by Germans and Swiss in 1710 and incorporated in 1723, in 1774 it was the first fixed capital in the American colonies. The Colonial Assembly convened here from 1745 to 1761, as did the first provincial convention in 1774, which chose it as capital. Its port, fortified by the Confederacy, fell to Union forces under Gen. S.E. Burnside in March 1862 during the Civil War. There are many fine examples of colonial architecture here, including the former British governor's Tryon Palace, badly burned in 1798 but now restored.

NEW BEVERLY. See BURLINGTON.

NEW BRANDENBURG. See NEUBRANDENBURG.

NEW BRAUNFELS (United States) City on the Guadalupe River, 32 mi NE of San Antonio, S central TEXAS. It was settled in 1845 by Prince Carl von Solms-Braunfels and a large group of German immigrants. A local historical museum houses many pioneer artifacts. Today it is a textile city, using massive hydroelectric power.

NEW BRITAIN [*German:* **Neu-Pommern**] (Papua-New Guinea) Largest island of the BISMARCK ARCHIPELAGO, SW Pacific Ocean. Discovered by the English in 1700, it was colonized by GERMANY in 1884. AUSTRALIA took it during World War I and retained it from 1920 to 1941 as a League of Nations mandate. In January 1942 JAPAN seized it, and it became the scene of bitter fighting during World War II from 1943 to 1945. It was subjected to heavy U.S. air raids on Japanese positions here, followed by U.S. invasions in late 1943 to March 1944.

NEW BRITAIN (United States) City, 9 mi SW of Hartford, central CONNECTICUT. Settled in 1686 and incorporated in 1870, it flourished in the 18th century as a center for the manufacture of tin and brass products and continued to develop as an early industrial city of NEW ENGLAND.

NEW BRUNSWICK (Canada) Maritime province, on the Atlantic Ocean. Estevan Gómez from PORTUGAL is said to have been the first European to sail along the coast, in 1525. Jacques Cartier of FRANCE landed at Point Escuminac in 1534, and the first settlement was established at the mouth of the SAINT CROIX RIVER in 1604 by Samuel Sieur de Champlain and the Sieur de Monts. Present NOVA SCOTIA and the coast of New Brunswick were considered one region, called ACADIA by the French and Nova Scotia by the English. The two nations contested for the region until 1713 when the Treaty of UTRECHT gave GREAT BRITAIN control.

Some French Acadians remained in New Brunswick, and in 1755 at the start of the French and Indian War the British attacked and then expelled them. Others fled to the interior, and today approximately 40 percent of the people are Acadian by descent. The Treaty of PARIS of 1763 confirmed British possession of all of New Brunswick. After many Loyalists fled to this area at the end of the American Revolution, New Brunswick was organized as a separate colony in 1784. Beginning in 1838, the AROOSTOOK War threatened violence between inhabitants of the U.S. state of MAINE and New Brunswick in a bitter border dispute. However, the boundary line was settled peacefully by the Webster-Ashburton Treaty of 1842. Dissatisfaction with a royal governor led to the granting of self-rule in 1849, and in 1867 New Brunswick was one of four colonies that established the Dominion of Canada.

NEW BRUNSWICK (United States) Manufacturing city on the Raritan River, 22 mi SW of Newark, central NEW JERSEY. Settled by the English in 1681 and incorporated in 1784, it served as headquarters for both the British and the Continental armies during the American Revolution. Gen. Washington retreated to the city in 1776 and began his campaign to YORKTOWN from here in 1781. Railroad magnate Cornelius Vanderbuilt and poet Joyce Kilmer lived here. The main campus of Rutgers University is here; and Camp Kilmer, a major U.S. Army base in World War II, is nearby.

NEWBURGH (United States) Port on the HUDSON RIVER, 58 mi N of New York City, SE NEW YORK State. Settled in 1709 and incorporated as a city in 1865, it was important during the American Revolution and was Washington's headquarters from April 1782 to August 1783. It was here that the Continental Army was disbanded, and here Washington received correspondence urging him to become king. Many colonial houses remain in this former whaling port.

NEWBURY (England) Town on the Kennet River, Berkshire, 53 mi W of London. It was a major center in the Middle Ages, and a 16th-century cloth hall is now the town's museum. Two Civil War battles were fought here on Sept. 20, 1643 and Oct. 26, 1644, both resulting in slight gains by Oliver Cromwell's army.

NEWBURY (United States) Town and summer resort near the S New Hampshire border, close to and S of NEWBURYPORT, NE MASSACHUSETTS. Settled before 1635 and incorporated in that year, it was one of the first colonial settlements in Massachusetts.

NEWBURYPORT (United States) Port and city, at the mouth of the MERRIMACK RIVER, 35 mi NE of Boston and close to the New Hampshire border. Settled in 1635, it was separated from nearby NEWBURY and incorporated in 1764. Its silverware and rum industries date from the colonial era, and it was an early whaling and commercial center of NEW ENGLAND. Shipping dropped off after Jefferson's Embargo Act of 1808 and the War of 1812, but the town continued for years to build clipper ships. Several old houses here date from the mid-17th century, and the Old South church dates from 1756. Abolitionist William Lloyd Garrison was born here in 1805.

NEW CALEDONIA, Canada. See BRITISH COLUMBIA.

NEW CALEDONIA [*French:* **Nouvelle Calédonie**] (France) Island group in the SW Pacific Ocean, approx. 700 mi E of Australia. The main island was discovered by Captain Cook in 1774 and was annexed in 1853 by France, which maintained a penal colony here from 1864 to 1898. Beginning in 1942 it was the main Allied base in the South Pacific during World War II. The islands became a French territory in 1946. The capital is at NOUMÉA.

NEWCASTLE [*former:* **King's Town**] (Australia) Port and industrial city on the Hunter River and the Pacific Ocean, 100 mi NE of Sydney, NEW SOUTH WALES. Founded as a penal colony in 1804, it became a free settlement in 1821 and a municipality in 1859.

NEWCASTLE (South Africa) Industrial town in W NATAL, 150 mi NW of Durban. It was the main British military base during their war against the Boers in 1880 and 1881.

NEW CASTLE (United States) Industrial town on the DELAWARE RIVER, 5 mi S of Wilmington, N DELAWARE. Founded in 1651 and incorporated in 1875, it served as the state capital during the early part of the American Revolution. Peter Stuyvesant and a group of Dutch settlers built Fort Casimir here in 1651, and William Penn took control of the region in 1682. As a principal port on the Delaware River, it was overshadowed by nearby WILMINGTON in the 18th century. It has many historic buildings at its center, and its courthouse is one of the oldest public buildings in the nation.

NEW CASTLE (United States) Industrial city, 18 mi S of Muncie, E central INDIANA. Prehistoric Indian mounds are located nearby. Aviation pioneer Wilbur Wright's birthplace is close by at Millville.

NEW CASTLE (United States) Industrial city on the Shenango River, 44 mi NW of Pittsburgh, W PENNSYLVANIA. Founded c.1800 and incorporated in 1869, it is the location of the White Homestead, a strategic antebellum Underground Railroad station for runaway slaves.

NEWCASTLE-UNDER-LYME (England) Town in the POTTERIES district of Staffordshire, just W of Stoke-on-Trent. It was chartered in 1173, and the ruins of its 12th-century castle are still standing. Roman remains are nearby at Chesterton. Keele University is close by.

NEWCASTLE UPON TYNE [*ancient:* **Pons Aelii**] (England) City in Tyne and Wear and admin. hq. of Northumberland, a large industrial city on the Tyne River, 83 mi N of Leeds. Growing up on the site of a Roman military station along HADRIAN'S WALL, it was chartered in 1216 and became a famous coal-shipping center after the 13th century, giving rise to the saying "bringing coals to Newcastle" to mean any superfluous action. Duke Robert of Normandy, the son of William the Conqueror, built the castle here in the 11th century that gave the town its present name. Parts of the castle, dating from 1177, still stand. Charles I was imprisoned in Newcastle in 1646.

NEW CREEK. See KEYSER.

NEW DELHI (India) City and capital of India, Delhi territory, on the Jumna River, 5 mi S of ancient DELHI. Built as the new capital of British India to replace CALCUTTA, it was designed on a grandiose plan by Sir Edwin Lutyens and others as an administrative center, with imposing avenues and the enormous Government House for the viceroy. Begun in 1912 by order of King George V and completed in 1929, it was officially opened in 1931, only 17 years before Great Britain gave India its independence and withdrew. Mahatma Gandhi was assassinated here by a Hindu fanatic in 1948.

NEW DORCHESTER. See WINDSOR.

NEW ECHOTA (United States) Former Indian town, now marked by a monument, NE of Calhoun, NW GEORGIA. It was the site of a village, the one-time capital of the Cherokee nation from 1819 to 1835. The Treaty of New Echota, forced on the Cherokees by the United States and signed on Dec. 29, 1835, provided for the removal of the Indians to the West and the taking over of the village as well as all Cherokee lands east of the MISSISSIPPI RIVER. The Cherokees, one of the Five Civilized Tribes, had published a newspaper, *The Cherokee Phoenix*, in New Echota in 1828, printed with the Cherokee alphabet devised by an Indian, Sequoyah.

NEW EDEN. See HARVARD, Massachusetts.

NEW ENGLAND (United States) Region in the extreme NE of the country, consisting of six states: CONNECTICUT, MAINE, MASSACHUSETTS, NEW HAMPSHIRE, RHODE ISLAND, and VERMONT. Known as Nurembega on early charts, Capt. John Smith, the English explorer, saw the region in 1614 and named it New England. It was the second region of permanent English settlement in North America, preceded only by VIRGINIA. The region was, in fact, officially named Northern Virginia by a grant of James I in 1606. In 1620 the Pilgrims established a colony at PLYMOUTH, in present Massachusetts. In 1686 the English government formed the Dominion of New England, comprising all the present states except Vermont, but this arrangement lasted only until 1689.

The enterprising New Englanders, who came to be called "Yankees," made the region a busy shipbuilding, trading, fishing, and whaling center. At the time of the American Revolution they were especially patriotic, but during the War of 1812, when commerce was hurt, a convention at HARTFORD, Connecticut considered secession; nevertheless New Englanders took an active part in the expansion into the NORTHWEST TERRITORY. America's Industrial Revolution began early here, along river courses such as the MERRIMACK or NAUGATUCK, and in textile centers such as LOWELL, Massachusetts or WATERBURY, Connecticut. For much of the 19th century, New England led the nation in culture, education, and devotion to humanitarian movements, such as the abolition of slavery, the area around BOSTON, Massachusetts being particularly rich in achievement.

Major cities in New England are: Hartford, NEW HAVEN, and Waterbury, Connecticut; AUGUSTA, BANGOR, and PORTLAND, Maine; Boston, SPRINGFIELD, and WORCESTER, Massachusetts; MANCHESTER and

PORTSMOUTH, New Hampshire; PROVIDENCE, Rhode Island; BURLINGTON, MONTPELIER, and RUTLAND, Vermont.

NEW FAIRFIELD. See BRIDGEPORT.

NEW FOREST (England) Wooded district in Hampshire, W of Southampton. In 1079 William the Conqueror placed it under forest laws, thus bringing it under the direct control of the crown. Its main use was as a royal hunting preserve, one of a number of such royal forests, but many warships were constructed from its tall oaks in subsequent years. New Forest is now in part a public park.

NEWFOUNDLAND (Canada) Province of the Dominion consisting of the island of Newfoundland in the Gulf of the SAINT LAWRENCE RIVER, and LABRADOR, a mainland area to the N. The Vikings reached both Labrador and Newfoundland c.1000 and probably spent the winter of 1001 on the island, where a settlement, L'ANSE AUX MEADOWS, has been excavated. The island was rediscovered in 1497 by John Cabot of ENGLAND. Gaspar Corte-Real of PORTUGAL may have touched on both Labrador and Newfoundland in 1500 and 1501, and Jacques Cartier of FRANCE was probably here in 1524. Sir Humphrey Gilbert claimed Newfoundland for England in 1583, by which time it had become an international fishing station, mostly for the cod fleet.

The first settlers arrived in 1610 under the leadership of John Guy, and in 1621 Sir George Calvert, Lord Baltimore, established a settlement at PLACENTIA on Placentia Bay. Later he settled at FERRYLAND, but in 1629 gave up his land in favor of a grant that became the state of MARYLAND after the American Revolution. The French and the English contested the island, which changed hands several times. It was granted to GREAT BRITAIN by the Treaty of UTRECHT in 1713, and possession was confirmed by the Treaty of PARIS in 1763. Newfoundland was governed by British naval officers until 1824. Some self-government was introduced in 1832 and more in 1855.

Newfoundland voters rejected union with the Dominion in 1869. The region was hard hit by the Great Depression of the 1930's; Newfoundland's government was suspended and Great Britain took control. On Aug. 14, 1941, on board a British battleship in Placentia Bay, President Franklin D. Roosevelt of the UNITED STATES and Prime Minister Winston Churchill of Great Britain signed the Atlantic Charter. In 1949 Newfoundland and Labrador became the 10th Canadian province.

NEW FRANCE (United States, Canada) The New World territory of FRANCE, prior to the Treaty of PARIS in 1763, by which these lands were ceded to SPAIN and GREAT BRITAIN. They lay mostly in E Canada and NE United States, although French explorers traveled through the American northwest and southwest. The region was a fur-trading center of the Company of New France from 1627 to 1663. It became a focus of British-French hostilities in North America, culminating in the French and Indian War from 1755 to 1763. See also ACADIA, CANADA, LOUISIANA PUR-

CHASE, MISSISSIPPI RIVER, NORTHWEST TERRITORY, ST. LAWRENCE RIVER.

NEW GEORGIA (Solomon Islands) Island group in the archipelago of the Solomon Islands, as well as its chief island, approx. 40 mi S of Choiseul Island. During World War II it was taken by JAPAN in 1942 and developed as a military base, especially at MUNDA. After severe fighting from June to August 1943, it was occupied by U.S. troops. Formerly a British protectorate, New Georgia became part of the independent nation of the Solomon Islands in 1978.

NEW GOA. See PANAJI.

NEW GRANADA Former Spanish viceroyalty of NW South America. It was conquered from 1536 to 1538 by Jiménez de Quesada and was subject to the rule of the viceroyalty of PERU. In 1717 it became an independent viceroyalty comprising COLOMBIA, ECUADOR, PANAMA, and VENEZUELA. In 1810 Simón Bolívar led the uprising for independence and by 1830 the Republic of New Granada, comprising Colombia and Panama, was formed. It became the Republic of Colombia in 1886, from which Panama seceded in 1903. See also GRAN COLOMBIA.

NEW GRANGE (Irish Republic) One of the finest passage graves of the Neolithic period, dating from c.2500 BC, one of many such monuments in the BOYNE RIVER valley, 25 mi N of Dublin. The immense cairn, built of stone, had a long passage leading into the corbelled burial chamber, a surrounding kerb of decorated slabs, and a circle of free-standing stones at a distance—somewhat similar, though smaller, than those at STONEHENGE. An opening over the passage entrance allows the sun to shine directly through the passage into the burial chamber only at the winter solstice, obviously for ritual purposes. New Grange is distinguished from the other tombs in the Boyne Valley by its elaborate pecked decoration covering many of the stones, similar to earlier passage graves in BRITTANY but found nowhere else in IRELAND. Another outstanding passage grave in the valley is at Knowth.

NEW GUINEA (Indonesia, Papua New Guinea) Island of the E Malay archipelago, W Pacific Ocean, N of Australia, one of the largest islands in the world. It is now divided into the Indonesian province of IRIAN BARAT in the west and independent Papua New Guinea in the east. It was first sighted by the Portuguese in the early 16th century; the Dutch annexed the western half of the island in 1828. In 1884 Germany took the northeast part of the island, while Great Britain made the southeast coast and islands a protectorate. The British holdings passed to AUSTRALIA in 1905 and were renamed Papua; and in World War I the Australians seized the German part to the north, the whole being mandated to Australia under the League of Nations in 1920, as the Territory of New Guinea. After fierce fighting throughout the area between JAPAN and the Allies during World War II, the Australian parts were returned to that nation as a Trust Territory under the United Nations. In 1963 Irian Barat in the west became

part of Indonesia, and the eastern sections were joined under the new nation of Papua New Guinea in 1975.

NEW HAARLEM. See HARLEM.

NEW HAMPSHIRE (United States) State in the NE corner of the nation, between Maine to the E, Vermont to the W, and Massachusetts to the S with a short seacoast in the SE on the Atlantic Ocean. It was the ninth of the 13 colonies to ratify the Constitution, on June 21, 1788, and it was the first colony to declare its independence and to establish its own government. The White Mts are its dominant geographical feature, and it has many lakes and streams.

Martin Pring in 1603 and Samuel Sieur de Champlain in 1605 were the first Europeans to explore the region. After the Council of NEW ENGLAND in 1620 received a royal grant that included present Maine and New Hampshire, Capt. John Mason in 1629 obtained rights to the area between the Piscataqua and the MERRIMACK rivers. He named it after his home county of HAMPSHIRE in ENGLAND. The first settlements were at DOVER and PORTSMOUTH c.1625. EXETER was established in 1638 by the Rev. John Wheelwright of MASSACHUSETTS, who was expelled from that colony for religious reasons. The same year a group of Puritans founded HAMPTON.

A long-standing dispute between New Hampshire and Massachusetts as to boundaries was not settled until 1741. Until that year, when Benning Wentworth was appointed governor, the British crown had named one man to rule both colonies. Wentworth and some friends became involved in a dispute with NEW YORK over lands east of the HUDSON RIVER, and this was not settled until Vermont became a state, although in 1764 a royal order had set the Connecticut River as New Hampshire's western boundary. The wars between GREAT BRITAIN and FRANCE, which did not end until 1763, delayed settlement of the western and northern parts of the state.

The people of New Hampshire were early opponents of British rule; and a patriot band in December 1774 seized heavily armed Fort William and Mary. A comparatively large number of soldiers joined and served with the Continental Army. In 1786, however, there was considerable civil unrest stemming from hard times and unequal taxation, but an uprising was put down without bloodshed. One of the landmark legal cases in U.S. constitutional history grew out of an attempt by the state legislature to take over Dartmouth College, contrary to its charter. Daniel Webster argued the case before the U.S. Supreme Court, which ruled in 1819 that the legislature's act was unconstitutional; and this, in a much broader context, upheld the legal standing of contracts. The Civil War found the state strongly pro-Union, and it supplied a significant number of soldiers to the Union armies.

In the decades after the war the state became heavily industrialized, textiles and shoes being leading products. Lumbering remained important, and the state is still 87 percent forested, although for some time the forests were being exploited without thought for the future. The Great Depression of the 1930's badly damaged industry, and in recent years there has been an attempt to broaden the economic base with newer industries, such as electronics. There is a U.S. naval base at Portsmouth. New Hampshire attracts national attention every four years because it holds the earliest of all the presidential primary elections. CONCORD is the capital, and MANCHESTER is the largest city. At Portsmouth is Strawberry Banke, a restored colonial community including a house that was built in 1664. NASHUA developed early as a textile town.

NEW HARMONY (United States) Town on the WABASH RIVER, 23 mi NW of Evansville, SW INDIANA. Established in 1814 by the Harmony Society under George Rapp, it was sold in 1825 to Robert Owen the British social reformer, who renamed it and established a Utopian community here. Internal disagreements ended the project in 1828, but the town maintained the high level of educational and intellectual innovation it had inherited. The first American kindergarten, first free library, and first free public school were all begun here.

NEW HAVEN [*former:* **Quinnipiac**] (United States) Industrial city on New Haven Harbor, 36 mi SW of Hartford, S CONNECTICUT. Theophilus Eaton and John Davenport led a group of Puritans here in 1638 and established it as Quinnipiac, the name it bore until 1640. It was the joint state capital, with HARTFORD, from 1701 to 1875. Incorporated in 1784, it was attacked by the British during the American Revolution, and its port was blockaded by them during the War of 1812. It developed as an important manufacturing center during the Civil War. Eli Whitney, Samuel Colt, Charles Goodyear, Samuel F. B. Morse, and other inventors made it a center of industrial innovation in the 19th century. Yale University was moved to the city in 1716, and New Haven's old colonial public green is the locus of three early 19th-century churches. Noah Webster (1758–1843), the famous lexicographer, was a Yale graduate in 1778 and lived here from 1798. He also died here.

NEW HEBRIDES [*French:* **Nouvelles Hébrides**] (Vanuata) Group of islands in the SW Pacific Ocean, E of Australia. Discovered in 1606 by the Portuguese explorer Pedro de Queirós, the group was visited by British missionaries in the early 19th century. In 1887 the islands were placed under joint British-French control to stop the enslavement of natives for Australian plantation labor. The group became a condominium in 1906 and housed an important U.S. naval base on ESPÍRITU SANTO Island during World War II. The islands became the independent Republic of Vanuata on July 30, 1980.

NEW HELVETIA. See SACRAMENTO.

NEW IBERIA (United States) Agricultural, industrial, and mining center, 126 mi W of New Orleans, on the Teche Bayou, in S LOUISIANA. Founded by Acadians fleeing NOVA SCOTIA c.1765, it was incorporated in 1839. Several historic plantation homes are located here, including David Weeks's Shadows-on-the-Teche from 1834 and Justine from 1822.

The shop and house of David Allinos in Newark, New Jersey, in 1825. Settled by Puritans in 1666, Newark has long been an industrial center.

NEW INVERNESS. See DARIEN.

NEW IRELAND [*former:* **Neu-Mecklenburg**] (Papua New Guinea) Island in the BISMARK ARCHIPELAGO, NE of New Guinea, SW Pacific Ocean. Discovered in 1616, it was a German protectorate from 1884 to 1914 before coming under Australian control in World War I. Its chief port, KAVIENG, was occupied in January 1942 by JAPAN; the island was bombed repeatedly during World War II until it was retaken in 1945. See also AUSTRALIA.

NEW JERSEY (United States) A Middle Atlantic state on the nation's East Coast, it was one of the 13 original colonies and the third to ratify the Constitution, in December 1787. New York State is to the N and E, Pennsylvania to the W, and Delaware to the S.

Settlers from the NETHERLANDS and SWEDEN were the first to come here, the Dutch basing their claims to the HUDSON RIVER and DELAWARE RIVER valleys on the explorations of Henry Hudson. He sailed into Newark Bay in 1609, and Cornelis Jacobsen explored the lower Delaware River in 1614. The Dutch West India Company offered land grants, and colonies were established at the present sites of JERSEY CITY, HOBOKEN, and GLOUCESTER CITY. After 1638 the Swedes and the Finns, who were then subject to Sweden, were domi-

nant in the Delaware Valley. NEW SWEDEN included parts of PENNSYLVANIA and DELAWARE. Relations with the Delaware, Leni Lenape, Indians were mainly peaceful.

In 1655 the Dutch under Peter Stuyvesant took over New Sweden by force, but in 1664 England seized these Dutch colonies and NEW NETHERLAND. James II then granted the land between the Hudson and Delaware rivers to Lord John Berkeley and Sir George Carteret. The region was named New Jersey for the Isle of JERSEY in the ENGLISH CHANNEL whence Carteret came. Berkeley and Carteret encouraged settlement by offering free land, but after some disputes the grant was divided into East and West Jersey.

The Berkeley interests sold West Jersey to a group of Quakers in 1674; William Penn and other Quakers took over in 1677; and in 1681 they bought East Jersey after Carteret died. Difficulties developed between these proprietors and the settlers, and in 1702 control reverted to the English crown. New Jersey was practically autonomous by then, but after 1738 the governor of NEW YORK was also the governor of New Jersey. Strong anti-British feeling prevailed in New Jersey at the time of the American Revolution. Because of its strategic position between New York and NEW ENGLAND to the north and the other colonies to the south and west, New Jersey was the scene of more than 90 engagements during the war. George Washington's army crossed it four times and wintered twice at MORRISTOWN. The most important of the battles, all American victories to a greater or lesser extent, were at TRENTON on Christmas Day 1776; PRINCETON in January 1777; and MONMOUTH COURT HOUSE in June 1778.

After the Revolution came a period of expansion when roads, canals, and railroads were built, making New Jersey a vital transportation link between North and South. The southern part of the state showed some sentiment for the Confederacy in the Civil War, but New Jersey as a whole supported the Union. After that struggle, rapid industrial growth put power in the hands of capitalists and entrepreneurs. After the 1870's, laws that favored corporations and provided for low taxes on business further encouraged industry. A reform movement came to power, however, during Woodrow Wilson's governorship from 1910 to 1912. For nearly a century New Jersey has been divided politically, and usually neither major party can be sure of victory. One of the nation's most powerful and long-lived political machines was that of Democrat Frank Hague of JERSEY CITY from 1913 to 1949. A six-day riot in NEWARK in 1967 was part of the unrest of the times.

Trenton has been the capital since 1790, and Newark is the largest city. Densely populated and the most heavily industrialized state, New Jersey has numerous cities: ELIZABETH, HACKENSACK, Hoboken, Jersey City, PASSAIC, and PATERSON.

NEW LANARK (Scotland) Industrial site near Lanark, 22 mi SE of Glasgow, in Strathclyde region. Here in 1785 David Dale, a cotton manufacturer and philanthropist, built cotton mills, establishing a model community with better than usual housing for his workers. In 1800 Robert Owen, reformer, socialist, and pioneer of the cooperative movement, came to Lanark. Married to Dale's daughter, he took over operation of the mills. Owen improved still further the housing and working conditions and established schools and nonprofit stores. He was also a leader in securing passage by the British parliament of the Factory Act of 1819, which was a landmark, although it did not go as far in protecting workers as he wished. In 1825 Owen established NEW HARMONY, INDIANA, in the UNITED STATES, a self-supporting cooperative agricultural community; but disagreements among its members brought it to an early end.

NEW LONDON (United States) Industrial city on LONG ISLAND SOUND, 43 mi E of New Haven, SE CONNECTICUT. Founded in 1646 and incorporated in 1784, it was a major whaling port for many years and a haven for smugglers and pirates during the American Revolution. During the war it was burned in 1781 by British troops led by Benedict Arnold, and it was blockaded by the British in the War of 1812. It flourished as a shipbuilding and whaling center in the 19th century and now houses a naval submarine base. It has several colonial buildings, including a mill built in 1650 by John Winthrop.

NEW MADRID (United States) City on the MISSIS-SIPPI RIVER, 28 mi N of Caruthersville, SE MISSOURI. Damaged by an earthquake in 1811/12, it was taken on July 28, 1861 by Confederate troops, who held it for almost a year.

NEWMARKET (England) Town and racing center in Suffolk, 56 mi NNE of London. Devil's Dyke, an earthwork located here, dates back to the Iron Age. The famous racecourse was established in the reign of James I (1603–25). Portions of Charles II's royal palace still stand.

NEW MARKET (United States) Town in S Shenandoah county, N VIRGINIA. Confederate troops directed by Gen. C. Breckinridge won a Civil War battle here on May 15, 1864.

NEW MEXICO (United States) State in the SW, bordering on Mexico to the S, Arizona to the W, Colorado to the N, and Texas and Oklahoma to the E. It was admitted to the Union in 1912 as the 47th state. The Spanish explorer Francisco de Ibarra named the region Nueva Mexico in 1562.

The area has been inhabited since prehistoric times; and the Indian pueblo of ACOMA, founded c.1200 AD atop a mesa, is thought to be the oldest continuously inhabited community in the United States. Prehistoric settlements were those of the Anasazi culture, ancestors of the Pueblo Indians who now occupy the area. Ruins of a 12th-century Pueblo town are at the Aztec Ruins National Monument, but have no connection with the Aztec culture. Another ancient site is at the GILA CLIFF DWELLINGS NATIONAL MONUMENT. The people who lived here were the ancestors of the Pima and Papago Indians. Apache Indians entered the area c.1100 AD, and Navaho Indians came from the north.

The explorer Cabeza de Vaca from SPAIN may have been in New Mexico in 1528 and again in 1536; while Fray Marcos de Niza, in 1539, thought the Zuñi towns were the fabled Seven Cities of CIBOLA. Francisco Vásquez de Coronado, arriving in 1540 to find Cibola, cruelly mistreated the Indians and made permanent enemies of them. The first colony, at SAN JUAN, was founded in 1598 by Juan de Oñate. The Indians revolted against the Spanish in 1599 but were defeated. In 1609 Pedro de Peralta was named governor and founded SANTA FE.

The Indians continued to rebel against Spanish rule, the Apaches rising in 1676 and the Pueblo Indians in 1680. The Spanish were driven out in this great Pueblo Revolt and did not return until 1692. Settlement then began; and farming, ranching, and mining enterprises started up. New Mexico developed a Spanish culture, still much in evidence. After MEXICO won its independence from Spain in 1821, New Mexico became a province, and trade with the United States began. The SANTA FE TRAIL to Missouri opened the next year. In 1846, during the Mexican War, Gen. Stephen W. Kearny captured Santa Fe, and the treaty ending the war in 1848 gave a large region, including New Mexico, to the United States. The Compromise of 1850 made New Mexico a territory, and a final small strip of land in southwestern New Mexico was added by the GADSDEN PURCHASE of 1853 to make up its present boundaries.

During the Civil War Confederate troops from TEXAS entered the territory, but Union forces drove them out in early 1862. After the war there was intermittent fighting with the Indians, who in the past had also battled each other. The Apache and the Navaho both fought the Anglo-Americans, the Navaho being subdued in 1863/64 when Kit Carson destroyed their sheep. The Apache fought until their Chief Geronimo surrendered in 1886. The coming of the Santa Fe Railroad in 1879 gave ranching a boost, but cattlemen fought the sheepholders as well as the farmers. One struggle between the cattlemen and the authorities became known as the Lincoln County War, and the gunman Billy the Kid fought in it in 1878.

In 1916 men belonging to a force headed by Francisco "Pancho" Villa, Mexican bandit and revolutionary, raided the village of Columbus and killed a number of Anglo-Americans. U.S. troops pursued the raiders into Mexico but could not catch them. LOS ALAMOS in 1942 became the site of experiments that led to the production of the first atomic bomb, which was set off in July 1945 at the WHITE SANDS Proving Ground. Santa Fe is the capital and ALBUQUERQUE the largest city of New Mexico. Since the late 1960's the state has shared in the prosperity of the Sun Belt, and its cities have begun to attract many emigrants from other parts of the country.

NEW MILFORD (United States) Industrial town in an agricultural area, on the HOUSATONIC RIVER, NW CONNECTICUT. Its town hall is on the site of the former home of Roger Sherman, who helped draft and signed the Declaration of Independence and was a strong proponent of the new U.S. Constitution. The town was settled in 1707 and incorporated in 1712.

NEW NETHERLAND (United States) Former Dutch colony. It was established in 1613 and taken in 1664 by the English, who separated it into the colonies of NEW YORK and NEW JERSEY. The colony's major settlement was at New Amsterdam on MANHATTAN ISLAND, now a part of NEW YORK CITY. Its last governor was the unpopular Peter Stuyvesant. See also DELAWARE.

NEW ORANGE. See NEW YORK CITY.

NEW ORLEANS (United States) Major commercial and industrial city and port on the MISSISSIPPI RIVER, 107 mi from its mouth, SE LOUISIANA. Founded in 1718 by de Bienville, it became the capital of the French colony of Louisiana in 1722. It was ceded to SPAIN by the Treaty of PARIS in 1763. Smuggling flourished at the port under Spanish rule, and more and more New Orleans became the key to control of the Mississippi River inland. In 1803 France regained the territory, but in the same year Napoleon, embroiled in his European wars, sold it to the United States in the LOUISIANA PURCHASE. The city was incorporated in 1805, and it became the capital of Louisiana when it entered the Union, remaining the capital from 1812 to 1849. The Battle of New Orleans, a crushing victory by Andrew Jackson over the British on January 8, 1815, closed the War of 1812 with a much-needed U.S. victory, even though it was fought after the signing of the peace treaty at GHENT.

New Orleans flourished as a river port for the cotton trade and entry point for the interior, via the early steamboats, during the period of western expansion in the early 19th century. It seceded from the Union in 1861, at the beginning of the Civil War. However, it was soon captured by the Union forces under Adm. David G. Farragut on April 25, 1862 and suffered heavily in the postwar occupation period under Gen. Benjamin Butler. Its recovery during the Reconstruction period was slow.

The famous French quarter is a part of the city and a center of the well-known Mardi Gras celebration. Many of the French Cajuns, exiled from ACADIA, settled here. New Orleans's exotic mix of history and peoples, its unique site and beautiful old buildings have made it a tourist haven. Jazz had its beginnings here among black musicians. The city has been subject to hurricanes and threatened by many Mississippi River floods but has not been inundated owing to upriver controls.

NEW PONCA. See PONCA CITY.

NEWPORT (England) Port and admin. hq. of the ISLE OF WIGHT, 10 mi SW of Portsmouth. Chartered in the 12th century, it has the remains of a Roman villa and a 17th-century schoolhouse. Carisbrooke Castle, located nearby, was the scene of Charles I's incarceration before his execution.

NEWPORT (United States) City on the OHIO RIVER, E of Covington, N KENTUCKY. Founded in 1791 and incorporated in 1835, it served as a station on the Underground Railroad for runaway slaves before the Civil War. Several reform movements were inaugurated here, including anti-vice societies.

NEWPORT (United States) A center of naval installations, city, and port in NARRAGANSETT BAY, approx. 30 mi SE of Providence, SE RHODE ISLAND, on S Aquidneck Island. Founded in 1639 by religious dissenters from Massachusetts Bay Colony, it was incorporated in 1784. A colonial haven for dissident or minority religious groups in the 17th century, it developed as an important commercial port due to a thriving trade with the WEST INDIES involving rum, slaves, and molasses. It was a center of anti-British sentiment and a popular harbor for privateers and smugglers prior to the American Revolution, during which it was occupied from 1776 to 1779 by British troops. In 1780 and 1781 it became the headquarters of French troops under Gen. Rochambeau but declined after the war. It was the state's joint capital with PROVIDENCE until 1900 and was a popular high-society resort during that period and into the 1920's, when its unique and beautiful location brought many wealthy Americans to build palatial summer houses here. It thrives still as a naval base, though the naval presence has much diminished since the 1970's. However its colonial section has been restored, leading to extensive tourism. It has numerous historic landmarks including the Touro Synagogue of 1763, the oldest in the nation, and the Wanton-Lyman-Hazard House of c.1675, which was the locus of the Stamp Act riot in 1765.

NEWPORT (Wales) Port and admin. hq. of Gwent, on the Usk River, 20 mi NW of Bristol. Chartered in the 14th century, it was the scene in 1839 of Chartist riots, as that workingmen's movement tried to force the government into political reform.

NEWPORT NEWS (United States) Major shipbuilding center, shipping port, and air complex, on the JAMES RIVER and HAMPTON ROADS, 11 mi NW of Norfolk, in SE VIRGINIA. First settled by Irish planters in 1621, it was incorporated in 1896. It developed in the late 19th century as an important shipbuilding center and the terminus of the Chesapeake and Ohio Railroad. It was held during the Civil War by Union troops who operated a prison here. The famous battle between the early ironclads, *Monitor* and *Merrimac*, was fought in 1862 off its coast. It was a point of embarkation for U.S. troops during both world wars. Old Fort Eustis is located in the city. Due to its peninsular location, it was a backwater during the industrial development of the country, but with the growth of aviation has become a large complex of military-industrial power.

NEW PROVIDENCE (Great Britain) Most important island in the British BAHAMA ISLANDS, containing its capital, NASSAU, 170 mi E of Florida, in the S Atlantic Ocean. Settled by English immigrants from BERMUDA in 1656, it accepted many exiled American Tories following the American Revolution. Great Britain established an air base here during World War II.

NEW QUEBEC. See UNGAVA.

NEW ROCHELLE (United States) Suburb of NEW YORK CITY, 16 mi S on LONG ISLAND SOUND, SE NEW YORK State. Settled in 1688 by Huguenot refugees from FRANCE, it was incorporated in 1899. Chief Justice John Jay was educated here; and Thomas Paine, colonial American patriot, was a resident in the home here that is still preserved as a city museum.

NEW ROMNEY (England) Town in the ROMNEY MARSH district of Kent. A member of the CINQUE PORTS, it preserves many important documents concerning that medieval defensive association of coastal cities. The church of St. Nicholas, located here, was built partly in Norman times.

NEWRY (Northern Ireland) Town on the Newry River, Newry and Mourne district, 32 mi SSW of Belfast. An abbey founded here in the 12th century by Maurice McLoughlin, king of IRELAND, became a collegiate church in 1543. Edward Bruce, fighting for Irish independence from ENGLAND, captured the Newry castle in 1315. Newry was partly burned in 1689 by the duke of Berwick in his retreat from the forces of William III. The first Protestant church in Ireland was St. Patrick's church, built here in 1578.

NEW SAINT ANDREW. See DARIEN, PANAMA.

NEW SALEM (United States) Restored village, 15 mi NW of Springfield, central ILLINOIS. Abraham Lincoln (1809–65), 16th president of the United States (1861–65), lived here from 1831 to 1837. He studied law while working in a store in the town. He allegedly courted Ann Rutledge until her death here in 1835; however, he was actually engaged to one of his good friends.

NEW SARUM. See SALISBURY.

NEW SIBERIAN ISLANDS [*Russian:* **Novosibirskiye Ostrova**] (USSR) Island group in the ARCTIC Ocean, NE Russian SFSR. First discovered in 1712, the islands were the site of prehistoric fossil mammoth remains found in the 1870's. Scientific research stations have been established here since the 1920's.

NEW SMYRNA BEACH (United States) Resort and shipping port on the Atlantic Ocean, 14 mi SE of Daytona Beach, NE FLORIDA. Founded in 1803, it was incorporated a century later. A Spanish Franciscan mission was established here in 1696 near the site of prehistoric Indian mounds and a 16th-century Spanish fort.

NEW SOUTH WALES (Australia) State in the SE. First visited in 1770 by Capt. James Cook of GREAT BRITAIN, its earliest settlement was at BOTANY BAY, a convict station, in 1788. This was transferred to its capital, SYDNEY. It developed as a wool industry center in the 19th century. The state's history closely parallels that of the country, and its progress toward statehood began in 1901. Originally an extensive territory, it included QUEENSLAND, VICTORIA, TASMANIA, and NEW ZEALAND, which became separate colonies in the mid-19th century.

NEW SPAIN (Mexico) Former Spanish New World viceroyalty, administered locally through MEXICO CITY from the 16th to 19th centuries. It included the southwestern UNITED STATES, the WEST INDIES, the PHILIPPINES, and northern CENTRAL AMERICA. By 1825 most of New Spain had been lost to SPAIN.

NEW SWEDEN (United States) Former colony stretching from TRENTON, New Jersey to the mouth of the DELAWARE RIVER. It was established in the New World by the New Sweden Company. Containing parts of what are now PENNSYLVANIA, DELAWARE, and NEW JERSEY, its history began when Peter Minuit founded Fort Christina in 1638 on the present site of WILMINGTON. Peter Stuyvesant led a Dutch force that captured the colony in 1655.

NEWTON (United States) City, 35 mi E of Hutchinson, SE central KANSAS. A terminus of the old CHISHOLM TRAIL, it was populated in the early 1870's by German Mennonites from RUSSIA. At that time they introduced a variety of hard winter wheat that is now the main crop in the state. Newton had been a thriving cattle town, and later became an important railroad center.

NEWTON (United States) Residential city, 7 mi W of Boston, NE MASSACHUSETTS. It was settled in the 1630's as part of CAMBRIDGE and was incorporated in 1873. John Eliot's "praying Indians" established a Christian church here in 1646. Horace Mann, educator; Mary Baker Eddy, founder of the Christian Science movement; and the writer Nathaniel Hawthorne lived here at different times in the 19th century.

NEWTOWN. See MACON, QUEENS.

NEWTOWNARDS (Northern Ireland) Town in North Down district, 9 mi E of Belfast, on the Strangford Lough. The ruins of an abbey founded c.550 AD by St. Finian are nearby. Those of a Dominican priory founded here by the earl of ULSTER in 1244 mark the original site of the town.

NEWTOWN BUTLER (Northern Ireland) Town in Fermanagh district, 63 mi SW of Belfast. A Jacobite army was defeated here in 1689 by a force of Protestants from Enniskillen during the contest between William III of ENGLAND and the forces of James II.

NEW ULM (United States) City on the Minnesota River, 90 mi SW of Minneapolis, S MINNESOTA. Settled by German immigrants in 1854, it was defended by forces led by Justice C.E. Flandrau during two attacks in the Sioux Indian uprisings of 1862. It was incorporated in 1876.

NEW WESTMINSTER (Canada) City, port, and suburb of VANCOUVER, on the Fraser River, SW BRITISH COLUMBIA. Founded in 1859, it was the capital of British Columbia from 1860 to 1866, when it was replaced by VICTORIA.

NEW WINDSOR. See WINDSOR.

NEW YORK (United States) Northernmost of the Middle Atlantic states, it lies W of NEW ENGLAND, with Vermont, Massachusetts, and Connecticut to the E, New Jersey and Pennsylvania to the S, and Canada to the N and W. It was the 11th of the 13 colonies to ratify the Constitution, doing so by a narrow margin in July 1788.

Before the arrival of Europeans, the area was inhabited by a number of Indian tribes: the Mohegan, Leni-Lenape, and Wappinger, living mostly in the HUDSON RIVER Valley and on LONG ISLAND; and the powerful Iroquois Confederacy, organized c.1570 and stretching across the state from the Hudson to LAKE ERIE. A Florentine in the service of FRANCE, Giovanni da Verrazano, visited New York Bay in 1524. The next two explorers of the region, both in 1609, were Samuel Sieur de Champlain of France, who entered from the north down Lake Champlain, and Henry Hudson, in Dutch employ, who sailed up the Hudson River nearly to present ALBANY. The first to settle were the Dutch in 1624, when they established their colony of NEW NETHERLAND and a small settlement, NEW AMSTERDAM, on MANHATTAN Island. They also established Fort Orange where ALBANY now stands.

The Dutch made large land grants, mostly along the Hudson River, to men who engaged to bring in settlers. Nevertheless, New Netherland did not prosper, and its last governor, Peter Stuyvesant, surrendered it to England in 1664. King Charles II granted the colony to his brother, the duke of York, for whom it was renamed. The colony prospered, and the long-lasting alliance of the English and the Iroquois Indians was formed. A little later, however, there was a conflict between the large landholders on the one hand and the small farmers, artisans, and merchants on the other. Out of this, in the 18th century, came a more representative government that suited both provincial and royal inter-ests. The colony continued to grow, although the western area remained largely unsettled because of warfare between the British and the French. The various Navigation Acts and the Stamp Act of 1765 were objected to vigorously by the commercially minded colony.

When the American Revolution began, however, New York was badly divided, and there were many Loyalists. In May 1775 Ethan Allen of VERMONT captured Fort TICONDEROGA, and CROWN POINT was also seized. In August 1776 Gen. Washington lost the Battles of LONG ISLAND and of HARLEM Heights, evacuated NEW YORK CITY, and in October was defeated at WHITE PLAINS. The British held New York City until the end of the war. In 1777 the British attempted to split the 13 colonies in half by a drive into New York from CANADA southward, another up the Hudson River, and a third east through the MOHAWK RIVER Valley. The campaign ended in failure when the British surrendered at SARATOGA in October.

After independence, New York City was the first capital of the new nation, in 1789/90, and the state prospered, although the Embargo Act of 1807 and the War of 1812 were setbacks. During this war, the British captured FORT NIAGARA, but U.S. forces won a naval victory on LAKE CHAMPLAIN. In the first half of the 19th century New York came to be called the Empire State, due chiefly to the completion in 1825 of the ERIE CANAL, which connected the Great Lakes at BUFFALO with the Hudson River and thence with New York City and the Atlantic Ocean. The canal traffic and the railroads, which appeared a few years later, made New York City the nation's commercial and financial center.

Slavery was abolished in the state in 1827, and the first women's rights convention in the United States met in SENECA FALLS in 1848. During the 19th century several million immigrants poured into the United States through New York City and made it a great "melting pot." The state made large contributions in men and money to the Union side in the Civil War, although there were bloody draft riots in New York City in 1863. Since the late 19th century the state has been in the forefront of reform and social welfare legislation, and it has provided outstanding leaders in politics and industry, including the Roosevelts, Rockefellers, the Vanderbilts, Morgans, Alfred Smith, and others.

Albany has been the capital since 1797, and other cities of consequence are ROCHESTER, ROME, SCHENECTADY, SYRACUSE, and UTICA.

NEW YORK CITY [colloquial: **Gotham**; former: **New Amsterdam, New Orange**] (United States) City and port in SE NEW YORK State at the mouth of the HUDSON RIVER on New York Bay. For nearly two centuries it has been not only the nation's largest city but also one of the world's busiest ports, its premier financial center, the leader in culture and entertainment, a foremost manufacturing and commercial center, a magnet for immigrants who turned it into the greatest assemblage of ethnic groups perhaps in the world, and a mecca for tourists. Giovanni da Verrazano was the first recorded European to visit the site, in

1524. Henry Hudson was here in 1609 and sailed up the Hudson River. The first settlers, however, were Dutch, who established the colony of NEW NETHERLAND in 1624 and founded New Amsterdam, the future metropolis, on the southern tip of the island of MANHATTAN. Tradition has it that the entire island was purchased from the Indians for trinkets worth approximately $24. In 1664 the colony was seized by ENGLAND and renamed for the duke of York. The Dutch briefly regained it in 1673/74 and renamed it New Orange.

New York and its commerce grew steadily in the late 17th and 18th centuries, when it was already a cosmopolitan city. Opposition to British rule was strong after the passage of the Stamp Act in 1765, and in 1775 the Sons of Liberty forced the colonial government to flee. In 1776, however, the British army defeated George Washington's Continentals in several engagements, including the Battle of Long Island in modern Brooklyn and the Battle of HARLEM Heights in Manhattan. Washington abandoned the city, which remained in British hands until the end of the American Revolution. New York was the first capital of the United States in 1789/90, and by then it was the nation's largest city. In 1825 the opening of the ERIE CANAL made New York City the seaboard entrance to a water route to the Great Lakes and crowned its position as the most important city in the nation.

New York supported the Union in the Civil War but was the scene, from July 13 to 16, 1863 of the bloody Draft Riots, when thousands protested against the Federal Conscription Act. Tammany Hall, the Democratic Party organization, dominated politics until the blatant corruption of the Tweed Ring was exposed in 1871. In the late 19th and early 20th centuries the city was the entry point for several million immigrants from Europe, who made ELLIS ISLAND famous as they poured through it on landing. As a result, New York became an enormous melting pot of ethnic neighborhoods and a center of labor and radical movements. The city was enlarged in 1898 when the separate city of BROOKLYN, and STATEN ISLAND and part of the BRONX, were combined with Manhattan to form the greater city. The southern part of the Bronx, the only section of the city on the mainland, had become part of New York City in 1875.

Early in the 20th century the city began to sprout skyscrapers, and in 1904 it opened one of the first subway systems in the country. Political corruption and reform have alternated, while the need for regional cooperation in the tri-state metropolitan region, comprising parts of NEW JERSEY and CONNECTICUT, resulted in the establishment in 1921 of what is now the Port Authority of New York and New Jersey. Since World War II New York has suffered the ills of modern urban areas and in 1975 was on the verge of bankruptcy. The city has lost population to its suburbs while the proportion of black and Hispanic residents has increased. Its school and transportation systems have been strained, its housing has deteriorated, and crime has increased. There were riots in the 1960's. Nevertheless, New York remains supreme for its skyscrapers, museums, arts, clothing and fashion industry, colleges and universities, churches, bridges, parks, zoos, medical facilities, corporate and financial operations, theaters, publishing and musical establishments, shops, Rockefeller Center, GREENWICH VILLAGE, Yankee Stadium, and Central Park. It is also the headquarters of the United Nations.

NEW ZEALAND Nation consisting of two main islands and some smaller islands in the S Pacific Ocean, SSE of AUSTRALIA. It is a member of the British COMMONWEALTH OF NATIONS. The two main islands are North Island, smaller but with the larger population, and South Island. New Zealand also includes Stewart Island, south of South Island, discovered by the British in 1808, and the Chatham Islands, east of New Zealand, discovered by the British in 1791. The earliest known inhabitants of the main islands were the Maoris, who probably arrived c.800 AD or earlier and represented the southernmost point of Polynesian expansion. A second wave of these people came c.1350. The first European to see New Zealand was the Dutch navigator, Abel J. Tasman, in 1642; while Capt. James Cook, a British navigator, circumnavigated the islands in 1769/70 and charted their coastlines.

The first settlers were escaped convicts from Australia and runaway sailors. Organized settlement began in the 1840's, and GREAT BRITAIN made New Zealand a colony in 1841. A treaty of 1840 with the Maoris opened large tracts of land to the settlers, and WELLINGTON, the capital, was founded that year, as was AUCKLAND, both on North Island. CHRISTCHURCH, on South Island, was settled in 1850. The Maoris resented the continuing encroachment on their lands and fought bitterly off and on against the British until 1870. The colony was granted self-government in 1852, and in the course of the 19th century it became a large producer of dairy and meat products.

New Zealand also pioneered in social welfare legislation. Its soldiers fought in the ANZAC corps for Great Britain in both world wars. The British Statute of WESTMINSTER in 1931 gave complete independence to the islands, but until 1947 New Zealand allowed Great Britain to conduct its foreign affairs. The wars with the settlers greatly reduced the Maori population, but it has since grown back to approximately 225,000. The islands are noted for their scenery, the comfortable life style of the people, and a variety of unusual animals, including the kiwi, albatross, and tuatara.

NEYSHĀBŪR. See NISHAPUR.

NEZHIN [Nyezhin] (USSR) Town in central Chernigov oblast, in the N UKRAINE 70 mi NE of Kiev. Established by the 11th century, it was the headquarters from 1649 to 1782 of the Nezhin Ukrainian Cossacks. In 1657 the Cossack hetman permitted Greek merchants to live here and it developed as a thriving mercantile and transport center in the 17th and 18th centuries.

NEZIB. See NIZIP.

NGANKING. See AN-CHING.

N'GELA ISLAND. See FLORIDA ISLAND.

NGESEBUS (United States) Small island, one of the

PALAU ISLANDS in the W CAROLINE ISLANDS group, U.S. Trust Territory of the PACIFIC ISLANDS. Held by JAPAN since 1914, the Palaus as a whole were taken by U.S. troops during World War II in September/October 1944. The marines landed on Ngesebus on Sept. 28, 1944. The islands were placed under trusteeship in 1947. See also PELELIU.

NHA TRANG (Vietnam) Port town on the South China Sea, 50 mi N of Phan Rang, S central Vietnam. A major U.S. military base was established here during the Vietnam War. The remains of a Cham temple are located in the neighborhood.

NIAGARA. See NIAGARA-ON-THE-LAKE.

NIAGARA FALLS (Canada, United States) Famous falls of the Niagara River, on the boundary between W NEW YORK State and ONTARIO. Father Louis Hennepin visited the falls in 1678 during an expedition in which he accompanied Robert Sieur de La Salle. On its banks they built FORT NIAGARA. It was captured by the British in 1759, taken by the Americans after the American Revolution, and regained by the British during the War of 1812 and held until its end. The falls were the source of early hydroelectric power, which has

since been increased. See also the cities of NIAGARA FALLS, Canada and United States.

NIAGARA FALLS (Canada, United States) Twin cities, above and below the great falls of the Niagara River (see NIAGARA FALLS), connected by two bridges across the river. Both cities are centers of hydroelectric power and other major industries. The U.S. city, settled on the site of a fort after 1800, was created out of three small settlements in 1892 and 1927. The Canadian city was founded in 1853. Named Clifton from 1856 to 1881, it was incorporated as Niagara Falls in 1904.

NIAGARA, FORT. See FORT NIAGARA.

NIAGARA-ON-THE-LAKE [Niagara] (Canada) Resort town on LAKE ONTARIO, at the mouth of the Niagara River, SE ONTARIO. Settled by American Tories in 1784, it was the first capital of Upper Canada from 1792 to 1796. Fort George protected the town, but it was taken by U.S. forces in 1813 during the War of 1812. The town was burned during the attack but was reoccupied by the British later that year. It is now a tourist and cultural center, with many carefully restored buildings of the 19th and early 20th centuries.

NIAMEY (Niger) River port and capital of Niger, on

Typical dramatic scenery in New Zealand, near New Plymouth, on North Island. Founded in 1841, New Plymouth is a prosperous center of dairying, one of the country's chief industries.

the NIGER RIVER, West Africa. An insignificant 19th-century French military post, it was the center of a rich agricultural region, and after it was made the capital of the country in 1926 it quickly became an important center of trade and light industry.

NIAS (Indonesia) Volcanic island in the INDIAN OCEAN, off the W coast of SUMATRA. The Dutch started trading here in 1669. The island contains many megalithic shrines from its precolonial past.

NICAEA, France. See NICE.

NICAEA [*former:* **Antigonia**] (Turkey) Ancient city of Bithynia, in Asia Minor. It was on the site of modern İznik. Built in 316 BC by Antigonus I, one of the successors of Alexander the Great of the MACEDONIAN EMPIRE, it was named for him until Lysimachus renamed it for his wife. It was an important trading center during the early BYZANTINE EMPIRE and the capital of BITHYNIA. The Nicene Creed of the Christian church was formulated here during an ecumenical council called by Constantine I in 325 AD, which asserted the equality of the Trinity and outlawed Arianism. The veneration, but not worship, of icons was approved in another council held here in 787, which suppressed the Iconoclast movement in the Byzantine Empire.

The city, destroyed by an earthquake at that time, was taken by the Crusaders from the Turks in 1097. When the Crusaders took CONSTANTINOPLE itself from the Byzantine Empire in 1204, Nicaea became the capital of one of the successor states, the Nicaean Empire, until 1261, when Michael Paleologus succeeded in retaking Constantinople and reconstituting the Byzantine Empire. Nicaea passed to the Turks of the later OTTOMAN EMPIRE in 1330. Parts of the ancient church of St. Sophia have been unearthed here, and the city's medieval walls still stand.

NICARAGUA Nation of CENTRAL AMERICA, with coastlines on both the Caribbean Sea and the Pacific Ocean. It takes its name from an Indian chief. El Salvador and Honduras are to the N and Costa Rica is to the S. The Spanish conquistador Gil González de Ávila conquered Nicaragua, HONDURAS, and COSTA RICA in 1522. The next year Francisco Fernández de Córdoba was sent to deprive González de Ávila of his claim to Nicaragua, and in 1524 he founded GRANADA and LEÓN. Under Spanish rule, Nicaragua was part of the captaincy general of GUATEMALA. In 1678 England declared a protectorate over the MOSQUITO COAST, the eastern coast of the country and made BLUEFIELDS the capital. Nicaragua won independence from SPAIN in 1821 and with the other Central American nations—Guatemala, Honduras, EL SALVADOR, and Costa Rica—became part of the Mexican Empire, over which Augustín de Iturbide ruled briefly as Emperor Augustín I. Between 1825 and 1838 the five nations formed the CENTRAL AMERICAN CONFEDERATION, with Manuel José Arce as the first president. Rivalries brought about dissolution of the confederation in spite of the efforts of a liberal dictator, Francisco Morazán.

The British occupied the town of SAN JUAN DEL NORTE (Greytown) on the Mosquito Coast in 1848, but a treaty of 1860 with Nicaragua gave this area autonomy.

Later, in 1894, President José Santos Zelaya seized the region by force. As early as 1826 the United States expressed interest in building a canal across Nicaragua. No canal was built, but in 1851 Cornelius Vanderbilt, the American shipping and railroad magnate, opened a route from the Atlantic coast to CALIFORNIA that included a system of land transit across Nicaragua. An American adventurer, William Walker, set out in 1855 to conquer Nicaragua, which he did, and proclaimed himself president in 1856. The next year he was ousted by other Central American countries, assisted by Vanderbilt.

The country enjoyed a period of quiet from 1857 to 1909, most of the time under conservative rule. In 1912, however, U.S. Marines were sent to aid the conservative side in a civil war. They were opposed by guerrilla forces led by Augusto César Sandino until the U.S. withdrawal in 1933. The Bryan-Chamorro Treaty of 1916 gave the UNITED STATES the right to build a canal, but the treaty was terminated in 1970. In 1936, with U.S. backing, Anastasio Somoza killed Sandino and overthrew the democratically elected President Juan Batista Sacassa. Somoza became the nation's dictator; he and two sons turned the country, for practical purposes, into the private property of the Somoza family, ruling by terror and repression until a revolution in July 1979 destroyed their power. The revolution was broad based and included factions from all parts of the political spectrum, including the Sandinistas, named for the guerrilla leader. Though the original revolutionary government included all these factions, it has since late 1980 moved toward full Sandanista control but includes members of the Roman Catholic clergy. They have been accused by U.S. officials of being communist-oriented and of receiving military aid from the USSR and CUBA. The United States has sought to isolate the country diplomatically and economically and to overthrow the regime. The Sandinistas, however, assert they favor pluralistic democracy and negotiated settlements to regional disputes. MANAGUA is the capital and largest city; León is the second largest.

NICARIA. See IKARIA.

NICE [*ancient:* **Nicaea**; *Italian:* **Nizza**] (France) Resort city and port on the Mediterranean Sea, capital of Alpes-Maritimes department, 98 mi NE of Marseilles. Settled by Greeks in the fifth century BC, it was the scene of the Roman's first occupation of GAUL. It was ravaged twice by Saracens in the ninth century AD. It passed to PROVENCE, then to SAVOY by 1388, and was sacked in 1543 by the Turks. It was taken in 1792 by France during the French Revolution, when it was a refuge for Royalists. It was returned to Savoy in 1814 and became French in 1860 following a plebiscite. The Italian patriot Giuseppe Garibaldi was born here in 1807. A former house of Napoleon's is in the city, as are several old churches dating as far back as the 12th century. See also RIVIERA.

NICEPHORIUM. See RAKKA.

NICOBAR ISLANDS. See ANDAMAN ISLANDS.

NICOMEDIA. See IZMIT.

NICOPOLIS, Bulgaria. See NIKOPOL.

NICOPOLIS [*Greek:* Nikópolis] (Greece) City of ancient Epirus; its ruins lie just N of modern Preveza. It was founded in 31 BC by Octavian, later Emperor Augustus, to celebrate his victory at neighboring AC-TIUM, and settled with the populations of Akarnania and Aetolia. It became the captial of EPIRUS and ACARNANIA. Host to the famous Actian Games, it was destroyed and rebuilt several times before it was abandoned. St. Paul wrote the Epistle to Titus here *c.*65 AD. Epictetus had a philosophical school here from *c.*60 to 140. The city was destroyed by Alaric, Genseric, and Totila; but it was rebuilt by Justinian I. The site contains remains of the city walls and citadel, a theater, odeum, stadium, and a museum.

NICOPOLIS, Turkey. See AFYONKARAHISAR.

NICOSIA [Nikosia] [*ancient:* **Ledrae**; *Greek:* **Leukosia, Levkosia**; *Turkish:* **Lefkosha**] (Cyprus) City and capital of Cyprus, on the Pedieos River. Founded before the seventh century BC, it was the capital of the island from the 10th century AD. The residence of the Crusader LUSIGNAN kings from FRANCE from 1192 to 1489, it then passed to VENICE, and in 1571 it fell to the forces of the OTTOMAN EMPIRE after a siege. From 1878 it was the center of British control of the island and was instrumental in the struggle for independence from TURKEY, finally achieved in 1960. It was torn by strife again after the Turkish invasion of the island in 1974. The 13th-century church of St. Sophia, which houses the Lusignan tombs, survives today as a mosque. See also FAMAGUSTA.

NICOYA (Costa Rica) Town on the Nicoya peninsula, on the Gulf of Nicoya. Colonized by SPAIN *c.*1530, it is thought to be the first Spanish settlement in Costa Rica.

NICTHEROY. See NITERÓI.

NIDAROS. See TRONDHEIM.

NIEDERÖSTERREICH. See LOWER AUSTRIA.

NIEMEN. See NEMAN RIVER.

NIEUPORT. See NIEUWPOORT.

NIEUWKERKE. See NEUVE-ÉGLISE.

NIEUWPOORT [Nieuport] (Belgium) Town and port on the Yser River and the North Sea, 10 mi SW of Ostend. Dating from as far back as the ninth century AD and dominated by a fortress, it was the site of many battles and sieges during the wars that swept over the Low Countries from the 14th through 17th centuries. In 1600 Maurice of NASSAU defeated the Spanish here. The commune was nearly obliterated during incessant warfare in 1914/15 during World War I.

NIEWENSTAT. See NEUSTADT AN DER WEIN-STRASSE.

NIEWIEZ. See NESVIZH.

NIĞDE (Turkey) Town and capital of Niğde province, central Turkey. It flourished before its capture in the mid-15th century by the OTTOMAN EMPIRE. From the 11th through 14th centuries it was held by the Seljuk Turks as part of the sultanate of RUM.

NIGEL (South Africa) Gold-mining town in the TRANSVAAL, and a suburb of JOHANNESBURG. Founded in 1909, it was named for the miner Nigel MacLeish. It is the site of Sub-Nigel, long one of the richest gold mines in the world.

NIGER Landlocked country of W central Africa, bounded by Libya and Algeria on the N, Benin and Nigeria on the S, Upper Volta on the SE, Mali on the W, and Chad on the E.

The region forming the modern country of Niger did not fall under a unified political dominion until FRANCE incorporated it as part of its colonial African empire in the late 19th century. Before then, the land was constantly subject to conflicts between various tribes and competing states. The medieval GHANA, MALI, and SONGHAI EMPIRES all claimed parts of the region at different times. In the early 19th century the FULANI EMPIRE in HAUSALAND struggled with the empire of BORNU for control.

By the time European explorers began to traverse the country in the mid-19th century there was no dominant political unit to oppose colonial annexation. The BERLIN conference of 1885 gave Niger to France. The French overcame resistance from the Tuareg Arabs, who were centered around AGADEZ. In 1900 they made Niger a territory within their holdings of Upper Senegal-Niger.

In 1922 Niger was split off and made a separate colony within FRENCH WEST AFRICA and governed as such until it was touched by the great wave of African nationalism that swept across the continent after World War II. In 1958 autonomy was granted, and in 1960 complete independence was gained under President Diori. His leadership lasted until the great SAHEL drought of 1968 to 1974 brought tremendous famine and suffering to the country. In 1974 a coup led by Lt. Col. Seyni Kountché toppled Diori, and a military government took power. Since then, major uranium finds promise to help finance Niger's desperately needy economy. In 1976 Kountché returned a large degree of civilian rule.

NIGER COAST PROTECTORATE. See NIGERIA.

NIGERIA The predominant country in West Africa, with boundaries arbitrarily set a century ago by British colonial rulers. Nigeria stretches from the western edge of the SAHARA Desert to the Atlantic Ocean and is the site of many different tribal cultures. Benin is to the W, Niger to the N, Chad to the E, and Cameroon to the S.

A flourishing Iron Age village and farming culture at NOK existed by 100 AD. By 800 AD the centralized state of KANEM-BORNU had established itself in the northeastern part of the country and prospered because of its key position on the trans-Sahara trading route. By the 13th century the lucrative Sahara traffic in goods and slaves led to the rise of seven states in HAUSA-LAND, which traded in competition with Kanem-Bornu. Islam became the dominant religion of the northern states by the 14th century. In the southern forests the Yoruba people had developed a complex culture by the

12th century, centered at IFE. Two major states sprang from Ife: OYO and BENIN.

Europeans began exploration and trade with Nigeria in the late 15th century and immediately initiated an extensive, long-lasting, and profitable traffic in slaves. The economy of Benin rested almost entirely on its delivery of captives to English slavers, and Hausaland in the north participated in the funneling of slaves to the coast. Many small coastal city-states arose; notably BONNY, OWOME, Okrika, and OLD CALABAR.

In 1804 a holy war led by a Fulani, the Muslim reformer Usman dan Fodio, erupted against the northern Hausa kings. By 1817 Hausaland had largely been conquered; and under the leadership of Dan Fodio's son the sultanate of SOKOTO flourished.

In 1807 GREAT BRITAIN abolished slavery and attempted to shut down the slave trade entirely, but traffic with slavers of other nations continued unabated. Only in the delta of the NIGER RIVER did the alternative export of palm oil replace human cargoes. In 1861 the British occupied LAGOS, a major center for slave export, and with the concurrent loss of the American market, slavery's importance declined.

The British exploited the palm oil trade and from 1884 to 1885 claimed Nigeria and slowly gained control of the region through negotiation and military force. In 1914 the entire country was first administered as a unified British protectorate. After World War II Great Britain began to grant Nigeria greater independence while trying to reconcile the different tribal peoples. In 1960 Nigeria became an independent state, but the government was unstable. In 1967 the independent republic of BIAFRA split off in the east, and three years of disastrous civil war killed many thousands of people before the secession was put down and reconciliation effected. In recent years the country has been prosperous because of oil reserves but with the oil glut of the 1980's the economy again declined. Nevertheless, the country gropes toward democracy after the ending of military rule in 1979.

NIGER RIVER Africa's third-largest river, it arises in the highlands of Guinea and flows NE inland through Mali, then between Timbuktu and Gao turns south through Niger, Benin, and Nigeria, a total of 2,000 mi emptying into the Gulf of Guinea, to the south of Nigeria. The river was an important source of water for the arid sub-Saharan medieval MALI and SONGHAI Empires. The city of TIMBUKTU arose along the riverbank near the great bend of the Niger, which sends it south to the Gulf of Guinea. The Niger was never a highway for trade and settlement, however, because of rapids, falls, shifting channels, and seasonal drops in flow.

In the 18th century European explorers began to probe the river. The widely held notion that the Niger flowed from east to west was dispelled by the Scotsman Mungo Park in 1805, when he sailed from Timbuktu to Bussa. In 1830 Richard Cander managed to sail from Bussa to the Niger's mouth in the Gulf of Guinea. He showed that the coastal region known as the OIL RIVERS was in reality the Niger's delta.

NIHAVAND. See NAHÁVAND.

NIHON. See JAPAN.

NIJMEGAN [Nimeguen] [ancient: Noviomagus; French: Nimègue; German: Nimwegen] (Netherlands) Town on the Waal River, 10 mi S of Arnhem, in the E Netherlands. An old Roman town and an important residence of Charlemagne and the Carolingian emperors in the ninth century AD, it was chartered in 1184 and later joined the HANSEATIC LEAGUE. Loyal to SPAIN during the Dutch struggle for independence in the 16th century, it was captured in 1591 by Prince Maurice of NASSAU. A series of treaties was signed here in 1678 and 1679, ending the Dutch Wars of Louis XIV of 1672 to 1678 and leaving France in a supreme political position. In September 1944, during World War II, the U.S. 82nd Airborne dropped troops here. They took the town but were unable to rescue the ground troops surrounded in ARNHEM nearby. The city suffered heavy damage at this time. A medieval church and the ruins of an eighth-century palace built by Charlemagne are here.

NIKARIA. See IKARIA.

NIKKO (Japan) City and religious center in Tochigi prefecture, central HONSHŪ, 72 mi N of Tokyo. Early Shinto Shrines and Buddhist temples from the eighth century are located here; but the city is famous for its ornate temples and mausoleums of the Yedo period of 1600 to 1868. The first and third Tokugawa shoguns, Ieyasu and Iemitsu, built temples here in the 17th century. The famous Gate of Sunlight is in the shrine of Ieyasu.

NIKOLAINKAUPUNKI, NIKOLAISTAD. See VAASA.

NIKOLAYEV [Vernoleninsk] (USSR) City and port on the BUG River, 70 mi NE of Odessa, in the UKRAINE. It was founded in 1784 AD near the site of the ancient Greek colony of OLBIA. Originally used as a naval fortress and shipbuilding center, it began to industrialize in the 20th century. The Germans captured the city in August 1941 during World War II and destroyed its naval base.

NIKOLSBURG. See MIKULOV.

NIKOPOL [ancient: Nicopolis] (Bulgaria) Commercial port on the DANUBE RIVER, 23 mi NE of Pleven. Founded in 629 AD by the Byzantine Emperor Heraclius, it flourished as a mercantile and cultural center. It has been the scene of countless historic battles. The Ottoman Turks defeated an army of Crusaders here in 1396, thus opening the path to a Muslim invasion of Europe. It was besieged by HUNGARY in 1444, and the forces of the OTTOMAN EMPIRE were defeated here in 1595 and 1598. It figured prominently in the Russo-Turkish wars of the 18th and 19th centuries and was burned by RUSSIA in 1877. See also BYZANTINE EMPIRE.

NIKOPOL (USSR) Town on the DNIEPER RIVER, in the E central UKRAINE. Founded in the 1630's, it flourished as a center of river trade. Once a fortified Zaporozhe Cossack station, it has seen much fighting

The largest ancient temple of Egyptian Nubia, half submerged in the flooding waters of the Nile. The temple, built in the time of Augustus, has since been moved.

throughout its history. From late 1941 to February 1944 it was held by GERMANY.

NIKÓPOLIS. See NICOPOLIS.

NIKOSIA. See NICOSIA.

NIKŠIĆ [*former:* **Ogonoste**] (Yugoslavia) Town in MONTENEGRO, approx. 27 mi SE of Titograd. A medieval Turkish fortress guarded the old town until it was taken by Montenegro in 1878. The town's cathedral was donated by Czar Nicholas II. A Roman bridge is located here, as are the ruins of the old fortress.

NILE RIVER [*ancient:* **Nilus;** *Arabic:* **Al-Bahr**] The world's longest, flowing N approx. 4,180 miles from its source near LAKE VICTORIA, to its Egyptian outlet on the MEDITERRANEAN SEA. EGYPT's early prosperity was based on the Nile, and the great cities of ALEXANDRIA, CAIRO, MEMPHIS and THEBES arose along its banks. The river's annual inundations fertilized Egypt's farmland and have provided unfailing irrigation from 4000 BC, turning the desert into a granary of the ancient world. The Blue Nile and the White Nile join at KHARTOUM to form its main stream. Further south, the cataracts of the middle Nile served as a barrier to easy travel and sheltered the SUDAN from invasion from the north. The kingdoms of KUSH and then of MEROË

flourished on the banks of the Nile until destroyed by invaders from ETHIOPIA.

The source of the Nile had been a matter of conjecture since antiquity, and in the middle of the 19th century British explorers began to search actively for it. In 1858 John Speke found Lake Victoria and two years later, accompanied by James Grant, discovered the Nile's source at its northern end. David Livingstone, Richard Burton, and Sir Samuel White Baker all provided detailed information about the Nile basin and its upper course as a result of their explorations. The Aswan High Dam, completed in 1971 south of ASWAN, now contributes to Egypt's hydroelectric power, but has stopped the flow of vital nutrients downstream and caused the silting of the delta. The vast majority of Egypt's population and towns are still centered along the Nile and in the delta.

NILES (United States) City in SW MICHIGAN, 48 mi SW of Kalamazoo. A Jesuit mission was established here in 1690, and Fort St. Joseph was built by the French seven years later. The fort fell to the British in 1761, to Chief Pontiac in 1763, and to the Spanish in 1780. The city was settled permanently in 1827 on a stagecoach route between DETROIT and CHICAGO and was incorporated in 1829.

NILES (United States) Industrial city on the Mahoning River, 8 mi NW of Youngstown, NE OHIO. William McKinley, 25th U.S. president (1897–1901), was born here in 1843. The city was settled in 1806 and incorporated in 1895.

NILUS. See NILE RIVER.

NIMÈGUE. See NIJMEGAN.

NIMEGUEN. See NIJMEGAN.

NÎMES [*ancient:* **Nemausus**; *former:* **Nismes**] (France) City and capital of Gard department, 64 mi NW of Marseilles. Founded in 28 BC by the emperor Augustus for his veterans, by the second century AD it was the principal city of the province of NARBONENSIS and one of the largest cities in Roman GAUL. At the close of the ROMAN EMPIRE it was invaded by barbarians, and later became a medieval viscounty. In 1271 it became part of France. A center of the Protestant Reformation, it was the scene of a massacre of Catholics on Sept. 29, 1567, and many of its citizens fled after the revocation of the Edict of NANTES in 1685.

A bloodless bull fight in the ancient Roman amphitheater of Nîmes, one of many splendid Roman monuments here. The Romans held this southern French city for five centuries.

The city has an extraordinary array of Roman ruins. Its first century AD amphitheater is one of the best preserved in the world, and is still used for bullfights. The small temple called the *Maison Carrée* was built by Agrippa in 16 BC and is almost perfectly preserved. A temple of Diana and a nymphaeum survive from the adornments of the healing spring of Nemausus. Two

city gates and a massive Roman tower also survive. The famous three-tiered aqueduct bridge, the *Pont du Gard*, is nearby.

NIMRUD. See CALAH.

NIMWEGEN. See NIJMEGAN.

NINEVEH [*ancient:* **Ninus**] (Iraq) Ancient capital of ASSYRIA. Its remains lie on the E bank of the TIGRIS RIVER, opposite modern MOSUL. Sargon II made it his capital in the late eighth century BC, succeeding Nimrud (CALAH); but Sennacherib, his successor, built it into the spectacular capital of the ancient Assyrian Empire, one of the great cities of the world. Ashurbanipal developed it further in the seventh century as a cultural center and collected a huge library of cuneiform tablets, containing the knowledge and learning of ancient SUMER, BABYLON, and AKKAD, some of which has been recovered in excavations.

Nineveh and the Assyrian Empire fell to Nabopolassar of Babylon and the king of MEDIA in 612 BC. Excavations on the site were begun by the pioneer archaeologist and explorer, Austen Layard, in 1845. The city wall, the foundations of the lavish palaces of Sennacherib and Ashurbanipal, and much else have been uncovered. See also MESOPOTAMIA.

NINGHSIA. See NINGSIA.

NINGHSIEN. See NING-PO.

NING-PO [*ancient:* **Ching-Yüan**; *former:* **Ninghsien**; *Portuguese:* **Liampo**] (China) City and port on Hangchow Bay, 100 mi S of Shanghai. Dating from 713 AD, it traded with the Portuguese in the 16th century, was occupied in 1841 by the British during the Opium War, and became a treaty port in the following year under the Treaty of NANKING. It was held by JAPAN from 1941 to 1945 during World War II. Called Ninghsien from 1911 to 1949, it fell to the communists in 1949. Several Buddhist temples and monasteries are located here.

NINGSIA [**Ninghsia**] (China) Former province of W INNER MONGOLIA. Part of the 13th-century MONGOL EMPIRES, it was split between Manchu and Mongolian rule in the 17th century. In 1958 it became part of Ningsia Hui Autonomous Region. The Yellow River (HUANG HO) flows through its southern part, on which is situated its capital, YIN-CH'UAN. See also KANSU.

NINGYUAN. See I-NING.

NINUS. See NINEVEH.

NIORO (Mali) Market center and town in W Mali, 200 mi NW of Bamako. It was a trading center of the SONGHAI EMPIRE in the 16th century and became the independent state of Kaarta in the following century. This fell to the Muslim leader Al-hajj Umar in 1854 and to FRANCE in 1891.

NIORT [*ancient:* **Novioritum**] (France) City and capital of Deux-Sèvres department, 83 mi SE of Nantes, W France. A Gallo-Roman town, it was restructured around a 12th-century Plantagenet castle. A Huguenot stronghold during the Protestant Reformation, it suffered from the revocation of the Edict of NANTES in

1685. Two towers remain from its medieval fortress. See also NÎMES.

NIPHON. See JAPAN.

NIPPON. See JAPAN.

NIPPUR (Iraq) City in ancient MESOPOTAMIA, 100 mi SE of Babylon on the EUPHRATES RIVER. A religious and cultural center of the Sumerians and Babylonians, it was especially sacred to the ancient earth god, En-lil. It was ruled later by PERSIA and PARTHIA. Many important archaeological remains and artifacts have been uncovered here, including a horde of Sumerian clay tablets illuminating Sumerian literature, temples dating from the third millennium BC, and the seventh-century ziggurat of Ashurbanipal. See also ASSYRIA, BABYLON, SUMER.

NIŠ [Nish] [*Greek:* **Nissa;** *Latin:* **Naissus, Naïssus**] (Yugoslavia) Transport center on the Nišava River, approx. 125 mi SE of Belgrade, in Serbia. An ancient Greek and Roman city on the Via Militaris through the Balkans, it was the birthplace of Constantine I the Great c.290 AD, and here Claudius II had defeated the OSTROGOTHS some 20 years earlier. The Huns ravaged Naïssus in 441 AD, but Justinian I of the BYZANTINE EMPIRE rebuilt it a century later as an important frontier fortress. It was also an important military center in the Balkans for the OTTOMAN EMPIRE from 1386 to 1878, when it passed to SERBIA. From 1941 to 1944 it was occupied by GERMANY during World War II. The town has a medieval fortress and the Tower of Skulls, built in memory of the Serbs who blew up the powder magazine in 1809, killing themselves and the attacking Turks.

NISH. See NIŠ.

NISHAPUR [Neyshābūr] (Iran) Market town in KHORĀSĀN, approx. 40 mi W of MASHHAD, NE Iran. Founded by Shapur I in the third century AD, it was rebuilt in the next century by Shapur II. It flourished as the capital of the Sassanid dynasty until the mid-fifth century and was rejuvenated during the Tahirid and Samanid dynasties of the ninth and 10th centuries. The Seljuk Turks made it a cultural center in the 11th and 12th centuries. Here the Islamic philosopher Al-Ghazali studied, and the mathematician and poet Omar Khayyam was born and is buried. It was destroyed by earthquakes and foreign invasion in the 13th century. Significant medieval archaeological finds have been unearthed here. See also PERSIA.

NISIBIN. See NUSAYBIN.

NISIBIS. See NUSAYBIN.

NISMES. See NÎMES.

NISSA. See NIŠ.

NISTRUL. See DNIESTER RIVER.

NITERÓI [*former:* **Nictheroy**] (Brazil) Industrial city and suburb across from the city of RIO DE JANEIRO, on Guanabara Bay. Settled by Indians in 1573 on a Portuguese land-grant site, it was chartered in 1671. By 1819 the Indians had gone, and it became the provincial capital in 1835.

NITRA [*German:* **Neutra;** *Hungarian:* **Nyitra**] (Czechoslovakia) Market center, town in Slovak SR, on the Nitra River. First a Roman town, it was a medieval religious center and fortress for four centuries before it became a free city in 1248. Its church and castle, dating from c.830 AD, are the oldest in SLOVAKIA.

NIVE (France) River, approx. 50 mi long, at the base of the PYRENEES MOUNTAINS. The British triumphed over the French in battles along the banks of the Nive in December 1813 during the Napoleonic Wars.

NIVERNAIS (France) Historic region of central France, now part of the Nièvre department, with its capital at NEVERS. The land of the Aedui in ancient GAUL, it later became a countship in the 11th century AD and passed to BURGUNDY and many other rulers before joining the duchy of the Gonzaga family in 1565. It was purchased by Cardinal Mazarin in 1659, who passed it on to his heirs, the Mancini family. They were dispossessed by the French Revolution in 1789.

NIZHNEVARTOVSK (USSR) City in N Siberian SSR, now a developing city in the oil area of western SIBERIA. It was a very small village until the discovery of one of the world's largest oil fields here in 1965 at nearby Lake Samotlar.

NIZHNI NOVGOROD. See GORKI.

NIZIB. See NIZIP.

NIZIP [*former:* **Nezib, Nizib**] (Turkey) Town in Gaziantep province, 22 mi E of Gaziantep. Ibrahim Pasha, directing the Egyptian campaign of Mehmet Ali against the Turks, won impressively here on June 24, 1839. See also OTTOMAN EMPIRE.

NIZZA. See NICE.

NO. See THEBES, Egypt.

NOAILLES [*former:* **Longvilliers**] (France) Town in central Oise department. Having belonged to the famous Noailles family, it took its present name from that family in the 17th century.

NOEMFOOR. See NUMFOOR.

NOGALES (Mexico) Railroad terminus and port of entry on the Arizona border, adjacent to the U.S. city of the same name, Sonora state, NW Mexico. A bloody border clash was fought here in 1918 as the city was occupied by Anglo-Americans from NOGALES, Arizona.

NOGALES [*former:* **Isaactown**] (United States) Mining center and city on the Mexican border, adjacent to the city in MEXICO of the same name, 60 mi S of Tucson, ARIZONA. Founded in 1880 and incorporated in 1893, it was the scene of several forays against Pancho Villa in 1916. The 1699 Tumacori Mission is preserved, but the Guevavi Mission, established here in 1692, is now in ruins, as is nearby Tubac, Arizona's first European settlement, dating from 1752.

NOGENT-LE-ROTROU (France) Town in W Eure-et-Loir department. A hospital located in the town houses the tomb of the duke of Sully (1560–1641), French statesman and close adviser to Henry IV.

NOGENT-SUR-SEINE (France) Town in NW Aube department, approx. 56 mi SE of Paris. A few miles away is the site of the monastery of the Paraclete established in 1123 by Peter Abélard, the famous logician, theologian, and philosopher instrumental in laying the foundation of the University of Paris. Originally a haven for Abélard's followers, the Paraclete was later given by Abélard to Héloïse, his pupil whom he had loved and secretly married. After Abélard had been castrated by her relatives for the union, Héloïse founded a sisterhood here in 1129, while Abélard himself entered a monastery and guided and consoled his wife at the Paraclete. It was here that Héloïse received Abélard's *History of My Calamities* c.1135. In 1136 she was made abbess of the house. Eventually it housed the tombs of both Héloïse and Abélard.

NOGINSK [*former:* **Bogorodsk, Rogozhi**] (USSR) City 35 mi E of Moscow, Russian SFSR. Founded in the 16th century as Rogozhi and later renamed Bogorodsk, it has been a major textile center since the 19th century.

NOK (Nigeria) Village of central Nigeria that has given its name to a culture that flourished from c.900 BC to 200 AD. Nok culture produced a wide variety of highly decorative and finely crafted terracotta figurines. Primarily an agricultural society, Nok was actively smelting and working iron deposits as early as 400 BC.

NOKUHIVA. See NUKU HIVA.

NOLA (Italy) Agricultural town in Napoli province, CAMPANIA region, 16 mi NE of Naples. The town was of Oscan origin but was settled by Etruscans before the fifth century BC and passed to the Samnites. It thrived as a possession of ROME after 313 BC, and as an early center of Christianity. Marcellus fought the great general Hannibal of Carthage here in 216 and 215 BC. Augustus, the first ruler of the ROMAN EMPIRE, died in this town in 14 AD. Roman ruins located here include an amphitheater, tombs, and an early Christian cemetery.

NOLICHUCKEY RIVER (United States) River, approx. 150 mi long, rising in the Blue Ridge Mts in W NORTH CAROLINA, and flowing NW across the TENNESSEE border to join the French Broad River. Its first settlement was founded in 1772, and the frontiersman Davy Crockett was born in 1786 along its banks at Limestone, near GREENVILLE, Tennessee.

NOMBRE DE DIOS (Panama) Spanish colonial settlement in N Panama, NE of Portobelo. Founded in 1510, it was abandoned toward the end of the 16th century because of its unhealthy location. For several years it was an important port of NEW SPAIN.

NOME (United States) City on S Seward peninsula, at the mouth of the Snake River, W central ALASKA. Only a small fishing village, it was founded in 1896 as a gold-mining camp. It boomed almost overnight as the center of the Alaskan gold rush from 1899 to 1903. It was almost entirely destroyed by fire in 1934 but has been rebuilt since.

NO-MEN-K'AN [**Nomonhan**] (China) Town of INNER MONGOLIA in NE China. The USSR was victorious in a battle fought here in 1939 against forces from

JAPAN penetrating China in the second Sino-Japanese War.

NOMONHAN. See NO-MEN-K'AN.

NONNEBAKKEN. See SLAGELSE, Denmark.

NOORDBRABANT. See NORTH BRABANT.

NOORDHOLLAND. See NORTH HOLLAND.

NOOTEN EYLANDT. See GOVERNORS ISLAND.

NOOTKA SOUND (Canada) Inlet of the Pacific Ocean, W VANCOUVER ISLAND, SW BRITISH COLUMBIA. Capt. James Cook discovered it in 1778, and the British established a trading post here in 1788. The Spanish seized it in 1789, opening a controversy settled by the Nootka Convention in 1790, which permitted British settlement in the region.

NOPH. See MEMPHIS, Egypt.

NORBA CAESARINA. See CÁCERES.

NORCIA [**Nursia**] (Italy) Market town in Perugia province, UMBRIA region, 41 mi SE of Perugia. An ancient Sabine center, it was colonized by ROME in 290 BC. St. Benedict, founder of the Benedictine monastic movement in the West, was born here c.480 AD. Medieval city walls and buildings, along with a 16th-century fortress, have survived a series of major earthquakes that first hit the area in the early 18th century and have continued in recent years.

NORDALBINGIA. See DITHMARSCHEN.

NORDEN (West Germany) Industrial port and city in EAST FRIESLAND in NW Lower SAXONY, 16 mi N of Emden. First mentioned in 1124, it is the oldest town in the East Friesland region.

NORDHAUSEN (East Germany) City in Erfurt district, 69 mi W of Leipzig. A royal residence as early as the 10th century AD, it was a free city from 1253 to 1803. It was a member of the HANSEATIC LEAGUE and passed to PRUSSIA in 1815. The infamous Nazi concentration camp Dora, and underground rocket production plants for the V-2 ballistic missile were located here during World War II, in which the city was badly damaged. A 12th-century Gothic cathedral has survived here along with a 17th-century town hall.

NÖRDLINGEN (West Germany) Picturesque walled town, once in SWABIA, now in BAVARIA. It was founded in the ninth century AD and became a free city in 1217. Two battles were fought here during the Thirty Years War. In 1634 imperial troops defeated a Swedish army directed by Duke Bernhard of SAXE-WEIMAR, partly facilitating France's entry into the war. The French defeated the imperial forces here in 1645. Nördlingen passed to Bavaria in 1803.

NORD-OSTSEE KANAL [*former:* **Kaiser Wilhelm Canal**] (West Germany) Canal, approx. 60 mi long, extending from the BALTIC SEA, through SCHESWIG-HOLSTEIN, to the NORTH SEA. Constructed between 1887 and 1895, it was a prime target of aerial attacks and bombings in World War II.

NORDRHEIN-WESTFALEN. See NORTH RHINE-WESTPHALIA.

NORE, THE (England) Sandbank in the THAMES

RIVER estuary, 3 mi NE of Sheerness. A historic mooring, it was the scene of a mutiny in the British fleet a short time after the 1797 SPITHEAD mutiny. This mutiny, unlike its predecessor, was unsuccessful; and its leader, Richard Parker, was executed.

NORFOLK (England) Maritime county in the E, on the NORTH SEA, with its admin. hq. at NORWICH. Inhabited in prehistoric times, it became part of the SAXON SHORE in late Roman times, and of the kingdom of EAST ANGLIA following the Anglo-Saxon invasions of Britain in the late fifth century AD. It was also included in the DANELAW. In the late Middle Ages it was a center of the English wool trade. See also GREAT YARMOUTH, KING'S LYNN, THETFORD.

NORFOLK (United States) Commercial and industrial city and a major port at the mouth of the JAMES RIVER in SE VIRGINIA. One of the largest cities in the state, with nearby PORTSMOUTH and NEWPORT NEWS it makes up the huge port of HAMPTON ROADS. Founded in 1682, at the onset of the American Revolution the town, which was a Tory stronghold, was attacked by patriots. It was subsequently almost entirely burned, except for St. Paul's Church, built in 1738, which still stands today. It was incorporated in 1845. In May 1862 the pioneer ironclad warships *Monitor* and *Merrimac* clashed here in nearby Hampton Roads in the same month that Union troops occupied the city during the Civil War. Norfolk was an important naval center during World War II and now contains many top naval and marine installations. This major military complex also includes aeronautical facilities.

NORFOLK ISLAND (Australia) Island in the S Pacific Ocean, NE of Sydney, 800 mi E of the mainland. Discovered by Capt. James Cook in 1774, it became a penal colony of GREAT BRITAIN between 1788 and 1855. In 1856 the prisoners were removed, many descendants of the ship *Bounty* mutineers were brought here from PITCAIRN ISLAND, and the island was placed under the jurisdiction of NEW SOUTH WALES. It was incorporated into Australia in 1913.

NORICUM (Austria) Ancient region and Roman province, S of the DANUBE RIVER and W of modern Vienna, in the E ALPS. An old Celtic area, it was captured in 16 BC by ROME and its iron ore was profitably mined. It flourished as an outpost of the ROMAN EMPIRE, but was overrun by barbarian invaders in the fifth century AD.

NORMAN (United States) Agricultural center and city, 18 mi S of Oklahoma City, OKLAHOMA. It was first settled on April 22, 1889 during the great homestead "run" when the government permitted a large strip of land to be settled on a first-come basis. It was incorporated in 1902.

NORMANDIE. See NORMANDY.

NORRIDGEWOCK (United States) Town on the KENNEBEC RIVER, 13 mi NW of Waterville, W MAINE. Close by was an Indian village inhabited by Algonquians, who had been in the northeast for several thousand years. This tribe, called Abnaki by the French, was driven out and the village destroyed by the British in 1774. They then settled among the French in CANADA. The word "wigwam" is from their language.

NORRISTOWN (United States) Town on the SCHUYLKILL RIVER, 17 mi NW of Philadelphia, SE PENNSYLVANIA. Purchased from William Penn in 1704 by Isaac Norris, the Quaker mayor of PHILADELPHIA, it was incorporated in 1812. Civil War General Winfield Scott Hancock, Democratic presidential candidate in 1880, was born and is buried here.

NORRKÖPING (Sweden) Industrial center and port on an inlet of the BALTIC SEA, Östergotland county, 30 mi SW of Stockholm. Dating from the Bronze Age, it was founded as a city in the mid-14th century and chartered in 1384. In 1719 it was burned by Russian troops during the Great Northern War. It has been an important textile center since that industry's inception in Sweden in 1621 and was the scene of the coronation of Gustavus IV in 1800.

NORTH ADAMS (United States) Industrial city on the Hoosic River, 22 mi NE of Pittsfield, NW MASSACHUSETTS. Founded in 1748, it was incorporated and separated from ADAMS in 1878. Portions of the old Indian MOHAWK TRAIL go through the area. Fort Massachusetts, now in ruins, was erected here in 1745 by the Bay Colony and was burned a year later by a force of Indians and French soldiers.

NORTHALLERTON (England) Town and admin. hq. of North Yorkshire, 31 mi NNW of York. The Battle of the Standard, fought here on Aug. 22, 1138, was the scene of an English triumph as King Stephen (1135–54) stopped an invasion by King David of SCOTLAND. The latter's forces marched in service of the English Queen, Matilda, who was at civil war with Stephen. The peace treaty following, however, gave NORTHUMBRIA to David.

NORTHAMPTON (England) Town and admin. hq. of Northamptonshire, 60 mi NW of London, on the Nene River. Once a Roman settlement, it was significant as a habitation of the Anglo-Saxons, beginning in the sixth century AD, and of the Danes from the ninth to the 11th centuries AD. Its Norman castle, razed in the 19th century, was the scene of parliamentary meetings from the 12th to 14th centuries, including the one that granted independence to SCOTLAND in 1328. It was also the scene of the trial and condemnation of Thomas à Becket in 1164. Henry VI was defeated and abducted by the Yorkists in a battle fought here in 1460 during the Wars of the Roses. The city, largely destroyed by fire in 1675, has Roman and Anglo-Saxon remains.

NORTHAMPTON (United States) Manufacturing city, 16 mi N of Springfield, on the Connecticut River, W MASSACHUSETTS. It was founded in 1654 and incorporated in 1883. The famous colonial pastor, Jonathan Edwards, preached here for 25 years. Calvin Coolidge, 30th president of the United States, was the city's mayor from 1910 to 1911. The Parsons House, built in 1658, is located here.

NORTHAMPTON, Pennsylvania. See ALLENTOWN.

NORTHAMPTONSHIRE [Northampton, Nor-

thants] (England) Agricultural county of the Midlands. The old Roman roads, WATLING STREET and ERMINE STREET, run through it. Later it was part of the Anglo-Saxon kingdom of MERCIA until the Danish occupation. The Danes were finally integrated into the kingdom in the 10th and 11th centuries, leaving many place names on the land. The county's admin. hq. is NORTHAMPTON. See also DANELAW.

NORTH ANDOVER (United States) Town on the MERRIMACK RIVER, 23 mi N of Boston, NE MASSACHUSETTS. Founded in 1646, it was set off from ANDOVER and incorporated in 1855. Anne Bradstreet (1612–72), one of America's first woman writers, lived here with her husband Simon, governor of the Massachusetts Bay Colony from 1679 to 1686 and 1689 to 1692. Samuel Phillips, educator and statesman, was born here in 1752. The town partook in the early textile growth in NEW ENGLAND, but it now has diversified industries and several well-known schools.

NORTH ANNA (United States) River in E central VIRGINIA, joining the South Anna River to form the Pamunkey River in N Hanover county. Union forces under Gen. Ulysses S. Grant were unable to drive Gen. R.E. Lee's Confederate army from its positions near the river's confluence with the Pamunkey. The Civil War battle here was fought from May 23 to 25, 1864 during Grant's campaign designed to capture RICHMOND.

NORTHANTS. See NORTHAMPTONSHIRE.

NORTH ATTLEBORO (United States) Town, 28 mi SW of Boston, SE MASSACHUSETTS. Founded in 1669 and set off from ATTLEBORO in 1887, it has been the site of a notable jewelry industry since 1807. The colonial Woodcock tavern of 1670 and Attleboro Falls are attractions here.

NORTH BORNEO. See SABAH.

NORTH BRABANT [*Dutch:* **Noordbrabant**] (Netherlands) Province of S Netherlands, bordered by Belgium to the S and West Germany to the E. It was part of BRABANT until its active participation in the struggle for Dutch independence from Spanish rule brought it under the UNITED PROVINCES after the Peace of Westphalia in 1648. It became a province in 1795.

NORTH BRADDOCK (United States) Town on the MONONGAHELA RIVER, a suburb of PITTSBURGH, SE PENNSYLVANIA. General Edward Braddock's troops were defeated here during the French and Indian War in 1755. It figured prominently in events leading up to the Whiskey Rebellion after the American Revolution. Andrew Carnegie inaugurated his first steel factory here in 1875.

NORTH CAROLINA (United States) State in the SE, on the Atlantic Ocean, with Virginia to the N, South Carolina and Georgia to the S, and Tennessee to the W. It was the 12th and next-to-last of the original states to ratify the Constitution, in November 1789, after the Constitution had gone into effect. The coast was explored by Giovanni da Verrazano in 1524, and Spanish navigators may have been in the area by the 1580's. Sir Walter Raleigh sent out colonists from ENGLAND in 1585 who settled on ROANOKE ISLAND but returned to England the next year. Two years later Raleigh sent out another group under John White. White went back to England for supplies, returned to Roanoke in 1591 and found all the colonists gone. Their fate and that of their Lost Colony has never been determined. Among them was Virginia Dare (b. 1587), the first child of English parents born in America. The first permanent settlement here was made in 1563 around Albemarle Sound.

In 1629 King Charles I granted a large area here to Sir Robert Heath, and it was named Carolina in the king's honor; but in 1663 Charles II reallocated the land to eight of his favorites. After 1691 the region was known as North Carolina and ruled by deputy governors appointed from CHARLESTON, South Carolina, until 1711. Growth was slow, and at this time there were only three towns. Also in 1711 a bitter war with the Tuscarora Indians broke out. They were defeated and in 1714 moved to NEW YORK and joined the Iroquois. After North Carolina was made a royal colony in 1729 it developed more rapidly, as more immigrants arrived.

An insurrection, put down with bloodshed by the militia, disturbed the colony from 1768 to 1771. This was the Regulator Movement, a protest of back-country farmers against domination by eastern coast aristocrats. In May 1775 the citizens of Mecklenburg county adopted anti-British resolutions that implied independence, but there is serious question as to the authenticity of the Mecklenburg Declaration of Independence, supposedly proclaimed that month. During the American Revolution, Carolina Loyalists were defeated in February 1776 at the Battle of MOORES CREEK Bridge, near WILMINGTON. In the Carolina Campaign of 1780/81, the British attempted to revive Loyalist support in both the Carolinas by invading the region. In North Carolina, at the end of the campaign, General Cornwallis won a battle at GUILFORD COURTHOUSE in March 1781 but felt compelled to retreat, first to Wilmington, and then to Virginia, where he was forced to surrender at YORKTOWN.

The state continued to be dominated by eastern planters until 1835, when the western part of the state, now the most populous, forced through a new constitution. The final removal of the Cherokee Indians began that year, too. The state made progress until the Civil War, passing an early public-school law in 1839. But it seceded in May 1861 at the start of the Civil War. At its end, on April 26, 1865, Gen. J.E. Johnston surrendered the last large Confederate force on North Carolina soil.

The state became involved in the struggle over Reconstruction; abolished slavery in 1868; then saw the conservatives regain control in 1871. Meanwhile, the state prospered, especially because of the increased demand for tobacco. An agrarian revolt, spearheaded by the Granger Movement, the Farmers' Alliance, and the Populist Party, created turbulence in the 1880's and 1890's. In the 20th century North Carolina has been progressive in supporting education and in developing agriculture and industry. The state leads the nation in the production of textiles, tobacco, and furniture. In the 1950's, and 1960's North Carolina made a more peaceful adjustment to school integration than most southern states. It is the site of the University of North Carolina at CHAPEL HILL and of Duke University at DURHAM. At Kitty Hawk, on the coast, the Wright brothers made the first controlled airplane flight in 1903. RALEIGH is the capital; and CHARLOTTE, GREENSBORO, and WINSTON-SALEM are the largest cities.

NORTH CHICAGO (United States) Industrial city on Lake Michigan, 5 mi S of the port of Waukegan, NE ILLINOIS. Incorporated in 1909, it was the scene of a sit-down strike engaged in by steelworkers in 1937. This led to a decision in 1939 by the Supreme Court outlawing such strikes.

NORTH DAKOTA (United States) State in the N central region, bordering on Canada to the N, Minnesota to the E, South Dakota to the S, and Montana to the W. It is in the geographical center of North America. It was admitted to the Union in 1889 as the 39th state. "Dakota" is the name of an Indian tribe of the western Sioux.

In 1738, when the French explorer and trader Pierre de la Vérendrye entered this region, he found the Mandan Indians farming on the banks of the MISSOURI RIVER. There were other tribes, some also agricultural, such as the Arikara and Hidatsa; some nomadic, such as the Cheyenne Cree, Sioux, Assiniboin, Crow, and Ojibwa. Two sons of Vérendrye arrived in 1742, seeking a route to the Far East. A few years later fur traders became active and in 1804/05 the Lewis and Clark Expedition spent the winter with the Mandans. Both the North West Fur Company and the Hudson's Bay Company set up trading posts in the Red River of the North Valley, but after 1828 John Jacob Astor's American Fur Company won control of the fur trade.

The first settlement was made at PEMBINA in 1812, and the arrival of the steamboat on the upper Missouri encouraged more settlement. However, the permanent population was still very small in 1861 when Dakota Territory was created, including both present North and SOUTH DAKOTA and part of MONTANA and WYOMING. In 1857 military posts began to be built to protect travelers and railroad workers; and the Homestead Act of 1862 promoted settlement. On the other hand, concern with the Civil War and Indian troubles discouraged many pioneers. War with the Sioux was ended by treaty in 1868 but broke out again in the Dakotas in 1876, when gold was discovered in the BLACK HILLS of South Dakota and prospectors refused to respect Indian rights to the land. In 1881 the Sioux under Sitting Bull fled to Canada, where they surrendered. They were returned to the United States and were placed on reservations.

In the 1870's agriculture bloomed in the Red River Valley, when the "bonanza" wheat fields, farms of 3,000 to 65,000 acres, were created. The flow of settlers increased as railroads were built in the 1870's and 1880's, the immigrants being mostly from SCANDINAVIA, GERMANY and CZECHOSLOVAKIA. When North Dakota's state boundaries were set, the northwestern

half came from the LOUISIANA PURCHASE, while the southeastern half was the result of the boundary adjustment of 1818 between the United States and GREAT BRITAIN.

Differences between agrarians and mining and railroad interests aroused political controversy. The Republicans were in power until the Farmers' Alliance grew in strength and elected a governor in 1892, with Democratic and Populist Party support. In 1915 the Non-Partisan League was formed by farmers to oppose the grain industry owners. The League achieved power in 1919 and brought about state ownership of grain elevators and the establishment of a state bank.

BISMARCK is the capital; other cities are FARGO, GRAND FORKS, and Minot. The Badlands, in the southwest, where Theodore Roosevelt owned a ranch and spent part of each year from 1883 to 1886, were long known as "Hell with the fires out," because the topography made travel so difficult.

NORTH-EAST NEW GUINEA. See BISMARCK ARCHIPELAGO, NEW GUINEA, PAPUA NEW GUINEA.

NORTHERN IRELAND. See IRELAND, NORTHERN.

NORTHERN NECK (United States) Region in colonial VIRGINIA between the RAPPAHANNOCK and POTOMAC rivers. It was inherited by Thomas Fairfax from his grandfather Baron Culpeper, colonial governor. The Fairfax proprietors held their grant through the American Revolution, and Thomas Fairfax was the only British peer in America at that time; he remained unharmed. In 1785 the state of Virginia cancelled the Northern Neck proprietorship.

NORTHERN RHODESIA Former British colonial possession of central Africa; now the republic of ZAMBIA. The early history of the region is conjectural. During the 16th and 17th centuries a flow of migrations to the area between Lake Malawi and the headwaters of the ZAMBEZI RIVER brought a mixed group of Bantu-speaking peoples together here. By the 19th century several tribes dominated major parts of the country. The Lunda controlled a large area in the north, the Bemba ruled east of them, and the Luyana dominated the far west along the Zambezi. In the middle of the 19th century the Ngoni became an important force as they crossed the Zambezi from the south. The Kololo left their native Basutoland and invaded Barotseland in the west from 1863 to 1864, when they were ousted by the LOZI KINGDOM.

European interest in the area began with the explorations of the Scottish missionary David Livingstone, though explorers from PORTUGAL had entered the northeastern part of the country more than 20 years earlier. Several missions were established here during the latter half of the 19th century, and in 1890 agents of the British South Africa Company, set up by Cecil Rhodes, who gave his name to RHODESIA, obtained treaties from some local tribal leaders. Using these as an excuse, GREAT BRITAIN claimed the area in 1891 and sent troops to subdue Lunda and Ngoni warriors who resisted their domination. In 1911 Great Britain consolidated its protectorates of Northeastern and Northwestern Rhodesia into the single protectorate of Northern Rhodesia.

In 1923/24 major copper reserves were discovered in Northern Rhodesia, and six years later a mining boom created cities and towns peopled by black and white workers drawn from across southern Africa. Segregation and racial discrimination were imported from SOUTH AFRICA, while Northern Rhodesia's Africans constantly fought for better conditions. Strikes and riots erupted in 1925, 1940, and 1956.

The first organized African nationalist political movement was formed following World War II and unsuccessfully resisted the formation of the white-dominated Federation of Rhodesia and Nyasaland. Harry Nkumbala was the first leader of the African nationalist movement, but in 1958 Kenneth Kuanda became prominent. By 1960 Great Britain had decided to implement the gradual transfer of power to the African majority, but violent opposition from Northern Rhodesia's 70,000 white occupants slowed the process. In 1964 the first open election with universal suffrage was held, and Kuanda took over as prime minister. Northern Rhodesia became the independent Republic of Zambia on October 24, 1964 with Kenneth Kuanda as its first president. See also LUNDALAND, MALAWI, ZIMBABWE.

NORTHERN TERRITORY (Australia) Territory in N Australia. Originally settled from 1825 to 1863 as part of NEW SOUTH WALES, it was under SOUTH AUSTRALIA from 1863 to 1911 and became a territory in 1931. Bombed by JAPAN in February 1942, it was subsequently placed under military control until the end of World War II.

NORTHFIELD (United States) City, 36 mi S of St. Paul, S MINNESOTA. Founded in 1855 and incorporated two decades later, it was the scene on Sept. 7, 1876 of an attempted bank robbery by the noted bandits Frank and Jesse James and their gang. Several people were killed as the robbery was aborted.

NORTH FRISIAN ISLANDS. See FRISIAN ISLANDS.

NORTH GERMAN CONFEDERATION (Germany) A league of 22 German states lying N of the MAIN RIVER, it replaced the GERMAN CONFEDERATION after the Austro-Prussian War of 1866. Created in 1867 by the Prussian Chancellor Bismarck and dominated by PRUSSIA, it marked the new supremacy of Prussia over AUSTRIA in German affairs. It was superseded by the GERMAN EMPIRE in 1871. See also GERMANY.

NORTH GRAHAM ISLAND. See GRAHAM LAND.

NORTH HOLLAND [*Dutch:* **Noordholland**] (Netherlands) Peninsular province in the NW, on the NORTH SEA. Separated from SOUTH HOLLAND in 1840, it had previously played a leading role in the struggle for Dutch independence from Spain from 1568 to 1648. Its capital is HAARLEM. See also AMSTERDAM, HOLLAND.

NORTH INGERMANLAND (USSR) N part of the historic region of INGRIA, which is presently contained in Leningrad oblast, Russian SFSR. It seceded in 1920 from the new revolutionary government set up after the Russian Revolution but was soon forced into submission.

NORTH KANARA. See KANARA.

NORTH KINGSTOWN [*former:* **Kingstowne**] (United States) Commercial town on NARRAGANSETT BAY, 18 mi S of Providence, S central RHODE ISLAND. Founded in 1641 by Roger Williams and incorporated in 1674 as Kings Towne, it was separated from SOUTH KINGSTOWN in 1723. Minutemen and British troops clashed here during the American Revolution. Painter Charles Gilbert Stuart (1755–1828) was born here. Many colonial buildings are located in the town.

NORTH KOREA. See KOREA.

NORTH LITTLE ROCK [*former:* **Argenta, Silver City**] (United States) Agricultural center and industrial city, on the Arkansas River, opposite LITTLE ROCK, central ARKANSAS. Settled by prospectors as Silver City c.1855, it was incorporated in 1903. It grew with the onrush of silver miners late in the 19th century and was part of Little Rock until its citizenry proposed a bill, passed by the state legislature in 1903, allowing it to secede. It was then briefly named Argenta.

NORTH OLMSTEAD (United States) Residential city and suburb of CLEVELAND, NE OHIO. It was settled in 1815 and incorporated in 1951. The first national intracity bus line was inaugurated here in 1931.

NORTH OSSETIAN AUTONOMOUS SOVIET SOCIALIST REPUBLIC (USSR) Republic in the N central CAUCASUS MOUNTAINS, SE Russian SFSR. Alans, descendants of the early Scythian tribes, had inhabited the region since the fifth century AD. Its people were converted to Christianity in the 15th century. The region was taken by RUSSIA in 1802. Its capital is ORDZHONIKIDZE. See also OSSETIA, OSSETIAN MILITARY ROAD, SCYTHIA, SOUTH OSSETIAN AUTONOMOUS OBLAST.

NORTH PLATTE (United States) City between the North Platte and South Platte rivers, central NEBRASKA. It was founded in 1866 and incorporated in 1910. Scouts Rest Ranch, for three decades the home of the army scout, Pony Express rider, and showman Buffalo Bill (William) Cody, is located nearby. See PLATTE RIVER.

NORTH PLATTE RIVER. See PLATTE RIVER.

NORTH POLE The N extremity of the earth's axis, not to be confused with the North Magnetic Pole off Ellef Ringnes Island in Canada or the North Geomagnetic Pole in NW Greenland in Inglefield Land. It was the goal of many explorers, including, for instance, the fatal trip of S.A. Andrée in a balloon in 1897, during which he lost his life. In the race to reach the pole overland, the American explorer Adm. Robert E. Peary, after a number of attempts, reached it on April 6, 1909. In 1926 Adm. Richard E. Byrd and Floyd Bennett flew over the pole, and in 1958 the pioneer atomic-powered submarine, the *Nautilus*, crossed the pole underwater. Another U.S. atomic submarine, the *Skate*, followed the same route and surfaced at the pole in 1960. In 1968 and 1969 a foot and dogsled expedition crossed over the pole for the first time. In 1971 Guido Monzino of Italy followed Peary's route here. In 1978 Naomi Uemura of Japan was the first man to reach the pole alone by dogsled. In 1977 the Soviet icebreaker *Arktika* reached it, and in 1979 a Soviet team reached it on skis. See also the ARCTIC.

NORTH RHINE-WESTPHALIA [*German:* **Nordrhein-Westfalen**] (West Germany) State in W Germany. Much of this region was badly destroyed during World War II. It was formed in 1946 by the amalgamation of the historic Prussian province of WESTPHALIA, the northern part of the former RHINE PROVINCE of PRUSSIA, and the former state of LIPPE.

NORTH SEA [German Ocean] [*ancient:* **Mare Germanicum**] Arm of the Atlantic Ocean between the European mainland and GREAT BRITAIN, the invasion route for the Angles, Saxons, and Jutes invading Britain in the late Roman Empire period, and for the Vikings in the ninth and 10th centuries. King Canute briefly joined the British Isles and Scandinavia across the North Sea in the 11th century. The cities of the HANSEATIC LEAGUE traded across its waters, and it has been a battleground for European nations from the 16th century on through both world wars. Important and extensive natural gas and oil fields have been discovered near its shores off NORWAY and SCOTLAND in recent years, and in 1970 oil was found under the ocean's floor. See also DOGGER BANK, JUTLAND, SCANDINAVIA.

NORTH SHORE. See DEVONPORT, New Zealand.

NORTH SLOPE. See ALASKA.

NORTH TARRYTOWN (United States) Residential village on the HUDSON RIVER, 26 mi N of New York City, SE NEW YORK State. It was founded in 1680 by the early Dutch settler, Frederick Philipse, whose restored manor house and mill are located here. The village provided the setting for Washington Irving's *Legend of Sleepy Hollow.* The Old Dutch Church of 1697 and the adjacent old Sleepy Hollow Cemetery are also in the village. See also TARRYTOWN.

NORTHUMBERLAND (England) Northernmost English county, bordering on SCOTLAND, with a coastal plain on the NORTH SEA, moors and hills inland, and an industrial area in the SE. The admin. hq., NEWCASTLE UPON TYNE, now in the independent metropolitan county of Tyne and Wear, was retained after reorganization. The Roman HADRIAN'S WALL crosses the county from Carlisle to Newcastle. In the sixth century AD the area was overrun by the Anglo-Saxons. Circa 600 AD the settlements of DEIRA and BERNICIA were united to form NORTHUMBRIA, which became under Edwin, Oswald, and Oswiu the dominant Anglo-Saxon kingdom in England, extending at one time from the Scottish lowlands south through YORKSHIRE. From the late seventh century Northumbria was a renowned center of the arts and learning, centering on monasteries at LINDISFARNE, WEARMOUTH, and JARROW. The Venerable Bede, (673–735) of Jarrow, was the greatest scholar of his age. Oswiu called the famous synod of WHITBY in 664.

Little survived from the Danish invasions of 867; and in the 10th century Northumbria came under the kings of WESSEX. The Normans ravaged the area after William I's conquest in 1066; but in the later Middle Ages, despite recurring border warfare, Northumberland flourished in the wool trade, hides, shipping, and in exporting coal for London. Shipbuilding, sheep-raising, and coal-based industries still dominate the economy today. BERWICK-UPON-TWEED is its most northerly city.

NORTHUMBERLAND (United States) Town on the SUSQUEHANNA RIVER, 28 mi SE of Williamsport, E central PENNSYLVANIA. Joseph Priestley (1733–1804), noted English scientist, clergyman, and theologian, was driven out of his home country in 1794 because of his revolutionary teachings and his sympathetic attitude toward the democratic revolutions in America and France. He found refuge in this town, which was his home for the last decade of his life.

NORTHUMBRIA (England) Anglo-Saxon kingdom. Formed in the late sixth century AD, its King Edwin of DEIRA (616–32) made it the supreme power in England and also converted it to Christianity. Oswald (633–41) introduced Celtic Christianity to the kingdom, which soon was subjugated by MERCIA. It throve as a cultural and religious center until the Danes conquered it in 867. It was annexed by WESSEX in 920. See also NORTHUMBERLAND.

NORTH VIETNAM. See VIETNAM.

NORTH-WEST FRONTIER PROVINCE (Pakistan) Province in the NW, on the border of Afghanistan. Strategically located near the KHYBER PASS, it was conquered c.325 BC by Alexander the Great, followed by many other rulers over the centuries. The Muslim Pathan tribes arrived here in the seventh century AD, and by the 12th century they controlled the region. They were subjugated by the MOGUL EMPIRE in the 16th and 17th centuries; then by the Afghan Durrani in the 18th century; then by the Sikhs in the 19th century; and finally by GREAT BRITAIN from 1849 to 1947, who had considerable difficulty in maintaining order among the rebellious tribesmen. Many ancient remains have been found in this province where the Buddhist Mahayana tradition was founded.

NORTHWEST PASSAGE Navigable water routes connecting the Atlantic and Pacific oceans via the ARCTIC archipelago off North America. Sir Martin Frobisher was the first to seek this passage, in 1576, in an attempt to reach the Far East. He was followed by John Davis in 1585 and Henry Hudson in 1610, who discovered HUDSON BAY, where he died in 1611 when mutineers set him afloat. The Hudson's Bay Company was chartered to find the passage. Explorations were later started from the Pacific coast. With the end of wars between France and England in the early 19th century, the effort was resumed. By 1854 the existence of the passage was proven. In 1845–1848 Sir John Franklin's expedition was frozen in and perished in Victoria strait. It was first navigated by the Norwegian explorer Roald Amundsen from 1903 to 1906. In 1969, spurred by the discovery of oil in ALASKA in the 1960's, the icebreaker *Manhattan* became the first commercial vessel to traverse the passage. See also NORTHWEST TERRITORIES.

NORTHWEST TERRITORIES (Canada) Governmental division encompassing all of the country north of the Canadian provinces, except YUKON TERRITORY. It includes the islands of the ARCTIC archipelago. Sir Martin Frobisher, who made three annual voyages beginning in 1576, was the first European to explore the region, in the area of lower BAFFIN ISLAND and Hudson Strait. Henry Hudson saw more of it when he discovered HUDSON BAY in 1610. The Hudson's Bay Company, established in 1670 by a grant from Charles II of ENGLAND, sent fur traders and explorers into the vast unknown land it controlled. Samuel Hearne reached the mouth of the Coppermine River in 1771 and Alexander Mackenzie the mouth of the Mackenzie River in 1789.

The region attracted explorers seeking the NORTHWEST PASSAGE around the mainland and through the many islands. Sir John Franklin carried out his first such expedition from 1819 to 1822, his second from 1825 to 1827, and disappeared on his final voyage in 1845. In 1870 the land of the Hudson's Bay Company was sold to the Dominion of Canada. This, with the Arctic islands transferred by GREAT BRITAIN to Canada in 1880, constituted the original Northwest Territories. Some of the land was transferred to ONTARIO, LABRADOR, and QUEBEC; and later the provinces of ALBERTA, MANITOBA, and SASKATCHEWAN were carved out of it, as was the Yukon Territory. The present boundaries were settled in 1912.

NORTHWEST TERRITORY (United States) Former governmental division, consisting of what became the states of ILLINOIS, INDIANA, MICHIGAN, OHIO, WISCONSIN, and part of MINNESOTA. As a geographical region it was earlier known as the Old Northwest, being then land W of PENNSYLVANIA, N of the OHIO RIVER, E of the MISSISSIPPI RIVER, and S of the Great Lakes. Europeans were attracted to it as rich fur country, and in 1634 Jean Nicolet of FRANCE was the first to enter the region. In 1749 the Ohio Company received a British land grant and was active in the Ohio River Valley. The British and French conflict for the region culminated in the French and Indian War of 1755 to 1763, which ended with a victory by GREAT BRITAIN. That same year a royal proclamation forbade settlement west of the ALLEGHENY MOUNTAINS, to pacify the Indians and protect the fur trade, but it angered the American colonists. Despite Great Britain's efforts, the Indians rose against them in Chief Pontiac's Rebellion from 1763 to 1766 but were defeated.

During the American Revolution George Rogers Clark led a successful American expedition, beginning in 1778, which gave the Americans control of the region. This was confirmed by the Treaty of 1783. CONNECTICUT, MASSACHUSETTS, NEW YORK State, and VIRGINIA claimed portions of the area, but between 1780 and 1786 they ceded them to the Federal government except for the Virginia Military District and the WESTERN RESERVE. In 1786 the Ohio Company of Associates was formed and in April 1788 began laying out MARIETTA, Ohio. With the Ordinance of 1787 Congress established a government that provided for the admission of states made from the region and prohibited slavery in them. Indian resistance continued, but Anthony Wayne defeated them in the Battle of FALLEN TIMBERS near Toledo, Ohio, on Aug. 20, 1794. The next year he negotiated the GREENVILLE Treaty by which the Indians ceded large tracts to the United States.

The British had not evacuated their posts in the area, but by Jay's Treaty of 1794 they promised to leave by June 1, 1796. In 1811 the Indians once more rebelled against the Americans, but their strength was broken by William Henry Harrison's troops at the Battle of TIPPECANOE on November 7. In the War of 1812 Americans and British once more fought for the Old Northwest, and at its conclusion the United States retained the region. Meanwhile, the territory began to be split up. Ohio was admitted as a state in 1803, and the other states were gradually formed. Government policy made it fairly easy for settlers to acquire land, and the region soon became a settled and prolific agricultural area.

NORTHWICH (England) Town in Cheshire, 19 mi SW of Manchester. Once the site of a Roman military camp, it has been the center of a salt-mining industry since antiquity.

NORWALK (United States) Industrial city on LONG ISLAND SOUND, 42 mi NE of New York City, in SW CONNECTICUT. Settled in 1640 and incorporated as a city in 1893, it had been burned by British troops in 1779, during the American Revolution. Over the centuries it has expanded to take in many nearby villages. It is now a major electronics and aircraft research center. The colonial home of Col. Thomas Fitch, who inspired the composition of *Yankee Doodle*, is located here. See also NORWALK, Ohio.

NORWALK (United States) City, 15 mi S of Sandusky, N OHIO. It was founded in 1816 by former residents of NORWALK, CONNECTICUT, who had been burned out of their homes by raiding British troops in 1779, during the American Revolution. Incorporated in 1881, it has a pioneer museum.

NORWAY Kingdom of N Europe, it is a long and narrow country that stretches along the NORTH SEA and the Norwegian Sea of the North Atlantic, in W SCANDINAVIA, from the Skagerrak in the S to the Barents Sea in the N. It is predominantly mountainous, and its coastline is indented by many inlets, or fjords. Its capital is OSLO. Under Danish and Swedish rule for much of its history, Norway has only been independent since the beginning of the 20th century. Since that time and because of the Norwegians' traditional reliance on the sea, Norway has developed into an important maritime nation with the fourth-largest merchant marine in the world.

During its early history Norway was divided politically into *fylker* or petty kingdoms. Circa 900 AD Harald Haarfager of the Yngling dynasty united these kingdoms and conquered the SHETLAND and ORKNEY ISLANDS but failed to establish lasting unity. While

Viking Norsemen raided western Europe from the late eighth to 11th centuries, Norway itself was split by civil strife. It was finally united under the rule of the Danish King Canute between 1028 and 1035. The rule of Sverre in the 12th century did much to assert the power of the monarchy, and in the 13th century the country enjoyed considerable peace and prosperity. By the Union of KALMAR in 1397, Norway, SWEDEN, and DENMARK were united under the Danish crown; and for the next four centuries Norway was ruled as a province of Denmark. Under Danish rule Lutheranism was introduced in the 16th century; and although land was lost to Sweden, which left the union in 1523, Norway developed economically and became a naval power. During the Napoleonic Wars of 1803 to 1815, Norway was blockaded by GREAT BRITAIN; and in 1814, by the Treaty of KIEL, it passed from Denmark to Sweden.

Although the Swedes allowed Norway its own constitution and parliament, the movement for an independent Norway grew in strength throughout the 19th century, fueled by the rapid expansion of Norway's commercial interests. In 1905 the Norwegian parliament dissolved the union, and after a plebiscite this decision was accepted peacefully by Sweden. Norway remained neutral during World War I; but during World War II, despite attempts at neutrality, it was invaded by GERMANY in April 1940. It remained occupied until the end of the war, although its merchant fleet, having escaped capture, played an important role in the Allied war effort.

After the war Norway made a rapid recovery, becoming one of the founding members of the United Nations. However, Norway rejected membership in the European Economic Community in 1972. The discovery of oil in the North Sea off Norway in the early 1970's has added a new impetus to the country's economy.

NORWICH (England) City and admin. hq. of Norfolk, on the Wensum River, 97 mi NE of London. Sacked by the Danes in the 11th century, the town founded its Norman cathedral in 1096 under its first bishop. After the Norman Conquest it became the site of a massive Norman castle. It suffered from the Black Death in 1348 as well as from Wat Tyler's peasant rebellion in 1381. The city was at the center of East Anglia's rich wool trade from the late Middle Ages on. Chartered in 1404, it flourished and was one of the largest cities in England from the 17th to 19th centuries and was also a cultural center. The castle now houses artifacts and artworks of the notable local art school of the 18th and

Early tourists embarking for a cruise up Norway's Nordfjord. A land of deep fjords and huge mountains, it is no wonder that Norway has always been a maritime nation.

19th centuries. Bombed during World War II, the city still has its public library, built in 1608, a medieval hospital, over 30 medieval parish churches, and a grammar school. The 19th-century social philosopher Harriet Martineau came from here.

NORWICH (United States) City at the confluence of the Yantic and Shetucket rivers, SE CONNECTICUT. Settled in 1659 and incorporated in 1784, it was the site of a great Indian battle between the Mohegan and the Narragansett tribes in 1643. A colonial industrial and shipbuilding center, it figured prominently in the War of 1812. The Revolutionary turncoat Benedict Arnold was born here. The old Leffingwell Inn has stood here since 1675.

NOTABILE. See MDINA.

NOTION. See NOTIUM.

NOTIUM [Notion] (Turkey) Ancient port for the city of COLOPHON, on the SW coast of Asia Minor, in IONIA. During the Peloponnesian Wars Lysander of SPARTA directed its navy to a victory in 407 BC over the fleet of ATHENS just off Notium. Notium later took the place of Colophon as the important city of the area, after the inhabitants of Colophon had moved to EPHESUS in 299 BC. It flourished thereafter on its own.

NOTRE-DAME-DES-ERMITES. See EINSIEDELN.

NOTTINGHAM (England) City and admin. hq. of Nottinghamshire, on the Trent River, 115 mi N of London. It was a Danish borough in the ninth century AD. Its 11th-century castle was built by William the Conqueror. Parliaments were held here in 1334, 1337, and 1357. The Civil War began when Charles I raised his standard here in 1642. The town was badly damaged by Oliver Cromwell's army in 1644, by fire during the Reform Bill riots of 1831, and by World War II bombings. According to tradition, Robin Hood was born here.

NOTTINGHAMSHIRE [Nottingham, Notts] (England) County in the Midlands. The remnants of SHERWOOD FOREST, famous as the haunt of the legendary Robin Hood and his merry men, are located in the county. Once a part of the old Anglo-Saxon kingdom of MERCIA, it was here that the Pilgrim Separatist movement first took shape in 1606, leading to the founding of PLYMOUTH Colony in America. William Booth, founder of the Salvation Army, was born in the county's admin. hq., NOTTINGHAM, in 1829.

NOTTS. See NOTTINGHAMSHIRE.

NOUAKCHOTT (Mauritania) Town and capital of Mauritania, a port on the Atlantic Ocean, West Africa. Once a village, it replaced St.-Louis as the national capital in 1957. The Muslims of the ALMORAVID Caliphate are believed by some to have departed from a nearby monastery as they began their conquests of North Africa and SPAIN in the 11th century.

NOUMÉA (France) Port and capital of the French Overseas Territory of NEW CALEDONIA, on the SW coast of the island, SW Pacific Ocean. Founded in 1854, it served as a French penal colony from 1864 to 1897. It harbored the Free French movement during World War II and was developed by the Allies as a major military base starting in 1942. A seaplane base is now across the harbor from the town.

NOUVELLE CALÉDONIE. See NEW CALEDONIA.

NOUVELLES HÉBRIDES. See NEW HEBRIDES.

NOVA CIVITAS. See NEUSTADT AN DER WEINSTRASSE.

NOVAESIUM. See NEUSS.

NOVANTIA. See GALLOWAY.

NOVARA [ancient: Novaria] (Italy) Town and capital of Novara province, in Piedmont region, 28 mi W of Milan. A Celtic town before its capture by ROME in the third century BC, it flourished as an important medieval city of the duchy of MILAN. It was the site of several early 16th-century battles during the Italian Wars. It passed to AUSTRIA in 1714 and to SARDINIA in 1738. King Charles Albert of Sardinia abdicated his power here following the defeat of his Piedmontese troops by the Austrians in the famous Battle of Novara on March 25, 1849. His son, Victor Emmanuel II, succeeded him during the Risorgimento, or movement for the independence and unification of Italy.

NOVARIA. See NOVARA.

NOVA SCOTIA (Canada) Maritime province consisting of a peninsula in the Atlantic Ocean and of CAPE BRETON ISLAND to the NE. The Abnaki and Micmac Indians lived in the area before Europeans came. John Cabot of ENGLAND may have landed on Cape Breton Island in 1497, by which time European fishermen were already stopping here. The Sieur de Monts of FRANCE, made the first settlement at Port Royal in 1605. This was unsuccessful and was succeeded by another in 1610. By 1710 the settlement had changed hands five times between the French and the English. That year a force of men from NEW ENGLAND captured it and changed its name to ANNAPOLIS ROYAL.

The French called the region ACADIA, but the English named it Nova Scotia after James I gave a grant to Sir William Alexander in 1621. By the Treaty of UTRECHT in 1713 Nova Scotia became British, but France retained Cape Breton Island. In 1720 the French began to build the fortress of LOUISBOURG on the island, which they named Île Royale. New Englanders captured it in 1745, it was returned to France in 1748 and retaken by the British in 1758. At the start of the French and Indian War in 1755, the British expelled the French Acadians from Nova Scotia, distributing them along the Atlantic Coast. By the Treaty of PARIS of 1763 both Nova Scotia and Cape Breton Island were ceded to GREAT BRITAIN.

In 1783/84, after the American Revolution, many Loyalists fled to Nova Scotia, and in 1784 it and Cape Breton Island were made separate provinces. In 1820 they were joined as one province. Nova Scotia became the first Canadian province of the British Empire to be granted responsible self-government, in 1848. In 1867 it was one of the first four provinces to be federated as the Dominion of Canada. HALIFAX is the capital.

WELIKI·NOVOGOROD
ODER
GROS·NAVGARD

fol. 121

The proud city of Great Novgorod. As Moscow's rival it once ruled all northern Russia and the famous Alexander Nevski was one of its princes. Later it was a leader in the Hanseatic League.

NOVA SOFALA [*former:* **Sofala**] (Mozambique) City in SE Mozambique, on the Mozambique Channel, approx. 25 mi S of Beira. Circa 1000 AD Arab and Swahili traders settled here and at other points on the coast in order to trade with the interior of Africa. Sofala became famous as a center for exporting gold and ivory. It had close ties with KILWA, on the coast in present TANZANIA, and at times was controlled by that town. In 1500 and 1502 two Portuguese navigators, Pedro Alvares Cabral and Sancho de Tovar, visited Sofala; and in 1505 another Portuguese explorer, Pedro de Anhaia, captured Sofala and built a fort. The town continued to be a starting point for expeditions into the interior, especially the region between the ZAMBEZI and the Save rivers, which was a rich source of gold. In 1574 a force of approximately 400 men under Vasco Fernandes Homen set out for the interior from Sofala to conquer inland areas, but most of the men were killed fighting black Africans.

NOVAYA ZEMLYA (USSR) Two large islands in the ARCTIC Ocean, between the Barents and Kara seas, N of the Arctic Circle. Travelers from NOVGOROD discovered the islands in the 11th or 12th century. Explorers searching for the NORTHWEST PASSAGE often sighted them. They have been used recently as a Soviet thermonuclear testing site and contain several settlements and scientific stations.

NOVÉ ZÁMKY [*German:* **Neuhäusel;** *Hungarian:* **Ersekújvár**] (Czechoslovakia) Town on the Slovak River, Slovak SR. A Hungarian fortress founded in 1561, it was important during the Turkish wars. It was occupied throughout World War II by HUNGARY but was returned to Czech rule in 1945.

NOVGOROD [*former:* **Velikiy-Novgorod**] (USSR) Principality and city with roots in the Middle Ages. As a principality from the 11th to 15th centuries it covered all of N RUSSIA from Lake Peipus and LITHUANIA to the URAL MOUNTAINS. The city that was its capital was built on both sides of the VOLKHOV RIVER just N of Lake Ilmen, approx. 110 mi S of the present city of Leningrad. Peopled by Slavs, from antiquity the city was a cultural and commercial center of medieval Europe. In 862 the Eastern Slavs invited Rurik, the prince of a Varangian or Viking band, to rule them. He accepted, and the city became the capital of the principality. Novgorod was the cultural equal of KIEV, some 600 to 700 miles to the south, but was dependent upon it until it obtained self-government in 997.

Finally it became the capital of the independent republic of Sovereign Great Novgorod in 1136, covering all of northern Russia to the Urals. It was ruled by Prince Alexander Nevski from 1238 to 1263, and it developed economically by its location on the major trade route from Russia to the Orient and CONSTANTINOPLE. With LÜBECK, BRUGES, and BERGEN it was one of the four key trading centers in the HANSEATIC LEAGUE. Novgorod fought off the Teutonic and the

Livonian Knights and SWEDEN and escaped the Mongol invasion of 1240 to 1242 because of its surrounding marshes. It reached its apex in the 14th century with famous fairs, great shops, and hundreds of churches. It rivaled MOSCOW, but by 1478 it was conquered by Ivan III, grand duke of Muscovy, and lost its independence. It was devastated by Ivan IV in 1570. In 1611 it was taken by the Swedes and held for seven years.

Novgorod retained its commercial supremacy until after the founding of St. Petersburg in 1703. Its architectural beauty gave it the name Museum City, but during World War II it was held by GERMANY from 1941 to 1944 and suffered great damage. Many of the buildings have been restored, but much of the artwork and frescoes have been irretrievably lost. Badly damaged but restored is the 12th-century kremlin containing the cathedral of St. Sophia, founded in 1045, with massive bronze doors dating from the 12th century.

NOVIBAZAR. See NOVI PAZAR.

NOVI LIGURE (Italy) Town in Alessandria province, 14 mi SE of Alessandria, in PIEDMONT region. It was the scene of a battle in 1799, during the Napoleonic Wars, in which a Russo-Austrian force led by Marshal Suvorov triumphed over French forces under Barthélemy Joubert, director of the French armies in Italy, who was mortally wounded.

NOVIODUNUM. See NEVERS, NOYON, NYON, SOISSONS.

NOVIOMAGUS, Netherlands. See NIJMEGAN.

NOVIOMAGUS, West Germany. See SPEYER.

NOVIOMAGUS LEXOVIORUM. See LISIEUX.

NOVIOMAGUS REGENSIUM. See CHICHESTER.

NOVIORITUM. See NIORT.

NOVI PAZAR [Novibazar] [*ancient:* Rascia; *former:* Rarka, Rašhka; *Turkish:* Yeni-Paza] (Yugoslavia) Town on the Raška River, in SERBIA. A trading center and the capital of Serbia from the 12th to 14th centuries, it was taken by the Turks in 1456. They made it the seat of the Turkish administrative district of Novibazar, which separated MONTENEGRO and Serbia. Occupied by AUSTRIA from 1879 to 1908, it was taken in 1912 by the Serbians in the First Balkan War. It became part of Yugoslavia in 1918 after World War I but was occupied by GERMANY in 1941 during World War II. The Turkish Altum-Alem mosque is located here, as are many oriental-style buildings.

NOVI SAD [*German:* Neusatz; *Hungarian:* Újvidék] (Yugoslavia) City and port on the DANUBE RIVER, 45 mi NW of Belgrade, in SERBIA. Known since the 17th century, it became a Serbian episcopal see in the next century. It developed as a commercial and cultural center of the Serbians into the 19th century, before it was destroyed during the revolution of 1849. It became part of Yugoslavia in 1918 but was occupied by Hungarian forces during World War II.

NOVI SLANKAMEN [Slankamen] [*Hungarian:* Szalánkemén] (Yugoslavia) Town on the DANUBE RIVER, in SERBIA. The margrave of BADEN, Louis William I, led his forces to a victory over the Turks in a battle fought here on Aug. 19, 1691. He had been battling the Turks since 1683.

NOVO-ALEKSANDROVKA. See MELITOPOL.

NOVOCHERKASSK (USSR) City, 21 mi NE of Rostov-na-Donu, SW Russian SFSR. Don Cossacks founded it in 1805 as the capital of the Don Cossack region after the old capital, CHERKASSY, was flooded by an arm of the DON RIVER. A stronghold of anti-Bolshevism, it was held from 1917 to 1920 by White armies before the final communist takeover. It was occupied in 1942/43 by German troops during World War II. The hetman's palace and a Don Cossack museum are in the city.

NOVOGEORGIEVSK. See MODLIN.

NOVOGRUDOK [*Polish:* Nowogródek] (USSR) Town, 77 mi SE of Vilnius, Belorussian SSR. Controlled at various times in its history by LITHUANIA, POLAND, and RUSSIA, it was occupied by GERMANY during World War II but was retaken by Soviet forces in the summer of 1944 and ceded to the USSR in 1945. The house of the Polish poet Adam Mickiewicz, born here in 1798, is now a museum.

NOVOKUZNETSK [Kuznetsk Sibirski] [*former:* Stalinsk] (USSR) City on the Tom River, Russian SFSR, 190 mi SE of Novosibirsk. The Cossacks established a fort here in 1617. It remained a small trading center until its industrialization in the 20th century under the Stalin regime.

NOVONIKOLAEVSK. See NOVOSIBIRSK.

NOVOROSIYSK. See DNEPROPETROVSK.

NOVOROSSIISK. See NOVOROSSIYSK.

NOVOROSSISK. See NOVOROSSIYSK.

NOVOROSSIYSK [Novorossiisk, Novorossisk] (USSR) Port city on the BLACK SEA, 700 mi SW of Rostov, Russian SFSR. A medieval Genoese colony in the 13th and 14th centuries and then a fortified Turkish town, it passed to RUSSIA in 1829. White armies led by Gen. Denikin occupied the city in 1919 and 1920 during the Russian Civil War, and GERMANY occupied it during World War II in 1942 and 1943.

NOVOSIBIRSK [*former:* Novonikolaevsk] (USSR) City and capital of Novosibirsk oblast, Russian SFSR, 390 mi E of Omsk. Originally founded in 1896 as a construction settlement by Trans-Siberian Railway crews, it became the capital of the West Siberian region. It received dismantled factories from the West during World War II and used them to develop into a notable industrial center itself. See also SIBERIA.

NOVOSIBIRSKIYE OSTROVA. See NEW SIBERIAN ISLANDS.

NOWA SÓL [Nowasól] [*German:* Neusalz an der Oder] (Poland) Industrial city and port on the ODER RIVER, Zielona Góro province, SW Poland. A medieval town, it was once incorporated in SILESIA in the state of Germany. Taken by the USSR at the end of World War II, it was assigned to Poland in 1945 by the POTSDAM Conference.

NOWOGRÓDEK. See NOVOGRUDOK.

NOWY SĄCZ [*German:* **Neusandez**] (Poland) Industrial town on the Dunajec River, 46 mi SE of Cracow. It was chartered in 1298, passed to AUSTRIA in 1772 and again to Poland in 1919. Its 14th-century palace was destroyed in World War II.

NOYON [*ancient:* **Noviodunum**] (France) Town on the Oise Canal, 65 mi N of Paris. An old Roman town, it became a bishopric in the sixth century AD. It was the scene of the Frankish coronations of Pepin the Short in 752 and of Charlemagne in 768, and of the election in 987 of Hugh Capet as king of France. Many battles occurred here during the Hundred Years War of 1337 to 1453. France and SPAIN signed a treaty in the town in 1516 during the Italian Wars. John Calvin, Protestant reformer, was born here in 1509. The city was devastated in both world wars, but its 15th-century library and 12th-century cathedral have survived.

NUBIA (Egypt, Sudan) Ancient state in the NILE RIVER valley, included today in Egypt and Sudan. From the 20th to the eighth century BC it was dominated by Egypt, but in the eighth and seventh centuries the Nubian kingdom of KUSH dominated the area. Subsequently, it was ruled by ASSYRIA, ETHIOPIA, and a powerful local tribe, the Nobatae. Its ancient capital of NAPATA was removed to MEROË *c.*530 BC by the Assyrians. Its Nobataen capital of DUNQULAH was a Christian stronghold from the fifth to the 14th century AD, before it finally fell to the Muslim Arabs. Much of the region was flooded during the construction of the High Dam at ASWAN in the 1960's. See also MAKURIA.

NU CHIANG. See SALWEEN.

NUESTRA SEÑORA DE LA ASUNCIÓN. See ASUNCIÓN.

NUESTRA SEÑORA DE LA PAZ. See LA PAZ, Bolivia.

NUEVA BUENOS AIRES. See BAHÍA BLANCA.

NUEVA CACERES. See NAGA.

NUEVA CARTAGO. See COSTA RICA.

NUEVA CÓRDOBA. See CUMANÁ.

NUEVA GALICIA (Mexico) Colony of NEW SPAIN, roughly corresponding to modern Jalisco and Nayarit states, and S Sinaloa. Conquered first by Nuño de Guzmán from 1529 to 1531 and then by Francisco Coronado, it obtained its own *audiencia* at GUADALAJARA in 1548. An Indian uprising was staged here in 1541 against Spanish rule. The Mixtón War, as it was called, ended with the bloody reinstatement of Spanish authority. The colony's importance waned with the rise of MEXICO CITY.

NUEVA SAN SALVADOR [*former:* **Santa Tecla**] (El Salvador) Coffee-growing center, city, and capital of La Libertad department, 8 mi NW of San Salvador, SW El Salvador. Founded in 1854 as an interim national capital following the earthquake destruction of SAN SALVADOR, it remained such for five years. Subsequently, it developed into a prestigious residential suburb.

NUEVA VISCAYA. See DURANGO.

NUEVA ZAMORA. See MARACAIBO.

NUEVO LAREDO (Mexico) Transportation center on the RIO GRANDE RIVER, opposite Laredo, Texas. Founded in 1755, it was part of LAREDO, Texas, until the conclusion of the Mexican War in 1848. An important participant during the Mexican revolution of 1910, it was badly damaged by fire in 1914. It is the terminus of the northern railroad and of the Inter-American Highway.

NUEVO LEÓN (Mexico) State in N Mexico with its capital at MONTERREY. Settled by the Spanish in the 16th century, it became a state in independent Mexico in 1824. A stronghold of opposition to advances by the UNITED STATES, it was occupied by U.S. forces during the Mexican War of 1846 to 1848.

NÛK. See GODTHÅB.

NUKUALOFA. See TONGA.

NUKU HIVA [**Nokuhiva, Nukahiva**] (France) Largest island of the MARQUESAS ISLANDS, in the S Pacific Ocean, E of the LINE ISLANDS. Nuku Hiva and others of the northern part of the Marquesas were discovered in 1791 by Capt. Joseph Ingraham, an American navigator. David Porter, an officer of the U.S. Navy, claimed it for the UNITED STATES in 1813, naming it Madison Island; but Congress did not act on the claim. France took possession of the island as part of FRENCH POLYNESIA, and established a settlement in 1842 that was abandoned in 1859. Copra is the chief export, Hakapehi (Taiohae) is the chief town.

NUMANTIA (Spain) Archaeological site and ancient Spanish town, on the Duero River, just N of modern SORIA. It was a stronghold of Celtiberian opposition to the conquest of Spain by ROME, and withstood many Roman offensives, especially between 143 and 133 BC, when it finally fell after an eight-month siege directed by Scipio the Younger, the destroyer of CARTHAGE. The 4,000 defenders resorted to cannibalism and mass suicide before yielding. Numantia has become a symbol of Spanish resistance in modern Spain, as MASADA is in ISRAEL. A series of Roman military camps dating from the 20-year campaign have been traced in the area; and Numantia itself, later a Roman town, has yielded rich remains.

NUMFOOR [*Dutch:* **Noemfoor**] (Indonesia) One of the SCHOUTEN ISLANDS, on Sarera Bay, N IRIAN BARAT. JAPAN established several strategic air bases here in World War II, but they were captured from July 1 to 6, 1944 by Allied forces.

NUMIDIA (Algeria) Ancient country in North Africa that occupied approximately the same area as modern Algeria. It was a long-time stronghold of CARTHAGE; its allegiance during the Second Punic War of 218 to 201 BC was split when a tribe led by Masinissa joined ranks with the Romans against Carthage. He later became king, and Numidia flourished under his rule and that of his successor, Micipsa (*c.*148–118 BC). Later, however, it suffered in a war against ROME from 111 to 106 BC incited by King Jugurtha, and was subdued in 46 BC by the Romans when King Juba I sided with Pompey during the Roman civil wars.

The country flourished under Roman rule but was

sacked and overrun by the Vandals in the fifth century AD and by the Arabs in the eighth century. Numidia's capital was at Cirta; and Hippo, the diocesan seat of St. Augustine, was its most important city. See ANNABA, CONSTANTINE.

NUPE (Nigeria) Former kingdom in Nigeria, centered on BIDA, in W central Nigeria, approx. 180 mi NE of Abadan. The founder and first king of Nupe was Tsoede (Edegi), who captured Bida *c.*1530 and made it his capital. Circa 1805 the kingdom was conquered by the FULANI, and Nupe became an emirate of that empire. From 1859 to 1873 Nupe was again a powerful kingdom in central Nigeria and established trade relations with GREAT BRITAIN in 1871. The Nupe occupied an area important for trade routes; but disputes over commercial relations led to war with Great Britain, which defeated the Nupe in 1897. In 1908 the Nupe region, then known as the Bida Emirate, was incorporated by the British into the province of Nigeria.

NUREMBEGA. See NEW ENGLAND.

NUREMBERG [*German:* **Nürnberg**] (West Germany) City on the Pegnitz River, 92 mi NW of Munich, BAVARIA. Founded by the mid-11th century and chartered in 1219, it flourished after the 12th century as a commercial link with ITALY and subsequently, in the 15th and 16th centuries, as the cultural center of the German Renaissance and a renowned center of early printing. Albrecht Dürer (1471–1528), the great and influential artist, was born here; and Humanists, scientists, and publishers congregated here. The Peace of Nuremberg of 1532 granted tolerance to Lutherans. Nuremberg declined after the Thirty Years War of 1618 to 1648 and passed to Bavaria in 1803.

In the 1930's it became a headquarters of the National Socialist (Nazi) movement directed by Adolf Hitler. The Nuremberg Laws and other anti-Semitic propaganda were created here, and it became the main industrial and political focus of Hitler's war effort. The Nuremberg Stadium was the scene of several massive Nazi assemblies. It was greatly damaged during World War II by Allied bombings and was the site of postwar judicial hearings on international war crimes. These Nuremberg Trials have become a legal precedent for, and symbol of, the right of the individual to resist unjust orders and his or her guilt in obeying them. Medieval churches, a Hohenzollern castle, and portions of its old city walls remain; and the old interior city has been reconstructed.

NÜRNBERG. See NUREMBERG.

NURSIA. See NORCIA.

NUSAYBIN [**Nisibin**] [*ancient:* **Nisibis**] (Turkey) Town on the Syrian border. An ancient frontier fortress and trading center, it was a royal residence of the kings

The reconstructed medieval core of Nuremberg. Once a liberal cultural center, it became the symbolic center of Nazism, and as such it was nearly destroyed in World War II.

of ARMENIA from the second century BC to the early second century AD. It was important to both PARTHIA and ROME and was a center of Nestorian Christianity for many years. In 1839 AD the Egyptians defeated the Turks here.

NUTTEN ISLAND. See GOVERNORS ISLAND.

NUUANU PALI (United States) Mountain pass and cliff leading into Nuuanu valley, near Honolulu, SE OAHU ISLAND, HAWAII. Kamehameha I, originator of the Kamehameha dynasty in Hawaii, sealed his conquest of Oahu with a victory here in 1795. He later allowed traders from America and Europe to settle in Hawaii.

NUWARA ELIYA (Sri Lanka) Resort town in ancient Ceylon, now Sri Lanka, high up on a plateau. According to tradition, it provided the setting for the imprisonment of Sita, wife of Rama, in the Sanskrit epic *Ramayana*. It was discovered and settled by the British in 1827 as a health resort.

NUZI (Iraq) Ancient site in N Iraq, near Kirkuk. Archaeologists have unearthed here a horde of clay tablets in the Akkadian language, dating from the third millennium BC, which have thrown a great deal of light on the laws and customs of the early biblical period in MESOPOTAMIA. See also AKKAD.

NYASALAND. See MALAWI.

NYBORG (Denmark) Port on FYN Island. Eric V in 1282 inaugurated the first constitution in Denmark's history at the 12th-century Nyborg Castle here, which now stands in ruins.

NYEMAN. See NEMAN RIVER.

NYEZHIN. See NEZHIN.

NYÍREGYHÁZA (Hungary) City, 30 mi N of Debrecen. Dating from the 13th century, it was leveled by invading Turks in the 16th century. Its renovation began in the 18th century.

NYITRA. See NITRA.

NYKÖPING (Sweden) Port on the BALTIC SEA, in Södermanland county. Founded in the 13th century, it was devastated by fire in 1665 and by RUSSIA in 1719 during the Great Northern War.

NYMPHAION, CAPE [Cape Nymphaeum] [*Greek:* **Akra Nimfaion**] (Greece) Cape thrusting into the AEGEAN SEA on the CHALCIDICE, Acte peninsula. In a campaign during the Persian Wars against the Greek city-states, the fleet of Darius of PERSIA commanded by Mardonius was wrecked in 492 BC by a storm in waters just off the cape.

NYMPHENBURG (West Germany) Former village, now a historic section of MUNICH, BAVARIA. The castle of the dukes of Bavaria, begun in 1664, is located here. By the terms of a secret pact endorsed here in 1741 during the War of the Austrian Succession, SPAIN allied itself to Bavaria against AUSTRIA.

NYON [*ancient:* **Noviodunum**; *German:* **Neuss**] (Switzerland) Resort commune in VAUD canton, 13 mi N of Geneva, W Switzerland. A 16th-century castle is located in this old commune, as are remains of the Roman town.

NYSA [*German:* **Neisse**] (Poland) City on the NEISSE RIVER, 47 mi SE of Wrocław. Founded in the early 13th century, it was occupied several times during the Thirty Years War. Earlier under SILESIA, it became part of PRUSSIA in 1742 and was occupied in 1807/08 by French forces during the Napoleonic Wars. It passed to Poland after World War II at the POTSDAM Conference.

NYSLOTT. See SAVONLINNA.

NYSSA (Turkey) Ancient town in the district of CAPPADOCIA, E Asia Minor, near the Halys River. A center of the cult of the Greek god Dionysus, it became the home of the noted Christian orthodox theologian, Saint Gregory of Nyssa (c.335–c.395).

NYSTAD. See UUSIKAUPUNKI.

O

OAHU (United States) Most important island of HAWAII. King Kamehameha I consolidated his power over Oahu by 1795 and over the rest of the Hawaiian Islands by 1810. Oahu was the seat of the Kamehameha dynasty in the 19th century. It is now an important U.S. military center, that includes the PEARL HARBOR naval base on the south coast.

OAKLAND (United States) Industrial city in W CALIFORNIA, adjacent to SAN FRANCISCO on the E coast of SAN FRANCISCO BAY. Spaniards settled here in 1820, followed by gold seekers in 1849. It served as a refuge for 65,000 people fleeing the great San Francisco earthquake of 1906. It was the home of writers Jack London and Robert Louis Stevenson. It became an important port and shipbuilding center during World War II.

OAK PARK (United States) Town in NE ILLINOIS, a suburb 10 mi W of CHICAGO. Novelist Ernest Hemingway was born here in 1899. It displays some 25 houses, as well as the Oak Park Unity Temple, built by architect Frank Lloyd Wright early in the 20th century.

OAK RIDGE (United States) City in E TENNESSEE, 17 mi W of Knoxville. It is active in highly secret nuclear research and radioactive isotope production. Founded by the United States government in 1942, it served until 1945 as a site for the secret development of uranium and plutonium needed for the atomic bomb project. It was incorporated as an independent city in 1959.

OARUS. See VOLGA RIVER.

OAXACA [Oaxaca de Juárez] [*Aztec:* **Huasyacac**] (Mexico) Commercial and tourist center and capital of Oaxaca state. Founded in 1486 by the Aztec Indians, it is near the ruins of the ancient Indian cities of MONTE ALBÁN and MITLA. The site of the monastery of Santo Domingo, the city has suffered strong earthquakes. A center of resistance against SPAIN during the Mexican revolution of 1810 to 1821, it is also the birthplace of Porfirio Díaz, Mexican dictator from 1877 to 1911.

OBAN (Scotland) Seaport in Strathclyde region, on the Firth of Lorne, 61 mi NW of Glasgow. Nearby are the ruins of 12th-century Dunollie castle. Among these stands a huge rock known as the Dog Stone, purported to be where Fingal's giant dog Bran was chained. Oban serves as background for Sir Walter Scott's work *Lord of the Isles*.

OBERAMMERGAU (West Germany) Resort town located 42 mi SW of Munich. It has gained international recognition for its performance each decade of the *Passion Play*. This is done in fulfillment of a vow made in 1633 celebrating deliverance of the village during a plague.

OBERDONAU. See UPPER AUSTRIA.

OBERHAUSEN (West Germany) Industrial city in North Rhine-Westphalia in the RUHR, 7 mi WNW of Essen. It became a city in 1874 and in 1929 absorbed the nearby towns of Sterkrade and Osterfeld. It has 14th- and 16th-century castles.

OBERHESSEN. See UPPER HESSE.

OBERHOLLABRUNN. See HOLLABRUNN.

OBERLIN (United States) Residential city in N OHIO, 30 mi WSW of Cleveland. Before the Civil War it was an antislavery center. Oberlin College, founded in 1833, was staffed largely by Congregationalists from New England and was one of the earliest coeducational colleges.

OBERÖSTERREICH. See UPPER AUSTRIA.

OBOCK [Obok] (Djibouti) Seaport village in E Africa, nearly opposite Djibouti City. The port became an entry point for France into East Africa in 1862 and was occupied in 1884.

OBOK. See OBOCK.

OB RIVER (USSR) River in W SIBERIA, rising in the Altai Mts, and flowing generally N across Siberia to empty into the Gulf of Ob, an arm of the ARCTIC Ocean. With its main tributary, the IRTYSH RIVER, its length is approx. 3,460 mi. It drains an area of more than 1 million sq mi. Although much of it is frozen nearly half the year, it is important as a trade and transportation route. The Ob was first visited by Europeans before 1667, and the lower Ob was studied by Russian scientists on the Great Northern Expedition of 1733 to 1743. NOVOSIBIRSK, the largest city on the Ob, was founded in 1893, while Barnaul was founded in 1738.

OCEAN GROVE (United States) Summer resort in E central NEW JERSEY on the Atlantic coast, adjoining ASBURY PARK. It was founded in 1869, as a site for religious revivals and conferences.

OCEAN ISLAND [Banaba] (Kiribati) Island in the W Pacific Ocean, approx 57 mi S of the equator. It was claimed by the British in 1900, was made part of the Gilbert and Ellice Islands Colony in 1916, and served as its capital for a time. It was occupied by the Japanese in 1942. It became independent in 1979 with the Gilbert Islands, now Kiribati.

OCEAN POND. See OLUSTEE (Fla.)

OCEANUS BRITANNICUS. See ENGLISH CHANNEL.

OCEANVIEW. See BERKELEY.

OCHAKOV [Greek: Alektor] (USSR) Important seaport of S Ukrainian SSR on the BLACK SEA between

Odessa and Kherson. It is the site of the ancient Greek city of Alektor of the seventh and sixth centuries BC, then near the Greek colony of OLBIA. A fortress called Kara-kerman was built here by a Tatar khan from the CRIMEA in 1492. Ochakov was contested by Ukrainian Cossacks and Turks in the 16th and 17th centuries, taken by RUSSIA in 1788 during the Russo-Turkish War, and occupied by the Allies during the Crimean War in 1855. See also UKRAINE.

OCHRIDA. See OHRID.

OCMULGEE RIVER (United States) A river, 255 mi long, in central GEORGIA, formed SE of Atlanta. It flows past the Ocmulgee National Monument, where one of the most important prehistoric Indian villages of the Southeast was found. The ruins here date after 1000 BC and include a restored council chamber. The national monument was established in 1936.

ODA. See KYŌTO.

ÖDENBURG. See SOPRON.

ODENDAALSRUS (South Africa) Town of ORANGE FREE STATE, 38 mi SW of Kroonstad. It grew rapidly after an important gold field was found nearby in 1946.

ODENSE (Denmark) Commercial, industrial and cultural center on FYN ISLAND. It was founded in the 10th century. There is an ancient shrine here dedicated to the Norse god Odin, as well as a 12th-century church and a 13th-century cathedral of St. Knud, who was murdered in the city in 1086 and canonized as patron saint in 1101. The house of the writer Hans Christian Andersen, who was born in the city in 1805, is now a museum. Odense was a center of Allied resistance against GERMANY during World War II.

ODENSVOLD. See UDDEVALLA.

ODER-NEISSE LINE (East Germany, Poland) Boundary line between East Germany and W Poland, adopted at the POTSDAM Conference in 1945. It is defined by the NEISSE RIVER from the Sudetic Mountains to its junction with the ODER RIVER, south of FRANKFURT, and then by the Oder flowing north to the Baltic Sea.

ODER RIVER [*Czech* and *Polish:* **Odra;** *Earlier:* **Viadua**] (Czechoslovakia, East Germany, Poland) River, 567 mi long, flowing through Czechoslovakia, along the border between Poland and East Germany and into the Baltic Sea. A transportation route for the Polish industrial economy, it has facilitated contact between southern and northern European peoples from ancient times. It allowed the introduction of Lusitanian cultures of the Bronze Age, which influenced the later evolution of the Slavic people. Internationalized by the Treaty of VERSAILLES in 1919, it was a common battle site during World War II and became part of the ODER-NEISSE LINE established at the POTSDAM Conference.

ODESSA [*Greek:* **Odessos, Ordas; Ordyssos;** *Tatar:* **Khadzhi-Bei**] (USSR) Industrial city, 25 mi NE of the mouth of the DNIESTER RIVER on Odessa Bay, in Odessa oblast, in the Ukraine. The city is said to be on the site of a Miletian Greek colony settled *c.*800 BC. The Russians gained it from the Turks in 1792 and estab-

lished it as a fort, naval base, and commercial port. It became important during the labor movement in the 19th century and spawned the abortive revolution of 1905, which included the mutiny on the battleship Potemkin here. It fell to GERMANY in 1941 after an epic defense but was liberated in 1944. See also UKRAINE.

ODESSOS. See ODESSA.

ODESSUS. See VARNA.

ODEYPORE. See UDAIPUR.

ODON (France) Small river in NORMANDY that flows into the Orne River at CAEN. There was heavy fighting along its banks in June and July 1944 after the landing in Normandy in World War II.

ODRA. See ODER RIVER.

OEA. See TRIPOLI.

OELS. See OLEŚNICA.

OELS IN SCHLESIEN. See OLEŚNICA.

OENGARAN. See UNGARAN.

OENOTRIA. See LUCANIA, Italy.

OESEL. See SAAREMAA.

OFFALY [*former:* **Kings;** *Gaelic:* **Ua bhFailghe**] (Irish Republic) County in the central part of the country. Much of the W boundary is formed by the SHANNON RIVER, and sections of the county are covered by the Bog of Allen. The area, with some adjacent land, made up the ancient Irish kingdom of Offaly. In 548 AD St. Kieran, one of the most active founders of monasteries in Ireland, established a house at CLONMACNOISE, a village on the Shannon. It became a notable center of learning and survived 10 centuries of raids and invasions but was destroyed by the English in 1552. Its ruins and those of other ancient buildings can still be seen. In 553 St. Columba, a prince of the O'Donnells of Donegal, founded DURROW Abbey, near Tullamore. Circa 700, the *Book of Durrow,* a copy of the Gospels, was written here. It is now in Trinity College Library, Dublin. The abbey was torn down in the 12th century.

OFFA'S DYKE (England, Wales) Remnants of an ancient dyke and ditch extending from Tidenham, Gloucestershire, on the Severn River, to Prestatyn, Clwyd, at the mouth of the Dee River. Built by Offa, king of the Mercians, who died in 796 AD, it served as a defense against the Welsh along the western border of MERCIA.

OFFENBACH [**Offenbach am Main**] (West Germany) Long an industrial center of HESSE, known for its leather goods, Offenbach lies on the Main River very close to FRANKFURT am Main. It first appears in history in the 10th century, and was taken over by Hesse-Darmstadt in 1816. Heavily damaged during World War II by bombing, it has been reconstructed.

OFFENBACH AM MAIN. See OFFENBACH.

OGADEN (Ethiopia) Region bordering on SOMALIA, in Harar province. It was claimed as a protectorate by ITALY in 1891, but recaptured the same year by Menelik II. It was coveted by Mussolini, and a contrived dispute at Walwal in 1934 was used as a pretext for the

Italian war against Ethiopia in 1935/36. Restored to Ethiopia in 1948, it has been involved in boundary disputes between Somalia and Ethiopia since 1960. A major Ethiopian offensive aided by CUBA and the USSR resulted in the withdrawal of Somali troops in 1978, but the rebels continue to oppose Ethiopian forces.

OGAKI (Japan) Town, Gifu prefecture, W central HONSHŪ, just W of Gifu and 20 mi NW of Nagoya. It first became prominent in feudal times and remained so under the shoguns until the 19th century. It was bombed in 1945 during World War II.

OGALLALA. See NEBRASKA.

OGASAWARA-GUNTO. See BONIN ISLANDS.

OGBOMOSHO (Nigeria) City in SW Nigeria, 50 mi NNE of Ibadan. It is a busy trading center. Founded as a military camp in the 17th century, it became important in the resistance to FULANI invasions. It grew after the influx of refugees from the Fulani in the early 19th century.

OGDEN (United States) Intermountain railway center between the ROCKY MOUNTAINS and the West Coast, 35 mi N of Salt Lake City, in N UTAH. Founded and planned by Brigham Young and the Mormons in 1847 and incorporated in 1851, it is the oldest community in Utah.

OGDENSBURG (United States) Industrial port city in NE NEW YORK on the ST. LAWRENCE RIVER, 55 mi NNE of Watertown. It was founded in 1749 as a mission for converted Iroquois and incorporated as a city in 1868. The British built Fort Presentation here during the Revolution and held it until 1796. The city was an important point of defense against the British during the War of 1812 and a center of American sympathizers during CANADA's brief rebellion against GREAT BRITAIN in 1837. In 1940 U.S. President Roosevelt and Canadian Prime Minister King met here to initiate studies of the defense problems of North America, resulting in the Ogdensburg Agreement.

OGDEN'S RIVER. See HUMBOLDT RIVER.

OGONOSTE. See NIKŠIĆ.

OGUMKIQUEOK. See LIVERPOOL, Canada.

OHIO (United States) State, in the Midwest between LAKE ERIE on the N and the OHIO RIVER on the S. Pennsylvania is on the E, Kentucky and West Virginia on the S, Indiana on the W, and Michigan on the N. It was the 17th state of the Union and the first to be admitted from the old Northwest Territory, in 1803. With its rich natural resources, thriving industry and agriculture, excellent transportation, and varied population, Ohio is considered to be the most representative state of the Union. Beginning with Gen. Ulysses Grant in 1869, it has furnished seven native-born presidents to the nation.

Plentiful remains of prehistoric Indian Mound Builders dot the state, but by the colonial era the area had become a battleground of later, intrusive tribes. FRANCE first explored it in the 17th century but met competition in the 1730's from traders from the British

colonies and the Virginia-based Ohio Company, which sent Christopher Gist to explore the region in 1750. Such rivalry led to the French and Indian War beginning in 1754, which ended in 1763 with control of the whole Northwest by GREAT BRITAIN. A major Indian uprising, Pontiac's Rebellion of 1763/64, foreshadowed the bitter fighting during the American Revolution between Indians, supported by the British at DETROIT, and the Americans based at FORT PITT. In 1783 the Northwest became American.

The land claims of the eastern states were ceded to Congress between 1781 and 1786, except the Virginia Military District and the WESTERN RESERVE, retained by VIRGINIA and CONNECTICUT for veterans. Congress then established a pattern for the subsequent western development of the nation through the Ordinance of 1785, which provided for an orderly survey and sale of government lands, and the great Ordinance of 1787, which created the NORTHWEST TERRITORY, with a territorial governor and provision for the admission of three to five states, when population growth warranted it, on equal terms with the original states. New Englanders of the Ohio Company of Associates made the first settlement at MARIETTA in 1788; New Jerseyites settled the SYMMES PURCHASE; and Virginians entered the Military District in the 1780's. Moses Cleaveland founded CLEVELAND in 1796. Indian resistance was finally broken by Gen. Anthony Wayne at FALLEN TIMBERS in 1794.

Statehood followed in 1803, with the capital finally located at COLUMBUS in 1816. In 1804 Ohio University became the first university west of the Allegheny Mts. In Ohio the War of 1812 was marked by Capt. Oliver H. Perry's naval victory on Lake Erie. After this the population grew rapidly, swelled by German, Irish, Swiss, and Welsh immigrants. The first railroad was opened in 1832, heavy steamboat traffic developed on the Ohio River; the NATIONAL ROAD was pushed across the state, toll roads were opened, canals dug, and the four main railroad systems were completed by 1850. Ohio was now the leading agricultural state of the Union, and the third most populous with approx. 2 million inhabitants. During the Civil War it contributed over 300,000 troops to the Union cause.

Between 1850 and 1880 industry grew rapidly, outstripping agriculture—though the latter is still important today—and after 1880, attracting a new wave of immigrants from southern and eastern Europe to increase the polyglot nature of the big cities, which also gained a substantial black population. Industrial growth brought political domination by the moneyed interests that made Ohio-born William McKinley President in 1896. It also brought bitter strikes and the 1894 march of "Coxey's Army" to WASHINGTON, D.C. to demand reforms.

In 1912, in a liberal reaction, the constitution of 1851 was amended, and in subsequent years much attention was paid to municipal reform and social legislation. During both world wars Ohio furnished considerable industrial might and manpower, and thereafter continued to reflect the problems and accomplishments of the nation: Lake Erie became badly polluted, there was racial strife in 1966 and the deaths of four students at Kent State University in a Vietnam War protest in 1970; but also the election of a black mayor of Cleveland in 1968, and new efforts to conserve natural resources and solve growing urban problems. See also ERIE CANAL.

OHIO AND ERIE CANAL (United States) Former waterway of OHIO, 307 mi long. This canal connected LAKE ERIE and the OHIO RIVER. It was built from 1825 to 1832. It flourished as a means of transporting freight between Ohio and the East in the first half of the 19th century. The canal helped to link Ohio economically and politically to the East instead of the South, also preparing the way for future railroad development along similar routes. Among the places it served were AKRON, CLEVELAND, and COLUMBUS.

OHIO RIVER (United States) River, 981 mi long that empties into the MISSISSIPPI RIVER at CAIRO, ILLINOIS. It forms in western PENNSYLVANIA at the joining of the Allegheny and Monongahela rivers, then flows northwest, southwest, and west. It was reached by the French explorer Robert Cavalier de La Salle in 1669 and became the site of the French Fort DUQUESNE in 1754 and the British Fort Pitt, 1758, both trading and military outposts. It became a major travel and commercial route linking East and West during the late 18th and early 19th centuries and was known as the Gateway to the West. Flatboats, steamers, and showboats became commonplace during this period. Prior to the Civil War it was a notable boundary between the slave and the free states. With the growth of the railroads its traffic fell off.

OHLAU. See OLAWA.

OHRID [Ochrida, Okhrida] [*Greek:* **Lychnidos;** *Latin:* **Lychnidus**] (Yugoslavia) Town on Lake Ohrid in S Yugoslavia. It is MACEDONIA's chief resort area. The ancient Greek colony of Lychnidos was founded here in the third century BC. In the second century AD it was taken by ROME and later served as an episcopal see. It was the seat of the Bulgarian patriarchate in the ninth century. It has been ruled by the BYZANTINE EMPIRE and by the OTTOMAN EMPIRE. It has numerous ancient churches, including the ninth-century cathedral of St. Sophia and the 13th-century cathedral of St. Clement and two 14th-century churches; also parts of a former Turkish citadel.

OIL CITY (United States) City in NW PENNSYLVANIA, approx. 50 mi SSE of Erie, on the Allegheny River, at the mouth of Oil Creek. It is on the site of a former Indian village. The city owes its founding in 1860 to the discovery of oil and the introduction of the first producing well in the United States the previous year near TITUSVILLE, approx. 12 mi to the north. Until 1870 Oil City was the chief shipping point for petroleum produced during the frantic boom period of the country's first oil field. It remains a center of the Pennsylvania oil region.

OIL RIVERS (Nigeria) A large area of vague boundaries centering around the delta of the NIGER RIVER, West Africa. In 1885 the British established a protectorate of this name, which in 1893 became the Niger Coast Protectorate. In 1886 they had established the Colony and Protectorate of LAGOS. The two were combined in 1899 into the Protectorates of Northern and Southern Nigeria. By 1914, when the area was renamed The Protectorate and Colony of Nigeria, the beginnings of modern Nigeria had taken shape.

OIROT AUTONOMOUS OBLAST. See GORNO-ALTAI AUTONOMOUS OBLAST.

OISE RIVER (Belgium, France) River, 186 mi long, which rises in the ARDENNES Mts of S Belgium, then flows SW through N France, joining the SEINE RIVER near Pontoise. Mostly navigable and linked to other rivers by canals, the Oise is an important transportation route. COMPIÈGNE on its banks was a gathering place for royalty from the seventh century AD. PONTOISE, which has a 12th-century cathedral, was often besieged in the 15th, 16th, and 17th centuries. The armistice ending World War I was signed at Compiègne on Nov. 11, 1918; in World War II Hitler forced France to surrender to Germany on the same spot on June 22, 1940. Several battles were fought on the banks of the Oise in World War I, and the Oise-Cambre Canal formed a battle line. LA FÈRE was occupied by the Germans from September 1914 to October 1918.

OITA (Japan) Rail hub and manufacturing center in NE KYŪSHŪ, Oita prefecture, 65 mi SE of Moji on Beppu Bay. A castle city controlling most of Kyūshū Island, it became the center of 16th-century Portuguese trade. It has remnants of early markets from this period.

OKAYAMA (Japan) Port and industrial center in SW HONSHŪ, on the Inland Sea. A former castle town of the Ikeda clan, the city has a 16th-century castle and the famous 18th-century Korakuen Park.

OKAZAKI (Japan) Town, Aichi prefecture, S HONSHŪ, 21 mi SE of Nagoya. This is the birthplace of Iyeyasu, founder of the Tokugawa shogunate, which ruled Japan through a feudal system and central bureaucracy from 1603 to 1867.

OKEECHOBEE, LAKE (United States) Lake in SE FLORIDA, N of the EVERGLADES, approx. 700 sq mi in area. Here on Dec. 25, 1837 the bloodiest battle of the Second Seminole War was fought as Gen. Zachary Taylor defeated a force of Seminole Indians. In 1926 it was struck by a disastrous hurricane. Recent construction of canals and a levee have reduced the flow of water from the lake into the Everglades, making these huge marshes subject to saltwater seepage and underground fires.

OKEL DAMA. See ACELDAMA.

OKHRIDA. See OHRID.

OKINAWA (Japan) An agricultural island in the N Pacific Ocean, 350 mi SW of KYŪSHŪ, part of the RYUKU ISLANDS chain. It was the scene of a successful but costly U.S. amphibious campaign, from April 1 to June 21, 1945, to establish air bases close to mainland Japan during World War II. One of the bloodiest campaigns of the war, it saw heavy damage done to the U.S. ships by suicide air attacks. The UNITED STATES returned the island to Japan in 1972 but retains some military bases.

OKLAHOMA (United States) State, in the SW, it has the Red River as its S boundary with Texas, New Mexico is on the W, Kansas on the N, and Arkansas on the E. It was admitted to the Union in 1907 as the 46th state. Oklahoma is a Choctaw word meaning "people-red," coined in 1866 by a chief for his tribe's land in Indian Territory.

The first Europeans in Oklahoma were those of Francisco Vasquez de Coronado's expedition in 1541, searching for the fabled land of QUIVIRA. Hernando de Soto reached here as did Juan de Oñate. Other Spanish and some French explorers also visited Oklahoma. At the time there were Osage, Kiowa, Comanche, and Apache Indians in the west and more sedentary Indians, such as the Wichita, in the east. The first European settlement was the post established by Jean Pierre Chouteau, a fur-trader from ST. LOUIS, Missouri, at Salina in 1796.

The LOUISIANA PURCHASE in 1803 made Oklahoma U.S. territory, and the Adams-Onis Treaty of 1819 with SPAIN made it the southwestern boundary of the nation. In the meantime, American explorers and travelers began to visit the region. These included Stephen H. Long, the scientist; Washington Irving, the author; and George Catlin, the painter. After the War of 1812 the United States tried to induce the eastern Indians to move west across the MISSISSIPPI RIVER, but by the 1830's force was being used; and the Cherokees and others of the Five Civilized Tribes were moved to Indian Territory, which included present Oklahoma, Kansas, and Nebraska. These Indians had been farmers settled in villages, including some plantations with slaves. They tried to reestablish their way of life in Oklahoma but with little success. They also clashed with the Plains Indians. In the Civil War most of the Indians sided with the Confederacy. There were no important battles but many skirmishes and considerable violence in the state.

After the war the Federal government punished the Indians by taking away some of their land, while cattle drives from TEXAS to KANSAS began and crossed Oklahoma on the CHISHOLM TRAIL. The railroads came too, beginning in 1870, and it became more difficult to keep white settlers out of Indian Territory. On April 22, 1889 a large area was thrown open to settlement, and people lined up at the border to rush in on signal at noon. Those who beat the gun became known as "sooners." By nightfall the area had 60,000 inhabitants. In 1890 the western section became Oklahoma Territory.

A Federal Law of 1906 was intended to break up Indian reservations into individually held units and so possibly open more land to settlers. When the state was formed in 1907, Oklahoma and Indian Territory were united. The state was ready for large-scale economic development, and in a few years World War I quickened a demand for agricultural products created by the country's rapid urban population growth. In the 1920's, drought, overplanting, and too much grazing brought hard times early to the state. Oklahoma was part of the DUST BOWL in the 1930's and became known for the "Okies," who abandoned their stricken farms and headed west. The New Deal's government price supports, irrigation projects, World War II, and postwar prosperity have brought back better times for farmers. Oklahoma has a long Democratic tradition but has voted Republican in recent presidential elections. OKLAHOMA CITY, settled during the land rush of 1889, is the capital and largest city. The other important city is TULSA, first settled as a Creek Indian village in the 1830's.

OKLAHOMA CITY (United States) Oil, agricultural, and aviation center and state capital in central OKLAHOMA. It was first settled by the five Indian nations of the Cherokee, Chickasaw, Choctaw, Creek, and Seminole, who had been forcibly evacuated from the east to the area in the 1830's in the tragic long death march. Although given to them as a reservation in the early 1880's, the area was opened to homesteaders on April 22, 1889 by presidential proclamation. Some 10,000 people had settled there overnight in the ensuing startling land rush. The city was incorporated in 1890 and became the state capital in 1910. When oil was discovered in December 1928, it became a major petroleum producing area.

OKMULGEE (United States) An oil and farming center in E central OKLAHOMA. It began as the capital of the Creek nation which existed from 1868 to 1907. The city has an Indian mission dating from 1882, and an original Creek council house built in 1878. It was incorporated in 1900. The town boomed with the discovery of oil in 1907.

ÖLAND (Sweden) Island in the Baltic Sea off the SE coast of Sweden. Stone Age burial monuments have been found here. They are formed of groups of rocks placed in the shape of ships. Öland first appeared in history in the eighth century. On the west coast are the ruins of a once magnificent Swedish castle begun in the 13th century, rebuilt, and enlarged in the 16th.

OLAWA [*German:* **Ohlau**] (Poland) City in E Wrocław province, on the ODER RIVER, 18 mi SE of Wrocław. Chartered as a city in 1291, it was taken by Soviet troops during World War II on Feb. 7, 1945, and was later assigned to Poland.

OLBIA (USSR) Excavation site on the right bank of the Bug River in Ukrainian SSR. As a leading Greek Milesian colony between the sixth and third centuries BC, it specialized in handicrafts, trade, and the export of wheat. In the second century BC it became a part of Scythian CRIMEA. It had disappeared by the sixth century AD. Hellenic towers, city gates, parts of a fortified wall, and temple from the Roman period have been found here. See also OCHAKOV, SARMATIA, UKRAINE.

OLCHIONIA. See SOROKI.

OLCINIUM. See ULCINJ.

OLD CALABAR. See CALABAR.

OLD CRIMEA. See STARY KRYM.

OLD DEER (Scotland) Village, 26 mi N of Aberdeen, in Grampian Region. The founding of a monastery here by St. Columba in the sixth century AD is described in the *Book of Deer* discovered in 1857 at Cambridge University. A manuscript copy of portions of the Gospels is included. While most of the book is in Latin Vulgate, marginal notes are in Gaelic; and this is the oldest Scottish document containing Gaelic. There are no remains of the abbey.

OLD DELHI. See DELHI.

OLDENBURG (West Germany) Former German state bounded by the North Sea, and elsewhere by the former Prussian province of HANOVER. Its history is mainly of dynastic importance. A part of SAXONY in the 12th century, it passed to DENMARK from 1676 to 1773, and to RUSSIA from 1773 to 1777. It was given to the bishop of LÜBECK who temporarily lost it to Napoleon but regained it in 1813. It joined the GERMAN CONFEDERATION in 1815, the GERMAN EMPIRE in 1871, and the WEIMAR Republic in 1918. Its capital is also Oldenburg.

OLD HARBOUR BAY. See PORTLAND BIGHT.

OLD HARRYSTOWN. See MANCHESTER.

OLD JHELUM. See JHELUM, Pakistan.

OLD LYME (United States) Town in SE CONNECTICUT at the mouth of the Connecticut River. Settled in 1665, it was incorporated in 1885. It has become a summer resort and residential town noted for many old homes of architectural interest. In addition to seaside homes, it has a Congregational church that was a subject for the American impressionist painter Childe Hassam.

OLD MACKINAC See MACKINAC.

OLD MARGILAN. See MARGILAN.

OLD MOSHI. See MOSHI.

OLD NORTHWEST. See NORTHWEST TERRITORY.

OLD PANAMA [*Spanish:* **Panamá Vieja**] (Panama) Former city on the S shore of the Isthmus of Panama. It was a port on the Pacific Ocean used by SPAIN in the 16th and 17th centuries. It was sacked by the buccaneer Henry Morgan in 1671. The ruined city is near the present city of PANAMA.

OLD SARATOGA. See SCHUYLERVILLE.

OLD SARUM [*Latin:* **Sorbiodunum**] (England) Former city 2 mi N of SALISBURY, Wiltshire, S England. Extensive ruins remain from its history as an ancient British fort, a Roman station, and a Saxon and Norman town. It was the seat of a bishopric between 1075 and 1220. The "Use of Sarum," a Liturgy, was formulated by Osmund, bishop from 1078 to 1099. The see was transferred to Salisbury along with materials from its great cathedral, in the 1220's. It was a "rotten borough," which, though deserted, retained its parliamentary representation until the Reform Bill of 1832.

OLD SAYBROOK. See SAYBROOK.

OLD SITKA. See SITKA.

OLD SPANISH TRAIL. See SANTA FE, UTAH.

OLD STURBRIDGE VILLAGE (United States) Recreated farm village in Sturbridge MASSACHUSETTS, 20 mi SW of Worcester. It shows the life, art, and handicrafts of NEW ENGLAND in the period of 1790 to 1840. It has over 35 original buildings.

OLDUVAI GORGE (Tanzania) Ravine in East Africa, 150 mi NW of Mt Kilimanjaro. It is the site of rich fossil beds. The ancient fossil skull of *Homo habilis*, 1.75 million years old, was discovered here in 1959 by British anthropologist L.S.B. Leakey. Anthropological explorations and discoveries have continued since then.

OLÉRON [Île d'Oléron] [*Latin:* **Uliarus Insula**] (France) Island W of France in the Bay of Biscay. It is a resort and oystering spot. The 12th-century Laws of Oléron, promulgated by Louis IX, form the basis for modern maritime law. It was a Protestant refuge during the Reformation. It is the site of prehistoric megalithic monuments.

OLEŚNICA [*German:* **Oels, Oels in Schlesien**] (Poland) Manufacturing city in E Wrocław province, 17 mi ENE of Wrocław. Founded in the 10th century, by the 14th century it was the capital of an independent principality. Poland acquired it during the POTSDAM Conference after World War II.

OLGIONIA. See SOROKI.

ÓLIMBOS. See OLYMPUS.

OLINDA (Brazil) City in Pernambuco state, N of RECIFE. A Jesuit seminary founded here in 1796 is the basis for its reputation as a center of learning. The city was burned to the ground in 1630 and then rebuilt by the Dutch during their occupation from 1630 to 1654. It has notable 16th- and 17th-century buildings.

OLISIPO. See LISBON.

OLIVA. See OLIWA.

OLIVES, MOUNT OF [Olivet] (Jordan) Ridge E of JERUSALEM on the Judaean Plateau, in Israeli-occupied Jordan. Its four peaks are scenes of biblical events: David's flight from the city, Ezekiel's theophany, Zechariah's prophecy, and the Ascension of Jesus. It is the site of ancient catacombs and of the Garden of GETHSEMANE. It is also the site of Hebrew University and of several churches.

OLIVET. See OLIVES, MOUNT OF.

OLIWA [*German:* **Oliva**] (Poland) Town, now part of GDAŃSK, Gdańsk province. A peace treaty signed here with SWEDEN on May 3, 1660 ended the war with Sweden begun in 1655, as John II Casimir of Poland gave up his claim to the Swedish throne.

OLMÜTZ. See OLOMOUC.

OLOMOUC [*German:* **Olmütz**] (Czechoslovakia) Moravian city on the Morava River, 40 mi NW of Brno. This industrial and cultural center was the capital of MORAVIA until 1640. The Conference of Olmütz in 1850 dissolved the German Union under the rule of PRUSSIA and therefore became known in that country as the "humiliation of Olmütz." It was a leading trading city in the 10th and 11th centuries and the scene of the coronation of the king of BOHEMIA in 1469. It has many intact examples of Gothic architecture.

OLONETS [*Finnish:* **Alavoinen**; *former:* **Aunus**] (USSR) City in the Russian SFSR on Olonets Isthmus near the E shore of LAKE LADOGA, 112 mi NE of Leningrad. It is famous for the ironworks established here by Peter the Great of RUSSIA (1672–1725).

OLONGAPO (Philippines) City and harbor on LUZON, on the NE coast of Subic Bay near the Bataan border. Once a U.S. naval station, it was occupied by the Japanese from December 1941 to February 1945 during World War II.

OLORON-SAINTE-MARIE [*former:* **Iloro**] (France) City in Pyrénées-Atlantiques department, SW France, 13 mi SW of Pau. It was an ancient city at the north end of a road across the Pyrenees. Destroyed by the Saracens and the Normans, it was rebuilt in 1080. It was also an episcopal see, founded in the fourth century, which lasted until 1790.

OLSZTYN [*German:* **Allenstein**] (Poland) Capital city of Olsztyn province, approx. 120 mi NW of Warsaw. It was founded by the Teutonic Knights in 1348, who built an impressive castle (14th century) which stands today. Ceded to Poland in 1772, it was taken over by PRUSSIA in 1772 and by GERMANY in 1920, but was finally returned to Poland in 1945 after the POTSDAM Conference, since it had long been a center of Polish nationalist movements. Although it was heavily damaged in World War II, the old city has been reconstructed.

OLTENIŢA [**Oltenitza**] [*Latin:* **Constantiola**] (Rumania) City in Ilfov county, on the Argeş River at its confluence with the DANUBE RIVER. It was the scene of a battle on Nov. 4, 1853 in which the Turks defeated the Russians during the preliminaries of the Crimean War.

OLTENITZA. See OLTENIŢA.

OLTRE GIUBA. See JUBALAND.

OLUSTEE (United States) Village in NE FLORIDA, 45 mi SW of Jacksonville. A Confederate force led by Gen. Joseph Finnegan defeated Union troops under Gen. Truman Seymour here in the battle of Ocean Pond, on Feb. 20, 1864. It was an important victory and the major military engagement of the Civil War in Florida.

OLYMPIA (Greece) Valley in ancient ELIS in the NW PELOPONNESUS on the N bank of the Alpheus River. Excavations here starting in the 19th century have unearthed the ruins of many temples and buildings indicating that it was once a religious sanctuary and the scene of the original Olympian Games in honor of Zeus. The games were first held in 776 BC. The games were held every four years thereafter, and while the athletes were competing the Greek city states stopped warring. It is the site of the temple of Olympian Zeus, now fallen, in which stood the statue of Zeus by Phidias. Part of the workshop of Phidias has been found, and Praxiteles' statue of Hermes is here.

OLYMPIA (United States) City in W WASHINGTON state, at the southern end of PUGET SOUND, capital of the state. Founded in 1846, it was made the capital of the new Washington Territory in 1853. It became the first port of entry on Puget Sound in 1851. Lumber products and fisheries are important to its economy.

OLYMPUS [*Greek:* **Ólimbos**] (Greece) Mountain range in THESSALY. The peak, overlooking the Vale of Tempe and enshrouded by clouds, was the mythic home of the Olympian gods.

OLYNTHUS (Greece) Excavation site on the CHALCIDICE peninsula at the head of the Toronaic Gulf. It was the most important of the Greek cities on the Macedonian coast. As the head of the Chalcidian League, in the late fifth century BC, it had to face severe opposition from ATHENS and SPARTA. It was captured by Sparta in 379 BC, and in 348 BC, despite Demosthenes' famous *Olynthiac* orations, was laid waste by Philip II of MACEDON. The only city on the Greek mainland with completely excavated city plans, because it was never re-established after its destruction, it offers a unique view of the great Greek cultural period of the fifth and fourth centuries BC.

OMAHA (United States) City 50 mi NE of Lincoln in E NEBRASKA, on the MISSOURI RIVER. It is an industrial and transportation hub today, as well as a major livestock and farming market, and is the headquarters of the U.S. Air Force's Strategic Air Command. A Mormon encampment in 1846, it was first permanently settled in 1854 and served as the capital of the Nebraska Territory from 1854 to 1867. In 1869 it became an important transportation and industrial center, linking the East and the West, as the eastern terminus of the Union Pacific portion of the first transcontinental railroad.

OMAHA BEACH (France) Code name during World War II for the W central portion of the NORMANDY coast. U.S. Army troops, with intensive air and naval protection, landed on these beaches on what was called D-Day, June 6, 1944, opening a major invasion of German-held Europe. There was prolonged and bitter fighting before the Allies gained their first landhold in northern Europe.

OMAN [*former:* **Masqat and Oman, Muscat and Oman**] Sultanate on the SE ARABIAN PENINSULA, on the Gulf of Oman and the Arabian Sea. Its capital is MASQAT. It was first Islamicized in the seventh century. In the 16th century it was subject to PORTUGAL. The most powerful Arabian state in the early 19th century, it controlled ZANZIBAR and much of the coast of Persia. After its fall from power in the 19th century, it became dependent upon the British government. It has been the scene of constant civil strife in the 20th century, including a civil war in the Dhofar region during the 1960's. Oil was discovered in commercial quantities in 1964.

OMBOS (Egypt) Ancient city on the NILE RIVER, S of Edfu. The city became important under the Ptolemies, who reigned from the fourth century BC until the Roman conquest of Egypt in the first century BC. Temples were erected here in honor of the crocodile-headed god Suchos and the falcon-headed god Horus.

OMDURMAN [*Arabic:* **Umm Durmān**] (Sudan) City on the left bank of the White NILE RIVER, opposite KHARTOUM. It is an important trading center. In January 1884 it became the military headquarters of the

Mahdi Muhammad Ahmad, who tried to make it the model African city after he had sacked Khartoum. The Mahdi's tomb, built in 1885, replaced MECCA briefly as the object of the obligatory Islamic pilgrimage, and the city flourished. The nearby battle of Karari on Sept. 2, 1898 saw the defeat of the Mahdist forces by Lord Kitchener's Anglo-Egyptian army. Most of the city was destroyed at this time, but the tomb survives, and the city has revived.

OMSK (USSR) City, industrial center, and capital of Omsk oblast in the Russian SFSR, at the confluence of the Om River and the Irtysh River. The only major town in the region, it was founded in 1716. In the 19th century it was headquarters for the Siberian Cossacks. During the civil war following the Revolution of 1917, it became the anti-Bolshevik headquarters of the armed forces of Adm. A.V. Kolchak. During World War II the government moved many factories from combat zones to Omsk, giving rise to its later industrial development.

OMUDA. See OMUTA.

OMUTA [Omuda] (Japan) Coal mining and chemical center in KYŪSHŪ, Fukuoka prefecture, on the Amakusa Sea. The city was heavily bombed in 1944 and 1945 during World II as the U.S. forces came within reach of Japan.

ON. See HELIOPOLIS.

ONEGA (USSR) Town at the SW end of the White Sea, at the mouth of the Onega River 90 mi S of Arkhangelsk. Settled in the 15th century, the medieval town became a lumbering center. The port is navigable only about half of the year when the sea is not frozen.

ONEGLIA. See IMPERIA, Italy.

ONEIDA (United States) City in NEW YORK State, 13 mi WSW of Rome. The city was founded in 1829 and became well known after 1848 when the Oneida Community was established by John Humphrey Noyes and his followers. Noyes first set up a Perfectionist community in Putney, Vermont in 1839, preaching that human beings can become sinless by right living. When he developed a complex marriage system, a form of polygamy, his neighbors' opposition forced him to flee. The people of the Oneida Community held all property in common, and children were raised in a community nursery. The community prospered, at first by manufacturing a trap for small animals, later by producing silverware. Unlike most utopian communities, this one lasted for three decades, but in 1879 opposition again forced Noyes to flee, this time to Canada. The communal life style was abandoned at Oneida, and in 1881 the group was reorganized as a business corporation. Oneida is now an industrial city.

ONEIDA COMMUNITY. See ONEIDA.

ONITSHA (Nigeria) Port and trading center on the NIGER RIVER, 135 mi from its mouth. Settlers from BENIN came here in the 16th century and were followed by Ibo tribesmen in the 17th century. In 1857 the British set up a trading station and a Christian mission here. The city became part of a British protectorate in 1884.

ONONDAGA, LAKE (United States) Lake in central NEW YORK, 5 mi long, 1 mi wide, NW of SYRACUSE. The Onondaga Indians guided a French missionary to salt springs along its shore in 1654. In 1795 New York State purchased these springs and the area around them, and a sizable salt industry developed that lasted until the mid-19th century. The Salt Museum in Syracuse displays many of the tools and processes of the industry, and there is also a museum on the lake shore near Liverpool.

ONTARIO (Canada) Province of the Dominion of Canada, in the E central region. Before Europeans appeared the region was inhabited by several Indian tribes, of which the Hurons were the largest. Étienne Brulé of FRANCE explored southern Ontario from 1610 to 1612. Henry Hudson's discovery of HUDSON BAY in 1610 resulted in his claiming for England what became part of Ontario. The French explorer Samuel de Champlain crossed to the eastern shore of LAKE HURON in 1615, and other Frenchmen reached LAKE ERIE in 1640. The French built a number of posts for defense, trading, and missionary work among the Indians in the 17th and 18th centuries. Meanwhile, the British built trading posts in the Hudson Bay area.

The French and British fought several wars for control of Canada until the French were forced to give up all the mainland in 1763 after the French and Indian War. In 1774 Great Britain combined Ontario and QUEBEC into one province. After the American Revolution, fleeing Loyalists increased Ontario's population, so that the British government in 1791 divided the two regions into Lower Canada (Quebec) and Upper Canada (Ontario). During the War of 1812 a number of engagements were fought on Ontario soil between the British-Canadians and the Americans, especially in the NIAGARA peninsula area. U.S. forces burned TORONTO in 1813.

In the 19th century conflict arose between the ruling aristocrats and conservatives, known as the Family Compact, and a group of reformers and radicals. The struggle led to an armed uprising in 1837 that was quickly suppressed. As a result of the conflict, however, Ontario and Quebec were once more joined as Canada West (Ontario) and Canada East (Quebec) in the new Province of Canada in 1849. In 1867, when the Dominion was formed, Ontario became one of the first four provinces. Its present boundaries, however, were not established until 1912.

ONTARIO, LAKE [*French:* **Lac Frontenac**] (Canada and United States) Easternmost and smallest of the Great Lakes, its W end is fed by the NIAGARA River while at its E end it forms the start of the ST. LAWRENCE RIVER. Two French explorers, Étienne Brulé and Samuel de Champlain, were the first Europeans to see Lake Ontario, in 1615. It was part of the vast region of North America that became controlled by GREAT BRITAIN after the French and Indian War in 1763. Following the American Revolution the border between Canada and the United States was drawn through the lake. The end of warfare speeded settlement and commerce around the lake. The Welland Ship

Canal, first opened in 1829 and enlarged since, together with the St. Lawrence Seaway project completed in 1959 have increased the importance of Lake Ontario as a shipping artery.

OODEYPORE. See UDAIPUR.

OOS-LONDEN. See EAST LONDON.

OOSTENDE. See OSTEND.

OOTHCALOGA. See CALHOUN.

OPAR. See MOROCCO.

OPAVA [*German:* **Troppau**] (Czechoslovakia) Moravian market center on the Opava River, approx. 15 mi NW of Ostrava. An important commercial center on the junction of trade routes from the Baltic Sea to the Adriatic Sea for centuries, it was founded in the 12th century and later became the capital of Austrian SILESIA. It was the site of the Congress of Troppau in 1820, at which several European powers adopted a policy of armed intervention to suppress the liberal movements that followed the Napoleonic Wars. The Czech population was driven from the city when it was taken in September 1938 by Nazi Germany, but the town was returned to Czechoslovakia after World War II.

OPELOUSAS (United States) Old farming and livestock center in S central LOUISIANA, 53 mi W of Baton Rouge. Settled in 1690, it was taken by the French in 1765. They established a military and trading post here. It was incorporated as a town in 1821 and served as state capital in 1863, during the Civil War.

OPEQUON (United States) Village at N end of SHENANDOAH VALLEY, N VIRGINIA, 60 mi NW of Washington, D.C. It is the site of a Civil War battle known also as the battle of WINCHESTER. Here on Sept. 19, 1864 Confederate forces under Gen. Jubal Sheridan were defeated by Union troops under Gen. Philip Sheridan, thus initiating his famous drive down the Shenandoah Valley.

OPHIR (Arabian Peninsula) Ancient seaport of unknown location, now considered to have been in SW Saudi Arabia or YEMEN. It has also been associated with northeast Africa. It was frequently mentioned in the Old Testament as a place from which the ships of Solomon brought gold in great quantities. Gems, sandalwood, apes, peacocks, and ivory were also part of their cargo.

OPIS (Iraq) Ancient town on the W bank of the TIGRIS RIVER, approx. 43 mi N of Baghdad. Here are the ruins of an Assyrian city, which was the site of a battle in 539 BC in which Cyrus the Great of PERSIA defeated the Babylonians. See also BABYLON.

OPOBO (Nigeria) A center for the palm oil trade in the NIGER RIVER delta. The town was founded in 1869 when a middleman in the trade named JaJa led a group of people there from nearby BONNY. The town grew, but Jaja antagonized European traders and was deported by the British in 1887. Opobo's trade later shrank, as did that of Bonny. See also PORT HARCOURT.

OPOLE [*German:* **Oppeln**] (Poland) City on the ODER RIVER, 190 mi SW of Warsaw. A 10th-century Slavic settlement, it became the capital of the Silesian duchy of Opole, ruled by a branch of the Polish Piast dynasty through the Middle Ages. It was under Bohemian and then Austrian Hapsburg rule from 1532. The city was taken by PRUSSIA in 1742 and remained under German rule until it was assigned to Poland in 1945 by the POTSDAM Conference. The 10th-century church of St. Adalbert is here. See also SILESIA.

OPORTO [*Iberian:* **Cale**; *Latin:* **Portus Cale**; *Portuguese:* **Pôrto**] (Portugal) Atlantic seaport and capital of Pôrto district, near the mouth of the DOURO RIVER, 170 mi NE of Lisbon. An ancient settlement of pre-Roman origin, it was captured in 716 AD by the Moors, who lost it to the Christians in 1092. It was the capital of northern Portugal until 1174. After the Methuen Treaty in 1703, it became a major wine exporter. In 1757 it was the scene of the Tipplers' Revolt, which involved the wine monopoly of the Marquês de Pombal. Portugal was conquered by the French in the Peninsular Campaign of 1808 to 1813, but Oporto was first to revolt in 1808 and was liberated in 1809. In the Miguelist Wars, Dom Pedro I of BRAZIL withstood a long siege of the city by his brother Dom Miguel in 1832. An abortive republican government was set up in the city in 1891.

OPPELN. See OPOLE.

OPPIDUM. See GERONA.

OPPIDUM UBIORUM. See COLOGNE.

OQAIR. See DAMMAM.

ORADEA [Oradea-Mare] [*German:* **Grosswardein**; *Hungarian:* **Nagyvárad**] (Rumania) Industrial city and seat of an Orthodox Eastern bishopric in Crişana-Maramureş. It was made a Roman Catholic bishopric in 1083 by King Ladislaus I of HUNGARY. Destroyed by the Tatars in 1241, it was rebuilt in the 15th century. Having passed to TRANSYLVANIA in 1556 for a short time and then to the Turks from 1660 to 1692, it became part of Rumania in 1919; it was occupied by Hungarian forces during World War II. Hungary ceded it to Rumania after the war.

ORADEA-MARE. See ORADEA.

ORAIBI (United States) Pueblo in the Hopi Indian Reservation in N ARIZONA, on a high mesa 60 mi N of Winslow. For many years the greatest and one of the oldest of Indian pueblos, it can be dated to c.1150 AD. It was discovered in 1540 during one of Francisco Coronado's expeditions. In 1629 a Franciscan mission was set up here, but it perished in 1680 when the Hopi revolted. Dissension and economic changes led to the pueblo's gradual abandonment. Those remaining went to Hotevila and Bakavi pueblos in 1907. The mesa is now mainly in ruins. At its foot is the village of Lower Oraibi.

ORAN (Algeria) Commercial port on the Gulf of Oran of the Mediterranean Sea, 225 mi W of Algiers. Settled in prehistoric times, it was built up in the 10th century by Moorish traders from ANDALUSIA. By the 15th century it was flourishing. Much of its prosperity was due to piracy, however, and in 1509 SPAIN took it from the Moors in a fierce battle and held it for two centuries. After earthquakes, famine, and disease had decimated it *c.*1790, the Bey of MASCARA established his capital there. FRANCE occupied it and made it a naval base in 1831, and it became an important economic center. Held by Vichy France during World War II, it was taken by the Allies on Nov. 10, 1942 at the beginning of the North African campaign. In the 1950's most of its European inhabitants left because of the violent activities of French terrorists and Algerian nationalists.

ORANGE [*Latin:* **Arausio**] (France) Town in Vaucluse department, 17 mi N of Avignon. Ancient capital of the Celtic Cavares, it saw the defeat of the Romans by the Cimbri and the Teutones in 105 BC. Later conquered by ROME, it became an episcopal see in the third century AD. By Charlemagne's time, *c.*800, it was an earldom. It was an independent city in the 11th century but was inherited by William the Silent of the house of NASSAU in 1554. French possession began when the city was conquered by Louis XIV in 1672 and was confirmed by the Treaty of UTRECHT in 1713; but the Dutch princes of Orange retained the title. The town has many Roman ruins, including a triumphal arch built in 26 AD and an amphitheater, still in use.

ORANGE (United States) Village in N OHIO. It was the birthplace of James A. Garfield, the 20th president of the United States.

ORANGEBURG (United States) Cotton trading and processing center in central SOUTH CAROLINA, on the Edisto River, 75 mi NE of Charleston. Among the oldest townships in the state, it was settled in 1732 and incorporated in 1883. German-Swiss immigrants on free land grants planned and carried out the settlement.

ORANGE FREE STATE [*Afrikaans:* **Oranje Vrystaat**] (South Africa) Province of the Republic of South Africa, S of TRANSVAAL, and N and E of CAPE PROVINCE. Before European settlers arrived in the early 19th century, the region was inhabited mainly and sparsely by people of the Bantu ethnic group. Beginning in the 1820's Boers, African colonists of Dutch and French Huguenot descent, began to enter the territory. This immigration increased during the Great Trek of 1835/36, when large numbers of Boers, using ox-drawn wagons, moved here to escape British rule in what is now Cape Province. In 1848, however, the British annexed the territory as the Orange River Sovereignty. This action led to armed conflict with the Boers, led by Andries Pretorius, but the British quickly prevailed. Nevertheless, in 1854, by the Bloemfontein Convention, Great Britain gave the territory its independence as the Orange Free State. Continuing tensions between Great Britain and the Boers of southern Africa led to the South African (or Boer) War, which began in 1899. The people of the Orange Free State sided with their fellow Boers in the struggle. By May 1900 the British controlled the region and that year annexed it again and named it the Orange River Colony. It was given self-government in 1907 and in 1910 was one of the provinces that founded the Union of South Africa. The capital is BLOEMFONTEIN, which was founded in 1846.

ORANIENBAUM. See LOMONOSOV.

ORANIENBURG [*former:* **Bötzow**] (East Germany) Center of a fruit-growing region on the Havel River in Potsdam district. The town was first mentioned as Bötzow in the 12th century. One of the earliest Nazi concentration camps was set up here in 1933.

ORANIYENBAUM. See LOMONOSOV.

ORANJE VRYSTAAT. See ORANGE FREE STATE.

ORASUL STALIN. See BRAŞOV.

ORBETELLO (Italy) Town in central Italy, on the Tyrrhenian Sea, 25 mi S of Grosseto. Site of ancient Etruscan ruins and a medieval cathedral. See also COSA.

ORCADES. See ORKNEY ISLANDS.

ORCHOE. See ERECH.

ORCHOMENUS (Greece) City of ancient BOEOTIA, NW of Lake Copais, 7 mi NE of Lebadea. A center of Mycenaean civilization from *c.*1600 BC, it was later eclipsed by THEBES. In 85 BC Sulla won a significant victory nearby, destroying the army of Mithridates VI. Settled by the Minyans of prehistory, the city has been extensively excavated. It has no connection to Orchomenus in ARCADIA. See MYCENAE, ROME.

ORDAS. See ODESSA.

ORDU. See COTYORA.

ORDYSSOS. See ODESSA.

ORDZHONIKIDZE [*former:* **Dzaudzhikau, Vladikavkaz**] (USSR) Trading center and the capital of NORTH OSSETIAN ASSR, 92 mi N of Tbilisi, on the upper Terek River. It was founded in 1784 as a fortress during the Russian conquest of the CAUCASUS. In 1861 it became a town and grew in importance when connected with TBILISI by the famous Georgian military road in 1864. Kazbek Peak, rising just above the city, was the farthest the German armies advanced into the Caucasus Mts from Nov. 10 to 19, 1942 during World War II.

ORDZHONIKIDZE KRAI. See STAVROPOL KRAI.

ÖREBRO (Sweden) The capital of Örebro county, on Lake Hjälmaren, 100 mi W of Stockholm. Known since the 11th century, it has been the site of many national diets, particularly that of 1529 marking the start of the Reformation in Sweden, and one in 1810 which saw Marshal Bernadotte, who later was Charles XIV, elected crown prince of Sweden and NORWAY. In 1854 it was almost completely rebuilt after a great fire. Swedish patriot Engelbrekt Engelbrektsson was born here. The Kungs Stuga, one of the most typical timber buildings remaining from ancient times, is here.

OREGON (United States) State in the far NW, on the Pacific Ocean to the W, Washington to the N, Idaho to the E, and Nevada and California to the S. It was admitted to the Union in 1859 as the 33rd state. The origin of its name is uncertain. Oregon was discovered during the search for the NORTHWEST PASSAGE, the hoped-for water route from Europe to the Far East. Spanish navigators sailed along the coast from the 16th to the 18th century, and in 1579 Sir Francis Drake may have sailed this far north and may have landed here. In 1778 Capt. James Cook charted some of the coastline. At this time RUSSIA was pushing south from ALASKA, and British fur traders were coming in through CANADA as the fur trade with CHINA became important.

Beginning in 1792, George Vancouver of GREAT BRITAIN spent considerable time navigating the area. Also that year, Robert Gray, the first American to circumnavigate the globe, made the first venture into the COLUMBIA RIVER. This established the U.S. claim to the region. The Lewis and Clark Expedition wintered near the mouth of the river from 1805 to 1806, calling their camp Fort Clatsop. John Jacob Astor's Pacific Fur Company founded ASTORIA at the river's mouth in 1811 but sold it to the North West Company of Canada in 1813. A treaty in 1818 between the United States and GREAT BRITAIN provided for joint occupation of the region, which included Oregon and what are now the states of WASHINGTON, IDAHO, part of MONTANA, and in Canada, BRITISH COLUMBIA.

The merger of the North West Company and the Hudson's Bay Company in 1821 gave Great Britain dominance of the fur trade, but the American presence was maintained by Jedediah S. Smith and other mountain men in the southeast. The eastern and midwestern United States showed great interest in this far-away land, and in 1829 Hall J. Kelley of NEW ENGLAND founded the American Society for Encouraging the Settlement of the Oregon Territory. One of his disciples, Nathaniel J. Wyeth, tried but failed to establish a colony in 1832. He returned in 1834 to found FORT HALL and to build Fort William on the Columbia River, but two years later he again gave up. The missionary Marcus Whitman arrived in 1836, however, and some of his party settled in the valley of the WILLAMETTE RIVER. "Oregon fever" struck the Midwest, and the lure of forests, water, and good soil started the wagon trains rolling over the OREGON TRAIL in 1842.

In 1846 the United States and Great Britain agreed on a boundary at 49° north, and Oregon Territory was formally established in 1848. In 1859 the state constitution excluded slavery but also forbade free blacks to enter. Agriculture prospered, and by 1867 a surplus from the wheat crop could be exported. Large cattle ranches were established. From the 1850's through the 1870's there was conflict with the Indians, but this was over by 1880. At that time railroads were built from both the east and the south to CALIFORNIA. The rails spurred lumbering on a large scale.

The 1880's also saw opposition to the influx of the Chinese, a feeling shown again in the 20th century against the Japanese. In politics, Oregon has been a leading state in inaugurating reforms, such as the initiative, the recall, and the referendum. A dispute in the 1930's over whether electric power should be developed by the state or by private interests was won by advocates of public power.

Important cities are SALEM, the capital; PORTLAND, the largest; and Eugene. See also OREGON COUNTRY.

OREGON CITY (United States) City in NW OREGON, on the WILLAMETTE RIVER, 11 mi S of Portland. Founded in 1829 at the terminus of the OREGON TRAIL, it was the first capital of the Oregon Territory, from 1849 to 1852.

OREGON COUNTRY (United States) Region, W North America, between the Pacific coast and the ROCKY MOUNTAINS, extending from the N border of CALIFORNIA to ALASKA, often so called in the early 19th century. The pioneer Marcus Whitman started a mission in the COLUMBIA RIVER valley in 1836 and was massacred there with his wife and others in 1847. The Oregon Territory was established in 1848 after GREAT BRITAIN had withdrawn its claim to land below the 49th parallel in 1846. See also OREGON.

OREGON TERRITORY. See OREGON.

OREGON TRAIL (United States) The way west for pioneer emigration to the OREGON COUNTRY, especially between 1842 and 1860. It extended 2,000 mi between the MISSOURI RIVER and the COLUMBIA RIVER and was the longest of the frontier routes. It was partially traveled by Lewis and Clark in 1805; a group led by Elijah White first reached Oregon on the Trail in 1842. The following year saw the "great emigration" of more than 900 persons and 1,000 cattle into the area. Travel declined with the advent of the railroads, and the trail was abandoned in the 1870's. Indian attacks, flooded rivers, and food and water shortages were common perils of the trail.

The route began in INDEPENDENCE, MISSOURI and went 600 mi to FORT LARAMIE en route to Oregon Country. The next stretch went 430 mi through the South Pass to FORT BRIDGER; this difficult mountain terrain is now littered with horse and oxen bones and the shallow graves of pioneers. It then continued 220 mi to FORT HALL on the Snake River where wagons were often abandoned for pack horses. The Grand Ronde Valley offered recuperation before the Blue Mts were encountered. Finally, the trail wound through Fort Walla Walla, down the Columbia River to Fort Vancouver and the WILLAMETTE Valley, center of the early settlement. See also OREGON.

OREKHOVO-ZUYEVO (USSR) Industrial city 54 mi E of Moscow, in Moscow oblast, on the Klyazma River. It was formed in 1917 by the merging of two adjacent 17th-century industrial villages, Orekhovo and Zuyevo. It had a textile industry dating from the 18th century, which made it an important industrial center in the 19th century. Numerous strikes and uprisings occurred here before the Bolshevik Revolution as the large working class in the city became a source of the labor and revolutionary movements.

OREL [Orlov, Oryol] (USSR) An important railroad junction and the capital of Orel oblast, SFSR, on the Oka River, 200 mi S of Moscow. Ivan IV founded the city in 1564 to protect the southern border of Muscovy from Tatar attacks from the CRIMEA. It was a trading center in the 18th and 19th centuries. Here was the northernmost point reached by Gen. Denikin's White Army in 1919 during the Russian civil war. Captured by GERMANY on Oct. 3, 1941, it was retaken by the Soviets in 1943 as the entire central front was cleared of German control by the battles of KURSK and Orel in World

War II. It was nearly destroyed during the war. The writer Ivan Turgenev was born here.

ORELLANA. See AMAZON RIVER.

ORENBURG [*former:* **Chkalov**] (USSR) Rail junction and capital of Orenburg oblast in Central Asian SSR on the Ural River. Founded at ORSK in 1735 as a Russian fort and outpost, it was moved 155 mi west in 1743. It was inhabited by Orenburg Cossacks who defended the country against invading nomads. In 1773/74 it resisted a siege by E.I. Pugachev, and after the Revolution of 1917 it saw severe fighting. A great famine swept it in 1920/21. It was temporarily renamed in honor of Valeri Chkalov, the aviator who made a nonstop flight from Moscow to Vancouver, Wash. in 1937.

ORENSE (Spain) Capital of Orense province, in GALICIA, on the Miño River, 250 mi NW of Madrid. It was originally a Roman settlement around popular hot sulfur and mineral springs. It was important as the capital of the kings of the Suevi under the Visigoths in the fifth and sixth centuries AD. Demolished by the Arabs in 713, it was rebuilt by Alfonso II in the ninth century. It

declined commercially after the expulsion of the Jews at the end of the Middle Ages.

ØRESUND [The Sound] [*Swedish:* **Öresund**] (Denmark, Sweden) A strait, approx. 45 mi long, between the Danish island of Sjaelland and the mainland of Sweden, connecting the Kattegat with the Baltic Sea. COPENHAGEN and MALMÖ are on the Øresund. It has always been a strategic passage, long contested between Denmark and Sweden.

ORIEL, KINGDOM OF. See LOUTH.

ORIENTALE. See HAUT-ZÄIRE.

ORIENTE [*former:* **Santiago de Cuba**] (Cuba) Easternmost and wealthiest Cuban province. This was the site of the first settlement and the starting point for the conquest of the island by SPAIN in the early 16th century. It has been a scene of fighting in all of Cuba's many political disturbances.

ORIHUELA (Spain) Agricultural city in Alicante province, on the Segura River, 30 mi SW of Alicante. The site has been inhabited from *c.*1500 BC. It was held by the Moors from 713 to 1264 AD. In 1829 it was rocked by an earthquake. There was a university here

The cultures of Africa, the Mediterranean, and Europe mingle in ancient Orihuela in Spain's Valencia region. The town was Moorish for over 500 years.

from 1516 to 1701, and a 14th-century cathedral and church can both be found here today.

ORILLIA (Canada) Town and resort on Lake Couchiching, 80 mi N of Toronto in SE ONTARIO. Samuel de Champlain explored this former Huron Indian territory in 1615. The first white settlers came in 1833, and the town was incorporated in 1875. A monument was erected in 1925 to commemorate Champlain's discovery.

ORINOCO RIVER (Venezuela) Major commercial river approx. 1,700 mi long. Beginning in the Parima highlands near the BRAZIL boundary, it flows NW to the border of COLOMBIA and then NE across Venezuela to the Atlantic Ocean. Christopher Columbus probably discovered the mouth in 1498, and Lope de Aguirre traveled most of its length in 1560. Its source was undiscovered until aerial explorations in 1944. Steamships run along the chief route between TRINIDAD and CIUDAD BOLÍVAR most of the year.

ORISKANY (United States) Village in central NEW YORK, on the MOHAWK RIVER, approx. 7 mi WNW of Utica. The Oriskany battlefield to the west was the site of a Revolutionary War battle on August 6, 1777. A British and Indian ambush here defeated an American force that refused, nonetheless, to be driven from the field. There were severe losses on both sides, and American Gen. Nicholas Herkimer was killed.

ORISSA (India) Agricultural and fishing state on the Bay of Bengal, 60,162 sq. mi. in area. For centuries it was the heart of the strong KALINGA kingdom. It was temporarily ruled by Asoka, c.250 BC, and held for almost a century by the MAURYA EMPIRE. Hindu dynasties then came to dominate. Afghan invaders took it in 1586, and it soon passed to the MOGUL EMPIRE. In 1803 it was taken by the British, who governed it through BENGAL until 1936 when it became a separate province. In 1950 it gained Indian statehood.

ORIZABA (Mexico) Agricultural and industrial city in Veracruz state, 65 mi SW of Veracruz. Originally an Indian village taken by the Aztecs and used as a garrison, it was conquered by SPAIN in the 1550's. It has been a chartered city since 1774. An inactive volcano, Orizaba Peak, the highest in Mexico, is nearby. It was known to the Aztecs as Citlaltépetl. In 1862 Benito Juarez held a conference here with foreign powers to try to limit their intervention in Mexico. He failed, and FRANCE later used the city as a base for invading Mexico. The Emperor Maximilian, who reigned with the support of France from 1864 to 1867, frequented Orizaba as a favorite resort.

ORKNEY ISLANDS [Orkneys] [*Latin:* **Orcades**] (Scotland) Archipelago in the Atlantic Ocean and the North Sea, separated from the N mainland of Scotland by the 6-mi-wide Pentland Firth, a group of seventy islands, many uninhabited. The islands were settled early by Picts and ruled from the ninth century AD by Norse earls. Scottish nobles had moved in by 1231, but the Orkneys remained the possessions of Norwegian and Danish kings. In 1468 they were promised as security for the dowry of Princess Margaret of DENMARK,

engaged to marry James III of Scotland. The dowry was never paid, but Scotland took the islands in 1472. SCAPA FLOW, south of Mainland island, was a major British naval base in World Wars I and II. The islands formed a county before 1975, and they are now an island area, with admin. hqs. at KIRKWALL, on MAINLAND island.

There are many prehistoric relics on the islands. On Hoy The Old Man of Hoy, a famous standing stone, and the Dwarfie Stone, a Neolithic sepulcher of sandstone; at Stennes the Ring of Brogar, famous standing stones, and MAES HOWE, one of the finest chamber tombs in Great Britain; at Rinyo on Rousay a broch, or Pictish fort; at SKARA BRAE, an extensive excavated Neolithic village of stone.

Skara Brae, a remarkable Neolithic village in the Orkney Islands. The houses and narrow alleyways, built of flagstone and shale, were once buried in debris for protection.

ORKNEYS. See ORKNEY ISLANDS.

ORLANDO (United States) City in E central FLORIDA, 78 mi NE of Tampa. Founded in 1843, it was first settled near Fort Gatlin. It was named for Orlando Reeves, a soldier who died in the Second Seminole War. Incorporated in 1875, it is close to Walt Disney World and is a tourist center for other attractions, such as CAPE CANAVERAL.

ORLANDO, CAPE (Italy) Point near NE point of SICILY. During World War II U.S. forces landed just east of the cape on August 12, 1943 as part of the invasion and conquest of Sicily prior to the invasion of Italy.

ORLÉANAIS (France) Region and former province on both banks of the LOIRE RIVER. During the Roman occupation of GAUL the Celts in the area revolted unsuccessfully against Julius Caesar in 52 BC. Its central lands, with the town of ORLÉANS, belonged to the French royal domain since the rule of Hugh Capet in the 10th century. The large, old forest of Orléans is here, as well as many châteaux and ruins of fortresses and churches from the Carolingian period. There are also many prehistoric remains. See also BLOIS, CHARTRES, FRANKISH EMPIRE.

ORLÉANS [*early:* **Genabum;** *Latin:* **Aurelianum**] (France) Important commercial town and capital of Loiret department. It is 70 mi SSW of Paris on the LOIRE RIVER in the heart of the château country. Once a market center for the Celtic Carnutes, it fell to Roman rule and was burned by Julius Caesar in 52 BC after a revolt. Orléans resisted attacks in 451 AD by Attila the Hun and in 471 by the German Odoacer; but it fell in 498 to Clovis I and by 511 became the capital of the FRANKISH kingdom of Orléans. Joan of Arc was called the Maid of Orléans after she broke the siege of the city by England in 1429 during the Hundred Years War of 1337 to 1453. It became a Huguenot stronghold during the Wars of Religion in the 16th century and was besieged by Catholic forces in 1563. It was given peace by the Edict of NANTES in 1598. Its famous university was founded in the 14th century, and the cathedral of Sainte Croix, destroyed by the Huguenots in 1567, was rebuilt by Henry IV and his successors. A large section of the city was damaged during World War II.

ORLÉANS, ÎLE D', Canada. See ORLEANS, ISLAND OF.

ORLÉANS, ÎLE D', United States. See ORLEANS, ISLE OF.

ORLEANS, ISLAND OF [Orleans Island] [*French:* **Orléans, Île d'**] (Canada) An island, 20 mi long, in the ST. LAWRENCE RIVER, 4 mi downstream from QUEBEC. Settled by the French in 1651, it became the site of one of Wolfe's camps in his attacks against Quebec in 1759 during the French and Indian War. It has remained largely agricultural and attracts many tourists.

ORLEANS, ISLE OF [*French:* **Orléans, Île d'**] (United States) District around NEW ORLEANS, LOUISIANA, approx. 2,800 sq mi in area, E of the MISSISSIPPI RIVER. It was ceded to SPAIN by FRANCE as part of the Treaty of Paris in 1763. France also ceded the balance of eastern Louisiana territory to GREAT BRITAIN at this time.

ORLEANS TERRITORY. See LOUISIANA.

ORLOV. See OREL.

ORMOC [MacArthur] (Philippines) City in Leyte province on the W coast of LEYTE Island, on Ormoc Bay, 36 mi SW of Tacloban. It was the main Japanese military supply base on Leyte during World War II. It was retaken by U.S. forces in bitter fighting on December 11, 1944.

ORMSKIRK (England) Town in Lancashire, 11 mi NNE of LIVERPOOL. Its church, with its tower arrayed for battle, contains the burial chapel of the earls of DERBY. The nearby ruins of the abbey of Burscough date from the 12th century.

ORMUZ. See HORMUZ.

ORO BAY (Papua New Guinea) Small inlet of Dyke Ackland Bay on NEW GUINEA Island, 20 mi S of Buna. By 1943, during World War II, it was an Allied base under constant attack by the Japanese.

OROLAUNUM. See ARLON.

ORONTES RIVER [*Arabic:* **Nahr Al-'Āṣī;** *Turkish:* **Asi Nehri**] (Lebanon, Syria, Turkey) River, approx. 250 mi long, rising in N Lebanon, flowing N through Syria, then W into S Turkey and to the Mediterranean Sea. An unnavigable river, it rises near the site of ancient BAALBEK. HAMA in Syria, the site of a Hittite settlement, is also on the river. Here are found huge medieval water wheels that are used to lift water from the river to irrigate the plains above.

OROTE. See APRA HARBOR.

ORRHOE. See URFA.

ORSHA [*former:* **Rsha**] (USSR) City in Vitebsk oblast, a port at the confluence of the DNIEPER RIVER and the Orshitsa River, 122 mi NE of Minsk. It was first mentioned in 1067 and by the 13th century belonged to LITHUANIA. By the 16th century it had become a Polish fortress and trading center, but in 1772 RUSSIA annexed it during the first partition of POLAND. GERMANY held it from 1941 to 1944, during World War II.

ORSK (USSR) Town in Orenburg oblast on the Ural River, 155 mi E of Orenburg, 309 mi SW of Chelyabinsk. It is the first site of ORENBURG, with which it became a fort in 1735. After Orenburg's move downriver in 1743 it continued to grow and was a town by 1866. It became important industrially and as a cattle-breeding center after it was joined by rail with Chelyabinsk and Orenburg in the late 19th century.

ORSONA. See OSUNA.

ORTELSBURG. See SZCZYTNO.

ORTHEZ (France) Town in N Pyrénées-Atlantiques department, on the Gave de Pau River, approx. 25 mi NW of Pau. It was the capital of BÉARN until the 15th century and later a center of the Protestant Reformation. A Calvinist university was founded here by Jeanne d'Albret, mother of Henry IV, but was suppressed by Louis XIII, who annexed Béarn in 1620. Marshal Soult was defeated here by the Duke of Wellington, on Feb. 27, 1814, during the Peninsular Campaign.

ORTONA (Italy) Seaside town and resort in ABRUZZI, on the Adriatic Sea, approx. 100 mi ENE of Rome. Originally the home of the Frentani, the town was under Roman rule by the fourth century BC. By the 11th century it was growing in importance, but in 1447 VENICE destroyed its fleet and arsenal. In the 18th century it was controlled by NAPLES. During World War II, among its historic buildings damaged were a 12th-century castle, now restored, and a 15th-century Aragonese castle. The British occupied it on Dec. 27, 1943.

ORURO [*Spanish:* **Real Villa de San Felipe de**

Austria] (Bolivia) Tin-mining city at an altitude of approx. 12,000 ft, and capital of Oruro department, 130 mi SE of La Paz. It was founded in 1595 to mine rich lodes of silver. It was fortified by SPAIN in 1820 and renamed in 1826, just after Bolivia had gained independence. With the drop in silver production in the 19th century it became almost deserted. Exploitation of other mineral deposits since then has rebuilt it.

ORVIETO [*Etruscan:* **Velsuna, Volsinii;** *Latin:* **Urbs Vetus**] (Italy) Town and pilgrimage center in UMBRIA, on the Poglia River, 29 mi WNW of Terni. It stands on the site of the Etruscan town of Volsinii, one of twelve cities of ancient ETRURIA. This was destroyed by Rome in 280 BC. After the fall of Rome it was ruled by Goths, Byzantines, and Lombards. It came under papal control in 1448. In the 12th to 14th centuries it was embroiled in constant strife between the papal (Guelph) and imperial (Ghibelline) parties. Its creativity is shown by its many superb Romanesque, Gothic, and Renaissance buildings, including its cathedral. Medieval mines are nearby, and an Etruscan necropolis was discovered here in 1874.

ORYOL. See OREL.

ŌSAKA [*former:* **Naniwa**] (Japan) Capital of Ōsaka prefecture in S HONSHŪ, 27 mi W of Kyoto, 20 mi E of Kobe, on Ōsaka Bay. It is one of the oldest cities in Japan and one of the greatest industrial cities of the Orient. Its imperial palaces date back to the fourth century AD when it was called Naniwa. There is a restoration of an imposing castle first built by the shogun Toyomoti Hideyoshi in 1583 and destroyed in a fire in 1868. This shogun united Japan under his rule. Ōsaka became his capital, and it prospered as a commercial city. It received a city charter in 1889 and was an important industrial center during World War II. It was therefore a target for devastating U.S. air raids, in 1944 and 1945. The city is a center of Japanese culture and theater and was the site of the 1970 World's Fair. The sixth-century Buddhist temple of Shitennoji is here.

OSAWATOMIE (United States) Farm and trading center in E KANSAS, on the Marais des Cygnes River, 45 mi SSW of Kansas City. It was founded in 1855 by the New England Emigrant Aid Company and was incorporated in 1883. Once a station on the Underground Railroad, it has a memorial park that contains the cabin where John Brown, "Old Brown of Osawatomie," lived in 1856. Here, in August 1856, Brown and his sympathizers fiercely battled supporters of slavery.

OSCA. See HUESCA.

OSCELA. See DOMODOSSOLA.

ÖSEL. See SAAREMAA.

OSETIA. See OSSETIA.

OSH (USSR) Capital of Osh oblast in Fergana Valley in Kirgiz SSR, approx. 30 mi SE of Andizhan. A very old settlement of central Asia, for centuries it was on a main trade route to INDIA. It later became a silk production center. The Oriental and Western sections adjoin. The rock called Takht-i-Sulaiman, or Solomon's throne, once a Muslim pilgrimage goal, is just west of the town.

OSHAWA [*former:* **Skea's Corners**] (Canada) Auto manufacturing city in SE ONTARIO, on LAKE ONTARIO, 33 mi ENE of Toronto. It was started as a French trading post in 1752. Settlement began after the building of the Toronto–Kingston military road in 1793. It was incorporated as a town in 1879 and as a city in 1924. The city has been producing automobiles since 1907. The Canadian Automotive Museum is here.

OSHKOSH (United States) Industrial city in E WISCONSIN, on the W shore of Lake Winnebago. Beginning as a French fur-trading post, it was settled in 1836 and named for a local Menominee Indian chief. It was incorporated as a city in 1853. In the later 19th century it grew as a major lumbering center, even though the downtown district was destroyed by fire in 1875. Today it is a woodworking and leather finishing center in the midst of a resort area.

OSHOGBO (Nigeria) Farming city in Western State, on a railroad line approx. 50 mi NE of Ibadan. Settled from Ibokun in the precolonial era, in the 17th century it was founded as a town in the Yoruba kingdom of ILESHA. In 1839 it was a battle site where the Yoruba city state of Ibadan halted the southward advance of the FULANI state of ILORIN. The victory sent many refugees into Oshogbo, which continued to pay tribute to Ibadan until 1951.

OSIJEK [*ancient:* **Mursa;** *German:* **Esseg;** *Hungarian:* **Eszek**] (Yugoslavia) City in N Yugoslavia, in CROATIA, approx. 130 mi ESE of Zagreb. The Roman colony and fortress of Mursa was established here early in the Christian era. On Sept. 28, 351 Constantius II, the Roman emperor of Asia Minor, Egypt, and Syria, defeated Magnentius, a German who had been a general in the western part of the ROMAN EMPIRE and was attempting to usurp the throne. Casualties were so heavy that they may have done permanent damage to the military strength of the empire as a whole. The battle also marked the first time heavy cavalry won out over the traditional foot soldiers of the Roman legion. The present city grew up around a castle, built in 1091 on the site of the Roman colony. The city was ruled by the OTTOMAN EMPIRE from 1526 to 1687, was later incorporated into the AUSTRO–HUNGARIAN EMPIRE, and became part of the new nation of Yugoslavia in 1918.

OSKALOOSA (United States) Farm and trading city in SE central IOWA, 55 mi ESE of Des Moines. A fort was established here in 1835, which became a post stop on a route west. Settled by Quakers in 1844, it was incorporated in 1852. Coal mining started more than a century ago, and a huge strip mining project is active now.

OSLO [*former:* **Christiania, Kristiania**] (Norway) Cultural and commercial center and capital of Norway, in Akershus county, at the N end of Oslo Fjord. Founded *c.*1050 by Harald III, it became the capital in 1299. It was dominated by the HANSEATIC LEAGUE from the 14th century on. Destroyed by fire in 1624, it was rebuilt as a Renaissance city by Christian IV and renamed Kristiania. The city was captured by SWEDEN in 1716. In the 19th century it replaced BERGEN as the main city in Norway, becoming the center of a cultural renaissance that was followed by a wave of nationalism. The movement resulted in Norway's split with Sweden in 1905. Renamed Oslo in 1925, the city was delivered up to GERMANY by Vidkun Quisling's group on April 9, 1940. It was occupied by the Nazis until the end of World War II. Its medieval architecture includes the Akerskirke of the 12th century; the Akershus, a 13th-century fortress; and the ruins of its first cathedral, St. Hallvard, erected for Harald III in the 11th century.

OSNABRÜCK (West Germany) Manufacturing city and inland port, Lower SAXONY, 30 mi NE of Münster. An episcopal see was founded here by Charlemagne in 793 AD on the site of an ancient Saxon settlement. A city since 1171, it became a member of the HANSEATIC LEAGUE and a leading linen center. It took part in the Reformation in 1543. From 1648, as a result of the Peace of WESTPHALIA, largely negotiated here, the see was occupied alternately by Catholic and Lutheran bishops until it was secularized and granted to HANOVER in 1803. It passed to the kingdom of Westphalia in 1807 and back to Hanover by order of the Congress of Vienna in 1815. In World War II it was badly damaged when bombed by the Allies in 1944 and 1945. It was captured in April 1945. Its three-towered cathedral was begun in 783, burned in 1254, and rebuilt soon after. The Gothic church of St. Mary is also here. Its city hall was built between 1487 and 1512.

OSNABURGH. See DAIRSIE.

OSORHEI. See TÎRGU-MURES.

OSORNO (Chile) City and capital of Osorno province, approx. 240 mi S of Concepción. It was founded in 1553 and destroyed by Araucanian Indians in 1602. Its reestablishment was ordered by Ambrosio Higgins in 1796. In the late 19th century many Germans swelled its population.

OSRHOENE. See OSROENE.

OSROENE [Osrhoene] (Syria, Turkey) Ancient kingdom in NW MESOPOTAMIA, E of the EUPHRATES RIVER, with its capital at EDESSA. Founded in the second century BC in a revolt from the Seleucids, it was later ruled by PARTHIA, ARMENIA, and ROME. The Roman Emperor Caracalla abolished it in 216 AD.

OSSETIA [Osetia] (USSR) Region of the central CAUCASUS in S European USSR, between the Black and Caspian seas. Administratively it is divided into the NORTH OSSETIAN AUTONOMOUS SOVIET SOCIALIST REPUBLIC, with its capital at ORDZHONIKIDZE, and the SOUTH OSSETIAN AUTONOMOUS OBLAST, with its capital at TSKHINVALI. The region takes its name from the Ossetians, an Iranian-Japhetic people. From the seventh century BC to the first century AD the region was generally under Scythian-Sarmatian domination. After that Ossetia was controlled by the Alani, a nomadic people from northeast of the BLACK SEA. The Tatars took control in the 13th century, and in the 17th Karbada princes ruled in the north. Beginning in the late

18th century RUSSIA started to conquer Ossetia and by 1806 had annexed all of it. In World War II the German invasion of the Soviet Union reached as far as northern Ossetia in November 1942. The OSSETIAN MILITARY ROAD runs through the region. See also SCYTHIA.

OSSETIAN MILITARY ROAD (USSR) Highway, approx. 170 mi long, across the CAUCASUS Mountains in S European USSR. Built in 1889 in a wild area inhabited by Ossetian tribesmen, it links KUTAISI with Alagir. It crosses the Caucasian crest through a pass at Mamison. See also OSSETIA.

OSSINING [former: Sing Sing] (United States) Town on the HUDSON RIVER in SE NEW YORK, 30 mi N of New York City. Settled c.1750, it was incorporated under the Indian name Sing Sing in 1813. It was renamed in 1901. It is the location of the Ossining Correctional Facility, formerly known as Sing Sing state prison, built by convicts from Auburn State Prison from 1825 to 1828. This institution was known for its extreme disciplinary regimen before reforms were initiated in the mid-20th century. The town also contains Maryknoll, worldwide headquarters for the Catholic Foreign Missions, and parts of a New York City aqueduct completed in 1839 but no longer used.

OSSORY (Irish Republic) Ancient kingdom in SW LEINSTER. Its borders are now largely those of the Roman Catholic diocese of Ossory. Its control was long disputed. In 1110, it was dissolved, and it became a part of Leinster under the Normans in the 12th century. By the mid-14th century it was a part of the earldom of Ormonde.

OSTEND [Oostende] [French: Ostende] (Belgium) Major commercial and fishing port on the North Sea in W Flanders province. A port by the 11th century, it was fortified in 1583 by William the Silent and became most important in the Dutch struggle for independence from SPAIN. A three-year siege ended in 1604 when the Spaniards finally took the nearly destroyed city. In the 19th century it became one of Europe's most fashionable social centers and remained so until it was occupied and used as a submarine base by the Germans in World War I. It was heavily bombed by the Allies during World War II. See also FLANDERS.

OSTERFELD. See OBERHAUSEN.

ÖSTERREICH. See AUSTRIA.

OSTFRIESLAND. See EAST FRIESLAND.

OSTIA [Ostia Antica] (Italy) Ancient town and the port for ROME at the mouth of the TIBER RIVER in LATIUM. The town was founded in the fourth century BC as protection for Rome. After 100 AD, with large harbor installations, it rivaled Puteoli, now PUZZUOLI, as Italy's major port. It declined after the third century AD and was abandoned c.850 in the face of malaria and Arab raids. The mouth of the Tiber here has since silted up, and the old town is 4 mi inland. It has been extensively excavated. The ruins graphically show the layout of an ancient Roman town and the life of its largely working class people. A modern village is just to the east.

OSTIA ANTICA. See OSTIA.

OSTIA ATERNI. See PESCARA.

OSTIAN WAY [*Latin:* **Via Ostiensis**] (Italy) Old Roman road from ROME to OSTIA following the TIBER RIVER. There are many ancient bridges along the modern road, which takes nearly the same course.

OSTPREUSSEN. See EAST PRUSSIA.

OSTRAVA [*former:* **Moravská;** *German:* **Märisch-Ostrau**] (Czechoslovakia) Industrial, cultural, and educational city in MORAVIA, near the junction of the ODER RIVER and the Ostravice River, 170 mi E of Prague. The town was known in the Middle Ages because of its location guarding the Moravian Gate, the pass to the Moravian lowlands. In the 19th century the opening of coal mines and railroad development made it important. Its industrial plants were damaged while the city was under Nazi martial law from 1939 to 1945, during World War II.

OSTRIHOM. See ESZTERGOM.

OSTROG (USSR) Town in W Ukrainian SSR, 59 mi SE of Lutsk, on the upper Goryn River. It was founded in the ninth century, and was an independent principality until the 17th century. It passed from RUSSIA to POLAND in 1921 and back to Russia in 1945. The first complete Slavonic bible was printed here in 1581.

OSTROGOTHIC KINGDOM (Italy) One of two kingdoms that evolved following the exodus of large numbers of Goths from the S of SWEDEN to the territory N of the Black Sea in the late second and early third centuries AD. In the late third and early fourth centuries they split into two groups, the Ostrogoths, or East Goths, occupying the UKRAINE and the Visigoths, or West Goths, settling in DACIA, now part of RUMANIA and HUNGARY.

Under Ermanaric's rule in the fourth century AD, the Ostrogoths were conquered by the Huns from the east and remained subjugated until the death of Attila in 453 AD. Following this, they moved west into the Roman province of PANNONIA, modern Hungary. With Theodoric, their king from 471 AD, they became allies of the Eastern Roman or BYZANTINE EMPIRE. The Byzantine emperor Zeno the Great instructed Theodoric to undertake the reconquest of Italy from Odoacer and the Lombards. He invaded Italy in 488, murdered Odoacer in 493, and founded the Ostrogothic kingdom of Italy, establishing its capital at RAVENNA.

The Ostrogoths' decline began with the death of Theodoric in 526 AD. He was succeeded by his daughter, Amalasuntha, who served as regent for her son Alaric. The Byzantine emperor Justinian I acted as her protector until she was assassinated in 535 AD. He then commanded his general, Belisarius, to reconquer Italy from the Ostrogoths. Although Belisarius was successful, Totila led the Ostrogoths in rebellion in 541 AD. He was defeated and killed in battle by the Byzantine General Narses. This signalled the end of the Ostrogothic kingdom as a definable political entity. Italy passed to the Byzantines and was then almost immediately overrun by the Lombards.

Although the Ostrogoths were always regarded by the Italians as outsiders, under the influence of Cassiodorus and Boethius they introduced a renewed appreciation of Classical culture and Roman institutions. They were converts to Arian Christianity by the 4th century AD. During this period St. Benedict laid the foundations of the Western monastic system which helped to nurture Christian and Western civilization through the Middle Ages. See also VISIGOTHIC KINGDOM.

OSTROŁĘKA [*Russian:* **Ostrolenka**] (Poland) Manufacturing town in NE Warszawa province, on the Narew River, 62 mi NNE of Warsaw. Chartered in 1427, it passed to PRUSSIA in 1795, RUSSIA in 1815, and Poland in 1920. It was the site of several battles involving FRANCE, Russia, and GERMANY in the 19th and 20th centuries.

OSTROLENKA. See OSTROŁĘKA.

OSTSEE. See BALTIC SEA.

OSUNA [*Latin:* **Gemina Urbanorum, Orsona, Urso;** *Moorish:* **Oxuna**] (Spain) Town in Sevilla, 52 mi ESE of Seville. Once an ancient Roman garrison post, it was taken by the Moors in 711 AD. Ferdinand III of León and Castile regained the town from the Moors in 1239. It has Roman ruins, a ducal castle, a 16th-century Gothic church, and remains of a university founded in 1549 but closed in 1820.

OSWEGO (United States) Port city on LAKE ONTARIO and the Oswego River, N central NEW YORK, 33 mi NNW of Syracuse. A Jesuit mission to the Iroquois Indians was founded here in 1653. This was followed by the British establishment of the first Great Lakes trading post here in 1722. It became a vital outlet for the ALBANY fur trade. Other forts were built in the strategic vicinity of Fort Oswego, including Fort George and Fort Ontario. All were greatly contested in the colonial wars of the 18th century. Fort Oswego was the last British foothold during the Revolution, held by them until 1796. Its importance as a lake port came with the completion of the Barge Canal in 1917 and the ST. LAWRENCE RIVER Seaway in 1959. Oswego provided the setting for James Fenimore Cooper's novel *The Pathfinder.* See also ERIE CANAL.

OSWESTRY (England) Market town and district in W central England in Salop, near the Welsh border, 16 mi NW of Shrewsbury. It was named for St. Oswald, a seventh century Northumbrian king killed in battle against Penda, king of MERCIA. In the 12th century the town was fortified by the Normans. Poet Wilfred Owen was born here.

OŚWIĘCIM See AUSCHWITZ.

OTAHEITE. See TAHITI.

OTAVALO (Ecuador) Manufacturing town high in the ANDES, in Imbabura province, in an Indian area approx. 42 mi NNE of Quito. It was settled in 1534 and was heavily damaged by an earthquake in 1868.

OTRANTO [*Greek:* **Hydrus;** *Latin:* **Hydruntum**] (Italy) Town of ancient Calabria now in SE APULIA, 29 mi SE of Lecce. It was originally a Greek settlement,

The unspoiled Ottawa River falls, an 18th-century view by Thomas Davies. Now at Ottawa, capital of Canada, they are used to generate hydroelectric power.

then a Roman port. It served as a center for trade with the Orient until 1480 when it was razed by the Turks. It was a supply base during World War II. The ruins of the 15th-century castle built here by the Aragonese is the setting for Horace Walpole's novel, *The Castle of Otranto.*

OTSEGO, LAKE (United States) Lake in N central Otsego county, central NEW YORK. COOPERSTOWN lies at the S end. It is the "Glimmerglass" of the novels in the Leatherstocking saga of James Fenimore Cooper.

ŌTSU [Ōtu] (Japan) City in W central HONSHŪ, capital of Shiga prefecture, approx. 10 mi from KYŌTO. A former castle town, it was a flourishing city and an imperial seat in the second and seventh centuries AD. It is the site of two famous Buddhist temples, the Ishiyamadera, and the seventh century Mii-dera. The grave of the famous poet Basho (1640–94) is here.

OTTAWA [*former:* Bytown] (Canada) Capital of Canada, SE ONTARIO, 100 mi W of Montreal. Reached by Samuel de Champlain in 1613, it was permanently settled by Col. John By following the construction of the Rideau Canal in 1827. Incorporated in 1854, it was selected by Queen Victoria as capital of Canada in 1858. There are numerous notable public buildings, foremost being the Gothic Parliament Buildings, built between 1859 to 1865. The University of Ottawa dates back to 1848.

OTTAWA (United States) City in N ILLINOIS, on the Illinois River, 40 mi WSW of Joliet. Fort Johnson was established here in 1832. The site was incorporated as a city in 1853. Here Abraham Lincoln first debated Stephen Douglas on Aug. 21, 1858.

OTTAWA (United States) Industrial center in rural E KANSAS on the Marais des Cygnes River, 37 mi SE of Topeka. It was named after Ottawa Indians from OHIO who settled here in 1832 after turning over their eastern lands to the Federal government. The city was incorporated in 1866, and in 1867 the Indians were removed to OKLAHOMA.

OTTAWA RIVER [*former:* Grand River] (Canada) River in SE ONTARIO and S QUEBEC, 696 mi long. It forms in the lower section of the boundary between Ontario and Quebec, continues E across S Quebec, and empties into the ST. LAWRENCE RIVER at MONTREAL. It was discovered by Jacques Cartier in 1535; Samuel de Champlain was the first European to explore it, from 1613 to 1615. For centuries it was a well-traveled route for the fur trade, and for exploration and missionary activity. Lumbering developed as an industry here in the 19th century.

OTTERBURN (England) Village in Northumberland, 29 mi NW of Newcastle upon Tyne, site of a battle in 1388 in which the English, led by Sir Henry Percy, Shakespeare's Hotspur, were defeated by the Scots under James Douglas. The battle is celebrated by the English ballad *Chevy Chase* and by the old Scottish ballad *The Battle of Otterburn*. In 1402, however, Percy won a famous victory over the Scots at HAMILDON HILL.

OTTOMAN EMPIRE Former empire, originating in Asia Minor. At its height it controlled the BALKANS, much of E Europe, the North African seaboard and the ARABIAN PENINSULA as far as the Persian Gulf. It dominated the eastern MEDITERRANEAN SEA and posed a serious threat to the countries of central Europe. When it collapsed after World War I, its place in Asia Minor was taken by the modern state of TURKEY.

The founders of the Ottoman Empire were the Osmanlis dynasty of a Turkish tribe that entered Asia Minor from Central Asia in the 13th century AD. The collapse of the empire of the Seljuk Turks at the hands of the Mongols in the 14th century saw the emergence of small principalities, of which the Ottomans emerged as the most powerful.

The Ottomans first entered the BYZANTINE EMPIRE as mercenaries, but later in the 14th century they expanded westward, consolidating their hold on the Byzantine Empire and taking BURSA in 1326 and ADRIANOPLE in 1361. By the end of the 14th century, all of Asia Minor and much of the Balkans lay under Ottoman control, though in the early 15th century, just as they were on the verge of taking CONSTANTINOPLE, their lands in Asia Minor were completely, though briefly, overrun by Tamerlane and his Mongol armies. With the withdrawal of Tamerlane, the Ottoman sultans recovered their territory and under Sultan Mahomet II in 1453 dealt the death blow to the Byzantine Empire by capturing Constantinople, which then became their capital of ISTANBUL. The remaining Venetian fortresses in Greece were formally surrendered in 1503.

The 15th and 16th centuries were years of rapid expansion, and the empire reached its zenith during the reign of Suleiman the Magnificent from 1520 to 1566. During the 1460's and 1470's BOSNIA and the Adriatic coast and the BLACK SEA area were taken. In the early 16th century SYRIA, CAIRO, and ALGIERS fell. The island of RHODES was wrested from the Knights Hospitalers after a long siege in 1522. HUNGARY was crushed at the Battle of MOHÁCS in 1526, Buda seized, and VIENNA itself laid under siege in 1529. In the meantime the forces of Suleiman were contesting the INDIAN OCEAN with the Portuguese. By 1562 AUSTRIA was paying tribute to the Turks in an attempt to maintain the peace. However, in a Christian victory the island of MALTA resisted a siege in 1565, and the myth of Ottoman invincibility was dealt a blow by the naval defeat at LEPANTO in 1571, at the hands of VENICE, SPAIN, and the Papacy.

All of this was carried out with a military force second to none. A characteristic was the use of massed artillery, both in the field and at sieges. Discipline was severely enforced, and the armies were often led by the fanatical corps of Janissaries, an elite guard made up of captured Christian slaves who were devoted to the sultan. The Turkish fleet was lavishly supported from its main base in the arsenal at Istanbul.

In 1638 the Ottoman Empire recovered from the setback of Lepanto and waged a successful campaign against PERSIA, a rival since the early 16th century. In 1683 the empire posed its greatest threat to Europe when VIENNA was again besieged. The war however turned against the Ottomans, and by the Treaty of KARLOWITZ of 1699 they were forced to cede Hungary.

From the 18th century the history of the empire is one of slow disintegration, hastened by unsuccessful wars against the increasing might of RUSSIA and by the growing nationalist aspirations of peoples within the empire. Nor were matters helped by an administration hampered by corruption and the antiquated nature of Ottoman society. In 1770 MOLDAVIA and WALACHIA fell to Russia; and during the Napoleonic Wars EGYPT, a province of the empire, was briefly under French rule. Thanks to the intervention of Russia and GREAT BRITAIN, the Ottomans were forced to recognize the independence of GREECE by the Treaty of Adrianople of 1828.

The collapse of the southern part of the empire followed in 1833, when the sultan was obliged to sign over Syria and Egypt to his rebellious vassal, Mehmet Ali. Although the empire was nominally victorious in the Crimean War, this campaign placed a further strain on an already floundering economy. Increasingly the sultans were only able to survive thanks to the political and economic support they received from European nations who favored bolstering the empire, "The Sick Man of Europe," in the interests of the balance of power.

The Russo-Turkish War of 1877/78 weakened the sultan's control over his remaining Balkan territories, and with growing political unrest in Istanbul, BULGARIA proclaimed her independence in 1908. LIBYA was lost to ITALY in 1912, and by 1913 the Balkan Wars had ended Turkish rule in Europe. Allied to GERMANY in World War I, the Turks effectively foiled the Allied GALLIPOLI venture; in Arabia, however, the campaign went badly and after the fall of BAGHDAD and JERUSALEM an armistice was signed in 1918 which marked the end of the Ottoman Empire.

OTTUMWA (United States) Commercial and industrial center of an agricultural area in SE IOWA, on both banks of the Des Moines River, 75 mi SE of Des Moines. It was incorporated in 1851. Its municipal airport was a large inland flying base for the Navy during World War II.

OTUMBA (Mexico) Town in NE Mexico state. A battle was fought here on July 7, 1520 on the plain of Otumba. Hernando Cortez and his forces, during their retreat from MEXICO CITY, here defeated a large Aztec army.

OUACHITA POST. See MONROE.

OUADAÏ. See WADAI.

OUAGADOUGOU [Wagadugu] (Upper Volta) Economic center and capital of Upper Volta, in West Africa. Founded in the 11th century as the capital of a

Mossi empire, it was a center of their power until the French took it in 1896.

OUARGLA [Wargla, Warqla] (Algeria) Town, oasis, and capital of Oasis department, approx. 90 mi SW of Touggourt, in the heart of a palm grove. It was settled *c.*1000 by Kharijite Muslims in flight from religious persecution. From the 16th century it paid tribute to the OTTOMAN EMPIRE until it was conquered by FRANCE in 1853. The Hassi Messaoud oil fields are nearby.

OUBANGI-CHARI. See UBANGI-SHARI.

OUBANGI-CHARI-TCHAD. See UGANGI-SHARI.

OUCHY (Switzerland) Port and shorefront of LAUSANNE, a village in Vaud canton, on LAKE GENEVA. The site of the preliminary Treaty of Ouchy, settling the Tripolitan War between Italy and the Ottoman Empire (May 1912), it is the former residence of two famous poets, Shelley and Byron.

OUDENAARDE [*French:* **Audenarde**] (Belgium) Town, textile center in East Flanders province, W Belgium, on the SCHELDE RIVER. The Battle of Oudenaarde on June 30 to July 11, 1708 saw the defeat of the French under the duke of Vendôme by the duke of Marlborough and Prince Eugene of Savoy here during the War of the Spanish Succession. The defeat completely undermined French military confidence and hastened their ultimate defeat. French and American troops took the town in November 1918 near the end of World War I. See also FLANDERS.

OUDH [Audh] (India) A province of former British India in a central and historic region, now a part of UTTAR PRADESH state. In ancient times Ajodhya was a sacred Hindu city, and capital of the kingdom of KOSALA, which was close to modern Oudh in area. It came under the Guptas in the fourth century AD, and was taken by Muslim invaders in the 11th century. It then became the center of the Rajput state of Kanauj. In the 16th century it was a province of the MOGUL EMPIRE and was later governed by the nawabs of Oudh. The British annexed it in 1856, raising the tension that erupted into the Indian mutiny in 1857/58. In 1877 it was joined with AGRA to form the United Provinces, governed by GREAT BRITAIN. In 1947 it became a state of India. See also GUPTA EMPIRE, RAJPUTANA.

OUDJDA. See OUJDA.

OUEZZANE. See WAZZAN.

OUIDAH [Whydah, Wida] (Benin) Seaport town in West Africa on a lagoon 23 mi W of Cotonou. Capital of a small state founded in the 16th century, it was a center of activity from the early 17th century for Portuguese, French, and Dutch traders. PORTUGAL built a fort here in 1788, which still stands. In the 18th and early 19th centuries it became an important point of export for African slaves. In the 1840's FRANCE established a substantial trade with Ouidah for palm oil and ivory and in 1866 annexed it.

OUJDA [Oudjda] [*Arabic:* **Ujda**] (Morocco) Commercial city of NW Africa, near the Algerian border. Founded in 944 AD, and ruled by Berbers and Arabs

for centuries, it was taken by Morocco in 1797. It was intermittently held by FRANCE in 1844, 1859, and 1907.

OULILI. See VOLUBILIS.

OULU [*Swedish:* **Uleaborg**] (Finland) Port, cultural center, and capital of Oulu province, on the Gulf of Bothnia at the mouth of the Oulu River, 320 mi N of Helsinki. The city grew around a castle built in 1590, was chartered in 1610, and destroyed by a fire in 1822. Long an important port for exporting tar from the forests of Finland, by the 19th century it became a major commercial center.

OURIQUE (Portugal) Town in Beja district, 31 mi SSW of Beja. The Moors suffered a great defeat nearby in 1139, leading to the establishment of the kingdom of Portugal by its earliest king, Alfonso I. He had already freed the country from the rule of LEÓN, and in 1147 he extended his power by taking SANTAREM from the Moors.

One of many fine baroque churches in Ouro Prêto, Brazil, an 18th-century town that began with silver mining and later became a cultural center.

OURO PRÊTO [*former:* **Vila Rica**] (Brazil) Town in Minas Gerais state, 40 mi SE of Belo Horizonte, 175 mi N of Rio de Janeiro. Founded in 1701 as a gold mining settlement, it became the Brazilian center of gold production in the 18th century. It was the core of Tiradentes' early and unsuccessful drive for independence at that time. The 18th century was also one of great cultural achievement here; and the town is noted for its many buildings, churches, and private homes that present examples of baroque colonial architecture. So many works of art are here that the town was made a national monument in 1933.

OUTER HEBRIDES. See HEBRIDES.

OUTER MONGOLIA. See MONGOLIAN PEOPLE'S REPUBLIC.

OUTER PROVINCES. See INDONESIA.

OUTREMER. See JERUSALEM, LATIN KINGDOM OF.

OVALAU (Fiji) Island in the Lomai Viti group, in the SW Pacific Ocean, approx. 12 mi off the E coast of Viti Levu. The capital of Fiji until 1882, it was a favorite residence of Europeans in the early days of its settlement.

OVERIJSSEL (Netherlands) Province between the IJsselmeer to the west and West Germany to the east. It once belonged to the bishop of Utrecht, but was sold in 1527 to Emperor Charles V. In 1579 it joined the Union of UTRECHT and became one of the UNITED PROVINCES of the Netherlands. Some of man's earliest settlements were probably located here. Traces of pre-Christian customs still remain.

OVERLAND TRAIL (United States) Routes across the United States traveled by emigrants and the U.S. Mail in the 19th century. The term is used for any of the trails between the Missouri-Mississippi river system and the Pacific Coast, but sometimes its application is to the central trails only. Best known of these was the trail that provided an alternate, more southern route to the OREGON TRAIL. It branched off from the Oregon Trail where the North and South Platte rivers join near North Platte City, Nebraska, followed the South Platte to present Julesberg, in northeastern Colorado, went overland to the North Platte, and rejoined the Oregon Trail east of FORT LARAMIE, in southeastern Wyoming.

Overland Trail is also the name of a trail that went to California, sometimes known as the California Trail. This one went west from FORT BRIDGER in southwestern Wyoming to the GREAT SALT LAKE, which meant that in part it followed the Mormon Trail. It then went on to SUTTER'S MILL near Sacramento, California. Another trail led southwest from SALT LAKE CITY, Utah, to LOS ANGELES, California. A southern route from ST. LOUIS, Missouri to SAN FRANCISCO, California swung southwest through EL PASO, Texas and TUCSON, Arizona.

The famous but short-lived Pony Express used the trails from ST. JOSEPH, Missouri, then the end of the telegraph line, to SACRAMENTO. Relays of riders took the U.S. Mail 2,000 miles in eight days. The service began in April 1860, but it did not last long after a transcontinental telegraph line opened in October 1861.

OVIEDO [earlier: **Asturias**] (Spain) Mining center and capital of Oviedo province, NW Spain, 230 mi NNW of Madrid, near the mines of the Cantabrian Mts. Founded c.760 AD as a monastery, it was important in the ninth century as the capital of the Asturian kings until it was replaced in 924 by LEÓN. Noted for its fierce defense of independence, Ovieda was sacked by

FRANCE in 1809 for disobedience during the Napoleonic era. It suffered during an uprising of Asturian miners in 1934 and again in a siege during the Spanish civil war of 1936 to 1939, when it was defended by the Nationalists. Its Gothic cathedral, begun in 1388, contains the tombs of the Asturian kings. Its university was founded in 1604. See also ASTURIAS.

OVIEDO PROVINCE (Spain) Coal mining province in NW Spain, on the Bay of Biscay. It is coextensive with the historical kingdom of ASTURIAS. A sanctuary in COVADONGA marks the defeat of the Arabs by the Christians in 772 AD. This was the beginning of the reconquest of the IBERIAN PENINSULA.

OVILAVA. See WELS.

OWATONNA (United States) Industrial city in S MINNESOTA, 15 mi S of Faribault. It was incorporated in 1854. A bank was built here in 1908 designed by Louis Sullivan, American architect, many of whose buildings were notable for their modern design. Sullivan designed several early skyscrapers.

OWENSBORO [former: **Rossboro, Yellow Banks**] (United States) City on the OHIO RIVER, in W KENTUCKY, 80 mi SW of Louisville. Founded in 1797 as Yellow Banks, it was renamed later for Col. Abraham Owens who died in the battle of TIPPECANOE. Settled c.1800, it was incorporated as a city in 1866. In 1864 Confederate guerrillas raided it during the Civil War.

OWO. See NIGERIA.

OWYHEE RIVER (United States) River, approx. 300 mi long, in SE OREGON. Formed in the SW corner of IDAHO, it flows NW across the Oregon boundary and empties into the SNAKE RIVER. It was named in 1826 for two Hawaiian employees of the Hudson's Bay Company who were killed by Indians. Gold and silver were discovered in the region in 1863, and many mining camps sprang up along the river. The river has now been dammed and is part of a reclamation project.

OXFORD [Latin: **Oxonia**] (England) City, admin. hq. of OXFORDSHIRE, and seat of Oxford University, on the THAMES RIVER, 52 mi WNW of London. It was first mentioned in 912 AD. By the 12th century it had a castle, an abbey, and the university, which is the oldest in England, founded in the 12th century. The seat of a bishopric from the 16th century, it was headquarters for the Royalists during the Civil War and was besieged for a time by the Parliamentarians. It became a manufacturing area after William R. Morris, Lord Nuffield, founded an automobile works at nearby Cowley in 1918. The university colleges, the Sheldonian Theatre, the Radcliffe Camera, the Observatory, and several medieval churches are here. The city cathedral is the chapel of Christ Church College.

OXFORD (United States) Residential town in central MASSACHUSETTS, 10 mi SSW of Worcester. Settled in 1687 by French Protestants, it was incorporated in 1693. Clara Barton, organizer of the American Red Cross, was born here in 1821.

OXFORD (United States) College town in N MISSISSIPPI, 70 mi SE of Memphis, Tennessee. It was founded in 1835, incorporated in 1837, and has been the home of the University of Mississippi since 1844. It was the scene of racial rioting when the first black university student was enrolled there in 1962. It was the home of the novelist William Faulkner.

OXFORDSHIRE [Oxford, Oxon] (England) Agricultural county in central England. The site of prehistoric monuments in the northern region, it was occupied by the Romans during the early years of their conquest of Britain, as evidenced by traces of riverside villas found here. In the Middle Ages it was part of the Anglo-Saxon kingdom of MERCIA. Norman kings hunted here, and during the English Civil War it was a stronghold of the Royalists after the 1642 battle of EDGEHILL. Historic WOODSTOCK is here, where Henry I built a palace. Here also is Blenheim Palace, seat of the dukes of Marlborough. Ardent Jacobites were large landowners here at the time of the "Forty-five," the Young Pretender's attempted restoration of the Stuarts in 1745. Since 1974 Oxfordshire has included a large area taken from Berkshire.

OXON. See OXFORDSHIRE.

OXONIA. See OXFORD.

OXUNA. See OSUNA.

OXUS RIVER. See AMU DARYA.

OXYRHYNCHUS [*Arabic:* **Al-Bahnasā, Behnesa**] (Egypt) Ancient site on the heights above Bahr Yusef, on the W bank of the NILE RIVER, approx. 54 mi S of AL-FAIYUM. The Oxyrhynchus papyri, discovered on the ancient site of what is now the village of Behnesa probably date from the first century BC to the 10th AD. Ptolemaic, Roman, and Byzantine, they include formerly lost literary works of famous Greek authors. They mention earlier settlements at this site, including a Greek colony and a later Christian monastic center. The papyri, discovered in 1897 and 1903, also contain fragments of the apocryphal sayings of Jesus, which probably date from the third century AD.

OYO (Nigeria) Farm town in Western State, approx. 32 mi N of Ibadan. It was founded *c.*1835 as the successor to Old Oyo or Katunga, the capital of the Yorubas of Oyo, which was destroyed in the Yoruba civil wars in the early 19th century. It came under a British protectorate in 1893.

OYSTER BAY (United States) Residential suburb of NEW YORK CITY. Town on LONG ISLAND SOUND on LONG ISLAND, NEW YORK. It is known as the home of President Theodore Roosevelt, although his Sagamore Hill estate is actually in nearby Cove Neck. Also here are several 18th-century homes and the Theodore Roosevelt bird sanctuary, which adjoins his grave site.

OYSTER RIVER. See DURHAM.

P

PAARDEBERG (South Africa) Battle site in W ORANGE FREE STATE, E central Republic of South Africa, on the Modder River, 23 mi SE of Kimberley. Gen. Piet Cronje and the Boers surrendered here to the British under Lord Roberts on Feb. 28, 1900 during the Boer War of 1899 to 1902.

PAARL (South Africa) Agricultural town in SW CAPE PROVINCE, S Republic of South Africa, 30 mi ENE of Cape Town, on the Berge River. Dutch farmers founded it in 1687, and French Huguenots came soon after.

PABIANICE [Pabjanice] (Poland) Industrial town in Łódź province, 10 mi SSW of Łódź, in central Poland. It was founded in the 13th century and flourished under Russian rule in the 19th century as a textile center. There is a castle and a 16th-century church in the town. The town was occupied by Germany in 1914 and was returned to Poland in 1919. The Germans captured it again in 1939.

PABJANICE. See PABIANICE.

PACHÁCAMAC (Peru) Ruins of a pre-Incan city, approx. 25 mi SE of Lima, near present La Mamacoma. Noted for its ancient Yuncan pyramidal temple with tombs and frescoes, it was also the site of an important later Inca temple. Francisco Pizarro attacked and plundered the city in 1523 during the Spanish conquest, stripping the gold from the temple.

PACHUCA [Pachuca de Soto] (Mexico) Silver-mining center, city, and capital of Hidalgo state, 50 mi N of Mexico City, central Mexico. Founded in 1534 on the site of an ancient Toltec city, it has been a silver-mining center since the Aztec period. Its silver deposits invited conquest by SPAIN in the 16th century. A royal tribute treasury was established here in 1670 at La Caja, and the church of San Francisco has stood in the city since 1596.

PACHUCA DE SOTO. See PACHUCA.

PACHYNUS PROMONTORIUM. See PASSERO, CAPE.

PACIFIC ISLANDS, TRUST TERRITORY OF THE (United States) A U.S. trust territory consisting of the CAROLINE, MARSHALL, AND MARIANA ISLANDS, except Guam. They were taken by JAPAN during World War I in 1914 but occupied by the United States during World War II in 1944. The islands became a U.S. trusteeship by approval of the United Nations in 1947.

PACKHOI. See PEI-HAI.

PACTOLUS (Turkey) A river in W central Turkey, joining the Hermus, the modern Gediz, after passing SARDIS. In antiquity gold was washed from its sands, providing great wealth to the Lydian kings.

PADANG (Indonesia) City, capital of West Sumatra province, a port on the W coast of SUMATRA ISLAND, on the Indian Ocean. Founded by the Dutch East India Company in the 1630's, it was fortified in 1667. It was briefly occupied by the British in the late 18th century. Its port was constructed toward the end of the 19th century. The city was held by JAPAN from 1942 to 1945 during World War II.

PADDY'S TOWN. See KEYSER.

PADERBORN (West Germany) Industrial city in North Rhine-Westphalia, 50 mi ESE of Münster. Charlemagne met with Pope Leo III here in 799 AD, prior to his coronation as emperor in Rome. It became an episcopal see six years later and was subsequently a center of imperial diets. It joined the HANSEATIC LEAGUE in the 13th century and became Prussian and secularized in 1803. The city was badly damaged during bombings in World War II. A 13th-century town hall and an 11th-century cathedral are located here. A theological school here was a Catholic university from 1614 to 1819.

PADOVA. See PADUA.

PADRE ISLAND (United States) Uninhabited island, S TEXAS, in the Gulf of Mexico, off the coast. Discovered in 1519, it gained a reputation as a death trap after a Spanish treasure fleet went aground here in 1553. A cattle ranch was founded on the island c.1800.

PADUA [ancient: Patavium; Italian: Padova] (Italy) Commercial town, capital of Padova province, Veneto region, NE Italy, 22 mi W of Venice. According to Livy, who was born here, the city was founded by the Trojans. The native Eugenei and Veneti were made Roman citizens in 89 BC. A wealthy Roman city, it was sacked by Goths and Huns in the fifth century and by the Lombards in 601 AD. An independent republic by 1164, it was commercially, politically, and culturally important in the Middle Ages, before it fell to VENICE in 1405. The University of Padua, called la Dotta, "The Learned," was founded in 1222 by students who left BOLOGNA and is the second-oldest in Italy. Galileo taught here, and Dante and Petrarch studied here. There are many churches and works of art remaining from the ancient and medieval periods. Giotto's famous frescoes in the Scrovegni Chapel are also here.

PADUCAH (United States) City, W KENTUCKY, approx. 100 mi SW of Owensboro, on the OHIO RIVER. Settled in 1827, it became a city in 1856. It was damaged during the Civil War as the Confederates raided Union supplies, and was flooded badly in 1884, 1913, and 1937.

PADUS. See PO RIVER.

PAEKCHE (Korea) Former kingdom occupying the SW part of the peninsula. According to tradition, Paekche was founded in 18 BC by a legendary leader, Onjo. By the third century AD Paekche was a fully developed kingdom under King Koi (234–80). In the mid-fourth century control was secured of the Han River basin in central Korea. In the late fifth century the rival northern kingdom of KOGURYO took away the Han territory and later advanced farther south. To attempt to regain this territory, Paekche allied itself with the SILLA kingdom of southern Korea, but later Silla, with Chinese help, conquered both Koguryo and Paekche, and the latter's dynasty came to an end in 660. Chinese Buddhism and culture initially came to JAPAN in the 6th century AD through Paekche.

PAEONIA (Yugoslavia) Ancient district N of Macedonia. Originally settled, according to tradition, by the Trojans, it was conquered by Phillip II of the MACEDONIAN EMPIRE in 358 BC. STOBI is its chief town.

PAESTUM [*ancient:* **Poseidonia**] (Italy) Ancient city on the Gulf of Salerno, in Salerno province, Campania region, approx. 22 mi SE of Salerno. Founded in the sixth century BC by Greeks from SYBARIS, it was later colonized by the Romans in 273 BC. Some of the best-preserved Greek Doric temples in existence can be found here. The city declined in antiquity and was abandoned after its destruction by Saracens in 871 AD.

PAG [*Italian:* **Pago**] (Yugoslavia) Agricultural and resort island in the Adriatic Sea off the N Dalmatian coast, W Yugoslavia. A palace and cathedral are located in its main village, also named Pag, dating back to Venetian times (1420–1797 AD). See also DALMATIA, VENICE.

PAGAN (Burma) Ruined city in Myingyan district, central Burma, on the IRRAWADDY RIVER, 92 mi SW of Mandalay. Founded in 847 AD, it was the capital of an important dynasty from c.1050 to 1298. Thousands of impressive pagodas and temples remain from the era of King Anawratha, when the introduction of Buddhism made this city a pilgrimage center of great religious importance. It is one of the great archaeological treasures of Southeast Asia.

PAGO. See PAG.

PAGO PAGO [*former:* **Pango-Pango**] (United States) Village and port on S Tutuila Island, capital of AMERICAN SAMOA, SW Pacific Ocean. Ceded to the United States in 1878, it was an important coaling and naval station until 1951. It became the capital in 1899 and was an important U.S. military staging area during World War II.

PAGUS VADENSIS. See VALOIS.

PAHANG (Malaysia) State on the SE coast of the MALAY PENINSULA. It was a vassal state under the control of various powers prior to the 16th century. After the fall of MALACCA in 1511, it became part of the Riau and Johor Sultanate until it came under British protection in 1888. It joined the Federated Malay States eight years later. It has been a state of Malaysia since 1963.

PAIMPOL (France) Fishing port, village in Côtes-du-Nord department, NNW of St.-Brieuc, on the Gulf of St. Malo, NW France. It was the setting of Pierre Loti's tale of Breton fishermen, *Pêcheurs d'Islande,* written in 1886.

PAISLEY (Scotland) Manufacturing town in Strathclyde region, 7 mi W of Glasgow. Scottish royalty are entombed in Paisley Priory, built in 1163, around which the town developed. The priory was burned by the English in 1307 and exists today in its 15th-century restored form. The town became a textile center in the 18th century and was once famous for its shawls.

PAKHOI. See PEI-HAI.

PAKISTAN Nation in the NW part of the Indian subcontinent, bounded on the W and N by Afghanistan, on the NE by China, on the E and SE by India, on the S by the Arabian Sea and on the SW by Iran. The many ethnic groups in the country are witness to the numerous peoples who have invaded the land over the centuries. Today the population is about 90 percent Muslim; and Urdu is the official language. Present Pakistan was part of British India from 1857 to 1947. Movements for freedom and for Muslim political rights in relation to the dominant Hindu population of India grew after the formation of the Muslim League in 1906. By 1930 there was increasing sentiment, led by the poet and statesman Muhammad Iqbal, for a separate Muslim nation. In 1940 Muhammad Ali Jinnah became the league leader and then the first head of the new nation when it received independence in 1947. The division of British India into the two nations, Pakistan and INDIA, was marked by bloodshed in fighting between Muslims and Hindus and much hardship as hundreds of thousands of people shifted their homes to be with fellow Muslims or Hindus.

Pakistan at that time was in two sections, separated by approximately 1,000 miles of Indian territory. Present Pakistan was called West Pakistan; and the eastern section, now BANGLADESH, was first known as East Bengal and then as East Pakistan. KARACHI was Pakistan's first capital. Pakistan and India went to war over the division of KASHMIR in 1947/48 and again in 1965. A boundary line was finally agreed on in December 1972. Dissatisfaction grew in East Pakistan, which felt the government favored the west, although most of the population was in the east. When East Pakistan won a majority in parliament in December 1970, the legislature was not allowed to meet and matters came to a head. In March 1971 East Pakistan declared its independence as Bangladesh. West Pakistan troops tried brutally to put down the revolt but were badly defeated by India when that nation entered the war in December. Pakistan finally recognized Bangladesh's independence in February 1974.

Tension on the AFGHANISTAN border heightened in December 1979, when Russia invaded that country. Although Pakistan is nominally a republic, it has been under martial law in recent years. Its relations with

India, although improved, are still far from cordial. ISLAMABAD, a completely new city begun in 1960, is now the capital.

PAKOKKU (Burma) Trading center, town, capital of Pakokku district, on the IRRAWADDY RIVER, 75 mi SW of Mandalay, central Burma. It gained commercial importance as a British protectorate in the 19th century. The nearby Yenangyuang oil fields have operated since the 1870's; they were badly damaged during World War II but have been rebuilt since. Pakokku was occupied by communist rebels from 1949 to 1955.

PAKSHITIRTHAM. See TIRUKKALIKKUNRAM.

PALAESTINA. See PALESTINE.

PALAESTINA SALUTARIS. See ARABIA, PROVINCE OF.

PALAIKASTRO (Greece) Archaeological site on the NE coast of CRETE. Excavations here have uncovered the ruins of a town that dates back to the Middle and Late Minoan periods.

PALANAN (Philippines) City in E Isabela province, LUZON. The Filipino revolutionary government under Gen. Emilio Aguinaldo had its headquarters here from 1900 to 1901. The general was captured by U.S. Gen. Funston on March 23, 1901, ending the rebellion against U.S. occupation following the Spanish-American War.

PALANTIA. See PALENCIA.

PALATINATE [*German:* **Pfalz**] (West Germany) Name derived from the title of its medieval lord, the Count Palatine, an office that existed under the Roman, Byzantine, and Holy Roman Empires and was used as well in Poland, Hungary and England. At present the name refers to two geographically separate but historically connected districts. The Lower or Rhenish Palatinate, the German Niederpfalz or Rheinpfalz, is part of the state of RHINELAND-PALATINATE and is situated on the E bank of the RHINE RIVER. It extends S to France and W to Saarland and Luxembourg. The Upper Palatinate, the German Oberpfalz, is located in NE BAVARIA and is bounded on the E by the Bohemian Forest. Their respective capital towns are NEUSTADT AN DER WEINSTRASSE and REGENSBURG.

In the 15th and early 16th centuries HEIDELBERG, then capital of the Rhenish Palatinate, flourished as a center of the German Renaissance. As electors of the HOLY ROMAN EMPIRE from the 14th century, the counts palatine were influential on both sides during the Protestant Reformation and the Catholic Counter-Reformation. Indeed, Elector Frederick V's acceptance of the Bohemian throne aroused such violent religious sentiments that it triggered the Thirty Years War, which eventually devastated the Palatinate.

The Palatinate again suffered devastation during the political wars beginning in the late 17th century and continuing through the Napoleonic Wars. However, Maximilian I Wittelsbach of Bavaria gained control of both Palatinates as constituent parts of Bavaria through shrewd negotiations with Napoleon and at the Congress of Vienna. Following World War II the Rhenish Palatinate became part of the new state of Rhineland-Palatinate, while the Upper Palatinate became part of the state of Bavaria.

PALATINE HILL (Italy) Most important of the seven hills on which ROME was built, on the E bank of the TIBER RIVER. It actually contains three summits, the Palatium, the Germalus, and the Velia. The name is traditionally attributed to Pales, the god of shepherds, whose feast day, April 21, is the traditional birthdate of Rome. According to legend Romulus founded Rome on the Palatine Hill in 753 BC. The rock-cut post holes of primitive Iron Age huts have been found on the slopes of the Palatine and are on display. Traces of occupation have been dated to the ninth century BC with certainty. Later all the hills of Rome were occupied by various tribes, since the low-lying areas were subject to malaria. They became the meeting ground of ancient Latins, Sabines, and Etruscans.

During the late Roman Republic and early empire the Palatine Hill was a favored location for upper class villas, including those of Catulus, Cicero, and Mark Antony. The House of Livia and of Augustus, her husband and first emperor, who was born here, has been excavated near the huts of Romulus. It contains well preserved frescoes and is on display. Later the hill became the site of the enormous imperial palaces, of which impressive remains survive.

Augustus began the building program, while Tiberius and Caligula demolished most of the other villas for the expansion of the Palatine villa, or "Palace." Augustus also built the Temple of Apollo, with Greek and Latin libraries, while the Temple of Augustus was built later. Under Domitian (81–96) the Palace was expanded on a grand scale to include an official area, a residence, and a stadium. Septimius Severus (193–211) extended the Palace to include an imperial box overlooking the Circus Maximus, the Septizonium, whose huge arches survive, and a bath complex.

With the fall of Rome the Palace became residence of the barbarian kings Odoacer and Theodoric, and of the Byzantine exarchs. In the early Middle Ages it fell into disrepair, while churches and monasteries sprung up on the hill. Roman nobles built castles on the ruins in the Middle Ages. In the 16th century the Farnese built a large garden here. Excavations were begun in 1724. See also ETRURIA, ROMAN EMPIRE.

PALATION. See MILETUS.

PALAU ISLANDS [*former:* **Pelew**] (United States) The largest cluster of the CAROLINE ISLANDS, in the W Pacific, U.S. Trust Territory of the Pacific Islands, 1,060 mi SE of Manila. It was controlled by SPAIN for three centuries preceding its purchase by GERMANY in 1899. It was taken by JAPAN in 1914 during World War I and held one of their most important naval bases during World War II. The base was occupied by the Allies on Oct. 13, 1944, following several months of bitter fighting. The Palaus became a U.S. trusteeship in 1947.

PALAWAN [*former:* **Paragua**] (Philippines) Agricultural island in SW Philippines. It was settled early by Muslims, who were followed by SPAIN in the 18th and

19th centuries. The Japanese occupied the island in 1942 during World War II and massacred a group of U.S. war prisoners here. The Allies regained it early in 1945 and developed a strategic air base here.

PALAZZOLO ACREIDE [*ancient:* **Acrae**] (Italy) Town in Siracusa province, 22 mi W of Syracuse, SE SICILY. Founded by ancient SYRACUSE as an outpost in 664 BC, the Greek colony here has been excavated, revealing a small Greek theater, a council chamber, an agora or main square, and a number of tombs.

PALEMBANG (Indonesia) Industrial and commercial city and port, capital of South Sumatra province, on the Musi River. The largest city of SUMATRA, it was the capital of the important Hindu-Sumatran kingdom of SRIVIJAYA in the eighth century AD. It became Islamic in the 17th century. The Dutch, who first settled here in 1617, abolished the sultanate in 1825 shortly after the sultan had massacred Dutch settlers here. It was occupied by JAPAN from 1942 to 1945 during World War II.

PALENCIA [*ancient:* **Palantia**] (Spain) Transportation center, city, and capital of Palencia province, León region, on the Carrión River, approx. 120 mi NW of Madrid, N Spain. A former Roman colony, it was sacked by the Visigoths in the sixth century AD and retaken by León from the Moors in the 10th century. A medieval residence of the Leónese royalty, it was the site of Spain's first university, founded *c.*1210, until its removal in 1238. It flourished in the Middle Ages but declined following Charles I's severe chastisement for its role in the Comuneros revolt of 1520. A 14th-century Gothic cathedral is here, as well as several notable churches.

PALENQUE (Mexico) Ancient city in N Chiapas state, S Mexico. A city containing exquisite examples of Mayan architecture and culture from the Classic period, it is the site of one of the best-preserved Mayan temples, the Temple of Inscriptions, famous for its hieroglyphic tablets.

PALERMO [*ancient:* **Panhormus, Panormus**] (Italy) Commercial city and port, capital of both Palermo province and SICILY, on the Bay of Palermo, 265 mi SE of Rome. The city has countless examples of Norman and Byzantine art and architecture, the most famous of which is the 12th-century Palatine Chapel. An ancient Phoenician settlement dating back to the eighth century BC, it was later occupied by the Carthaginians and by the Romans in 254 BC. It was ruled by the Byzantines and Arabs before becoming the prosperous capital of Norman Sicily from 1072 to 1194 AD. It was a center of commercial and cultural wealth during the Hohenstaufen period until their defeat by Charles of ANJOU in 1266. It overthrew its French rulers in the Sicilian Vespers insurrection, which started here in 1282. It then offered the Sicilian crown to ARAGON. The city reflects its Spanish history under the Aragonese, Hapsburgs and Bourbons, until the revolutions and reunification of the 19th century. Garibaldi made it part of Italy in 1861, and it suffered great damage in World War II before the Allied takeover on July 30, 1943. Since the war Palermo's recovery has been slow, due both to the agricultural basis of Sicilian life, the great damage done to its port, and government inability to bring investment south. See also CARTHAGE, PHOENICIA, ROME.

PALESTINE [*biblical:* **Canaan;** *Latin:* **Palaestina**] Ancient region of the Middle East, much of which is now part of modern ISRAEL. Extending inland from the eastern shore of the Mediterranean Sea, its shifting boundaries generally reached east to the JORDAN RIVER. It has been inhabited since the Paleolithic age, and discoveries have shown that its earliest people were much like the Neanderthal Men of Europe. In the prehistoric period and in the earliest years of Middle Eastern civilization, Palestine, with SYRIA to the north, was a crossroads of influences from all the great early civilizations, Egyptian, Babylonian, and Hittite. It was also a crossroads of trade from east, north, and south as part of the FERTILE CRESCENT, the terminus of caravan routes from the ARABIAN PENINSULA, and the locus of the earliest extensive navigation and maritime trade in the MEDITERRANEAN SEA. The first fully developed civilization in the area was that of CANAAN, consisting of a group of fortified city states, such as HAZOR or MEGIDDO. The nomadic Hebrews first entered Canaan when their patriarch, Abraham, led his people westward from MESOPOTAMIA *c.*1900 BC. The region was then dominated by the Hyksos and the Egyptians. When Canaan was conquered by EGYPT in 1479 BC, many of the Hebrews were taken to Egypt in enslavement.

Moses led a group of these Hebrews back into Canaan in the 13th century BC, beginning the slow Hebrew conquest of the country. Much of the superior Canaanite culture was absorbed by the Hebrews as they settled down in the Promised Land. Circa 1225 BC the Philistines (Pulesti), a branch of the piratical Sea Peoples who ravaged the eastern Mediterranean after the breakup of the earliest civilizations around the AEGEAN SEA, invaded the southern coastal region called after them, PHILISTIA, and for a time subjugated the Hebrews. The Sea Peoples brought iron tools and weapons with them, destroying the HITTITE EMPIRE and subduing such powerful coastal city states as TYRE and UGARIT.

The Hebrews fought back under Saul and their great king, David, and defeated the Philistines, whose enmity had done much to awaken a national consciousness among the Hebrews themselves. The new Hebrew kingdom, established *c.*1000 BC, grew powerful under David and his son, Solomon, and was distinguished in the Palestinian region for its devotion to a monotheistic religion. Solomon's death brought the division of the kingdom into Israel in the north and JUDAH in the south, with its capital at JERUSALEM. The conquest of Israel by ASSYRIA in 721 BC and the taking of Judah in 586 by BABYLON and the exiling of the Judaeans to BABYLONIA ended the first great period of Hebrew history. Babylonia soon fell to Cyrus the Great (*c.*600–529 BC) of PERSIA, who allowed many of the Jews to return to Palestine, where they maintained their national and religious identity by compiling a strict code of social and religious conduct enshrined in the Old Testament of the Bible.

Once more they were submerged by the conquering armies of Alexander the Great of MACEDON in 333 BC and by his successors, the SELEUCID EMPIRE and the empire of the Ptolemies of Egypt. The Seleucid attempt to impose Hellenism on the Jews forged a new unity among them and inspired a revolt under the Maccabean family that led to the founding of a new Maccabean Jewish state in 142 BC. This endured until the Roman conquest of Palestine under Pompey in 64/63 BC, after which Palestine was put under the rule of the puppet kings, the Herods. From c.5 BC to 29 AD, during the lifetime of Jesus Christ, Palestine was part of the Roman province of Syria. Once more the Jews arose in the great revolt of 66 to 73 AD, which was ruthlessly suppressed by the Roman Vespasian and his son Titus, who destroyed the temple in Jerusalem and vanquished the last desperate Jews in the fortress of MASADA. The Diaspora that followed, or exodus of Jews to all the countries of the known world, made them an international people, held together as always by their strict religion and laws. A second revolt in 135 AD, under the Roman Emperor Hadrian, led to further destruction in Palestine and the rebuilding of Jerusalem as the Roman city of Aelia Capitolina.

Following Constantine's recognition of Christianity in 313 AD, Palestine flourished as an important center of Christianity and pilgrimage. Under the BYZANTINE EMPIRE many of the cities were refortified and the Christian holy sites richly endowed. Taken by the Sassanian Persians in 614, Palestine was recovered briefly by the Byzantines under Heraclius before falling to Muslim Arabs by 640 AD. Then came the territorial contention between the Muslim Ummayad and AB-BASID Caliphates in the late eighth century, the conquest of Palestine by the Egyptian Fatimids in the ninth, domination by the Seljuk Turks after 1071, and the capture of Jerusalem by the Christian Crusaders in 1099, when the LATIN KINGDOM OF JERUSALEM was established. The Crusaders suffered a disastrous defeat at the Battle of HATTIN in 1187, and were finally expelled by the armies of the Egyptian MAMLUK EMPIRE in 1291.

The defeat of the Mamluks by the OTTOMAN EMPIRE in 1516 isolated Palestine for more than three centuries until 1831, when the Egyptian viceroy opened the region to European influence. In 1882 the first Russian Jews arrived with the goal of establishing a Jewish homeland there. At the same time the first stirrings of Arab nationalism developed in opposition to Turkish rule. Both Jews and Arabs received encouragement from the British, who eventually found themselves compromised by their dual policy. During World War I the Arabs aided the British in gaining control of Palestine.

The scientist-statesman, Chaim Weizman, persuaded Great Britain to support the establishment of a national home for the Jews. The Balfour Declaration of 1917 formalizing this was approved by the League of Nations in 1922, and GREAT BRITAIN was appointed to govern Palestine as a mandate. Increased Jewish immigration between the wars met resistance by Arabs already resident there, and from the British. During World War II both Arabs and Zionists supported the Allied side, but extremist groups were emerging within each. Hitler's genocide against the Jews generated a wave of sympathy for the establishment of a Jewish state, and survivors of the Nazi terror emigrated to Palestine in great numbers. By 1947 the British considered their mandate unmanageable and passed the problem to the United Nations in February. At this time the Palestinian population was composed of 1,091,000 Muslim Arabs, 614,000 Jews and 146,000 Christians. The Palestinian territory was divided in 1948 to form the state of Israel, with the western portion going to JORDAN. The solution was not a happy one. Arab-Israeli relations have existed in a state of tension with sporadic fighting and occasional wars to the present. In the 1967 War, Israel acquired the entire territory of the former League mandate.

The plight of the Palestinian refugees displaced by the establishment of Israel were brought to world attention by their charismatic leader, Yasir Arafat. At the same time relations between Israel and Egypt entered a new, conciliatory phase, thanks largely to the initiatives of former President Carter of the United States, Egypt's President Anwar Sadat, and Israel's Prime Minister Menachem Begin. However, current fears over arms supplies and military superiority, the assassination by Muslim extremists of Egypt's far-sighted president, Anwar el-Sadat, and the recent Israeli siege of the Palestinian guerrillas in Beirut, LEBANON, sustain tension throughout the Palestinian region.

PALESTRINA [*ancient:* **Praeneste**] (Italy) Agricultural town, in Roma province, LATIUM region, central Italy, approx. 25 mi E of Rome. It flourished before the eighth century BC but was conquered by ROME following the Latin War of 340 to 338 BC. Sulla seized it from Marius's troops and destroyed it in 82 BC. The city and its sanctuary of Fortuna Primigenia were rebuilt by Sulla in recompense, and have been excavated and restored. The town prospered greatly under the ROMAN EMPIRE, and it was famous for its oracles.

Taken by the Lombards in 752 AD, it passed to the counts of Tusculum, and then to the Colonna family in 1043. It was a major stronghold for them during their resistance to Cola di Rienzi, the tribune of Rome between 1348 and 1354. The composer Giovanni Pierluigi da Palestrina was born here c.1525. The town has a notable museum of antiquities.

PALGHAT [Pulicat] (India) Trading center and town in central KERALA, on the Ponnani River, 112 mi WNW of Madurai, SW India. Strategically located at the entrance to the Western Ghats, the passageway known at the Palghat Gap, it became a thriving center of East-West trade in India. It was of great strategic importance in the British wars with Hyder Ali and passed to GREAT BRITAIN in 1790.

PALIA. See SIVRIHISAR.

PA-LI-CH'IAO [Palikao] (China) Village in Hopeh province, near Peking. A British and French expeditionary force defeated the Chinese here in 1860 en route to the capture of PEKING.

PALIKAO. See PA-LI-CH'IAO.

PALLAVA EMPIRE (India) Ancient realm in S India, established by the Pallava dynasty. They rose to power in the fourth century AD and made KANCHIPURAM their capital. The strength and wealth of the Pallavas reached a peak between *c.*600 to 630 AD during the reign of Mahendravarman I. They fought regularly with the CHALUKYA dynasty and in the eighth century lost their power to the CHOLA dynasty. The Pallavas were noted patrons of Dravidian architecture, especially in MAHABALIPURAM, a religious center founded by their kings in the seventh century.

PALMA [Palma de Mallorca] (Spain) Agricultural and commercial town, capital of both Baleares province and MAJORCA Island, on the Bay of Palma. It was probably founded in the second century BC and later fell to the Moors, who lost it to James I of ARAGON in 1229 AD. There is an impressive Gothic cathedral begun in 1230 in the town. There are also several ancient churches and the royal Moorish palace known as the Almudaina.

PALMA DE MALLORCA. See PALMA.

PALMA SORIANO (Cuba) City in Oriente province, E Cuba, 18 mi NW of Santiago de Cuba. French Haitians came here during the 19th century and developed it into the commercial center of an important coffee-growing region.

PALMERSTON. See DARWIN.

PALM SPRINGS [*former:* **Agua Caliente**] (United States) Resort city in Coachella Valley, approx. 100 mi SE of Los Angeles, SE CALIFORNIA. Well known in the 18th century to the Spanish for its hot springs, it became popular as a stagecoach stop in the late 19th century. It was settled in 1884 and incorporated in 1938.

PALMYRA [*ancient:* **Tadmor**] (Syria) Ancient city, in an oasis on the N edge of the Syrian Desert, 135 mi NE of Damascus. Reputedly founded by Solomon, it flourished as a center of trade between Syria and BABYLONIA after it came under Roman control *c.*30 AD. It became the capital of an empire of its own during the reign of Queen Zenobia, who succeeded her husband, Septimius Odenathus, in the third century AD. Aurelian destroyed the city in 273, and its rich ruins were first discovered in the 17th century. A temple to Baal, a theater, a civic center and many tombs were found, dating back to its days of glory. See also ROMAN EMPIRE.

PALMYRA (United States) Village in W NEW YORK State 21 mi E of Rochester. Nearby is the glacial drumlin, Hill Cumorah, where the gold plates that were the source of the *Book of Mormon* were reputedly unearthed in 1827 by the Mormon founder, Joseph Smith.

PALMYRA ISLAND (United States) Tiny atoll, one of the LINE ISLANDS, SW of Honolulu in the central Pacific Ocean. It was discovered by an American, Capt. Sawle, in 1802. It was later claimed by the kingdom of

Triumphal arch in Palmyra, desert capital of Queen Zenobia, who briefly wrested the eastern empire from Rome. For her pains she ended up in Rome in chains in 273 AD.

HAWAII in 1862, by Great Britain in 1889 and by the United States in 1898. Formerly part of the Hawaiian Islands, it was excluded from the newly-formed state in 1960. Now privately owned, it is administered by the U.S. Department of the Interior.

PALO ALTO (United States) Residential city in W CALIFORNIA, 32 mi SE of San Francisco. It was established in 1889 by an associate of Leland Stanford, who founded Stanford University nearby in 1885. Incorporated in 1894 and known for an ancient redwood tree for which the city was named, it has developed as a naval aviation center.

PALO ALTO (United States) Battlefield in S TEXAS, 12 mi NE of Brownsville. United States forces under Gen. Zachary Taylor here defeated a Mexican force led by Gen. Mariano Arista in the first battle of the Mexican War on May 8, 1846.

PALOS. See PALOS DE LA FRONTERA.

PALOS DE LA FRONTERA [Palos] (Spain) Town and former port of Huelva province, on the Rió Tinto River in SW Spain. Columbus set sail from here on his initial voyage in 1492, and it was the site of his reembarkation a year later. Hernando Cortés landed here in 1528 following his conquest of Mexico. The port has since silted up.

PALWAL (India) Town in the PUNJAB, approx. 35 mi S of Delhi, in NW India. Palwal is a town of great antiquity that according to the earliest Aryan traditions was important under the name of Apelava, part of the Pandava kingdom of Indraprastha.

PAMIR [The Pamirs] (Afghanistan, China, USSR) Mountain region in central Asia, mostly in TADZHIK SSR, bordering on parts of China, India, and Afghanistan. Marco Polo traveled along its Terak Pass in 1271 en route to China. The first north-south expedition across the Pamirs was led by the French explorer, Pierre Bonvalot, in 1886.

PAMIRS, THE. See PAMIR.

PAMPANGA (Philippines) Province in central LUZON. The ancient home of the once prosperous Pampangan tribe, it was overcome by the neighboring city of LEGASPI in 1572 after bitter fighting. Since then it has been a province and was one of the first to join the revolution of 1896 against SPAIN. It was recaptured from Japan by U.S. forces in February 1945 during World War II.

PAMPELUNA. See PAMPLONA.

PAMPHYLIA (Turkey) Ancient district and Roman province in S Asia Minor, between LYCIA and CILICIA. It was subject to several rulers of the area but first became a political unit following its capture by the Romans, who defeated Antiochus III in 188 BC. See also PISIDIA.

PAMPLONA [*ancient:* **Pompaelo;** *former:* **Pampeluna**] (Spain) Commercial and communications center, city, and capital of Spanish Navarre, on the Arga River, N Spain, 196 mi NNE of Madrid. An ancient Basque metropolis, it was founded by Pompey as a Roman colony in 75 BC. Taken by the Visigoths and Moors, it became the capital of the kingdom of NAVARRE in 824 after its capture from the Moors by Charlemagne. It remained the capital following the kingdom's union with CASTILE in 1512, effected by Ferdinand V. It was captured by the French in 1808 and by the British in 1813 during the Peninsular campaign. The city is dominated by its citadel, built by Philip II in 1571. There is also a 14th-century Gothic church here built on the site of a Romanesque sanctuary.

PANAJI [Pangim, Panjim, New Goa] (India) Town, port, and capital of territory of GOA, DAMAN, AND DIU, W India, on the Arabian Sea. The capital of former Portuguese India, it became their viceroy's residence in 1759. It was annexed by India in 1962.

PANAMA [*former:* **Darién;** *Spanish:* **Panamá**] A nation occupying the Isthmus of Panama, which connects South America and Central America. Cuna Indians inhabited the region when Europeans arrived. The coast was first seen by navigators from SPAIN, Rodrigo de Bastidas in 1501 and then Christopher Columbus, who anchored near present PORTOBELO in 1502. Circa 1510 Diego de Nicuesa attempted to found a colony on DARIÉN, the eastern part of Panama. He was followed by Martín Fernández de Enciso, but it was Vasco Núñez de Balboa, another conquistador, who stabilized the colony in 1510. In 1513 Balboa crossed the isthmus and on September 13 became the first European to see the Pacific Ocean. PANAMA CITY, founded in 1519 by Pedro Arias de Avila, became the transshipment port for Andean gold on its way to Spain.

The Darién Scheme was an attempt by a Scottish company to establish a colony on Darién. Two expeditions, in 1698 and 1699, founded New Saint Andrew, but the scheme was a disastrous failure. Until 1717 Panama was part of the Spanish viceroyalty of PERU but in 1739 it became permanently part of the viceroyalty of NEW GRANADA, which also included modern COLOMBIA, VENEZUELA, and ECUADOR. When independence from Spain was won in 1821, Panama became part of GRAN COLOMBIA, comprising the same territory as the viceroyalty. After Venezuela and Ecuador seceded in 1830, Panama remained part of Colombia.

A treaty between Colombia and the United States resulted in the building of a railroad across the isthmus between 1850 and 1855. The route was much used by Americans on their way to the CALIFORNIA gold fields and the OREGON Territory. In 1903 another treaty with Colombia gave the United States the right to build a canal across the isthmus, but the Colombian senate refused to ratify the treaty. On November 3, aided by U.S. warships, Panama declared its independence from Colombia. The Hay-Bunau-Varilla Treaty quickly established the Panama CANAL ZONE and provided for a lump sum payment and an annuity to Panama. The PANAMA CANAL was constructed by the United States between 1904 and 1914. In the early 20th century there were many changes of government; and in 1908, 1912, and 1918 the United States sent armed forces to Panama to restore order. By another treaty in 1936 the United States gave up its protectorate over Panama and increased the annual canal payments.

From the 1930's until late into the 1950's, first Arnulfo Arias and then José Antonio Remon dominated politics. In early 1969 Omar Torrijos Herrera emerged as ruler and remained so until August 1981, when he died in a plane crash. For many years there was strong and at times violent agitation in Panama for revision of the treaties concerning the canal. In 1967 the presidents of the United States and Panama agreed on a treaty that would have given Panama rule over the Canal Zone, among other terms, but neither country ratified it. New negotiations began in 1973 and were completed in 1978, at which time two treaties were ratified that provide for turning the canal over to Panama at the end of 1999.

Panama City is the capital and largest city; Colon and DAVID are the next largest.

PANAMA CANAL (Panama) Artificial waterway crossing the Isthmus of Panama and connecting the CARIBBEAN SEA and the Atlantic Ocean with the Pacific Ocean. From shore to shore the canal is 40 mi long, and the Pacific end is E of the Caribbean end. Three sets of locks raise and lower ships in their transit as they go through Gatun Lake, Gaillard (formerly Culebra) Cut, and Miraflores Lake. The city of Balboa is at the Pacific end, and Colon at the Atlantic end. Almost as soon as the narrow Isthmus of Panama was discovered in the 16th century, men proposed cutting a canal across it and thus shortening the water voyage from the

Atlantic to the Pacific, which otherwise took ships around CAPE HORN at the southern tip of South America. After the United States acquired CALIFORNIA in 1848, interest in a canal increased. Great Britain also had designs on such a waterway, and the Clayton-Bulwer Treaty of 1850 provided that neither nation would have exclusive rights to a canal.

The first attempt to dig a canal began in 1881 when a French company undertook the task. Disease, inadequate planning, and lack of funds brought this effort to an end in 1889. In 1901 the Hay-Pauncefote Treaty between Great Britain and the United States gave the latter the right to build a canal. The Hay-Herrán treaty of 1903 between the United States and COLOMBIA, of which the isthmus was then a part, would have allowed the work to proceed, but the Colombian Congress refused to ratify the treaty. Revolution in the Panama region broke out and was encouraged by President Theodore Roosevelt. Panama's independence was quickly recognized, and on November 17 the Hay-Bunau-Varilla Treaty allowed the United States to go ahead. Panama received $10 million and an annual rent of $250,000. The United States obtained a CANAL ZONE five miles wide on each side of the canal.

Work began in 1904 after plans had been made to control disease, especially yellow fever. The canal, one of the great engineering feats of all time, was opened on Aug. 15, 1914. It was at once of enormous benefit to merchant shipping and was a prime strategic asset to the United States since it allowed U.S. Navy ships to move from one ocean to another. In 1921 the United States paid Colombia $25 million, and the latter finally recognized the independence of Panama. Over the years the terms of the treaty have been made more favorable to Panama, and improvements have been made in the canal. Nevertheless, since the 1960's there has been increasing agitation in Panama for more control over the canal and the zone. This movement culminated in a treaty of 1978 by which, on Oct. 1, 1979 the zone was returned to Panama and the canal itself is to become Panamanian property in 1999. The United States retains the right to protect the canal against attack.

PANAMA CANAL ZONE. See CANAL ZONE.

PANAMA CITY (Panama) Manufacturing city, capital of Panama, on the Gulf of Panama. Founded in 1519, it was a prosperous colonial port until it was raided and leveled for its gold stores by Sir Henry Morgan in 1671. It was refounded five miles west of the original site in 1673 but declined as its Andean gold sources diminished. Revived during the California gold rush and the construction of the trans-Panama railway in the mid-19th century, it was the center of the revolt against Colombia in 1903. Its university, founded in 1935, is a recognized center of inter-American affairs. See also COLOMBIA, PANAMA CANAL.

PANAMÁ VIEJA. See OLD PANAMA.

PANAY (Philippines) City in Capiz province, Panay Island in the VISAYAN ISLANDS, 3 mi SE of Roxas. In 1569, the old town was the site of the first Spanish colony on the island and the second settlement in all the Philippines. During World War II the island was attacked in September 1944 by the Allies, who occupied it between March 18 and 20 of the following year.

PANČEVO [*Hungarian:* **Pancsova**] (Yugoslavia) Industrial city in SERBIA, NE Yugoslavia, on the DANUBE RIVER, opposite BELGRADE. A trading center since the 12th century, it has been under Turkish and then Austrian rule. It was occupied from 1941 to 1944 by the Axis forces during World War II. It has an old church that is a monument of Serbian art, culture, and religion.

PANCHAVATI. See NASIK.

PANCSOVA. See PANCEVO.

PANDERMA. See BANDIRMA.

PANDHARPUR (India) Town in SE Maharashtra, on the Bima River, 185 mi ESE of Bombay, W India. A famous temple to Vishnu located here attracts large numbers of Hindu pilgrims triannually.

PANDOSIA (Italy) Ancient town in S Italy. According to tradition, Alexander I of EPIRUS was killed here in a battle in 326 BC on an attempted invasion of Italy. A half century later Pyrrhus of Epirus had considerably more success on his invasion of Italy.

PANEVEZHIS. See PANEVĖŽYS.

PANEVĖŽYS [*Russian:* **Panevezhis**] (USSR) Industrial city in Lithuanian SSR, 55 mi NNE of Kaunas. An important trading center since the 14th century, it became Russian in 1795. It joined LITHUANIA in 1918 but passed to the USSR in 1940. It was occupied by Germany from 1941 to 1944 during World War II.

PANGASINAN (Phillipines) Province in N central LUZON. It was probably an ancient kingdom. Spanish explorers and missionaries arrived here in the 16th century, and it became a province by 1611. Revolts were staged here in 1660 and 1765, and a civil government was created in February 1901, following the Spanish-American War. The Japanese occupied it through most of World War II, until the U.S. takeover in January 1945.

PANGIM. See PANAJI.

PANGKOR (Malaysia) Island in the Strait of Malacca, off the W coast of S MALAY PENINSULA. Formerly part of PERAK, it came under British protection in 1826, was incorporated into the Dindings in 1874, and was returned to Perak in 1935.

PANGO-PANGO. See PAGO PAGO.

PANHORMUS. See PALERMO.

PANIPAT (India) Market town in Haryana, 53 mi N of Delhi, NW India. A very old town, it was the site of three decisive battles. In 1526 the DELHI SULTANATE was defeated by Babur, who went on to forge the MOGUL EMPIRE. Thirty years later that rule was reinforced with Akbar's victory over the Afghans. In 1761 the Afghans were victors over the MARATHAS here.

PANJĀB. See PUNJAB.

PANJDEH [**Penjdeh**] (USSR) Village in TURKMEN

SSR, on the Kushka River. A boundary dispute resulted in a battle here on March 30, 1885 between RUSSIA and AFGHANISTAN. The Afghans were defeated, and the boundary was settled the following year, narrowly averting a war between Russia and Great Britain.

PANJIM. See PANAJI.

PANKOW (East Germany) Industrial district of East BERLIN, E central East Germany, on the Panke River. The seat of the government of East Germany, it has several noteworthy castles.

PANMUNJOM (Korea) Village in N South Korea, on the boundary of North Korea, in the demilitarized zone set up after the Korean War. Peace negotiations were held in the village in October 1951, during the war. A truce was ultimately signed here on July 27, 1953.

PANNONIA (Austria, Hungary, Yugoslavia) Ancient Roman province W of the DANUBE RIVER, Central Europe. It was conquered by the Romans between 39 BC and 9 AD and was incorporated as a province of the empire with ILLYRIA. It was divided c.105 AD into Lower Pannonia and Upper Pannonia and included the important towns of Vindobana (VIENNA) and Aquincum (BUDAPEST). It was the scene of much resistance against the barbarian invasions but was abandoned by the Romans after 395. See also ROMAN EMPIRE.

PANOPOLIS. See AKHMIM.

PANORMOS. See BANDIRMA.

PANORMUS. See PALERMO.

PANTELLERIA [ancient: Cossyra, Cosyra; Italian: Isola di Pantelleria] (Italy) Island in the Mediterranean Sea, between Sicily and Tunisia, forming part of Trapani province, SICILY. It was inhabited in the Neolithic age and megalithic tombs were built here. It was ruled by the Phoenicians in the seventh century BC, by CARTHAGE, and then by ROME from 217 BC and by the BYZANTINE EMPIRE until c.700 AD. The Muslims controlled the island until the 13th century, when it fell to the kingdom of the TWO SICILIES. Strategically located, it was strongly fortified by Italy prior to World War II but surrendered to the Allies on June 11, 1943 after heavy attack.

PANTICAPAEUM. See KERCH.

PAO-TING [Paoting] [former: Tsingyuan] (China) Commercial port, city in central Hopeh province, approx. 90 mi SSW of Peking, NE China. The wall around the city was built during the Ming dynasty (1368–1644). Captured by the communists on Nov. 22, 1948 during the Chinese civil war, it was the capital of HOPEH province until 1958.

PAO-T'OU [Paotow] (China) Industrial town in central INNER MONGOLIA, on the YELLOW RIVER, approx. 300 mi NW of Peking, N China. The city is enclosed by a nine-mi-long earthen wall constructed during the reign of Ch'ing Emperor T'ung Chih (1861–75). During World War II it was occupied by JAPAN from 1937 to 1945. Two nuclear reactors are near the city.

PAOTOW. See PAO-T'OU.

PÁPA (Hungary) Commercial city in Veszprém county, 80 mi W of Budapest, W Hungary. A castle was built here by Count Maurice Esterházy in the 18th century.

PAPAL STATES [Pontifical States, States of the Church] [former: **Patrimony of St. Peter**; Italian:**Lo Stato della Chiesa**] (Italy) Territorial possessions of the papacy, land holdings donated to the bishops and church of Rome, which existed early in the church's history. The properties grew from that time by endowments and gifts until by the fifth century AD they extended to all parts of Italy, the Mediterranean islands, Gaul, Africa, and the Balkans. With the disintegration of the empire, they were gradually confined to Italy but became more directly controlled by the popes, especially Gregory I, the Great (590–604). Discord with the BYZANTINE EMPIRE brought a further loss of territory in the south, so that papal holdings eventually centered around ROME, which, with its neighboring territories, was regarded as the realm of the Apostle Peter and his papal successors.

By the eighth century AD the popes, facing the threat of a Lombard invasion, sought the protection of the Frankish princes, Pepin the Short and his son Charlemagne. In 754 Pepin presented to Pope Stephen II the exarchate of RAVENNA, which he had reconquered from the Lombards. This famous DONATION OF PEPIN laid the basis for the Papal States. In return Pepin received the pope's endorsement as the legitimate king of the Franks. Charlemagne confirmed his father's donation in 774. To provide greater force to papal authority, a forged document, entitled the Donation of Constantine, seems also to have been issued in the eighth century. This document purported to have recorded the donation by the Emperor Constantine of the Western Empire to the papacy upon his departure to Constantinople and was used as a support for many later papal claims to temporal power.

As papal authority was established, so lay political power became more ensconced, with the inevitable result of conflicting interests in the realm of worldly possessions and authority. With the Babylonian Captivity at AVIGNON between 1305 and 1378 and the Great Schism between 1378 and 1417, the Papal States fell into chaos. Several attempts were made to pacify the states, now the region between Ravenna and Rome, most notably by Giles Albornoz, the cardinal general (1360–67), but not until the 16th century did real papal control return; but this was at the price of rampant nepotism epitomized by the career of Cesare Borgia (1476–1507), son of Pope Alexander VI. Nepotism ceased only with the Catholic Reformation later in the 16th century. Throughout the Renaissance the Papal States played a major role in the military and diplomatic balance of power, first in Italy, and then Europe, but the political power of the papacy declined as it fell under the sway of the surrounding power of the Hapsburgs as Holy Roman Emperors and Spanish kings of NAPLES. Spanish rule in Italy in the 17th and 18th centuries preserved the states in a weakened position. By the time Napoleon invaded Italy in the late 18th century, the papal mercenary troops offered little resistance, and Popes Pius VI and VII twice endured occupation and the abolition of their states between 1796 and 1814.

The states were returned to the papacy in 1815 and placed under Austrian protection by the terms of the Congress of Vienna. The papacy was initially sympathetic to the 19th-century nationalist and revolutionary movements, but as nationalism emerged as a threat to papal power, the popes' enthusiasm waned. French intervention in Rome following Garibaldi's revolution of 1848/49 prevented the confiscation of the Papal States during the early phases of the Risorgimento, but Austria's departure from BOLOGNA and ROMAGNA allied these two with the kingdom of SARDINIA in the push toward unification. During the final unifying stages, Garibaldi invaded the remaining Papal States but was twice prevented from taking Rome by Victor Emmanuel II, in 1862, and by Napoleon III in 1867. However, the fall of Napoleon III in 1870 left the way open for Victor Emmanuel II to occupy ROME. Pius IX refused to recognize the loss of his temporal domain and remained, along with his successors, a prisoner in the Vatican until the Lateran Treaty of 1929, negotiated with Benito Mussolini, established VATICAN CITY as the temporal center of the papacy, and an independent state—thereby settling the so-called Roman Question.

PAPANTLA [Papantla de Olarte] [*former:* **Papantla de Hidalgo**] (Mexico) Town in Veracruz state, approx. 70 mi NNW of Jalapa, E Mexico. The ruins of TAJÍN are nearby, dating back to pre-Columbian times and referred to as Classic Veracruz.

PAPANTLA DE HIDALGO. See PAPANTLA.

PAPANTLA DE OLARTE. See PAPANTLA.

PAPEETE (France) Commercial port, capital of both FRENCH POLYNESIA and the SOCIETY ISLANDS, on the NW coast of TAHITI. Capt. James Cook led a scientific expedition that anchored nearby in 1768, and Capt. Bligh of H.M.S. *Bounty* visited the harbor in 1788, before the famous mutiny. Papeete was the commercial and cultural center of Tahiti in the 18th century, especially as part of the French protectorate in the 19th century. A French nuclear laboratory is located here today.

PAPHLAGONIA (Turkey) Ancient country of N Asia Minor, on the BLACK SEA. The major settlement here in antiquity was at the Ionian town of SINOPE. It was part of the Lydian and Persian empires before being occupied by the kings of BITHYNIA, then by the kings of PONTUS. It was colonized by the Romans in 63 BC. It became a Roman province, and was occupied by the Turks in the Middle Ages.

PAPHOS [*modern:* **Baffo, Neo Paphos**] (Cyprus) Ancient city in Paphos district, 1 mi S of Ktima. Old Paphos, approx. 10 mi to the SE, was probably founded by Phoenicians. The present town, New Paphos, was founded *c.*1200 BC probably by Greeks from MYCENAE and was famous for its worship of Aphrodite. It suffered from several tremendous earthquakes. The new town became capital of Cyprus from the middle of the

Hellenistic period until the end of the ROMAN EMPIRE. It was visited by St. Paul in the first century AD. It was destroyed by Arabs in the 10th century, only to be revived in recent times. Excavations have revealed many Hellenistic and Roman remains, including a theater, the elaborate tombs of Hellenistic kings, a large Roman villa, and much more.

PAPIA. See PAVIA.

PAPUA NEW GUINEA Nation in the SW Pacific Ocean, independent since 1975, occupying the eastern half of the island of NEW GUINEA and including a number of islands: the BISMARCK ARCHIPELAGO, the D'ENTRECASTEAUX ISLANDS, the Louisiade archipelago, Samarai Island, the TROBRIAND ISLANDS, and the northernmost SOLOMON ISLANDS of Buka and BOUGAINVILLE. Largely tropical, New Guinea is a land of rugged mountains and thick forests, containing exotic plant and animal life. Much of it is still unexplored. Native arts and crafts have attracted attention in recent years; and although cannibalism and headhunting seem to have disappeared, tribal warfare still goes on. There are some 700 linguistic groups in the area, and so pidgin English has become the lingua franca. Agriculture and the mining of various metals are the main industries, wooden digging sticks and mammoth mining machines both being in use. PORT MORESBY is the capital and a modern city that contrasts sharply with the primitive tribal villages of the interior.

New Guinea was probably first sighted in 1511 by an explorer from PORTUGAL, Antonio d'Abreu, and named for its resemblance to the Guinea coast of West Africa. Papua, the southern section of Papua New Guinea, was annexed by QUEENSLAND in 1883, and the next year the British proclaimed a protectorate over it. In 1905 it came under the control of AUSTRALIA as the Territory of Papua. The northern region became German New Guinea in 1884, was occupied by Australian forces in World War I, and became an Australian mandated territory in 1920 as the Territory of New Guinea. In 1949 the two territories were merged for administrative purposes. During World War II the region was the scene of an intense struggle between the Japanese and the Allies. JAPAN captured LAE and RABAUL in early 1942, but the latter was so heavily bombed that it was of little use to the Japanese, while Lae was retaken by the Australians in September 1943. Port Moresby was the chief Allied base on New Guinea. On Dec. 1, 1973 the two sections became self-governing as Papua New Guinea, which on Sept. 16, 1975 became completely independent and a member of the COMMONWEALTH OF NATIONS.

PAQUIMÉ. See CASAS GRANDES.

PARÁ (Brazil) State in N Brazil, bisected by the AMAZON RIVER. Long a haven for smugglers, it was settled by PORTUGAL in the early 17th century. Captive Indians worked the sugar and coffee fields in the next century, and from the mid-19th to the early 20th century an impressive rubber industry flourished. The capital is Belém.

PARACALE (Philippines) City on an inlet of the N

coast of Camarines Norte, approx. 16 mi NW of Daet, in LUZON. The Spanish were attracted here because of its rich gold mines, which they exploited for two centuries.

PARACEL ISLANDS [*Chinese:* **Hsi-sha;** *Japanese:* **Hirata Gunto**] (China) Group of small islands in the South China Sea. Occupied by JAPAN in 1939, they reverted to China at the end of World War II. They were claimed and occupied during the VIETNAM War by South Vietnam and then by reunited Vietnam until Chinese forces recaptured them in 1974.

PARADISE (United States) Unincorporated town, in the foothills of the Sierra Nevada range, N of Sacramento, N CALIFORNIA. Gold was discovered nearby in 1859 during the great California gold rush.

PARAGUA. See PALAWAN.

PARAGUARÍ (Paraguay) Agricultural town, capital of Paraguarí department, 35 mi SE of Asunción, S central Paraguay. The town was founded in 1775. Argentine forces from BUENOS AIRES were defeated here in 1811 by Paraguayan patriots during the wars of independence.

PARAGUAY A landlocked nation in S central South America, bounded on the N and NW by Bolivia; on the NE and E by Brazil; and on the SE, S, and W by Argentina. Sebastian Cabot, in the service of SPAIN, explored the Paraguay River in 1527, hoping it would lead him to Peru. Circa 1535 the Spanish Juan de Ayolas and Domingo Martínez de Irala sailed up the Paraguay River for the same reason. The first settlement was made at ASUNCIÓN c.1535 by Juan de Salazar and Gonzalo de Mendoza, and Irala became not only the first governor of what was later Paraguay, but also the first freely elected governor in the Americas. In 1542 Alvar Núñez Cabeza de Vaca was appointed governor of the RIO DE LA PLATA area, which then included Paraguay.

As governor of Rio de la Plata, Hernando Arias de Saavedra succeeded in having Paraguay, then called Guaira, made a separate province in 1617. He gave territorial rights to the Jesuits who established *reducciones*, settlements of Indians, mostly Guarani, for the purpose of using their labor as well as converting them to Christianity. The Jesuits went on to establish their own nearly independent country here until the order was dissolved in 1773. The colonial fight for freedom from Spain began in 1721, with the revolt of the *comuneros*, citizens organized to defend their rights. They were led by José de Antequera y Castro, a Peruvian; and although he was captured and beheaded in 1731, the *comuneros* effectively ruled for nearly 10 years. In 1776 the whole region was made part of the Spanish viceroyalty of Rio de la Plata.

In 1810 another revolt, beginning in ARGENTINA, spread to Paraguay, and the next year independence was declared. José Gaspar Rodriquez Francia, who took part in the revolt, declared himself dictator in 1814 and ruled until his death in 1840. Known as El Supremo, he was a just despot, isolating Paraguay from the world and making it more self-sufficient. After his death, Carlos Antonio López became much the same kind of dictator. However, his son, Francisco Solano López, who ruled from 1862 to 1870, considered himself the Napoleon of South America. He pushed the country into the War of the Triple Alliance against BRAZIL, Argentina, and URUGUAY in 1865 and led the nation to devastating defeat in 1870.

Liberal forces ultimately secured control in 1904 and ruled for 20 years, but the Great Depression of the 1930's brought economic problems and unrest. The Chaco War of 1932 to 1935 was fought over the GRAN CHACO, a lowland plain in Paraguay, BOLIVIA, and Argentina. The boundary had long been disputed, and the discovery of oil caused war between Paraguay and Bolivia. At the end both sides were badly worn down. A treaty in 1938 gave three-fourths of the disputed area to Paraguay, while Bolivia received a corridor to the Paraguay River. Higinio Morínigo, president in 1940, established a military dictatorship but was ousted in 1948. After a series of short-lived governments, Alfredo Stroessner led a coup and became president in 1954. Although virtual dictator, he continues to hold elections and to campaign vigorously. He has been reelected several times and in 1978 was sworn in for a sixth consecutive term. There have been charges of abuses of human rights by this right-wing government, but Stroessner insists that order and prosperity outweigh abuses. Asunción is the capital and largest city; Encarnación is also an important center.

PARAHIBA. See PARAÍBA.

PARAHYBA DO NORTE. See PARAÍBA.

PARAÍBA [*former:* **Parahiba, Parahyba do Norte**] (Brazil) State in NE Brazil, on the Atlantic Ocean. It was settled in the late 16th century by Portuguese, but the resistance of the large native population of Indians delayed development for nearly a century. Although Paraíba prospered in the 17th century, the Indians continued their efforts, and the Dutch occupied the area between 1634 and 1654. There was a nationalist uprising here in 1710. Violence continued into the 19th century, when slavery was abolished. There have been many severe droughts leading to massive migrations from the countryside.

PARAMARIBO (Surinam) Port, city, and capital of Surinam, on the Surinam River, in what was formerly Netherlands Guiana. The French settled here on the site of an Indian village in 1640, and the English made it the capital of their settlement ten years later. A Jewish refuge for many years, it came under Dutch control in 1815 and was partly destroyed by fire in 1821 and 1832. There is a fine Dutch church and museum in the city.

PARAMUS (United States) City, NE NEW JERSEY, 12 mi W of NEW YORK CITY, NEW YORK State. It was settled in 1668 and incorporated in 1922. A colonial Dutch church is located here.

PARAMUSHIR (USSR) Island, part of the Kuril Islands, Russian SFSR. A well-defended naval base was operated here by JAPAN during World War II. It came under U.S. aerial attack in 1943 and 1944 and was taken by the USSR in 1945.

PARANÁ [*former:* **Bajada de Santa Fe**] (Argentina)

A visualization of the Temple in medieval Paris, center of the Knights Templar. The Templars, formed in the Crusades, were abolished in 1314.

Agricultural center, city, and capital of Entre Rios province, 250 mi W of Buenos Aires, on the Paraná River, NE Argentina. It was founded in the late 16th century by settlers from nearby Santa Fé who called it Bajada. It served as Argentina's capital from 1852 to 1862. The bishop's palace and a museum of fine arts are located here.

PARANAGUÁ (Brazil) Town and port, on the Atlantic Ocean, Paraná state, SE Brazil. One of Brazil's chief export centers, it was founded in 1560. Many fine examples of colonial architecture can be found in the town.

PARAN, WILDERNESS OF (Egypt) Desert region in NE SINAI peninsula, SE of Kadesh. According to the Bible, the Israelites settled here for 38 years before continuing on to the Promised Land. Ishmael and David both settled here at various times. It is mentioned in the Old Testament books of Genesis, Numbers, and I Samuel.

PARAY-LE-MONIAL (France) Manufacturing town, Saône-et-Loire department, approx. 55 mi NNW of Lyons, E central France. St. Margaret Mary established the cult of the Sacred Heart of Jesus here in the 17th century. Made famous by the nun's visions, it has since become an important French pilgrimage site. The 12th-century Romanesque basilica of Paray-le-Monial is located in the town.

PARCHIM (East Germany) Town in Schwerin dis-trict, 23 mi SE of Schwerin. Founded in 1210, it flour-ished as a trading center in the 14th century but de-clined after the Thirty Years War.

PARDUBICE [*German:* **Pardubitz**] (Czechoslova-kia) Industrial town, Czech SR, 60 mi E of Prague, on the ELBE RIVER, NW central Czechoslovakia. Dating from the 13th century, the town was refurbished in the Renaissance style in the 16th century by the Pernstejn family. Swedish forces attacked and razed it in 1645. The town has many fine examples of Gothic and Renais-sance architecture, including a 13th-century church and a royal castle.

PARDUBITZ. See PARDUBICE.

PARENZO. See POREČ.

PARIS [*ancient:* **Lutetia, Lutetia Parisiorum**] (France) City and river port, capital of France, on both banks of the SEINE RIVER, 110 mi ESE of Le Havre, and 107 mi from the English Channel, NE central France. It is economically, culturally, and politically the nucleus of the nation and has for centuries been one of the leading cultural and intellectual centers of the world. It is an important transportation center for its region, and as a city it preserves a unique atmosphere that for centuries has attracted artists, writers, stu-dents, and tourists from all over the world.

Originally concentrated on the ÎLE DE LA CITÉ, it began as a small Gallic fishing village of the Parisi tribe, called Lutetia Parisiorum by the Romans. On an important bridgehead, it was conquered by Julius Caesar in 52 BC. It expanded under the Roman occupation, and in the sixth century AD it became important as the capital of the Frankish Merovingian kings. The city started to develop as a cultural center during the reign of Charlemagne (764–814), but soon after it came under the devastating attacks of the Norsemen. The city was burned in 845 and again in 856 and 866. Finally in 885 its rebuilt walls and fortified bridges across the Seine halted the Vikings.

With the accession of Hugh Capet in 987, Paris became acknowledged as the center of the remnant of the royal domain, the ÎLE DE FRANCE, and expanded along with the fortunes of the French monarchy. After his defeat at FRÉTEVAL and the destruction of most of his traveling archives, King Philip II (1180–1228) made Paris his permanent capital. Soon the *curia regis*, or king's council, expanded into the *Parlément*, which began to meet at Paris under Louis IX (1214–70). The first known meeting of the Estates General was held here under Philip IV in 1302.

The 12th and 13th centuries saw the blossoming of the city's economic and cultural life as French court circles, wandering scholars, and members of the monastic and cathedral schools mingled together in the city. At first the schools were a center of the liberal arts, but with the introduction of Aristotle's recovered works, the University of Paris, chartered in 1200, became the European center of the new logical, theological, and scientific studies called Scholasticism. Paris became the home of such scholars as Abélard, Albert the Great, Thomas Aquinas, Jean Buridian, and Nicolas of Cusa. The Gothic cathedral of Nôtre Dame, the gem-like Sainte Chapelle, the fortress-palace of the Louvre, and a new, larger ring of walls were built during this period of growth.

By the Peace of Paris in 1259, King Louis IX had eased the relationship between the French crown and its major vassal, the king of ENGLAND. Under the terms of the treaty King Henry III of England renounced his claims to NORMANDY, MAINE, ANJOU, and POITOU and did personal homage for AQUITAINE and GASCONY. This uncomfortable arrangement eventually led to the Hundred Years War of 1337 to 1453 between the two countries. During this period the city suffered the ravages of the Black Death in 1348 and of the peasants' revolt called the Jacquerie in 1358.

In 1407, during the virtual civil war between the dukes of BURGUNDY and ARMAGNAC, the craftspeople of Paris overthrew the city's government with the help of the duke of Burgundy. In 1413 they forced the Estates General to enact civil reforms known as the Ordonnance Cabochienne, but the revolt was soon overthrown by the duke of Armagnac. The city was occupied by England from 1419 to 1436 and saw English King Henry V reign as king of France. In the Wars of Religion of 1562 to 1598 Paris became the scene of the Massacre of St. Bartholomew's Day in 1572 in which French Protestants were slaughtered by the Catholics.

As the cradle of the outstanding achievements of the French classical period, Paris in the late 17th and 18th centuries came to be the acknowledged cultural center of Europe. The French court, which moved to nearby VERSAILLES in 1682, was a model for foreign monarchs and the arbiter of fashions of every kind. By the 18th century Paris had become the second-largest city in Europe, after LONDON. The Peace of Paris, which ended the worldwide Seven Years War, was signed here in 1763. During this period the city became the center of the Enlightenment as its salons played host to the Philosophes and Encyclopaedists, thinkers like Montesquieu (1689–1755), Voltaire (1694–1778), Rousseau (1712–78), Diderot (1713–84), and Condorcet (1743–94).

Paris played a key role in the French Revolution and centered some of the principal events of the period: the storming of the Bastille on July 14, 1789, the meeting of the National Assembly from October 1789 to September 1791, the Paris Commune of 1792, the execution of the king and queen in 1793, and the Terror of 1793/94. Paris was also the seat of the revolutionary Jacobin party and of the Directory of 1795 to 1799. Under Napoleon I the city became the focal point of a considerable empire and was suitably embellished. After Napoleon's defeat at WATERLOO in 1815 it was occupied by the Allies, who also met here in 1814/15 to forge the Peace of Paris.

With industrialization, Paris expanded rapidly in the 19th century. The resulting social and political problems, allied with democratic ideals, brought about revolutions here in 1830 and 1848 that were significant for all of Europe. Under Napoleon III the city began to assume its modern aspect, thanks largely to the work of Baron Haussmann, who constructed the wide radiating boulevards and circular plazas for which Paris is famous. In 1856 another Peace of Paris settled the Crimean War. During the Franco-Prussian War of 1870/71 there was a bitter four-month siege of the city by PRUSSIA, during which the Parisians set up a republic, the Commune. After the withdrawal of the Prussians, bloodshed and atrocities on both sides marked the suppression of the Commune, many of the leaders of which were the new socialists.

In the 20th century Paris was the scene of the Peace of Paris in 1919, which settled World War I with five treaties, the most famous of which is the Treaty of Versailles. During World War II the city was occupied by the Germans from 1940 to 1944, but suffered only slight damage, escaping total annihilation when German officers refused Hitler's order to leave the city in ashes. The Paris Peace Conference of 1946 assembled the Allied victors of that war. The headquarters of NATO from 1950 to 1967, Paris was the scene of unrest among students and workers in 1968 that nearly caused the fall of the Fifth Republic. Today the city's old aspect has changed somewhat with the appearance of new skyscrapers and expressways along the banks of the Seine.

PARKERSBURG (United States) Manufacturing city in W WEST VIRGINIA, at the confluence of the Ohio and Little Kanawha rivers, approx. 65 mi N of Charleston. Settled in 1773, it was incorporated in 1820. Nearby BLENNERHASSET ISLAND was the scene of

Aaron Burr's conspiracy in 1805 to form a Southwest empire.

PARKINSON'S FERRY. See MONONGAHELA.

PARMA (Italy) Commercial and industrial town, capital of Parma province, Emilia-Romagna region, 75 mi SE of Milan, N Italy. Founded as a Roman city in 183 BC as a station on the AEMILIAN WAY, it had previously been occupied by Etruscans and Celts. It was made a bishopric in the fourth century AD and was a Ghibelline republic from the 11th to 14th centuries. It was added to the PAPAL STATES in 1531. It came under the rule of the Farnese line by papal bestowal in 1545 as part of the duchy of Parma and PIACENZA, which in the 18th century passed to the house of Bourbon-Parma until 1801. Ruled by the French from 1815 to 1859 it became part of the kingdom SARDINIA in 1860, then of united Italy. It was severely damaged by Allied bombings during World War II. It was the home of a famous painting school after the arrival of Correggio c.1520 and produced the painter Parmigianino. Palazzo della Pilotta was built for the Farnese c.1585 to 1622 and restored after 1944. The city also has a 11th-century cathedral and a university founded in 1064. The conductor Arturo Toscanini was born here in 1867.

PARNASSÓS. See PARNASSUS.

PARNASSUS [*Greek:* **Parnassós**] (Greece) Mountain, N of the Gulf of Corinth, central Greece. It was sacred to Apollo, Dionysus, and the Muses in antiquity. DELPHI is located at its foot, between its flanks called the "Shining Rocks," and the sacred Castalian Spring is on its slopes. The mountain has long been a favorite subject of painters and poets.

PARNU [**Pernov, Pyarnu**] [*German:* **Pernau**] (USSR) Industrial port, ESTONIAN SSR, on Parnu Bay. Founded in 1251 by the Livonian Knights, it later joined the HANSEATIC LEAGUE. It was occupied by SWEDEN in the 17th century and was taken by Peter the Great of RUSSIA in 1710. It was incorporated into an independent Estonia in 1918.

PAROPAMISUS. See HINDU KUSH.

PÁROS (Greece) Island in the AEGEAN SEA, in the CYCLADES Islands, 6 mi W of Naxos. Its marble was a favorite material of ancient sculptors. Founded by Ionians from Athens, it flourished as a maritime and commercial center of the Aegean from the seventh century BC until 479 BC. At that time it was captured by ATHENS during the Persian Wars. One of the Arundel marbles, the Parian Chronicle, an inscription recounting pre-Hellenistic events, was discovered here in 1627.

PARRAL. See HIDALGO DEL PARRAL.

PARRAMATTA (Australia) City, near Sydney, New South Wales, SE Australia. Founded in 1788 and incorporated in 1861, it is Australia's second-oldest settlement.

PARRAS. See PARRAS DE LA FUENTE.

PARRAS DE LA FUENTE [**Parras**] (Mexico) Wine-producing center in S Coahuila state, approx. 120 mi WSW of Monterrey, N Mexico. It was occupied in 1846 by U.S. forces during the Mexican War. When FRANCE intervened in Mexican affairs in the 19th century, a French force met defeat at the hands of the Mexicans in a battle fought here in 1866.

PARRIS ISLAND (United States) Island, part of the SEA ISLANDS chain, off the S coast of SOUTH CAROLINA, S of Port Royal Island. A U.S. Marine Corps training station was established here in 1915.

PARROT'S BEAK (Kampuchea) Region of SE Kampuchea, formerly Cambodia. Communist Vietnamese forces used the region as a military staging area for raids on SAIGON and the Mekong Delta region during the VIETNAM War. South Vietnamese and U.S. troops invaded the stronghold in April 1970. The invasion and bombings of a third country by U.S. forces caused a massive outcry in the United States and calls for an investigation and the resignation of then President Richard M. Nixon.

PARRSBORO (Canada) Lumbering port town, Cumberland county, NOVA SCOTIA, on the N shore of Minas Bay, 119 mi NW of Halifax. It was once a noted ship-building center. Many important geological discoveries have been made here, including one of fossilized animal footprints.

PARR TOWN AND CARLETON. See SAINT JOHN.

PARRY ISLANDS. See QUEEN ELIZABETH ISLANDS.

PARS. See FARS.

PARSA. See PERSEPOLIS.

PARSNIP RIVER (Canada) River, rising in E central BRITISH COLUMBIA, flowing NW to join the Finlay River and going on to form the PEACE RIVER. It was discovered in 1793 by Sir Alexander Mackenzie during the first overland journey across North America north of Mexico, ending at the Pacific Ocean. The Parsnip subsequently became an important route used by fur traders.

PARTHENOPE. See NAPLES.

PARTHENOPEAN REPUBLIC. See NAPLES.

PARTHIA [*ancient:* **Regnum Parthorum**] (Iran, Iraq) Ancient country of W Asia, approximately the same as modern KHORASAN province, NE Iran. It was part of the Assyrian and Persian empires before being taken by Alexander the Great in 334/33 BC. After the end of the SELEUCID EMPIRE, the Arsaces dynasty founded a new Parthian kingdom c.250 BC, which flourished in the first century BC but later fell to Ardashir, the first Sassanid ruler of PERSIA, in 226 AD. In its greatest days between c.65 and 150 AD the Parthian empire stretched from the EUPHRATES RIVER on the west to the OXUS RIVER on the east and challenged the power of the Romans in the East. It fought with Rome over ARMENIA between 53 and 63 and stalemated a Roman invasion in 114 and 115.

PARTHIAN EMPIRE. See PARTHIA, PERSIA.

PASADENA (United States) Industrial city in SE TEXAS, 10 mi S of Houston. Founded in 1895 and incorporated in 1929, it was the site of Gen. Antonio Santa Anna's capture in 1836 following the battle of

SAN JACINTO, a turning point of the Texas Revolution.

PASAI. See INDONESIA.

PASARGADAE (Iran) Ruins of an ancient city in PERSIA, 54 mi NE of Persepolis. Cyrus the Great founded his capital here, where he had defeated Astyages in 550 BC. In 522 BC, after Darius I the Great came to power, it was succeeded by PERSEPOLIS as the dynastic home. Alexander the Great captured it in 336 BC. The ruins include a temple, a palace, and the impressive tomb of Cyrus.

PASAY (Philippines) City in Rizal province, LUZON, on Manila Bay. It was almost destroyed by Japanese attacks on the city in December 1941 during World War II.

PASCAGOULA (United States) Commercial and resort city in SE MISSISSIPPI, on the Mississippi Sound, 18 mi E of Biloxi. It was founded in 1634. A 19th-century lumbering center, it was incorporated in 1907. The homes of Adm. David Farragut and poet Henry Wadsworth Longfellow, who resided here in 1850, are in the city, as is the Old Spanish Fort, built in 1718, around which Pascagoula developed.

PASCO (United States) Commercial river city, at the junction of the Columbia and Snake rivers, 185 mi SE of Seattle, SE WASHINGTON. Founded in 1880 and incorporated in 1891, it was developed as a supply center during World War II for the nearby HANFORD Works, constructed by the Atomic Energy Commission.

PAS-DE-CALAIS (France) Maritime department in NE France, on the STRAIT OF DOVER. A battleground through much of French history, the department has an old fortified town called Petit-Fort-Philippe and a fortified medieval castle at St. Pol. It was occupied by GERMANY in 1940 and 1944 and suffered from heavy fighting in both world wars. See also ARRAS and BOULOGNE.

PASSAIC [*former:* **Acquackanonk**] (United States) Industrial city in NE NEW JERSEY, on the PASSAIC RIVER, 4 mi S of Paterson. It was settled by Dutch traders in 1678 and incorporated in 1873. Washington crossed the Passaic River at this point during his retreat of 1776 through the state during the American Revolution. Several important labor strikes have occurred here, especially in 1926.

PASSAIC RIVER (United States) River, approx. 80 mi long, which rises near Morristown in NE NEW JERSEY and follows a winding course, first NE and then S, to Newark Bay and the city of NEWARK. The Passaic has played a role in both the military history and the industrial development of the nation. At the city of PASSAIC, George Washington led the Continental Army across the river as he retreated from New York City in 1776, pursued by Lord Cornwallis and his British troops. The river has supplied both water and power to its region, most importantly at PATERSON. Here are the Great Falls, 70 ft high, around which Alexander Hamilton, Washington's secretary of the treasury, organized a company in 1791 to use the water power and to create America's first important industrial center; the first step in the nation's road to independence in manufac-

turing. In 1970 the area around the falls was designated a national historic site. Poet William Carlos Williams used the course of the river as a metaphor in his poem, *Paterson*, published between 1946 and 1958.

PASSARO, CAPE. See PASSERO, CAPE.

PASSAROWITZ. See POŽAREVAC.

PASSAU [*ancient:* **Bojodurum, Castra Batava**] (West Germany) Commercial city in BAVARIA, SE West Germany, 93 mi NE of Munich, at the confluence of the Danube, Inn, and Ilz rivers. Of ancient Celtic origin, it was once a Roman outpost and was made an episcopal see in 738 AD. A religious center in the Middle Ages, it was the site of the signing of the Treaty of Passau in 1552, leading to the religious freedom of the German states. There are a 15th-century cathedral, a 14th-century city hall, a baroque palace, and an eighth-century Benedictine monastery in this city.

Passau, a major port on the Danube, with its Oberhaus Castle. A powerful episcopal see in the early Middle Ages, Passau is associated with the German Nibelungen legend.

PASSCHENDAELE (Belgium) Commune in West Flanders province, NW Belgium. Heavy fighting occurred here in October and November 1917 during World War I.

PASSERO, CAPE [Cape Passaro] [*ancient:* **Pachynus Promontorium**] (Italy) Cape, SE SICILY, projecting into the Mediterranean Sea. In a naval battle here on Aug. 11, 1718 during the War of the Quadruple Alliance an entire Spanish fleet was destroyed by the British under Adm. George Byng. The British landed here on July 10, 1943, initiating their Sicilian invasion during World War II.

PASSO DEL BRENNERO. See BRENNER PASS.

PASTO (Colombia) Commercial city, capital of Nariño department, at the foot of the Galeras volcano, SW Colombia. Founded in 1539 by a Spanish conquistador, it was a royalist stronghold during the struggle for independence from SPAIN until this was achieved in 1819. It was occupied by ECUADOR in 1831 but gained separate status in the following year by the terms of a peace treaty signed here. There are many colonial churches in the city.

PATAGONIA (Argentina, Chile) Wild region in South America, mostly in extreme S Argentina. It was explored by Magellan in 1520, but hostile natives discouraged settlement in the next two centuries. The area was visited by Charles Darwin in the mid-19th century during the voyage of the *Beagle*. Following the lead of the Argentine General Julio Roca, Europeans began ranching in the region in the late 19th century.

PATALIPUTRA. See PATNA.

PATAN [Pattan] (India) Town in Gujarat, on the Saraswati River, 65 mi NNW of Ahmadabad, W India. It is located on the site of Anhilwara, the ancient GUJARAT capital, captured by Mahmud of GHAZNI in 1024 AD. Many Jain temples housing important Jain manuscripts are here.

PATAN [Lalitpur] (Nepal) City in central Nepal, 5 mi S of Katmandu, on the Bagmatti River. Founded in the seventh century AD, it became the capital of a local kingdom in the 17th century. It was plundered in 1768 by Prithvi Narayan Shah and the Gurkhas and declined steadily thereafter. There are a palace and several Buddhist temples in the city.

PATANI. See PATTANI.

PATAN SOMNATH. See SOMNATH.

PATARA (Turkey) City of ancient LYCIA, S Asia Minor, just E of the mouth of the Xanthus River, on the Mediterranean Sea. An ancient port, it was a Dorian colony and a center of the worship of Apollo. St. Paul came to the city, as mentioned in the New Testament book of Acts 21:1. See also XANTHUS.

PATAVIUM. See PADUA.

PATAY (France) Town, Loiret department, N central France, NW of Orléans. During the Hundred Years War, Joan of Arc won a major victory over the English here on June 18, 1429, shortly after their unsuccessful siege of ORLÉANS.

PATERNÒ (Italy) Town in Catania province, E SICILY, on the S slope of MT ETNA, 12 mi WNW of Catania. An 11th-century castle was rebuilt here in the 14th century. It is probably the site of ancient Hybla. It was heavily bombed during the Sicilian campaign of World War II, when it was taken by the British in August 1943.

PATERSON (United States) Industrial city in N NEW JERSEY, on the PASSAIC RIVER, 14 mi N of Newark. It was founded on a site chosen by Alexander Hamilton in 1791 for the development of independent American industry. The first Colt revolvers (1835) and the first successful submarine (1881) were built in this city, which became the silk center of the world in the second half of the 19th century. There were several serious labor strikes here, especially in the 1930's. There are many historical buildings and restorations here, evoking life and society during the Industrial Revolution.

PATIALA [Puttiala] (India) Manufacturing city in N India, approx. 125 mi NW of New Delhi. It is the foremost of three Phulkian centers in PUNJAB. Founded by a Sikh chieftain c.1765, it came under British protection in 1809. The capital of the former state of Patiala, it was incorporated into Punjab in 1956. It is still a major Sikh center and was the seat of the maharajahs of Patiala.

PATMO. See PÁTMOS.

PÁTMOS [Patmos] [*Italian:* **Patmo**] (Greece) An island of the DODECANESE, approx. 28 mi SSW of Samos, in the Aegean Sea, SE Greece. St. John supposedly wrote the Apocalypse or Book of Revelation during his exile here c.95 AD. The 11th-century monastery of St. John, located on the island, has a valuable library of early Christian manuscripts.

PATNA [*ancient:* **Pataliputra;** *former:* **Putna**] (India) Commercial center, city, and capital of both BIHAR state and Patna division, on the GANGES RIVER, 290 mi NW of Calcutta, NE India. It was founded in the fifth century BC as Pataliputra. It became the Mauryan capital of Asoka between 270 and 30 BC and is the site of this emperor's impressive palace, in addition to having many other ruins from the period. Abandoned by the fourth century AD, it regained importance as Putna, the 16th-century viceregal capital of the Moguls. A 15th-century mosque remains from this time. The place of Guru Gobind Singh's birth in 1666, it is still a sacred Sikh city. See also MAURYA EMPIRE, MOGUL EMPIRE.

PATOS (Venezuela) Island in W Dragon's Mouth, a strait between NW Trinidad and NE Venezuela. Venezuela was given sole possession of the island by GREAT BRITAIN in 1942, ending a century and a half of conflict between the two nations.

PATRAE. See PÁTRAI.

PÁTRAI [Patras] [*ancient:* **Colonia Augusta Aroë Patrensis, Patrae**] (Greece) Port city on the Gulf of Pátrai, capital of Achaea department, NW PELOPONNESUS, S Greece. An important commercial center by the fifth century BC, it joined with ATHENS in the Peloponnesian Wars and was an important member of the Second Achaean League in the third century BC. It was revived and colonized by Roman Emperor Augustus late in the first century BC. The Apostle Andrew preached here and may have been martyred here in the first century AD.

The city became commercially important again in the Middle Ages. It was besieged by the Saracens in 805, and was taken by the Latins in 1205, after the fall of

CONSTANTINOPLE to the Crusaders on the Fourth Crusade. The Latins founded an archbishopric and a barony here, which was sold to VENICE in 1408. The city fell to a revived BYZANTINE EMPIRE in 1429, and in 1460 it was taken by the OTTOMAN EMPIRE. The first Greek city to revolt against the Turks, in 1770, it was also the first to revolt in the Greek War of Independence, but was destroyed by the Turks in 1821. The city was rebuilt eight years later. See also ACHAEA.

PATRAS. See PÁTRAI.

PATRIMONY OF ST. PETER. See PAPAL STATES.

PATTAN. See PATAN.

PATTANI [Patani] (Thailand) Town and capital of Pattani province in SW Thailand, 50 mi ESE of Songkhla. The medieval seat of Sailendra power on the MALAY PENINSULA, it was one of the first ports in Siam (Thailand) to be opened to Portuguese trade in the 16th century. It rebelled several times against the royal courts of AYUTTHAYA and BANGKOK. It was given provincial status in the 19th century.

PÁTZCUARO (Mexico) Lake and town in Michoacán state, W Mexico. It was a center of the brilliant pre-Columbian Tarascan Indian civilization, which the Aztecs could not conquer. The lake's shores are still dotted with their villages.

PAU (France) Tourist center, city, and capital of Pyrénées-Atlantiques department, on the Gave de Pau, 109 mi S of Bordeaux, SW France. Founded by the viscounts of BÉARN in the 11th century AD, it became their capital in the 15th century and the royal residence of NAVARRE after 1512. It was a center of learning in the 16th century. Henry IV was born here in 1553. There is a 12th-century castle here. Charles XIV, Bernadotte, of Sweden was born in the city in 1763.

PAUGUSSET. See DERBY.

PAULSBORO (United States) City in SW NEW JERSEY, 10 mi SSW of Camden. It was settled in 1681. There is a battleground nearby, where the colonists and Hessians clashed during the American Revolution. Shortly after the war it was the headquarters of a notorious group of counterfeiters.

PAUTANIA. See KYUSTENDIL.

PAVIA [*ancient:* **Ticinum;** *former:* **Papia**] (Italy) Manufacturing town, capital of Pavia province, LOMBARDY region, 19 mi S of Milan, N Italy. It was an important Roman municipality and, in the sixth century AD, the capital of the Lombards. Here were crowned Charlemagne as king of Lombardy in 774, Berengar as king of Italy in 888, and Frederick I Barbarossa as king of Italy in 1155. The city was Ghibelline in the disputes between pope and emperor in the 12th and 13th centuries.

It fell to the Visconti in 1359 and flourished in the following centuries under their rule. Its 15th-century cathedral, 14th-century castle, monastery (Certosa di Pavia), and church were all built during this era. At the Battle of Pavia in 1525 Holy Roman Emperor Charles V defeated Francis I of FRANCE nearby during the Italian Wars, which ruined much of the city. It was ruled by

several European powers before its liberation in 1859 by the kingdom of PIEDMONT. Lanfranc (1005–89), archbishop of CANTERBURY in England and noted scholar, was born here. See also HOLY ROMAN EMPIRE.

PAVLODAR (USSR) Agricultural town, capital of Pavlodar oblast, NE KAZAKH SSR, on the Irtysh River, approx. 240 mi SE of Omsk. It was founded in 1720 as a Russian fort and was incorporated as a town in 1861. It became the capital of the oblast in 1938.

PAVLOVSK [*former:* **Slutsk**] (USSR) Resort town, Leningrad oblast, Russian SFSR, approx. 15 mi S of LENINGRAD. Catherine the Great founded the town in 1777. It became the royal summer residence of St. Petersburg, now Leningrad, in the 19th century and was the scene of concerts conducted by Johann Strauss and other famous musicians during the same century. It was heavily damaged during World War II. It has many fine examples of Russian classical architecture, including its 18th-century palace and park pavilions and the Pil Tower.

PAWHUSKA (United States) City, approx. 40 mi from Tulsa, N OKLAHOMA. In 1906 it was given to the Osage Indians, who have since profited from the discovery of oil here. There is a fine museum of Osage culture in the city.

PAWNEE (United States) Agricultural city in N OKLAHOMA, 30 mi SSE of Ponca City. The Pawnee Indians left their homelands in Nebraska to settle here and were granted the right to individual ownership of property. The seat of the Pawnee Agency was established in 1876; the city was settled in 1893.

PAWTUCKET (United States) Industrial city, 4 mi NE of Providence, on the Blackstone River, at Pawtucket Falls, N RHODE ISLAND. Originally deeded in 1638 to Roger Williams, the area was a colonial center of religious freedom. Settled in 1671 and incorporated in 1851, it became a textile center after Samuel Slater built and operated the nation's first successful water-powered cotton mill here in 1790. The mill now exists as a museum.

PAX AUGUSTA. See BADAJOZ.

PAX JULIA. See BEJA, Portugal.

PAYERNE [*German:* **Peterlingen**] (Switzerland) Town in Vaud canton, approx. 10 mi W of Fribourg. Bertha of Burgundy, the wife of Robert II of France, founded an abbey in the town in the 10th century.

PAYSANDÚ (Uruguay) Commercial city and port, capital of Paysandú department, on the Uruguay River, 210 mi NW of Montevideo, W Uruguay. It was founded in 1772 by a Christian missionary and his Indian converts.

PAZARDZHIK [*former:* **Tatar Pazardzhik**] (Bulgaria) Commercial center, city, and capital of Pazardzhik province, on the Maritsa River, S central Bulgaria. Controlled by the Turks from the 15th to 19th centuries, it has an old church with an impressive store of icons and religious artifacts.

PAZIN [*German:* **Mitterburg;** *Italian:* **Pisino**] (Yugoslavia) Village and commune in NW Yugoslavia, S central ISTRIA peninsula, 27 mi NE of Pula. A part of Italy until 1947, Pazin is an ancient cultural center of the Istrian Croats. There is a 16th-century castle and a cathedral built in 1266.

PAZYRYK (USSR) An eastern extension of the area once occupied by the Scythians. It lies in the Gorno-Altai region of southern SIBERIA. In this arctic area the tombs of their chieftains, from c.500 to 600 BC, have been discovered completely frozen, so that archaeologists have been able to preserve their clothes, food, weapons, and trade goods. These people were nomadic traders who were in contact with the great civilizations on their borders, from CHINA to HUNGARY and south to the upper limits of MESOPOTAMIA. See also SCYTHIA.

PEABODY [*former:* **South Danvers**] (United States) Industrial city, 18 mi N of Boston, NE MASSACHUSETTS. Settled in the 1630's, it was originally part of SALEM and was incorporated as South Danvers in 1855. In 1868 it was renamed in honor of George Peabody, the philanthropist who was born and buried in the city. Glass-making began here in 1638, and tanning was introduced shortly after the American Revolution. The tanning industry is still operating here.

PEACE RIVER (Canada) River, 1,195 mi long, formed by the confluence of the Finlay and PARSNIP RIVERS, E central BRITISH COLUMBIA, flowing E into Alberta, then NE to join the Slave River. Discovered c.1775 by the American fur trader Peter Pond, it was first explored by Sir Alexander MacKenzie in 1792/93. A log fort built by MacKenzie at the present town, named Peace River, was the first settlement along its banks. It was an important fur-trading route in the 19th century.

PEACH TREE CREEK (United States) Creek in GEORGIA, joining the Chattahoochee River, near Atlanta. Gen. John Hood and his Confederate troops were unable to stop Gen. William Sherman's march to ATLANTA here during the Civil War. The Union army continued on its way, following three days of battle between July 20 and 22, 1864.

PEA RIDGE (United States) City in NW ARKANSAS. The Union Army under Gen. Samuel R. Curtis won its first victory west of the Mississippi here between March 6 and 8, 1862 during the Civil War. The battle was initiated by Gen. Earl Van Dorn, and his Confederate troops.

PEARL COAST (Panama) Coastal region in the NE, along the Isthmus of Darien. Alonso de Ojeda of Spain received a settlement grant for this area in 1508. Its first successful community was established two years later at DARIÉN with the help of Vasco Balboa and Francisco Pizarro.

PEARL HARBOR (United States) Inlet on the S coast of OAHU Island, HAWAII, 6 mi W of Honolulu, near the Pacific Ocean. The United States was granted permission in 1887 by the kingdom of Hawaii to use the harbor as a repair station. It was not until after Hawaii's annexation in 1900 that a naval base was constructed here. It was attacked on Dec. 7, 1941 by Japanese planes. Thousands of military personnel were killed or wounded, several battleships sunk, and the Pacific Fleet crippled. The following day the United States declared war on JAPAN, thus entering World War II.

PEARY LAND [**Pearyland**] (Greenland) Region of N Greenland, on the Arctic Ocean. It was first explored by Adolphus Greely and James Lockwood in 1881/82 but was named after Adm. Robert E. Peary who explored it in 1892 and 1900.

PEĆ [**Pech, Petch**] [*Turkish:* **Ipek**] (Yugoslavia) Agricultural town in SERBIA, S Yugoslavia, approx. 75 mi NW of Skopje. It was the seat of the Orthodox Serbian patriarchs from 1346 to 1766. There are Turkish mosques and a notable 13th-century cathedral in the town.

PECH. See PEĆ.

PECHENGA [*Finnish:* **Petsamo**] (USSR) Territory forming a 135-mi-long strip, also a copper-mining port and village, in Murmansk oblast, Russian SFSR, on the ARCTIC Ocean, 60 mi W of Murmansk. The village was first settled by Russian monks and became a Muscovite trading port in the 16th century. FINLAND took the region, known popularly as the Pechenga Corridor, in 1920 when it became independent of the USSR. Its warm-water port was the object of the USSR's interest, and it regained the territory in 1939. It became part of the USSR again in 1944 following German occupation of 1940 to 1944 and use of the port as a military base during World War II.

PECOS (United States) Oil-producing city in W TEXAS, 40 mi S of the New Mexico border, on the PECOS RIVER. Founded in the 1880's as a cattle town, it was incorporated in 1903. Its annual rodeo, which began in 1883, was the first in the world. There is a museum dedicated to the lawman, Judge Roy Bean.

PECOS RIVER [**Rio Pecos**] (United States) River, 500 mi long, rising in E New Mexico and emptying into the RIO GRANDE in SW Texas. In the early days of settlement in the Southwest, in the second half of the 19th century, the Pecos became an unofficial dividing line between law-abiding civilization and the Wild West. The area identified as "west of the Pecos" was first tamed by the famous lawman, Judge Roy Bean. See PECOS.

PÉCS [*German:* **Fünfkirchen**] (Hungary) Coal-mining center, city in Baranya county, 106 mi W of Budapest, S Hungary. It was once a Celtic settlement. Emperor Hadrian (117–138 AD) made it the capital of the Roman province of Lower PANNONIA. The Hungarians took it in the ninth century AD and made it an episcopal see by 1009. In 1367 the first Hungarian university was founded here. Occupied by the Turks from 1543 to 1686, it became a free city in 1780. There is an 11th-century cathedral here, a palace, and former Turkish mosques.

PEDDA VEGI. See ELURU.

PEEKSKILL (United States) Commercial city in SE NEW YORK State, on the HUDSON RIVER, 41 mi N of New York City. Founded in 1764 and incorporated in 1816, it was strategically significant during the American Revolution and was burned by the British in 1777. St. Peter's Church of 1767 has been restored. Camp Smith, a National Guard center, is in the area.

PEEL (England) Resort town on the W coast of the ISLE OF MAN, 6 mi NW of Douglas. A medieval chapel dedicated to St. Patrick is here, as are the ruins of an old castle and cathedral.

PEENEMÜNDE (East Germany) Village on USE-DOM Island, at the mouth of the Peene River, 58 mi NW of Szczecin (Stettin). During World War II it was a major German rocket research and experimentation center. When the V-1 rocket bomb was being developed here, the village was heavily bombed by the Allies on Aug. 18, 1943. The raid killed many scientists and delayed use of the bomb. The village was captured by the USSR in April 1945.

PEGASAE. See IOLCUS, VOLOS.

PE GEWAT. See CANOPUS.

PEGU (Burma) Town, capital of Pegu division, 47 mi NE of Rangoon. Founded by the Mons *c.*825 AD, it was the capital of Burma for many centuries. The Talaing capital was established here in the 18th century and was destroyed by the Burmese in 1757. It became a British protectorate in 1852 and was occupied by JAPAN during most of World War II. There are many ancient Buddhist pagodas in the city, including the famous Shwemawdaw.

PEHTANG. See PEI-T'ANG.

PEI-HAI [Pakhoi] [*former:* **Packhoi**] (China) Port in SW Kwangtung province, SE China. Located in the area of China's most bountiful pearl beds, it was opened as a treaty port in 1877.

PEIPING. See PEKING.

PEIPSI. See PEIPUS LAKE.

PEIPUS, LAKE [*Estonian:* **Peipsi**; *Russian:* **Chudskoye Ozero**] (USSR) Lake in E ESTONIAN SSR and W Pskov oblast, NW USSR. The Teutonic Knights were defeated by Alexander Nevsky on the iced-over lake in a great battle fought in 1242. It was later the scene of heavy World War II fighting.

PEI-T'ANG [Pehtang] (China) Town, 10 mi N of Ta-ku, on the Gulf of Chihli, Hopeh province, NE China. British and French expeditions landed here in 1860 in an effort to take TAKU, one year after a peace treaty was signed in this town.

PEIWAR KOTAL. See PEIWAR PASS.

PEIWAR PASS [Peiwar Kotal] (Afghanistan, Pakistan) Pass through the W Safed Koh mountains, connecting NW Pakistan with Afghanistan, SE of Kabul. Lord Roberts defeated the Afghans here during the Second Afghan War in December 1878.

PEKALONGAN (Indonesia) Important port and city in N central JAVA, capital of Pekalongan regency, 55 mi W of Semarang. A Dutch fort was built here in 1753. The Buddha Stairs in the city have survived from the Hindu period.

PEKAN (Malaysia) Commercial port and town, on the Pahang River, E Pahang state. Formerly the residence of the sultan, it was the capital of PAHANG until 1898.

PEKIN (United States) Commercial city in central ILLINOIS, on the Illinois River, 10 mi S of Peoria. Incorporated in 1839, it was settled in 1824 by pioneers from Virginia, Kentucky, and Tennessee. Its courthouse was the scene of cases argued by Abraham Lincoln as a young lawyer.

PEKING [*former:* **Cambaluc, Peiping**] (China) City in NE China, the capital of the People's Republic of China and its political and cultural center, as well as an important industrial and financial hub. While the region has been inhabited since prehistoric times, Peking was the site of a number of cities with various names dating from 723 BC. In the second century BC it was the capital of the Yen kingdom, and the Han dynasty (206 BC–220 AD) built a new town here. Under the Khitan Tatars, Peking was an important city from the 10th to 12th centuries. Its greatest period, however, came after Kublai Khan, the MONGOL conqueror, deposed the Sung dynasty and between 1260 and 1290 built a new city on the site, which he called CAMBALUC. It was this city that the famous traveler from VENICE, Marco Polo, reached in 1275. Peking, under that name, was the capital of China from 1421 to 1911. It was captured in 1644 by the Manchus from MANCHURIA who established the Ch'ing, or Manchu, dynasty, the last in China.

In the 19th century European nations began to put pressure on China for trade and other concessions, and in 1860 this led to a battle between the Chinese and the British and French at Pa-li-ch'iao, a village near Peking. The Europeans won and received the right to station diplomats at Peking's imperial court. This and other signs of European arrogance resulted in the Boxer Rebellion, led by an antiforeign secret society, which in June 1900 besieged the foreign quarter of the city. The siege was lifted in August by an international military force that fought its way into the city. Peking changed hands several times during the civil wars that ensued after China became a republic in 1911. The Second Sino-Japanese War began at the MARCO POLO BRIDGE, nine miles southwest of Peking, on July 7, 1937 when a clash between troops of the two nations was used by the Japanese as an excuse to occupy the city. In January 1949 Peking was taken by the Chinese communists, who made it their capital. In the late 1960's and early 1970's Peking became the focus of the Cultural Revolution. In February 1972 the city hosted a Summit Meeting between U.S. President Richard Nixon and Mao Zedong and Premier Zhou Enlai, which resulted in a communique promising closer relations between the two countries.

Peking consists of two districts that once were completely walled and had monumental gates. They are the Outer or Chinese City and the Inner or Tatar City. Within the Inner City is the Forbidden City where the emperor lived, the Imperial City with its government offices, and the legation quarter for foreign diplomats. The Forbidden City is now a museum. One of Peking's many interesting and spectacular sights is the Temple

The merchants' quarter of old Peking, imperial capital of China. Still China's capital, Peking today preserves the magnificent Forbidden City, an imperial palace built in the 15th century.

of Heaven, dating from the 15th century, with a white marble altar.

PELAGIAN ISLANDS [*Italian:* **Isole Pelagie**] (Italy) A small group of mostly uninhabited Mediterranean islands S of Sicily, between Malta and Tunisia, in Agrigento province, Italy. A penal colony once existed on one of the islands, LAMPEDUSA. The islands were captured by the Allies in June 1943 during World War II.

PELÉE, MOUNT [*French:* **Montagne Pelée**] (France) Volcano on N MARTINIQUE Island, part of the Windward Islands, in the French WEST INDIES. It erupted in 1792, 1851, 1902, and 1929. In the 1902 eruption the town of SAINT PIERRE, along with its entire populace of nearly 40,000, was buried, except for one prisoner in a deep dungeon.

PELELIU (United States) Island at the S end of the PALAU group of the CAROLINE ISLANDS, in the W Pacific Ocean, United States Trust Territory. U.S. forces landed on this Japanese stronghold on Sept. 15, 1944 during World War II. Severe fighting and bombings ensued until the Japanese were finally displaced in November.

PELEW. See PALAU ISLANDS.

PELHAM MANOR (United States) Residential suburb of New York City, village in SE NEW YORK State, on LONG ISLAND SOUND. It was settled by Thomas Pell in 1654. The Battle of Pell's Point occurred here in 1776 during the early stages of the American Revolution.

PELLA (Greece) Ruins of an ancient city of Greek MACEDONIA approx. 24 mi NW of modern THESSALONÍKI. The capital of Macedon in the fourth century BC, it declined following the kingdom's conquest by the Romans in 168 BC. It was the birthplace of Alexander the Great in 356 BC. Many ancient buildings have been excavated here. See also MACEDONIAN EMPIRE.

PELLA, Syria. See APAMEA AD ORONTEM.

PELL'S POINT, BATTLE OF. See PELHAM MANOR.

PELOPIA. See AKHISAR.

PELOPÓNNESOS. See PELOPONNESUS.

PELOPONNESUS [*former:* **Morea**; *Greek:* **Pelopónnisos, Pelopónnesos**] (Greece) Region consisting of a peninsula in S Greece linked to central Greece by the Isthmus of Corinth. On the E it is bounded by the Aegean Sea, and on the S and W by the Ionian Sea. Its ancient divisions were ACHAEA, ARCADIA, Argolis, CORINTH, ELIS, and LACONIA and MESSENIA, which made up LACEDAEMONIA. Chief cities included ARGOS, CORINTH, MEGALOPOLIS, and SPARTA.

The original inhabitants were Leleges and Pelasgians, who reputedly built MYCENAE and TIRYNS. In the

14th and 13th centuries BC the Achaeans appeared and by about 1250 BC ruled the region. They were displaced by the Dorians, probably between 1150 BC and and 950 BC. Except for Achaea and Argos, the peninsula participated in the Persian Wars of 500 to 449 BC. The Peloponnesian War of 431 BC to 404 BC not only ruined ATHENS but also left Sparta in control of a land empire that included almost all the peninsula. Spartan power was broken by Epaminondas, a Greek general of THEBES, who defeated the Spartans in 371 BC. However, the kingdom of MACEDON under Philip II (reigned 359–336 BC) overran the Peloponnesus as well as the rest of Greece.

ROME conquered the region in 146 BC and from then until the fourth century AD the Peloponnesus made up the larger part of the province of Achaea. After the division of the ROMAN EMPIRE in 395 AD, the Peloponnesus became part of the BYZANTINE EMPIRE, but during this time it was often invaded by Bulgars, Petchenegs, and Slavs. When the Latin Empire of CONSTANTINOPLE temporarily replaced the Byzantines in 1204, the peninsula, except for some ports held by VENICE, became the principality of Achaia under a noble French family, the Villehardouin, who ruled from 1210 to 1278. This was a period of prosperity and cultural activity, a mixture of Hellenic and French civilizations. The principality then passed to the Angevin dynasty of NAPLES, next to various nobles, and in 1383 to some Navarrese adventurers. Meanwhile, the Byzantines, centered around their despotate of MISTRA, were gradually regaining control of the peninsula, which they achieved in 1432, but by 1460 the Ottoman Turks had crushed the Byzantines here. In the course of wars between Venice and the Turks until 1718, Venice held parts of the region at times and the whole region from 1687 to 1715. Finally, after the Greek war of independence against the Turks from 1821 to 1829, the Peloponnesus became part of a free Greece.

OLYMPIA, in Elis in the northwestern Peloponnesus, was an important center of worship of Zeus, the chief Greek god, and the site of the Olympic Games, which were first staged in 776 BC. BASSAE, EPIDAURUS, and PYLOS are other ancient sites. METHONE, MONEMVASÍA, NAUPLÍA, and PÁTRAI are important medieval centers. KALAMATA in the south is a major port and agricultural center.

PELOPÓNNISOS. See PELOPONNESUS.

PELOTAS (Brazil) Manufacturing and commercial port, city in SE Rio Grande do Sul state, 29 mi NNW of Rio Grande, in S Brazil. Settled by colonists from the AZORES in the late 18th century, it developed commercially in the 19th century as an inland port on the São Goncalo canal. It was founded in 1830 and incorporated in 1835.

PELOUSIOU. See PELUSIUM.

PELUSIUM [*biblical:* **Sin;** *Greek:* **Pelousiou**] (Egypt) Ancient city on a branch of the NILE RIVER; its ruins are E of the Suez Canal, approx. 20 mi SE of modern Port Said, on the Bay of Pelusium. An important frontier post, it was the scene of the Persian victory of Cambyses over Psamtik III in 525 BC. Ro-

man remains have been discovered here. It is said to be the birthplace of the astronomer Claudius Ptolemy of the second century AD.

PEMBA (Tanzania) Agricultural island in NE Tanzania, in the INDIAN OCEAN, E Africa. Settled in the 10th century AD by local traders, it was occupied by the Portuguese in the 16th century and by the Omani Arabs by 1698. In the early 19th century it became part of the sultanate of ZANZIBAR, which passed to GREAT BRITAIN in 1890. It merged with TANGANYIKA in 1964, forming an independent Tanzania.

PEMBINA (United States) City, approx. 22 mi NE of Cavalier, NE NORTH DAKOTA. A trading post established here in 1797 was the first in the state's history. It was also the site of the first pioneer settlement in the state.

PEMBROKE (Canada) Manufacturing town in SE ONTARIO, on Allumette Lake, 98 mi NW of Ottawa. It was the westernmost point of Samuel Sieur de Champlain's exploration of this area in 1613. Settled in the early days of the timber trade it was incorporated in 1858.

PEMBROKE (Wales) Port and tourist center in Dyfed, 42 mi W of Swansea. The earls of Pembroke built fortifications on this site, and the town was used as a base for the English invasion of IRELAND. Here are ruins of an impressive 11th-century castle in which Henry VII was born in 1457 and which fell to Oliver Cromwell during the English Civil War. There is also a 11th-century Benedictine priory in the town.

PEMBROKESHIRE [Pembroke] (Wales) Former county in SW Wales. Many prehistoric megalithic remains have been found here. Conquered by the Normans in the 11th century AD, it is the location of Saint David's Cathedral, one of the most famous in Welsh history. It is now incorporated in Dyfed.

PENANG [Pinang] (Malaysia) A state of Malaysia, MALAY PENINSULA, on the Strait of Malacca. It consists of Penang Island, formerly George Town, and PROVINCE WELLESLEY. The first British settlement in Malaysia, it was ceded to the British East India Company in 1786 by the sultan of KEDAH. The sultan failed to recapture it five years later, and it soon became part of the British colony known as the STRAITS SETTLEMENTS and flourished as a commercial center. It was bombed and captured in 1941 by Japanese forces during World War II. The state joined the Federation of Malay States in 1948.

PENANG ISLAND [Pinang] [*former:* **George Town, Prince of Wales Island**] (Malaysia) Island off the W coast of Malaysia on the Strait of Malacca. With PROVINCE WELLESLEY, a strip of land adjacent to it on the Malay peninsula, it forms the state of Penang. George Town on the island, also known as Penang, is the capital of the province and is Malaysia's chief port. The first British settlement on the MALAY PENINSULA was made here in 1786 by the British East India Company. This was by agreement with the sultan of KEDAH who, however, tried unsuccessfully to retake the island in 1791. The island became part of the British STRAITS

SETTLEMENTS in 1826, of the Malayan Union in 1946, of the Federation of Malaya in 1948, and of the Federation of Malaysia in 1963. The Japanese occupied the island in December 1941 during World War II.

PEN-CH'I [Penhsihu, Penki] (China) Town in S Liaoning province, 48 mi SE of Mukden, NE China. Coal mines, worked here since the 18th century, were exploited and modernized by the Japanese following the Russo-Japanese War of 1904/05. A steel plant was constructed soon after, but both the plant and the coal mines suffered setbacks during World War II. Since the communist takeover in 1949, however, they have been vastly improved.

PENCO. See CONCEPCIÓN.

PENDELIKON [Pentelicus] (Greece) Mountain, 10 mi NE of ATHENS, E central Greece. Its fine marble was quarried in antiquity for use in the construction of many Athenian buildings.

PENDLETON (United States) Trading city in NE OREGON, on the Umatilla River, approx. 209 mi E of Portland. Founded in 1868 and incorporated in 1880, it was originally an important junction on the OREGON TRAIL between Fort WALLA WALLA in Washington and California. It was an important cattle center in the 1870's and 1880's.

PENETANGUISHENE (Canada) Resort town in SE ONTARIO, approx. 84 mi N of Toronto, on an inlet of Georgian Bay. The Jesuits settled here on the site of a Huron Indian community, in 1634. It was an early fur-trading post; its harbor was a fortified British naval station during the War of 1812 to guard the Great Lakes.

P'ENG-HU [*former:* Mako, Makun, Makung] (Taiwan) Town on P'eng-hu Island, PESCADORES, on the Formosa Strait. Utilized by the Japanese as a naval base in World War II, it passed to CHINA after the war and to Taiwan in 1949.

PENGWERN. See SHREWSBURY.

PENHSIHU. See PEN-CH'I.

PENINSULA, THE (United States) A region in SE VIRGINIA, between the James and York rivers. It was an area of intense activity during the Peninsular campaign of April 4 to July 1, 1862 during the Civil War. Directed by the Union armies at RICHMOND to the northwest, the campaign included Gen. Robert E. Lee's offensive at MECHANICSVILLE and battles at GAINES' MILL and MALVERN HILL. The Confederates held off the Union assault.

PENJDEH. See PANJDEH.

PENKI. See PEN-CH'I.

PENMARCH (France) Village in Finistère department, 18 mi SW of Quimper, NW France. Nearby is the site of a port that flourished as a commercial center from the 14th to 16th centuries.

PENNSYLVANIA (United States) Middle Atlantic state in the eastern United States, one of the original 13 colonies and the second to ratify the Constitution, in December 1787. New York State is to the N; New Jersey to the E; Delaware, Maryland, and West Virginia to the S, and Ohio to the W. Lake Erie is on the NW.

In the early 17th century the English, Dutch, and Swedes competed for possession of the DELAWARE RIVER Valley, and the first permanent settlement was made on Tinicum Island in the SCHUYLKILL RIVER in 1643 by Johan Printz, governor of NEW SWEDEN. Another settlement was started at Uppland (now CHESTER), in 1644. The Dutch gained control of the region in 1655, but the English took it from them in 1664. In 1681 Charles II granted what is now Pennsylvania and most of DELAWARE to William Penn, a Quaker, in payment of a debt he owed Penn's father. Charles is said to have named the grant Penn's Woods (in Latin "Pennsylvania") against Penn's wishes.

Penn envisaged the area as a haven for religious dissenters and sent men to lay out PHILADELPHIA, the "City of Brotherly Love." He arrived in 1682 and signed a treaty with the Delaware Indians that achieved a goodwill that was only occasionally disrupted. His constitution called for religious freedom and humane penal laws but left him firmly in control of the government. In 1692 Penn was accused of treason, and the colony was put under New York, but it was restored to Penn in 1694. The colony grew as Germans, locally known as Pennsylvania Dutch, took up eastern farm lands; and the hardy Scotch-Irish went west. Nevertheless, it was badly hit by the French and Indian War. Gen. Edward Braddock's army was routed when it attempted to capture FORT DUQUESNE, modern Pittsburgh, in July 1755. The Quaker-controlled legislature did little to aid the frontier, causing conflict between the proprietary rulers and the settlers.

A more democratic constitution was forced through by western inhabitants when the American Revolution began. In September 1777 Washington's army was forced to retreat after the Battle of BRANDYWINE CREEK, and the British then captured Philadelphia. In October the Americans attacked unsuccessfully at GERMANTOWN, after which Washington led his army to VALLEY FORGE for the dreary winter of 1777/78. In the WYOMING VALLEY Massacre of 1778, many Americans lost their lives to a force of British rangers, Loyalists, and Indians. Philadelphia was host to the two Continental Congresses in 1774 and 1789; the Declaration of Independence was signed there in 1776; the Constitutional Convention met there in 1787; and from 1790 to 1800 it was the capital of the United States.

After the revolution, the Whiskey Rebellion broke out in the western counties in 1794 in protest against a new Federal excise tax, but troops put down the rioting. The state was growing, especially around PITTSBURGH and ERIE, aided by turnpikes (the LANCASTER was the first in 1792), canals, and eventually the railroads. Pennsylvania was a Union state in the Civil War; and one of the decisive battles of the war was fought at GETTYSBURG in July 1863, after which Gen. Robert E. Lee was forced to retreat south.

The second half of the 19th century witnessed a remarkable economic boom, including the discovery of oil in 1859 and the development of such industries as the efficient steel mills of Andrew Carnegie. Industrial growth brought labor troubles between the coal-mine owners and the radical Molly Maguires in the 1870's; between steel mill owners and workers in the HOMESTEAD Strike of 1892, in which there were a number of deaths; between the operators and the anthracite miners in 1902; and in the steel strike of 1919, which the union lost. By 1941, however, the steel mills and the mines were organized, and the unions were strong. The state's economy has been hurt by the decline in coal use since the 1940's, and most recently by the recession of the 1980's, which hit Pennsylvania's industry especially hard.

HARRISBURG is the capital and Philadelphia and Pittsburgh are the largest cities; others are Allentown, Bethlehem, Chester, Erie, Reading, Scranton, and Wilkes-Barre.

PENN YAN (United States) Resort village in W NEW YORK State, on Lake Keuka, approx. 50 mi SE of Rochester. Settled c.1800 and incorporated in 1833, it is the site of the Oliver House and Garrett Chapel. Jemima Wilkinson's Jerusalem colony of 1790 to 1819 was established and operated here.

PENNYCOMEQUICK. See FALMOUTH, England.

PENOBSCOT BAY (United States) Large inlet of the Atlantic Ocean in S MAINE. Claimed for France by Samuel Sieur de Champlain in 1604, its possession was contested by the British, French, and Americans for many years. Trading posts and missions were established here in the colonial era; and it became a shipbuilding center in the 19th century.

PENOBSCOT RIVER (United States) River, 350 mi long, in central MAINE, flowing S into PENOBSCOT BAY. Samuel Sieur de Champlain explored it in 1604, and the Pilgrims of MASSACHUSETTS established a trading post, Pentagoet, on its bay in the 1620's. It marked the border between the French and British possessions in the New World.

PENSACOLA (United States) Manufacturing city in NW FLORIDA, on the Gulf of Mexico, 10 mi E of the Alabama border. Settled by the Spanish in the 16th century, it was captured by U.S. forces under Andrew Jackson in 1814 during the War of 1812. It became part of the United States in 1821 in the Spanish cession of Florida. It was incorporated in 1822. Occupied by the Confederates early in the Civil War, it was taken by Union forces in 1862. There are several old forts here from the 1780's and 1830's.

PENSHURST (England) Village, 4 mi WSW of Tonbridge, Kent. Sir Philip Sidney (1554–86), an illustrious author and diplomat who exemplified Elizabethan court life and manners, was born at the family mansion here.

PENTAPOLIS. See CYRENAICA.

PENTELICUS. See PENDELIKON.

PENTHIÈVRE (France) Former medieval countship in BRITTANY, now included in Côtes-du-Nord department. Lamballe, capital city of its counts from 1134 to 1420, was succeeded by GUINGAMP. Penthièvre became an independent duchy in 1569.

PENTUCKET. See HAVERHILL.

PENYDARREN. See MERTHYR TYDFIL.

PENZA (USSR) Industrial city, capital of Penza oblast, at the confluence of the Penza and Sura rivers, 225 mi W of Kuibyshev. Established in 1666, it was taken during Stenka Razin's revolt in 1670 and E.I. Pugachev's revolt in 1774. It was burned several times. An agricultural center through most of its history, the city was industrialized after the communist revolution.

PENZANCE (England) Resort and seaport in Cornwall, on the ENGLISH CHANNEL, 65 mi WSW of Plymouth. Founded in the 14th century and incorporated in 1614, it flourished as a trading port in the 15th century. It was ravaged by the Spanish in 1595 and was the victim of pirate raids until the 18th century. Scientist Sir Humphry Davy was born here in 1778.

PEOPLES DEMOCRATIC REPUBLIC OF YEMEN. See YEMEN.

PEOPLE'S REPUBLIC OF BULGARIA. See BULGARIA.

PEOPLE'S REPUBLIC OF CHINA. See MIDDLE KINGDOM.

PEORIA [*former:* **Fort Clark**] (United States) Industrial and transportation center, city in NW central ILLINOIS, on the Illinois River, 130 mi SW of Chicago. Fort Crèvecoeur was established here by the French in 1680, and it developed as a trading post. Fort Clark was built here in 1813 during the War of 1812; and Peoria was incorporated in 1845.

PEPPERELLBORO. See SACO.

PEQUONNOCK. See BRIDGEPORT.

PERAEA [**Perea**] A section of ancient PALESTINE, it was part of the earlier region of GILEAD. It formed part of the Tetrarchy of Herod Antipas. In Roman times it was the region east of the JORDAN RIVER, between the SEA OF GALILEE and the DEAD SEA.

PERAK (Malaysia) A state in Malaysia, on the W coast of the MALAY PENINSULA. A vassal state of local powers prior to the 16th century, it was conquered by the Siamese in 1818. Having fallen into anarchy some years later, it became a British protectorate in 1874. In 1896 it joined the Federated Malay States and in 1963 became part of Malaysia. See also THAILAND.

PERCÉ (Canada) Unincorporated resort village on E GASPÉ PENINSULA, SE QUEBEC. Missionaries settled here in the 18th century; and a well-known bird sanctuary is located on nearby Percé Rock.

PERCHE (France) Former county and ancient region in N France. It is presently included in the departments of Orne, Eure-et-Loir, and Eure. Well known for its local breed of Percheron horses, which were used by knights of the Middle Ages, it was joined to the French crown in 1525.

PEREA. See PERAEA.

PEREKOP, ISTHMUS OF [*ancient:* **Taphros**] (USSR) Isthmus connecting the Crimean oblast, UKRAINE, with the mainland. Strategically located, it has ruins of Greek and Tatar fortifications. Russian since 1783, it was the site of a decisive Red Army victory in 1920 over Gen. P.N. Wrangel during the Civil War. It was occupied by German forces from November 1941 to November 1943 during World War II. See also CRIMEA.

PEREMYSHL. See PRZEMYŚL.

PERESLAVL-ZALESSKI [*former:* **Pereyaslavl-Zalesski**] (USSR) Industrial town on Lake Pleshcheyevo, S YAROSLAVL oblast, Russian SFSR. Founded in 1152, it was the capital of an independent principality from 1175 until it became part of MOSCOW in 1302. Peter I began to develop the first Russian navy on the lake. The ruins of a 12th-century fortress and cathedral are here, as well as the remains of a 16th-century cathedral.

PEREYASLAV. See PEREYASLAV-KHMELNITSKI.

PEREYASLAV-KHMELNITSKI [*former:* **Pereyaslav**] (USSR) Agricultural town in E Kiev oblast, Ukraine, 50 mi SE of Kiev. Founded before 907 AD, it was the ancient capital of Pereyaslav principality. Destroyed by the Mongols in 1239, it became the headquarters of Bogdan Chmielnicki and his band of Cossacks during the early stages of the Cossack Wars of 1648 to 1712. The UKRAINE became a Russian protectorate by a treaty signed here in 1654. The remains of an 11th-century cathedral are in the town, as well as a 17th-century monastery and cathedral.

PEREYASLAVL-RYAZAN. See RYAZAN.

PEREYASLAVL-ZALESSKI. See PERESLAVL-ZALESSKI.

PERGA [*modern:* **Murtana**] (Turkey) Principal city of ancient PAMPHYLIA, S Asia Minor, 10 mi NE of modern Antalya, Turkey. The seat of the cult of an Asian nature goddess, it was visited by St. Paul on his first mission, as recorded in Acts 13:3, 14:25. Its ruins include a theater and a stadium.

PERGAMON. See PERGAMUM.

PERGAMOS. See PERGAMUM.

PERGAMUM [**Pergamus**] [*Greek:* **Pergamon**, **Pergamos**; *modern:* **Bergama**] (Turkey) Ancient city of NW Asia Minor, Mysia province, in modern Turkey. Ruled by PERSIA in the fifth century BC, it flourished as a Hellenistic city under Eumenes I and the Attalids from 263 to 133 BC. Bequeathed to Rome, it became Christian and was known as one of the Seven Churches of Asia, according to the book of Revelations. Under Greek rule it was famous for its sculpture, most notably for the Great Altar of Zeus, its library, palaces, and fortifications. The word "parchment," a writing material first used here, is derived from its name. Here remain impressive ruins of the city, which have been called a text for the study of Hellenistic art.

PERGAMUS. See PERGAMUM.

PÉRIERS (France) Town in Manche department, 14 mi NW of Saint-Lô, NW France. It was captured by the Allies during their attack on SAINT-LÔ in mid-July 1944, during the battle of NORMANDY in World War II.

PÉRIGORD (France) Former region of N Guienne province, in SW France, now in Dordogne and Lot-et-Garonne departments. Under the Carolingians Périgord became a county in the ninth century AD. It passed to the dukes of AQUITAINE and then to ENGLAND with the marriage of Eleanor of Aquitaine to Henry II in 1152. It passed back to France c.1370 and to the Bourbons in 1574. Inherited by Henry IV of France, it was incorporated as part of GUIENNE province in 1607. There are many Paleolithic cave sites in the area.

PÉRIGUEUX [*ancient:* **Vesuna**] (France) Commercial town, capital of Dordogne department, 66 mi ENE of Bordeaux, SW central France. An important Roman settlement of the Gallic Petrocorii, it was sacked by the Saracens in 730 AD and by the Normans in 844, before becoming the capital of PÉRIGORD in the ninth century. In the later Middle Ages it developed around an abbey and suffered as a Protestant stronghold in the 16th century in the Wars of Religion. Roman remains include several arenas and an amphitheater, and there are also a number of medieval Romanesque churches here, including the domed church of Saint-Front of c.1120, modeled on the church of the Holy Apostles in CONSTANTINOPLE, and Saint-Etienne-en-La-Cité, of slightly earlier date.

PERIM [*Arabic:* **Barim**] (Yemen) Island in Bab al-Mandab Strait, between the Red Sea and the Gulf of Aden, Southern Yemen. Strategically situated at the southern entrance to the RED SEA, it was garrisoned in 1799 by GREAT BRITAIN and policed by ADEN. It became part of the British colony of Aden in 1937. It served the British navy as a coaling station between 1883 and 1936, until oil replaced coal as the primary ship fuel.

PERLIS (Malaysia) A Malaysian state in central MALAY PENINSULA, on the Andaman Sea. Once controlled by KEDAH, then by SIAM from 1841, it came under British protection in 1909. One of the Unfederated Malay States, it became a state of Malaya in 1936.

PERM [*former:* **Brukhanovo, Molotov**] (USSR) Manufacturing city, capital of Perm oblast, W of the S central Ural Mts, Russian SFSR. An early frontier settlement inhabited by the Finnic Permiaks, it was occupied by Russian merchants in 1568. Copper and salt were mined here soon after. Political prisoners from RUSSIA were banished to Perm in the 17th and 18th centuries, and the city underwent rapid industrial expansion in the 19th century.

PERNAMBUCO. See RECIFE.

PERNAU. See PARNU.

PERNOV. See PARNU.

PÉRONNE (France) Commercial center, town in Somme department, approx. 35 mi N of Amiens, N France. The Frankish kings resided here in the 10th century. BURGUNDY under Charles the Bold captured it in 1468. Strategically located, it was taken by Holy Roman Emperor Charles V in 1536 and by the British under the duke of Wellington in 1815. It was almost totally destroyed during World War I after five months of bitter combat in 1916. There is a restored 16th-century church in the town.

PÉROUSE. See PERUGIA.

PERPIGNAN (France) Resort city, capital of Pyrénées-Orientales department, 96 mi S of Toulouse, on the Tet River, near the Mediterranean Sea, S France. Founded in the 10th century, it was the capital of Spanish ROUSSILLON, and a major city of the kingdom of MAJORCA after 1276. It was captured by Louis XIII of France in 1642. Its university was founded in 1349 and functioned for five centuries. It has a 13th-century citadel and a castle and cathedral from the 14th century. King Robert the Wise of Naples (1278–1343) was married to the Infanta Sancia of Majorca (1286–1345) here in 1304.

PERRYVILLE (United States) City, 40 mi SW of Lexington, E central KENTUCKY. An indecisive battle was waged here during the Civil War on October 8, 1862 between the Confederates under Gen. Braxton Bragg and the Union forces under Gen. Don Carlos Buell.

A fallen capital amidst the columns of the Audience Hall at Persepolis, huge ceremonial center of the early Persian Empire, which includes the palaces of Darius and Xerxes.

PERSEPOLIS [Parsa] [*modern:* **Takht-e Jamshid**] (Iran) An ancient Persian capital, its ruins lie approx. 30 mi NE of SHIRAZ, SW central Iran. There are impressive remains from Achaemenid PERSIA, including the massive palaces of Darius I, Xerxes, and later kings, and a treasury looted by Alexander the Great, all on a massive platform, and the rock tombs of Darius and others at nearby Naksh-i-Rustam. A Neolithic village

has also been discovered near the site. Persepolis was burned and partly destroyed by Alexander in 330 BC. It has been excavated and partially restored.

PERSIA [*modern:* **Iran**] Ancient empire and modern nation in SW Asia. TEHERAN is the capital. This region was the home of the ancient civilizations of ELAM and MEDIA as well as of Persia. In the seventh century BC the Persians aided the Medes in their struggle with ASSYRIA. In the next century Cyrus the Great founded the Persian Empire and established the Achaemenid dynasty that ruled from c.550 to 330 BC. He conquered Media, BACTRIA, LYDIA, BABYLONIA, some Greek city-states and returned the exiled Jews to PALESTINE. By 500 BC the Persian Empire extended from North Africa, including EGYPT, eastward to the INDUS RIVER and from the CAUCUSUS in the north to the INDIAN OCEAN. Under Darius I, who reigned from 521 to 486 BC, an extraordinarily efficient centralized government administered the affairs of this extensive empire. The Achaemenids were also noted for their art and architecture, as exemplified in the great palaces of PERSEPOLIS.

The period from 500 to 449 BC was marked by the Persian Wars between the empire and the Greek city-states. Persia conquered THRACE and MACEDONIA in 492 but ATHENS, leading the forces of GREECE, defeated Darius in 490 BC. In 480 and 479 BC Xerxes I tried again, and although he captured Athens he was later defeated. Trouble in the empire appeared near the end of the fourth century when Cyrus the Younger rebelled against Artaxerxes II, but he was defeated in 401 BC. The Corinthian War of 395 to 386 BC pitted various Greek city-states against each other, with Persia aiding Athens. The Peace of Antalcidas, ending the war, was a victory for Persia, which recovered CYPRUS and the city-states in ASIA MINOR. In 334 BC Alexander the Great of MACEDON invaded the empire and in battles that year, in 333, and in 331 BC defeated the Persians and brought an end to the Persian Empire.

After Alexander's death in 323 BC, one of his generals inherited part of his empire and, as Seleucus I, established a kingdom that included Persia. In 250 BC, however, PARTHIA threw off SELEUCID rule and created an empire. At its height in the first century BC, it ruled Persia and challenged the power of ROME in the East. Parthian power ended in 226 AD when Ardashir I, a native prince, overthrew the Parthians and established a new Persian Empire under the Sassanid dynasty. Under Khosru I Persia extended its territory east, west, and north and fought successfully against the BYZANTINE EMPIRE. The Sassanids ruled in splendor and with efficiency, but between 636 and 642 the rapidly rising Arab Muslim Empire, under its founder, the Caliph Umar, conquered the empire. The Arabs carried the Islamic religion to Persia. The Shiite sect developed here, while Persian culture dominated the Arab ABBASID dynasty at BAGHDAD. The Arabs ruled until the early 11th century, when the Seljuk Turks conquered Persia. They were followed by the Mongols who controlled Persia by 1260 and who, under Tamerlane, invaded again in the late 14th century (see MONGOL EMPIRES).

Foreign control ended in 1502 when Shah Ismail founded the Safavid dynasty, which ruled until 1736. This dynasty reached its peak under Shah Abbas I, who reigned at ESFAHAN from 1587 to 1628, established trade relations with GREAT BRITAIN, and fought frequently with the Turks. The Afghans brought about the fall of the Safavids after overthrowing Shah Husein in 1722, but Nadir Shah established the short-lived Afshar dynasty in 1736. He was a successful conqueror, bringing back spectacular spoils from India. Shortly after Nadir Shah's death, Karim Khan founded the Zand dynasty, which lasted from 1750 until 1794. SHIRAZ was the Zand capital, which was beautified with mosques and other buildings. The dynasty, however, declined and was overthrown by Aga Muhammad Khan, who founded the Kajar dynasty, which ruled from 1794 until 1925 but under which the nation lost power and prestige.

Persia had to give up the Caucasus to RUSSIA in the early 19th century and was forced to recognize AF-GHANISTAN'S independence in 1857. After oil was discovered in the early 20th century, the already existing rivalry between Russia and Great Britain for influence over Persia increased. It was settled in 1907 by an agreement between the two nations that divided the country into separate spheres of influence. During World War I Russia and Great Britain occupied the country. An army officer, Reza Khan, staged a coup in 1921, overthrew the last Kajar shah and in 1925 became the head of a new dynasty, the Pahlevi, as Reza Shah Pahlevi. He instituted reforms to modernize the country, and changed its name to Iran in 1935.

In World War II the shah was suspected of German sympathies and in August 1941 British and Soviet troops again occupied Iran. The next month the shah abdicated in favor of his son, Muhammed Reza Shah Pahlevi. When the war ended the USSR tried to stir up trouble in the north and refused to remove its troops from the country. Iran protested to the United Nations, and in May 1946 the Soviets left. In 1951 a militant nationalist movement resulted in the nationalization of the oil industry. There was much unrest, stemming from economic hardship and antiforeign sentiment, but in 1957 martial law came to an end after 16 years. Iran joined the Central Treaty Organization for the defense of the Middle East and established close ties with the United States, which provided military and economic assistance. In 1963 the shah initiated a series of reforms, including land redistribution, and the emancipation of women. With the aid of large oil revenues, he also tried to make Iran the strongest military power in the region.

Nevertheless, dissatisfaction with the shah's rule grew, resulting partly from his harsh methods of repression, partly from continued poverty of most of the people, and partly from a resurgence of conservative Islamic forces that opposed the Westernization of the country. The shah's support dwindled to such an extent that on Jan. 16, 1979 he fled the country. Within a short time power came into the hands of the Islamic religious leaders, headed by the Ayatollah Ruhollah Khomeini, and an Islamic republic was established. Anti-American feeling became intense and culminated in the seizure on November 4 of the American Embassy in TEHERAN and its personnel. The embassy hostages were not released until Jan. 20, 1981. In September 1980 Iran's neighbor IRAQ attacked it in a dispute over territory. After some advances into Iran, the war bogged down with several unsuccessful Iranian offensives. Teheran is the capital; other important cities include MASHHAD in the northeast, TABRIZ in the northwest, HAMADAN in the west, ESFAHĀN in the central west, and ABĀDĀN and SHIRAZ in the southwest. The strategic strait of HORMUZ separates Iran from OMAN in the south and commands the PERSIAN GULF'S access to the Gulf of Oman and the INDIAN OCEAN.

PERSIAN EMPIRE. See PERSIA.

PERSIAN GULF [Arabian Gulf] [*ancient:* **Sinus Persicus;** *Arabic:* **Khalij al 'Ajam;** *Persian:* **Khalij-i-Fars]** Strategic body of water in Asia, an arm of the Arabian Sea. It extends approx. 600 mi SE from the Shatt el-Arab delta to the Strait of Hormuz, and at its maximum is approx. 200 mi wide. In antiquity, when MESOPOTAMIA to the north, drained by the TIGRIS and EUPHRATES rivers, was the center of dominant civilizations, the gulf was an important trade route. Its importance declined after the Mongols ravaged Mesopotamia in 1258. Arabs, Persians, Turks, Russians and Western Europeans contested control of the area in later centuries.

In 1853 the Arab sheikhdoms of the gulf signed the Perpetual Maritime Truce, by which they agreed not to attack British shipping in the Arabian Sea and to recognize Britain's dominant position in the area. This position was confirmed in 1907 by an international agreement, no longer in force, which placed the gulf in the British sphere of influence. The gulf attracted worldwide attention in the 1930's when it became clear that here, in the Middle East, were to be found the largest petroleum reserves in the world. Since World War II the region has been the most productive oil center on earth, and today the industrial world depends on the Persian Gulf to provide a vital traffic lane for a never-ending procession of oil tankers. The revolution in Iran in 1979, the Soviet invasion of AFGHANISTAN in the same year, the Iran-Iraq War over the Shatt el-Arab from 1980, and an attempted pro-Iranian coup in Bahrain in 1981 have alerted the oil-consuming nations of the West to the vulnerability of the Gulf. The Arab Gulf States, meanwhile, have formed their own military, political, and economic alliances to promote peace in the area and to forestall superpower interference. The states on the gulf are: BAHRAIN, IRAN, IRAQ, KUWAIT, QATAR, SAUDI ARABIA and the UNITED ARAB EMIRATES (formerly the Trucial States).

PERTH (Australia) Commercial city and capital of Western Australia, on the Swan River, SW Australia. Founded in 1829, it became prominent in the 1890's during the COOLGARDIE gold rush, which coincided with the development of its port at FREMANTLE. It was incorporated in 1856.

PERTH [*former:* **St. Johnstown**] (Scotland) Industrial city in Tayside region, 32 mi NNW of Edinburgh, on the Tay River. An early Roman settlement, it was made a royal burgh by David I in 1210 AD and was the capital of Scotland from the 11th to the 15th centuries. In 1437 James I of Scotland was assassinated here, and in the church of St. John in 1559 John Knox condemned idolatry in one of his most famous sermons. A conspiracy was formed in 1600 at the Gowrie House to kidnap James I of England, who later opened the church-state conflict by issuing the Five Articles of Perth in 1618. There is a prison here that was built in 1812 to house French prisoners of war.

PERTH AMBOY (United States) Industrial city and port, on the Raritan River, 17 mi SSW of Newark, central NEW JERSEY. Deeded to local Indians in 1651, it was bought soon afterwards by English settlers. It was the capital of East Jersey from 1684 to 1702. The city was incorporated in 1718. The former mansion of Gov. William Franklin here was headquarters for Gen. William Howe's Continental army during the American Revolution.

PERTHSHIRE (Scotland) Former county in central Scotland, now incorporated in Tayside and Central regions. In 1689 Viscount Dundee, "Bonnie Dundee" of the famous ballad, defeated William of Orange in the name of James II at the Pass of KILLIECRANKIE. The kings of Scotland were crowned at SCONE for many years. See also PERTH.

PERU A nation in western South America, bordering on the Pacific Ocean in the W, on Ecuador and Colombia in the N, on Brazil and Bolivia in the E, and on Chile in the S. Peru was the site of several distinctive Indian cultures before Europeans arrived. The Chavin was probably the earliest, flourishing from c.700 to 200 BC. In turn came the Paracas culture, the Nazca culture, developing in the first millennium AD, and then the Mochica, the Aymara, and the Chimu. The most highly developed was the INCA EMPIRE, whose people settled around CUZCO in the 12th century. By the mid-15th century they had conquered the other Indians of most of Peru and Ecuador, as well as parts of Bolivia, Chile, Argentina, and Colombia.

Led by Francisco Pizarro, Spanish conquistadors arrived in Peru in 1532 and treacherously captured the Inca ruler, Atahualpa, and had him murdered in 1533. Pizarro founded PIURA in 1532 but abandoned it; LIMA and its port, CALLAO, were founded in 1535. The Incas revolted in 1536 and tried unsuccessfully to retake Cuzco. The next year another conquistador, Diego de Almagro, claimed Cuzco and seized it. Pizarro's brother Gonzalo and half-brother Hernando fought Almagro and defeated him. In 1541 Cristóbal Vaca de Castro was sent from Spain to restore order.

Blasco Núñez Vela arrived in 1544 as the first Spanish viceroy, with instructions to enforce the New Laws. These laws resulted from agitation by the missionary Bartolomé de Las Casas to protect the Indians. Under the *encomienda* system, conquistadors were granted the right to use the labor of groups of Indians, a right that resulted in many abuses. Opposing the enforcement of the laws, Gonzalo Pizarro revolted and defeated the viceroy, but in turn was subdued by a new viceroy in 1548. Another viceroy in 1551 refused to enforce the New Laws; the next one, however, Francisca de Toledo, broke the power of the estate owners. In the 17th century the viceroyalty of Peru was expanded to include all of Spanish South America except Venezuela, but in the 18th century it was reduced by the creation of two new viceroyalties.

Peru's independence from SPAIN was due largely to outside leaders; Simón Bolívar and Antonio José de Sucre from Venezuela and José de San Martín from Argentina. Independence was proclaimed on July 28, 1821 and was established by two military victories in 1824: near JUNÍN on August 6 and near AYACUCHO on December 9. Andres Santa Cruz, president of BOLIVIA, emerged as ruler of Peru by combining the two countries. Fearing Santa Cruz, CHILE declared war and defeated him in 1839. Ramón Castilla served as president of Peru from 1845 to 1851 and 1855 to 1862 and brought some order and prosperity to the country.

Seeking to collect alleged damages, Spain seized Peru's Chincha Islands in 1863. War was declared; and Peru was joined by Chile, ECUADOR, and Bolivia. The Spaniards were defeated at Callao in 1866, and in 1879 Spain finally acknowledged Peru's independence. From 1879 to 1884 Peru and Bolivia were again at war with Chile, in the War of the Pacific, this time over nitrate deposits. At the end of the war Peru had to cede one province and yield two others for ten years. The Tacna-Arica Controversy over these provinces was not settled until 1929, when TACNA—but not ARICA—was returned to Peru.

The late 19th and early 20th centuries were dominated by presidents Nicolás de Piérola (1859–99) and Augusto Bernardino Leguía (1908–12 and 1919–30). Some economic progress was made, but the Great Depression of the 1930's brought a struggle between left and right. Border disputes with Ecuador over the Marañón River area led to war in 1942, by which Peru extended its northeastern border to its present line. Socialist reform groups won the 1962 election, but the army refused to accept the results. It deposed the next elected president, Fernando Belaúnde Terry, in 1968, but when elections were held in 1980, Belaúnde won again. In January 1981 a 165-year-old border dispute with Ecuador over the Amazonian headwaters in the Marañón River area resulted in armed clashes. The Organization of American States won a cease-fire in March and an agreement to mediate.

Lima is the capital and largest city; others include AREQUIPA and TRUJILLO.

PERUGIA [*ancient:* **Augusta Perusia, Perusia,** *French:* **Pérouse**] (Italy) Industrial and commercial town, capital of Perugia province, UMBRIA region, 85 mi N of Rome, central Italy. A major Etruscan city, it was taken by ROME in 310 BC, and destroyed in the civil wars in 41/40 BC. Augustus rebuilt the city as Augusta Perusia. It was captured by the Lombards in 592 AD. Nominally part of the PAPAL STATES in the

Middle Ages, it was finally subdued by the papacy in 1540. Pope Paul III fortified the city with a strong citadel, the Rocca Paolina, after 1540. The city fell to the French in 1809 who renamed it Pérouse. It was retaken by the papacy in 1815 and liberated in the Italian unification of 1860. There is an Etruscan cemetery and an arch in the city, as well as a university, founded in 1308. The 13th-century Palazzo dei Priori houses some of the great paintings of the Umbrian school that flourished here between the 13th and 16th centuries. Perugino (1446–1523) is its greatest exemplar. See also ETRURIA.

PERUSIA. See PERUGIA.

PESARO [*ancient:* **Pisaurum**] (Italy) Agricultural and industrial center, port, and capital of Pesaro e Urbino province, Marches region, on the Adriatic Sea, 85 mi ENE of Florence, central Italy. An ancient fortified city, it was settled by Etruscans and others before it was colonized in 184 BC by ROME. It was one of the cities of the Pentapolis from the fifth to 11th centuries AD, before passing to the Malatestas in 1285, to the Sforzas in 1445, to the Della Roveres in 1512, and to the PAPAL STATES in 1631. It was incorporated into a unified Italy in 1860. Here is the ducal Sforza palace from the 15th century, as well as the Villa Imperiale with 16th-century frescoes. Its Biblioteca Oliveriana houses many important medieval and Renaissance manuscripts.

PESCADORES [*Chinese:* **P'eng-hu;** *Japanese:* **Hoko Gunto, Hoko Shoto**] (Taiwan) Group of islands in Formosa Strait between Taiwan and mainland CHINA. Ceded to JAPAN in 1895 after the First Sino-Japanese War, they were returned to China in 1946 after World War II and have been controlled by Taiwan since 1949. The town of P'ENG-HU was a Japanese naval base during World War II.

PESCARA [*ancient:* **Aternum, Ostia Aterni**] (Italy) Industrial and commercial port and resort, capital of Pescara province, ABRUZZI region, on the Adriatic Sea, 98 mi ENE of Rome, central Italy. Fortified in 1867, it was heavily bombed during World War II and was taken by the Allies in June 1944. The soldier and poet Gabriele D'Annunzio (1863–1938) was born here.

PESCHIERA DEL GARDA [*ancient:* **Arilica;** *former:* **Peschiera sul Garda, Piscaria**] (Italy) Town in Verona province, Veneto region, on an island at the mouth of the Mincio River, on Lake Garda, 14 mi W of Verona, NE Italy. A fortress town, now no longer of military value, it played an important part as a frontier town, especially during the Napoleonic Wars. It became one of the Quadrilateral cities, together with VERONA, LEGNANO, and MANTUA, which formed the center of Austrian rule in Italy. The town was taken by the forces of PIEDMONT in 1848. See also AUSTRIA.

PESCHIERA SUL GARDA. See PESCHIERA DEL GARDA.

PESCIA (Italy) Town, Pistoia province, Tuscany region, 14 mi W of Pistoia, central Italy. A 16th-century cathedral is located here, as are the remains of its ancient city walls. The paper industry has flourished here since the 15th century. The 14th-century church of San Francesco contains a series of paintings on the life of the saint done soon after his death.

PESHAWAR [*former:* **Purushapura**] (Pakistan) Strategically located city, at the S entrance to the KHYBER PASS, capital of Peshawar division and district, on the Bara River, 240 mi NW of Lahore. Once the capital of the ancient Greco-Buddhist center of GANDHARA, it was the capital of the KUSHAN EMPIRE in the first and second centuries AD. The 18th-century residence of the Afghan Durrani rulers, it was captured by the Sikhs a short time before the British takeover in 1848. It became the center of British military operations against the Afghans and the Pathan tribes. There is a second-century Buddhist stupa here.

A picturesque alley in old Peshawar, at the foot of the Khyber Pass. Nearby was the Kushan capital of Purushapura (second century AD) where Buddhist and Hellenistic elements mingled.

PESSINUS (Turkey) Ancient city of GALATIA in Asia Minor. A major shrine was dedicated here to the Anatolian nature goddess Cybele.

PETACH TIKVA [Petah Tiqwa] (Israel) Town, 7 mi NE of Tel Aviv-Jaffa. Founded in 1878 as the first village and agricultural settlement of the Jews returning to PALESTINE, it was incorporated in 1937.

PETAH TIQWA. See PETACH TIKVA.

PETALUMA (United States) Agricultural city on the Petaluma River, 38 mi NW of San Francisco, W CALIFORNIA. Settled by Mexican officers in 1833, it is one of the nation's oldest dairy centers. Old Adobe, the house of Gen. Mariano Vallejo, is the oldest existing house in the area. The city was incorporated in 1858.

PETCH. See PEČ.

PETCHABUN. See PHETCHABUN.

PETÉN (Guatemala) Department of N Guatemala. Hernando Cortés visited here on his march to Honduras in 1524/25, but the local Itzá tribe was not driven out until 1697. There are many Mayan ruins in the area.

PETERBORO. See PETERBOROUGH.

PETERBOROUGH [*former:* **Scott's Plains**] (Canada) Industrial city in SE ONTARIO, 70 mi NE of Toronto, on the Otonabee River and Trent Canal. The city was first settled in 1818. A large group of Irish colonists arrived seven years later. The city was incorporated in 1905 and has important Indian sites nearby.

PETERBOROUGH [*former:* **Medeshamstede**] (England) Industrial city in Cambridgeshire, 75 mi N of London, on the Nene River. Having developed around a seventh-century Benedictine abbey, it was chartered in the 13th century and incorporated in 1894. The abbey was destroyed by the Danes in the 10th century, was burned again in 1116, and was damaged by Oliver Cromwell's army in 1643. The chapels of St. Nicholas and Thomas à Becket survive from the abbey. Queen Catherine of Aragon, the first wife of Henry VIII, is buried here.

PETERBOROUGH [Peterboro] (United States) Resort town, 16 mi E of Keene, S NEW HAMPSHIRE. Settled in 1749, it was here that Brigham Young was chosen as the head of the Mormon Church following the assassination of Joseph Smith in 1844.

PETERHEAD (Scotland) Port and town in Aberdeen county, 30 mi NE of Aberdeen, NE Scotland. George Keith founded the town in 1593. James Francis Stuart, the Old Pretender, landed here secretly on Christmas Day, 1715 to head the uprising against ENGLAND.

PETERHOF. See PETRODVORETS.

PETERLINGEN. See PAYERNE.

PETERSBURG (United States) Commercial city, 22 mi S of Richmond, on the Appomattox River, SE VIRGINIA. Fort Henry was established here in 1646 on the site of an Indian village. The town was incorporated in 1784, shortly after Gen. Charles Cornwallis departed from here en route to YORKTOWN toward the end of the American Revolution. It was an important battle site during the Civil War, as Gen. Robert E. Lee's Confederate troops withstood a Union siege directed by Gen. Ulysses S. Grant in an attempt to approach RICHMOND. Trench warfare lasted for months. The siege, which began in June 1864, was finally successful in April 1865 after the victory at FIVE FORKS. Richmond fell the same day, and Lee surrendered at APPOMATTOX Courthouse on April 9, 1865. Much of the battle site has been preserved. There is also a Confederate cemetery here.

PÉTERVÁRAD. See PETROVARADIN.

PETERWARDEIN. See PETROVARADIN.

PETIT CHARENTON. See SAINT-MAURICE.

PETRA [*biblical:* **Sela**] (Jordan) A ruined, rock-hewn city in SW Jordan, just W of modern Wadi Musa. It was the ancient capital of the Edomites, then of the kingdom of NABATAEA, beginning *c.*300 BC, before its Roman colonization in 106 AD. It flourished for centuries as the center of a rich caravan trade between Arabia, the Far East, and the West. It declined as the trade routes changed, and was taken by the Muslims in the seventh century AD, then by the Crusaders in the 12th century. Its ruins were discovered in 1812. Hellenistic temples and tombs have been discovered, as well as a huge theater and inscriptions celebrating local deities.

A rock-cut Classical temple at Petra in eastern Jordan, one of many carved out in the early centuries AD by the Nabataeans, who prospered from the caravan trade.

PETRIKAU. See PIOTRKÓW TRYBUNALSKI.

PETRODVORETS [*former:* **Leninsk, Peterhof**] (USSR) Town on Neva Bay, 12 mi W of LENINGRAD, NW Leningrad oblast, Russian SFSR. Founded in 1711 by Peter the Great as the site of imperial palaces, it was designed to rival VERSAILLES as one of the greatest courts in Europe. The palaces were converted into museums under the Soviet regime. Peter the Great's Grand Palace of 1720 was the most lavish, and all the palaces created here were famous for their gardens and fountains. The town was badly damaged in World War II.

PETROGRAD. See LENINGRAD.

PETROKOV. See PIOTRKÓW TRYBUNALSKI.

PETROKREPOST [*former:* **Shlisselburg;** *German:* **Schlüsselburg**] (USSR) Transportation center, town in NW Leningrad oblast, on the Neva River and Lake Ladoga, Russian SFSR. A fortress built here by the Novgorodians in 1323 fell to SWEDEN in 1611 and then to Peter the Great in 1702. The fortress soon declined in military importance and was used as a political prison until the Bolshevik revolution. It was recaptured from the Germans by Soviet troops in 1943 during World War II, opening land access to LENINGRAD. See also NOVGOROD.

PETRONELL. See CARNUNTUM.

PETROPAVLOVSK. See PETROPAVLOVSK-KAMCHATSKI.

PETROPAVLOVSK-KAMCHATSKI [*former:* **Petropavlovsk**] (USSR) Port, town, and capital of Kamchatka oblast, at S end of KAMCHATKA PENINSULA, Russian SFSR. Its port, founded in 1740 by Vitus Bering, was attacked by the French and British navies several times during the Crimean War of 1853 to 1856.

PETRÓPOLIS (Brazil) Residential city in Rio de Janeiro state, 27 mi N of Rio de Janeiro, SE Brazil. Founded in 1745, it was the royal summer residence of Emperor Dom Pedro II and others; the old imperial palace is now a musuem. An inter-American security conference was held here from Aug. 15 to Sept. 2, 1947.

PETROVARADIN [*German:* **Peterwardein;** *Hungarian:* **Pétervárad**] (Yugoslavia) Town in NE SERBIA, on the DANUBE RIVER, opposite Novi Sad. Peter the Hermit, religious leader of the First Crusade, met here with his followers in 1096. Prince Eugene of Savoy, in the service of Charles VI and the HOLY ROMAN EMPIRE, soundly defeated the Turks here on Aug. 5, 1716 during a war against the OTTOMAN EMPIRE between 1714 and 1718.

PETROVSK. See MKHACHKALA.

PETROZAVODSK [**Kalininsk**] (USSR) Industrial city, capital of Karelian ASSR, on Lake Onega, 185 mi NE of Leningrad. Novgorodian iron works operated here in the Middle Ages; and Peter the Great founded a metal factory here in 1703, making it the industrial center of the region for the next two centuries. It was damaged considerably during World War II. See also KARELIA, NOVOGOROD.

PETSAMO. See PECHENGA.

PETWORTH (England) Village, 42 mi SSW of London, West Sussex. Petworth house, located in the village, was once owned by the Percy family, the earls and later dukes of Northumberland. It later passed to the dukes of Somerset. Largely built in the late 17th century, it was often visited by the artist J.M.W. Turner in the early 19th century and has a large collection of his paintings of the house and grounds as well as Grinling Gibbons wood carvings.

PEVENSEY (England) Resort village, in East Sussex, on the ENGLISH CHANNEL, 5 mi NE of Eastbourne. The site of a Roman fort, it was the landing place of William the Conqueror in 1066. A former CINQUE PORT, the town contains a 12th-century Norman castle built inside the Roman fortress. See also SAXON SHORE.

PÉZENAS (France) Small town in Hérault department, 13 mi NE of Béziers, S France, chiefly distinguished by the fact that the great French dramatist Jean Baptiste Molière lived here in 1655/56 and wrote one of his comedies here, *Les Précieuses Ridicules*.

PFALZ. See PALATINATE.

PFORTA. See SCHULPFORTE.

PFORZHEIM [*ancient:* **Porta Hercyniae**] (West Germany) Manufacturing and commercial city, Baden-Württemberg state, 16 mi SE of Karlsruhe. Once a Roman settlement and a medieval commercial center, it was the residence of the BADEN margraves from the 13th century until 1565. It was nearly destroyed by the French in 1689 in the War of the Grand Alliance and again in World War II. There is an 11th-century church here.

PHAESTOS [*Latin:* **Phaestus**] (Greece) Ancient city, SW of Knossos, S CRETE. Occupied as early as the fourth millennium BC, it was the site of an ancient Minoan palace. Phaestos throve in the Classical and Hellenistic periods, but it declined after the advent of the Roman Empire. The ruins of the palace have been excavated.

PHAESTUS. See PHAESTOS.

PHALERON [*Latin:* **Phalerum**] (Greece) Town on Phaleron Bay, an inlet of the Saronic Gulf in the Aegean Sea, close to Athens and E of Piraeus. Phaleron served as the port of ancient ATHENS in the Archaic period, until Themistocles had the port of PIRAEUS constructed nearby in *c.*470 BC to serve the growing fleet and the maritime interests of Athens.

PHALERUM. See PHALERON.

PHANAR [**Fanar**] (Turkey) Greek quarter of CONSTANTINOPLE, now ISTANBUL, on the Bosporus Strait, Istanbul province, NW Turkey. The Phanariots, a group of prominent Greek families from the 17th to 19th centuries, resided here under the OTTOMAN EMPIRE. Their political influence waned after the war of Greek independence in the 1820's.

PHARNAKE. See APAMEA AD ORONTEM.

PHARNUCIA. See GIRESUN.

PHAROS (Egypt) Peninsula in Lower Egypt, extending into the Mediterranean Sea, now part of the city of ALEXANDRIA. Originally an island, it was connected to the mainland by an earth construction built by Alexander the Great. A lighthouse constructed here *c.*280 BC was one of the seven wonders of the ancient world but was destroyed by earthquake in the 14th century.

PHARSALA. See PHARSALUS.

PHARSALIA, BATTLE OF. See PHARSALUS.

PHÁRSALOS. See PHARSALUS.

PHARSALUS [**Pharsala**] [*Greek:* **Phársalos**]

(Greece) Ancient city in E THESSALY, S Larissa department, NE Greece. Caesar defeated Pompey here on Aug. 9, 48 BC in the famous battle.

PHARUS. See HVAR.

PHASIS. See POTI, RIONI.

PHAZANIA. See FEZZAN.

PHEASANTS, ISLE OF [Île de la Conférence, Île des Faisans] (Spain) Island in the Bidassoa River, 10 mi SE of Irún, in Navarra province, on the N frontier of Spain. It has several times been the site of international negotiations. Francis I of FRANCE, the prisoner of the Emperor Charles V, was exchanged for his two children here in 1526. The Treaty of the Pyrenees was signed here on Nov. 7, 1659. It settled the French position after the Thirty Years War in Roussillon, Artois, Flanders, and areas to the east of France; while Spain renounced its Hapsburg claims to Alsace, and France abandoned claims to Catalonia. Queen Maria Theresa of France also gave up her claims to the Spanish succession by the treaty.

PHENICIA. See PHOENICIA.

PHENIX CITY (United States) Manufacturing city in E ALABAMA, on the Chattahoochee River, opposite Columbus, Georgia. Incorporated in 1883, it was placed under martial law for five months in 1954 because of municipal corruption. The site of Fort Mitchell, built between 1811 and 1837, is nearby.

PHERAE [Pherai] (Greece) Ancient town of SE THESSALY, approx. 27 mi SE of Larissa, NE Greece. Its rulers controlled Thessaly in the first half of the fourth century BC. Lykophron II was defeated by Philip of Macedon in 352 BC. Antiochus the Great took the city in 191 BC; but he was, in turn, defeated by the Roman M. Acilius Glabrio soon after. The city walls, towers, acropolis, a temple to Hercules, the Larissan Gate and other remains have been excavated. It was the mythological home of Admetus.

PHERAI. See PHERAE.

PHETCHABUN [Bejraburana, Petchabun, Phetchbun] (Thailand) Town, capital of Phetchabun province, on the Sak River 70 mi SE of Phitsanulok. Because of its central location in the country, this small town was made the capital of Thailand by the Japanese, during their occupation of the country between 1944 and 1945, during World War II.

PHETCHBUN. See PHETCHABUN.

PHIGALIA. See BASSAE, Greece.

PHILADELPHIA, Jordan. See AMMAN.

PHILADELPHIA, Turkey. See ALASEHIR.

PHILADELPHIA (United States) City in SE PENN-

The Old State House in Philadelphia, where the Second Continental Congress met in 1775. With Independence Hall and other monuments, it is now a prime tourist attraction.

SYLVANIA, on the DELAWARE RIVER. For nearly three centuries from the colonial era on, the "City of Brotherly Love" has been a leading city in population, commerce, industry, and culture. During the American Revolution, it was the birthplace of the nation. The first Europeans to settle here were Swedes in the 1640's. In 1681 William Penn, who had been granted the region that became the colony of Pennsylvania, founded the city as a Quaker town. Philadelphia progressed rapidly in the colonial era and by the time of the American Revolution was second only to London in population in the English-speaking world. Benjamin Franklin was its leading citizen.

The First Continental Congress met here in 1774 and the second in the following year. In 1776 the Congress formally adopted the Declaration of Independence here on July 4. The British captured the city in September 1777 and held it until June 1778. After the Revolution, the Constitutional Convention met in Philadelphia and on Sept. 17, 1787 adopted the Constitution of the United States, subject to ratification by the states. The city was the capital of the nation from 1790 to 1800 and was the state capital until 1799. As it lost its political leadership to WASHINGTON, D.C.; it was also losing its commercial, financial, and cultural leadership to NEW YORK CITY. Philadelphia, however, was the seat of the government-sponsored Banks of the United States, which were active from 1791 to 1811 and from 1816 to 1836. The city was strongly Unionist in the Civil War.

In 1876 the Centennial Exposition was held here, bringing visitors from all over the world. For a century since then, Philadelphia has remained a major port, manufacturing, banking, and insurance center. It has many points of interest, such as Independence Hall, the Liberty Bell, and the Betsy Ross House. The city is the home of a U.S. mint and of the American Philosophical Society, the first scientific society in the country, founded in 1743.

PHILAE (Egypt) Former island in the NILE RIVER, Upper Egypt. It is the site of many temples dating from 600 BC to 600 AD, most notably the one dedicated to Isis by the early Ptolemies. Most of the monuments were partially flooded after the building of the old Aswan Dam in 1907 and completion of the Aswan High Dam, but have been preserved.

PHILIPHAUGH (Scotland) Village in Borders region, 31 mi NNW of Edinburgh. After the Scottish intervention in the English Civil War, the earl of Montrose and his Royalist Highlander force captured Scotland. They held it until their defeat on Sept. 13, 1645 at Philiphaugh by David Leslie of Oliver Cromwell's army.

PHILIPPEVILLE. See SKIKDA.

PHILIPPI [Filippoi] (Greece) Ruined city in Drama department, N central MACEDONIA. It was once inhabited by Thracians and Thasians. Philip II of Macedon (382–336 BC) enlarged and fortified it. Octavian and Mark Antony defeated Ceasar's assassins, Brutus and Cassius, here in 42 BC. It was the first place in Europe to hear the Gospel preached by St. Paul.

PHILIPPI (United States) Industrial and mining city, 19 mi ESE of Clarksburg, N WEST VIRGINIA. During the Civil War a battle took place here in 1861, in which the Union army triumphed.

PHILIPPINE ISLANDS. See PHILIPPINES, REPUBLIC OF THE.

PHILIPPINE SEA Part of the W Pacific Ocean, just E of the PHILIPPINES. There was an important naval battle in its southern waters on June 19/20, 1944 during World War II. A Japanese fleet was routed by U.S. air attacks from nearby carriers.

PHILIPPINES, REPUBLIC OF THE [Philippine Islands] [*Filipino:* **Republika ng Pilipinas;** *Spanish:* **Islas Filipinas, República de Filipinas**] Nation in the SW Pacific Ocean, off SE Asia, occupying the Philippine Archipelago and the smaller Sulu Archipelago to the SE. It consists of over 7,000 islands in all, of which 11 account for 95 percent of the land and most of the population. Called Filipinos, the inhabitants are mostly of the Malay group. The first inhabitants were Negritos, negroid pygmies who are thought to have migrated from Borneo, Sumatra, and Malaya approximately 30,000 years ago; they were followed later by Malayans. In the 14th century Arab traders introduced Islam. Europeans first reached the islands in 1521 in the course of the round-the-world voyage of Ferdinand Magellan for SPAIN. Spanish conquest began in 1564; and MANILA, now the capital, was founded in 1571.

Between 1600 and 1663 there were wars with the Dutch; the Moros of the islands continued to resist Spain; and Manila was captured and held by the British in 1762/63. Spain kept control until 1896 when Spanish oppression sparked a revolt. In 1898 the Spanish-American War began, stemming from American concern over Spanish rule of Cuba, and on May 1 George Dewey's U.S. fleet defeated the Spanish fleet in MANILA BAY. Meanwhile, the Filipinos were successful on land. In December a treaty ending the war ceded the Philippines to the UNITED STATES. Filipinos who had fought for freedom refused their new rulers and carried on a ferocious guerrilla war against the United States until 1901, when their leader, Emilio Aguinaldo, was captured.

A U.S. act of 1916 provided some self-rule, while a further law in 1934 promised independence in 1946 and established the Commonwealth of the Philippines on Nov. 15, 1935. On Dec. 8, 1941 JAPAN invaded the Philippines and held sway over the islands until U.S. forces landed on LEYTE on Oct. 20, 1944. By July 5, 1945 the islands were free; and independence came, as promised, on July 4, 1946. However, communist-dominated guerrillas, the Hukalahap, known as Huks, fought the government until 1954. They rose again in 1969; and there has also been fighting with the Moros, Muslim separatists, which continued into 1982. Although presumably a democracy, the Philippine nation has, in effect, had one-man rule since September 1972 under dictator Ferdinand E. Marcos, who was first elected president in 1965.

PHILIPPOPOLIS. See PLOVDIV.

PHILIPSBURG. See ST. MARTIN, West Indies.

PHILISTIA Country in ancient SW PALESTINE, partly in S CANAAN, along the Mediterranean coast. It was the focus of an important commercial route between Egypt and Syria and was settled by invading Sea Peoples, the Pulesti, c.1100 BC, who founded five coastal cities. The Israelites were subjected by the Philistines, but King David eventually conquered the area. ASSYRIA captured it during Sennacherib's Palestinian invasion c.700 BC.

PHILLIPSBURG (United States) Industrial town on the DELAWARE RIVER, 40 mi NW of Trenton, NW NEW JERSEY. It was settled in 1739 on the site of a Delaware Indian Village and incorporated in 1861. Its importance resulted from its position as the western terminus of the Morris and Essex Canal, built in the mid-19th century.

PHILOMELION. See AKŞEHIR.

PHINTIAS. See LICATA.

PHITSANULOK [Bisnulok, Pitsanulok] (Thailand) Town and capital of Phitsanulok province, in N central Thailand, 75 mi N of Nakhon Sawan, on the Nan River. The old city, dating back to the 13th century, once rivaled AYUTTHAYA in size and importance. There are several temples of interest located in the town.

PHLIUS (Greece) In antiquity it was an important town of a small district of NE PELOPONNESUS, SSW of Sicyon. A frequent ally of SPARTA, it was the home of a chief disciple of Pyrrho, Timon of Phlius (c.320–230 BC), who was a poet and sceptic philosopher.

PHLÓRINA. See FLÓRINA.

PHNOM PENH [Pnompenh] (Kampuchea) Commercial and educational center, city, and capital of Kampuchea (formerly Cambodia), at the confluence of the Mekong and Tonle Sap rivers, SE Asia. Founded in the 14th century, it became the Khmer capital in 1434 and the Cambodian capital in 1865. It was occupied by Japanese forces during World War II. The city was repeatedly besieged in the early 1970's during the civil war in Cambodia. During the same conflict, early in 1975, it was heavily bombed and totally deserted as the new Khmer Rouge government forcibly evacuated the population for labor in the countryside. The city came back to life in 1979. It has a dynastic palace and a Buddhist shrine and university.

PHOCAEA [modern: Foca] (Turkey) Ancient city, W coast of Asia Minor, on the Aegean Sea, in present Turkey. It flourished in the first half of the first millennium BC as an Ionian commercial and maritime state. Involved in early colonizing explorations, the Phocaeans founded Massilia, modern MARSEILLES. The city was captured by the Persians in 540 BC and never regained prominence. See also ELEA.

PHOCIS [modern: Fokis] (Greece) Ancient region in central Greece. The region exercised control over the oracle at DELPHI. It lost that control c.590 BC and regained it in 457 BC during the successive Sacred Wars. It came under Theban rule in the fourth century

and was defeated by Philip II of MACEDON in the Third Sacred War of 355 to 346 BC. It was controlled thereafter by the Aetolian League.

PHOENICIA [Phenicia] Ancient territory on the W Syrian coast. A group of city-states controlled by EGYPT since the 16th century BC, it gained independence in the 12th century BC and flourished for centuries thereafter as the leading maritime trader of the ancient Mediterranean world. The Phoenicians founded several important colonies in North Africa, including CARTHAGE and UTICA, and they introduced the alphabet to Europe through its adoption by the Greeks. The commercial and cultural empire fell prey to the Assyrians in the eighth century BC, to the Persians by 500 BC and to Alexander the Great in 332 BC, and eventually became a Roman province in 64 BC. See also BYBLOS, SIDON, TYRE.

PHOENIX (United States) Commercial and industrial city, capital of ARIZONA, on the Salt River, in the SW central part of the state. Settled in 1867 on the site of old Indian canals, it was incorporated in 1881, became the territorial capital in 1889 and the state capital in 1912. It developed rapidly after the completion of the Roosevelt Dam in 1911 and boomed with the advent of three airfields during World War II. There are significant Indian and pioneer relics here at the Pueblo Grande Museum and the Arizona museum, respectively.

PHOENIX ISLANDS (Kiribati) Group of eight islands, central Pacific Ocean, N of Samoa, discovered by British and American explorers in the early 19th century. They were jointly claimed by both Great Britain and the United States; but the two nations agreed in 1939 to jointly administer CANTON ATOLL and Enderbury for 50 years. The remaining islands became part of the British Gilbert and Ellice Islands Colony, then of Kiribati. Some attempts were made to settle three of these the islands from 1938 to 1940, but by 1963 this experiment had failed, and they are now uninhabited.

PHOENIXVILLE (United States) Industrial town on the SCHUYLKILL RIVER, approx. 24 mi NW of Philadelphia, SE PENNSYLVANIA. It was settled in 1720 and incorporated in 1849. Iron deposits have been worked here for many years. The town was the westernmost point of the British advance into Pennsylvania in 1777 during the American Revolution. There are several 18th-century stone houses here.

PHRADA. See FARAH.

PHRA NAKHON SI AYUTTHAYA. See AYUTTHAYA.

PHRYGIA (Turkey) Ancient country in W central Asia Minor, now central Turkey. A kingdom was established here c.1200 BC, and it flourished between the eighth and sixth centuries BC until it finally fell to the Cimmerians in 585 BC. It fell to Alexander the Great in 333 BC, to the Gauls in the third century BC, and to the Romans in 133 BC. Kings Midas and Gordius had their splendid royal residences at GORDIUM. The cult of Cybele was located here. The Phrygian cap, a cocked hat that was a symbol of the cult, later made its way into Roman art and into the European symbolism of the French Revolution.

PHUKET [Bhuket, Puket] [*former:* **Junkceylon, Salang**] (Thailand) Island and province off the W coast of the MALAY PENINSULA, in the Andaman Sea, SW Thailand. It has been a tin-mining region since antiquity. Its capital, Phuket, was founded by settlers from INDIA in the first century BC. The Siamese and Burmese struggled for control of the island in the 18th century, and it was taken by Thailand in the following century.

PHULKIAN STATES (India) PATIALA, Nabha, and JIND, former states of E and SE PUNJAB, presently part of Punjab state. Controlled mostly by the Sikhs by the 18th century, it was a federation of feudal states until united as a Sikh state under Ranjit Singh early in the 19th century. It came under British rule following the Sikh Wars.

PHYLAKOPI. See MELOS.

PHYLE (Greece) Ruins of an ancient fortress, 11 mi NNW of Athens, ATTICA department. It was the base of Thrasybulus's military operations against the Thirty Tyrants in 404/03 BC.

PIACENZA [*ancient:* **Placentia**] (Italy) Agricultural and commercial center, town, and capital of Piacenza province, EMILIA-ROMAGNA region, on the Po River, 40 mi SE of Milan. It was founded by the Romans in 218 BC as a defensive outpost against the Gauls. After its occupation in the early Middle Ages by the Goths, Lombards, and Franks, it became part of the Lombard League in the 12th century AD and witnessed peace negotiations between the league and Frederick Barbarossa. It was controlled by the Visconti family beginning in 1337, the Sforza family, and the PAPAL STATES, beginning in 1512. In 1545 it was given to the Farnese family as part of the duchy of PARMA and Piacenza. It was the first city in Italy to join Piedmont, by plebiscite in 1848, and was incorporated in 1860 into a unified Italy. There is a 13th-century Lombard Gothic town hall, a Lombard Romanesque cathedral of 1122 to 1233, a 16th-century Farnese palace, and several medieval and later churches in the town.

PIALI. See TEGEA.

PIANOSA [*ancient:* **Planasia**] (Italy) Island in the Tuscan Archipelago, Livorno province, in the Tyrrhenian Sea, SW of Elba. A place of exile in Roman times, it was part of PISA and GENOA during the Middle Ages. Inhabitants from PIOMBINO settled here in the 15th century until they were driven off by the Barbary pirates, leaving the island deserted by the 16th century. A penal colony was established here in 1855.

PIATIGORSK. See PYATIGORSK.

PIAVE (Italy) River in NE Italy, 137 mi long, rising in the Carnic Alps and flowing SE into the Adriatic Sea, 22 mi ENE of Venice. After the Italians were defeated at CAPORETTO in 1917 during World War I, they made the river their chief line of defense. The Austrians tried several times to break the line here until they were overwhelmed by a combined Allied offensive in October 1918.

PI-BESETH. See BUBASTIS.

PICACHO PASS. See ARIZONA.

PICARDIE. See PICARDY.

PICARDY [*French:* **Picardie**] (France) Former region of N France, bounded on the W by the English Channel, now included in the Somme, Oise, and Aisne departments. First mentioned in the 13th century, it had a military government *c.*1350 under the Valois family. It was taken by BURGUNDY in 1435 and then acquired by France in 1477. It remained a province until the French Revolution. Picardy was hotly contested during the Hundred Years War, from 1337 to 1453. The Battle of Picardy was fought in the region during World War I in March 1918.

PICHINCHA (Ecuador) Volcano, NW of QUITO, N Ecuador. It was the scene of a battle on May 24, 1822, in which the Spanish Royalists were defeated decisively by the patriots under Antonio José de Sucre. This victory freed the area that eventually became Ecuador.

PICKENS, FORT. See FORT PICKENS.

PICQUIGNY (France) Town, 8 mi NW of Amiens, Somme department, N France. During his invasion of France, Edward IV of England came to easy terms with King Louis XI of France and signed a treaty here on Aug. 19, 1475.

PICTAVIA. See MORAY.

PICTOU (Canada) Resort town on Northumberland Strait, N NOVA SCOTIA, Pictou county. It was settled in 1763 by colonists from Philadelphia and later became a refuge for Scottish Highlands immigrants. It was the starting point in 1833 of the first transatlantic steamboat crossing, accomplished by the *Royal William*. It was incorporated in 1873.

PIEDMONT [*Italian:* **Piemonte**] (Italy) Region in NW Italy, bordering on France to the W, Switzerland to the N, Lombardy to the E, and Liguria to the S. Part of the ROMAN EMPIRE by the first century BC, it became known as the Piedmont by the 13th century AD. Established in the 10th century, it passed to SAVOY in 1045 and was partly feudalized in the 12th century. The counts of Savoy were made dukes by the Holy Roman Emperor in 1391, and Piedmont continued as a nominal fief of the HOLY ROMAN EMPIRE throughout the later Middle Ages. It was often a battleground, especially during the Italian Wars of the 15th and 16th centuries.

Piedmont was held by the house of Savoy throughout the early modern period. Duke Victor Amadeus II was named king of Sicily in 1713 and in 1720 exchanged this title for that of king of SARDINIA. This kingdom was destroyed in the French Revolutionary Wars. The Congress of Vienna in 1814/15 placed the Piedmont in a newly-created kingdom of Savoy, with TURIN as its capital, and the region became a hotbed of Italian unification sentiment during the Risorgimento of the 19th century. King Victor Emmanuel II and his chief minister, Count Cavour, defeated the Austrians in 1859 and absorbed LOMBARDY into the kingdom. Turin then became the capital of the new kingdom of Italy from 1861 to 1864. Thereafter the history of Piedmont became that of Italy.

PIEDRAS NEGRAS (Guatemala) Ruined Mayan city, on the right bank of the Usumacinta River, NW Guatemala, NW PETÉN. Some of the finest pre-Columbian sculptural art and stonework has been discovered in this former center of Mayan civilization. It flourished during the Classic era from 300 to 900 AD. See also MAYA EMPIRE.

PIEDRAS NEGRAS [*former:* **Ciudad Porfirio Díaz**] (Mexico) Mining center, city in Coahuila state, on the RIO GRANDE RIVER, NE Mexico. It was once an international shipping center and was founded in 1849. There is an international bridge here connecting it with EAGLE PASS, TEXAS.

PIEMONTE. See PIEDMONT.

PIERIA (Greece) A region of ancient MACEDONIA, W of the Thermaic Gulf, now known as the Gulf of Thessaloníki. Mt Pierus, in this region, was an early center of the worship of Orpheus and the Muses, sometimes called the Pierides. The Pierian Spring, a traditionally sacred fountain of the Muses, is located here.

PIERRE (United States) Agricultural city and capital of SOUTH DAKOTA, in the central portion of the state, on the MISSOURI RIVER. Once the fortified home of the Aricara Indians, it was an important commercial junction on the Missouri River from 1822 to 1855. It became a steamboat terminus dealing in Black Hills gold from 1876 to 1885 and then a railroad terminus serving a huge agricultural and ranching area.

PIERREFONDS (France) Town near COMPIÈGNE, E Oise department, N France. The town has a famous château dating from the late 14th to the early 15th century. Destroyed by King Louis XIII in the 17th century, in 1858 it was restored by Viollet-le-Duc, well known for his restorations of medieval French buildings. See also CARCASSONNE.

PIETARSAARI [*Swedish:* **Jakobstad**] (Finland) Port city in Vaasa province, on the BALTIC SEA, W Finland. Founded in 1652, it was the birthplace in 1804 of the national poet Johan Ludvig Runeburg.

PIETAS JULIA. See PULA.

PIETERMARITZBURG (South Africa) Manufacturing town and capital of NATAL, 40 mi W of Durban, E South Africa. Founded in 1838 and named after two Boer leaders of the Great Trek, it was the capital of the former Voortrekker Republic of Natal. There are a 19th-century church and British fort here.

PIETERSBURG (South Africa) Commercial city in N central TRANSVAAL, 150 mi NNE of Pretoria, NE South Africa. Founded in 1884, it was the capital of both Transvaal and ORANGE FREE STATE for a short period during the Boer War. The headquarters of Boer forces during the war, it was occupied by the British in 1901.

PIETOLA. See VIRGILIO.

PIGNEROL. See PINEROLO.

PIG'S EYE. See SAINT PAUL.

PIHKVA. See PSKOV.

PIKE CREEK. See KENOSHA.

PIKES PEAK (United States) Mountain in the Front Range of the ROCKY MOUNTAINS, just W of COLORADO SPRINGS at the edge of the Great Plains, E central COLORADO. One of the most famous of the Rocky Mountain summits, it was discovered by U.S. explorer Zebulon M. Pike in 1806. The slogan "Pikes Peak or Bust" made it a symbol of the gold rush of 1859.

PILA [*German:* **Schneidemühl**] (Poland) Industrial city in Poznań province, approx. 55 mi N of Poznań, NW Poland. Chartered in 1380, it was formerly the capital of Grenzmark Posen-West Prussia. It was incorporated as a city in 1513, was taken by PRUSSIA in 1772, and by the Soviets on Feb. 14, 1945 during World War II. It was returned to Poland later in 1945 by the Potsdam Conference.

PILATUS (Switzerland) Mountain in FOUR FOREST CANTONS, central Switzerland, in the Alps. According to legend, Pontius Pilate, who presided over the trial of Jesus, supposedly committed suicide in Rome; his body was then thrown into a lake on the mountain.

PILE O'BONES. See REGINA.

PILIBHIT (India) Trading center, town in N Uttar Pradesh, approx. 50 mi N of Shahjahanpur, N India. It was the seat of the Muslim kingdom of Rohilla toward the end of the 18th century. There is a mosque from this period in the town.

PILLOW, FORT. See FORT PILLOW.

PÍLOS. See PYLOS.

PILOT KNOB, BATTLE OF. See IRONTON, Missouri.

PILSEN. See PLZEŇ.

PILTDOWN [Pilt Down] (England) Site in East Sussex, approx. 7 mi N of Lewes. The skull and jawbone fragments of what was thought to be an early Pleistocene man were discovered here in 1908 but were proven some years later to be a clever fake.

PIMERÍA ALTA (Mexico, United States) Region in SW United States and N Mexico, mostly in ARIZONA and SONORA. It was the homeland of the Pima Indians. Father Eusebio Kino directed a missionary effort in the region in the late 17th and early 18th centuries.

PIMLICO (England) District of the inner LONDON borough of Westminster. It was a well-known resort in the days of Queen Elizabeth I and her court, from 1558 to 1603 and was famous for its ale.

PINANG. See PENANG, PENANG ISLAND.

PINCIACUM. See POISSY.

PÍNDHOS ÓROS. See PINDUS MOUNTAINS.

PINDUS MOUNTAINS [*Greek:* **Píndhos Óros**] (Albania, Greece) Prominent mountain range in NW Greece, extending partly into S Albania. It was the traditional boundary between EPIRUS and THESSALY during Greece's classical era.

PINE BLUFF [*former:* **Mount Marie**] (United States) Industrial city on the Arkansas River, 43 mi SE of Little Rock, SE central ARKANSAS. Founded *c.*1820, it was incorporated in 1839. Confederate forces attacked a Union army here on Oct. 25, 1863 during the Civil War. The Pine Bluff Arsenal, established during World War II, still functions here.

PINEROLO [*French:* **Pignerol**] (Italy) Industrial town in PIEDMONT region, 22 mi SW of Turin, Torino province, NW Italy. First mentioned in 996 AD, it was well fortified when it came under the control of SAVOY in the 13th century, and was an important textile center in the 14th century. It was under French rule during much of the Middle Ages. A state prison in its citadel once held Nicholas Fouquet from the court of Louis XIV, who died here in 1680, as well as the "Man in the Iron Mask," of the late 17th century. There are royal palaces and an 11th-century cathedral in the town.

PINES, ISLE OF [*former:* **Evangelista;** *Spanish:* **Isla de Pinos**] (Cuba) Island in the NW Caribbean Sea, S of the W Cuba coast, La Habana province. It was discovered by Columbus in 1494. A penal colony developed here; and a political prison near Nueva Gerona held Fidel Castro in 1953. He has used it extensively for political prisoners since then.

PINES, ISLE OF [Kunie] [*French:* **Île des Pins**] (France) Island in the SW Pacific Ocean, 32 mi SE of, and part of, NEW CALEDONIA. It was formerly a French penal colony.

PINE TREE HILL. See CAMDEN.

PINEVILLE (United States) Town in S NORTH CAROLINA, 11 mi S of Charlotte. James K. Polk, the 11th president of the United States from 1845 to 1849, was born nearby in 1795. He lived here until 1806.

P'ING-CH'ANG. See TA-T'UNG.

PINGKIANG. See HARBIN.

PINGVELLIR. See THINGVELLIR.

PINKIANG. See HARBIN.

PINKIE (Scotland) Battleground in Lothian region, 6 mi E of Edinburgh. The duke of Somerset, sent by King Henry VIII to enforce a royal marriage, defeated the Scots here on Sept. 10, 1547.

PINSK [*Polish:* **Pińsk**] (USSR) Industrial town at the confluence of the Pina and Pripet rivers, 103 mi E of Brest, Brest oblast, Belorussian SSR. Part of the principality of KIEV in 1097, it became the capital of the duchy of Pińsk in the 13th century. It was taken by LITHUANIA in 1320 and by POLAND in 1569. It became Russian during the second partition of Poland in 1793, then Polish again between 1918 and 1945. Its considerable Jewish population was almost entirely exterminated during World War II, when it was under German occupation.

PINSK MARSHES. See POLESYE.

PIOMBINO (Italy) Industrial town, Livorno province, Tuscany region, 76 mi SW of Florence, on the Tyrrhenian Sea, central Italy. It was controlled by PISA from the 12th to the 14th centuries before being sold in 1399 to the Visconti. It then passed to other local ruling families, before being incorporated into TUSCANY in 1815. It was a French republic briefly during the Napoleonic era.

PIOTRKÓW TRYBUNALSKI [*German:* **Petrikau;** *Russian:* **Petrokov**] (Poland) Manufacturing town in Łódź province, 28 mi SSE of Łódź, central Poland. It was the seat of many Polish diets between 1347 and 1578 and of tribunals between 1578 and 1792. The town was taken by RUSSIA in 1815 and served as the capital of Petrokov province from 1867 to 1915. It was returned to Poland in 1919 and is the site of several old churches and the ruins of a castle established by Casimir the Great (1310–70), the last ruler of the Polish Piast dynasty.

PIPESTONE (United States) Trading center, city in SW MINNESOTA, 38 mi NE of Sioux Falls, South Dakota. There is a quarry nearby from which the local Indians once obtained the pipestone needed to make their ceremonial peace pipes, or calumets. A national monument was erected here in 1937.

PIQUA (United States) Manufacturing city, 27 mi N of Dayton, W OHIO, on the Miami River. Several battles in the French and Indian War were fought nearby, where Indian villages were once situated. Settled in 1797 and chartered in 1929, it was a supply base during the War of 1812 and a prominent 19th-century canal port.

PIRAEUS [*Greek:* **Piraiévs**] (Greece) Port city on the Saronic Gulf, 5 mi SW of Athens, capital of Piraiévs department. Planned by the Athenian naval commander Themistocles *c.*490 BC, its Long Walls connected it with ATHENS. Its fortified port was the Athenian supply base during the Peloponnesian War from 431 to 404 BC. Its arsenal, built from 347 to 323 BC, was destroyed by the Roman Sulla in 86 BC. The modern city was severely damaged by German aerial attacks in World War II.

PIRAIÉVS. See PIRAEUS.

PIRAN [*Italian:* **Pirano**] (Yugoslavia) Port, approx. 45 mi WNW of Rijeka, SLOVENIA. Frederick Barbarossa and the forces of GENOA lost a naval battle here in 1177 to VENICE. A 14th-century cathedral is located here.

PIRANO. See PIRAN.

PÍRGOS. See PYRGOS.

PI-RI'AMSESE. See RAAMSES.

PIRINEOS. See PYRENEES.

PIRMASENS (West Germany) Manufacturing city in North Rhineland-Palatinate, 40 mi WNW of Karlsruhe. Established in the eighth century, it was held by the counts of HANAU-Lichtenburg until 1736, then by HESSE-Darmstadt and later by BAVARIA. The French were beaten here on Sept. 14, 1793 by the duke of Brunswick during the French Revolutionary Wars. The city was badly damaged during World War II, before the U.S. takeover on March 22, 1945.

PIRNA (East Germany) Manufacturing city in Dresden district, 11 mi SE of Dresden, on the Elbe River.

Founded in 1240, it came under BOHEMIA in 1298 and then under MEISSEN in the 15th century. The Saxons surrendered here in 1756, during the Seven Years War fought against PRUSSIA. A Gothic church, Sonnenstein castle, and a town hall have survived here since the 16th century.

PIROT (Yugoslavia) Town on the Nišava River, approx. 33 mi ESE of Niš, SERBIA, E Yugoslavia. It was incorporated into Serbia in 1878 but was occupied by BULGARIA in 1885 and again at the beginning of World War II.

PISA (Greece) The central region of an area known as Pisatis, surrounding OLYMPIA in ancient Greece. Its inhabitants were routed in the early sixth century BC by an army from ELIS and SPARTA as they vied for control of the Olympic games.

PISA [*ancient:* **Pisae**] (Italy) Commercial city, capital of Pisa province, in TUSCANY region, 43 mi SW of Florence, on the Arno River. An Etruscan city, it became a Roman colony in 180 BC and flourished from the ninth to 11th centuries AD as a great maritime power. It conquered the BALEARIC ISLANDS, SARDINIA, and CORSICA from the Saracens in the 11th century and rivaled AMALFI, which it destroyed in 1135. Its commercial empire suffered after it was crushed by the Genoese in the naval battle of Meloria off LEGHORN in 1284. The city was long a Ghibelline stronghold and warred with FLORENCE incessantly for a century and a half. It took LUCCA in 1342 and extended its power in Tuscany before it was conquered by the Florentines in 1406. Pope Alexander V was elected by the Council of Pisa in 1409, which deposed two other claimants. The city fell again to Florence in 1509. Heavy fighting from July 31 to Sept. 2, 1944 in World War II damaged the city. The birthplace of Galileo in 1564, it had been a center of the arts and education since the Middle Ages. Its famous Leaning Tower was begun in the 12th century, and there is also a Tuscan Romanesque 11th-century cathedral, a 12th-century baptistry, 14th-century university and cloistered cemetery, the Camposanto, containing frescoes and other works of art, and many old churches in the city.

PISAE. See PISA.

PISAGUA (Chile) Port in Tarapacá province, approx. 40 mi N of Iquique, N Chile. Chilean forces won a battle here in 1879 during the Nitrate War, or War of the Pacific, waged against PERU and BOLIVIA.

PISAURUM. See PESARO.

PISCARIA. See PESCHIERA DEL GARDA.

PISCATAQUA. See KITTERY.

PÍSEK (Czechoslovakia) Industrial town in Czech SR, 55 mi SW of Prague, on the Otava River, W Czechoslovakia. Established in the 13th century, it was badly damaged in the Thirty Years War. It has some Gothic churches, a 13th-century palace, and a 14th-century stone bridge.

PISGAH. See NEBO, MOUNT.

PISHIN (Pakistan) District in N BALUCHISTAN, N of Quetta. Once controlled by AFGHANISTAN, it was ceded to the British in 1879.

PISHPEK. See FRUNZE.

PISIDIA Ancient country of S Asia Minor, N of PAMPHYLIA. Its bellicose native tribes were never dominated by the ancient powers of the region, including the Persians, Macedonians, and Romans. It was, however, included in the Roman province of CILICIA in the first century AD and later in GALATIA.

PISINO. See PAZIN.

PISIQUID. See WINDSOR.

PISKI (Rumania) Village in S TRANSYLVANIA, on the Mureşul River, SW of Alba Iulia. The Hungarians under Bem defeated the Austrians here in February 1849 in their war for independence from AUSTRIA.

PISTOIA [*ancient:* **Pistoria, Pistoriae**] (Italy) Manufacturing town, capital of Pistoia province, Tuscany region, 17 mi NW of Florence, W Italy. It was under Roman rule at the time when it was the scene of Catiline's death in a battle here in 62 BC. A banking, manufacturing, and cultural center in the 12th and 13th centuries, it was taken by FLORENCE in 1306, by Castruccio Castracani in 1315, and again by Florence by 1329. It passed to the grand duchy of TUSCANY in 1530. There are many notable buildings and churches here, including the Pisan-Romanesque cathedral of the 13th century, the Ospedale del Ceppo of the 14th century, a 13th-century convent, and three 12th-century churches. Cino da Pistoia (1270–1336), the poet and friend of Dante, was born here, as was Pope Clement IX (1667–69).

PISTORIA. See PISTOIA.

PISTORIAE. See PISTOIA.

PITCAIRN ISLAND (Great Britain) Island in the S Pacific Ocean, SE of the Tuamotu Archipelago. The volcanic island was discovered in 1767 by a British ship named for Midshipman Robert Pitcairn who was the first to sight it. It has been a British colony since 1898. In April 1789 the British ship *Bounty*, commanded by Capt. William Bligh on a mission in this region, was the scene of a mutiny of most of the crew, led by the mate, Fletcher Christian. Bligh and others were put adrift, eventually reaching safety. The mutineers sailed the *Bounty* to Pitcairn Island where they settled with Tahitian wives. Their whereabouts were unknown until 1808, when American whalers came to the island.

In 1831 the remaining mutineers and their descendants were moved to Tahiti but later returned to Pitcairn. By 1856 overpopulation became a problem, and so the people were sent to Norfolk Island, approximately 1,000 mi NE of Sydney, Australia. However, some of them soon returned to Pitcairn, and the island is still inhabited by a small group of *Bounty* mutineer descendants. The remains of the *Bounty*, which the original mutineers had sunk, were discovered in 1957 at the south end of the island. Adamston is the only settlement.

PITHECUSA. See ISCHIA.

Volcanic Pitcairn Island today, a remote British outpost halfway between Australia and South America. In 1980 there were 63 inhabitants, all descendants of the mutineers of the H.M.S. *Bounty.*

PITHECUSAE. See ISCHIA.

PITHOM (Egypt) Treasure city of ancient Egypt, in the E part of the NILE RIVER delta, the same as or near ancient Succoth. It was presumably built for the pharoah by the Hebrews. The walls of its storage chambers can still be seen.

PIT RIVER (United States) River, approx. 200 mi long, N CALIFORNIA, flowing SW from NE California to the Sacramento River. The Pit River Indians, also called the Palaihnihan, lived in brush dwellings along its banks in the 19th century.

PITSANULOK. See PHITSANULOK.

PITT ISLAND. See MAKIN.

PITTSBURG [*former:* **Black Diamond**] (United States) Industrial city at the confluence of the Sacramento and San Joaquin rivers, W CALIFORNIA. It was founded in 1835. Coal was discovered and mined here in the 19th century. It includes the site of Camp Stoneman, a major port of embarkation in World War II and the Korean War. It provided the setting for some of Jack London's *Tales of the Fish Patrol.*

PITTSBURGH (United States) Major industrial city at the confluence of the Allegheny and Monongahela rivers, at the formation of the OHIO RIVER, SW PENNSYLVANIA. Founded on an old Indian village site, it became a fur-trading post in the 17th century. The French built FORT DUQUESNE here in 1753. In 1754 Lt. Col. George Washington's Virginia militia were defeated at Great Meadows near here. Later in the year British Gen. Braddock's force and another Virginia detachment under Washington were surprised and soundly defeated by a force of French and Indians from Fort Duquesne near here on July 9. Braddock died of his wounds and three-quarters of the British force were killed or wounded in this first battle of the war. The fort was captured by the British in 1758 and renamed Fort Pitt. The University of Pittsburgh was established here in 1787, and the city was incorporated in 1816. Pittsburgh developed its famous steel industry in the 19th century. The city was a focal point of urban renewal projects in the 20th century. Pittsburgh was the site of a disastrous flood in 1936.

PITTSBURG LANDING. See SHILOH, BATTLE OF.

PITTSFIELD (United States) Resort city and cultural center 40 mi WNW of Springfield, on the Housatonic River, W MASSACHUSETTS. Incorporated in 1761, it was the home of American jurist Oliver Wendell Holmes (1841–1935) and author Herman Melville, who resided at Arrowhead from 1850 to 1863.

PIURA (Peru) Commercial city and capital of Piura department, 35 mi SE of Paita, its port, on the Piura River, NW Peru. Founded by the conquistador Francisco Pizarro in 1532, it was Peru's first settlement. It was badly damaged in 1912 by an earthquake.

PIZZO [**Pizzo di Calabria**] (Italy) Port on the Tyrrhenian Sea, approx. 55 mi NE of Reggio di Calabria, Catanzaro province, central CALABRIA region, S Italy. Joachim Murat, the French marshal who first betrayed and then rejoined Napoleon, was tried and executed here on Oct. 13, 1815 after an unsuccessful attempt to regain NAPLES.

PIZZO DI CALABRIA. See PIZZO.

PLACENTIA [*former:* **Plaisance**] (Canada) Fishing town on Placentia Bay, 62 mi WSW of St. John's, SE NEWFOUNDLAND. Founded and fortified by the French in 1660, it was their Newfoundland headquarters until the Treaty of Utrecht in 1713, when Newfoundland passed to GREAT BRITAIN.

PLACENTIA, Italy. See PIACENZA.

PLACENTIA BAY (Canada) Inlet of SW NEWFOUNDLAND on the Atlantic Ocean. Used as a naval anchorage since the early 17th century, it was the scene of the signing of the Atlantic Charter on Aug. 14, 1941 by Prime Minister Winston Churchill and President Franklin Roosevelt aboard the British ship *Prince of Wales.*

PLACILLA. See CONCÓN.

PLAINFIELD (United States) Town in NE CONNECTICUT, on the Quinebaug River. Settled in 1689 and incorporated in 1699, it has been a center of the textile industry since the early 19th century.

PLAINFIELD [*former:* **Milltown**] (United States) Industrial city, 11 mi WSW of Elizabeth, NE NEW JERSEY. Settled in the 18th century, it was incorporated in 1869. During the American Revolution George Washington supposedly used nearby Washington Rock as a military lookout and established his headquarters at the Nathaniel Drake House, built here in 1746. The Martine House of 1717 and a Friends meeting house of 1788 are also in the city.

PLAIN OF SARON. See SHARON, PLAIN OF.

PLAINS OF ABRAHAM. See ABRAHAM, PLAINS OF.

PLAINVIEW (United States) Agricultural city, 42 mi N of Lubbock, NW TEXAS. It was founded in 1886 and incorporated in 1907. Relics from a late Ice Age hunting culture were unearthed here in 1944/45, along with remains of the giant prehistoric beasts that were hunted.

PLAINVILLE (United States) Manufacturing town on the Quinnipiac River, central CONNECTICUT. Settled in 1657 and incorporated in 1869, it became a manufacturing center shortly after the installation of the New Haven-Northampton Canal in the 1840's. There are a few 18th-century buildings here.

PLAISANCE. See PLACENTIA.

PLÁKA, CAPE [Cape Salmone] (Greece) Cape, S of Cape Sidero, E CRETE. It was mentioned in the New Testament book of Acts 27:7 as visited by St. Paul during his fourth journey.

PLANASIA. See PIANOSA.

PLANT CITY (United States) Agricultural trading center, city, 20 mi E of Tampa, W central FLORIDA. Incorporated in 1885, it was settled on the site of an Indian village and grew during the age of the railroads in the late 19th century as a shipping junction.

PLASSEY (India) Village, approx. 80 mi N of Calcutta, on the Bhagirathi River, NE India. The British Indian Empire was initiated here with Robert Clive's victory on June 23, 1757 over a much larger force led by the local nawab of BENGAL.

PLATAEA [Plataeae] (Greece) Ancient city in SE BOEOTIA, 9 mi S of Thebes, E central Greece. It was allied with ATHENS during the Persian Wars of 500 to 449 BC and aided the city in the battle of MARATHON in 490 BC. It was destroyed in 480 BC by the Persians, who were routed here a year later by the Greeks under Pausanias. It was attacked in 431 BC during the Peloponnesian War by THEBES, from which it had separated before the Persian Wars. The Thebans besieged the city between 429 and 427 BC and finally captured and leveled it. It was rebuilt and then razed a third time by Thebes in 373 BC. Alexander the Great furthered its development, but thereafter it became an insignificant town.

PLATAEAE. See PLATAEA.

PLATA, RIO DE LA [*English:* **River Plate**] Estuary in SE South America, formed by the Paraná and Uruguay rivers, approx. 170 mi long, separating SW URUGUAY from Buenos Aires province of ARGENTINA. The estuary is the last section of the second-largest river system of the continent, the Uruguay River being approximately 1,000 miles long and the Paraná River approximately twice that. The latter is joined upstream by the Paraguay River, which is approximately 1,300 miles long. Dredging of the estuary permits large ships to use it. The estuary's first European visitor was Amerigo Vespucci in 1501, followed by Juan Diaz de Solis in 1516 and Ferdinand Magellan in 1520. Starting in 1526, Sebastian Cabot spent several years exploring La Plata and the other rivers. Settlement on its banks began in 1536, when BUENOS AIRES was founded, although it had to be abandoned in 1541 and refounded in 1580. COLONIA and MONTEVIDEO, in present Uruguay, were first settled by Portuguese from BRAZIL in 1680 and 1717, respectively, but were later taken over by SPAIN. In one of the first naval engagements of World War II, the Battle of the River Plate on Dec. 14, 1939, British warships drove the German pocket battleship *Admiral Graf Spee* into the river's mouth, where it was scuttled.

PLATTE RIVER (United States) River system, approx. 930 mi long. The main Platte River starts at the conjunction of the North and South Platte rivers in SW central NEBRASKA and flows E into the MISSOURI RIVER below OMAHA, Nebraska. The North and South Platte rivers both rise in the COLORADO ROCKY MOUNTAINS and flow east to join in Nebraska. The entire route was followed by the westward-bound pioneers during the great migration of the 19th century, both the OREGON TRAIL and the OVERLAND TRAIL (or Mormon Trail) following the Platte and its branches west across the GREAT PLAINS. The explorer Robert Stuart, who joined John Jacob Astor's ASTORIA venture, was the first to lead a party east across the later route of the Oregon Trail, in 1812/1813. Later, the original Pony Express traveled the route in 1860, followed by the transcontinental telegraph and then the railroads.

PLATTSBURG. See PLATTSBURGH.

PLATTSBURGH [Plattsburg] (United States) Industrial city in NE NEW YORK State, on LAKE CHAMPLAIN, approx. 20 mi S of the Canadian border. It was settled in 1767 and incorporated in 1902. The British won a naval battle off the coast of nearby VALCOUR ISLAND, on Oct. 11, 1776 during the American Revolution. Plattsburgh was the scene of a later American victory on Sept. 11, 1814 over the British in a naval engagement fought here during the War of 1812. The Kent-DeLord house of 1797 now serves the city as a museum.

PLAUEN [*former:* **Plauen in Vogtland]** (East Germany) Manufacturing city in Karl-Marx-Stadt district, 29 mi SW of Zwickau, on the Weisse Elster River, S East Germany. Founded in the 12th century, it passed to BOHEMIA in 1327 and then to SAXONY in 1466. Once the capital of Vogtland, it has been a textile center since the 15th century. It was badly damaged during World War II. It has a medieval church and castle.

PLAUEN IN VOGTLAND. See PLAUEN.

PLEASANT HILL (United States) Town in W LOUISIANA, 60 mi S of Shreveport. Union forces were raided here by Maj. Gen. Richard Taylor and his Confederate troops in a battle fought on April 9, 1864 during the Civil War.

PLEASANT ISLAND. See NAURU.

PLEASANT VALLEY SIDING. See DICKINSON.

PLESKOV. See PSKOV.

PLEVEN [Plevna] (Bulgaria) Manufacturing city, capital of Pleven province, 85 mi NE of Sofia, N Bulgaria. Located near rich oil fields, it was once a Roman settlement but flourished as a Turkish commercial center in the later Middle Ages. It was severely damaged during the course of a long Russian siege in 1877 during the Russo-Turkish War. It finally fell to the Russians.

PLEVNA. See PLEVEN.

PŁOCK [*German:*** Plozk]** (Poland) Industrial town in Warszawa province, on the Vistula River, NE central Poland. A bishopric since 1075, it was the capital from 1138 to 1351 of a duchy. It was controlled by PRUSSIA between 1793 and 1806 and by RUSSIA from 1815 to 1918 before being returned to Poland in 1921. It was under German occupation throughout World War II. There is a 12th-century cathedral here that houses royal Polish tombs from the 11th and 12th centuries.

PLÖCKEN [*Italian:*** Monte Croce]** (Austria, Italy) Mountain pass in the Carnic Alps between the upper Drava River valley in Austria and N Italy. It figured significantly in a campaign carried out in this region in 1917 during World War I.

PLÖERMEL (France) Town in Morbihan department, approx. 25 mi N of Vannes in BRITTANY, NW France. A fine 16th-century church contains several tombs of the dukes of Brittany. Both the church and the town were named for St. Armel (Plöermel means the people of Armel), a hermit who lived here in the sixth century AD. The ancient Estates of Brittany met several times in Plöermel.

PLOESTI. See PLOIESTI.

PLOIEŞTI [Ploeşti] (Rumania) Important petroleum-industry center, city in WALACHIA, 35 mi N of Bucharest, SE central Rumania. Founded in 1596 by a local prince, it bloomed into an important oil center in the 19th century. It was damaged by an earthquake in 1940. An important wartime source of German oil during World War II, it was damaged by heavy Allied bombing attacks in August 1943 and captured a year later by Soviet troops.

PLOMBIÈRES [Plombières-les-Bains] (France) Town in Vosges department, approx. 15 mi S of Épinal, NE France. Its spas were used by the Romans, and it provided the setting for Camillo Bensodi Cavour's agreement, concluded here with Napoleon III in 1858, to give SAVOY and NICE to France.

PLOMBIÈRES-LES-BAINS. See PLOMBIÈRES.

PLOVDIV [*ancient:*** Eumolpias, Philippopolis, Pulpudeva, Trimontium]** (Bulgaria) Commercial and manufacturing city, capital of Plovdiv province, on the Maritsa River, 80 mi SE of Sofia, S central Bulgaria. An old Thracian settlement, it was taken in 341 BC by Philip II of MACEDON and in 46 BC by the Romans, who made it the capital of THRACE. It was ravaged several times in the Middle Ages, was taken by the Turks in 1364 AD, and became the Russian capital of Eastern RUMELIA from 1878 to 1885. In 1885 it joined Bulgaria. It has been shaken by earthquakes on several occasions, especially in 1818 and 1928. The ruins of its ancient city walls and a 13th-century fortress remain.

PLOZK. See PŁOCK.

PLYMOUTH (England) Resort city of Devon, on the ENGLISH CHANNEL, 190 mi SW of London. It has been an important naval station since the 14th century and was the first town incorporated by Parliament, in 1439. It was a port of departure for exploratory voyages by Sir Francis Drake and others, and for the English fleet when it sailed against the Spanish Armada in 1588. The Pilgrim Fathers put in here before sailing for America. It was a Parliamentarian stronghold during the English Civil War from 1642 to 1648. The city was heavily bombed in the early part of World War II. There are several Renaissance churches here.

PLYMOUTH (United States) Resort and fishing town on Plymouth Bay, approx. 35 mi SE of Boston, SE MASSACHUSETTS. The Pilgrims landed here in 1620 and established the first European settlement in NEW ENGLAND and one of the earliest in the New World. Having arrived on the *Mayflower*, these settlers had forged an ad hoc government on board confirmed in a document called the Mayflower Compact. It set a precedent for the formation of later goverments in this and other colonies. There are many 17th-century houses in the town, as well as graves of the original settlers and a reconstruction of the early Plymouth Village.

PLYMOUTH (United States) Village, approx. 14 mi SE of Rutland, E VERMONT. John Calvin Coolidge, the 30th president of the United States (1923–29), was born in the village in 1872.

PLZEN [*German:*** Pilsen]** (Czechoslovakia) Industrial city in Czech SR, 50 mi SW of Prague, W Czechoslovakia. A medieval commercial center of BOHEMIA, it was a Catholic town during the 15th-century Hussite Crusade and became Gen. Albrecht Wallenstein's German headquarters in 1633/34 in the Thirty Years War. Heavily industrialized since the 19th century, it was a major armaments producer in World War I and especially in World War II. It was occupied by GERMANY in 1939 but reverted to Czechoslovakia at the end of World War II. There are medieval churches and abbeys and a 16th-century town hall in the city.

PNOMPENH. See PHNOM PENH.

POCASSET. See PORTSMOUTH, Rhode Island.

POCATELLO (United States) Manufacturing and trading city, 60 mi N of the Utah border, SE IDAHO. Founded in 1882, it became an important railroad junction and was incorporated seven years later. The site of FORT HALL, built in 1834, is nearby, as is the Fort Hall Indian Reservation.

PODGORICA. See TITOGRAD.

PODGORITSA. See TITOGRAD.

PODIUM ANICENSIS. See LE PUY.

PODOLIA [*Russian:*** Podolsk]** (USSR) Fertile agricultural region in W UKRAINE, W central European USSR. It was part of KIEV in the 10th century before being annexed by POLAND in 1430. In the next centuries it belonged to Poland, AUSTRIA, and RUSSIA at different times and was taken by the USSR in 1939. It was occupied by German forces, who practically annihilated its large Jewish population during World War II.

PODOLSK (USSR) Industrial town in Moscow oblast, 25 mi S of Moscow, on the Pakhra River, central European USSR. A medieval fief of the Danilov monastery in MOSCOW, it received an independent charter in 1781. It was a popular site for meetings where Lenin and others exchanged revolutionary ideas. Leo Tolstoy's former estate is here, along with the former castle of Prince Golitzyn.

PODOLSK. See PODOLIA.

POELCAPELLE. See POELKAPELLE.

POELKAPELLE [Poelcapelle] (Belgium) Town in West Flanders province, NNE of Ypres, NW Belgium. On Sept. 11, 1917 French Captain Georges-Marie Guynemer, a famous aerial ace, was killed here in action in World War I. Early the next month the town was captured by British troops, marking their biggest advance during the Third Battle of YPRES.

POICTIERS. See POITIERS.

POINT BARROW (United States) The northernmost location in the United States on the ARCTIC coast, N ALASKA. Discovered in 1826, it has become a focal point of expeditions into the region. Will Rogers, an American actor and humorist, died to the south of this point in an airplane crash in 1935.

POINT DE GALLE. See GALLE.

POINTE-À-PITRE (Guadeloupe) City on Grand Terre Island, in the WEST INDIES, the largest city and major commercial port of Guadeloupe. It was founded in the mid-17th century and is said to be named for a sailor, Pietre, who brought Dutch refugees here from Brazil in 1654. It is a picturesque town, with a cathedral, a bishop's palace, and old houses, the lower floors of which are of stone and the upper of wood.

POINTE LEVI. See LÉVIS.

POINTE-NOIRE (Congo) Commercial city and port in SW Congo, on the Atlantic Ocean, 230 mi SW of Brazzaville. Founded in 1883, it developed commercially with the construction of a port between 1934 and 1939 and a railroad in 1948. It was the capital of Middle Congo from 1950 to 1958.

POINT PLEASANT (United States) Village on the OHIO RIVER, SW OHIO. Ulysses S. Grant (1822–85), commander-in-chief of the Union army during the Civil War and the 18th president of the United States from 1869 to 1877, was born here.

POISSY [ancient: Pinciacum] (France) Town in Yvelines department, on the SEINE RIVER, 11 mi NW of Paris, N France. The baptism of St. Louis IX took place in 1215 in a church located in the town.

POITIERS [ancient: Limonus; former: Poictiers] (France) Commercial city, capital of Vienne department, and formerly of ancient POITOU, 219 mi SW of Paris, at the confluence of the Boivre and Clain rivers, W central France. Founded by the Gallic Pictones, or

Pictavi, it later became a Roman town, and in the fourth century AD was the religious center of Gaul under its bishop, St. Hilarius. It was a Visigoth capital before it fell to the Franks in 507. In 733 Charles Martel, the Carolingian major domus of the Merovingian Frankish kings, met and defeated the Muslims here in the furthest expansion north of Islam. The battle traditionally marks the shift in Frankish tactics from foot to cavalry, an important milestone in the development of feudalism. The brilliant 12th-century court of Eleanor of AQUITAINE was located here, as was the later court of Charles VII (1423–36), who founded the university here in 1431. Earlier, during the Hundred Years War, the Battle of Poitiers was fought here on Sept. 19, 1356 at nearby Maupertius, in which Edward the Black Prince of ENGLAND defeated John II of France. The Edict of Poitiers, signed in the city in 1577, granted religious freedom during the Wars of Religion. Poitiers is of great architectural interest, with many medieval palaces and churches, Roman baths, and the tombs of Christian martyrs.

POITOU (France) Former province in W France, since 1790 in Vienne, Deux-Sèvres, and La Vendée departments. Inhabited by the Gallic Pictones or Pictavi, it was later conquered by the Romans and incorporated into AQUITAINE. Charles Martel stopped the Muslim advance into Europe in 733 AD, when he defeated them between TOURS and the capital city of POITIERS. Possession of Poitou was frequently disputed between the French and ENGLAND. Charles VII made Poitou a French province in 1416. It was divided with the advent of the French Revolution. Part of it, the VENDÉE, was the site of peasant antirevolutionary rebellions between 1793 and 1796.

POKROVSK. See ENGELS.

POKROVSKAYA SLOBODA. See ENGELS.

POLA. See PULA.

POLAND [Polish People's Republic] [*Polish:* Polska] Nation in N central Europe with borders on East Germany to the W, the USSR to the E, Czechoslovakia to the S, and the Baltic Sea to the N. Few nations have had more changes of boundaries, status, and rulers than has Poland. It has appeared on maps, disappeared, and reappeared. It has shrunk and expanded, been strong and weak; but always the Polish people have clung to their ethnic and national heritage.

The area of Poland was inhabited by the Ostrogoths in the mid-fourth century AD. The Slavs arrived c.400 and were then absorbed by the Huns from c.435 to c.455 and by the Avars c.560 to c.625. The kingdom of Great MORAVIA controlled southern Poland c.890. Beginning in 960 the Piast dynasty provided the first rulers of the area that makes up modern Poland. Prince Mieszko I was baptized a Roman Catholic and accepted the overlordship of the German emperor in 967. Boleslav III Wrymouth was the first to take the title of king in 1025. He conquered the pagan Pomeranian Poles of the Baltic coast.

Beginning in 1138, the kingdom broke up into several smaller principalities; the Mongols devastated the country in 1241. Reunification began *c.*1320. Ladislaus II (reigned 1386–1434) began the Jagiello dynasty, which lasted until 1572. During this time the Teutonic Knights, a German crusading order, gained some of northern Poland but were defeated at the Battle of TANNENBERG in 1410. In the 16th century Poland entered a golden age. Closely allied with LITHUANIA, it dominated an empire that reached from the Baltic Sea to the Black Sea. With the end of the Jagiello dynasty, however, the nobles, among whom there was seldom agreement on public issues, made the establishment of another strong monarchy impossible.

In the 17th century Poland was involved in numerous wars with Russia, Sweden, and the Ottoman Turks; and by the end of this period it was virtually at the mercy of RUSSIA, PRUSSIA, and AUSTRIA. Poland was ravished several times during the Great Northern War of 1700 to 1721, and suffered further in the War of the Polish Succession of 1733 to 1735. In 1772 Russia, Prussia, and Austria partitioned Poland, taking most of its territory. Again in 1792 these three nations carved up the country, leaving only a central part independent, and in 1795 Poland disappeared entirely. In 1814 the Congress of Vienna shifted boundaries so as to give Russia more power over the dismembered land. The Poles revolted in 1830, but Russia defeated them in 1831. Insurrections broke out in 1846, 1848, and 1863, but all were put down.

The defeat of Germany and Austria-Hungary in World War I, together with the military collapse of Russia, gave Poland independence once more on Nov. 9, 1918. Poland fought Russia in 1920 and by a treaty in 1921 gained some territory. Caught between the communist USSR and Nazi Germany, and allied with France and Great Britain, Poland was invaded by GERMANY on Sept. 1, 1939 after refusing Hitler's demand to give up the port city of GDAŃSK (Danzig). On September 17 the USSR, having cynically made a treaty with the Nazis in August, invaded from the east, and Poland was partitioned again for the remainder of World War II. There was strong resistance, especially in the WARSAW uprising of August to October 1944, but Poland was not freed until early 1945.

Poland's boundaries were changed after the war, with the USSR retaining some prewar territory in the east and Poland receiving German land in the west. Russian domination of this part of Europe prevented any democratic processes from developing in establishing a new government, and in 1952 Poland became a communist state. Since then its domestic and foreign policies have been close to those of the USSR. After mass demonstrations in 1956 there was some relaxation of the oppressive rule, but in the 1960's Communist Party controls were strengthened. Although there was much industrialization after World War II, agriculture lagged, and the economy suffered from high prices and shortages. This led to rioting in late 1970 and some reforms. Ten years later similar unrest resulted in strikes and the formation of a labor union, Solidarity, which the government felt forced to recognize in August 1980, a most unusual step for a communist government. However, as debate heightened over labor's political and economic rights, the government declared martial law on Dec. 13, 1981, jailed union leaders, and reinstituted a repressive government. In October 1982 Poland's martial-law government banned Solidarity, but demonstrations, strikes, and opposition continued despite repression.

POLDHU (England) Point in CORNWALL, on Mount's Bay, 13 mi SW of Falmouth. The first transatlantic radio message was sent from here to Newfoundland in 1901 by the inventor, Guglielmo Marconi.

POLESYE [Pinsk Marshes, Pripet Marshes, Pripyat Marshes] (USSR) Swampy lowlands in S Belorussian SSR and NW Ukraine, on both sides of the Pripyat River, formerly in Poland. The largest swamp in Europe, it has long been a major obstacle to military operations and migratory movements in POLAND and Russia. It was the scene of much fighting in World War I, especially in 1914 and 1915. In World War II it was an obstacle to troop advances for both Germany in 1941 and the USSR in 1943/44.

POLISH CORRIDOR (Poland) A narrow strip of land, no more than approx. 50 mi wide. The area was first colonized by the Polish, but was taken by the Teutonic Knights in 1309. It was given to Poland under the Treaty of Versailles in 1919, which gained access to the Baltic Sea and the great port of GDAŃSK (then Danzig). It separated the German provinces of EAST PRUSSIA and POMERANIA and was therefore a bone of contention between Poland and GERMANY. When Hitler's demand for the cession of the free city of Danzig was refused, he sent his troops into Poland on Sept. 1, 1939, precipitating World War II. The area was returned to Poland, along with Gdańsk, in 1945 after World War II.

POLISH PEOPLE'S REPUBLIC. See POLAND.

POLLENTIA. See POLLENZA.

POLLENZA [*ancient:* Pollentia] (Italy) Town in Macerata province, S central MARCHES region, central Italy. Stilicho, the Vandal general commissioned to protect the ROMAN EMPIRE against the Visigoths, repulsed them here in 403 AD but allowed their leader, Alaric, to escape with his troops into the mountains. Seven years later Alaric sacked Rome.

POLLONARRUA [Polonnaruwa] (Sri Lanka) Ancient city and capital of Sri Lanka, formerly Ceylon. The capital of Ceylon since the late eighth century, it flourished under the last king of the Singhalese dynasty, Parakrama Bahu I (1164–97). It held a lavish court and was the center of Buddhist worship during this time. There were several impressive images of Buddha. The city was conquered by the Hindu Tamils in the 13th century.

POLONNARUWA. See POLLONARRUA.

POLOTSK (USSR) Commercial and manufacturing center, city in Vitebsk oblast, Belorussian SSR, 60 mi NW of Vitebsk, on the Western Dvina River. First mentioned in 862 AD, it was the capital of the former principality of Polotsk from the 10th to 13th centuries. A significant commercial center, it was controlled by

LITHUANIA from the 13th century until it attained independence in 1498. It was taken by RUSSIA in 1772 and was badly damaged in World War II. A medieval monastery and the 11th-century cathedral of Sofia are in the city.

POLSKA. See POLAND.

POLTAVA [Pultova, Pultowa] [*former:* **Ltava**] (USSR) Manufacturing city, capital of Poltava oblast, Ukrainian SSR, on the Vorskla River, 81 mi SW of Kharkov. A Slavic settlement existed here in the eighth century, and it was mentioned as Ltava in 1174. It passed to LITHUANIA in 1430 and was a stronghold of Chmielnicki's Cossack troops in the 17th century. RUSSIA under Peter the Great defeated Charles XII of SWEDEN here on July 8, 1709 in an important battle of the Great Northern War. The city flourished in the 18th and 19th centuries as a commercial, cultural, and nationalistic center. It was damaged extensively during World War II. The author, Nikolai Gogol (1809–52), made this area the setting for much of his work. There are a 17th-century monastery and several 18th-century churches in the city.

POLTORATSK. See ASHKHABAD.

POLYDORION. See BURDUR.

POLYNESIA (Pacific Ocean) Islands forming one of the three main groupings of Oceania in the Pacific Ocean. The other groups are MELANESIA and MICRONESIA. Polynesia consists of islands in the central and southern Pacific between 30° N and 47° S lat. European explorers began to discover them in the 16th century, but it was the late 18th century before all the important ones were located and explored. The islands of Polynesia include: the COOK ISLANDS, EASTER ISLAND, FRENCH POLYNESIA, the HAWAIIAN ISLANDS, the LINE ISLANDS, the PHOENIX ISLANDS, the SAMOA ISLANDS, the TOKELAU ISLANDS, the TONGA ISLANDS, and TUVALU. NEW ZEALAND is ethnologically, but not geographically, Polynesian because of its native Maori.

POLYNESIA, FRENCH. See FRENCH POLYNESIA.

POLYNÉSIE FRANÇAISE. See FRENCH POLYNESIA.

POMARIA. See TLEMCEN.

POMERANIA [*German:* **Pommern**; *Polish:* **Pomorze**] Region in N central Europe, along the BALTIC SEA from the VISTULA RIVER in Poland westward to the area of STRALSUND in East Germany. Slavic tribes living here in the 10th century AD were its first recorded inhabitants. Mieszko I, founder of the Piast dynasty and ruler of POLAND from 962 to 992, conquered Pomerania. The region, however, gained independence in the 11th century but became Polish territory again in the 12th when Boleslav III, duke of Poland from 1101 to 1138, reconquered it. In 1135 he signed a treaty at Meresburg by which he received Pomerania as a fief of Lothair II, the Holy Roman emperor. Eastern Pomerania, becoming known as POMERELIA, achieved independence, and after the early 14th century its history was different from that of the rest of Pomerania. Pomerania continued as a duchy of the HOLY ROMAN EMPIRE until 1367, with the island of RÜGEN added in 1325. During the Thirty Years War, SWEDEN invaded Pomerania in 1630. By the Treaty of Westphalia that ended the war in 1648, Sweden received Hither Pomerania, the western part, while Frederick William, elector of BRANDENBURG, received Farther Pomerania to the east.

In 1675 Frederick William defeated Charles XI of Sweden and occupied Swedish Pomerania, but by the Treaty of Saint-Germain in 1679, at the end of the Third Dutch War, he had to restore his conquests to Sweden. In the Great Northern War, Sweden lost approximately half of its part of Pomerania to PRUSSIA, then encompassing Brandenburg, in 1720 but held the rest until the Napoleonic period, when the French overran it. France restored it when peace was concluded in 1809. In 1814, in the Treaty of Kiel, Sweden gave Pomerania to DENMARK in exchange for NORWAY, but a year later at the Congress of Vienna Denmark exchanged Pomerania with Prussia for the duchy of LAUENBURG. Until the end of World War I Pomerania remained in Prussian hands. Then, as a result of Germany's defeat, part of Pomerania was transferred to Poland. The Soviets overran Pomerania toward the end of World War II, and at the Potsdam Conference of 1945 the Allies agreed to give Pomerania east of the ODER RIVER to Poland. Much of the German-speaking population was expelled. The remainder of the area is now part of East Germany. Among Pomerania's cities, some of which were important members of the HANSEATIC LEAGUE, are GDAŃSK (formerly Danzig), Stralsund, and SZCZECIN (formerly Stettin).

POMERELIA [*German:* **Pommerellen**] (Poland) Medieval district on the Baltic Sea, formerly part of POMERANIA. Inhabited by pagan Pomerianian Poles in the 12th century AD, it was conquered by Boleslav III Wrymouth (1101–38) and set off from Pomerania. It was ruled by the Teutonic Knights, who took it from rebellious vassals of Ladislaus the Short and refused to surrender it to him. It was finally incorporated into Poland in 1466. It became a possession of PRUSSIA following the partition of Poland in the late 18th century, but was returned to Poland after World War I.

POMMERELLEN. See POMERELIA.

POMMERN. See POMERANIA.

POMONA. See MAINLAND.

POMORZE. See POMERANIA.

POMPAELO. See PAMPLONA.

POMPEIOPOLIS. See SOLI.

POMPTON LAKES (United States) Residential city in NE NEW JERSEY, 20 mi NW of Newark. Founded in 1682 by the Dutch, it was incorporated in 1895. It has many dwellings remaining from the colonial era.

PONAPE [*former:* **Ascension**] (United States) Island of the Senyavin Islands, E CAROLINE ISLANDS, U.S. Trust Territory, in the W Pacific Ocean. There are significant ruins here from previous inhabitation, including stone walls and dikes. It was fortified by JAPAN during World War II.

PONCA CITY [*former:* **New Ponca**] (United States) Commercial city on the Arkansas River, 105 mi NE of Oklahoma City, N OKLAHOMA. It was founded in 1893 during one of the nation's greatest land rushes, following the opening of the CHEROKEE Strip to pioneer settlement. It was incorporated six years later and now has both a pioneer and an Indian museum, as well as the Ponca Indian Reservation.

PONCE (Puerto Rico) Commercial and industrial city, 4 mi from its Caribbean port of Playa, S Puerto Rico. One of the oldest European cities in the New World, it was founded in the early 16th century. Once a colony of SPAIN, it was named after Puerto Rico's first governor, Ponce de León (1509–12). It has an 18th-century fort and a Spanish cathedral.

PONDICHERRY [*French:* **Pondichéry**] (India) Port and industrial city, capital of Pondicherry territory and of former FRENCH INDIA, approx. 95 mi SW of Madras. Granted to the French East India Company, it was founded in 1683 but was captured ten years later by the Dutch, who returned it in 1697. The British made several attempts to gain control of the city, but it became a French possession until 1954 by the terms of the Treaty of Paris in 1814. It was taken by India in 1954.

PONDICHÉRY. See PONDICHERRY.

PONNANI (India) Town and port, at the mouth of the Ponnani River, 38 mi S of Calicut, central Kerala, S India. Tippoo Sahib, sultan of Mysore from 1782 to 1799, carried on the war against the British in this region started by his father, Haidar Ali, and was routed by them in a battle fought here in November 1782.

PONS AELII. See NEWCASTLE UPON TYNE.

PONS MILVIUS. See MILVIAN BRIDGE.

PONS MULVIUS. See MILVIAN BRIDGE.

PONS VETUS. See PONTEVEDRA.

PONT-À-MOUSSON (France) Industrial town in Meurthe-et-Moselle department, on the MOSELLE RIVER, 12 mi NNW of Nancy, NE France. Founded in the 13th century, it was the seat of a university from 1572 to 1768. A crown possession since 1632, it was a significant battle site in World War I. U.S. troops initiated their drive in the battle of ST-MIHIEL from this point on Sept. 12, 1918.

PONT DU GARD. See NÎMES, France.

PONTEFRACT (England) Town in West Yorkshire, 13 mi SE of LEEDS. An Anglo-Saxon fort once stood on the site of Pontefract Castle, built in 1080. Here Richard II of England was imprisoned and was probably murdered in 1400. Incorporated in 1484, the city was besieged repeatedly during the English Civil War. The first parliamentary election utilizing the secret ballot was held here in 1872. The first licorice industry began here in 1760.

PONTEVEDRA [*ancient:* **Duos Pontes, Pons Vetus**] (Spain) Manufacturing city and capital of Pontevedra province, 65 mi SW of Lugo, NW Spain. It was known as Duos Pontes to the Romans. The *Santa*

Maria was built here in the late 15th century for Columbus. A Roman bridge and the Gothic church of Santa Maria are in the city.

PONTHIEU (France) Ancient region in PICARDY, N France. Ruled by local nobility by at least the ninth century, it passed to CASTILE in 1251 and, through royal marriage, to ENGLAND from 1272 to 1336 and again from 1360 to 1369. It became a French possession in 1690.

PONTIAC (United States) Industrial city, 25 mi WNW of Detroit, SE MICHIGAN, on the Clinton River. Founded in 1818 and incorporated in 1837, it became a carriage-production center toward the end of the century and was converted into an automobile-manufacturing center in the beginning of the next. Ottowa Indian Chief Pontiac, who died in 1766, is said to be buried here.

PONTIAE. See PONZA ISLANDS.

PONTIANAK (Indonesia) Commercial city, port, and capital of West Kalimantan province, approx. 390 mi E of Singapore, W BORNEO. The Dutch East India Company operated a trading post in a sultanate established in 1772, of which Pontianak was the capital. The city flourished later as Borneo's major port for gold exports. It was occupied from 1942 to 1945 by Japanese troops during World War II.

PONTIFICAL STATES. See PAPAL STATES.

PONTINA. See PONTINE MARSHES.

PONTINE ISLANDS. See PONZA ISLANDS.

PONTINE MARSHES [*Italian:* **Agro Pontino, Pontina**] (Italy) Marshy region between the Tyrrhenian Sea and the Appenine Mts., Latina province, S LATIUM region, central Italy, stretching from Cisterna di Latina on the N to Terracina on the S. The region is named after the lost ancient town of Pontina. Crossed by the famous Roman road, the APPIAN WAY, by 213 BC, this once fertile area degenerated into marshland even during the imperial period, and remained a malarial wasteland through the Middle Ages. Popes Leo X (1513–21), Sixtus V (1585–90), and Pius VI (1775–99) attempted to reclaim it, but it remained uninhabitable until 1928, when drainage projects were begun and new towns founded. The area was again flooded because of damage during the ANZIO invasion of January and February 1944, in World War II. The destruction was repaired immediately after the war.

PONTISARAE. See PONTOISE.

PONTIVY (France) Town in Morbihan department, 30 mi NW of Vannes, NW France. Napoleon built the new town of Napoléonville here and utilized it as his military headquarters in BRITTANY.

PONTOISE [*ancient:* **Briva Isarae; Pontisarae**] (France) Residential town, capital of Val-d'Oise department, 18 mi NNW of Paris, on the OISE RIVER, N France. A French possession since 1064 and once the capital of French VEXIN, it was the meeting site for the Parlement of Paris in 1652, 1720, and 1753. The town has a medieval cathedral and a Renaissance church.

PONTUS (Turkey) Ancient country in NE Asia Minor, on the coast of the BLACK SEA, in modern Turkey. Established as a kingdom in the fourth century BC, it expanded its borders slowly and flourished as a strong power under Mithradates VI (c.131–63 BC). Pompey defeated the army of Mithradates in 66 BC, and Pontus was incorporated into the ROMAN EMPIRE soon after. It was a Christian center in the first century AD. See also AMASYA.

PONTUS EUXINUS. See BLACK SEA.

PONTYPRIDD (Wales) Town in Mid-Glamorgan, 11 mi W of Cardiff. It was named after a famous bridge built here in 1756 across the Taff River. The bridge still exists.

PONY EXPRESS. See OVERLAND TRAIL.

PONZA ISLANDS [Pontine Islands, Ponziane Islands] [*ancient:* **Pontiae**] (Italy) Island group in the Tyrrhenian Sea, Napoli province, Campania region, SW Italy. The most significant island of the group, Ponza, has many Roman remains and dates back to Greek colonization. It was the site of many early Christian monasteries. In 1435 a naval fleet from GENOA crushed another from ARAGON here, but frequent invasions of the island led to its abandonment by the 16th century. An ancient place of banishment, it was used for this same purpose by Mussolini in the 20th century.

PONZIANE ISLANDS. See PONZA ISLANDS.

POOLE (England) Town in Dorset, 97 mi SW of London, on the ENGLISH CHANNEL. Originally chartered by the Crown in 1258, it became independent in the following century and was incorporated in 1569. It flourished as a commercial port in the 18th century.

POONA [Pune] (India) Industrial city, capital of both Poona district and division, at the confluence of the Mula and Mutha Rivers, 80 mi ESE of Bombay, central W India. Once the capital of the MARATHAS in the 17th and 18th centuries, it has several temples and palaces from that era. It came under British protection in 1818, and was later a military and administrative center. The Hindu temple of Parvati and the National Defense Academy are in the city.

POOTOO. See P'U-T'O SHAN.

POPAYÁN (Colombia) Cultural center, city, and capital of Cauca department, 110 mi S of Cali, SW Colombia. Founded in 1536, it was a center of religious and commercial activity before the wars of independence in the early 18th century. Populated mostly by Spanish aristocrats during the colonial era, it was also a cultural oasis that housed a university established in 1640. Many eminent persons were born here, including national presidents, writers, and naturalist Francisco José de Caldas. There are several colonial Spanish churches and monasteries in the city.

POPOCATÉPETL (Mexico) Famous volcanic mountain, 40 mi SE of Mexico City, Puebla state, SE central Mexico. Hernando Cortés's soldiers gouged sulfur from its crater for use in making gunpowder. Its peak was first ascended in 1522. It has been dormant since 1702.

POPPI (Italy) Town in Arezzo province, E TUSCANY region, on the Arno River, central Italy. Mino da Fiesole, a sculptor of the early Renaissance, was born in this town in 1429. There is also an old castle here.

POPULONIA. See POPULONIUM.

POPULONIUM [Populonia] [*ancient:* **Pufluna, Pupluna**] (Italy) Ancient town of ETRURIA, on the Ligurian Sea, N of Piombino. An ancient metal-crafting center, it was besieged and sacked by the Roman general Sulla in 82 BC, by the Ostrogoth King Totila (d. 552 AD), and a few years later by the Lombards. A medieval castle was constructed on this site, and many ancient ruins remain here, some from the Iron Age.

PORBANDAR (India) Town in Gujurat state, on the Arabian Sea, 275 mi NW of Bombay, W central India. It was the capital of the former state of Porbandar. Mohandas Karamchand Gandhi (1869–1948), also known as Mahatma, was born here.

PORDENONE [*German:* **Portenau**] (Italy) Manufacturing town and capital of Pordenone province, Friuli-Venezia Giulia region, 37 mi SW of Udine, NE Italy. Destroyed in a battle between warring neighbors, in 1233, it passed to VENICE in 1508 and was returned to united Italy in 1866.

POREČ [*Italian:* **Parenzo**] (Yugoslavia) Town on ISTRIA peninsula, on the Adriatic Sea, 30 mi NW of Pula, NW Yugoslavia. A basilica in this town dates back to the sixth century AD. Poreč was part of Italy prior to World War II.

PORI [*Swedish:* **Björneborg**] (Finland) Manufacturing city and port, Turku ja Pori province, 135 mi NW of Helsinki, near the Gulf of Bothnia, SW Finland. Founded at the mouth of the Kokemäki River in 1365, it was removed to its present site in 1558 and was chartered in 1564. It was once a member of the HANSEATIC LEAGUE. The city had the largest commercial fleet in the nation by the mid-19th century. It was destroyed by fires in the 17th and 19th centuries.

PO RIVER [*ancient:* **Eridanus**; *Latin:* **Padus**] (Italy) River, the longest in Italy, flowing through the most important commercial and agricultural region of the country, approx. 405 mi long, rising on the border of France in the Cottian Alps in NW Italy and flowing generally E in a wide valley until it reaches the Adriatic Sea. The Po flows through, or forms a boundary of, several of Italy's historic regions: PIEDMONT, LOMBARDY, EMILIA-ROMAGNA, and VENETO. On its banks and those of its tributaries lie many historic towns.

TURIN was the most important Roman town in the western Po valley and later capital of Piedmont. ALESSANDRIA, just south of the river on the Tanaro River, was founded by Pope Alexander III (1159–81) and the Lombard League as a fortress against the Holy Roman Emperor, Frederick I Barbarossa. Where the TICINO RIVER joins the Po was the scene of Hannibal's victory for CARTHAGE over the Romans in 218 BC. PAVIA on the Ticino was the capital of the Lombard kings. MILAN, although not on the river, is in the heart of the Po basin, the second-largest city in Italy, important since Roman times. PIACENZA was an important town throughout the Middle Ages and a center of the Farnese duchy of PARMA and Piacenza. CREMONA is famous for its families of violin makers, such as the Stradivari; FERRARA was the site of the brilliant Renaissance court of the Este family.

The Po delta, also watered by the ADIGE RIVER, is now a well-drained and rich agricultural area. It was the scene of intense resistance by Italy's partisans against both the Germans and Italian fascists during World War II.

The Po River, Italy's longest river, near its Alpine source on Monte Viso. Its valley in northern Italy is rich in agriculture and industry, as well as in history.

PORKKALA PENINSULA (Finland) Peninsula, on the Gulf of Finland, 20 mi SW of Helsinki, S Finland. It was leased for fifty years to the USSR in exchange for HANGÖ, according to the Russo-Finnish armistice of Sept. 4, 1944. The Soviets used it as a naval base before returning it to Finland in 1956.

PÓROS (Greece) Island in the AEGEAN SEA, SE Greece. On the island are the remains of a temple of Poseidon, where Demosthenes committed suicide in 322 BC. An international conference was held here in 1828, shortly after the Greek War of Independence, to discuss the new nation's political course.

PORRENTRUY [*German:* **Pruntrut**] (Switzerland) Town in N Bern canton, NW Switzerland. The residence of the prince-bishops of BASEL from 1528 to 1792, it has been a thriving watchmaking town for many years.

PORSGRUND. See PORSGRUNN.

PORSGRUNN [*former:* **Porsgrund**] (Norway) Industrial town and port in Telemark county, 100 mi SW of Oslo, S Norway. A customs station in the mid-17th century, it was a leader in Norway's industrial revolution in the early 19th century.

PORTAGE (United States) Manufacturing city, 97 mi NW of Milwaukee, at the confluence of the Fox and Wisconsin rivers and the Portage Ship Canal, S central WISCONSIN. Explored in 1673 by Jacques Marquette and Louis Jolliet, it was the site of Fort Winnebago in 1828 and was settled in 1835. Historian Frederick Jackson Turner (1861–1932) was born and lived here. The ruins of Fort Winnebago and the restored Indian Agency House of 1832 are located in the city.

PORTAGE LA PRAIRIE (Canada) Shipping center and city, on the Assiniboine River, 54 mi W of Winnipeg, S MANITOBA. In 1738 the French established Fort La Reine here, where fur traders crossed the river to Lake Manitoba. The city was founded in 1853 and incorporated in 1907 and was the site of a Canadian Air Force training post during World War II.

PORTA HERCYNIAE. See PFORZHEIM.

PORTALEGRE (Portugal) Town and capital of Portalegre district, 100 mi NE of Lisbon, E central Portugal. Once a Roman town, it has several 16th and 17th-century edifices, including a cathedral begun in 1556 and extended considerably in the 18th century.

PORT ANGELES (United States) City and port of entry, 65 mi WNW of Seattle, on Juan de Fuca Strait, opposite VICTORIA, Canada, NW WASHINGTON. Designated a federal city by President Abraham Lincoln in 1862, it is the only one in the nation outside of Washington, D.C.

PORT APRA. See APRA HARBOR.

PORT ARTHUR, Canada. See THUNDER BAY.

PORT ARTHUR [*Chinese:* **Lü-shun;** *Japanese:* **Ryojun**] (China) City in Liaoning province, NE China, at the S tip of the Liao-tung peninsula. The site has been a port and a strongpoint for more than 2,000 years. The Han dynasty used it in the process of extending its sway over KOREA in the second century BC. Other Chinese dynasties fortified it, but in 1633 it was captured by the Manchus. Briefly occupied by the British in 1858, in 1880 it was strongly fortified by the Chinese and became the chief base of that country's first modern fleet. In 1898 Russia was given a leasehold on the peninsula that included Port Arthur. On Feb. 8, 1904, without warning, the Japanese attacked the Russians here, bottling up the czarist fleet and, after a siege, capturing Port Arthur on Jan. 2, 1905. It remained in Japanese hands until 1945 when, at the end of World War II, it became the headquarters of a joint Sino-Soviet administration. Ten years later the Chinese assumed exclusive control. Since then Port Arthur has been combined for administrative purposes with TALIEN (Dairen) as the joint municiplaity of Lü-ta.

PORT ARTHUR (United States) Industrial city and port on Sabine Lake, connected by canal with the Gulf of Mexico, 105 mi E of Houston, SE TEXAS. Settled in 1853, it was incorporated in 1898. It gained importance after Arthur Stilwell made it the southern terminus of the Kansas Southern Railroad in 1894. It became a boom town after oil was discovered in 1901 at Spindletop. See BEAUMONT, Texas.

PORT-AU-PRINCE (Haiti) Commercial port, city, and capital of Haiti, on the Gulf of Gonave, HISPANIOLA ISLAND, WEST INDIES. Founded by the French in 1749, it became the capital of the French colony of Saint-Domingue in 1770 and remained its capital when it gained independence and was renamed Haiti in 1804. It suffered severe damage from earthquakes, fire, and civil strife and lost much of its appeal and importance. The old French quay of 1780 is located here.

PORTBAIL (France) Town in Manche department, W COTENTIN PENINSULA, NORMANDY, NW France. It was taken by Allied troops on June 18, 1944, during World War II, thus making possible a cross-peninsular advance.

PORT BLAIR (India) Town and port on the SE coast of South ANDAMAN Island, in the Bay of Bengal, the capital of Andaman and Nicobar Islands territory. It was occupied by the British in 1789 but a few years later was deserted until a penal colony was established here from 1858 to 1945. The town was under Japanese occupation from 1942 to 1945 during World War II.

PORTCHESTER (England) Town and Roman fort of the SAXON SHORE, in Hampshire, on Portsmouth harbor, 13 mi ESE of Southampton. The entire defensive wall of this massive fortress of the third century AD and 14 of the original 20 semicircular towers survive in one of the most impressive Roman sites in Britain. A Norman keep was built into the northwest corner. An 11th-century timber hall has been excavated west of the Augustinian priory church here, founded in 1133, which lies in the southeastern corner of the old fortress. See also PEVENSEY, RICHBOROUGH.

PORT CHESTER [*former:* **Sawpit**] (United States) Industrial suburb, village on LONG ISLAND SOUND, 25 mi NE of New York City, SE NEW YORK State. Settled c.1660, it was known as Sawpit until 1837 and was incorporated in 1868. Gen. Israel Putnam, who lost several battles to the British in the Hudson Highlands, made his headquarters here in 1777/78 during the American Revolution. Some colonial dwellings still stand here.

PORT CLARENCE. See MALABO.

PORT CONWAY (United States) Village in S King George county, on the Rappahannock River, NE VIRGINIA. James Madison (1751–1836), fourth president of the United States, from 1809 to 1817, was born here.

PORT DALRYMPLE (Australia) Port on the mouth of the Tamar River, N TASMANIA. One of the island's oldest permanent communities, it was first settled in 1804. It was a military post until 1846.

PORT ELIZABETH (South Africa) Industrial and commercial town and major port on Algoa Bay, SE CAPE PROVINCE, approx. 410 mi E of Cape Town, S South Africa. Fort Frederick was established here in 1799, and the town was founded by a group of settlers from GREAT BRITAIN in 1820. It progressed industrially with the advent of the railroad in the late 19th century. See also KIMBERLEY.

PORTENAU. See PORDENONE.

PORT-EN-BESSIN (France) Small coastal village on the Bay of the Seine, Calvados department, NORMANDY, NW France. This town separated the U.S. and British forces' landing sites during the invasion of Normandy, on June 6, 1944, in World War II.

PORT GIBSON (United States) Industrial town, 28 mi S of Vicksburg, SW MISSISSIPPI. A battle fought here from April 30 to May 1, 1863 was part of Gen. Ulysses S. Grant's march on VICKSBURG, a campaign designed to secure Union control of the MISSISSIPPI RIVER.

PORT GLASGOW (Scotland) Commercial port on the Firth of Clyde, Strathclyde region, 17 mi WNW of Glasgow. Founded as GLASGOW's port in 1668, it was an important trading junction and became a city in 1775. Its dry dock of 1762 was one of Scotland's first; the ruins of 16th-century Newark Castle are also located here.

PORT HARCOURT (Nigeria) City in SE Nigeria, West Africa, a major port on the Bonny River, approx. 40 mi from the Gulf of Guinea. It was founded in 1912 on the site of an abandoned village, Obomotu, and is named for Viscount Lewis Harcourt, who was British secretary of state for colonies from 1910 to 1915.

PORT HUDSON (United States) Village on the MISSISSIPI RIVER, SE central LOUISIANA. Union Gen. Nathaniel Prentiss Banks coordinated his siege of Port Hudson with Gen. Ulysses S. Grant's siege of VICKSBURG as part of the Union campaign to gain control of the Mississippi River. The village was battered for six weeks before falling on July 9, 1863, shortly after Vicksburg was taken.

PORT HUENEME [**Hueneme**] (United States) City on Santa Barbara Channel, approx. 40 mi W of Los Angeles, near Point Hueneme, S CALIFORNIA. It was founded in 1870 and incorporated in 1948. The U.S. Navy operated a training base here in World War II and now maintains a guided missile range and a Seabee center in the city.

PORT HURON [*former:* **Fort Gratiot**] (United States) Manufacturing city, at the confluence of the St. Clair River and LAKE HURON, 57 mi NE of Detroit, SE MICHIGAN. It was first settled in 1686 and incorporated in 1857. A French fort was established here in 1685, followed by the construction of a U.S. fort in 1814 during the War of 1812. Thomas Edison spent his youth here, and the Fort Gratiot lighthouse, built in the early 19th century, is the oldest one existing on the Great Lakes.

PORT JEFFERSON. See LONG ISLAND.

PORT JERVIS (United States) Manufacturing and resort city approx. 60 mi NW of New York City, on the DELAWARE RIVER, SE NEW YORK State. Settled by the Dutch c.1700, it was incorporated in 1907. Destroyed in 1779 by Joseph Brant and his army of Indians during the American Revolution, it gained commercial importance with the completion of the Delaware and Hudson Canal in 1827.

PORT LA JOIE. See CHARLOTTETOWN.

PORTLAND (England) Town, 4 mi S of Weymouth, in Dorset. Adm. Robert Blake commanded an English fleet that won a major naval battle against the Dutch, just off the Isle of Portland, a naval base, on Feb. 18, 1653, during the first of the Dutch wars. A 16th-century castle is located here, and stone from the area has been quarried for the building of some London landmarks.

PORTLAND (United States) City, 26 mi NE of Muncie, E INDIANA. Elwood Haynes, the American inventor, was born here in 1857. He built one of the nation's first automobiles, and one of his vehicles, now on display at the Smithsonian Institution, is the oldest existing automobile in the United States.

PORTLAND [former: **Falmouth**] (United States) Commercial center, port, and city, approx. 100 mi NE of Boston, Massachusetts, on the Atlantic Ocean, SW MAINE. Founded in 1632, it was known as Falmouth until it was independently incorporated in 1786. It was destroyed by Indian raids in 1676 and 1690 and again by British attacks in 1775 during the American Revolution. The naval battle between the *Enterprise* and the *Boxer* was fought off its coast in 1812 during the War of 1812.

It served as the state capital from 1820 to 1832 and has been Maine's major port and commercial center since the early 18th century. The city was almost leveled by a great fire in 1866. A lighthouse erected here in 1791 was the first one on the Atlantic Coast, and it still stands. Henry Wadsworth Longfellow, eminent American poet, was born in the city in 1807.

PORTLAND, Ohio. See SANDUSKY.

PORTLAND (United States) Industrial city and important commercial port, on the WILLAMETTE RIVER, NW OREGON. Founded by pioneers from New England in 1844, it was incorporated in 1851. It became a boom town in the second half of the century as a supply center for Northwest goldrushers and as a rail and lumber center.

PORTLAND BIGHT [former: **Old Harbour Bay**] (Jamaica) Gulf on the SE coast of Jamaica in the WEST INDIES, S of Cuba. On Sept. 2, 1940 Great Britain leased part of its coastal region to the United States for naval and air bases later used in World War II.

PORT LAVACA [former: **La Vaca**] (United States) City and port on a bay in the Gulf of Mexico, 110 mi SW of Houston, S TEXAS. Founded by the Spanish in 1815, it was developed in 1840 by settlers fleeing the aftermath of a Comanche raid on nearby Linnville. Incorporated in 1907, it attracted more attention when oil was discovered here.

PORT LAWRENCE. See TOLEDO.

PORT LOUIS [former: **Île de France**] (Mauritius) Commercial port, city, and capital of Mauritius, 500 mi E of Madagascar, in the Indian Ocean. Inhabited in the early 18th century by Dutch *maroons*, or runaway slaves, it was first permanently settled in 1735 by the French and became a British colony during and after the Napoleonic Wars. There was a large influx of emigrants from INDIA in the early 19th century. The imposing city citadel was constructed in 1838.

PORT LOUIS, Trinidad and Tobago. See SCARBOROUGH.

PORT LYAUTEY. See KENITRA.

PORT MAHON. See MAHÓN.

PORT MORESBY (Papua New Guinea) Important port and capital of Papua New Guinea, on the SE coast of the Gulf of Papua, in the SW Pacific Ocean. Founded in 1873 by John Moresby, in 1883 it became the capital of British NEW GUINEA. A major Allied base in World War II, it was the object of a Japanese offensive in December 1942 and January 1943.

PORT NATAL. See DURBAN.

PORT NELSON (Canada) Location on the N end of the mouth of the Nelson River, NE MANITOBA. The Hudson's Bay Company established Manitoba's first fur-trading post here in 1670.

PÔRTO. See OPORTO.

PÔRTO ALEGRE (Brazil) Important commercial port, city, and capital of Rio Grande do Sul state, 175 mi NE of Rio Grande. Founded in 1742 by a group of Portuguese from the AZORES, it became the capital of the state in 1807. It developed as an important commercial and trading port in the 19th century and began to industrialize after World War I. There are many buildings and streets that date from its colonial era.

PORTO BARDIA. See BARDIA.

PORTO BELLO. See PORTOBELO.

PORTOBELO [Porto Bello, Puerto Belo] (Panama) Village, 20 mi NE of Colón, on the CARIBBEAN SEA coast, central Panama. Founded in 1597, it was a rich and flourishing port in the great days of the Spanish-American Empire in the 17th and 18th centuries, transshipping cargos from the Spanish fleets across the isthmus. Sir Francis Drake died of illness here while trying to capture the city in 1596. English buccaneers succeeded in this endeavor in 1601, 1688, and 1739. The city declined rapidly with the advent of the railroad in the mid-19th century, and especially after the construction of the PANAMA CANAL in the early 20th century.

PORTO D'ANZIO. See ANZIO.

PORTO DI MISENO. See MISENUM.

PORTO EDDA. See SARANDË.

PORTOFERRAIO (Italy) Resort town and port, Livorno province, Tuscany region, 48 mi S of Leghorn, N ELBA Island, in the Tyrrhenian Sea. The Medici family fortified this former Roman town from the 16th to 18th centuries, and it was under French siege from May 1801 to June 1802 during the Napoleonic Wars. Napoleon lived in the town during his banishment in 1814/15. His residence, the Villa dei Mulini, is now a museum. Portoferraio has been incorporated into TUSCANY since 1547.

PORTOFINO (Italy) Village in Genova province, LIGURIA region, NW Italy, on the Mediterranean Sea 16 mi SE of Genoa. It is a fishing and tourist center. Nearby is the monastery of Cervara, dating from 1361. Francis I of France was held prisoner in it by the Holy Roman Emperor Charles V after the battle of PAVIA in 1525. The church of St. Giorgio contains what are said to be relics of St. George, who probably lived in the fourth century and who became the patron saint of Genoa as well as England. The relics were brought here by Crusaders from the Holy Land. The town is now a major resort on the Italian Riviera.

PORT OF SPAIN [*former and Spanish:* **Puerto de España**] (Trinidad and Tobago) City and capital of Trinidad and Tobago, island nation just N of the Orinoco River delta of Venezuela. The city is in the northwestern section of the island of Trinidad and is the center of the nation's economy. After settling the island earlier in the 16th century, in 1595 the Spanish made this the capital, locating Puerto de España on the site of an Indian village, Conquerabia. The British seized Trinidad in 1797 and anglicized the name of the town.

PORTO GRANDE. See CHITTAGONG.

PORTO MAURIZIO. See IMPERIA, Italy.

PORTO-NOVO (Benin) Commercial town, port, and capital of Benin, formerly Dahomey, 55 mi W of Lagos, West Africa. It was founded in the 16th century. There was a Portuguese trading post here in the 17th century that dealt in the slave trade. The capital of a local kingdom of the same name, the town accepted French protection against GREAT BRITAIN in 1863 and was the capital of the colony of Dahomey by 1900.

PORTO-NOVO (India) Port town near Madras, Tamil Nadu, SE India. The British under Sir Eyre Coote won an important military victory here in July 1781 over the forces of the MYSORE Empire, led by Haidar Ali.

PORTO RICO. See PUERTO RICO, COMMONWEALTH OF.

PORTO SANTO (Portugal) Island in the Madeira group, NE of Madeira Island, Funchal district. The first of the MADEIRA ISLANDS to be sighted by João Zarco in 1418, it was reached by Columbus c.1480.

PORTO TORRES [*ancient:* **Turris Libisonis**] (Italy) Port in Sassari province, NW SARDINIA. There are Roman ruins here, including those of a temple and an aqueduct.

PORT RADIUM [*former:* **Eldorado**] (Canada) Mining village, E shore of GREAT BEAR LAKE, NORTHWEST TERRITORIES. Pitchblende mines were opened here in 1930. They were exploited extensively for their uranium to help Canada's atomic energy production effort in World War II. The mines were closed in 1960.

PORTREE. See SKYE.

PORT REPUBLIC (United States) Village in the Shenandoah Valley, NW VIRGINIA. Gen. Stonewall Jackson and his Confederate troops defeated Union forces here on June 9, 1862 during the Civil War. It was the final battle of Jackson's campaign that enabled him to secure the SHENANDOAH VALLEY.

PORT REX. See EAST LONDON.

PORT RICHMOND (United States) Commercial center on the N shore of STATEN ISLAND, New York City, SE NEW YORK State. It was the home of Thomas Jefferson's vice-president, Aaron Burr (1800–1804), who died here in 1836.

PORT ROSSIGNOL. See LIVERPOOL, Canada.

PORT ROYAL, Canada. See ANNAPOLIS ROYAL.

PORT ROYAL (Jamaica) Town on Kingston harbor, SE Jamaica, WEST INDIES. An old fortified capital of Jamaica, it was frequented by pirates in the colonial era. Destroyed on several occasions by earthquakes, it was used by both the British and U.S. navies during World War II.

PORT ROYAL [*former:* **Santa Eleana**] (United States) Resort town on Port Royal Island, in Port Royal Sound, S SOUTH CAROLINA. Settled by Jean Ribaut and a group of French Huguenots in 1562, it became an important Union naval base during the Civil War, after Commodore Samuel DuPont secured the fortifications guarding the sound in November 1861.

PORT ROYAL DES CHAMPS. See TRAPPES, France.

PORT SAID [*Arabic:* **Bur Sa'īd**] (Egypt) Commercial city and port, on the Mediterranean Sea and the SUEZ CANAL, NE Egypt. Founded in 1859 at the entrance to the Suez Canal, it was once the world's largest coaling station. It has been the target of many Israeli military raids since the 1967 Arab-Israeli War.

PORT SAVIOUR. See LIVERPOOL, Canada.

PORT SENIOR. See LIVERPOOL, Canada.

PORTSMOUTH (England) Major naval base, port, and city on Portsea Island, in Hampshire, on the ENGLISH CHANNEL, 65 mi SW of London. Dating from the 12th century, Portsmouth received a royal charter in 1627, and became a city in 1888. A 12th-century cathedral and 16th-century castle are located here, as is Buckingham House, where the first duke of Buckingham was murdered in 1628. Writer Charles Dickens was born here in 1812, and there was a royal marriage in the city in 1662. Lord Nelson's flagship, the *Victory*, is now preserved here in drydock. Portsmouth's famous naval dockyard, established in 1494, attracted heavy German bombing during World War II. Recently, the 16th-century warship *Mary Rose*, was recovered from its harbor.

PORTSMOUTH (United States) Industrial city and port, on the Piscataqua River, at its entrance into the Atlantic Ocean, SE NEW HAMPSHIRE. The oldest community in the state and a shipbuilding center since the 17th century, it was settled in 1624 and was made a provincial capital in the colonial era. The Treaty of Portsmouth, signed here in 1905, ended the Russo-Japanese War. There are many old buildings in the city, including the Richard Jackson house of 1664 and the John Paul Jones house of 1758. Daniel Webster practiced law in Portsmouth from 1806 to 1816.

PORTSMOUTH (United States) Industrial and manufacturing city, at the confluence of the Ohio and Scioto rivers, 90 mi S of Columbus, S OHIO. Founded in 1803 and incorporated in 1814, it has prehistoric relics and Indian mound remains that were discovered here at Mound Park. It gained some importance in 1832 as a terminus of the Ohio Canal.

PORTSMOUTH [*former:* **Pocasset**] (United States) Resort town on the Sakonnet River, on Aquidneck Island, 18 mi SE of Providence, SE RHODE ISLAND. Founded in 1638 by Anne Hutchinson and others fleeing from the Massachusetts Bay Colony, it was incorporated into the PROVIDENCE plantations six years later. The first provincial general assembly convened here in 1647. British general Richard Prescott was arrested at his headquarters here in 1777. The following year, the American Revolutionary Battle of Rhode Island took place here.

PORTSMOUTH (United States) Commercial and industrial city and port, on the Elizabeth River, opposite NORFOLK, SE VIRGINIA. It was founded in 1752 by a local landowner on an old Indian village site. A private shipyard built here in 1767 was used by the patriots during the American Revolution, was burned by the British in 1779, and was established as a U.S. naval base in 1801. The yard was also used in the Civil War by the Confederates, was again burned by Union troops in 1861 and retaken in 1862. The city suffered a disastrous fire in 1821 and a yellow fever epidemic in 1855. It was incorporated in 1858. Trinity Church of 1762 is located here. See also HAMPTON ROADS. The shipyard has an historic naval hospital and the nation's first dry dock, and it figured prominently in both world wars. The first U.S. battleship, the *Texas* in 1892, and aircraft carrier, the *Langley* in 1922, were constructed here.

PORT TOWNSEND (United States) Manufacturing city and port, on PUGET SOUND, 43 mi NW of Seattle, W WASHINGTON. Founded in 1851 and incorporated in 1860, it soon developed into a thriving lumbering center and port. Old Fort Townsend is located in the city.

PORTUGAL [*ancient:* **Lusitania**] Nation in SW Europe, occupying most of the western side of the IBERIAN PENINSULA. It also includes the MADEIRA ISLANDS and the AZORES. One of the earliest colonial powers in the modern world, Portugal is now a small nation. The region was first settled after 1000 BC by a Celtic people, the Lusitanians. In the second and first centuries BC they offered strong resistance to the Romans but were overcome. Portugal and part of western SPAIN became the province of LUSITANIA until the early fifth century AD, when the Visigoths overran the whole peninsula. The VISIGOTHIC KINGDOM, in turn, was defeated in 711 by the Moors, who then took over all of Portugal. For centuries thereafter the people of the Iberian peninsula fought to expel the Moors, and out of this long struggle Portugal emerged as a nation. Having defeated the Moors in 1139, Alfonso Henriques proclaimed himself King Alfonso I. Freedom was at last achieved by the victory of Alfonso II in 1212 at Las NAVAS DE TOLOSA and by Alfonso III in 1249 when he reconquered ALGARVE, the last Moorish stronghold.

In 1385 John I defeated CASTILE to confirm Portugal's independence and to inaugurate its most powerful and resplendent era. Beginning with an observatory at

SAGRES in 1419, Prince Henry the Navigator, as patron of exploration, sent out expeditions along the west coast of Africa. Gold, slaves, and geographical knowledge were brought back and an attempt made to find Christian kingdoms and outflank the Muslim control of Eastern trade routes. Later, under Manuel I, Vasco da Gama was the first European to reach INDIA by sea around Africa on his voyage from 1497 to 1499. BRAZIL was claimed by Portugal in 1500 after its discovery by ships en route to India. During the reign of John III (1521–27) the Portuguese Empire reached its peak, a power and prosperity sung in Luis Vaz de Camões's epic poem, *The Lusiads*. The empire included Brazil, the coast of ANGOLA, the coast of MOZAMBIQUE, GOA in India, and settlements in INDONESIA and on the coast of CHINA. The nation's resources were not strong enough

Typical seaside fishing town in Portugal. Always a maritime nation, this tiny country carved out the first world-wide colonial empire but was too weak to sustain it.

to support its empire, and the domestic economy was neglected for the "get-rich-quick" attractions of new lands. In 1580 SPAIN conquered Portugal, trade was cut off, the Dutch attacked the overseas territories, and Portugal never again ranked as a great power.

Revolt against Spain was successful in 1640, and an alliance with ENGLAND, which had begun in the 14th century, was revived to the advantage of trade. Portugal was involved in the War of the Spanish Succession of 1707 to 1714 without any gain. There then ensued a period of absolutist rule, marked by the unpopular efforts of the Marquês de Pombal to effect economic and other reforms. Napoleon I invaded Portugal in 1807, and the royal family fled to Brazil. During the Peninsular campaign of 1808 to 1814 the French were driven out of Portugal by 1811. Brazil declared its independence in 1822, but for a time in 1826 the emperor of Brazil was also king of Portugal. After a revolt in 1906 Charles I (reigned 1889–1908) established a dictatorship, which brought on another revolt that ended with his assassination. His son and successor, Manuel III, was dethroned in October 1910, and a republic was proclaimed.

The first president was Téofilo Braga. In World War I Portugal entered on the side of the Allies in 1916. Before and after the war economic conditions were poor, and both leftist and rightist groups attempted revolts. A military coup in 1926 was followed by the accession to power in 1932 of Antonio de Oliveira Salazar, who headed an authoritarian state until 1968. In 1962 India annexed the Portuguese territories of Goa, Daman, and Diu. A repressive government continued at home, and dissatisfaction was heightened by the government's attempt to hold by force its remaining African colonies. Finally, on April 25, 1974 a military coup, the "Happy Revolution," brought into power a reformist government with a policy of decolonization, granting independence to Mozambique in 1974 and to Angola in 1975. In 1976 Indonesia seized Portuguese East TIMOR. Since 1974 political violence has subsided and the country has steadily consolidated its leftist direction. LISBON is Portugal's capital and largest city; OPORTO is the major port.

PORTUGUESE EAST AFRICA. See KENYA, MALINDI, MOZAMBIQUE.

PORTUGUESE GUINEA. See GUINEA-BISSAU.

PORTUGUESE WEST AFRICA. See ANGOLA.

PORTUS BLENDIUM. See SANTANDER, Spain.

PORTUS CALE. See OPORTO.

PORTUS MAGNUS. See ALMERIA.

PORTUS MAGONIS. See MAHÓN.

PORTUS VICTORIAE. See SANTANDER.

PORT VILA (Vanuata) Port, town, and capital of Vanuata, formerly New Hebrides Islands, SW Efate Island, SW Pacific Ocean. Port Vila was developed into a strategic naval and air base for the Allies during World War II.

PORVOO [*Swedish:* **Borgå**] (Finland) Port on the Gulf of Finland, Uusimaa province, near Helsinki, S Finland. Founded in 1346, it was the scene of Finland's formal vow of allegiance to Alexander I of RUSSIA in 1809. Poet Johan Runeberg was born here in 1804. The town is the site of a 15th-century cathedral.

POSADAS (Argentina) Agricultural town, capital of Misiones province, on the Paraná River, at the border of Paraguay, NE Argentina. Founded in 1849, it was

once visited and inhabited by Jesuit missionaries whose history can be traced through the 17th-century ruins found nearby.

POSEIDONIA. See PAESTUM.

POSEN. See POZNAŃ.

POTAISSA. See TURDA.

POTCHEFSTROOM (South Africa) Mining and agricultural town in S TRANSVAAL, 75 mi SW of Johannesburg, NE South Africa. The oldest town in the province, founded in 1838, it was the capital until 1860. A Boer civil war took place here in 1862, and the British were defeated here in 1881 during the Transvaal Rebellion. The British occupied the town in 1900 during the Boer War. Gold was discovered nearby in 1933.

POTENTIA. See POTENZA.

POTENZA [*ancient:* **Potentia**] (Italy) Agricultural town, capital of both Basilicata region and Potenza province, 84 mi SE of Naples, S Italy. Founded by Rome in the second century BC, it was controlled by many medieval rulers, and was nearly destroyed in the 13th century AD. It initiated the expulsion of Bourbon rule in southern Italy in 1860. It was destroyed by earthquakes in 1273, 1694, 1857, and 1910. A 13th-century church is here.

POTI [*ancient:* **Phasis**] (USSR) Industrial town and port on the BLACK SEA and the Batumi River, 450 mi NW of Baku, W GEORGIAN SSR. A Greek trading city as far back as the fifth century BC, it was fortified by the Turks in 1578 and taken by RUSSIA in 1828.

POTIDAEA [*former:* **Cassandreia**] (Greece) Ancient city in MACEDONIA, near Olynthus, NE Greece. Founded in 609 BC, it was a Corinthian colony. It led a revolt against Persian occupation during the Persian Wars and was also a member of the Delian League headed by ATHENS. Its revolt against Athens in 432 BC was crushed three years later, but the conflict became one of the causes of the Peloponnesian Wars. Destroyed by Philip II of Macedon in the mid-fourth century BC, it was rebuilt in 301 BC by Cassander and renamed Cassandreia. It repulsed a Roman fleet during the Third Macedonian War of 171 to 168 BC. It was taken and destroyed by the Huns in the fifth century AD.

POTOMAC RIVER (United States) River, 285 mi long, formed near CUMBERLAND, Maryland by the joining of its north and south branches. It flows SE into CHESAPEAKE BAY, forming part of the Maryland-West Virginia boundary and the Virginia-Maryland and District of Columbia boundary, with WASHINGTON, D.C. on its E bank at the head of navigation. It is a beautiful river area with historical associations that go back to the earliest days of settlement. MOUNT VERNON, the home of George Washington, is on the river south of the city of Washington. The home of George Mason, a Founding Father, is at Gunston Hall further down river. The Chesapeake and Ohio Canal runs along the river's north bank. In 1608, colonist John Smith recorded the Indian name *Patawomeck* from which the name "Potomac" was derived.

POTOSÍ (Bolivia) Industrial and mining city, capital

of Potosí department, approx. 50 mi SW of Sucre, SW Bolivia. Founded in 1547, its mines were SPAIN's greatest source of silver, and it grew into one of the richest cities in the world, supplying Europe with much of the silver responsible for the great inflation of the 16th century. By the 18th century the mines had become too difficult and expensive to work, and the city rapidly declined, not regaining importance until the discovery of tin nearby in the late 19th century. There are fine examples of colonial architecture here, including the Mint House of 1753 and a palace and courthouse from the 16th century. Its university was founded in 1571.

POTSDAM (East Germany) Industrial city and capital of Potsdam district, 16 mi SW of West BERLIN, on the Havel River. A 10th-century Slavic settlement, it was chartered in the 14th century. It became a Prussian royal residence under the Hohenzollerns, beginning with Frederick the Great, who built the palace of Sans Souci here from 1745 to 1747. Other palaces were added in subsequent years. It has been a military center since the 18th century when it was under Frederick William I. Badly damaged in World War II, it was the site of the Potsdam Conference in 1945, which provided for the restoration of POLAND, the postwar administration of GERMANY, and the determination of U.S. and Soviet spheres of influence in Europe. The Garrison Church of 1731 to 1735 and part of the German Empire's archives are located here.

POTTERIES, THE (England) District in Staffordshire, around Stoke-on-Trent, 15 mi NNW of Stafford. The area was long a manufacturing center for china and pottery, especially under the Wedgwood firm in the 18th century and later. Arnold Bennett, a famous regional novelist who depicted urban life in early 20th-century England, is best known for his novels, including a trilogy, about this district, often referred to as the "Five Towns."

POTTSGROVE. See POTTSTOWN.

POTTSTOWN [*former:* **Pottsgrove**] (United States) Industrial city, 35 mi NW of Philadelphia, on the Schuylkill River, SE PENNSYLVANIA. It was planned in 1735 by John Potts, an ironmaster whose home is still here. Pottsgrove Manor, located here, was George Washington's headquarters in 1777 during the American Revolution. Incorporated in 1815, Pottstown was home to the state's first iron industry, which had flourished since the preceding century.

POTTSVILLE (United States) Coal-mining city on the SCHUYLKILL RIVER, 28 mi NNW of Reading, E central PENNSYLVANIA. Destroyed by Indians in 1780, it was resettled *c.*1795 and incorporated in 1828. The Molly Maguires, a secret labor organization, tried to improve conditions in the mines here in the late 19th century. Their activity resulted in some of their members being brought to trial and eventually executed by hanging.

POUGHKEEPSIE (United States) Manufacturing city on the HUDSON RIVER, 65 mi N of New York City, SE NEW YORK State. Settled by the Dutch in 1687, it was incorporated in 1854. It was interim capital of the state in 1777, and the U.S. Constitution was ratified by the state on July 26, 1778 in this city. Vassar College for women was established here in 1861 and still flourishes.

PÓVOA DE VARZIM (Portugal) Town and port on the Atlantic Ocean, Porto district, 20 mi NW of Oporto, NW Portugal. José Maria Eça de Queiroz, a novelist whose usual subject was French culture and society, was born here in 1843.

POŽAREVAC [*German:* **Passarowitz**] (Yugoslavia) Trading town in SERBIA, 35 mi ESE of Belgrade, E Yugoslavia. Turkey, Austria, and Venice endorsed the Treaty of Passarowitz here on July 21, 1718, ending a war between VENICE and the OTTOMAN EMPIRE. Captured by the Serbs in 1804, the town was occupied by the Germans in World War II.

POZNAŃ [*German:* **Posen**] (Poland) Industrial city and capital of Poznań province, on the Warta River, 167 mi W of Warsaw, W central Poland. Made the first Polish episcopal see in 968 AD, it was also a royal Polish residence until 1296. A prosperous member of the HANSEATIC LEAGUE, it survived two disastrous fires in the 16th century but lost its commercial significance after the Great Northern War of 1700 to 1721. It was controlled alternately by PRUSSIA and Poland until it passed permanently to the latter in 1918. It was damaged considerably during World War II while it was occupied by German forces between 1939 and 1945, and has since been rebuilt. In June 1956 it was the scene of the famous Poznań Riots, which resulted in political liberalization and the installation of a new Polish regime under Wladyslaw Gomulka. There are a Renaissance town hall, a Gothic cathedral, a 15th-century church, and an 18th-century episcopal palace in the city.

POZSONY. See BRATISLAVA.

POZZUOLI [*ancient:* **Puteoli**; *Greek:* **Dikaerchia**] (Italy) Fishing village in Napoli province, Campania region, on the Bay of Pozzuoli, 6 mi W of Naples, S Italy. Founded by Greek settlers from SAMOS, it was taken by Greeks from CUMAE *c.*530 BC. It was colonized by the Romans in 194 BC, renamed, and flourished as a commercial center of the ROMAN EMPIRE. Christianized early, it was visited by St. Paul, an event recounted in Acts 28:13. It declined in importance after falling prey to barbarian invasions in the fifth century and volcanic destruction in the Middle Ages. There are many Roman remains here, including portions of a temple, an ancient market called the Serapeum, baths, an amphitheater, and remains of Roman docks off the present waterfront. The cathedral, rebuilt in 1643, contains elements of a temple built for Augustus.

PRAENESTE. See PALESTRINA.

PRAESIDIUM JULIUM. See SANTARÉM.

PRAG. See PRAGUE.

PRAGUE [*Czech:* **Praha**; *German:* **Prag**] (Czechoslovakia) City of central Europe, once capital of the kingdom of BOHEMIA and present capital of Czechoslovakia, on the banks of the VLTAVA River, 150 mi NW of Vienna. Its colorful and exciting history begins in the mists of legend with the traditional tale of Prince Krok, his daughter Princess Libusa, and her peasant husband, Přemysl. The chronicles of Cosmos name Libusa as the founder of one of two settlements around which Prague grew—the castle on Hradčany Hill overlooking the Vltava River.

The initiative of King Wenceslaus I of Bohemia in establishing settlers from GERMANY here in 1232 introduced a long period of economic well-being. This culminated in a cultural flowering under Holy Roman Emperor Charles IV, in the 14th century, who founded one of Europe's oldest universities, the Charles, or Prague, University here in 1347.

The religious controversies of the 15th century touched Prague profoundly through the influence of John Huss, rector and theologian at the university and a follower of John Wycliff of England. Huss spoke against special clerical power and privilege, for moral reform, and against the pope. He was convicted and burned at the stake as a heretic in 1415, his martyrdom prompting the Hussite Wars that followed.

As dual capital with Vienna of the HOLY ROMAN EMPIRE from the 14th to 17th centuries, crucially located at a hub of European trade routes and boasting a university that attracted prominent scholars from all parts of Europe, Prague's greatest flowering came in the Hapsburg reign of Rudolph II (1576–1612), a patron of the sciences. During this period, the astronomers Tycho Brahe (1546–1601) and Johannes Kepler (1571–1630) made some of their fundamental observations at Charles University.

The Protestant Czech nobles, however, felt the hand of Catholic Hapsburg authority too heavily and responded with the "Defenestration of Prague" in 1618, in which several Hapsburg officials were tossed out of the windows of Hradčany Castle. The event helped ignite the Thirty Years War of 1618 to 1648, which wrought terrible destruction through much of central Europe. Further destruction followed in the 18th century with the War of the Austrian Succession and the Seven Years War, during which Frederick the Great of PRUSSIA defeated AUSTRIA in the battle at Prague in May 1757. Despite these upheavals Prague remained one of Eastern Europe's prominent cultural centers.

The 19th century saw the birth of Czech nationalism and its attempted suppression following the abortive revolution of 1848. In the later 19th and early 20th centuries Prague again emerged as a cultural capital, attracting the musicians Dvořák and Smetana, and the writers Karel Capek, R.M. Rilke and Franz Kafka. With Czech independence following World War I, Prague became the capital of the new republic of Czechoslovakia.

The Nazi occupation and anti-Semitic policies of World War II sowed mistrust and hatred among various elements of a population that had lived in harmony for centuries—German-Jewish, Czech, and German. Following the Allied victory and Soviet domination after World War II, Prague became the capital of the Czechoslovak People's Republic. Social and political discontent were manifest in demonstrations and culminated in a thwarted revolt in 1968, suppressed by Soviet troops, but the situation in the early 1980's appeared relatively stable.

Despite centuries of war, Prague is an architectural treasurehouse. As one of the oldest cities in Europe, it has Roman remains and a seventh-century AD Jewish cemetery. Hradčany castle, the home of royalty and elected Czech presidents, still looms preeminent over old Prague which is separated from the "new" city by the Vtlava. Since 1589 the 14th-century Gothic Cathedral of St. Vitus has housed the tombs of royalty. The 14th-century Gothic Tyn cathedral was a principal Hussite church and is the burial place of Tycho Brahe. In old Prague's Mala Strana the 14th-century Charles Bridge is perhaps the most notable of the city's thirteen bridges. The Old Town Hall dates from 1381, and the famed Powder Tower is one of the portals to the old city. The 18th century brought a burst of notable Baroque buildings designed by Italian architects, most notably the churches of Our Lady of Victory, St. Nicholas, the palace built for the Hapsburg General Wallenstein, and the Czernia Palace.

PRAHA. See PRAGUE.

PRAIRIE DU CHIEN (United States) Manufacturing city on the MISSISSIPPI RIVER, 53 mi S of La Crosse, SW WISCONSIN. It was settled by French fur traders in 1781. John Jacob Astor established a fur-trading post here before the War of 1812. During that war there was a battle here. The British occupied the city and Fort Shelby from 1814 to 1816. The site of the latter is now an historical museum. The Brisbois House of 1808 is one of the oldest in the state.

PRAIRIE GROVE (United States) Town, 11 mi SW of Fayetteville, NW ARKANSAS, in the Ozarks. Union forces under Francis Herron won a battle here on Dec. 7, 1862 during the Civil War. The Confederates were forced to retreat.

PRAMBANAN [Brambanan] (Indonesia) Hindu religious center in S central JAVA, approx. 12 mi ENE of Jogjakarta. The largest complex of temples in all of Indonesia, it was completed c.900 AD. Loro Jonggrang is the largest temple of many of outstanding architectural interest here.

PRATAS ISLAND [*Chinese:* **Tungsha**] (China) Island in the South China Sea, approx. 200 mi SE of Hong Kong, Kwangtung province, SE China. Occupied by JAPAN from 1907 to 1909 and again from 1939 to 1945 during World War II, it came under Chinese administration in 1950.

PRATICA DI MARE. See LAVINIUM.

PRATO [Prato in Toscana] (Italy) Manufacturing town in Firenze province, TUSCANY region, 11 mi NW of Florence, W Italy. A former Etruscan settlement, it was first mentioned in the ninth century AD and became an independent town in the 12th century and developed its famous and ongoing woolens industry in the 13th century. It passed to FLORENCE in 1351 and was sacked in 1512 by the Spanish in league with the pope. It was incorporated in 1653. There are a 12th-century cathedral here with noteworthy art work, a

13th-century palace and town hall, and medieval city walls.

PRATO IN TOSCANA. See PRATO.

PRATTVILLE (United States) City, 12 mi NW of Montgomery, central ALABAMA. Settled in 1816, in 1838 it became an early manufacturer of cotton gins that helped revolutionize the Southern economy before the Civil War.

PRAVDINSK [*German:* **Friedland**] (USSR) Town, 27 mi SE of Kaliningrad, (once known as Königsberg), Kaliningrad oblast, Russian SFSR; formerly in EAST PRUSSIA, Germany. Napoleon's French troops won a victory here on June 14, 1807 en route to their occupation of Königsberg. The march was part of the French emperor's attempt to subdue RUSSIA during the Napoleonic Wars.

PRAYAG. See ALLAHABAD.

PREBEZA. See PREVEZA.

PREDAPPIO [*former:* **Dovia**] (Italy) Village near Forli, Forli province, SE Emilia-Romagna region, N Italy, approx 18 mi E of Cesena. The Italian fascist dictator, Benito Mussolini (1883–1945), was born here. The village was elevated into a commune in 1925 and embellished with public buildings in the fascist style. It was liberated by Polish troops in October 1944. Mussolini's remains were interred here in 1957.

PRENZLAU (East Germany) Industrial city in Potsdam district 30 mi SE of Neubrandenburg. A city since 1234, it passed to BRANDENBURG in 1250. The forces of PRUSSIA surrendered here to the French in 1806 during the Napoleonic Wars.

PRERAU. See PŘEROV.

PŘEROV [*German:* **Prerau**] (Czechoslovakia) Manufacturing town in Czech SR, approx. 40 mi NE of Brno, central Czechoslovakia. It was an important trading center in the 11th century. The Žerotín castle has been here since the 16th century and is now preserved as a museum.

PRESCOTT [*former:* **Johnstown**] (Canada) Manufacturing town in SE ONTARIO, 113 mi W of Montreal, on the ST. LAWRENCE RIVER. Founded in 1797 and incorporated in 1849, it maintains a museum at Fort Wellington, which dates from the War of 1812. At nearby Windmill Point the British held off an American raid in 1838. See also OGDENSBURG, New York.

PRESCOTT (United States) Trading city, 78 mi NNW of Phoenix, central ARIZONA. Founded in 1864 shortly after the discovery of gold in the area, it was the territorial capital from 1864 to 1867 and again from 1877 to 1889. There is a Smoki Indian museum in the city and a long-standing annual rodeo.

PREŠOV [*Hungarian:* **Eperjes**] (Czechoslovakia) Industrial town in Slovak SR, 20 mi N of Košiče, E central Czechoslovakia. Founded in the 12th century and later a royal free town, it was leveled by a fire in 1887. There is an 18th-century cathedral here.

PRESQUE ISLE (United States) Agricultural city, 240 mi NE of Portland, N MAINE. A strategic air base was established here to service U.S. aircraft en route to Great Britain in World War II. The city was incorporated in 1939.

PRESSBURG. See BRATISLAVA.

PRESTON (England) Port on the Ribble River, Lancashire, 27 mi NNE of Liverpool. Represented in Parliament since 1295, it was a Royalist stronghold during the Civil War, during which Oliver Cromwell scored a victory in this town in 1648. The Jacobites surrendered here following the collapse of their revolt in 1715. The town was incorporated in 1889. It was the birthplace in 1732 of spinning frame inventor Richard Arkwright. There is a Gothic town hall here.

PRESTONPANS (Scotland) Mining town in Lothian region, 8 mi E of EDINBURGH. In 1745, during the second Jacobite rebellion, Prince Charles Edward and his army of Scots won a decisive battle here against forces directed by Sir John Cope.

PRESTWICK (Scotland) Town in Strathclyde region, 29 mi SW of Glasgow. Dating back to the 10th century AD, it is one of the oldest towns in the country. Its famous golf course has been the scene of the British Open championship series since 1860.

PRETORIA (South Africa) Industrial city, capital of TRANSVAAL and administrative capital of South Africa, 34 mi N of Johannesburg. It was visited in *c.*1840 by Boer immigrants during the Great Trek. It was founded in 1855 by a Boer leader, Andries Pretorius, whose son became the first president of the SOUTH AFRICAN REPUBLIC. The city was made the republic's first capital in 1860. Occupied by British troops during the Boer War, it was the scene of the peace treaty that ended it on May 31, 1902. It was chosen as the administrative capital of the newly formed Union of South Africa in 1910. S.J.P. Kruger, president of the republic from 1883 to 1900, lived and was buried here.

PREVEZA [**Prebeza**] [*ancient:* **Berenikia**] (Greece) Commercial town and port, capital of Preveza department, on the Ambracian Gulf, W Greece. Founded in 290 BC by Pyrrhus of EPIRUS, it was ruled by VENICE from 1499 before passing to the Turks by the Treaty of Carlowitz in 1699. It was retaken by Venice in 1717 and in 1797 it passed to France. It was taken by the OTTOMAN EMPIRE a year later. The Greeks regained control of it in 1912. In a narrow strait that separates Preveza from ACTIUM, Octavius Augustus defeated Mark Antony in 31 BC to become the first Roman emperor.

PRIBILOF ISLANDS [**Fur Seal Islands**] (United States) Archipelago in the SE BERING SEA, approx. 300 mi SW of ALASKA. Explored in 1786 by the Russian, G. Pribylov, it has been inhabited since then by Aleuts who were shipped here by RUSSIA. The islands were purchased along with Alaska by the United States in 1867. Commercial fishing almost exterminated the seal population here until an international conference of Russia, Japan, Canada, and the United States agreed in 1911 to allow the United States to regulate seal hunting in this area.

PŘÍBRAM (Czechoslovakia) Town in Czech SR, 33 mi SW of Prague, W Czechoslovakia. Gold and silver

Pretoria in the Transvaal in 1872, still a small Boer town. The Transvaal became South African only after the Boer War (1899-1902). Pretoria is now an industrial metropolis.

were extracted regularly from its ancient mines, among the oldest in Bohemia.

PRIEGO DE CÓRDOBA (Spain) Manufacturing town in Córdova province, 48 mi SE of Córdova, S Spain. Once a Roman settlement, it was fortified by the Moors during the period of Islamic expansion. An ancient castle and a medieval church are located here.

PRIENE [*modern:* **Samsun Kale**] (Turkey) Ancient Greek city in W Asia Minor, near the mouth of the MENDERES RIVER. In the fifth century BC it figured in the ill-fated Ionian revolt against the king of PERSIA, Darius I. It was destroyed and was rebuilt in the next century, when its temple to Athena Polias was established. It was under Roman and Byzantine rule before being subjugated by the Turks in the 13th century AD. Many revealing excavations have been made at this site.

PRILEP (Yugoslavia) Commercial city in S MACEDONIA, 47 mi S of Skopje, SE Yugoslavia. It was the birthplace of Serbian hero Marko Kraljevič (c.1335–94). It was the capital of the medieval empire of SERBIA, and it has a monastery and churches from this period, as well as the ruins of Kraljevič's castle. It was occupied in 1941 by BULGARIA during World War II.

PRIMORSK [*former:* **Koivisto**] (USSR) Town on the E end of the Gulf of Finland, Leningrad oblast, Russian SFSR. Formerly part of southeastern Finland, it was captured in March 1940 by Soviet troops following bitter fighting here during the Russo-Finnish War.

PRINCE ALBERT (Canada) Commercial city in S central SASKATCHEWAN, on the North Saskatchewan River, approx. 213 mi NW of Regina. Settled in 1866 by Presbyterian missionaries serving a nation of Cree Indians, it was incorporated in 1904.

PRINCE EDWARD ISLAND [*former:* **Île-St-Jean, Isle St. John**] (Canada) One of the Maritime Provinces of the Dominion of Canada, it is in the Gulf of SAINT LAWRENCE, in eastern Canada. Micmac Indians were living here when the first Europeans appeared. Jacques Cartier of France landed in 1534 and Samuel Sieur de Champlain, who named it Île St. Jean, arrived in 1603. The French made the first settlement in 1719 and followed it with others in the 1720's. They fought with the British for control of the island, but in 1758 the latter expelled many of the French settlers, called Acadians. By the Treaty of Paris of 1763 FRANCE ceded the island to GREAT BRITAIN; the British annexed it to NOVA SCOTIA but made it a separate colony in 1769. In the 1770's Scottish and English settlers arrived, and the island was renamed Prince Edward in 1799. The earl of Selkirk brought more Scottish settlers in 1803.

Responsible government was granted in 1851, and in 1864 the conference that resulted in the formation of the Dominion was held in CHARLOTTETOWN. Prince Edward Island, however, did not join the confederation until 1873. See also ACADIA.

PRINCE GEORGE (Canada) Agricultural city in central BRITISH COLUMBIA, approx. 315 mi N of Vancouver, at the junction of the Fraser and Nechako rivers. In 1807 a fur-trading post was established here at Fort George. It passed to the Hudson's Bay Company in 1821. The city prospered with the advent of the railroad into this region in the early 20th century and was incorporated in 1915.

PRINCE OF WALES ISLAND. See PENANG ISLAND.

PRINCE RUPERT (Canada) Fishing city and port, W BRITISH COLUMBIA, on the Pacific Ocean, approx. 460 mi NW of Vancouver. Founded in 1906 as the western terminus of the Grand Trunk Pacific Railway, it became a major supply base for U.S. troops stationed in nearby ALASKA in World War II.

PRINCE RUPERT'S LAND. See RUPERT'S LAND.

PRINCES ISLANDS. See KIZIL ISLANDS.

PRINCETON [former: **Stony Brook**] (United States) Town, 11 mi NE of Trenton, W central NEW JERSEY. Settled by Quakers in 1696, it was the scene of the first state legislature in 1777 and of the Continental Congress in 1783 from June to November. During the American Revolution the British Gen. Charles Cornwallis made his headquarters here at Morven house. At the battle of Princeton on Jan. 2/3, 1777 Gen. George Washington defeated the British with a surprise attack. Rocky Hill Mansion, Washington's residence in 1783, is in the city as is the Bainbridge House, Gen. Howe's headquarters. Princeton University was founded here in 1746.

PRINCETON (United States) Manufacturing and agricultural city in S WEST VIRGINIA. Founded in 1826, it was the scene of combat on May 16, 1862 during the Civil War. It was later burned by the Confederates as they were pushed back toward the South.

PRINCIPALITY OF LIECHTENSTEIN. See LIECHTENSTEIN.

PRIOZERSK [**Keksgolm**] [*Finnish:* **Käkisalmi;** *Swedish:* **Kexholm**] (USSR) Trading town on LAKE LADOGA, 75 mi N of Leningrad, Leningrad oblast, Russian SFSR. A medieval Swedish fortress, it passed to FINLAND in 1811, and to the Soviet Union in the treaty of March 12, 1940 following the Russo-Finnish War. Occupied by the Germans and Finns early in World War II, it was eventually retaken by the USSR.

PRIPET MARSHES. See POLESYE.

PRIPYAT MARSHES. See POLESYE.

PRISHTINA. See PRIŠTINA.

PRISTA. See RUSE.

PRIŠTINA [**Prishtina**] (Yugoslavia) City in SERBIA, approx. 48 mi NNW of Skopje, S Yugoslavia. A capital of the medieval Serbian empire, it has a 14th-century monastery located in the area. See SERBIA.

PRIVAS (France) Town and capital of Ardèche department, 107 mi NW of Marseilles, SE France. It was a Protestant citadel during the Wars of Religion in the 16th century.

PRIZREN (Yugoslavia) Trading center, city in SERBIA, approx. 40 mi WNW of Skopje, S Yugoslavia. It flourished in the Middle Ages as a commercial metropolis and was Stephen Dušan's capital of Serbia from 1376 to 1389. Dušan is now buried in the city. There are many mosques and monasteries here, dating from his reign. The Serbian headquarters in World War I, it was occupied by ITALY during World War II.

PROCHYTA. See PROCIDA.

PROCIDA [*ancient:* **Prochyta**] (Italy) Island in the NW Bay of Naples, CAMPANIA region, S Italy. John of Procida, lord of the island in the 13th century, attempted to wrest it from Charles of Anjou, king of NAPLES and Sicily, its rightful ruler by conquest and papal decree. John eventually helped Peter III of Aragon win the throne of SICILY in 1283. The islanders attempted a revolt against the Bourbons in 1799. Antonio Scialoia (1817–77), a leader of the new Italian state, died here.

PROME. See PYĖ.

PROMONTORIUM SACRUM. See SAINT VINCENT, CAPE.

PROMONTORY POINT (United States) Southern point of a peninsula protruding into the N end of the GREAT SALT LAKE, NW UTAH. The "golden spike," driven nearby on May 10, 1869 where the Central Pacific and the Union Pacific railroads met, was the final link in the building of the nation's first transcontinental railway.

PROPHETSTOWN (United States) Shawnee Indian village at the confluence of the Tippecanoe and Wabash rivers, approx. 7 mi NNE of Lafayette, W INDIANA. A U.S. expeditionary force led by Gen. William Henry Harrison leveled the village while quelling Indian uprisings in the area in the battle of TIPPECANOE on Nov. 7, 1811.

PROPONTIS. See MARMARA, SEA OF.

PROSKUROV. See KHMELNITSKI.

PROSSNITZ. See PROSTĖJOV.

PROSTĖJOV [*German:* **Prossnitz**] (Czechoslovakia) City in Czech SR, approx. 30 mi NE of Brno, central Czechoslovakia. An old Moravian trading center, it has a 14th-century church and a Renaissance city hall. It developed around its huge and impressive 16th-century Castle Leichtenstein, which still stands above the city.

PROVENCE [*ancient:* **Provincia**] (France) Region and former kingdom in SE France, bounded by the Mediterranean Sea on the S, the Alps on the E, Burgundy on the N, and the Rhône River on the W. The area was inhabited by Celto-Ligurians as late as the arrival of the Phoenicians and of the Greeks c.600 BC.

Its coast was colonized in the second century BC by the Romans and became part of Gallia Narbonensis, part of GAUL, in the first century BC. It became a center of Christianity just before the onset of the barbarian invasions of the fifth to eighth centuries AD.

Provence first became a kingdom in 855 with the death of the Carolingian Lothair; it extended from ARLES in the south to BASEL in the north, including VIENNE. Lothair's son, Charles, was unsuccessful in holding it together; and after his death in 863 Boso, a local noble, subdued most of the region. In 879 he assumed the title King of Provence and defied Carolingian attempts to oust him. Circa 950 Emperor Otto the Great united it with the Kingdom of BURGUNDY, but localism and Saracen Muslim invasion soon tore it apart. In 972 the Saracens were finally ousted from their stronghold of Fraxinetum.

King Rudolf III (933–1032) united Provence and Trans-Jurane Burgundy and bequeathed it to Emperor Henry II. Emperor Conrad II (1024–39) seized the area, however, and used it to buffer Italy from French intervention. In 1226 the Albigensian Crusade, named for ALBI, introduced French control of the area and resulted in the transfer of AVIGNON and the marquessate of Provence to the papacy. It was later taken by the French crown and passed as an appanage to Charles of Anjou, brother of King Louis IX. The region belonged to the house of ANJOU for most of the 13th to 15th centuries. It was rejoined to France in 1481.

Provençal civilization was a major force in the Middle Ages and combined Greek, Roman, Muslim, Spanish, and French influences in a unique and sophisticated way. The area was long a haven of unorthodox religious and social views, while the Provençal language, spread by the troubadors, was a major literary force, influencing French, Spanish, and Italian. Dante and Petrarch were heavily indebted to it.

PROVIDENCE, Maryland. See ANNAPOLIS.

PROVIDENCE (United States) Industrial city and port, capital of RHODE ISLAND, approx. 45 mi SW of Boston, Massachusetts. Founded as a center of religious freedom by Roger Williams in 1636, it was chartered in 1644 and incorporated in 1832. Partly burned in King Philip's War of 1675/76, it flourished in the following century as a commercial center, particularly in the West Indies triangle of trade in rum, sugar, and slaves. The general assembly of Rhode Island met here at the old statehouse from 1762 until 1900, when the city became the sole state capital and it moved to a new statehouse. Providence became a thriving textile center in the 19th century, especially under the Brown brothers. It has many historical landmarks, including one of the nation's oldest libraries, the Atheneum of 1753, and several homes from the American Revolutionary period. Brown University was established here in 1764. It is also home of the Rhode Island School of Design.

PROVIDENCE ISLAND. See UJELANG.

PROVINCETOWN (United States) Resort town on N CAPE COD, 50 mi SE of Boston, SE Massachusetts. It was the first continental landing site, in 1620, of the Pilgrims before they settled at PLYMOUTH. The Mayflower Compact was written in the harbor here on Nov. 21, 1620. Provincetown was incorporated as a township in 1627 and as a town in 1727. The Pilgrim House Tavern here has been a popular retreat for artists. The Provincetown Players, an influential little theater group that staged Eugene O'Neill's work, flourished here from 1915 to 1929.

PROVINCE WELLESLEY (Malaysia) Mainland portion of PENANG state, opposite George Town. One of the former STRAITS SETTLEMENTS, it was sold to Great Britain in 1800 by the sultan of KEDAH. It was incorporated into the state of Penang in 1957.

PROVINCIA. See PROVENCE.

PROVINS (France) Resort town, approx. 25 E of Melun, E Seine-et-Marne department, N France. Founded by the Romans, it was an important medieval commercial town from the ninth to 13th centuries and played host to one of the famous fairs of CHAMPAGNE. It was devastated by the plague in the 14th century and was attacked and conquered in 1592 by Henry IV's troops during the Wars of Religion. There are medieval ramparts and churches in the town.

PROVO (United States) City on the Provo River, 38 mi SSE of Salt Lake City, N central UTAH. Spanish explorers reached here as early as 1776, but the Mormons were the first to settle it, in 1849. It was incorporated in 1851. It survived an Indian war from 1865 to 1868. The railroad made it an important transportation center of a thriving mining region.

PRUDNIK [*German:* **Neustadt**] (Poland) Industrial city in SW Śląsk province, W of Zabrze, S Poland. Battles in 1745, 1760, and 1779 were fought here between PRUSSIA and AUSTRIA during the Silesian Wars and the War of Bavarian Succession. Held by GERMANY, the city became part of Poland following World War II.

PRUNTRUT. See PORRENTRUY.

PRUSA. See BURSA.

PRŮSMYK DUKELSKY. See DUKLA PASS.

PRUSSIA. Former state of N central Europe, it eventually occupied most of N GERMANY, stretching from Poland to Belgium. Without political significance today, Prussia is now divided between WEST GERMANY and EAST GERMANY, while East Prussia is in POLAND and the USSR. With its capital at BERLIN, Prussia was the largest and most powerful state of Germany during the 19th century and was the driving force behind the creation of the GERMAN EMPIRE. Because of its military tradition, Prussia came to embody that spirit of militarism that was to lead Germany to war twice during the 20th century.

Prussia originally consisted of the area later known as EAST PRUSSIA, which was colonized by the Teutonic Knights in the 13th century and which passed to the Hohenzollern electors of BRANDENBURG during the Reformation. The electors gradually extended their lands to the west and east so that when the Hohenzollern elector adopted the title King of Prussia in 1701,

Prussia came to designate a large part of northern Germany.

The foundations of the modern Prussian state were laid between 1720 and 1740 by Frederick William I, who enlarged the army and strengthened the central government. Under his son, Frederick the Great, Prussia emerged as a major European power, taking SILESIA from AUSTRIA during the War of the Austrian Succession of 1740 to 1748 and later participating in the three partitions of Poland, of 1772, 1793, and 1795.

During the Napoleonic Wars Prussia was defeated by FRANCE at JENA and AUERSTEDT. By the Treaty of TILSIT in 1807 it ceded valuable territories, including its lands west of the Elbe River. In 1813, however, Prussia rose again against France, defeating Napoleon at LEIPZIG and playing an important part in the Allied victory at WATERLOO in 1815.

In the 19th century Prussia took the lead in the unification of Germany, initially through the introduction of a customs union or Zollverein. Under her chancellor, Otto von Bismarck, Prussia snatched SCHLESWIG-HOLSTEIN from DENMARK in 1862 and humiliated Austria in the Austro-Prussian War of 1866. This victory confirmed Prussia as the leader of the German states and resulted in the creation of the NORTH GERMAN CONFEDERATION, from which Austria was excluded. Prussia's victory against France in the Franco-Prussian War of 1870/71 completed the process of unification and saw the creation of the German Empire. Prussia continued as a constituent state of the German Empire and later of Germany until 1934, when Hitler abolished the political significance of the separate German states.

PRUT [*German:* **Pruth**] (Rumania, USSR) River forming the E boundary of Rumania, 565 mi long, rising in SW UKRAINE and flowing SSE into the DANUBE RIVER at Reni. AZOV was returned to the Turks in accordance with the terms of the Treaty of Pruth, which was signed on the river's banks on July 21, 1711.

PRUTH. See PRUT.

PRZEŁĘCZ DUKIELSKA. See DUKLA PASS.

PRZEMYŚL [*Russian:* **Peremyshl**] (Poland) Trading center, city in E Rzeszów province, approx. 200 mi SE of Warsaw, on the San River, SE Poland. Founded in the eighth century AD, it was ruled by KIEV for some time before 1340, when it passed to Poland. It has since then passed from AUSTRIA to Poland to RUSSIA several times, and it was occupied by GERMANY during World War II. It was an important Austrian military post during World War I and was besieged twice by Russia. There are a 15th-century cathedral and the remains of a 14th-century castle in the city.

PSILORITI. See IDA, MOUNT, Greece.

PSKOV [*ancient:* **Pleskov;** *Estonian:* **Pihkva**] (USSR) Transportation center, city, and capital of Pskov oblast, Russian SFSR, 155 mi SW of Leningrad, on the Velikaya River. An ancient outpost of NOVGOROD, it dates back to the eighth century AD. A rich medieval commercial center, it gained independence in 1347 and was the capital of the Pskov Republic from

then until its fall to MOSCOW in 1510. It declined soon after and was the scene of sieges in 1581 and 1615. Czar Nicholas II abdicated at the city's railroad station in 1917. The city was occupied by GERMANY in both world wars and was severely damaged in World War II. Located in a region rich in historical landmarks, it has a medieval kremlin and a 17th-century cathedral.

PTERIA. See BOGAZKÖY.

PTOLEMAÏS. See ACRE.

PUCKLECHURCH [*Old English:* **Puclan Cyrcan**] (England) Ancient locality in Avon, 8 mi E of Bristol. Edmund I, king of England from 939 to 946, was killed here in a brawl.

PUCLAN CYRCAN. See PUCKLECHURCH.

PUDJUT POINT [*Dutch:* **Sint Nicolaas Punt;** *former:* **Saint Nicholas Point**] (Indonesia) Cape on NW JAVA, projecting into the Sundra Strait at its junction with the Java Sea. The U.S.S. *Houston* and H.M.A.S. *Perth* were destroyed by the Japanese in the waters just off Pudjut Point in a naval battle fought here on Feb. 28, 1942 during World War II.

PUDSEY (England) Industrial town in West Yorkshire, 6 mi W of Leeds. Moravians settled the area in the 18th century and established a school at nearby Fulneck.

PUEBLA [**Puebla de Zaragoza**] [*former:* **Puebla de los Angeles**] (Mexico) Manufacturing city and capital of Puebla state, 75 mi SE of Mexico City, SE central Mexico. Founded in 1532 by the Spanish, it was important militarily as a junction on the route to MEXICO CITY. UNITED STATES forces under Gen. Winfield Scott captured it in 1847 during the Mexican War. Ignacio Zaragoza led his compatriots in several battles against French imperialism, and he won an important victory here on May 5, 1862 against the French. The French occupied the city the next year but were driven out by Porfirio Díaz in 1867. There is an important 16th-century cathedral here, as well as the convent of Santa Monica and an 18th-century theater.

PUEBLA DE LOS ANGELES. See PUEBLA.

PUEBLA DE ZARAGOZA. See PUEBLA.

PUEBLO (United States) Industrial city on the Arkansas River, 40 mi SE of Colorado Springs, SE central COLORADO. A trading post and Mormon and Mexican settlements were here a few years before it was founded in 1860 during the gold rush. Incorporated in 1885, it was damaged by severe flooding in 1921.

PUEBLO BONITO. See CHACO CANYON.

PUEBLO GRANDE (United States) Pueblo, 5 mi E of Phoenix, SW central ARIZONA. It was the site of a prehistoric Pueblo Indian cliff-dwelling community. Its huge mound has been partially excavated, revealing remains of a civilization that flourished between the ninth and 12th centuries AD.

PUERTO BELO. See PORTOBELO.

PUERTO CABELLO (Venezuela) City and port on the CARIBBEAN SEA, Carabobo state, 70 mi W of Caracas, N Venezuela. As a Spanish colony it was a frequent target of pirate raids from the 16th to 18th centuries and was a popular stop for Dutch smugglers. During the Venezuelan struggle for independence it remained a royalist stronghold until it was finally taken in 1823 by José Antonio Páez.

PUERTO DE ESPAÑA. See PORT OF SPAIN.

PUERTO DE SANTA MARIA DE BUEN AIRE. See BUENOS AIRES.

PUERTO LIMON. See LIMON, Costa Rica.

PUERTO ORDAZ. See SANTO TOMÉ DE GUAYANA, Venezuela.

PUERTO PLATA [*former:* **San Felipe de Puerto Plata**] (Dominican Republic) Port, city, and capital of Puerto Plata province, on the Atlantic Ocean. It was supposedly founded by Christopher Columbus. The late 15th-century ruins of his first New World settlement are located nearby.

PUERTO PRINCESA (Philippines) Commercial city and capital of PALAWAN ISLAND, E central coast of the island. A Spanish penal colony during the colonial era, it became the capital c.1905. It was taken by U.S. forces on Feb. 28, 1945 toward the end of World War II.

PUERTO RICO, COMMONWEALTH OF [*former:* **Porto Rico, St. Juan de Porto Rico**] (United States) A self-governing territory under the ultimate authority of the United States. It is an island in the WEST INDIES, approx. 1,000 miles SE of Miami, Florida. Formerly called Porto Rico, the name was officially changed in 1932 and means "rich port." The island also appears on old maps as St. Juan de Porto Rico.

The inhabitants are descendants of Spanish colonists, mixed with Indians and blacks. The official language is Spanish. Before the Spanish came, Puerto Rico was inhabited by the Arawak Indians who called it Borinquén or Boriquén. Christopher Columbus discovered the island in 1493 and Juan Ponce de León landed at SAN JUAN harbor in 1508. The first settlement was made here in 1521. Disease and mistreatment by the Spanish wiped out the Arawaks, and African slaves were imported to take their place. Gold resources were exhausted by the 1530's, and the Spanish then developed the cultivation of sugar cane and production of sugar for export.

In the 16th and 17th centuries the English and the Dutch attempted to seize Puerto Rico, but SPAIN made the island a mighty fortress. Beginning in the 1820's there were unsuccessful rebellions against Spanish rule. Slavery was abolished in 1873, and the Spanish constitution of 1876 gave Puerto Rico representation in the Spanish Parliament. In 1898 some degree of autonomy was granted, but that same year U.S. troops landed in July in the course of the Spanish-American War, and by treaty the island became a U.S. possession.

Under a law of 1900, Puerto Rico was ruled by an U.S.-appointed governor, an appointed legislative upper house and an elected lower house, with laws subject to review by the U.S. Congress. In 1917 the people were declared U.S. citizens and allowed to elect all legislators, but the U.S. governor could veto legislation. World War I and the rapid population growth on the

mainland gave the sugar industry a boost, but as more land was taken from farm land for sugar cane, food shortages developed. The depressed sugar market of the 1930's caused hardships, although the New Deal produced measures for recovery. World War II and Operation Bootstrap in the 1940's successfully encouraged industry with higher demand, tax exemptions, low interest loans, and other incentives. After World War II many Puerto Ricans immigrated to the industrial cities of the mainland Northeast to seek economic opportunity.

The granting of power to elect the governor, beginning in 1948, and commonwealth status in 1952 have not ended agitation for statehood or independence, even though in 1967 a large majority voted for the status quo. The 1970's brought many large industrial projects to the island, stemming emigration but causing increased concern for environmental risks. Terrorist activities have increased, and there have been many bombings on the island and on the mainland by groups seeking independence. In November 1980 a prostatehood governor was narrowly reelected. San Juan is the capital; other major cities are BAYAMON, Mayaguez and PONCE.

PUFLUNA. See POPULONIUM.

PUGET SOUND (United States) Arm of the Pacific Ocean in NW WASHINGTON. It is connected with the ocean by JUAN DE FUCA STRAIT and is entered through Admiralty Inlet. It then extends, in two arms, approx. 100 mi S. Spanish navigators arrived in nearby waters as early as 1774. An English sailor, Charles William Barkly, discovered the Juan de Fuca Strait and the Sound in 1787; but it was another Englishman, George Vancouver, who in 1792 was the first to explore it. He named it for his aide, Peter Puget. The Sound has a number of important cities and port facilities, especially SEATTLE, TACOMA, OLYMPIA and the U.S. Navy shipyard at BREMERTON.

PUGLIA. See APULIA.

PUKAPUKA. See DANGER ATOLL.

PUKET. See PHUKET.

PULA [**Pulj**] [*ancient:* **Pietas Julia**; *Italian:* **Pola**] (Yugoslavia) Commercial city on the Adriatic Sea, CROATIA, 45 mi SW of Rijeka, NW Yugoslavia. A Roman trading port and military base, it was leveled by the Illyrians in 39 BC. Although rebuilt, it was insignificant in the Middle Ages and was controlled by VENICE from 1148 to 1797 AD. The Genoese destroyed it in 1379 when they won a battle here against the Venetians. It was the center of Hapsburg naval activity in the 19th century, after passing to AUSTRIA in 1797. It became Italian after World War I and Yugoslavian after World War II. The temple of Augustus, an impressive amphitheater, and other Roman ruins are preserved here.

PULASKI, FORT. See FORT PULASKI.

PULAU TERNATE. See TERNATE.

PULAU TIDORE. See TIDORE.

PUƚAWY (Poland) Industrial town on the Vistula River, Lublin province, WNW of Lublin, E Poland. It

Pula, now in Yugoslavia, was already an important Roman naval station when this wonderfully preserved amphitheater was built under the early empire. Pula is still a naval base.

was once the residence of the Czartoryskis, a princely Polish family that dominated much of Poland in the 18th century.

PULE 'ANGA TONGA. See TONGA.

PULICAT (India) Town on S Pulicat Lake, Tamil Nadu, S India. The site of a Dutch fort established here in the early 17th century, it remained the center of the Dutch settlement of the COROMANDEL COAST until it passed to the British in 1825.

PULICAT. See PALGHAT.

PULJ. See PULA.

PULLMAN (United States) Former suburb of Chicago, ILLINOIS, incorporated into CHICAGO in 1889. It was founded by G.M. Pullman in 1880 as an experimental community for his sleeping-car company employees. It was the scene of a major wage-protest strike led by Eugene V. Debs in 1894.

PULO CABALLO. See CABALLO.

PULPUDEVA. See PLOVDIV.

PULTOVA. See POLTAVA.

PULTOWA. See POLTAVA.

PUŁTUSK (Poland) Industrial town, on the Narew River, Warszawa province, 32 mi N of Warsaw, NE central Poland. Charles XII of SWEDEN defeated the Saxons here on Apr. 21, 1703 as he established Swedish supremacy in the Baltic lands during the Great North-

ern War. The Russians lost a battle to the French here in 1806 during the Napoleonic Wars. The town was captured by the Germans during both world wars.

PUNAKA [Punakha] (Bhutan) Town and traditional capital of Bhutan, NW Bhutan. Founded in 1577, it has fortifications and a significant Buddhist monastery.

PUNAKHA. See PUNAKA.

PUNDRAVARDHANA. See BOGRA.

PUNE. See POONA.

PUNJAB [*Hindu:* **Panjāb**] (India) Region in the NW Indian subcontinent, former province of British India. Its capital is LAHORE, and its summer capital is SIMLA. A center of the prehistoric INDUS RIVER Valley civilization, it was ruled by Alexander the Great in the fourth century BC and then by Asoka and the MAURYAN EMPIRE in the next century. From the eighth century AD to the 18th century it was ruled by Muslims, and it flourished as a cultural center under the MOGUL EMPIRE. East Punjab remained a Hindu stronghold during this time. The Sikhs took over the area in the late 18th century, but the British annexed it in 1849, following their victory in the two Sikh Wars of 1846 and 1849. The province was reorganized into several states, beginning in 1947.

PUNT Ancient area in Africa, S of EGYPT, probably along the coast of SOMALIA. A flourishing trade in slaves, gold, incense, and myrrh existed between ancient Egypt and Punt following the expedition sent to it by Queen Hatshepsut in the 15th century BC. The visit is recorded in temple reliefs at DEIR AL-BAHRI in western THEBES.

PUNTA ARENAS [Magallanes] (Chile) Commercial port, city, and capital of Magallanes province, Brunswick Peninsula, S. Chile. A penal colony was established here in 1843. Six years later the town was founded to substantiate the Chilean claim to the STRAIT OF MAGELLAN. One of the world's southernmost cities, it has one of the best museums in South America.

PUNTA DAR ZOYARA. See ZUWARĀH.

PUNTA DEL ESTE (Uruguay) Resort town on the Atlantic Ocean, Maldonado department, 70 mi E of Montevideo, S Uruguay. The German battleship *Graf Spee* was badly battered in 1939 by a British attack just off the coast during World War II. Inter-American conferences were held here in 1961, 1962, and 1967. In 1962 the decision was made here to suspend Cuba's membership in the Organization of American States (OAS).

PUPLUNA. See POPULONIUM.

PURA. See IRANSHAHR, Iran.

PURBECK, ISLE OF (England) Peninsula on the SE coast of DORSET. Originally an island, it was joined to the mainland by silting. The district was a popular hunting ground, frequented by Anglo-Saxon and Norman royalty. It is the site of the ruined Corfe Castle, built between the 11th and 13th centuries and later destroyed by Parliamentarians during the Civil War. Purbeck is the source of the black marble used in the elegant interior of Canterbury Cathedral.

PURI [Jagannath, Juggernaut] (India) Port town in E Orissa, on the Bay of Bengal, 260 mi SSW of Calcutta, E India. It is the location of an important center of Hindu worship to Juggernaut, a Krishna form of Vishnu. A major pilgrimage is directed toward the town annually, and many festivals are held at that time, mainly the Rathayatra celebration in which a huge Juggernaut image is venerated. The imposing 12th-century Sri Jagannath Temple dominates the site. The custom of many devotees to hurl themselves to death beneath the wheels of a massive rolling image of Juggernaut, a practice observed by the Franciscan Oderic as early as 1320, has given rise to the English term for any terrible, irresistible force.

PURIGERE. See MYSORE.

PURPLE ISLANDS. See MADIERA ISLANDS.

PURPURIARAE (PURPLE ISLANDS). See MADIERA ISLANDS.

PURUSHAPURA. See PESHAWAR.

PUSAN [*Japanese:*** Fusan]** (Korea) Major commercial center, port, and city on the Korea Strait, 200 mi SSE of Seoul, capital of South Kyŏngsang province, SE South Korea. A thriving port of the Chinese Empire, its castle was captured in 1592 by a Japanese expeditionary force that was recalled six years later. Its harbor was greatly improved while under the rule of JAPAN

from 1910 to 1945, and the town became a stronghold of U.S. and U.N. troops protecting South Korea in 1950 during the Korean War.

PUSHKAR LAKE (India) Lake in E central Rajasthan, 5 mi W of Ajmer, NW central India. The only Brahmanic temple in India is located on its banks, and an annual pilgrimage is directed in October and November toward its sacred waters and temple.

PUSHKIN [*former:*** Detskoye Selo; Tsarskoye Selo]** (USSR) Residential town in NW Leningrad oblast, Russian SFSR, 16 mi S of Leningrad. This 17th-century Finnish village was converted in 1708 by Peter the Great into one of the most magnificent royal residences in the world. Palaces and lavish gardens were constructed here by Peter between 1748 and 1762 and by Alexander I between 1792 and 1796. Czar Nicholas II was its last royal resident in 1917. Severe damage was done to the city and its palaces during World War II, and extensive restoration has ensued. The town has undergone many name changes.

PUSZCZA BIAŁOWIESKA. See BIALOWIEZA FOREST.

PUTEOLI. See POZZUOLI.

PUT-IN-BAY (United States) Bay in South Bass Island, LAKE ERIE, OHIO. Commodore Oliver H. Perry won a naval victory here against the British on Sept. 10, 1813 during the War of 1812.

PUTNA. See PATNA.

PUTNEY (England) District of the inner LONDON borough of Wandsworth. Thomas Cromwell (1485–1540), notorious for his role in the confiscation of monastic lands, was born here, as was historian Edward Gibbon (1737–94). Statesman William Pitt lived here. Two duels were fought here, one between William Pitt and George Tierney in 1798, and another between Robert Castlereagh and George Canning in 1809.

PUTO. See P'U-T'O SHAN.

P'U-T'O SHAN [Pootoo, Puto, Puto Shan] (China) Island member of Chou-shan archipelago, Chekiang province, E China. One of China's centers of Buddhism, it has many temples and an impressive monastery. It was once a pilgrimage center as well.

PUTTIALA. See PATIALA.

PUTUMAYO (Brazil, Colombia, Peru) River in NW South America, approx. 980 mi long, rising in SW Colombia, flowing SE into the AMAZON RIVER in Brazil. The river valley boomed as a center of the rubber business in the late 19th and early 20th centuries. It became the focus of international indignation when reports of grossly inhumane treatment of native workers were made public.

PUYALLUP (United States) Lumbering center, city on the Puyallup River, 8 mi ESE of Tacoma, W central WASHINGTON. It was founded in 1877, in an area once frequented by the local Puyallup Indians, by Ezra Meeker. His 19th-century mansion, Pioneer Park, is still intact.

PUY DE DÔME (France) Extinct volcano in the AUVERGNE Mts., central France. The remains of an ancient temple dedicated to the Roman Mercury are located at its summit. A famous experiment confirming Evangelista Torricelli's air-pressure theory was carried out here in 1648, under the direction of Blaise Pascal.

PUYÉ. See SANTA CLARA, New Mexico.

PUY, LE. See LE PUY.

PYARNU. See PARNU.

PYATIGORSK [Piatigorsk] (USSR) Resort city in Stavropol Krai, Russian SFSR, approx. 200 mi NW of Tbilisi, SW USSR. Founded in 1780, its famous health spa has been operated since 1803. The Russian poet M. Y. Lermontov was shot here in 1841 in a duel. A museum in the city is devoted to his work.

PYDNA (Greece) Ancient town in S MACEDONIA, near the Gulf of Salonica, N Greece. The kingdom of Macedonia was destroyed when its King Perseus was defeated here in 168 BC by a Roman army under Aemilius Paulus.

PYÈ [Prome] (Burma) Commercial town and port on the IRRAWADDY RIVER, 150 mi NW of Rangoon, capital of Pyè district, in Pegu, S central Burma. Founded in the eighth century AD, it was the capital of Pyu state until conquered by the Burmese Mon Kingdom in the following century. Its ruins are located near the modern town, which became part of British Burma in 1852 and was occupied by the Japanese during World War II.

PYEITAWINZU MYANMA NAINGUGANDAW. See BURMA.

PYLOS [*former:*** Navarino;** *Greek:* **Pílos]** (Greece) Ancient port on a bay of the Ionian Sea, MESSINA, SW Greece, now a fishing town. A great Mycenaean palace dating from the 13th century BC was unearthed not far from here recently and may have been the residence of King Nestor, of Homer's *Iliad*. An Athenian stronghold during the Peloponnesian War, Pylos was the scene of an Athenian naval victory in 425 BC against a Spartan fleet. The modern town, once called Navarino, is near the site of the naval battle of Navarino Bay, where a Turkish and Egyptian fleet was overcome on Oct. 20, 1827 during the Greek War of Independence, by a fleet commanded by Great Britain's Sir Edward Codrington.

PYŎNGYANG [*Japanese:*** Heijo]** (Korea) Industrial and commercial city, capital of North Korea, on the Taedong River, approx. 125 mi NW of Seoul. Formerly the capital of Korea and of the Koguryu dynasty (*c.*35

BC–668 AD), it was settled even earlier, perhaps as far back as 1122 BC. In early modern times it was captured by JAPAN in 1592 during its abortive invasion of Korea. The Japanese planned to invade CHINA from this base, but in the fighting the city was destroyed. Pyŏngyang was razed again in 1894 during the Sino-Japanese War and a third time in 1904. It was industrialized under Japanese rule between 1910 and 1945, and after World War II it became the capital of newly formed North Korea in 1948. It was occupied in 1950 by U.N. troops during the Korean War, but was retaken after being severely damaged. Among the few landmarks that have survived its violent history are ancient tombs from the first century BC and some old Buddhist temples.

PYRENAEI MONTES. See PYRENEES.

PYRENEES [*ancient:*** Pyrenaei Montes;** *French:* **Pyrénées;** *Spanish:* **Pirineos]** (France, Spain) Mountain range, along the Spanish-French border, extending approx. 250 mi from the Bay of Biscay on the W to the Gulf of Lions on the Mediterranean Sea on the E. The main passes are the Somport, the Poterla, the Puymorens, and Roncevalles. The Col de Pert (or Perthus) was a popular Roman passage.

Prehistoric cave paintings have been found at ALTAMIRA and AURIGNAC in the region. In 788 AD the massacre by Basques of a Carolingian rear guard returning from Spain in the pass of RONCEVALLES was the historical basis for the medieval epic, the *Song of Roland.* The Spanish border was set at the Pyrenees by the Treaty of the Pyrenees, negotiated on the ISLE OF PHEASANTS here in 1659.

The mountain passes were often used by pilgrims in the Middle Ages on their way to the shrine of SANTIAGO DE COMPOSTELA in northwestern Spain. The mountains were also a major route for the clandestine movement of heretics in the late Middle Ages, for Republicans and their sympathizers during the Spanish civil war, and now for terrorists in the north of Spain.

The kingdom of NAVARRE, astride the mountains, played a major role in the conflicts between Spain and France from the eighth to 17th centuries. The principality of ANDORRA has survived in the mountains since the eighth century.

PYRGOS [*Greek:*** Pírgos]** (Greece) Commercial town and capital of Elis department, PELOPONNESUS, 120 mi W of Athens, SW Greece. It was attacked and plundered by the Ottoman Turks in the early 19th century, during the Greek War of Independence.

PYTHO. See DELPHI.

Q

QABIS. See GABES.

QADAS. See CADASA.

QAFSAH [Gafsa] [*ancient:* **Capsa**] (Tunisia) Town and oasis in W central Tunisia, 50 mi NW of the city of Gabès. Built on the site of ancient Capsa, it was once a Numidian town and later came under Roman rule. Artifacts of the upper Paleolithic (Capsian) culture of North Africa and southern Europe have been found on the site. See also NUMIDIA.

QAIROUAN. See KAIROUAN.

QAIRWAN. See KAIROUAN.

QALUNIYA. See MOZAH.

QANAT AS SUWAYS. See SUEZ CANAL.

QANDAHAR. See KANDAHAR.

QANTARAH, AL [El Kantara] (Egypt) Town on the E bank of the SUEZ CANAL, NE Egypt. Founded on an ancient military route between Egypt and SYRIA, it became the terminus of the rail line to PALESTINE, built during World War I for the British Expeditionary Force. Captured by ISRAEL during the Arab-Israeli War of 1967, the town was evacuated in 1969 and was returned to Egypt in 1974. There are Egyptian and Roman ruins in the area.

QARAQORUM. See KARAKORUM.

QARQAR. See KARKAR.

QARS. See KARS.

QARTHADASHT. See CARTHAGE, Tunisia.

QĀRŪN, LAKE [*ancient:* **Moeris**] (Egypt) Lake in Al Fayyum governorate, S of Cairo, in N Upper Egypt. Described by Herodotus in the fifth century BC, the lake is now much reduced in size. The Ptolemies, Greek rulers of ancient Egypt, made their residence at Crocodilopolis, which was later known as ARSINOË. In the 1920's an ancient irrigation system was unearthed in the area. See also FAIYUM.

QATAR [Katar] Sheikhdom in E Arabia, on a 100-mi-long peninsula on the PERSIAN GULF. Its capital is Doha, also known as Bida. Invaded by the Persians in 1783, the area was occupied by forces of the OTTOMAN EMPIRE in 1871, which maintained some control until World War I. Qatar maintained treaty relations with GREAT BRITAIN until it became independent in 1971. The state has developed rapidly since oil production began in 1949.

QATNA [Katna] [*modern:* **al-Mashrafah, el-Meshrife, el-Michirfe, Mecherfe, Mishrifeh, Mushrife**] (Syria) Ancient city, approx. 10 mi NE of Homs. Qatna flourished in the second millennium BC and was the site of a temple dedicated to the Sumerian goddess Nin-E-Gal, which was excavated from 1924 to 1929. A stone sphinx consecrated by Ita, daughter of the Egyptian ruler Amenemhet II (1929–1895 BC), and Mycenaean vases are evidence of foreign trade with the city. The Hittite king Suppiluliumas razed Qatna in 1375 BC. See also EGYPT, HITTITE EMPIRE, MYCENAE, SUMER.

QAZVĪN. See KASVIN.

QIFT. See COPTOS.

QINA [Keneh] [*ancient:* **Caene, Caenepolis**] (Egypt) Town and capital of Qina governorate, on the NILE RIVER, E central Egypt. Founded on the site of the ancient trading center of Caene, the town has many remains of the original settlement.

QIRGHIZ. See KAZAKH SOVIET SOCIALIST REPUBLIC.

QISARAYA. See CAESAREA PALESTINAE.

QOM [Kum, Qum] (Iran) City in Teheran province, 75 mi S of Teheran, NW central Iran. Long a pilgrimage center of the Shi'ite Muslims, it is the site of the shrine of Fatima, sister of the Imam Riza, the important saint of Shiite Islam, who died in 816 AD. It was invaded by the Mongols in 1221 and by the Afghans in 1722. In the 1970's it became known as the seat of the Ayatollah Khomeini, the religious and political leader of Iran.

QOMUL. See HAMI.

QUAI D'ORSAY (France) Quay, situated along the left bank of the SEINE RIVER, between the Eiffel Tower and the Palais Bourbon, in PARIS. Named after a French general, it is the location of the French ministry of foreign affairs, which is also referred to as the Quai d'Orsay.

QUANTICO (United States) Town, Prince William county, on the POTOMAC RIVER near Fredericksburg, VIRGINIA. Founded as a base for servicing colonial vessels during the American Revolution, it became a permanent Marine Corps training base in 1918.

QUATRE BRAS (Belgium) Village, Brabant province, approx. 20 mi SSE of Brussels. Two days before the defeat of Napoleon at WATERLOO, British troops under the duke of Wellington repulsed the French forces under Marshall Ney here on June 16, 1815.

QUEBEC [*French:*** Québec]** (Canada) City in S QUEBEC province, on the N bank of the ST. LAWRENCE RIVER where it is joined by the St. Charles River. Its name may be derived from an Algonquin word meaning narrows. The first European here, the French explorer Jacques Cartier, who spent the winter of 1535/36 in the area, found the Indian village of Stadacona on the site. Quebec, itself, the first permanent settlement in Canada, was established in 1608 as a trading post by another French explorer, Samuel Sieur de Champlain. In 1663 it officially became a city and the capital of NEW FRANCE.

The English captured Quebec in 1629, but it was returned to France in 1632. It withstood English sieges in 1690 and 1711, but on Sept. 19, 1759, during the French and Indian War, the city surrendered to the British for the last time during the French and Indian War, after the Battle of the PLAINS OF ABRAHAM five days earlier. In 1763 all of French Canada, including Quebec, was ceded to GREAT BRITAIN. During the American Revolution an American army failed in an attempt to take the city in 1775/76.

Quebec was the capital of Lower Canada from 1791 to 1841, and of the Province of Canada from 1851 to 1855 and again from 1859 to 1865. It has been the capital of the Province of Quebec since 1867. In October 1864 the second of two conferences resulting in the confederation that became the present Dominion of Canada was held here. During World War II, in August 1943 and September 1944, meetings to plan Allied strategy were held here between President Franklin D. Roosevelt of the UNITED STATES and Prime Minister Winston Churchill of Great Britain, together with other leading military and civilian figures.

Old fortifications and buildings from the colonial era make Quebec a picturesque city, popular with tourists.

The old fort, La Citadelle, has been restored as it was between 1820 and 1832. The population is overwhelmingly of French descent and is French-speaking.

QUEBEC (Canada) A province of the E Dominion of Canada. The first European in the region was Jacques Cartier of France, who landed on the GASPÉ PENINSULA in 1534. The next year he explored the SAINT LAWRENCE RIVER. In 1608 Samuel Sieur de Champlain, also of France, established a trading post on the site of QUEBEC city; and from this earliest Canadian settlement traders, explorers, and missionaries began their daring journeys into the unknown interior of North America. In 1663 Louis XIV of France made the region, known as NEW FRANCE, a royal colony. A long struggle followed, first against the Iroquois Indians and then against the British. The latter captured Quebec city in 1759 and took MONTREAL in 1760. In 1763 at the end of the French and Indian War, France ceded the region to GREAT BRITAIN.

In 1774, as a conciliatory measure, Great Britain's Quebec Act allowed French residents to keep their religion and laws. The territory of Quebec was extended to include the land east of the MISSISSIPPI RIVER and north of the OHIO RIVER. During the American Revolution, a colonial army in 1775 captured Montreal but failed to take Quebec city, and in 1777 the British were defeated in an attempted invasion of NEW

Quebec on its rocky hill, in the 18th century. French for almost 155 years, it fell to Great Britain in 1759, but the city is still French in culture today.

YORK State. In 1791 Great Britain detached the part of Quebec west of the OTTAWA RIVER and created Upper Canada, now ONTARIO; while Quebec became Lower Canada. In 1837 some leaders of the French community revolted against the British and the ruling French group, known as the Château Clique, but the rebellion was crushed. The result was the formation in 1841 of the Province of Canada, consisting of Canada East (Quebec) and Canada West (Ontario). A measure of self-government came in 1849, and in 1867 Quebec was one of the four founding provinces of the Dominion. French culture remained dominant, and in 1974 French was made the sole official language in the province. A group advocating independence arose in the 1960's, but in a referendum in May 1980 Quebec voted against secession.

QUEDLINBURG (East Germany) City, Halle district, 33 mi SSW of Magdeburg, W East Germany. One of Germany's oldest cities, it was fortified by the German King Henry I, the Fowler, in 922 AD. The city was a member of the HANSEATIC LEAGUE until 1477 and passed to BRANDENBURG in 1698. It has a castle, church, and convent built between the 10th and 14th centuries.

QUEEN CHARLOTTE ISLANDS (Canada) Group of islands off the coast of BRITISH COLUMBIA, between Alaska and Vancouver Island. The archipelago was visited by Juan Pérez in 1774 and by Capt. James Cook in 1778. Capt. George Dixon surveyed the islands in 1787 and named them for his ship. The population consists mainly of Haida Indians.

QUEEN ELIZABETH ISLANDS [*former:* **Parry Islands**] (Canada) Group of islands in the northern part of the ARCTIC archipelago, Franklin district, NORTHWEST TERRITORIES, N Canada. Discovered in 1819/20 by the British explorer Sir William Parry, the islands bore his name until 1954. Since the 1960's they have become a source of oil.

QUEEN MAUD MOUNTAINS (New Zealand) Mountain range in ANTARCTICA, in the S Ross Dependency, S of Ross Ice Shelf. The range was discovered in 1911 by Roald Amundsen, a Norwegian explorer, and contains three of the world's great glaciers: Amundsen, Liv, and Thorne.

QUEENS (United States) Borough of NEW YORK CITY, on the W end of LONG ISLAND, across the East River from the borough of MANHATTAN. Originally part of NEW NETHERLAND, it was settled by the Dutch in 1635. Some of its early settlements were Flushing Bay, founded in 1636, Newtown in 1642, Far Rockaway in 1644, FLUSHING in 1645, and Jamaica in 1656. Peter Stuyvesant surrendered the area to the English in 1664. After the Battle of LONG ISLAND in 1776, during the American Revolution, British troops controlled the area. Many of the inhabitants were Tories and chose to emigrate to NEWFOUNDLAND after the Revolution. With the construction of the Queensborough Bridge in 1909 and a railroad tunnel in 1910, Queens expanded rapidly. It was twice the site of World's Fairs, in 1939 and 1964.

QUEENSLAND (Australia) State, covering the entire NE part of the Australian continent, with its capital at BRISBANE. The coastal area was explored by Capt. James Cook in 1770. Under the jurisdiction of NEW SOUTH WALES, it was a penal colony from 1824 to 1843. In 1901 Queensland was made one of the states of the Australian Commonwealth.

QUEENSTON [Queenstown] (Canada) Village and battle site in Lincoln county, ONTARIO, just N of Niagara Falls. It was the scene of a battle on Oct. 13, 1812, during the War of 1812, in which invading U.S. troops under Maj. Gen. Stephen Van Rensselaer were defeated by British forces under Maj. Gen. Isaac Brock. The conflict is often called the Battle of Queenston Heights.

QUEENSTOWN. See QUEENSTON.

QUELIMANE [Kilimane, Kilmain, Quilimane] (Mozambique) Town, port, and capital of Zambézia district, E central Mozambique. Founded as a trading post in 1544 by the Portuguese, it became a major center of the slave trade in the 18th and 19th centuries.

QUELPART ISLAND. See CHEJU.

QUEMADOS DE MARIANAO. See MARIANAO.

QUEMOY [*Mandarin:* **Chin-men, Kinmen**] (Taiwan) Island group in the Formosa, or Taiwan, Strait, off Fukien province of the People's Republic of China, approx. 150 mi W of Taiwan. The main island was held and heavily fortified after 1949 when the Nationalist Chinese government was forced off the mainland to Taiwan. China claims it as well as MATSU Island, farther north on the China coast near Foochow, and Taiwan. When China shelled Quemoy in 1955, the U.S. government gave a qualified promise to Taiwan to defend it. Again in 1958 there was intensive bombardment, and the U.S. Seventh Fleet was sent to the area. Quemoy and Matsu were made a major issue in the 1960 U.S. presidential election. In recent years neither China nor Taiwan has made an issue of the islands.

QUENGIANFU. See SIAN.

QUERA. See CHUR.

QUERCY [Cahorsin] (France) Region and former county, in the area now occupied by the Lot and Tarn-et-Garonne departments, SW France. CAHORS is its chief city. Dating from Gallo-Roman times, the region came under the counts of TOULOUSE in the ninth century AD. Quercy was the subject of fierce conflict during the Hundred Years War of 1337 to 1453 and the Wars of Religion from 1562 to 1598. It was united with the French crown in 1472 and included in GUIENNE province.

QUERÉTARO (Mexico) City and capital of Querétaro state, 160 mi NW of Mexico City, central Mexico. Inhabited by the Otomi-Chichimec Indians, Querétaro was made part of the AZTEC EMPIRE in 1446 and was conquered by SPAIN in 1531. The city was the scene of a conspiracy that led to Mexico's revolt against Spain in 1810. The execution of Austrian-born Hapsburg Emperor Maximilian of Mexico took place here in 1867.

QUETTA (Pakistan) City in Baluchistan province, 450 mi WSW of Lahore. It lies in a strategic region near the Bolan pass, which controls the trade and invasion route from AFGHANISTAN to S Pakistan, the INDUS RIVER valley, and INDIA. The British occupied Quetta in the First Afghan War of 1839 to 1842 and annexed it after the Second Afghan War in 1876. They made a strong fortress of it. The city was almost entirely destroyed by an earthquake in 1935 but was rebuilt.

QUEZALTENANGO (Guatemala) City and capital of Quezaltenango department, in the W highlands, SW Guatemala. Once the center of the ancient Quiché kingdom of Xelaju, it is today the second city of Guatemala. Its name means "palace of the quetzal" and refers to a native tropical bird of great symbolic importance to the Maya and now the national symbol of Guatemala.

QUEZON CITY (Philippines) City on Luzon Island, adjacent to MANILA. Once a private estate, the site was chosen as the new official capital of the Philippines, replacing Manila in 1937, and was named for President Manuel Quezon.

QUIBERON BAY (France) Bay on Quiberon peninsula, Morbihan department, in BRITTANY, NW France. It was the scene of a naval battle during the Seven Years War, on Nov. 20, 1759, in which the French fleet was defeated by the British under Lord Hawke, thus ending the French plan to invade GREAT BRITAIN. On July 20/21, 1795, during the French Revolutionary Wars, an invading party of French Royalists was landed in the area by British ships but was repulsed.

QUILIMANE. See QUELIMANE.

QUILON [Kollam] [*former:* Coilum, Elancon, Kaulam Mall] (India) Town, SE Kerala state, 130 mi SW of Madurai, on the MALABAR COAST, S India. The oldest city on the Malabar Coast, it was said to be the southernmost area of Nestorian Christian influence in the seventh century AD. Quilon was inhabited by the Portuguese in the 17th century and was occupied by the Dutch in 1662. Soon after it came under the control of the British East India Company.

QUIMPER [*Breton:* Kemper] (France) Town and capital of Finistère department, in BRITTANY, near the Bay of Biscay, NW France. It was the medieval capital of the Breton county of Cornouaille, inhabited in the sixth century AD by Britons from CORNWALL fleeing the Anglo-Saxons. The town became the seat of a bishopric in 495 and joined the duchy of Brittany in the 11th century.

QUINCY [*former:* Bluffs] (United States) City, seat of Adams county, W ILLINOIS, on the E bank of the MISSISSIPPI RIVER. Founded in 1822, it was renamed on March 4, 1825 for President John Quincy Adams. It was an important stop for escaping slaves on the Underground Railroad to Canada in the 1830's, and it was the site of the sixth Lincoln-Douglas debate on Oct. 13, 1858.

QUINCY (United States) City, Norfolk county, 8 mi S of Boston, E MASSACHUSETTS. It was founded as a trading post by the anti-Puritan Thomas Morton *c.*1625 and was resettled in 1634. Presidents John Adams and John Quincy Adams were born here and are buried in the First Parish Church in the city. Quincy was the site of the laying of the first railroad tracks in the United States in 1826.

QUI NHON [Quinhon] (Vietnam) City and port in SE Vietnam, on the South China Sea. Once a capital of the ancient kingdom of CHAMPA, its small port was opened to trade with France in 1874. In 1965, during the Vietnam War, the UNITED STATES developed the port for military use.

QUINHON. See QUI NHON.

QUINNIPIAC. See NEW HAVEN.

QUINTANA ROO (Mexico) A state of Mexico in the densely-forested half of the YUCATAN PENINSULA. This region contains a number of Mayan and late Mayan archaeological sites, including the very late settlement of Tulum and the great center of Coba, which has been little excavated. Mayan resistance and heavy forests made Spanish invasion impossible during the 16th century.

QUIRIGUÁ (Guatemala) Ancient city and archaeological site in the Motagua valley, E Guatemala, near the border of Honduras. It is the site of a ruined city dating from the Late Classic epoch of the Maya in the eighth century AD. The site, not impressive architecturally, is known for its carved monoliths and stone steles.

QUIRINAL. See SEVEN HILLS OF ROME.

QUITO [Villa de San Francisco de Quito] (Ecuador) City and capital of Ecuador and Pichincha province, approx. 114 mi from the Pacific coast and 170 mi NE of Guayaquil. Once inhabited by Quito Indians, it was taken by the Incas in 1487 and by Sebastián de Benalcázar for SPAIN in 1534. The city was freed from Spanish rule by Antonio José de Sucre in 1822. It has many fine examples of Spanish colonial architecture. See also GRAN COLOMBIA, INCA EMPIRE, NEW GRANADA, PICHINCHA, BATTLE OF.

QUIVIRA (United States) Area said to be located near Great Bend, central KANSAS. Quivira was the land sought and found in 1541 by Francisco Vásquez de Coronado and later explored by the Spanish in 1593 and 1601.

QUM. See QOM.

QUMRAN (Jordan) Village in ancient PALESTINE, on the NW shore of the DEAD SEA, in the West Bank region occupied by Israel in 1967. The village was inhabited by a group of religious Jews, probably Essenes, from the second century BC until the Romans destroyed it in 68 AD. In 1947 the first group of manuscripts written by the sect were discovered in nearby caves and came to be known as the Dead Sea Scrolls.

R

RAAMSES [*Egyptian:* **Pi-Ri'amsese**] (Egypt) Biblical name for the ancient city of Pi-Ri'amsese, built by Hebrew slave labor under the pharaohs of ancient Egypt. It was destroyed and then rebuilt under Ramses II (1292–1225 BC). The site is presumed to be in the eastern part of the Nile River delta, near Qantir or Tel el-Dab'a, and close to AVARIS, the lost capital of the Hyksos invaders. At Qantir remains of a palace and other structures dating from the time of Ramses II have been turned up.

RAANANA [**Ra'anana**] (Israel) Settlement in the PLAIN OF SHARON, 9 mi NE of Tel Aviv, W Israel. A large reception camp for Jewish immigrants was founded here in 1921, as well as an Orthodox Jewish children's community.

RAB [*Italian:* **Arbe**] (Yugoslavia) Island off the coast of CROATIA, W Yugoslavia, in the Adriatic Sea. A Catholic bishopric since the 10th century, it was under the rule of VENICE from the 10th to 18th centuries. The island has ruins of ancient walls, the Venetian governor's palace, and a 12th-century cathedral.

RABAT (Morocco) City and capital of Morocco, on the Atlantic Ocean coast, 57 mi NE of Casablanca, at the mouth of the Bou Regreg estuary, opposite Salé. Once a Muslim fortress, built *c.*700 AD, it was formally founded in the 12th century by Abd-al-Mumin, originator of the ALMOHAD dynasty, and served as a base for voyages to SPAIN. A pirate fortress in the 17th and 18th centuries, it was made a French protectorate in 1912 and became independent in 1956.

RABAUL (Papua New Guinea) Town and port, on NE NEW BRITAIN Island, in the BISMARCK ARCHIPELAGO, W Pacific Ocean. Founded as the capital of German NEW GUINEA in 1910, it was the capital of the Territory of New Guinea from 1920 to 1941. It was taken by JAPAN in January 1942, during World War II, and became an important naval and air base for the planned attack on Australia. Destroyed by Allied raids between 1943 and 1945, it was reconstructed after the war.

RABBATH. See AMMAN.

RABBATH AMMON. See AMMAN.

RACCONIGI (Italy) Town in Cuneo province, SW Piedmont region, 24 mi S of Turin, NW Italy. The château here was the summer residence of the kings of Italy from 1900.

RACIBÓRZ [*German:* **Ratibor**] (Poland) Town on the ODER RIVER, 42 mi SSE of Opole, near the Czechoslovakian border, S Poland. Granted a charter in 1217 AD, it was made the capital of an independent principality in 1288. In 1526 it passed to the house of Hapsburg

Storks nesting on the old fortifications of Rabat, capital of Morocco. Founded by the fanatical Berber Almohads, who briefly ruled medieval Spain, Rabat was later a pirate base.

and to PRUSSIA in 1742. Between 1822 and 1840 it was the capital of Ratibor principality and then of the duchy of Ratibor between 1840 and 1918. It was returned to Poland in 1945.

RACINE (United States) City in SE WISCONSIN, on LAKE MICHIGAN, 23 mi S of Milwaukee. The first permanent settlement was made here in 1834. The improvement of the harbor 10 years later, combined with the coming of a railroad in 1855, stimulated the economy. There are three buildings here designed by Frank Lloyd Wright, and Racine retains a Danish cultural heritage from early settlers.

RACOVA, BATTLE OF. See VASLUI, Rumania.

RADASBONA. See REGENSBURG.

RADAUTI [**Radautsi**] [*German:* **Radautz**] (Rumania) Town in Suceava province, 20 mi NW of Suceava. A 14th-century cathedral in the town contains tombs of the Moldavian princes. See also MOLDAVIA.

RADAUTSI. See RADAUTI.

RADAUTZ. See RADAUTI.

RADNOR (United States) Town in Delaware county, 12 mi NW of Philadelphia, SE PENNSYLVANIA. The Welsh founded Radnor in 1685 and in 1715 built St. David's Church, which still stands. It is the burial place of the American Revolutionary general, Anthony Wayne.

RADOM (Poland) City in Kielce province, 37 mi NE of Kielce, E central Poland. One of the oldest towns in Poland, dating from c.1155 AD, it is believed to have developed as a meeting place for local diets. In 1187 the first church was built here, and Radom was the seat of diets and tribunals from the 14th to 18th centuries, as well as of the Confederation of Radom of 1767. The city came under the rule of AUSTRIA in 1795, of RUSSIA in 1815, and was finally returned to Poland after World War I.

RAETIA [Rhaetia] (Austria and Switzerland) Roman province S of the DANUBE RIVER, conquered in 15 BC by the Romans after overcoming fierce resistance on the part of the Raetic tribes. It included most of what now comprises the TYROL of western Austria; the Austrian province of Vorarlberg; and Graubunden, a Swiss canton that made up the largest part of the province. Raetia was bounded by the Roman provinces of VINDELICIA on the north, NORICUM on the east, Gaul on the west, and by Italy on the south. Under the Romans Raetia was important because its network of highways connected Italy, the Danube River region, GAUL, and the Balkans. Its boundaries varied from time to time, depending on the amount of pressure exerted on the Roman defenses by Germanic tribes. By 450 AD Rome controlled only the Alpine area.

RAETIA SECUNDA. See VINDELICIA.

RAFA [Rafiah] [ancient: **Raphia**; Egyptian: **Er Rafa, Rafah**] (Israel) Town on the SINAI peninsula, on the border between Gaza and EGYPT, and comprising two adjacent towns, which were combined after the Arab-Israeli War of 1967. Here in 720 BC the Philistines and Egyptians were defeated by Sargon II of ASSYRIA. In 217 BC another great battle was fought here between Antiochus III, king of SYRIA and King Ptolemy IV of Egypt, who was victorious. Rafa was a British military base during World War I. See also PHILISTIA, SELEUCID EMPIRE.

RAFAH. See RAFA.

RAFIAH. See RAFA.

RAGES. See RHAGES.

RAGUSA [ancient: **Hybla Heraea**] (Italy) City and capital of Ragusa province, 32 mi SW of Syracuse, SE SICILY, not to be confused with Ragusa in Dalmatia, now DUBROVNIK. It is the site of ancient necropolises, containing prehistoric weapons and artifacts, and of Greek tombs. The old quarter of the town has walls and a castle built in the Byzantine period. Ragusa was the seat of an independent county in the 12th century.

RAGUSA, Yugoslavia. See DUBROVNIK.

RAGUSAVECCHIA. See CAVTAT.

RAGUSIUM. See DUBROVNIK.

RAHWAY (United States) City in Union county, on the Rahway River, 5 mi SSW of Elizabeth, NE NEW JERSEY. It was settled c.1720 as part of Elizabethtown, now known as ELIZABETH, and was incorporated in 1858. In 1777, during the American Revolution, the British were defeated here in several skirmishes.

RAI. See RHAGES.

RAIDESTOS. See TEKIRDAĞ.

RAISIN RIVER (United States) River, approx. 115 mi long, flowing from S MICHIGAN to LAKE ERIE at Monroe, Michigan. Gen. James Winchester and his U.S. troops were defeated here by British and Indian forces during the War of 1812, when Winchester tried to recapture Frenchtown (MONROE). On Jan. 22, 1813 the Indians massacred the remaining Americans after having promised them safety.

RAJAGRIHA. See RAJGIR.

RAJAHMUNDRY (India) City in NE Andhra Pradesh state, on the Godavari River, 30 mi W of Cocanada, E India. A fortress of the VIJAYANAGARA and Bahmani kingdoms in the 15th century, it was captured by the Muslims in 1470 AD, passed to the Hindus early in the 16th century, and was retaken by the Muslims in 1572. The French held it from 1753 to 1758, when it was taken by the British. Today it is the site of the Pukharam religious festival.

RAJASTAN. See RAJASTHAN.

RAJASTHAN [Rajastan] [former: **Union of Rajasthan**] (India) State in NW India, bordered on the W by Pakistan, with its capital at JAIPUR. It was created in 1948 out of several former principalities of the old region of RAJPUTANA, and in 1956 other areas were added to the state. The inhabitants are 75 percent Hindu.

RAJGIR [ancient: **Rajagriha**] (India) Village in PATNA district, N central Bihar, 43 mi SSE of Bihar, NE India. In the seventh century BC it was the first capital of the MAGADHA kingdom, under the rule of Bimbisara. Gautama Buddha (c.563–483 BC) lived here for many years, and the first Buddhist monastery was founded in Rajgir, which became an important Buddhist pilgrimage center.

RAJMAHAL [ancient: **Agmahal**] (India) Town on the GANGES RIVER, E Bihar, 55 mi ESE of Bhagalpur. It was the capital of BENGAL under the Mogul Emperor Akbar in the 16th century. See also MOGUL EMPIRE.

RAJPAT. See KAMATAPUR.

RAJPUTANA (India) Region in NW India, roughly the same as RAJASTHAN state, extending partly into Gujarat and Madhya Pradesh states. The region was ruled by the Rajput tribes between the seventh and 13th centuries AD. Muslim invasions began in the 11th century, and in 1568 the area came under the MOGUL EMPIRE, which controlled it from AJMER until the early 18th century. It was under the Marathas from c.1750 to

1818, when it came under the domination of Great Britain. See MARATHA CONFEDERACY.

RAKATA. See KRAKATAU.

RAKKA [Raqqa] [*ancient:* **Nicephorium;** *Arabic:* **Ar Raqqah, El Rashid**] (Syria) Town on the EUPHRATES RIVER, 100 mi SE of Aleppo, N central Syria. A prosperous town in antiquity, it was a residence of the Abbasid caliph Harun al-Rashid (c.764–809) and the home of al-Battani (Albatenius), the Arab astronomer and mathematician. It was razed by the Mongols in the early 13th century. See also ABBASID CALIPHATE, MONGOL EMPIRES.

RALEIGH [*former:* **Bloomsbury**] (United States) City and state capital, seat of Wake county, E central NORTH CAROLINA. Founded in 1788 on a site chosen for the capital, it was occupied on April 14, 1865, during the Civil War, by Union troops under Gen. William T. Sherman. Andrew Johnson, 17th president of the United States, was born here in 1808.

RAMADI [Ramadie, Rumadiya] [*Arabic:* **Ar Ramadi**] (Iraq) Town on the EUPHRATES RIVER, 60 mi W of Baghdad, central Iraq. Settled in 1869, it is the starting place of a highway crossing the desert to the Mediterranean Sea. During World War I the British defeated the Turks here in a major battle fought on Sept. 28/29, 1917. See OTTOMAN EMPIRE.

RAMADIE. See RAMADI.

RAMBOUILLET (France) Town in Yvelines department, 28 mi SW of Paris, N central France. The château here, built between the 14th and 18th centuries, was the site of the death of King Francis I in 1547 and the abdication of King Charles X in 1830. It is presently the official summer residence of the presidents of France.

RAMILLIES. See RAMILLIES-OFFUS.

RAMILLIES-OFFUS [Ramillies] (Belgium) Village in Brabant province, 13 mi NE of Namur, central Belgium. Nearby is the site of the battle of Ramillies, fought from May 12 to 23, 1706 during the War of the Spanish Succession. French forces under the duke of Villeroi were defeated by combined British, Dutch, and Danish troops led by the duke of Marlborough, whose brilliant tactics allowed the allies to take ANTWERP, GHENT, and BRUGES and to invade the SPANISH NETHERLANDS.

RAMITHA. See LATAKIA.

RAMLA [Er Ramle, Ramle, Ramleh] (Israel) Town and capital of Central district, 12 mi SE of Tel Aviv-Jaffa. Probably settled by the Arabs c.715 AD, Ramla was the capital of PALESTINE and was the object of much conflict during the Crusades. Captured by the Muslim Sultan Saladin in 1187, it became the base of Richard the Lion-Hearted of ENGLAND in 1191. In 1799 Napoleon made the town his headquarters during the Palestine campaign. See FRANCE.

RAMLE. See RAMLA.

RAMLEH. See RAMLA.

RÂMNICUL-SĂRAT. See RÎMNICU-SĂRAT.

RAMPUR. See UTTAR PRADESH.

RAMSGATE (England) Port and seaside resort on the ISLE OF THANET, Kent, on the North Sea, 17 mi N of Dover. A fishing village trading with Baltic ports in the early 18th century, it was the girlhood home of Queen Victoria (1819–1901). In 1940, during World War II, troops evacuated from DUNKIRK were landed here.

RANCAGUA (Chile) City and capital of O'Higgins province, 48 mi S of Santiago, central Chile. Founded in 1743, it was the site of a battle on Oct. 1/2, 1814 during the war of independence. Chilean revolutionists led by Bernardo O'Higgins made an heroic but unsuccessful attempt to defend the city against a larger Spanish Royalist force.

RANDERS (Denmark) City and port, E Jutland peninsula, 22 mi NNW of Århus. Settled in the 11th century, it became an important medieval trading center. It has a 15th-century Gothic church and an 18th-century town hall.

RAND, THE. See WITWATERSRAND.

RANGOON (Burma) City, capital of Burma and its largest city, on the Rangoon River, near the Gulf of Martaban. It is the site of an ancient Buddhist shrine, the tall, gold-spired Shwe Dagon Pagoda dating from c.590 BC, around which the city developed. A Mon fishing village in the sixth century AD, it became the capital of King Alaungpaya in 1752. The city was occupied by GREAT BRITAIN in 1852 during the Second Burmese War and by JAPAN from 1942 to 1945 during World War II, in which it was heavily damaged.

RANKOVICEVO. See KRALJEVO.

RANKOVICHEVO. See KRALJEVO.

RANN OF KUTCH. See KUTCH.

RAPALLO (Italy) Town in NW Italy, on the Ligurian Sea, approx. 16 mi ESE of Genoa. It was first mentioned in 964. By a treaty signed here on Nov. 12, 1920, Italy and Yugoslavia agreed to establish RIJEKA (Fiume) as a free state, although an Italian fascist coup seized it in 1922. On April 16, 1922 GERMANY and the USSR signed a treaty here by which the former gave de jure recognition to the Soviet government, the first time any government had done so since World War I. The agreement renounced all claims stemming from World War I, cancelled prewar debts, and made trade arrangements. By secret agreements, the treaty allowed Germany to experiment with, and produce, in the USSR arms that it was forbidden to have by the Treaty of VERSAILLES.

RAPA NUI. See EASTER ISLAND.

RAPHIA. See RAFA.

RAPPAHANNOCK RIVER (United States) River, 212 mi long, rising in the Blue Ridge Mts of N VIRGINIA and flowing SE to CHESAPEAKE BAY. It was the scene of much fighting during the Civil War, especially in November 1863. See also CHANCELLORSVILLE, FREDERICKSBURG, WILDERNESS.

RAQQA. See RAKKA.

RARKA. See NOVI PAZAR.

RAS AL-KHAIMAH. See UNITED ARAB EMIRATES.

RASCIA. See NOVI PAZAR, SERBIA.

RASHID. See ROSETTA.

RAŠHKA. See NOVI PAZAR.

RASHT [Resht] (Iran) City and capital of Gilan province, near the Caspian Sea, NW Iran. English trade expeditions from RUSSIA reached the city in the late 16th century, and it prospered in the 17th and 18th centuries. The eldest son of Shah Abbas I (1557–1629) was murdered here, and the city was sacked in 1636 by Stenka Razin and his Cossacks. See also PERSIA.

RASTADT. See RASTATT.

RASTATT [Rastadt] (West Germany) City in Baden-Württemberg, 14 mi SW of Karlsruhe, near the French border, SW West Germany. First described in 1247 AD, it was razed by the French in 1689 and rebuilt shortly thereafter. The margraves of BADEN-BADEN made it their residence between 1705 and 1771. The Treaty of Rastatt was signed here in March 1714 and, together with the treaties of UTRECHT and BADEN, ended the War of the Spanish Succession. Between 1797 and 1799 the city was the scene of a congress of states of the HOLY ROMAN EMPIRE.

RATAE CORITANORUM. See LEICESTER.

RATHENOW (East Germany) City in Potsdam district, on the Havel River, 33 mi NW of Potsdam. Founded early in the 13th century and chartered in 1284, the city was ravaged during the Thirty Years War, especially between 1631 and 1641. Swedish forces under Elector Frederick William occupied it briefly in 1675. See also SWEDEN.

RATIBOR. See RACIBÓRZ.

RATISBON. See REGENSBURG.

RATISBONA. See REGENSBURG.

RAT PORTAGE. See KENORA.

RAU. See VOLGA RIVER.

RAUCOUX. See ROCOURT.

RAUMA [*Swedish:* Raumo] (Finland) City and port in Turku ja Pori province, on the Gulf of Bothnia, SW Finland. Chartered in 1445, it became a trading center noted for its lace. The British fleet shelled the city in 1855 during the Crimean War. Rauma harbored one of Finland's largest sailing fleets in the late 19th century.

RAUMO. See RAUMA.

RAVENNA (Italy) City and capital of Ravenna province, Emilia-Romagna region, 61 mi NE of Florence, N Italy. Thought to have been founded by the Sabines, in 191 BC it developed under the Romans as part of Gallia Cisalpina. Its port, Classis, founded by Augustus, harbored the Roman Adriatic fleet. The name *Classis* is the Latin word for fleet. The capital of the Western Empire after 402 AD under Honorius, it was also the seat of the OSTROGOTHIC kings Odoacer and Theodoric. In the sixth century it became the capital of the Exarchate of Ravenna, the territory of the BYZANTINE EMPIRE in northern Italy, until its capture by the Lombards in 751. It was an independent commune by 1177.

Ravenna was ruled by the pope, by the Polenta family from the 13th to 15th centuries, by VENICE from 1441, and was added to the PAPAL STATES in 1509. It was sacked in 1512 following the Battle of Ravenna between Louis XII of France and the Holy League. In 1860 it became part of the kingdom of Italy. The city is famous for its beautiful Byzantine mosaics, for its Roman and Byzantine buildings, and for the tombs of Theodoric and Dante. See also GAUL, ROMAN EMPIRE.

RAVENSBRÜCK (East Germany) Village in Brandenburg, East Germany, N of Fürstenberg. It was the site of an infamous concentration camp for women under the Hitler regime.

RAVENSBURG (West Germany) City in Baden-Württemberg, 47 mi SSW of Ulm, West Germany. Little changed since the Middle Ages, it was founded in the 11th century under the aegis of the Welf (Guelph) family. A free imperial city from 1276 to 1803, it joined the Swabian League in the 14th century and passed to BAVARIA in 1803.

RAWALPINDI (Pakistan) City and capital of Rawalpindi division and district, N Punjab, 90 mi ESE of Peshawar. Founded by Sikhs in 1765, it became an important British military station after their occupation of the PUNJAB in 1849. On Aug. 8, 1919 a treaty was signed here by GREAT BRITAIN and AFGHANISTAN that ended the Third Afghan War. It was the temporary capital of Pakistan between 1959 and 1970.

RAY. See RHAGES.

READING (England) Town in Berkshire, at the confluence of the Kennet River and the Thames River, 39 mi W of London. It was occupied in 871 AD by the Danes, who put it to the torch in 1006. In 1121 King Henry I founded a Benedictine abbey here, and later several parliaments met within its confines. During the Civil War Reading surrendered to the Parliamentarians under the third earl of Essex in 1643. Among the many literary figures associated with the city are Jane Austen and Oscar Wilde, whose *Ballad of Reading Gaol* was based on his stay in prison here.

READING (United States) City on the SCHUYLKILL RIVER, 50 mi WNW of Philadelphia, SE PENNSYLVANIA. Founded in 1733 by the British and later settled by Germans, it was an early center of iron production and manufactured cannons during the American Revolution. During the Civil War it was a Union ordnance depot.

REAL VILLA DE SAN FELIPE DE AUSTRIA. See ORURO.

REATE. See RIETI.

REBEL CREEK, BATTLE OF. See INDEPENDENCE, Kansas.

RECIFE [*former:* Mauritzstad, Pernambuco] (Brazil) City and port, capital of Pernambuco state, at the mouth of the Capibaribe River, at the easternmost point of South America. Often called the Venice of Brazil, it was founded in 1548 by the Portuguese and served as the port for nearby OLINDA. English buccaneers sacked the city in 1595; and from 1630 to 1654 it was held by the Dutch. Later it became the capital of the Pernambuco captaincy.

RECITA. See REŞIŢA.

RECKLINGHAUSEN (West Germany) City in North Rhine-Westphalia, 30 mi SW of Münster, W West Germany. Once inhabited by the Saxons, it was chartered c.1230 and was controlled by the archbishopric of COLOGNE from 1236 to 1803. In 1316 it became a member of the HANSEATIC LEAGUE. PRUSSIA acquired the city in 1815.

RED RIVER (United States) River with two branches, approx. 1,200 mi long, southernmost of the large tributaries of the MISSISSIPPI RIVER, flowing E and S from New Mexico to Louisiana. In the mid-19th century the Great Raft, a centuries-old log jam stretching for 160 miles, was cleared from the river to facilitate navigation. In 1864, during the Civil War, Union forces under Gen. N.P. Banks and Adm. Porter tried to open the route to Texas by way of the river, but were defeated at SABINE CROSSROADS.

RED RIVER SETTLEMENT (Canada) Colony on the banks of the Red River of the North, near the mouth of the Assiniboine River, in present MANITOBA. Thomas Douglas, fifth earl of Selkirk and a Scottish philanthropist, obtained a grant from the Hudson's Bay Company in 1811 to establish the colony. Opposition from the North West Company led to the massacre of Seven Oaks on June 19, 1816, in which many colonists were killed. Frequent conflict occurred until the union of the two companies in 1821. Louis Riel's 1809 rebellion originated in the area.

RED SEA [ancient: **Sinus Arabicus**; Arabic: **Al Bahr al Ahmar**; medieval: **Mare Rubrum**] Narrow sea, approx. 1,200 mi long, between the ARABIAN PENINSULA and NE Africa. A major trade route in antiquity, it declined in importance after the rounding of the CAPE OF GOOD HOPE in 1488 and the decline of Mediterranean trade in the 17th century. After the inauguration of the SUEZ CANAL in 1869, it again became a major shipping route between Europe, the Far East, and Australia.

REGENSBURG [Celtic: **Radasbona**; English: **Ratisbon**; former: **Ratisbona**; Latin: **Castra Regina, Reginum**] (West Germany) City in BAVARIA, on the DANUBE RIVER, 65 mi NNE of Munich, SE West Germany. One of Germany's oldest cities, it was settled by the Celts c.500 BC and became a Roman frontier post in 179 AD. It was then dominated by the Alemanni, Thuringians, and Bavarians. In 739 it was made an episcopal see and fell to Charlemagne in 788, who incorporated it into FRANCONIA. It became a free imperial city in 1250. The township converted to Protestantism in 1542. It was the meeting place for the imperial diet between 1532 and 1806, and was the seat of the Eternal Diet after the Thirty Years War. Attacked by Napoleon in 1809, the city came under Bavaria in 1810 and was made the capital of the Upper PALATINATE. It was heavily damaged by Allied bombs in World War II. The city has Roman remains, including the Porta Praetoria, Christian tombs from the Roman period, the Gothic cathedral of St. Peter, the Baumburger Tower of c.1260, the abbey of St. Emmeran, and many other Romanesque, Gothic, Renaissance, and Baroque buildings.

REGGIO. See REGGIO NELL'EMILIA.

REGGIO CALABRIA. See REGGIO DI CALABRIA.

REGGIO DI CALABRIA [Reggio Calabria] [ancient: **Regium, Rhegion, Rhegium**] (Italy) City, port, and capital of Reggio di Calabria province, in CALABRIA region, on the Strait of Messina opposite Sicily, S Italy. Founded in the eighth century BC by Chalcidian and Messenian Greeks, it was the sister city to ancient Zancle (MESSINA). Dionysius the Elder of SYRACUSE razed the city in 387 BC, and it came under ROME in 270 BC. Its strategic location invited frequent invasion between 410 and 1282 AD, and the area was devastated by earthquakes in 1783 and 1908.

REGGIO EMILIA. See REGGIO NELL'EMILIA.

REGGIO NELL'EMILIA [Reggio, Reggio Emilia] [ancient: **Regium Lepidum**] (Italy) City and capital of Reggio nell'Emilia province, in Emilia-Romagna region, N central Italy. Established by ROME in the second century BC, it was a member of the Lombard League in the 12th century AD before passing to the Este family in 1409. The Este dukes of MODENA controlled it until 1796. It became part of Italy in 1860. There are fine examples of medieval and Renaissance art and architecture here. See also LOMBARDY.

REGILLUS, LAKE (Italy) Battle site in ancient LATIUM, a few miles SE of ROME. Here, probably in 495 BC, the Romans achieved supremacy in Latium by defeating the Latins. The exact site is uncertain, but it presumably was near FRASCATI, a town approximately 12 miles southeast of Rome and near the site of ancient TUSCULUM. See also ARICCIA.

REGINA [former: **Pile o'Bones**] (Canada) City and capital of SASKATCHEWAN province, 350 mi W of Winnipeg. Settled on the site of a Cree Indian hunting ground, the city was founded in 1882 with the coming of the railroad, and named in honor of Queen Victoria. The capital of the NORTHWEST TERRITORIES between 1883 and 1905, Regina became the capital of the new province of Saskatchewan in 1905. It is presently the headquarters of the Royal Canadian Mounted Police.

REGINUM. See REGENSBURG.

REGIUM. See REGGIO DI CALABRIA.

REGIUM LEPIDUM. See REGGIO NELL'EMILIA.

REGLA (Cuba) City and suburb of HAVANA, in La Habana province, W Cuba. It developed in the late 17th century around the hermitage of Nuestra Señora de Regla and was formally founded in 1765. Regla was a base for smugglers during the colonial era.

REGNUM PARTHORUM. See PARTHIA.

REHOBOTH. See REHOVOT.

REHOVOT [Rehoboth, Rehovoth] [biblical: **Ruheiba**] (Israel) Town, approx. 4 mi SW of Ramla, central Israel. It was settled by immigrant Jews from Russia in 1890 and was the home of Israel's first president,

Chaim Weizmann, from 1922 to 1948 during the term of the British mandate. Weizmann is buried here.

REHOVOTH. See REHOVOT.

REI. See RHAGES.

REICHENAU (West Germany) Island in the W arm of Lake Constance, 4 mi W of Constance, West Germany. A Benedictine abbey was founded here in 724 AD; and later in the Middle Ages Reichenau became an artistic, literary, and cultural center. Wall paintings dating from the 10th century in St. George's Church are the oldest in Germany. Charles III, the Fat, of France (839–88), emperor of the West as Charles II (881–87), is buried in the church of Mittelzell. Reichenau was independent until 1540. The abbey was secularized in 1799. See also FRANKISH EMPIRE.

REICHENBACH. See DŻIERZONIÓW.

REICHENBERG. See LIBEREC.

REICHSHOF. See RZESZÓW.

REIKJAVIK. See REYKJAVÍK.

REIMS. See RHEIMS.

REMAGEN (West Germany) Town in North Rhineland-Palatinate, on the RHINE RIVER, 20 mi NW of Koblenz, W West Germany. Probably settled in the 11th century, it is the location of the Ludendorff Bridge built during World War I. The bridge was the only Rhine bridge not destroyed at the time of the Allied advance into Germany, near the end of World War II. It was taken on March 8, 1945, permitting the Allies to cross the river.

REMI. See RHEIMS.

RENDSBURG (West Germany) City and port in SCHLESWIG-HOLSTEIN, on the Kiel Canal, 13 mi S of Schleswig, N West Germany. Probably founded in the late 12th century, it came under the counts of HOLSTEIN in 1252. From 1848 to 1851 it was the provisional capital of Schleswig-Holstein during the conflict with the Danes. It was annexed by PRUSSIA in 1866.

RENFREW. See CLYDE RIVER.

RENNES [ancient: **Condate**; Breton: **Roazon**] (France) City and capital of Ille-et-Vilaine department, at the junction of the Ille and Vilaine rivers, NW France. Once a major Gallo-Roman town, it was made the capital of the Breton county of Rennes in the 10th century and in 1196 of the duchy of BRITTANY. From 1561 to 1675 it was the seat of the parliament of Rennes. It suffered much damage during the Hundred Years War and in World War II.

RENO [former: **Lake's Crossing**] (United States) City and Washoe county seat, on the Truckee River, 20 mi N of Lake Tahoe, NEVADA. First inhabited in 1859 as a campsite on the DONNER PASS route to California, it developed after the coming of the Union Pacific Railroad in 1868. It has prospered due to the legalization of gambling in 1931 as well as state laws allowing quick divorce.

RENSSELAER (United States) City in Rensselaer county, on the HUDSON RIVER, opposite ALBANY, E NEW YORK State. It was founded in 1630 after Kiliaen Van Rensselaer was granted land by the Dutch West India Company. British surgeon Richard Shuckburg is thought to have composed *Yankee Doodle* at the 17th-century Fort Crailo here, now restored.

REPTON (England) Town in Derbyshire, 5 mi NE of Burton-upon-Trent. It was a principal town of Anglo-Saxon MERCIA and the site of a monastery. It was also seat of the Mercia bishopric. The town was founded in the seventh century and destroyed in the ninth century by the Danes. A public school for boys was established here in 1557 and still functions. Repton has a 10th-century church and ruins of a priory dating from 1172.

REPÚBLICA DE FILIPINAS. See PHILIPPINES, REPUBLIC OF THE.

REPUBLICA SOCIALISTĂ ROMÂNIA. See RUMANIA.

REPUBLIC OF IRELAND. See IRELAND.

REPUBLIC OF THE RIO GRANDE. See LAREDO, Texas.

REPUBLIEK VAN SUID-AFRIKA. See SOUTH AFRICA, REPUBLIC OF.

REPUBLIKA NG PILIPINAS. See PHILIPPINES, REPUBLIC OF THE.

RÉPUBLIQUE CENTRAFRICAINE. See CENTRAL AFRICAN REPUBLIC.

RÉPUBLIQUE DU SÉNÉGAL. See SENEGAL.

RÉPUBLIQUE FRANÇAISE. See FRANCE.

RÉPUBLIQUE GABONAISE. See GABON.

RÉPUBLIQUE MALGACHE. See MADAGASCAR.

REQUENA (Spain) Town in Valencia province, 36 mi W of Valencia, E Spain. It was taken by the Spanish soldier and hero Rodrigo Diaz de Bivar, known as El Cid, c.1095. Later conquered by the Moors, it was recaptured in 1219 by King Alfonso VIII of CASTILE.

RESACA DE LA PALMA (United States) Battle site in Cameron county, 4 mi N of Brownsville, S TEXAS. On May 9, 1846, in the second battle of the Mexican War, Anglo-American troops under Gen. Zachary Taylor defeated the Mexican forces led by Gen. Mariano Arista here and drove them from Resaca across the RIO GRANDE.

RESHITSA. See REŞIŢA.

RESHT. See RASHT.

RESICZABÁNYA. See REŞIŢA.

RESISTENCIA (Argentina) City and capital of Chaco province, on the Paraná river, facing CORRIENTES, N Argentina. The location of an Indian community and a Jesuit mission in the 18th century, it was a major military post during the wars against the Indians.

REŞIŢA [Recita, Reshitsa] [Hungarian: **Resiczabánya**] (Rumania) City in the BANAT, 65 mi SE of Arad, SW Rumania. A mining center for precious metals in Roman times, the city was officially founded in 1768 when the dowager empress Maria Theresa of AUSTRIA established a foundry here.

REST HILL. See KINGSTON.

RETHEL (France) Town in Ardennes department, on the AISNE RIVER, 23 mi NE of Rheims. From the 10th to 16th centuries it was the seat of a countship, held first by the counts of CHAMPAGNE and in 1384 by the house of BURGUNDY. Elevated to a duchy in 1581, it was bought by the Mazarin family in 1663. The town's strategic position resulted in heavy damage during World Wars I and II.

RETHONDES (France) Village in Oise department, 6 mi E of COMPIÈGNE, in the Forest of Laigue, N France. On Nov. 11, 1918 the armistice ending World War I was signed here. In 1940, during World War II, it was the site of the signing of an armistice between France and Germany by Hitler.

RÉUNION [Bonaparte] [*former:* **Bourbon**] (France) Island in the MASCARENE ISLANDS group, in the Indian Ocean, approx. 430 mi E of Madagascar. It was discovered by the Portuguese in 1513 and remained uninhabited until France claimed it in 1638. Colonized as Bourbon in 1662 under the aegis of the French East India Company, it was renamed Réunion in 1793 and Bonaparte in 1806. During the Napoleonic Wars it was occupied by GREAT BRITAIN between 1810 and 1815 and became an overseas department of France in 1946. The population is largely French Creole.

REUSS (East Germany) Two former principalities in THURINGIA, central Germany. Dating from the 12th century, with a very complicated genealogy, the House of Reuss was divided into the Reuss Older Line, with its capital at GREIZ, and the Reuss Younger Line, with its capital at GERA to the north. In 1673 the heads of both the Older and the Younger lines were made counts of the HOLY ROMAN EMPIRE, and later both became princes. The two principalities joined the CONFEDERATION OF THE RHINE in 1807, the GERMAN CONFEDERATION in 1815, and the GERMAN EMPIRE in 1871. After Germany's defeat in World War I, both principalities were briefly free states but were merged as the People's State of Reuss in 1919. A year later they were incorporated into the new state of Thuringia.

REUTLINGEN (West Germany) City in Baden-Württemberg, 19 mi S of Stuttgart, SW West Germany. Established before 1090 AD, it became a free imperial city from 1240 until it passed to WÜRTTEMBERG in 1802. Duke Ulrich of Württemberg was defeated here in 1377 by the Swabian League. It was the first city in SWABIA to join the Protestant Reformation in the 16th century, and was the birthplace of the 19th-century economist Friedrich List.

REVAL. See TALLINN.

REVEL. See TALLINN.

REVESSCO. See SAINT-PAULIEN.

REY. See RHAGES.

REYKJAVÍK [Reikjavik] (Iceland) City, port, and capital of Iceland, on the SW coast. It was founded by Ingolfur Arnarson c.870 and remained a village until the 18th century. Granted a charter in 1786, it became the headquarters of the Danish administration in 1801. Reykjavík was made the Icelandic capital in 1918 and is the seat of the parliament (*Althing*) and of the Lutheran bishop. It was a vital Allied base in World War II.

The bleak northern port of Reykjavik, Iceland's capital. A country of huge glaciers and active volcanoes, Iceland was settled *c.*874 AD by Norse Vikings, who later discovered America.

REZAIYEH [*former:* **Urmia, Urumiyeh**] (Iran) City and capital of West AZERBAIJAN province, near Lake Rezaiyeh, NW Iran. Founded before the ninth century AD, it was taken by the Oghuz Turks in the 11th century, by the Seljuks in 1184, and later by the Ottoman Turks. In the 19th century it was a center of Christian missionary endeavor, and until 1918, 40 percent of the inhabitants were Christian. The city is said to be the birthplace of Zoroaster, the religious prophet of ancient PERSIA.

RĒZEKNE [*former:* **Ryezhitsa**; *German:* **Rositten**] (USSR) Town in E Latvian SSR, on the Rezekne River, NW European USSR. Founded in 1285 at the site of a castle built by the Livonian Knights, it was controlled by the Polish-Lithuanian state from 1560 to 1772, when it passed to RUSSIA. Rezekne became part of independent LATVIA in 1918, and during World War II it was occupied by GERMANY between 1941 and 1945 before being absorbed into the USSR. See also LITHUANIA, POLAND.

RHA. See VOLGA RIVER.

RHADAMES. See GHUDAMIS.

RHAEDESTUS. See TEKIRDAĞ.

RHAETIA. See RAETIA.

RHAGAE. See RHAGES.

RHAGES [Rages] [*ancient:* **Rhagae**; *Greek:* **Europus**; *Persian:* **Rai, Ray, Rei, Rey**] (Iran) Ancient and medieval city of PERSIA, at the site of modern Rai, approx. 5 mi SE of Teheran. One of the great cities of antiquity, it is believed to have been founded c.3000 BC. It was a capital of the ancient empire of MEDIA and in the Middle Ages prospered under the Seljuk Turks, until it was destroyed by Genghis Khan in 1220 AD. The city was abandoned c.1400. It is an important archaeological site with many impressive ruins.

RHEGION. See REGGIO DI CALABRIA.

RHEGIUM. See REGGIO DI CALABRIA.

RHEIMS [Reims] [ancient: **Durocortorum**; former: **Remi**] (France) City in Marne department, on the Vesle River, in the CHAMPAGNE region, NE France, approx. 82 mi ENE of Paris. The ancient capital of the Gallic Remi tribe, it was conquered by the Romans and became an important and prosperous city of Roman GAUL. It was made an archiepiscopal see in the third century AD and was the site of the crowning of Clovis I as king of all the Franks in 496, and of all the kings of France since the 12th century, including that of Charles VII in 1429. Charles's coronation took place here at the insistence of Joan of Arc and symbolized the intention of the French crown to regain northern France from ENGLAND. The present Rheims cathedral, built in the 13th and 14th centuries, is an outstanding example of French Gothic architecture, and its cathedral school was a center of learning in the 12th century. The city was severely damaged during World Wars I and II; and on May 7, 1945 GERMANY signed an unconditional surrender at Allied headquarters here.

RHEIN. See RHINE RIVER.

RHEINFELD. See RHEINFELDEN.

RHEINFELDEN [Rheinfeld] (Switzerland) Town in Aargau canton, on the RHINE RIVER, N Switzerland, opposite the German town of the same name. A free imperial town in the Middle Ages, it was a frequent battle site during the Thirty Years War of 1618 to 1648. On Feb. 28, 1638 the imperial troops were defeated here by Bernhard of SAXE-WEIMAR, and the Huguenot leader Duke Henri de Rohan was fatally wounded.

RHEINLAND. See RHINELAND.

RHEINLAND-PFALZ. See RHINELAND-PALATINATE.

RHEINPROVINZ. See RHINE PROVINCE.

RHEINSBERG (East Germany) Town in Potsdam district, on the Rhine River, 12 mi NNE of Neuruppin, N central East Germany. Known to exist in 1335 AD, it later became the residence of King Frederick II the Great of PRUSSIA from 1736 to 1740, while he was crown prince.

RHENUS. See RHINE RIVER.

RHIN. See RHINE RIVER.

RHINEBECK (United States) Village in SE NEW YORK State, near the E bank of the HUDSON RIVER, 16 mi N of Poughkeepsie. It was settled some time before 1700. What is said to be the oldest hotel in the United States, the Beekman Arms, is still operated here. There is also a pre-Revolutionary Dutch Reformed Church and cemetery.

RHINELAND [German: **Rheinland**] (West Germany) Region W of the RHINE RIVER, in West Germany, with COLOGNE as its chief city. Sometimes used to refer only to the former RHINE PROVINCE of PRUSSIA, the name "Rhineland" may also include the Rhenish PALATINATE, Rhenish and southern HESSE, and western BADEN. It was controlled by the Allies after World War I until 1930. In defiance of the terms of the Treaty of Versailles of 1919 and the Locarno Pact of 1925, the Hitler government remilitarized the region from 1936 and built the SIEGFRIED LINE, an extensive chain of almost impenetrable fortifications.

RHINELAND-PALATINATE [German: **Rhineland-Pfalz**] (West Germany) State, mainly W of the RHINE RIVER, with its capital at MAINZ. Once part of the French zone of occupation after World War II, it was created in 1946 by uniting the Rhenish PALATINATE, Rhenish HESSE, the southern part of the former RHINE PROVINCE of PRUSSIA, and a small portion of the former Prussian province of Hesse-Nassau. See also SPEYER, TRIER, WORMS.

RHINE PROVINCE [German: **Rheinprovinz**] (West Germany) Former province of PRUSSIA, in W West Germany, of which KOBLENZ was the capital. It was created from the area west of the RHINE RIVER ceded to FRANCE in 1801 and the area east of the Rhine that became the duchy of BERG. Both areas passed to Prussia at the Congress of Vienna of 1814/15, and the Rhine Province was formed in 1824. It was a center of Roman Catholic activity in Germany.

RHINE RIVER [ancient: **Rhenus**; Dutch: **Rijn**; French: **Rhin**; German: **Rhein**] Major river of Europe and a principal waterway, approx. 820 mi long, rising in the Swiss Alps and flowing to the NORTH SEA, contiguous to Austria, France, Liechtenstein, Netherlands, Switzerland, and West Germany. During the expansion of ROME, the legions under Julius Caesar reached the Rhine in 56 BC and built the first bridge, of wood, across it. The Romans continued to move into Germany until the disastrous massacre of Roman legions in the TEUTOBURG FOREST by Germanic tribes in 6 AD, after which Augustus established the river as the boundary of the ROMAN EMPIRE. Thereafter the Rhine area became a flourishing part of the empire, until on Dec. 31, 406 a mixed force of barbarian Vandals, Suevi, Alans, and Burgundians crossed through the barrier of the Rhine, over the frozen river, to begin the breakup of the Western Roman Empire.

As Europe recovered during the Dark Ages and Middle Ages, the Rhine valley was gradually cleared for agriculture and opened for trade, becoming a major trade route linking northern Italy and the Mediterranean through the Alpine passes to lower Germany, the Low Countries, and the North Sea. During the Middle Ages and the early modern period the river was dotted with the castles and toll stations of petty lords, who exacted heavy duties on its commerce. Nevertheless, the river played an important part in the rejuvenation of urban activity, especially in the Low Countries.

The Rhine was opened to international navigation only in 1868. It was taken as the "natural boundary" of France since the 17th century; the victory of the Allies over Germany in World War I enabled them to reassert this boundary with the reward of ALSACE and LORRAINE to FRANCE. Before World War II the Rhine area was the site of the German SIEGFRIED and French MAGINOT defensive lines, which played an important part in the early stages of the war. In March 1945 U.S. troops succeeded in crossing the Rhine at REMAGEN, shortly before the end of the war.

The major trading towns along its route, many of them Roman foundations, include BASLE, BONN, COLOGNE, FREIBURG, KARLSRUHE, KOBLENZ, MAINZ, MANNHEIM, SPEYER, STRASBOURG, UTRECHT, and WORMS.

RHINOCOLURA. See AL-'ARISH.

RHODAMUS. See RHÔNE RIVER.

RHODE ISLAND (United States) State in the NE, in SE New England, the smallest state in the Union. Massachusetts is to the N and E and Connecticut to the W. It was the last of the 13 colonies to ratify the Constitution, in May 1790. Its capital is PROVIDENCE.

The first European to see the area was Giovanni da Verrazano in 1524. He may also be responsible for its name, having reported seeing an island about the size of the island of RHODES in the Aegean Sea. The area was explored in 1614 by a Dutchman, Adriaen Block, who also may have given Rhode Island its name, using the Dutch word for "red," with respect to the soil. Settlement began when Roger Williams, banished from MASSACHUSETTS Bay Colony for religious dissent, established a colony near modern Providence in 1636. In 1638 Anne Hutchinson and some other dissenters, also banished, bought the island of Aquidneck in NARRAGANSETT BAY and established PORTSMOUTH. This group split over religion, and some of them founded NEWPORT in 1639. WARWICK was settled in 1642.

Williams received a patent in 1644 from the English parliament, and in 1647 the four towns organized a government. King Charles II in 1663 issued a liberal charter that continued religious freedom. This situation, uncommon at the time, had already drawn diverse settlers, including Jews in 1654 and Quakers soon after. Rhode Island was not admitted to the NEW ENGLAND Confederacy because of its religious freedom, but it was in the thick of King Philip's War of 1675/76, which almost wiped out the Indians in southern New England. In the Swamp Fight near KINGSTON in 1675, the Narragansett Indians lost nearly 1,000 warriors.

From 1750 to 1770, Providence and Newport contended for control of the colony. Newport was the commercial center, profitably engaged in the rum, molasses, and slave trade. The British Navigation Acts, especially the Molasses Act, were hated and often violated. The colony was a haven for smugglers; and a British revenue cutter was burned in 1772 as a protest, an event that many in the state consider the beginning of the Revolution. During the American Revolution, British troops occupied part of Rhode Island from 1776 to 1779, the Americans and the French trying unsuccessfully in 1778 to force them out. Rhode Island refused to cooperate with the Continental Congress, and no delegates were sent to the Constitutional Convention of 1787. Resistance to ratifying the Constitution continued until the new Federal government threatened to cut all commercial ties.

Worthless paper currency and many bankruptcies caused economic difficulties, and the Embargo Act of 1807 was hard on a shipping economy. Rhode Island was also feeling competition from other New England ports. However, the start of the textile industry, with the first mill opening in PAWTUCKET in 1790, was a help. Dorr's Rebellion, led by Thomas Wilson Dorr in 1842, was an attempt to secure suffrage without property qualifications and was partially successful. Rhode Island, strongly antislavery, gave aid to the Union during the Civil War.

Into the 20th century the state's politics and economy were dominated by the mill owners, with many immigrant workers living in company towns. A long textile strike after World War I and the movement of textile mills to the South were injurious. The state was controlled by the Republicans until the 1930's but now usually votes Democratic nationally.

RHODES [Ródhos] [*Greek:* **Rhodos, Rodos;** *Italian:* **Rodi;** *Latin:* **Rhodus**] (Greece) City and capital of the island of RHODES and of the Dodecanese department, situated at the NE tip of the island. Founded in 408 BC according to the design of Hippodamus of Miletus, it was controlled at different times by SPARTA, ATHENS, CARIA, and Alexander the Great of MACEDON. Rhodes was attacked in 305 BC by Demetrius I of Macedon. After resisting the siege, the citizens of the city created the Colossus of Rhodes, a huge bronze statue of Helios, which was one of the seven wonders of the ancient world. It was later destroyed in an earthquake. The city lost importance after the rise of DELOS as a free port in the second century BC, but it remained an important center of learning and the arts throughout the Hellenistic and Roman periods. Held by the BYZANTINE EMPIRE until 1204, it was conquered c.1280 by the religious order, the Knights Hospitalers, who held it as their principal base after the fall of the Crusader States to the Muslims at Acre in 1291. They then became known as the Knights of Rhodes. It fell to the OTTOMAN EMPIRE, after a long siege, in 1522. Italy captured the island from the Ottoman Turks in 1912 and ceded it to Greece in 1947. Much of the old city was built under the Knights and includes the restored Palace of the Grand Masters.

RHODES [Ródhos] [*ancient:* **Rhodus;** *Greek:* **Rhodos, Rodos;** *Italian:* **Rodi**] (Greece) Island, largest of the DODECANESE group, in the SE Aegean Sea near Turkey. It was settled by Dorians from ARGOS before 1000 BC and was dominated in the seventh century BC by three city-states, including LINDUS. It founded colonies in the Mediterranean, the largest of which was GELA, in Sicily, and remained independent until the Persian invasion of the sixth century BC. Allied with ATHENS before 411 BC and taken by MACEDON in 322 BC, Rhodes flourished after the death of Alexander the Great and became a major cultural and literary center. After a period of decline in the second century BC, it was sacked in 43 BC by Caius Cassius, the conspirator. Part of the BYZANTINE EMPIRE until 1204 AD, it was headquarters for the Knights Hospitalers before falling to the OTTOMAN EMPIRE in 1522. ITALY captured Rhodes from the Ottoman Turks in 1912 and ceded it to Greece in 1947.

RHODES FERRY. See DECATUR, Alabama.

RHODESIA [Southern Rhodesia, Zimbabwe-Rhodesia] A landlocked country of south-central Africa, bordered by Zambia on the north, Mozambique on the east, Botswana on the west, and South Africa to the south. Its capital is at HARARE, formerly Salisbury.

A flourishing culture centered around the massively built center of GREAT ZIMBABWE, south of Fort Victoria, which flourished in the 14th century. Zimbabwe may have been the capital of the Shona kingdom of Guruuswa, which traded extensively with the coastal city-states of TANZANIA. By the middle of the 15th century Zimbabwe had lost its preeminence to the emergent northern kingdom of MWANAMUTAPA (Monomotapa), which actively developed the region of the Zambezi river.

Portuguese explorers discovered Mwanamutapa in the 16th century and actively began to trade for gold; at the same time they sought to dominate the kingdom. In the early 17th century their efforts had weakened the kingdom's control over its interior regions, and in 1630 Portuguese machinations culminated in the installment of a puppet king on the throne. This coup opened the door for an influx of settlers and Catholic missionaries, forming a European group that successfully resisted attempts by succeeding kings to oust it. By 1700 Mwanamutapa's influence had been destroyed.

The next invasion of outsiders into the region came as a result of the devastating success of King Shaka in ZULULAND during the 1820's. A general of Shaka's named Mzilikazi decided to carve out his own principality and easily conquered the region north of the Vaal river. However, Afrikaners from the CAPE COLONY moved in to contest Mzilikazi's dominion and in 1837 forced him and his followers to head north in search of new land. They settled in what became Rhodesia and established their capitals at Inyati and BULAWAYO. Mzilikazi and his Ndebele tribesmen established a powerful and efficient conquest state that totally dominated the native Shona peoples.

GREAT BRITAIN became interested in Rhodesia during the latter part of the 19th century and in 1890 a colonizing party of British and European South Africans entered Rhodesia from BECHUANALAND under the aegis of Cecil Rhodes's British South Africa Company. Ousting the native Shona, the invaders established Fort Salisbury deep in Rhodesian territory. An increasing flow of South African settlers followed, and they began to press the Ndebele. In 1893 the settlers forced the Ndebele to accept an exploitative treaty and proceeded to take all the choicest land. Three years later Ndebele anger exploded in a bloody rebellion, and they were joined by the Shona in attacks on the European settlers. After a year of fierce fighting both tribes were resubjugated.

The British South Africa Company administered the largely autonomous British protectorate of Southern Rhodesia until 1923, when the European settlers opted for independent home rule as a British colony. Southern Rhodesia's mining and agricultural interests prospered, with a firm racist policy reserving all advantages for the white minority. Increasingly repressive laws patterned on South Africa's apartheid policy were enacted, restricting African freedom. In 1953 Great Britain established the Federation of Rhodesia and Nyasaland, which lasted until 1964. In 1965 an ultra-conservative government headed by Ian Smith reacted to British pressure to make concessions to African nationalists by unilaterally declaring Rhodesia's independence of Great Britain, which viewed this as unlawful rebellion and quickly moved, with U.N. Security Council backing, to clamp down a punitive trade embargo. Smith's government easily continued in power, with economic backing from South Africa and Portugal, and in 1970 declared Rhodesia to be an independent republic.

African nationalist forces stepped up guerrilla activity against the white minority regime, and fighting escalated throughout the 1970's. In 1978 the Smith government formulated a plan for black majority rule with moderate African leaders that would protect many white privileges. The guerrilla leaders rejected this and continued their warfare, even after the election of Abel Muzorewa as the first prime minister of Zimbabwe-Rhodesia in 1979. Fighting halted when Muzorewa agreed to turn rule over to Great Britain, pending a new general election, and in 1980 Robert Mugabe became the prime minister of the new republic of ZIMBABWE.

RHODESIA AND NYASALAND, FEDERATION OF. See MALAWI, ZIMBABWE.

RHODOS. See RHODES.

RHODUS. See RHODES.

RHÔNE RIVER [*ancient:* **Rhodamus**] (France, Switzerland) River, approx. 500 mi long, rising in the Swiss Alps and flowing through LAKE GENEVA into S France, to the Mediterranean Sea W of Marseilles. One of Europe's major waterways, it has links with the RHINE and SAÔNE river systems, and from antiquity it has been an important route for trade and migrations. It was explored and settled by Greek colonists and Romans and became an important part of Roman GAUL. It was the center of the early kingdom of BURGUNDY, and its lower valley was the cradle of the medieval culture of PROVENCE. The Rhône itself was important in transporting the thriving culture of LANGUEDOC to northern France, GENEVA, and GERMANY and, in reverse, in facilitating the eventual dominance of northern France over the south. Important cities of the Rhône valley include ARLES, AVIGNON, GENEVA, LYONS, MARSEILLES, NÎMES, and VIENNE.

RHUDDLAN (Wales) Town and parish in Flintshire, Clwyd administrative county, N Wales, approx. 25 mi WNW of Chester. In 1277 AD King Edward I of ENGLAND built a castle here, which was later destroyed in 1646 by the Parliamentarians during the Civil War. The castle was the scene of Edward's enactment of the

Statute of Rhuddlan of 1284, which established the government of conquered Wales.

RIAD. See RIYADH.

RIAZAN. See RYAZAN.

RIBE (Denmark) City and capital of Ribe county, on the Ribe River, SW Denmark. One of Denmark's oldest cities, it was first described in 862 AD and in 948 was made an episcopal see. It prospered greatly during the Middle Ages and today has fine buildings dating from that period.

RIBEIRA GRANDE. See CAPE VERDE ISLANDS.

RIBEIRÃO PRÊTO (Brazil) City in N central São Paulo state, 180 mi NNW of São Paulo, SE Brazil. It developed in the late 19th century with the arrival of the railroad and a large number of Italian immigrants. Until the 1930's it was known as the coffee capital of Brazil.

RIBNICA. See TITOGRAD.

RICHBOROUGH [*ancient:* **Rutupiae**] (England) Former port in KENT, on the Stour River, 5 mi SW of Ramsgate, now silted up. It is on the site of the Roman port of Rutupiae, whose excavated remains are on view. These include the earthen ramparts thrown up by the invading Romans in 43 AD, the enormous concrete base of a victory morument erected somewhat later, and the third-century buildings and massive walls of the later fort of the SAXON SHORE. There are also the foundations of an Anglo-Saxon church within the fortress. Rutupiae was the starting point of the Roman road, WATLING STREET. The conversion of the victory monument into a lookout post, surrounded by ditches, *c.*275, is evidence of the increasing vulnerability of the Saxon Shore to barbarian raids.

RICHLAND (United States) City in SE WASHINGTON, on the COLUMBIA RIVER, 10 mi WNW of Pasco. Settled in 1892 and incorporated in 1910, Richland was a quiet farming community until World War II. At that time the U.S. government took over thousands of acres of land and between 1943 and 1945 built the Hanford Works nearby for research and production of the atomic bomb. Housing was built for the thousands of workers. In 1958 the housing was turned over to private enterprise.

RICHMOND (United States) City in E central KENTUCKY, 24 mi SSE of Lexington. Settled in 1784, it is the center of a tobacco and livestock-producing area. During the Civil War the battle of Richmond was fought here on Aug. 30, 1862, resulting in a victory for the Confederates under Kirby Smith, who on May 26, 1865 became the last southern general to surrender to Union forces. The 1849 courthouse was used as a hospital. Mt Zion Church, where the battle began, can still be seen. Nearby is White Hall, built in 1864 around a 1787 house. Cassius M. Clay, diplomat, abolitionist, and U.S. minister to Russia, is buried here.

RICHMOND, New York City. See STATEN ISLAND.

RICHMOND (United States) City, port of entry, and capital of the state of VIRGINIA, on the JAMES RIVER.

It was settled in 1637 and grew as a trading post around Fort Charles. Planned in 1737, the city was the site of the second and third Virginia Conventions in 1775, during which Patrick Henry made his famous *Give me liberty or give me death* speech. Richmond became the capital of Virginia in 1779 and was the Confederate capital during the Civil War, when it was a frequent target of the Union forces. Captured in 1865 after the fighting around PETERSBURG, it was burned during the Confederate retreat. The state capitol building of 1785 was designed by Thomas Jefferson.

RICHMOND UPON THAMES (England) Outer London borough, on the THAMES RIVER. Richmond is one of England's most historically interesting small areas because of its long association with royalty. It was the site of the palace of Sheen, residence of kings Edward III, Richard II, Henry V, and Henry VII, who changed its name to Richmond. Queen Elizabeth I died here. Cardinal Wolsey, powerful chancellor under Henry VIII, began building HAMPTON Court Palace as his private residence in 1514. Following Wolsey's downfall Henry took it over, and it remained a royal residence until the time of George II in the 18th century. Prior to that, William III had had part of it torn down and rebuilt by England's most noted architect, Christopher Wren.

The Hampton Court Conference of 1604, held here to consider reforms of the Anglican Church, authorized the new Bible translation that became the King James Version. The author Horace Walpole acquired Strawberry Hill, near Twickenham, in 1747 and built a pseudo-Gothic castle that became a showplace of the new Romantic style. The Royal Botanic Gardens, popularly known as KEW Gardens, was founded in 1761, while the Kew Observatory was constructed for George III in 1768. Most of the annual Oxford-Cambridge boat race is rowed on the part of the Thames within Richmond.

RICH MOUNTAIN (United States) Battle site in E central WEST VIRGINIA, near Beverly. Here on July 11, 1861 a Union force under William S. Rosecrans defeated a Confederate force. The battle was part of Rosecrans's successful campaign, in what was then part of the seceded state of VIRGINIA, which lasted from July 1861 to April 1862.

RICOMAGUS. See RIOM.

RIEKA. See RIJEKA.

RIETI [*ancient:* **Reate**] (Italy) Town in central Italy, in Rieti province, Latium region, 42 mi NNE of Rome. It was an important center of the Sabines, an ancient people of this region, who were conquered by the Romans in 290 BC. In the 12th century AD the town belonged to the Guelphs, the pro-papal faction of the later Middle Ages. The town is often associated with St. Francis of Assisi, and it was a center of the Franciscan Order and of investigations by the Inquisition into heretical Franciscans in the 1340's. To the northwest is Greccio, a sanctuary where St. Francis created the first Christmas *presepio*, or Nativity scene, in 1223. Rieti became part of the PAPAL STATES (States of the

Church), the temporal domain of the papacy, in 1354 and remained so until annexed to Italy in 1870. The town was badly damaged in World War II. It is surrounded by 13th-century walls and was the birthplace in 116 BC of Marcus Terentius Varro, Roman man of letters. The Palazzo Comunale contains a museum of classical and medieval art.

RIFF. See RIF MOUNTAINS.

RIF MOUNTAINS [Riff] [*Arabic:* **Er Rif, Er Riff**] (Morocco) Range of the Atlas Mts, extending along the Mediterranean coast from Ceuta to Melilla, NE Morocco. In this isolated region, once part of Spanish Morocco, the fierce Berber tribes rose up against the Spanish and French from 1921. Abd el-Krim and his Berber forces were put down in 1926 by a combined Spanish and French military expedition, and he was exiled to RÉUNION.

RIGA (USSR) City, port, and capital of Latvian SSR, on the Western Dvina River, near the Gulf of Riga. Inhabited by Baltic tribes before the 12th century, it was settled by German merchants in 1158. In 1201 Bishop Albert of LIVONIA formed the Livonian Brothers of the Sword in Riga, and in 1282 the city joined the HANSEATIC LEAGUE. Following the breakup of the order of Livonian Knights in 1561, the city was the scene of religious upheaval and was contested by POLAND and RUSSIA until it was taken by SWEDEN in 1621. A century later it passed to Russia after the Great Northern War, by the Treaty of NYSTAD. Riga developed into a major industrial city in the 19th century and was occupied by Germany in 1917 during World War I. The independence of LATVIA was proclaimed here in 1918, but Latvia fell to the Soviet Union in 1940, when Riga was made capital of the Latvian SSR. After renewed German occupation in World War II, it was returned to the Soviets in 1944.

RIJEKA [Rieka] [*ancient:* **Tarsatica;** *German:* **Sankt Veit am Flaum;** *Italian:* **Fiume**] (Yugoslavia) City and port in Croatia, on the Adriatic Sea, 40 mi SE of Trieste, NW Yugoslavia. Once a Roman settlement, it was ruled between the ninth and 14th centuries by the dukes of CROATIA. Later it passed at various times to AUSTRIA, HUNGARY, and FRANCE. Because of its large Italian population, it was claimed by ITALY after World War I but was awarded to Yugoslavia. After being seized by a free corps under the poet Gabriele D'Annunzio in September 1919, Fiume became a free state until it was annexed by Italy in 1924, following a fascist coup in 1922. Yugoslavia was given Fiume's suburb, Sušak. During World War II, Yugoslavia liberated Fiume from the Germans, united it with Sušak, and began developing it into a major industrial city, a commercial center, and port.

RIJN. See RHINE RIVER.

RIJSWICK. See RYSWICK.

RIKITEA. See GAMBIER ISLANDS.

RILEY, FORT. See FORT RILEY.

RIMINI [*ancient:* **Ariminum**] (Italy) City and port in Forlì province, Emilia-Romagna region, on the Adriatic Sea, 27 mi ESE of Forlì, N Italy. In an area settled by the Umbrians in antiquity, the Romans established a colony here in 268 BC at the meeting place of the FLAMINIAN and AEMILIAN Ways. Rimini served as a Roman military post during the Second Punic War of 218 to 210 BC. A papal city in the eighth century AD, it was taken by the Guelph Malatesta family in the 13th century and held until 1509, when it came directly under the PAPAL STATES. It fell to Venice but was retaken in 1512. Rimini was heavily damaged in World War II. It has impressive Roman remains and Renaissance buildings.

Rimini was the home of Francesca da Rimini, the tragic lover recalled in Dante's *Inferno*. It is also the birthplace of film maker Federico Fellini and figures as the backdrop in many of his films. It is now a popular seaside resort.

RÎMNICU-SĂRAT [Râmnicul-Sărat] (Rumania) Town, 20 mi NE of Buzau, SE central Rumania. It was frequently the site of battle between the Moldavians and Walachians and of fighting between the Turks and Walachians, Austrians, and Russians. Destroyed by fire in 1854, it has since been rebuilt. See also MOLDAVIA, WALACHIA.

RINGSTED (Denmark) City in Vestsjaelland county, 34 mi SW of Copenhagen, E Denmark. An ancient place of pagan worship in Sjaelland, it developed into a major medieval town and Christian center, noted for its 12th-century Benedictine monastery with tombs of several Danish kings.

RINGWOOD (United States) Town in N NEW JERSEY, in the Ramapo Mts, near the New York State line, 15 mi NNW of Paterson. Ringwood Manor was the headquarters of Peter Hasenclever's mines and iron works, established in 1764, where munitions for the American Revolution were produced by his successor, Robert Erskine.

RIO AMAZONAS. See AMAZON RIVER.

RIOBAMBA (Ecuador) City and capital of Chimborazo province, 110 mi S of Quito, central Ecuador. It was founded in 1798 after the original city nearby, dating from *c*.1530, was completely leveled by an earthquake. On Aug. 14, 1836 the first constitution of the republic of Ecuador was declared here.

RIO BRANCO. See RORAIMA.

RIO BRAVO. See RIO GRANDE.

RIO BRAVO DEL NORTE. See RIO GRANDE.

RIO DE JANEIRO (Brazil) City and capital of Rio de Janeiro state, in SE Brazil, on the Atlantic Ocean. One of the world's most glamorous cities, Rio is known everywhere for its Copacabana Beach, its frenetic pre-Lenten Carnival, and its Sugar Loaf Mt, and Corcovado Mt topped by a gigantic statue of Christ. It is Brazil's second-largest city, its major port, and from 1763 to 1960 was successively the capital of the Portuguese colony, the Portuguese empire in exile, the Brazilian empire, and the independent republic. According to tradition the area was first seen by Europeans in January 1502, when Portuguese explorers arrived. Thinking

Guanabara Bay the mouth of a river, they named it Rio de Janeiro to mark the month of their arrival. It is quite likely, though, that the site was first seen in 1504 by Gonçalo Coelho.

French Huguenots established a colony here in 1555 and called it Antarctic France. After a struggle of several years they were driven out in 1567 by Mem de Sá, governor general of Brazil. The Portuguese had started one settlement in the area in 1565; but in 1567, at Mem de Sá's direction, his cousin moved the settlement to the present site. It was formally named São Sebastião do Rio de Janeiro. The French returned in 1711 to capture the town and hold it for ransom for a time. Rio prospered in the 18th century when it became the shipping port for gold and diamonds that came from the interior region of Minas Gerais. It became capital of Brazil colony in 1763, of the Brazilian empire in 1822, and of the republic from 1889 to 1960, when it was replaced by BRASILIA.

Today Rio is the cultural center of the nation and of major importance in finance, commerce, and transportation. From one of the largest and best harbors in the world, it exports metal ores, cotton, coffee, meat, and other products. It manufactures a great variety of goods from foodstuffs to chemicals. There are many attractions for tourists: a warm climate, wide streets, museums, beaches, parks, gardens, one of the largest sports stadiums in the world, and both modern and old architecture, including a 16th-century monastery, a 17th-century convent, and the 18th-century church of Nossa Senhora de Glória. See also PORTUGAL.

RIO DE LA PLATA. See PLATA, RIO DE LA.

RIO DE LAS AMAZONAS. See AMAZON RIVER.

RIO DE ORO. See MOROCCO.

RIO DO ESPIRITO SANTO. See LIMPOPO RIVER.

RIO GARONA. See GARONNE RIVER.

RIO GRANDE [*Spanish:* **Río Bravo, Río Bravo del Norte**] (Mexico, United States) River, approx. 1,880 mi long, rising in SW Colorado and flowing S and E to the Gulf of Mexico, forming part of the border between TEXAS and Mexico. It was visited by Spanish explorer Francisco Vásquez de Coronado in 1540, when Pueblo Indians were using its water for their irrigation systems. In 1848, at the end of the Mexican War, the treaty of GUADALUPE HIDALGO stipulated that it would be the international boundary.

RIO GRANDE DE CHIAPAS. See GRIJALVA.

RIOM [*ancient:* **Ricomagus**] (France) Town in Puy-de-Dôme department, 8 mi N of Clermont-Ferrand, S central France. Of Gallo-Roman origin, it was the old capital of the dukes of AUVERGNE. From Feb. 19 to April 2, 1942, during World War II, the VICHY government brought Edward Daladier, Léon Blum, and others to trial here on charges of having led France into war unprepared. The case was dismissed after the burden of guilt was placed on the accusers.

RIO MUNI. See EQUATORIAL GUINEA.

RION. See RIONI.

RIONI [Rion] [*ancient:* **Phasis**] (USSR) River, 180 mi long, rising in the Caucasus Mts and flowing S and W to the BLACK SEA at Poti. For a brief time considered the boundary between Europe and Asia, it played a role in ancient Greek legends of the Argonauts and the Golden Fleece. The Argonauts sailed up this river after their arrival in Colchis. This has given rise to the expression "sailing to the Phasis" to describe dangerous voyages.

RIO PECOS. See PECOS RIVER.

RIO SALADO. See SALADO, RIO.

RIPON (England) City in the Yorkshire Dales, in North Yorkshire, 23 mi N of Leeds. St. Cuthbert founded a monastery here *c.*660 AD, and the Ripon cathedral was built between the 12th and 15th centuries over an Anglo-Saxon crypt. The city is in the center of the medieval wool-producing area of Yorkshire that supported such monastic houses as Bolton Abbey, Fountains Abbey, and Jervaulx Abbey, now all in ruins. Fountains is approximately 3 miles to the southwest. A treaty signed here in 1640 brought to an end the Second Bishops' War.

RIPON [*former:* **Ceresco**] (United States) City in Fond du Lac county, 20 mi W of Fond du Lac, E WISCONSIN. Settled in 1844 by followers of the French social philosopher Charles Fourier, it was incorporated in 1858 and renamed. On March 20, 1854 a meeting held here led to the formation of the Republican Party.

RISHON LE TSIYON. See RISHON LE-ZION.

RISHON LE-ZION [Rishon le Ziyyon, Rishon le Tsiyon] (Israel) Town, approx. 8 mi SE of Tel Aviv-Jaffa, W central Israel. Established in 1882, it was one of the first modern Jewish communities in PALESTINE.

RISHON LE ZIYYON. See RISHON LE-ZION.

RIVAS [*former:* **Nicaragua**] (Nicaragua) Town and capital of Rivas department, on the W shore of Lake Nicaragua. It was the center of an Indian civilization at the time of the Spanish conquest. Strategically positioned on the route across Nicaragua during the California Gold Rush, it was the site of the defeat of filibuster William Walker that ended in his surrender to the U.S. Navy in May 1857.

RIVER PLATE. See PLATA, RIO DE LA.

RIVERSIDE (United States) City and Riverside county seat, 10 mi SSW of San Bernardino, S CALIFORNIA. Famous for its orchards of navel oranges introduced here in 1873, it was the site of the first marketing cooperative in 1892, which led to the formation of the California Fruit Grower's Exchange.

RIVIERA [Côte d'Azur] (France, Italy) Famous coastal strip between the ALPS and the MEDITERRANEAN SEA, in NW Italy and SE France, long a tourist area and fashionable playground. A scenic highway, the CORNICHE, runs along the entire seaboard. Well-known cities of the Riviera include CANNES, MONTE CARLO, NICE, PORTOFINO, RAPALLO, and SAINT-TROPEZ. See also LIGURIA, PROVENCE, SEPTIMANIA.

RIVNE. See ROVNO.

RIVOLI VERONESE (Italy) Town in Verona province, on the Adige River, 14 mi NW of Verona, NE Italy. On Jan. 15, 1797 Napoleon and his forces defeated the Austrians here during the French Revolutionary Wars.

RIYADH [Er Riad, Riad] (Saudi Arabia) City and capital of Saudi Arabia, in the E central Ad-Dahnā region, approx. 235 mi from the Persian Gulf. In 1818 the city replaced Deraya (DERAIYEH) as the center of Wahabism, an Arab Islamic reform movement. Between 1891 and 1902 it came under the Rashid family of Hail. It was reconquered by Ibn Saud and served as his headquarters for the takeover of the region that later became Saudi Arabia.

RJUKAN (Norway) Town in Telemark county, on the Måne River, S Norway. It was occupied by Germany during World War II. A plant producing heavy water was destroyed by Norwegian commandos here in February 1943 to halt German efforts to make an atomic bomb.

ROANNE [ancient: **Rodumna**] (France) Town in Loire department, on the LOIRE RIVER, 40 mi WNW of Lyons, SE central France, a major industrial center. Mentioned in the writings of the geographer Ptolemy in the second century AD, it was a crossroads in Gallo-Roman times and today has Roman and medieval remains. See GAUL.

ROANOKE [former: **Big Lick**] (United States) Independent city on the Roanoke River, 40 mi W of Lynchburg, SW VIRGINIA. Settled in 1740, it was a village that began to develop after the arrival of the railroad in 1882. It was incorporated in 1884 and is today a major commercial and industrial city.

ROANOKE ISLAND (United States) Island near the S entrance to Albemarle Sound, NE NORTH CAROLINA. It was settled in 1585 by colonists sent by Sir Walter Raleigh, but was unable to prosper. A second colony, the "lost colony," was established in July 1587 under Capt. John White, but when White returned here after a trip to England for supplies, the colonists had disappeared. On Feb. 8, 1862, during the Civil War, Union troops took the island. See also JAMESTOWN, Virginia.

ROATÁN [Coxen Hole, Coxin's Hole] (Honduras) Town and capital of Bay Islands department, on Roatán Island, N Honduras. A pirate stronghold in the 17th century, it was under British control between 1848 and 1859 when the Bay Islands were garrisoned. Remnants of 17th-century pirate fortifications survive.

ROAZON. See RENNES.

ROBBEN ISLAND (South Africa) Island in SW CAPE PROVINCE, at the entrance to Table Bay, 6 mi NNW of Cape Town. Once a mail drop for Dutch ships en route to the Indies, it was later a prison for native chiefs and a leper colony. It is now a military reservation.

ROBESON CHANNEL. See ARCTIC, THE.

ROCAMADOUR (France) Village in Lot department, 12 mi ENE of Gourdon, SW France. Built on the side of a cliff under the remains of a medieval fortress, it has long been a pilgrimage site. Its ramparts date from the 12th to 15th centuries.

ROCCABRUNA. See ROQUEBRUNE.

ROCCASECCA (Italy) Village in Frosinone province, Latium region, 5 mi NW of Aquino, S central Italy. St. Thomas Aquinas was born in the castle here in 1225. In 1411, during the dynastic struggles for the crown of NAPLES, the village was the site of the defeat of the Hungarian claimant King Ladislas of Naples by Louis II of Anjou, the French and papal candidate.

ROCHDALE (England) Town in Greater Manchester, on the Roch River, 10 mi NNE of Manchester. The modern cooperative movement was launched here with the founding of the Rochdale Society of Equitable Pioneers in 1844 by 28 local weavers.

ROCHEFORT [Rochefort-sur-Mer] (France) City and port in Charente-Maritime department, 17 mi SSE of La Rochelle, W France. Fortified as early as 1047 AD, it was developed by the statesman Jean Baptiste Colbert in 1666 with shipyards and a naval arsenal. The marquis de Lafayette embarked from here on his first trip to America. Napoleon surrendered in 1815 to a British warship off the coast at Rochefort. BREST later replaced Rochefort as the chief naval base.

ROCHEFORT-SUR-MER. See ROCHEFORT.

ROCHELLE, LA, See LA ROCHELLE.

ROCHESTER [ancient: **Durobrivae**] (England) City in Kent, on the Medway River, 28 mi ESE of London. Founded by the Romans and later an important Anglo-Saxon town, it was the site of a mission and bishopric founded in 604 AD by St. Augustine of Canterbury. The city was an important stop on the pilgrimage way from London to Canterbury described in Chaucer's *Canterbury Tales*. In 1688 King James II fled to France from here. The town has many 11th- and 12th-century remains, including a notable cathedral, and is dominated by the keep of its Norman castle. Gadshill, the home of novelist Charles Dickens, is here.

ROCHESTER (United States) City and Olmsted county seat, 70 mi SSE of St. Paul, SE MINNESOTA. It is the site of the Mayo Clinic, founded by Dr. W.W. Mayo and his sons in 1889 and now known throughout the world.

ROCHESTER (United States) City and port of entry, on the Genesee River and LAKE ONTARIO, 70 mi ENE of Buffalo, W NEW YORK State. Founded in 1812 by Col. Nathaniel Rochester, it expanded after the opening of the ERIE CANAL and again during the Civil War. The abolitionist Frederick Douglass lived and worked here, as did George Eastman of the Kodak firm, founded here in 1888. Rochester also became known in the late 19th century for its horticulture.

ROCHFORD (England) Town in Essex, 3 mi N of Southend-on-Sea. It was the site of Rochford Hall, home of the Boleyn family and possibly the birthplace of Anne Boleyn c.1510. Parts of the hall survive.

ROCKIES. See ROCKY MOUNTAINS.

ROCK ISLAND [*former:* **Stephenson**] (United States) City and county seat, on the MISSISSIPPI RIVER, 78 mi NW of Peoria, NW ILLINOIS, settled in 1826. Arsenal Island, joined to the city by a bridge, was fortified during the War of 1812 by the British and in 1816 by U.S. forces. In 1862 the Union built a large arsenal here, and during the Civil War Arsenal Island served as a northern military prison. It is still one of the largest arsenals in the world.

ROCK SPRINGS (United States) City in Sweetwater county, 40 mi N of the Utah border, SW WYOMING. It developed in the 1860's around a trading post and stagecoach stop on the OREGON TRAIL. It expanded with the arrival of the railroad and the opening of mines in the area.

ROCKY HILL (United States) An old town in central CONNECTICUT, on the Connecticut River. It was settled in 1650. From 1700 to *c.*1820 it was an important river port and has since become known for its synthetic textiles.

ROCKY MOUNTAIN HOUSE [*former:* **Blackfoot Post**] (Canada) Town in S central ALBERTA, at the foot of the Rocky Mts. Once a fortified post established by the North West Company in 1799 in Blackfoot Indian territory, it was acquired in 1821 by the Hudson's Bay Company who ran it until 1875. Today it is a center for big-game hunting.

ROCKY MOUNTAINS [**Rockies**] (Canada, United States) Mountain system of W North America that runs for more than 3,000 miles from New Mexico to Alaska. On the east are the GREAT PLAINS and on the west a number of basins and plateaus. Geologically complex, the Rockies were lifted up over millions of years and then eroded. They form the Continental Divide that separates streams that drain W to the Arctic Ocean and the Pacific Ocean from those that drain E to the Gulf of Mexico and the Atlantic Ocean. Recognized today for their beauty and majesty and visited by thousands every year, the Rockies, nevertheless, were a heartbreaking barrier to the pioneers who first sought to cross them. It was many years before hope was given up of finding some low and easy passage.

The Spanish explorer Francisco Vásquez de Coronado led an expedition north from Mexico in 1540 into what is now ARIZONA and NEW MEXICO and first sighted the Rockies. Far to the north in CANADA, Louis Joseph and François Verendrye, French explorers, may have seen them in 1742/43. Alexander Mackenzie, a fur trader active in Canada, made an expedition in 1793 that took him over the Continental Divide and on to the Pacific coast; he was the first European to make the overland journey across North America north of Mexico.

The Lewis and Clark Expedition of 1803 to 1806, sent out to explore the newly acquired LOUISIANA PURCHASE, crossed the Rockies in 1805 in the northwestern United States and followed the COLUMBIA RIVER to its mouth. In 1806/07 Zebulon Pike, explorer and U.S. Army officer, reached the site of PUEBLO, Colorado and sighted the peak named for him. In Canada David Thompson and Simon Fraser blazed new paths across

the mountains in 1807/08. Stephen Long and Benjamin de Bonneville, both U.S. Army officers, gathered much information about the Rockies from their expeditions that began in 1819 and 1832 respectively. John C. Frémont, political leader as well as explorer, headed an expedition in 1842; while geologist Ferdinand Hayden spent two years in the Rockies, beginning in 1854. His explorations led to the creation of YELLOWSTONE NATIONAL PARK, the nation's first, in 1872.

Best known of the passes through the Rockies is SOUTH PASS, in southwestern WYOMING, at an altitude of approximately 7,550 feet. In 1832 de Bonneville's expedition was the first to take wagons through it, and the first emigrant train used it in 1841. It became famous as the route of the OREGON TRAIL and was also used by the Mormon and California trails. Raton Pass, in southeastern Colorado, was part of the SANTA FE TRAIL. In Canada Yellowhead Pass and Kicking Horse Pass provide rail and highway routes over the Continental Divide.

ROCOUR. See ROCOURT.

ROCOURT [**Rocour**] [*former:* **Raucoux**] (Belgium) Town in Liège province, just N of Liège, E Belgium. A battle took place here on Oct. 11, 1746 during the War of the Austrian Succession, in which the French, led by Marshal Maurice de Saxe, defeated the combined British and Austrian forces under Prince Charles of Lorraine.

ROCROI [**Rocroy**] (France) Town in Ardennes department, near the Belgian frontier, NE France. The duke of Enghien, known as the Great Condé, led his French forces to a decisive victory here over SPAIN in a battle fought on May 19, 1643 during the Thirty Years War.

ROCROY. See ROCROI.

RODEZ [*ancient:* **Ruthena, Segodunum**] (France) City and capital of Aveyron department, on the Aveyron River, 78 mi NE of Toulouse, S France. An episcopal see since 401 AD, it had been capital of the Rutheni, and was the capital of the ROUERGUE countship until 1789. It was a center of Catholic activity during the Wars of Religion of 1562 to 1598.

RÓDHOS. See RHODES.

RODI. See RHODES.

RODIGO. See ROVIGO.

RODOMUM. See ROUEN.

RODOS. See RHODES.

RODOSTO. See TEKIRDAĞ.

RODRIGUES. See RODRIGUEZ.

RODRIGUEZ [**Rodrigues**] (Mauritius) Island in the MASCARENE ISLAND group, in the Indian Ocean, approx. 350 mi E of Mauritius. The Portuguese discovered it in 1645. It was held by the Dutch between 1691 and 1693, was colonized by the French from Mauritius in the 18th century, and was ruled by GREAT BRITAIN from 1810 to 1968. It is now a dependency of independent MAURITIUS.

RODUMNA. See ROANNE.

ROERMOND (Netherlands) Town in Limburg province, at the confluence of the Maas (Meuse) and Roer rivers, SE Netherlands. A major town and trading center of Upper GELDERLAND in the Middle Ages, it was badly damaged in January and February 1945 during World War II.

ROESELARE [*former:* **Rousselaere;** *French:* **Roulers**] (Belgium) City in W FLANDERS province, NW Belgium. A battle took place here in 1794, during the French Revolutionary Wars, in which the French under Gen. Charles Pichegru defeated the Austrians. Germany occupied the city in World War I between October 1914 and October 1918.

ROFREIT. See ROVERETO.

ROGER SIMPSON ISLAND. See ABEMAMA ATOLL.

ROGOZHI. See NOGINSK.

ROHILKHAND [**Bareilly**] (India) Ancient region in N central Uttar Pradesh, N India. Subject to invasion from the Rajputs, Afghans, Moguls, Pathans, and Marathas, it was held since the early 18th century by the Afghan Rohilla tribe. In 1749 the region was divided, and the Rohillas were driven out by British forces assisted by the nawab of OUDH. See also PILIBHIT, UTTAR PRADESH.

ROHILLA, KINGDOM OF. See PILIBHIT, ROHILKHAND, India.

ROMA. See ROME.

ROMAGNA [*medieval:* **Romania**] (Italy) Region in N central Italy, now included in the region of Emilia-Romagna and parts of the Marches. It was the seat of Byzantine rule in Italy from 540 to 751 AD, with the exarchs residing at RAVENNA. Although it was a province of the PAPAL STATES from the eighth century, several factions vied for control of the region. It became largely independent in the later Middle Ages as urban communes shook off papal and feudal control. Bologna, Imola, Ravenna, Rimini, Faenza, Forlì, and Cesena were among these. The Maletesta, Montefeltro, and the Gonzaga were among the *condottieri*, or mercenary captains, who at times served the papacy, at times their own interests, in subduing the region in the early Renaissance. It was taken by Cesare Borgia in 1501 as a personal principality, but Pope Julius II soon after brought it directly under the papacy, and papal rule continued until 1860, broken only by the French occupation between 1797 and 1814. See also RIMINI.

ROMAGNE-SOUS-MONTFAUCON (France) Village in Meuse department, 18 mi NW of Verdun, NE France. The largest U.S. military cemetery in France is here, with the graves of more than 14,200 soldiers killed in World War I.

ROMAN (Rumania) Town in Bacau province, Moldavia, 28 mi N of Bacău, NE Rumania. Described as early as 1392, it was established at that time by the ruling prince of MOLDAVIA. It was put to the torch by Hungarian troops in 1467, although its 15th- and 16th-century churches have survived. Roman was occupied by the Soviet Union in 1944 during World War II.

ROMAN EMPIRE One of the greatest empires in history, based on the city of ROME, at its peak the Roman Empire comprised all the countries around the MEDITERRANEAN SEA, and western Europe as far north as SCOTLAND. The rule of Rome brought to the Mediterranean basin, and to a lesser extent to Europe, a strong and cohesive government with a superb communications network that fostered the growth of trade and internal movement, a uniform code of law, sophisticated aesthetics, religion, philosophy, and civic life that bestowed enormous benefits on the people concerned. The legacy of the Roman achievement remains with us today. Roman law forms the basis of the law of many European states, the Romance languages are derivations of Latin, and Europe is sprinkled with archaeological monuments that testify to the technical genius of the Romans and have influenced western artistic styles to this day. Western civilization is still inspired by Roman notions of justice, concord, and the beneficial role of the state in human life.

The beginning of the empire can be conveniently dated from 31 BC, when Octavius Caesar defeated Mark Antony and Cleopatra of EGYPT at ACTIUM and assumed complete power over Rome and her dominions, which then stretched from SPAIN to the PERSIAN GULF. As Emperor Augustus, Octavius added new holdings to the empire, including the provinces of GALATIA, RAETIA, NORICUM, and PANNONIA. His reign marked the beginning of two centuries of peace, the Pax Romana, within the empire. Under Claudius I (41–54 AD) the Roman conquest of BRITAIN was begun and later completed in 84 by the general Agricola. Augustus united the empire under the loose institutions of the Roman Republic, with Roman administrators presiding over provinces and city-states, with due regard to local traditions and laws. The cities of the empire were allowed to have their own councils, the administration of local laws, and the local administration of justice. Nevertheless, he and his successors were unable to solve the serious defects in the imperial system, such as the mode of imperial succession, the role of the army in state affairs, the defense of the empire's vast frontiers, and the establishment of a sound economy independent of the takings from wars and booty.

The empire reached its greatest extent during the reign of Trajan (98–117), who pushed eastward into the ARABIAN PENINSULA and acquired lands in ASIA MINOR from the Parthians of PERSIA, and in DACIA. His work was consolidated under his successors Hadrian (117–138) and Marcus Aurelius (161–180). The third century was a period of unrest both within and on the frontiers of the empire. Rome was engaged in wars with the Goths, Alemanni, and Persians; while the murder of Alexander Severus in 235 initiated 30 years of anarchy, during which time the administration foundered and the frontiers were breached.

The reign of Claudius II (268–70) saw a brief period of recovery, but anarchy set in again after his death as each rival for the imperial title led his legions against his enemies and tore the empire apart. The impossibility of holding together such a vast empire became increasingly apparent. Diocletian (284–305) divided the empire into the four prefectures of GAUL, ILLYRIA, ITALY, and the East, while making himself Augustus of the East, the wealthiest part, and Maximilian, Augustus of Italy. Their appointed successors became Caesars of the two other prefectures. However, with the abdication of both Augusti in 305 in favor of their successors, anarchy broke out again until the empire was finally reunited by Constantine the Great in 324. The empire, however, was redivided again under Valentinian (364–375) into the empires of the East and the West, and this division became permanent under Theodosius in 395.

The Western Empire, with its capital at MILAN, gradually disintegrated under the impact of the barbarian invasions of Goths, Huns, Franks, Burgundians, Vandals, and others. The Roman legions were withdrawn from Britain, and Gaul was overrun in the early fifth century. Rome itself was sacked by Visigoths in 410, and in 415 SPAIN fell to them. Africa was lost to the Vandals in 429 and in 476 the last Roman emperor was overthrown, although his office had long ceased to hold any real power. However, the Eastern Empire, later the BYZANTINE EMPIRE, survived through several drastic changes for 1,000 years until the fall of CONSTANTINOPLE in 1453. In the West the notion of the Roman Empire continued to fascinate the Germanic successor states, until the revival of the Roman Empire became a central theme of the Middle Ages. See also HOLY ROMAN EMPIRE, VISIGOTHIC KINGDOM.

ROMANIA, Italy. See ROMAGNA.

ROMANIA. See RUMANIA.

ROMANS. See ROMANS-SUR-ISÈRE.

ROMANS-SUR-ISÈRE [Romans] (France) Town in Drôme department, on the Isère River, 11 mi NE of Valence, SE France. In 837 AD St. Barnard established an abbey here, and during the Middle Ages it became an important town of the DAUPHINÉ.

ROME [*Italian and Latin:* **Roma**] (Italy) Capital city of Italy, in Roma province, Latium region, on the Tiber River, near its mouth on the Tyrrhenian Sea. Dating from the eighth century BC, Rome was the capital of the Roman Republic and of the ROMAN EMPIRE, and as such was for many centuries the greatest city in the Western world. Today it is still a major cultural and intellectual center. The VATICAN City, a separate state within Rome, is the seat of the pope and arbiter of the worldwide Roman Catholic Church. Rome is renowned for the architectural and archaeological wonders that testify to the richness of its history and the genius of its inhabitants.

According to tradition, Rome was founded by Romulus in 753 BC. We know now that the site was originally a cluster of separate villages on the SEVEN HILLS OF ROME overlooking the meandering, swampy TIBER RIVER. A ford, and later a bridge, over the Tiber attracted trade, and the marshy area that is now the Roman Forum was early drained and made into a common meeting place for the nascent city. Certainly by the eighth century BC Rome was an Etruscan city; though by c.500 BC the Etruscan kings were driven

out, and an independent republic was established. A semi-democratic government, divided by tribes, ensured representation by patricians and a voice in the assembly for the common people. In the fifth and fourth centuries, by virtue of its disciplined citizen army, Rome had expanded throughout LATIUM and by the third century had conquered much of central and southern Italy. Roman territorial expansion led to war with CARTHAGE, which was eventually defeated in the three long Punic Wars of 264 to 146 BC. Rome itself had been briefly threatened during the wars by the bold Carthaginian general, Hannibal.

In the course of the struggle Rome acquired SPAIN, North Africa, SICILY, SARDINIA, and CORSICA; and during the second century it also expanded eastward, gaining MACEDONIA and much of ASIA MINOR. At home, however, success led to acute social tensions, erupting in a series of slave revolts and the increasing discontent of the common citizen, who was gradually debarred from the economic and social benefits of the state. The social revolution of the Gracchus brothers in the 130's and 120's followed; and the Social War erupted from 90 to 88 BC, in which recently subjected peoples in Italy itself revolted against their Roman masters.

In the first century BC civil war broke out, first between Marius and Sulla, and then between Pompey, Sulla, Crassus, and Caesar. With Pompey's defeat at PHARSALUS in 48 BC, Julius Caesar became sole master of Rome. A further struggle for power followed his assassination in 44 BC, from which Caesar's nephew, Octavius, emerged supreme after the Battle of ACTIUM in 31 BC as the first emperor of the Roman Empire. For the next three centuries Rome was to be the capital of the empire, and as such its institutions and amenities came to reflect the might of the emperors. The city had long outgrown the original seven hills and the construction of Aurelian's Wall from 270 to 275 AD also enclosed several other hills north of the city and across the Tiber.

The decline of Rome's political importance began in 330 AD, when Constantine the Great moved the capital of the empire to CONSTANTINOPLE. After the division of the empire in 395, RAVENNA was made capital of the West, and the once imperial city was sacked by Alaric the Visigoth in 410 and again by Gaiseric the Vandal in 455. Although Rome was recovered by the BYZANTINE EMPIRE in 552 and made a duchy, after the collapse of the Roman Empire the Romans looked more and more to the bishops of Rome, or popes, for civic guidance and some sense of continuity after all the upheavals. When the Lombard invaders threatened Rome in the eighth century, the popes called in the Franks to subdue them. The Franks then recognized the right of the popes to the so-called Patrimony of St. Peter, and this laid the foundation of the PAPAL STATES. Rome's new importance was further recognized when Charlemagne was crowned in the city in 800, setting a precedent for the papal crowning of the emperors of the HOLY ROMAN EMPIRE for centuries to come.

During the Middle Ages Rome, as a symbol of great earthly and spiritual power, became a shining goal of pilgrimage; but the actual city, sacked in 846 by Saracens and in 1084 by Normans, was beset with internal feuds and attacks from outside. With a consequent decline in trade and population, it became a shadow of itself. Fighting between Guelphs and Ghibellines in the 13th and 14th centuries further damaged the city, which also lost much prestige when the popes moved to AVIGNON in FRANCE between 1309 and 1354. By the 14th century, on the eve of the Italian Renaissance, Rome had shrunk almost to the size of a village centering around the present Piazza Navona-Pantheon area, Trastevere, and the Vatican. The Aurelian walls now enclosed little but farms, vineyards, and cattle markets. An abortive attempt was made by Cola di Rienzi to reestablish the Roman Republic between 1347 and 1354, but it was not until the end of the 15th century that the papacy succeeded in subduing the commune and the independent barons and restoring order.

St. Peter's under construction in the early 16th century, with the other great churches of Rome. The print suggests how medieval Rome had shrunk within its third-century Aurelian walls.

Although the city was plundered by the emperor Charles V in 1527, the late 15th and 16th centuries saw a new flowering of cultural life in Rome under the popes, who began to sponsor the revival of letters and the great artists and architects of the Renaissance, including Michelangelo, Raphael, Perugino, Bramante, and others. In the next century Rome became the Catholic capital of Europe and of the Catholic Counter Reformation. Great palaces of the princes, cardinals, and bankers were built, as well as magnificent baroque churches. By the 16th century Rome had become more or less the city we know today as Pope Sixtus V (1585–90) laid out its great avenues and major squares. With such an artistic heritage, the city became the center of Europe's cultural life in the 17th century and in the 18th century the most important stop on the Grand Tour.

During the French Revolutionary Wars Rome was occupied by the French armies, and a republic estab-

lished in 1798; while the Papal States were annexed by France in 1809 and the pope exiled. The pope was able to return in 1814 at the fall of the Napoleonic empire. During the 19th century the liberal and nationalist aspirations that were growing throughout Italy had repercussions in Rome, which became a center of reaction under Pope Pius IX. Giuseppe Garibaldi established another republic in the city in 1848, but it was overthrown the next year with the help of French troops. It was not until 1871 that Rome became the capital of the new, united kingdom of Italy. In the early 20th century Rome grew rapidly as new urban projects—and new archaeological discoveries—transformed the city. The advent of Mussolini in 1922 marked the beginning of the fascist era. Rome escaped relatively unscathed during World War II, although occupied by the Germans, and was liberated by the Allies in 1944.

ROME (United States) City and Floyd county seat, 55 mi NW of Atlanta, NW GEORGIA. Founded in 1834 on the site of a Cherokee Indian village, it was named for the seven surrounding hills. In November 1864, during the Civil War, the city was burned by Gen. William T. Sherman's Union forces.

ROME (United States) City and Oneida county seat, on the Mohawk River, 15 mi WNW of Utica, central NEW YORK State. It was founded c.1785 on the site of FORT STANWIX, which had played a strategic role in the French and Indian War and the American Revolution. It was the scene in 1768 of the Six Nation Treaty. The building of the ERIE CANAL was started in Rome in 1817 and contributed to the city's expansion.

ROME, THE SEVEN HILLS OF (Italy) The seven hills, originally quite steep and of volcanic origin, on which ancient ROME was founded. The traditional date was 753 BC. It is certain that in the eighth century BC there were separate settlements on most of the hills, which combined during that period to create Rome. The original Roman settlement was on the PALATINE HILL, later the site of the imperial palaces, where the foundations of early Iron Age huts have been found. Later the watery area of the forum was gradually drained and filled in, and the Palatine settlement combined with others in the neighboring hills to use the forum as a common meeting place. The CAPITOLINE and Quirinal hills were the first to join with the Palatine. It is thought that Tullus Hostilius (673–641 BC) added the Caelian Hill and Ancus Marcius (641–616 BC) the Aventine. Servius Tullius (578–534 BC) brought in the Esquiline and Viminal hills and around all seven built the famous Servian wall, parts of which survive. The Capitoline, which eventually became the political and religious center of the city, consisted of two peaks, the Tarpeian Rock and the Arx, where the original temple of Jupiter was built. The Capitoline gave its name to any political or culture "capital," the Palatine to our word "palace," and the Quirinal, traditionally named after Quirinus, or Romulus, shared its origin with the Roman synonym for its citizens, the *Quirites*.

ROMNEY MARSH (England) Historic area of pasture land, famous for its sheep and many fine churches, which was once a marshy tract extending approximately 10 miles inland along the coast of KENT, northeast of RYE and southwest of FOLKESTONE. Up to the 13th century the Rother River flowed through it to the sea. It was long ago drained and is now very productive. In Roman times it was protected by a seawall.

ROMORANTIN. See ROMORANTIN-LATHENAY.

ROMORANTIN-LATHENAY [**Romorantin**] (France) Town in Loir-et-Cher department, approx. 24 mi SE of Blois, N central France. The 15th-century château here was the scene of the signing of the Edict of Romorantin in 1560 by King Francis II, which prohibited the Inquisition in France.

ROMSDAL. See ROMSDALEN.

ROMSDALEN [Romsdal] (Norway) Valley, 60 mi long, in Møre og Romsdal county, flanked by the Dovrefjell Mts, SW Norway. An ancient mountain route between the western coast and southern Norway, it was the site of a massacre during the KALMAR War with Denmark in the early 17th century. Scottish mercenaries attempting to join King Gustavus II of SWEDEN were slaughtered here by Norwegian peasants.

RONCAGLIA (Italy) Village in Piacenza province, Emilia-Romagna region, part of the commune of PIACENZA. Roncaglia was a stopping point for German emperors of the HOLY ROMAN EMPIRE, especially Frederick I, on their way to ROME. From 1155 onwards a number of diets or meetings of the Holy Roman Empire were held here, as were frequent reviews of their troops by the emperors.

RONCEVALLES [*French:* **Roncevaux**] (Spain) Mountain pass in the PYRENEES, between Pamplona in Spain and St.-Jean-Pied-de-Port in France. It was here that Roland, Charlemagne's famous commander on the Breton border, met his death at the hands of the Basques in 778 AD, when the rearguard of Charlemagne's army was ambushed after the emperor's futile attempt to begin the reconquest of Spain from the Moors and his strengthening of the border, or Spanish March. The pass was often used in the Middle Ages as a route for invasions and for pilgrims on their way to SANTIAGO DE COMPOSTELA. According to the medieval *Song of Roland*, the battle was transformed into a cosmic struggle between the Christian forces under Charlemagne and those of the Muslims of Spain and North Africa, aided by the entire non-Christian world. Roland died awaiting reinforcements from the French host. In the song, Charlemagne went on to defeat the Muslims and convert their queen.

RONCEVAUX. See RONCEVALLES.

RONDA (Spain) Town in Málaga province, ANDALUSIA, 40 mi W of Málaga, S Spain. Dramatically located on two hills separated by a ravine, it consists of an old town, San Miguel, probably of Roman origin, and a newer town, Mercadillo, founded by Ferdinand the Catholic in 1485 after he had conquered the town. It was the scene of a Moorish revolt in 1501. There are interesting Roman and Moorish remains.

The bull ring in picturesque Ronda, an old Moorish stronghold dramatically situated high in the mountains of Andalusia's Sierra de Ronda. It is now a resort and tourist center.

ROOSEBEKE [Rozebeke] (Belgium) Village in East Flanders province, W Belgium, near Roeselare. Resenting French domination, taxation, poor working conditions, and lack of political power, Flemish workers, led by weavers, rebelled in 1381 under the leadership of Philip van Artevelde. On Nov. 27, 1382 at Roosebeke the French Army under Philip the Bold, duke of BURGUNDY, and Oliver de Clisson defeated the insurgents. Van Artevelde was killed. See also FLANDERS, FRANCE.

ROPSHA (USSR) Village in W central Leningrad oblast, Russian SFSR, 8 mi W of Krasnoye Selo. The castle here was built by Peter the Great. It was a favorite residence of Czarina Elizabeth and the site of the assassination of Peter III in 1762, who was succeeded by his wife, Catherine the Great.

ROQUEBRUNE [Roquebrune-Cap-Martin] [*Italian:* **Roccabruna**] (France) Picturesque mountain-side village, in Alpes-Maritime department, near the coast, between Monaco and Menton, SE France. Roquebrune, together with neighboring MENTON, was ruled by the prince of MONACO until 1848, when its citizens rebelled. The resulting period of independence lasted until it became part of France in 1860. See RIVIERA.

ROQUEBRUNE-CAP-MARTIN. See ROQUEBRUNE.

RØRAAS. See RØROS.

RORAIMA [*former:* **Rio Branco**] (Brazil) Mountaintop, ranching territory on the border of Venezuela and

Guyana, NW Brazil, with its capital at Boa Vista. Slave traders explored the area in the 17th century, after which it was partly fortified by the Portuguese against incursions by the Spanish, English, and Dutch. In 1943 it became a federal territory created from lands that once belonged to Amazonas state.

RØROS [*former:* **Røraas**] (Norway) Village in central Norway, Sør-Trøndelag county, close to the Swedish frontier. It has been the copper-mining center of Norway since the first mines were opened in 1644.

ROSARIO (Argentina) City and port in Santa Fe province, on the Paraná River, 190 mi NW of Buenos Aires, E central Argentina. Established in 1725, it developed after 1859 when it was made the official port for the confederation of the upper provinces and became a great trading center. It is the second-largest city in Argentina.

ROSCOMMON (Irish Republic) Town in N Central Ireland, the county capital of Roscommon, 80 mi WNW of Dublin. It is a tourist and market center with the ruins of a castle from 1268 and a Dominican priory from 1257.

ROS CRÉ. See ROSCREA.

ROSCREA [*Gaelic:* **Ros Cré**] (Irish Republic) Town in NE county Tipperary, 10 mi SSE of Birr, S Irish Republic. A priory was founded here in the seventh century, and this medieval town contains the remains of a castle built in 1213 by the Ormonde family, as well as a ruined Franciscan friary dating from 1490.

ROSEAU. See DOMINICA.

ROSELLE (United States) City in Union county, 2 mi W of Elizabeth, NE NEW JERSEY. It was the location of the inventor Thomas Alva Edison's laboratory, and its streets were the first anywhere to be lit by electric light. Abraham Clarke, one of the signers of the Declaration of Independence, was born here.

ROSETTA [*Arabic:* **Rashid**] (Egypt) City in Beheira governorate, in the NILE RIVER delta, 35 mi NE of Alexandria. It was established in the ninth century AD and later became a major port and trading center before trade was diverted by a canal to ALEXANDRIA. In 1799 Napoleon's troops discovered the Rosetta Stone here, a piece of black basalt trilingually inscribed by priests of Ptolemy V. It enabled the scholar Jean Champollion to decipher ancient Egyptian hieroglyphics for the first time.

ROSITTEN. See RÉZEKNE.

ROSKILDE (Denmark) City and capital of Roskilde county, on the Roskilde fjord, E Denmark. From the 10th century to 1443 it was Denmark's capital and remained a center of ecclesiastical activity from the 11th century until the Reformation in 1536. The cathedral, built *c.*1200, houses the tombs of many Danish kings. In 1658 the Treaty of Roskilde was signed here between Denmark and SWEDEN. A Viking ship museum here displays the remains of five Viking ships recovered from the nearby fjord in 1962.

ROSLAVL (USSR) City in W central European USSR, on the Oster River, approx. 65 mi SE of Smo-

lensk. Dating from the 14th century, it was granted a charter under the rule of LITHUANIA in 1408 and in 1667 passed to RUSSIA. Roslavl was occupied by German forces during World War II between August 1941 and September 1943.

ROSS AND CROMARTY (Scotland) Former county, which included Lewis Island in the Outer HEBRIDES, now part of the Western Islands region, and a mainland area now incorporated in the Highland region. Originally two separate counties inhabited by feuding local clans, they were joined in the 17th century by the earl of Cromartie.

ROSSBACH (East Germany) Village in Halle district, 8 mi SW of Merseburg, S central East Germany. On Nov. 5, 1757, during the Seven Years War, a battle was fought here in which Frederick II, the Great, of PRUSSIA defeated the Austrians and French. See also LEUTHEN.

ROSSBORO. See OWENSBORO.

ROSSIYA. See RUSSIA.

ROSS SEA. See ANTARCTICA.

ROSTOCK [**Rostock-Warnemünde**] (East Germany) City, port, and capital of Rostock district, on the Warnow River, 8 mi from the Baltic Sea. Founded on the site of an old Slavic fortress in 1189 AD, it was granted a charter in 1218 and became a leading member of the HANSEATIC LEAGUE in the 14th century. The university here, dating from 1419, was a major educational center for northern Germany and Scandinavia. During World War II Rostock was severely damaged by Allied bombs.

ROSTOCK-WARNEMÜNDE. See ROSTOCK.

ROSTOV [*former:* **Rostov-Veliki, Rostov-Yaroslavski**] (USSR) City in the Russian SFSR, on Lake Nero, 35 mi SW of YAROSLAVL. It is one of Russia's oldest cities, dating from *c.*860 AD, and in 1207 was made the capital of the principality of Rostov-Suzdal, which included SUZDAL, VLADIMIR, Tver, and MOSCOW. Acquired by the grand duchy of Moscow in 1474, it was commercially active between the 16th and 19th centuries. It has an ancient kremlin, a 13th-century cathedral and several churches from the same period. See also KALININ.

ROSTOV-NA-DONU [*English:* **Rostov, Rostov-on-Don**] (USSR) City and capital of Rostov oblast, SE Russian SFSR, on the DON RIVER, near the Sea of Azov. In 1749 a customs post was established here, and settlement began in 1761 with the building of a Russian fortress named after St. Dmitri of the older city of ROSTOV. A strike center during the revolution of 1905, it was the scene of fighting during World War II because of its position as the "gateway to the CAUCASUS." It is now a major industrial city.

ROSTOV-ON-DON. See ROSTOV-NA-DONU.

ROSTOV-SUZDAL. See ROSTOV.

ROSTOV-VELIKI. See ROSTOV.

ROSTOV-YAROSLAVSKI. See ROSTOV.

ROTHENBURG OB TER TAUBER [*medieval:*

Rotinbure] (West Germany) Town in BAVARIA, on the Tauber River, 31 mi SSE of Würzburg, S West Germany. Known as early as the ninth century, it grew around a Hohenstaufen fortress and was a free imperial city from the late 13th century until it passed to Bavaria in 1803. The old walls dating from the 14th and 15th centuries are intact, and the town has many fine examples of medieval architecture.

ROTHERHAM (England) Town in South Yorkshire, at the confluence of the Don and Rother rivers, 6 mi NE of Sheffield. In the vicinity there are Bronze and Iron Age barrows, and at Templebrough there are traces of a Roman fort. In the middle of a bridge over the Don is a 15th-century chantry chapel, now reconstructed. During the English Civil War Royalists captured Rotherham in 1643, but after the battle of MARSTON MOOR the town was surrendered to the Parliamentarians. Ironworks were established in 1746 at Masborough, on the other side of the Don; and steel, iron, and brass continue to be the source of this area's productivity.

ROTHESAY (Scotland) Town on the island of Bute, in the Firth of CLYDE, now part of Strathclyde region, 32 mi W of Glasgow. It is the site of Rothesay Castle, said to have been built in the 11th century, which was partly destroyed by Oliver Cromwell in 1650, further damaged by the earl of ARGYLL in 1685, and restored in 1871. The title of Duke of Rothesay dates from 1398,

when King Robert III of Scotland bestowed it on his eldest son.

ROTINBURE. See ROTHENBURG OB DER TAUBER.
ROTOMAGUS. See ROUEN.

ROTTENBURG (West Germany) Town in S Württemberg, on the Neckar River, 6 mi SW of Tübingen. The town dates from the Middle Ages. It was the capital of the Austrian county of Hohenberg until 1805, when it became part of WÜRTTEMBERG.

ROTTERDAM, Indonesia. See MAKASAR.

Second city of the Netherlands and a major port, Rotterdam was brutally destroyed by German bombing in May 1940, several hours after it had surrendered. It has been entirely rebuilt.

ROTTERDAM (Netherlands) City and port, South Holland province, on the Nieuwe Maas, approx. 15 mi from the North Sea, W Netherlands. Founded in the 13th century and chartered in 1328, it prospered greatly in the late 16th and 17th centuries. From 1795 to 1813 it was occupied by FRANCE. In 1830, after the separation of BELGIUM from the Netherlands, the city benefited from the shifting of trade from ANTWERP. It grew rapidly after 1866 with the opening of the New Waterway, which gave ocean-going ships access to its port, which in turn tapped the RHINE RIVER trade from Germany. On May 14, 1940, during World War II, much of Rotterdam was leveled by German bombs, and many old buildings were destroyed. It has been reconstructed on a new plan and is now one of the largest and most modern ports in the world.

The kremlin walls and 13th-century cathedral of old Rostov in Russia, founded in the ninth century. It gave its name to the newer city of Rostov-on-Don.

ROUBAIX (France) City in Nord Department, 7 mi NE of Lille, N France. Chartered in 1469, it has been a textile center since its early days. In the late 18th century it was given the right, already granted to nearby LILLE, to produce textiles in the English style, and it developed rapidly in the 19th century, along with its nearby twin textile city of TOURCOING. The city was occupied by GERMANY during World War I and suffered damage.

ROUEN [*ancient and medieval:* **Rodomum, Rotomagus**] (France) City and capital of Seine-Maritime department, a major river port on the SEINE RIVER, 70 mi NW of Paris, N France. Established in pre-Roman times as the center of the Rotomagi, it was invaded in the ninth century AD by the Normans, who settled around it, and in the 10th century it became the ducal capital of NORMANDY. ENGLAND occupied it between 1418 and 1449 during the Hundred Years War, and Joan of Arc was tried and executed here in 1431. It was taken by the Huguenots in 1562 during the Wars of Religion. The city was held by GERMANY in 1870 during the Franco-Prussian War. The famous Gothic cathedral of Rouen, damaged in World War II, has since been restored, and many 13th-, 14th-, and 15th-century buildings remain.

ROUERGUE (France) Ancient province of S France, in the area now comprising Aveyron department, with its capital at RODEZ. Originally a dependency of the feudal counts of TOULOUSE, it came under the French crown in 1271, passed to ENGLAND in 1360 by the Treaty of BRÉTIGNY, and in 1368 was returned to France. Later the region was acquired by the Bourbon family and formed part of the inheritance of King Henry IV in 1607.

ROULERS. See ROESELARE.

ROUMANIA. See RUMANIA.

ROUMELIA. See RUMELIA.

ROUND TOP. See CEMETERY RIDGE.

ROUSSELAERE. See ROESELARE.

ROUSSILLON (France) Region and former province, bordering on Spain along the PYRENEES and on the Mediterranean Sea, roughly coextensive with Pyrénées-Orientales department, with its capital at PERPIGNAN. Inhabited by Iberians from the seventh to third centuries BC, it was conquered by the Romans *c.*120 BC and became part of Gallia NARBONENSIS. After enduring frequent changes of rule, it was taken from SPAIN in 1642 by King Louis XIII, and its acquisition sealed in 1659 by the Treaty of the Pyrenees.

ROVEREDO. See ROVERETO.

ROVERETO [*former:* **Roveredo;** *German:* **Rofreit**] (Italy) Town in Trento province, Trentino-Alto Adige region, on the Adige River, 13 mi SSW of Trent, N Italy. Once part of the bishopric of TRENT, this picturesque town was taken by VENICE in the 15th century and later passed to AUSTRIA in 1517. On Aug. 15, 1796 Napoleon defeated the Austrians here. The town was recaptured by Italy during World War I.

ROVIGNO. See ROVINJ.

ROVIGNO D'ISTRIA. See ROVINJ.

ROVIGO [*former:* **Rodigo**] (Italy) City and capital of Rovigo province, Veneto region, 36 mi SW of Venice, NE Italy. Known to exist as early as 838 AD, it was a part of the Este family lands between 1194 and 1482, when it was acquired by VENICE. It came under AUSTRIA in 1797 and was annexed to Italy in 1866. A walled town, its buildings include the ruins of a 10th-century castle, the 16th-century octagonal church of the Madonna del Socorso, and several Renaissance palaces.

ROVINJ [*Italian:* **Rovigno, Rovigno d'Istria**] (Yugoslavia) Town and port in CROATIA, on the Istrian coast of the Adriatic Sea, NW Yugoslavia. VENICE ruled the town between 1283 and 1797, when it became part of AUSTRIA. In 1918 ITALY took the town and held it until 1947 when it was returned to Yugoslavia. Rovinj Cathedral contains the purported sarcophagus of St. Euphemia.

ROVNO [*German:* **Rowno;** *Polish:* **Równe;** *Ukrainian:* **Rivne**] (USSR) City and capital of Rovno oblast, UKRAINE, approx. 110 mi NE of Lvov. Originally a Ukrainian community dating from *c.*1280, it prospered as a trading center in the later Middle Ages. Part of RUSSIA in 1793, it reverted to POLAND in 1921 but was taken over by the Soviets in 1939. It was held by the Germans from 1941 to 1944 during World War II.

RÓWNE. See ROVNO.

ROWNO. See ROVNO.

ROXBURGH. See ROXBURGHSHIRE.

ROXBURGHSHIRE [**Roxburgh**] [*former:* **Teviotdale**] (Scotland) Former county in Scotland, with its county town at Jedburgh. The Cheviot Hills are to the south, Teviotdale to the north and west. At one time included in the ancient kingdom of NORTHUMBRIA, the county is filled with the ruins of border warfare between ENGLAND and Scotland. It became part of the Borders region in 1975. Jedburgh Abbey is on the Jed Water just South of Jedburgh; Dryburgh Abbey and Melrose Abbey are on the outskirts of MELROSE.

ROYAN (France) Town in Charentes-Maritime department, on the Atlantic Ocean, at the mouth of the Gironde River, W France. Once a famous resort community, it was almost completely destroyed between January and April 1945 by the Allies as they attempted to dislodge a German garrison during World War II.

ROZEBEKE. See ROOSEBEKE.

RSHA. See ORSHA.

RUANDA. See RWANDA.

RUANDA-URUNDI [*former:* **Belgian East Africa**] (Burundi, Rwanda) Former colonial territory in central Africa, now divided into the independent states of RWANDA and BURUNDI, with its capital at Usumbura (now BUJUMBURU). Inhabited by pygmies before the 12th century AD and later by the Hutu and the Tutsi tribes in the 15th century, it was explored by Germans in the late 19th century. The area became part of German East Africa in the early 20th century, until its conquest by BELGIUM in 1916 during World War I. As a mandate of the League of Nations in 1924, it remained under Belgian rule and in 1946 was made a trust territory of the United Nations. With the coming of independence on July 1, 1962 it was divided into two separate countries.

RUBI. See RUVO DI PUGLIA.

RUBICO. See RUBICON.

RUBICON [Rubicone] [*ancient:* **Rubico**] (Italy) Small river flowing into the Adriatic Sea, just N of RIMINI, N central Italy. It was once the ancient boundary between Italy proper and Cisalpine GAUL, south of which no military commander was allowed to cross with his troops. It was crossed by Julius Caesar in 49 BC in his civil war against Pompey and the Senate. Caesar's act of audacity gave rise to the expression "to cross the Rubicon," or to make a conquer-or-perish decision.

RUBICONE. See RUBICON.

RÜDESHEIM [Rüdesheim am Rhein] (West Germany) Town in HESSE, on the RHINE RIVER, 16 mi WSW of Wiesbaden, central West Germany. Known to exist as early as 864 AD, it is the site of the 10th-century castle of Brömserburg, which was a residence of the archbishops of MAINZ.

RÜDESHEIM AM RHEIN. See RÜDESHEIM.

RUDOLSTADT (East Germany) City in Gera district, on the Saale River, 18 mi S of Weimar, S East Germany. Established before the ninth century, it was the home of the rulers of Schwartzburg-Rudolstadt from 1574 to 1918. There is a 17th-century church here, as well as a castle and palace dating from the 18th century.

RUEIL-MALMAISON (France) Town in Hauts-de-Seine department, on the SEINE RIVER, 8 mi W of Paris. The Merovingian kings used the town as a resort from the fifth to seventh centuries AD. Cardinal Richelieu purchased it in the early 17th century and built a château here, Malmaison, which later became the residence of Napoleon from 1800 to 1804 and of the Empress Josephine after her divorce. Josephine and her daughter Hortense are buried here.

RUGBY (England) Town in Warwickshire, on the Avon River, 28 mi ESE of Birmingham. It is the location of Rugby School, for boys, founded in 1567, which became known through Thomas Arnold, famous educator and its headmaster from 1827 to 1842 and the father of poet Matthew Arnold. Thomas Hughes's classic novel *Tom Brown's School Days* is based on life at Rugby. Rugby football also originated here.

RÜGEN (East Germany) Large island in the BALTIC SEA, part of Rostock district, N East Germany. Once inhabited by the Rugieri and Slavonic Wends, it was taken by DENMARK in 1168, came under POMERANIA in 1325, and passed to SWEDEN under the Treaty of Westphalia in 1648. In 1815 it was acquired by PRUSSIA.

RÜGENWALDE. See DARLOWO.

RUHEIBA. See REHOVOT.

RUHR (West Germany) Region, approx. 1,300 sq mi, along and north of the Ruhr River, W West Germany. Some of its major cities are BOCHUM, DORTMUND, DUISBERG, and ESSEN. The center of the huge coal and steel empires of Krupp and Thyssen that developed in the 19th century, it was occupied from 1923 to 1925 after World War I by Belgian and French forces during the conflict over Germany's postwar reparations. The French occupation offered Hitler the excuse to rise against the Weimar Republic in the unsuccessful "beer-hall *Putsch*" of 1923. Between 1942 and 1945, during World War II, the region was a chief arsenal for Germany and was almost completely leveled by Allied bombs. Control of the Ruhr remained in the hands of international authorities from 1949 to 1954, when it was returned to West Germany.

RUIKIU. See RYUKYU ISLANDS.

RULLION GREEN, See MIDLOTHIAN.

RUMADIYA. See RAMADI.

RUMANIA [Romania, Roumania] [*Rumanian:* **Republica Socialistă România**] Nation in SE Europe bounded by Hungary and Yugoslavia on the W, Bulgaria on the S, the USSR on the N, and the Black Sea on the E. Modern Rumania comprises roughly what was once the ancient region of DACIA, which under that name was a province of ROME in the first and second centuries AD. The modern name *Rumania* means "land of the Romans." Latin-speaking Roman colonists provided the foundation for the Rumanian language, a Romance tongue. After the Romans departed in 270 AD, the region was invaded by a succession of peoples: the Visigoths in the fourth century; the Huns who soon pushed the Goths farther into Europe; the Avars, nomads who plundered the Balkan peninsula in the sixth century; the Bulgars in the next century; and the Magyars in the late ninth century, who were then forced farther on to settle HUNGARY. The Mongols (see MONGOL EMPIRES) ruled the region in the 13th century, and after that the history of Rumania is chiefly that of the principalities of MOLDAVIA and WALACHIA and of TRANSYLVANIA.

Moldavia, in the northwest, was a strong state that at its height in the 15th century included BUKOVINA and BESSARABIA. By 1504, however, the OTTOMAN EMPIRE had made Moldavia a tributary state. Walachia in the south suffered much the same fate. Its ruler Vlad the Impaler, also called Dracula, or son of the Devil, was defeated and killed by the Ottomans in 1476. In Transylvania, in northwest and central Rumania, the rulers were also under Turkish suzerainty. Michael the Brave, prince of Walachia, fought both the Ottomans and the HOLY ROMAN EMPIRE successfully and controlled all three regions by 1600. However, after his death the next year, the Turks resumed control of Moldavia and Walachia, and AUSTRIA took Transylvania.

In the late 18th and early 19th centuries RUSSIA and Turkey fought over Moldavia and Walachia. After the Russo-Turkish War of 1828/29 both remained officially under Turkish control but actually were protectorates of Russia. Following the Crimean War, the Congress of Paris in 1856 recognized the two states as quasi-independent and awarded southern Bessarabia to Moldavia. In 1859 both principalities elected the same prince, Alexander John Cuza. On Dec. 23, 1861 the two states merged and formed the nation of Rumania, with BUCHAREST as the capital. Rumania joined Russia in war against Turkey in 1877 and at the Congress of Berlin in 1878 was recognized as fully independent. However, Rumania had to cede Bessarabia to Russia, receiving the DOBRUJA, a historic region in southeastern Rumania and northeastern BULGARIA, in return. At this time the kingdom was mostly in turmoil, the result of corruption in government, lack of land reform, and violent anti-Semitism. As a result of the Second Balkan War in 1913, Rumania gained some territory from Bulgaria. In World War I Rumania remained neutral until 1916, when it joined the Allies. It was, however, overrun by Austrian and German forces and in 1918 was forced to submit to harsh peace terms. Allied victory in November changed the situation, and the treaties of Saint-Germain in 1919 and the Grand Trianon in 1920 gave Rumania Transylvania, Bukovina, and part of the BANAT in western Rumania; but Russia refused to recognize the seizure of Bessarabia.

For protection against Bulgaria's and Hungary's desire to get back certain territory, Rumania joined the Little Entente with CZECHOSLOVAKIA and YUGOSLAVIA in 1920 and the Balkan Entente in 1934 with Yugoslavia, GREECE, and Turkey. In the late 1920's and 1930's, there was dissension over the succession to the throne, tense controversy between political parties, and frequent changes of government. The Iron Guard, a fascist organization formed in 1927, became increasingly powerful. In his contest with it, King Carol II in 1938 established a royal dictatorship. At the start of World War II Rumania remained neutral, but in 1940 it was powerless to resist the Soviet demand for Bessarabia and northern Bukovina or Bulgarian and Hungarian demands for southern Dobruja, the Banat, and part of Transylvania.

In June 1941 Rumania joined GERMANY in war on the USSR, only to suffer defeat. King Michael then overthrew the fascist regime, surrendered to the USSR, and joined the Allies. By a 1947 treaty Rumania recovered all its territory except Bessarabia, northern Bukovina, and southern Dobruja. A communist-dominated government took office in 1945, forced Michael to abdicate in December 1947, and proclaimed Rumania a people's republic. The nation became closely attached to the USSR, joining the Council of Mutual Economic Assistance in 1949 and the Warsaw Pact Treaty Organization when it was formed in 1955. However, Rumania became more independent of the USSR in foreign policy after 1963, especially under Nicolas Ceausescu, who has been the head of the communist regime since 1967. It maintained diplomatic relations with China and Albania and with Israel. It has also criticized the Soviet invasion of Afghanistan and made friendly diplomatic and cultural gestures toward the United States. Treatment of dissidents at home, however, remains harsh.

RUMELI. See RUMELIA.

RUMELIA [Roumelia] [*Turkish:* Rumeli] (Bulgaria) Region between the Balkan and Rhodope mountains, S Bulgaria. It was the name applied to the Balkan territories of the OTTOMAN EMPIRE, especially THRACE and MACEDONIA. It comprised part of modern YUGOSLAVIA, Bulgaria, European TURKEY, northern GREECE, and part of ALBANIA. Until 1828 SOFIA was the administrative center. In 1878 the Congress of Berlin divided Bulgaria into three areas, of which one was EASTERN RUMELIA.

RUMFORD. See CONCORD, New Hampshire.

RUM, SULTANATE OF (Turkey) Former kingdom, comprising at its peak all of ASIA MINOR except the W section and the N and S coastal areas. It was a realm of the Seljuk Turks who, with the Ottomans, were the most important Turkish peoples to invade western Asia. Asia Minor was part of the BYZANTINE EMPIRE when in 1066 Alp Arslan, Seljuk sultan of PERSIA from 1063 to 1072, invaded it. In 1071 he defeated the Emperor Romanus IV at MANZIKERT (now Malazgirt), to increase the Seljuk realm. When the Seljuk empire began to break up, the Sultanate of Rum, (the Turkish pronunciation of the Byzantine Empire), was one of its successor states. In 1099 Iconium, now KONYA, became its capital. The state was sometimes known as the sultanate of Iconium. It flourished until the late 13th century, when it was overrun by the Mongols. Much of its territory passed to KARAMAN.

RUNCORN (England) Town in Cheshire, on the Mersey River, 10 mi ESE of Liverpool. It was fortified in 916 AD by Aethelflaed, daughter of King Alfred the Great of WESSEX. The modern city developed mainly after the building of the pioneer Bridgewater Canal in the 18th century.

RUNNIMEDE. See RUNNYMEDE.

RUNNYMEDE [Runnimede] (England) Meadow in Surrey, on the S bank of the THAMES RIVER, 19 mi WSW of London, near Egham. On June 15, 1215 King John is said to have signed the Magna Carta either here or on the nearby Charter Island in the Thames. Part of the island is now a memorial to President John F. Kennedy.

RUPELLA. See LA ROCHELLE.

RUPERT HOUSE [Rupert's House] [*former:* Fort Charles, Fort Rupert] (Canada) Village on the Rupert River, James Bay, W QUEBEC. The oldest fur-trading station of the Hudson's Bay Company, it was founded in 1668. The French took it in 1686, and it changed hands several times during the conflict between the English and French in Canada. It was returned to the company in 1713 by the Peace of UTRECHT.

RUPERT'S HOUSE. See RUPERT HOUSE.

RUPERT'S LAND [Prince Rupert's Land] (Canada) Region in N and W Canada, comprising the drainage basin of HUDSON BAY. In 1670 King Charles II of England granted a charter to the Hudson's Bay Company for the area, which includes modern ONTARIO, part of QUEBEC, MANITOBA, SASKATCHEWAN, part of ALBERTA and the NORTHWEST TERRITORIES, along with part of MINNESOTA and NORTH DAKOTA in the United States. Most of the area was bought by the Dominion of Canada in 1869.

RUSADDIR. See MELILLA.

RUSCHUK. See RUSE.

RUSE [Russe] [*ancient:* **Prista;** *Turkish:* **Ruschuk, Rustchuk**] (Bulgaria) City and capital of Ruse province, on the DANUBE RIVER, approx. 155 mi NE of Sofia, N Bulgaria. Established by the Romans in the second century BC as a Danube naval station, it was razed by barbarians in the seventh century AD. It became a military post under Turkish rule between the 15th and 19th centuries.

RUSICADA. See SKIKDA.

RUSSE. See RUSE.

RUSSELLAE. See GROSSETO, Italy.

RUSSIA [*Russian:* **Rossiya**] (Asia, Europe) Former empire, now replaced by the UNION OF SOVIET SOCIALIST REPUBLICS. The name is also applied to the RUSSIAN SOVIET FEDERATED SOCIALIST REPUBLIC. The world's largest nation, the empire occupied Europe from the eastern European nations on the west to the Pacific Ocean on the east, taking in northern Asia, or SIBERIA. Many peoples have inhabited parts of Russia at different times; Scythians in southern Russia in the seventh century BC, who were replaced in the third century by Sarmatians. The Russian steppes were invaded by Goths in the third century AD, by Huns in the next century, by Avars in the sixth, by Khazars in the seventh, by Bulgars in the Volga River region in the eighth, and by Slavs in the ninth. The foundations of a Russian state were not laid, however, until the ninth century when the Varangians, Scandinavian Viking warriors and traders, established themselves at NOVGOROD *c.*860 under their leader Rurik. Oleg, Rurik's successor, transferred his headquarters to KIEV in 882. The Kievan state flourished until a Tatar, or Mongol, invasion in 1237 ended its power.

In eastern and southern Russia the Tatars established the EMPIRE OF THE GOLDEN HORDE, which lasted until 1480; while BELORUSSIA and most of the UKRAINE became part of LITHUANIA. Meanwhile, the MOSCOW area grew in strength, especially after Dmitri Donskoi defeated the Golden Horde at the battle of KULIKOVO in 1380. The grand duchy of Moscow, or Muscovy, gained supremacy over other principalities. An era of expansion followed, and in 1547 Ivan IV, the Terrible, was crowned the first czar of all Russia. By the late 16th century Russia was able to conquer Siberia, the first expedition for this purpose being led by a

THE GROWTH OF RUSSIA, 1689–1725

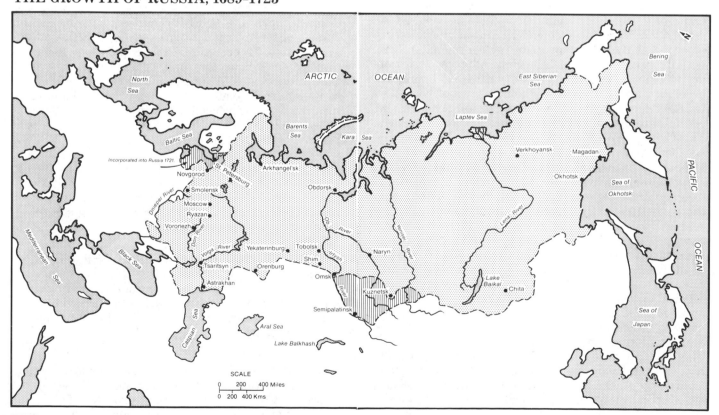

Russia

Territory gained 1689–1725

Cossack, Yermak, in 1581. The first Romanov became czar in 1613, founding the dynasty that lasted until the fall of the empire; but Russia lagged far behind Western Europe in all respects and was hardly considered a European nation. Serfdom, here especially a system of peasant slavery, became legal in 1649.

Russia changed greatly in the late 17th and early 18th centuries under the rule of Peter I, the Great, who forced on his people military, economic, governmental, and cultural modernization. He founded St. Petersburg (now LENINGRAD) and made it his capital; won LIVONIA, Ingermanland (INGRIA), ESTONIA, and other areas as a result of the Great Northern War of 1700 to 1721; and founded a navy with an outlet on the BALTIC SEA. Russia now took an active part in European affairs, fought PRUSSIA successfully in the Seven Years War of 1756 to 1763, and under Catherine II, the Great (reigned 1762–96), became the strongest power of continental Europe. Russia's territory increased with her participation in the three partitions of POLAND in 1772, 1793, and 1795; the annexation of the CRIMEA in 1783 and of KURLAND in 1795; and the acquisition of large regions in the south and west as a result of wars with the OTTOMAN EMPIRE. As an "enlightened despot," Catherine encouraged the arts and stimulated a cultural development that continued through the 19th century, despite despotic rulers.

Under Alexander I, Russia annexed FINLAND in 1809, took BESSARABIA in wars with TURKEY and PERSIA in 1812, and parts of the CAUCASUS in 1813. Meanwhile, Russia had opposed and then been allied with Napoleon I, changing sides again when the French emperor invaded Russia in 1812, only to be repulsed. As a result of Napoleon's downfall, Russia and AUSTRIA emerged as the chief powers of the continent. In 1815, with Prussia, they formed the Holy Alliance, a reactionary attempt to maintain a conservative and oppressive order in Europe. However, the accession of Nicholas I in 1825 triggered the Decembrist Conspiracy, an unsuccessful attempt to secure some measure of democracy. The Crimean War of 1854 to 1856, in which Turkey, GREAT BRITAIN, and FRANCE fought Russia, revealed the basic weaknesses of the Russian system.

Some reforms were achieved under Alexander II (reigned 1855–81), especially his edict of 1861 freeing the serfs. Russia also continued to expand, taking the rest of the Caucusus and, during 1864/65, what is now Soviet Central Asia, including TURKISTAN, as well as some far eastern territory from CHINA. The Pacific had been reached; and the construction of the Trans-Siberian Railroad from 1891 to 1905 began to open Siberia to exploitation and settlement. Shifting alliances marked European diplomacy in the late 19th and early 20th centuries. Russia, GERMANY, and Austria-Hungary formed the Three Emperors' League in 1872. This was replaced in 1887 by a Russian-German alliance. In the meantime, the Congress of Berlin of 1878 awarded southern Bessarabia to Russia. Russia shifted sides again in 1894, forming an alliance with France and concluding an arrangement with Great Britain that resulted in the Triple Alliance of these nations in 1907.

In the Far East, Russian and Japanese competition over MANCHURIA and KOREA led to the Russo-Japanese War of 1904/05 in which JAPAN captured PORT ARTHUR (Lü-shun) and MUKDEN (Shen-yang) and destroyed the Russian fleet. This disaster brought about the Revolution of 1905, which forced Nicholas II to grant a constitution and establish a parliament; but little came of this gesture toward democracy. World War I, into which Russia was immediately drawn in 1914, partly as the professed defender of Slavs everywhere, was another disaster. Many military defeats were suffered at the hands of Germany and Austria-Hungary, the economy could not support a modern war, and food shortages developed.

Revolution broke out in February 1917, and Nicholas abdicated on March 15. A provisional government was organized which in May admitted socialists and which in July made Aleksandr F. Kerensky its head. This government wanted to continue fighting the unpopular war and was unable to manage the economy. As a result, on November 7 it was overthrown by the Bolsheviks, the dominant faction of Russian socialism, led by Vladimir E. Lenin. The Russian Empire was thus succeeded by the USSR, the first government based on Marxist socialism.

RUSSIAN SOVIET FEDERATED SOCIALIST REPUBLIC (USSR) One of the 15 constituent republics of the USSR, by far the largest and most important economically. It occupies most of eastern Europe and northern Asia (SIBERIA), an area of approximately 5,000 miles from the Baltic Sea in the west to the Pacific Ocean in the east. The URAL MOUNTAINS are usually taken as the boundary between the European and Asian sections. The RSFSR contains a little more than three-quarters of the land area of the USSR and approximately 54 percent of the population. Some 60 nationalities inhabit this land, nearly twice the size of the United States. After the Bolsheviks seized control of Russia in November 1917, they organized a government on Marxist principles and in January 1918 established the RSFSR, which occupies what was the principal part of the overthrown empire. In 1922 the RSFSR was united with the UKRAINE, BELORUSSIA, and TRANSCAUCASIA to form the USSR. It has almost every kind of natural resource, and the Soviets have put a great deal of capital and effort into developing it economically. Today much of it is highly industrialized. MOSCOW is the capital of the RSFSR as well as of the USSR.

RUSTAVI (USSR) City in Georgian SSR, approx. 15 mi SE of Tbilisi, SE European USSR. It was founded in the 1940's near the site of the ancient town of Rustavi, destroyed by Tamerlane c.1400. Shota Rustaveli, Georgia's national poet, was born here in the 13th century.

RUSTCHUK. See RUSE.

RUTHENA. See RODEZ.

RUTHENIA (USSR) Former autonomous region, now constituting the Transcarpathian oblast, in the Ukraine. A latinized form of the word "Russia," it was used in the Middle Ages when the princes of GALICIA declared themselves the kings of Ruthenia. It was later used by Austria-Hungary to designate the Ukrainian inhabitants of the northeast CARPATHIAN MOUNTAINS. After 1918 it was the name given to the easternmost province of CZECHOSLOVAKIA. In 1945 all Ruthenians were included in the Soviet UKRAINE.

RUTHERGLEN (Scotland) Town in Strathclyde region, on the CLYDE River, 3 mi SE of Glasgow. Made a royal town in 1126, it was the scene of a truce signed between ENGLAND and Scotland in 1297, prior to the betrayal of Sir William Wallace. The Covenanters published their Declaration and Testament here before the battles at Drumclog and BOTHWELL Bridge.

RUTHIN (Wales) Town in Clwyd, 14 mi WNW of Wrexham. The castle here, now in ruins, was stormed in 1400 by Owen Glendower, leader of a revolt against English domination, after a dispute with his English neighbor Lord Grey of Ruthin.

RUTHWELL (Scotland) Village in Dumfries and Galloway region, near Solway Firth, 9 mi SE of Dumfries. Its church contains the early medieval 18-foot-high Ruthwell Cross with runic inscriptions. To the SW are the ruins of the Conlongon Castle.

RUTLAND (United States) City and Rutland county seat, 22 mi E of the Poultney River entrance on LAKE CHAMPLAIN, W VERMONT. It was chartered by NEW HAMPSHIRE in 1761 and founded c.1770 and was the site of two forts during the American Revolution. Between 1784 and 1804 it was the seat of the Vermont legislature. Rutland became a center of marble quarrying c.1845.

RÜTLI [Grütli] (Switzerland) Meadow in Uri canton, on the shore of LAKE LUCERNE, central Switzerland. The League of the Three Forest Cantons of SCHWYZ, UNTERWALDEN, and URI, soon joined by LUCERNE, was supposedly created here in 1307, as told in the legend of William Tell. A document unearthed in the 19th century, detailing the alliance and dated Aug. 1, 1291, has since challenged the legend. See also FOUR FOREST CANTONS.

RUTUPIAE. See RICHBOROUGH, SANDWICH, England.

RUVO DI PUGLIA [ancient: Rubi] (Italy) Town in Bari province, APULIA region, 9 mi W of Bari, SE Italy. An ancient town, famous for its ceramics during the fifth to second centuries BC, it is now a bishopric and has a 13th-century cathedral of Apulian Romanesque style.

RWANDA [former: Ruanda] A landlocked African nation bordered by Uganda on the N, Burundi on the S, Tanzania on the E, and Zaire on the W, with its capital at Kigali. The grassy uplands and hills of Rwanda have been intensively grazed for centuries. Now the most densely populated nation in Africa, Rwanda suffers from severe erosion and soil exhaustion.

Originally the home of the pygmy Twa people, Rwanda was settled by a Bantu people named the Hutu, who had migrated from the Congo Basin. By the 15th century the Hutu had become the feudal underlings of the Tutsi (Watusi), an extremely tall warrior people who may have originated in ETHIOPIA. The Tutsi maintained their exploitative domination unchal-

lenged until 1885, when GERMANY claimed the region. In 1916 Belgian forces from the Congo overthrew the German colonial forces, and after World War I the country became part of the BELGIUM-administered League of Nations mandate of RUANDA-URUNDI.

Belgian rule did little to affect the Tutsi hold on power. The rise of African nationalism in the 1950's, however, brought to the subjugated Hutu a desire for freedom from minority rule. From 1955 to 1958 Tutsi repression was extreme and sought to thwart the growing Hutu movement. In 1959 a massive and bloody Hutu uprising put an end to the Tutsi monarchy and forced 120,000 Tutsi to flee the country. In 1962 Rwanda was granted full independence. A year later the exiled Tutsi attempted to reconquer the country but were repulsed, resulting in the massacre of 12,000 resident Tutsi.

A military clique seized power in 1973. Rwanda continues to struggle with the problems caused by its isolation, poverty, and dense population.

RYAZAN [Riazan] [former: Pereyaslavl-Ryazan] (USSR) City and capital of Ryazan oblast, Russian SFSR, on the Oka River, 120 mi SE of Moscow. One of the oldest cities in Russia, it was settled in 1095 AD and was made the capital of Ryazan principality after the destruction of Old Ryazan by the Mongols in 1237. It passed to MOSCOW in 1521 and became a city in 1778. Ryazan has many examples of medieval architecture, including a kremlin wall, a palace, a cathedral, and two former monasteries dating from the 15th to 17th centuries.

RYBINSK [former: Rybnaya Sloboda, Shcherbakov] (USSR) City and port in Yaroslavl oblast, Russian SFSR, on the VOLGA RIVER and the Rybinsk Reservoir. Mentioned as early as 1137, it has been a center of river traffic between ARKHANGELSK and MOSCOW for four centuries and since the 1870's has been a shipping link to LENINGRAD. Birthplace of the Bolshevik leader Shcherbakov, the city was renamed in his honor between 1946 and 1958.

RYBNAYA SLOBODA. See RYBINSK.

RYBNIK (Poland) Town in Katowice province, 20 mi SW of Katowice, S Poland. Founded c.1100 and once a fish hatchery famous for its carp, it was granted a charter in the 14th century. It was briefly under Germany and in 1921 was restored to Poland.

RYE (England) Town in East Sussex, on the Rother River, 10 mi NE of Hastings. One of the "ancient towns" added to the CINQUE PORTS during the reign of Henry III in the 13th century, it was incorporated in 1289. The town prospered in the 17th century but declined after the recession of the sea in the early 19th century. The Ypres Tower here dates from c.1160, and there are remains of an ancient friary. The novelist Henry James lived here for several years.

RYE (United States) City in Westchester county, on LONG ISLAND SOUND, 24 mi NE of New York City, SE NEW YORK State. Established in 1660 by settlers from CONNECTICUT before state boundaries were determined, it was a stopping place on the old Boston Post

Road. Its Square House Inn was frequented during the American Revolution by many important figures. Chief Justice John Jay is buried here.

RYEZHITSA. See RĒZEKNE.

RYLSK (USSR) City in W Kursk oblast, Russian SFSR, 65 mi WSW of Kursk. Founded in the ninth century, it received a charter in 1152 and was made the capital of Rylsk principality in the 12th and 13th centuries. In 1503 it was acquired by MOSCOW.

RYO JUN. See PORT ARTHUR, China.

RYSSEL. See LILLE.

RYSWICK [Rijswick] (Netherlands) City in South Holland province, a suburb of THE HAGUE, NW Netherlands. On Sept. 20, 1697 the Treaty of Ryswick was signed here by FRANCE on one side and ENGLAND, the Netherlands, and SPAIN on the other. This marked the end of the War of the Grand Alliance between England and France, recognized William III as king of England, and acknowledged the autonomy of SAVOY.

RYUKYU ISLANDS [Loo-Choo, Luchu, Nansei, Ruikiu] [*Japanese:* **Ryukyu Retto**] (Japan) Archipelago, extending in a 600-mi-long arc between Taiwan and Japan, E of the East China Sea, in the W Pacific Ocean, with its chief town at Naha on Okinawa Island. It is composed of three main island groups: the Amami, the OKINAWA, and the SAKISHIMA Islands. Okinawa was the home of an ancient autonomous kingdom. CHINA invaded the islands in the seventh century AD and by the 14th century exercised political influence over them. The Japanese prince of SATSUMA attacked them in the 17th century and exacted tribute from the islanders and the resident Chinese. The Ryukyus became part of Japan in 1879 but were neglected by Japan until World War II, when Japan and the UNITED STATES fought for their possession. Controlled by the United States after the war, the islands were not completely restored to Japan until May 1972, although the Amami group had been returned by 1953.

RYUKYU RETTO. See RYUKYU ISLANDS.

RZESZÓW [*German:* **Reichshof**] (Poland) City and capital of Rzeszów province, approx. 95 mi E of Cracow, SE Poland. Founded *c.*1340, it was later given to a nobleman by Casimir the Great of Poland in return for military assistance against the invading Mongols. From 1772 to 1918 it was under the rule of AUSTRIA and was returned to Poland in 1919. GERMANY occupied the city from October 1941 to March 1943 during World War II.

RZHEV (USSR) City in S Kalinin oblast, Russian SFSR, on the banks of the VOLGA RIVER, 70 mi SW of Kalinin. Under the control of the principality of SMOLENSK in the 12th century, it was taken by NOVGOROD in 1216 and became a trading center on the route between Novgorod and KIEV. In 1390 it passed to MOSCOW. GERMANY occupied the city for two years during World War II and fortified it as part of their northern line of defense.

S

SAALFELD [Saalfeld an der Saale] (East Germany) City in the SE, on the Thuringian Saale River, 25 mi S of Weimar. The site was first mentioned in 899 AD as a royal palace. A Benedictine monastery was built here in 1074. Founded *c.*1200 and capital of the duchy of Saxe-Saalfeld from 1680 to 1735, the city was passed in 1826 to the duchy of SAXE-MEININGEN by the duke of SAXE-COBURG in exchange for GOTHA. It was the site in 1806 of a French victory over PRUSSIA in the Napoleonic Wars. The city retains much of its historical architecture, including a 13th-century church, a 16th-century castle, a Franciscan monastery, now a museum, a 14th-century church, a 16th-century city hall, and an 18th-century castle.

SAALFELD AN DER SAALE. See SAALFELD.

SAAR. See SAARLAND.

SAARBRÜCKEN [*French:* Sarrebruck] (West Germany) Capital city of SAARLAND, in the W, on the Saar River, near the French border, 39 mi E of Trier. A Saar crossing in Roman times, it has Roman remains from the first and third centuries AD. Later settled by German Frankish kings, the city developed around a Frankish castle of 999 AD. It was chartered by 1321. It became the capital of the counts of NASSAU-Saarbrücken from 1381 to 1793, when it was occupied by the French. The city eventually passed to PRUSSIA in 1815. It served as the capital of the French-administered Saar Territory after the end of both world wars, from 1919 to 1935 and from 1945 to 1957. Besides the Frankish castle, there are the remains of a Roman fortress, a 15th-century Gothic church, and an 18th-century town hall. See also FRANKISH EMPIRE.

SAARE. See SAAREMAA.

SAAREMAA [Sarema] [*German:* Oesel; *Russian:* Ezel, Saare; *Swedish:* Ösel] (USSR) Island in the E BALTIC SEA, off the W coast of ESTONIAN SSR NW of the Gulf of Riga. Conquered by Teutonic Knights of the Sword in 1227 AD, it was ruled by Livonian knights until 1560, when it passed to DENMARK and then to SWEDEN in 1645. United with RUSSIA when it became part of LIVONIA in 1721, it joined Estonia in 1918.

SAARGEBIET. See SAARLAND.

SAARLAND [Saar, Saar Territory, Westmark] [*French:* Sarre; *German:* Saargebiet] (West Germany) State in the SW, between France and Germany, drained by the Saar River. Its capital is SAARBRÜCKEN. It became the tenth state of the Federal Republic of Germany in 1957.

Previously there had been little political unity in the region. In 1797 the Treaty of CAMPO FORMIO ceded to FRANCE territory that had been French, the country of Saarbrücken, and the Palatinate duchy of ZWEI-BRÜCKEN, but the Treaty of Paris in 1815 divided that territory between BAVARIA and PRUSSIA. In 1919 the area's coal mines were assigned to France for 15 years under the administration of the League of Nations. Returned to Germany by plebiscite in 1935, it became the Saarland province. Hitler annexed the land, with LORRAINE, in 1940 and called it Westmark. It was the scene of heavy fighting in World War II, particularly in December 1944 along the Saar River. Occupied by France in 1945, it was the subject of negotiations with France concerning economic union, but it has been economically integrated into West Germany since 1957.

SAARLAUTERN. See SAARLOUIS.

SAARLOUIS [*former:* Saarlautern, Sarrelibre; *French:* Sarrelouis] (West Germany) Town in SAARLAND, near the French border on the Saar River, 12 mi NW of SAARBRÜCKEN. It is named for Louis XIV of France, who founded it in 1680 as a fortress. Designed by Vauban, it became the capital of the French Sarre and was called Sarrelibre during the French Revolution. Ceded to PRUSSIA in 1815, the fortress was razed in 1889. It was known as Saarlautern from 1936 to 1945. The town was the birthplace of Michel Ney, marshal of Napoleon's armies.

SAAR RIVER. See SAARLAND.

SAAR TERRITORY. See SAARLAND.

SAAZ. See ZÁTEC.

SABA (Netherland Antilles) Island, 5 sq mi, one of the NW Leeward Islands, in the NE WEST INDIES, 16 mi NW of ST. EUSTATIUS. The island is actually the cone of an extinct volcano. Its chief settlement, The Bottom, is in the crater of the volcano. It was first settled by the Dutch in 1632. Fishing and shipbuilding are the main industries.

SABA, Yemen. See SHEBA.

SABADELL (Spain) City of Barcelona province, in CATALONIA, 8 mi NW of Barcelona. A leading textile center today, Sabadell has manufactured wool and cotton since the 13th century.

SABAH [*former:* British North Borneo, North Borneo] (Malaysia) State at the N tip of BORNEO, on the South China Sea. The area was visited by the English as early as the 17th century. There were vain attempts at settlement until Sir James Brooke made a local arrangement in 1841. With the organization of the North Borneo Company in 1881, the sultans of BRUNEI and SULU made more extensive concessions, until in 1888 the territory was proclaimed a British protectorate. The company, however, administered it up to the beginning of World War II, when it was occupied by the Japanese from 1941 to 1945. It was made a British colony in 1946 and joined the Federation of Malaysia as a state in 1963, when it took its present name. See also SARAWAK.

SABANG (Indonesia) Important free port on the island of Weh, approx. 14 mi off the NW tip of SUMATRA. Occupied by Japanese troops during World War II, it came under heavy Allied air attack in 1945, the last year of the war.

SABARIA. See SZOMBATHELY.

SABASTIYAH. See SAMARIA.

SABINE CROSSROADS (United States) Battle site near Mansfield, LOUISIANA, 40 mi S of Shreveport. It was the scene of the Battle of Sabine Crossroads on April 8, 1864, an important Confederate victory for forces under Gen. Richard Taylor over Union forces under Gen. Nathaniel P. Banks.

SABKHAT AL-KURZĪYAH [Sebkret El Kourzia] (Tunisia) Lake in N central Tunisia, in North Africa. Heavy fighting occurred here in April and May 1943 in World War II. On May 12, 1943 the Allied troops finally defeated the Axis powers in the critical African campaign.

SABLE ISLAND (Canada) An island, 25 mi long, off SE NOVA SCOTIA, 110 mi SSE of Canso. The island is the visible part of an extremely hazardous sand shoal, earning the island its name as the Graveyard of the Atlantic by mariners. Despite lighthouses at either end of the island, it has been the scene of over 200 reported shipwrecks. It was the location of a fortified French settlement between 1598 and 1603. See also LOUISBOURG.

SABRATA [Abrotonum, Sabratha] (Libya) One of three ancient cities of Tripolitana, in Roman Africa, on the Mediterranean coast, 48 mi W of TRIPOLI, near modern Sabratah. Founded by the Carthaginians in the fourth century BC as a trading post, it passed under Roman rule after the fall of CARTHAGE in 146 BC. The city fell into serious decline under Vandal rule in the fifth century AD. By the Arab Conquest in 643, it had almost ceased to exist. There is an archaeological museum, the ruins of Roman temples, forts, a theater, a forum, and two Byzantine Christian basilicas. Flavia Domitilla, wife of Emperor Vespasian, came from Sabrata, and it was where Lucius Apuleius stood trial for witchcraft.

SABRATON (United States) Former town, part of MORGANTOWN, WEST VIRGINIA since 1949. Thomas Decker established a settlement here in 1758, but Mingo Indians ravaged it a year later.

SABRINA. See SEVERN RIVER.

SABUCINO. See CALTANISSETTA.

SACHSELN (Switzerland) Town in UNTERWALDEN canton, near Sarnen, central Switzerland. The birthplace of Nicholas von der Flüe (1417–87), noted hermit and Swiss patriot, is nearby. Nicholas was instrumental in the united canton's struggle for freedom from AUS-

TRIA, and he helped preserve the resulting peace by his intervention at the Diet of Stans in 1481.

SACHSEN. See SAXONY.

SACHSEN-ALTENBURG. See SAXE-ALTENBURG.

SACHSEN-COBURG. See SAXE-COBURG.

SACHSEN-GOTHA. See SAXE-GOTHA.

SACHSENHAUSEN (East Germany) Village in Brandenburg, East Germany, approx. 5 mi N of Berlin. It was the site of a Nazi concentration camp, one of the six major ones already in operation by 1939. In April 1945, with the Soviet army rapidly advancing on BERLIN, the Germans evacuated the camp, forcing its 40,000 ill and starving inmates to march out of the path of the Soviets.

SACHSEN-MEININGEN. See SAXE-MEININGEN.

SACHSEN-WEIMAR. See SAXE-WEIMAR.

SACKETS HARBOR (United States) Resort village on LAKE ONTARIO, 11 mi SW of Watertown, in N NEW YORK State. Settled in 1801, it was developed as a U.S. naval base during the War of 1812. Several battles were fought here during that war.

SÄCKINGEN (West Germany) Town in SW Baden-Württemberg, on the RHINE RIVER, E of Basel. St. Fridolin founded a monastery here in the sixth century. Säckingen was the setting, and its 17th- and 18th-century castle the focus, of Scheffel's 1853 epic poem, *The Trumpeter of Säckingen.*

SACKVILLE (Canada) Town of SE NEW BRUNSWICK at the head of Chignecto Bay, an arm of the Bay of Fundy, near the Nova Scotia boundary, 25 mi SE of Moncton. It was settled in 1760 by French Acadians who diked and reclaimed the Tantramar marshes here for agriculture. The first Baptist church in Canada was established here in the 1770's. See ACADIA.

SACO [former: Pepperellboro] (United States) City of York county, SW MAINE, on the Saco River. Settled in 1631, it was incorporated as Pepperellboro in 1762 but was renamed Saco, a Sawatucke Indian word meaning "burnt pine," in 1805. Saco was incorporated as a city in 1867.

SACRALIAS. See ZALAKA.

SACRAMENTO [former: Fort Sutter, New Helvetia] (United States) Commercial center, city, and capital of CALIFORNIA, on the SACRAMENTO RIVER, 72 mi NE of San Francisco. John Sutter led the establishment of a settlement here in 1839. A fort was built in 1840, and by 1848 it was a mecca for newly arrived immigrants. The town began to prosper from the discovery of gold at nearby SUTTER'S MILL. It became an important trading center, the western end of the Pony Express route, and in 1854 was made the state capital. Four businessmen from Sacramento created the Central Pacific railroad and set up the state's influential Republican party here. Sutter's fort still stands.

SACRAMENTO RIVER (United States) Largest river in CALIFORNIA, flowing 360 mi SW from Mt Shasta to SAN FRANCISCO BAY and running into the San Joaquin river. It drains one of California's most fertile valleys. The river, and the Mother Lode Country in the foothills to the east, was the scene of the famous California Gold Rush of 1848 that stimulated the growth of towns along its banks, of which SACRAMENTO is the largest.

SACRIFICIOS [Islos de los Sacrificios] (Mexico) Island in the Gulf of Mexico, 3 mi S of Veracruz. Believed to be an ancient Aztec center for human sacrifice, it still has remains of ancient temples.

SACRO MONTE. See AMECAMECA, Mexico.

SACSAHUAMAN (Peru) Huge Inca fortress guarding the former Inca capital of CUZCO, situated just outside the city. It was built in the 15th century of huge monoliths. These single blocks of stone were transported to the site without the aid of wheeled vehicles and perfectly fitted together. Its remains are still impressive. During the Indian rebellion of Manco Capac in 1536/37 after the fall of the INCA EMPIRE, a Spanish garrison besieged in Cuzco managed to capture the fortress, enabling them to defeat the Indians.

SADIYA (India) Town in Arunachal Pradesh in the NE. It became a supply station in World War II and an important terminus of transportation routes into CHINA following the loss of the BURMA ROAD in 1942.

SADO [*Japanese:*** Sado-Shima]** (Japan) Large island, off the NW coast of the island of HONSHŪ. It has been a gold- and silver-mining center since 1601. The island is famous as a place of exile for prominent Japanese. Emperor Juntoku was in exile here from 1197 to 1242, and the priest Nichiren was here from 1222 to 1282.

SADO-SHIMA. See SADO.

SADOVA [Sadowa] [*German:*** Königgrätz]** (Czechoslovakia) Village in the N, in BOHEMIA, near Hradec. It was the site of the Battle of Sadowa, or Königgrätz, during the Austro-Prussian War, which PRUSSIA won decisively on July 3, 1866. See also HRADEC KRALOVÉ.

SADOWA. See SADOVA.

SAENA JULIA. See SIENA.

SAFAD [Safed] [*Hebrew:*** Zefat; ***Talmudic:*** Tzefiya]** (Israel) Town in the NE, 7 mi NNW of the SEA OF GALILEE, 30 mi ENE of Haifa. One of the four holy cities of PALESTINE and a center of Jewish culture and mysticism, Safad was founded c.70 AD and fortified by the Jewish historian and general Flavius Josephus. It was an important 12th-century Crusader castle. Jews expelled from Spain in 1492 established Safad as a seat of rabbinical and cabalistic studies, setting up the first Hebrew press in 1563. In 1776 an influx of Russian Hasidim repopulated the city after it had been damaged by a violent earthquake in 1769. Jews were forced to leave by the Arabs in 1929, but they returned in 1948 after World War II and the declaration of the State of Israel. Ruins of the 12th-century castle are here.

SAFAQIS. See SFAX.

SAFED. See SAFAD.

SAFETY ISLANDS [Îles du Salut] (French Guiana) Archipelago in the Atlantic Ocean, 7 mi off the N coast of French Guiana. Of the three islands in the group, DEVIL'S ISLAND is the most famous thanks to its notorious penal colony, which was founded in 1852 and phased out between 1938 and 1951.

SAFFI. See SAFI.

SAFFRON WALDEN (England) Town in Essex, 41 mi NNE of London. It was named for the saffron cultivation that thrived from the time of Edward III (1327–77) until the 18th century. There are Roman ruins, the remains of a 12th-century castle, and a 15th-century church containing the tomb of Lord Audley, the chancellor of Henry VIII. Audley End, the great Jacobean mansion, lies approximately 1 mile west of the town.

SAFI [Asfi, Saffi] (Morocco) City of NW Africa, on the Atlantic Ocean, SW of Casablanca, 85 mi NW of Marrakech. It was fortified during the 13th century. It became a Portuguese holding and was made the chief port of MARRAKECH in 1660. U.S. troops landed here in November 1942 during World War II. An old citadel from the period of Portuguese occupation survives. See also PORTUGAL.

SAGA (Japan) Capital city of Saga prefecture in W KYŪSHŪ, on the E Hizen peninsula, 43 mi NE of Nagasaki. Formerly part of the feudal province of Hizen, it was a castle town known for the porcelain made here. In 1874 it was the headquarters of insurrectionists. Traces of the castle survive.

SAGAING (Burma) Town, capital of the S division, and district of Upper Burma, 10 mi SW of Mandalay, on the right bank of the IRRAWADDY RIVER, opposite ruined AVA. A trading center, Sagaing was the capital of a petty Shan kingdom in the 14th century before it was dominated by PEGU in the 16th century. It became the capital of Burma in the 18th century. The important Ava Bridge here was the object of a successful Japanese attack during World War II.

SAGAMI-NADA. See SAGAMI SEA.

SAGAMI SEA [*Japanese:*** Sagami-nada]** (Japan) Bay on the SE coast of HONSHŪ, SW of Tokyo in Kanagawa prefecture. A U.S. naval raid was staged here in the summer of 1945 during World War II.

SAGAN [Zagan] [*Polish:*** Żagán, Żegán]** (Poland) Town of Lower Silesia, in Zielona Gona province in the W, on the Bobrawa River, 35 mi NNE of Görlitz. Founded in the 12th century, it was the capital of an independent principality from 1274 to 1472. From 1628 to 1635 it was the property of Gen. Albrecht Wallenstein, who built the late Gothic church out of a former Franciscan monastery in 1629. It passed to PRUSSIA in 1745. The town was the site of a prison camp in World War II. It was included in Poland after 1945.

SAGAULI. See SEGAULI.

SAGHALIEN. See SAKHALIN.

SAG HARBOR (United States) Village in Suffolk County, SE NEW YORK State, at the E end of LONG ISLAND, midway on the South Fork, on Gardiner's Bay, 25 mi W of Montauk. It was settled between 1720 and 1730. An active whaling center in the 19th century, it is a summer resort and fishing and yachting center today. Long Island's first newspaper, the *Long Island Herald,* was published here in 1791. There is a whaling museum.

SAGINAW [*former:* **East Saginaw, Fort Saginaw, Saginaw City**] (United States) City in Saginaw county, S MICHIGAN, on the Saginaw River, 32 mi NNW of Flint. A port of entry off LAKE HURON and an industrial center, it was settled in 1816 in an area laced with Indian trails and villages. The city was the site where Lewis Cass negotiated a treaty with the Indians in 1819 to gain much of Michigan for the United States. Important as a fur-trading and pine-lumbering center in the 19th century, in 1889 it merged with East Saginaw, a settlement across the river, to form the present city.

SAGINAW CITY. See SAGINAW.

SAGRES (Portugal) Village in the extreme SW of Portugal, 3 mi SE of Cape Vincent. Here in 1416 Prince Henry of Portugal established a base for naval exploration of the west coast of Africa. His ships used the nearby port of LAGOS. Henry became Europe's most famous patron of exploration, and his captains pioneered in voyages that led to world-wide discoveries less than a century later.

The MADEIRA ISLANDS, in the Atlantic Ocean off Morocco, had been known to the Romans but were rediscovered between 1418 and 1420 by some of Henry's navigators. The AZORES, approximately 900 miles west of Portugal, were found in 1427 or 1431. Gradually the west coast of Africa was explored, and from 1444 to 1446 some 30 or 40 ships took this route. Finally in 1460 a ship reached a point near present SIERRA LEONE. When gold and slaves began to be brought back, Henry's explorations were vindicated, and Portugal's standing among European nations was greatly enhanced.

Henry, who became known as Prince Henry the Navigator, attracted the attention of many of Italy's new Humanists, including Poggio Bracciolini, but he was not himself a man of great learning. His main contribution rests in his bringing together the practical knowledge and skills of mariners and fishermen with that of scholars. A staunchly pious and idealistic leader, he forbade the kidnapping of blacks in 1455. He built at Sagres a naval arsenal, an observatory, and a school for the study of geography and navigation. The activities at Sagres led directly, after Henry's death in 1460, to the rounding of the Cape of GOOD HOPE and the discovery of a sea route to INDIA by Vasco da Gama and the founding of the Portuguese Empire.

SAGUNTO [*ancient:* **Murbiter, Saguntum;** *Arabic:* **Murviedro**] (Spain) Town of Valencia province, 15 mi NNE of Valencia. It was originally a Greek colony. An ally of ROME, it was conquered by the Carthaginians under Hannibal in 219/18 BC leading to the Second Punic War. After the Roman victory in 214, Sagunto was made a municipium. After resistance, Sagunto was conquered by the Moors in 713 and called Murviedro until 1877. Besides Roman and Greek remains, there are medieval fortifications and a Moorish citadel. The restoration of the Bourbon dynasty to Spain was proclaimed here in 1874. See also CARTHAGE.

SAGUNTUM. See SAGUNTO.

SAHAGÚN (Spain) Town of León province, in the NW, 33 mi ESE of LEÓN. It was a center of Castilian culture from the 10th to 15th centuries. Here are ruins of a Benedictine abbey where Alfonso VI is buried. It also saw the beginning of Sir John Moore's retreat to CORUNNA during the Peninsular campaign of the Napoleonic Wars, in December 1808, after he had failed to assist the Spanish in their vain attempt to defend MADRID.

SAHARA [*Arabic:* **Sahra**] (Africa) Desert, largest in the world, extending more than 3,000 mi from the Red Sea on the E, westward to the Atlantic Ocean. On the N are the Atlas Mts, the Mediterranean Sea, and some steppeland. The Sahara extends approx. 1,200 mi S to the SAHEL, a semiarid region running from SENEGAL on the W to ETHIOPIA on the E.

Weathered rock in the awesome Sahara Desert. Until occasional camel caravans penetrated its vast expanse, the Sahara largely isolated Black Africa from the ancient civilizations of North Africa.

The climate of the Sahara is extremely harsh, with very little rainfall, very high temperatures, and little vegetation except in scattered oases. The permanent population has always been small, consisting in ancient times mostly of black Sudanese. After the camel was introduced, probably in the first century AD, Berbers and Arabs took over. They improved oases by drilling for water and by planting date palm trees. The Sahara became a sea of sand on which caravans traveled like ships crossing an ocean. The medieval peoples and kingdoms of West Africa, such as the FULANI, the HAUSA, MALI, BORNU, and SONGHAI, participated in this trade, which carried slaves, gold, salt, ivory, and other goods in all directions. The north-south route between the mysterious and fabled city of TIMBUKTU, in present Mali, and ALGERIA on the Mediterranean was particularly prosperous until the slave trade was suppressed in the 19th century.

Today specially equipped motor vehicles have mostly replaced the camel as the ship of the desert. Beginning in the early 19th century the Sahara attracted many European explorers anxious to prove their mettle by crossing it and curious to find some of the ancient cities in it and around its edges. The earliest adventurers were Friedrich Hornemann in 1805 and Mungo Park in 1806. One of the first to make the full crossing was René Caillié of France, who was also the first European to visit Timbuktu. Others were Heinrich Barth, a German in British service; Gustav Nachtigal, a German who visited the central Sahara in 1869 and reached KHARTOUM; Hugh Clapperton of Great Britain, one of the first Europeans to see Lake Chad, mostly in present CHAD; and Dixon Denham of Great Britain who reached the Bornu region in 1823. From west to east the Sahara covers all or most of the modern nations of Senegal, Mauritania, Western Sahara, Algeria, Mali, Niger, Tunisia, Libya, Chad, Egypt, and Sudan.

SAHARANPUR (India) City of Uttar Pradesh state on the Dharmanta River, 100 mi NNE of Delhi. Founded c.1340, it was the summer resort of the Mogul court and is now the district administrative center. See also MOGUL EMPIRE.

SAHEL (Africa) Region between the SAHARA DESERT to the N, the savannas of the S, Senegal on the W, and Ethiopia to the E. A prolonged drought in the late 1960's wiped out meager water supplies and the entire agricultural economy here, causing massive starvation and a general migration to the south.

SAHRA. See SAHARA.

SAIDA. See SIDON.

SAIGON [Sai Gon] [*French:* Saïgon; *modern:* Ho Chi Minh City] (Vietnam) Capital city of South Vietnam, on the right bank of the Saigon River, between the Mekong River delta and the South China Sea. The country's largest and most important city, it began as an ancient Khmer settlement. Occupied in the 1680's by Vietnamese who had lived in the north for 15 centuries, it was captured by the French in 1859 and ceded to FRANCE in 1862. Compared to Cholon, a city that was merged with Saigon in 1932 and which has a very strong Chinese influence, Saigon reflects its French background and is very European in its architecture and city plan. Capital of the Union of INDOCHINA from 1887 to 1902, the joined cities were included in the new prefecture of Saigon in 1956, after Saigon became the capital of the new state of South Vietnam in 1954. Headquarters for U.S. and South Vietnamese troops during the Vietnam War, Saigon was severely damaged during the Tet offensive in 1968 and was inundated

after the war with millions of rural refugees, now numbering nearly 13,000 persons per square mile. Under the victorious North Vietnamese the city was renamed Ho Chi Minh City.

SAIGON RIVER. See MEKONG RIVER.

SAIKYO. See KYŌTO.

SAILLY-SAILLISEL (France) Village of Somme department, in the N of Péronne. Major combat took place here in World War I between 1916 and 1918, especially as the Allies made small advances on German positions during the great battle of the SOMME from July 1 to Nov. 18, 1916.

SAINT-ACHEUL (France) Hamlet and gravel pit in Somme department, in the N, near AMIENS. The Paleolithic remains found here were named after this location. The Acheulian Period refers to the last part of the Lower Paleolithic Period, c.50,000 to 30,000 BC.

SAINT ALBANS [*ancient:* **Verulamium**] (England) City of Hertfordshire, 20 mi NNW of London. It is the site of Roman VERULAMIUM and of an abbey established in 793 by the king of MERCIA to house the relics of St. Alban, martyred here in 303 AD. Prominent throughout the Middle Ages, the abbey included a school replaced by St. Albans School in the 16th century. During the Middle Ages St. Albans and its Chronicles produced a school of brilliant historians, among them Roger of Wendover, Mathew Paris (d. 1259), and Thomas Walsingham. Upon the abbey's dissolution, St. Albans town received its first charter in 1553. The abbey houses the first version of the Magna Carta (1215). It was the scene of a great peasant uprising in 1381. The 11th to 14th century abbey church, built by Paul of Caen, the first Norman abbot, incorporating Roman materials, has one of the longest Gothic naves in the world. During the Wars of Roses, St. Albans was the scene of a Yorkist victory in 1455 and a Lancastrian victory in 1461. Holywell House here was the birthplace of the first duchess of Marlborough, Sarah Jennings. The Fighting Cock Inn here is one of the oldest inhabited houses in England.

SAINT ALBANS (United States) City in NW VERMONT, near Lake Champlain, 25 mi N of Burlington. The region was French territory from the time of a grant in 1664 until Great Britain took possession in 1763 at the end of the French and Indian War. The town was chartered that year and organized in 1788. In the early 19th century it was an active base for smuggling goods between the United States and Canada.

On Oct. 19, 1864 a group of approximately 25 Confederate soldiers, who had made their way to CANADA, infiltrated the town. Announcing they were annexing it to the CONFEDERATE STATES, they robbed three banks of approximately $200,000, tried to burn the town, and killed one man. When they fled back to Canada, they were chased by a sheriff's posse, and all but five of them were captured and turned over to Canadian officials. A Canadian judge, however, released them, thus damaging United States-Canadian relations.

In 1870 a group of Fenians, members of a secret order pledged to use force to secure Ireland's independence from Great Britain, attempted to stage a raid on Canada from St. Albans. Many of them were arrested, including their leader, John O'Neil.

SAINT-AMAND [Saint-Amand-les-Eaux] (France) A small manufacturing city and resort, with hot springs, in Nord department, 22 mi E of Lille. Saint-Amand was widely known for its production of faience in the 18th century. It grew up around an abbey established in 647 AD.

SAINT-AMAND-LES-EAUX. See SAINT-AMAND.

SAINT ANDREWS [former: Kilyrmount, Mucross] (Scotland) Town of Fife region, on St. Andrews Bay, 11 mi SE of Dundee. Originally a Celtic settlement, it was the archibishopric and ecclesiastical center of Scotland from 908 AD to the Reformation, receiving its charter in 1160. Its university, founded in 1410, is the oldest in Scotland. Protestant reformers Patrick Hamilton and George Wishart were burned here for heresy, and the bishop's palace was held by Protestant reformers for over a year in 1546 in resistance to the French. The Royal and Ancient Golf Club, established in 1754, is where the rules of golf were established. Ruins of the 12th-century cathedral and of the bishop's palace are here.

SAINT ANN'S BAY [former: Santa Gloria] (Jamaica) Town and bay in St. Ann parish, on the N coast of the island of Jamaica, in the WEST INDIES. Columbus discovered the island for SPAIN on May 4, 1494, but it was on his second voyage, later in 1494, that he named St. Ann's Bay Santa Gloria. The fort, built in 1777, is now a slaughterhouse.

SAINT ANTHONY FALLS. See MINNEAPOLIS.

SAINT ASAPH (Wales) Town in Clwyd, on the Clwyd River and the Elwy River, 24 mi NW of Wrexham. It was the probable site of a bishopric c.560 AD. Its ancient monastery of Llanelywe was renamed to honor Asaph, a sixth-century abbot. Its first cathedral was twice destroyed in the 13th century by the English. The 15th-century cathedral, one of the smallest in Great Britain, contains a collection of early bibles. Morgan, the translator of the Bible into Welsh, was a bishop here.

SAINT AUGUSTINE (United States) City in NE FLORIDA, on a peninsula between the Mantanzas and San Sebastian rivers, 35 mi from Jacksonville. A port of entry and the oldest city in the United States, it was founded in 1565 by the Spanish explorer Pedro Avilés near where Ponce de León discovered Florida in 1513. The Spanish destroyed the later French colony of Fort Caroline, built on the site of an ancient Indian village. It was named for the feast day of Saint Augustine, the day Avilés entered the harbor. It was burned and sacked by English buccaneers under Sir Francis Drake in 1586 and Capt. John Davis in 1665. The city resisted capture in 1740 by James Oglethorpe, the founder of GEORGIA. It passed to Great Britain in 1763 at the end of the French and Indian War and became a Tory refuge during the American Revolution. It reverted to Spain in 1783. In 1821 Spain turned over the city to the United States, and it grew rapidly until the Seminole War of the 1830's and the occupation by Union troops during the Civil War.

Retaining much of its Spanish colonial atmosphere, the city contains the Castillo de San Marcos, built between 1672 and 1696, the oldest masonry fort in the country, Fort Matanzas of 1742, old city gates, the oldest house in the United States, dating from the 16th century, a slave market, and an 18th-century cathedral. In 1937 the Carnegie Institute began restoration of the city's historical landmarks.

SAINT AUSTELL WITH FOWEY. See FOWEY.

SAINT BERNARD PASSES (France, Italy, Switzerland) The name of two Alpine passes: the Great St. Bernard (called in antiquity *Alpis Poenina* and *Mons Jovis* after a temple of Jupiter here) on the Swiss-Italian border connects VALAIS canton with VALLE D'AOSTA in Italy. The Little St. Bernard, the ancient *Alpis Graia*, links the Savoie department of France with the Valle d'Aosta. Both passes have been used since antiquity.

The Great St. Bernard has seen the passage of Gauls, Romans, Charlemagne, Emperor Henry IV, Frederick Barbarossa, and Napoleon, who led 40,000 men over it in 1800 on the way to his Italian campaign. It received its present name in the 12th century. It is the site of a 11th-century hospice for Augustinian friars built by St. Bernard of Menthon, where the famous St. Bernard dogs were bred to look for lost travelers. The Little St. Bernard may have been the route used by Hannibal and his elephants on invading Italy in the autumn of 218 BC. It also has a hospice supposedly built by St. Bernard of Menthon in the 11th century.

SAINT BONIFACE (Canada) City in SE MANITOBA, on the RED RIVER, opposite WINNIPEG. It was named for the German saint by Swiss mercenaries who had earlier attempted to establish a colony here. Founded in 1818 as a Roman Catholic mission, it included a mission school, St. Boniface College. Today it is a major Roman Catholic center of Canada.

SAINT BOTOLPH'S TOWN. See BOSTON, England.

SAINT-BRIEUC (France) Town, capital of Côtes-du-Nord department, in the NW, on the Gouet River, near the English Channel, 55 mi NW of Rennes. It is named for St. Brieuc, a Welsh monk of the fifth century who built a monastery on the site. An episcopal see since the ninth century, it was also the meeting place for the provincial estates of BRITTANY in the 17th and 18th centuries. A fortress and a recently restored Gothic cathedral from the 13th century have survived sieges in 1375 and 1394.

SAINT CATHARINES [former: Shipman's Corner] (Canada) City of S ONTARIO, on the Welland Ship Canal, S of Lake Ontario, 25 mi NW of Buffalo. A Church of England mission was established in 1792 on the site of the present city after St. Catharine's University was opened in 1790. An industrial and agricultural center today, St. Catharines is a resort with mineral springs and the site of an old tuberculosis sanitarium.

SAINT CHARLES (Canada) Village of S QUEBEC, on the Richelieu river, 14 mi WNW of St. Hyacinthe. It was the center of the Lower Canada Rebellion in 1837. The Confederation of Six Counties was proclaimed here in October 1837, before British troops defeated the insurgents and burned the village.

SAINT CHARLES (United States) City and seat of St. Charles county, in E MISSOURI, along the N bank of the MISSOURI RIVER, 20 mi NW of St. Louis. The earliest permanent European settlement on the river, it began as a trading post, settled by French traders in 1769. It then became a starting point west on Daniel Boone's Lick Trail. The capital of Missouri Territory, it was the capital of the state from 1821 to 1826. The old state capitol building remains.

SAINT CHRISTOPHER. See SAINT KITTS-NEVIS.

SAINT-CLAUDE (France) Town of Jura department in the E, in FRANCHE-COMTÉ, at the confluence of the Bienne and Tacon rivers, 19 mi NW of Geneva. An ancient town with Gallo-Roman origins, it was named after Bishop Claude of Besançon who died here in the seventh century. The 14th to 18th-century cathedral contains late 15th-century choir stalls that came from a fifth-century abbey, now destroyed.

SAINT CLEMENT'S ISLAND. See BLAKISTONE ISLAND.

SAINT-CLOUD (France) Town of the Hauts-de-Seine department, a suburb of PARIS, on the SEINE RIVER. It was named after the grandson of Clovis I, St. Clodoald, or Cloud, who built a monastery here in the sixth century. There are the remains of a royal palace built in 1572 that was the residence of many French rulers, including Charles X, Napoleon, and Napoleon III. It was the scene of the murder of Henry III in 1589. Napoleon proclaimed the empire from the palace here in 1804; and the town served as the headquarters in 1815 of Marshal Gebhard von Blücher during the Waterloo campaign of the Napoleonic Wars. The palace was destroyed in 1870 during the Franco-Prussian War.

SAINT CLOUD (United States) City and seat of Stearns county, in central MINNESOTA, on the MISSISSIPPI RIVER, 58 mi NW of Minneapolis. Settled in 1851 and named after the French city, it was for a time a terminus of the Hudson's Bay Company. Fortified during the Sioux Wars of 1862, it took in thousands of fleeing homesteaders. This region has been famous since 1868 for its granite quarrying and fine granite finishing.

SAINT CROIX [Santa Cruz] (United States) Largest of the U.S. VIRGIN ISLANDS, 40 mi S of St. Thomas and St. John. It was inhabited by Carib Indians until Columbus discovered the island on his second voyage in 1493. He overcame fierce native resistance to Spanish invasion and named the island Santa Cruz. Occupied throughout the 17th century by Holland, France, Spain and England, it was held from 1651 to 1665 by the Knights of Malta and was purchased by DENMARK in 1733, when it became known as the Garden of the Danish West Indies. There were slave revolts in the 19th century. The United States purchased the island in 1917, and it is now a luxury vacation resort.

SAINT CROIX RIVER (Canada, United States) River, 75 mi long, flowing from the Chiputneticook lakes SE of Passamaquoddy Bay, forming part of the U.S.-Canadian border. In a territorial dispute in 1798 the British mistook the St. Croix River for the PENOBSCOT RIVER to the west and therefore not the international boundary. Discovery of the ruins of the first settlement in ACADIA on St. Croix island—established by Champlain in 1604 and abandoned the next year for PORT ROYAL after an outbreak of scurvy—verified the river as the St. Croix, and the British agreed to assign the island to the United States.

SAINT-CYR-l'ÉCOLE (France) Town of Yvelines department, 3 mi W of Versailles. It was established in 1685 by Louis XIV and Mme. de Maintenon as a school for the daughters of noble but impoverished families. Napoleon turned it into a military academy in 1808. Destroyed in World War II, the school was moved to Coëtquidan in BRITTANY after the war.

SAINT DAVID, FORT. See FORT SAINT DAVID.

SAINT DAVID'S [medieval: **Menevia**] (Wales) City in Dyfed, 60 mi WNW of Swansea. Tradition has it that Menevia was founded in the sixth century AD by St. David, the patron saint of Wales. Its transitional Norman cathedral is the most famous in Wales, and there is a 13th-century shrine to St. David. Long a pilgrimage center, it has remains of medieval walls enclosing the monastic buildings, as well as the remains of a 14th-century bishop's palace. Prehistoric megalithic monuments are abundant in the area of St. David's.

SAINT-DENIS (France) Port and capital city of the island of RÉUNION, an overseas department of France, on the Indian Ocean, at the mouth of the St.-Denis River, on the N coast, 10 mi ENE of Pointe-des-Galots. St.-Denis was founded in the late 17th century as a French way station on the way to the Orient. There is a noteworthy cathedral in the city, and beautiful colonial gardens. It exports sugar and rum today.

SAINT-DENIS [ancient: **Catulliacum**] (France) Industrial city of Seine department and a suburb, 7 mi NNE of PARIS, on the right bank of the SEINE RIVER. It developed around a Benedictine abbey built by the Merovingian ruler, Dagobert I, in 626 AD over the tomb of St. Denis, patron saint of France. The abbey, where Abélard became a monk and Joan of Arc blessed her weapons, was the wealthiest and most prominent in France in the Middle Ages and housed a famous scriptorium from the eighth century. Its famous abbot, Suger (c.1081–1151), was one of the most influential figures in the politics and culture of France in the high Middle Ages. Abbot from 1122, he became a member of the royal court in 1124 and regent of France from 1147 to 1149 when Louis VII was on the Second Crusade. He made St. Denis fabulously wealthy and was a key figure in formulating the new Gothic architecture, of which St. Denis was the first example. The east end of this 12th-century basilica, built at the abbey, became the standard for later Gothic cathedrals, such as at CANTERBURY and CHARTRES. The basilica contains the tombs of many kings of France, including Francis I and Henry II. Louis XVI and Marie Antoinette are buried in the crypt. The abbey's banner, the Oriflamme, was also the royal standard of France from the 12th through the 18th century and was housed here from 1120 with the rest of the royal insignia.

The historical St. Denis, the first bishop of Paris, was decapitated in the third century AD. In legend he soon became confused with St. Dionysius (Denis) the Areopagite, the disciple of St. Paul. By the 12th century the confusion of fact and legend caused the abbots of St. Denis to establish a school for the study and translation of the works of this Pseudo Dionysius from the Greek. According to some, these mystical works influenced Abbot Suger in his design for the new Gothic basilica. The town was damaged during the Hundred Years War, and in 1567 it was the scene of a battle in the Wars of Religion. In the French Revolution many of the abbey tombs were vandalized. The town was briefly renamed Franciade during the early years of the Revolution. The abbey was rebuilt during the 18th century and is now a school for the daughters of the Legion of Honor. The area has yielded many medieval artifacts, which are now on display in a local museum here.

SAINT-DENIS-LE-GAST (France) Town, in Manche department, 12 mi N of Avranches. U.S. armored forces, directed by Gen. George Patton, staged a significant breakthrough here on July 30, 1944 during the Allied Normandy campaign of World War II.

SAINT-DIÉ (France) City of Vosges department, in LORRAINE, on the Meurthe River, 25 mi ENE of Épinal. The city's historical architecture—a seventh-century monastery built by St. Deodatus, a Romanesque and Gothic cathedral, 14th- to 16th-century cloisters, and a 17th-century episcopal palace—were largely destroyed in World War II, when most of the population was massacred or deported. In 1507 Martin Waldseemüller printed here the first geographical work that referred to the newly discovered continent of America by that name.

SAINT-DIZIER [*ancient:* **Desiderii Fanum**] (France) Town of Haut-Marne department, in the NE, on the MARNE RIVER, 39 mi N of Chaumont. It was once a Roman settlement. Besieged and taken in 1544 during the interminable wars between the emperor Charles V and Francis I of France, it was also the scene of a battle in 1814, during the Napoleonic Wars. St. Dizier's museum displays Roman and early Christian artifacts, and the town has many noteworthy buildings from the 15th to 18th centuries.

SAINT-DOMINGUE. See HAITI.

SAINTE-ADRESSE (France) Town near Le Havre, in Seine-Maritime department, in the N. It served as the headquarters, from Oct. 13, 1914 to December 1918, of Belgium's displaced government during World War I.

SAINTE-ANNE DE BEAUPRÉ (Canada) Village in S Quebec, on the ST. LAWRENCE RIVER, 21 mi NE of Quebec, opposite Île d'Orléans. It is the site of a shrine erected in 1620 by shipwrecked sailors and of a chapel built in 1658. The large church contains relics, and the shrine and chapel have supposedly been the scene of miraculous cures. This makes the village a popular pilgrimage center.

SAINTE ANNE DE BELLEVUE (Canada) Town in S Quebec, on Montreal Island, 20 mi WSW of Montreal. Originally a fur-trading post, it also served as the departure point for canoes heading west. It was referred to in Thomas Moore's poem *Canadian Boat Story*.

STE. ANNE'S POINT. See FREDERICTON.

SAINTE-BAUME (France) Mountain chain in Bouches-du-Rhône and Var departments, SE France. La Grotte de Sainte Madeleine, where by tradition Mary Magdalene lived out her last days, is a pilgrimage center here.

SAINT EDMUND'S BURY. See BURY SAINT EDMUNDS.

SAINTE-GENEVIEVE. See MISSOURI.

SAINTE-MARIE-AUX-MINES [*German:* **Markirch**] (France) Small town at the crest of the VOSGES Mts, in Haut-Rhin department, NE France. It is now a textile center. The mines in its vicinity were worked for copper, silver, and lead well up into the 18th century.

SAINTE-MENEHOULD (France) Town in the NE, in Marne department, on the AISNE RIVER. Occupied by the Germans early in World War I, it was later recaptured by the French, who utilized it as their ARGONNE headquarters.

SAINTE-MÈRE-ÉGLISE (France) Town in NW Manche department, approx. 20 mi SE of Cherbourg, Normandy. During the Allies' Normandy campaign of World War II, U.S. paratroopers raided this town between June 6 and 10, 1944, capturing it.

SAINTES [*ancient:* **Mediolanum Santorum**] (France) Town of Charente-Maritime department, in the W, on the Charente River, 40 mi SE of La Rochelle. Most likely the ancient capital of the Celtic Santones, it was taken by ROME in the first century BC. It became the capital of the medieval province of SAINTONGE. The Roman amphitheater and triumphal arch date from the first century AD, while the partially restored Romanesque church of St. Eutrope dates from the 11th and 12th centuries. In 1242 Louis IX of France defeated the forces of Henry III of ENGLAND here.

SAINTES, BATTLE OF (France) Island group of French overseas department of GUADELOUPE, WEST INDIES. Off these islands on April 12, 1782 British Admiral George Rodney defeated French Admiral Comte De Grasse in a brilliant victory in which Rodney captured De Grasse himself. The battle helped to offset the surrender of British forces at YORKTOWN in 1781, which ended the American Revolution.

SAINT-ÉTIENNE (France) Capital city of Loire department in the SE, in the Massif Central, 31 mi SW of Lyons. With LYONS and ROANNE, Saint-Étienne forms the industrial triangle of France and has been known for its textiles since the 11th century. Francis I ordered firearms from here in the 16th century, and the industrial city was not surprisingly the terminus of the first railroad in France in 1827. In addition to a medieval church and abbey, there is a 17th-century cathedral and a palace of art in the city.

SAINT EUSTATIUS [*Dutch:* **Sint Eustatius;** *local:* **Statia**] (Netherlands) One of the islands of the NETHERLANDS ANTILLES, in the CARIBBEAN, 8 mi NW of St. Kitts-Nevis, the WEST INDIES. Although settled by the French in 1625, it became Dutch after 1632. It was a strategic port for contraband trade with the American colonies through the American Revolution. Its was reputedly the first government to recognize the American flag in 1776. Saint Eustatius was also a famous smuggling center for West Indies pirates. It went into decline after the British sacked it in 1781.

SAINT GALL [*French:* **Saint-Gall;** *German:* **Sankt Gallen**] (Switzerland) Canton in the NE surrounding the canton of APPENZELL, with Lake Constance on the N and the Rhine River to the E. Its capital city is also St. Gall, 39 mi E of Zurich. Named after a Celtic abbey founded by St. Columbarus between 585 and 615 on the site of the hermitage of St. Gall, an early missionary Irish monk, both the city and the canton became an important center of learning north of the Alps in the early Middle Ages. The house was refounded in 750. Famous medieval manuscripts are still preserved in its libraries. One of the most famous of these is the *St. Gall Plan*, a comprehensive design for a completed monastic community based on Roman urban planning. Completed *c.*675, it incorporates the new planning ideas of the Middle Ages for work, living, cooking, drainage and sewage, hospital, administrative, and intellectual functions that are a model for modern design.

Ruled by the abbots of St. Gall until the early 13th century, the area then became a free imperial city, and the abbots were made princes of the HOLY ROMAN EMPIRE. St. Gall rebelled against the abbots in 1453 and allied itself with the Swiss Confederation. Under Napoleon's Act of Mediation in 1803, St. Gall was consolidated as a canton of the Swiss Confederation and has been a bishopric since 1846. It has been famous for its textiles since the Middle Ages.

SAINT GEORGE (Great Britain) Town on the S coast of St. George's Island in BERMUDA. Founded in 1621 as the first settlement on the island, it was the capital of Bermuda until 1815, when it was replaced by HAMILTON. During the U.S. Civil War, it was a refuge for Confederate blockade-runners.

SAINT GEORGE, Greece. See SKYROS.

SAINT GEORGE, Grenada. See SAINT GEORGE'S.

SAINT GEORGE [*former:* **Fort Saint George**] (United States) Town of Knox county, in S MAINE, on an Atlantic Ocean inlet, 36 mi ESE of Augusta. In an area first explored in 1605, a trading post was established here in 1630. Fort St. George, built in 1719/20, was frequently under Indian attack in the 18th century and fell to the British in 1809 in a battle of the War of 1812.

SAINT GEORGE'S [**Saint George**] (Grenada) Town and capital of Grenada, in the WEST INDIES, 90 mi N of Port of Spain, Trinidad. A picturesque port town and previous capital of the former British colony of the Windward Islands, St. George's was first established nearby in 1650 by French settlers. The present site dates from 1705, as do most of the old buildings, including St. George's Church. In 1783 Great Britain seized control, and St. George's later became the center of government for all the Windward Islands.

SAINT GEORGE'S CAY (Belize) Small island in the Caribbean Sea, off the NE coast of Belize, 50 mi NE of Nassau. It was the scene of the defeat of the Spanish by British settlers on Sept. 10, 1798, marking the end of Spanish claims in British Honduras.

SAINT-GERMAIN-EN-LAYE (France) Town in the Île de France, on the SEINE RIVER, 11 mi WNW of PARIS. A resort today, it has a museum of pre-Christian antiquities that was a château that served as a royal residence until the French Revolution. Louis XIV was born here. It was used by the exiled Mary Stuart and James II of ENGLAND, who is buried here. The edifice had originally been built in the 12th century by Louis VI. It was burned by the English in 1346 and restored. Several treaties were signed here, in 1570, 1632, 1679, most recently the 1919 Treaty of Saint-Germain, which ended World War I for AUSTRIA. It was the birthplace of Claude Debussy.

SAINT-GILLES (France) Town of Gard department, in the S, 12 mi SSE of Nîmes. It was under the rule of the counts of TOULOUSE in the Middle Ages. The Knights of St. John of Jerusalem founded the first priory in Europe here. Only the west front and crypt remain of the 12th-century church.

SAINT-GOBAIN (France) Village of Aisne department, in the N, 7 mi NW of Laon. Famous for its mirror and optical glass factories, established in 1685, it was also an important World War I German fortification point on the HINDENBURG LINE, until October 1918.

SAINT-GOND. See SÉZANNE.

SAINT GOTTHARD. See SZENTGOTTHÁRD.

SAINT GOTTHARD PASS [*German:* **Sankt Gotthard**] (Switzerland) Mountain pass in the Lepontine Alps, in the SE, the source for the Reuss, Rhine, Ticino, and Rhône rivers. An important and well-traveled pass since the Middle Ages, its approaches were originally guarded by the League of the Three Cantons. At least by the 14th century, a hospice was established here to give aid to travelers. Destroyed by the French in 1800, it was reconstructed but burned down completely in 1905.

SAINT HELENA (Great Britain) Island in the S Atlantic, 1,200 mi W of Africa. Discovered by a Portuguese explorer in 1502, it was annexed by the Dutch in 1633, then was taken over and occupied by the English East India Company from 1659, except for one day in January 1673 when the Dutch retook the island. Napoleon I was exiled here in 1815 and lived under guard near JAMESTOWN until his death in 1821. It was made a British crown colony in 1834. Boer prisoners were held here during the Boer War from 1899 to 1902. The island was a British naval base in both world wars. Astronomer Edmund Halley had an observatory here from 1676 to 1678.

SAINT HELENA ISLAND. See SEA ISLANDS.

SAINT HELIER (Great Britain) Town and capital of JERSEY, in the CHANNEL ISLANDS, on St. Aubin's Bay, 122 mi SSW of Southampton. In addition to the parish church, partially from the 14th century, there is on an adjacent island a 16th-century castle and the ruins of a chapel on a rock, believed to have been the sixth-century hermitage of St. Helier. The Royal Square in the town was the scene of a battle in 1781 when France tried unsuccessfully to regain Jersey. Victor Hugo lived here from 1852 to 1855.

SAINT HONORAT. See CANNES.

SAINT-HUBERT (Belgium) Town of Luxembourg province in the SE, in the ARDENNES, 17 mi W of Bastogne. The town is a tourist resort today. There is a seventh-century Benedictine abbey with attached older buildings, which are now a juvenile reformatory. St. Hubert, patron saint of the hunt, is buried in the 16th-century abbey church here.

ST. IAGO DE LA VEGA. See SPANISH TOWN.

SAINT IGNACE. See MACKINAC, Michigan.

SAINT JEAN [Saint Johns] [*former:* **Fort St. Jean**] (Canada) City of S Quebec, on the Richelieu River, 21 mi SE of Montreal. Fort St. Jean, built 1748, and an earlier fortification on the site were important in the 17th and 18th centuries, especially as a British base during the American Revolution. British soldiers here checked Gen. Richard Montgomery's advance in 1775, during the unsuccessful QUEBEC campaign. St. Jean was also the terminus of the first railroad in Canada, which was run from LAPRAIRIE in 1836.

ST-JEAN-D'ACRE. See ACRE.

SAINT-JEAN-D'ANGÉLY (France) Town, in Charente-Maritime department, in the W, on the Boutonne River, 15 mi NNE of Saintes. A commercial center today, this town played an important role in the Wars of Religion of the 16th century. A Protestant stronghold, it was finally taken after a siege by Louis XIII in 1621. The town has a 15th-century clock tower and a Renaissance fountain.

SAINT-JEAN-DE-LUZ (France) Resort town, in Pyrénées-Atlantiques department, in the SW, on the Bay of Biscay. Near the Spanish border, it was a prosperous commercial center in the Middle Ages and an important fishing and trading port from the 14th to 17th centuries. Its Basque fishermen were the first to exploit the NEWFOUNDLAND codfish banks, in 1520. In 1660 Louis XIV married Maria Theresa of Austria in this town. There is a 16th-century Basque church here. See BASQUES PROVINCES.

SAINT-JEAN-DE-MAURIENNE (France) Town, in Savoie department, in the SE, 28 mi SE of Chambéry. The old capital of the Alpine Maurienne valley, this was an ecclesiastical town from the sixth century and is an episcopal see. An Allied conference was held here April 19, 1917. The town has a 15th-century cathedral.

SAINT-JEAN-PIED-DE-PORT [*Basque:* **Dona-**

jouna] (France) Village, in Pyrénées-Atlantiques department, in the SW, on the Nive River, 26 mi SSE of Bayonne. During the Middle Ages this village was the northern terminus of the road to Spain via the RONCEVALLES Pass, 11 miles to the southwest. The village's ramparts and citadel were built by Marshal Vauban. In 1589, after passing to France, it became the capital of French NAVARRE.

SAINT JOHN [*former:* **Parr Town and Carleton**] (Canada) Port city of S NEW BRUNSWICK, at the mouth of the ST. JOHN RIVER, on the Bay of Fundy. Champlain visited the site in 1604, but it was not until between 1631 and 1635 that Fort St. Jean and a trading post were established here by Charles de la Tour. Fought over in the struggle for ACADIA between the British and French, it became a British possession in 1713, and in 1758 Fort Frederick and a permanent colony arose here. Then known as Parr Town, it expanded with the arrival of 4,000 Loyalists fleeing from the American Revolution, who had been rewarded for their loyalty to the British with land grants. In 1785 the village incorporated with nearby Carleton and was named St. John, after the river, becoming the first incorporated city in Canada. Benedict Arnold, in exile from the United States, lived here from 1786 to 1791. A major fire in 1877 nearly destroyed the city, but the courthouse and other important buildings remain.

SAINT JOHN ISLAND (United States) Island of the U.S. VIRGIN ISLANDS, 4 mi E of St. Thomas, 80 mi E of San Juan. Discovered by Columbus on his second voyage in 1493, it was taken by DENMARK in 1684 but was only settled in 1716 by black slaves brought in for sugarcane planting. They revolted in 1773. During the 17th and 18th centuries it was a popular base for pirates. The Virgin Island National Park, covering most of St. John, was established in 1956 and contains prehistoric Carib Indian sites and the remains of Danish colonial sugar plantations. See also ST. CROIX.

SAINT JOHN RIVER (United States, Canada) River, 418 mi long, flowing from N MAINE to NEW BRUNSWICK, and then SE to the Bay of Fundy at ST. JOHN. Discovered by Champlain in 1604, it has been called the Rhine of North America. Forming a 70-mile boundary between New Brunswick and Maine, it was an important route in the 17th and 18th centuries for French, Indian, and English traders who developed posts along the river. See also FREDERICTON.

SAINT JOHN'S (Antigua) Principal city and capital of independent ANTIGUA, in the WEST INDIES, 285 mi ESE of San Juan, Puerto Rico. A commercial center at the head of a harbor, St. John's today thrives on tourism. In the 18th century, however, it was the headquarters for the British Royal Navy in the WEST INDIES and is still flanked by old fortifications, such as Fort James and Goat Hill Fort, and has a magnificent 17th- and 18th-century cathedral.

SAINT JOHN'S (Canada) City and provincial capital, in SE NEWFOUNDLAND, on the NE coast of the Avalon peninsula. It is one of the oldest settlements in North America: John Cabot entered the harbor in 1497 and by the early 16th century fishermen from DEVON had begun to settle here. It was an important fishing fleet anchorage, and in 1583 Sir Humphrey Gilbert took it for ENGLAND. Changing hands between the French and British, it was made a permanent British possession in 1762, becoming an important British naval base in the American Revolution and the War of 1812. Closer to Europe than any other North American city, it was here that Marconi's first transatlantic message was heard in 1901. The first nonstop transatlantic flight left here in 1919. Newfoundland was made a province in 1946, and St. John's was made the capital.

SAINT JOHNS. See SAINT JEAN.

ST. JOHNSTOWN. See PERTH.

SAINT JOSEPH (United States) City and seat of Berrien county, in SW MICHIGAN on LAKE MICHIGAN, at mouth of the St. Joseph River, 49 mi WSW of Kalamazoo. It was first visited by Europeans c.1670 when Jacques Marquette and Robert Cavalier de la Salle came through the region. It has been the site of Indian villages prior to 1830, of a Jesuit mission, of Fort Miami, a French army and trading post built by La Salle in 1679, and of a later fur-trading post.

SAINT JOSEPH (United States) City and seat of Buchanan county, in NW MISSOURI, on the MISSOURI RIVER, 50 mi NNW of Kansas City. Known as "St. Joe," this city was laid out in 1843 after the Indians sold lands here that they had considered sacred. It was the site of a trading post founded by French fur trader Joseph Robidoux in 1826. It was involved in the long wars of gang raids and border conflicts before the Civil War. Made the eastern terminus of the Pony Express in 1860, it still has Pony Express stables and the house where Jesse James was killed in 1882.

ST. JUAN DE PORTO RICO. See PUERTO RICO, COMMONWEALTH OF.

SAINT JUST [Saint Just-in-Penwith] (England) Town in CORNWALL, 7 mi W of Penzance. In addition to the Ding Dong mine, one of the oldest in England, there is a 15th-century church with one of the earliest pre-Christian tombs in England. The St. Just Round, an outdoor amphitheater here, saw miracle plays produced in the Middle Ages.

SAINT JUST-IN-PENWITH. See SAINT JUST.

SAINT KITTS-NEVIS [Saint Christopher] Island state in the Leeward Islands of the WEST INDIES, W of Antigua. The state consists of the islands of St. Kitts, or St. Christopher, Nevis, ANGUILLA, and smaller Sombrero. Columbus discovered the islands in 1493 and named one St. Christopher for his patron saint. When English settlers first arrived in 1623 they shortened the name to St. Kitts. This was the first successful English colony in the West Indies. The French came two years later, and in 1628 the British settled Nevis.

The Treaty of Paris of 1783 gave the islands to Great Britain. From 1871 to 1956 they were part of the colony of the Leeward Islands. From 1958 to 1962 they joined the short-lived Federation of the West Indies, and in 1967, together with Anguilla, they became a self-

governing state, associated with Great Britain. Anguilla withdrew in the same year, but has returned. Alexander Hamilton, the first U. S. secretary of the Treasury, was born on Nevis in 1755. Basseterre on St. Kitts, founded in 1627, is the capital.

SAINT-LAURENT-SUR-MER (France) Town on the Bay of the SEINE RIVER, 8 mi NW of Bayeux, in Calvados department. It was a U.S. beachhead on June 6, 1944 during the invasion of NORMANDY in World War II. It was served by a large artificial harbor, towed from England, which was greatly damaged by a severe gale two weeks later.

SAINT LAWRENCE ISLAND (United States) Island, 90 mi long, off W ALASKA, in the BERING SEA, 150 mi S of the Bering Strait. It was discovered by Vitus Bering on St. Lawrence's Day, 1728. It is inhabited by an isolated Eskimo society of great interest to anthropologists and archaeologists, who have been able to study over 2,000 years of Eskimo culture on the island.

SAINT LAWRENCE RIVER (Canada, United States) River, approx, 750 mi long. The outlet of the Great Lakes, it begins at the NE end of LAKE ONTARIO and flows NE to the Gulf of St. Lawrence. For part of its course it forms the U. S.-Canada border. One of the most important rivers of North America, the St. Lawrence played a leading role in the exploration of the continent and, later, in its commercial life. Its valley was a major battlefield in the British-French struggle for control of a large part of North America, which did not end until 1763.

The river was discovered in 1534 by Jacques Cartier, who claimed possession of the region for FRANCE. Its discovery led to speculation that Cartier had found the fabled NORTHWEST PASSAGE, a shortcut from the Atlantic to the Orient around the Americas. On a second voyage in 1535/36, Cartier went up the river to the vicinity of present QUEBEC, then on to Hochelaga, an Indian village on the site of present MONTREAL. On his third voyage of 1541/42, he reached the LACHINE Rapids. Many other French fur traders, missionaries, and explorers used the river, usually starting at Montreal. The French and British fought and besieged each other along the river and later, during the American Revolution, the American colonists tried to detach Canada from Great Britain by taking Quebec and Montreal and thus controlling the waterway.

Since 1825, when the first Lachine Canal was opened to get around the Lachine Rapids near Montreal, work has been undertaken to make the river more easily navigable and capable of carrying larger ships. Such work culminated in the St. Lawrence Seaway, a joint project of the United States and Canada, which was completed in 1959 and makes it possible for ocean-going vessels to sail from the north of the St. Lawrence to LAKE SUPERIOR.

SAINT LAWRENCE SEAWAY. See ST. LAWRENCE RIVER.

SAINT-LÔ [ancient: **Briovera, Laudus**] (France) Town of NORMANDY, capital of Manche department, in NW France, 34 mi W of Caen. A town as far back as

Broadway in St. Louis in 1858, lined with the covered wagons of pioneers. St. Louis in this period was truly "The Gateway to the West."

Gallo-Roman times, St.-Lô has always been a communications hub. It was fortified by Charlemagne, Frankish emperor from 800 to 814, pillaged by Norsemen in 889, captured by Geoffrey Plantagenet, count of ANJOU, in 1141, and by Edward III of ENGLAND in 1346. In the 16th century a massacre of French Protestant Huguenots took place here during the Wars of Religion.

After the Normandy landings in June 1944 in World War II, the town was a major objective of the Allies. It was attacked by U.S. troops on July 7 and taken on the 18th, after it was heavily bombed. This broke one end of the German line and enabled the Allies to begin their advance across France.

SAINT-LOUIS (Senegal) City and port in NW Senegal, West Africa, on an island in the SENEGAL RIVER. In 1638 the French established a post at the mouth of the river and in 1659 founded Saint-Louis on the island. It is the oldest French colonial settlement in Africa and was prosperous in slave-trading days. The British held Saint-Louis from 1758 to 1759, during the Seven Years War, and from 1809 to 1815 during the Napoleonic Wars. When Senegal became a French colony in 1895, Saint-Louis became its capital until 1902, when Senegal was made part of FRENCH WEST AFRICA.

SAINT LOUIS (United States) City in E MISSOURI, on the MISSISSIPPI RIVER, approx. 10 mi S of where the MISSOURI RIVER flows into the Mississippi. It is one of the great river ports of the country and the largest city in the state. In the mid-19th century it was the gateway through which thousands of settlers from the east and from Europe passed on their way west. The city was established in 1764 by the French pioneer Pierre Laclède, whose firm held a monopoly on fur trading in a large region. It was named after Saint Louis (King Louis IX). The small town was part of the area that France ceded to Spain in 1770 and that Spain secretly retroceded to France in 1800. In 1803 St. Louis became part of the LOUISIANA PURCHASE when the United States acquired the whole vast territory.

French influence was then still strong, but it dwindled after the War of 1812 as St. Louis became the supply point for settlers and traders moving west. Although there was southern sentiment in Missouri in the Civil War, the city was strongly Unionist. St. Louis benefited as the railroads spread over the trans-Mississippi region; the first bridge over the river was built in 1874. In the 20th century St. Louis has remained a leading transportation, commercial, and banking center but had lost its role as a rail center by the early 20th century. In recent years it has suffered more from urban decay than some other cities but has taken steps to restore the economy and prestige of its urban core. These include the establishment of the Jefferson National Expansion Memorial National Historic Site, which features the stainless steel Gateway Arch, 630 feet high, symbolizing St. Louis's place in U.S. history.

SAINT LUCIA Island nation, second largest of the Windward Islands, in the WEST INDIES between Martinique and St. Vincent. It was probably discovered by Columbus in 1502. In the early 17th century the English tried to colonize it, but the Carib Indians beat them off. The French settled here in 1650 and 10 years later made a treaty with the Caribs. The French and British fought over St. Lucia until the early 19th century; it became permanently British in 1803. During World War II Great Britain leased a naval base here to the United States.

From 1958 to 1962 the island was part of the Federation of the West Indies, and in 1967 it became one of the six Associated States of the West Indies with internal self-government. St. Lucia became independent, and a member of the COMMONWEALTH OF NATIONS, in 1979. French culture remains strong. The population, mostly of black African descent, speak a French patois. Castries is the capital.

SAINT-MAIXENT-L'ECOLE (France) Town in Deux-Sèvres department, NE of Niort, in the W. The old abbey church here was reconstructed in the 17th century, having been destroyed by Protestant Huguenots in 1568 during the Wars of Religion. The abbey dates back to the 12th century.

SAINT-MALO (France) Town of BRITTANY, on the ENGLISH CHANNEL, 40 mi NNW of Rennes. In the sixth century Welsh monks built a monastery nearby, and in the ninth century refugees from Saint-Servan, also nearby, fled to the site to escape Norman raiders. St.-Malo became part of France in 1491. It was a prosperous port in the 15th century and in the 17th and 18th centuries it benefited from numerous navigators, traders, and privateers who used its port in spite of English efforts to get rid of the pirates.

In World War II German troops, who held the city as a stronghold, burned it before retreating in August 1944 in the face of the Allied advance. Old ramparts and 17th-century architecture make St.-Malo interesting. Jacques Cartier (1491–1557), discoverer of the ST. LAWRENCE RIVER, and François René de Chateaubriand (1768–1848), the author, were born here.

SAINT MARTIN [*Dutch:* **Sint Maarten**] Island of the Leeward Islands, in the WEST INDIES, E of Puerto Rico. It received its name from Columbus, who discovered it on St. Martin's day in 1493. The Dutch and the French both occupied it in the 1640's, and it has been equitably divided between them ever since. The Dutch part, slightly smaller but more valuable, takes up the southern section of the island and belongs to the NETHERLANDS ANTILLES. The French part in the north is associated governmentally with GUADELOUPE. Marigot is the capital of the French area and Philipsburg the chief town of the Dutch section. With a climate and scenery that attracts many tourists, the island produces cotton, sugar cane, and tropical fruits.

SAINT MARTINVILLE (United States) Town in S LOUISIANA, 45 mi SW of Baton Rouge. It was settled *c.*1760. Beginning in 1755, after the British expelled the French Acadian settlers from NOVA SCOTIA and other parts of eastern Canada, St. Martinville became the best known of the regions along the Atlantic Ocean and Gulf of Mexico coastal areas to which they were exiled.

The Acadians in the south became known as Cajuns, and still retain their own customs.

The Evangeline Oak here marks the supposed meeting place of the two Acadian lovers who were the models for the hero and heroine of the well-known poem, *Evangeline*, by Henry Wadsworth Longfellow, published in 1847. See also ACADIA.

SAINT MARYS (United States) City on the Kansas River, 24 mi SW of Topeka, in NE KANSAS. One of the earliest towns in Kansas, it was the site of a Catholic mission that was established here in 1847/48 to work with the Potawatomi Indians.

SAINT MARY'S CITY (United States) Village of St. Mary's county, in S MARYLAND, on the St. Mary's River, 14 mi ESE of Leonardtown. English colonists under Leonard Calvert arrived here in the ships *Ark* and *Cove* in 1634 and purchased the village from the Piscataway Indians. They renamed it and built Fort St. George. It was the first town in Maryland. In 1635 the first state assembly met here. The village served as provincial capital until ANNAPOLIS replaced it in 1694, marking the beginning of its decline. It was restored for a tercentenary celebration in 1934.

SAINT MARY'S ISLAND. See SCILLY ISLANDS.

SAINT MATHIAS ISLANDS. See EMIRAU.

SAINT-MAUR-DES-FOSSÉS (France) City of Val-de-Marne department, on the MARNE RIVER, a suburb SE of PARIS. It is famous for the treaty signed by Louis XI with the members of the League of the Public Weal here in 1465. The 12th- to 14th-century church of St. Nicholas contains a statue of Our Lady of Miracles, long an object of pilgrimage.

SAINT-MAURICE [*former:* **Petit Charenton**] (France) Town of Seine department, just SE of PARIS, on the right bank of the MARNE RIVER. A Protestant stronghold from 1606 to 1685, it is also known for the large insane asylum here known as Charenton. One of its most famous inmates was the Marquis de Sade.

SAINT-MAURICE [*Celtic:* **Agaunum**] (Switzerland) Town of VALAIS canton in the SW, on the RHÔNE RIVER, 17 mi W of Sion. Renamed after the fourth-century martyr, Saint-Maurice, it is distinguished for its Augustinian abbey, the oldest convent in Switzerland, founded in 515 AD. Its 17th-century church was built on the site of a fourth-century one.

SAINT-MAXIMIN-LA-SAINTE-BAUME (France) Town of Var department, in the Lower Provence Alps, 23 mi N of Toulon. It is named for the grotto of Sainte-Baume, 9 mi SSE in the Sainte-Baume Range, where Ste. Madeleine lived in penitence. The town itself contains the 13th- to 16th-century provençal Gothic church, where Ste. Madeleine is buried, and 14th- to 15th-century buildings that once housed a famous Dominican monastery.

SAINT MICHAEL (United States) Village in W ALASKA, on St. Michael Island, off the SE shore of Norton Sound, 110 mi NE of the mouth of the Yukon River, SW of Unalakleet. Strategically located as a supply center for the YUKON, it was established in 1831 as a trading post of the Russian America Company.

SAINT MICHAEL'S MOUNT (England) Small rocky island in CORNWALL, 3 mi E of Penzance, connected to the mainland at Marazion at low tide. By tradition a fisherman saw a vision of St. Michael here in 495 AD, and a priory was built on the site. The present St. Aubyn's Castle stands on the site of the priory. In 1047 the island became a monastic fortress, traditionally given to MONT-SAINT-MICHEL in Normandy, France by King Edward the Confessor of England. Rebuilt in the 12th century, it was returned to England by Henry V and thereafter figured in a number of rebellions against the crown. In 1660 it was sold to the St. Aubyn family. The National Trust inherited it in 1954. The 12th-century refectory and the 15th- to 17th-century additions remain a tourist attraction.

SAINT-MIHIEL (France) Town of Meuse department, in LORRAINE, on the MEUSE RIVER, 9 mi W of Commercy. It developed around a Benedictine abbey founded in 709 AD. It is famous for the battle, late in World War I, of Sept. 12 to 14, 1918, when U.S. forces under Gen. Pershing, in their first major battle, brilliantly captured the town from the Germans, who had held it since 1914.

SAINT MORITZ [*German:* **Sankt Moritz;** *Romansh:* **San Murezzan**] (Switzerland) Town of Grisons canton in the SE, in the Upper Engadine, on the Inn River, 28 mi SSE of Chur. A popular winter-sports and year-round resort with mineral springs, it has been known since the 15th century. In 1928 and 1948 the Olympic winter games were held here. Of interest is the leaning tower of a Romanesque church in St. Moritz-Dorf.

SAINT-NAZAIRE [*ancient:* **Carbilo**] (France) Major port at the base of Brittany, on the LOIRE RIVER estuary and the BAY OF BISCAY, approx. 30 mi WNW of Nantes. It is thought to lie on the site of the ancient Gallo-Roman settlement of Carbilo, where Julius Caesar built a fleet in 56 BC before invading Britain. In the late Middle Ages it belonged to the dukes of BRITTANY.

During World War II it was a German submarine base from 1940 to 1944 and in 1942 was the object of a strong commando raid by the British. Nearly destroyed by Allied bombing, it was isolated by the advancing Allies by August 1944 but did not fall until the following May. Rebuilt, St.-Nazaire today is a metallurgical and shipbuilding center and channels a heavy export trade to Latin America.

SAINT NEOTS (England) Town in Cambridgeshire, on the Ouse River, approx. 50 mi N of London. Saint Neot, reputed brother or other relative of King Alfred, founded the abbey for which the town is named. It was long an agricultural market with iron foundries and paper mills. The first modern papermaking machine was invented here in 1799. In addition to the abbey, there is a 15th-century church and a 14th-century bridge.

SAINT NICHOLAS POINT. See PUDJUT POINT.

SAINT-OMER (France) City of Pas-de-Calais department, in FLANDERS, on the Aa River, 22 mi SE of Calais. It developed around a seventh-century monastery founded by St. Omer, bishop of Thérouanne, whose tomb is now enclosed within the basilica of Notre Dame. During the ninth century the Flemish built a fort and walled settlement here. During the later Middle Ages, with its abbey of St. Bertin, now in ruins, it was a famous center of learning and also of the Flemish wool trade with ENGLAND. It did not become part of France until 1677, when Louis XIV annexed it after a long history of sieges. During World War I it was one of the principal headquarters of the British army, and it was heavily bombed and shelled in both world wars.

SAINTONGE (France) Historic province of W France, on the BAY OF BISCAY, now part of Charente-Maritime department, with its capital at SAINTES. The area was inhabited by the Gallic Santones before coming under ROME. It was occupied by the barbarian Visigoths in 419 and was taken by Clovis I, the Merovingian Frankish king, in 507.

In 1154 it became part of ENGLAND along with AQUITAINE after the marriage of Eleanor of Aquitaine to Henry of Anjou, later Henry II of England. Reconquered by the French in 1371, it was joined to France in 1375, and during the Wars of Religion of 1562 to 1598 it was a Protestant stronghold, especially its city of LA ROCHELLE. Thereafter it was a province of France until the French Revolution.

SAINT OSYTH (England) Village in Essex, 4 mi W of Clacton-on-Sea. East Saxon Queen Osyth was murdered here by the Danes *c.*870 AD in what is now the 12th-century St. Osyth's Priory.

SAINT-OUEN (France) City of Seine department, suburb N of PARIS, on the SEINE RIVER, 4 mi from Notre Dame Cathedral. It was formerly the site of a castle where Louis XVIII signed the Declaration of Saint-Ouen in 1814, near the end of the Napoleonic Wars, declaring himself a constitutional monarch. A villa from the Merovingian period remains.

SAINT PANCRAS (England) Former borough in LONDON, N of the THAMES RIVER, 2 mi N of Charing Cross. The area was centered on an early medieval church, rebuilt in 1848, named for a fourth-century Roman boy martyr popular in medieval England. Now incorporated with HAMPSTEAD and Holborn into the Inner London borough of CAMDEN, NW. Euston, King's Cross, and St. Pancras were its three famous train stations.

SAINT PATRICK'S PURGATORY (Irish Republic) Pilgrimage site on Station Island, in Lough Derg county, Donegal. It is a desolate area long thought to be where St. Patrick had his vision of Purgatory. Although this legend is disputed by modern scholars, it has been a pilgrimage site since the Middle Ages. The site, a narrow cave thought to be the entrance to Purgatory, is the subject of a 12th-century English poem, *Saint Patrick's Purgatory,* about a knight who entered the cave, experienced many adventures and sufferings, and reemerged purer and wiser. The poem is a noted offshoot of the Irish *imram,* or fantastic journey story.

SAINT PAUL [*former:* **Pig's Eye**] (United States) City in E MINNESOTA, on the MISSISSIPPI RIVER, across the river from MINNEAPOLIS, with which it forms the Twin Cities. In the early 19th century a fur-trading post was established at Mendota, approximately 6 miles southwest of the present city. In 1805 Lt. Zebulon Pike obtained this region from the Sioux Indians, and Fort Snelling was soon built, where a pioneer named Pierre Pig's Eye Parrant had first settled in 1838. It took its name from St. Paul Church, which had been established in 1841 by a French priest, Lucian Galtier.

St. Paul became the territorial capital in 1849, and it was named the state capital when Minnesota was admitted to the Union in 1858. The city profited as a transportation center when the railroad arrived in 1862. Beginning in 1878 James J. Hill started to build his railroad empire, which gave St. Paul a connection with Canada and, later, with the Pacific Coast. The city remains a busy transportation and commercial center.

SAINT-PAULIEN [*ancient:* **Revessco**] (France) Village of Haute-Loire department, in the Monts du Velay, 7 mi NNW of Le Puy. Once the ancient capital of a Gallic tribe, the Vellaves, it was also the seat of the bishops of Velay until the sixth century. It is known today for its lacemaking and brickworks.

SAINT PAUL'S BAY (Malta) Village in the NE, on St. Paul's Bay. St. Paul is believed to have been shipwrecked here. The 16th-century church of St. Paul was bombed in World War II. The Wignacourt Tower of 1610 was one of the fortifications on the bay. There is a megalithic temple near the village.

SAINT PETERSBURG. See LENINGRAD.

SAINT-PIERRE (France) Town, on the island of MARTINIQUE, in the WEST INDIES, 11 mi NW of Fort-de-France. Established by French settlers under Esnambuc in 1635, it was a thriving center of commercial activity until it was buried under the volcanic eruption of Mount Pelée in 1902, leaving one survivor out of 28,000 people. The ruins are visited by tourists today.

SAINT PIERRE AND MIQUELON [*French:* **Saint-Pierre-et-Miquelon**] (France) A French overseas territory, an archipelago of nine islands off Newfoundland to the S, of which Saint Pierre and Miquelon are the largest. Believed to have been first settled by Basque fishermen because of its proximity to the GRAND BANKS, it is still primarily a fishing area. Colonized by France in 1604, the territory was taken several times by the British before it was restored to France through the Treaty of Paris in 1814. Bootlegging was a profitable activity here during the U.S. Prohibition era of the 1920's and 1930's. The islands were granted local autonomy in 1935.

SAINT-PIERRE-ET-MIQUELON. See SAINT PIERRE AND MIQUELON.

SAINT-PIERRE-LE-MOÛTIER (France) Village of Nièvre department, 14 mi S of Nevers. Fortified in the Middle Ages and the site of a 12th-century church, the village was captured from the English by Joan of Arc in the 15th century.

SAINT-QUENTIN [*ancient:* **Augusta Viroman-**

duorum] (France) City of Aisne department, in the N, on the SOMME RIVER, 80 mi NE of Paris. Of Roman origin, the town was later renamed for one of the third-century martyrs buried here. It was chartered in 1080 and made the capital of VERMANDOIS in the Middle Ages, becoming part of the royal French domain in 1191. It was famous throughout the Middle Ages for its art and literature, as well as for its flourishing wool industry.

The city was the scene of numerous military actions through history, particularly a battle with Spain in 1557 during the Wars of Religion, two important battles in 1870 and 1871 during the Franco-Prussian War, and the British breakthrough of the German lines here in September/October 1918, during World War I, which was so decisive that an armistice was soon sought by Germany. Saint-Quentin's Gothic church dates from the 13th to 15th centuries, and the town hall is from the 16th century. The city was the birthplace of the pastel artist Maurice Quentin de la Tour.

SAINT RADEGUND [**Sankt Radegund**] (Austria) Village, in Upper Austria, in Innviertel, approx. 30 mi N of Salzburg, near Braunau-am-Inn. It was founded *c.*1370 under the patronage of Duke Stephen the Elder of Bavaria. A Cistercian monastery was built here in 1420. In 1943 it witnessed the defiance of Franz Jägerstätter, a villager who refused to be drafted into the German army under the Nazis and was executed in Berlin later that year. There is a memorial in the village to Jägerstätter.

SAINT-RAPHAËL (France) Town of Var department, in the SE, on the French RIVIERA, 18 mi SW of Cannes. A fashionable resort today, it has a port built by the Romans. It was Napoleon's landing point on his return from EGYPT in 1799. The town was the scene of heavy fighting during the Allied invasion of southern France in August 1944.

SAINT REGIS RESERVATION (Canada, United States) Indian settlement on both sides of the U.S.-Canadian border, partly in QUEBEC and partly in NEW YORK State, on the ST. LAWRENCE RIVER. Established *c.*1755 by Catholic Iroquois Indians from Caughnawaga, Quebec, it was named after the French priest, St. John Francis Regis (1597–1640), who was canonized in 1735.

SAINT-RÉMY [**Saint-Rémy-de-Provence**] (France) Town of the Bouches du Rhône department, in the SE, 12 mi NE of Arles. Nearby are the excavated ruins of a complete, small Hellenistic-Roman town, founded originally as a colony of Greek MARSEILLES. The town has the remains of two first century AD monuments of Roman Glanum, part of a city gate, and a tall memorial to two grandsons of the emperor Augustus, both adorned with fine sculpture in relief.

SAINT-RÉMY-DE-PROVENCE. See SAINT-RÉMY.

SAINT-SAUVEUR-LE-VICOMTE (France) Village of Manche department, in the NW, 18 mi SSE of Cherbourg. An old Norman town, once in the possession of Sir John Chandos of ENGLAND, its 12th-century castle was damaged by U.S. troops driving across the

COTENTIN PENINSULA in June 1944 in the invasion of NORMANDY during World War II.

SAINT-SERVAN. See SAINT-MALO.

SAINT SIMONS ISLAND (United States) One of the SEA ISLANDS, in Glynn county, SE GEORGIA, off the coast, 13 mi long. Although a resort island today, it was the scene of much early American history. The ruins of FORT FREDERICA, built for the defense of the Georgia colony by Gen. James Oglethorpe between 1736 and 1754, still remain. Nearby is the site of the Battle of Bloody Marsh in June 1742, a British victory over SPAIN, which settled British claims over much of the present southeastern United States.

SAINT STEPHEN (Canada) Town of SW NEW BRUNSWICK, on the San Croix River, opposite Calais, Maine. The two towns, connected by an international bridge, form a single community. Founded by United Empire Loyalists after the American Revolution, it is now known for its manufacturing and cotton milling.

SAINT STEPHENS (United States) Hamlet in Washington county, SW ALABAMA, on the Tombigbee River, 60 mi N of Mobile. In 1818 the first territorial legislature of Alabama met at this settlement, which included a Spanish fort built in 1789 and a trading post of 1803.

SAINT THOMAS (United States) Island, 32 sq mi, the second-largest of the U.S. VIRGIN ISLANDS in the WEST INDIES, 40 mi E of Puerto Rico, 2 mi W of ST. JOHN Island. Originally inhabited by Caribs and Arawaks, it was discovered and named by Columbus in 1493 on his second voyage. Attempts at colonization by the Dutch in 1657 and the Danes in 1666 were met with hostile resisistance until 1672, when the Danes were able to settle permanently at St. Thomas Harbor, one of the best anchorages in the West Indies. Held by the British from 1801 to 1802 and from 1807 to 1815, it became a U.S. possession in 1917. Slavery was abolished on the island in 1848. CHARLOTTE AMALIE is capital of the island and of the U.S. Virgin Islands.

SAINT THOMAS'S MOUNT. See MADRAS.

SAINT THOMÉ. See MADRAS.

SAINT-TROND. See SINT-TRUIDEN.

SAINT-TROPEZ (France) Town in SE France, 37 mi ENE of Toulon, on the Mediterranean Sea and part of the RIVIERA, a narrow coastal strip in France and Italy between the sea and the Alps that is noted for its mild climate and natural beauty. The town is both a fishing port and a popular resort. The region became a favorite playground for the rich and the "smart set" beginning in the 1920's. Expatriate Americans favored the Riviera, and it is the setting of F. Scott Fitzgerald's novel *Tender Is the Night*. During World War II it was heavily damaged during Allied landings in August 1944. Saint-Tropez became noted for the brevity of the beachwear worn here.

SAINT UBES. See SETUBAL.

SAINT-VAAST-LA-HOGUE (France) Town of Manche department, in the NW, on the COTENTIN PENINSULA, 16 mi ESE of Cherbourg. Fort La Hogue,

slightly to the south, was built by Vauban in the 17th century on what was then an island; and nearby Tatihou Island was also fortified. In the Battle of LA HOGUE here the French fleet under Tourville was defeated by the English and the Dutch in 1692.

SAINT-VALÉRY-SUR-SOMME (France) Part of Somme department, in the N, on the SOMME RIVER, 11 mi NW of Abbeville. William the Conqueror left from here in 1066 on his second and successful attempt to cross the English Channel and invade England. The upper town still contains medieval fortifications and the ruins of a 13th-century abbey.

SAINT VINCENT AND THE GRENADINES Island nation in the WEST INDIES, in the Windward Islands, including the island of St. Vincent and the small Grenadine Islands to the N. The capital is KINGSTOWN. After Columbus discovered the island in 1498, European efforts at colonization were met with fierce resistance from the native Carib Indians. The island was not settled until 1762 by the British. Captured by the French in 1779, it was returned to Great Britain in 1783. The British finally deported most of the Caribs to ROATÁN ISLAND off Honduras in 1797 and into the 19th century introduced Portuguese, East Indian, and black African slave labor to work the plantations.

Volcanic eruptions by Mt. Soufrière in 1902, and again in 1979, destroyed much of the economy. Part of the West Indies Federation from 1958 to 1962, the islands have formed a self-governing state under Great Britain since 1969 and gained independence in 1979.

SAINT VINCENT, CAPE [*ancient:* **Promontorium Sacrum;** *Portuguese:* **Cabo de São Vincente**] (Portugal) Promontory in the extreme SW of Portugal, considered by ancient geographers to be the westernmost point of Europe. It was the scene of several sea battles, particularly the victory of the British under Adm. Sir John Jervis on Feb. 14, 1797 over the Spanish under Don José de Córdoba. The Spanish were on their way to join the French for an invasion of GREAT BRITAIN. As a young commodore, Horatio Nelson, victor of TRAFALGAR, took part in the battle.

The cape is also associated with the Portuguese patron of exploration, Prince Henry the Navigator, whose center of navigation research lay nearby at SAGRES. Today a lighthouse rises above the ruins of a 16th-century monastery on the promontory.

SAINT-VITH [*German:* **Sankt Vith**] (Belgium) Town of Liège province, in the Malmédy district, near the border of West Germany, 35 mi SE of Liège. Formerly German, it was awarded to Belgium in 1919 and became an important road and railroad junction in World War II. Captured by the Germans in the Battle of the Bulge in December 1944, it was retaken by U.S. forces in January 1945.

SAINT YVES. See SETÚBAL.

SAIPAN [*former:* **Saypan**] (United States) Volcanic island, 47 sq mi, in the W Pacific in the MARIANA ISLANDS, part of U.S. Trust Territory of the Pacific Islands. Under Spanish possession from 1565 to 1899 and German from 1899 to 1914, it was mandated to

JAPAN with the other Marianas in 1920 by the League of Nations. An important Japanese air base in World War II, it was captured in 1944 by U.S. forces and was used as a base for attacking the Japanese mainland. Taiwanese guerrillas used the island for a training base from 1953 to 1962.

SAÏS (Egypt) Ancient city and capital of Lower Egypt, in the W central region of the NILE RIVER delta, 55 mi SE of Alexandria. It was a royal residence of the kings of the 26th dynasty, who ruled from 663 to 525 BC when a Persian invasion under Cambyses ended their reign. It was a center of the worship of Neith and Osiris, two Egyptian gods important during this dynasty. The latter became a major deity in the Roman world.

SAISHU TO. See CHEJU.

SAKAI (Japan) City of Ōsaka prefecture, S HONSHŪ, on Ōsaka Bay, at the mouth of the Yamato River, 6 mi S of Ōsaka. it was an important port in antiquity and during the 15th to 17th centuries, when it carried on trade with China and Portugal. The city declined after 1635 when its harbor silted up, preventing the entry of large vessels. There are a number of massive early tomb mounds in the vicinity, notably that of Emperor Nintoku of the fifth century AD.

SAKALA. See SIALKOT, Pakistan.

SAKARTVELO. See GEORGIAN SOVIET SOCIALIST REPUBLIC.

SAKASTAN. See SEISTAN.

SAKHALIN [*former:* **Saghalien;** *Japanese:* **Karafuto**] (USSR) Island off the coast of the SOVIET FAR EAST, between the Sea of Okhotsk and the Sea of Japan. Under Chinese influence until 17th-century Russian exploration, it was colonized by RUSSIA and JAPAN in the 18th and 19th centuries. It was jointly controlled under the Treaty of SHIMODA in 1855 until 1875, when Japan gave it up for the KURIL ISLANDS. It was originally inhabited by the Ainu, possibly the first inhabitants of Japan. The population became mostly Russian after 1875, and Sakhalin became a czarist place of exile as well as the vital center of the Soviet Far East. The southern part of Sakhalin was ceded to Japan in 1905 after the Russo-Japanese War; the rest was occupied from 1918 to 1924. The Japanese part was returned to the USSR after World War II.

SAKHALYAN. See AIGUN.

SAKHARA. See SAQQARA.

SAKISHIMA ISLANDS (Japan) Group of islands in the S RYUKYU ISLANDS, off the coast of N Taiwan. Several Japanese air bases were situated on the islands in World War II. They were bombed heavily by Allied aircraft between April and June 1945.

SAKKARA. See SAQQARA.

SALACA. See ZALAKA.

SALACIA IMPERATORIA. See ALCÁCER DO SAL.

SALADO, RIO (Spain) River in Cádiz province in the S, near TARIFA. The Battle of Salado was fought on its banks on Oct. 30, 1340, as Alfonso XI of CASTILE joined forces with PORTUGAL, NAVARRE, and ARAGON to win a major decision for the Christian world against the Moors.

SALAMANCA (Mexico) City of Guanajuato state, 30 mi S of Guanajuato. It was the site of the first battle between the Liberals and Conservatives during the 19th-century War of the Reform in Mexico.

SALAMANCA [*ancient:* **Helmantica, Salmantica**] (Spain) Capital city of Salamanca province, in León, on the Tormes River, 110 mi WNW of Madrid; artistically and historically one of the most important cities in Spain. The ancient city was seized from the Romans by Hannibal in 220 BC, later became Roman, was occupied by the Visigoths in the sixth century AD, by the Moors in the eighth century, and by Christians in the 11th. It was famous for its university, founded in the early 13th century by Alfonso IX, which helped introduce Arabic philosophy to western Europe. Salamanca soon became a center of Spanish culture and philosophy. In the late 15th and 16th centuries it was a center of Renaissance Humanist learning. Its printing presses specialized in editions of classical and of Spanish Humanist authors.

The French, who occupied it in 1808, badly damaged it before being defeated here by the British under Wellington in 1812, during the Peninsular campaign. From 1937 to 1938 it served as the Insurgent capital in the Spanish civil war. There is a Roman bridge, an exceptional Renaissance square, the Plaza Major, a 12th-century Gothic cathedral, and the famous university, which has a valuable manuscript library.

SALAMAUA (Papua New Guinea) Town on W Huon Gulf, approx. 19 mi S of Lae, on NEW GUINEA Island. The Japanese captured it on March 8, 1942 and developed it into a military base in World War II. Heavy fighting then took place here before the Allies finally took it on Sept. 11, 1943.

SALAMIS (Cyprus) Ancient city in the E, on Famagusta Bay, 6 mi N of Famagusta. Probably of Mycenaean origin and reputedly founded by Teucer, a Trojan War hero, it was a Greek stronghold and an important harbor for trade with PHOENICIA, EGYPT, and CILICIA. Nearby Enkomi, its predecessor, has important Mycenaean remains. It was the scene of a brilliant naval victory in 306 BC when Demetrius I of the Antigonid house of MACEDON defeated Ptolemy I of Egypt.

Visited in the first century AD by St. Paul and St. Barnabas, a native whose tomb is nearby, it decayed after the Muslim invasion of 647/48. Excavations of the extensive site have unearthed a Greek theater and many other Greek and Roman remains, including spectacular royal tombs of the eighth and seventh centuries BC.

SALAMIS [**Koulouri, Kuluri**] (Greece) Island in the Saronic Gulf, W of Athens. Belonging originally to the nearby island of AEGINA, it passed to ATHENS except when briefly occupied by MEGARA c.600 BC. A promontory on the NE of the island, Cynosura, is famous for the naval battle of September 480 BC, probably fought in the narrow channel between it and Artemisium on the mainland. While the island itself harbored refugees from the evacuated city of Athens, the Greek allied fleet, led by Themistocles, defeated the invading Persians under Xerxes who watched the battle from the shore. When MACEDON replaced Athenian rule, the island was fortified by Cassander in 318 BC, but Athens retook it in 229. A Greek naval base now occupies the island. See also PERSIA, THERMOPYLAE.

SALANG. See PHUKET.

SALARIAN WAY [*ancient and Italian:* **Via Salaria**] (Italy) Ancient Roman road, 150 mi long, running from ROME NE through Reate (RIETI) and Asculum Picenum (ASCOLI PICENO) to the Adriatic Sea coast. Before it became a Roman road it was used by the Sabines to bring their salt from the sea, hence its name, from *sal,* the Latin word for salt.

SALAS DE LOS INFANTES (Spain) City, in Burgos province, in the N, on the Arlanza River, 30 mi SE of Burgos. In 1924 the urns of the much-venerated seven infants of Lara, which were in the Santa Maria Church here, were moved to BURGOS Cathedral. Other historical points of interest include the Siete Salas Palace, two famous monasteries, and an ancient Benedictine convent founded in the sixth century AD and known for its beautiful cloister.

SALDAE. See BEJAÏA.

SALDUBA. See SARAGOSSA.

SALÉ [*Arabic:* **Sla**] (Morocco) City in the NW, on the Atlantic Ocean, at the mouth of the Bou Regreg, opposite RABAT. Founded in the 11th century AD, it was a leading port along Morocco's coast in the Middle Ages. During its period as an independent republic in the 17th century it became a popular base for Barbary pirates, known as Sallee Rovers. It was unsuccessfully attacked by the English and the French. See BARBARY STATES.

SALEM (United States) Manufacturing city, 13 mi NE of Centralia in S central ILLINOIS. It was the birthplace of William Jennings Bryan (1860–1925), the famous orator, revivalist, newspaper editor, U.S. secretary of state, and unsuccessful U.S. presidential candidate in 1896 and 1900. Bryan made his famous *Cross of Gold* speech in Chicago in 1896.

SALEM (United States) City in NE MASSACHUSETTS, on an arm of Massachusetts Bay, 14 mi NE of Boston. It was founded in 1626 by Roger Conant, who had come to PLYMOUTH, Massachusetts from England in 1623, when he led a group from Cape Ann to this location. The Indians called it Naumkeag. Although they were only part of its long history, the witchcraft trials of 1692 have left a blot on Salem's reputation. In that year a group of young girls accused a family slave of witchcraft. When she confessed and accused two other women, a chain reaction began and those accused in turn accused others. A special court was set up, and before the trials were over, 19 persons had been hanged, 14 of them women, and one man pressed to death, while 55 had pleaded guilty. When prominent personages began to be accused, the colonial assembly ended the proceedings and released the prisoners.

During the American Revolution and the War of 1812 Salem was a bustling base for privateers, and in the early 19th century its trade with CHINA made many shipowners and captains wealthy. Salem was the birthplace in 1804 of Nathaniel Hawthorne, the novelist, who held the post of surveyor of the port from 1846 to 1849. The house of his birth, dating from the 17th century, survives, as does the House of Seven Gables of 1668, which he made famous. Here are also Pioneer Village, a reproduction of a 1630 settlement, the 1819 Custom House, and the Salem Maritime National Historic Site.

SALEM (United States) Town of Rockingham county, in SE NEW HAMPSHIRE. Part of HAVERHILL, Massachusetts until 1741, it was settled in 1652 and incorporated in 1750. It is best known for Mystery Hill, the site of prehistoric structures believed to date from as early as 2000 BC and presumably made by an early Indian culture.

SALEM (United States) City and seat of Salem county, in SW NEW JERSEY, on Salem Creek, 3 mi from the DELAWARE RIVER, 16 mi WNW of Bridgeton. Settled in 1641, the site was under Swedish, Dutch, and English control before English Quakers led by John Fenwick founded it in 1675. It became a port of entry for vessels in 1682 and was incorporated as a village in 1695. During the American Revolution it was the scene of much fighting and plundering. The Hancock House, where an American militiaman was murdered by the British, is four miles from Salem.

SALEM (United States) City of Columbiana county, in NE OHIO, 17 mi SW of Youngstown. Settled by Quakers in 1803, it became an early center of the Abolitionist movement and functioned as an important station on the Underground Railroad, which aided the movement and resettlement of slaves escaped from the South.

SALEM [*Indian:* **Chemeketa**] (United States) City of Marion county, and state capital, in NW OREGON, on the WILLAMETTE RIVER, 44 mi SSW of Portland. The second-largest city in the state, it was founded by Methodist missionaries under Jason Lee in 1840/41. The city became the capital of the Oregon territory in 1851 and of the state in 1859.

SALEMI [*ancient:* **Halycyae**] (Italy) Town of Trapani province in W SICILY, 21 mi SE of Trapani. It is known for its olive oil and nearby sandstone deposits. There are also relics of a third- to sixth-century Christian basilica and the ruins of a Norman castle. Garibaldi declared himself dictator of Sicily here on May 14, 1860.

SALERNO [*ancient:* **Irnthi, Salernum**] (Italy) Capital city of Salerno province, Campania region, on the Gulf of Salerno, 29 mi ESE of Naples. Originally a Greek settlement, it became a Roman colony c.195 BC. Its name derives from the Latin word *sal,* for salt, and Irno, its river. It was part of the Lombard duchy of BENEVENTO in the sixth century and the seat of an independent principality in the ninth century before it fell to the Norman Robert Guiscard in 1076. Guiscard enriched the renowned school of medicine here, which was founded by the 10th century and flourishing by the 11th century. It was a major university from the 12th century to 1817. The *Regimen Sanitatis Salernitatum (Salerno Health Diet)* written c.1150 was a major "best-seller" in the Middle Ages. Many of its maxims, such as "After breakfast walk a mile, after dinner rest a while," have survived. The city was destroyed by Emperor Henry VI in 1198. The ninth-century Sicilian-Norman cathedral with its 11th-century bronze doors and 12th-century pulpit contains the tombs of Pope Gregory VII, who died here in flight from Rome in 1085, Margaret of Anjou, and, traditionally, of St. Matthew the Apostle. Concentrated fighting between the Germans and Allies took place over the beaches of Salerno in September 1943 after the Allied landing.

SALERNUM. See SALERNO.

SALFORD (England) Town of Greater Manchester on the Irwell River, 3 mi W of Manchester. A free town from 1230 AD, it was settled c.1360 by Flemish weavers, who made it a leading textile center. Salford included MANCHESTER in the Middle Ages, and its docks serve the Manchester Ship Canal today. Salford also contains the first free municipal library in England. Neolithic tools and traces of Roman habitation have been found in the city.

SALINA (United States) City of Saline county, central KANSAS, on the Smoky Hill River, 75 mi NNW of Wichita. Established by an antislavery group in 1858, it was a trading center for Indians and Fort Riley cavalry. It grew with the coming of the railroad in 1867. There is an important Indian burial pit nearby.

SALINA, Oklahoma. See OKLAHOMA.

SALISBURY [New Sarum] (England) City on the AVON RIVER, 17 mi NW of Southampton, in WILTSHIRE. Successor to OLD SARUM, 1 mi N, and chartered in 1220, the city was laid out in a grid pattern and is a good example of medieval city planning. It grew around its famous 13th-century cathedral, which has the nation's tallest spire, and is one of the best examples of Early English Gothic. It is unique in England for its unified plan and uninterrupted construction. Many building materials used to construct the cathedral were taken from the earlier cathedral in Old Sarum. The city received the bishopric from Old Sarum in 1220. Surviving are the 13th-century Old Deanery and palace of the bishops, St. Thomas's Church, St. Martin's Church, with restored frescoes, several medieval inns and houses, and the Poultry Cross. The inhabitants were finally freed from episcopal rule by James I in 1612. The city was laid out with several canals to link the rivers Avon, Bourne, Nadder, and Wylye and to aid its cloth trade, which prospered from the 15th century. The canals, filled in 1852, gave the city the name "The English Venice." The city figures as "Manchester" in novels by Thomas Hardy, and in Dickens's *Martin Chuzzlewit.* STONEHENGE is ten miles to the north.

SALISBURY (United States) City of W central NORTH CAROLINA, in the Piedmont industrial area, 32 mi SSW of Winston-Salem. Settled in 1751, it was the scene of engagements between British Gen. Cornwallis and the American general Nathanael Greene in 1781, just before the Battle of GUILDFORD COURTHOUSE. This historical city contains 18th- and 19th-century buildings, a courthouse from 1857, a fort from the French and Indian War, and a national cemetery, which is on the site of one of the largest Confederate prison camps in the Civil War; 11,700 Federal soldiers were buried here. Andrew Jackson studied law here from 1784 to 1787.

SALISBURY, Zimbabwe. See HARARE.

SALISBURY PLAIN (England) An open plateau, approx. 300 sq mi, in WILTSHIRE N of SALISBURY. A sheep pasture and the site of military camps, this area is best known for STONEHENGE and other prehistoric megalithic monuments.

SALMANTICA. See SALAMANCA.

SALODURUM. See SOLOTHURN.

SÁLONA. See AMPHISSA.

SALONA [Solim] [*ancient and Byzantine:* **Salonae**] (Yugoslavia) Ancient city of DALMATIA, 3 mi NE of modern SPLIT, its successor. An important Roman colony, founded in 78 BC, and capital of ILLYRICUM in the first century BC, this port on the Adriatic Sea was later the residence of Emperor Diocletian (305–313 AD), whose palace in Spalatum (now Split), 3 miles to the south, was a refuge for inhabitants fleeing the Avar invasion in 639. The extensive ruins of Salona have been partially excavated.

SALONAE. See SALONA.

SALONICA. See THESSALONÍKI.

SALONIKA. See THESSALONÍKI.

SALONIKI. See THESSALONÍKI.

SALOP (England) County, formerly SHROPSHIRE, on the border of Wales. Its admn. hq. is SHREWSBURY.

SALOPSBURY. See SHREWSBURY.

SALSETTE [*Marathi:* **Sashti]** (India) Island, 250 sq mi, in the Arabian Sea, off BOMBAY, now connected to the mainland by causeways and railroad embankments. Occupied by the Portuguese in the 17th century, the island was annexed by the British in 1782. Four miles southeast of BORIVLI are the famous Kanheri Buddhist temples.

SALSK (USSR) Transportation center and town of S Rostov oblast, Russian SFSR. With an eye on the rich oil fields of Caucasia, the Germans captured this town on July 31, 1942, during their campaign from July to November 1942 in World War II. Soviet troops regained it in 1943.

SALTA (Argentina) Capital city of Salta province in the NW, in the Lerma Valley, 140 mi NW of San Miguel de Tucumán. An important commercial center today, Salta was founded in 1582 as a fortress against Indian attacks and became an important colonial town. It still retains its colonial atmosphere, with its ruins of 17th-century buildings, a bishop's palace, and a theater. Gen. Manuel Belgrano decisively defeated Spanish Royalists here in 1813.

SALTCOATS (Scotland) Town in Strathclyde region, on the Firth of CLYDE, 26 mi SW of Glasgow. It is famous for shipbuilding and salt mines. The saltworks here were established by James V of Scotland in the 16th century.

SALTEE ISLANDS (Irish Republic) Islands in St. George's Channel, off Crossfarnoge Point, County Wexford, E of Waterford. Great Saltee Island was the hiding place for leaders of the 1798 insurrection in IRELAND.

SALTILLO (Mexico) Capital city of Coahuila State, in the NE, 430 mi NNW of Mexico City. Still an agricultural and commercial center, Saltillo was famous in the colonial era for its annual fair, where Spanish and Philippine imports were exchanged for Mexican goods. Taken by Gen. Zachary Taylor's army in the Mexican War of 1846 to 1848, it was also briefly occupied by French troops during the French intervention in Mexico in the 1860's.

SALT LAKE CITY [*former:* **Great Salt Lake City**] (United States) State capital and city in N central UTAH, approx. 10 mi E of the southern end of GREAT SALT LAKE. Founded by the Mormons under the leadership of Brigham Young, it was carefully planned to be the hub of Mormon life, both religious and economic. The city was a supply center after 1849 for settlers and prospectors headed for California. During the Utah War of 1857/58 there was considerable hostility toward the Mormons. To keep order an army fort, Camp Floyd, was established nearby; in 1862 Fort Douglas was erected above the city.

In 1870 Salt Lake City was connected with the first transcontinental railroad by way of a line to OGDEN. It is the heart of an irrigated farming area, which also contains minerals. The great temple, built over a period from 1853 to 1893, is world famous. The home of Brigham Young has been restored to its condition in 1877.

SALT SEA. See DEAD SEA.

SALUAFATA (Western Samoa) Harbor on the N coast of UPOLU Island, Western Samoa, in the SW Pacific Ocean. A coaling station for German ships was operated here from 1879, before Western Samoa became a German colony in 1899. More recently, the harbor was a U.S. naval station until the independence of the country in 1962.

SALUCES. See SALUZZO.

SALUCIAE. See SALUZZO.

SALÛM [**As-Sallüm, Sollum**] [*ancient:* **Catabathmus Magna;** *Arabic:* **El Sollum**] (Egypt) Village

Old church in Salvador, once the chief city and capital of colonial Brazil. The many slaves imported here have left a strong African imprint on the modern city.

in the NW, on the Gulf of Salûm, an inlet of the Mediterranean Sea, 275 mi W of Alexandria. An important desert camp during the North African campaigns of World War II, it was taken by ITALY, GREAT BRITAIN, GERMANY, and again by Great Britain.

SALUZZO [*ancient:* **Saluciae;** *French:* **Saluces**] (Italy) Town, in Cuneo province, Piedmont region, in the NW, 18 mi NW of Cuneo. It was capital of the marquisate of Saluzzo from 1175 to 1548, when it passed to France. The town was also an important bishopric. Its Gothic cathedral built between 1481 and 1511 contains the tombs of the marquises. In 1601 it passed to PIEDMONT under the house of SAVOY. A 13th-century castle is among many notable buildings. The astronomer Giovanni Schiaparelli was born here in 1835.

SALVADOR [**São Salvador da Bahia de Todos os Santos**] [*former:* **Bahia, São Salvador**] (Brazil) Capital city of Bahia state in the E, and a commercial port on the Atlantic. Founded in 1549 by Thomé de Sousa of PORTUGAL, Salvador developed as the center of colonial Brazil with the import of black African slaves for the expanding sugar plantations. Capital of the Portuguese colony in Brazil from 1549 to 1763, except when under Dutch occupation in 1624/25, it was replaced by RIO DE JANEIRO in 1763. A bishopric since 1551, it has many buildings and forts from the colonial era, including a 16th-century cathedral and many churches. It was the early 19th-century center for the Brazilian independence movement. The city was damaged in 1912 by federal forces.

SALWEEN [**Salwin**] [*Chinese:* **Nu Chiang;** *Thai:* **Mae Nam Khong;** *Tibetan:* **Chiama Ngu Chu**] (Burma, China, Thailand, Tibet) River in SE Asia, rising in the Tibetan plateau and flowing E through Tibet, then S through China and into Burma, and finally into the Gulf of Martaban at Moulmein in Lower Burma. During World War II fighting took place along its lower course in 1942 and along its banks in Northern Burma in May 1944.

SALWIN. See SALWEEN.

SALZBURG [*ancient:* **Juvavum**] (Austria) City in SW Austria, 71 mi ESE of Munich, West Germany. An old city in a picturesque setting and with many notable buildings, it is today a major music center and a favorite of tourists. The site was long visited as a source of salt, *Salzburg* meaning "salt fort." The Celtic settlement here became the town of Juvavum in the Roman province of NORICUM. A Benedictine abbey was founded late in the seventh century AD, and the city became the seat of an archbishopric in 798. Salzburg was ruled for nearly 1,000 years by these autocratic archbishops, who were made princes of the HOLY ROMAN EMPIRE in 1278. They were among the most prominent ecclesiastics of the German-speaking world, but they were extremely intolerant, expelling the Jews in the 15th century and persecuting Protestants so that thousands of them left in the 18th century.

The Peace of Schönbrunn of 1809, imposed by Napoleon I, allotted Salzburg to BAVARIA, but the Congress of Vienna in 1815 returned it to Austria. Among the

city's historical and architectural treasures are the Benedictine abbey, the 11th century fortress, the former archepiscopal palace, and the modern concert hall. Wolfgang Amadeus Mozart was born in Salzburg in 1756 and twice held concertmaster posts here but received little recognition from his native city in his lifetime. The Salzburg Festival, an annual event featuring both music and drama, was started in 1920, a descendant of festivals that were held irregularly from 1877 on. The Swiss physician and alchemist, Philippus Aureolus Paracelsus, died here in 1541. The original saltworks, a short distance from the city, can still be visited.

SALZKAMMERGUT (Austria) Resort area in the W, in Styria and Salzburg provinces. Renowned for its beautiful lakes and mountains, it has been famous for its salt mines since prehistoric times, although they were forbidden to visitors until the 19th century for fear of salt being smuggled out. SALZBURG is its principal city. Cultural remains from antiquity have been found in some of the outlying towns. See also BAD ISCHL, HALLSTATT, SANKT WOLFGANG.

SALZWEDEL (East Germany) City of Magdeburg district, 55 mi NNW of Magdeburg. Founded in the eighth century, there are remains of a castle thought to have been built by Charlemagne c.780 AD. First mentioned in 1117, it was where Albert the Bear started off in his conquest of BRANDENBURG in 1134. By 1247 it had received a charter, and it joined the HANSEATIC LEAGUE by the mid-13th century. This city is known for its 13th- to 15th-century churches.

SAMAIPATA (Bolivia) Capital town of Florida province in Santa Cruz department, 55 mi SW of Santa Cruz. Founded in 1620, it is important for its oil deposits and the nearby ruins of a pre-Incan civilization.

SAMAKOV. See SAMOKOV.

SAMAR (Philippines) Island of the Visayan Islands in the E Philippines. The first of the VISAYAN ISLANDS to be discovered, in 1521, by Spanish explorers, it was frequently raided by Moro pirates for several centuries. Taken by Japanese forces in 1942 during World War II, it was liberated by U.S. troops late in 1944.

SAMARA. See KUIBYSHEV.

SAMARAI (Papua New Guinea) Commercial township on Samarai Island. It was totally destroyed during World War II by Japanese forces in January 1942.

SAMARANG. See SEMARANG.

SAMARIA [**Sebaste**] [*modern:* **Sabastiyah**] (Jordan) Ancient city of PALESTINE on a hill NW of NABLUS, ancient Shechem, in Israeli-occupied Jordan. Named for Shemer, who owned the land, it was founded in 887 BC by King Omri of Israel and was the southern capital of the northern kingdom of ISRAEL. Influenced by the rich civilization of nearby PHOENICIA, it was reviled in the Bible as corrupt and idolatrous because of the activities of Omri's son, Ahab, and his Phoenician queen, Jezebel. After it fell to Sargon II of ASSYRIA in 721 BC, its inhabitants were deported, giving rise to the legend of the Lost Tribes of Israel. Finally destroyed in 107 BC by John Hyrcanus of the Maccabean dynasty, it was rebuilt by Herod the Great of JUDAEA and named Sebaste.

The purported burial place of St. John the Baptist, it has the remains of a Crusader church. Excavations in the early 20th century uncovered the fortifications and palace of Omri and Ahab, as well as Roman remains. The original city, as a holy place of the Samaritans, was the source of the tale of the Good Samaritan. See also GERIZIM.

SAMARKAND [*ancient:* **Maracanda**] (USSR) Famous ancient city, the oldest in central Asia, now an industrial center and capital of Samarkand oblast in the Uzbek SSR, 180 mi SW of Tashkent. The city, known as Maracanda by the Greeks, arose on the site of Afrosiab, a prehistoric settlement possibly as old as the fourth millennium BC, and became the chief city of SOGDIANA. It was captured by Alexander the Great in 329 BC. Always a meeting point for trade and culture between East and West, it became an important post on the great SILK ROAD between CHINA and the West that had developed by the time of the ROMAN EMPIRE. The Arabs took it in the eighth century AD, and under the ABBASID CALIPHATE in particular it became an important center of Islamic culture in central Asia, mentioned by a traveler *c.*1160 as a prosperous city with 50,000 Jews. Although destroyed by the Mongol Genghis Khan in 1221, it was rebuilt and was again an important city when Marco Polo of VENICE visited it *c.*1270. It reached its apogee of splendor as the capital of Tamerlane after 1370 and was adorned with magnificent parks, mosques, and avenues under Tamerlane and his Timurid successors. Thereafter it withered away, came under the Uzbeks for several centuries after the late 15th century, then under the emirate of BUKHARA, and was finally taken by RUSSIA in 1868. Many fine buildings from the Timurid period remain, including the mausoleum of Tamerlane. Remnants of the ancient Greek settlement may be seen outside the present city. See also MACEDONIAN EMPIRE, MONGOL EMPIRES.

Remnants of Tamerlane's huge mosque of Bibi Khanum in Samarkand, built in 1399 when the world conqueror had just returned from India. It was named for a favorite wife.

SAMARRA (Iraq) Ancient city of N central Iraq, on the TIGRIS RIVER, 65 mi NNW of Baghdad. The city was founded in 836 AD by one of the Abbasid caliphs to replace BAGHDAD as capital, where the court had been at the mercy of Turkish mercenary guards. The caliphs lived in Samarra until 876, when the court was moved back to Baghdad and the city abandoned. The impressive ruins extend for 20 miles along the Tigris River with a great minaret still dominating the center. There is also a 17th-century mosque here with a golden dome, sacred to Shiite muslims. Samarra was also a prehistoric site, and its name is used to describe a type of Neolithic pottery from the fifth millennium BC. See also ABBASID CALIPHATE.

SAMBHAI (India) Town in NW central Uttar Pradesh, 80 mi E of Delhi, in the N. It flourished as a significant Muslim capital in the 15th century. Here are a fort, the tomb of a Muslim saint, and a 16th-century mosque built over the ruins of a Hindu temple.

SAMBODJA (Indonesia) Oil field in East Kalimantan province, near BALIKPAPAN, on the E coast of BORNEO. Occupied by Japan during World War II, it was liberated on July 18, 1945, during a major Australian offensive from May 1 to Aug. 14, 1945, which began at TARAKAN.

SAMBRE RIVER (France, Belgium) Short river rising in the Aisne department in N France and flowing NE to join the MEUSE RIVER at Namur in Belgium. The Sambre is remembered as the site of an important British victory toward the end of World War I, in November 1918.

SAM HOUSTON, FORT. See FORT SAM HOUSTON.

SAMINA. See SEMNĀN.

SAMNAN. See SEMNĀN.

SAMNIUM (Italy) Ancient region of central and S Italy, mostly in the S Apennines, E of CAMPANIA and LATIUM and NW of present APULIA. This ancient country was inhabited by an Italic people who entered Italy along with the Latins and were descended from the Sabines. The Samnites spoke a dialect of Oscan and originally inhabited hilltop forts and unwalled villages in the central Apennines. When their population increased they began to expand westward against the Greek settlements in the fifth century BC. They soon became enemies of the Romans, whose attempts to expand into Samnium led to the Samnite Wars of 343 to 290 BC and their defeat at Sentinum (Sassoferrato) and eventual absorption by ROME in 290 BC. During the war the Romans built the APPIAN WAY (*via Appia*) to replace the LATIN WAY (*via Latina*), which ran too close to Samnium. See also CAUDINE FORKS, SENTINUM, VENOSA.

SAMO. See SLOVENIA.

SAMOA. See AMERICAN SAMOA, WESTERN SAMOA.

SAMOGITIA [*Lithuanian:* **Žemaitija**] (USSR) Historic region now comprising most of modern LITHUANIA, N of the Neman River. Inhabited in the Middle Ages by a Lithuanian tribe known as the Samogitians, it was held by the Teutonic Knights in the 14th century and surrendered to POLAND by the Treaty of Thorn (TORÚN) in 1411. The Teutonic Knights waged a long and brutal war of extermination against the Samogitians, who fought them from their forest settlements. The Knights practiced indiscriminate genocide and torture, destroyed crops and forests, burned down villages, deported peasants or resettled them by force until resistance ended and the area was "converted" to Christianity.

SAMOKOV [Samakov] (Bulgaria) City of Sofia province, on the Isker River, 27 mi SSE of Sofia. A textile and agricultural center today, it is a showpiece of Bulgarian Renaissance architecture with its old churches, monasteries, and other buildings. Stock trading was important here when it was under Turkish rule from the 15th to 19th centuries. See also the OTTOMAN EMPIRE.

SAMOS [Turkish: Susam-Adasi] (Greece) One of the Sporades Islands, in the AEGEAN SEA, near Turkey. Inhabited since the third millennium BC and into the Bronze Age, the island was colonized by Ionian Greeks in the 11th century BC. Under the rule of Polycrates in the sixth century BC, it flourished to become one of the principal commercial and cultural centers of Greece. Residents during that period included the poet Anacreon, the sculptor Rhoecus, and the legendary fabulist, Aesop. It was also the birthplace of Pythagoras and Conon. Conquered by PERSIA toward the end of the sixth century BC, it became independent in 479 BC and joined the Delian League, supporting ATHENS in the Peloponnesian Wars. In 390 BC the island revolted against Athens, which recaptured it in 365 BC and deported the entire population. The Samians resettled the island in 321 BC by permission of Alexander the Great.

The island then passed back and forth among Antigonids of MACEDON, Ptolemies of EGYPT, and PERGAMUM. In 129 BC it was joined to the Roman province of ASIA. It was plundered several times by Roman governors or factions of the first century BC. It was part of the eparchy of the CYCLADES under the BYZANTINE EMPIRE. During much of the later Middle Ages it was held by GENOA until it was conquered by the OTTOMAN EMPIRE in 1475. Before it passed to Greece in 1913, it was a semi-independent principality from 1832. See also IONIA.

SAMOSATA [Samsat] (Syria) Ancient city in N Syria on the EUPHRATES RIVER, 30 mi NNW of Urfa. Originally an important river crossing followed by a frontier fort and caravan station, Samosata became the important capital of the Hellenistic kingdom of COMMAGENE under the Seleucids in the third century BC. Taken by the Romans in 72 AD, it remained relatively important until it was captured by the Arabs in the seventh century. It was the birthplace of Lucien, the satirist, and of Paul of Samosata. This bishop of Antioch was condemned in 268 AD and deposed from his see in 272 for his heresy, which held that Jesus Christ was not God but a man inhabited by God's spirit, the *Logos*. See also SELEUCID EMPIRE.

SAMOTHRACE [ancient: Samothracia; Greek: Samothrake, Samothraki] (Greece) Island in the NE AEGEAN SEA, off the Marifsa River mouth, 28 mi SSW of Alexandroupolis. It is an important island in Greek history and legend, with the highest peak in the Aegean Islands. It was where Poseidon surveyed the plain of TROY in the *Iliad* and was supposedly the home of Dardanus, founder of Troy. In antiquity it was a Pelasgian center of worship of the Cabiri and known for its legendary Cyclopean temple. Its extensive ruins today date back to the sixth century BC. The island was inhabited by Thracian peoples in the Neolithic and Bronze ages. Their religious traditions survived the arrival of the Greeks from LESBOS *c.*700 BC and into the first century BC. Samothrace sent a contingent to the Greek fleet at SALAMIS, but it declined in the fifth century BC, despite the fame of its mystery cult. It was a base for Athens, the Antigonids, Ptolemies, and Seleucids before falling to Rome after the Battle of Pydna in 168 BC.

In 1444 it was taken by GENOA. The island was ceded to Greece in 1913 by the OTTOMAN EMPIRE, which had conquered it in 1456. The famous winged Nike (Victory) statue of Samothrace, erected in 306 BC to commemorate a Greek naval victory at Cyprus over the Egyptians, was discovered here in 1863 and is now in the Louvre Museum in Paris. Samothrace was the first stop in St. Paul's Macedonian itinerary.

SAMOTHRACIA. See SAMOTHRACE.

SAMOTHRAKE. See SAMOTHRACE.

SAMOTHRAKI. See SAMOTHRACE.

SAMSAT. See SAMOSATA.

SAMSON ISLAND. See SCILLY ISLANDS.

SAMSUN [ancient: Amisus] (Turkey) Capital city of Samsun province, one of Turkey's most important ports on the BLACK SEA, 110 mi NNW of Sivas. Founded in the sixth century BC by Greek colonists, it became one of the principal Greek cities of the Black Sea, with nearby SINOPE, and was a major city under the kingdom of PONTUS and the ROMAN EMPIRE, being frequently used as a trade channel to central Asia. In the 16th century it fell to the OTTOMAN EMPIRE after having been held by the BYZANTINE EMPIRE, the Seljuk Turks, GENOA, and the Empire of TREBIZOND. On May 19, 1919 Kemal Atatürk landed here to rally support and supplies for the Turkish nationalist movement.

SAMSUN DAĞI. See MYCALE.

SAMSUN KALE. See PRIENE.

SAMYE [Chinese: Sang-yüan Ssu] (Tibet) Lamasery in the SE, near the Brahmaputra River, 36 mi SE of Lhasa. Famous as the residence of the Tibetan oracle, this large monastery, built in the eighth century AD, is also the oldest of its kind.

SANA [San'a, Sanaa] [former: Azal, Umal] (Yemen) Capital city of the Yemen Arab Republic, connected by road to the RED SEA port of HODEIDA, 40 mi away. It is the largest city on the S ARABIAN PENINSULA, and an important Islamic cultural center. It was founded before the first century AD when the fortress of Ghumdan was erected. Its ancient origins are obscured in legend. A walled city with eight gates and mosques, it fell under Ethiopian control in the sixth century AD, and in the eighth century it was the target of nomad raids.

When Yemen became independent from Turkey in 1918, Sana was made the capital for the imam of Yemen and was named capital of the Yemen Arab Republic in 1962.

SANAA. See SANA.

SANABADH. See MASHHAD.

SANABPUR. See MULTAN.

SAN AGUSTÍN DE LAS CUEVAS. See TLALPÁN.

SAN AGUSTÍN DE TALCA. See TALCA.

SĀN AL-HAJAR AL QIBLIYAH. See TANIS.

SAN ANDRÉS TUXTLA [Tuxtla] (Mexico) Town in Veracruz state, 90 mi SE of Veracruz in the E. Carved relics dating back to the early civilization of the MAYA EMPIRE c.300 to 600 AD have been discovered here.

SAN ANGELO (United States) City in W central TEXAS, 77 mi SSW of Abilene. The city grew up around Fort Concho, built in 1866 and now restored as a museum. In the 1870's San Angelo was a lively frontier town amidst cattle trails and overland traffic. It grew more rapidly after the coming of a railroad in 1888. It is a market center for livestock; in the area are irrigated farms and oil and gas fields.

SAN ANTONIO (Philippines) City in SW Zambales province, LUZON, approx. 65 mi NW of Manila. An area between here and San Narciso was the invasion site of a U.S. military expedition, which landed on Jan. 29, 1945 during World War II.

SAN ANTONIO [*former:* **San Antonio de Béjar**] (United States) City in S central TEXAS, approx. 75 mi SW of Austin. It is the commercial center of a large agricultural area and is in the midst of an unusually large number of military installations, but it retains a decidedly Spanish flavor. Although an Indian village here was long known to the Spanish, there was no settlement until 1718, when Martin de Alarcón founded a presidio, Béjar, and a mission, San Antonio de Valero, later THE ALAMO.

The first civilian community was established in 1731 as San Fernando, and c.1795 the three settlements were combined as San Antonio. Anglo Texans took the town during the Texas Revolution in 1835, but in early 1836 the Mexicans besieged the Anglos in the Alamo, which had become a garrison. It fell, and all of its defenders were killed. The Mexicans briefly held the city in 1842. When the railroad arrived after the Civil War, San Antonio became a rowdy cow town for a while. There is a large Mexican-American population. Remnants of the Spanish period, such as the governor's palace, built c.1750, and the Alamo, survive.

SAN ANTONIO DE BÉJAR. See SAN ANTONIO, United States.

SAN AUGUSTIN DE ISLETA. See ISLETA, New Mexico.

SAN AUGUSTINE (United States) Town, in E TEXAS, 37 mi ENE of Lufkin. It was the site of a Spanish mission dating from 1716 to 1719 and 1721 to 1773, and of a fort from 1756 to 1773 that protected the Spanish-French border. It was settled in 1818 by Anglo-Americans.

SAN BERNARDINO (United States) City, in S CALIFORNIA, in the San Bernardino Valley, 55 mi E of Los Angeles. First explored in 1772, it was named in 1810 by Spanish explorers and planned in 1853 by Mormons, who had arrived in 1851. Today it is well known for its Rim of the World Drive, 5–7,000 feet high in the San Bernardino Mountains. It is surrounded by several large military installations.

SAN BERNARDINO STRAIT (Philippines) Strait between S Sorsogon province of LUZON, and N SAMAR Island. It formed a significant water passageway during World War II. Portions of a Japanese fleet were routed in a naval battle fought here on Oct. 24/25, 1944. Early in 1945 U.S. troops captured several islands in the strait.

SAN BERNARDO DE TARIJA. See TARIJA.

SAN BONIFACIO DE IBAGUÉ. See IBAGUÉ.

SAN BUENAVENTURA. See VENTURA.

SANCHI (India) Village in W Madhya Pradesh, approx. 23 mi NE of Bhopal, in the N. It is the site of some of the earliest and finest monuments of primitive Buddhism, some of the oldest buildings in India. These include a number of stupas, designed to house Buddhist relics, in particular the Great Stupa, whose oldest parts date from the third century BC and the reign of Asoka of the MAURYAN EMPIRE. Others are later, around the turn of the Christian era. They are ornamented with some of the finest sculptural reliefs to be found in India.

SAN CLEMENTE (United States) City in SW CALIFORNIA, SE of Los Angeles. Richard M. Nixon, the 37th U.S. president from 1969 to 1974, maintained the western White House here before he was forced to resign from office on Aug. 9, 1974.

SAN CRISTOBÁL (Dominican Republic) City in the S, 25 mi WSW of Santo Domingo. Founded in 1575 by Spanish settlers who discovered gold here, it was important as the site of the 1844 signing of the first Dominican constitution and as the birthplace of the dictator Rafael Trujillo in 1891.

SAN CRISTÓBAL DE LA HABANA. See HAVANA.

SAN CRISTÓBAL DE LAS CASAS [*former:* **Ciudad Real**] (Mexico) City in CHIAPAS state, in the S, in Sierra de Hueytepec, 32 mi E of Tuxtla. Founded in 1530 and named Ciudad Real, it was later named for Bartolomé de las Casas, a protector of the Indians and the first bishop of the diocese. The church of Santo Domingo dates from 1547. Other noteworthy buildings include the theater, an institute of arts and sciences, and a cathedral. The city was the state capital until 1891 and is perhaps most famous for its silver saddles.

SANCTI SPIRITUS (Cuba) Town, in E Las Villas province, 45 mi SE of Santa Clara. This oldest inland city of Cuba, founded in 1516, retains many colonial streets, plazas, and churches. It was here in 1516 that Bartolomé de las Casas advocated tolerance toward the Indians. Considered one of Cuba's leading cities in the 19th century, it was the first to be captured by Castro's troops in 1958.

SAN CUICUILCO. See TLALPÁN, Mexico.

SANDAKAN (Malaysia) Port town of SABAH, in North BORNEO, on Sandakan Harbor, an inlet of the Sulu Sea, 140 mi E of Jesselton. This town was the capital of British North Borneo, now Sabah, until 1947, when it was replaced by Jesselton, now KOTA KINABALU. It was occupied by the Japanese and nearly destroyed in World War II.

SAND CREEK (United States) Battle site in Colorado, near Fort Lyon. It was the setting of a controversial massacre of Indians. On Nov. 29, 1864, in spite of Cheyenne Chief Black Kettle's offer of peace, which was ignored, Col. John M. Chivington led his troops in a ruthless surprise attack.

SANDGATE (England) Town in Kent, on the ENGLISH CHANNEL, 2 mi W of Folkestone. A popular seaside resort today, the area is known for the remains of a castle built by Henry VIII and for its function as an important military base during World War II.

SANDHILLS. See DENILIQUIN.

SANDHURST (England) Village in Berkshire, 30 mi SW of London. The famous Royal Military College, established at Sandhurst in 1799, became part of the Royal Military Academy in WOOLWICH in 1946.

SAN DIEGO (United States) City on the Pacific Ocean, in S CALIFORNIA, near the Mexican border. A Portuguese explorer serving Spain, Juan Rodriguez Cabrillo, discovered San Diego Bay, which he called San Miguel, in 1542 and claimed the area for SPAIN. Don Sebastian Viscaino of Spain reached here in 1602. Caspar de Portolá, leading an expedition from MEXICO, visited the site in 1769. Father Junipero Serra, who was with him, founded the first of a system of Californian missions here. A fort, the first in the area, was also built, as Indian attacks were feared. Gradually the settlement expanded, and trade in cattle hides began.

Commodore Robert Field Stockton captured San Diego for the United States in 1846, and it became a permanent part of the country by the treaty of 1849 ending the Mexican War. In 1849/50 a large party of Mormons traveled overland from Utah to settle here. The town was incorporated in 1850 at a time when whaling was beginning to be an important enterprise. The whaling boom ended c.1870. A busy port, San Diego is today the site of a major base of the U.S. Navy, and of many aerospace and electronic installations, and is also a popular retirement area. Parts of the original town and the restored mission are noteworthy.

SANDOMIERZ [*Russian:* **Sandomir**] (Poland) Town on the VISTULA RIVER, 52 mi SE of Kielce, in Kielce province, in the SE. Strategically located, it was one of the first fortresses of the Little Poland area and became the capital of a duchy in 1139. Destroyed several times by Mongol invasions in the 13th century, it throve as a commercial and cultural center during the Reformation era. Polish Protestants were united by the Consensus Sandomiriensis, held here in 1570. Nearly destroyed by SWEDEN in 1656, it passed to AUSTRIA in 1772, to RUSSIA in 1815, and again to Poland in 1919. In addition to the medieval castle, Renaissance church, and Gothic cathedral, there is a 13th-century town hall here.

SANDOMIR. See SANDOMIERZ.

SANDRINGHAM (England) Village near the Wash, in NORFOLK, 7 mi NE of King's Lynn. Sandringham House, a notable royal residence, is situated in the village. Purchased in 1861 by Edward VII, the house is currently being used by Queen Elizabeth II. George VI was born and died here.

SANDUSKY [*former:* **Portland**] (United States) City and port of entry in N OHIO, 50 mi W of Cleveland, on Sandusky Bay, LAKE ERIE. A fort erected here in 1763 was burned by Wyandot Indians on May 16, 1763 during Pontiac's Rebellion. In the War of 1812 the naval battle of PUT-IN-BAY, or Lake Erie, was fought by Comm. Perry in 1813 approximately 12 miles from the site. Sandusky was laid out as Portland in 1817, incorporated in 1824, and was called Sandusky after 1844. A popular tourist and resort center since the 19th century, Sandusky now has an extensive lake trade.

SANDWIC. See SANDWICH, England.

SANDWICH [*Anglo-Early English:* **Lundenvic**; *Middle English:* **Sandwic**] (England) Port in Kent, on the Stour River, 12 mi E of Canterbury. The oldest of the CINQUE PORTS, it was most important militarily in the late 15th century, before silting ruined the harbor in the 16th century. The medieval buildings include a 12th-century hospital and an ancient wall with gates from the 14th to the 16th century. The chief Roman port in Britain, Rutupiae, lies in ruins 2 miles north in a suburb of RICHBOROUGH.

SANDWICH (United States) Town in SE MASSACHUSETTS, on CAPE COD BAY, at the base of the cape and the end of the Cape Cod Canal, 11 mi WNW of Barnstable. One of the earliest settlements on the Cape, founded in 1636, Sandwich is famous for its glass produced from 1825 to 1888. Hoxie House, the oldest in the town, dates partially from 1637.

SANDWICH ISLANDS. See HAWAII.

SANDY HOOK (United States) Peninsula in Monmouth county, NE NEW JERSEY, between Sandy Hook Bay and the Atlantic Ocean, 15 mi S of Manhattan, New York City. Explored by Henry Hudson in 1607, Sandy Hook was the logical site for Fort Hancock, built to protect New York Harbor. During the American Revolution it was held by the British. The Sandy Hook Lighthouse, built in 1763, is the oldest still in use in the United States.

SAN ELIZARIO (United States) Village in El Paso county, W TEXAS, 13 mi SE of El Paso, on the RIO GRANDE RIVER. One of the oldest settlements in Texas, it was established in the 1680's as a presidio town. In 1877 it was the scene of local violence in the Salt War, a riot between Mexican-Americans and Anglo-Americans over the use of nearby salt lakes. San Elizario was formerly the capital of El Paso county.

SAN FELIPE [*Aconcagua*] (Chile) Capital town of Aconcagua province and San Felipe department, 50 mi N of Santiago. A colonial town founded in 1740, San Felipe played an important role during the war of independence.

SAN FELIPE (United States) Pueblo in Sandoval county, N central NEW MEXICO, on the W bank of the RIO GRANDE RIVER, 33 mi SW of Santa Fe. Settled c.1700 by Pueblo Indians of the Kerensian linguistic group, it is well known for its ceremonial dances held in May and December.

SAN FELIPE (United States) Town of Austin county, in S TEXAS, on the Brazos River, 45 mi W of Houston. Founded in 1823 as the headquarters of Steven Austin's colony, it was the site of conventions held here in 1832, 1833, and 1835 before the Texas Revolution. It was burned in 1836 during the revolution, but was rebuilt.

SAN FELIPE APÓSTOL DEL ARECIVO. See ARECIBO.

SAN FELIPE DEL RIO. See DEL RIO.

SAN FELIPE DE PUERTO PLATA. See PUERTO PLATA.

SAN FERNANDO (Philippines) Name of two different municipalities on LUZON; one is capital of Pampanga province, 35 mi NW of Manila; the other is the capital of La Union province, 45 mi N of Dagupan. Both were captured by Japanese forces early in World War II and liberated by U.S. forces in January 1945, during the recapture of the Philippines.

SAN FERNANDO [*former:* **Isla de León**] (Spain) City, in Cádiz province, SW Spain, in ANDALUSIA, 7 mi SE of Cádiz. A maritime city of great tradition, it is known for its naval academy, arsenal, naval workshop, and observatory. The Cortés met here in the city's theater in 1810.

SAN FERNANDO (United States) City, Los Angeles county, S CALIFORNIA, in the San Fernando valley. Although the city was not founded until 1874 and was incorporated in 1911, it is still the oldest in the valley. First explored in 1769, it developed on a travel route to northern California, particularly after gold was discovered there in 1842. The San Fernando Mission of 1797 was founded by the Spanish and still stands. In 1971 San Fernando was damaged by an earthquake.

SAN FRANCISCO [*former:* **Yerba Buena**] (United States) City in W central CALIFORNIA, on a peninsula between the Pacific Ocean and San Francisco Bay. The English explorer, Sir Francis Drake, was in the general area in 1579, but the Spanish explorer; Gaspar de Portolá, was the first to sight land within the bay on an expedition from Mexico in 1769. In 1776 the Spanish, led by Juan Bautista de Anza, founded a presidio and mission on the peninsula. As a village it was called Yerba Buena, and it came under Mexican control after 1821; from 1806 to 1841 Russian fur traders tried unsuccessfully to gain a foothold here. On July 9, 1846 Comm. John D. Sloat captured it for the United States, and it became part of the territory ceded to the United States in 1848, when the Mexican War ended. The name was changed that year to San Francisco.

In this same year, too, gold was discovered in California, and the subsequent rush of prospectors raised San Francisco from a village of approximately 800 to a city of 25,000 in only two years. It was a period of lawlessness and riotous living for many on the city's infamous Barbary Coast. The city became a cosmopolitan center, Chinese being among the first to arrive as laborers. Their efforts and cultural tradition live on in America's best-known Chinatown. The pace of business and industrial development increased after the first transcontinental railroad was completed in 1869.

Refugees in a merry mood watch the great fire of 1906 in San Francisco. A mere village in 1848, earthquakes and fire have never stopped its phenomenal growth.

On April 18, 1906 the city suffered a major setback when an earthquake, followed by a three-day fire, almost completely destroyed it. The city, however, was soon rebuilt and continued growing. The opening of the San Francisco-Oakland Bay Bridge in 1936 and the Golden Gate Bridge in 1937 added further to its prosperity and reputation. In World War II it was a major embarkation and supply point for the war in the Pacific. A picturesque city of hills, with its charming architecture and its moderate climate, San Francisco has become world famous. With its large population of European immigrants the city early became a cosmopolitan center for the West, attracting artistic, musical, and other cultural institutions. The city is also the center of banking and finance, insurance, and other industries for the West Coast. During the 1960's its Haight-Asbury district was the center of the "hippie" movement, which culminated in the 1967 "Summer of Love." See also Oakland.

SAN FRANCISCO BAY (United States) Bay, 50 mi long, 3 to 13 mi wide, in W CALIFORNIA. Important in the early exploration of this area, the bay was discovered by Sir Francis Drake in 1579, sighted by Gaspar de Portolá in 1769, and entered by Juan Manuel Ayala in 1775. Its natural harbor is one of the finest in the world, now with an underwater transit tube designed to absorb earthquake tremors. Treasure Island and ALCATRAZ are well-known islands in the bay. SAN FRANCISCO, BERKELEY, OAKLAND, and SAN MATEO are the major cities on its shores. San Jose is approximately 12 miles to the southeast. San Pablo Bay is to the north, leading to the Napa Valley.

SAN FRANCISCO DE LA SELVA. See COPIAPÓ.

SAN GABRIEL (United States) City, Los Angeles county, S CALIFORNIA, 9 mi E of downtown Los Angeles. San Gabriel's Arcángel Mission, founded in 1771 as a starting point for colonizers, contains many rare paintings and relics. Rebuilt in 1812 after an earthquake, it is the scene of an annual festival.

SAN GERMÁN (Puerto Rico) Town in the SW on the Guanajibo River, 10 mi SE of Mayagüez. A Spanish settlement, its site was selected by Columbus's son Diego. It grew around the Porta Coeli Convent, built in 1511, one of the oldest religious establishments in the Americas. San Germán was also the birthplace of the first American saint, St. Rose of Lima.

SAN GERMANO. See CASSINO.

SAN GIMIGNANO (Italy) Town, in Siena province, TUSCANY region, 18 mi SW of Siena. A picturesque medieval town named for the fourth-century bishop who freed the area from barbarian control, San Gimignano has 13th-century walls, its Palazzo del Popolo, Palazzo del Podestà, 13 medieval towers remaining of an original 72, palaces, an art-filled 12th-century cathedral, and frescoes by Benozzo Gozzoli in the 13th-century church of St. Augustine. In the 12th and 13th centuries, during the wars between Florence, Pisa, and Siena for control of Tuscany, San Gimignano managed to retain a balanced independence. The city had fallen under the domination of FLORENCE by 1250 but again managed to gain its freedom. At the heart of the Guelph-Ghibelline conflicts, it was where Dante delivered a speech supporting the Guelphs in 1300. By 1350 it was again under Florentine control. Its towers, built by its rival noble families as symbols of their power, still combine to resemble a modern American city seen from a distance.

SANG-YÜAN SSU. See SAMYE.

SAN ILDEFONSO [La Granja] (Spain) Town of Segovia province, in old CASTILE, 38 mi NW of Madrid. La Granja is the name of the royal summer residence built here by Philip V between 1721 and 1723 to imitate Versailles. Philip's abdication in 1724 took place in the palace, as did the signing of the treaty of 1796, an alliance of FRANCE and Spain against GREAT BRITAIN

in the French Revolutionary Wars; a secret treaty of 1800 giving LOUISIANA to Napoleon I in exchange for lands in Italy; the revocation of the Pragmatic Sanction by Ferdinand VII in 1832; and the acceptance of the Cádiz constitution by Queen Regent Christina in 1836. A fire partially destroyed the palace in 1918.

SAN ISIDRO (Philippines) Municipality on the NW coast of LEYTE Island, in Leyte province, 45 mi NW of Tacloban. United States aircraft scored a resounding victory in San Isidro Bay on Dec. 7, 1944, when they destroyed an entire Japanese convoy in World War II.

SAN JACINTO RIVER (United States) Battle site, approx. 16 mi E of Houston, TEXAS, on the San Jacinto River, near its mouth on Galveston Bay. At this site, now a national historical landmark, Mexican troops under Santa Ana were decisively defeated by Sam Houston's Anglo-Texan troops on April 21, 1836, winning independence for Texas. See also DEER PARK, Texas.

SAN JOSÉ [*former:* **Villa Nueva**] (Costa Rica) Capital city of Costa Rica, 50 mi E of the Pacific port of Puntarenas. Founded in 1738, it became independent from SPAIN in 1821 and was made a capital in 1823, replacing Cartago after the two cities fought each other. Tobacco was replaced by coffee in commercial importance as the city began to develop in the 19th century and overtake older colonial centers. The mixture of North American and Spanish architecture makes San José a charming city.

SAN JOSE [*former:* **El Pueblo de San José de Guadalupe**] (United States) City of W CALIFORNIA, 40 mi SE of San Francisco, in the fertile Santa Clara Valley. The first city founded in California, in 1777, it was taken over by the United States in 1846, and was the site of the first meeting of the state legislature in 1849. It was the state capital from 1849 to 1851. To the west and north of the city are two missions: Mission Santa Clara de Asís of 1777, and Mission San José de Guadalupe of 1797.

Today it is the fastest-growing city in the United States, as the Santa Clara Valley, formerly the center of the cultivation of cherries, apricots, and raisins for drying, has given way to the microcomputer industry. The success of this new industry has renamed the area the Silicon Valley, now the center of high-technology industry and young professional affluence. Only 10,000 of the original 100,000 acres of orchard land survive.

SAN JOSÉ [San José de Mayo] (Uruguay) City of S Uruguay, on the San José River, 50 mi NW of Montevideo. Founded in 1783 by Spanish settlers, it was the provisional capital of Uruguay in 1825/26. It is distinguished for its early architecture, especially a church, administrative buildings, and a theater.

SAN JOSE DE CÚCUTA. See CÚCUTA.

SAN JOSÉ DE GUASIMAL. See CÚCUTA.

SAN JOSÉ DE MAYO. See SAN JÓSE, Uruguay.

SAN JUAN [*former:* **San Juan de la Frontera**] (Argentina) Capital city of San Juan province, 600 mi NW of Buenos Aires. A stronghold against the Indians, San Juan was founded in 1562 and moved to its present site in 1593. It played an important role in the 19th-century civil wars. It was also the birthplace of many Argentinian statesmen, including Domingo Faustino Sarmiento, president of Argentina from 1868 to 1874. Most of the city was destroyed in an earthquake in 1944.

SAN JUAN (Puerto Rico) Capital and chief city of Puerto Rico, WEST INDIES, approx. 1,000 mi ESE of Havana. The island was named Porto Rico by Ponce de León, who founded a settlement at nearby CAPARRA in 1508. It was moved to its present site in 1521. Fortified to resist attacks, it became the most formidable Spanish stronghold in the New World. A major port of the West Indies, it is also an export center to the United States. The city has the oldest church in continuous use in the Western Hemisphere and several colonial churches, including one containing the tomb of Ponce de León. El Morro and San Cristóbal fortresses remain.

SAN JUAN (United States) Pueblo, in N NEW MEXICO, on the RIO GRANDE RIVER, 26 mi NNW of Santa Fe. The first permanent Spanish settlement in New Mexico was founded here on the site of an Indian village by Juan de Oñate in 1598. It later became a Franciscan mission. It was the home of Popé, the medicine man who led the Indians in the Pueblo Revolt of 1680.

SAN JUAN BAUTISTA TUXTEPEC. See TUXTEPEC.

SAN JUAN CAPISTRANO (United States) Town in S CALIFORNIA, 20 mi SE of Santa Ana. Father Junipero Serra named the mission he founded here in 1776 after the Franciscan missionary and preacher St. John of Capistrano (1386–1456), from whom the town also took its name. It is famous for the swallows that come to the mission church ruins in the spring and leave on October 23, the anniversary of the saint's death.

SAN JUAN DE LA FRONTERA. See SAN JUAN, Argentina.

SAN JUAN DE LA FRONTERA DE LOS CHACHAPOYAS. See CHACHAPOYAS.

SAN JUAN DEL NORTE [*former:* **Greytown**] (Nicaragua) Town in the SE, on the CARIBBEAN SEA, 75 mi S of Bluefields. Positioned as the eastern terminus of the Cornelius Vanderbilt Trans-isthmian Transport Company, this small town prospered after its previous occupation in 1848 by the British who were then trying to secure much of the MOSQUITO COAST. It was attacked in 1854 by the UNITED STATES as reprimand for Nicaraguan aggression toward Anglo-Americans and their property. See also SAN JUAN DEL SUR.

SAN JUAN DE LOS ESTEROS. See MATAMOROS.

SAN JUAN DEL SUR (Nicaragua) Town of Rivas department, in the SW, 14 mi S of Rivas. This port was important during the California Gold Rush as the Pacific terminus of the Cornelius Vanderbilt Trans-isthmian Transport Company. See also SAN JUAN DEL NORTE.

SAN JUAN HILL (Cuba) Battle site in Oriente province, E of SANTIAGO DE CUBA. It was the scene of a battle on July 1, 1898 in the Spanish American War, in which Theodore Roosevelt and the Rough Riders took part and, with other U.S. and Cuban troops, captured the hill from the Spanish.

SAN JUANICO STRAIT (Philippines) Strait, 25 mi long, between SW SAMAR and NE LEYTE, connecting the Samar Sea and San Pedro Bay. In October 1944 U.S. forces posted military watchposts along its banks to secure the occupation of Leyte during World War II. Its shores are dotted with pueblos.

SAN JUAN ISLANDS [Haro Islands] (United States) Archipelago of 172 islands in NW WASHINGTON, E of Vancouver Island. Discovered and named by Spanish explorers in 1790, these scenic islands were the subject of bitter controversy and invasion by armies of both nations in the San Juan Boundary Dispute between Great Britain and the United States. It was finally arbitrated in 1872 by the emperor of Germany.

SAN JUAN TEOTIHUACÁN. See TEOTIHUACÁN.

SAN JULIÁN (Argentina) Port in Santa Cruz province, in the S. Portuguese navigator Ferdinand Magellan spent the winter here from March to August 1520 during his famous around-the-world voyage. Several of his officers staged an unsuccessful mutiny during this time. See also PATAGONIA.

SANKISA. See FARRUKHABAD, India.

SANKT GALLEN. See SAINT GALL.

SANKT GOAR (West Germany) Town of the Rhineland Palatinate, on the left bank of the RHINE RIVER, 8 mi SE of Boppard, opposite Sankt Goarshausen, and near the LORELEI. This old town is dominated by a fortress, Rheinfells, which was dismantled by the French in 1797. It passed to HESSE in 1497 before it became part of independent Hessen-Rheinfels from 1567 to 1583. It was later divided between Hesse-Darmstadt and Hesse-Kassel.

SANKT GOTTHARD. See SAINT GOTTHARD PASS.

SANKT JOACHIMSTAL. See JÁCHYMOV.

SANKT MORITZ. See SAINT MORITZ.

SANKT PÖLTEN [*ancient:* **Aelium Cetium**] (Austria) City, 30 mi W of Vienna. On the site of a Roman town arose an abbey dedicated to St. Hippolytus. The city was chartered in 1159 and made the seat of a bishopric. There is a Romanesque cathedral, built in the 11th century and rebuilt in the 18th, as well as a 16th- to 17th-century town hall.

SANKT RADEGUND. See SAINT RADEGUND.

SANKT VEIT AM FLAUM. See RIJEKA.

SANKT VEIT AN DER GLAN (Austria) Town in the S, on the Glan River, 10 mi N of Klagenfurt. Serving as capital of CARINTHIA until the 16th century, the walled town has a 14th-century church, a city hall built in 1468 and an important museum. One of its fountains, the Schüsselbrunnen, has a large marble basin from the Roman town of Virunum. In the area are many noteworthy castles, including Burg Hochosterwitz, atop and part of a high rock; it has 14 gateways and was built as protection against Turkish invaders.

SANKT VITH. See SAINT-VITH.

SANKT WOLFGANG (Austria) Town of Upper Austria, in the SALZKAMMERGUT, on the shore of picturesque Sankt Wolfgangsee, 8 mi W of Bad Ischl. Famous for its White Horse Inn, it also contains a Gothic church with an altar elaborately carved by Michael Pacher in 1481. It is situated on the old Pilgrim's Way.

SANLÚCAR DE BARRAMEDA [*ancient and Arabic:* **Luciferi-Fani**] (Spain) City, in Cádiz province in the S, 17 mi N of Cádiz. Of Roman origin, it, or nearby Coto de Doñana, may be the site of ancient TARTESSUS, an early Iberian-Phoenician port, which was the center of a kingdom before the absorption of southern Spain by Carthage. It flourished with the discovery of America when ships passed through to SEVILLE. Columbus sailed from here in 1498, on his third voyage, as did Magellan in 1519. It has a medieval castle and a 14th-century church.

SAN LUIS [*former:* **San Luis de la Punta**] (Argentina) Capital city of San Luis province, 400 mi WNW of Buenos Aires. San Luis was founded by Martín de Loyola in 1596. Although largely destroyed by the Indians in 1712 and 1720, it has many historical buildings from the colonial era.

SAN LUIS D'APRA. See APRA HARBOR.

SAN LUIS DE LA PUNTA. See SAN LUIS.

SAN LUIS OBISPO (United States) City, in S CALIFORNIA near San Luis Obispo Bay, 80 mi NW of Santa Barbara. After capturing the city for the United States in 1846, Gen. John C. Frémont and his troops escaped heavy storms by finding refuge in the Franciscan mission of San Luis de Tolosa built here in 1772. There are still historical buildings on the mission plaza.

SAN LUIS POTOSÍ (Mexico) Capital city of San Luis Potosí state, 225 mi NW of Mexico City. Founded in 1576 as a Franciscan mission, this city was strategically important in the colonial era as well as during the Mexican Revolution. When briefly imprisoned here in 1910, the patriot Francisco I. Madero drew up the Plan of San Luis Potosí—the social and political program of the Mexican revolution. The city still retains much colonial character in its architecture and narrow cobbled streets.

SAN MARCOS DE ARICA. See ARICA.

SAN MARINO (San Marino) City and capital of the republic of San Marino in N central ITALY. Probably founded in the fourth century by St. Marinus, a Dalmatian Christian fleeing persecution, the city developed around a hermitage founded on Mt Titano. Made formally independent in 1637 by the Pope, the republic has been attacked several times, notably in the 16th and 18th centuries but has remained free. While it has many treaties of friendship with Italy, it was neutral in World War II and was heavily bombed on one occasion.

The state claims to be the oldest continuous republic in the world. It has its own Council General of 60 members, a 10-member executive Congress of State, a 12-member Court of Appeal, two Regent captains, mint, post, police, and 1,000-member army.

SAN MARTÍN DEL REY AURELIO (Spain) Town in Oviedo province, 7 mi SE of Oviedo. The cathedral contains the tombs of the medieval kings of ASTURIAS, including that of Aurelio of Oviedo.

SAN MATEO (United States) City of San Mateo county, in W CALIFORNIA, on SAN FRANCISCO BAY, approx. 17 mi from downtown San Francisco. Named by Spanish explorers for St. Matthew in 1776, it was a Mexican colony from 1822 to 1846. The coming of the railroad in 1863 accelerated its growth, as did the influx of people homeless after SAN FRANCISCO's 1906 earthquake. The San Mateo Bridge links it with the eastern shore of San Francisco Bay.

SAN MIGUEL. See CEBU.

SAN MIGUEL DE IBARRA. See IBARRA.

SAN MIGUEL DE TUCUMÁN [**Tucumán**] (Argentina) Capital city of Tucumán province, on a tributary of the Dulce River, 665 mi NW of Buenos Aires and 500 mi WSW of Asunción, Paraguay. Founded in 1565, this old colonial town became part of the viceroyalty of LA PLATA in 1776, and was the scene of Gen. Balgrano's victory over the Spanish royalists in 1812, at the Battle of Tucumán. Argentina's independence was declared here at the first congress of the republic on July 9, 1816.

SAN MINIATO (Italy) Town, in Pisa province, TUSCANY region, 21 mi WSW of Florence. The town was the birthplace in 1046 of Countess Matilda of Tuscany, who supported the papacy against the German emperors during the Investiture Conflict in ITALY. The town became the seat of the imperial vicariate in Tuscany and was fortified by Emperor Frederick II, who strengthened its citadel. A bishopric with a 12th-century cathedral and a 16th-century palace, both damaged in World War II, it is probably best known for the church of San Domenico of 1330, which contains terracotta work by Giovanni della Robbia. The town was the scene of a massacre of its inhabitants by the retreating Germans in July 1944 during World War II.

SAN MUREZZAN. See SAINT MORITZ.

SANNAR. See SENNAR.

SAN NARCISO. See SAN ANTONIO, Philippines.

SAN PABLO ETLA. See ETLA.

SAN PANTALEO. See MOTYA.

SAN PASCUAL. See SAN PASQUAL.

SAN PASQUAL [**San Pascual**] (United States) Battle site, approx. 40 mi NE of San Diego in SW CALIFORNIA. A battle was fought here on Dec. 6, 1846 during the Mexican War. U.S. troops led by Gen. Stephen Kearny were attacked and suffered heavy losses before they were relieved by Comm. Robert Stockton, and thus eventually were able to reach SAN DIEGO.

SAN PEDRO DE DURAZNO. See DURAZNO.

SAN PEDRO DE TACNA. See TACNA.

SAN PEDRO SULA (Honduras) Capital city of Cortés department, in the NW, 24 mi SSW of Puerto Cortés. Founded in 1536 east of its present site, this colonial city with its banana and sugar plantations has become one of the principal ports and historic centers for western and northwestern Honduras.

SANQUHAR (Scotland) Village in Strathclyde region, 24 mi NW of Dumfries. A monument marks the site of the cross where the Sanquhar Declarations were posted. These were the public disavowal of allegiance to Charles II and James VII by the Covenanters Richard Cameron in 1680 and James Renwick in 1685. There is a ruined castle in the village of Eliock, 2 miles to the south-southeast.

SAN REMO [*Italian:* **Sanremo**] (Italy) City of Imperia province, LIGURIA region, 27 mi ENE of Nice, on the Gulf of Genoa. It is a port and important year-around resort. The city's old town has a 12th-century Romanesque church and a 15th-century palace that was ruined in World War II. The city was the site of an international conference from April 19 to 26, 1920, when representatives of countries involved in World War I met to ratify the decisions made at the Paris Peace Conference of May 1919. Decisions made here also led to the Treaty of SÈVRES.

SAN RIVER (Poland) River, 247 mi long, flowing NW from the CARPATHIAN MOUNTAINS to the VISTULA RIVER in the SE. During World War I several battles were fought in May 1915 across the line formed by the river.

SAN SALVADOR, Angola. See SÃO SALVADOR.

SAN SALVADOR [*former:* **Guanahani, Watling, Watlings Island**] (Bahamas) Island in the British WEST INDIES, 200 mi ESE of Nassau. Known as Guanahani to the Indians, the island was renamed San Salvador by Columbus. Its discovery by Columbus on Oct. 12, 1492 was the explorer's first landfall in the New World. The White Cliffs of High Cay on the southeast were the first sight of land. A cross on the southwestern shore marks Columbus's actual landfall.

SAN SALVADOR (El Salvador) Capital and largest city in the country, 23 mi from the port of La Libertad, and 110 mi SE of Guatemala City. Founded in the early 16th century on a volcanic slope, San Salvador has suffered many earthquakes; a particularly disastrous one was in 1854. Capital of the Central American Federation from 1831 to 1838, it has been the capital of El Salvador since 1841, except for a period between 1854 and 1859. It is the financial, commercial, and industrial center of the country. Near here on Dec. 4, 1980 three nuns from the United States were murdered by government forces. Despite the suspension of aid by the U.S. Carter administration and repeated inquiries under the Reagan administration, the crime had yet to be punished in early 1983.

SAN SALVADOR DE BAYAMO. See BAYAMO.

SAN SALVADOR DE JUJUY. See JUJUY.

SANSAPOR (Indonesia) Village on the NW coast of Doberai peninsula, in NW IRIAN BARAT on NEW GUINEA Island. United States forces landed here on July 30, 1944, during World War II. Using the element of surprise, they quickly captured the village and moved on to take MOROTAI shortly thereafter.

SAN SEBASTIÁN (Spain) Capital city of Guipúzcoa province, in the N, on the BAY OF BISCAY, 48 mi E of Bilbao and 220 mi NNE of Madrid. First mentioned in 1014 and chartered in the late 12th century, San Sebastián was the summer residence of Spanish royalty until the 20th century and is still one of the leading resorts in Spain. Burned and severely damaged in the battle between Wellington and the French in 1813, during the Peninsular campaign, it was rebuilt throughout the 19th century. The San Sebastián Pact, a Republican manifesto that preceded the fall of the Spanish monarchy, was signed here in 1930.

SAN STEFANO. See YESILKÖY.

SANTA ANA (El Salvador) Capital city of Santa Ana department, 32 mi NW of San Salvador. The second-largest city of El Salvador, it is a commercial and industrial center as well as an historically important city. Known as Santa Ana since 1708, it became the capital of the department in 1855. Besides the Spanish Gothic cathedral and El Calvario church, other historic buildings include the city hall, a theater, an art school, and a garrisoned fortress. CHALCHUAPA is 9 miles to the west.

SANTA ANA DE CORIANA. See CORO.

SANTA ANA DE CUENCA. See CUENCA.

SANTA BARBARA (United States) City of S CALIFORNIA, on the Pacific Ocean, 85 mi WNW of Los Angeles. In an area discovered, explored, and named by Juan Cabrillo in the 16th century, it was an important city in early Californian history. The remains of a Spanish presidio date from 1782, and a mission built in 1786 is considered to be one of the most beautiful in California. The architecture is largely Spanish in flavor, as exemplified by a courthouse resembling a Moorish castle. The harbor was attacked in 1942 by Japanese submarines. The area is rich in early Indian artifacts, many housed in the city's Museum of Natural History.

SANTA BARBARA ISLANDS [**Channel Islands**] (United States) Chain, 150 mi long, of eight rugged islands along the S CALIFORNIA coast, stretching from Point Conception to San Diego. The islands were discovered by the Portuguese explorer Juan Cabrillo in 1542, and he is reputedly buried here on San Miguel Island. A 1969 oil slick destroyed much of the aquatic life in the area. See also SANTA CRUZ, SANTA ROSA.

SANTA CLARA [**Villa Clara**] (Cuba) Capital city of Las Villas province, 165 mi ESE of Havana. On a site occupied by the ancient Cubanacan Indians, it was believed to have been the residence of Kublai Khan by Columbus, who thought that he had reached Cathay by sailing west around the world. Founded in 1689, it expanded from cattle trading to sugar-cane growing and tobacco processing in the 19th century. Well known for its beautiful buildings, Santa Clara was captured by guerrilla forces in 1958 during Castro's revolution against Batista.

SANTA CLARA (United States) Indian pueblo in Rio Arriba, Sandoval, and Sante Fe counties, N NEW MEXICO, 21 mi NW of Sante Fe. Noted for its pottery, the village was settled in 1700. Nearby are the Puyé ruins, remains of a 15th-century Tewa pueblo, including cliff dwellings, kivas, and four-terraced communal houses on the mesa tops. Pictographs and pottery artifacts offer abundant information about the former inhabitants. It was in the center of the Anasazi cultural area from *c.*600 AD to the arrival of the Spanish in the 16th century.

SANTA CROCE CAMERINA. See CAMARINA, Sicily.

SANTA CRUZ (Bolivia) Capital city of Santa Cruz department, on the Piray river, 180 mi NE of Sucre. Founded in 1560 by Ñuflo de Chávez as a Jesuit missionary center, it was moved to its present site in 1595 after repeated Indian attacks. One of the earliest revolutionary centers, it declared itself independent in 1811 before it was temporarily recaptured by the Spanish. A trading and processing center today, it contains many historical buildings and is the site of a rail line, built in 1962, that allows access to both the Pacific and the Atlantic oceans.

SANTA CRUZ, Morocco. See AGADIR.

SANTA CRUZ (United States) City and seat of Santa Cruz county, in W CALIFORNIA, at the N end of Monterey Bay, 60 mi S of San Francisco. This city was founded in 1791 on the site of the Santa Cruz Mission, built in 1791, and of the Branciforte Colony of 1797, a model, planned settlement. Outstanding points of interest are the replica of the mission, the University of California, Santa Cruz branch, and the huge municipal wharf, which was built in 1913.

SANTA CRUZ, U.S. Virgin Islands. See SAINT CROIX.

SANTA CRUZ DE TENERIFE (Spain) Capital, city, and port of TENERIFE province, in the W CANARY ISLANDS. Founded in 1494, it was attacked by English forces first in 1657 and again in 1797, during which battle Adm. Horatio Nelson lost his arm. It was here that Gen. Franco organized an uprising that developed into the Spanish civil war. A 16th-century church stands here.

SANTA CRUZ ISLANDS (Solomon Islands) Remote island group, in the SW Pacific Ocean, N of the New Hebrides. They were discovered in 1595. The U.S. aircraft carrier *Hornet* was destroyed in a naval battle fought here on Oct. 26, 1942, during World War II. U.S. forces defeated the Japanese in the battle, however.

SANTA ELEANA. See PORT ROYAL.

SANTA FE [*former:* **Santa Fe de Vera Cruz**] (Argentina) Capital city of Sante Fe province, 240 mi NW of Buenos Aires. Because it is an inland river port, connected by canal to the Paraná River, it is an important shipping point for NW Argentina. Founded in 1573 by the Spanish explorer Juan de Garay, it became a center for Jesuit missions and an outpost against the Indians. In 1853 the first constitutional assembly met here to draft the Argentinian constitution. In addition to the historical churches and the university, there are notable buildings grouped around two large plazas.

SANTA FE, Colombia. See BOGOTÁ.

SANTA FE (Philippines) Village in Nueva Vizcaya province, on LUZON, N of Balete Pass, approx. 25 mi SW of Bayombong. Heavy fighting occurred here as U.S. forces invaded Luzon in World War II. The capture of the village on May 27, 1945 permitted access to the CAGAYAN valley.

SANTA FE (United States) City in N central NEW MEXICO, the capital of the state, and the oldest capital in the United States. Modern Santa Fe is an administrative center, a popular tourist resort, and a commercial outlet for various products, including Indian wares. The Spanish founded the town on the site of Indian ruins *c.*1610, and it was a trading point for the Spanish and Indians for more than 200 years. In 1680 the Indian Pueblo Revolt drove out the Spanish inhabitants, who did not return for a dozen years.

After MEXICO became independent in 1821, extensive commerce with the United States developed over the SANTA FE TRAIL to the east, which terminated in the city. During the Mexican War, troops under Stephen W. Kearny occupied the city without resistance, and it was part of the large region ceded to the United States in 1848. The city was briefly occupied by Confederate troops during the U.S. Civil War. Among points of historic interest are San Miguel Church, built *c.*1635; Cristo Rey Church, the largest adobe building in the United States; and the Palace of the Governors, built *c.*1610 and used by Spanish, Indian, Mexican, and Anglo-American officials before becoming a museum in 1914.

SANTA FE DE BOGOTÁ. See BOGOTÁ.

SANTA FE DE VERA CRUZ. See SANTA FE, Argentina.

SANTA FE TRAIL (United States) A commercial route, 780 mi long, in the W, extending from INDEPENDENCE, MISSOURI to SANTA FE, NEW MEXICO. Originally used by small trapping parties that were forbidden to trade in Spanish-ruled Santa Fe, the trail became a bonanza for traders when MEXICO became free in November 1821 and Mexican Sante Fe welcomed trade. Over $5 million in goods were traded in 1855 alone. A monthly stage line, established in 1850, preceded the Santa Fe Railroad, which was opened in 1880.

SANTA GLORIA. See SAINT ANN'S BAY.

SANTA ISABEL, Equatorial Guinea. See MALABO.

SANTA ISABEL [Isabel] [*Spanish:* **Ysabel**] (Solomon Islands) One of the Solomon Islands, in the W Pacific Ocean. It was controlled by Germany from 1886 to 1899. A Japanese military base was developed at Rekata Bay on the NW coast during World War II until 1943.

SANTA MARIA (Portugal) Island in Ponta Delgada district, in the SE AZORES, approx. 800 mi off the mainland coast of Portugal. Columbus first stopped here during his return from the New World, on his initial voyage. It was developed into an Allied military base during World War II.

SANTA MARIA ANTIGUA DEL DARIEN. See DARIEN.

SANTA MARIA CAPUA VETERE. See CAPUA.

SANTA MARIA DE BELÉM DO GRÃO PARÁ. See BELÉM.

SANTA MARIA DE PUERTO PRINCIPE. See CAMAGÜEY.

SANTA MARTA (Colombia) Coastal city and capital of Magdalena department, 450 mi N of Bogotá. One of the oldest cities in South America and the oldest in Colombia, it was founded by the Spanish explorer Rodrigo de Bastidas in 1525 and has functioned as a banana-shipping center since the late 19th century. It was attacked by corsairs in the 16th century, remained Royalist during the revolution before it was liberated in 1821, and at one time contained in its cathedral the tomb of Simón Bolívar. Fort San Fernando and the ruins of the Santo Domingo monastery survive. CARTAGENA is nearby.

SANTA MAURA. See LEUKAS.

SANTANDER [*ancient:* **Portus Victoriae**] (Spain) Capital city of Santander province, in the N, on the BAY OF BISCAY, Old Castile, 212 mi N of Madrid, and approx. 47 mi WNW of Bilbao. An ancient port, sometimes identified with the Roman colony of Portus Blendium, Santander has been the historical and commercial capital of Old Castile since the Middle Ages. After the discovery of America it became the busiest port in northern Spain. It was devastated by the French in 1808. A former royal summer palace remains on the nearby peninsula of Magdalena. The 13th-century cathedral and business district, which were destroyed by fire in 1941, have been restored. The famous prehistoric cave of ALTAMIRA is nearby.

SANT' ANTIOCO [*ancient:* **Sulci**] (Italy) Town on the island of Sant' Antioco, The ancient Plumbaria Insula, SW of SARDINIA. An old Carthaginian town, it retains the ruins of its ancient walls, as well as Roman and Carthaginian tombs and other remains.

SANTARÉM [*ancient:* **Praesidium Julium;** *Arabic:* **Scallabis**] (Portugal) Capital town of Santarém district, above the right bank of the Tagus river, 43 mi NE of Lisbon. An important town since Roman times for its proximity to LISBON, it was a Moorish stronghold from 715 to 1093, and was recaptured from the Moors in 1147 by the first king of Portugal, Alfonso I. Besides the 13th-century church, there is a seminary from the 17th century.

SANTA ROSA (United States) City, 50 mi NW of San Francisco in W CALIFORNIA. Settled in 1868, the city is known for the Jack London Wolf House, and the preserved gardens of Luther Burbank (1849–1926), who once lived here. Old Fort Ross is nearby.

SANTA ROSA DE COPÁN. See COPÁN, Mexico.

SANTA TECLA. See NUEVA SAN SALVADOR.

SANTIAGO [Santiago de Chile] [*former:* **Santiago del Nuevo Estremo**] (Chile) Central industrial city and capital of both Chile and Santiago province, on the Mapocho river, 70 mi SE of Valparaíso. Founded in 1541, it has been a leading cultural center of Chile since the colonial era. The city has been the victim of many disasters, including an Indian massacre in 1541, an earthquake in 1647, many floods and political riots, and the fire in 1863 that destroyed the Campania Church and its 2,000 worshipers. President Allende was killed here in September 1973, during a coup d'etat that overthrew his socialist government and installed a right-wing military dictatorship over Chile.

SANTIAGO [Santiago de los Caballeros] (Dominican Republic) Capital city of Santiago province, on the Yaque del Norte River, 85 mi NW of Santo Domingo. This colonial city, today the second-largest city in the Dominican Republic, was founded *c.*1500 AD by Bartholomew Columbus and was rebuilt after the 1564 earthquake. Important buildings include the San Luis Fort, a cathedral and churches, and a municipal palace. A battle fought here on March 30, 1844 was a turning point for Dominican independence.

SANTIAGO, Spain. See SANTIAGO DE COMPOSTELA.

SANTIAGO DE CHILE. See SANTIAGO, Chile.

SANTIAGO DE COMPOSTELA [Santiago] [*ancient:* **Campus Stellae**] (Spain) City of La Coruña province, in the NW, in GALICIA, on the Sar River, 32 mi SW of La Coruña. According to legend, the tomb of St. James the apostle was miraculously discovered here in the ninth century, and the sanctuary built by Alfonso II of Asturias on the site became one of the three major shrines and pilgrimage centers of western Christianity. The site became such a popular pilgrimage goal that the symbol of St. James, the scallop shell, became the normal badge for any pilgrim, worn in his or her cap, like a hiking badge today. The routes to Compostela were well provided with pilgrim hospices; and the Cluniac order especially founded houses and churches along the major road from southern France across the PYRENEES, to BURGOS, and on to Compostela. The route to Compostela later became a major Crusader road during the *Reconquista* of Spain from the Moors.

A beautiful Romanesque cathedral was built between 1077 and 1122 to replace the sanctuary after it had been destroyed by a Moorish attack in the 10th century. The cathedral was augmented by the Hospital Reál of 1501 to 1511 for pilgrims and the 16th-century Colegio Fonseca, a part of the university. The art and architecture of Compostela shares much in common with the Cluniac churches of St. Martial in Limoges, St. Sermin in Toulouse, Cluny itself, and St. Foix at Conques.

SANTIAGO DE CUBA (Cuba) Seaport, city, and capital of Oriente province, in the SE, 460 mi ESE of Havana. Founded in 1514 by Diego de Velázquez, who is buried in the cathedral, Santiago was moved to its present site in 1522 and was the capital of Cuba until 1589. Hernando Cortés, its first mayor, left here in 1518 with the expedition that conquered MEXICO. A smuggling center of the WEST INDIES, it was captured many times by French and British buccaneers.

During the Spanish-American War of 1898 its harbor was blockaded by the United States because of its proximity to SAN JUAN HILL to the east. The Spanish fleet was destroyed here on July 3, 1898. Fidel Castro tried unsuccessfully to take it in July 1953 and was imprisoned here. It finally fell to his forces in 1959. The

The Romanesque cathedral at Santiago de Compostela in Spain, one of the great pilgrimage goals for all of Europe during the Middle Ages.

narrow streets and historical architecture reflect the city's colonial background. See also ORIENTE.

SANTIAGO DE GUAYAQUIL. See GUAYAQUIL.

SANTIAGO DE LEÓN DE CARACAS. See CARACAS.

SANTIAGO DEL ESTERO (Argentina) Capital city of Santiago del Estero province, 575 mi NW of Buenos Aires and 90 mi SE of San Miguel de Tucumán. Founded in 1553 and moved to its present site in 1556, it is the oldest continuous settlement in Argentina. There are many notable buildings here, including two 16th-century churches and administrative buildings.

SANTIAGO DEL NUEVO ESTREMO. See SANTIAGO, Chile.

SANTIAGO DE LOS CABALLEROS. See SANTIAGO, Dominican Republic.

SANTIAGO DE LOS CABALLEROS DE GUATEMALA LA NUEVA. See GUATEMALA.

SANTIPONCE. See ITALICA.

SANTI QUARANTA. See SARANDË.

SANTO DOMINGO [*former:* **Ciudad Trujillo**] (Dominican Republic) City in the S part of the republic, on the CARIBBEAN SEA. It is the capital, largest city, and chief port. The city was founded on Aug. 4, 1476 by Bartholomew Columbus, brother of Christopher, and is the oldest continuously inhabited settlement in the Western Hemisphere. In 1511 Diego de Velázquez, Spanish conquistador, was dispatched from here to conquer CUBA. Before Mexico and Peru were conquered, Santo Domingo was the headquarters for Spanish administration of its New World colonies, and the first viceroyalty was established here in 1509. The

English seaman, Sir Francis Drake, sacked the city in 1586, but in 1655 the city repelled another English attack.

Santo Domingo became the capital when the Dominican Republic won independence in 1844. Almost totally destroyed by a hurricane in 1930, it was rebuilt and renamed Ciudad Trujillo for the then dictator, Rafael Trujillo Molina, but its former name was restored in 1961. The city was the scene of fighting in 1965 during a civil war in which U.S. troops were sent to restore the status quo before the leftist rebellion. The first cathedral in the Western Hemisphere was completed here in 1521 and is reputed to contain the tomb of Christopher Columbus. The first university in the New World was established here in 1538.

SANTO DOMINGO (United States) Pueblo of Sandoval county, in N central NEW MEXICO, on the RIO GRANDE RIVER, 26 mi SW of Sante Fe. Inhabited by Pueblo Indians of the Eastern Kerensan linguistic family, it was founded *c.*1700 after a flood destroyed an earlier pueblo. The pueblo is known for its agriculture and distinctive pottery as well as for the ceremony of the Green Corn Dance, held on the feast of St. Dominic every year.

SAN TOMÁS DE LA NUEVA GUAYANA DE LA ANGOSTURA. See CIUDAD BOLÍVAR.

SANTORIN. See THERA.

SANTORINI. See THERA.

SANTOS (Brazil) City of São Paulo state, the thriving port for SÃO PAULO, 40 mi SE of that city. It is located on the island of São Vicente just off the SE coast of Brazil, close to its suburb, São Vicente, one of Brazil's earliest settlements, founded in 1532. The most important coffee port in the world today, Santos was founded *c.*1540. Both it and nearby São Vicente were sacked by the English privateer Thomas Cavendish in 1591. Tucked in and around the cosmopolitan commercial center and resort of Santos are 16th- and 17th-century buildings, reflecting its colonial heritage.

SANTO TOMAS. See CHICHICASTENANGO.

SANTO TOMÉ DE GUAYANA [Ciudad Guayana] (Venezuela) City and industrial and port complex in NE Bolívar state, E Venezuela, at the confluence of the Orinoco and Caroni rivers, approx. 70 mi ENE of Ciudad Bolívar. The area was claimed for Spain in 1532 by the explorer Diego de Ordaz and first settled in 1576. Puerto Ordaz, the hub of the region now united as Santo Tomé de Guayana, was established in 1947. In 1961 it was combined with other towns and economic activities in the area in a planned complex that includes iron and gold mining, steel production, port facilities, and dams and hydroelectric plants. There are specified residential, recreational, industrial, and commercial sections that extend over an area with a radius of 100 miles.

SANT-TU-AO [Santuao] (China) Port on the N coast of Fukien province, in the SE, on Sant-tu Island, 48 mi NE of Foochow. This city's importance centered around its tea trade, which flourished after the opening of foreign trade in 1899.

SÃO FRANCISCO (Brazil) River, approx. 1900 mi long, rising in the Brazilian plateau and flowing N, NE, and then E to the Atlantic Ocean. One of the great rivers of South America, it has been involved in many incidents—legendary and real—of stream piracy. Recently constructed dams along sections of the river have improved the economic conditions of the drought-ridden region.

SÃO JOSÉ DO RIO NEGRO. See MANAUS.

SÃO LUIS [*former:* **Maranhão, São Luiz do Maranhão**] (Brazil) Port, city, and capital of Maranhão state on São Luis Island, in the Atlantic Ocean, 300 mi ESE of Belém. The birthplace of many Brazilian writers and poets, it is known as the Athens of Brazil. Founded by the French in 1612 and named for Louis IX, it was taken by the Portuguese in 1615 and was under the control of the Dutch from 1641 to 1644. Under a commercial trading monopoly from 1682 to 1780 it flourished as a merchant's center and had developed into a cultural center by the 19th century. Today it serves as the trading and distribution outlet for the state's agricultural and industrial products. A 17th-century cathedral reflects Portuguese colonial life.

SÃO LUIZ DO MARANHÃO. See SÃO LUIS.

SAÔNE RIVER [*ancient:* **Arar**] (France) River, 268 mi long, which rises in the Vosges Mts in E France, near Épinal, and flows SW, joining the Rhône River at Lyons. It is an important transportation route between Paris and Marseilles and is connected by canals to the Loire, Marne, Moselle, and Yonne rivers. The Saône flows past some of France's famous vineyards. Among cities on its banks are CHALON-SUR-SAÔNE, the scene of 10 church councils, the most notable being the one the Emperor Charlemagne convoked in 813; GRAY, which gave its name to a well-known English family of Grey or de Grey; and MÂCON, a 16th-century Huguenot stronghold and the birthplace in 1790 of Alphonse Lamartine, poet and novelist.

SÃO PAULO (Brazil) Capital city of São Paulo state, in the SE, on the Tiete River, 45 mi NNW of SANTOS, its port. The largest city in South America, this ultramodern metropolis of some 10 million is the industrial, financial, and commercial center of Brazil. Until the large-scale cultivation of coffee in the 1880's, São Paulo was a typical Brazilian colonial settlement. Founded by Jesuit priests on Jan. 24, 1554 on the site of an old Indian village, it had become a base for expeditions into Brazil by the 17th century, the administrative capital of the area by 1681, and an important city by 1711. Independence from Portugal was declared here by Brazil's emperor, Dom Pedro I in 1822. The site is marked by the Ypiranga museum. This set the stage for the city's explosive growth and massive European immigration, following the beginning of the exportation of coffee in the 1880's.

SÃO PAULO DE LUANDA. See LUANDA.

SÃO SALVADOR [San Salvador, São Salvador do Congo] (Angola) Town of N Angola, in SW Africa. Between the 16th and the 18th centuries it served as capital of the former African kingdom of the KONGO, a modern district of ZAIRE. The kingdom was largely controlled then by Portuguese slave traders.

SÃO SALVADOR, Brazil. See SALVADOR.

SÃO SALVADOR DA BAHIA DE TODOS OS SANTOS. See SALVADOR.

SÃO SALVADOR DO CONGO. See SÃO SALVADOR.

SÃO TOMÉ AND PRINCIPE [São Thomé e Principe] Republic in West Africa, in the Gulf of Guinea, consisting of five islands, of which São Tomé and Principe are the most important. São Tomé is the chief town and capital. The uninhabited islands were discovered in 1471 by Portuguese explorers Pedro Escobar and Jaôa Gomes. A settlement was founded on São Tomé in 1483. The islands were declared a province of PORTUGAL in 1522 and after a period of Dutch occupation between 1641 and 1740, they were recaptured by the Portuguese. They were an overseas province from 1951 until independence was granted on July 12, 1975. A plantation economy was established in the 18th century on these volcanic and highly fertile islands. They continue to produce and export coffee, cacao, and coconuts.

SÃO VICENTE. See SANTOS, Brazil.

SAPPHAR. See ZAFAR.

SAPPORO (Japan) Capital city of Hokkaidō prefecture on HOKKAIDŌ Island, 177 mi NE of the port of Hakodate. The Japanese government founded Sapporo in 1871 as a center for development of the island, and today it is one of Japan's most rapidly growing urban centers. It is the site of well-known botanical gardens and of Hokkaidō University, founded in 1918. Its cold and snowy climate made it an ideal choice for the 1972 Winter Olympic Games.

SAQQARA [Sakhara, Sakkara, Saqqarah] (Egypt) Necropolis of ancient MEMPHIS, capital of early Egypt, on the NILE RIVER, approx. 15 mi S of Cairo. There are the remains here of several pyramids from the fifth and sixth dynasties, as well as the famous Step Pyramid, the earliest true pyramid in Egypt, built for King Zoser of the third dynasty c.2630 BC by his prime minister and architect, Imhotep. The nearby tombs of the sacred bulls, called the Serapeum, are from a later period.

SAQQARAH. See SAQQARA.

SARAFAND. See ZAREPHATH.

SARAGOSSA [*ancient:* **Caesarea Augusta, Salduba**; *Arabic:* **Sarakosta, Sarakusta**; *Spanish:* **Zaragoza**] (Spain) Capital city of Zaragoza province, in the NE, on the EBRO RIVER, 170 mi NE of Madrid. Known as Salduba, this Celtiberian settlement became important under ROME in the late first century BC and was renamed Caesarea Augusta by the Emperor Augustus. Falling to the Visigoths in the fifth century AD and to the Moors c.715, it resisted an attack by Charlemagne in 778. With the collapse of the emirate of Córdova in 1031, Saragossa became the center of a new emirate in the northeast of Spain, which resisted both

Christians to the north and the Berber ALMORAVIDES of North Africa. Aragon slowly pressed it from the north, and it was finally reconquered by Alfonso I of ARAGON in 1118. It remained the capital of Aragon until the end of the 15th century. By the Treaty of Saragossa on April 23, 1529 Emperor Charles V renounced all Spanish claims to the Spice Islands in favor of PORTUGAL.

In Byron's poem *Childe Harold* reference is made to Saragossa's heroic resistance against the French in the Peninsular campaign of 1808/09. The birthplace of the early Christian poet, Aurelius Publius Clemens Prudentius, in 348 AD, it has always been a center of culture, known for its art and its churches.

SARAJEVO [Serajavo] [*ancient:* **Vrh-Bosna;** *Turkish:* **Bosna-Seraj**] (Yugoslavia) Capital city of BOSNIA AND HERZEGOVINA, in the S, on the Bosnia River, 125 mi SW of Belgrade. Originally the site of a Roman military station, it was not until the citadel fell to the Turks in 1429 that it began to develop as an important military and commercial power, peaking in prosperity in the late 16th century. Burned in 1697 by Eugene of Savoy, it was assigned to Austrian rule in 1878 and grew as the center of the Serb nationalist movement. Archduke Francis Ferdinand and his wife were assassinated here on June 28, 1914, precipitating World War I. It passed to Yugoslavia in 1918. The architecture of the city is largely Muslim, with over 100 mosques. The ruins of a 13th-century Hungarian castle are perched on a hill above the town.

SARAKOSTA. See SARAGOSSA.

SARAKUSTA. See SARAGOSSA.

SARANA (United States) Valley and a mountain pass on NE Ahu Island, in the W ALEUTIAN ISLANDS, ALASKA. It was the scene of heavy combat between U.S. and Japanese forces in May 1942 during World War II.

SARANAC LAKE (United States) Village in NE NEW YORK State, in the Adirondack Mts, 36 mi S of Malone. A popular summer and winter resort today, Saranac Lake was known in the 19th century as a health resort for the tubercular. Edward Trudeau founded his famous outdoor sanitorium and research laboratory here in 1884. It closed in 1954, although research continues here.

SARANDË [*former:* **Porto Edda, Santi Quaranta**] (Albania) Commercial port and capital of Sarandë province, on the Adriatic Sea, in the S. The Italians invaded and conquered Albania in 1939; they built up Sarandë as a commercial port during World War II.

SARAPUL (USSR) City, E European USSR, in Urdmurt ASSR, on the Kama River, 35 mi SE of Izhevsk. Founded in the late 16th century, it was destroyed in the Pugachev rebellion in 1773 and then rebuilt. An important industrial and transportation point for this agricultural area, Sarapul is a railroad junction on the Moscow-Sverdlovsk line and was a trading center on the route to SIBERIA in the early 19th century.

SARATOGA. See SCHUYLERVILLE.

The minarets of Sarajevo's numerous mosques rise amidst modern buildings. Now a major industrial center, Sarajevo was Turkish for many centuries. Its population is still largely Muslim.

SARATOGA, BATTLE OF. See BEMIS HEIGHTS, FREEMAN'S FARM, SARATOGA SPRINGS.

SARATOGA SPRINGS (United States) City of Saratoga county, in E NEW YORK State, W of the Hudson River, 33 mi N of Albany. Named after the Indian word Saraghoga, meaning "place of swift water," the city land was ceded by the Indians to the Dutch in 1684. In the 17th century it was frequently the scene of battles between English and French and Indian forces. The last battle of the Saratoga campaign—and the first and perhaps most decisive victory of the American Revolution—took place 12 miles east of the city, near Stillwater, on BEMIS HEIGHTS in 1777. Here at Freeman's Farm New England forces under Gen. Benedict Arnold decisively beat British troops under Gen. John Burgoyne on September 19. Surrounded, Burgoyne again attacked at Freeman's Farm on October 7. Once again Arnold routed his forces. The British surrendered on October 17. Most the credit for the Battle of Saratoga, however, went to Arnold's commander, Gen. Horatio Gates. The great American victory was thus a bitter slight for Arnold.

The mansions and historical buildings date from the 19th century when the town was the playground of the rich, with horse racing, gambling, sporting events, and the carbon mineral waters of the health resort giving it its reputation. President Grant spent the last weeks of his life nearby writing his memoirs, and Edgar Allan Poe wrote the first draft of *The Raven* here in 1843.

SARATOV (USSR) City and capital of Saratov oblast, in E European Russia, on the VOLGA RIVER, 220 mi N of Volgograd. Founded as a Russian sentry post on the Volga c.1590, between Samara and the present Volgograd, it was reestablished near the original site in 1674. Its military importance dwindled as its trade increased, especially when the railroad tied Saratov to central European Russia in the 19th century. It is now a large and important industrial center.

SARATOV OBLAST (USSR) Oblast in Russian SFSR. Probably inhabited in prehistoric times, it was later held by the Scythians. It was ruled in the eighth and ninth centuries AD by the Khazars and has been a Russian possession since the 18th century and an oblast since 1934. See also KHAZAR EMPIRE, SCYTHIA.

SARAWAK (Malaysia) State on the NW of the island of BORNEO, on the S China Sea. Known since 1841 as the Land of the White Rajahs because of a three-generation rule by an English family, the Brookes, it became a British protectorate in 1888 under the Brookes. Occupied by Japan in World War II, it was ceded to Great Britain as a crown colony in 1946. Until 1963, when Malaysia was formed, Sarawak was the center of anti-Malaysian rebellions. Kuching, founded 1839 and formerly called Sarawak, is its capital.

SARBINOWO. See ZORNDORF.

SARDEGNA. See SARDINIA.

SARDES. See SARDIS.

SARDICA. See SOFIA.

SARDINIA [*Italian:* **Sardegna**] (Italy) Region and former kingdom, consisting of the island of Sardinia and some nearby small islands in the Mediterranean Sea, S of CORSICA, and W of the Italian mainland. The capital is CAGLIARI. Traces of prehistoric settlement abound, especially the remains of the Nuraghi culture, whose origins are uncertain. The Nuraghi built stone towers of unusual design of which approximately 6,500 exist. The Phoenecians were in Sardinia c.800 BC and the Carthaginians c.500 BC. The latter were conquered by the Romans in 238 BC, and Sardinia became an important source of grain and salt for Rome.

The Vandals occupied the island c.455 AD and in 533/34 were driven out by the BYZANTINE EMPIRE. The Goths took the island briefly, but it was recovered by the Byzantines in 552. The popes claimed suzerainty over Sardinia and were active in repelling Arab attacks that lasted from the eighth to the 11th centuries. PISA and GENOA allied to take it from the Muslims between 1016 and 1022. From then to the 14th century the two cities often fought over it. In 1297 Pope Boniface VIII awarded Sardinia to the house of ARAGON, a family that would later rule much of SPAIN and southern Italy, and Alfonso IV conquered Sardinia between 1323 and 1334.

In 1713, by the Peace of Utrecht, Spain ceded the island to AUSTRIA, but in 1717 a Spanish force occupied it. By agreement it was given to Victor Amadeus II of

SAVOY, who ruled as king of Sardinia from 1720 to 1730. At this time TURIN was the capital of the kingdom of Sardinia, which included Savoy, PIEDMONT, and NICE. LIGURIA, including Genoa, was added in 1815. This period, known as the Risorgimento, was one of activism in cultural and political affairs that led to the unification of Italy. The movement fomented an uprising in Sardinia in 1821, and in 1848 the kingdom of Sardinia took the leadership of the Risorgimento. Victor Emmanuel II, king of Sardinia from 1849 to 1861, defeated the Austrians with French help in 1859. In 1860 other parts of Italy joined Sardinia, and in 1861 Victor Emmanuel was proclaimed the first king of a united Italy.

Sardinia was used as an air base by the Germans in World War II. They left in September 1943, after Italy surrendered to the Allies. Giuseppe Garibaldi, a leading figure in the Risorgimento, is buried on the island of CAPRERA, NE of Sardinia. See also BYZANTINE EMPIRE, CARTHAGE, PHOENICIA, ROME.

SARDIS [Sardes] (Turkey) Famous ancient city of Asia Minor, in the Hermus Valley, 35 mi NE of modern Izmir. Once the capital of the ancient kingdom of LYDIA, the site was not rediscovered until 1958 and has been extensively excavated. The first coins were minted here in the seventh century BC. Considered the political and cultural center of Asia Minor from c.650 BC until its peak under Croesus of Lydia, it was conquered by Cyrus of PERSIA in 547 BC. Thereafter it remained part of the Persian Empire until "liberated" by Alexander the Great. It formed part of the kingdom of Antigonus from 323 BC, of the SELEUCID kingdom from 301 BC, of PERGAMUM after 190 BC, and of the ROMAN EMPIRE after the last king of Pergamum willed his state to it in 133 BC.

One of the Seven Churches of Asia Minor in New Testament times, it was an early seat of Christianity under the Roman Empire and passed to the BYZANTINE EMPIRE. After surrendering to the OTTOMAN EMPIRE in 1390, it was destroyed by Tamerlane in 1402. The widespread ruins include a Lydian marketplace and necropolis, the remains of the Hellenistic Temple of Artemis, an acropolis, and several enormous Roman bath complexes.

SAREMA. See SAAREMAA.

SARGASSO SEA Part of the Atlantic Ocean, 2 million sq mi, between the WEST INDIES and the AZORES, so named for the sargassum (floating seaweed) on the surface. Important in ancient legends of ships becoming entangled in the seaweed, it was a phenomenon that Christopher Colubus reported on his voyages.

SARI BAIR [*Turkish:* **Sari Bayir**] (Turkey) Hilly region in the central GALLIPOLI PENINSULA. From August 6 to 10, 1915 ANZAC forces raided a Turkish stronghold here during World War I, during the Gallipoli campaign, but they were turned back.

SARIKAMIS [Sarikamish] (Turkey) Town, in SW Kars province, in NE Turkey, 30 mi SW of Kars and formerly in Russian ARMENIA. The Russians decisively defeated the Turks here in an important battle of World War I in December 1914.

SARIKAMISH. See SARIKAMIS.

SARIM BATIM. See CONSTANTINE.

SARK [*French:* **Sercq**] (Great Britain) One of the CHANNEL ISLANDS, 2 sq mi, in the ENGLISH CHANNEL, E of Guernsey. Divided into Great Sark and Little Sark by an isthmus, this island retains a medieval feudal system of government with a governing hereditary seigneur under Great Britain. It was given by William the Conqueror to MONT-SAINT-MICHEL c.1040 and changed hands frequently thereafter. It was damaged during the 14th century and became finally English in 1558. It was occupied by the Germans in World War II.

SARMATIA (USSR) The Roman name of an ancient region between the VISTULA RIVER and the Caspian Sea, inhabited by the Sarmatians from the third century BC to the second century AD. Traces of a local culture east of the Urals dating from the fourth century BC have been associated with the early Sarmatians. In the second half of the third century BC these people, related to the Scythians and of Iranian origin, crossed from the area north of the Aral Sea to the Russian steppes west of the Volga. They pushed the Scythians west in their advance. Polybius mentions their power in 179 BC. The Sarmatians were horsemen who wielded spears, wore coats of plate mail and conical helmets, in appearance quite like the knights of William the Conqueror. In the third century their art combined Greco-Roman style with oriental flower and geometrical motifs, an art which they handed on to the Goths and Germanic tribes of the early Middle Ages. This nomadic, pastoral group lived to the E of the DON RIVER until 200 BC where they came into conflict, and then alliance, with the Romans. Trajan's Column in ROME depicts a battle between Romans and Sarmatians in full armor c.105 AD. Today, this area constitutes central and S Russia. See also SCYTHIA.

SARMI (Indonesia) Village on the N coast of IRIAN BARAT, 175 mi W of Djajapura. During World War II the Allies took this village from the Japanese in an invasion on May 17, 1944.

SARMIZEGETUSA [*ancient:* **Ulpia Traiana**] (Rumania) Ancient mountain capital of DACIA, ESE of modern Lugoj in W Rumania. It was besieged and taken by the Romans under Trajan in 102 AD during the Dacian wars of 101 to 106 AD. The Dacian king Decebalus committed suicide here along with his court rather than be captured. The young Hadrian participated in the campaign, which is recorded on Trajan's Column in ROME.

The name was later transferred to the new Roman capital of Ulpia Traiana, now Sarmizegetusa. The ruins of the Dacian capital have been excavated. Sarmizegusta Regia, approximately 30 miles to the northeast, is today the city of Grŭdiştea Muncelului, which some identify with the Dacian capital.

SARNATH (India) Religious site, in the N, approx. 3 mi N of Varanasi, Uttar Pradesh. Gautama Buddha is thought to have first taught in the Deer Park here. The ruins include the court of the monastery, the stupa of Emperor Asoka, 130 feet high, and the remains of Asoka's memorial pillar. See also MAURYA EMPIRE.

SARNEN. See SACHSELN.

SARPSBORG (Norway) Port city of Østfold county, in the SE, on the Glama River, near its mouth in the Oslofjord, 45 mi SSE of Oslo. Founded by Olaf II (St. Olaf) in 1016, this city was burned by SWEDEN in 1567. It was rebuilt in 1839 on the site of the medieval town. Nearby is the Skjeberg Church, a medieval stone structure.

SARRE. See SAARLAND.

SARREBRUCK. See SAARBRÜCKEN.

SARRELIBRE. See SAARLOUIS.

SARRELOUIS. See SAARLOUIS.

SARSINA (Italy) Town of ancient N UMBRIA, now in Forli province, Emilia-Romagna region, on the Savio River, approx. 24 mi WSW of Rimini. Plautus (254–184 BC), the famous Roman poet and dramatist, was born in this mountain town. It has a small museum with Roman tombs from the Republic and early Empire. The town is on a major route over the Apennines between the headwaters of the Tiber River and those of the Savio and RUBICON rivers.

SARZANA (Italy) Town of La Spezia province, LIGURIA region, 7 mi E of La Spezia, in the NW. A fortress at least by the 11th century, it was probably founded by refugees from LUNA when it was destroyed by the Saracens. A 14th-century cathedral stands in this old commune.

SASEBO (Japan) Port city on outer Omura Bay, in Nagasaki prefecture, on NW KYŪSHŪ, 55 mi NNW of Nagasaki. In 1886 this small village with its deep harbor was selected as the headquarters for the Third Naval District and functioned as the chief Japanese base for the wars with China in 1894/95, Russia in 1904/05 and Germany from 1914 to 1918. The city was rebuilt after it was heavily bombed in 1944/45 during World War II.

SASENO. See SAZAN.

SASHTI. See SALSETTE.

SASKATCHEWAN (Canada) One of the Prairie provinces of the Dominion of Canada, in the western part of the country. Before the Europeans arrived there were Chipewyan, Blackfoot, and Assiniboin Indians in the region. When Charles II of ENGLAND made a grant of a very large area to the Hudson's Bay Company in 1670, it included most of present Saskatchewan. Henry Kelsey of the company was probably the first European here, in 1691, but the French were the first to establish fur-trading posts c.1750. The first permanent settlement was Cumberland House, established in 1874 by Samuel Hearne for the British company. Other trading stations were set up over the years.

In 1868 the Rupert's Land Act returned it to the British crown. In 1870, when the Dominion took over the former Hudson's Bay Company lands, this area became part of the NORTHWEST TERRITORIES. Indians and *métis* (mixed race) rose in rebellion in 1884/85, under the leadership of Louis Riel, because they feared losing title to the lands they had settled. The rebellion was put down by armed force. The area became a province in 1905 by the Saskatchewan Act. REGINA is the capital.

SASKATOON (Canada) City of S central SASKATCHE-WAN, on the S Saskatchewan River, 150 mi NW of Regina. Founded in 1883 as the administrative center of a temperance colony, it was named after the Cree Indian word for a local berry. The arrival of the railroad in 1890 influenced its growth. Today it is the second-largest city in the province and the primary manufacturing and distribution center for central and northern Saskatchewan.

SASON. See SAZAN.

SASSANID EMPIRE. See PERSIA.

SASSARI [*former:* **Tathari**] (Italy) Capital city of Sassari province, on the island of SARDINIA, 110 mi NNW of Cagliari. Known as Tathari in the Middle Ages, it was first held by GENOA in 1284 and then by ARAGON in 1323. There is an Aragonese castle and an 11th- to 13th-century cathedral with a baroque facade. In 1718 the city passed to PIEDMONT, and today is an agricultural, mining, and trading center for Sardinia. It was seriously damaged during World War II.

SASSOFERRATO. See SENTINUM.

SATALIA. See ANTALYA.

SATARA (India) Town, 120 mi SE of Bombay, in S Maharashtra, in the W. Overrun by the Muslims in the 14th century, it flourished as a capital for the MARATHA CONFEDERACY. It came under British protection in the mid-19th century. A fort from the 12th century is here.

SATGAON (India) Ancient village in E India, West Bengal state, approx. 26 mi NW of Calcutta. Satgaon flourished for approximately 1,500 years as the commercial capital of lower BENGAL. It declined in the 16th century when the Hooghly River, on which it was located, changed its course. In 1537 its decline prompted the Portuguese to found Hooghly, now the joint municipality of HOOGHLY-CHINSURA, six miles southeast. The site of Satgaon is marked by tombs and the ruins of a mosque.

SATSUMA (Japan) Former province and peninsula, in Kagoshima prefecture, on SW KYŪSHŪ. Best known for the 16th-century porcelain of the same name, Satsuma was a feudal province under the powerful rule of the Shimazu clan until the Meiji Restoration in 1869, when the samurai, eager to support the emperor's efforts to end feudalism and forge internal solidarity, ceded all of their lands. Their only rebellion occurred in 1877 and was the last serious threat to the Meiji Restoration.

SATU-MARE [*Hungarian:* **Szatmár, Szatmár-Németi**] (Rumania) City of Baia-Mare province, in the NW, near the Hungarian border, on the Somes River, 295 mi NW of Bucharest. First mentioned in the 14th century, Satu-Mare became a Roman Catholic bishopric and a commercial and cultural center. The conquest of TRANSYLVANIA from Hungary by the Walachians began here. An old palace, three large churches, and a

Vincentian monastery still stand. The Peace of Szatmár was signed here in 1711, providing religious rights for HUNGARY after the Hungarian rebellion against AUSTRIA. See also WALACHIA.

SAU. See SAVA RIVER.

SAUDI ARABIA A nation that occupies most of the Arabian peninsula. It is bounded on the W by the Gulf of Aqaba and the Red Sea; on the E by the Persian Gulf and the Gulf States of Bahrain, Qatar, and the United Arab Emirates; on the N by Jordan, Iraq, Kuwait, and two neutral zones; and on the S by Oman, the Republic of Yemen, the Yemen Arab Republic, and the Rub 'al-Khali desert. In the 18th century the Wahabi sect arose in the ARABIAN PENINSULA as a divisive, reforming movement within Islam. Although the Wahabis were crushed in 1811 and again in 1891, the movement was revived at the beginning of the 20th century by ibn Saud, a descendant of one of the first Wahabi rulers. In 1902 he captured the city of RIYADH and in 1906 overcame the NEJD. By 1914 he had taken the AL HASA region from the OTTOMAN EMPIRE and extended his control even further. Although pro-British, he played little part in World War I despite British pressures. In 1925 ibn Saud took the HEJAZ, with the holy cities of MECCA and MEDINA, and in 1926 combined it with the Nejd to form the kingdom of Saudi Arabia, so named in 1932, with Riyadh as its capital.

After the discovery of rich oil reserves in Saudi Arabia in 1936, the country rapidly became a significant economic and political power. Remaining neutral until nearly the end of World War II, it finally declared for the Allies and after the war became a charter member of the United Nations. Ibn Saud died in 1953 and was succeeded by his oldest son, Saud, who leaned heavily on Crown Prince Faisal in economic and foreign affairs. Saud severed relations with EGYPT's Nasser over his pan-Arab alliance and joined King Hussein of JORDAN in sending troops to the YEMEN ARAB REPUBLIC in 1962 to support the royalist regime against the attempt of pro-Egyptian revolutionaries to establish a republic. Saud was deposed by Faisal in 1964, who was assassinated in 1975. King Khalid succeeded until his death in 1982, when King Fahd became the ruler.

Saudi Arabia played only a minor part in the wars between ISRAEL and the Arab nations, although it gave large financial aid to the enemies of Israel. The country played a leading role however in the oil embargo of 1973/74 against the Western nations and has been a moderating influence in the councils of the oil producers' organization, OPEC. The country obtains a great deal of revenue from the many Muslim pilgrims who come from all over the world to Mecca each year.

SAUER RIVER (Belgium, Luxembourg, West Germany) River, 107 mi long, rising in SE Belgium and flowing E to Luxembourg and into the Moselle River 2 mi S of Trier, West Germany. It was the scene of severe fighting in the Battle of the Bulge from December 1944 to January 1945, during World War II.

SAUGAS. See LYNN.

SAUGATUCK. See WESTPORT.

SAUGUS (United States) Town of Essex county in NE MASSACHUSETTS, 8 mi N of Boston. Settled before 1637, Saugus established the first successful ironworks in the country in the 17th century. They were restored in 1954. Saugus separated from LYNN in 1815.

SAUK CENTRE (United States) City, in Stearns county, in central MINNESOTA, on the Sauk River, at the S end of Sauk Lake, 40 mi WNW of St. Cloud. Settled in 1856, Sauk Centre was the birthplace of Sinclair Lewis, who used the city as the setting for his novel *Main Street*.

SAUK CITY (United States) Village, in Sauk county, in central WISCONSIN, on the Wisconsin River, 21 mi NW of Madison. Dating from c.1840, it became known as a settlement for liberal European refugees, including Haraszthy de Mokcsa, from Hungary, who founded the town and then went on to found the grape and wine industry in CALIFORNIA.

SAULT DE GASTON. See SAULT SAINTE MARIE.

SAULT SAINTE MARIE [*former:* **Sault de Gaston**] (Canada) City of S central ONTARIO, connecting LAKE HURON and LAKE SUPERIOR, opposite SAULT SAINTE MARIE, Michigan, 300 mi N of Detroit. A mission, founded here in 1668, became a fur-trading post in 1738. U.S. forces destroyed the post and a lock built in 1798 in the War of 1812. A busy port and tourist center developed in 1887 on the site. A canal and lock to bypass the St. Mary's rapids was built in 1898. A railroad bridge was built in 1887, and replaced 1913, to connect the city to its namesake in Michigan. The two cities have shared much of their history ever since.

SAULT SAINTE MARIE (United States) City and seat of Chippewa county, in N MICHIGAN, on the falls of the St. Mary's River, opposite SAULT SAINTE MARIE, Canada, 300 mi N of Detroit. Founded by Father Marquette as a Jesuit mission in 1668, it became a French and English fur-trading post until the discovery of mineral deposits in the area opened new possibilities for growth. It was French until 1763, when the British took over.

Ceded to the United States in 1783, it was not occupied until 1820, when Fort Brady was built. Known as the Soo Locks, the Sault Sainte Marie Canal was constructed in 1855. Since then it has been enlarged and elaborated many times. It links lakes SUPERIOR and HURON and is famous as the world's busiest lock system. Sault Sainte Marie suffered an economic decline in the 1960's when many of its larger industries closed down, but it still is an important tourist attraction.

SAUMUR (France) Town of Maine-et-Loire department in the W, on the LOIRE RIVER, 27 mi SE of Angers. Originally a Roman settlement, Saumur became the center of Protestantism in France until the revocation of the Edict of NANTES in 1685 by Louis XIV drove the Huguenots overseas. The VENDÉE army defeated the Republicans here in 1793, and the town was heavily damaged in World War II. Its importance during the Renaissance is reflected in its many Renaissance structures, art, and tapestries. Its 14th-century château incorporates a decorative arts museum. There are prehistoric caves nearby.

SAURASHTRA. See KATHIAWAR.

SAURASTRENE. See KATHIAWAR.

SAVAGE'S STATION (United States) Battle site, 8 mi E of RICHMOND, VIRGINIA. One of the Seven Days' Battles in the Civil War, Savage's Station was the scene of an unsuccessful attack by the Confederates on Union troops under Gen. Edwin Sumner on June 29, 1862; the Confederates tried again at FRAYSER'S FARM to deter the enemy from reaching the JAMES RIVER. See also MALVERN HILL.

SAVANKALOK. See SAWANKHALOK.

SAVANNAH (United States) City in SE GEORGIA, near the mouth of the Savannah River, across from South Carolina. James Oglethorpe, British general and philanthropist, was granted land in June 1732 to establish a buffer colony between SOUTH CAROLINA and Spanish FLORIDA and to found a New World haven for debtors. He brought 116 colonists with him and on Feb. 12, 1733 founded Savannah, the oldest city in Georgia. During the American Revolution the British captured Savannah and held it from December 1778 until July 1782. A combined force of French and Americans attempted to retake the city in 1779, but their assault on October 9 was decisively beaten off.

Savannah was the capital of Georgia from 1782 to 1785 and gradually became an important commercial center as well. The *Savannah*, the first U.S. steamship to cross the Atlantic, made the trip from here to LIVERPOOL, England in 1819. In the Civil War the city fell to Union troops on Dec. 21, 1864 as Gen. William T. Sherman completed his march to the sea from ATLANTA. Although Savannah is now a busy shipping and industrial city, it is justly proud of its wide streets, its parks, and its many old homes and other early buildings, including churches. The Herb House, built in 1754, is the oldest building in Georgia. In 1966 the old section of the city was designated a national historic landmark.

SAVANTVADI [**Sawantwadi**] (India) Former Indian state, 937 sq mi, now part of Maharashtra state, W India. The history of this Maratha state dates from the sixth century AD. It suffered much from the rivalry of the Portuguese at GOA in the 16th and 17th centuries. See also MARATHA CONFEDERACY.

SAVARIA. See SZOMBATHELY.

SAVA RIVER [*ancient:* **Savus**; *German:* **Sau**; *Hungarian:* **Száva**] (Yugoslavia) River, longest in Yugoslavia, approx. 580 mi, rising in the Julian Alps in the N part of the country and flowing generally SE into the DANUBE RIVER at BELGRADE. It drains nearly half of Yugoslavia and is navigable for 362 miles. On it besides Belgrade, Yugoslavia's capital, are a number of ancient and modern cities, including LJUBLJANA, SISAK, Sremska Mitrovica, and ZAGREB.

SAVENAY (France) Village of Loire-Inférieure department, in the W, 13 mi ENE of St.-Nazaire. It was the scene of General Kléber's decisive victory over the army of the VENDÉE in 1793.

SAVERDUN (France) Village of Ariège department, in the S, on the Ariège River, 8 mi N of Pamiers. Formerly one of the strong towns under the old countship of FOIX, Saverdun later became a center of Protestantism in the south.

SAVERNE [ancient: **Tres Tabernae**; German: **Zabern**] (France) Town of Bas-Rhin department, in E France, 21 mi NW of Strasbourg, Alsace. Important in Roman times as Tres Tabernae, Saverne today is remembered for the Zabern Affair of 1913, when a German lieutenant made insulting remarks about Alsatians in public that led to rioting and the arrest of 29 civilians. The incident became an international affair. Though the German Reichstag voted 293 to 55 to censure the army, Chancellor Bethmann-Hollweg and Kaiser William II ignored the vote. Saverne, long known for its metals, quarry, and glass, is the site of an 18th-century castle and has many distinctive old houses.

SAVO, Italy. See SAVONA.

SAVO (Solomon Islands) One of the SE Solomon Islands, 18 mi W of Florida Island in the W Pacific Ocean. It was the scene of heavy fighting during the GUADALCANAL campaign of World War II. On August 8/9, 1942 Allied forces lost four cruisers, but on Nov. 12/13, 1942 they gained a hard-fought victory here over the Japanese.

SAVOIA. See SAVOY.

SAVOIE. See SAVOY.

SAVONA [ancient: **Savo**] (Italy) Major port on the Gulf of Genoa, capital of Savona province, Liguria region, in the NW, 3 mi WSW of Genoa. This Gallo-Roman center was first mentioned c.205 BC during the Second Punic War as a Carthaginian base. It was destroyed by the Lombards in 641 AD before becoming the seat of a marquisate in the Middle Ages. In continuous rivalry with GENOA, it finally fell to that city in 1528. Under French rule from 1805 to 1815, during the Napoleonic period, it passed to SAVOY in 1815. Savona contains a distinctive 16th-century castle and a cathedral partially from the 16th century.

SAVONLINNA [Swedish: **Nyslott**] (Finland) City, in Mikkeli province, in the SE, 55 mi E of Mikkeli. Located on a large island, the city was chartered in 1639. Savonlinna was built around the fortress of Olavinlinna of 1475, which was important in the Russo-Swedish wars until 1812.

SAVOY [French: **Savoie**; Italian: **Savoia**] (France and Italy) Historical region embracing SE France and NW Italy; now included in the French departments of Savoie and Haute Savoie, and the PIEDMONT region of Italy. Ruled by the counts of Savoy from the 11th century as part of the kingdom of ARLES, it became in effect independent, and it eventually expanded to include the Piedmont plain and much of the LAKE GENEVA area. Involved in many wars, the region was alternately allied with France, SPAIN, or Italy. Joining the Grand Alliance in 1704, it gained SICILY by the Treaty of Utrecht in 1713 and held it until 1720 when it was exchanged for SARDINIA. The kingdom of Sardinia was then formed to include Piedmont, Savoy, and the island of Sardinia. When Sardinia sided with the Royalists in the French Revolution, it first lost Savoy in 1792 and then Piedmont in 1796. Both were restored to Victor Emmanuel I by the Congress of Vienna, with the addition of GENOA. In 1860 Sardinia, Piedmont, and Genoa joined other Italian states to form the kingdom of Italy headed by the house of Savoy. But Savoy itself, including NICE, went to France. See also CHAMBÉRY.

SAVUS. See SAVA RIVER.

SAWANKHALOK [Savankalok, Swankalok] (Thailand) Town, in Sukhothai province, in the N, 20 mi N of Sukhothai, on the Yom River. Founded c.1800 on its present site, it is 10 miles south of the former Thai capital of the SUKHOTHAI period in the 14th century, which is known for one of the three most important temples in Thailand.

SAWANTWADI. See SAVANTVADI.

SAWHAJ [Sohag] (Egypt) Capital town of Sawhaj governorate, on the NILE RIVER, 190 mi NNW of Aswan. This densely populated agricultural region is the site of two Coptic monasteries, as well as a mastaba (tomb) at nearby Bayt Khallaf famous under King Zoser of the Third Dynasty of ancient Egypt.

SAWPIT. See PORT CHESTER.

SAXA RUBRA (Italy) Town of ancient ETRURIA, on the FLAMINIAN WAY, 9 mi N of Rome, and W of the Tiber River. Maxentius, in retreat from a battle here with the victorious Constantine in 312 AD, tried to escape to ROME over the TIBER RIVER and drowned crossing the MILVIAN BRIDGE. The battle was named after the bridge. According to the Christian historian Eusebius, Constantine had a vision of a luminous cross in the sky with the words "in this conquer." The flaming cross depicted in legend and art supposedly symbolized Constantine's later conversion to Christianity.

SAXE. See SAXONY.

SAXE-ALTENBURG [German: **Sachsen-Altenburg**] (East Germany) Former duchy of THURINGIA. Ruled from 1329 by the house of Wettin as a separate duchy, Saxe-Altenburg passed to SAXE-GOTHA in 1672, was again separate from 1826 to 1918, and was included in Thuringia in 1920. See also ALTENBURG, SAXONY.

SAXE-COBURG [German: **Sachsen-Coburg**] (East Germany) Former duchy, belonging since 1353 to the Ernestine branch of the house of Wettin. It passed through family lines to the duke of SAXE-SAALFELD, whose descendants ruled the duchy until 1918. A redivision of possessions in 1826 resulted in Saalfeld joining SAXE-MEININGEN and SAXE-GOTHA joining Saxe-Coburg. Ernest I, duke of Saxe-Coburg-Gotha, brother of Leopold I of BELGIUM, and father of Prince Albert of Great Britain, founded the British dynasty that changed its name to Windsor in World War I, for British public relations purposes. In 1920 Saxe-Gotha was incorporated into THURINGIA and Saxe-Coburg into BAVARIA. See also COBURG, SAXONY.

SAXE-GOTHA [German: **Sachsen-Gotha**] (East

Germany) Former duchy in THURINGIA. A possession of the Ernestine branch of the house of Wettin, it was ruled from the 16th century by the dukes of SAXE-WEIMAR. In the territorial redivision of 1826, Ernest I received Saxe-Gotha-COBURG-MEININGEN and SAALFELD, and inherited SAXE-ALTENBURG. See also GOTHA, SAXONY.

SAXE-LAUENBURG. See SAXONY.

SAXE-MEININGEN [*German:* **Sachsen-Meiningen**] (East Germany) Former duchy of THURINGIA. It was a possession of the house of Wettin. With the extinction of the male line in 1825 and the redivision of the Ernestine lands, the duke of Saxe-Meiningen received Saxe-Saalfeld from the duke of SAXE-COBURG, and the duke of Saxe-Coburg received SAXE-GOTHA. In 1866 Saxe-Meiningen sided with AUSTRIA in the Austro-Prussian War. The last duke abdicated in 1918, and the duchy was incorporated into Thuringia in 1920. See also SAXONY.

SAXE-SAALFELD. See SAXE-COBURG, SAXE-MEININGEN, SAXONY.

SAXE-WEIMAR [*German:* **Sachsen-Weimar**] (East Germany) Former duchy of THURINGIA. The most important of the Thuringian principalities belonging to the house of Wettin, Saxe-Weimar under Duke Charles Augustus was considered one of the most cosmopolitan capitals of Europe. Bernard of Saxe-Weimar, one of the sons of Frederick I of Saxony, who inherited the newly divided duchies in 1547, later figured prominently in the Thirty Years War. With the failure of the family line, EISENACH was joined with Saxe-Weimar in 1741. Saxe-Weimar-Eisenach was raised to a grand duchy in 1815. Its last duke abdicated in 1918, and it was incorporated into Thuringia in 1920. See also SAXONY.

SAXE-WITTENBERG. See SAXONY.

SAXON SHORE, THE (England) A series of late Roman forts, erected along the SE coast of England, the Saxon Shore, in the third century AD to defend Britain from Anglo-Saxon raids. The fortresses, of which the best surviving examples are PEVENSEY, PORTCHESTER, and RICHBOROUGH, had massive 30-foot high walls with projecting bastions.

The system was begun during the reigns of the usurpers Carausius and Allectus, who revolted from Rome and ruled Britain and Belgica separately between 287 and 296. The series of forts ran from Norfolk to the Isle of Wight and was integrated with a fleet of *pictae*, small camouflaged picket boats that dogged the steps of the Anglo-Saxon pirates and reported them to the Roman fleet.

So effective was this defense system that it took the unusually concerted efforts of the Anglo-Saxons, Picts, and Scots to make an attack on the shore in 367. They killed the count of the Saxon Shore and the duke of the Britains, the Roman coastal and inland commanders, and opened the way to later Angle, Saxon and Jute conquest. Similar forts were built in the west, and a reconstructed example of the enormous walls and towers can be seen at CARDIFF. See also ROMAN EMPIRE.

SAXONY [*French:* **Saxe**; *German:* **Sachsen**] (East Germany) Historic region and former duchy, whose boundaries have varied greatly over the centuries. It was initially the land of the Germanic Saxons, who in the eighth century occupied northwest GERMANY roughly between the Elbe and Ems rivers. Charlemagne, emperor of the West, conquered the Saxons between 772 and 804, and the first duchy of Saxony was established late in the ninth century. It included somewhat more territory than the original Saxony and was one of the original "stem" duchies of medieval Germany. Henry I, duke of Saxony, was elected German king in 919 and his son Otto I, the first Holy Roman emperor, gave Saxony to a Saxon nobleman, Hermann Billung, in 961. In 1106 it was taken over by the man who in 1133 became Emperor Lothair II, who in turn bestowed it on Henry the Proud. The latter's son, Henry the Lion, however, lost Saxony in 1180, and the large duchy was broken up into many separate fiefs. The title of Duke of Saxony went to Bernard of Anhalt, who founded the Ascanian line, which after 1260 held the widely separated territories of Saxe-Lauenburg and Saxe-Wittenberg.

In 1356 Saxe-Wittenberg became known as Electoral Saxony, and in 1423 it was conquered by Margrave Frederick the Warlike of the house of Wettin, which already held large parts of LUSATIA and THURINGIA. Thus the name "Saxony" now applied to lands in east-central and eastern Germany rather than northwestern Germany. In 1485 Ernest, founder of the Ernestine line of the Wettins, received Electoral Saxony. His successors in the 16th century defended Martin Luther and the Reformation. The Schmalkaldic League, formed in 1531 by Protestant princes including the Elector John Frederick I, was defeated in 1547 by the Emperor Charles V; and John Frederick lost the electorate. Duke Maurice of Saxony, of the Albertine line, became the elector, and his branch of the Wettins retained the title until the end of the HOLY ROMAN EMPIRE in 1806. During the Thirty Years War of 1618 to 1648, Electoral Saxony was ravaged several times, but by the Peace of Westphalia in 1648 Elector John George I became one of the two most powerful of German Protestant princes.

Frederick II of PRUSSIA invaded Saxony in 1756 at the start of the Seven Years War, and although its boundaries were restored by treaty in 1763, Saxony's prestige declined, and its union with Poland was ended. In the Napoleonic era, Saxony first opposed FRANCE, changed sides in 1806, and as a result, after Napoleon's downfall, lost nearly half its territory at the Congress of Vienna in 1815. It was on the losing side again in the Austro-Prussian War in 1866 and had to pay a large sum to Prussia and join the NORTH GERMAN CONFEDERATION. Saxony was part of the GERMAN EMPIRE from 1871 until its destruction in 1918, after which it became a state in the WEIMAR Republic. Since World War II the territory has been in the German Democratic Republic.

LEIPZIG, long an intellectual center, and DRESDEN, beautified by Saxony's rulers and the home of the famous Meissen china, are leading cities. See also FRANKISH EMPIRE, SAXE-ALTENBURG, SAXE-COBURG, SAXE-GOTHA, SAXE-MEININGEN, SAXE-WEIMAR, SCHMALKALDEN.

SAY (Niger) Town on the NIGER RIVER, approx. 30 mi SE of NIAMEY, in West Africa. It was the boundary between British and French territory from 1890, before being annexed in 1898 by FRANCE.

SAYBROOK [Old Saybrook] (United States) Town in Middlesex county, CONNECTICUT, on the W bank of the Connecticut River, at Long Island Sound, opposite OLD LYME. It was a Dutch outpost of 1623 in the early colonial era but was definitely settled and fortified by New Englanders under Governor Winthrop of MASSACHUSETTS Bay Colony in 1635 as the Saybrook settlement. It was incorporated in 1854. A school founded here in the early 18th century became the nucleus of Yale University in nearby NEW HAVEN.

SAYBROOK. See DEEP RIVER.

SAYDĀ. See SIDON.

SAYPAN. See SAIPAN.

SAZAN [*ancient:* **Sason;** *Italian:* **Saseno**] (Albania) Small island, 4 mi long, in the Strait of Otranto, at the entrance to the harbor of VLORË, opposite the heel of Italy. Seized by ITALY in 1914, this island was held as a naval base until a treaty was signed in 1947 returning it to Albania.

SBEÏTLA [*ancient:* **Sufetula**] (Tunisia) Town in North Africa, approx. 100 mi NW of Sfax. It throve as a Roman town, especially during the reign of Marcus Aurelius from 121 to 180 AD. Occupied by the Germans in February 1943 during World War II, it was liberated by U.S. troops several weeks later. The ruins of a Roman forum and several temples are in the town.

SCALDIS. See SCHELDE.

SCALLABIS. See SANTARÉM.

SCAMPA. See ELBASAN.

SCANDIA. See SCANDINAVIA.

SCANDINAVIA [*ancient:* **Scandia**] Historic region in N Europe, consisting principally of DENMARK, NORWAY, and SWEDEN, although FINLAND and ICELAND are usually considered part of it. Norway and Sweden occupy the Scandinavian peninsula. It was from this region that the Vikings or Norsemen, Scandinavian warriors, raided the coasts of Europe and the British Isles for about two centuries, beginning in the ninth century AD and sailed to Iceland, GREENLAND, and North America, as well as down the rivers of RUSSIA. They were excellent shipbuilders and sailors driven by overpopulation, internal political troubles, and a thirst for adventure and trade. Sometimes they established settlements, conquering the local inhabitants, as in ENGLAND and FRANCE. In the latter they became known as Normans.

From 1018 to 1035 Canute, a Dane, was king of England, Denmark, and Norway; but Norway recovered its independence in 1035. Meanwhile, Sweden warred many times with the Danes and Norwegians and in the 12th century conquered Finland. Iceland came under Norwegian suzerainty in the 13th century, and Greenland also acknowledged its rule, while Denmark ruled southern Sweden. Sweden and Norway were united under King Magnus VII in 1319, but he was forced in 1343 to surrender the Norwegian crown to his son Haakon VI. In 1397, by the KALMAR Union, Margaret I of Denmark united the crowns of Denmark, Norway, and Sweden; and while Sweden became separate in 1523, Norway was ruled by the Danes until 1814. Iceland went from Norwegian to Danish control in 1380. In the 17th century Denmark and Sweden were at war several times, until by the Treaty of Copenhagen in 1660 Denmark was forced to return southern Sweden, and the boundaries of all three nations were settled along lines still in existence. In 1809 Sweden was compelled to turn Finland over to Russian rule, but in 1814 by the Treaty of Kiel it gained Norway from Denmark. The union of Norway and Sweden was ended peacefully in 1905, and in 1918 Iceland became independent, although sharing its king with Denmark. In World War II the Germans seized Denmark and Norway by force in April 1940, while Sweden remained neutral, and Finland was dominated by the USSR. Iceland's union with Denmark ended entirely in 1944.

The oldest Germanic literature, Old Norse, flourished in Scandinavia from *c.*850 to *c.*1350. It has survived mostly in Icelandic writings. The major cities of Scandinavia are: In Denmark, ÅLBORG, ÅRHUS, COPENHAGEN, and ODENSE; in Finland, HELSINKI; in Iceland, REYKJAVÍK; in Norway, BERGEN, NARVIK, OSLO, STAVANGER, and TRONDHEIM; in Sweden, GÖTEBORG, MALMÖ, STOCKHOLM, and UPPSALA. North Cape (Nordkapp), on an island just off northern Norway, is the northernmost point of Europe.

SCAPA FLOW (Scotland) Sea basin in the ORKNEY ISLANDS, off the N coast of Scotland. It was a major British naval base in both world wars. It was closed in 1956. The British *Vanguard* was torpedoed here in 1917, and in 1919 the surrendered German fleet was scuttled here by its crews. The *Royal Oak* was sunk here by a German submarine in October 1939, causing a temporary closing of the base.

SCARABANTIA. See SOPRON.

SCARBOROUGH (England) Seaport and resort in North Yorkshire, 37 mi N of Hull, on the NORTH SEA. Because of its location, a Roman watchtower was built in what was then a village, which actually dates from the Bronze Age. The village was chartered in 1181. The church here dates from 1198, and there is a 12th-century castle. George Fox (1624–91), founder of the Society of Friends, was imprisoned here.

SCARBOROUGH [*former:* **Port Louis**] (Trinidad and Tobago) Capital town of Tobago Island in the WEST INDIES, 65 mi NE of PORT OF SPAIN. Scarborough replaced Georgetown, now Mount St. George, as the capital in 1796. The ruins of Fort King George of 1770 and the Government House remain.

SCARPANTO. See KARPATHOS.

SCARSDALE (United States) Village in WESTCHESTER COUNTY, SE NEW YORK State, 20 mi N of New York City. Settled *c.*1700, it takes its name from Scarsdale Manor, the estate of Caleb Heathcote, who came from Scarsdale, Derbyshire, England. A section of the town is still known as Heathcote. In 1717 Heathcote is said to have erected the building that became the Wayside Inn and was run by the Varian family for 75 years. In 1776, during the American Revolution, British commander Sir William Howe made his headquarters in the Jonathan Griffin farmhouse before the Battle of WHITE PLAINS. Modern Scarsdale is often cited as a typical affluent American suburb.

SCATTERY ISLAND (Irish Republic) Island in the SHANNON RIVER estuary, in SW county Clare, SW of Kilrush. Queen Elizabeth I gave this island to LIMERICK citizens, who built a castle here near the existing ruins of six early medieval churches and an ancient round tower.

SCEAUX (France) Town of Seine department, a suburb SSW of PARIS. The château built here by Jean Baptiste Colbert in the 17th century was destroyed in the French Revolution. The present château was built on the same site in the 19th century. The impressive park of the château was made into a public garden in 1922.

SCHAAN (Liechtenstein) Town near the Rhine River and the Swiss border, approx. 3 mi NNW of Vaduz. This early settlement of probable Celtic origin is known for its Roman and Allemanic remains. In addition to the Dux chapel, there is a graveyard, a Romanesque belfrey, and a convent.

SCHAFFHAUSEN [Schaffhouse] [*former:* **Villa Scafhusun**] (Switzerland) Capital city of Schaffhausen canton, 23 mi N of Zurich, on the RHINE RIVER. The first settlement in the canton, this picturesque town was very important in the Middle Ages, and its medieval architecture—a Benedictine abbey of 1050, and 11th-century town hall, gates, tower and castle—reflect that period. By 1208 it had become a free city of the HOLY ROMAN EMPIRE. It was ruled successively by its abbots, the Hapsburgs, and finally local trade guilds until it joined the Swiss Confederation in 1501.

SCHAFFHOUSE. See SCHAFFHAUSEN.

SCHÄSSBURG. See SIGHISOARA.

SCHAUENBERG. See SCHAUMBURG-LIPPE.

SCHAULEN. See SIAULIAI.

SCHAUMBURG-LIPPE [*former:* **Schauenberg**] (West Germany) Former state in N West Germany, E of the Weser River. This region encompassed much of WESTPHALIA in the 12th century, before HOLSTEIN was acquired by Count Adolph in 1111. When the family line died out in 1459, most of the area was divided between DENMARK, BRUNSWICK-LÜNEBERG, and HESSE-KASSEL. The rest went to Count Philip of LIPPE. Thereafter known as Schaumburg-Lippe, it became a principality in 1807.

SCHEEMDA (Netherlands) Town, in Groningen province, in the NE, 4 mi NW of Winschoten. This town was the site of the first battle in the Netherlands' struggle for independence against SPAIN, in 1568.

SCHELDE [Scheldt] [*ancient:* **Scaldis**; *French:* **Escaut**] (Belgium, France, Netherlands) River of W Europe rising near Aisne in N France, flowing N and E

through W Belgium to Antwerp, thence NW to the North Sea through the East and West Schelde estuaries. It is connected with a thick network of canals in France and Belgium. From 1648 until 1863, except during the Napoleonic period, the Dutch held the right to close the Schelde estuary to navigation, thereby throttling the trade of the city of ANTWERP. In 1839, when the Netherlands and Belgium were separated, Holland fixed the toll and obtained the assent of the other powers to the arrangement. In 1863 Belgium bought up the rights, and each of the powers involved in trade contributed its quota; thereafter the navigation of the Schelde was declared free.

SCHELDT. See SCHELDE.

SCHENECTADY (United States) City and seat of Saratoga county, in E NEW YORK STATE, on the MOHAWK RIVER and the Barge Canal, 13 mi NW of Albany. Founded by Arent Van Curler in 1661, the settlement was destroyed in an Indian massacre in 1690. Growth came in the early 19th century with the opening of the ERIE CANAL and the arrival of the railroad. By the 1850's the city became the center of American locomotive building, and later of the electrical industry. St. George's Church is from the early 18th century, as is the old stockade.

SCHENSTOCHAU. See CZESTOCHOWA.

SCHEVENINGEN (Netherlands) Seaside resort and part of THE HAGUE in South Holland province, 2 mi NW of The Hague. In 1653 this bathing and fishing resort was the scene of an English naval victory over the Dutch fleet under Admiral Tromp. It was heavily damaged in World War II.

SCHIEDAM (Netherlands) Town of South Holland province, in the SW, 3 mi W of Rotterdam, near the Meuse River. Chartered in 1275, it was a fish and grain trading center during the Middle Ages before it was replaced by ROTTERDAM. There are ruins here of a 13th-century castle. The town also has a 15th-century church and a 17th-century town hall.

SCHIEFFERSTADT (West Germany) Village, in SE Rhineland-Palatinate, in the RHINE RIVER Valley, 7 mi SSW of Ludwigshafen am Rhein. Many Roman remains have been excavated near this village.

SCHIERATZ. See SIERADZ.

SCHLESIEN. See SILESIA.

SCHLESWIG [*former:* **Sliaswic, Sliesthorp**; *Danish:* **Slesvig**] (West Germany) Port city of Schleswig-Holstein, in the N, on an inlet of the BALTIC SEA, 70 mi NNW of Hamburg. One of the oldest cities of northern Germany, Schleswig has played an important role in German-Danish history since *c.*800 AD. It succeeded the Viking trading town of HEDEBY nearby in the 11th century. After being a town of the German or HOLY ROMAN EMPIRE, it was ceded to DENMARK in 1027. In the later Middle Ages, although a fief of Denmark, it fell again under the German Empire as a part of HOLSTEIN; later it came under the royal house of Denmark again.

In the meantime, from 947 until the Reformation in the 16th century it was an episcopal see and the residence of the dukes of Schleswig, as well as the dukes of Holstein-GOTTORP, who lived in the Gottorp Castle from 1514 to 1713. It was the Danish capital of Schleswig-Holstein from 1721 to 1848, and the capital of the duchy under Prussia from 1866 to 1917, when it was replaced by KIEL.

Its ambiguous status led in the 19th century to the SCHLESWIG-HOLSTEIN question, which involved GERMANY, PRUSSIA, Denmark, and AUSTRIA. It was finally settled by agreement when Schleswig came under the administration of Prussia in the 1860's. In 1920, by plebiscite, the northern part of Schleswig was awarded to Denmark, though the city remained in Germany. The Gothic cathedral of the 12th to the 15th century contains the tomb of Frederick I of Denmark.

SCHLESWIG-HOLSTEIN [*Danish:* **Slesvig**] (West Germany) State in West Germany, occupying the southern part of the Jutland peninsula, with the North Sea on the W, the Baltic Sea on the E, and Denmark on the N. Schleswig, the southern part, is a former duchy created in 1115 as a hereditary fief held from the kings of Denmark; while HOLSTEIN became a county of the HOLY ROMAN EMPIRE in 1111. For more than six centuries the two territories had many different rulers and were at different times combined or divided in various ways. After 1773 the kings of DENMARK held both duchies. They were full sovereigns of Schleswig and ruled Holstein as princes of the Holy Roman Empire. The Congress of Vienna in 1815 confirmed this status with the GERMAN CONFEDERATION, organized that year, which succeeded the extinct Holy Roman Empire. The population of Schleswig-Holstein was predominantly German, and growing nationalism made a touchy issue of the relation of the region to Denmark. The Germans feared Schleswig would be fully incorporated into Denmark.

In 1848 Frederick VII of Denmark declared such a complete union, and revolt broke out in both duchies. Led by PRUSSIA, the German Confederation occupied the duchies in support of the revolutionaries. An armistice was arranged, but fighting resumed in 1849 and ended inconclusively in 1850. The question of the succession to the rule of Schleswig-Holstein was the subject of a conference in London in 1852 that resulted in a treaty guaranteeing the integrity of Denmark's territory; it also conferred the succession to the Danish throne and both duchies on the Glucksburg branch of the Danish royal house. Denmark promised to keep the duchies united and their status that of a personal union through the Danish crown. In 1855, however, under Danish nationalist pressure, Frederick VII declared that the Danish constitution applied to the duchies. The German Confederation protested, and the proclamation was withdrawn in 1858. In 1863, however, a common constitution for Denmark and Schleswig was signed by Frederick's successor, Christian IX. The German diet objected, and in January 1864 Prussia and AUSTRIA declared war on Denmark, which was quickly defeated. Austria favored recognizing a claim to the duchies by the duke of Augustenburg, but Prussia, under the leadership of Otto von Bismarck, was determined to annex the duchies.

The Treaty of Gastein in 1865 placed Holstein under Austrian control and handed over Schleswig to Prussian administration. As Bismarck had hoped, this dual control caused friction that helped him maneuver Austria into war in 1866. The Austro-Prussian War ended in seven weeks with victory for Prussia, and the two duchies were annexed to Prussia, along with the duchy of LAUENBURG, which became part of the province of Schleswig-Holstein. Following World War I a plebiscite was held in 1920 in which the Danish majority of nothern Schleswig voted to join Denmark. The leading cities of Schleswig-Holstein are FLENSBURG; KIEL, the capital; LÜBECK; and SCHLESWIG, one of the oldest cities in West Germany.

SCHLETTSTADT. See SÉLESTAT.

SCHLÜSSELBURG. See PETROKREPOST.

SCHMALKALD. See SCHMALKALDEN.

SCHMALKALDEN [**Schmalkald, Smalcald, Smalkald**] (East Germany) Town in the Suhl district, of SW East Germany, 30 mi SW of Erfurt. First mentioned in 874 AD, this medieval metal-working center was chartered in 1227 and joined HESSE-KASSEL in 1583, with which it passed to PRUSSIA in 1866. In the early Reformation period, the League of Schmalkalden of the Protestant German princes and free cities was founded in the town hall here in 1531 to counteract the Catholic forces of Emperor Charles V. Their union won the financial and diplomatic support of the Catholic king of France, Francis I. Their defiance led eventually to the Schmalkaldic War between the opposing sides. The league forces under the Elector John Frederick of SAXONY were defeated at the Battle of MÜHLBERG, near Leipzig, on April 24, 1547. The emperor's triumph was short-lived, however; and the league managed to bring him to a stalemate. This, the power politics of France, and Charles's desire to unite Germany against the Turks, led to the Peace of Augsburg of 1555, which recognized the legitimacy of the Protestant princes and the principle that each prince would determine the religion of his own state.

In Schmalkalden are the 15th-century town hall and the restored Crown Inn, where Martin Luther drew up the Schmalkaldic Articles representing the Protestant point of view in 1536. There is also a medieval fortress here, and the 15th-century church of St. George.

SCHMÖLLN (East Germany) Industrial city in Leipzig district, 12 mi E of Gera. Chartered in 1320, this German city became a paper- and leather-manufacturing center. Its town hall was built in the 16th century, and there is a 15th-century church.

SCHNEEBERG (East Germany) City, in Karl-Marx-Stadt district, 22 mi SW of Karl-Marx-Stadt. This city grew in importance with the discovery of silver deposits in 1477 and eventually became a metal and lace-making center for Germany. Its 16th-century church contains paintings by Lucas Cranach the Elder.

SCHNEIDEMÜHL. See PILA.

SCHOENBRUNN VILLAGE STATE MEMORIAL (United States) Historical site in E OHIO, S of New Philadelphia. The first town in Ohio, this site was settled by a Moravian missionary and his Indian converts in 1772. The village was abandoned during the American Revolution because of an Indian threat, and was later burned by the Indians. The site was restored as a museum in 1923.

SCHOONEVELDT (Netherlands) Battle site on the S shore of the mouth of the SCHELDE River in Zeeland, in the SW. During the Dutch Wars it was the scene of a naval battle in 1673 between the Dutch fleet commanded by Adm. de Ruyter and the combined English and French fleets.

SCHOUTEN ISLANDS [Misore Islands] (Indonesia) Island group off IRIAN BARAT, NEW GUINEA. It is comprised of BIAK, NUMFOR and other islands. It was first explored by the Dutch navigator Willem Schouten on his successful voyage into the Pacific for the Dutch East India Company in 1616. Biak was occupied by U.S. troops during World War II on May 27, 1944, after severe fighting, and Numfor on July 6. After years of dispute, this area was taken over by Indonesia in May 1963.

SCHRAALENBURGH. See DUMONT.

SCHULPFORTA. See SCHULPFORTE.

SCHULPFORTE [Pforta, Schulpforta] (West Germany) Village in N HESSE, 2 mi SW of Naumburg, on the Saale River. This village is the site of a school established by Elector Maurice of SAXONY in 1543 in the buildings of a former monastery founded in 1134. From it Klopstock, Fichte, Ranke, and Nietzsche graduated. It became a Nazi Party school after 1933.

SCHUYLER. See NEBRASKA.

SCHUYLERVILLE [Old Saratoga, Saratoga] (United States) Village, in Saratoga county, in E NEW YORK State, on the W bank of the HUDSON RIVER, 32 mi N of Albany. When it was settled in 1689, this village was originally named Saratoga. During the American Revolution it was the scene of Gen. John Burgoyne's surrender on Oct. 17, 1777 to Gen. Horatio Gates in the Saratoga campaign. Gates had replaced Philip Schuyler as commander when the latter assumed supreme command. Burgoyne's defeat has been attributed to Benedict Arnold. See also SARATOGA.

SCHUYLKILL RIVER (United States) River, approx. 130 mi long, which rises in E central PENNSYLVANIA and flows mostly SE into the DELAWARE RIVER at PHILADELPHIA. Along its banks are some of the early industrial cities of the United States, such as Conshohocken, NORRISTOWN, POTTSTOWN, POTTSVILLE, and READING. Also on the river is VALLEY FORGE, where the Continental Army spent the bitter winter of 1777/78.

SCHWABACH (West Germany) City, in N Bavaria, 8 mi SSE of Nuremberg. First mentioned in 1117, it was chartered in the late 14th century. It was ceded to PRUSSIA in 1791 and to BAVARIA in 1806. The Articles of Schwabach of 1529 led to the drafting of the 1530 AUGSBURG Confession of the Protestant Lutheran faith. Notable buildings include a 16th-century city hall and a 15th-century Gothic church.

SCHWABEN. See SWABIA.

SCHWABISCH-GMÜND. See GMÜND.

SCHWÄBISCH-HALL [Hall] (West Germany) City of Baden-Württemberg in the S, on the Kocher River. The settlement developed around salt springs. It was chartered in the 12th century and was an important free city until 1803. There is a former fortified Benedictine abbey of 1075 nearby, a baroque town hall, and a 15th-century church in the city. See also SWABIA.

SCHWANGAU (West Germany) Village in SW Bavaria, 2 mi ENE of Füssen. This is the site of two important castles: the Hohenschwangau, formerly known as Schwanstein and renovated in the 19th century, which passed in 1567 from the Welfs to the dukes of BAVARIA, and the famous Neuschwanstein, built by Louis II "The Mad King" of Bavaria between 1869 and 1886.

SCHWARZA (West Germany) Town, in THURINGIA, on the Saale River, 3 mi SSW of Rudolstadt. In October 1806 the French army under Launes and Angereau defeated the Prussians under Prince Louis Ferdinand in this town. See also PRUSSIA.

SCHWARZWALD. See BLACK FOREST.

SCHWECHAT (Austria) A suburb SE of VIENNA, on the Leitha River. Although its modern boundaries were formed by the incorporation of 28 towns in 1938, the original Schwechat was the scene of a Hungarian defeat in 1848 by Prince Windisch-Grätz, who crushed revolutions against the Hapsburgs in PRAGUE, BOHEMIA, and all around Vienna. The next year the Hungarians were victorious at Gödöllö near BUDAPEST, HUNGARY, costing Windisch-Grätz his command.

SCHWEDT. See SCHWEDT AN DER ODER.

SCHWEDT AN DER ODER [Schwedt] (East Germany) City, in Frankfurt district, 50 mi NE of Berlin. Founded in 1265, it passed to BRANDENBURG in 1469. Tobacco was introduced by the French Huguenots who settled the area in the 17th century. The city suffered extensive damage in World War II. See also FRANCE.

SCHWEIDNITZ. See SWIDNICA.

SCHWEINFURT (West Germany) City, in Lower Franconia, NW BAVARIA, on the Main River, 66 mi E of Frankfurt. First mentioned in 791, it became a free imperial city in 1280 and passed to BAVARIA in 1803. Because it was the center of the German ball-bearing industry, it was severely bombed in World War II by Allied aircraft between 1942 and 1945. The Allies suffered disastrous losses in planes. The 15th-century church and the 16th-century town hall remain.

SCHWERIN (East Germany) Capital city of Schwerin district in the NW, on Lake Schwerin, 110 mi NW of Berlin. A commercial and industrial center today, Schwerin was first mentioned in 1018 and was chartered by Henry the Lion in 1160, when it also became an episcopal see. The Reformation was introduced in 1524, and the town was occupied by Roman Catholic imperial forces under Wallenstein from 1624 to 1631 during the Thirty Years War. There is a 14th- to 15th-century cathedral and a 19th-century ducal palace on an island in the lake. Schwerin was the capital of what was the MECKLENBURG state.

SCHWETZINGEN (West Germany) Town of Baden-Württemberg, 5 mi WSW of Heidelberg. The medieval castle here was rebuilt c.1700 to serve as the summer residence of the electors palatine between 1720 and 1777. It has a notable castle park created in the 18th century that includes a rococo theater.

SCHWYZ [*former:* **Suittes**] (Switzerland) Canton between the lakes of Zurich in the N and Lucerne in the S, and its capital town, 22 mi E of Lucerne. One of the oldest towns in Switzerland, it was passed to the counts of Hapsburg in the early 13th century, and in 1240 Emperor Frederick II made it a direct fief of the HOLY ROMAN EMPIRE. Rudolf I of Hapsburg revoked its charter in 1274, and in 1291 Schwyz joined URI, UNTERWALDEN, and later LUCERNE in a pact forming the FOUR FOREST CANTONS, which became the basis of Swiss independence. The original document is now housed in the Swiss federal archives here. Its name is the source of Schweiz or Switzerland. Schwyz's attempt to dominate EINSIEDELN led to an unsuccessful Austrian counterattack and the Battle of MORGARTEN in 1315. It acquired various lands over the next centuries and was involved in battles at SEMPACH and KAPPEL. A Catholic canton, its territorial jurisdiction was finalized in 1848, after the Sonderbund war against the Protestant cantons, and in 1898. Notable buildings include a 16th-century town hall, a medieval convent, rebuilt in the 17th century, several baroque churches, and houses from the 17th and 18th centuries.

SCIACCA (Italy) Port town of Agrigento province, in SW SICILY, on the Mediterranean Sea, 30 mi NW of Agrigento. An important royal town in the Middle Ages, it has town walls dating from 1330 and the ruins of castles, a palace, and a medieval cathedral.

SCILLA. See SCILLIUM.

SCILLIUM [**Scilla**] (Tunisia) Ancient town in North Africa near modern Sbeïtla, Tunisia. The execution of 12 Christians from this town in CARTHAGE on July 17, 180 AD is the earliest recorded Christian martyrdom in the Roman province of AFRICA PROCONSULARIS. The Scillitan Martyrs, seven men and five women, refused to renounce their faith and to repudiate "The sacred books and the letters of a righteous man named Paul" that they carried in a satchel. The proconsul Saturnius offered them a month to recant, but they refused and were executed.

SCILLY ISLANDS [**Isles of Scilly**] (England) Archipelago of more than 150 islands in CORNWALL, off SW England, 25 mi SW of Lands End. The scene of many shipwrecks through the centuries, this area, because of its flower growing, is known as the Flower Garden of England. Five of the islands are inhabited and contain historical buildings. Samson Island has ancient stone monuments. Tresco has remains of an abbey from the 10th century and Oliver Cromwell's Tower. The main island, St. Mary's, is where Prince Charles (Charles II) stopped during his flight from the English Civil War in 1645.

SCIO. See CHIOS.

SCITUATE (United States) Town, in Providence county, in N RHODE ISLAND, W of Cranston, 11 mi W of Providence. It was settled in 1710. Cannon were manufactured here for the American Revolution. The town was also the birthplace of Stephen Hopkins (1707–85), governor of Rhode Island and revolutionary patriot. Scituate separated from PROVIDENCE in 1731.

SCODRA. See SHKODËR.

SCOGLITTI (Italy) Town in Ragusa province, in the S of SICILY, approx. 15 mi SE of Gela. It served as a beachhead during the Allied invasion of Sicily from July 9 to Aug. 8, 1943 during World War II.

SCONE (Scotland) Village in Tayside region, 35 mi N of Edinburgh. It was the residence of the kings of Scotland from 1157 to 1488. The abbey here founded in 1115 and destroyed by Protestants in 1559 contained the Stone of Scone, or the Stone of Destiny, upon which the kings sat for coronation. It was brought to Westminster Abbey by Edward I in 1297 and now sits beneath the English coronation throne there.

SCONSET. See SIASCONSET.

SCOPUS, MOUNT [*Hebrew:* **Har Hazofim**] (Israel) Peak, a N extension of the Mount of Olives, NE of Jerusalem. Strategically important in the defense of JERUSALEM throughout its history, it was a camp site for Roman legions in 70 AD, during the Jewish revolt, and for the Crusaders in 1099 when they captured Jerusalem. Until the Israeli capture of all of Jerusalem in 1967, it was Israeli-held land in Jordanian territory.

SCOTIA. See SCOTLAND.

SCOTLAND Country of Great Britain. It lies N of ENGLAND and includes the HEBRIDES, ORKNEY, and SHETLAND Islands. Much of the country consists of the sparsely populated Highlands, renowned for their scenic beauty, while the bulk of the population is centered in the central Lowlands around the capital, EDINBURGH, and GLASGOW in the W. United with England under one parliament since 1707, Scotland retains a distinct legal system and has preserved intact its cultural traditions.

Inhabited originally by Picts, Scotland was invaded though never subdued by the Romans. By the end of the second century AD, the Romans had been forced to retreat south of the ANTONINE WALL, which marked the northern border c.140 AD, into northern England where they had built the defensive HADRIAN'S WALL by 126 AD. By c.400 the Picts of Galloway had been converted to Christianity by St. Ninian. By 565 St. Columba had converted northern Scotland from the monastery of IONA.

In the sixth century the country was invaded by Scots from IRELAND, and in 844 the Picts and Scots united under the Scottish king Kenneth I of DALRIADA. From the 8th to 12th centuries, Scotland was continually prey to invasions by Norsemen. Under David I (1084–1153), the power of the crown was consolidated and trade began to develop. As a result of his participation in the rebellion against Henry II of England in 1173/74, the king of Scotland became a vassal of the English monarch. By 1263, the Norse invaders had been finally repulsed from the Scottish mainland. Under Alexander III (1249–86) the Hebrides and the Isle of Man had been taken from Norway. In 1290, however, Alexander's last heiress, Margaret, the "Maid of Norway," died childless. More than a dozen claimants to the throne therefore appealed to Edward I of England, who claimed the Scottish throne for himself, owing to his position as feudal lord of many Scottish holdings. In the following struggle, known as the "Great Cause," the Baliols contested the throne with the Bruces. After the rule of a Baliol, a Wallace, and Edward I, Robert the Bruce won a decisive victory over the English at BANNOCK-BURN in 1314, which was strengthened by an alliance with FRANCE throughout the Hundred Years War. England was forced to recognize Scottish independence in 1328, but relations between the two countries remained poor. Edward III defeated the Scots at HALIDON HILL in 1333, but the victory was fruitless. Scotland was torn by civil strife in the 14th century, and one third of its population succumbed to the plague of the Black Death.

The reign of James IV saw some return to order, but this ended prematurely when he was killed by the English at the Battle of FLODDEN Field in 1513. The 16th century was a period of religious turmoil, with the arrival of the Protestant Reformation clashing with Scotland's traditional ties with Catholic France. In the 1550's John Knox brought Calvinism to the country, where it developed into Presbyterianism, the official religion. These differences came to a head during the reign of Mary Stuart, Queen of Scots, who lost her throne in 1567 owing to a rebellion by nobles. She was imprisoned by Elizabeth I of England and executed in 1587.

Order was restored under her son James VI who in 1603 ascended the throne of England as James I, thus uniting the two countries. During the English Civil War, Scotland's religious sympathies caused her to favor the Parliamentarians. The rebellion against Charles I began in Edinburgh, in 1637, after attempts to impose Anglicanism there, but the execution of Charles I in 1649 alienated Scottish feelings, so that Oliver Cromwell's Protectorate was not popular in Scotland.

The Scots welcomed the Restoration of Charles II in 1660 and, by the Act of Union in 1707 the Scottish and English parliaments were merged. With the death of Queen Ann, the last reigning Stuart, in 1714, and under the Hanoverian dynasty, the Jacobites claimed that the Stuarts were the rightful kings of Scotland as well as England. They rebelled unsuccessfully in 1715 and again, with French help, during the war of the Austrian Succession. After their defeat at CULLODEN MOOR in 1745, however, the Jacobites' cause was finally dead. English troops were thereafter quartered in the Highlands for years, roads were pushed through the moors, the chieftains lost their power, and the clans were dissolved as political and landholding units. For thirty years wearing of the kilt was forbidden. During the 18th century, however, despite cultural repression, Scotland made an important contribution to the Enlightenment in Europe with the writings of David Hume, Adam Smith, and others, as Edinburgh became a European capital. The enclosure system caused the depopulation of the Highlands and prompted mass emigration after 1750 to the new industrial cities, including Glasgow and Edinburgh, and to America and Australia.

Throughout the 19th and 20th centuries Scotland developed peacefully as an integral part of the UNITED KINGDOM, with the Lowlands benefiting from the industrial revolution. The exploitation of oil in the NORTH SEA, off the Scottish coast, enhanced Scotland's economic position in the 1970's and brought renewed demands from nationalists that Scotland become self-governing. Since 1975 the 33 counties of Scotland have been regrouped into 12 administrative regions. Other important cities are DUNDEE, ABERDEEN, and PAISLEY.

SCOTTSBLUFF (United States) City in W NEBRASKA, on the North PLATTE RIVER, 20 mi E of the Wyoming border. It is named for a nearby butte, a landmark on the Mormon and OREGON trails. Robert Stuart, courier from John Jacob Astor's fur-trading post in Oregon, was among the first Europeans to see it. Fort Mitchell was established here in 1864 as an outpost for FORT LARAMIE. It is the site of the Oregon Trail Museum.

SCOTTSBORO (United States) Town in NE ALABAMA, 30 mi E of Huntsville, the scene in 1931 of one of the most controversial and highly publicized criminal trials in the history of the United States. Nine black male youths were indicted here, charged with having raped two young white women. In several trials the young men were found guilty, some of them being sentenced to death, others to long prison terms. The U.S. Supreme Court twice overturned the convictions on procedural grounds, including the fact that no blacks had served on the juries. In 1937 the charges against five were dropped, in 1940 three of the men were set free, and a fourth escaped to Michigan in 1946. In 1976 a pardon was granted this man, the last known survivor of the nine.

Liberals and radicals came to the defense of the nine, doubting that they were guilty and believing they were the victims of racial prejudice. One of the women recanted her earlier testimony against the youths at the second trial.

SCOTT'S PLAINS. See PETERBOROUGH.

SCRANTON (United States) City in NE PENNSYLVANIA, on the Lackawanna River, in the center of an anthracite coal region. Settlement in the area began in 1788, and iron was first forged here in 1797. In 1840 George W. Scranton, for whom the city is named, combined with other entrepreneurs to secure large tracts of coal land, including the site of the present city. By 1842 he had developed the use of anthracite coal in smelting iron ore, and ever since the city has been an industrial center. There is a model coal mine in Nay Aug Park, where historic blast furnaces can be viewed.

SCROBBESBYRIG. See SHREWSBURY.

SCROOBY (England) Village of Nottinghamshire, 18 mi E of Sheffield. It was the home of William Brewster and other founding members of a group later called the Pilgrims, who founded the PLYMOUTH colony in New England in 1620. See also MASSACHUSETTS.

SCUPI. See SKOPJE.

SCUTARI, Albania. See SHKODËR.

SCUTARI, Turkey. See USKUDAR.

SCYROS. See SKYROS.

SCYTHIA (USSR) Ancient country that included parts of Eurasia from the Danube River in the W to the borders of China in the E. It was inhabited by a barbaric, nomadic people from the Ural River, of Iranian background, living chiefly in the steppes north and northeast of the BLACK SEA and the region east of the Aral Sea. They were mentioned from the seventh century BC, when they overwhelmed the Medes and replaced the Cimmerians. This group was then driven out of MEDIA by King Cyaxares. They were apparently the same people as the Sakas east of the Caspian. Circa 615 BC they allied with the Medes and Babylonians to sack Nineveh in 612 BC. Darius campaigned against them in Europe c.515 BC and halted their expansion. They annihilated the army sent against them in 325 BC by Alexander the Great of MACEDON, but in 300 BC they were driven out of the Balkans by the invading Celts. They were centered north of the Caspian from c.700 to 550 BC and in the CRIMEA from 550 BC on. They are identified with the use of the bow in battle and superior horsemanship. They were noted for their pointed caps, flowing robes, and trousers. In the second century BC they were conquered by the Sarmatians, became part of SARMATIA, and disappeared shortly after. Long in contact with the Greek colonies of the Black Sea coast, the Scythians developed a unique gold- and metal-working art of fine detail and fluid line, which fused Hellenistic, Celtic, and Central Asian motifs with great vigor. Artifacts reveal the influence of Mesopotamian, Siberian, and Chinese motifs as well. See also PAZYRYK.

SCYTHOPOLIS. See BETH-SHAN.

SEA ISLANDS (United States) Island chain off the Atlantic coast of SOUTH CAROLINA, GEORGIA, and FLORIDA, including ST. HELENA ISLAND, South Carolina and ST. SIMONS, Georgia. They were discovered and first settled by the Spanish, who set up missions and garrisons in the 16th century. The British advanced into the region in the early 18th century. James Oglethorpe, founder of the Georgia colony, built Fort Frederica on St. Simons Island. The islands were the first important cotton-growing region in the United States and became the site of large plantations in the 19th century. Invaded by Union forces during the Civil War, following the war the land was distributed to the former slaves who, in relative isolation, developed distinct customs and dialects, as exemplified by the Gullah language. There are antebellum plantations here, abandoned during the Union takeover.

SEA OF CHINNERETH. See GALILEE, SEA OF.

SEA OF THE PLAIN. See DEAD SEA.

SEATTLE (United States) Largest city of WASHING-TON State, situated between Elliot Bay in PUGET SOUND and Lake Washington. It is the commercial and industrial capital of the Pacific Northwest. The city was settled in 1851 and successfully withstood Indian attacks in 1856. It enjoyed its first real growth in 1884 with the coming of the railroad. From 1897 Seattle became an important commercial center during the ALASKA gold rush. The opening of the PANAMA CANAL, the industrialization of the West, and World War I brought further expansion as a port. In World War II it became a center of the aircraft industry. For many years a center of the labor movement, in 1919 it was the scene of a general strike organized by the Industrial Workers of the World (IWW).

SEBASTE, Israel. See SAMARIA.

SEBASTE, Turkey. See SIVAS..

SEBASTIA. See SIVAS.

SEBASTOPOL. See SEVASTOPOL.

SEBASTOPOLIS. See SUKHUMI.

SEBENICO. See ŠIBENIK.

ŞEBINKARAHISAR [*ancient:* **Colonia, Karahissar**] (Turkey) Town of Giresun province, in the NE, approx. 85 mi SW of Trabzon and 280 mi ENE of Ankara. Originally a Roman colony, it grew up around a fortress and was later a Byzantine frontier outpost. It was taken by the Turks in 1465. See also OTTOMAN EMPIRE.

SEBKRET EL KOURZIA. See SABKHAT AL-KURZĪYAH.

SEBTA. See CEUTA.

SECUNDERABAD [**Sikandarabad**] (India) Town and military post in N Andhra Pradesh, part of HYDER-ABAD. Founded in 1806, it was among the largest of British military bases until it was turned over to India in December 1945. It is still a major army base.

SECYON. See SICYON.

SEDALIA (United States) City of W central MIS-SOURI. Throughout the Civil War it was a Union military post on the Missouri-Kansas-Texas railroad. It was held for one day, Oct. 15, 1864, by a Confederate detachment from Sterling Price's raiding column.

SEDAN (France) Town of ARDENNES department, in the NE, on the MEUSE RIVER, 11 mi ESE of Mézières. Through the 16th and 17th centuries it was a strong Protestant center with a well-known Calvinist academy. The site of several battles, it saw the defeat of France and the surrender of Napoleon III on Sept. 2, 1870 in the Franco-Prussian War. Occupied by GER-MANY with heavy fighting in World War I, it was again taken by the Germans in May 1940 at the start of their invasion of France in World War II.The town was held by them until the Allied liberation on Aug. 31, 1944. It has an exceptionally large 15th-century castle. See also METZ.

SEDGEMOOR (England) Marshy tract of moorland in Somerset, 3 mi SE of Bridgwater. On July 6, 1685 it was the scene of the defeat of the rebelling duke of Monmouth by the forces of James II under Feversham and Churchill. The latter was named the first duke of Marlborough for his valor here and became a famous commander, victor of BLENHEIM.

SEDLEZ. See SIEDLCE.

SEDUNUM. See SION.

SÉES (France) Town of Orne department, in the NW, 13 mi NNE of Alençon. It was a fortified town in the 4th century AD when St. Lain was named its first bishop. In the ninth century it fell to the Normans, and from 1356 it was in the possession of the counts of ALENÇON. Changing hands several times in the wars of Henry II of ENGLAND and his sons, it was one of the first towns of NORMANDY to fall to the English in 1418 during the later phase of the Hundred Years War. Sacked by the Protestants during the Wars of Religion, it nevertheless attached itself to the Holy League in 1589 and voluntarily surrendered to Henry IV in 1590. Its outstanding cathedral dates from the 13th and 14th centuries.

SEGAULI [Sagauli] (India) Town of NW Bihar, in the NE, 85 mi N of Patna. A former British military base, on March 3, 1816 it was the site of the signing of a treaty that established British relations with NEPAL.

SEGESTA [*Greek:* Egesta] (Italy) Ruins of an ancient city in NW SICILY, in Trapani province, approx. 17 mi ESE of Trapani. Traditionally considered a Trojan colony and long the rival of SELINUS, it allied with Athens from 415 to 413 BC for the unsuccessful war against SYRACUSE during the Peloponnesian Wars. It then gained the alliance of CARTHAGE, sacked Selinus in 409 BC, and became a Carthaginian dependency. In 307 BC it suffered an attack and massacre by the tyrant of Syracuse, Agathocles, who changed its name briefly to Dicaeopolis. Besieged by Carthage in the First Punic War, it eventually overcame the Carthaginians and turned to ROME. It went into decline in the first century BC and was eventually destroyed by the Vandals in the fifth century AD. Its ruins include an outstanding unfinished temple of the fifth century BC and a rock-cut theater.

SEGESVÁR. See SIGHISOARA.

SEGODUNUM. See RODEZ.

SEGONTIUM. See CAERNARVON.

SÉGOU [Segu] (Mali) Port town in the SW, on the NIGER RIVER. Developed in the late 17th century as the capital of a BAMBARA kingdom, it reached its peak in the 18th century. It was taken in 1861 by Al-hajj Umar, a militant Muslim reformer who ruled until 1864, when he was succeeded by his son, Ahmadu. The latter made Ségou his capital and ruled until 1890. The town was occupied by the French from that year and was their headquarters for development on the Niger River, beginning in 1932.

SEGOVIA (Spain) City and provincial capital, approx. 45 mi NW of Madrid, on a rocky hill in Old CASTILE overlooking the Eresma River. Of ancient origin, it became a flourishing city in Roman times. After 714 AD it frequently changed hands between Moors and Christians until finally reconquered by Alfonso VI in 1079. It was a Moorish textile center, and then a favored residence of the kings of Castile and LEÓN. The great Alcázar on its rock saw the proclamation of Isabella I as queen. Ravaged by the French in 1808, Segovia also saw much fighting at the beginning of the Spanish civil war. A walled town, Segovia has the restored 14th and 15th century Alcázar, a 16th-century Gothic cathedral, and several Romanesque churches and medieval palaces. It has a Roman aqueduct, still in use, dating probably from the first century BC and one of the outstanding engineering monuments of the period.

SEGU. See SÉGOU.

SEGUIN (United States) City and county seat in S TEXAS, on the Guadalupe River, 33 mi ENE of San Antonio. Founded in 1831 by members of the Texas Rangers, it was named after Col. Juan Seguin, a hero of the Texas Revolution. Once a plantation center, it retains the character given it by later German settlers.

SEGUSIO [*modern:* Susa] (Italy) Ancient Roman town, on the Dora Riparia River, in Torino province, Piedmont region, approx. 30 mi W of Turin. It was the capital of the Cottii in northern ancient LIGURIA. Cottius, the son of King Domus, ruled as imperial prefect here over the 14 tribes his father had ruled, and erected a triumphal arch honoring Augustus, in 9/8 BC. The town was captured by Constantine in the fourth century AD in his campaign against Maxentius. It was assaulted unsuccessfully by Frederick Barbarossa in 1168 and burned by him in 1176. The town also contains an 11th-century church, now a cathedral, and the 13th-century church of San Francesco. See also SUSA, Italy.

SEICHEPREY (France) Hamlet in the Meurthe-et-Moselle department, E of St. Mihiel. The remains of trenches here commemorate one of the earliest advances by U.S. troops, newly entered into World War I on the side of the Allies. The battle occurred in the ST. MIHIEL sector on April 20, 1918.

SEINE RIVER [*ancient:* Sequana] (France) River, 482 mi long, rising in the Plateau de Langres, in the Côte d'Or department in the E and flowing NW past TROYES, through PARIS, and meandering through NORMANDY, past ROUEN, until it empties into the ENGLISH CHANNEL near LE HAVRE. It is navigable for approximately 350 miles.

Along its course it flows through or bounds on the departments of Côte d'Or in Burgundy; Aube and Marne in Champagne; Seine-et-Marne, Essonne, Paris, Yvelines in the Île-de-France; and Eure and Seine-Maritime in Normandy. It rises near the village of Chanceaux, approximately 22 miles northwest of Dijon. An enclosed spring with a sculpted tablet marks its source. The small plot within the enclosure belongs to the city of Paris. Along its route it is joined by the Aube, Yonne, MARNE, and OISE rivers.

An important route inland since Roman times, it was used by Viking raiders who sacked Paris in the ninth century, and with its tributaries is responsible for the richness of the entire Paris basin and the cities along its banks. The Seine formed the Allied defensive line east of Paris after Gen. von Kluck advanced past the Marne from Aug. 17 to Sept. 3, 1914 during World War I.

SEISHIN. See CHONG-JIN.

SEISTAN [Sistan] [*ancient:* **Drangiana, Sakastan**] (Afghanistan and Iran) Lowland and delta region of SW Afghanistan and E Iran, fed mainly by the flood of the HELMAND RIVER. It was a former province in eastern Iran, corresponding to ancient DRANGIANA. The capital was at Nasratabad (now Zabōl, Iran). It was held by the eastern Scythians or Sakas and called Sakastan in the second and third centuries AD. From the fourth to the seventh century the region was a center of Zoroastrian worship. From the eighth century until 1383 and the arrival of Mongol conquerors, it flourished under the Arabs. The Mongols destroyed the river control system and ended Seistan's prosperity. Under the Safavids from 1502 to 1736, the region was a source of dispute between PERSIA and Afghanistan and continued to be so until the 20th century, most intensively in the 19th century.

SEKHET-AM. See SIWAH.

SEKIGAHARA (Japan) Town of SW Gifu prefecture, on central HONSHŪ, 16 mi WSW of Gifu. In 1600 it was the scene of a crucial battle, following which Shogun Iyeyasu gained complete control of the government. He then initiated the Tokugawa Shogunate, under which Japan was closed to foreign penetration until the mid-19th century.

SEKONDI-TAKORADI (Ghana) Commercial city and port in the Western Region of the SW, 110 mi WSW of Accra. The two parts of this city developed around forts dating from the 17th century, English and Dutch in Sekondi, the older and larger of the two, and Swedish in Takoradi. In 1872 the region was ceded by the Dutch to the British; and Sekondi became the main port of the Gold Coast. The two sections merged in 1946 and were made a city in 1963. The reconstructed Fort Orange changed hands peacefully between the Dutch, British, and French and is now in ruins in the Sekondi area.

SELA. See PETRA.

SELANGOR (Malaysia) State on the W coast of the S MALAY PENINSULA, on the Strait of Malacca. Under various powers before the 16th century, it was ruled after the fall of MALACCA in 1511 by the sultans of Riau and JOHORE. Conquered by Bugis tribesmen from MAKASAR in the Celebes in the early 18th century, it was overrun by the Dutch in 1783/84. A commercial treaty with the British in 1818 preceded British control as a protectorate in 1874, after the outbreak of civil war. Part of the Federated Malay States from 1895 and part of the independent Federation of Malaya from 1957, it became a state of Malaysia in 1963. KUALA LUMPUR is capital of Selangor and of Malaysia itself.

SELAT TEBRAU. See JOHORE STRAIT.

SÉLESTAT [*German:* **Schlettstadt**] (France) Town of Bas-Rhin department, in the NE, near the Ill River, 34 mi SW of Strasbourg. A free city under the Hohen-staufens, it was taken in 1632 by SWEDEN during the French intervention in the Thirty Years War. It was captured by the French in 1634. Their rule continued following the Peace of Westphalia in 1648. An object of dispute in 1815, it was captured by the Germans in 1870 during the Franco-Prussian War and remained under their control until the end of World War I, when it was returned to French rule.

SELEUCIA (Iraq) Ancient city on the W bank of the TIGRIS RIVER, opposite Ctesiphon, approx. 20 mi SSE of Baghdad. Founded by one of Alexander the Great's generals, Seleucus I of the SELEUCID EMPIRE, c.310 BC, it became its chief city and eastern capital, overshadowing BABYLON. Connected by canal to the EUPHRATES RIVER, it became a bustling commercial center, reaching a population of some 600,000 by the first century AD. Although conquered by the Parthians in 140 BC, it remained a Hellenistic city until the first century AD. The Parthians then built up CTESIPHON as a rival and their capital. Seleucia was burned by Trajan in 162 AD during his war against Parthia, rebuilt, then finally destroyed by the Romans in 164 AD. The site, known as Tel Umar, was extensively excavated in the 1930's.

Here the Persian religious leader, Mani, began preaching c.240 AD. He taught a dualist religion of an eternal conflict between the forces of Good and Evil, Light, and Darkness. His followers, later called Manicheans, influenced heretical Christian sects, among them the Cathars of LANGUEDOC, centered around ALBI. See also PARTHIA, ROME, ROMAN EMPIRE.

SELEUCIA PIERIA [*modern:* **Süveydiye**] (Turkey) Ancient port of ANTIOCH, in ancient SYRIA, now in SW Hatay in S Asian Turkey, on the ORONTES RIVER near Süveydiye. A strongly fortified city, founded by Seleucus I c. 300 BC near the border of CILICIA, it was especially important in the third century BC when the Seleucid and Egyptian successors of Alexander the Great of Macedon were vying for control of the region. Seleucia disappeared in the sixth century AD. Roman and Hellenistic shrines and temples, the city walls, and a necropolis for Roman sailors have been found here. St. Peter, who sailed from the port on his voyages, is supposed to have preached to the first Gentile Christian converts in the little St. Peter's Church in the outskirts of the city. See also APAMEA AD ORENTEM, LAODICEA, SELEUCID EMPIRE.

SELEUCIA TRACHEOTIS [**Trachea**] [*modern:* **Silifke**] (Turkey) Ancient city in CILICIA, in SE Asia Minor, SW of Tarsus on the Calycadmus River, now the Göksu. It was one of a number of cities founded by Seleucus I (c.358–28 BC), founder of the SELEUCID EMPIRE, including his capital, SELEUCIA, on the Tigris. Some ruins of the ancient town remain. See also SELEUCIA PIERIA.

SELEUCID EMPIRE Ancient empire founded by Seleucus I, one of Alexander the Great's generals, after Alexander's death in 323 BC and the breakup of the MACEDONIAN EMPIRE. At its greatest extent it included ASIA MINOR, SYRIA, MESOPOTAMIA and reached east into INDIA as far as the Indus River. After

BABYLONIA was awarded to Seleucus in 312 BC he founded a capital at SELEUCIA on the banks of the TIGRIS RIVER, approximately 20 miles southeast of the future site of Baghdad, which rapidly became a major Greek metropolis and continued to flourish as such well into the period of domination by PARTHIA, until the first century AD. Seleucus also founded ANTIOCH in Syria and other important Greek colonies.

Ruled by four kings named Seleucus and 13 named Antiochus, the empire waxed and waned during the dynastic wars of the successors of Alexander, but after the second century BC it began rapidly to break up until its remnants were taken over by the Romans under Pompey in 64 BC and eventually became part of the ROMAN EMPIRE.

SELIMIYE. See SIDE.

SELINOUS. See SELINUS.

SELINUS [*Greek:* **Selinous**] (Italy) Ancient Greek colony and city on the S coast of SICILY in Trapani province. Its ruins are approx. 7 mi SSE of Castelvetrano. It was founded by Dorian Greeks in the seventh century BC. Facing Africa on the south coast, and near the Carthaginian center of MARSALA (Lilybaeum) it early chose accommodation with CARTHAGE, and thus prospered during the sixth and fifth centuries BC. This period saw the construction of the seven splendid Doric temples, all toppled by earthquakes, whose ruins can be seen today. It was often at war with SEGESTA. The Carthaginians turned on Selinus in 409 BC and held the city until 250 BC, when they destroyed it and moved the inhabitants to Lilybaeum. Approximately 15 miles to the east is the site of Aquae Selinuntiae, now SCIACCA.

SELKIRK (Canada) Town of SE MANITOBA, on the Red River, just S of Lake Winnipeg. It is named for the fifth earl of Selkirk who established the RED RIVER SETTLEMENT in the region in 1812.

SELKIRK [**Selkirkshire**] (Scotland) Former county and town in Borders region. The town is 31 mi SSE of Edinburgh. Once under the Anglo-Saxon kingdom of NORTHUMBRIA, it became part of Scotland in 1018 and suffered extensively in the lengthy border wars between England and Scotland. The 12th-century castle at Selkirk, no longer standing, was taken by the English in 1333 after the Battle of HALIDON HILL. The county was the royal hunting forest for many years and has literary associations with Sir Walter Scott, who served as sheriff of Selkirk for 33 years, and with Scott's discovery, poet James Hogg, known as the "Ettrick Shepherd." A five-mile ancient earthwork and Roman ruins are found here. The ruins of several medieval abbeys, including Melrose, Dryburgh, and Jedburgh, are in the area. See also FLODDEN.

SELKIRKSHIRE. See SELKIRK, Scotland.

SELLASIA (Greece) Town of ancient LACONIA, in the SE Peloponnesus, approx. 5 mi N of Sparta. In 222/21 BC it was the site of a battle in which Antigonus Doson, the king of MACEDON, defeated the Spartans under Cleomenes III. The site is now occupied by the chapel of St. Constantine. See also SPARTA.

SELMA [*former:* **Moore's Bluff, Moore's Landing**] (United States) Industrial city and county seat of Dallas county, ALABAMA, on the Alabama River, 40 mi W of Montgomery. Incorporated in 1820, it served as a Confederate arsenal and supply depot in the Civil War and was captured and seriously damaged by Union troops in 1865. One hundred years later, in 1965, it was the scene of large-scale, nonviolent, civil rights demonstrations in a black voter registration drive under the leadership of Dr. Martin Luther King, Jr. There had been several previous incidents of violence and the killing of Rev. James Reeb of Boston during earlier organizing attempts.

SEMARANG [**Samarang**] (Indonesia) Port, city, residency, and capital of central Java province, on JAVA, on the N coast, approx. 225 mi E of Jakarta. Under Dutch rule from *c.*1750, it was once a fortified town surrounded by a moat. During World War II it was occupied by the Japanese from February 1942 until September 1945. See also DEMAK.

SEMENDRIA. See SMEDEREVO.

SEMINARA (Italy) Town in Reggio di Calabria province, near the W coast of Italy, approx. 20 mi NE of Reggio di Calabria. This small town is known chiefly for a battle fought here in 1503 during the destructive wars released by the invasion of Italy by Charles VIII of FRANCE. In the battle the Spanish under García de Paredes defeated a French army. Seminara also witnessed a number of other battles.

SEMIPALATINSK (USSR) City and oblast in Central Asian USSR, on the Irtysh River, 560 mi NNE of Alma-Ata. It was founded in 1718 as a Russian frontier post and was moved to its present site in 1778 to escape frequent flooding. It long owed its importance to its position on the caravan routes from Mongolia to RUSSIA and from SIBERIA to central Asia. It profited economically when the Turkistan-Siberia railroad reached it in 1906. The Semipalatinsk oblast was organized in 1939. The city takes its name, meaning "seven palaces," from the ruins of a Buddhist monastery. The novelist Feodor Dostoyevsky was stationed here from 1854 to 1859 as a soldier in exile.

SEMMERING PASS (Austria) Mountain pass in the Eastern Alps, 23 mi SW of Wiener Neustadt. It is the site of the world's first mountain railroad, built from 1848 to 1854. It passes through 15 tunnels and over 16 viaducts.

SEMNĀN [**Samnan**] [*ancient:* **Samina**] (Iran) City and governorate of Māzanderān province, 110 mi E of Teheran, S of the Elburz Mts. An ancient town mentioned by the geographer Ptolemy in the second century AD, it was destroyed by the Oghuz Turks in 1036 AD and was laid waste by the Mongols in 1221. There are, nevertheless, the remains of several castles, parts of a 12th-century mosque, and of a 12th-century minaret.

SEMPACH (Switzerland) Town in Lucerne canton, on the Lake of Sempach, 8 mi NW of Lucerne. Here on July 9, 1386 the Swiss confederates defeated the Austrian Hapsburg army under Duke Leopold. The battle helped to consolidate Swiss independence from the Hapsburgs. There is a monument here to Arnold von Winkelried, who purportedly sacrificed himself to lead his Swiss compatriots to the victory. See also NÄFELS.

SENA (Mozambique) Town in SE Africa, on the right bank of the ZAMBEZI RIVER, approx. 125 mi SE of Tete. Founded by the Portuguese in the 16th century, it is the site of an 18th-century fort and a railroad bridge across the Zambezi.

SENA GALLICA. See SENIGALLIA.

SENDAI (Japan) Capital city of Miyagi prefecture, on N HONSHŪ, near the E coast, 180 mi N of Tokyo. At present an important cultural center, it has the ruins of a 16th-century castle and a monument to Date Masamune, a powerful feudal lord in the 17th century who made the city his headquarters. His successors ruled the city for nearly 300 years. The Osaki Hachiman Shrine dates from 1606.

SENECA FALLS (United States) Manufacturing village in W central NEW YORK State, on the Seneca River, 11 mi W of Auburn. The first women's rights convention in the United States was held here in 1848. The name reflects the importance throughout this area of the Seneca, an Iroquois tribe very powerful in the 17th and 18th centuries as far as Ohio. British allies in the American Revolution, they had many of their villages destroyed by American troops in 1779.

SENEGAL [*French:* **République du Sénégal**] A republic of West Africa bordered by the Atlantic Ocean on the W, Mali on the E, Mauritania on the N, and Guinea and Guinea-Bissau on the S.

Senegal was formerly the center of FRENCH WEST AFRICA, and its capital city of DAKAR was the commercial and administrative hub of the French African empire.

The first Europeans to reach the region were the Portuguese, who in the mid-15th century established several factories here, as did the French in 1638 and then briefly the Dutch. The British captured the then French posts during the Seven Years War of 1759 to 1763, and again during the Napoleonic Wars. French influence steadily increased, until Senegal officially became a colony in 1895.

In 1945 Senegal became a republic within the French community, led by President Leopold Senghor. A brief union with the Sudanese Republic as the Federation of Mali lasted from 1959 to 1960, after which Senegal became an independent state. Senghor continued to be the dominant figure in the country and maintained close ties with France. He also kept a tight rein on internal politics. Its economy, resting almost entirely on peanut production, was devastated by the great sub-Saharan drought of 1973; and many thousands died from starvation. Senegal is currently trying to diversify its agricultural output with U.S. assistance. In 1979 ground was broken for a three-nation, $550 million project to harness the SENEGAL RIVER for power and irrigation, in an attempt to provide a long-term solution to the country's continuing economic problems. In 1981 it joined with GAMBIA to form the new nation of Senegambia. See also GORÉE, SAINT-LOUIS, TEKRUR.

SENEGAL RIVER (Africa) River, approx. 1,000 mi long. It is formed in MALI by the confluence of the Bafing and Bakoy rivers, which rise in the Fouta Djallon, a highland region of Guinea. The river flows north, then west, forming the border between SENEGAL and MAURITANIA. It enters the Atlantic Ocean at Saint-Louis, Senegal. The Tukolor people settled in the Senegal valley in the ninth century and between the 10th and 14th centuries ruled the strong state of TEKRUR. They were conquered by the MALI EMPIRE in the 14th century. Portuguese explorers reached the mouth of the river in 1444/45. They established a trading post and used the river as a trade route, exchanging cloth and metal goods for gold dust, gum arabic, ivory, and slaves. The French displaced the Portuguese in 1638 and in 1698 established St. Joseph de Galam, a post 400 miles upstream. Kayes, in western Mali, is an administrative and business center at the upper limit of navigation.

SENEGAMBIA Confederation of West Africa agreed upon by the countries of SENEGAL and GAMBIA on Dec. 17, 1981. It was also the name for a short-lived British colony in the 18th century, Britain's first in Africa.

SENGLEA. See COSPICUA, VITTORIOSA.

SENIGALLIA [*ancient:* **Sena Gallica**; *former:* **Sinigaglia**] (Italy) Port on the Adriatic Sea, in central Ancona province, in the Marches region, 18 mi NW of Ancona. It was a capital of the ancient Gallic Senones before it was captured by the Romans in 289 BC and turned into a Roman military outpost. During the Punic Wars Hasdrubal of CARTHAGE was defeated at the Metaurus River in the vicinity by the Romans in 207 BC. One of the cities of the Pentapolis under the BYZANTINE EMPIRE in the sixth century AD, it was part of the lands given by Pepin the Short to the popes in the eighth century. Although a free town in the 12th century, it became a papal fief. It was sacked by Arab raiders in 1264, then rebuilt. It is mentioned by Dante in the *Divine Comedy* as a typical victim of the Guelph-Ghibelline Wars. It had a regional fair from the 13th to the 19th centuries. The town's castle and city walls date from the 15th century, and it has two Renaissance churches of note. Pope Pius IX was born here in 1792. See also PAPAL STATES, ROME.

SENKADAGALA MAHANUWARA. See KANDY.

SEN KINGDOM. See NABADWIP, India.

SENLAC. See HASTINGS.

SENLIS (France) Ancient town of Oise department, in the N, 28 mi NNE of Paris. Here on May 23, 1493 Charles VIII and Emperor Maximilian I signed a treaty by which Charles relinquished the FRANCHE-COMTÉ. The town has Gallo-Roman walls, medieval fortifications, and the outstanding early Gothic cathedral of Notre Dame, a masterpiece dating from between 1150 and the early 13th century. There is also a 15th-century town hall and the ruins of a château used as residence by the earlier kings of France.

SENNAAR. See SENNAR.

SENNAR [Sannar, Sennaar] (Sudan) Region, town,

and ancient kingdom in the E, mainly between the White and Blue Nile rivers. The uninhabited old town, on the Blue NILE RIVER, south of Wad Madani, served as capital of the former Muslim kingdom of Sennar, or Sannar, founded in the 16th century and known as the Black Sultanate. At its most extensive, it occupied much of the eastern part of the present Sudan. The 18th century brought decline and eventual absorption into the OTTOMAN EMPIRE in 1821. The town was sacked after a siege by the Mahdists in 1883 and has been replaced by the modern town nearby.

SENS [Sens-Sur-Yonne] [*ancient:* **Agedincum, Agendicum**] (France) Ancient city of Yonne department, in the NE, on the Yonne River, 32 mi NW of Auxerre. An ancient capital of the Gallic Senones, it was taken by the Romans in the first century BC and became an important town of Roman GAUL. Made a bishopric in the fourth century AD, it became an archiepiscopal see in the eighth century and had Chartres, Orléans, and, until 1622, Paris itself under its jurisdiction. Attacked by the Saracens in 731 and the Normans in 886, it went to the French crown in 1055. A council held here in 1121 saw Bernard of Clairvaux attack the teachings of Peter Abélard. At the Synod here in 1152 the annulment of the marriage of King Louis VII and Eleanor of Aquitaine was decreed. Pope Alexander III took refuge here during his exile from Italy in 1163/64. It became a stronghold of the Holy League during the 16th century Wars of Religion and suffered a massacre of Huguenots in 1562.

The High Gothic cathedral of Saint-Étienne, begun c.1130, was mostly the work of William of Sens, a master builder who also contributed to the reconstruction of CANTERBURY cathedral in England. It is the first completely Gothic cathedral and the first to use Gothic ribbed vaulting throughout.

SENS-SUR-YONNE. See SENS.

SENTA [*Hungarian:* **Zerta**] (Yugoslavia) City in the Vojvodina region of SERBIA, in the NE, on the right bank of the Tisza River, approx. 80 mi NNW of Belgrade. Here on Sept. 11, 1697 Prince Eugene of Savoy won a decisive victory over the Turks who had controlled the area for over 100 years. This contributed to the Turkish acceptance of the Treaty of Passarowitz (see POŽAREVAC) and made AUSTRIA the foremost power in central Europe. See also OTTOMAN EMPIRE.

SENTINUM [*modern:* **Sassoferrato**] (Italy) Ancient town in UMBRIA, now in Ancona province, Marches region, on the Sentino River, near Sassoferrato, approx. 33 mi SW of Ancona. A climactic battle was fought here in 295 BC between the Romans under Publius Decius Mus and the combined forces of the Samnites, Etruscans, and Gauls in which the victorious Romans firmly established their power in central Italy. Sentinum was sacked by Octavius Augustus in 41 BC, but it was later restored as part of the ROMAN EMPIRE. A few ruins and the city walls survive. Many of the elements of the site were used in the construction of the 12th-century church of Santa Croce near here. The Museo Civico here has archaeological finds from the Umbrian town. See also ROME.

SEOUL [Kyongsong] [*Japanese:* **Keijo**] (South Korea) Capital city of the nation and of Kyonggi province, 40 mi E of INCHON, its port. The industrial, commercial, and cultural center of the country, it served as capital of the Korean Yi dynasty from 1392 to 1910. Under Japanese rule from 1910 to 1945, it was extensively modernized and, with the partition of the country in 1945, was made the headquarters for the U.S. military government until Aug. 15, 1948, when it became capital of the Republic of KOREA. Occupied by communist forces only three days after their crossing of the 38th parallel, it endured two occupations in the Korean War—from June 28 to Sept. 29, 1950 and from Jan. 4 to March 14, 1951—following which U.N. forces retook the city. It became headquarters for the U.N. command in the war. Badly damaged, it has been largely rebuilt since 1953. It retains three gates of the ancient city wall and three imperial palaces, including the Chanduk and Ducksoo.

SEPETON. See SHEPTON MALLET.

SEPHAR. See ZAFĀR.

SEPPHORIS. See ZIPPORI.

SEPTIMANCA. See SIMANCAS.

SEPTIMANIA (France) Medieval territory extending from the mouth of the RHÔNE RIVER to the PYRENEES Mts on the S, and NW to the CÉVENNES Mts. Until the first century BC the region roughly corresponded to the Roman province of Transalpine Gaul, reorganized after Caesar's conquest into Gallia Narbonensis. By the fifth century AD Septimania had emerged as a Roman province. It became part of Visigothic Gaul by 414 and was retained by Visigothic Spain in 507, when Theodoric, the Ostrogoth king of Italy, intervened to prevent Clovis's Franks from conquering it. In 720 it was overrun by the Muslims from Spain. Reconquered by Charlemagne in 759, it then merged into the FRANKISH EMPIRE, later sharing the history of PROVENCE. See also VISIGOTHIC KINGDOM.

SEQUANA. See SEINE RIVER.

SERADZ. See SIERADZ.

SERAFIMOVICH (USSR) Town of Volgograd oblast, on the DON RIVER, NW of Volgograd, in SE Russian SFSR. Near the end of the unsuccessful 66-day siege of Stalingrad (now VOLGOGRAD) by the German invaders during World War II, this town was the scene of the first offensive of the Soviet armies in November 1942, in the counterattack that ultimately led to the victorious end of the war as a whole.

SERAJAVO. See SARAJEVO.

SERAM. See CERAM.

SERAMPORE. See SERAMPUR.

SERAMPUR [Serampore] [*Danish:* **Frederiksnagar**] (India) Town of West Bengal, in the NE, on the right bank of the Hooghly River, 13 mi N of Calcutta. In a region occupied by the Danes in 1755, it was founded in 1799 and was the center of Danish colonialism in India until 1845, when Great Britain purchased the town from DENMARK. It is the site of an important Baptist mission that was also responsible for the first introduction of typesetting and newspapers in an Indian alphabet.

SERAN. See CERAM.

SERANG. See CERAM.

SERBIA [*Serbo-Croatian:* **Srbija**] (Yugoslavia) Constituent republic of Yugoslavia, in the E part of the country, the largest of six republics and the most influential. The Serbs are South Slavs who first settled in the BALKAN PENINSULA during the sixth and seventh centuries AD when the region was controlled by the BYZANTINE EMPIRE. Rascia, the first organized Serbian state, was probably founded early in the 10th century. This state expanded, and in 1159 Stephen Nemanja founded a dynasty that ruled for two centuries, at first under Byzantine suzerainty. BELGRADE became Serbia's capital in the 12th century. Under Stephen Dusan, who became king in 1331 and czar in 1346, Serbia rose to be the most powerful nation in the Balkans as well as the economic and cultural leader.

After Stephen's death in 1355, Serbia declined in the face of assaults by the OTTOMAN EMPIRE. The climax came in 1389 at the Battle of KOSOVO Field in which the Serbs were defeated, thereafter losing territory and their independence. Sultan Muhammad II completed the annexation of Serbia in 1459. For nearly four centuries Serbia suffered under extremely harsh Turkish rule, which did not end until 1812 when a revolt led by Karageorge, beginning in 1804, gained Serbian autonomy within the Ottoman Empire. This situation lasted only a short time, but in 1829, with help from RUSSIA, the Turks were forced out of most of Serbia.

From this time on the course of events in Serbia was governed largely by feuding between the Karageorge and Obrenovic families, who sought to control the government. Miloš Obrenović, who ruled twice between 1817 and 1860, was the founder of his dynasty as well as of modern Serbia. Although the last Turkish soldiers left Serbia in 1867, the nation declared war on the Turks in 1876, only to be defeated until Russia again came to its aid.

The Congress of BERLIN in 1878 recognized an entirely free Serbia and added to its territory, but the prestige thus gained was partly lost in an unsuccessful war with BULGARIA in 1885. The Obrenović dynasty ended in 1903 when King Alexander was assassinated, to be succeeded by Peter I of the Karageorge dynasty. He made the parliament more powerful and revived the economy. To offset the power of AUSTRIA-HUNGARY and Turkey, Serbia led in the formation of the Balkan League, which included MONTENEGRO, Bulgaria, and GREECE. With Russian assistance the league defeated Turkey in 1912 in the First Balkan War. Dissatisfied with its spoils, Serbia warred on its former ally, Bulgaria, in 1913 in the Second Balkan War.

When the heir to the Austro-Hungarian throne was assassinated by a Serbian on June 28, 1914 at SARAJEVO, the empire served Serbia with an ultimatum that led to the start of World War I. Serbia was overrun by the Central Powers in November 1915, but after the Allied victory in 1918 Serbia became part of the Kingdom of the Serbs, Croats and Slovenes, renamed Yugoslavia in 1929. In 1945, at the end of World War II, Peter II, the last of the Karageorges, lost his throne when Yugoslavia became a republic.

SERCQ. See SARK.

SERDICA. See SOFIA.

SERENDIP. See SRI LANKA.

SERES. See SERRAI.

SERGIEV. See ZAGORSK.

SERGIEVO. See ZAGORSK.

SERGIEVSKI POSAD. See ZAGORSK.

SERGIYEV. See ZAGORSK.

SERGIYEVO. See ZAGORSK.

SERGIYEVSKI POSAD. See ZAGORSK.

SERICA (China) Ancient regional name applied to an area of E Asia, roughly that of China today. It was used by the Greeks and Romans to refer to the land peopled by the Seres, who were then renowned for their silk manufacture. These were placed by Lucan (39–65 AD) at the sources of the Nile, near Ethiopia. The word later came to denote all silk products and garments.

SERINAGAR. See SRINAGAR.

SERINGAPATAM (India) Town of Mysore state, in the S, 8 mi N of Mysore. The state's former capital under Tipu Sahib, whose fort and palace were on an island in the Cauvery River, it was the scene in 1792 of the signing of a treaty with the British. Seven years later, in the Fourth MYSORE War, it was besieged and captured by the British, and Tipu was killed. It is the site of Tipu's mausoleum and that of his father, Haidar Ali.

SERMIONE. See SIRMIONE.

SEROWE (Botswana) S African town in the E, approx. 160 mi N of Gabarone. It has been the seat of the Ngwato tribe since 1902, when they arrived from Palapye. It is the site of a memorial to Khama III, chief of the Ngwato in the late 19th and early 20th centuries.

SERPUKHOV (USSR) City on the Oka River, 56 mi S of Moscow. A fortress town and outpost for MOSCOW since 1339, it was officially founded in 1374. It was attacked and damaged by Tatars in 1382 and 1408 and refortified by Ivan the Terrible c.1550. The site of a stone kremlin from the 16th century, it also contains the 16th-century church of St. Gregory and St. Dmitri and the 17th-century Vysotsk monastery.

SERRAE. See SERRAI.

SERRAI [Seres, Serres] [*ancient:* **Serrae, Serrhae, Siris, Sirrhae;** *Greek:* **Sérrai**] (Greece) Ancient city and present capital of Serrai department in the NE, near the end of Lake Ahinou, approx. 42 mi NE of Thessaloníki in MACEDONIA.

It was capital of its district by the fifth century BC, when Herodotus mentioned it. Xerxes passed through it in his invasion of Greece in 480 BC.

As a fortress of the BYZANTINE EMPIRE it was sacked by the Bulgars in 1195/96. Taken by the Latin Franks in 1204 during the Fourth Crusade, it was besieged and occupied in 1205 by the Vlach Johannica.

It was retaken soon after by Boniface of Montferrat. Captured by Stephen Dušan of SERBIA, it was occupied by the Serbians from 1345 to 1371, who made it their capital.

Held by the OTTOMAN EMPIRE from 1383 to 1913, it then passed to Greece. Occupied and damaged by the Bulgarians before and during World War I from 1916 to 1918, it was the center of a revolt in 1935. During World War II it was again held by the Bulgarians from 1941 to 1944. See also BULGARIA.

SERRES. See SERRAI.

SERRHAE. See SERRAI.

SERT. See SIIRT.

SESSA AURUNCA [*ancient:* **Suessa Aurunca;** *later:* **Colonia Julia Felix Classica**] (Italy) Town of Caserta province, CAMPANIA region, 33 mi NNW of Naples. When the leading city of the Aurunci, it was damaged for failing to pay tribute to the Romans. With its name changed, it was later an Augustan colony. It is the site of Roman ruins and a 12th-century cathedral, which incorporates Roman elements.

SESTOS (Turkey) Ancient town on the Thracian shore of the DARDANELLES (Hellespont), at the straits' narrowest point, opposite Abydos. It was the north end-point of Xerxes's daring bridge of boats across the Hellespont, made c.480 BC for his invasion of Greece via Thrace. The king's engineering feat was a wonder to the ancient world. According to Aeschylus's play, *The Persians,* Xerxes was punished by the gods for his act of *hubris,* or overweening pride, in attempting to bridge the straits. Later controlled by Athens and important in Roman times, Sestos declined after the founding of Byzantium, later CONSTANTINOPLE.

SETABIS. See JÁTIVA.

SÈTE [*former:* **Cette**] (France) One of the most important commercial and fishing ports in the S, in Hérault department, LANGUEDOC, on the Mediterranean, 18 mi SSW of Montpellier. A town laced by canals, its harbor was designed by Colbert in 1666 and built by Vauban and Riquet under Louis XIV. It is the birthplace and burial place of Paul Valéry, poet and philosopher.

SÉTIF [*ancient:* **Sitifis**] (Algeria) Department and town built by the French on the ruins of a Roman town, 60 mi NW of Constantine. Founded in the first century AD, it was an important provincial capital under both the Romans and the Byzantines. There are remains of the large Byzantine fortifications and a Roman mausoleum.

SETÚBAL [*former English:* **Saint Ubes, Saint Yves**] (Portugal) Major port of Portugal and district capital on the bay of Setúbal, at the mouth of the Sado River, 19 mi SE of Lisbon. Sétubal was important in the former wine trade with England. It was a royal residence under John II from 1481 to 1495. A 17th-century castle and several noteworthy churches are about the only survivors of the great earthquake of 1755. Across the estuary from Setúbal are the ruins of Roman Cetobriga, half submerged, with huge concrete tanks for drying fish.

SEVASTOPOL [**Sebastopol**] [*ancient:* **Chersonesus;** *medieval:* **Akhtiar**] (USSR) Port city on the Crimean peninsula and the Bay of Sevastopol, 40 mi SW of Simferopol. A major Russian naval base and strategic fortress since the 19th century, it stands near the ruins of the ancient Greek colony of CHERSONESUS. After Chersonesus was destroyed by the Tatars in 1399, they founded a settlement called Akhtiar here on the site.

Modern Sevastopol was founded by Catherine II as a naval base on the same site in 1783/84. In the Crimean War the city resisted the Allied invasion and assault from October 1854 until Sept. 11, 1855. During the Russian civil war it was headquarters for the White Army under Gen. Wrangel. In World War II it fell to the Germans after another heroic siege from October 1941 to July 1942 and was severely damaged. The city was recaptured by the Soviets on May 10, 1944. See also CRIMEA, UKRAINE.

The great Russian Black Sea port and naval base at the time of the Crimean War. Catherine the Great established Sevastapol after she annexed the Crimea in 1783.

SEVENEH. See ASWAN.

SEVEN GOLDEN CITIES OF CIBOLA. See CIBOLA.

SEVEN HILLS. See ROME, SEVEN HILLS OF.

SEVEN ISLES OF IZU. See IZU-SHICHITO.

SEVERN RIVER [*ancient:* **Sabrina;** *Welsh:* **Hafren**] (England, Wales) River rising in Plinlimmon, Wales and flowing approx. 180 mi E and NE to Shrewsbury and thence SE, S, and SW through an estuary to the Bristol Channel. Although the river is second only to the Thames in length, its direct distance from source to mouth is only approximately 80 miles. It has many tributaries, including the WYE and the AVON; and over much of its length the countryside is noted for its beauty. The mouth of the Severn at the Bristol Channel is some 10 miles wide, and the lower river formed a formidable barrier between England and the coal-mining and industrial area of Wales surrounding CARDIFF. In the mid-17th century a bridge was built spanning it near Sharpness, but it was not until 1886, when the Severn railroad tunnel was completed under the estuary, some 14 miles south of the bridge, that significant relief was provided. Rail time for passengers, and more importantly for freight, was cut in half between the Cardiff area and BRISTOL, England. A new suspension bridge across the estuary was opened in 1966.

SEVILLA. See SEVILLE.

SEVILLE [*ancient:* **Hispalis;** *Spanish:* **Sevilla**] (Spain) City and provincial capital, in the SW, on the Guadalquivir River, 62 mi NNE of Cádiz. An ancient Iberian city and important in Phoenician times, and now the leading city of ANDALUSIA, it prospered under the Romans, who made it the judicial center of BAETICA province and who built the nearby city of ITALICA where both Hadrian and Trajan were born. Sustained as the chief city of the south under the Vandals and the Visigoths, from the fifth to eighth centuries, it was captured in 712 AD by the Moors under Musa and until 1248 was an independent emirate under the Abbadids, and a cultural and commercial center under the ALMORAVIDS and the ALMOHADS. In 1248 it was besieged and captured by Ferdinand III of León and Castile, and after 1492 was the center of Spanish colonial trade. In the 16th century it was a major center of Spain's cloth industry. Decline began in the 17th century through rivalry with Cádiz. During the Napoleonic Wars it was occupied by the French under Soult from 1808 to 1812. The center of a well-known school of painting, it was the birthplace of both Velázquez and Murillo. Its Gothic cathedral of 1401 to 1519 houses the tomb of Christopher Columbus and is a structure rich in art treasures. It is on the site of a former mosque, two parts of which remain—the Giralda tower and the Court of Oranges. The city is rich in Roman and Moorish remains and maintains a distinctly Moorish character.

Isidore, bishop of Seville from *c.*570 to 636, was the most learned man in Europe during his lifetime. His *Etymologies* are a vast encyclopedia of ancient learning, organized by field of study. The book was a major source of learning throughout the Middle Ages.

SÈVRES (France) Town of Hauts-de-Seine department, in the N, on the SEINE RIVER, 6 mi SW of Paris. In 1920 a treaty was signed here between the Allies and the Turks, in effect ending the OTTOMAN EMPIRE. The aggressions of a second Turkish government necessitated a new treaty, signed in 1923 at LAUSANNE. Sèvres is also the site of the national porcelain factory, transferred from VINCENNES in 1756.

SEYCHELLES, REPUBLIC OF Island group and republic in the Indian Ocean, approx. 1,000 mi E of Mombasa, Kenya. Its chief islands are Mahé, Praslin, La Digue, Silhouette, and Curieuse. Known to Arabs and Europeans long before it was claimed by the French in 1744, it was first colonized in 1768 by French planters and slaves from MAURITIUS. Taken by the British in 1794 and made a dependency of Mauritius in 1810, the islands came under British control by the Treaty of Paris in 1814. Made a crown colony in 1903, they became independent in 1976. The capital and port city is Victoria. In 1982 a group of mercenaries from South Africa tried unsuccessfully to capture the islands and topple its left-leaning government.

Seville, chief city of southern Spain since Roman times, with many Moorish remains. Following Columbus's discovery of America, it was the principal port for the New World.

SEYMOUR ISLAND (Ecuador) One of the GALÁPAGOS ISLANDS, in the Pacific Ocean, approx. 600 mi W of the Ecuador coast. By special arrangement with the government of Ecuador, it was the site of a U.S. air base during World War II from December 1941 to July 1, 1946, when it was evacuated by U.S. troops.

SÉZANNE (France) Town of SW Marne department, in the NE. Its surrounding countryside was the scene of Marshal Foch's victory in the first battle of the MARNE on Sept. 9, 1914, when French forces drove the Germans into the marshes of St.-Gond to the northeast.

SFAX [**Safaqis**] [*ancient:* **Taparura, Thaenae**] (Tunisia) Port city, 78 mi S of Sousse, on the N shore of the Gulf of Gabès. It became an important trading port from the 11th century, was taken by the Sicilians in the 12th century, the Spanish in the 16th century, and was bombarded by the French as they prepared to invade Tunisia in 1881. During World War II it was heavily damaged by Allied bombing in 1942/43. It was occupied by British troops on April 10, 1943. Ninth-century fortifications and a 10th-century mosque are of interest here.

SHABA [*former:* **Katanga**] (Zaire) Copper-rich province in the S, bordered by Angola, Zambia, and Lake Tanganyika. Its capital and chief city is LUBUMBASHI. It was generally controlled by the LUBA EMPIRE and LUNDALAND from the 17th to 19th centuries. It became a kingdom founded in the late 19th century by a Nyamwezi trader named M'Siri, who came from what is now TANZANIA. It lasted until he was killed in 1891 by the Belgians, who ruled here from 1884 to 1960. With Zaire's independence Katanga attempted, with Belgian support, to secede in July 1960 and declare itself an independent republic, but a U.N. force helped ease the tension and finally ended the movement by routing Moise Tshombe's forces in 1963. In 1966 the government nationalized the Belgian firm that had controlled most of the mining interests here.

SHAF-SHAWAN. See CHECHAOUÉN.

SHAFTESBURY (England) Market town in Dorset, 18 mi WSW of Salisbury. This site was probably first occupied in Anglo-Saxon times, and there are traces of Roman presence. Alfred the Great, who reigned from 871 to 899, founded an abbey here in 880, which was destroyed by the Danes along with the town. Its remains can still be seen. Shaftesbury was first granted a charter in 1252.

SHAHDARA (Pakistan) Suburb, approx. 5 mi NW of LAHORE and across the Ravi River, in the PUNJAB. It is the site of the tomb of the Mogul Emperor Jahangir (1569–1627) who furthered his father Akbar's territorial expansion; he also allowed English and Portuguese commercial interests to acquire power in India. See also MOGUL EMPIRE.

SHAHJAHANABAD. See DELHI.

SHAHJAHANPUR (India) City of central Uttar Pradesh, in the N, approx. 100 mi NW of Lucknow. It was founded in 1647 by Nawab Bahadur Khan, a Pathan leader. It was named in honor of the reigning emperor, Shah Jahan, at the height of his success in the conquest of DECCAN and KANDAHAR. See also MOGUL EMPIRE.

SHAHO. See AN-SHAN.

SHA HO [Shaho] (China) Town and small river, a tributary of the Liao, 15 mi S of Mukden, in the NE. On this river, in October 1904, the Japanese defeated the Russians in one of a series of victories during the Russo-Japanese War of 1904/05. Brought on by aggressive Russian policies and the occupation of MANCHURIA, despite Japanese attempts at mediation, the war culminated in the Japanese capture of PORT ARTHUR and the disastrous naval defeat of the Russians at TSUSHIMA, both in 1905.

SHAHR. See COMANA.

SHAKER HEIGHTS (United States) Residential suburb in Cuyahoga county, N OHIO, approx. 8 mi E of CLEVELAND. It takes its name from the North Union Shaker community, which existed here from 1822 until 1889. It is the site of a Shaker historical museum. In the 20th century it has become famous as a wealthy suburban community. It is mentioned in Leonard Bernstein's *Trouble in Tahiti* from 1952.

SHAKHTY [*former:* **Aleksandrovsk-Grushevski**] (USSR) City in SW Rostov oblast, approx. 35 mi NE of Rostov-on-Don. This mining center in the eastern Donets coal region was founded in 1839. In 1928 it was the scene of a "show" trial in the Stalin period of engineers accused of collaboration with the Germans by sabotaging production. The trial was followed by terrorism against all technicians.

SHALAMAR GARDENS [Shalimar Gardens] (Pakistan) Outstanding gardens 6 mi E of LAHORE. They were laid out in 1637 by the Mogul Emperor Shah Jahan, who was also the moving force behind the construction of the Taj Mahal at AGRA and much of DELHI. See MOGUL EMPIRE.

SHALIMAR GARDENS. See SHALAMAR GARDENS.

SHANDI. See SHENDI.

SHANGHAI [Shang-Hai] (China) Major port and China's largest city, of SE Kiangsu province, on the Huang P'u River, 13 mi from its mouth, and 150 mi SE of Nanking. Next to Peking, it is the country's foremost educational center. Now a major manufacturing city as well, it was founded in the 11th century but was of little import until it was opened in 1842 as one of the first five treaty ports, when it took on a distinctly European look and culture. It was taken by the Chinese Nationalists in 1927. In the Sino-Japanese wars it was attacked and bombed from January to March 1932 by the Japanese, who withdrew in May. The saturation bombing of civilian targets spurred shocked protests from Europe and the United States. Again from August to November 1937 it was the scene of heavy fighting in the renewed Japanese offensive. With the coming of World War II, the foreign settlement was occupied by the Japanese in 1941 and the city was under complete Japanese control after December of that year. Great Britain and the United States renounced their claims to the city in 1943, and France followed suit in 1946 after it had been restored to China following World War II. Shanghai fell to the communists in May 1949. The term "shanghai," the drugging and forceable kidnapping of crews for the long voyage to China, grew from this widespread practice, especially on the U.S. West Coast, beginning in the 1870's.

SHANGRI-LA. See CATOCTIN MOUNTAIN.

SHAN-HAI-KUAN [Linyu, Shanhaikwan] [*former:* **Hai-yang**] (China) Town of Hopeh province, in the NE, on the Gulf of Liaotung, at the E end of the GREAT WALL, approximately half-way between Peking and Mukden. A centuries-old, strategic border town, it suffered from numerous invasions and battles. It was the first Chinese city to be occupied by the Manchus in 1644. In 1900 it was the scene of intense activity during the Boxer rebellion.

SHAN-HSI. See SHANSI, SHENSI.

SHANIDAR (Iraq) Cave and archaeological site in the Zagros Mts, NW of Rawanduz, 80 mi ENE of Mosul. Excavators found here a long cultural sequence beginning with Neanderthal remains and moving up in time through the Paleolithic period of ancient man, with crude blades and microliths. The upper levels of the ninth millennium BC showed evidence for the first gathering of wild plant foods that led to the Neolithic period. This tendency is continued up to the borders of the true Neolithic period in the nearby settlement site of ZAWI CHEMI-SHANIDAR, where evidences of domesticated sheep and the sickles and other equipment used in the preparation of food from grains were found.

SHANNON RIVER (Irish Republic) River in N central and SW Ireland, approx. 230 mi long, the longest river in the country. It rises in County Cavan and flows S to Limerick, then W into a large estuary. The Shannon drains a land of farms and peat bogs. In the early 19th century it was a very important part of Ireland's waterways system and was connected with eastern Ireland by the Royal Canal and the Grand Canal. In west-central Ireland the Shannon flows through Lough Derg, an expansion of the river. In it is Holy Island, or Iniscaltra, with ruins of churches and a round tower. On the river are ATHLONE, whose castle was often besieged, and LIMERICK, with a long history including occupation by Norsemen in the ninth century. Near Limerick is the Shannon Airport Industrial Estate, a duty-free international terminal, which was opened in 1945.

SHANSI [Shan-Hsi] (China) Province in the NE between Inner Mongolia and the rich plain of N China, bounded on the W and S by the Yellow River with its capital at T'AI-YÜAN. Mostly fertile loess land, it was part of the heartland of ancient China, with SHENSI, where the first civilizations arose. It is bounded on the north by sections of the GREAT WALL. It has been the center of all the many north Chinese kingdoms. After the revolution of 1911 Shansi was taken over by a war lord, Yen Hsi-Shan, who ruled it as an almost independent "model province" up to the communist takeover of 1949. During the Sino-Japanese War of 1937 to 1945 it was partially occupied by the Japanese, and in the disturbed 1940's it suffered from much guerrilla and communist activity because of its strategic position in the northeast. It is also the site of the sacred peak, long a pilgrimage goal, WU-T'AI SHAN.

SHAN STATE [Shan States] [*former:* **Federated Shan States**] (Burma) Region of E central Burma with its capital city at Taunggyi. Dominating most of Burma from the 12th to 16th centuries, it then fragmented into a group of petty states paying tribute to the Burmese king. Under British control from 1887, the states were ruled by their *sawbwas*, or hereditary chiefs, under feudal tenure to the British crown. Joined as the Federated Shan States in 1922, a single state was established by the Burmese constitution in 1947, and in 1959 the *sawbwas* gave up much of their power to the Burmese government.

SHAN STATES. See SHAN STATE.

SHAN-T'OU. See SWATOW.

SHANTUNG [Shan-Tung] (China) Coastal province in the NE, bounded by Hopeh, Honan, and Kiangsu. Occupied by Chinese cultivators from early times, it was influential in Chinese history as the birthplace of the philosophers Confucius and Mencius. It became a province during the Ming dynasty of 1368 to 1644. Its chief port of CHEFOO was opened as a treaty port in 1863. Great Britain leased WEI-HAI-WEI, and Germany the Kiaochow district in 1898. During World War I it was a hotbed of intrigue due to the Japanese capture of TSINGTAO in 1914 and the accompanying secret demands made on China. Returned to China in 1922, it

was again occupied by Japan in 1937, was returned to China in 1945, and finally fell to communist forces with the capture of TSINAN in September 1948.

SHAOHING. See SHAO-HSING.

SHAO-HSING [Shaohing] (China) Ancient city in N Chekiang province, 40 mi ESE of Hangchow. In the fifth century BC it was the seat of a powerful king of Yüeh.

SHAPUR. See BISHAPUR.

SHARJAH (United Arab Emirates) Emirate and former British protectorate on the PERSIAN GULF. It was the site of a British base until 1971, when Great Britain withdrew from the Persian Gulf area and Sharjah joined the federation of emirates. Next to ABU DHABI, its capital town of Sharjah is the largest in the federation.

SHARM ASH-SHAYKH. See SHARM EL-SHEIKH.

SHARM EL-SHEIKH [Sharm Ash-Shaykh] [*Hebrew:* **Mifraz Schlomo**] (Egypt) Strategic bay at the S end of the SINAI peninsula, opposite Tiran Island. A former Egyptian military base and an Israeli naval base, it was captured by ISRAEL in 1956 and restored to Egypt in 1957. From 1957 until 1967 a United Nations Emergency Force was stationed here until Egypt requested its departure—whereupon the base was again captured by Israel during another Arab-Israeli war in that year. The Egyptian flag was again raised here on April 25, 1982, marking the completion of the Israeli pullout, begun in 1979 according to the terms of the Camp David Accords of 1978.

SHARON, PLAIN OF [Plain of Saron] (Israel) Coastal plain, approx. 50 mi long by 10 mi wide, between the Samarian Hills of central Israel and the Mediterranean Sea. Famous for its fertility in antiquity, it later became a swampland. Zionist efforts in the 20th century have returned it to farmland.

SHARPSBURG. See ANTIETAM.

SHARQAT [As Sharqāt] [*ancient:* **Ashur**] (Iraq) Village on the TIGRIS RIVER, 60 mi S of Mosul. It lies at the site of the ancient settlement of ASHUR, once the religious capital of the empire of ASSYRIA. Here, in October 1918, the British won a final victory over the Turks in World War I, just before the signing of the armistice with TURKEY on Oct. 30, 1918.

SHATT DIJLA. See TIGRIS RIVER.

SHAULYAI. See SIAULIAI.

SHAWNEETOWN (United States) City of SE ILLINOIS, near the Ohio River, 10 mi below its confluence with the Wabash River. Named after an Algonquin Indian tribe that came here in the 17th century, it is the site of very much earlier prehistoric Indian mounds.

SHCHERBAKOV. See RYBINSK.

SHEBA [Saba] [*Arabic:* **Saba'**] Ancient country in the S ARABIAN PENINSULA, probably including the two Yemens and the HADHRAMAUT. Inhabited by the Sabaeans, a Semitic race of ancient culture, it was a political entity from the 10th century BC when it had colonized ETHIOPIA. Wealthy and commercially strong because of its position on the India-Africa trade routes, its culture reached its height from the sixth to the fifth century BC, as shown by such engineering feats as the great dam near MARIB, the capital. In the fourth century AD Ethiopia occupied Sheba and in 572 it became a province of PERSIA. As it came under Islamic control it lost its identity. The story of the Queen of Sheba's visit to Solomon is told in the Old Testament in I Kings 10.

SHEBOYGAN (United States) City in E WISCONSIN, a port on the W shore of LAKE MICHIGAN, approx. 50 mi N of Milwaukee. The North West Company set up a fur-trading post here in 1795, and permanent settlement began in 1835. Lumbering was important in the 19th century. Many residents are of German descent, and there is a German festival in August. South of the city are Indian mounds with excavated burial sites.

SHECHEM. See NABLUS.

SHEERNESS (England) Seaport and town in Kent, on the Isle of Sheppey, where the MEDWAY estuary joins the THAMES RIVER, 38 mi E of London. It is the site of a fort built by Charles II, which was taken by the Dutch fleet under De Ruyter on July 10, 1667 in the second Dutch War.

SHEFFIELD [*former:* **Escafeld**] (England) City in South YORKSHIRE, on the Don River, 68 mi NNE of Birmingham. A manufacturing center, it is the former site of Sheffield Castle, a Norman stronghold where Mary, Queen of Scots, was imprisoned between 1570 and 1584. From the early 18th century the city developed as a center of the cutlery and steel industry.

SHEKI [*former:* **Nukha**] (USSR) Town of Azerbaijan SSR, at the foot of the Caucasus Mts, 55 mi NE of Kirovabad. At present a center of the silk industry, as Nukha it was the capital of a Tatar khanate under the Persian Empire. It was annexed by Russia between 1805 and 1819. See PERSIA, RUSSIA.

SHELBY. See KINGS MOUNTAIN.

SHELBYVILLE (United States) City of Bedford county, in central TENNESSEE, 25 mi S of Murfreesboro. One of the country's earliest planned cities, it is the site of numerous notable 19th-century buildings and was named in honor of Gen. Isaac Shelby of Kentucky. The surrounding region is known for its breeding of the Tennessee walking horse.

SHEMAKHA (USSR) Ancient town of E Azerbaijan SSR, 65 mi WNW of Baku, on the S slopes of the E Caucasus Mts. A commercial center cited by the geographer Ptolemy in the second century AD, it was the early capital of the medieval khanate of Shirvan. It was controlled by the Persian Empire until the 17th century. Important as a silk center in the 16th century, with an extensive Venetian trade, the town was overrun and destroyed by Nadir Shah of PERSIA in 1742. After being rebuilt it was annexed by RUSSIA in 1805. It was badly damaged in an earthquake in 1902 and during the Russian Revolution in 1917. The ruins of the tombs of the Shirvan shahs are here.

SHENANDOAH VALLEY (United States) Valley in VIRGINIA, between the Allegheny and Blue Ridge mountains extending SW from Harpers Ferry. Its location made it a natural route for the Confederacy's push northward during the Civil War, and so it was the site of several important campaigns. These include CEDAR CREEK, HARPER'S FERRY, MARTINSBURG, and WINCHESTER, and Gen. Philip Sheridan's famous ride from Winchester to Cedar Creek, where his presence turned a previous defeat into a Union victory. See also STAUNTON, WAYNESBORO.

SHENDI [**Shandi**] (Sudan) Ancient town of Berber province, on the right bank of the NILE RIVER, approx. 100 mi NNW of Khartoum. It lies within the Island of Meroê. Invaded by EGYPT in 1820, it submitted to Ismail Pasha, the son of the Egyptian leader, Mehmet Ali. The citizens revolted and killed him, only to have their city burned and themselves massacred in retaliation.

SHENGKING. See MUKDEN.

SHENSI [*Mandarin:* **Shan-Hsi**] (China) Province in the N central region, bounded on the N by Inner Mongolia. Its capital, SIAN, generally under the name of Ch'ang-an, was from the earliest times China's imperial capital down to the 12th century AD. The founders of both the Chou and T'ang dynasties built their power in this province, with the Manchus giving it its present boundaries. It suffered great damage during the Muslim rebellion of 1861 to 1876. From 1935 to 1949, it was the seat of the Chinese communists, serving from 1937 as headquarters, at YEN-AN, for the communist Eighth Route Army against the Japanese.

SHEN-YANG. See MUKDEN.

SHEPERDSTOWN. See WEST VIRGINIA.

SHEPPEY, ISLE OF. See SHEERNESS.

SHEPTON MALLET [*medieval:* **Sepeton**] (England) Town of Somerset, 16 mi SW of Bath. A possession of the abbots of GLASTONBURY for 400 years before passing to the Norman Roger de Courcelle, it is the site of a church with a 13th-century oak roof made of 350 individually-designed panels. An outstanding 50-foot high market cross here dates from 1500.

SHERIDAN (United States) City in N WYOMING, on Goose Creek, E of the Bighorn Mountains. Named after Gen. Philip Sheridan, who led troops in the area, it is near the site of the Fetterman Massacre by a group of Indians of a force of 80 soldiers under William Fetterman. The inn, now a national historic landmark, dates from 1893. Fort MacKenzie was located here, and a restoration of Fort Phil Kearny is nearby. See also MASSACRE HILL.

SHERIFFMUIR (Scotland) Battlefield in central region, just W of the Ochil Hills, 23 mi SW of Perth. On Nov. 13, 1715 it was the scene of an indecisive battle between the Royalists under John Archibald Campbell and the Jacobites, or Stuart supporters, under John Erskine, earl of Man. The Jacobites withdrew but were soon after defeated at PRESTON. The entire Jacobite rebellion of this period has been called the Sherramoor, or Sherrymoor, Rebellion after this battle.

SHERSHELL. See CHERCHELL.

'sHERTOGENBOSCH [*French:* **Bois-le-Duc**] (Netherlands) Provincial capital of North Brabant province, in the S, at the confluence of the Aa and Dommel rivers. Chartered in 1184/85, it was a fortress city until 1874 and is the site of the beautiful Gothic St. John's Cathedral, the Janskerk. It was also the birthplace of painter Hieronymus Bosch c.1450.

SHERWOOD FOREST (England) Former royal forest, dating from the time of Henry I, located chiefly in Nottinghamshire. Only remnants of it remain today near MANSFIELD, Hucknall, and Rotherham and vicinity, but in its prime it was celebrated as the haunt of Robin Hood and his band. Though the first traces of the Robin Hood legend come from the 14th century, it refers to the reign of Kings Richard II and his brother John in the late 12th and early 13th centuries.

SHETLANDS [Zetland] [*Norse:* **Hjaltland**] (Scotland) Administrative region and archipelago off the N coast, 50 mi NE of the Orkney Islands. Its main islands are UNST, Fetlar, Whalsay, MAINLAND, FOULA, Papa Stour, and Yell, with the admin. hq. at LERWICK. It was occupied by the late ninth century by Norsemen, traces of whose customs and Norn speech survive. It was taken over by Scotland in 1472, when King Christian I of NORWAY and DENMARK failed to fulfill his dowry pledge for his daughter, Margaret, who married James III of Scotland. Famous for its ancient relics, it has Pictish forts scattered throughout the islands. At JARLSHOF on Mainland Island a Bronze Age village has been unearthed.

SHEWA [Shoa] (Ethiopia) The country's southernmost province. From the mid-10th to the end of the 13th century it was the residence of the Abyssinian sovereigns, who had been driven out of their previous capital of AXUM. Conquered and damaged by Muslim invaders in 1528, it was reconquered by an Abyssinian chief in 1682, but it remained independent of northern Ethiopia until 1855. In that year it was subjugated by Emperor Theodore. In 1889, on the death of Emperor John, Menelik II made himself master of all Abyssinia, now Ethiopia, and built ADDIS ABABA as his capital.

SHIBENIK. See ŠIBENIK.

SHIEL, LOCH (Scotland) Lake between the former counties of Invernessshire and Argyllshire, now in Highland region, 80 mi NW of Glasgow. At Glenfinnan, at the head of Loch Shiel, Prince Charles Edward Stuart raised his standard in 1745. A medieval chapel is on St. Finnans Isle.

SHI-FU. See KASHGAR.

SHIGATSE. See JIH-K'A-TSE.

SHIKOKU (Japan) The smallest of the four principal islands, S of Honshū and E of Kyūshū. Held by various feudal families from early times, it was subjugated c.1590 by Hideyoshi and was subdivided by him. The daimiate of TOSA, an old province in the southern region, was powerful until the 1868/69 Meiji Restoration.

SHILLA. See SILLA.

SHILLONG (India) Capital town of Assam and Meghalaya states, a summer resort, high in the Khasi hills region of NE India. In 1864 the town was made the headquarters of the Khasi and Jaintia Hills district under the British. It became the capital of Assam in 1874 after that province had been set up.

SHILOH [*Arabic:* **Khirbat Saylūn;** *modern:* **Khirbet Seilun**] (Jordan) Village of ancient PALESTINE, NNE of Jerusalem, 15 mi E of the Jordan River, on the E slope of Mt Ephraim. The home of the prophets Ahijah and Eli, it was the sacred repository of the Ark of the Covenant after the conquest of JUDAH. It was also a general meeting place of the Israelites until the Philistines captured the Ark of the Covenant and destroyed the town.

SHILOH CHURCH (United States) Civil War battle site, 3 mi SSW of Pittsburgh Landing near Shiloh Church, in TENNESSEE. The battle here occurred on April 6/7, 1862. After the fall of FORT DONELSON to the Union Army, Grant established headquarters for the Army of the Tennessee at Savannah. At the same time Gen. D.C. Buell and the Army of the Ohio marched west from Nashville to join Grant. On the Confederate side, Generals A.S. Johnston and Pierre Beauregard planned to overwhelm Grant before Buell's arrival and staged a surprise attack in which Johnston was killed. Beauregard assumed command but failed to take Pittsburgh Landing or to cut off the Union retreat. The arrival of 20,000 reinforcements as well as advance divisions of Buell's army led to a Union offensive on April 7. The outnumbered Confederates withdrew to CORINTH, Mississippi, which was in turn abandoned one month later. In the last analysis Shiloh was considered a Union victory because of the subsequent Union successes, but it was one of the bloodiest of the Civil War battles, with losses to each side of over 10,000.

SHIMABARA (Japan) Peninsula on W KYŪSHŪ, E of Nagasaki. Christianity found one of its first bases here, although the inhabitants and those on the near island of Amakusa were frequently persecuted. Rebelling in 1637/38, 37,000 Christians were massacred at the local castle on orders from Iyemitsu, the Tokugawa shogun, who was an implacable enemy of foreigners and Christianity.

SHIMODA (Japan) Port town of Shizuoka prefecture, S HONSHŪ, on the SE coast of the Izu peninsula. It was visited by Comm. Perry in 1854 and opened to U.S. trade that year. The town was the site of the first U.S. consulate in Japan, opened in 1856/57 under the direction of Townsend Harris. His residence, the Gyokusenji Temple, is now a memorial here. The town's poor harbor brought the consulate's closing in 1859 and a switch of U.S. trade to YOKOHAMA.

SHIMOGA (India) Town of central Mysore, in the S, on the Tunga River, 150 mi WNW of Bangalore. It was plundered by the Marathas in 1798. It was brought under British control in 1830 after the Maratha insurrection of that year. See MARATHA CONFEDERACY.

SHIMONOSEKI [*former:* **Akamagaseki, Bakan**] (Japan) Port city of Yamaguchi prefecture, in SW HONSHŪ, on Shimonoseki Strait opposite Kitakigūshū. It was the site of the historic naval battle at DANNOURA, at the eastern end of town, in 1185 when the Minamoto clan led by Yoshitsune defeated Emperor Antoku and the Taira clan. From Sept. 5 to 8, 1864 Shimonoseki was bombarded by British, Dutch, French, and U.S. warships in retaliation for Choshu daimio's firing on foreign ships. The shogun paid indemnities, but the U.S. portion was refunded in 1883. The Treaty of Shimonoseki was signed here April 17, 1895, ending the first Sino-Japanese War, following which severe terms were imposed on China after its humiliating defeat.

SHINAR. See SUMER.

SHINGŪ (Japan) Town on the S coast of HONSHŪ Island, 55 mi SE of Wakayama. There is an ancient Shinto shrine here that, along with a series of other shrines in Honshū, has been a place of pilgrimage since at least the ninth century AD. There are also the ruins of a castle.

SHINKYO. See CH'ANG-CH'UN.

SHIPCHENSKI PROKHOP. See SHIPKA PASS.

SHIP ISLAND (United States) Island in the Gulf of Mexico, off the SE coast of Harrison county MISSISSIPPI. A harbor and base for French exploration of the Gulf coast in the 18th century, it served as a British naval base in the War of 1812. Later a U.S. military base, it was fought over in the Civil War and was a Confederate prison camp. A quarantine station and lighthouse here date from 1878/79.

SHIPKA PASS [Sipka Pass] [*Bulgarian:* **Shipchenski Prokhop**] (Bulgaria) Strategically located mountain pass in the Balkans between Gabrovo to the N and Kazanlŭk, on the route through STARA ZAGORA. It was the scene of several battles in the Russo-Turkish War. The Russians and Bulgarians took it on July 19, 1877, holding it during August and September despite heavy Turkish attacks. After the Turkish defeat at PLEVEN, the Russians advanced here and received the surrender of Gen. Vessil Pasha near Gabrovo on Jan. 9, 1878.

SHIPMAN'S CORNER. See SAINT CATHARINES.

SHIRAZ (Iran) Capital city of Fars province, in the central SW. It has been an important city from the late seventh century AD. Shirazi traders were active along the African coast in the 10th century. Although sacked by Tamerlane in the late 14th century, the city was rebuilt by the Safavids, and attacked and damaged in the early 18th century. Under Karim Khan it served as capital of PERSIA from 1750 to 1779. Its decline began when Karim's successor, Aga Muhammad Khan, moved the capital to TEHERAN. It was the birthplace of the Persian poet Saadi and is the burial place of both Saadi and the poet Hafiz. The tombs of two brothers of Imam Riza, who died here in the ninth century, are a place of pilgrimage. Nearby are the ruins of PERSEPOLIS.

SHIRPURLA. See LAGASH.

SHIRVAN. See SHEMAKHA.

SHITTIM (Jordan) Valley on the W side of lower Jordan, N of the DEAD SEA, E of JERICHO. In biblical times it was the last camping site for the Israelites before reaching the Holy Land.

SHIZUOKA [Sizuoka] [*former:* **Sumpu**] (Japan) Capital city of Shizuoka prefecture, 55 mi SW of Tokyo, near the W shore of Suruga Bay. Once a defense-point for Tokyo, it is also the site of the castle that housed the last of the Tokugawa shoguns. A statue of Ieyasu, founder of the Tokugawa shogunate, is in a Buddhist temple here.

SHKODËR [Shkodra] [*ancient:* **Scodra**; *Italian:* **Scutari**; *Serbo-Croatian:* **Skadar**; *Turkish:* **Iskenderiye**] (Albania) Town and province between the Drin River and Lake Scutari. The capital of ancient ILLYRIA, it was made a Roman colony in 168 BC. It came under the BYZANTINE EMPIRE in the fourth century AD and was conquered by the Serbs in the seventh century. Until the fall of SERBIA in the 14th century it was the seat of the princes of Zenta or MONTENEGRO, who gave it to VENICE in 1396 in exchange for financial help in the war against the Turks. Nevertheless, the Turks under Sultan Muhammad II captured it in 1479. Under the Turks it was the seat of a pashalik. Turkish rule ended in 1913 when it was occupied by Montenegrin troops in the Balkan War, but in the peace settlement it was given to newly independent Albania. Shkodër was the scene of fighting in World War I and was occupied by Austria between 1916 and 1918. A Venetian citadel here dates from the 15th century.

SHKODRA. See SHKODËR.

SHKUP. See SKOPJE.

SHLISSELBURG. See PETROKREPOST.

SHOA. See SHEWA.

SHOLAPUR (India) Former fortress town of SE Maharashtra, 170 mi W of Hyderabad. Taken by the Moguls in 1668, it passed to HYDERABAD in 1723 and to the Marathas in 1795. It was captured by the British in 1818. It is the site of a 14th-century Muslim fort that played an important role in the DECCAN wars. PANDHARPUR, a Hindu pilgrimage site, is 33 miles to the west. See also MARATHA CONFEDERACY.

SHONAN. See SINGAPORE.

SHORKOT. See JHANG-MAGHIANA, India.

SHQIPERI. See ALBANIA.

SHQIPNI. See ALBANIA.

SHQIPRI. See ALBANIA.

SHREVEPORT (United States) City in NW LOUISIANA, on the Red River, 18 mi E of the Texas border. Named the Confederate capital of Louisiana in 1863, it is the site of the ruins of the Confederate Fort Humbug, which during the Civil War was defended with logs made to look like cannons. See also SABINE CROSSROADS.

SHREWSBURY [*ancient:* **Pengwern**; *Anglo-Saxon:* **Scrobbesbyrig**; *Middle English:* **Salopsbury**, **Sloppesbury**] (England) Town and admin. hq. of SALOP, on the SEVERN RIVER, near the Welsh border, 40 mi WNW of Birmingham. Founded in the fifth century AD, it was an Anglo-Saxon stronghold that in the late eighth century became part of the kingdom of MERCIA. One of the oldest Norman earldoms in England, it was granted in 1071 to Roger de Montgomery, who established an abbey here, and it was the scene of extensive fighting with the Welsh. In 1403 Henry IV defeated and killed the rebel Henry Percy, known as Hotspur, on a nearby plain and displayed his body to the townspeople. The Shrewsbury School, founded in 1552 by King Edward VI, was attended by Sir Philip Sidney, Fulke Greville, and Charles Darwin, who was born in Shrewsbury. Many half-timbered houses dating from the 15th, 16th, and 17th centuries embellish the town, and much of the original wall survives. An early Norman church with noteworthy stained glass is here, as is an 11th-century castle. The nearby site of the Roman city of Uriconium or Vironconium at WROXETER has yielded many archaeological treasures.

SHROPSHIRE [Salop] (England) Former county, on the border of WALES, now officially called SALOP. In Anglo-Saxon times it was part of the kingdom of MERCIA. Following the Norman conquest, it was an important part of the Welsh Marches and was the scene of great border conflicts. There are earthworks from the Bronze Age, early Iron Age forts, Roman remains, ruins of numerous medieval castles, as well as many monastic remains. A.E. Houseman's *Shropshire Lad* describes the beauty of the county's landscape. See also BRIDGNORTH, LUDLOW, OFFA'S DYKE, SHREWSBURY, WROXETER.

SHTIP. See ŠTIP.

SHU [Shu-Han] (China) Ancient kingdom comprised of modern Szechwan and most of Kweichow and Yunnan; one of three kingdoms formed on the breakdown of the Han empire in 220 AD, on the death of Emperor Hsien. Under the kingdom, which lasted until 264 AD, the Szechwan area was rapidly developed. The kingdom's capital was at CH'ENG-TU.

SHUFU. See KASHGAR.

SHU-HAN. See SHU.

SHUMEN [Shumla] [*former:* **Kolarovgrad**] (Bulgaria) Provincial capital of Shumen province, approx. 50 mi W of Varna. Founded in 927 AD, it was fortified under Turkish rule from the 15th to 19th centuries. It was a strategically important stronghold, often under attack in the Turks' various wars. The city was surrendered to RUSSIA on June 22, 1878 toward the end of the Russo-Turkish War. It was briefly renamed Kolarovgrad in 1950, in honor of the Bulgarian communist leader who was born here. The town is the site of the largest mosque in Bulgaria, built in 1649.

SHUMLA. See SHUMEN.

SHURUPPAK [*modern:* **Fara**] (Iraq) Ancient city of SUMER in the SE, approx. 55 mi NW of An Nasiriya. Probably a dependent of LAGASH, it disappeared from ancient records c.2300 BC, but excavations here have revealed much information of an advanced culture existing here at least by 4000 BC. In legend it is the site of the great flood, which left one survivor, King Ziusudra, who was ordered to build an ark and recreate a living world. The legend is associated with Greek and other epics, including that of Noah in the Bible.

SHŪSH. See SUSA, Iran.

SHUSHA (USSR) Town and former fortress in the Transcaucasian Federation, on a rocky outcropping, 170 mi SE of Tiflis. Once the capital of the khanate of Kara-bagh, it acquired a fortress in 1789. It withstood a siege by Aga Muhammed of PERSIA in 1795, but surrendered two years later. In 1805 Ibrahim Khan of Kara-bagh sought the protection of RUSSIA, which annexed it in 1822.

SHUSHAN. See SUSA, Iran.

SHŪSHTAR (Iran) Town in Khūzestān province, in the SW, on the Kārūn River, 50 mi N of Ahvāz. In 260 AD Shapur I of the Sassanid Empire employed the captives taken from his great victory over the Roman emperor, Valerian, in building elaborate hydraulic works including a dam spanning the Kārūn. Shūshtar flourished under the Mongols in the 13th and 14th centuries, but it was captured by Tamerlane in 1393 and by Shah Ismail of PERSIA, founder of the Safavid dynasty, in 1508. Although it declined in importance after the 18th century, it has long been a stronghold of both the Kharijites and the Shiites. The ruins of a large citadel and relics of an ancient canal system survive. It is assumed that the Minau Canal here was built by Darius I in the fifth century BC. See also MONGOL EMPIRES, ROMAN EMPIRE.

SHWEBO (Burma) Town and district capital in Upper Burma, 50 mi NNW of Mandalay. The birthplace and capital of Alompra, who founded the last Burmese dynasty, it was captured by the British on Jan. 9, 1945 toward the end of World War II.

SIA HSIA. See TANGUT KINGDOM.

SIALKOT (Pakistan) District and its capital city, in the PUNJAB, near the left bank of the Chenab River, 70 mi N of Lahore. A fortress built in 1181 by Muhammad of Ghor still stands here. It is also the site of the mausoleum of Guru Nanak, the 16th-century founder of the Sikh religion, and was the birthplace of the philosopher-poet Muhammad Iqbal. Sialkot may be the site of Sakala, ancient capital of an Indo-Greek kingdom.

SIAM. See THAILAND.

SIAN [Hsi-An, Signan, Singan] [*former:* **Ch'ang-an, Hsien-yang, Ken-zan-fu, Quengianfu, Siking**] (China) Provincial capital of Shensi province, on the banks of the Wei River, 80 mi above its junction with the Yellow River. The site was an imperial capital for 11 Chinese dynasties, beginning with the very first emperor, Shih Huang Ti, the unifier of China in 221 BC. It became Ch'ang-an under the Han, and under the T'ang dynasty in the eighth and ninth centuries AD became a huge, cosmopolitan capital of some 2 million people, with Nestorian Christian, Buddhist, and Muslim quarters and a bustling commercial life involving trade with Arabia, Africa, and Rome.

The city, known to Marco Polo as Ken-zan-fu, or Quengianfu, was visited by him in the 13th century.

During the Muslim Rebellion it withstood a siege from 1868 to 1870, and during the Boxer Rebellion of 1900 to 1902 it served as refuge for the Empress Dowager and the Emperor Kuang Hsü. In December 1936, in the Sian incident, Chiang Kai-shek of the Nationalists was kidnapped and imprisoned here by the communists in a successful effort to make him agree to cooperate with them against the invading Japanese.

Of the ancient capital cities little is left except two T'ang pagodas, a palace platform, remnants of the Ming dynasty walls, and miles of mounds with some excavation. There is a museum containing stone-carved T'ang tablets.

SIASCONSET [Sconset] (United States) Village and summer resort on NANTUCKET Island, MASSACHUSETTS. The first wireless telegraph station in the United States was constructed here in 1901, shortly after the inventor, Guglielmo Marconi, had received the first transatlantic message to be sent from Europe to America at his station in NEWFOUNDLAND. The station at Siasconset was dismantled in 1918.

SIAULIAI [*German:* **Schaulen,** *Russian:* **Shaulyai**] (USSR) Old city in the Lithuanian SSR, 75 mi NNW of Kaunas. The site of a Lithuanian victory over the Livonian Knights in 1236, it was under the Polish crown from 1589 to 1772, and passed to RUSSIA in 1795. Following World War I, in November 1919, a Lithuanian-Lett army defeated the German Free Corps here. Passing to newly independent Lithuania in 1920, it was next held by the Germans from 1941 to 1944 during World War II. See LITHUANIA.

ŠIBENIK [Shibenik] [*Italian:* **Sebenico**] (Yugoslavia) Port city of CROATIA, 30 mi NW of Split, on the Adriatic Sea. Founded in the 10th century, it was captured by VENICE in 1117. Under Hungarian rule from 1180 to 1322 and 1351 to 1412, it was returned to Venice until it passed to AUSTRIA in 1797. It remained under Austria until 1918 and was incorporated into Yugoslavia in 1922. The fine cathedral of St. Jacob of 1431 to 1455 and a town hall with a Renaissance loggia of 1542 are from the Venetian period. The carved Venetian Lion of St. Mark is evident everywhere.

SIBERIA [*Russian:* **Sibir**] (USSR) Region in Asia, most of it politically in the Russian Soviet Federated Socialist Republic. Siberia consists of the northern third of Asia, from the Ural Mts eastward to the Pacific Ocean. It is bounded on the N by the Arctic Ocean and on the S by the Kazakh Soviet Socialist Republic, the Mongolian People's Republic, and China. This vast region has almost every variety of climate, all kinds of natural resources, long rivers, high mountains, and steppes. From early historic times Siberia has been the heartland of nomadic hordes, such as the Huns, Mongols, and Manchus, who periodically overran Europe and Asia. In the mid-15th century the Tatar khanate of Sibir was established here. Russians traded with Siberian tribes as early as the 13th century, but the expansion of RUSSIA into Siberia, then a khanate, by conquest began in 1581 with an expedition led by the Cossack Ermak Timofeev. In 1582 he captured the town of ISKER, or Sibir (near present TOBOLSK), capital of the

khanate. The remainder of the khanate was conquered in 1598.

By 1640 Cossack adventurers had reached the Sea of Okhotsk, an arm of the Pacific, and by the late 18th century Russians had founded such towns and fortresses as YAKUTSK, IRKUTSK, TOMSK, OMSK, and Barnaul. Siberia was a rich source of furs and raw materials that soon made the colony profitable, but after the early 18th century mining became the most important economic activity. From the early 17th century Siberia had also been used as a penal colony and a place for exiled political dissidents. The leaders of the Decembrist Conspiracy of 1825 were sent to CHITA. Settlement, however, was slow until the construction of the Trans-Siberian Railroad, between 1891 and 1905.

After the Russian Revolution of 1917, an autonomous Siberian government was formed early in 1918, but it was overthrown by counterrevolutionary forces under Aleksandr V. Kolchak. His forces, known as the Whites in contrast to the communist Reds, held most of Siberia for a time. They were aided by an Allied expeditionary force that landed in the Far East; but by 1920 Kolchak was defeated, and Siberia came under communist control. The communist regime proclaimed it part of the RSFSR in January 1918. During the first Five-Year Plan of 1928 to 1933, the USSR put great emphasis on the development of Siberia's resources, expanding mining and industry, especially in the Kuznetsk Basin. During World War II entire industrial plants were moved to Siberia to prevent capture by the Germans. Since then development has continued at a rapid pace, with much labor supplied by convicts and political dissidents.

SIBIR. See ISKER, SIBERIA.

SIBIU [*ancient:* **Cibinium;** *German:* **Hermannstadt;** *Hungarian:* **Nagyszeben**] (Rumania) City at the N foot of the Transylvanian Alps. Originally the site of a Roman colony, it was refounded in the 12th century by German colonists from SAXONY. Destroyed by the Tatars in 1241, in the 14th century it became the administrative center for the German communities in TRANSYLVANIA. After suffering in the Turkish wars, it came under AUSTRIA in 1699. The city retains considerable medieval character and still has a significant German minority, although many were forced to flee following World War II.

SIBONEY (Cuba) Town on the S coast, just E of SANTIAGO DE CUBA. During the Spanish-American war the American troops landed at Siboney Bay, near this town, on June 20, 1898 and at DAQUIRI to the east, before their march on Santiago and the victories of EL CANEY and SAN JUAN HILL, which led to the investment of the city.

SICCA VENERIA. See LE KEF.

SICILIA. See SICILY.

SICILIES, THE TWO. See TWO SICILIES, KINGDOM OF.

SICILY [*ancient:* **Thrinacria, Trinacria;** *Italian:* **Sicilia**] (Italy) Island, region, and former kingdom. The largest island in the Mediterraean Sea, it forms a triangle, from which is derived its ancient name *Trinacria* (three-pointed) and its symbol, a gorgon head inside three revolving legs. It is separated from the Italian mainland by the narrow Strait of Messina and bounded elsewhere by the Ionian Sea to the SE and Tyrrhenian Sea to the N. The region includes a number of other islands and island groups. PALERMO is the capital.

Stone Age inhabitants of Sicily were the Sicani, the Elymi, and the Sicels, or Siculi, who immigrated from the toe of Italy *c.*1000 BC and gave their name to the island. Between the eighth and sixth centuries BC the Greeks founded a number of cities in the south and east, including AGRIGENTO, CATANIA, HIMERA, MESSINA, and SYRACUSE, which gained supremacy over the others. In the west the Carthaginians seized control of more than half the island *c.*400 BC and founded Lilybaeum (MARSALA) in 396. For about a hundred years the Greeks and the Carthaginians fought for control, after which the struggle was between the Carthaginians and the Romans. The latter won almost all of Sicily by *c.*215 BC. The Romans further Hellenized Sicilian culture, but their rule was often corrupt and drained the economy. Sicily became a major source of wheat for the city of Rome and is still a major supplier. After Rome declined, the island was controlled by the Vandals in the mid-fifth century AD; by the Goths in 493; by the Byzantines in 535; and was conquered by the Arabs between 850 and 925.

Between 1061 and 1091, the Normans took Sicily from the Arabs, and in 1127 Roger II became the first king of Sicily. His realm, which he received as a fief from the pope, included NAPLES, the southern part of the Italian mainland. With the death of the last Norman ruler in 1189 Sicily was inherited by the German Hohenstaufens. Under the Normans and the Hohenstaufens Sicily was the center of a brilliant cultural renaissance that combined Greco-Roman, Byzantine, Muslim, French, and German influences in a unique way. Sicily was home to English, French, African, and Greek scholars, and a hybrid architecture which survives at Palermo and the palace and cathedral at MONREALE, with its brilliant mosaics. It became a center for the study of law, languages, and science, and of religious toleration and philosophical speculation and debate.

After the death of the Holy Roman Emperor Frederick II in 1250, there were several claimants to the throne, and in 1266 Pope Clement IV crowned Charles I of ANJOU as king of both Sicily and Naples after his defeat of the Hohenstaufens at BENEVENTO. His rule was unpopular and led to the Sicilian Vespers, an uprising so named because it broke out at Palermo at the start of Vespers on Easter Monday, March 30, 1282, resulting in the massacre of the French on the island and the eventual proclamation as king of Peter of Aragon, the son-in-law of Manfred. He was the last Hohenstaufen king of Sicily. A 20-year war followed between the Angevin kings of Naples, which supported by the papacy, proclaimed a crusade to regain its fief, and the Aragonese kings of Sicily. In 1302 the kingdom of Sicily and the kingdom of Naples were separated, the Aragonese ruling the former and the Angevins the

latter. In 1442 Alfonso V of ARAGON reunited the two kingdoms and called himself king of the TWO SICILIES. The island then passed to the crown of SPAIN after the marriage of Ferdinand and Isabella united Aragon to León and Castile in 1469. Sicily was then inherited, with Spain, by the Hapsburgs, and was under a harsh and corrupt Spanish rule from 1504 to 1713.

By the Peace of Utrecht in 1713 Sicily was given to SAVOY, which in 1720 exchanged it with Emperor Charles VI of AUSTRIA for SARDINIA. After the War of the Polish Succession both Sicily and Naples became realms of the Bourbons of Spain in 1735. In the Napoleonic period the French held Sicily from 1806 to 1815. The next year, over Sicilian protests, Naples and Sicily were again merged under Ferdinand III of Bourbon who became king of the Two Sicilies as Ferdinand I. The Sicilian desire for independence and Ferdinand's repressive policies resulted in revolt in 1820. In 1848/49 Sicily took part in the general revolutionary movement of Europe. Giuseppe Garibaldi, the Italian patriot, conquered Sicily in 1860, and the next year it became part of the unified kingdom of Italy. In World War II the Allies invaded Sicily on July 9, 1943, and completed its conquest on August 8.

Sicily has never fully recovered from the devastation of World War II. To this is added official indifference and national disdain for the South. The island is also beset by corruption and the widespread influence of organized crime under the leadership of the Mafia. Of uncertain origin, the Mafia is believed to have been born in the numerous secret societies and sworn brotherhoods of brigands, revolutionaries, and patriots opposed to foreign oppression, but has since been devoted exclusively to crime. The highest volcano in Europe, Mt ETNA, approximately 10,900 feet high, is on Sicily. Its first recorded eruption was in 475 BC. See also BYZANTINE EMPIRE, CARTHAGE, HOLY ROMAN EMPIRE, ROME.

SICYON [Secyon] [*Greek:* **Mekone, Sikion, Sikyon**; *Ionian:* **Aegialeia**] (Greece) Ancient city of the S, in the NE PELOPONNESUS, 10 mi NW of Corinth, and S of the Gulf of Corinth. Settled since Mycenaean times, it figures in Homer's lists for the Trojan expedition. Under the control of ARGOS for several hundred years, it includes the hero Adrastus among its kings. The city was most powerful under the tyrant Cleisthenes in the sixth century BC. Generally following SPARTA after 555 BC and CORINTH after 500 BC, it was captured by the Thebans *c.*370. Demetrios Poliorketes destroyed the city in 303 BC and rebuilt it. Under the leadership of Aratus in the third century BC, it joined the Achaean League. It was briefly powerful following the destruction of Corinth by the Romans in 146 BC but declined soon after. Modern Sikionia, site of an early Christian church, is two miles to the northeast of the ruins of the ancient city. Sicyon was famous for its painting and pottery in the Archaic period, of 625 to 480 BC, and thereafter a Sicyonic school of painting founded by Eupompus produced artists, such as Pamphilus and Apelles. Its school of bronze sculpture included such masters as Polykleitos and Lysippos.

SIDDHPUR. See SIDHPUR.

SIDE [*modern:* **Selimiye**] (Turkey) Ancient city on the Bay of Antalya, 49 mi E of Antalya. A Greek colony founded in the seventh century BC, it was most important in Roman imperial times. The remains include the walls, colonnaded streets, two agoras, temples, private houses, and an aqueduct. The huge theater has been partly restored. The splendid sculpture from the site is housed in a museum built inside the fifth-century AD baths.

SIDERS. See SIERRE.

SIDHPUR [Siddhpur] (India) Ancient city of E Gujarat state, in the W, on the Saraswati River, 63 mi N of Ahmadabad. Long an object of pilgrimage, it is the site of the ruins of the ancient temple of Rudra Mala.

SĪDĪ BARRĀNI (Egypt) Village on the NW coast of Egypt, E of Buqbuq and W of Marūh. The scene of severe fighting during the North African campaign in World War II, it was captured by the Italians in September 1940, then taken by the British on December 11 of that year, and next taken by Gen. Rommel in 1941. It was retaken by the British on Nov. 11, 1942 as Rommel retreated.

SIDI-BEL-ABBÈS (Algeria) Town of Oran department, in the NW, 40 mi S of Oran. Founded in 1843 and named for the nearby tomb of a saint, it developed around a French camp. Until Algerian independence in 1962 it was the headquarters of the French Foreign Legion.

SIDON [Zidon] [*Arabic:* **Saydā**; *French:* **Saida**] (Lebanon) Ancient Phoenician port, 22 mi N of its daughter city and rival, Tyre. Founded *c.*3000 BC, it was one of the great cities of PHOENICIA from the third millennium BC, and at times all Phoenicians were called Sidonians. Traditionally noted for its glass manufactures and its purple dyes, extracted from a sea creature here, it was ruled successively by the major ancient powers: ASSYRIA, BABYLONIA, EGYPT, the Persian Empire, under which it reached its greatest prosperity, the MACEDONIAN EMPIRE of Alexander the Great, and its successors the SELEUCID EMPIRE, and ROME. Herod the Great lavished much building and development on the city.

It often changed hands during the period of the Crusades, was sacked by the Mongols in 1260, but prospered again under the OTTOMAN EMPIRE from 1517. It declined in the 18th century, especially after the expulsion of French traders in 1791 and a destructive earthquake in 1837. Sidon was ultimately overshadowed by its own colony, TYRE, but was always an important port in antiquity. The city was heavily damaged in June 1982 during the Israeli invasion of Lebanon. Some slight excavation has been carried out in the heavily populated modern city.

SIEBENBÜRGEN. See TRANSYLVANIA.

SIEDLCE [Syedlets] [*German:* **Sedlez**] (Poland) Industrial town of Warszawa province, 55 mi ESE of Warsaw. Chartered in 1557, it was occupied by AUSTRIA in 1795. From 1809 to 1815 it was part of the duchy of WARSAW, finally passing to RUSSIA in 1918. During World War II it was the locus of several German concentration camps.

SIEGEN (West Germany) Industrial city of North Rhine-Westphalia, 6 mi N of Bonn. From 1606 to 1743 it was the residence of the princes of NASSAU. It suffered extensive damage in World War II. Surviving notable buildings include the Nikolaikirche from the 13th century and two castles. The artist Peter Paul Rubens was born here in 1577.

SIEGFRIED LINE [Westwall] (West Germany) Defense system constructed by Nazi GERMANY in the 1930's, extending from the Swiss border to German KLEVE, opposite the Netherlands. In general it ran parallel to the RHINE RIVER, and in the south it was opposite the MAGINOT LINE, the French defense system. It was constructed with strong-point defense in depth, and the approaches to it consisted of thick mine fields. In World War II the Allies finally penetrated it after heavy fighting between September 1944 and April 1945. The system took its name from Siegfried, an important folk hero of early and medieval Germany and of Wagner's *Ring* cycle.

SIENA [*ancient:* **Saena Julia**] (Italy) City and capital of Siena province, in W TUSCANY region, 33 mi S of Florence, famous for its treasures of art and architecture. An Etruscan city, it later became an ally of ROME between 298 and 263 BC. It fell to the Lombards in the sixth century AD. It was already a flourishing medieval town when it warred with FLORENCE in 1082. It established a commune in 1125, with its bishop and citizens allying against the Aldobrandeschi and other noblemen in the city and in the *contado*, or neighboring countryside. In the next century it developed into a prosperous trading and manufacturing center. As a Ghibelline center it extended its rule over the *contado* and came into conflict with Guelph Florence.

After the Peace of CONSTANCE of 1183 settled the Guelph-Ghibelline struggle in Italy, civil war broke out between Siena's rival factions. In 1186 Frederick Barbarossa besieged the city unsuccessfully. War with Florence continued, and in 1260 Siena decisively defeated its rival at Montaperto. Despite external successes and attempts at compromise between different political and social groups, civil strife continued unabated. In 1270, therefore, Siena opened its gates to Charles of Anjou, king of NAPLES, who established an aristocratic oligarchy of wealthy merchants under the Council of Nine, and forced the city to join the Guelph party. However, party war between the *grandi*, or wealthy merchants, and the *populo minuto*, or craftsmen and workers, continued. By 1318 the oligarchy was in firm control, and by 1350 an aristocratic *signoria* had taken power.

Despite the ravages of the Black Death in 1348, Siena remained a great city and embarked on its most flourishing period of artistic and cultural life. Along with Florence, LUCCA, and VENICE, it continued to be one of Italy's four great republics. The Council of the Nine was overthrown in 1355, in 1368, and again in 1371. In 1384, however, the nobility reacted and gave power to

The Piazza del Campo, the center of Siena, in the 18th century. Here, in one of Italy's loveliest medieval cities, the famous Palio horserace is run twice each summer.

several great families, including the Salimbene, the Malavolti, Piccolomini, Tolomei, and Usurgieri. In 1399 the weakened city fell to Gian Galeazzo Visconti, the duke of MILAN.

From 1487 to 1523 the city was ruled by the Petrucci family, after which it became embroiled in the wars between France and the Hapsburgs for the control of Italy. In 1523 it defeated Florence but in 1530 was taken by Spain. Absorbed by the Hapsburg-backed Medici dukes of Florence and Tuscany, in 1552 Siena revolted and ousted its imperial garrison. Despite promises of help from Henry II of France, the city finally fell to Duke Cosimo I de Medici in 1555; only one fifth of the population remained alive after the siege. From then on Siena's political history became that of Florence and Tuscany. During World War II Siena was occupied by the Allies without a struggle on July 3, 1944.

Its notable structures include its medieval walls and 16th-century Medici fortress, a Tuscan Gothic cathedral built between 1196 and 1215, its late 13th- and early 14th-century Palazzo Pubblico with its 14th-century campanile, and many other buildings and palaces, including the Palazzo Piccolomini, now a museum, and a fountain described in detail in Dante's *Inferno*. The

main square, or *campo*, on the site of the Roman forum, is a key monument in the history of urban design. Built in the shape of a scallop shell, it affords the perfect setting for the city's social life and has been widely imitated. Here every year the *Palio* horse race, first run in 1656, recreates Siena's medieval past.

Among the city's famous citizens are Pope Alexander III, St. Catherine of Siena, Pope Pius II (Aeneas Sylvius Piccolomini), the noted Renaissance Humanist; sculptors Tino di Camaino and Jacopo della Quercia; and painters Duccio di Buoninsegna, Simone Martini, the Lorenzetti, and Sassetta. The city is also the center of the Chianti wine region.

SIERADZ [*German:* **Schieratz;** *Russian:* **Seradz**] (Poland) Town in Lodz province, 35 mi WSW of Lodz. The town was once the seat of an independent medieval prince. Later it became the residence and base of a local Polish lord, and the Polish diet, or national assembly, met here. During World War II it was overrun and held by the Germans.

SIERRA LEONE A nation of West Africa bounded by Guinea to the N and E, Liberia to the S and E, and the Atlantic Ocean on the W.

The coast of Sierra Leone was discovered by the

Portuguese explorer Pedro da Cintra in 1460. English colonists came to the coastline in the 17th century, but they quickly abandoned their settlement because of the unhealthy climate. Sierra Leone soon became known as the "white man's grave." The slave trade was very active until the 18th century and was controlled by small local chiefdoms. In 1787 a group of British abolitionists founded the colony of FREETOWN to resettle freed British-owned slaves. Freetown's population was boosted in 1792 by the addition of 1,200 fugitive slaves from Canada and the Bahamas. In 1808 it became a crown colony. Great Britain declared a protectorate over the interior of the country in 1896.

Nationalist aspirations surfaced after World War I and slowly gathered momentum during the 20th century. In 1951 a new constitution provided a blueprint for decolonization, and ten years later Sierra Leone achieved independence as a member of the British Commonwealth. The new country's stability was interrupted in 1967 when a military clique seized power from newly elected Prime Minister Siaka Stevens. In a second coup, in April 1968 led by noncommissioned officers, constitutional civilian rule was restored and Stevens reinstated. In 1971 the government was threatened by another army-inspired coup, but Stevens gained the upper hand, and Sierra Leone was declared a republic. Despite criticisms for autocratic methods, Stevens has been repeatedly elected president, most recently in 1978. The nation's economic development of its substantial mineral resources is progressing, with heavy commercial investment from the United States.

SIERRA MAESTRA (Cuba) Mountain range in Oriente province, in the SE, extending along the coast. In the 1950's these mountains served as Fidel Castro's base of operations for the eventually successful guerrilla operations against the Batista dictatorship in Cuba.

SIERRE [German: **Siders**] (Switzerland) Town in VALAIS canton, approx. 55 mi E of Geneva. Picturesquely situated in the middle of the RHÔNE RIVER valley, it has a 13th-century tower, a 16th-century castle, which was once the residence of the poet Rainer Maria Rilke, and the buildings of a monastery.

SIEVERSHAUSEN (West Germany) Village of Lower Saxony, 15 mi E of Hanover. Here on July 9, 1553 Albert Alcibiades was defeated by Maurice of SAXONY who in turn was mortally wounded. This battle stemmed from Maurice's conflicts with Holy Roman Emperor Charles V over the treatment of Philip of Hesse. See also HOLY ROMAN EMPIRE, PASSAU.

SIFNÓS. See SIPHNOS.

SIGHISOARA [German: **Schässburg;** Hungarian: **Segesvár**] (Rumania) City in TRANSYLVANIA, 45 mi NE of Sibiu. Colonized by Saxons in the 13th century, it was the scene on July 31, 1849 of the defeat of the Hungarian revolutionists under Bem by a vastly superior Russian force under Gen. Lüders, an aftermath of the revolutions of 1848. The Hungarian poet Petöfi is believed to have died in this battle. The old town, topped by a citadel, is surrounded by medieval walls.

SIGIRI. See SIGIRIYA.

SIGIRIYA [**Sigiri**] (Sri Lanka) Fortified rock in the N central region, N of Kandy. As Ceylon's ancient Buddhist capital, it served as King Kasyapa's refuge in the fifth century AD. There are ruins of a palace and baths.

SIGMARINGEN (West Germany) City of Baden-Württemberg, on the DANUBE RIVER, 30 mi S of Reutlingen. Chartered in the 13th century, it came under the control of the Hohenzollerns in 1535. It is the site of the castle that was their ancestral home. It is now an outstanding museum.

SIGNAN. See SIAN.

SIGTUNA (Sweden) Town of Stockholm county, in the E, on Lake Skarven, near STOCKHOLM. Founded c.1000 AD, it was one of Sweden's first towns and was the nation's first capital. Because it was a center of Christian missionary activity, Sweden's first coin, with the motto: "Sigtuna Dei" (God's Sigtuna), was minted here. Sacked by Finnish or Estonian pirates in 1187, it declined rapidly afterwards, but today is a popular tourist resort. Ruins of 11th-century churches here show the influence of English stonework.

SIIRT [**Sert**] [ancient: **Tigranocerta**] (Turkey) Capital town of Siirt province, on a tributary of the Tigris River, 85 mi E of Diyarbakir. In its great period it was a fortified city founded by Tigranes, king of ARMENIA, who made it his capital. Tigranes was defeated here in 69 BC by the Roman general Lucullus. Ten years later it was captured by the Roman Corbulo. Later Siirt became an important commercial center under the OTTOMAN EMPIRE.

SIKANDARABAD. See SECUNDERABAD.

SIKANDRA (India) Village of Uttar Pradesh, in the N, 6 mi NW of Agra. It is the site of the tomb of Akbar (1542–1605), who reigned as Mogul emperor of India from 1556 until his death. He greatly expanded the empire and also furthered the arts and religious unity. See also DELHI, FATEHPUR SIKRI, MOGUL EMPIRE.

SIKAR (India) Walled town and market center of Rajasthan state, in the NW. It is the site of the Harasmath temple dating from c.1000 AD.

SIKASSO (Mali) Town in West Africa, approx. 190 mi SE of Bamako, near the Ivory Coast border. Founded in the 1870's, it was once the fortified capital of a leading trading state. It was attacked in the 1880's and 1890's by Samory, a Muslim leader. The town was conquered by the French in 1898 and absorbed into FRENCH WEST AFRICA.

SIKING. See SIAN.

SIKION. See SICYON.

SIKKIM Constitutional monarchy associated with INDIA. Sikkim lies in the NE of the Indian subcontinent, on the S slopes of the Himalayas, and is bounded by China to the N, Bhutan to the E, India to the S, and Nepal to the W. Its capital is Gangtok. In 1642 a Tibetan king founded a hereditary line of rulers of Sikkim, which had been settled by Tibetans in the 16th century. Sikkim is still officially a Buddhist state. It was invaded several times in the 18th and 19th centuries by Gurkhas from Nepal, but the British forced the Gurkhas out and in the 1830's and in the 1840's exacted a number of territorial concessions from the Sikkimese. It then became a British protectorate and remained so until the independence of India in 1947. A treaty of 1949/50 made it an Indian protectorate. Assisted in modernization by India, in 1975 the *chogyal*, or ruler, was pressured into accepting a constitution making Sikkim an associated state of India and reducing the monarchy to a titular position.

SIKYON. See SICYON.

SILBURY HILL (England) Prehistoric mound near AVEBURY, Wiltshire. The largest man-made mound in Europe, it has been dated by radiocarbon methods to *c.*2600 BC for its first phase. It is approximately 130 feet high. Presumably a burial mound, it has been extensively excavated, but nothing has been revealed in its interior except evidences of careful engineering with wooden beams against slippage.

SILCHESTER [*ancient:* **Calleva Atrebatum**] (England) Archaeological site in Hampshire. Excavations here from 1889 to 1909 revealed the ruins of the ancient Roman town, founded in the last quarter of the first century AD, which was locus of a major road system. The entire roughly octagonal plan of the city, with its outside walls, baths, a forum, an amphitheater, a Christian church, and several temples on native plans is now evident. The excavations have revealed our most complete picture of a Romano-British town of the third and fourth centuries. Many archaeological finds are housed in the museum at READING.

SILESIA [*Czech:* **Slezsko;** *German:* **Schlesien**] (Czechoslovakia, East Germany, Poland) District and former Prussian province in E central Europe, traversed by the ODER RIVER and earlier divided by PRUSSIA into Lower Silesia and Upper Silesia. Traditionally, it was inhabited by the Vandal Silingars from the third century BC to the third century AD. By the early sixth century AD it had been occupied by Slavic peoples and was absorbed by Poland by the 11th century. Under King Boleslaus III and the Polish Piast dynasty, it underwent many feudal divisions by inheritance; thus political and territorial cohesiveness was lost.

From the 13th century Silesia pursued a policy of encouraging colonization by GERMANY and introducing a strong German influence. In the 14th century, by acknowledging the sovereignty of the king of BOHEMIA, the Silesian nobility gained stature as minor princes of the HOLY ROMAN EMPIRE. The Hussite Wars in the early 15th century separated Silesia and MORAVIA from Bohemia, but they were united again under Hapsburg rule. In 1523 the Hohenzollerns of BRANDENBURG acquired some territory in Silesia, thereby laying the foundation for a strong Prussian influence in the region. With the onset of the Thirty Years War in 1618, the Silesians endured terrible suffering at the hands of the Swedes, the Hapsburgs, and the Saxons. With the

Peace of WESTPHALIA in 1648 Silesia returned to Hapsburg rule.

The 18th century saw Frederick the Great of Prussia challenging Maria Theresa of AUSTRIA and the Hapsburgs for the possession of the region. Frederick prevailed, following the War of the Austrian Succession of 1742 to 1745 and continued in control after the Seven Years War of 1756 to 1763. The Industrial Revolution of the late 18th and early 19th centuries brought a more intensive exploitation of Silesia's rich iron and coal deposits and the further development of a flourishing textile industry. It also brought crippling disputes between Polish workers and German management.

Following World War I, most of Silesia became part of Poland. Taken by the Nazis in World War II, it was invaded by the Soviets in 1945, but was assigned to Poland by the POTSDAM Conference in 1945. After World War II continuing Polish-German tensions resulted in a massive expulsion of German-speaking peoples from the Silesian sector. A dispute over rights of habitation smoldered until 1972, when WEST GERMANY renounced all claims to Silesia in signing a nonaggression pact with Poland.

SILHOUETTE. See SEYCHELLES.

SILIFKE. See SELEUCIA TRACHEOTIS.

SILISTRA [**Silistria**] [*ancient:* **Durostorum;** *Bulgarian:* **Drstr, Drustur;** *medieval:* **Dristra**] (Bulgaria) Provincial capital and province in the NE, on the DANUBE RIVER, 70 mi ENE of Ruse. Founded in 29 BC as the Roman camp Durostorum, it became an important town of MOESIA and remained important under Byzantine and Bulgar rule. Under the Bulgarian czar Simeon it was successfully defended in 893 AD against the Magyars and the Greeks. Taken by Turkey in 1388, it was heavily fortified and prospered under Turkish rule. Captured by the Russians in the Russo-Turkish War of 1877/78, it was ceded to Bulgaria. Transferred to RUMANIA in 1913, it was returned to Bulgaria in 1940. Several mosques and the ruins of the ancient fortress survive. See also OTTOMAN EMPIRE.

SILISTRIA. See SILISTRA.

SILKEBORG (Denmark) City of Århus county, on the E JUTLAND peninsula, 27 mi W of Århus. It is the site of a memorial honoring the playwright Kaj Munk, who was murdered here by the Nazis in 1944.

SILK ROAD [**Silk Route**] (China, India, Turkistan) Historic trade route from E China through the Wei Valley, Kansu, and Sinkiang in the W, dividing into the N and S caravan routes at the oasis town of TUN-HUANG and passing through the S mountains to Turkistan. The caravan trails were named after their use in the conveyance of Chinese silk to western markets and as routes for statesmen, missionaries, and those on religious pilgrimages.

In the first century BC the Hsiung-nu (Huns) and the Chinese fought for its control. The Chinese Han dynasty won control and restored its eastern reaches in the first century AD. Under the second Han dynasty China extended its control of the Silk Road to the Oases of the Tarim Basin. In the West the Macedonian trader

Maes Titianos explored the route in the first century AD, while the geographer Ptolemy described it in the second century AD.

The ancient route stretched from ANTIOCH in Syria, across the EUPHRATES RIVER at Hieropolis (Menbij), entered PARTHIA at Ectabana (HAMADAN), and then aimed north and east through RHAGAS, HECATOMPY-LOS (Shahrud), MERV, Bactra (BALKH), to the Pamirs Mts. Here it converged with the routes from the East at the Stone Tower, where Levantine goods were exchanged for silks. At KASHGAR to the east the road then forked into a northern and southern road.

The northern road headed through Central Asia to YÜM-EN Kuan, where it entered China. The southern route passed through Kashgar, YARKAND, KHOTAN, Niya, and Miran. The two routes then reunited at the oasis of Tun-huang (the Greco-Roman Throana) in China.

During the barbarian invasions the Huns, UIGURS, and others closed the road. The Chinese under T'ai-tsung reestablished their control c.650 AD. Marco Polo followed the road east c.1270 in the wake of its consolidation under the MONGOL EMPIRE, and several Franciscan missionaries used it in the 14th century to establish and maintain missions in China. Under the Mongols another route was forged from Tana in the CRIMEA to SARAI on the Volga River, then on to KARAKORUM in Central Asia and to SUCHOW. Further south another route started in TREBIZOND, went south to Lajazzo in CILICIA, and then on to TABRIZ and the old Silk Road.

The Silk road has carried the Hellenistic art of Alexander the Great's successors and Greco-Roman merchants to the East; and Han dynasty generals to PERSIA and the Roman Orient. The maintenance of the Silk Road was a cornerstone of Chinese rulers from the Han to Kublai Khan. Buddhism traveled the road east in late antiquity, as did Buddhist-Hellenistic art. Roman coins from the reign of Valens (364–78) have been found at Yotkan, Roman seals at Niyang, and Greco-Roman art at Rawak, east of Khotan.

SILK ROUTE. See SILK ROAD.

SILLA [Shilla] (Korea) Once powerful early kingdom of Korea, in the SE part of the peninsula, probably established in the third century AD. Unlike PAEKCHE, a hostile neighbor state that formed a channel to JAPAN for Chinese culture, Silla was constantly at odds with early Japan and with CHINA. Between the fourth and sixth centuries there is evidence of an invasion of Japan by horse-riding nobles from Silla, and later there were several Japanese attempts to conquer Silla. The last, in 661, was turned back by a Chinese-Sillan force and ended Japanese attempts on the peninsula for many centuries thereafter. Silla at one time eliminated Chinese influence, adopted Buddhism in 528, and eventually conquered all Korea and ruled it from 670 to 935 AD.

SILL, FORT. See FORT SILL.

SILPIA [ancient: Ilipa] (Spain) Town of ancient BAETICA, now in S Spain, N of the Guadalquivir River. In 206 BC Scipio Africanus Major defeated the Carthaginian General Mago in a battle here toward the end of the three-year conquest of southern and eastern Spain by ROME.

SILVER CITY. See NORTH LITTLE ROCK.

SILVES (Portugal) Town on the S coast, 18 mi NNW of Faro. Alphonse III (1210–48) took it from the Moors. It was destroyed by Ferdinand I of CASTILE and then by the great earthquake of 1755. It has a fine Gothic cathedral and a Moorish castle. See also LISBON.

SIMANCAS [ancient: Septimanca] (Spain) Old town in Valladolid province, 8 mi SW of Valladolid. Occupied by the Moors in the ninth century, in 934 it was the scene of a bloody battle between the Christians and the Moors in which Ramiro II defeated Caliph Abder-Rahman. A castle houses the national archives, moved here by Philip II in 1563.

SIMBIRSK. See ULYANOVSK.

SIMFEROPOL [ancient: Neapolis; former: Ak Mechet] (USSR) Capital city of the Crimean oblast, in the UKRAINE, in the S, on the Sebastopol-Kharkov railway. Dating from the third century BC, it was originally a town and fortress of SCYTHIA. Later it became a Tatar town as Ak Mechet in the 16th century, was captured by RUSSIA in 1736, and in 1784 was refounded and fortified as Simferopol. In 1918 it served as capital of the Crimean Tatar nationalist government, and in 1920 was the capital of Gen. P.N. Wrangel's White government. From 1921 to 1946 it served as capital of the Crimean Autonomous SSR. See also CRIMEA.

SIMLA (India) Capital town of Himachal Pradesh state, in the W Himalayas, 53 mi NE of Ambala. A resort town high in the mountains, Simla was famous as the summer capital and social center of British India during the Raj. It was established as a rest home for troops in 1819, after the Gurkha War. It is now the headquarters of the Indian army.

SIMONSTAD. See SIMONSTOWN.

SIMONSTOWN [Simonstad] [former: Simon's Town] (South Africa) Town and naval base in SW CAPE PROVINCE, on the W shore of False Bay, 20 mi S of Cape Town. Established by the Dutch as a military depot in 1741, it was named for Simon van der Stel, the governor of Cape Colony from 1679 to 1697. Made a base for the British South Africa Naval Squadron in 1814, it was transferred to South African jurisdiction in 1957, but the British continue to use it. It took on a new importance for shipping with the Arab-Israeli war of 1967 and the temporary closing of the SUEZ CANAL. It is the site of the oldest English church in South Africa, consecrated in 1814 and rebuilt in 1834.

SIMPLON PASS (Switzerland) An Alpine pass in SW Switzerland marking the dividing line between the Pennine and Lepontine ALPS, running from BRIG, in Switzerland, to Iselle, in NE Italy, approx. 10 mi N of DOMODOSSALA. The pass is crossed by the Simplon road, which was built between 1800 and 1806 by Napoleon I. Its usage fell drastically after the completion of the Simplon railway tunnel in 1906. The tunnel connects the same towns as the pass, but is approximately 13 miles long, while the road winds through 29 miles. The

Simplon tunnel is the longest in the world.

SIMSBURY (United States) Town of Hartford County in N CONNECTICUT, S of Granby. Incorporated in 1670, it was abandoned in 1675 during King Philip's War, was destroyed by Indians in 1676, but was resettled the following year. The first colonial copper coins, known as Higley coppers, were minted here in 1737 and 1739.

SIN. See PELUSIUM.

SINAIA (Rumania) Town in SE Prahova county, in WALACHIA, 21 mi S of Braşov, in the Transylvanian Alps. A summer residence of the kings of Rumania from the 1850's until King Michael's abdication in 1947, it is the site of two former royal palaces. One in the Renaissance style houses an internationally famous art collection. There are also a former royal hunting lodge, a 17th-century monastery, and a castle here.

SINAI, MOUNT [*Arabic:* **Jabal Musa**] (Egypt) Mountain in the S SINAI PENINSULA of NE Egypt. It is approx. 7,500 ft high. Mt Sinai is reputed to be the place where Moses, the Hebrew lawgiver who led his people out of bondage in Egypt in the 13th century BC, received the Ten Commandments on two tablets of stone. In the Bible the account is in Exodus 19 and 20 and in Deuteronomy 5. On the north slope of the mountain is the Greek Orthodox monastery of St. Catherine, founded *c.*250 AD and rebuilt by Justinian *c.*530. It is named for the martyr, Catherine of Alexandria, whose body supposedly was miraculously transported to this site. In 1844 Lobegott F. K. von Tischendorf, a German biblical scholar, found in the monastery a few pages of a very old Greek manuscript of the Old Testament. Later, in 1859, he found an early manuscript of the New Testament, now known as the Codex Sinaiticus, and secured it for the czar of Russia. In 1933 the British museum purchased the Codex Sinaiticus from the USSR. The monastery retains the Codex Syriacus, a Syrian text of the gospels dating from *c.*400. There are also icons dating from before the eighth century and the period of Iconoclasm under the Byzantine Empire, when images of the divinity were ordered destroyed in a religious reform drive. In the Bible Horeb is another name for Mt Sinai.

SINAI PENINSULA (Egypt) Arid peninsula lying between the Gulf of Suez on the W and the Gulf of Aqaba on the E, much disputed throughout history. Copper mines at Magharah here supplied predynastic Egypt. At Sarabit el Khādim turquoise mines have yielded hieroglyphics from *c.*1500 BC. In biblical times Moses received the Ten Commandments on a peak in the Sinai, identified with Mt Sinai, and here the Israelites wandered for 40 years. The Wilderness of Etham is believed to have been to the west, at the head of the Gulf of Suez, the Wilderness of Sin further south, north of Mt Sinai, and the Wilderness of Param to the northeast, west of Elath. In classical antiquity Sinai was ruled by the Arabs of PETRA, but it was for the most part under the jurisdiction or influence of Egypt until it became a part of the ROMAN EMPIRE, most of it lying in the province of ARABIA. Emperor Justinian of the BYZANTINE EMPIRE rebuilt the famed St. Catherine's monastery here *c.*530 AD. Between 1517 and the end of World War I, in 1918, the peninsula was under the OTTOMAN EMPIRE, and several battles of World War I took place here.

After the creation of ISRAEL in 1948 it was disputed between Israel and Egypt and in the wars of 1956, 1967, and 1973 was generally held by Israel. In 1974 U.N. troops were inserted between the Egyptians, who held a narrow strip on the east bank of the Gulf of Suez, and the armies of Israel. In 1978 the CAMP DAVID agreements provided for the gradual withdrawal of Israeli troops from the peninsula and the reestablishment of diplomatic relations between the two countries. In April 1982 the last part of the Sinai was returned to Egypt. See also MOUNT SINAI, PARAN, RAFA, SHARM EL-SHEIKH.

SIND [Sindh] (Pakistan) Historic province in the SE, bounded by India on the E and S and by the Arabian Sea on the SW, with its capital at Karachi. It consists largely of the lower INDUS RIVER valley, in which arose the early Indus Valley Civilization of MOHENJO-DARO and HARAPPA. Later in history the area came under PERSIA of the Achaemenian kings in the fifth century BC, and from them passed to Alexander the Great of the MACEDONIAN EMPIRE in 325 BC. It was held by the MAURYAN EMPIRE in the third century, was overrun by the Huns in 165 BC, and came under the KUSHAN EMPIRE. The Arabs who invaded Sind in 711 AD were the first Muslims to settle in the subcontinent.

Sind remained under the rule of Arab rulers until the 11th century, when it was conquered by the Turkish Ghaznavids. Akbar of the MOGUL EMPIRE ruled the region briefly, but it soon passed to local emirs until they were defeated by Sir Charles Napier of Great Britain in 1843, after which it was administered as part of the BOMBAY Presidency until 1937, when it was made an autonomous province. With Pakistan's independence in 1947, KARACHI became the national capital, and HYDERABAD the new capital of Sind.

SINDER. See ZINDER.

SINDH. See SIND.

SINDHU. See INDUS RIVER.

SINFENG. See HSIN-FENG.

SINGAN. See SIAN.

SINGAPORE [*Japanese:* **Shonan;** *Javanese:* **Temasek**] City and independent republic of SE Asia, comprising Singapore Island and several adjacent islands at the S tip of the MALAY PENINSULA. It was first colonized by a ruler from PALEMBANG, and a CHOLA ruler later named it City of Singhs in the 11th century. It then became a Malay city of some size until it was destroyed by the Javanese in 1365. It remained in ruins until refounded by the British Sir Thomas Raffles in 1819. Until 1823 it was part of the British settlement of BENKOELEN, when it became the property of the East India Company in 1824 and was joined with the new colony of the STRAITS SETTLEMENTS in 1836. It was named the capital in 1836.

The fall of Singapore to the Japanese during World

War II on Feb. 15, 1942, after a ruthless assault in December 1941 to January 1942, shocked the world. The Japanese renamed it Shonan. It was bombed by the Allies in 1944 and 1945 and finally recaptured in September 1945. A British colony again in 1946, it became part of the new state of MALAYSIA from 1963 to 1965, after which it became an independent republic.

Singapore today is the fourth-largest and second-busiest port in the world. It is a center of commerce, finance, communications, and oil refining. Its population of well-educated, skilled citizens comes from all over south and southeast Asia and has one of the highest standards of living in the world.

SINGHASARI. See SINGOSARI.

SINGIDUNUM. See BELGRADE.

SINGOSARI [Singhasari] (Indonesia) Former kingdom in E JAVA, now a village N of Malang. From 1222 to 1292 it was a powerful kingdom dominating eastern Java, with its capital at Singosari. It is referred to in numerous Javanese legends.

SING SING. See OSSINING.

SINIGAGLIA. See SENIGALLIA.

SINING. See HSI-NING.

SINKIANG [Chinese Turkistan, Eastern Turkistan, Hsin-Chiang, Sinkiang-Uighur] (China) Autonomous region in the W, bounded by the Mongolian People's Republic, Kansu province, Tibet, and the USSR. The western and central sections correspond to Chinese or Eastern Turkistan. Its capital is URUMCHI. A very early cradle of mankind inhabited from ancient times by nomad tribes, it first came under Chinese control in the first century BC. It was lost to the UZBEK Confederation in the second century AD and was not reoccupied by China until the seventh century. A strategic and politically sensitive region, it was particularly important in Chinese history as the region traversed by the SILK ROAD. Conquered by the Tibetans in the eighth century, it was next overrun by the Uigurs and was subsequently invaded in the 10th century by the Arabs. It passed to the Mongols under Genghis Khan in the 13th century, following which anarchy reigned until the Manchus reestablished some order in 1756.

In the 19th century unrest was encouraged by both Great Britain and Russia with a view to protecting India and Siberia. Following the Russian Revolution in 1917 it came under Soviet influence until 1942, when it was established as a Chinese province. Rebellion and civil war ensued from 1944 to 1945, and in 1949 its people yielded to the Chinese communists without a struggle.

SINKIANG-UIGHUR. See SINKIANG.

SINOP [ancient: Sinope] (Turkey) Port and provincial capital of Sinop province in the N, on the BLACK SEA, approx 187 mi NE of Ankara. The area may have been first settled c.1200 BC. On the site of an ancient city founded by Greek colonists from MILETUS in the eighth century BC, it was destroyed in the seventh century by Cimmerians and was rebuilt to become politically and commercially important, on the route from the Black Sea to the EUPHRATES RIVER. It established numerous colonies on the Black Sea shores. It fell c.185 BC to the kings of PONTUS and became their capital and the most important port on the Black Sea. In the Third Mithriditic War of 74 to 63 BC, the Romans under Lucullus took it and made it a free city. Sacked by Pharnaces II, it was restored by Julius Caesar and under the Romans enjoyed great prosperity, which continued under the BYZANTINE EMPIRE.

On the breakup of that empire in 1204 after the conquest of Constantinople during the Fourth Crusade, it joined the Greek empire of TREBIZOND. By 1230 it was occupied by the Seljuk Turks, sultanate of Iconium, who brought about its decline. From c.1350 it belonged to the emirate of Kastamien.

On Nov. 30, 1853 a surprise attack and the destruction of a large part of the OTTOMAN EMPIRE's fleet by a Russian naval squadron here helped bring about the Crimean War. Much of the town was also destroyed. In March 1980 a defense agreement between Turkey and the United States placed Diogenes Station here, an important base of U.S. intelligence operations, operated under their joint control. Sinop was also the birthplace of the Greek philosopher Diogenes and of Mithridates the Great of Pontus.

SINOPE. See SINOP.

SINT EUSTATIUS. See SAINT EUSTATIUS.

SINT MAARTEN. See SAINT MARTIN.

SINT NICOLAAS PUNT. See PUDJUT POINT.

SINTRA [former: Cintra] (Portugal) Town of Lisboa district, in the W, 12 mi NW of Lisbon. In 1509 the Sintra Convention laid out regions of overseas exploration to be pursued by Portugal and by Spain. In 1808 it was the scene of the signing of a convention by British, French, and Portuguese military leaders during the Peninsular campaign. It is the site of a large Moorish castle, a 12th- to 15th-century palace, and a convent. Its scenery was celebrated by Byron in his *Childe Harold.*

SINT-TRUIDEN [French: Saint-Trond] (Belgium) Town of Limburg province, in the NE, 20 mi NW of Liège. Growing around a seventh-century abbey founded by St. Trudo, it was conquered by Charles the Bold in the 15th century. It was more recently captured by the Germans in 1914 during World War I. This town has a 13th-century Beguinage, the 15th-century church of Notre Dame, and a 17th-century belfry on the town hall.

SINUS AELANITICUS. See 'AQABA, GULF OF.

SINUS ARABICUS. See RED SEA.

SINUS PERSICUS. See PERSIAN GULF.

SIN, WILDERNESS OF (Egypt) Desert region of the SW SINAI PENINSULA in the NE, on the E side of the Gulf of Suez. It was one of the wildernesses crossed by the Israelites during their Exodus from Egypt.

SIN-YANG. See HSIN-YANG.

SION, Israel. See ZION, Israel.

SION [ancient: Sedunum; German: Sitten] (Switzerland) Capital town of VALAIS canton, on the RHÔNE

RIVER, 50 mi S of Bern. Dating from Roman times, it was made an episcopal see in 580 AD. In 999, when King Rudolf III of BURGUNDY made the bishop a count of the Valais, the latter thereby became the temporal as well as the spiritual lord of the canton. Mentioned as a city in 1179, it is the site of the pilgrimage church of St. Catherine, and has a 13th-century castle, a late Gothic cathedral, and a 17th-century town hall.

SIOUX FALLS (United States) City and county seat in SE SOUTH DAKOTA, on the Big Sioux River, approx. 75 mi N of Sioux City, Iowa. First settled in 1856/57, it was abandoned during the Sioux rebellion in 1862, but it was resettled in 1865 following the establishment of Fort Dakota, which provided protection to the area.

SIPHNO. See SIPHNOS.

SIPHNOS [Siphno] [*modern Greek:* **Sifnós**] (Greece) One of the CYCLADES Islands, in the AEGEAN SEA, it lies 30 mi SW of Syra. Its present town of Kastro is built on the site of the ancient town of Siphnos, inhabited since the eighth century BC, believed to have been settled by Ionians from Athens. In 480 BC the island sent a ship to fight on the Greek side at SALAMIS. Its gold and silver mines gave Siphnos prosperity until they were flooded in the first century AD. Under the BYZANTINE EMPIRE the school of Siphnos, or School of the Holy Tomb, founded by refugees from Constantinople during the iconoclastic persecutions of the eighth century, became a great cultural center for the Greek world. The island was occupied by VENICE in 1207 and changed hands several times before becoming a part of the OTTOMAN EMPIRE in 1617.

SIPKA PASS. See SHIPKA PASS.

SIPONTUM. See MANFREDONIA.

SIPPAR [Sippara] [*Sumerian:* **Zimbir**] (Iraq) Ancient city of BABYLONIA, on the E bank of the EUPHRATES RIVER, 16 mi SSW of Baghdad. It was one of the chief cities of SUMER and later one of the capitals of Sargon of AKKAD (c.2637–2582 BC). Excavations begun in the late 19th century have revealed the remains of a large temple dedicated to the Sumerian god Shamash and a horde of inscribed clay tablets. The temple had been rebuilt in the ninth and seventh centuries BC. Sippar had often been sacked, starting with two partial destructions in the 12th century BC. It was peacefully taken by Cyrus the Great of PERSIA after the defeat of the last Babylonian king at OPIS in 539 BC.

SIPPARA. See SIPPAR.

SÍRACUSA. See SYRACUSE, Italy.

SIRHIND (India) Town of Patiala state in the N, in the PUNJAB, 21 mi N of Patiala. Of early but uncertain origin, it flourished under the Moguls. Its extensive ruins include mosques, and two domed tombs from the 14th century, believed by the Sikhs to be cursed because of the murder of the son of Guru Govind by the Muslim governor here in 1704. See also MOGUL EMPIRE.

SIRIS. See SERRAI.

SIRMIO. See SIRMIONE.

SIRMIONE [*ancient:* **Sirmio;** *former:* **Sermione**] (Italy) A promontory, village, and port extending into Lake Garda at its S end, in Brescia province, LOMBARDY region. There is a 13th-century castle and Roman ruins, including those of a large villa above the modern village, believed to be the country home of the poet Catullus.

SIRMIUM (Yugoslavia) Ruins of an important ancient city of Pannonia, in the NE, on the Sava River, near modern Sremsk Mitrovica. In a strategic location, it became important following the Roman conquest of PANNONIA in the first century BC. The city continued to be prominent as the chief center of Lower Pannonia in the third and fourth centuries AD, when it was often an imperial residence. It was destroyed by the Avars in 589 AD.

SIROS. See HERMOUPOLIS, SYROS.

SIRRHAE. See SERRAI.

SIS [*modern:* **Kozan**] (Turkey) Ancient city in S central Turkey, 40 mi NE of Adana. The former capital of Armenian CILICIA, it was first mentioned in Byzantine history when it was unsuccessfully besieged by Arabs in 704 AD. Sis often changed hands between the BYZANTINE EMPIRE and Muslim forces until the 12th century. At that time Leo II of Armenian Cilicia transferred his capital here and constructed many new buildings. His castle and cathedral have survived. Sis was attacked frequently by the Mamluks of Egypt, who occupied it in 1375, and in 1488 it was captured by the Turks. The city long held an important place in the ecclesiastical history of Christian ARMENIA. The head of the church, the Catholicus, resided here from 1249 to 1439. Between 1915 and 1920 Turkey forced the Armenian population out. One of those expelled was the then current head of the church, Sahag II.

SISAK [Sisek] [*ancient:* **Siscia;** *German:* **Sissek;** *Hungarian:* **Sziszek**] (Yugoslavia) Ancient town of CROATIA, in the N, on the Sava River, 30 mi SE of Zagreb. In the third century AD it was the site of the principal mint and treasury of the ROMAN EMPIRE. The scene of Turkish defeats in 1593 and 1641, it became part of the AUSTRO-HUNGARIAN EMPIRE from 1641 to 1918.

SISAPON. See ALMADÉN.

SISCIA. See SISAK.

SISEK. See SISAK.

SISSEK. See SISAK.

SISSONNE (France) Village of Aisne department, in the N, 12 mi E of Laon. The site of a military camp, it served as a German stronghold in World War I, until it was retaken in October 1918.

SISTAN. See SEISTAN.

SISTOVA. See SVISHTOV.

SITIFIS. See SÉTIF.

SITKA [*former:* **New Archangel**] (United States) Capital city of Greater Sitka Borough, on the W coast of Baranof Island, approx. 100 mi SSW of Juneau, ALASKA. Historically the most notable settlement in

Alaska, it was preceded by Fort Archangel Gabriel, referred to as Old Sitka, and founded as New Archangel in 1799 by Aleksandr Baranov. It was the principal town of Russian America. After it was destroyed by the Tlingit Indians in 1802, it was quickly rebuilt and continued as the capital of Alaska under U.S. rule from 1867 to 1906. Once the principal commercial center of the territory, its decline began following the transfer of the capital to JUNEAU in 1906. Sitka Historic Park here commemorates an important battle between the Indians and the Russians in 1804. The Russian Orthodox Cathedral of St. Michael dates from 1844 to 1848, and Castle Hill was the site of the transfer of Alaska to the United States.

SITOWIR. See ZITTAU.

SI-TSANG. See TIBET.

SITTANG (Burma) River, 260 mi long, in E central Burma, flowing S into the Gulf of Martaban. There was extensive fighting here between the Allies and the Japanese early in 1942 and again in May 1945 during World War II.

SITTEN. See SION.

SITTINGBOURNE (England) Town in Kent, on Milton Creek, 39 mi ESE of London. Adjacent to the ancient royal borough of Milton Regis, it is located on the Roman WATLING STREET and on the former route followed by pilgrims on their way to CANTERBURY. Nearby are Castle Rough, an earthwork dating from the ninth century AD believed to have been erected by Hasten the Dane, and the ruins of Tong Castle.

SIVAS [ancient: **Cabira, Sebaste,Sebastia**] (Turkey) Capital town of Sivas province, on the right bank of the upper Kizil Irmak, 225 mi E of Ankara. It was a principal city of Armenia Minor under Diocletian and the ROMAN EMPIRE. It became especially prosperous under the BYZANTINE EMPIRE until it came under Muslim rule in 1071 AD with the defeat of the Byzantines by the Seljuk Turks at MANZIKERT. It became part of the Seljuk empire of RUM in the late 12th century and was then destroyed by Tamerlane in 1400. Restored under the OTTOMAN EMPIRE in the mid-15th century, it was the site of an important nationalist congress held by Kemal Atatürk in 1919. Here are the remains of 13th-century schools and tombs.

SIVRIHISAR [ancient: **Justinianopolis, Palia;** former: **Sivri-Hissar**] (Turkey) Town of Eskisehir province, 58 mi ESE of Eskişehir. Important as a fortress town on the BYZANTINE EMPIRE's military road to the east, it was refounded and renamed Justinianopolis by the Emperor Justinian (524–65). Circa 700 it became the chief city of Galatia Salutaris.

SIVRI-HISSAR. See SIVRIHISAR.

SIWA. See SIWAH.

SIWAH [Siwa] [ancient: **Ammonium,Sekhet-am**] (Egypt) Oasis in Matrūh governorate, N of the Libyan desert, 350 mi WSW of Cairo. It was the ancient seat of the oracle of Jupiter Ammon, or Zeus Amon, portrayed in the Hellenistic period by Zeus with the horns of Amon. It was visited by Alexander the Great after his conquest of Egypt, and here, according to accounts, he underwent a private illumination. Traces of the temple may still be found in the towns of Siwah and Aghurmi.

SIZUOKA. See SHIZUOKA.

SKADAR. See SHKODËR.

SKAGWAY (United States) City of SE ALASKA, at the head of the Lynn Canal, 80 mi N of Juneau. Founded in 1896/97, it was a boom town during the KLONDIKE gold rush of 1897/98 when it was the departure point for the White Pass to the YUKON.

SKANEATLES (United States) Village in the Finger Lakes region of central NEW YORK State in Onondago county, at the N end of Skaneatles Lake, 8 mi E of Auburn. Settled before 1800, this village is now a resort. In the period before the Civil War it was a hotbed of abolitionist sentiment and activity.

SKARA (Sweden) City of Skaraborg county, in the S. Dating from the ninth century and perhaps earlier, it is one of the country's oldest cities. Sweden's first bishopric was established here in the 11th century. The town has been an educational center since 1641. A notable cathedral, restored in 1894, dates from the 12th century.

SKARA BRAE (Scotland) Prehistoric village on MAINLAND Island, in the ORKNEY ISLANDS. Preserved under a sand dune until it was uncovered by a storm in 1851, the Neolithic period village dates from c.2000 to 1500 BC and consists of seven underground rooms complete with fireplaces, stone beds, dressers, and tables made of flat slates. The site is in a remarkable state of preservation.

SKATCHIA. See XANTHI.

SKEA'S CORNERS. See OSHAWA.

SKIERNIEWICE (Poland) Town of Łódź province, 42 mi SW of Warsaw. Chartered in 1463, it was the residence of the bishops of GNIEZNO in the 17th and 18th centuries and still has their palace. In 1844 it was the scene of a meeting between the emperors of Germany, Austria, and Russia.

SKIKDA [ancient: **Rusicada;** former: **Philippeville**] (Algeria) Port of Constantine department, in the NE, on the Gulf of Stora in the Mediterranean Sea, approx. 210 mi W of Tunis. It was founded by the French in 1838 as a port for CONSTANTINE, on the site of the Carthaginian colony of Rusicada, which was also a flourishing port under the Romans.

SKIPTON MOOR, BATTLE OF. See YORKSHIRE.

SKÍROS. See SKYROS.

SKOPJE [Skoplje] [Albanian: **Shkup;** ancient: **Justina Prima, Scupi;** Turkish: **Üsküb, Üsküp**] (Yugoslavia) Capital city of Macedonia province, 200 mi SSE of Belgrade. Dating from Roman times, it was the capital of Dardania in the fourth century AD and was rebuilt after an earthquake in 518. It was first taken by the Serbs in 1189. The city was the capital of medieval SERBIA and was the site of Stephen Dušan's coronation as czar of Serbia in 1346. Taken by the Turks in 1392, it remained under the OTTOMAN EMPIRE until 1913, and until the capture of Constantinople in 1453 was considered the second city of the Turkish empire.

Conquered by the Serbs in the Balkan War of 1912/13, it became part of Yugoslavia in 1918. The Germans occupied it during World War II. Numerous landmarks, some rebuilt after a major earthquake in 1963, include the Stephen Dušan Bridge, probably Roman in origin, a Turkish citadel, the 15th-century mosques of Mustafa Pasha and Sultan Murad, and a famous oriental bazaar.

SKOPLJE. See SKOPJE.

SKÖVDE (Sweden) City of Skaraborg county, in the S, between Lake Vänern and Lake Vättern. During the Middle Ages it was a place of pilgrimage to the shrine of St. Elin (Helen), canonized in 1164. The nearby Gothic church of a former Cistercian monastery of Varnhem is the burial place of several Swedish kings.

SKYE (Scotland) Largest island of the Inner HEBRIDES, in Highland region. At Dunvegan on the W coast is the castle of the Macleod clan, and on the N end of the island are the ruins of the Castle Duntulm, which belonged to the rival Macdonalds. Prince Charles Edward Stuart took refuge here at Portree, now the capital, after his defeat at CULLODEN MOOR in 1746. Flora Macdonald, who helped Charles escape, is buried at Kilmuir near Dunvegan.

SKYROS [Scyros] [*Greek:* **Skíros**] (Greece) Largest of the N SPORADES Islands, in the AEGEAN SEA, off the coast of THESSALY. Prominent in Greek legends of Theseus, the hero of ATHENS, it was conquered in 476 BC by the Athenians under Cimon who returned the presumed bones of Theseus to Athens in triumph. Cimon also deported the inhabitants, sold them into slavery and replaced them with Athenians.

Skyros was taken by Philip of Macedon in 322 BC and remained under MACEDON until 196 BC, when the Romans took it from Philip V and restored it to Athens. In 269 AD it was sacked by an army of barbarian Goths, Heruli, and Peucini. The World War I English poet Rupert Brooke died and was buried here in 1915. The modern town of St. George occupies the site of the ancient town of Skyros. In tradition Achilles also had been disguised and hidden here by his mother Thetis to keep him from the Trojan War, but he was discovered by Odysseus and followed him to the war.

SLA. See SALÉ.

SLAGELSE (Denmark) Town of S central Vestsjaelland county, on E Zealand island, approx. 55 mi SW of Copenhagen. It is the site of an 11th-century church. Nearby is the great Viking fortress of Trelleborg, one of four constructed between 950 and 1000 AD by Harold Bluetooth or Sweyn Forkbeard of Denmark as military camps for the massive invasion of England. They were also used as settlements and refuges in times of trouble. The others are Fyrkat, Aggersborg, and Nonnebakken. These circular earthworks contained barracks and storehouses along intersecting streets. At Trelleborg there were over 30 boat-shaped barracks, each over 100 feet long, one of which has been reconstructed.

SLANKAMEN. See NOVI SLANKAMEN.

SLAVE COAST (West Africa) Coastal region along the Bight of Benin, on the Gulf of Guinea, between the Benin River and VOLTA RIVER, now Nigeria, Benin, and Togo. From the 16th to mid-19th centuries most of the slaves brought to Europe or the Americas were taken from this region.

SLAVKOV. See AUSTERLITZ.

SLAVKOV U BRNA. See AUSTERLITZ.

SLAVONIA [*Serbo-Croatian:* **Slavonija**] (Yugoslavia) Historic region now part of Croatia state, in the N. Once in the Roman imperial provinces of Illyricum and PANNONIA, it became a Slavic state in the seventh century. Both Croatia and Slavonia united with HUNGARY in 1102, and the region came under Turkish rule in the 16th century. Returned to Hungary by the Treaty of Karlowitz in 1699, it was made an Austrian crown land following the 1848 revolution. Restored to the Hungarian crown and united with CROATIA in 1868, it has been part of Yugoslavia since 1918.

SLAVONIJA. See SLAVONIA.

SLEAFORD (England) Market town of Lincolnshire, on the Slea River, 32 mi E of Nottingham. It is the site of Roman and Anglo-Saxon settlements. A Norman castle built by Alexander, bishop of Lincoln, became one of the main episcopal strongholds in the region.

SLEEPY HOLLOW (United States) Valley and historic district on the HUDSON RIVER, near TARRYTOWN, NEW YORK State. Made famous by Washington Irving's *Legend of Sleepy Hollow*, it is at the heart of the region farmed by the first Dutch settlers. Here are Irving's burial place and several historic restorations.

SLESVIG. See SCHLESWIG, SCHLESWIG-HOLSTEIN.

SLEZSKO. See SILESIA.

SLIASWIC. See SCHLESWIG.

SLIESTHORP. See SCHLESWIG.

SLIGEACH. See SLIGO.

SLIGO [*Gaelic:* **Sligeach**] (Irish Republic) Port and county town of Sligo county, on Sligo Bay, at the mouth of the Garavogue River, approx. 108 mi NW of Dublin. It is the site of a 13th-century castle, several times destroyed and restored, and the remains of the 13th-century Dominican monastery, Sligo Abbey, built by Maurice Fitzgerald, earl of KILDARE. Destroyed in 1414, it was rebuilt and was destroyed again in 1641 when Parliamentarians attacked the town. At nearby Carrowmore are megalithic remains and at Knocknaerea the traditional burial place of Queen Mab, identified with an early queen of CONNAUGHT. Sligo is the site of the notable church of St. John, a Roman Catholic cathedral, and a bishop's palace. It was the birthplace of W.B. Yeats, the poet.

SLIVEN [Slivno] (Bulgaria) Provincial capital city and province in E RUMELIA, 60 mi W of Burgas, at the foot of the Balkan Mts. Its strategic importance at the entrance to the Balkan passes made it a center of conflict between Bulgaria and the BYZANTINE EMPIRE in the Middle Ages and between the OTTOMAN EMPIRE and RUSSIA in the 19th century, when it was a center for the Bulgarian independence movement. It is the seat of an Eastern Orthodox metropolitan.

SLIVNICA [Slivnitza] (Bulgaria) Town in Sofia province, in the W, 19 mi NW of Sofia. Here, from Nov. 17 to 19, 1885 a battle took place in which the Serbs, who had declared war against Bulgaria over the question of EASTERN RUMELIA, were defeated by the Bulgarians. The Bulgarians went on to invade SERBIA but were forced to withdraw by AUSTRIA. Peace was made on March 6, 1886.

SLIVNITZA. See SLIVNICA.

SLIVNO. See SLIVEN.

SLONIM [*Polish:* Słonim] (USSR) Town of Grodno oblast, in W Belorussian SSR, on the Shchara River, 43 mi SSW of Novogrudok. First mentioned in 1040 when Yaroslav, prince of KIEV, defeated the Lithuanians nearby, it was destroyed by the Mongol hordes in 1241. Formerly part of Poland, from Sept. 13 to 18, 1915 it was the scene of a battle in which the Germans defeated the Russians during World War I.

SLOPPESBURY. See SHREWSBURY.

SLOT, THE (Solomon Islands) Long open-water passage in the W Pacific Ocean, running 300 mi NW to SE. Its name was given by U.S. forces in World War II, to the usual route taken by Japanese ships and planes en route to their garrisons on GUADALCANAL between August 1942, and January 1943. It saw much military action.

SLOVAKIA [*former:* **Slovene;** *Slovak:* **Slovensko**] (Czechoslovakia) Component state of Czechoslovakia, bordered by the Ukraine on the E, Austria on the W, Hungary on the S, and Poland on the N. Its capital is the important DANUBE RIVER port of BRATISLAVA. Settled by Slavic Slovaks in the sixth and seventh centuries AD, by the mid-seventh century it was threatened by the Avars from the east and then by the Franks from the west before being absorbed by the Bulgar khanate by 830 and the kingdom of MORAVIA by 890. It was in the Moravian period that St. Cyril and St. Methodius converted the Slovaks to Christianity.

From the 10th century until 1918 Slovakia was dominated by the Magyars, who subjected the pastoral Slovaks to the harsh rule of the kingdom of Hungary by 1001. Following the Turkish defeat of Louis II of HUNGARY and BOHEMIA at MOHÁCS in 1526, Slovakia came under Hapsburg control. As a regional Hapsburg capital, Bratislava made Slovakia politically important, but the forceful Magyar landowners continued to mistreat the Slovaks. In the 18th century Joseph II and Maria Theresa of AUSTRIA encouraged some reform but also fostered Germanic influences in the region. Reacting to these Germanizing policies, the Catholic clergy led a movement aimed at developing a Slovak national consciousness. This continued in the 19th century under the leadership of Lúdovít Štúr, founder of the modern Slovak literary movement.

Early 20th century immigration of Slovak peasants to new communities in the UNITED STATES brought a reaction in North America favoring Slovak nationalism. In May 1918 Czechs and Slovaks in the United States promulgated the Pittsburgh Declaration, which proposed a united Czechoslovak republic assuring the Slovaks a marked degree of independence. By October 1918 the Slovak National Council had declared the region's independence from Hungary and incorporation with the Czechs. However, continued territorial claims by Hungary rendered Czechoslovak unity precarious. Moreover, the Slovaks consistently asserted they were being denied their autonomous right by the Czech government. Father Jozef Tiso continued the demands for Slovak autonomy, and after the MUNICH Pact in 1938 he actually became premier of Slovakia in a reconstructed Czecho-Slovakia. When he was removed from his post by the government in PRAGUE, he turned to Hitler of GERMANY who used the unstable situation as a pretext for establishing a German "protectorate" over Moravia, SILESIA, and Bohemia, while assuring Slovakia's independence under German "protection." Tiso subsequently allowed Hitler to occupy Slovakia and cooperated with him in World War II.

A pro-Allied underground developed in reaction, joining the invading Soviet forces in 1944 to force the Germans out. Slovakia became a component state of Czechoslovakia in 1948, but was to retain its independent government agencies. Subsequently, Alexander Dubcek's liberal communist regime caused such uneasiness on the part of the Soviets that they invaded and crushed the Czech government in 1968. The new Socialist Federal Republic of Czechoslovakia came into existence Jan. 1, 1969. Under its aegis, both the Czech and Slovak republics have responsibility for the conduct of local and state affairs, with a central government controlling the principal areas of defense, foreign policy, taxation, and finance for the two republics.

SLOVAK SOCIALIST REPUBLIC. See SLOVAKIA.

SLOVENE. See SLOVAKIA.

SLOVENIA [*ancient:* **Samo;** *Serbian:* **Slovenija**] (Yugoslavia) Constituent republic in the NW, with its capital at LJUBLJANA. Settled by Slovenes in the sixth century AD as the state of Samo, it was later under the Franks and the Bavarians. After 1335 most of the Slovene territory came under AUSTRIA, except for 1809 to 1813, when it was part of the Slavic ILLYRIAN PROVINCES created by Napoleon. In 1918 Slovenia joined other South Slavs in creating the Kingdom of the Serbs, Croats and Slovenes or, after 1931, Yugoslavia. During World War II Slovenia was divided between Hungary, Italy, and Germany. It became a constituent republic in 1946. See also CELJE, MARIBOR.

SLOVENIJA. See SLOVENIA.

SLOVENSKO. See SLOVAKIA.

SLUIS. See SLUYS.

SŁUPSK [*German:* **Stolp**] (Poland) City in the NW, 39 mi ENE of Koszalin. First mentioned in 1180, it was chartered in 1310 and became a member of the HANSEATIC LEAGUE. In 1648 it passed to BRANDENBURG. Captured by the Soviet Union on March 9, 1945 toward the end of World War II, it was later assigned to Poland by the Potsdam Conference. Historic structures include a 16th-century castle and 14th-century town gates.

SLUTSK. See PAVLOVSK.

SLUYS [Sluis] [*French:* Écluse, L'Écluse] (Netherlands) Town of Zeeland province, on the Belgian border, now connected by canal to the sea. On June 24, 1340 it was the scene of a naval battle in which Edward III of England, commanding in person, nearly destroyed the French fleet of Philip VI in the first major battle of the Hundred Years War. During the Revolt of the Netherlands it fell to the Spanish in 1587, but the Dutch retook it in 1604.

SMALCALD. See SCHMALKALDEN.

SMALKALD. See SCHMALKALDEN.

SMEDEREVO [*ancient:* **Mons Aureus;** *German:* **Semendria**] (Yugoslavia) Serbian town in the E, on the DANUBE RIVER, 25 mi ESE of Belgrade. Dating from Roman times, it served as the capital of SERBIA from 1430 to 1459, when Belgrade was held by the Turks. Its famous vineyards are believed to have been planted by the Roman Emperor Probus. In the 15th century George Brankovich became lord of Tokay and made Semendria both his residence and the capital of SERBIA. Vines from the town transplanted to his estate produced the famous Tokay wine. In 1429 Brankovich erected an unusual triangular castle with 19 towers here, modeled after the walls of Constantinople. Taken by the Turks in 1456, it still stands. The town was occupied by the Germans in World War II.

SMITHWICK. See FALMOUTH, England.

SMOKE THAT THUNDERS, THE. See VICTORIA FALLS.

SMOLENSK (USSR) Capital city of Smolensk oblast, on the left bank of the DNIEPER RIVER. It came into prominence in the ninth century and became an important town on the trade route from Constantinople to the Baltic Sea. Allied first with the principality of KIEV, it served as capital of Smolensk principality from the 12th to 14th centuries. In 1240 it was pillaged by the Tatars. LITHUANIA took it over in 1408, and it then became a bone of contention between POLAND and Russia for a quarter century before being finally ceded to RUSSIA in 1686. During Napoleon's invasion of Russia in 1812 it was burned on August 17/18 and was again virtually destroyed in heavy fighting during World War II. Taken by the Germans in 1941, it was retaken by the Soviets in 1943. Restored historic structures include a citadel and the town walls, the Uspensky Cathedral of 1677 to 1679, several 12th-century churches, and monuments to Gen. Kutuzov and to the composer Glinka.

SMYRNA. See İZMIR.

SNAKE RIVER [*former:* **Lewis River**] (United States) River in the NW, 1,038 mi long. The chief tributary of the COLUMBIA RIVER, it rises in NW Wyoming in YELLOWSTONE NATIONAL PARK. The Snake follows a twisting course, flowing first into Idaho and NW to a junction with the Henrys Fork River; then making a bend into Oregon, where it turns N to form the Idaho-Oregon and Idaho-Washington boundaries. After LEWISTON, Idaho, it flows mostly W until it joins the Columbia near Pasco, Washington.

The river was discovered by the Lewis and Clark Expedition of 1803 to 1806. Headed by Meriwether Lewis and William Clark, this was sent by President Jefferson to explore the LOUISIANA PURCHASE and to reach the Pacific Ocean overland. The expedition found the Snake in 1805 where the Clearwater River joins it, camped here at the site of present Lewiston, and then followed it to the Columbia. In 1834, near present Pocatello, Idaho, FORT HALL, an important military and trading post, was established on the Snake. Idaho Falls, Idaho, was originally a fording point used by miners to cross the Snake. Along the river's course are a number of very large irrigation, navigation, and hydroelectric projects.

SNOWDOUN. See STIRLING.

SOBA The capital city of the ancient Nubian kingdom of ALWA, on the upper NILE RIVER. It was destroyed by the FUNJ in 1504 AD. See also NUBIA.

SOBRAON (India) Village of the PUNJAB, in the NW, on the right bank of the Sutlej River. On Feb. 16, 1846 it was the scene of a decisive battle on the opposite river bank in which the British under Sir Hugh Gough defeated the Sikhs, thereby concluding the First Sikh War.

SOCĂ. See ISONZO RIVER.

SO-CH'E. See YARKAND.

SOCIALIST PEOPLES' LIBYAN ARAB REPUBLIC. See LIBYA.

SOCIETY ISLANDS (France) Island group and overseas territory in W FRENCH POLYNESIA, S Pacific Ocean. The Tahitian town of PAPEETE is the capital, and TAHITI the most important island. First reported by the Portuguese navigator Pedro Fernandes de Quierós in 1607, they were claimed for Great Britain by Samuel Wallis in 1767 and for France by Louis de Bougainville in 1768. They were next visited and named by Captain Cook in 1769 on his *Endeavour* expedition. Made a protectorate of France in 1843, the islands became a colony in 1880 and were made an overseas territory in 1946.

SOCOTRA [Sokotra] [*Arabic:* **Suqutra**] (Yemen) Island at the mouth of the Gulf of Aden, in the Indian Ocean, 150 mi off the African coast. Known to the ancient Egyptians and Greeks, it may have been the Iskuduru conquered by Darius of PERSIA. In legend it was associated with eternal life and unearthly happiness and was thus visited by early explorers seeking paradise. It became a possession of the sultans of Qishn and shared the history of the ARABIAN PENINSULA, except for a Portuguese occupation from 1507 to 1511. The East India Company of Great Britain took it over in 1834, and it was the subject of a treaty between Great Britain and the local sultan in 1876. It became part of Great Britain's Aden protectorate in 1886. In 1967 it was joined to the new state of South Yemen.

SÖDERTÄLJE [*former:* **Tälje**] (Sweden) City of Stockholm county, in the S, and a suburb of STOCKHOLM. One of Sweden's earliest cities, as Tälje it was a trading center during the Viking era from the ninth to the 11th century. It was damaged by fires in the 14th, 17th, and 18th centuries. It is the site of an 11th-century church and of Gripsholm Castle.

SODOM [Sodoma] (Israel and Jordan) City of ancient PALESTINE, in the plain of the JORDAN RIVER, probably now beneath the S portion of the DEAD SEA. It was the most important of the biblical Cities of the Plain, the others being GOMORRAH, Admah, Zeboiim, and ZOAR. According to the Bible, only Zoar was spared destruction by the fire from heaven sent as punishment for their sins.

SODOMA. See SODOM.

SOERABAJA. See SURABAJA.

SOERAKARTA. See SURAKARTA.

SOEST [*medieval:* Sosat] (West Germany) One of Germany's oldest cities, in North Rhine-Westphalia, 30 mi E of DORTMUND. Chartered in 1144, it was the chief town of WESTPHALIA in the Middle Ages and a prosperous member of the HANSEATIC LEAGUE. Under the archbishop-princes of COLOGNE until the 15th century, it then passed to the county of Mark under the duke of KLEVE and in 1614 came under the house of BRANDENBURG. Notable buildings surviving severe damage in World War II include the Romanesque cathedral of St. Patroclus, once used as an armory, and the Romanesque Nicholas Chapel, both 12th century, a massive gate tower with an important collection of weapons, numerous medieval and Renaissance houses, and part of the old town wall.

SOFALA. See NOVA SOFALA.

SOFIA [Sophia] [*ancient:* Serdica, Sardica; *Bulgarian:* Sofiya; *Byzantine:* Triaditsa; *former:* Sredets] (Bulgaria) The nation's capital, on a high plain surrounded by the Balkan Mts. Originally a Thracian settlement, it was taken by the Romans in 29 AD and founded as Serdica or Sardica. It prospered under Trajan and was a favorite residence of Constantine the Great. Destroyed by the Huns in 447, it was rebuilt in the sixth century by the Byzantine Emperor Justinian I, who renamed it Triaditsa. Part of the first Bulgarian kingdom from 809 to 1018, it then reverted to the Byzantines until 1186, when it became part of the second Bulgarian kingdom which lasted until 1382.

Known as Sredets under the Bulgars, it was renamed Sofia in 1376. Passing to the OTTOMAN EMPIRE in 1382, it became the residence of the Turkish governors of RUMELIA until 1877/78, when it was taken by the Russians in the Russo-Turkish War. It became capital of the newly independent Bulgaria in 1879. After the city suffered severe bombing damage in World War II, the Soviets took it from the Germans and established a communist government. Notable buildings include the parliament, the state opera house, the former royal palace, the church of St. George from the third, fourth, and fifth centuries, the church of St. Sofia from the sixth and seventh centuries, and the Banya Bashi Mosque of 1474.

SOFIYA. See SOFIA.

SOGDIANA (USSR) Province of the ancient Persian Empire, in central Asian Russia, between the Oxus and Jaxartes rivers. SAMARKAND, then Maracanda, was its capital. Conquered by Cyrus the Great in 525 BC, it became a satrapy under Darius I and was invaded by Alexander the Great between 329 and 327 BC. It was next conquered by Diodotus, a satrap of BACTRIA and was later taken by PARTHIA and by PERSIA. Sogdiana roughly corresponded to the later emirate of BUKHARA. See also TRANSOXIANA and UZBEK SSR.

SOHAG. See SAWHAJ.

SOHO (England) Once fashionable quarter of the borough of Westminster, Inner LONDON, S of Oxford Street, centering around Soho Square. The name derives from a medieval hunting cry, first mentioned in 1636. Soho Square was laid out in 1681, and soon after French Huguenot refugees, fleeing from the revocation of the Edict of Nantes, flocked to the area. The quarter was first one of great mansions, of embassies, and fashionable restaurants. It was also the home of London's scientific community in the 18th century, where Priestley, Cavendish, and others worked and met. Since 1685 it has been chiefly a foreign quarter, known for its restaurants and theaters. Popular among writers and artists in the 19th century, its famous residents included John Dryden, William Blake, and Thomas De Quincey. Mozart taught music here for a while in 1764. William Hazlitt and Karl Marx also lived here. The first television demonstration was presented here by J.L. Baird in 1926.

SOIGNIES [*Flemish:* Zinnik] (Belgium) Town in SW Belgium, 23 mi SSW of Brussels. The Romans constructed a fortress here, and the town is said to have been founded in the seventh century AD by St. Vincent, who built a monastery on the site. The 11th-century Romanesque church is the dominant feature of Soignies. Nearby is the ancient Forest of Soignies.

SOISSONS [*ancient:* Augusta Suessionum, Noviodunum] (France) Ancient and important town of Aisne department, in the N, on the Aisne River, 18 mi SW of Laon. A principal town of the Suessiones of Belgian GAUL, it became an important Roman city. Clovis I, one of the Merovingian founders of the FRANKISH EMPIRE, defeated the troops of a Gallo-Roman enclave here under Syagrius in 486 AD. The town later became the seat of several Merovingian kings. Charles Martel defeated the forces of NEUSTRIA here in 716/17, and the hapless Childeric III, last of the Merovingians, was dethroned here by the Carolingian Pepin the Short in 751. A church council held here in 1092 condemned the nominalism of Roscellinus, which by extension denied the real existence of universal ideas, such as the Church or the Trinity.

Chartered in 1131, Soissons was attacked and sacked during the Hundred Years War in 1414, and later in 1544 and 1565. During the Franco-Prussian War it was captured by the Prussians in 1870, and during World War I suffered terrible German bombardments and was captured by the Germans in 1914 and 1918. Taken by the Germans again in 1940 at the beginning of World

War II, it was recaptured by the Allies on Aug. 27/28, 1944.

The Gothic cathedral of St. Gervais and St. Protais was built between 1176 and 1250 and clearly shows the influence of CHARTRES Cathedral. It was severely damaged in World War I, but demolition of a section of the nave revealed the engineering brilliance of its High Gothic design. Flying buttresses here were shown to have been built to counterbalance both the thrust of the vaulting and to stabilize the wind pressure on the roof. The cathedral now has stained glass windows by Rubens. Here are also the ruins of the abbey of St. Jean des Vignes, where St. Thomas à Becket lived for a time. The nearby abbey of St. Médard was a burial place of Merovingian kings.

SOKOTO (Nigeria) Former sultanate that included most of northern Nigeria, now in Sokoto State. Under Berber and Arab influences from the 12th to 18th centuries, it was comprised of many small kingdoms under Muslim rulers. It was subdued between 1801 and 1804 by Fulah tribes under Usuman dan Fodio, who established the Fulah (Muslim) Empire and sultanate with its capital at the town of Sokoto. Its decline followed a treaty in 1885 with the British, who took over in 1903. They put down a religious uprising here in 1906. The tomb of dan Fodio and other shrines make Sokoto town a Muslim pilgrimage center.

SOKOTRA. See SOCOTRA.

SOLESMES (France) Village of Sarthe department, on the Sarthe River, approx. 23 mi SW of Le Mans. It is the site of the well-known Benedictine abbey of St. Pierre de Solesmes, dating from 1010, which was a pilgrimage site and which, in the late 19th century, led in the revival of the pure Gregorian chant, or plain song. The Solesmes chant was eventually adopted by the Roman Catholic Church as a whole. This monastery has frequently been involved in controversy and suppression; most recently its monks were forced to relocate to the Isle of Wight between 1901 and 1922. The abbey church has a collection of priceless 15th and 16th century sculptures.

SOLEURE. See SOLOTHURN.

SOLFERINO (Italy) Village of Mantova province, in SE LOMBARDY region, 5 mi W of the Mincio River. On June 24, 1859, during the Risorgimento, or unification of Italy, it was the scene of a bloody but indecisive battle between the French and Sardinians under Napoleon III and the Austrians under the Emperor Francis Joseph. Prompted by the terrible losses in the battle, Napoleon III soon arranged a meeting with Francis Joseph to end the war. J. Henry Dunant, a Swiss philanthropist and witness to the battle, was inspired by it to promote the founding of the Red Cross in 1864.

SOLI [Soloi] [later: **Pompeiopolis**] (Turkey) City of ancient CILICIA, on the southern coast of Turkey, 3 mi SW of Mersin. Founded in 700 BC by colonists from Argos and Rhodes, it became an important port in the time of Alexander the Great. Destroyed in the first century BC by Tigranes of ARMENIA in the Mithridatic War, it was rebuilt by the Roman Pompey, who named it Pompeiopolis. The English word "solecism," meaning incorrectly spoken, derives from Soli because of the poor Greek spoken here.

SOLIM. See SALONA.

SOLINGEN (West Germany) Industrial city of North Rhine-Westphalia, in the Ruhr Valley, 14 mi ESE of Düsseldorf. Chartered in 1374, it is the home of Solingen steel and has been known for its excellent cutlery since the Middle Ages. Belonging to the duchy of BERG until 1600, it passed to PRUSSIA in 1815. It suffered heavy bombing and damage in World War II but has been rebuilt.

SOLKHAT. See STARY KRYM.

SOLLUM. See SALÛM.

SOLNA (Sweden) City and N suburb of STOCKHOLM, in the E. Settled since antiquity, it has Viking remains, including runic stones. It is the seat of the Nobel Institute and of several scientific institutes. Since 1792 the Swedish War Academy has been housed in Karlsberg Castle, one of several here.

SOLO. See SURAKARTA.

SOLOI. See SOLI.

SOLOMON ISLANDS (Solomons) Nation of six large and many small islands, in a 900-mi chain, in the W Pacific, E of New Guinea, including Choiseul, GUADALCANAL, BOUGAINVILLE, and NEW GEORGIA islands. Honiara, on Guadalcanal, is the capital. Discovered by Alvaro de Mendaña of Spain in 1567, they were next seen by Europeans on Louis Bougainville's visit in 1768. D'Urville's arrival between 1837 and 1840 was then followed by visits from missionaries and traders from 1845 to 1893. An 1886 agreement completed in 1899 divided the islands between Great Britain and Germany. With the outbreak of World War I the German group was taken by the Australians in 1914 and became part of the Australian mandate under the League of Nations in 1920, as a portion of the Trust Territory of New Guinea. Mostly occupied by the Japanese during World War II, they were the scene of a bloody battle beginning Aug. 7, 1942 when the U.S. forces landed, eventually occupying Guadalcanal in February 1943. They are now entirely independent.

SOLOTHURN [ancient: **Salodurum**; French: **Soleure**] (Switzerland) Cantonal capital of Soluthurn Canton, in the NW, on the Aare River, 19 mi N of Bern. Developing from the Roman settlement of Salodurum, it became a free town of the HOLY ROMAN EMPIRE in 1218. In 1481 it was admitted to the Swiss Confederation. It successfully resisted attempts by the Hapsburgs to take control and joined in the SEMPACH War, which resulted in ridding the confederation of Hapsburg influence. Developing as a cultural center, until 1797 it was the residence of the French ambassadors to the Swiss Diet. It retains much of its historic quality, with a 13th-century clock tower, old fortifications, a 15th-century town hall and the 18th-century cathedral of St. Ursus and St. Victor.

SOLOVETS. See SOLOVETSKI ISLANDS.

SOLOVETSKI ISLANDS [Solovets] [*Russian:* **Solovetskiye Ostrova**] (USSR) Archipelago of Arkhangelsk oblast, in the SW White Sea, 30 mi E of Kem and approx. 160 mi W of Archangel. From the days of Ivan IV the Terrible (1530–84) until 1956 the islands and their forced labor camps were a place of exile for criminals and political and religious prisoners. A former monastery on the largest island, dating from 1429, was used in the 16th and 17th centuries as a fortress against the Swedes.

SOLOVETSKIYE OSTROVA. See SOLOVETSKI ISLANDS.

SOLTĀNĪYEH [Sultānīyah] (Iran) Village, approx. 20 mi SE of Zanjan city, and approx. 90 mi NW of Kasvin. Once capital of PERSIA, it was founded in the late 13th century largely by Öljeitü, one of the Mongol Il-khans. His magnificent mausoleum, with its enormous dome and inlaid faience decoration, though little known, is one of the great monuments of early medieval Persia. See also MONGOL EMPIRES.

SOLUTRÉ-POUILLY (France) Village in Saône-et-Loire department, near Mâcon, which gives its name to the Solutrean epoch of Paleolithic culture. A cave discovered here in 1867 revealed both human remains and unusually fine chipped stone implements. The Solutrean, dated *c.*19,000 to *c.*15,000 BC, preceded the final period of Paleolithic culture, the Magdalenian, which was distinguished by its famous cave art. See also LA MADELEINE.

SOLWAY MOSS (England) Former moorland district in Cumbria, near the Scottish border, NW of the Esk River. In a brief border war between England under Henry VIII and Scotland, James V of Scotland, father of Mary, Queen of Scots, was defeated here in a battle on Nov. 25, 1542 on the moor. James V died shortly thereafter.

SOMALIA [Somali Democratic Republic] Nation in East Africa, bordered on the N and E by the Gulf of Aden and the Indian Ocean, and on its landward side by Djibouti (formerly French Somaliland) to the NW, Ethiopia to the W and N, and Kenya to the W and S. The capital and largest city is MOGADISHO. The region was part of what the ancient Egyptians called Punt, "the land of aromatics and incense." They sent expeditions here to obtain slaves, gold, and incense. Arabs and Persians set up trading posts on the coast between the seventh and 10th centuries AD, while Somali warriors fought for Muslim sultans in the 15th and 16th centuries in battles with ETHIOPIA, which was Christian. In the 19th century Great Britain, France, and Italy brought their imperialistic ambitions to the region. EGYPT had occupied much of the area in the 1870's; and when its troops withdrew in 1884 the British moved in. They entered into agreements with local chiefs and established a protectorate in 1887. Meanwhile, the French had acquired some territory here in the 1860's. Italy came on the scene in 1889 by establishing a small protectorate in the central zone. JUBALAND, an area east of the Juba River, became part of the Italian colony in 1925 by cession from Great Britain.

After Italy conquered Ethiopia in 1936, ITALIAN SOMALILAND became a province of Italian East Africa. In World War II the Italians invaded British Somaliland in August 1940, but the British took it back in 1941 and seized Italian Somaliland as well. The region was ruled by Great Britain until 1950, when Italian Somaliland became a United Nations Trust territory controlled by the Italians. The two Somalilands became an independent state in mid-1960 as the United Republic of Somalia. The OGADEN region, now in southeastern Ethiopia, had been returned to that country in 1954 by Great Britain, much to the displeasure of the Somalis, who claimed it on ethnic grounds.

War between Somalia and Ethiopia broke out in 1964 over the Ogaden; ended temporarily in 1967; broke out again in 1977; and guerrilla warfare continues. Somalia's close relationship with the USSR was threatened by Somali support of the Ogaden rebels. In 1977 Somalia finally expelled all Soviet military and diplomatic personnel. In November 1981 the United States began using a naval base granted it at BERBERA.

SOMALIA ITALIANA. See ITALIAN SOMALILAND.

SOMALI DEMOCRATIC REPUBLIC. See SOMALIA.

SOMALILAND. See DJIBOUTI, ETHIOPIA, SOMALIA.

SOMBRERO. See SAINT KITTS-NEVIS.

SOMERSET [Somersetshire] (England) County on the Bristol Channel. The area was conquered by the Romans in 43/44 AD, and some of the most interesting Roman remains in England have been found at BATH, now in Avon. Contested by Welsh and Anglo-Saxons, eventually it became part of the Anglo-Saxon kingdom of WESSEX and has strong associations both with the legendary King Arthur and with King Alfred the Great. The town of GLASTONBURY is important in England's religious history and legend, and the cathedrals of Bath and of WELLS are outstanding among numerous notable churches. In 1974, in a reorganization of counties, the new county of Avon was created out of a northern section. The admin. hq. of Somerset is TAUNTON. See also MENDIP HILLS.

SOMERSETSHIRE. See SOMERSET.

SOMERS ISLANDS. See BERMUDA.

SOMERVILLE [*former:*** Cow Commons]** (United States) City in MASSACHUSETTS, 3 mi NW of Boston, on the Mystic River. Settled in 1630, it was important in the history of the American Revolution. Gen. Israel Putnam raised the first flag of the United Colonies in 1776 on Prospect Hill Tower, which also served as a prison camp in the Civil War. It is the site of the Old Powder House used in the American Revolution, and of Ploughed Hill, one of the fortified hills used in the siege of Boston in 1776 by the Americans.

SOMME (France) Battle site and river in the N, rising in Aisne department and flowing W to Amiens, then NW past Abbeville and into the English Channel. From July 1 to Nov. 18, 1916 it was the scene of one of World War I's greatest and bloodiest battles, involving a series of encounters in which the Allies, mainly under Marshal Haig and Gen. Henry Rawlinson, made only minor advances against the Germans. During World War II the Somme valley was occupied by the Germans in May and June 1940 and was recovered by the Allies in August 1944.

SOMNATH [Patan Somnath] (India) Ancient port on the S coast of Gujarat state, in the W, near Veraval. Settled at least 3,000 years ago, it is important in Hindu legends as the place where Krishna was shot by the Bhils. One of several ancient temples here was looted by Mahmud of Ghazni in 1024 when the Gates of Somnath were carried off to his capital. Twice reconstructed, the Temple of Shiva was again destroyed during the 13th-century Muslim conquest. In 1842 what were believed to be the same Somnath gates were brought back to AGRA by Lord Ellenborough.

SØNDERBORG (Denmark) Seaside resort town on Swais Island, off the SE coast of JUTLAND, 17 mi NE of Flensburg. Part of the duchy of SCHLESWIG, it developed around a 13th-century castle. After being deposed, Christian II was held prisoner here from 1532 to 1549. Christian III (1534–49) created the duchy of Sønderborg for his son from which the present Danish dynasty of Schleswig-Holstein-Sønderborg-Glücksburg is descended. The town was held by PRUSSIA from 1864 to 1920. A museum here houses a collection of military objects, including many used in the battle at nearby DYBBØL.

SONGDO. See KAESŎNG.

SONGHAI [Songhay, Songhoi, Sonrhai] A great trading empire of 15th- and 16th-century West Africa. Its territory extended from the Atlantic Ocean to modern Nigeria and was centered in what is now the nation of MALI along the bend of the Niger River.

The Songhai capital of Gao was originally settled c.800 and prospered because of its position on the lucrative trans-Saharan trade route. The empire of MALI won possession of Gao from 1325 to 1375 and established it as a center of Muslim scholarship. After breaking Mali's hold, Songhai maintained a precarious independence until Sonni Ali ascended the throne c.1465 and strengthened its position. By 1476 he had successfully campaigned against the hostile Dogon, FULANI, and Tuareg and seized control of the cities of TIMBUKTU and DJENNÉ.

In 1493 Muhammad I Askia seized the throne and aggressively pursued a course of expansion that brought the center of the Western SUDAN under the firm control of the Songhai Empire. His rule was characterized by a strong central administration and a flourishing of commerce and Muslim scholarship. In the late 16th century the Moroccan Sultan Ahmed al-Mansur began to apply pressure to Songhai's northern border. In 1591 a Spanish-Portuguese army equipped with firearms entered Songhai from MOROCCO and easily captured Gao and Timbuktu. Songhai's army was destroyed and its government and national identity were fatally shattered.

SONGHAY. See SONGHAI.

SONGHOI. See SONGHAI.

SONORA (Mexico) State in the NW, on the Gulf of California, S of Arizona. Following Coronado's expedition in 1540, systematic exploration of the area was begun by Cristóbal de Oñate. Spanish missionaries arrived in the 17th century and were active in colonizing and dealing with hostile Indian tribes. Sonora was significantly involved after 1910 in the Mexican revolution. HERMOSILLO is its capital.

SONRHAI. See SONGHAI.

SONTIUS. See ISONZO RIVER.

SOOCHOW. See SUCHOU.

SOPHIA. See SOFIA.

SOPOT [*German:* Zoppot] (Poland) Seaside resort town of old Prussia, on the Gulf of Danzig and the Baltic Sea. First mentioned in the 13th century, from 1283 to 1807 it belonged to the city of Danzig, now GDAŃSK. Passing to PRUSSIA in 1814, it was developed as a resort from 1823 and remained German until 1919, when it joined the Free City of Danzig. It passed to Poland in 1945 after World War II.

SOPRON [*ancient:* Scarabantia; *German:* Ödenburg] (Hungary) City in NW Hungary, not far from the Austrian border, 140 mi W of Budapest. It is first heard of as a Celtic and Roman settlement called Scarabantia, a military outpost that in the 10th and 11th centuries was settled by Hungarians and made into a significant fortress. King Ferdinand III of Hungary and BOHEMIA, later Holy Roman emperor, was crowned here in 1625, and the Hungarian parliament met here in 1681.

Lying in the BURGENLAND, it was transferred to AUSTRIA after World War I, but after a plebiscite in 1921 its part of Burgenland was returned to Hungary. Long a cultural center, it has a university, several important churches, and a palace.

SORA (Italy) Ancient Samnite town of Latium, in Frosinone province, approx. 58 mi SE of Rome. It was captured by the Romans three times, in 345, 314, and 305 BC before being finally annexed in 303 BC. In 209 BC it was one of several colonies that refused further contributions to the Punic War against Hannibal. The castle of Sorella, above the town, was a Hohenstaufen stronghold in the Middle Ages. Charles I of Anjou made the town a duchy in the late 13th century. It was courageously defended against Cesar Borgia (1475–1507) by Giovanni de Montefeltro. It was the ancient birthplace of the Decii, Attilius Regulus, and Lucius Mummius. Cesare Baronio (1538–1607), the church historian, was also born here.

SŎRABŎL. See KYONGJU.

SORAU [Sorau in der Niederlausitz] [*modern:* Zary] (Poland) Ancient town of Lower LUSATIA, 54 mi SE of Frankfurt an der Oder. An important salt market during the Middle Ages, it passed to SAXONY in 1785 and to PRUSSIA in 1815, and was almost entirely destroyed in World War II. It was assigned to Poland by the Potsdam Conference of 1945. A number of medieval buildings survive, including a 13th-century town hall and a 15th-century church.

SORAU IN DER NIEDERLAUSITZ. See SORAU.

SORBIODUNUM. See OLD SARUM.

SORIA (Spain) Medieval town of Soria province on the Duero River, 155 mi NE of Madrid. Rebuilt after the Moors conquered the area, it is the site of two outstanding Romanesque churches, of Santo Domingo and of San Nicolas, and the cloisters of the convent of San Juan. The ruins of an old citadel and remnants of the 13th-century town wall still stand. Nearby was the Iberian and Carthaginian city of NUMANTIA, captured by the Romans in 133 BC. See also CELTIBERIA.

SORIANO. See URUGUAY.

SOROCA. See SOROKI.

SOROKI [*ancient:* **Olgionia;** *former:* **Olchionia;** *Rumanian:* **Soroca**] (USSR) Town in NE Moldavian SSR, in BESSARABIA, on the right bank of the DNIESTER RIVER, 30 mi SE of Mogilev-Podolski. The town of Olgionia in pre-Christian times, it became a trading colony of GENOA under the name of Olchionia. There are the remains of a 13th-century Genoese fortress. Stephen the Great of MOLDAVIA also built a fortress and a castle here in the 15th century. Subsequently the town was often passed between POLAND, RUSSIA, and the OTTOMAN EMPIRE. It was captured by Peter the Great of Russia in 1711 but was returned to the Turks until 1812. During World War II it was held by the Axis powers under Germany.

SORRENTO [*ancient:* **Surrentum;** *Neapolitan:* **Surriento**] (Italy) Port and summer resort in Napoli province, CAMPANIA region, on the S side of the Bay of Naples, 17 mi SE of Naples. Famed for its beauty, its origins are unclear. It may have been a colony of the Greeks, Etruscans, or Pelasgians. The Romans made it a popular resort. It is the site of Roman ruins and more recent churches and palaces of note. During World War II, during the SALERNO campaign, it was occupied by Allied forces in September 1943. It was the birthplace of poet Torquato Tasso in 1544.

SORVIODURUM. See STRAUBING.

SOSAT. See SOEST.

SOUCHEZ (France) Village of Pas de Calais department, in the N, 4 mi SW of Lens. It was captured by the French in a battle on Sept. 25, 1915, during World War I.

SOUDAN. See SUDAN.

SOUEÏDA. See AS-SUWAYDĀ'.

SOULI. See SULI.

SOUND, THE. See ØRESUND.

SOUR. See TYRE.

SOUSSE [*Susa, Susah*] [*ancient:* **Hadrumetum**] (Tunisia) Ancient seaport and city, in the NE, on the Gulf of Hammamet, on the Mediterranean Sea, approx. 78 mi SE of Tunis. Founded in the ninth century BC by the Phoenicians, it fell to CARTHAGE and later to ROME and continued to be an important port until destroyed by the Vandals in 434 AD. Rebuilt by Emperor Justinian I (527–65) of the BYZANTINE EMPIRE, it survived the Arab conquest of the seventh century and continued to be a significant port up to the 11th century, when it declined. As a center of the fertile coastal SAHEL region, it took on new importance during the 13th century.

After it had become a French protectorate in 1881 it developed even more rapidly. During World War II it was taken by the British in April 1943 during the Tunisian campaign. Early Christian catacombs are among the ancient remains here.

SOUTH AFRICAN REPUBLIC [*Dutch:* **Zuid Afrikaansche Republiek**] (South Africa) Former independent republic, now coextensive with TRANSVAAL. Settlement began by the Dutch or Boers after the Great Trek of 1836. It was formed in 1856. The discovery of diamonds in the area led to the loss of GRIQUALAND WEST in 1871 and eventual annexation by the British in 1877. The republic was restored in 1881 after a Boer rebellion but was once more annexed, as Transvaal, by the British in 1900. The Transvaal joined the Union, now Republic, of South Africa in 1910.

SOUTH AFRICA, REPUBLIC OF [**Republiek van Suid-Afrika**] [*former:* **Union of South Africa**] Occupying the southern tip of Africa between the South Atlantic Ocean and the Indian Ocean, South Africa is bordered on the north from west to east by Namibia, Botswana, Zimbabwe, Mozambique and Swaziland.

The maintenance of white racial dominance *(apartheid)* has been integrally bound in with the development of South African nationhood. The long-standing conflict between the Afrikaners, Dutch-descended Boers, Germans, and French Huguenots of the TRANSVAAL and ORANGE FREE STATE and the British of the CAPE PROVINCE was finally resolved in 1910 when the Union of South Africa was formed.

The scars of the Boer War of 1899 to 1902 still remained, but a union based on the legal and social maintenance of white supremacy gained widespread approval among the colonists, spurred on by an unsuccessful African rebellion in NATAL in 1906. The new nation consolidated its position as a bastion of white minority domination with ever-increasing legal barriers to equality or advancement erected against all nonwhites. In 1948 the newly elected Afrikaaner National Party officially adopted apartheid as national policy and enforced rigid racial segregation in all aspects of life.

In 1959 the white government initiated a program designed to isolate the nonwhite majority of its inhabitants in less valuable, closed regions, the old colonial "native reserves." "Bantustans" were to be set up, which would be quasi-independent African enclaves wholly surrounded by white South Africa. In 1963 Transkei was the first segregated territory to be created. It was declared independent in 1976 and was followed by Bophuthatswana in 1977 and Venda in 1979. Ciskei became independent in December 1981. Black resistance to this repressive treatment was widespread and continuous, but was brutally and bloodily suppressed by South Africa's formidable army and security forces.

In 1961 the Republic of South Africa was proclaimed, and the nation formally left the British Commonwealth.

England's premier port, Southampton was known to many travelers as the port of call for the big ocean liners. It has been an important city since Anglo-Saxon days.

South Africa's dominant economic position, bolstered by its enormous reserves of gold and diamonds, enabled it to ignore widespread world condemnation of its policies. Its refusal to release NAMIBIA, the League of Nations and United Nations protectorate of South-West Africa, to U.N. control was ruled illegal by the World Court in 1971, but that judgment was ignored. Since 1976 South African troops have been engaged in limited yet bitter warfare against SWAPO guerrillas in Namibia, based in ANGOLA. South African troops have repeatedly bombed and invaded Angola. Since the late 1970's its racist social policies and poor treatment of black workers, its curbs on speech and press freedom for white critics, and the repeated threat of black guerrilla war have heightened tensions.

SOUTHAMPTON [*ancient:* **Clausentum**; *Early English:* **Hanwih**; *Middle English:* **Hamtune, Suhampton, Suth-Hamtun**] (England) Port city of Hampshire, at the head of Southampton Water, 70 mi WSW of London. Located on the site of early Roman and Anglo-Saxon settlements, it was the embarkation point for the Crusaders under Richard I, for Henry V on his expedition to FRANCE in 1415, and for the Pilgrims leaving to found PLYMOUTH Colony, Massachusetts. It had a flourishing trade with VENICE throughout the late Middle Ages until the discovery of a new trade route to the East. As a major U.S. naval base in World War II, it was severely damaged by German bombing. It is at present England's chief port for transatlantic passenger ships. Of historic interest is King John's Palace, 14th-century town gates, and St. Michael's Church.

SOUTHAMPTON, United States. See LONG ISLAND.

SOUTH ARABIA, FEDERATION OF (Southern Yemen) Former federation in the S ARABIAN PENINSULA, formed by the merger of the British colony of ADEN with the Federated Emirates of the South, a British protectorate. This was opposed by the people of Aden; and the National Liberation Front, emerging as the dominant nationalist opposition force, brought the collapse of the federation and the withdrawal of British forces in November 1967. Aden and South Arabia then merged to become the independent state of Southern Yemen.

SOUTH AUSTRALIA (Australia) State in S central Australia, bounded on the S by the Indian Ocean. It was probably first visited in 1627 by a Dutch expedition under F. Thyssen. In 1802 the British explorer Matthew Flinders noted possible places for settlement. In 1830 Captain Sturt opened up the southern part, and with the passage of the South Australian Colonization Act in 1834, the way was open to settlement. The first colonists arrived in 1836 and proclaimed the region a colony. Unlike WESTERN AUSTRALIA, convicts were not admitted as settlers. It included the NORTHERN TERRITORY from 1863 to 1901, when it became a federated state. Here in 1894 the franchise was extended to women, who first voted in the 1896 election. See also ADELAIDE.

SOUTH BEND (United States) City in N INDIANA, approx. 75 mi ESE of Chicago, Illinois, on the St. Joseph River. It is an industrial city in a farming region. The Sieur de La Salle, the French explorer, camped in the area in 1679 while making a portage from the St. Joseph to the Kanakee River. The American Fur Company, organized by John Jacob Astor and the largest American enterprise of the kind, established a trading post here c.1820 on the site of an earlier French mission and post. In 1831 a town was laid out on the site of a Miami Indian village. The Studebaker Brothers Manufacturing Company, which went from producing horse-drawn carriages to automobiles, opened here in 1852. There is a museum in the 1855 St. Joseph Courthouse. Notre Dame University, founded in 1842, is nearby.

SOUTH CADBURY CASTLE. See CAMELOT.

SOUTH CAROLINA (United States) State in the southeastern part of the country, on the Atlantic Ocean to the E. North Carolina is to the N, Georgia to the S and W. It was the eighth of the original 13 colonies to ratify the Constitution, in May 1788.

The first attempt at a European settlement on the Atlantic Coast was possibly made in the Carolinas by Lucas Vásquez de Ayllon in 1526, but it was abandoned the same year. Hernando de Soto reached the Savannah River region in 1540; and a Frenchman, Jean Ribaut, started a short-lived Huguenot settlement on PARRIS ISLAND in Port Royal Sound in 1562. Spanish missions spread north from Florida almost to present CHARLESTON, but Charles I of England made a grant of the region of the Carolinas in 1629, and the region was named for him. In 1663 Charles II regranted the land to some favorites, and a settlement was made in 1670 at Albemarle Point. Ten years later the colonists moved and established Charles Town, now Charleston.

The colony began to prosper, with a plantation and slave economy. Tobacco was cultivated, and rice was introduced c.1680. In 1713 the colony was divided into North and South Carolina. In 1715/16 an attack by the once friendly Yamasee Indians was defeated. Protests of the small farmers and newer immigrants against the planter aristocracy of the coast led to the Regulator Movement of the late 1760's, which brought about some reforms.

South Carolinians resented such laws as the British Stamp Act and gave the American Revolution strong support. The British failed to capture Charleston in 1776 but succeeded in 1780. They held it until 1782. In the Carolina campaign during the Revolution the British attempted to win North and South Carolina. The Americans were routed at CAMDEN in August 1780, were victorious at KINGS MOUNTAIN in October 1780, won again at COWPENS in January 1781, were defeated at HOBKIRK'S HILL in April 1781 and were barely victorious at EUTAW SPRINGS in September 1781. The British eventually withdrew to Charleston. During the Revolution guerrilla warfare against the British was carried on by such men as Francis Marion, the "Swamp Fox."

In the early 19th century the recently-invented cotton gin encouraged cotton production, and the planters continued to dominate the state. In response to a Federal Tariff Act of 1832, which they disliked, the South Carolinians passed a Nullification Act, declaring the tariff null and void in the state and expressing the states' rights doctrine against Federal authority. President Jackson prepared to use troops, and Congress granted him power, but a compromise tariff in 1833 let the state save face.

Meeting Street in old Charleston, South Carolina's most handsome city. Here promenaders used to walk, displaying themselves and their finery. St. Michael's church looms in the background.

In December 1860 South Carolina was the first state to secede from the Union, and the Civil War began on April 12, 1861 at Charleston when Confederate forces fired on FORT SUMTER, forcing it to surrender. At the end of the war Sherman's army marched through the state in 1865, inflicting immense damage and burning COLUMBIA. After the war a carpetbagger government came to power, and the state was readmitted to the union in 1868. This government built schools and railroads, but there was much corruption and waste. The

Democrats regained control in 1877, and white supremacy returned.

The state was badly hurt economically by the war and later by the Panic of 1873. In 1890 the rural Democrats took control from the conservatives and enacted some reforms, but also passed Jim Crow laws. Agriculture suffered in the 1920's and 1930's, but textile manufacturing grew. In the 1950's blacks gradually achieved the vote, but school integration was strongly resisted by the whites. Some progress was made in the 1960's and 1970's. Long Democratic, the state began voting Republican in the 1960's.

Columbia is the capital and largest city; Charleston is an important port; others are Greenville and SPARTANBURG.

SOUTH DAKOTA (United States) State in the north Central region. It was admitted to the Union in 1889 as the 40th state. Its name is that of a branch of the Sioux Indians. North Dakota is to the N, Minnesota and Iowa to the E, Nebraska to the S, and Montana and Wyoming to the W.

The agrarian Arikara and the nomadic Sioux inhabited the region when the Europeans first came, although the Sioux drove the others out by the 1830's. Sons of the French explorer and trader the Sieur de la Vérendrye, reached the area in 1742/43. After the region became part of the United States through the LOUISIANA PURCHASE of 1803, the Lewis and Clark Expedition of 1804 to 1806 explored the area around the MISSOURI RIVER. Fort Pierre, established in 1817, was the first of the trading posts set up by Pierre Chouteau and the American Fur Company. The introduction of the steamboat along the upper Missouri in 1831 helped the fur trade, but it was not until the 1850's that any real settlement began, with farmers and land speculators moving west from Minnesota and Iowa.

By 1856 there were two land companies in SIOUX FALLS; and in 1859 YANKTON, Bon Homme, and Vermillion were laid out. At this time a treaty with the Sioux opened to settlement the land between the Missouri and the Big Sioux. Dakota Territory was formed in 1861, including both North and South Dakota, as well as eastern Montana and Wyoming. Plagues of insects, drought, and fear of Indians slowed settlement; but after the railroad reached Yankton in 1872 immigrants began arriving, mostly from Germany, Scandinavia, and Russia. Two years later gold was discovered in the BLACK HILLS, and although a treaty of 1868 reserved the land to the Sioux, white men pushed in. By 1876 such famous mining towns as DEADWOOD had been founded and became noted for frontier characters, such as Wild Bill Hickok and Calamity Jane. The gold rush led to Indian wars, which did not end until the infamous fight at WOUNDED KNEE in December 1890. The Sioux had fled to the BADLANDS after Chief Sitting Bull was killed while allegedly resisting arrest. They were brought to bay at Wounded Knee by soldiers who encircled and killed 200 mostly unarmed men, women, and children.

Mining stimulated ranching to provide food, and the period from 1878 to 1886, a time of more railroad

building, witnessed a continuing land boom. However, the good times ended with the terrible winter of 1886/87, which destroyed cattle herds and ruined the bonanza ranches. Hard times brought into being the Farmers' Alliance and the Populist Party, whose forces won the election of 1896 and put through reforms. In 1898 South Dakota was the first state to adopt the initiative and the referendum.

Prosperity returned, aided by the transcontinental railroad, but a new drought from 1901 to 1911 revived reform politics. There was even an attempt to regulate the railroads and to experiment with state ownership of some facilities. With drought and the Great Depression, the 1920's and 1930's were also hard times, but World War II and the return of peace brought about relief with higher farm prices and agricultural prosperity as many farms were combined into larger units. Beginning in 1968 South Dakota has voted Republican in four presidential elections. In February 1973 members of the American Indian Movement seized the trading post at Wounded Knee and demanded hearings in the United States Senate on Indian treaties. With some violence, they held the post until May.

PIERRE is the capital; other cities are Aberdeen, Rapid City, and Sioux Falls. Mt Rushmore National Memorial is in the western part of the state.

SOUTH DANVERS. See PEABODY.

SOUTHERN CARPATHIANS. See TRANSYLVANIAN ALPS.

SOUTHERN COOK ISLANDS. See COOK ISLANDS.

SOUTHERN RHODESIA. See RHODESIA, ZIMBABWE.

SOUTHERN YEMEN. See YEMEN, PEOPLE'S DEMOCRATIC REPUBLIC OF.

SOUTH GEORGIA ISLANDS. See FALKLAND ISLANDS.

SOUTH GLAMORGAN (Wales) County in the S, on the Bristol Channel. Created from part of the former county of Glamorganshire, its admin. hq. is CARDIFF.

SOUTH GRAHAM ISLAND. See GRAHAM LAND.

SOUTH HADLEY (United States) Town in W MASSACHUSETTS, approx. 12 mi N of Springfield. Settled in 1684 as part of HADLEY, it was separately incorporated in 1753. One of the earliest canals in the United States, approximately two miles long, was dug here between 1792 and 1796. Mt. Holyoke College, an early educational institution for women, was chartered in 1836 and opened here in 1837 as Mt. Holyoke Female Seminary. Its founder was Mary Lyon, who was also its head for 12 years.

SOUTH HOLLAND [*Dutch:* **Zuidholland**] (Netherlands) Province in the W bounded by the NORTH SEA, with its capital at THE HAGUE. United with NORTH HOLLAND as Holland until 1840, it has been central in the history of the Netherlands. Other major cities in the province include ROTTERDAM, LEIDEN, DELFT, and GOUDA.

SOUTH KINGSTOWN (United States) Town of SE Washington county, RHODE ISLAND. It was once a stronghold of the Narragansett Indians; in King Philip's War they made their last stand at nearby Great Swamp. Wakefield House here, now a museum, was the birthplace of naval hero Oliver Hazard Perry (1785–1819).

SOUTH KOREA. See KOREA.

SOUTH MOLLUCAN REPUBLIC See AMBOINA, INDONESIA.

SOUTH MOUNTAIN, BATTLE OF. See BURKITTSVILLE, Maryland.

SOUTH OSSETIA. See SOUTH OSSETIAN AUTONOMOUS OBLAST.

SOUTH OSSETIAN AUTONOMOUS OBLAST [South Ossetia] (USSR) Autonomous subdivision of N GEORGIAN SSR, a plateau region on the S slopes of the CAUCASUS MOUNTAINS. See NORTH OSSETIAN ASSR, OSSETIA.

SOUTH PASS (United States) Designated national historic landmark in SW central WYOMING, at the S end of the WIND RIVER RANGE. It is part of the historic OREGON TRAIL, discovered in 1824 and first used by wagons in Captain Benjamin Bonneville's exploring party of 1832.

SOUTH PLATTE RIVER. See PLATTE RIVER.

SOUTH POLE Southern end of the earth's axis, on ANTARCTICA, lying at 90°S latitude and 0° longitude so that from it the only direction is north. The South Magnetic Pole was found in 1909 by two British geologists, Sir T.W.E. David and Sir Douglas Dawson, who located it at 72°15′S and 155°16′E. That same year another Briton, Sir Ernest Shackleton, reached a point only 97 miles from the South Pole. The race to be the first here was won by Roald Amundsen, a Norwegian. He reached the pole on Dec. 14, 1911. He was followed on Jan. 18, 1912 by Robert F. Scott of England who, with his four companions, died on the return trip. On Nov. 29, 1929 Richard E. Byrd and Bernt Balchen of the United States were the first to fly over the pole. As scientific exploration of Antarctica increased, U.S. Operation Deep Freeze of 1955/56 established a number of stations, one of which was at the pole and was supplied entirely by air. In 1958 a British Commonwealth expedition led by Vivian Fuchs accomplished the first complete crossing of the continent by land, going by way of the pole.

SOUTHPORT. See KENOSHA.

SOUTH PORTLAND (United States) City in SW MAINE, a suburb of PORTLAND. Settled in 1633, it was the site of Fort Preble, built before the War of 1812. Portland Head Light near the fort is the oldest lighthouse on the Maine coast.

SOUTH SHETLAND ISLANDS (Great Britain) Island group in the British Antarctic Territories, off the ANTARCTIC peninsula, and separated from it by the Bransfield Strait. It was discovered in 1819 by British mariner William Smith. Since 1946 its jurisdiction has been disputed between Great Britain and the republics of CHILE and ARGENTINA. See also GRAHAM LAND.

SOUTH SHIELDS (England) Admin. hq. and seaport of Tyne and Wear, on the North Sea, at the mouth of the Tyne River, 10 mi E of Newcastle upon Tyne. It was founded in the 13th century. The remains of a Roman fort lie on Lawe Hill. The town was the scene in 1790 of the launching of the first unsinkable, self-righting lifeboat by William Wouldhave.

SOUTH VICTORIA LAND. See VICTORIA LAND.

SOUTH VIETNAM. See VIETNAM.

SOUTHWELL (England) Town and bishopric in Nottinghamshire, 12 mi NE of Nottingham. Since 1884 it has been the cathedral town of NOTTINGHAMSHIRE. The present cathedral, begun c.1110, is on the site of a church said to have been founded in the seventh century by Paulinus. The King's Arms, now the Saracen's Head, was the site of Charles I's surrender to the Scots in 1646.

SOUTH-WEST AFRICA. See NAMIBIA.

SOUTHWOLD (England) Seaside town and resort of Suffolk, 29 mi NE of Ipswich. On May 28, 1672 Southwold (or Sole) Bay was the scene of a naval battle in which the English under James, duke of York, defeated the Dutch under Adm. De Ruyter.

SOUTH YEMEN. See YEMEN, PEOPLE'S DEMOCRATIC REPUBLIC OF.

SOVETSK [former: Tilsit] (USSR) Town in the NW European Soviet Union, on the NEMAN RIVER, 37 mi NNW of Gusev. Developing around a castle built by the Teutonic Knights in 1288, it was chartered in 1552. On June 25, 1807 it was the scene of an historic meeting following Napoleon's victory at Friedland, now PRAVDINSK. On a raft in the Neman River, Alexander I of RUSSIA, and William III of PRUSSIA met with Napoleon to conclude the Treaties of Tilsit, signed on July 7 and 9. In the first treaty Russia recognized the grand duchy of WARSAW and promised to mediate between FRANCE and Great Britain. Russia gained a carte blanche against the Swedes in FINLAND. The second treaty seriously reduced the size of Prussia and in effect rendered her a vassal of France until 1813. The Russo-French alliance collapsed in 1812. During World War II the town was occupied by the Soviets and was assigned to them by the Potsdam Conference of 1945. It has a notable 18th-century town hall.

SOVIET FAR EAST [former: Far Eastern Region, Far Eastern Republic, Far Eastern Territory] (USSR) Region in NE Asia, part of SIBERIA, and administratively of the Russian SFSR. It is bounded on the S by China, on the SW by the Yablonovy Mts, on the NW by the Yakutsk Autonomous SSR, on the W by the East Siberian Sea, on the NE by the Bering Sea, and on the S by the Sea of Japan. RUSSIA began colonization of the area with Cossack forts and settlements in the late 16th century. During a period of Chinese weakness, in 1856/57, the Russians occupied the territory north of the AMUR RIVER and in 1860 took the land lying east of the USSURI River. China has never accepted these seizures.

Russia acquired all of SAKHALIN Island, which had formerly been under joint Russian-Japanese control, by agreement in 1875 but lost the southern part to Japan by the Treaty of PORTSMOUTH in 1905. In 1917, after the Russian Revolution, an Allied force of British, French, Japanese, and U.S. troops landed at VLADIVOSTOK to support anti-Bolshevik forces under Adm. Kolchak and, at first, to help deny any possible access to the region's resources by Germany. The communists, however, were victorious by 1920, and all but the Japanese withdrew.

The Far Eastern Republic was then formed to be a buffer state between Japan and the Soviets. When the Japanese withdrew in 1922, the republic came to an end and was absorbed into the USSR. The area was called the Far Eastern Territory from 1926 to 1938, and it has also been known as the Far Eastern Region. In recent years the Russo-Chinese border area has been the scene of repeated armed clashes.

SOVIET UNION. See UNION OF SOVIET SOCIALIST REPUBLICS.

SOWETO. See JOHANNESBURG.

SOZOPOL. See APOLLONIA.

SPA (Belgium) Town and watering place of Liège province, in the ARDENNES. It was the site of the Spa Conference of July 1920, when the Allies met with representatives from Germany, present for the first time since the Treaty of Versailles. They accepted the German plan for paying war reparations and directed the reduction of German arms. The town's therapeutic mineral springs, known since the 16th century, were most popular as a watering place in the 18th and 19th centuries. The generic name "spa" originated with this popular resort.

SPAIN [*Spanish:* **España**] Country of SW Europe, on the IBERIAN PENINSULA, off the coast of Morocco in NW Africa. France is to the N across the Pyrenees Mts, Portugal is to the W. At one time the most powerful nation in Europe and the center of a vast empire, Spain remains one of the poorest countries in Western Europe, despite the economic advances of recent years. The country has always been inhabited by people of many races, and this is mirrored in the rich diversity of its cultural heritage. On the other hand, Spanish history is stamped by the attempts of its rulers to unite the country, to channel the self-discipline and zeal of its people, to establish an orthodoxy and uniformity of thought, and to exert the authority of its central government, which even today is challenged by strong separatist movements. MADRID is the capital.

Spain's Iberian population appeared as early as 8500 BC. By 670 BC the Celts had occupied the northeast and had moved into the central plateau by 560 BC. The country's strategic importance on the Strait of GIBRALTAR has been recognized since antiquity, as were its deposits of tin and precious metals and its fertile fields. There were Phoenician colonies in ANDALUSIA as early as the ninth century BC. Celto-Iberian contact with them gave rise to the kingdom of TARTESSUS in the south between c.650 and 550 BC. Between 500 BC and 220 BC the Greeks established some colonies, but CARTHAGE extended its control over most of the southeastern peninsula. Eventually it came into conflict with ROME around the Ebro River and at the town of Saguntum (now SAGUNTO), a Greek colony allied with Rome. In the Second Punic War of 218 to 201 BC Carthage was finally dislodged from Spain. Rome occupied the south and east of the peninsula and gradually conquered CELTIBERIA of the center and north between 197 BC and 14 BC. The Scipios, Pompey, Caesar, and Augustus all advanced Roman control.

Under the ROMAN EMPIRE Spain enjoyed prosperity, unity, and peace. It was divided into the Roman provinces of BAETICA in the south and west, TARRACONENSIS in the north and east, and part of LUSITANIA in the west. Its population soon became romanized, and both the emperors Trajan and Hadrian were born here. The barbarian invasions saw the eruption of the Suevi, the Alans, and the Vandals from the north; but it was the Visigoths who emerged as masters of the peninsula in the sixth century AD. They beat off both the Franks to the northeast and the BYZANTINE EMPIRE in the south, which had reconquered most of Andalusia during a civil war in 554, and held on to portions of the southern coast until 631. The VISIGOTHIC KINGDOM, ruling over a people of mixed cultural loyalties, at first established a centralized monarchy, with a uniform code of law and the support of the Catholic hierarchy. But disunity eventually set in, so that when the Moors invaded the country from Africa in 711, the kingdom collapsed.

With its capital at CÓRDOVA, the Moorish Ummayad emirate conquered all of Spain except ASTURIAS, from which emerged the kingdom of GALICIA, the Carolingian Spanish March, and the Basque country. The March developed into the county of BARCELONA by 900. It was these lands that were to form the nucleus for the *Reconquista*, the gradual Christian reconquest of Spain. The Moorish cities of Spain reached a high level of civilization, their chief cities of Córdova, TOLEDO, and SEVILLE becoming famous throughout Europe for their learning and their industries and developing agricultural techniques of unparalleled efficiency.

By 925 the Kingdom of LEÓN had developed in the northwest. NAVARRE grew from the Basque country by 1000 and by 1037 León was conquered by CASTILE. By 1092 ARAGON had united with Navarre, and by 1175 the country of Barcelona had developed into the kingdom of Aragon.

With the collapse of the caliphate of Córdova in 1031, Muslim Spain disintegrated into several emirates, reunited by the ALMORAVIDS by 1110. The Almoravids were replaced from North Africa in 1145, by the ALMOHADS. In 1212 Christian Spain, united under Castile, won a decisive victory over the Almohad dynasty at Las NAVAS DE TOLOSA, leaving only the emirate of GRANADA in Moorish hands. The Christian position was consolidated further by the union of the kingdoms of LEÓN and Castile in 1230 and by the union of Aragon and Castile in 1479. Meanwhile, Aragon extended its rule eastward to SARDINIA in 1323, the BALEARIC ISLANDS in 1349, SICILY in 1409, and finally NAPLES in 1435 and 1442.

Spain was united under Ferdinand II of Aragon and

Isabella of Castile in 1469. With the fall of Granada in 1492 the reconquest was complete, and in the same year Columbus discovered America. With the ensuing flow of wealth from the New World in the 16th century, Spain became the foremost power in Europe with a vast overseas empire and with substantial territories in Europe, acquired after the crowning of the Hapsburg heir to Spain, Charles I, as Holy Roman Emperor Charles V in 1519. The 16th century also saw the increasing power of the Counter-Reformation and the Inquisition. Despite the War of the Comunidades of 1520 to 1521, a rebellion in which the cities attempted unsuccessfully to retain their autonomy against the centralizing policies of Charles V, Spain became the bulwork of Catholicism and of Christianity, supplying men and treasure against Protestants and Turks.

The period from 1550 to 1650 has been called the Golden Age (siglo de oro) for Spain. Under Charles V and Philip II (1556–98) Spain saw its domains stretch from Sicily to the NETHERLANDS and, while Philip's marriage to Queen Mary of ENGLAND was recognized, to England. Its realm also included all of the Americas from the Rio de LA PLATA to CHILE, from PERU to COLORADO and across the Pacific to the PHILIPPINES. It also included any English claims in North America during Philip's marriage to Mary. This was also the age of Ignatius Loyola, of Cervantes, Murillo, Velasquez, Lope de Vega, and Suarez. Until 1567 Catholic Spain held the initiative in Europe. At LEPANTO in 1571 it led the Christian fleet that defeated the Turks. At the Massacre of St. Bartholemew in FRANCE in 1572 it rejoiced at the defeat of the Protestants. But already in the reign of Philip II Spain faced repeated bankruptcies. Continued revolt in the SPANISH NETHERLANDS from 1566 to 1579 and the disastrous defeat of the Spanish Armada in 1588 by England proved a great drain on an economy already undermined by the overextension of agricultural land to sheep raising, the misguided expulsion of the Jews (1492) and Moors (1609) and the flight of the riches of the New World to northern mercantile countries. After the Thirty Years War of 1618 to 1648 it was France that emerged as master of Europe. Annexed by Spain in 1580, PORTUGAL became independent in 1640. France took the FRANCHE-COMTÉ in 1678; and in the War of the Spanish Succession of 1702 to 1713, Spain passed to the Bourbons of France. For a time it was torn by civil war, and it lost many of its European territories, including Gibraltar and Minorca to Great Britain, MILAN, Naples, and Sicily to AUSTRIA; and Sardinia to SAVOY.

Although reforms were introduced in the 18th century, Spain's position remained weak. The Bourbons regained the separate kingdom of the TWO SICILIES from Austria in the War of the Polish Succession. Spain also aided the colonies in the American Revolution. In 1808, having placed his brother Joseph on the Spanish throne, Napoleon occupied Spain. In the Peninsular campaign the British under Wellington were aided by Spanish insurgents, who fought behind the lines in "small wars" from which we get the term guerrillas. They forced the French out of Spain by 1814. In 1812 a new liberal constitution was drawn up in CÁDIZ. After the war, however, the nationalist and liberal aspirations of the war years flared again in 1820 but were stifled by a period of reactionary government. In 1823 the Conservatives welcomed a French invasion to reestablish their rule. By 1825 Spain had finally lost most of her American empire, and on the death of Ferdinand VII in 1833 the first of the dynastic Carlist Wars of 1833 to 1839 split the country. After peace was restored, Spanish politics remained dogged by instability throughout the 19th century, with left-wing and separatist movements increasingly active, especially in CATALONIA and the BASQUE PROVINCES. The Spanish-American War of 1898 brought further setbacks abroad with the loss of CUBA, PUERTO RICO, and the Philippine Islands.

Spain remained neutral during World War I but was plunged into civil war in 1936 following a right-wing military uprising under Gen. Francisco Franco. Aided by the fascist governments of Italy and Germany, Franco unleashed the developing technology of World War II in fascist aerial bombings of Madrid and Barcelona. He forced the Loyalist government to surrender in 1939 and established a dictatorship. Over 600,000 Spanish died in the war, which left bitter feelings for two generations. Despite Spain's neutrality in World War II, the Western powers were reluctant to recognize the legitimacy of its fascist government, and it was not until 1955 that Spain was admitted to the United Nations. However, despite the oppressive regime of the postwar years, Spain made considerable economic progress under Franco. With his death in 1975, the monarchy was reestablished under Juan Carlos, who has steered a course toward constitutional government and gradual liberalization through Spain's volatile political scene. In June 1977 a centrist government under Adolfo Suarez was elected. In December 1978 Spain's parliament (Cortés) approved a new constitution. In 1982 Spain joined NATO (North Atlantic Treaty Organization). In October 1982 a new Socialist administration, the first since 1936, was voted in. It pledged to bring Spain further along the path of democracy and economic growth. Spain has announced its intention of joining the European Common Market by 1984.

SPALATO. See SPLIT.

SPALATUM. See SPLIT.

SPANDAU (West Germany) District of WEST BERLIN, at the confluence of the Havel and Spree rivers. It was chartered as a town in 1232. In the period 1560 to 1594 the electors of BRANDENBURG built an important fortress on the Havel. Occupied by the Swedes in the Thirty Years War and by the French in the Napoleonic Wars of 1806 to 1813, it became a political prison where in modern times several Nazi war criminals were imprisoned following the NUREMBURG trials of 1945/46. It became part of West Berlin in 1945.

SPANISH GUINEA. See EQUATORIAL GUINEA.

SPANISH MAIN Region on the mainland of South America on the CARIBBEAN SEA, particularly the coastal area from the Isthmus of PANAMA south to the mouth of the ORINOCO RIVER in VENEZUELA. In the colonial era the Spanish fleets carrying back the treasures of the New World sailed from ports in this area. As a result, English pirates, sallying from hideaways on the coast and from WEST INDIES islands, attacked these tempting prizes. The words "Spanish Main" came to symbolize the supposed romance of piracy and were applied to the whole Caribbean area in which the buccaneers operated. These pirates sacked MARACAIBO, Venezuela, five times in the 17th century; while PANAMA CITY, from which Inca treasure was dispatched to Spain, attracted all the leading English privateers: Sir Francis Drake, William Parker, Sir Henry Morgan, and Admiral Edward Vernon. PORTOBELO, Panama, was sacked three times, the first time in 1572.

SPANISH MOROCCO. See MOROCCO.

SPANISH NETHERLANDS (Belgium) Approximately the same area as modern Belgium. It comprised the former southern provinces of the NETHERLANDS, which remained under Spanish control in 1579, when the seven northern provinces formed the Union of Utrecht. The area became the independent kingdom of Belgium in 1830.

SPANISH SAHARA (Africa) Former Spanish overseas province, part of the SAHARA DESERT in NW Africa bounded by Morocco, Algeria, Mauritania, and the Atlantic. In the Middle Ages Berber tribes here began to be supplanted by Bedouin. After a Portuguese navigator reached the coast in 1434, the Spanish established a trading post here in 1476 but abandoned it in 1524. Not until 1884 did Spain proclaim a protectorate over the region, and in 1900 and 1912 boundary agreements were concluded with FRANCE. The capital is El Aaiún. In 1958 its status changed from colony to overseas province made up of Rio de Oro and Saguia el Hamra. A partially elected assembly was formed in 1967. Granted independence in 1976, part of the territory was seized by MAURITANIA, then yielded to MOROCCO, which annexed the whole territory in that year. However, Polisario guerrilla resistance continues.

SPANISH TOWN [*Spanish:* **St. Iago de la Vega, Villa de la Vega**] (Jamaica) Town in the SE, on the Cobre River, 20 mi W of Kingston. It was founded *c.*1525. Following the earthquake destruction of PORT ROYAL in 1692 it was Jamaica's leading city and capital until 1872.

SPARNACUM. See ÉPERNAY.

SPARTA [**Lacedaemon, Lakedaimonia**] [*modern Greek:* **Spárti**] (Greece) Ancient capital of LACONIA, in the central Laconian plain of the PELOPONNESUS, on the Eurotas River. Though some late Helladic remains have been found on the acropolis here, Homeric Sparta was probably at Menalaion, approx. 3 miles away. The city-state was of Dorian origin. Lycurgus was its traditional lawgiver. He lived possibly as early as the ninth century BC. With ATHENS, Sparta gradually became one of the leading cities of Greece. During the eighth and seventh centuries BC the city slowly conquered Laconia and MESSENIA, despite a major Messenian revolt from 685 to 668 BC, and a war with TEGEA between *c.*600 and 560 BC. Both made the Spartans distrustful of their neighbors and subjects, so that the

defeated populations were thereafter reduced to virtual slavery as helots, completely under the Spartans' control.

Using the helots as agricultural laborers and thus assured of a material basis, the Spartans developed a high culture in the seventh century BC noted for its pottery, music, theater, and temple building. But by the sixth century BC Sparta had begun to develop into the rigid militaristic state for which it was notorious in antiquity. The state was characterized by a strict separation of castes. There were the Spartans themselves, whose only occupation was war and who were subjected to the strictest discipline, sexual segregation, and physical hardship from youth. Deformed children were routinely exposed and left to die, while discipline and absolute obedience were enforced by the *krypteia*, or secret police, who also rounded up disloyal helots. Another class, the *periokoi* lived as freemen in the surrounding areas and supplied hoplite infantry for Sparta's wars. The state itself was ruled by two hereditary kings and by an Oligarchic council of ephors.

This Lycurgan constitution, however, did not really take effect until the fifth century BC, after another Messenian revolt of 464 BC. Becoming the leading state in the Peloponnesus, the city finally conquered ARGOS *c.*495 BC. Though it took no part in the first Persian War, it joined Athens and the other allies in repelling the second invasion in 480 BC. In that year 300 Spartans under King Leonidas blocked the narrow pass at THERMOPYLAE and held off the might of all PERSIA until betrayed, surrounded, and killed to a man. Afterwards Sparta fought at PLATAEA. With the Persian defeat, Sparta became the paramount city in the Peloponnesian League and the leading champion against the growing power of Athens. Conflict between the two cities led to the protracted Peloponnesian Wars of 460 to 404 BC, in which, with the eventual help of Persia, Sparta eventually defeated Athens. In 395, however, Athens allied with THEBES, CORINTH, and Argos to defeat Sparta at CNIDOS in 394 BC.

Sparta's hegemony was further checked by Thebes at LEUCTRA in 371 BC. The Thebans then ringed Laconia with a series of garrison forts and created the Achaean League to prevent the city's reemergence. After the creation of the MACEDONIAN EMPIRE and its successor states, Demetrios Poliorcetes of Macedonia defeated the Spartan army in 295 BC and took the city. In 272 BC King Pyrrhus of EPIRUS also defeated the Spartans, but spared the city. An attempt to revive Sparta's might under Cleomenes III met final defeat by King Antigonus Doson of Macedon at SELLASIA in 222/21 BC.

In 192 BC the city-state was forced to join the Achaean League, to raze her walls, and to abolish the Lycurgan constitution. Her power continued to weaken, and she was torn by civil war until absorbed by the Roman province of ACHAEA in 146 BC. The Romans revived the oligarchic Lycurgan system and restored the city's economic life.

Plundered and destroyed by the Goths in 395/96 AD, Sparta was finally deserted in the ninth century during the Slavic invasions. Its people fled to the Mani in the southern Peloponnesus. The city was refounded and renamed Lakedaimonia by the BYZANTINE EMPIRE, though by the time of the Fourth Crusade and the Latin conquest of Greece in 1204/05, it was gradually overshadowed by nearby MISTRA, and finally deserted. The meager ruins of the ancient city lie north of the modern regional center of Spárti.

SPARTANBURG (United States) Town and county seat in NW SOUTH CAROLINA, at the foot of the Blue Ridge Mts, 30 mi ENE of Greenville. In a region that endured 11 major battles in the American Revolution, both the city, established as a village in 1785, and its county are named for the Spartan Regiment of Revolutionary troops from this area. During the Civil War it was a supply and manufacturing point. Nearby are the COWPENS and KINGS MOUNTAIN battlefields.

SPÁRTI. See SPARTA.

SPASSK-RYAZANSKI (USSR) Port city in the E European Soviet Union, on the Oka River. Founded in 1778, it is across the river from the well-preserved ruins of Old RYAZAN, or Staraya-Ryazan, founded in the ninth or 10th century and pillaged by the Mongols in 1237.

SPEICHERN. See SPICHEREN.

SPEYER [*ancient:* **Augusta Nementum, Civitas Nementum, Noviomagus;** *English:* **Spires;** *medieval:* **Spira**] (West Germany) City of Rhineland-Palatinate, on the RHINE RIVER, 22 mi N of Karlsruhe. An important Celtic settlement, it was developed by the Romans and was destroyed by the Huns *c.*450 AD. Rebuilt in the seventh century, it eventually became an episcopal see, and under Emperor Otto I (936–73) its bishops were granted extensive secular powers. It was a major trading center by the 11th century. In 1146 it was a scene of the preaching of the Second Crusade by Bernard of Clairvaux. In May 1199 at Speyer the German princes wrote to the pope, ignoring the need for his approval and announcing their election of Philip of SWABIA as emperor. In December 1273 the Diet of Speyer ended the imperial interregnum in Germany by ordering the return of all usurped lands to Rudolf of Hapsburg, the new emperor. It was an early center of the art of printing. At the Diet of Speyer of 1529 the Lutheran princes protested the policies of Emperor Charles V.

Destroyed by the French in the War of the Grand Alliance in 1689, it was occupied by the French during the French Revolutionary Wars and was ceded to them by the Treaty of CAMPO FORMIO in 1797. The settlement of the Congress of Vienna in 1815 gave Speyer and its surrounding episcopal lands to BAVARIA. Incorporated into the Rhenish PALATINATE, it was its capital until 1945. Notable structures include the outstanding Romanesque imperial cathedral begun by Conrad II in 1030 and completed in 1061. After a fire in 1159 the church was substantially rebuilt. It houses the tombs of eight emperors, and a historical museum of pre-Roman and Roman artifacts.

SPEZIA, LA. See LA SPEZIA.

SPICE ISLANDS. See MOLUCCAS.

SPICHEREN [Spickeren] [*German:* **Speichern, Spichern**] (France) Battle site near a village in the Moselle department, E of Forbach. One of the three German armies that invaded France during the opening stages of the Franco-Prussian War met a French army here under Gen. Charles Frossard and defeated it. This victory on Aug. 6, 1870 under Gen. Karl Friedrich von Steinmetz preceded the final defeat and capitulation of France at SEDAN on September 1.

SPICHERN. See SPICHEREN.

SPICKEREN. See SPICHEREN.

SPINA (Italy) Ancient Etruscan port city on the ADRIATIC SEA, in Ferrara province, Emilia-Romagna region, between the mouths of the PO RIVER and Ravenna, 20 mi N of Ravenna at Camacchio. One of the northern cities of the Etruscan League of ETRURIA, it flourished as a port and commercial center until destroyed in the Gallic invasion of the fourth century BC. Excavations have shown that it was laid out in a regular grid pattern on a network of canals, much like later VENICE. The houses also were built on piles, and there was a "grand canal" leading out to the sea. Two cemeteries have been found with burials containing quantities of imported goods, especially Attic vases of the classical period from 480 to 360 BC. The coastline has now moved to the east due to the silting of the Po delta.

SPINDLETOP. See BEAUMONT, Texas.

SPION KOP (South Africa) Hill and battle site in NATAL, 24 mi WSW of Ladysmith. During the Boer War Gen. Sir Redvers Buller, in his attempt to reach and relieve LADYSMITH, crossed the Tugela River and seized this hill on January 25, 1900, but he was forced back by the Boers. Ladysmith was finally reached by the British on February 28.

SPIRA. See SPEYER.

SPIRES. See SPEYER.

SPIRIT LAKE. See IOWA.

SPITHEAD (England) Body of water comprising the eastern part of the Solent, off the ENGLISH CHANNEL, between the ISLE OF WIGHT and HAMPSHIRE, on the S coast of England. Since the 18th century it has often been used as a rendezvous for the British fleet. Here in 1797 a mutiny occurred on the ships in the channel when British seamen, protesting their miserable living conditions, brutal punishment, and the way they were pressed into service, forced their officers ashore while they ran the ships. Order was restored when the government met most of the seamen's demands. At about the same time, while Great Britain was at war, another part of the fleet mutinied and sailed its ships to the NORE in the THAMES RIVER estuary. In 1853 Queen Victoria reviewed the fleet at Spithead, just before the Crimean War, and the ships gathered here again when she died in 1901, on the Isle of Wight, and her body was transported to the mainland. In June 1953 Spithead was the scene of a review of ships of many nations in connection with the coronation of Queen Elizabeth II.

SPITSBERGEN [*former:* **Vestspitsbergen**] (Norway) Large island and archipelago in Svalbard county, in the ARCTIC Ocean, 360 mi N of Norway. Probably known to the Vikings, the islands were later discovered in June 1596 by William Barents. By the Treaty of Svalbard they officially became part of Norway on Aug. 14, 1925. The treaty also allowed equal access to the islands' resources to 40 other countries, including the USSR, whose citizens outnumber the Norwegians here. It was held by the Allies in World War II. Several towns were severely damaged by German bombing. Spitsbergen was the starting point for numerous early polar expeditions, including those of Nobile and Byrd, both in 1926.

SPLIT [*ancient:* **Spalatum**; *Italian:* **Spalato**] (Yugoslavia) Port of CROATIA, on the Adriatic Sea, approx. 105 mi WSW of Sarajevo. Split grew up in and around the vast palace of the Roman emperor Diocletian, a native of the area, who retired to the palace in 305 AD and died here. Imitating a Roman fort town, it was built near the Roman colony of SALONA, founded 78 BC, of which extensive ruins survive. When Salona was destroyed by the Avars in the early seventh century AD, the inhabitants took refuge in the nearby palace. The settlement took the name of "palace" or *Palatium,* which became Split. A flourishing port of medieval DALMATIA, Split was held by the BYZANTINE EMPIRE from 812 to 1069 and eventually fell into the hands of VENICE in 1420.

Under the Treaty of CAMPO FORMIO in 1797 it was given to AUSTRIA, and following the Napoleonic Wars the Congress of Vienna returned it to Austria. In 1918 it was included in the newly formed state that was to become Yugoslavia. The palace of Diocletian is one of the great monuments of the ROMAN EMPIRE. Covering almost eight acres, its fabric is remarkably complete, despite the city huddled within it. The mausoleum of Diocletian, now a cathedral, a baptistry, once a Roman temple, and other elements survive. Split was occupied by Axis troops during World War II from 1941 to 1945.

SPOKANE [*former:* **Spokane Falls**] (United States) City in E WASHINGTON, approx. 15 mi W of the Idaho border. It is known as the capital of the Inland Empire because it is the business, industrial, and transportation center of a region that is very productive, both in agriculture and in manufacturing. A fort and trading post was established here in 1810 in a valley formerly inhabited by the Spokane Indians, but civilian settlement did not begin until 1871. A fire destroyed most of the town in 1889, but the city was soon rebuilt.

SPOKANE FALLS. See SPOKANE.

SPOLETIUM. See SPOLETO.

SPOLETO [*ancient:* **Spoletium**] (Italy) Town of Perugia province, UMBRIA region, 30 mi SE of Perugia. Begun by the Umbrians, it was taken by the Etruscans and then by the Romans in 242 BC. In 217 BC Hannibal vainly besieged it. Marius and Sulla both attacked it. Flourishing under the Romans as a key city on the FLAMINIAN WAY, it became an episcopal see in the fourth century AD. In 571 AD it became the seat of an important Lombard duchy. It was one of the principal cities of Charlemagne's donation to the church in the eighth century. It was destroyed by Emperor Frederick I in 1155. Rebuilt, the city came under direct papal control from 1354 until 1860. Its Roman ruins include a bridge, the Arch of Drusus of 21 AD, a theater, and an amphitheater. It is the site of the notable fourth-century basilica of San Salvatore, and of the cathedral of Santa Maria Assunta, begun by Frederick I, which has frescoes by Fra Filippo Lippi, who is buried here, and by Pinturicchio. The 14th-century castle, La Rocca, is now a prison. A sixth-century BC bronze chariot, excavated here, is housed in New York's Metropolitan Museum. Spoleto is now the site of the Festival of Two Worlds, a major annual arts festival organized mainly by the composer Gian Carlo Menotti. See also PAPAL STATES.

SPORADES (Greece) Two groups of islands, E and S of mainland Greece, in the AEGEAN SEA. In its broadest sense the name is sometimes applied to all the Greek islands of the Aegean except the CYCLADES. The most important islands of the Northern Sporades, or *Voriai Sporadhes,* are: Iliodhrómia, LEMNOS, LESBOS, Skiathos, Skopelos, and SKIROS; of the Southern Sporades or *Notiai Sporadhes,* CHIOS, IKARIA, Kalymnos, KARPATHOS, KOS, PATMOS, RHODES, and SAMOS.

SPOTSYLVANIA (United States) Village, county, and Civil War battle region in NE VIRGINIA. The village is 11 mi SW of FREDERICKSBURG, and the county was formerly part of the estate of Alexander Spotswood, a colonial governor of Virginia. From May 8 to 21, 1864 it was the site of the battle of Spotsylvania Court House, fought to a standoff between the Union army under Gen. Grant and the Confederates under Gen. Lee. This included the battle of Bloody Angle on May 12. Other engagements took place at Fredericksburg, CHANCELLORSVILLE, and the WILDERNESS. All were part of the Wilderness campaign.

SPRINGFIELD (United States) State capital of ILLINOIS on the Sangamon River, 185 mi SW of Chicago. Settled c.1820, it was the home of Abraham Lincoln from 1837 to 1861, who was instrumental in making it the state capital. Lincoln is buried here. It is now a National Historic site. It was in the old capitol building, dating from 1837, that Lincoln made his famous *House Divided* speech.

SPRINGFIELD (United States) City in SW MASSACHUSETTS, on the Connecticut River, 5 mi N of the state border. Settled in 1636 by Puritans under William Pynchon, it was burned in 1675 during King Philip's War. In 1786/87 it was one of the sites of Shays's Rebellion. A U.S. armory, established here from 1794 to 1966 and famous for the development of the Springfield and Garand army rifles, is now an arms museum.

SPRINGFIELD, Missouri. See WILSON'S CREEK.

SPRINGFIELD (United States) Battle site, now a residential town in NE NEW JERSEY, approx. 6 mi NW of Elizabeth. On June 23, 1780 during the American Revolution Gen. Nathanael Greene forced the British to retreat here. It is also the site of a Revolutionary era cemetery.

SPRINGFIELD (United States) City in SE VERMONT, on the Black River, approx. 37 mi SE of Rutland. A charter was granted for the area in 1761 by NEW HAMPSHIRE and in 1762 by NEW YORK, both colonies at that time claiming title to the Vermont region. Settlement began in 1772, and two years later a sawmill began operations, using waterpower from the Black River. Springfield became an early center of American machine-tool production, and this industry remains its most important one. The cascades of the river here were an important Indian meeting place.

SRBIJA. See SERBIA.

SREDETS. See SOFIA.

SREMSKI KARLOVCI [*German:* **Carlowitz; Karlowitz;** *Hungarian:* **Karlocza**] (Yugoslavia) Serbian town, in the NE, on the right bank of the DANUBE RIVER. Here on Jan. 26, 1699 the Treaty of Karlowitz was signed by AUSTRIA, the OTTOMAN EMPIRE, POLAND, and VENICE, signifying the suppression of Turkish power in Europe and the passing of her lands to Austria and Poland.

SRIJIVAYA EMPIRE (Indonesia) Former empire, centered in SUMATRA, which flourished in the Malay archipelago from the seventh to 13th centuries AD. PALEMBANG was its capital, and it was a center of Mahayana Buddhism. Under the Sailendra dynasty Srijivaya extended its rule over other areas, such as JAVA and much of the MALAY PENINSULA, while it was influential in Siam and INDOCHINA. On the peninsula the empire's seat of power was the city of PATTANI, and it maintained a large naval base in the state of KEDAH. Srijivaya controlled the sea trade over an extensive region, much of its power coming from this control. It traded with INDIA and CHINA. In the 11th century, however, the CHOLA dynasty of the COROMANDEL COAST of India conquered Srijivaya's Malayan territory and in 1025 seized Palembang, taking away treasure as well as capturing the king. By the end of the 12th century Srijivaya was merely a small kingdom in Sumatra, and in the next century it came to an end when invaded by the MADJAPAHIT Kingdom of Java.

SRI LANKA [Lanka] [*ancient:* **Taprobane;** *Arabic:* **Serendip;** *former:* **Ceylon**] Independent island state in the Indian Ocean, just S of the S tip of India, with its capital at COLOMBO. Inhabited originally by aboriginal

The rich tropical highlands of Sri Lanka, or Ceylon. The island was long disputed between native Sinhalese, Indian Tamils, Portuguese, Dutch, and the British. It is now independent.

Veddas, it was conquered in the sixth century BC by the Sinhalese, whose capital at ANURADHAPURA became one of the chief world centers of Buddhism after the third century BC. The island suffered many Hindu Tamil invasions from INDIA, and the Tamils still form a large element in the population. It was visited in the 12th and 13th centuries AD by Arabs, attracted by the island's spices. The *Travels of John Mandeville*, written in the late Middle Ages, cited Taprobane as the source of immense wealth. In Europe the existence of a large island or group of islands south of India, called Taprobane, was known to the soldiers of Alexander the Great. Under the Seleucids a mission actually reached southern India and recorded the island. It appears as a huge island in Ptolemy's geography of the second century AD.

Ceylon was therefore avidly sought by Renaissance Europeans and was settled in 1505 by the Portuguese, in 1658 by the Dutch, and in 1796 by the British. It became a British crown colony in 1798 and was granted independence on Feb. 4, 1948. Armed rebellion against the government of Mrs. Bandaranaike broke out in April 1971 but was quelled with foreign aid. Ceylon became the Republic of Sri Lanka on May 22, 1972. Economic decline and corruption have plagued the nation. In elections held in 1977 Junius Richard Jayawardene defeated Bandaranaike to become president, naming Ranasinghe Premadasa prime minister. See also KANDY.

SRINAGAR [Kashmir South; Serinagar] (India) Summer capital city of Jammu and Kashmir, in the Vale of KASHMIR, on the Jhelum River, 170 mi N of Amritsar. It was founded in the sixth century AD. In 1948 it became capital of the Indian portion of Jammu and Kashmir. The seventh-century temple of Sankaracharya, a 16th-century fortress built by Akbar, numerous mosques, the notable Shalimar gardens built by the Moguls, and several palaces are here. There are extensive Buddhist ruins nearby. It was the setting of Thomas Moore's *Lalla Rookh*. See also MOGUL EMPIRE.

SRIRANGA PATNA (India) Town of Karnataka state, in the S, on an island in the Cauvery River. It is a former capital of MYSORE, and most of its buildings date from the 17th and 18th centuries. Tippoo Sahib was its greatest builder, leaving a summer palace, a mosque, and a mausoleum where he and his father, Hyder Ali, are buried. The town declined in importance after its capture by the British in 1799, a battle in which Tippoo was killed. Certain Hindu monuments here date from the 13th century.

SSU-CH'UAN. See SZECHWAN.

SSU-MAO. See FU-HSING-CHEN.

STAATEN EYLANDT. See STATEN ISLAND.

STABIAE. See CASTELLAMARE DI STABIA.

STABLO. See STAVELOT.

STABROEK. See GEORGETOWN.

STACY'S MILLS. See TRENTON.

STADE (West Germany) Town of Hanover, 20 mi NW of Hamburg. Though legend says that Stade was the oldest town of the Saxons, built in 321 BC, it has a recorded history only from 988 AD. Passed to BREMEN in the 13th century, it joined the HANSEATIC LEAGUE and became commercially important. Under the Swedes in 1648 at the end of the Thirty Years War, it was made capital of Bremen principality. It was ceded to HANOVER in 1719.

STADTLOHN (West Germany) Town of North Rhine-Westphalia, W of Münster near the Netherlands border. In a battle here on Aug. 6, 1623 the Catholic League led by the Count of Tilly defeated the Protestant forces under Christian of Brunswick in the early stages of the Thirty Years War.

STAFFORD (England) Admin. hq. of Staffordshire, on the Sow River, 25 mi NNW of Birmingham. It was founded by a daughter of Alfred the Great. A castle in Stafford, built by William the Conqueror, was captured and dismantled by the Parliamentarians in 1643 during the English Civil War. Stafford was the birthplace of Izaak Walton in 1593; his cottage at Shallowford is now a museum.

STAFFORDSHIRE (England) Industrial county of the Midlands, which includes the POTTERIES around STOKE-ON-TRENT. It formerly included the BLACK COUNTRY between Birmingham and Wolverhampton, which is now in West Midlands. The admin. hq. is STAFFORD.

STAGIRA [Stagiros] (Greece) Town of ancient MACEDONIA, on the E CHALCIDICE peninsula, in the Strymonic Gulf. It was known chiefly as the birthplace of the ancient Greek philosopher Aristotle (384–322 BC), a student of Plato, whose writings on philosophy, rhetoric, and science had a vast influence on the emerging thought of medieval and Renaissance Europe. He was often referred to as the Stagirite.

STAGIROS. See STAGIRA.

STAKHR. See ISTAKHR.

STALIN, Bulgaria. See VARNA.

STALIN, USSR. See DONETSK.

STALINGRAD. See VOLGOGRAD.

STALINGRAD OBLAST. See VOLGOGRAD OBLAST.

STALINO. See DONETSK.

STALINSK. See NOVOKUZNETSK.

STAMFORD (England) Town in Parts of Kesteven, Lincolnshire, on the Welland River, 35 mi SE of Nottingham. The site of Anglo-Saxon, Danish, and Norman settlements, it is the supposed scene of a battle in 449, in which the Anglo-Saxons defeated the Picts and the Scots. A Danish fort here became one of the five Danish boroughs. Of interest is the gate of Brasenose College, founded in 1333, when Stamford was an important seat of learning. There are parts of a seventh-century church, and numerous 17th- and 18th-century buildings of Lincolnshire limestone. The 16th-century Burghley House nearby was the home of Lord Burghley, an Elizabethan statesman and member of the Cecil family.

STAMFORD (United States) City in SW CONNECTICUT, on LONG ISLAND SOUND. It was settled in 1641 by

28 people who moved from WETHERSFIELD, Connecticut. Three years later about a third of them moved on to Long Island. The settlement became part of the colony of Connecticut in 1662. In 1893 a city government was formed within the township of Stamford, and in 1949 the two governments were merged into one. The First Presbyterian Church, built in 1958, is notable because it is in the form of a fish, an ancient Christian symbol. It was designed by two well-known American architects, Wallace K. Harrison and Max Abramovitz. In recent years a number of large corporations have moved to Stamford and made it an important center of industrial activity.

STAMFORD BRIDGE (England) Village of Humberside, 8 mi ENE of York. Here King Harold II, just elected king of England, defeated his brother Tostig, who with Harold Hardrada, the Norwegian king, had invaded England in an attempt to dislodge the new king. If they had succeeded, the later fortunes of England might well have lain with Scandinavia rather than with Western Europe. But Harold of England, in a forced march north, defeated and killed Hardrada at this site on Sept. 25, 1066, then marched down to the ENGLISH CHANNEL coast to confront the invading William the Conqueror at HASTINGS. Harold was killed, and the Norman-French took over England.

STANDERTON (South Africa) Town of SE Transvaal in the NE, on the Vaal River, 90 mi ESE of Johannesburg. There was much fighting in and around the town in the First Boer War of 1880/81, after the Boers of the TRANSVAAL had revolted against the British and had set up an independent republic. At first the British attempted to quell the revolt, but by the Treaty of PRETORIA in April they agreed to grant the new SOUTHAFRICAN REPUBLIC virtual independence. See also MAJUBA HILL.

STANIMAKA. See ASENOVGRAD.

STANISŁAÓW. See IVANO-FRANKOVSK.

STANISLAU. See IVANO-FRANKOVSK.

STANISLAV. See IVANO-FRANKOVSK.

STANLEY. See FALKLAND ISLANDS.

STANLEYVILLE. See KISANGANI.

STANS. See SACHSELN.

STANWIX, FORT. See FORT STANWIX.

STAPLES, THE. See FARNE ISLANDS.

STARAYA RUSSA (USSR) City in W Russian SFSR, 15 mi S of Lake Ilmen. A health resort and former salt-mining center, it is known to have existed as early as 1167, making it one of Russia's oldest settlements. In the 12th century it was under the rule of NOVGOROD, and there is a monastery dating from that period. Staraya Russa was damaged in wars in the Middle Ages and again in World War II, when it was occupied by the Germans from 1941 to 1944.

STARA ZAGORA [ancient: **Augusta Traiana, Beroe**; Turkish: **Eski-Zagra, Yeski-Zagra**] (Bulgaria) Departmental capital of EASTERN RUMELIA, 70 mi NW of Adrianople. Originally the large Thracian settlement of Beroe, it was renamed Augusta Traiana by the Ro-

mans. In 1370 it was taken by the Turks, who named it Eski-Zagra or Yeski-Zagra. The town was nearly destroyed in the Russo-Turkish War of 1877/78. During the reconstruction period that followed, important Thracian, Roman, Byzantine, and Turkish antiquities were discovered. See also OTTOMAN EMPIRE.

STARGARD. See BURG STARGARD.

STARGARD IN MECKLENBURG. See BURG STARGARD.

STARGARD IN POMMERN. See STARGARD SZCZECIŃSKI.

STARGARD SZCZECIŃSKI [Szczeciński] [former: Stargard in Pommern] (Poland) Town of POMERANIA, once in old PRUSSIA, on the Ihna River, 20 mi ESE of Szczecin. Once a Slavic fortress, it was destroyed by the Poles in 1120. It was rebuilt and became the capital of eastern Pomerania and a prosperous early member of the HANSEATIC LEAGUE. It endured several sieges during the Middle Ages and in the Thirty Years War in 1633 and passed to BRANDENBURG in 1648. It was heavily damaged before being occupied by the Soviet Union on March 5, 1945. It was assigned to Poland by the Potsdam Conference following World War II. Notable structures include the medieval walls and gates and a 13th-century church.

STARODUB (USSR) Old town of W Bryansk oblast, Russian SFSR, 80 mi SW of Bryansk. A Russian medieval town, it was sacked by the Mongols in the 13th century, after which the Russians, Lithuanians, and Poles vied for its control until it became Russian in 1686. It was held by the Germans from 1941 to 1943 during World War II.

STARVED ROCK (United States) Cliff and national historic landmark in ILLINOIS, on the S bank of the Illinois River, 90 mi SW of Chicago. It was visited by Marquette and Jolliet in 1673 on their return from exploring the MISSISSIPPI RIVER and in 1679 by La-Salle and Tonti, who built Fort St. Louis here from 1680 to 1683. The fort was abandoned in 1702 and burned by the Indians in 1721. An unconfirmed legend tells of the Ottawa Indians driving a band of Illinois Indians onto the cliff here, where they died of starvation. It is now part of the oldest state park in Illinois.

STARY. See MARGILAN.

STARY KRYM [Krym] [former: Old Crimea, Solkhat, Surkhat] (USSR) City of the UKRAINE, in the SE European USSR, in CRIMEA. From the 13th to 15th centuries, as Surkhat or Solkhat, it was the residence of the Crimean khans of the GOLDEN HORDE and was a major caravan center. It languished when the capital of the Crimean khans was moved to Bakchisaray. The ruins of several 14th-century mosques, and a caravansary survive.

STATEN ISLAND [Dutch: Staaten Eylandt; former: Richmond] (United States) Island and borough of NEW YORK CITY, in New York Bay, NEW YORK State. It was first visited by Henry Hudson in 1609. Part of the island was granted to David De Vries by the Dutch West India Company in 1636. The first settlement, quickly destroyed by Indians, was in 1641. A permanent settlement was finally established at Oude Dorp in 1661, when the island was part of NEW JERSEY. It became part of New York in 1668, a borough of New York City in 1898, and in 1975 the official name of the borough was changed from Richmond back to Staten Island. Of the numerous older buildings the most noteworthy is the Billopp or Conference House, built before 1688, where Lord Howe unsuccessfully negotiated with colonial patriots in 1776 on the eve of the American Revolution. The house where the Italian patriot Garibaldi lived in the 1850's also survives, and the older settlement is preserved as an outdoor museum called Richmondtown.

STATE OF VATICAN CITY. See VATICAN CITY.

STATES OF THE CHURCH. See PAPAL STATES.

STATIA. See SAINT EUSTATIUS.

STATION ISLAND. See SAINT PATRICK'S PURGATORY.

STATO DELLA CITTÀ DEL VATICANO. See VATICAN CITY.

STAUNTON (United States) City of N central VIRGINIA, 35 mi WNW of Charlottesville, in a rich agricultural area in the SHENANDOAH VALLEY. Staunton was the capital of Virginia during the American Revolution, in 1781. During the Civil War it was a bone of contention and was twice held by Union Forces. Woodrow Wilson, twenty-eighth president of the United States, was born here.

STAVANGER (Norway) Port and seat of Rogaland county, in the SW, on the Stavangerfjord. Probably founded in the eighth century AD, it was an episcopal see from c.1125 to 1682. In World War II it was occupied by the Germans on April 9, 1940. The 12th-century cathedral of St. Swithin is noteworthy.

STAVELOT [*Flemish:* **Stablo**] (Belgium) Town of Liège province, in the E, in the ARDENNES. It arose after the founding c.650 of a Benedictine abbey whose abbots became princes of the HOLY ROMAN EMPIRE until the French Revolutionary Wars. Until 1815 it included the MALMÉDY region, which then came under PRUSSIA. Stavelot passed to the Dutch and then to Belgium. In December 1944, during the Battle of the Bulge in World War II, the Germans pushed as far as Stavelot and massacred a number of U.S. prisoners of war held nearby.

STAVROPOL [*former:* **Voroshilovsk**] (USSR) Capital city of STAVROPOL KRAI or Territory in Kuibyshev oblast, in the S Russian SFSR. Founded and fortified by Field Marshall Aleksandr Suvorov in 1777, it served as an important base for the subsequent Russian conquest of CAUCASIA.

STAVROPOL KRAI [*former:* **Ordzhonikidze Krai**] (USSR) Territory in SE Russian SFSR, its eastern part the traditional area of the Terek Cossacks. Part of the khanate of the GOLDEN HORDE in the Middle Ages, it was conquered by MOSCOW in the 16th century. It was organized as a territory in 1924 and was recognized 20 years later under its present name.

STĘBARK. See TANNENBERG.

STEENKERKE [**Steenkerque, Steinkirk**] (Belgium) Village and battle site, in Hainaut province, in the SW. From July 23 to August 3, 1692 it was the site of a battle during the War of the Grand Alliance, in which the English under William III were defeated by the French under Marshal François Henri, the duke of Luxembourg.

STEENKERQUE. See STEENKERKE.

STEIER. See STEYR.

STEIERMARK. See STYRIA.

STEINAMANGER. See SZOMBATHELY.

STEINKIRK. See STEENKERKE.

STEINKJER (Norway) Town in the N central region, N of Levanger, at the head of TRONDHEIM Fjord. In the early months of World War II the British and the Germans waged several battles here in April 1940 during the abortive British invasion.

STELLALAND (South Africa) Former Boer republic, now part of CAPE PROVINCE. Created in 1882 in W TRANSVAAL as the Boers pushed westward, its capital was at VRYBURG. It was dissolved in 1885. GOSHEN was another such republic.

STENAY (France) Ancient town of N Meuse department, in the NE, on the MEUSE RIVER, 26 mi NNW of Verdun. Once the royal seat of Frankish AUSTRASIA, it was held briefly by the Spanish in the mid-17th century and was taken by siege for France in 1654. In World War I it was captured by U.S. troops on Armistice Day, Nov. 11, 1918.

STENDAL (East Germany) City in the W, on the Uchte River, 32 mi NNE of Magdeburg. Founded in 1151 by Albert the Bear on the site of a Wendish settlement, it grew to flourish as a member of the HANSEATIC LEAGUE. It is also a former capital of medieval Altmark. Notable Gothic buildings here include a basilica from 1188, city gates from the 13th to the 15th century, and a city hall from the 15th century. The French writer Stendhal, born Marie Henri Beyle, took his pen name from the city.

STENNESS, LOCH OF (Scotland) Lake on MAINLAND Island, in the ORKNEY ISLANDS, off the N coast. On an isthmus between Lochs Stenness and Harray are the Standing Stones of Stenness, two prehistoric stone circles dating from c.3000 BC. One has 12 stones, two of which still stand; and the large Ring of Brogar has approximately 60 stones, 20 of which remain standing. See also MAES HOWE, SKARA BRAE.

STEPHENSON. See ROCK ISLAND.

STEPNEY (England) District of Inner LONDON borough of Tower Hamlets, part of the East End. Here in 1381 at Mile End, during the Peasants Revolt, the rebels from ESSEX under the leadership of Wat Tyler gathered to negotiate with King Richard II. The area of docks and shipping warehouses was severely damaged by bombing in World War II.

STETTIN. See SZCZECIN.

STEUBENVILLE (United States) City on the OHIO

RIVER, 50 mi S of Youngstown, OHIO. Fort Steuben, built here in 1786, was named for Baron von Steuben, the Prussian officer who helped shape the Continental Army in the American Revolution. The fort was abandoned in 1790, but the town was permanently laid out by Pennsylvania land speculators in 1797, making it one of the oldest settlements in Ohio. One of the first Federal government offices to sell public lands in the NORTHWEST TERRITORY was opened in Steubenville in 1800. Edwin M. Stanton, secretary of war in President Lincoln's Civil War cabinet, was born here in 1814.

STEYR [Steier] (Austria) Industrial city of Upper Austria, on the Steyr River, at its confluence with the Enns, 16 mi SSE of Linz. It was an iron-working center from the Middle Ages to the present. Its numerous historic structures include the Lamberg Castle of 991 AD, restored in 1727, a 15th-century Gothic church, and an 18th-century town hall, which is Austria's outstanding rococo building.

STIKLESTAD (Norway) Village on Trondheim Fjord, NE of Trondheim. Here in 1030 King Olaf II (St. Olaf) of Norway was killed in battle while attempting to regain the Norwegian crown.

STILLWATER. See SARATOGA SPRINGS, New York State.

STINGRAY HARBOR. See BOTANY BAY.

ŠTIP [Shtip] [*Turkish:* **Ishtob, Istib, Istip**] (Yugoslavia) Town of Macedonia, in the SE, 40 mi SE of Skopje. An old town that early belonged to the Byzantines, it became an important center of the Serbian and Bulgarian empires in the Middle Ages. It belonged to the Turks from 1389 to 1913. It is the site of a 14th-century monastery and has the ruins of a castle. See also BULGARIA, BYZANTINE EMPIRE, OTTOMAN EMPIRE, SERBIA.

STIRLING [*former:* **Snowdoun]** (Scotland) Strategically located admin. hq. of central region, on the FORTH River, 31 mi WNW of Edinburgh. A Roman station, then a Pictish settlement, it was chartered in 1130. Stirling Castle, a majestic fortress above the Forth, dominates the town. It long vied with EDINBURGH Castle as a royal residence. The birthplace of James II and, probably, of James III and IV, it was the site of the coronations of both the infant Mary, Queen of Scots, and of James VI of Scotland (James I of England). The Parliament House, built in the castle by James III, was the scene of many assemblies. The castle was frequently besieged during Scotland's battle for independence and was held by the English in 1296 and from 1304 to 1314. On Sept. 11, 1297, at the battle of Stirling Bridge, Sir William Wallace defeated an English army under the earl of Surrey. See also BANNOCKBURN.

STIRLINGSHIRE (Scotland) Former county of central Scotland, with its county town at STIRLING, now part of Central administrative region. It was the scene of many important battles in Scottish history: the battle of Stirling Bridge in 1297, the first battle of FALKIRK in 1298, the battle of BANNOCKBURN in 1314, KILSYTH in 1645, and the second battle of Falkirk in 1746. The county is crossed by the Roman wall of Antoninus.

STOBI (Yugoslavia) Ancient town of Paeonia dating from the sixth century BC, now part of Yugoslavian Macedonia, approx. 50 mi SE of Skopje. An important center in ancient MACEDONIA, it became prominent in the ROMAN EMPIRE and in the BYZANTINE EMPIRE until destroyed by an earthquake in 518 AD and not rebuilt. It was capital of the Roman province of Macedonia. Its ruins, lying near modern BITOLA, constitute one of the most important ancient sites in Macedonia. Extensive excavations have revealed a marble theater, streets, walls, a gate, baths, numerous once-rich villas, and several basilicas. Most of the ruins, open to the public, date from the fourth to the sixth century AD.

STOCKACH (West Germany) Town of Baden-Württemberg, NW of Constance. It was the scene of two historic battles during the Napoleonic Wars, one on March 25, 1799 in which archduke Charles Louis of AUSTRIA defeated the French under Gen. Jean Baptiste Jourdan; and the second on May 3, 1800 in which Gen. Jean Moreau defeated the Austrians.

STOCKBRIDGE (United States) Town and summer resort of W MASSACHUSETTS, 12 mi S of Pittsfield. It was founded in 1734 by John Sergeant as a mission for the Housatonic Indians, who were moved here by the colonial settlers of their Hudson Valley homeland and who were known as the Stockbridge Indians thereafter. The original mission house of 1739 is now a museum. Jonathan Edwards, the noted Puritan, was head of the Indian school here from 1750 to 1757, during which time he finished his masterwork, *The Freedom of the Will.* Nearby are Indian burial grounds. The Old Corner House, dating from the 18th century, contains numerous Norman Rockwell paintings.

STOCKHOLM (Sweden) Port, capital, and largest city in Sweden, in the S, on the Baltic Sea. Tradition says it was founded *c.*1250 by one Birger Jarl. Developing on several islands and peninsulas in the Baltic, it had become an important town by 1288 and was soon allied with, and dominated by, the HANSEATIC LEAGUE. In 1520 Christian II of DENMARK and NORWAY proclaimed himself also king of Sweden. When the Swedish nobles gathered for his coronation, Christian incited a massacre of the anti-Danish nobility. This coalesced the national spirit and provoked a successful revolt led by Gustavas Vasa, who was crowned Gustavus I. Reigning from 1523 to 1560, he broke the power of the Hanseatic merchants. Made the nation's capital in 1634, under Queen Christina Stockholm became a leading European intellectual center, attracting such luminaries as Descartes. Known as the Venice of the North, its historic buildings include the Ridarkyrka, burial place of kings and the country's outstanding citizens, the Nobel Institute, the royal palace of 1754, city hall, national museum, a 17th-century cathedral, and medieval streets and houses in the Old Town area.

STOKE-ON-TRENT (England) City of Staffordshire, 38 mi N of Birmingham. The center of the development and growth of the British pottery industry from the 18th century, it was the home of Josiah Wedgwood, Josiah Spode, and Thomas and Herbert Minton, all famous potters. It was also the birthplace and burial

A charming city of islands and wandering waterways, Stockholm, Sweden's capital, is loved by tourists. It was founded *c.*1250 AD on the island in the background.

place of the writer Arnold Bennett, whose novels were often set here. See also POTTERIES.

STOLP. See SŁUPSK.

STONEHENGE (England) Impressive megalithic monument on SALISBURY PLAIN, Wiltshire. The monument, consisting of two main circles of huge stones and an outer bank and ditch, was completed in much its present form in the Bronze Age, *c.*2000 BC, but was developed gradually over a period of some 1,500 years. Outside the ditch is the Heelstone, aligned exactly on the rising of the midsummer solstice sun. The monument is surrounded by a complex of burial mounds and ritual sites scattered over several miles.

Stonehenge was certainly a religious center of major importance, perhaps of a sun cult connected with the calendrical phases of the agricultural season. In many ways it was also thus an astronomical observatory for calculating the phases of the moon and the occurrences of eclipses, again connected with the local agricultural cult. See also AVEBURY.

STONES RIVER. See MURFREESBORO, Tennessee.

STONEY CREEK (Canada) Town and battle site, near HAMILTON, in SE ONTARIO, at the W end of LAKE ONTARIO. During the War of 1812, on June 6, 1813, the Americans under Generals Chandler and Winder suffered a defeat here by the British under General Vincent.

STONINGTON (United States) Town in SE CONNECTICUT, on LONG ISLAND SOUND, E of Groton. Settled in 1649, it was once an important whaling and shipbuilding center, and in both the American Revolution and the War of 1812 was attacked by the British. It is the site of numerous outstanding sea captains' houses. Incorporated in the township is Mystic, which has a noted maritime museum in the Mystic Seaport.

STONY BROOK. See PRINCETON.

STONY POINT (United States) Village in Rockland County, SE NEW YORK State. Named for a rocky promontory on the HUDSON RIVER, during the American Revolution it was an American blockhouse from 1776 to 1779, when it was taken by the British on May 31 and converted into a strong fort. It was also an anchoring point for the massive chain strung across the Hudson to hinder passage of the British fleet. The fort was retaken by the Americans under Gen. Anthony Wayne on July 15 and 16 and shortly thereafter abandoned, although the victory led to the driving of the British from the upper Hudson area. In 1780 Gen. Benedict Arnold secretly arranged to betray WEST POINT to the British at Stony Point.

STORKYRO. See ISOKYRÖ.

STRAIT OF JUAN DE FUCA. See JUAN DE FUCA STRAIT.

STRAITS SETTLEMENTS (Malay Peninsula) Historic and collective name for several former British colonies in southeast Asia, including PENANG, SINGAPORE, MALACCA, and LABUAN. Territories of the British East India Company from 1826, they then passed under British Indian control and in 1867 were made a crown colony administered by the Colonial Office. Labuan became a separate colony in 1912. In 1946, after Japanese occupation in World War II, the original crown colony was dissolved. Singapore and its dependencies were made a separate crown colony; Penang and Malacca evolved to become part of MALAYSIA; while Singapore became independent in 1965.

STRAITS, THE. See BOSPORUS, DARDANELLES.

STRALSUND (East Germany) Industrial city of the Rostock district, on the Strelasund inlet of the Baltic Sea, opposite Rügen Island. Founded in 1209, it became a prominent member of the HANSEATIC LEAGUE in the late 13th century and in 1370 was the site of the signing of the Treaty of Stralsund between DENMARK and the league. A prominent city of POMERANIA, it withstood a siege during the Thirty Years War by Wallenstein in 1628, but it passed to SWEDEN with the Peace of Westphalia in 1648. Changing hands numerous times up to the Napoleonic Wars, it was taken by the French in 1807 and ultimately passed to PRUSSIA through the Congress of Vienna. The town was severely damaged in World War II. Several notable buildings survive, including the 13th- and 14th-century city hall, and the 13th- to 14th-century church of St. Nicholas.

STRASBOURG [*ancient:* **Argentoratum;** *German:* **Strassburg;** *medieval:* **Strateburgum**] (France) Franco-German city, the capital of Bas-Rhin department, in the NE, in a strategic location on the Ill River, approx. 2 mi W of its confluence with the RHINE RIVER, and 83 mi SW of Metz. First a Celtic settlement, it was then taken by the Romans and as Argentoratum was important on a major crossroads of Northern Europe. Sacked by Attila and his Huns in the fifth century AD, it was rebuilt by the Franks as Strateburgum. In 842 it was the scene of the Oath of Strasbourg in which Charles the Bald, later Carolingian Emperor Charles II, and Louis the German swore alliance against their brother, Emperor Lothair I and confirmed the dissolution of the FRANKISH EMPIRE of Charlemagne. As part of the German and later HOLY ROMAN EMPIRE, from 923 it was ruled by its local bishops, until its citizens managed to have it made a free imperial city in 1262. It became linked to GERMANY through the homage of the duke of Lorraine to Henry I and became a leading Protestant city during the Reformation. Severely damaged in the Thirty Years War, it was occupied by the French in 1681 and was ultimately ceded to them by the Treaty of Ryswick in 1697. Bombarded by the Germans in the Franco-Prussian War in 1870/71, it came under German rule from 1871 to 1918. Returned to France in 1919, it was taken again by Germany in 1940 and suffered considerable damage in World War II. It is the seat of the Council of Europe. Historic buildings include the 11th- to 15th-century cathedral with its astronomical clock, a governor's palace, the town hall, and an episcopal palace.

STRASSBURG. See STRASBOURG.

STRATEBURGUM. See STRASBOURG.

STRATFIELD. See BRIDGEPORT.

STRATFORD-UPON-AVON [*Middle English:* **Aetstretfordae**] (England) Town on the AVON RIVER, in Warwickshire, 21 mi SSE of Birmingham, made famous through its association with William Shakespeare. The place of his birth in 1564, it is also the site of his grave beside that of his wife, Anne Hathaway, whose cottage is nearby. Both are buried in the old church of the Holy Trinity, parts of which date to the 12th century. Stratford has become a bustling tourist center. It also houses the Shakespeare Memorial Theatre.

STRATHCLYDE (Scotland) Modern region and ancient Celtic kingdom, S of the Clyde River. Believed to have been established in the mid-fifth century AD, the kingdom was conquered by Anglo-Saxon NORTHUMBRIA and by the Picts in 756, plundered by the Norse Vikings a century later, and defeated by the Anglo-Saxons, despite Scottish and Norse allies, at the Battle of Brunanburh in 937 AD. It was finally taken by King Edmund of ENGLAND in 945, who awarded it to King Malcolm of Scotland. Its capital was DUMBARTON. The modern region incorporated Ayrshire, Bute, Dumbartonshire, Lanarkshire, Renfrewshire, and parts of Argyll and Stirlingshire. The admin. hq. is GLASGOW. See also CUMBRIA.

STRATTON AND BUDE. See BUDE-STRATTON.

STRAUBING [*ancient:* **Sorviodurum**] (West Germany) City of BAVARIA, on the DANUBE RIVER, 23 mi ESE of Regensburg. A Roman town was founded here on the site of prehistoric and Celtic settlements. A new town developed around St. Peter's Church, built in 1180. Made the capital of the duchy of Bavaria-Straubing in 1353, it was ruled by a branch of the Wittelsbach family. Historic buildings include a 12th-century church, a Gothic city hall from 1382, and the 15th- and 16th-century Gothic church of St. Jacob.

STRELITZ. See MECKLENBURG, NEUSTRELITZ, East Germany.

STREONSHALH. See WHITBY.

STRESA (Italy) Resort town and conference site in Novara province, in NE Piedmont region, on the W shore of Lake Maggiore. It was the scene of two historic conferences in the 1930's. The first, from Sept. 5 to 20, 1932, included the representatives of 15 countries who met to discuss European economic collaboration. Their recommendations were submitted to the Commission of Inquiry for European Union. The second involved representatives of France, Great Britain, and Italy, who met from April 11 to 14, 1935 to demonstrate their opposition to German rearmament that had begun in violation of the Treaty of Versailles. Their decision to maintain a common posture was never implemented.

STRIGONIUM. See ESZTERGOM.

STRUMICA [**Strumitsa, Strumnitza**] [*ancient:* **Tiberiopolis**] (Yugoslavia) Ancient town of MACEDONIA, on the Strumica River, approx. 75 mi SE of Skopje. A battle site in both the Balkan Wars and World War I, it was earlier under Turkish rule. Ceded to BULGARIA in 1913, it passed to Yugoslavia in 1919. Of historic interest are the ruined fortress built by the Roman Emperor Tiberius and a 14th-century Serbian castle.

STRUMITSA. See STRUMICA.

STRUMNITZA. See STRUMICA.

STRY [*Polish:* **Stryj**] (USSR) Ukrainian city on the

Stry River, in the Carpathian foothills, 44 mi NW of Ivano-Frankovsk. A settlement chartered in 1431, it reached its pinnacle in the 15th and 16th centuries. It passed to Austria in 1772. During World War I the Russians were repulsed by German forces here from May to June 1915. Stry was ceded to Poland in 1919 and finally passed to the UKRAINE in 1939.

STRYJ. See STRY.

STUART. See ALICE SPRINGS.

STUHLWEISSENBURG. See SZÉKESFEHÉRVÁR.

STUTTGART (West Germany) Industrial city and capital of Baden-Württemberg state on the Neckar River, 38 mi ESE of Karlsruhe. Settled since prehistoric times and the site of a Roman fort, it was founded c.950 as a fortified manor and stud farm. It developed into a town, was chartered in the 13th century, and in 1320 became the residence of the counts, later dukes, and from 1806 kings, of WÜRTTEMBERG. It became capital of the duchy in 1495 and of the kingdom in 1806. It was the seat of the Reichstag and National Assembly at the time of the Kapp Putsch in 1920. An industrial center severely damaged by bombing in World War II, it was occupied by the French on April 22, 1945. Historic buildings include the 12th-century Stiftskirche, the 18th-century rococo Solitude Palace, the New Palace of 1746 to 1807, now an administration building, and the Rosenstein Palace of 1824 to 1829.

STYRIA [*German:* **Steiermark**] (Austria) State in mountainous central and SE Austria, bordering on Yugoslavia to the S. Its capital town is GRAZ. There are traces of Paleolithic habitation in this area, which was first permanently settled by the Celts. It was part of NORICUM and Roman PANNONIA and was overrun by Germans in the fifth century AD and then by the Slavs. The Bavarians gained control c.780. Made part of CARINTHIA, it became the duchy of Steiermark in 1180 and passed to the Austrian house of Babenberg in 1192. Under Ottocar II of BOHEMIA it was successfully held against Bela IV of HUNGARY, in 1260, but at the battle of MARCHFELD in 1278 Ottocar was defeated and killed by Ruldolf I of Hapsburg, who then made Styria, Austria, and CARNIOLA Hapsburg possessions. By the Treaty of St. Germain in 1919 the southern portion was ceded to YUGOSLAVIA, but this was restored to Austria in 1941.

SU. See KIANGSU.

SUBIACO [*ancient:* **Sublaqueum**] (Italy) Town and monastic site in Roma province, Latium region, 50 mi E of Rome. The site derives its name from the village built for workers on Nero's pleasure palace. It was downstream from the lake (*sub laqueum*) formed by his damming of the Aniane River here. The dam burst in 1305, but remnants of it and the palace survive. The first monastery founded by St. Benedict of Nursia c.505 is in the cliff walls on Mt Taleo above the valley. Sta. Scholastica, sister of St. Benedict, established a monastic community for women here, and the monastery of Sta. Scholastica is further down the mountainside from St. Benedict's hermit cave, the *Sacro Speco.*

The upper monastery contains ninth-century frescoes, St. Gregory's Chapel, and a fresco of St. Francis of Assisi, probably done during his lifetime after his visit here in 1210. The monastery was a haven for Franciscan heretics in the 1320's and 1330's. It also housed the first printing press in Italy, established here in 1464. Sta. Scholastica today houses a priceless collection of medieval manuscripts and early printed books. The town contains the 14th-century St. Francis Bridge and church of St. Francis, and the Rocca Abbeziale, a palace and papal residence.

SUBLAQUEUM. See SUBIACO.

SUCCANESSET. See FALMOUTH, Massachusetts.

SUCEAVA [**Suczawa**] (Rumania) Town of BUKOVINA, in the NE, on the Suceava River. From 1388 to 1565 it was the first capital of MOLDAVIA until it was succeeded by IAŞI. The 16th-century St. George Church here is a historic shrine and place of pilgrimage. Nearby is the famed 17th-century Dragomirna Monastery.

SUCHOU [**Soochow**] [*former:* **Wuhsien**] (China) City of S Kiangsu province, in the E, on the GRAND CANAL. Founded c.525 BC, it was capital of the kingdom of Wu, dating from 513 to 473 BC. Its present name derives from the sixth-century AD Sui dynasty. Partly destroyed by the Mings in the 14th century, it was restored under Emperor K'anghsi in 1662 whose town walls survive. Badly damaged in the Taiping Rebellion, it was again rebuilt and was opened as a treaty port in 1896. It was captured by the Japanese in 1937 and held by them in World War II. The city passed to the communists in 1949. Noted for its beauty, it is the site of numerous palaces, canals, temples, gardens, and the Great Pagoda, one of the largest in China.

SUCRE [*former:* **Charcas, Chuquisaca, La Plata**] (Bolivia) The constitutional capital, 260 mi SE of LA PAZ, which is the actual legislative capital as part of a compromise settlement following civil war over the removal of the capital from here in 1898. Founded as Chuquisaca in 1538, it was the scene on May 25, 1809 of the outbreak of the Bolivian revolt against Spanish rule. Renamed in 1840 in honor of the first president of Bolivia, it is the seat of the national supreme court and of the University of San Francisco Xavier, founded c.1625, which specializes in law. It is known as City of Four Names; Charcas was the name of an Indian tribe that originally inhabited the area.

SUCZAWA. See SUCEAVA.

SUDAK (USSR) Ukrainian town and resort on the BLACK SEA, in the CRIMEA. Founded in the third century AD as a Greek settlement it passed to NOVGOROD c.800 and thereafter became an important port for Mediterranean and Asiatic trade. Marco Polo passed through here in the 13th century, followed by Venetians who established a community here. After suffering a series of Tatar attacks in 1289, 1322, and 1327, it was taken and fortified by GENOA in 1365. Both Genoa and the Crimean Tatars, from 1475, brought decline until its acquisition by RUSSIA in 1783. See also UKRAINE.

SUDAN [*Arabic:* **Bilād-es-Sudan;** *French:* **Soudan**] (Africa) Historic region of N central Africa, extending from the W coast S of the Sahara and the Libyan desert, 4,000 mi E to the mountains of Ethiopia. It occupies the basins of the NIGER, NILE, and SENEGAL rivers and the Lake CHAD area. Ethnically an area populated by black African peoples under Muslim influence, in the Middle Ages it was the site of the black African states of BORNU, FULANI, and SONGHAI.

SUDAN, DEMOCRATIC REPUBLIC OF [*Arabic:* **Jum hūrīyat as-Sūdān ad-Dīmuqratīyah**] The largest country in Africa, lying S of Egypt, bordered on the E by Ethiopia and the Red Sea; on the S by Kenya, Uganda, and Zaire; on the W by the Central African Republic, Chad, and Libya.

The ancient kingdom of KUSH occupied the region of NUBIA that is now Sudan, as did EGYPT, which had begun to colonize this northern section at least by 3000 BC. MAKURIA and ALWA inherited control from Kush and ruled as Coptic Christian kingdoms until the 15th century AD, when they were converted to Islam. After the 16th century there was no dominant state in the region until the early 19th century, when Ottoman Egyptian forces occupied the country.

By the middle of the century there had been considerable European exploration of this area, often referred to as Ethiopia or Nubia, and a considerable trade in slaves and ivory had begun. A violent religious war of rebellion erupted in 1881, led by Muhammad Ahmal al-Mahdi, an Islamic messianic leader. The Mahdi's troops repelled the Ottoman Egyptian forces and destroyed a punitive expedition sent by Great Britain. Egypt abandoned the Sudan, and in 1884 Charles George Gordon was sent to KHARTOUM to relieve the remaining troops. Gordon was besieged there and killed in 1885 shortly before a relief column arrived.

Thereafter a Muslim Sudanese state ruled until 1898, when a British army led by Gen. H.H. Kitchener reconquered the region. In 1899 it became the ANGLO-EGYPTIAN SUDAN, a joint condominium of Egypt and Great Britain. The latter dominated the condiminium, and after Egyptian troops rebelled in 1924 Great Britain assumed sole control of the Sudan.

Nationalism became a strong movement after World War II, and in 1956 Sudan became an independent republic. The new country underwent several coups and changes of government and faced rebellion from black Sudanese guerrillas from the southern part of the country. In 1971 a coup led by Col. Jafaar al-Nimeiry seized power, and he was subsequently elected president and has survived several assassination and coup attempts. Sudan moved to establish close ties with the United States in the late 1970's, following the lead of neighboring Egypt and threats from neighboring Libya.

SUDBURY (England) Town on the Stour River, 13 mi NW of Colchester, in Suffolk, East Anglia. Flemish weavers introduced the woolen industry to Sudbury in the 14th century. A grammar school was founded in 1491, and the town has three 15th-century churches and a town hall of the same period. Thomas Gainsborough, the landscape and portrait painter, was born here in 1727.

SUDBURY (United States) Town in NE MASSACHUSETTS, 18 mi W of Boston. It was settled in 1638, only a few years after the founding of the Massachusetts Bay Colony, and saw action during the American Revolution. The Wayside Inn, still preserved here and once known as the Howe or Red Horse Tavern, formed the setting for Henry W. Longfellow's *Tales of a Wayside Inn.*

SUDETENLAND Historic region originally comprising the mountainous borderlands on the N of BOHEMIA and SILESIA, which had generally been inhabited by German-speaking peoples. During the Sudentenland Crisis of 1938/39, the area was widened to include the similar borderlands of MORAVIA as well. After the MUNICH Agreement of 1938 between Germany and Great Britain, France, and Italy, these areas were seized by the Nazi German government in 1939 and absorbed into the German Reich, in effect partitioning Czechoslovakia. They were returned to Czechoslovakia in 1945 after World War II.

SUESSA AURUNCA. See SESSA AURUNCA.

SUESSULA (Italy) Ancient Samnite town of Campania in the S, N of modern Caserta. During the short First Samnite War, in 343 BC, there was a battle here. The three Samnite wars between ROME and the Samnites eventually secured control of CAMPANIA and all of central and southern Italy for Rome. See also CAUDINE FORKS, SAMNIUM.

SUEZ [*ancient:* **Clysma; Kolzum;** *Arabic:* **As-Suways**] (Egypt) City at the N end of the Gulf of Suez and the S terminus of the SUEZ CANAL. It was first a Greek settlement. As Kolzum, it was the terminal point connecting the RED SEA with the NILE RIVER in the seventh century AD. Under the OTTOMAN EMPIRE in the 16th century it became a naval and commercial port and later a base for pilgrims on their way to MECCA via JIDDA. It became a major port in 1869 after the completion of the Suez Canal but in recent years has suffered economically with the Arab-Israeli wars and the periodic closing of the canal.

SUEZ CANAL [*Arabic:* **Qanat as Suways**] (Egypt) Ship canal across the Isthmus of Suez in the NE, extending more than 100 mi from PORT SAID to Port Tawfiq and connecting the MEDITERRANEAN SEA with the Gulf of Suez and the RED SEA. As early as the 19th century BC the ancient Egyptians built a canal here. It was used until the eighth century AD, when it was abandoned. The present one was built between 1859 and 1869 according to the plans of the French engineer Ferdinand de Lesseps. It opened Nov. 16, 1869 and remained under French-British ownership until the creation of a British protectorate over Egypt in 1882.

In 1888 the Convention of Constantinople declared the canal neutral, to be administered by the Suez Canal Company. The canal was nationalized by the Egyptian government under Nasser in 1956, inciting Anglo-French intervention in November and the closing of the canal until April 1957. The Arab-Israeli wars of the late

1960's and early 1970's brought Egyptian-Israeli fighting to the canal banks, and its periodic closing forced shipping to use alternate sea routes. A 1974 agreement provided for the disengagement of Egyptian and Israeli forces and the withdrawal of the Israelis to the SINAI. The canal was reopened in 1975.

SUFETULA. See SBEÏTLA.

SUFFOLK (England) Coastal county in the E. With NORFOLK it formed the ancient kingdom of the Iceni, whose queen, Boadicea, led a revolt against the Romans in 60 AD. Meaning "south folk," in Anglo-Saxon, it was part of the kingdom of EAST ANGLIA in the early Middle Ages. It became the center of a large wool industry in the late Middle Ages. The admin. hq. is IPSWICH. See also BURY ST. EDMUNDS, COLCHESTER, LOWESTOFT, MILDENHALL.

SUFFOLK (United States) Town of SE VIRGINIA, on the Nansemond River, 18 mi WSW of Portsmouth. Founded in 1742, it was burned by the British in 1779 during the American Revolution. The town was taken by Union forces in 1862 during the Civil War.

SUGBU. See CEBU.

SUHAMPTON. See SOUTHAMPTON.

SUITTES. See SCHWYZ.

SUKARNAPURA. See DJADJAPURA.

SUKHOTHAI [Sukotai] (Thailand) Town in the W, 30 mi NW of Phitsanulok. From 1256 to 1350 the town was the capital of the first Thai state, under the same name, to be set up independently of the Khmers. It is also the site of one of Thailand's most impressive temples. See also AYUTTHAYA.

SUKHUM. See SUKHUMI.

SUKHUMI [*ancient:* **Dioscurias, Sebastopolis;** *former:* **Sukhum**] (USSR) Port and provincial capital of Abkhaz ASSR, in the Georgian SSR, on the BLACK SEA, 100 mi NW of Kutaisi. Originally the Greek colony of Dioscurias, founded in the sixth century BC, the town, with its sulfur baths, continued to flourish as Sebastopolis under ROME and the BYZANTINE EMPIRE.

The Roads at Port Said, photographed on the very day of the opening of the Suez Canal, Nov. 17, 1869. The canal revolutionized maritime access to the Far East.

It had become the Turkish fortress of Sukhum-Kale before its acquisition by RUSSIA in 1810. There are the remains of Byzantine fortifications here.

SUKOTAI. See SUKHOTHAI.

SULAWESI [*former:* **Celebes**] (Indonesia) The largest of the four Greater Sunda Islands of East Indonesia, separated from the east of Borneo by the Makasar Strait. The earliest evidences of human habitation are stone implements of the Toalian culture. Muslim sultanates had already arrived before the first Europeans, the Portuguese, visited it in 1512. The Portuguese subsequently settled in Macassar, now MAKASAR, in 1625. The Dutch took over in 1660 and with the establishment of MANADO in 1667 extended their influence over the west and south, but the sultanate in the southeast was not conquered until 1905. During the 17th and 18th centuries there was intermittent war between the Dutch and the local settlers as well as the Buganese pirates. In World War II Celebes was occupied by JAPAN in January 1942. The Japanese finally surrendered to Australian forces in September 1945. Celebes was governed by the Dutch as part of the Netherlands East Indies until 1946, when East Indonesia was founded, joining the Republic of Indonesia in 1950.

SULCI. See SANT' ANTIOCO.

SULGRAVE (England) Village of Northamptonshire, 15 mi SW of Northampton. It is the site of Sulgrave Manor, a modest Tudor mansion, once the home of George Washington's ancestors from 1539 until 1610. It has been restored and is open as a museum.

SULI [**Souli**] (Greece) Small, mountainous district in EPIRUS, in the N. The Suliotes, a tough mountain people, managed to remain independent during most of the Ottoman Turks' occupation of Greece. From 1790 to 1802 they held out against Ali Pasha, the Turkish governor of IOÁNNINA, until they were duped by a false truce concluded in 1803 by Ali, who then massacred many of them. They suffered heavily in another rebellion in 1820, and many took refuge on the Ionian islands.

SULMO. See SULMONA.

SULMONA [*ancient:* **Sulmo**] (Italy) Town of Aquila province, ABRUZZI region, in the Apennines, 35 mi SE of L'Aquila. Historic structures here include the Gothic-Renaissance Palazzo dell'Annunziata and the cathedral of San Panfilo. It was the birthplace of Ovid and of Pope Innocent VII.

SULPHUR ISLAND. See IWO JIMA.

SULTĀNĪYAH. See SOLTĀNÍYEH.

SULU. See JOLO.

SULU (Philippines) Province and archipelago of many islands, SW of Mindanao, between the Celebes and Sulu seas and extending almost to Borneo. It is inhabited by the Moros, a fiercely independent Muslim people, much feared in the past as pirates, who maintained their freedom from Spain into the 19th century. Of Malayan stock, they were converted to Islam in the 14th and 15th centuries. The Moro Sultanate, dating from the 16th century, came under U.S. control after the

Spanish-American War in 1899 and was only abolished in 1940, when Sulu became part of the Philippine Commonwealth.

SULUAN (Philippines) Island and ships' landmark, 10 mi E of Homonhon Island, 13 mi S of the S point of Samar. It was the site, with HOMONHON, of the first landing of U.S. troops on their return to the Philippines on Oct. 19, 1944 during World War II.

SUMATERA. See SUMATRA.

SUMATRA [**Sumatera**] (Indonesia) Island of W Indonesia, S of the Malay peninsula. Long known due to trading between China and India, it was in early contact with Hindu civilization. By the seventh century AD a widespread Hindu-Sumatran kingdom, SRIVIJAYA, had evolved based, on the island. Under the house of Sailendra, with its capital near PALEMBANG, it controlled a large part of Indonesia and the MALAY PENINSULA and successfully held off attacks from JAVA. Marco Polo, the first recorded European to visit Sumatra, arrived in 1292, during Srivijaya's hegemony. Its power declined by the 14th century, and the Javanese kingdom of MAJAPAHIT took control. Meanwhile, Arabs arrived in the 13th century and established the sultanate of ATJEH, which flourished in the 17th century.

The Portuguese arrived in 1509, followed in 1596 by the Dutch, who gained control of the native states including Atjeh, despite sporadic competition from the English and Portuguese. An Atjehnese revolt against the Dutch in 1873 was not subdued until 1904. Occupied by the Japanese in early 1942 and throughout World War II, Sumatra became part of the Republic of Indonesia in 1949. The Atjehnese have continued their separatist activity. In 1958 dissident army officers launched a full-scale rebellion on the island, which was finally suppressed.

SUMER (Iraq) Ancient region and civilization in the S part of MESOPOTAMIA. The people of Sumer, who spoke a non-Semitic language, may have come from outside Mesopotamia. Building upon a long development of increasingly sophisticated cultures in Mesopotamia and to the north, not long before 3000 BC they produced what is still accounted the world's earliest urban civilization, which was shortly to be followed by the rather different civilization of ancient EGYPT, and finally by that of the INDUS VALLEY. The Sumerians were responsible for the development of a written language known as cuneiform; for their extensive irrigation and canal-building achievements; for their exceptional artistry in gold, silver, and precious minerals; as well as for their massive religious architecture.

Flourishing as a series of independent city-states, the Sumerians finally united with the Semitic-speaking inhabitants of Mesopotamia from AKKAD, and it was Sargon of Akkad who finally imposed a political unity on the whole of Mesopotamia c.2340 BC. Invading barbarians from the north brought about the collapse of Akkad c.2180 BC, although one great ruler of a Sumerian city state, Gudea, held out in Lagash.

Sumer was able to regain some of its political power and prestige under the Third Dynasty of Ur (c.2060–

1950 BC), but Ur was destroyed by ELAM. With the rise of BABYLONIA under Hammurabi, the Sumerians disappeared as a distinct nation, although their culture as a whole was carried on for thousands of years, from Babylonian times into those of ASSYRIA and PERSIA. The chief cities of Sumer, many of which have been excavated, lay near the lower EUPHRATES RIVER and included ERECH, LARSA, LAGASH, KISH, NIPPUR, and UR.

SUMPU. See SHIZUOKA.

SUMTER, FORT. See FORT SUMTER.

SUNBURY. See BANGOR.

SUNGARIA. See DZUNGARIA.

SUNG-CHIANG [Sungkiang] (China) Town in the E, on the Huang-p'u River, 25 mi SW of Shanghai. It is the burial place of Gen. Frederick T. Ward, U.S. adventurer and leader of the Ever-Victorious Army, which he organized at the time of the Taiping Rebellion to aid the central government against the rebels. He was wounded and died in 1862. A temple dedicated to him was erected by the Chinese in the town.

SUNGKIANG. See SUNG-CHIANG.

SÜNTEL [Süntelberg] (West Germany) Battle site and mountain in Lower Saxony, on the N bank of the Weser River. In 782 AD it was the scene of a battle in which the Saxon leader Widukind defeated a Frankish army sent out by Charlemagne, killing many of them, including two generals. In revenge Charlemagne later massacred 4,500 defenseless Saxons at VERDEN on the Aller River. See also FRANKISH EMPIRE.

SÜNTELBERG. See SÜNTEL.

SUNWUI. See HSIN-HUI.

SUOMENLINNA [former: Viapori; Swedish: Sveaborg] (Finland) Fortress in the harbor of HELSINKI. Built by the Swedes in 1749, it was surrendered, along with 110 ships, 2,000 cannon and 7,000 men, to RUSSIA in 1808. In 1855, during the Crimean War, it was bombarded by the Franco-British fleet.

SUPERIOR (United States) City in NW WISCONSIN, at the end of LAKE SUPERIOR, opposite DULUTH, Minnesota. It shares an excellent harbor with Duluth and has large docks used in shipping coal and iron. The area was visited in 1661 by Pierre Radisson, a French explorer and fur trader, and in 1679 by the Sieur Duluth, another French explorer who was heading an expedition to conquer the Indians and put an end to the Ojibwa-Sioux War. There was a late 18th-century fur-trading post here, but civilian settlement did not begin until 1852. The discovery of very large iron-ore deposits in the region in 1883 led to the growth of Superior.

SUPERIOR, LAKE [French: Lac Supérior] (Canada, United States) Largest of the Great Lakes and the largest freshwater lake in the world, it is bordered on the W by Minnesota, on the N and E by Ontario, and on the S by Michigan and Wisconsin. The lake is the western terminus of the 2,343-mile-long Great Lakes-St. Lawrence Seaway and can be reached by ocean-going vessels. Pierre Radisson and Médard des Groseil-liers in 1659, and Étienne Brulé, in 1622, were the first Europeans to see the lake. French traders used it for transporting furs, and missions were established in the region in the 17th century. The French Jesuit Claude Jean Allouez made a canoe trip around the lake in 1667 that provided data for the first map of the region. Ceded to the British in 1763, it remained in British control until 1817. The U.S. Canadian border runs through the lake.

SUQUTRA. See SOCOTRA.

SUR. See TYRE.

SURA (Iraq) City on the EUPHRATES RIVER, formerly in BABYLONIA, just W of THAPSACUS. It was fortified by the Romans during their wars with PERSIA. From 609 to 1038 AD it was well known for its Talmudic school.

SURABAJA [Dutch: Soerabaja] (Indonesia) The country's second-largest city and provincial capital of E JAVA, on Surabaja Strait, at the mouth of the Kali Mas River. Before the 17th century it was a small trading kingdom, which was then taken by the MATARAM Sultanate in 1625. Under Dutch control from 1743, it was capital of a residency and the main Dutch naval base in the East Indies until occupied by the Japanese from 1942 to 1945, in World War II. During this time it suffered extensive bombing damage. It was a center of rebellion against the Dutch and British during the country's war of independence from 1945 to 1949. The city is the site of a large 19th-century mosque.

SURAJPUR. See SURAT.

SURAKARTA [Solo] [Dutch: Soerakarta] (Indonesia) City of S central JAVA, 50 mi SE of Semarang. Founded in 1755 at the break-up of the MATARAM Sultanate, it was the seat of a Dutch-protected principality in the former Netherlands East Indies. Occupied by the Japanese from 1942 to 1945, it is the site of a vast, walled sultan's palace, a veritable town in itself. The picturesque European section includes a Dutch fort dating from 1799.

SURAT [former: Surajpur, Suryapur] (India) City of SE Gujarat state, in the W, on the Tapti River, near its mouth, 150 mi N of Bombay. Destroyed by the Portuguese in 1512, 1530, and 1531, it was conquered by Akbar in 1573. Under him, Jahangir, and Shah Jahan it became a large city and the chief port of India. The first English factory in India was established here in 1608, marking the beginning of the British Empire in India. Sacked by the Marathas in 1664, it declined thereafter. Nevertheless it remained the seat of the English Indian government until 1687. See also MARATHA CONFEDERACY, MOGUL EMPIRE.

SURESNES (France) Suburb of PARIS on the W, and on the SEINE RIVER, Hauts-de-Seine department. In 1593 it was the site of a conference between Protestants and Catholics that resulted in Henry IV's embracing Catholicism. MT VALÉRIEN here is the site of a fort important in the defense of Paris.

SURIGAO (Philippines) One of the country's oldest Spanish towns and a province in NE MINDANAO. It was explored in the mid-16th century. Missions were established here in 1597 but were subject to harassment by the Muslim Moro pirates from SULU. A particularly serious attack occurred in 1752. Military government was finally established in 1860, and civil government was introduced by the United States in May 1901.

SURIGAO STRAIT (Philippines) Channel between Leyte and Dinagat islands, connecting the Pacific Ocean with the Mindanao Sea. During the U.S. invasion of the Japanese-held Philippines in World War II, a U.S. fleet under the command of Gen. Douglas MacArthur sailed through the strait toward the first landing on LEYTE on Oct. 20, 1944. After the landing there was a major air and sea engagement here from October 23 to 25 that was part of the larger Battle of LEYTE GULF, or Second Battle of the Philippine Sea, in which the U.S. fleet and aircraft destroyed the Japanese fleet in one of the most important battles of the war.

SURINAM. See SURINAME.

SURINAME [Surinam] [former: **Dutch Guiana, Netherlands Guiana**] Independent republic, former autonomous territory under the Dutch crown, on the Atlantic Ocean in N South America. Its capital is PARAMARIBO. First permanently settled by the English under Lord Willoughby of Parham in 1650, it then capitulated to the Dutch and was ceded to them under the Treaty of Breda in 1667 in exchange for New Netherland (NEW YORK). The British and French again sought to establish claims here, and it was held by the British from 1799 to 1802 and from 1804 to 1816, but the Congress of Vienna in 1815 reaffirmed Dutch possession. Suriname was granted a parliament in 1866 and full autonomy in 1954. Its independence came in 1975. In a military coup in February 1982 a National Military Council took power.

SURKHAT. See STARY KRYM.

SURRENTUM. See SORRENTO.

SURREY (England) County in the SE, with its admin. hq. at Kingston-upon-Thames. One of the home counties around LONDON, in Anglo-Saxon times it was held at various times by MERCIA and WESSEX, until invaded by Viking Danes in the ninth century. At RUNNYMEDE here in 1215 King John signed the Magna Carta. The region is known for its Iron Age earthworks, notably at Lingfield.

SURRIENTO. See SORRENTO.

SURYAPUR. See SURAT.

SUSA [Biblical: **Shushan**; modern: **Shūsh**] (Iran) Capital city of ELAM, in the SW, 15 mi S of Dezful. Settled very early, from the fourth millennium BC it was under the cultural influence of MESOPOTAMIA. Destroyed in the seventh century BC by Assurbanipal of ASSYRIA, it was revived in the Achaemenid Empire of PERSIA. Made the capital by Cyrus the Great, it was the winter residence of the Achaemenian kings until the conquest by Alexander the Great of the MACEDONIAN EMPIRE. It became a flourishing Hellenic city under the SELEUCID EMPIRE and PARTHIA. Excavations of the huge site have uncovered much from all periods, including the early stele of Naram-Sin and the Code of Hammurabi, among many objects taken by the Elamites from BABYLONIA. Susa was the setting of the biblical story of Esther, the Jewish queen of the Persian King Ahasuerus. According to Muslim tradition, Daniel is buried here.

The remains of ancient Susa in Iran, which date back to the fourth millennium BC. An archaeological treasure house, it was once the resplendent capital of Persia.

SUSA (Italy) City of the Turin province, PIEDMONT region, 33 mi W of Turin. In the 10th century it became the capital city for Adelaide, countess of Savoy and mistress of all Piedmont. In 1176 Frederic Barbarossa set fire to Susa while retreating from LEGNANO. It became important again in the 16th century when it was heavily fortified by Emmanuel Philibert, but its fortifications were dismantled in 1796 by Napoleon I. See also SEGUSIO.

SUSA, Tunisia. See SOUSSE.

SUSAH. See SOUSSE.

SUSAM-ADASI. See SAMOS.

SUSIANA. See ELAM, KHUZESTAN.

SUSQUEHANNA LOWER FERRY. See HAVRE DE GRACE.

SUSQUEHANNA RIVER (United States) River, 444 mi long, which rises in OTSEGO LAKE in central New York State, then flows SE and SW through E central Pennsylvania to CHESAPEAKE BAY near Havre de Grace, Maryland. Its chief tributary is the West Branch, rising in W Pennsylvania. The river is not suitable for navigation but is useful for producing hydroelectric power. Being in an anthracite coal area, the river has mining and industrial cities on its banks, such as Binghamton, New York, and HARRISBURG, Pittston, and WILKES-BARRE, Pennsylvania. The WYOMING VALLEY, a 20-mi-long region on the river in northeastern Pennsylvania, was the scene of the Wyoming Valley massacre in 1778.

In 1779, during the American Revolution, John Sullivan led an expedition up the Susquehanna into western New York State to retaliate against the Iroquois Indians for their raids on settlers. He was joined on the way by James Clinton, who brought another force down the river from Otsego Lake. In June 1972 the river was flooded by rains from Hurricane Agnes, and did enormous damage to cities and towns on its banks. In March 1979 the worst nuclear power reactor accident in history occurred on Three Mile Island in the river near Harrisburg.

SUSSEX (England) Former discrete English county, now divided into East Sussex, with its admin. hq. at LEWES, and West Sussex with its admin. hq. at CHICHESTER. It was also a medieval Anglo-Saxon kingdom, traditionally founded by the Saxon king Aelle in the late fifth century AD. Defeating the Romano-British, the kingdom remained independent until subject at various times to KENT and MERCIA in the sixth and seventh centuries. Conquered in 771 by Offa of Mercia, it remained under Mercia until Egbert of WESSEX brought it under his sway in 825. In 1066 William the Conqueror landed here at PEVENSEY and defeated King Harold of England at HASTINGS. The area has numerous prehistoric remains and Iron Age hill forts.

SUSSEX, EAST. See SUSSEX.

SUSSEX, WEST. See SUSSEX.

SUTH-HAMTUN. See SOUTHAMPTON.

SUTTER'S MILL (California) Former settlement, founded by John A. Sutter, a pioneer who received a Mexican land grant in 1839 that included the site of present SACRAMENTO. Another pioneer, James W. Marshall, undertook to build a sawmill for Sutter on his grant on the AMERICAN RIVER. On Jan. 24, 1848, while building it, Marshall discovered gold in the water. Although an attempt was made to keep the news secret, word leaked out, and by 1849 a gold rush involving the whole nation was under way. Prospectors invaded Sutter's land, killed his cattle, and destroyed his mill, so that by 1852 he and Marshall were both ruined. In the meantime, however, Sacramento had been founded and SAN FRANCISCO's population had grown from approximately 800 to 25,000. The village of Coloma, 36 miles northeast of Sacramento, occupies the site of Sutter's mill.

SUTTON HOO (England) Rich archaeological site on the Deben River in Suffolk, opposite Woodbridge, 8 mi ENE of Ipswich. Here, before and after World War II, a boat burial of a seventh-century AD king of EAST ANGLIA was uncovered. Apparently no body was ever laid here, hence it was probably a memorial cenotaph, possibly for King Redwald. The grave goods have been called the richest treasure ever found in Great Britain. The finds in the Anglo-Saxon boat included jewelry, a helmet, a standard, a gold-embellished sword, a decorated shield, Merovingian coins, a great silver dish of Byzantine workmanship, and other implements, weapons, and utensils. Garnets, gold, and silver were much in evidence. The finds are in the British Museum.

SUVALKAI. See SUWAŁKI.

SUVALKI. See SUWAŁKI.

SÜVEYDIYE. See SELEUCIA PIERIA.

SUWAŁKI [*Lithuanian:* **Suvalkai;** *Russian:* **Suvalki**] (Poland) Region and city in the NE, E of the Masurian Lakes. During World War I it was the scene of several battles in the first half of 1915, with particularly intense fighting on February 7–14. Divided after 1919, the northern part of Suwalki went to LITHUANIA, and the southern to Poland. Assigned to GERMANY in 1939, it was retaken by the Soviets in 1944 during World War II. It was part of Belorussian SSR until reassigned to Poland in August 1945.

SUZDAL (USSR) City of the central European Soviet Union, near Moscow. Founded after 1000 AD as a fortress town and soon merged with ROSTOV, in the 11th and 12th centuries it developed as a principal city of the grand duchy of Vladimir-Suzdal and became an important center of northeastern RUSSIA. It was sacked by the Tatars in 1238 and thereafter declined, falling to the grand duchy of MOSCOW in 1451. Historic structures include the kremlin, a cathedral, a monastery, and several episcopal palaces dating from the 15th to 18th centuries. See also VLADIMIR.

SVALBARD (Norway) Island group, including SPITSBERGEN, in the Arctic Ocean, approx. 400 mi N of the Norwegian mainland. Known to the Norse by 1194, it was then forgotten until its rediscovery in 1596 by the Dutch navigator William Barents. After Henry Hudson reported good whaling here in 1607, the area became a subject of dispute between English and Dutch whalers that was eventually resolved by compromise. Fifty years after the discovery of coal, Norway, Sweden and Russia negotiated for the islands, and they became a Norwegian possession by a treaty signed at Paris in 1920 with several nations, including the USSR, allowed mining concessions. In World War II Svalbard was raided in 1941 by the Allies who evacuated the civilian population to Great Britain. A subsequent German garrison was forced out in 1942 by Norway, and in September 1943 the area's mines were bombarded by the German battleships *Tirpitz* and *Scharnhorst*. The coal-mining operations have been revived, with Soviet mining concessions taking one-third of the coal produced.

SVEABORG. See SUOMENLINNA.

SVERDLOVSK [*former:* **Ekaterinburg, Yekaterinburg**] (USSR) Capital city of Sverdlovsk oblast, in the E foothills of the central Urals on the Iset River. Founded in 1721 by Peter the Great as a fort and metallurgical factory, in 1723 it was named Ekaterinburg in honor of Peter the Great's wife, later Empress Catherine I. During the Russian Revolution, Czar Nicholas II and his family were imprisoned here in 1917 and shot by the Bolsheviks on July 16, 1918. The city was renamed in 1924 for the Bolshevik leader Y.M. Sverdlov.

SVERIGE. See SWEDEN.

SVIR (USSR) River in Leningrad oblast, flowing from Lake Onega to Lake Ladoga. In World War II it served as a battle line between the Finns and the Soviets in 1941 and between the Germans and the Soviets in 1944.

SVISHTOV [Sistova, Svištov] (Bulgaria) River port town of Tŭrnovo province in the N, on the DANUBE RIVER. Dating from Roman times, it was under Turkish rule from the 15th to 19th centuries. On Aug. 4, 1791 it was the site of the signing of the Treaty of Sistova, which set the boundary between AUSTRIA and the OTTOMAN EMPIRE.

SVIŠTOV. See SVISHTOV.

SWABIA [*former:* **Alamannia;** *German:* **Schwaben**] (West Germany) Medieval duchy of widely shifting boundaries and rulers, covering modern Baden-Württemberg and SW Bavaria in S West Germany. AUGSBURG is the chief city in the E, STUTTGART in the W. It borders on Switzerland and Austria to the S and France to the SW. The name is still used locally within Germany. Settled in the third century AD, its original Germanic inhabitants were the Suevi and Alammani, and until the 11th century it was also known as Alamannia. It once included ALSACE and part of SWITZERLAND.

Conquered in the fifth and sixth centuries by the Franks, it was made a duchy in the 10th century, then became a fief of Emperor Henry IV, and was ruled by the Hohenstaufen dukes, kings, and emperors from 1105 to 1254. Leagues of virtually independent Swabian cities, chief of which were Augsburg, FREIBURG, CONSTANCE and ULM, were formed to protect trade and to maintain regional peace, the most important of them in 1331 and from 1488 to 1534. At the Diet of REGENSBURG of 1801 to 1803, held under the influence of Napoleon I, many of the small feudal and ecclesiastical holdings were absorbed by BAVARIA, BADEN, and WÜRTTEMBERG. See also HOHENZOLLERN, REUTLINGEN.

SWANENDAEL. See LEWES.

SWANKALOK. See SAWANKHALOK.

SWANSEA (United States) Village of SE MASSACHUSETTS, 3 mi NW of Fall River, on an inlet of Mount Hope Bay. Settled in 1632, it was the site of the first important battle in King Philip's War in 1675, when many of its inhabitants were massacred.

SWANSEA (Wales) Seaport and admin. hq. of West Glamorgan, at the mouth of the river Towe. It was once occupied by the Romans and later was associated with the Danes. Early in the 12th century the Norman Henry de Newburgh built a castle here that has since disappeared. A borough existed here as early as 1135. Bishop Henry of St. David's built a castle and founded St. David's hospital in 1331. The ruins still remain. The Knights Hospitallers, a medieval Crusading order, held a church in the parish of Church St. Mary. By the middle of the 19th century Swansea was almost the only British copper smelting town, and its Metal Exchange was the center of the world trade in copper. The heart of the city was destroyed by German bombing in 1941 in World War II but has since been rebuilt. The poet Dylan Thomas was born here in 1914.

SWATOW [Shan-T'ou] (China) Town of Kuangtung province, in the SE, on the S side of the mouth of the Han Shui River, 170 mi NW of Hong Kong. It grew from a village after it was made a treaty port in 1869, following the Second Opium War. During World War II it was taken and held by the Japanese until 1945.

SWAZILAND Kingdom in S Africa, bordering on Mozambique and the Republic of South Africa. Its capital is Mbabane. Bantu people were here in the 16th century. It was settled in the 1880's by the Swazi branch of the Zulu nation, whose aggressions they fled. Its independence was guaranteed in 1881 and 1884 by the British and Transvaal governments. Following the Boer War of 1899 to 1902, it was administered by the British governor of the TRANSVAAL. In 1906 his powers were transferred to a British High Commissioner. The Swazi Paramount Chief gained full internal authority in 1941. In 1949 Great Britain rejected South Africa's request for control over Swaziland, and in 1963 limited self-government was introduced. Independence was granted in 1968. King Sobhuza II began his reign in 1921, strengthened his power in 1973, and died in 1982. The Swazis continue to resist union with South Africa, desired by the Afrikaner minority here. A rubber-stamp parliament was opened in 1979.

SWEDEN [*Swedish:* **Sverige**] Kingdom of N Europe, it lies in E Scandinavia between Norway to the W and the Gulf of Bothnia and the Baltic Sea to the E; it is generally mountainous in the north and low-lying in the south. It is today one of the world's most highly industrialized nations, with a population enjoying great material prosperity. Although Sweden now follows a policy of cautious nonalignment in foreign affairs, the country has a proud military tradition and was at one time the chief power of northeastern Europe. The nation's capital is STOCKHOLM.

Sweden was originally inhabited by the Svear and Gotar people who merged in the sixth century AD when the Svear defeated the Gotar. Swedish Vikings were active in trading and colonizing in RUSSIA, down to the BLACK SEA. In the following centuries, Swedes were engaged in wars with their Danish and Norwegian neighbors. In the 12th century southern Sweden was united under a king. Royal authority however remained weak due to the strength of the nobility and the power of the country's cities. Meanwhile the Swedes were slowly converted to Christianity between the ninth and 12th centuries.

By the Union of KALMAR of 1397 Sweden was united with DENMARK and NORWAY under Queen Margaret I of Denmark. However the Danes were unable to control the Swedes, and following the massacre known as the Stockholm Blood Bath of 1520, by which the Danes tried to assert their dominance, the Swedes declared their independence in 1523.

Gustavus I, who reigned from 1523 to 1560, is traditionally regarded as the founder of modern Sweden.

Under him Lutherism became the state religion. Under Gustavus Adolphus (reigned 1611–32), Sweden reached its zenith, becoming a great European power and winning INGRIA and KARELIA from RUSSIA in 1617 and most of LIVONIA from POLAND. In the Thirty Years War Sweden won victories at BREITENFELD in 1631 and LÜTZEN in 1632 and by the Treaty of Westphalia of 1648 gained POMERANIA and BREMEN.

Sweden's southern provinces were recovered from Denmark in 1660, but in the 18th century Sweden's fortunes waned. Despite initial successes in the Great Northern War of 1700 to 1721, the country was later defeated and by the Peace of Nystad of 1721 lost most of her possessions in continental Europe. Sweden's relations with FRANCE became close.

During the Napoleonic Wars Sweden fought first against France, then Russia, to which country she lost FINLAND in 1809. After 1810 French Marshal Bernadotte, adopted heir of the king and later Charles XIV, dominated Swedish affairs. He founded the present reigning dynasty. Sweden was again at war with Napoleon in 1813 and by the Treaty of Kiel in 1814 gained Norway from Denmark. The personal union of the crowns of Norway and Sweden was dissolved in 1905.

In the late 19th and early 20th centuries, Sweden experienced widespread industrialization, which was met by a comprehensive program of social welfare legislation, initiated by the growing Social Democrat Party. Over 1 million Swedes emigrated to the United States between the 1870's and World War I. In foreign affairs, Sweden pursued a consistent policy of armed neutrality throughout the 20th century, thus avoiding involvement in both world wars. She became a member of the United Nations in 1946, but in furtherance of her policy of nonalignment refused membership in both NATO and the European Economic Community. See also SCANDINAVIA.

SWELLENDAM [Zwellendam] (South Africa) Town of SW CAPE PROVINCE, 115 mi E of Cape Town, in the Bree River valley. Founded in 1745, it is one of the oldest towns in South Africa. In 1795 it initiated a rebellion against the Dutch East India Company, proclaiming a "free republic," but calling for the "absolute enslavement of all Hottentots and Bushmen." It quietly surrendered to the British a short time later.

SWIDNICA [German: Schweidnitz] (Poland) City of S central Wrocław province, 33 mi SW of Wrocław. Founded in the first part of the 13th century, it was one of the first residences of the Piast dukes of SILESIA and became a leading center of commerce. Passed with its principality to BOHEMIA in the late 14th century, it endured suffering and severe damage in the Hussite Wars of the 15th century and in the Thirty Years War. Ceded to PRUSSIA in the 1740's, it was again victimized in the Silesian Wars, particularly during the sieges of 1757 to 1759 and 1761/62. It was assigned to Poland by the Potsdam Conference of 1945. Historic buildings include a 14th-century church and a 13th-century town hall.

SWINEMÜNDE. See ŚWINOUJŚCIE.

ŚWINOUJŚCIE [German: Swinemünde] (Poland) Port city on the Baltic Sea, on the N coast of Usedom Island, at the mouth of the Świna River, 37 mi NNW of Szczecin. Chartered in 1765, it was part of the Prussian province of POMERANIA. In World War II the German battleship *Lützow* was sunk in the harbor of this German naval base during a bombing raid in April 1945. Captured by the Soviets May 5, 1945, the port was assigned to Poland by the Potsdam Conference of 1945.

SWISS CONFEDERATION. See SWITZERLAND.

SYBARIS (Italy) Archaeological site, near modern Terranova de Sibari, in Cosenza province, N CALABRIA region, on the Gulf of Tarentum. The oldest Greek colony in MAGNA GRAECIA, founded by Achaeans c.720 BC, it prospered on trade and agriculture and became famous in history and literature for its size, wealth, and luxurious ways, the origin of the word "sybaritic." It was utterly destroyed and buried, by diverting a stream over its ruins, by its sister colony CROTONE in 510 BC and was never rebuilt. Athens established a new colony, THURII, near the site in 443 BC. The ruins of Sybaris were rediscovered far beneath the river mud by a U.S. expedition in the 1960's after eight years of arduous exploration. One of Sybaris's colonies was PAESTUM.

SYCAMINUM. See HAIFA.

SYDNEY (Australia) The country's largest city and capital of NEW SOUTH WALES in the E, on Port Jackson inlet, on the Pacific Ocean. The first British settlement in Australia, it was founded in 1788 as a penal settlement on Botany Bay and was named after Captain Cook's benefactor, Viscount Sydney. A major Allied military base in World War II, Sydney has notable buildings, including the State Parliament House of 1811 to 1817, the Old Mint Building of 1811, Government House of 1837 to 1845, the Town Hall of 1889, and the Sydney Opera House of 1974, designed by Joern Utzon of Denmark.

SYDNEY (Canada) City on CAPE BRETON ISLAND, NOVA SCOTIA, in Sydney Harbor, an inlet of the Atlantic Ocean. Founded in 1783 by United Empire Loyalists, exiles from the American Revolution, it was the capital of Cape Breton province from 1784 to 1820. St. George's Church here dates from 1786 and is one of the oldest Anglican churches in Canada.

SYEDLETS. See SIEDLCE.

SYENE. See ASWAN.

SYLT. See FRISIAN ISLANDS.

SYMMES PURCHASE. See OHIO.

SYRA. See SYROS.

SYRACUSAE. See SYRACUSE, Italy.

SYRACUSE [ancient: Syracusae; Italian: Siracusa] (Italy) Ancient city of MAGNA GRAECIA, in SE SICILY, on the Ionian Sea, 130 mi SE of Palermo. The principal city of Greek colonial expansion into Sicily, it was founded in 734 BC by colonists from CORINTH and grew rapidly, founding colonies of its own. In 485 BC Gelon took possession of the city without opposition, suppressing democratic government and making it the seat

The magnificent harbor of Sydney, Australia, in 1907. The harbor is now graced by the fantastically modern opera house of 1974. Sydney was founded as a penal colony.

of his power. Under his generally benign rule, Syracuse became the principal Greek city of the West, gaining fame in 480 BC for a decisive victory over CARTHAGE at HIMERA.

Gelon's brother and successor, Hiero I (478–467 BC), made Syracuse one of the great centers of Greek culture. The dramatist Aeschylus and the poet Pindar lived at his court. Soon after Hiero's death, democracy was reestablished, and Syracuse extended her control over eastern Sicily. In a famous battle in 414 BC it defeated an Athenian expedition under Nicias, Alcibiades, and Lamachus and in 413 BC won a stunning victory over the Athenian fleet, humiliating the once invincible empire of ATHENS, and assuring the eventual Spartan victory in the Peloponnesian Wars. The Athenian captives were held in the quarries here, which can still be seen today.

The city reverted to tyranny in 406 BC, when Dionysius the Elder acceded to power. Under him Syracuse achieved the highest point of its power, expansion and grandeur, dominating the whole of southernmost Italy, and enjoying a period of cultural brilliance. The philosopher Plato was to visit it several times as an adviser, and it was the birthplace of both the poet Theocritus and, later, the mathematician-physicist Archimedes.

Following the death of the elder Dionysius in 367 BC, the heroic Greek figure Timoleon appeared just as a menace was rising from Carthage. He led Syracuse to a decisive victory over Carthage and acceded to power briefly, ruling benevolently. Upon his death, however, Syracuse returned to tyranny under Agathocles (317–280 BC).

The city then reverted to democratic government for several decades until Hiero II reestablished tyranny in the late fourth to early third centuries BC. He made an alliance with ROME that continued through the First Punic War. Syracuse, however, unwisely abandoned its Roman alliance in favor of one with Carthage. As a result, in the Second Punic War the city was destroyed in 212 BC by the Roman consul Marcellus, ending its long period of cultural hegemony. It was while directing the defense of Syracuse in this war that Archimedes perished.

Under the BYZANTINE EMPIRE from 535 AD, Syracuse became the capital of Sicily. Destroyed by Saracens in 878 AD, it was next conquered by the Normans in 1085, when it became part of the Norman kingdom of Sicily; but it remained unimportant in the Middle Ages. During World War II it was taken by the British on July 12, 1943.

Most outstanding of its historic remains are an Archaic Greek temple, the fountain of Arethusa, the ruins of a temple to Apollo, a cathedral from the seventh century AD, and a 13th-century castle built by Emperor Frederick II—all on the island of Ortygia, the oldest part of the ancient city. On the mainland are a Greek theater from the fifth century BC, still used for performances; a Roman amphitheater from the second century AD; the large Greek fortress of Euralus; the extensive catacombs of St. John, dating from the fifth to sixth centuries AD, and the grotto of Dionysius, in a grove behind the theater.

SYRACUSE (United States) City in central NEW YORK State, approx. 10 mi S of Lake Oneida. It was established in the heartland of the Iroquois Confederation, which was founded in part by Hiawatha and was eventually called the Six Nations. French explorers visited the site in 1615. After 1654, when salt was discovered in the area, it began to be known, and a mission and fort were established in 1655. The first civil settlement began with a trading post in 1786, and a few years later salt works were established. The production of salt became the town's chief industry until after the Civil War, when the effects of competition began to be felt.

Earlier, Syracuse had begun to prosper when the ERIE CANAL reached it in 1819. The Oswego Canal, opened in 1838, joined the Erie here. With the coming of the railroad, manufacturing became the city's main activity. Syracuse was named after SYRACUSE in ancient Sicily when classical names were popular for new towns in upstate New York.

SYRIA, Greece. See SYROS.

SYRIA [Syrian Arab Republic] [*Arabic:* **Ash Shām**] Ancient country and modern republic. Historic crossroads at the E end of the Mediterranean Sea, its modern counterpart belies the vastness and complexity of Syria's long history. It was dominated by the early empires of AKKAD and SUMER before 1900 BC, while the Semitic Amorites established several kingdoms in Syria, notably at ALEPPO. Meanwhile the Indo-European HITTITE EMPIRE, moving south from Asia Minor *c.*1800 BC, clashed with the empire of EGYPT between 1750 and 1000 BC on Syrian soil. The two eventually divided the Syrian region between their spheres of influence. Nevertheless large city states, such as UGARIT, flourished in this period, nurturing the earliest writing and the arts. South of Syria, in PALESTINE, the Canaanites were subdued by the wandering Hebrews, but their northern branch became the seafaring people of the maritime empire of PHOENICIA, based on the Lebanese coast of Syria.

From the 11th to the seventh centuries BC the various empires of ASSYRIA to the east invaded the area several times, capturing DAMASCUS in 732 BC. Within a century the succeeding empire of Babylon conquered Syria again, only to be displaced by Cyrus the Great, who took BABYLONIA in 538 BC and united the Middle East under the new empire of PERSIA until 333 BC, when Alexander the Great of the MACEDONIAN EMPIRE defeated Darius III of Persia at ISSUS. Near the site of his victory Alexander founded ANTIOCH, which became the new political and cultural center of Syria. The division of Alexander's empire among his generals in 323 BC gave most of the East to Seleucus, who founded the SELEUCID EMPIRE, based on Syria. It introduced Hellenistic civilization to the area and ruled Syria until the first century BC. Invasions from ARMENIA and PARTHIA ended the dynasty. In 64 BC the

Romans under Pompey conquered the Near East and incorporated Syria into a Roman province.

Under the ROMAN EMPIRE Christianity took root in the area, soon penetrating north from Palestine into Syria. While traveling to Damascus in this period, St. Paul, a Roman civil servant, was converted to Christianity. The first use of the word "Christian" to describe the new religion was used in Antioch. Syria flourished under the empire, contributing emperors and eastern cults to the amalgam that was Roman culture. It then became part of the BYZANTINE EMPIRE, but in 636 AD was lost to Islam when religious schism between Antioch and Constantinople alienated its population and the resurgent Arab hosts defeated the Byzantines at the Battle of the YARMUK. From 661 to 750 the Muslim Umayyad dynasty, ruling from Damascus in Syria, carved out an empire that eventually stretched from SPAIN to INDIA. Syria lost its central position in Islam, however, when the ABBASID CALIPHATE replaced the Umayyad in 750 and moved the center of power to BAGHDAD in Iraq.

In the Middle Ages Syria continued to be a crossroads of dissension as the Crusaders struggled to gain the Holy Land. In 1098 they took Antioch on the First Crusade and expanded east to EDESSA and Aleppo but were forced to defend them against the Byzantine Empire, Fatimids of Egypt, the Seljuk Turks, and finally the great Saladin, sultan of Egypt and Syria. Saladin emerged victorious, but after his death in 1193 AD Syria fell into disarray and in 1260 was devastated by the Mongols. They sacked Damascus and Aleppo, whose inhabitants they massacred. But in the same year the MAMLUK EMPIRE of Egypt defeated the Mongols and dominated Syria until 1516, when the OTTOMAN EMPIRE took over the region. For 400 years the Turks held sway over Syria, interrupted only by a French invasion under Napoleon I in 1798/99, two brief incursions by Egypt from 1831 to 1833 and 1839/40 and an insurrection in 1860/61. Turkish rule weakened and collapsed during World War I as the Arabs of the HEJAZ, acting with those of Syria and supported by the British under Lord Allenby and the legendary Lawrence of Arabia, threw off their yoke.

The Syrian region was made a French mandate under the League of Nations in 1920, and in 1925 Damascus and Aleppo were united to form modern Syria, which became a republic in 1930. In the meantime by agreement LEBANON was carved out of the area as an independent state in 1926. In World War II Syria was at first under the control of the collaborationist French Vichy government. It was captured by the British and Free French in June/July 1941, and the French mandate was brought to an end. In 1944 the Syrian Arab Republic achieved independence, although French troops did not leave the country until 1946.

The nation united briefly with Egypt in 1958 as the United Arab Republic, which was dissolved at Syrian insistence in 1961. In the first Arab-Israeli War of 1948/49 the Syrian armies were defeated, as they were again in 1967 and 1973, by ISRAEL, which occupied the strategic Golan Heights on the border of both countries and formally annexed them in 1981. Syria's invasion of

Lebanon in 1976 to put down the civil war was followed by a ceasefire, which was broken in 1981 by more dissension. While Syrian troops remained in the country, Israel invaded it in June 1982 in pursuit of the Palestine Liberation Organization guerrillas and clashed with the Syrians. A series of uneasy ceasefires were again imposed through 1982 and 1983, while protracted negotiations for the withdrawal of both armies from Lebanon continued. See also CANAAN, MONGOL EMPIRES.

SYRIAN ARAB REPUBLIC. See SYRIA.

SYROS [*Syra*] [*ancient:* **Syria;** *Greek:* **Siros**] (Greece) The major island of the CYCLADES group, in the AEGEAN SEA, with its capital at HERMOUPOLIS. Held by VENICE in the Middle Ages, it was taken from the Venetians by the Turks in 1537 and was part of the OTTOMAN EMPIRE until 1832. During the Greek war of independence from 1821 to 1829, the island was protected by the French and maintained its neutrality, becoming a haven and home for many Greek refugees and of a large Roman Catholic population here since the Middle Ages. Thereafter it became a commercial center of some importance. Hermoupolis is the capital of the island and of the Cyclades nome.

SYUT. See ASYUT.

SZALÁNKEMÉN. See NOVI SLANKAMEN.

SZATMÁR. See SATU-MARE.

SZATMÁR-NÉMETI. See SATU-MARE.

SZÁVA. See SAVA RIVER.

SZCZECIN [*German:* **Stettin**] (Poland) Major port and provincial capital, in the N, near the mouth of the ODER RIVER, 125 mi NE of Poznán. Settled for over 2,000 years, before the ninth century AD it had a Slavic fortress and was already of commercial importance. Made part of the Polish state at the end of the 10th century, by 1124 it was the largest city in POMERANIA and from the 12th to the 17th centuries was the residence of the dukes of Pomerania. In 1360 it joined the HANSEATIC LEAGUE. The peace of Stettin, ending the Northern War between Denmark and Sweden, was signed here in 1570. Passed to SWEDEN by the Peace of Westphalia in 1648 at the end of the Thirty Years War, it was ceded to PRUSSIA in 1720, at the end of the Great Northern War. It was held by France during the Napoleonic Wars from 1806 to 1813. In World War II it was heavily bombed in 1944 and 1945 and was taken by the Soviets on April 6, 1945 after a long battle and siege. The Potsdam Conference of 1945 assigned it to Poland, and the German inhabitants were expelled. It has a Renaissance castle and many other fine old buildings.

SZCZECINEK [*German:* **Neustettin**] (Poland) City and resort in Koszalin province, 41 mi SE of Koszalin. A foundation of the dukes of POMERANIA, it was chartered in 1310. Before World War II it was in EAST PRUSSIA. During that war fierce fighting here destroyed a large part of the town, which finally fell to Soviet troops in January 1945. It was assigned to Poland after the war at the Potsdam Conference of 1945.

SZCZECIŃSKI. See STARGARD SZCZECIŃSKI.

SZCZYTNO [*German:* **Ortelsburg**] (Poland) City of Olsztyn province, in the N, 27 mi SE of Olsztyn. Formerly part of EAST PRUSSIA in Germany, it was founded in the 13th century. In World War I it was captured and destroyed by the Russians in 1914. During World War II it fell to the Soviets in January 1945, and was assigned to Poland by the Potsdam Conference.

SZECHUAN. See SZECHWAN.

SZECHWAN [**Szechuan**] [*Mandarin:* **Ssu-ch'uan**] (China) Province in the SW, bounded on the far W by Tibet. Its capital is CH'ENG-TU. Subject to several cultural and ethnic influences, in early Chinese history it was populated entirely by non-Chinese. Often an independent kingdom, it was long ago a center of Thai culture. The Burma-Yunnan trade route introduced an Indian influence, but by the third century AD the region was part of the Chinese empire under the Chin dynasty. During the 1930's the Chinese communists controlled much of Szechwan, and it served as a refuge during the Long March. In the Sino-Japanese War of 1937 to 1945, it was the capital of the Nationalist Government and military headquarters. It sustained Japanese bombing from 1938 to 1945. See also CHUNG-KING.

SZEGED [*German:* **Szegedin**] (Hungary) Port city on the Tisza River, in the S, on the Yugoslav border. In the ninth or 10th century, it was a heavily fortified trading center and was the site of the first national assembly of the Magyar tribes under their chief, Arpad. Ravaged by the Tatars in the 13th century, it was under Turkish rule from 1542 to 1686. The city was damaged by a flood in 1879. Surviving historic structures include a striking 13th-century Romanesque tower.

SZEGEDIN. See SZEGED.

SZÉKESFEHÉRVÁR [*ancient and medieval:* **Alba Regia;** *German:* **Stuhlweissenburg**] (Hungary) City and seat of Fejér county, in the W central region. Settled in Roman times, it was the first capital of the Magyar kings and capital of Hungary until the 14th century. During the Middle Ages it was still called Alba Regia. It was an important fortress town. Many of its buildings were destroyed at the end of the Turkish occupation of Hungary between 1686 and 1688. The town was rebuilt in the 18th century but was again severely damaged during World War II. The foundations of the medieval cathedral, where the kings of Hungary were crowned and were buried, and the royal palace have been excavated and are on view.

SZE-MAO. See FU-HSING-CHEN.

SZENTGOTTHÁRD [*English:* **Saint Gotthard**] (Hungary) Town in the W, on the Rába River, near the Austrian border. On Aug. 1, 1664 it was the scene of a battle in which the Turks were defeated for the first time in Hungary, by the imperial forces under Gen. Montecuccoli. The battle led to the Treaty of VASVÁR, with its twenty-year truce.

SZIGETVÁR (Hungary) Town in the S, W of Pécs.

As a medieval fortress it was heroically defended in 1566 by Miklós Zrinyi and approximately 3,000 men against the Turks under Sultan Sulayman I, who was killed during the siege. Zrinyi was then himself killed, and the fortress fell to the Turks. It is the site of a mosque built for Sulayman I, which is now a church.

SZISZEK. See SISAK.

SZOLNOK (Hungary) River port, city, and county seat, 55 mi SE of Budapest, where the Tisza and Zagyva rivers meet. Its fortress was much fought over by the Magyars and Turks. It is an old settlement that had a prosperous trade in salt from the beginning of Arpad Magyar rule in the late ninth century until the 19th century.

SZOMBATHELY [*ancient:* **Sabaria, Savaria;** *German:* **Steinamanger**] (Hungary) City and seat of Vas county, in the W, near the Austrian border. It was founded as Sabaria in 48 AD by the Roman Emperor Claudius, and from the third century it was the Roman capital of PANNONIA. In 193 AD Septimius Severus was proclaimed emperor here. The birthplace of St. Martin of Tours *c.*315 AD, it was destroyed by the Huns in the fifth century but was rebuilt.

There are an 18th-century cathedral here, an episcopal palace, and Dominican church. Recent excavations have revealed the remains of various Roman buildings, including a bath, a sanctuary of Zeus, and a temple of Isis, now partly restored as an open-air theater. In the center of the city sections of Roman roads, a basilica of the fourth century AD, and the foundations of a medieval castle have been exposed.

SZTALINVAROS. See DUNAÚJVÁROS.

T

TAANACH [*modern:* **Tell ti Innik**] (Israel) Ancient city of CANAAN, 5 mi SE of MEGIDDO, in the Israeli-occupied West Bank. According to Judges 5:19 in the Old Testament, the Canaanite general Sisera was defeated here by the Israelites under Barak and Deborah. An important royal city during the time of Solomon, it has remains dating from the 26th century BC.

TABARCA [**Tabarka**] [*ancient:* **Thabraca**] (Tunisia) Town, port, and capital of Tabarca district, on the Mediterranean Sea, 55 mi E of Bône, NW Tunisia. Famous in Roman and early Christian times as a marble-shipping port, it is the site of a 17th-century Genoan castle and two Turkish forts.

TABARISTAN. See MAZANDERAN.

TABARIYA. See TIBERIAS.

TABARKA. See TABARCA.

TABASCO (Mexico) State in E Mexico on the Gulf of Campeche. With a hot, wet climate, Tabasco's economy rests mainly on tropical agriculture, but the discovery of oil along the coast is bringing change. The first European in the area was Juan de Grijalva in 1518, followed in 1519 by Hernando Cortés, who fought the Indians here on his way to TENOCHTITLAN (Mexico City) and the conquest of the AZTEC EMPIRE. Tabasco was conquered for SPAIN in 1530 by Francisco de Montejo. ENGLAND contested its possession with Spain in the 17th and 18th centuries. After Mexican independence Tabasco became a state in 1824. Villahermosa is the capital, and nearby are many Olmec stone sculptures. Frontera is the principal port.

TABGHA. See TABIGHA.

TABIGHA [**Tabgha**] [*Greek:* **Heptapegon**] (Israel) Locality in NW PALESTINE, on the N shore of the Sea of Galilee, 6 mi N of Tiberias, in Northern district, NE Israel. Inhabited since Paleolithic times, it is the site of the church of the Multiplication of the Loaves commemorating Christ's feeding of the Five Thousand, which is reputed to have taken place here.

TABLE BAY. See CAPE PROVINCE, GOOD HOPE, CAPE OF.

TABLE MOUNTAIN [*Afrikaans:* **Tafelberg**] (South Africa) Mountain in SW Cape Province, overlooking CAPE TOWN and Table Bay, S South Africa. The mountain is famous for its flat summit and is often shrouded in a mist known as the Table Cloth. Gold was mined here in the 1850's.

TABOR (Czechoslovakia) Town in S BOHEMIA, 55 mi S of Prague, W Czechoslovakia. Founded in 1420 by John Žižka, it became a stronghold of the Taborites, the extreme chiliastic wing of the Hussites who believed that they were the elect prophesied in the Book of Revelation. They named their center after the biblical site of Israelite victories and Christ's prediction of his Second Coming. They set up an egalitarian, sexually promiscuous, and communal society here in expectation of the destruction of all towns in the world, save their own.

The Taborites set out on a program of massacring the unjust around them. By October 1421 Žižka and the moderate Hussites had turned on the Taborites and destroyed them here. The town was damaged during the Thirty Years War and declined thereafter.

TABOR, MOUNT [*Arabic:* **Jabal at-Tur;** *Hebrew:* **Har Tavor**] (Israel) Mountain near the edge of the Plain of Esdraelon, 6 mi SE of Nazareth, in Northern district, N Israel. Mentioned in Egyptian inscriptions of the 13th century BC, it was the scene of the victory of the Israelites led by Barak over the Canaanites led by Sisera in the 11th century BC. Traditionally it is the site of the Transfiguration of Christ and where he predicted his Second Coming. See also ESDRAELON, PLAIN OF; TAANACH.

TABORA (Tanzania) Town and capital of Tabora region, 430 mi WNW of Dar es Salaam, W central Tanzania. Founded by Arab traders c.1820, it became an important trading center. Captured by the Germans in 1891, it was made the administrative center of German East Africa. During World War I it was captured by Belgian forces on Sept. 19, 1916.

TABRIZ [**Tabrīz**] [*ancient:* **Tauris**] (Iran) City and capital of East AZERBAIJAN, 350 mi WNW of Teheran, NW Iran. The fourth-largest city of Iran, it enjoyed a strategic position on the old trade route between Russia and Turkey. The capital of ARMENIA in the third century AD under King Tiridates III, it was captured by Seljuk Turks in 1054. Under Ghazan Khan, the Mongol ruler of PERSIA, it was made the administrative center of a considerable empire in 1295 but was captured by Tamerlane in the 14th century. Tabriz became the capital of the empire of Shah Ismail in the early 16th century and was occupied by the OTTOMAN EMPIRE in 1514 and again frequently thereafter. After 1918 it was a stronghold of the Nationalist movement and the scene of a revolution in 1946, when the Soviet-supported Tudeh Party held power for a few months. It has few historical remains because of frequent earthquakes.

TACAPE. See GABÉS.

TACLOBAN (Philippines) City, port, and capital of Leyte province, on NE LEYTE Island, on an inlet of Leyte Gulf. A port since 1874, it fell to the Japanese in 1942 during World War II. United States troops landed here in the first stage of their campaign to liberate the Philippines and recaptured the city on Oct. 21, 1944. It then became the temporary capital of the Philippines until the fall of MANILA.

TACNA [*former:* **San Pedro de Tacna**] (Peru) Town and capital of Tacna department, S Peru, 40 mi N of Arica, Chile. A prosperous colonial city, it became famous in 1826 during the wars of independence from SPAIN as the Heroic City of Tacna. It passed to Chile in 1880 during the War of the Pacific, following the Chilean defeat of Peruvian and Bolivian forces nearby. It was returned to Peru in 1929.

TACOMA [*former:* **Commencement City**] (United States) City and port in W central WASHINGTON State, 26 mi S of Seattle, on Commencement Bay and Puget Sound. A major port and one of the chief industrial cities of the Northwest, it was once considered the lumber capital of America. Settled in 1864, it was reached by the Northern Pacific Railroad in 1873. An air force base and army training center are nearby.

TACUBA (Mexico) Suburb NW of MEXICO CITY, in Federal District, central Mexico. Tacuba was founded by Tepaneca Indians and later became part of the Aztec Confederacy. It was partly destroyed following its occupation by the Spanish in 1521. There are many archaeological remains in the area. See also AZTEC EMPIRE.

TADCASTER (England) Village in North Yorkshire, 9 mi SW of York. It was the site of the Roman military station Calcaria.

TADMOR. See PALMYRA.

TADOUSSAC (Canada) Village in S QUEBEC, 117 mi NE of Quebec, at the confluence of the St. Lawrence and Saguenay rivers. Visited by Jacques Cartier in 1535, it later was the home of the oldest Christian mission in Canada and a major fur-trading post.

TADZHIKISTAN. See TADZHIK SOVIET SOCIALIST REPUBLIC.

TADZHIK SOVIET SOCIALIST REPUBLIC [**Tadzhikistan, Tajikistan, Tajik SSR**] (USSR) Constituent republic of the USSR, in SE Soviet Central Asia, N of Afghanistan. Dushanbe is the capital. A chiefly mountainous region, rich in mineral resources, it is named after the Tadzhiks, an Iranian people who established themselves here by the 10th century AD. Conquered by Mongols in the 13th century, it became part of the khanate of BUKHARA in the 16th century. It was ruled by various weak khanates in the 19th century and fell prey to Russian expansion in the 1880's and 1890's. The Tadzhiks rebelled against Russian rule in 1917 but were put down by the Red Army in 1921. Tadzhikistan became a constituent republic of the Soviet Union in 1929.

TAEGU [*Japanese:* **Taiku, Taikyu**] (South Korea) City and capital of North Kyŏngsang province, on the Kum River, 55 mi NNW of Pusan, SE South Korea. Inhabited as early as the eighth century AD, it was one of three major market cities under the Yi dynasty (1392–1910). During the Korean War it was important in the defense of the PUSAN beachhead and became the temporary capital of South Korea in August 1950.

TAEJON [*Japanese:* **Taiden**] (South Korea) City in W central South Korea, 70 mi NW of Taegu. It was an old but poor village until the early 20th century, when rail lines were built. It was the temporary capital of the Republic of KOREA for a time during the Korean War of 1950 to 1953, in which it was damaged.

TAENARUM. See MATAPAN, CAPE.

TAFELBERG. See TABLE MOUNTAIN.

TAFILALT [**Tafilet**] (Morocco) Saharan oasis in Ksar es-Souk province, stretching 30 mi along the Ziz River, S of the High Atlas Mts, S Morocco. The old capital of the oasis was the Berber stronghold of Sijilmassa, which was founded on a Saharan caravan route in 757 AD. It became a prosperous city but was destroyed in 1363 and again in 1818 by Ait Atta nomads. Although the French occupied it after 1917, they did not completely subjugate the region until the 1930's. Today the oasis is the site of fortified villages and palm groves.

TAFILET. See TAFILALT.

TAGANROG (USSR) City and port in SW Russian SFSR, on the N coast of Taganrog Gulf, on the Sea of Azov, 45 mi W of Rostov-on-Don. Originally the site of a colony of PISA, it was sacked by Mongols in the 13th century. It was established in 1698 by Peter the Great as a fortress and naval base but was continually captured by the Turks until it passed to RUSSIA in 1769. Czar Alexander I died in the imperial palace here in 1825. Anton Chekhov the dramatist was born here.

TAGAUNG (Burma) Village in Sagaing division, upper Burma, on the IRRAWADDY RIVER, 110 mi N of Mandalay. Founded in the sixth century BC by a MANIPUR prince, it is reputedly Burma's oldest capital. There are extensive remains of the ancient city.

TAGINAE (Italy) Ancient village and battlefield in Perugia province, UMBRIA region, near Gubbio, central Italy. In 552 AD the Byzantine General Narses defeated and killed the Gothic King Totila here. See BYZANTINE EMPIRE.

TAGLIACOZZO (Italy) Town and battlefield in L'Aquila province, ABRUZZI region, 21 mi SSW of L'Aquila, central Italy. Conradin, the last of the Hohenstaufens, was defeated here by Charles I of Anjou on Aug. 25, 1268 during Charles's conquest of the kingdom of NAPLES.

TAHEIHO. See AIGUN.

TAHITI [*former:* **King George III Island, Otaheite;** *French:* **Taïti**] (France) Island of the Windward Group, SOCIETY ISLANDS, in the central South Pacific Ocean. The largest of the islands of FRENCH POLYNESIA, it is famous as a South Seas island paradise and is known to many through the paintings of Paul Gauguin. Settled by Polynesians in the 14th century, it was discovered in 1767 by a captain of the British Navy and visited several times by Capt. James Cook. The Tahitian Queen Pomare IV was forced to accept the establishment of a French protectorate in 1842, and the island became a French colony in 1880.

TAHLEQUAH (United States) City in E central OKLAHOMA, in the foothills of the Ozarks, 26 mi ENE of

Muskogee. Settled by Cherokee Indians, it was the capital of the old Cherokee Nation from 1839 to 1907. It has many old Indian buildings.

TAHPANHES. See DAPHNAE.

TAHURE (France) Village, hill, and battleground in Marne department, 30 mi ESE of Rheims, NE France. It was the scene of two battles during World War I: the first took place on Oct. 7, 1915 when it fell to the Germans; and the second occurred on Sept. 25, 1918 when it was recaptured by the Allies.

T'AI-CHOU. See LIN-HAI.

TAIDEN. See TAEJON.

TAIF. See AT-TA'IF.

TAIHOKU. See TAIPEI.

TAIKU. See TAEGU.

TAIKYU. See TAEGU.

T'AI, MOUNT [*ancient:* **Tai-Tsung, T'ai-Yüeh;** *Chinese:* **Tai Shan, T'ai Shan**] (China) Mountain in W central Shantung province, NE China, S of Tsinan. It is one of the five holy peaks of China, revered by Buddhists and Taoists. It was the scene of important sacri-fices under the Han and T'ang dynasties and was worshiped as a deity in its own right. The mountain was believed to control man's fate on earth. Its slopes are covered with temples and shrines.

T'AI-NAN [Tai-nan] [*former:* **Dainan, T'ai-wan, T'ai-yüan, Ta-yüan**] (Taiwan) City on the Taiwan Strait, SW Taiwan. One of the oldest cities of Taiwan, it was settled in 1590 by the Chinese and was the headquarters of the Dutch from 1624 until 1662, when they were expelled by Koxinga (Cheng Ch'eng-kung), who made the city the capital of Taiwan. It remained the political center of the island until the government was moved to Taipei in 1885. Today it is Taiwan's third-largest city.

TAINARON, CAPE. See MATAPAN, CAPE.

TAIOHAE. See HAKAPEHI.

TAIPEH. See TAIPEI.

TAIPEI [Taipeh, T'ai-Pei] [*former:* **Daihoku, Taihoku**] (Taiwan) City and capital of Taiwan, in the N of the island, 121 mi SE of the Chinese mainland. The largest city of Taiwan, it was founded in the 18th century by immigrants from Fukien province in China.

Street in thoroughly modern Taipei, capital of Taiwan. Though a Chinese island, Taiwan has been separated from China for the larger part of a century, much of it under the Japanese.

It developed after becoming the capital of Taiwan in 1885 and expanded further under Japanese rule from 1895 to 1945. It became the provisional capital of the Chinese Nationalists in 1949.

TAISHA (Japan) Town in Shimane prefecture, SW Honshū, 5 mi NW of Izumo, on the Sea of Japan. It is the location of Izumo Taisha, said to be the oldest Shinto shrine in Japan. The grounds of the shrine cover 20 acres, and there are 68 smaller shrines in the vicinity.

TAI SHAN. See T'AI, MOUNT.

TAÏTI. See TAHITI.

TAI-TSUNG. See T'AI, MOUNT.

T'AI-WAN. See T'AI-NAN.

TAIWAN [*Portuguese:* **Formosa**] (Taiwan) Autonomous island state in the Pacific Ocean, separated from the mainland of S CHINA by the 100-mi wide Taiwan Strait. Its capital is TAIPEI. Settled by the Chinese in the seventh century AD, it was colonized by various European powers before passing under Dutch control in 1641. The Dutch were expelled in 1662 by Koxinga (Cheng Ch'eng-kung), who established an independent kingdom that fell to the Manchus in 1683. The island was industrialized following its acquisition by JAPAN in 1895. Returned to China in 1945, it became the refuge of the Chinese Nationalists under Chiang Kai-shek in 1949. In the following years the territorial status of the so-called Republic of China remained an important issue between the major powers, and Taiwan was often protected from feared communist invasion by the UNITED STATES, while its economy boomed. The 1970's saw a decline of the republic's international position as the United States sought friendlier relations with China and as other governments recognized the communist government of mainland China as its legitimate government. In 1971 Taiwan lost its seat on the United Nations. Since the late 1970's Taiwan and Chinese officials have made several overtures toward the eventual reunification of the province with the mainland. The Peking government in 1982 offered Taiwan a directing role in the reunited China's government.

T'AI-YÜAN [**Taiyüan, Yang-Ku**] (China) City and capital of Shansi province, 265 mi SW of Peking, on the Fen River, NE China. An ancient walled city, it was a center of Buddhism in the sixth century AD and became a heavily fortified military base. In 1949 it was taken by the communists after a siege during which thousands starved. Today it is a mining and smelting center in one of the richest coal and iron areas in the world.

T'AI-YÜAN, Taiwan. See T'AI-NAN.

T'AI YÜEH. See T'AI, MOUNT.

TAIZ. See TA'IZZ.

TA'IZZ [**Taiz**] (Yemen) Town and capital of Ta'izz province, in the S Yemen Highlands, 85 mi NW of Aden, Yemen Arab Republic. It was the capital of the Ayyūbid dynasty under Tūrān Shāh, the brother of Saladin, during the 12th century, but the capital was later moved to San'a. It was under Ottoman control from the 16th century until 1918 and was the administrative capital of the Yemen Arab Republic from 1948 to 1962.

TAJIKISTAN. See TADZHIK SOVIET SOCIALIST REPUBLIC.

TAJIK SSR. See TADZHIK SOVIET SOCIALIST REPUBLIC.

TAJIN (Mexico) Ruined city of the Totonac Indians, 6 mi W of PAPANTLA de Olarte in E Mexico. The ruins, only slightly excavated, are those of a pre-Columbian civilization that flourished from *c.*400 to 900 AD, during the Meso-American Classic period. The centerpiece of the ruins is a pyramid 60 feet high. It is in seven tiers and is 82 feet square at the base. Carved stone objects of unusual shape, whose use is unknown, have been found here.

TAKAO. See KAO-HSIUNG.

TAKHT-E JAMSHID. See PERSEPOLIS.

TAKORADI. See SEKONDI-TAKORADI, Ghana.

TAKOW. See KAO-HSIUNG.

TAKSAŚILĀ. See TAXILA.

TAKU [**Ta-Ku**] (China) Town in E Hopei province, 37 mi E of Tientsin, at the mouth of the Hai River, NE China. Once the location of fortresses guarding the outskirts of TIENTSIN, it was besieged by foreign troops in 1860 and again in 1900 during the Boxer Rebellion. The forts were destroyed in 1902.

TALABRIGA, Portugal. See AVEIRO.

TALABRIGA, Spain. See TALAVERA DE LA REINA.

TALAKAD [**Talkad**] (India) Town in Mysore district, 25 mi ESE of Mysore, on the Cauvery River, S India. To the south is the site of an ancient city with ruined Dravidian temples dating from the sixth century AD. Other later temples are notable examples of Chalukyan art. See CHALUKYA.

TALANA HILL. See DUNDEE, South Africa.

TALAS. See DZHAMBUL.

TALAVERA DE LA REINA [*ancient:* **Caesarobriga, Talabriga**] (Spain) Town in Toledo province, on the Tagus River, 41 mi WNW of Toledo, Castile, central Spain. An old Roman town, it was taken from the Moors in 1082 by King Alfonso VI and was an important town in the 16th century, noted for its silk and wool. During the Peninsular campaign of the Napoleonic Wars, on July 28, 1809, the French under Joseph Bonaparte were defeated here by the British and Spanish under Gen. Arthur Wellesley, who was made Viscount Wellington as a result of the victory.

TALCA [*former:* **San Agustín de Talca**] (Chile) City and capital of Talca province and department, 150 mi SSW of Santiago, central Chile. Founded in 1692, it was here that Bernardo O'Higgins formally declared Chilean independence on Feb. 12, 1818. The city was destroyed by an earthquake in 1928.

TALCAHUANO (Chile) City and port in Concepción province, on Concepción Bay, 8 mi NNW of Concepción, S Chile. It is a major port and Chile's main naval station. In its harbor is anchored the Peruvian ironclad vessel *Huáscar,* whose capture in 1879 during the War of the Pacific established the supremacy of the Chilean navy.

TA-LI [Da-Li, Tali] [*former:* **Tungchow**] (China) City in W central Yunnan province, 180 mi W of K'un-Ming, S China. An ancient city strategically placed on the trade route to Burma and northern India, it was the capital of an independent state from the early ninth century until the Mongol conquest of 1253. It is famous for its marble.

TA-LIEN [*Japanese:* **Dairen;** *Russian:* **Dalny**] (China) Major Chinese port in MANCHURIA, on the S coast of Liao-tung peninsula, 20 mi E of PORT ARTHUR, with which it is joined in a common municipality called Lü-ta. In 1899, then under RUSSIA, it became the terminus of the South Manchurian Railroad and a commercial free port. Occupied by JAPAN in 1904 during the Russo-Japanese War, it was a free port again by 1906. The city suffered some damage during World War II and was taken by Soviet troops in August 1945. However, by a treaty with Nationalist China, renewed with Communist China, the Chinese retained sovereignty, but the USSR holds port privileges. The Soviet troops withdrew in 1955.

TALIKOT. See TALIKOTA.

TALIKOTA [Talikot] (India) Town and battlefield in N Mysore, 50 mi SE of Bijapur, W India. The Hindu Raja of VIJAYANAGARA was defeated here in January 1565 by the Muslim sultans of the DECCAN. This defeat led to the breakup of the Vijayanagara Empire.

TALIN. See TALLINN.

TÄLJE. See SÖDERTÄLJE.

TALKAD. See TALAKAD.

TALLADEGA (United States) City and battle site in NE central ALABAMA, in the foothills of the Appalachian Mts, 44 mi E of Birmingham. An army of Creek Indians was defeated here on Nov. 9, 1813 by Andrew Jackson's Tennessee Volunteers. The Creeks were subsequently moved west.

TALLAHASSEE (United States) City and capital of FLORIDA, 210 mi NNW of Tampa. The site of an Indian settlement when discovered by Hernando De Soto in 1539, it was settled by Spanish missionaries but was destroyed by the governor of South Carolina during Queen Anne's War of 1702 to 1713. Tallahassee was founded as the capital of Florida Territory in 1824. The secession resolution was adopted here in 1861, though the city was never captured by Union forces during the Civil War.

TALL AL-'AJJUL (Israel) Ancient site in SW PALESTINE, just S of GAZA on the Gaza Strip, S Israel. The ancient town reached the height of its development between 2300 and 1550 BC, in the Bronze Age; and remains dating from 2100 BC have been discovered here. The largest palace of this period in Palestine was found here, one of five successive palaces excavated.

TALL AL-DAFANA. See DAPHNAE.

TALL AL FAR'AH (Israel) Ancient site in SW PALESTINE, near GAZA, on the Gaza Strip, S Israel. It is thought to be the site of Sharuhen, an important Egyptian fortress dating from the late 17th and early 16th centuries BC. Following the collapse of Hyksos rule in EGYPT it resisted a three-year-long siege by anti-Hyksos Egyptians. It was also an important town of CANAAN and of the Philistines. See PHILISTIA.

TALL AL FUL. See GIBEAH.

TALL AL-KABĪR [Tell El-Kebir] (Egypt) Village and battlefield in Sharqiva governorate, near Zagazig. On Sept. 13, 1882 the British defeated the Egyptians here.

TALL AL-KHALIFĀH. See EZIONGEBER.

TALL AL MUQAYIR. See UR.

TALL AL-UHAIMER. See KISH.

TALL AL WARNA. See ERECH.

TALL BASTA. See BUBASTIS.

TALL BIRĀK (Syria) Ancient site in al-Hasakah governorate, NE Syria. Inhabited from c.3200 to 2200 BC, it was the site of a royal residence built during the reign of the Akkadian King Naram-Sin (2254–2218 BC). It is the location of the Eye Temple where thousands of small stones called eye idols were found. See AKKAD.

TALL-E BAKUN (Iran) Prehistoric site near PERSEPOLIS, in Fārs province, SW central Iran. Inhabited from c.4200 to 3000 BC, it is the most ancient settlement yet discovered in that part of Iran. The painted pottery found here has contributed much to the study of early Iranian art.

TALL HALAF [Tell Halaf] [*former:* **Bit-Bahiani**] (Syria) Ancient Syrian city near Ra's al-'Aya, in al-Hasakah governorate, NE Syria. It developed in prehistoric times, producing exquisite painted pottery, and during the first millennium BC became an Aramaean town known as Bit-Bahiani. Adad-nirari III of ASSYRIA destroyed the city in 808 BC and made the area a province of the Assyrian Empire. It is mentioned in the Old Testament as Gozan, and it was to this place that the Israelites were deported in 722 BC after the Assyrian capture of SAMARIA.

TALL IBRAHIM. See CUTHAH.

TALLINN [*former:* **Revel;** *German:* **Reval;** *Russian:* **Talin**] (USSR) City, port, and capital of the ESTONIAN SSR, on the Gulf of Finland, 200 mi W of Leningrad, W European USSR. The site of a fortified settlement from the first millennium BC, it fell to the Danes in 1219 AD and joined the HANSEATIC LEAGUE in 1285. Sold to the Teutonic Knights in 1346, it passed to SWEDEN in 1561 and was captured by Peter the Great of RUSSIA in 1710 during the Great Northern War. Capital of independent Estonia from 1918 to 1940, it became part of the Soviet Union in 1940 but was under German occupation from 1941 to 1944. Today it is a major Baltic port and industrial center.

TALL SANKARAH. See LARSA.

TAMATAVE [Toamasina] (Madagascar) City, port, and capital of Tamatave province, on the E coast of Madagascar. The chief port of the island, it was settled in the 18th century around a Portuguese trading post. Radama I captured it in 1817 and made it the chief port of the Hova kingdom. In 1894, under French occupation, it was used as a base for the French conquest of the interior. It was rebuilt after being destroyed by a hurricane in 1927.

TAMAULIPAS (Mexico) State in NE Mexico, on the Gulf of Mexico, bordered on the N by Texas. The interior is elevated, while the lowlands and coastal areas are humid. Although agriculture is important, petroleum deposits are the major source of wealth. The Spanish began exploring the region in 1519 and conquered it as they spread out after the fall of the AZTEC EMPIRE in 1521. Settlement did not begin until 1747. Ciudad Victoria, founded in 1750, is the capital. TAMPICO, one of Mexico's major ports, was the site of the Indian kingdom of the Huastec.

TAMBOV (USSR) City in central Russian SFSR, 260 mi SE of Moscow, on the Tsna River. Founded in 1636 as a fortress against the Crimean Tatars on the BELGOROD defense line, it became the capital of a province in the late 18th century.

TAMESA. See THAMES RIVER, England.

TAMESIS. See THAMES RIVER, England.

TAMIL NADU [*former:* **Madras**] (India) State of SE India, on the Bay of Bengal, with its capital at MADRAS. This was an ancient cultural center of the Dravidian peoples; its remains are among the finest in southern India. It was the seat of the CHOLA Empire from the 10th to 13th centuries and of the VIJAYANAGARA Kingdom from 1335 to 1565. Colonized by Europeans in the 16th century, it eventually came under the control of the British, who enlarged its boundaries. Made an autonomous province in 1937, it became part of the Republic of India in 1947, though greatly reduced in size.

TAMLŪK [**Tāmraliptā, Tumluk**] (India) Town and port at the mouth of the GANGES RIVER, in West Bengal, NE India, 30 mi SW of Calcutta. The ancient capital of the Hindu kingdom of Tāmraliptā, or Suhma, it was a Buddhist center in BENGAL by the fifth century BC.

TAMMERFORS. See TAMPERE.

TAMPA (United States) City and port of entry at the mouth of the Hillsborough River, in W central FLORIDA, 210 mi SSE of Tallahassee. Visited by Pánfilo de Narváez in 1528, it was shunned by Europeans for 200 years because of Indian hostility and was only settled in 1823. During the Civil War it was captured by Union forces in May 1864, and in 1898 was the embarkation point for Col. Theodore Roosevelt's Cuba-bound troops. It expanded industrially in the late 19th century and today is Florida's third largest city.

TAMPERE [*Swedish:* **Tammerfors**] (Finland) City and lake port in Häme province, 105 mi NNW of Helsinki, SW Finland. An important trading center since the 11th century, it developed industrially during the 19th century under Russian rule. During the Finnish war of independence, White Russian forces defeated Finnish Bolsheviks here in 1918.

TAMPICO (Mexico) City and port in Tamaulipas state, on the Pánuco River, 6 mi from the Gulf of Mexico, 220 mi NE of Mexico City, NE Mexico. The site of the pre-Columbian Huastec Kingdom, it was settled by Franciscan friars in the 1530's but was destroyed by pirates in 1683. During the Mexican War of 1846 to 1848 it was occupied by U.S. troops. In 1862 it was taken by French forces. The discovery of oil at Tampico c.1900 made it one of the greatest oil ports in the world.

TAMRA-GUK. See CHEJU.

TĀMRALIPTĀ. See TAMLŪK.

TAMSHUI. See TANSHUI.

TAMWORTH (England) Town in Staffordshire, 15 mi NE of Birmingham. Fortified in the eighth century by Offa of MERCIA, it was burned by the Danes in the ninth century but rebuilt by Queen Aethelflaed in the 10th century. In 1834 Sir Robert Peel, member of parliament for Tamworth, issued the *Tamworth Manifesto*, which stated the principles of British Conservative Party policy.

TANA, India. See THANA.

TANA, USSR. See AZOV.

TANAGRA [*Greek:* **Tanágra**] (Greece) Ancient city of E BOEOTIA, 14 mi E of Thebes, E central Greece. An important city of ancient Greece, it was first inhabited by the Gephyreans, an Athenian clan, and later became a major town of the eastern Boeotians. During the first Peloponnesian War, in 457 BC, the Spartans defeated the Athenians here in a battle that marked the beginning of the city's decline. Now in ruins, Tanagra became famous in 1874 after the discovery of many life-like terracotta figurines produced here in antiquity.

TANAÏS. See AZOV.

TANAIS. See DON RIVER.

TANAMBOGO (Solomon Islands) Small island in the SE Solomon Islands, W Pacific Ocean, attached by a causeway to Gavutu Island. The site of a Japanese base during World War II, it was captured by U.S. Marines on Aug. 7/8, 1942.

TANANARIVE [**Antananarivo, Antannarivo**] [*former:* **Analamanga**] (Madagascar) City and capital of Madagascar and of Tananarive province, 135 mi WSW of Tamatave. Established in the 17th century, it was for a long time the capital of the Hova rulers. Captured by the Imerina kings in 1794, it was controlled by them until 1895, when it fell to FRANCE.

TANCHOW. See CH'ANG-SHA.

TAN-CHU [**Tanchuk**] (China) Town in SE Kwangsi Chuang province, 60 mi W of Wu-Chow, on the Hsi River, SE China. The location of a U.S. air base during World War II, it was abandoned to the Japanese on Nov. 1, 1944. The Chinese recaptured it on July 9, 1945.

TANCHUK. See TAN-CHU.

TANDJOENGPINANG. See TANJUNGPRIOK.

TANDJUNGPRIOK. See TANJUNGPRIOK.

TANGA (Tanzania) Port, city, and capital of Tanga region, 120 mi N of Dar es Salaam, on the Indian Ocean,

E Tanzania. The country's third-largest city, it was founded in the 14th century by Persian traders and came under German rule in the 1890's. During World War I it was taken by the British in 1916. It declined with the growth of Dar es Salaam as a rival port.

TANGANYIKA A former British colonial possession in East Africa, now part of the nation of TANZANIA.

The coast of Tanganyika was the scene of active trade with the ARABIAN PENINSULA and INDIA by the first century AD. Arab traders settled in several coastal towns. These trading posts were undisturbed until Portuguese explorers arrived in the late 15th century and slowly became the dominant coastal power. In the early 18th century the coastal Arabs allied with the powerful sultan of MASQAT and displaced the Portuguese. In 1776 FRANCE revived the slave trade from the coastal town of KILWA, and Arab traders began to explore the unknown interior of Tanganyika as they searched for slaves and ivory. In the mid-19th century European missionaries entered Tanganyika, and their discoveries spurred exploration by Great Britain's Richard Burton, John Hanning Speke, David Livingstone, and Henry M. Stanley, among others.

In 1884 GERMANY moved to establish a colonial territory on the mainland, bypassing the narrow coastal strip controlled by the sultan of ZANZIBAR. An Anglo-German agreement in 1886 set up British and German spheres of influence over the interior, with the Germans controlling Tanganyika as part of German East Africa. The sultan of Zanzibar's territory was limited to a narrow coastal strip that was leased by Germany in 1888. In 1891 the entire area of Tanganyika was declared a German protectorate, and railways were built to encourage the development of valuable new crops of sisal, coffee, rubber, and cotton.

World War I saw the end of Germany's colonial ambitions as the British occupied the country. The League of Nations gave Great Britain a mandate to the Tanganyika territory. The British administrators moved to revive the economy, largely destroyed by the collapse of German control during the war, by building up local government and securing African land rights. The Great Depression of the 1930's slowed the country's development, and World War II was a time of struggle for self-sufficiency.

In 1947 Great Britain placed Tanganyika under United Nations trusteeship, and nationalism slowly gathered strength owing largely to the efforts of Julius Nyerere. He served as the first prime minister when Tanganyika became independent in 1961. A year later he was elected president by a large majority, and Tanganyika entered the British Commonwealth as a member republic. In 1964 the Republic of Tanganyika joined with the newly independent People's Republic of Zanzibar to form a new country named Tanzania, still under Nyerere.

TANGANYIKA, LAKE (Africa) Lake, the second-largest in Africa, approx. 420 mi long. It is in E central Africa, and the states of Burundi, Tanzania, Zaire, and Zambia border on it. The first Europeans to see the lake, in 1858, were two British explorers, Sir Richard Burton and John Hanning Speke. They were seeking the source of the NILE RIVER. David Livingstone, the Scottish missionary and explorer, came upon the lake in 1866 while also looking for the Nile's source. When Livingstone seemed to be lost, Henry Morton Stanley, a journalist, set out to find him, and they met on Nov. 10, 1871 at UJIJI on the lakeshore, where Stanley uttered his now famous words, "Dr. Livingstone, I presume." The two explored the lake, reaching its northern end. Another British traveler, Verney L. Cameron, mapped the lake in 1873. He determined that the Lukuga River, which flows into the CONGO RIVER, is the outlet of Tanganyika. During World War I, when Great Britain and Germany had rival colonies in the region, several small naval battles were fought on the lake.

T'ANG EMPIRE. See CHINA.

TANGER. See TANGIER.

TANGERMÜNDE (East Germany) Town in Magdeburg district, 30 mi NNE of Magdeburg, on the ELBE RIVER, W East Germany. Founded c.1010, it was Albert the Bear's stronghold in the 11th century and later became the seat of the margraves of BRANDENBURG from 1412 until the end of the 15th century. It changed hands several times during the Thirty Years War and was heavily damaged.

TANGIER [Tangiers] [ancient: Tingis; Arabic: Tanjah; French: Tanger; Spanish: Tánger] (Morocco) City, port, and capital of Tangier province, on a bay of the Strait of Gibraltar, 140 mi NNE of Rabat, N Morocco. Probably founded by Phoenicians in the 15th century BC, it was a free city under ROME and became the capital of the province of MAURETANIA Tingitana. It was the chief port and commercial center of Morocco until the founding of FÈS in 808 AD. Captured from the Moors by the Portuguese in 1471, it was transferred to England in 1662 as part of Catherine of Braganza's dowry. Abandoned by the English in 1684, it became the diplomatic center of Morocco by the mid-19th century. From 1923 to 1924 it was part of an internationally administered zone and was returned to international control following World War II, during which it was administered by Spain. Returned to the kingdom of Morocco in 1956, it is now an important port.

TANGIERS. See TANGIER.

TANGUT KINGDOM [Chinese: Hsia Hsia, Sia Hsia] Former kingdom, in NW China, in the region of the former province of Ningsia in W Inner MONGOLIA and of Kansu province. The capital was Halachar, near the present Tingyüanying. Founded c.1000 AD, the Tangut realm was one of several kingdoms created in this general region, the others being the Khitai and the Jurchen. China, then under the Sung dynasty, considered them barbarians. In 1207, the year after he became great khan of the Mongols, Genghis Khan invaded the Tangut kingdom. Then and in 1209 he devastated the land, and King Li An-ch'uan became his vassal. The khan found, however, that his dashing horse soldiers were not much use against fortified cities. He invaded the Tangut realm again in 1225, and his troops killed so

Tangier, ancient Moroccan city, in 1803 at the time of the United States Tripolitan War against the Barbary pirates of the North African coast.

many people that "the fields were covered with human bones." The Mongol ruler died in 1227 while the Tangut capital was still under siege, and when it fell everyone in it was killed in accordance with one of the khan's last commands. See also MONGOL EMPIRES.

TANIS [*biblical:* **Zoan;** *modern:* **Sān al-Hajar al Qibliyah**] (Egypt) Ancient city of Lower Egypt, in modern Sharqiya governorate, 20 mi ESE of El Manzala, N Egypt. Once the capital of the 14th province of Lower Egypt, it is identified with Avaris, the capital of the invading Hyksos, who established their rule in Egypt *c.*1720 BC. Tanis was made the capital of Egypt by the pharaohs of the Twenty-first Dynasty in 1085 BC. It was abandoned after the sixth century AD.

TANJAH. See TANGIER.

TANJONG PUTRI. See JOHOR BAHARU.

TANJORE. See THANJAVUR.

TANJUNGPRIOK [**Tandjoengpinang, Tandjungpriok**] (Indonesia) Port for JAKARTA, 5 mi NE of the city, on Jakarta Bay, NW JAVA. The development of the port began in 1877. It was used as a temporary base by the U.S. Navy in February 1942 during the battle of the Java Sea in the early months of World War II.

TANNENBERG [*Polish:* **Stębark**] (Poland) Village and battleground in Olsztyn province, 15 mi SE of Ostróda, N Poland. On July 15, 1410 the Teutonic Knights were defeated here by the Lithuanians and Poles under Wladislaw Jagiello. This defeat, also known as the Battle of Grünfelde, marked the start of the decline of the order. The Second Battle of Tannenberg

was fought here during World War I, from Aug. 26 to 30, 1914 when the Germans under Paul von Hindenburg defeated the Russians under Gen. P.K. Rennenkampf, causing heavy Russian losses. Hindenburg was buried here in 1934, though his body was later removed.

TANNU TUVA. See TUVA ASSR.

TANSHUI [**Tamshui**] (Taiwan) Town and port in T'ai-pei county, 10 mi N of Taipei, on the N coast of Taiwan, at the mouth of the Tanshui River. The oldest of the port settlements of northern Taiwan, it was occupied sucessively by the Spanish, the Dutch, and by the pirate Koxinga (Cheng Ch'eng-kung) in the 17th century. In 1683 it passed under Chinese control and in the 19th century became a center of the tea industry. Its importance has declined in modern times because of the silting of the Tanshui River.

TANTA (Egypt) City of the NILE RIVER delta, capital of al-Gharbīyah governorate, 52 mi NNW of Cairo, N Egypt. It is an important pilgrimage center and seat of Arab learning and is the location of the mosque and tomb of the 13th-century holy man, Ahmad al-Badawī. In 1895 the patriarch of Alexandria made the city a Coptic bishopric.

TANYANG. See NANKING.

TANZANIA Lying on the east coast of Africa, the United Republic of Tanzania was formed by the union of TANGANYIKA and ZANZIBAR in 1964. Julius Nyerere of Tanganyika became the new country's president; and Sheik Abeid Amani Karune, Zanzibar's leader, became his vice-president. Tanzania emerged as a one-party state, and in 1967 its leaders announced their intention to guide the nation along a socialist developmental path. Much of the country's industry and agriculture was nationalized. Although sympathetic to Soviet and Chinese communism, Nyerere retained open relations with the United States. Massive Chinese aid built a rail line linking the Tanzanian port capital of DAR ES SALAAM with LUSAKA, the inland capital of ZAMBIA.

The seizure of power in neighboring UGANDA by Idi Amin in 1971 was bitterly opposed by Tanzania. Border clashes and constant invective between the two nations became commonplace. Disputes over roads and boundaries with KENYA and Zambia also caused friction. In 1976 President Nyerere, then serving a fourth term, opened Tanzania's borders to guerrilla fighters seeking the overthrow of white-controlled RHODESIA, now ZIMBABWE. The simmering dispute with Amin blazed into full-scale war in 1978 when Ugandan troops invaded northeastern Tanzania. A counteroffensive captured KAMPALA, Uganda, in 1979 and caused Amin to flee to Libya. A Tanzanian military presence in Uganda was maintained until elections in December 1980. Troops were withdrawn in May 1981.

TAORMINA [*ancient:* **Tauromenium**; *Arabic:* **Mu'izzīyah**] (Italy) Town in Messina province, E SICILY, between Messina and Catania, at the foot of MOUNT ETNA. A native settlement of the eighth century BC, it was first settled by the Greeks in *c.*405 BC after the destruction of NAXOS, and prospered under the Greeks and the Romans, who rebuilt it in the second century BC. Burned by the Arabs in 902 AD, it fell to the Normans in 1078. Today it is a world-famous winter resort with Roman and medieval remains and is the site of the second-largest Greek theater in Sicily.

TAOS [**Don Fernando de Taos**] (United States) Town in N NEW MEXICO, 55 mi NNE of Santa Fe, in the Sangre de Cristo Mts. It was settled by the Spanish in the early 17th century near an ancient Indian pueblo that still thrives. In 1680 the Taos and other Pueblo Indians banded together in a revolt against Spain, called the Pueblo Revolt, which forced the Spanish out. A second uprising occurred here in 1849 when the Indians, incited by the Mexican-Americans killed the U.S. governor Charles Brent. Today Taos is a resort for artists and writers.

TAPARURA. See SFAX.

TAPHROS. See PEREKOP, ISTHMUS OF.

TAPOCHO. See TAPOTCHAU.

TAPOTCHAU [**Tapocho**] (United States) Mountain ridge on central SAIPAN Island, Mariana Islands, U.S. Trust Territory of the Pacific Islands. The ridge was the scene of bitter fighting in June 1944 during World War II, when U.S. forces captured the island from JAPAN.

TAPPAN (United States) Village in SE NEW YORK State, 6 mi SSW of Nyack, on the New Jersey line. It is the site of the De Wint Mansion, which served George Washington as headquarters in 1780 and 1783. Maj. John André, a British spy during the American Revolution, was executed here in 1780.

TAPPEH HESAR DAMGHAN. See TEPE HISSAR.

TAPROBANE. See SRI LANKA.

TARA (Irish Republic) Village in County Meath, 22 mi NW of Dublin. A symbol of Irish nationalism, the Hill of Tara was the seat of the high kings of IRELAND from antiquity until the sixth century AD. The Danes were defeated here in 980, as were the Irish insurgents in 1798. It was the site of a mass meeting addressed by Daniel O'Connell in 1843. There are Bronze Age tombs here.

TARABALUS. See TRIPOLITANIA.

TARABALUS AL-GHARB. See TRIPOLI, Libya.

TARABULUS. See TRIPOLI, Lebanon.

TARABULUS ESH SHAM. See TRIPOLI, Lebanon.

TARAHTI. See KALINJAR.

TARAKAN (Indonesia) Island in the E Celebes Sea, off the NE coast of BORNEO. After the Dutch destroyed its oil wells, the island was taken by JAPAN between Jan. 10 and 12, 1942 during World War II. It was retaken between May 1 and 19, 1945 by the Australians.

TARANCÓN (Spain) City in Cuenca province, New Castile, 45 mi SE of Madrid, central Spain. The French were defeated here during the Peninsular campaign of the Napoleonic Wars, in 1809. It is also the site of the palace of the dukes of Riánsares.

TARANTO [*Greek:* **Taras**; *Latin:* **Tarentum**] (Italy) City, port, and capital of Taranto province, APULIA region, on the Gulf of Taranto, 156 mi SE of Naples, SE Italy. Founded in the eighth century BC by colonists from SPARTA, it was a leading town of MAGNA GRAECIA and resisted ROME until 272 BC. Destroyed by the Arabs in 927 AD, it was rebuilt by the Byzantines in 967. As a principality of the kingdom of NAPLES it was the victim of frequent Turkish attacks in the 16th and 17th centuries. Important as a naval base in World Wars I and II, it is today the second-most important military port of Italy.

TARAPACÁ. See ANCÓN.

TARARORI, BATTLE OF. See AJMER.

TARAS. See TARANTO.

TARASCON (France) Town in Bouches-du-Rhône department, 9 mi N of Arles, SE France, on the RHÔNE RIVER. It is the site of a 12th-century château built on the remains of a Roman fortress, which became the 15th-century residence of René I, count of PROVENCE and titular king of Naples. The town was made famous by Alphonse Daudet's novel *Tartarin de Tarascon.*

TARAWA (Kiribati) Island and capital of Kiribati, in the W central Pacific Ocean, 2,800 mi NE of Australia. Once the capital of the former British crown colony of the Gilbert and Ellice Islands, it was the site of a bloody battle from Nov. 22 to 24, 1943 when the U.S. Marines captured it from Japanese occupying forces during World War II.

TARAZ. See DZHAMBUL.

TARBATU. See TARTU.

TARBES [*ancient:* **Bigorra**] (France) City and capital of Hautes-Pyrénées department, on the Adour

River, 23 mi ESE of Pau, SW France. Important under the ROMAN EMPIRE, it became the capital of the earldom of Bigorre in the 10th century and fell to the English during the Hundred Years War of 1337 to 1453. During the Napoleonic Wars the French were defeated near the city in 1814 by the British under the duke of Wellington. Poet Théophile Gautier and Marshal Ferdinand Foch were born at Tarbes.

TARCHNA. See TARQUINIA.

TARCHUNA. See TARQUINIA.

TARENTUM. See TARANTO.

TARGOVISHTE [*former:* **Eski Dzhumaya**] (Bulgaria) City in Kolarovgrad district, on the Vrana River, 17 mi W of Kolarovgrad, E Bulgaria. Under the rule of Turkey, it emerged as a cultural center of Bulgarian Muslims. It was ceded to Bulgaria after its capture by the Russians in 1878. See also OTTOMAN EMPIRE.

TÂRGOVISTE. See TÎRGOVISTE.

TÂRGU-JIU. See TÎRGU-JIU.

TÂRGUL-NEAMȚ. See TÎRGU-NEAMȚ.

TÂRGU-MUREȘ. See TÎRGU-MUREȘ.

TÂRGU-NEAMȚU. See TÎRGU-NEAMȚ.

TARIFA [*ancient:* **Julia Joza, Julia Traducta**] (Spain) Town and port in Cádiz province, Andalusia, 51 mi SE of Cádiz, on the Strait of Gibraltar, S Spain. The most southerly city of mainland Europe, it was settled by the Greeks and later was made the first Roman colony in Spain. Captured in 711 AD by the Berber leader Tarik for the Moors, it was recaptured in 1292 by Sancho IV. During the Peninsular campaign of the Napoleonic Wars it was attacked in 1812 by the French.

TARIJA [*former:* **San Bernardo de Tarija**] (Bolivia) City and capital of Tarija department, 180 mi SSE of Sucre, S Bolivia. Founded by the Spanish in 1574 as a trading center, it is one of the oldest settlements in Bolivia. During its early history it suffered continual Indian attacks.

TARNOPOL. See TERNOPOL.

TĂRNOVO. See TIRNOVO.

TARNÓW (Poland) City in Kraków province, 45 mi E of Cracow, SE Poland. Founded in 1330 as a fortified town by the Tarnowski family, it was completely leveled by fire in the 15th century. Once rebuilt, the city became a cultural center in the 16th century. After passing to AUSTRIA in 1772, it was returned to Poland after World War II, during which its industrial plant was destroyed. Its 14th-century cathedral contains tombs considered to be among Poland's finest Renaissance treasures.

TARN RIVER (France) River in S France, rising in the Cévennes Mts, and flowing approx. 235 mi W and SW to join the GARONNE RIVER. Tourists are attracted by its deep gorges. ALBI on the Tarn gave its name to the Albigenses, a religious Cathar sect of southern France in the Middle Ages who were declared heretics and were persecuted for their dualist beliefs and practices, which included strict vegetarianism, sexual abstinence, and refusal to swear oaths. GAILLAC is the site

of a Benedictine abbey founded in 960, while MILLAU was a Huguenot stronghold in the 16th century. Robert Louis Stevenson, the popular Scottish author, wrote about a trip he took in the region in *Travels with a Donkey in the Cévennes*, published in 1879.

TAROUDANT [**Tarudant**] (Morocco) Town and oasis in W Morocco, 45 mi E of Agadir. An ancient settlement, it was inhabited by the ALMORAVIDS, the Berber conquerors of Morocco, in the 11th century and was later the seat of the Saadian sultans. The French captured the area in 1917.

TARQUINIA [*Etruscan:* **Tarchna, Tarchuna;** *former:* **Corneto;** *Latin:* **Tarquinii**] (Italy) Town in Viterbo province, LATIUM region, 4 mi from the Tyrrhenian Sea, just N of Civitavecchia, central Italy. It was an important member of the Etruscan confederation against ROME. The Romans took the city in 311 BC and made it a colony in 181 BC. After a period of decline under the late ROMAN EMPIRE, the site was moved two miles southwest in the ninth century AD. The town itself has many medieval and Renaissance buildings, including the 16th-century cathedral and the Gothic-Renaissance Palazzo Vitelleschi of 1436 to 1439, which is now the National Tarquinian Museum and houses a large collection of antiquities. The first recorded archaeological dig in modern times took place in this town in 1489. Nearby, in the renowned necropolis of Tarquinii, are Etruscan painted tombs dating from the sixth to fourth centuries BC. See also ETRURIA.

TARQUINII. See TARQUINIA.

TARRACINA. See TERRACINA.

TARRACO. See TARRAGONA.

TARRACONENSIS, PROVINCE OF. See TARRAGONA.

TARRAGONA [*ancient:* **Colonia Julia Victrix Triumphalis, Tarraco**] (Spain) City, port, and capital of Tarragona province, 54 mi WSW of Barcelona, in CATALONIA, NE Spain. Originally an Iberian town, it was captured in 218 BC during the Second Punic War by Gnaeus and Publius Scipio for ROME. The earliest Roman fortress in Spain, it became the capital of the province of Tarraconensis under Emperor Augustus and was one of the richest ports of the ROMAN EMPIRE, drawing praise from Martial and Pliny the Elder. Traditionally it is the site of St. Paul's founding of the Christian church in Spain in 60 AD. Razed by the Moors in 714, it was recaptured by Christians in the 12th century and became an important city of ARAGON. During the Spanish civil war, it was one of the last cities to fall to Gen. Francisco Franco in 1939. It has Roman remains and a 14th-century cathedral with one of the finest cloisters in Spain.

TARRYTOWN (United States) City, on the HUDSON RIVER, 24 mi N of New York City, SE NEW YORK State. Founded by Dutch settlers in the 17th century, it developed as a river port after the American Revolution. It was the home of author Washington Irving, whose residence, Sunnyside, is preserved near here. See also NORTH TARRYTOWN.

TARSATICA. See RIJEKA.

TARSHISH. See TARTESSUS.

TARSUS (Turkey) City in İçel province, Cilicia, on the Tarsus River, 23 mi W of Adana, S Turkey. Inhabited since Neolithic times, it was the capital of CILICIA and one of Asia Minor's most important cities, strategically situated at the southern end of the Cilician Gates. It flourished greatly under Roman rule and in 41 BC was the site of the first meeting of Mark Antony and Cleopatra. It was the birthplace of St. Paul. Razed by the Arabs c.660 AD, it was recaptured by the BYZANTINE EMPIRE and the Crusaders and was part of Cilician ARMENIA in the 13th and 14th centuries. It fell to the OTTOMAN EMPIRE in 1515. Extensive remains of the ancient city can be seen today.

TARTESSOS. See TARTESSUS.

TARTESSUS [Tartessos] [biblical: Tarshish] (Spain) Ancient kingdom and town of SW Spain, in ANDALUSIA, around the mouth of the Guadalquivir River. The exact location of the town is not known. Established c.1200 BC, it prospered in the silver and tin trade and was later expanded by the Phoenicians and Greeks. It was destroyed, possibly by the Carthaginians, in 480 BC. See also CARTHAGE, PHOENICIA.

TARTOUS. See TARTUS.

TARTU [ancient: Tarbatu; former: Yuryev; German: Dorpat] (USSR) City and port of E ESTONIAN SSR, on the Ema River, 100 mi SE of Tallinn, W European USSR. It was founded in 1030 AD on the site of a fifth-century settlement by Yaroslav I, grand prince of KIEV. It was seized by the Teutonic Knights in 1224 and prospered as a member of the HANSEATIC LEAGUE until captured by RUSSIA in 1558. It fell to SWEDEN and POLAND before finally passing to Russia in 1704, during the Great Northern War. Soviet peace treaties with Estonia and FINLAND were signed here in 1920. The city suffered severely during the German occupation of World War II. Its university was founded in 1632 by Gustavus II of Sweden.

TARTUS [Tartous] [ancient: Antaradus, Tortosa] (Syria) Town, port, and capital of Tartus governorate, 42 mi S of Latakia, on the Mediterranean Sea, W Syria. Built in 346 AD by Constantius II on the site of ancient Antaradus, it was under Byzantine control from 968 to 1099 and was held by the Crusaders from 1102 to 1291. It declined following the Ottoman conquest and only revived in the 20th century. See also BYZANTINE EMPIRE.

TARUDANT. See TAROUDANT.

TARUM. See MUŞ.

TARVISIUM. See TREVISO.

TASHKENT (USSR) City and capital of Uzbek SSR, in the foothills of the Tien Shan Mts, 1,800 mi SE of Moscow, central Asian USSR. First described in the first century BC, it was under Arab rule in the seventh century AD and in the 12th century passed to the Turkish shahs of KHWARIZM. It fell to the Mongols Genghis Khan and Tamerlane, and it became part of the khanate of KOKAND in 1814. In 1865 it fell to RUSSIA and was made the capital of the UZBEK SSR in 1930. A meeting was held at Tashkent in 1966 between India, Pakistan, and the Soviet Union in an attempt to solve the KASHMIR dispute. The city was damaged by an earthquake in the same year. Today it is the fourth-largest city of the Soviet Union and the economic and cultural center of Soviet Central Asia.

TASHKURGHĀN [Tashkurgan, Tash-Kurgan] [ancient: Aornos] (Afghanistan) Town in Samāngan province, 30 mi E of Mazār-i-Sharīf, N Afghanistan. Established c.1750, it was a major center of trade between BUKHARA and INDIA. The ruins of ancient Khulm are 3 miles to the north.

TASMANIA [former: Van Diemen's Land] (Australia) Island and state of Australia, in the S Pacific Ocean, 150 mi S of the state of Victoria, across the Bass Strait. HOBART is its capital. Discovered by the Dutch navigator Abel Tasman in 1642, in 1803 it passed to the British, who established a penal colony on the island. It was the scene of the Black War at the beginning of the 19th century between European settlers and the now extinct aborigines. It became a colony separate from New South Wales in 1825. Renamed Tasmania in 1853, it became a state of the Commonwealth of Australia in 1901.

TATAR AUTONOMOUS SOVIET SOCIALIST REPUBLIC [Tatariya, Tatarstan] (USSR) Autonomous republic of E central Russian SFSR, around the confluence of the Volga and Kama rivers, E European USSR. KAZAN is its capital. The indigenous Bulgars were displaced from this region in the 13th century AD by the Tatars, offspring of the Mongols of the GOLDEN HORDE. In the 15th century the area was split into several states including the Kazan Khanate, which engaged in a long struggle with MOSCOW, ending in 1552 when Ivan the Terrible captured Kazan. In 1920 the republic was formed as one of the first autonomous areas created by the Soviet government.

TATARIYA. See TATAR AUTONOMOUS SOVIET SOCIALIST REPUBLIC.

TATAR PAZARDZHIK. See PAZARDZHIK.

TATARSTAN. See TATAR AUTONOMOUS SOVIET SOCIALIST REPUBLIC.

TATHARI. See SASSARI.

TATTA [Thato, Thatta] (Pakistan) Town in Sind province, 55 mi ESE of Karachi. A flourishing Muslim city between the 15th and 17th centuries, it became the capital of the Samma dynasty in the 16th century. The Portuguese destroyed Tatta in 1555. It has numerous medieval remains, and there is a large necropolis in the nearby Makli Hills.

TA-T'UNG [Tatung] [former: P'ing-Ch'ang] (China) City in N Shansi province, 180 mi W of Peking, NE China. An important industrial and railway center, it was the capital of the T'o-pa Wei Kingdom from the fifth to sixth centuries AD. Under the Ming dynasty (1368–1644) the city was an important part of the defensive line against Mongol invaders. Nearby are the Yung-Kan limestone grottoes containing fifth- and sixth-century Buddhist art.

TAUBERBISCHOFSHEIM (West Germany) Village in Baden-Württemberg, 11 mi SSE of Wertheim, SW West Germany. During the Austro-Prussian War, in 1866, the WÜRTTEMBERG army was decisively defeated here by the Prussians. See also PRUSSIA.

TAUCHIRA. See TOCRA.

TAUNTON (England) Admin. hq. of Somerset, on the Tone River, 38 mi SW of Bristol. It was founded by the Anglo-Saxon King Ine in the eighth century. Its castle was attacked three times by Royalists during the Civil War. Following the rebellion of the duke of Monmouth in 1685, Judge Jeffreys conducted the infamous Bloody Assizes here, condemning many of the rebels to death.

TAUNTON (United States) City on the Taunton River, 30 mi S of Boston, SE MASSACHUSETTS. Its site was purchased from the Indians in 1638 by Elizabeth Poole, and it was the scene of operations between Indians and colonists in King Philip's War in 1675/76. It was an iron-working center from 1656 to 1876.

TAURAGE [*German:* **Tauroggen**] (USSR) Town in Lithuanian SSR, 65 mi WNW of Kaunas, W European USSR. Dating from the 13th century, it was the scene of the signing of the Convention of Tauroggen in 1812, which dealt with problems of neutrality between Russia and her neighbors. See also LITHUANIA.

TAURASIA. See TURIN.

TAURIS, Iran. See TABRIZ.

TAURIS, USSR. See CRIMEA, THE.

TAUROGGEN. See TAURAGE.

TAUROMENIUM. See TAORMINA.

TAURUS MOUNTAINS [*Turkish:* **Toros Dağlari**] (Turkey) Mountain chain of S Turkey, running parallel to the Mediterranean coast and forming the S border of the Anatolian plateau as well as a natural barrier between Anatolia and the Levant. The Cilician Gates, the main pass through the mountains, has been used by caravans and armies since antiquity.

TAUS. See DOMAZLICE.

TAVASTEHUS. See HÄMEENLINNA.

TAVAU. See DAVOS.

TAXCO [**Taxco de Alarcón**] (Mexico) City in Guerrero state, 70 mi SSW of Mexico City, S central Mexico. Its mines were worked in pre-Columbian times, and Indians settled here in the mid-15th century. In 1528 Hernando Cortés and the Spanish founded the town, which grew rich from the silver deposits. It has been declared a national monument, thanks to the many buildings remaining from its colonial days.

TAXCO DE ALARCÓN. See TAXCO.

TAXILA [**Taksaśilā**] (Pakistan) Ancient ruined city and important archaeological site in the PUNJAB, 22 mi NW of Rawalpindi, central Pakistan. Situated on three major trade routes, it was the site of a flourishing city from the seventh century BC to the fifth century AD, which absorbed Indian, Greek, and Iranian culture and was famous as a center of learning. Taken by Alexander the Great in 326 BC, it flourished under the empire of Asoka. Overrun by Kushans in the first and second

centuries AD, when it became a Buddhist center, it fell to the Persian Sassanid dynasty in the fourth century and was destroyed by Huns in the fifth century. See also INDIA, MAURYAN EMPIRE, PERSIA.

TAYDULA. See TULA, USSR.

TAYIF. See AT-TA'IF.

TAYSAFUN. See CTESIPHON.

TAYSIDE (Scotland) Region composed of the former counties of Angus, Kinross, and a large part of Perthshire, Scotland's longest river, the Tay, crosses it. The admin. hq. is DUNDEE.

TA-YÜAN. See T'AI-NAN.

TAZA (Morocco) City in Taza province, 55 mi ENE of Fès, N central Morocco. Established as a Berber fortress in the 11th century AD, it was taken in 1914 by the French.

TAZOULT. See LAMBESSA.

TBILISI [**Tiflis**] (USSR) City and capital of the GEORGIAN SSR, on the Kura River, 280 mi WNW of Baku, S European USSR. Strategically situated on the route between west and east TRANSCAUCASIA, it has had a turbulent history. Inhabited as early as the fourth century BC, it was founded as the capital of the Georgian kingdom in 458 AD but later fell to the Persians, Byzantines, and Arabs. A Muslim stronghold from the eighth to 11th centuries, it was restored to its position as the capital of an independent Georgia by David II, the Builder of Georgia, in 1122. Captured by the Mongols in 1234 and by Tamerlane in 1386, it was put to the torch by the Persians in 1795 and fell to RUSSIA in 1801. It became the capital of the Georgian republic in 1921 and is now a major cultural and educational center and a principal industrial city of the Soviet Union. Joseph Stalin studied at the Orthodox seminary in Tbilisi. See also MONGOL EMPIRES, PERSIA.

TCHAD. See CHAD.

TCHESME. See CHESMÉ.

TCHONGKING. See CHUNGKING.

TCZEW [*German:* **Dirschau**] (Poland) Town and major river port in Gdańsk province, on the Vistula River, 20 mi SSE of Gdańsk, N central Poland. The site of a Pomeranian fortress built in 1252, it was annexed in 1282 by Poland and was held by the Teutonic Knights from 1308 to 1466. In 1772 it passed to PRUSSIA and was only returned to Poland after World War I.

TEATE MARRUCINORUM. See CHIETI.

TEBESSA [*ancient:* **Theveste**; *French:* **Tébessa**] (Algeria) Town in Annaba department, 146 mi S of Bône, in the Atlas Mts, NE Algeria. In the seventh century BC it was an outpost of CARTHAGE and in 146 BC became a strategic Roman garrison town. Tebessa lost importance in the fifth and sixth centuries AD, and little is known about it until 1840, when the French established their rule in Algeria and developed the town.

TÉBOURBA (Tunisia) Town and battle site in N Tunisia, 32 mi W of Tunis. During World War II the

British captured Tébourba from the Germans between May 4 and 8, 1943.

TECPAM. See TECPÁN GUATEMALA.

TECPÁN GUATEMALA [*former:* **Tecpam**] (Guatemala) Town in Chimaltenango department, 15 mi WNW of Chimaltenango, S central Guatemala. In 1524 Guatemala's first capital was founded here at the site of Iximché, the former Indian capital.

TEGEA [*modern:* **Piali**] (Greece) Ancient city of S Greece, in Arcadia department, 4 mi SE of Tripolis, in the Peloponnesus. Under Spartan domination from the sixth century BC until the defeat of SPARTA at LEUCTRA in 371 BC, it allied itself with its old rival MANTINEA against Sparta in 362 BC but later opposed Mantinea again. It prospered under the Byzantines from the fourth century AD and the Franks after 1204. The remains of the temple of Athena Alea, adorned by the sculptor Scopas, can be seen today.

TEGUCIGALPA (Honduras) City and capital of Honduras and of Francisco Morazán department, in the mountains of S central Honduras, 120 mi WNW of San Salvador. Founded in 1579 as a center of gold and silver mining, it became a Liberal stronghold following its independence from Spain in 1821 and was made the permanent capital of the republic in 1880. It is one of the only capitals in the world without a railroad.

TEGUTUM. See TEIGNMOUTH.

TEHERAN, Albania. See TIRANË.

TEHERAN [**Tehran**] (Iran) City and capital of Iran, one of the major cities of the Middle East, capital of Teheran province, on the S slopes of the Elburz Mts, 440 mi NE of Baghdad. Originally overshadowed by its neighbor RHAGES, Teheran became more important in the 13th century AD when the inhabitants of Rhages migrated here after the destruction of their city by the Mongols in 1220.

In 1788 it became the capital of PERSIA and was considerably modernized from 1925 to 1941 by Reza Shah Pahlevi. Occupied by the Allies in 1941, during World War II, it was the site of the Teheran Conference from Nov. 26 to Dec. 2, 1943 attended by Joseph Stalin, Franklin Roosevelt, and Winston Churchill, which guaranteed Iranian independence after the war and planned an offensive against Germany's eastern flank.

As the focal point of Iran's recent Islamic revolution, the city witnessed massive demonstrations against the rule of Shah Mohammed Reza Pahlevi in September 1978, demanding the return from exile of Ayatollah

Teheran, Iran's capital and now a sprawling metropolis, as it looked in the mid-19th century. Lovely Mount Demavend, here exaggerated in shape and height, rises behind the city.

Ruhollah Khomeini. With the city torn by continued demonstrations, strikes, and riots, the shah abandoned the country in January 1979, opening the way for the return of Khomeini, the Islamic revolution, and the theocratic reign of terror that followed, including the November 1979 capture by radicals of the staff of the U.S. embassy.

TEHRAN. See TEHERAN, Iran.

TEHRI [Tehri Garhwal] (India) District of NW Uttar Pradesh state, in the HIMALAYAS, N of the GANGES RIVER, N India. Its administrative headquarters is at Narendranagar. Established as a princely state by the British in 1815 after the war with NEPAL, it was merged with the United Provinces in 1947. It contains the sources of both the Ganges and the Yamuna rivers and hence has many places of pilgrimage.

TEHRI GARHWAL. See TEHRI.

TEHUANTEPEC (Mexico) Town in S Mexico, Oaxaca state, 110 mi SE of Oaxaca and on the Isthmus of Tehuantepec. The people are largely Zapotec Indians whose territory consists chiefly of the isthmus. They had a developed civilization here more than 2,000 years ago and captured Tehuantepec from the Zoquean and Huavean Indians. When the Aztec nation invaded the region in the mid-15th century, the Zapotec withstood a long siege on Giengola, a mountain that overlooks Tehuantepec. The society here is matriarchal, and the women are famous both for their beauty and their industry. Nearby JUCHITÁN is Tehuantepec's rival as a center of Zapotec culture. See also AZTEC EMPIRE.

TEIGNMOUTH [ancient: Tegutum] (England) Town on the ENGLISH CHANNEL, 12 mi S of Exeter, in DEVON. It was the site of an Anglo-Saxon settlement destroyed by the Danes in 970. The town was damaged by French raids in 1338 and 1690.

TEISHEBAINI (USSR) Ancient Urartian fortress town in ARMENIAN SSR, near Yerevan, on the hill of Karmirblur, S European USSR. Excavations here have revealed a citadel, probably destroyed in the early sixth century BC, containing many items including gold and silver jewelry, wooden stools, and bronze war gear. See also URARTU.

TEJUCO. See DIAMANTINA.

TEKIRDAĞ [ancient: **Bisanthe, Raidestos, Rhaedestus;** Italian: **Rodosto**] (Turkey) City, port, and capital of Tekirdağ province, on the SEA OF MARMARA, 78 mi W of Istanbul, W Turkey. Founded by Greeks from SAMOS in the seventh century BC, it was an important city of the Thracian kingdom in the first century BC. Captured by the Ottoman Turks in 1360, it fell to RUSSIA in 1877, to BULGARIA in 1912, and to GREECE in 1920. It was formerly the port for Adrianople. See also EDIRNE, THRACE.

TEKRIT. See TIKRĪT.

TEKRUR An ancient empire named after its capital city, which held power in the western SUDAN, in what is now modern MAURITANIA. Tekrur rose in competition with the neighboring empire of GHANA in the third to the sixth century AD. The capital was the terminus of a major trans-Saharan caravan route originating in MARRAKECH. But Ghana had subjugated Tekrur by the tenth century and exacted tribute from its rulers. When the ALMORAVID EMPIRE attacked Ghana in the 11th century, it was quickly aided by Tekrur, which was one of the earliest black African kingdoms to embrace Islam.

Independence was regained when Ghana fell, and it lasted until the empire of MALI began its irresistible expansion in the late 13th century and resubjugated Tekrur. Islam continued to be a dominant force in the kingdom, and the Fulani peoples of Tekrur eventually rode the crest of a holy jihad to form the 19th-century FULANI EMPIRE.

TEL ASHQELON. See ASHQELON.

TELAV. See TELAVI.

TELAVI [former: **Telav**] (USSR) City in E GEORGIAN SSR, 35 mi NE of Tbilisi, S European USSR. Possibly inhabited as early as the 13th century AD, it was the 17th-century capital of KAKHETIA in the wine-producing region of Georgia and has the remains of a medieval fortress.

TEL AVIV-JAFFA [Tel Aviv-Yafo] (Israel) City and port in Tel Aviv district, W central Israel, on the Mediterranean Sea, 35 mi NW of Jerusalem. Founded by Jews from JAFFA in 1909, its population expanded in the 1920's and following Hitler's rise to power in Germany, as well as after World War II. Tel Aviv was the capital after Israel was declared an independent state on May 14, 1948 until the capital was officially moved to Jerusalem in 1980. Several countries continue to maintain official embassies here. The city merged with Jaffa in 1950 to form Tel Aviv-Jaffa, the largest city in Israel and the country's commercial, financial, and cultural center.

TEL AVIV-YAFO. See TEL AVIV-JAFFA.

TEL CHAI. See TEL HAY.

TEL EL-AMARNA. See TELL AL-AMARNA.

TEL HAI. See TEL HAY.

TEL HASI (Israel) Archaeological site of SW PALESTINE, E of Gaza, in Southern district, S Israel. There is evidence that this site was first inhabited c.2600 BC. The first stratigraphical excavation in Palestine was carried out here between 1892 and 1894 by Sir Flinders Petrie.

TEL HAY [Tel Chai, Tel Hai] (Israel) National memorial and former settlement of Upper Galilee, in Northern district, near Qiryat Shemona, N Israel. Occupied occasionally from 1905, it was one of the earliest Jewish communities in northern Palestine and was permanently settled in 1918. On March 1, 1920 the resistance of the settlement to Arab attack gave it an immortal place in Jewish history. It also caused the boundaries between the trust territories of Great Britain and France to be shifted northward so that Upper GALILEE passed under British and, eventually, Israeli control. Today Tel Hay is a pilgrimage center and is the place where the Israelis killed in the Arab-Israeli wars are buried.

TELL AL-AMARNA [Tel El-Amarna, Tell El-Amarna] (Egypt) Ancient locality of upper Egypt, in al-Minyā governorate, near the Nile River, 60 mi N of Asyut. It was the site of King Akhenaton's (Amenhotep IV) capital, Akhetaton, built anew in 1375 BC but abandoned c.1360 BC when the court was forced to return to THEBES. One of the few cities of ancient Egypt to have been excavated, in 1887 it yielded 400 tablets with inscriptions in Akkadian cuneiform that have thrown much light on the history of ancient Egypt and the Middle East.

TELL ÂN-NEBĪ MEND. See KADESH.

TELL ASMAR [ancient: Eshnunna] (Iraq) Archaeological site in E Iraq, 33 mi ENE of Baghdad. Many Sumerian stone statuettes and copper objects dating from c.3000 to 2700 BC were found here. See also SUMER.

TELL ATCHANA. See ALALAKH.

TELL DOTHAM. See DOTHAIM.

TELL ED-DUWEIR. See LACHISH.

TELL EL-AMARNA. See TELL AL-AMARNA.

TELL EL-FAR'A. See TIRZAH.

TELL EL-KEBIR. See TALL AL-KABĪR.

TELL EL-QADI. See DAN.

TELL HALAF. See TALL HALAF.

TELLICHERRY (India) Town and port on the Malabar Coast, NW Kerala state, S India, 168 mi WSW of Bangalore. Established by the English East India Company in 1683 for trade in pepper and cardamom, it was their first settlement on the MALABAR COAST. Hyder Ali unsuccessfully besieged the fort here from 1780 to 1782.

TELL JOKHA. See UMMA.

TELLOH. See LAGASH.

TELL QASSILA (Israel) Locality of W PALESTINE, in Tel-Aviv district, just N of Tel-Aviv-Jaffa, W Israel. Excavations undertaken here in 1949 revealed the remains of several strata of ancient buildings dating from Philistine and later periods. It is believed that materials for the temple in Jerusalem were shipped from here. See also PHILISTIA.

TELL TI INNIK. See TAANACH.

TEL MEGIDDO. See MEGIDDO.

TELO MARTIUS. See TOULON.

TELTOWN (Irish Republic) Village in County Meath, 35 mi NW of Dublin. It was the site in antiquity of annual pagan revelry in honor of Tailte, the foster mother of the god Lug. The festival was revived in Dublin in 1924 as the Tailtean Games.

TEMASEK. See SINGAPORE.

TÉMBI. See TEMPE, VALE OF.

TEMESVÁR. See TIMIŞOARA.

TEMIR-KHAN-SHURA. See BUINAKSK.

TEMPELHOF (West Germany) District of West Berlin, West Germany. The site of West Berlin's principal airport, it was enlarged in 1948/49 during the Soviet blockade of West Berlin and was the main western Allied terminus for airlifting supplies into the beleaguered city. See BERLIN.

TEMPE, VALE OF [Greek: Témbi] (Greece) Narrow valley gorge between Mt Olympus and Mt Ossa, in NE THESSALY, Greece. In antiquity it was sacred to Apollo, and its beauty was extolled by poets, including Virgil in the *Georgics*. It was also of strategic importance as an access route from MACEDONIA and was used by the armies of Xerxes in 480 BC and of Alexander the Great in 336 BC. It was fortified under the ROMAN and BYZANTINE Empires. During World War II it was briefly held against the Germans on their advance south. The vale was recreated by Hadrian at his palatial villa at TIVOLI. The Greek vale was a favorite subject for late Renaissance, classical revival, and Romantic painters.

TEMUCO (Chile) City and capital of Cautín province, 100 mi NNE of Valdivia, S central Chile. It was founded in 1881 as a frontier station following a treaty signed nearby between Chile and the Araucanian Indians that put an end to the Indian wars. Temuco was settled principally by German immigrants.

TENBY [Welsh: Dinbych-y-Pysgod] (Wales) Market town in Dyfed, on Carmarthen Bay, 33 mi W of Swansea. The site of a Danish fishing settlement, it became the home of Flemish weavers in the 12th century.

TENEDOS. See BOZCAADA.

TÉNÈS [Tenez] [ancient: Catenna] (Algeria) Town and port in el-Asnam province, on the Mediterranean Sea, 24 mi N of Orléansville, N central Algeria. It was established c.875 AD by colonists from Spain at the location of the former Roman and Phoenician colonies of Catenna. It was occupied by TLEMCEN from 1299 until 1517, when it fell to the corsair Barbarossa. FRANCE occupied it in 1843.

TENEZ. See TÉNÈS.

TENNESSEE (United States) State in the south central region, admitted to the Union as the 16th state in 1796. Its name is that of a Cherokee Indian town, first written as Tinnase. Virginia and Kentucky are to the N; North Carolina to the E; Mississippi, Alabama, and Georgia to the S; Arkansas and Missouri to the W.

There are remains of the Mound Builders here, who were succeeded by the Cherokee, Chickasaw, Shawnee, and Creek Indian tribes. Hernando De Soto, in 1540, was the first European in the region. French explorers traveling down the Mississippi claimed the area, and c.1680 Robert Sieur de La Salle built Fort Prudhomme. The French erected other posts, and English trappers from Virginia and the Carolinas entered the region. In 1756 British troops and men from South Carolina established Fort Loudon on the Little Tennessee River, but the garrision was massacred by the Cherokees in 1760.

France lost its claim to the area in 1763; and the first permanent settlement was made in 1769 in the WATAUGA River Valley by Virginians, who were followed by North Carolinians. The first attempt at government was made in 1772 when these pioneers formed the

Watauga Association; and in 1777, at their request, North Carolina organized the settlements into a county. JONESBORO, founded in 1779, became the county seat. That year, too, the Cherokees ceded a large area to the settlers, but some Cherokees refused to recognize the agreement and made war. The settlers objected when North Carolina ceded the region to the Federal government and in 1784 they set up their own State of FRANKLIN. Four years later North Carolina again took charge, and in 1790 Tennessee became part of the Southwest Territory.

Pioneers came in from the Carolinas, Virginia, and Pennsylvania especially, and the state prospered in the 19th century as canals and railroads were built. MEMPHIS was laid out in 1819, and more settlers arrived after the Cherokees and Chickasaws were moved west in the 1830's. In early 1861 a referendum rejected secession; but another in June, after the Civil War began, approved it. Tennessee turned out, after Virginia, to be the bloodiest battleground of the war. The capture of FORT HENRY on the TENNESSEE RIVER in February 1862 and of FORT DONELSON on the Cumberland the same month were the first major Union victories. In April the Battle of SHILOH, near Pittsburg Landing, was a narrow victory for Union Gen. Ulysses S. Grant. At the end of 1862 the Battle of MURFREESBORO began, ending in a Confederate retreat. Several battles marked the CHATTANOOGA Campaign of August to November 1863, in which the Union army finally took the city. When the Confederates attempted to regain the state in 1864 they were defeated at FRANKLIN in November and decisively beaten at NASHVILLE in December.

After the war Tennessee was the first state to be readmitted to the Union, in March 1866. That year the Ku Klux Klan was organized in Tennessee, but the Radical Republicans controlled the government until 1870, after which some of their reforms were undone. The farm tenancy system that replaced the large slave-manned plantations was not successful, but gradually industry increased and economic conditions improved. The Tennessee Valley Authority, started in 1933 by the Federal government, has been of vital importance to the state in providing waterways, irrigation, and hydroelectric power. Material for the first atomic bombs was produced at OAK RIDGE in the early 1940's. School integration caused some disruption in the 1960's. In July 1980 there were riots in Chattanooga after members of the Ku Klux Klan, on trial, were acquitted.

Nashville is the capital. Memphis is the largest city, and others are Chattanooga and KNOXVILLE.

TENNESSEE RIVER (United States) River of SE United States, it is formed just N of Knoxville, TENNESSEE and follows a U-shaped course S into N Alabama and then N to the Ohio River at Paducah, Kentucky. The principal tributary of the Ohio River, it is 650 miles long. Formerly navigable only by flatboats, it has increased in importance as a waterway since the 1930's, when the Tennessee Valley Authority converted it into a chain of lakes by the construction of nine dams. During the Civil War it presented an obvious route to the Union for an invasion of the western

Confederacy and was followed by Gen. Ulysses S. Grant's army in February 1862 in capturing FORT HENRY and FORT DONELSON on the way to VICKSBURG. See also CHATTANOOGA, SHILOH.

TENOCHTITLÁN (Mexico) Ancient city and capital of the AZTEC EMPIRE, it existed on the site of MEXICO CITY, in Federal District, Mexico. Founded c.1345 AD on a marshy island in Lake Texcoco, it became a flourishing city of between 200,000 and 300,000 inhabitants, with a unique system of waterways and dikes, and a great central plaza with palaces and temples. The Spanish under Hernando Cortés reached it in 1519 when it was Emperor Montezuma's capital, but they were forced to retreat under heavy Aztec attack on June 30, 1520. Cortés returned the following year and captured and razed the city after a three-month siege. Mexico City was later founded by the Spanish on the ruins.

TENTYRA. See DENDERA.

TEOS (Turkey) Ancient city of Asia Minor, on the S coast of the İzmir peninsula, 2 mi W of Seferihisar, in İzmir province, W Turkey. It was one of the 12 cities of IONIA, a religious league, and was the birthplace of the Greek lyric poet Anacreon. Only its ruins remain today.

TEOTIHUACÁN [San Juan Teotihuacán] (Mexico) Ruined city in México state, 30 mi NE of Mexico City, central Mexico. An ancient religious and commercial center, it is the largest and most impressive urban site of ancient America, covering some eight square miles. Dating from the second century AD, the city was planned formally at the start of the Christian era, though little is known of the origins of its inhabitants or of the extent of their political power. Archaeological evidence has revealed that the people of Teotihuacán had a complex religious system and had developed sculpture to a high degree. The city was sacked and burned by the Toltec c.750 AD. Extensive ruins remain, including the vast Pyramid of the Sun, the largest and highest pyramid in Mexico.

TEOTITLÁN DEL VALLE (Mexico) Town in Oaxaca state, 17 mi ESE of Oaxaca, S Mexico. It was the 11th- and 12th-century capital of the Zapotec Indians, and today it is a weaving center.

TEOZAPOTLÁN. See ZAACHILA.

TEPE GAWRA (Iraq) Ancient settlement of MESOPOTAMIA, an important archaeological site, in al-Mawsil governorate, E of the Tigris River, 15 mi NE of Mosul, N Iraq. Inhabited from c.4500 BC until the mid-second millennium BC, the site has revealed 26 layers of cities and gives its name to the northern Mesopotamian Gawra period. It clearly shows the development of early farming villages into more sophisticated settlements with elaborate temples. The city was invaded by non-Semites and Hurrians c.1700 BC.

TEPE HISSAR [Tappeh Hesar Damghan] (Iran) Ancient site in Semnan province, SW of Shahrud, N Iran, near DĀMGHĀN. A site of continuous habitation from c.3900 BC to c.1900 BC, it is near the remains of a large Sassanian palace.

TEPELENA. See TEPELENË.

TEPELENË [Tepelena] [*ancient:* **Antigonea;** *Italian:* **Tepeleni**] (Albania) Town in S Albania, 30 mi ESE of Valona. Built on the site of ancient Antigonea, it grew into a flourishing commercial center under the Turkish governor, Ali Pasha. It lost importance following the Balkan Wars and suffered in an earthquake in 1920.

TEPELENI. See TEPELENË.

TEPEXPÁN (Mexico) Village in México state, near Texcoco, central Mexico. In 1947 a skeleton between 10,000 and 11,000 years old was found here. Known as the Tepexpán Man, it may be the oldest human skeleton yet discovered in the Western Hemisphere.

TEPE YAHYA (Iran) Ancient and important archaeological site in Kermān province, NE of Dowlatābād, Iran. It was almost continuously inhabited from the fifth millennium to the end of the third millennium BC and from c.1000 BC to 400 AD. It had an important economic position in the third millennium BC, exporting steatite bowls to MESOPOTAMIA and the INDUS RIVER Valley.

TEPLICE [*former:* **Teplice-Šanov;** *German:* **Teplitz-Schönau**] (Czechoslovakia) City and spa in N Bohemia, 56 mi NNW of Prague, NW Czechoslovakia. The site of radioactive springs known to the Romans, it was the location of a convent established in 1156 by Queen Judith of BOHEMIA. The famous meeting between writer Johann Wolfgang von Goethe and composer Ludwig van Beethoven took place here in 1812. In the 19th century the waters were believed to heal gunshot wounds. Teplice's German population was expelled after World War II.

TEPLICE-ŠANOV. See TEPLICE.

TEPLITZ-SCHÖNAU. See TEPLICE.

TERAMO [*ancient:* **Interamna**] (Italy) City and capital of Teramo province, ABRUZZI region, 82 mi NE of Rome, central Italy. Originally occupied by the pre-Roman Praetuttii tribe, it was part of the duchy of SPOLETO in the Middle Ages, and was included in the kingdom of NAPLES, first under the Normans, and then from 1814 to 1860. It has the remains of a Roman theater.

TERENGGANU. See TRENGGANU.

TEREZIN [*German:* **Theresienstadt**] (Czechoslovakia) Town in Severočeský region, 11 mi SSE of Usti nad Labem, in N Bohemia, NW Czechoslovakia. Founded by Maria Theresa of AUSTRIA as a fortress, it was occupied by GERMANY during World War II and was the site of an infamous Nazi concentration camp.

TERGESTE. See TRIESTE.

TERMEZ (USSR) City in Uzbek SSR, on the Afghan frontier, 160 mi S of Samarkand, Central Asian USSR. An ancient town, it prospered in the first century BC as part of the kingdom of BACTRIA and was razed at the end of the 17th century AD. The modern city was founded on the site of a Russian fort built in 1897.

TERMINI IMERESE [*ancient:* **Thermae Himerenses**] (Italy) Town and port on the N coast of SICILY, in Palermo province, 22 mi ESE of Palermo. Said to be the site of a Phoenician port, it contained famous thermal springs celebrated by the poet Pindar in the sixth century BC. Agathocles, the tyrant of SYRACUSE, was born here in 361 BC. There are Roman remains.

TERMINUS. See ATLANTA.

TERMONDE. See DENDERMONDE.

TERNATE [*Indonesian:* **Pulau Ternate**] (Indonesia) Island of the Molucca Islands group, in the Molucca Sea, off the W coast of Halmahera Island, in Maluku province, E Indonesia. It was an important center of the spice trade for centuries and a major island in the MOLUCCAS group. Ternate accepted Islam early and was a sultanate from the 12th to the 17th century. Following the expulsion of the Portuguese in 1574, the island passed under Dutch rule in 1606. The sultan gave the Dutch a spice monopoly, and his power declined after popular revolts in 1650 and 1683. The Dutch remained in control of the island until after World War II, when an independent Indonesia was established.

TERNI [*ancient:* **Interamna Nahars**] (Italy) City and capital of Terni province, in UMBRIA region, on the Nera River, 49 mi NE of Rome, central Italy. Originally an ancient Umbrian town, it was possibly the birthplace of the Roman historian Tacitus. Emperor Gallus was murdered here in 253 AD. It passed to the papacy in the 14th century and was the scene of a battle during the French Revolutionary Wars in 1798, when the Neapolitans were defeated by the French. Half the city was destroyed during World War II. It has Roman ruins and the remains of a Neolithic village. See also PAPAL STATES.

TERNOPIL. See TERNOPOL.

TERNOPOL [*Polish:* **Tarnopol;** *Ukrainian:* **Ternopil**] (USSR) City in the UKRAINE, on the Seret River, 70 mi ESE of Lvov, SW European USSR. Once a Polish town, it was razed by the Tatars in 1524. It became part of AUSTRIA in 1772 and was returned to POLAND in 1920. It passed to the Soviet Union in 1939 and was severely damaged during World War II.

TERRACINA [*ancient:* **Anxur, Tarracina**] (Italy) Town in Latina province, LATIUM region, approx 58 mi SE of Rome, on the Gulf of Gaeta, W of Gaeta, S central Italy. Originally a town of the Volsci tribe, it came under ROME c.400 BC and was a major city on the APPIAN WAY. Here the road, previously running straight southeast across the Pontine Marshes, suddenly turns east as it reaches the sea and cuts through the seaside cliffs. The Roman aristocracy made it a resort, and ruins of the villas of the emperors Tiberius, Galba, and Vitellius can be seen here today. The temple of Jupiter Anxurus crowns the cliffs above the town and dates back to the Volscian period. Emperor Galba was born here in 3 BC. The town has an archaeological museum.

TERRANOVA DI SICILIA. See GELA.

TERRE HAUTE (United States) City in W INDIANA, on the Wabash River, 67 mi WSW of Indianapolis. Built on the site of an old Indian meeting place, it was originally the site of Fort Harrison, which was frequently attacked by Tecumseh's Shawnee Indians. Planned in 1816 in a coal-mining region, it is remembered in labor history for its militant union activity. Eugene V. Debs, the organizer of the country's first industrial union, the Brotherhood of Locomotive Firemen, lived and got his start here.

TERRITOIRE DES COMORES. See COMOROS.

TERRITORIOS ESPAÑOLES DEL GOLFO DE GUINEA. See EQUATORIAL GUINEA.

TERRITORY OF NEW GUINEA. See NEW GUINEA, PAPUA NEW GUINEA.

TERTRY [*former:* Testry] (France) Village in Somme department, N France. Pepin of Herstal became ruler of all the Franks by conquering NEUSTRIA here in 687 AD. See also FRANKISH EMPIRE.

TERUEL [*ancient:* Turba] (Spain) Town and capital of Teruel province, in ARAGON, at the confluence of the Guadalaviar and Alfambra rivers, 138 mi E of Madrid, E central Spain. Originally the site of the Iberian settlement of Turba, it was destroyed by the Romans in 196 BC. It became a center of Moorish power after the eighth century AD but was conquered in 1171 by Alfonso II of Aragon. The town was the scene of intense fighting during the Spanish civil war from 1936 to 1939, during which it was largely destroyed.

TESCHEN [Český Těšín] [*Czech:* Těšín; *Polish:* Cieszyn] (Czechoslovakia, Poland) Former principality, now in N central Czechoslovakia and S central Poland, centered around the twin towns of Cieszyn and Český Těšín. At one time a duchy in the Polish province of SILESIA, it passed to BOHEMIA in 1335 and to the Hapsburgs in 1526. As one of the most prosperous areas of AUSTRO-HUNGARY, it was claimed by both Poland and Czechoslovakia following the collapse of the Hapsburg Empire after World War I. In January 1919 the Czechs took much of Teschen by force, and the arbitration of the Conference of Ambassadors of the Allies was needed to settle the dispute peacefully by dividing the region between the two claimants along the Olse River. Poland accepted the decision grudgingly and occupied Teschen in October 1938 after the MUNICH Conference. Following World War II the Soviet Union reestablished the 1920 to 1938 boundary.

TĚŠÍN. See TESCHEN.

TESSIN. See TICINO.

TESTRY. See TERTRY.

TETON PASS. See WYOMING.

TÉTOUAN [Tetuán] (Morocco) City and capital of Tétouan province, on the Martin River, 25 mi S of Ceuta, N Morocco. Built in the 14th century at the location of an earlier town, it was razed by Castilians *c.*1400 because of its use as a pirate base. Reestablished by Muslim refugees from SPAIN in 1492, it was captured by the Spanish in 1860 and was the capital of Spanish Morocco from 1913 to 1956.

TETSCHEN. See DĚČÍN.

TETUÁN. See TÉTOUAN.

TEUCHIRA. See TOCRA.

TEUTOBURGER WALD. See TEUTOBURG FOREST.

TEUTOBURG FOREST [*German:* **Teutoburger Wald**] (West Germany) Hilly range in North Rhine-Westphalia and Lower Saxony, N central West Germany, extending roughly from Osnabrück to Paderborn. Its highest point, near DETMOLD, was the scene of a battle in 9 AD when the Roman legions under Varus were annihilated by German tribes under Arminius. This defeat is said to have prevented the Romanization of Germany between the Rhine and Elbe rivers and left millions of Germans on Rome's borders unconquered. The late eighth-century war between the Saxon Widukind and Charlemagne occurred here. See also FRANKISH EMPIRE, ROMAN EMPIRE.

TEVERE. See TIBER RIVER.

TEVERYA. See TIBERIAS.

TEVIOTDALE. See ROXBURGHSHIRE.

TEWKESBURY (England) Town in Gloucestershire, on the Severn and Avon rivers, 10 mi NNE of Gloucester. An ancient market town, it was the location of a monastery built in the eighth century and reestablished in the 12th century. It grew to be one of England's most famous Benedictine abbeys. During the Wars of the Roses, on May 4, 1471, the Yorkist king Edward IV finally defeated his Lancastrian adversaries here at the Battle of Tewkesbury. The town has many fine old houses and a splendid abbey church.

TEXAS (United States) A state in the southwestern part of the country. It was admitted in 1845 as the 28th state. Texas is derived from the word *Teyas,* as some local Indians were known. The word means "friends." It has a 1,000-mile border with Mexico to the S. New Mexico is to the W, Oklahoma to the N, and Arkansas and Louisiana to the E.

Cabaza de Vaca, shipwrecked off the coast in 1528, passed through the region in the 1530's; Francisco Vásquez de Coronado was probably here in 1541, and Hernando De Soto's men came in 1542. The first Spanish settlement was at Ysleta, near present EL PASO, in 1682. Missions were established; but the Comanche, Apache, and other Indians were unfriendly. Robert Sieur de La Salle, representing FRANCE, was in east Texas in 1685. To hold the region the Spanish established more missions, at SAN ANTONIO in 1718, NACOGDOCHES in 1719, and GOLIAD in 1749.

The cession of Louisiana by France to SPAIN in 1762 removed the French threat but brought contact with the British. Spain unsuccessfully attempted settlements in the north and on the Gulf of Mexico. After the United States acquired the LOUISIANA PURCHASE in 1803, Anglo-Americans began to show interest in Texas. Moses Austin received a grant from Spain in 1821 and later that year his son Stephen led the first 300 Anglo-American families to Texas. MEXICO, now independent, made more grants, more Anglo-American settlement followed, and by 1830 there were more Anglo-Americans than Mexicans in Texas. Mexico attempted to stop further immigration.

Relations worsened, and in 1835 a revolution began. Mexican troops were driven out, and in March 1836 the Texan Americans declared their independence as the REPUBLIC OF TEXAS. The Mexican dictator Antonio Lopez de Santa Anna attacked the ALAMO in San Antonio, killing its defenders, and several hundred others were massacred at Goliad. In April 1836 at the Battle of SAN JACINTO near HOUSTON, Santa Anna was crushed, and Texas' independence was achieved. The Anglos wanted annexation to the United States, but antislavery forces fought it, and annexation did not take place until July 1845. This triggered the Mexican War, the first two battles of which, on Texas soil, were U.S. victories.

An early photograph of the Mexican market in San Antonio, Texas. Mexican-Americans still play a part in Texas, which now enjoys fabulous wealth from its oil fields.

After the war settlers poured in, and the planter class prospered. Texas seceded in February 1861, but in the Civil War it was the only Confederate state not overrun by Union troops. Radical Republicans controlled the state government for several years after the war, and there was considerable lawlessness. Texas was readmitted to the Union in 1870. The Democrats recaptured control in 1874 and have held on to it, except for the results of some recent presidential elections. Texas did not suffer as much in the Civil War as other rebellious states, nor was the cotton plantation system, destroyed by the war, as important. Stock raising expanded, and the cattle drives north began.

In the 1880's, through the Farmers' Alliance and the Greenback Party, there were demands for reform, especially of the practice of granting large areas of public land to the railroads. The economy changed drastically after 1901 with the discovery of the SPINDLETOP oil field near BEAUMONT. The 1920's were a boom period of industrialization, and the Great Depression of the 1930's was less severe in the south than in the Panhandle region and elsewhere. The rich East Texas oil field was discovered in 1930. World War II, with its demand for goods and its many military installations in the state, further spurred the economy. Since 1954 school integration has made progress, and since 1965 a Federal law has increased the number of black voters. Since the late 1960's Texas has been at the heart of the Sun Belt and its economic boom. Houston has been one of

the fastest-growing and richest cities in the nation, attracting thousands yearly. Rapid expansion and lack of planning have begun to show their effects on the state, however.

AUSTIN is the capital. Among many growing cities are DALLAS, El Paso, FORT WORTH, Houston, and San Antonio.

TEXAS CITY (United States) City and port in SE TEXAS, on Galveston Bay, 9 mi NW of Galveston. An industrial city with giant oil refineries, it was developed after 1893. Most of the city was destroyed and over 500 people killed on April 16, 1947 when a nitrate-laden freighter blew up, causing many secondary explosions on shore.

TEXAS, REPUBLIC OF Former independent nation whose territory occupied essentially the same area as the present state of TEXAS in the UNITED STATES. Until 1835 it was part of MEXICO. In that year Anglo-American settlers who had emigrated from the United States, beginning in 1821, set up a provisional government and in 1836 declared their independence. The Anglo-Americans and others were dissatisfied with what they felt was tyrannical and arbitrary Mexican rule. They were also slaveholders, while the Mexican government was against slavery. War broke out, and after initial defeats the Anglos won independence by a victory at the Battle of SAN JACINTO on April 21, 1836.

Sam Houston, who had led the troops, became president, and the city named for him was the capital until 1839, when the capital was transferred to AUSTIN. The new nation found it impossible to get foreign loans, and it had to create armed forces, including the Texas Rangers, to combat raids from Mexico and occasional Indian forays. As early as 1836 the Texans had voted for annexation by the United States, but antislavery forces here fought the move bitterly. Great Britain also wanted an independent Texas to block further westward expansion by the United States, and at one point it seemed Texas might give up slavery in return for British support. This possibly had some effect in the United States, and by a joint resolution of Congress of Feb. 28, 1845 annexation was approved, and Texas's 10 years as a separate nation ended.

TEXCOCO [Texcoco de Mora, Tezcuco] (Mexico) Town in México state, on the side of Lake Texcoco, NE of MEXICO CITY, central Mexico. It was an important town in Aztec times; its rulers were the first Nahuatl leaders to gain control over the Valley of Mexico. By the 15th century Texcoco was paying tribute to the rulers of Azcapotzalco and later in the century came under the shadow of the Aztec rulers of TENOCHTITLÁN as one of the three pueblos of the Aztec Confederation. The Spanish under Hernando Cortés used Texcoco as a base from which to attack Tenochtitlán. See also AZTEC EMPIRE.

TEXCOCO DE MORA. See TEXCOCO.

TEXEL, BATTLES OF (Netherlands) Naval battle site off the most southerly of the West FRISIAN ISLANDS, in the North Sea. It was the scene of two significant battles during the Anglo-Dutch wars of the 17th century. Between July 31 and August 9, 1653 the

Dutch were defeated by the English in the First Battle of Texel. Then in 1673, following his appointment as Lord High Admiral of England, Prince Rupert, formerly count Palatine of the Rhine and duke of Bavaria, met defeat by the Dutch after a battle that raged from August 11 to 21. The English were prevented by the defeat from landing troops in Holland and were forced to quit their blockade of the Dutch coast.

TEZCUCO. See TEXCOCO.

THABA BOSIU (Lesotho) Village and mission in Maseru district, 12 mi E of Maseru, NW Lesotho. In 1831 Chief Moshesh defeated the Matabele here and founded the Basuto nation, with Thaba Bosiu as his headquarters. In 1866 the Treaty of Thaba Bosiu gave part of Basutoland to the ORANGE FREE STATE.

THABRACA. See TABARCA.

THAENAE. See SFAX.

THAILAND [former: **Siam**] A constitutional monarchy occupying the center of INDOCHINA, with seacoasts on the Gulf of Thailand and the Andaman Sea. Thailand's central position has led to continual conflict with neighboring BURMA, KAMPUCHEA, and VIETNAM as their contending empires sought control of the region.

Early Thailand was thinly settled and remained largely vacant for much of its history. Two Indian-influenced cultures developed in the region; the Mons in lower Burma and central Thailand and the Khmers in the MEKONG RIVER valley. The stronger KHMER EMPIRE displaced the Mons from all their territory except a small state of Haripunjaya in central Thailand and then found their own power and influence rapidly eroding. Beginning in the 13th century AD, Thai settlers moved southward from CHINA and established small states throughout Indochina. In Thailand two major states became established: SUKHOTHAI and CHIANG MAI. Sukhothai was founded after a successful revolt against a Khmer-controlled outpost c.1220, and it ruled Thailand's central plain. In the north, Chiang Mai was founded in 1296 after the defeat of Haripunjaya. In the early 15th century Sukhothai was absorbed by the emerging kingdom of AYUTTHAYA.

Ayutthaya differed from Sukhothai in its effective use of centralized power through an organized and efficient governmental bureaucracy. The Thai state prospered and traded with China, Vietnam, INDIA, JAVA, and MALACCA while conducting continual wars of expansion. Ayutthayan expansion in the 14th century encroached on Kampuchean territory, and by the 15th century an often contested but durable link of vassalage held Kampuchea under Thai domination. The Ayutthaya kings tried repeatedly to dominate the northern Thai kingdoms of Chiang Mai and LAOS but never succeeded.

The only major threat to Ayutthayan dominance emanated from Burma. In the 16th century Burmese troops briefly succeeded in reducing Siam to vassalage. During the 17th century European trading and religious influences began to affect Siam. The Dutch established an early stranglehold on trade, and the Thais welcomed missionaries from FRANCE as a counterbalance. When the French used this welcome to establish a large armed mission in 1687, Thai mistrust led to an anti-Western coup that served to keep Siam aloof from further Western contact for the next 150 years.

In 1767 a second Burmese invasion broke the Ayutthayan state by sacking the capital city of Ayutthaya. A noble named Taksin succeeded in routing the Burmese and set up a new capital at THON BURI. In 1781 he was deposed after losing his mind, and Siam's leading general, Chao Phraya Chakkri, assumed the throne and founded the royal Chakkri dynasty that still heads the country. He immediately moved the capital across the Chao Phraya river to BANGKOK, and he and his successors proceeded to restore Siam's power over its vassal states, including Kampuchea, the MALAY PENINSULA, and the Lao kingdom of Wiangchan (VIENTIANE).

Most of Siam's trade was with China, and an enormous surge of Chinese immigration to Bangkok found the city half Chinese by the middle of the 19th century. The Chinese brought advanced commercial acumen to Siam, and Western countries demanded an end to the century-and-a-half of isolation. During the 1850's the kingdom granted both free trade and consular representation to leading Western powers. King Mongkut (1851–68) and his son Chulalongkorn (1868–1910) saw little hope of resisting increasing Western demands for concessions and grudgingly gave up Kampuchea and Laos to FRANCE and Malaysia to Great Britain. Internally, Siam's monarchy successfully worked to reform and strengthen their governement on a Western model, better to retain their independence.

In World War I Siam fought on the Allied side and in return received favorable treaty provisions. In 1932 a coup established a constitutional government, ending absolute monarchy in the country. Thailand allied itself with Japan in World War II, and since then the nation has been dominated by military leadership, under the influence of the United States, interspersed with brief interludes of civilian rule. Since the Vietnam War the country has moved steadily toward democracy. Thailand resumed civilian rule in 1975, but it saw a military coup in 1976. Several military premiers have followed, most recently Prem Tinsulanonda in 1980, who rules through a parliamentary coalition that faces increasing political opposition.

THAMES RIVER (Canada) River rising NW of Woodstock, S ONTARIO and flowing past London and Chatham to Lake St. Clair. During the War of 1812, U.S. forces under Gen. William H. Harrison defeated a British and Indian army under Brig. Gen. Henry A. Procter and the Indian leader Tecumseh near CHATHAM on Oct. 5, 1813. Tecumseh was killed, the Indian confederacy that he had formed against the UNITED STATES was destroyed, and U.S. control of the Northwest was restored.

THAMES RIVER [ancient: **Tamesa, Tamesis**] (England) River of S England rising in four headstreams in the Cotswold Hills, E Gloucestershire, and flowing S and E through LONDON to the North Sea at the NORE. It is 210 mi long and is navigable by barge as far as Lechlade, though the upper part is generally used only for fishing and pleasure. London, founded as a Roman town, grew up around the only bridge in the area; and the lower river, including the port of London, has always been of great importance to shipping, especially since the 17th century. The Thames valley is the heart of southern England, and the river itself has many historical and literary associations. Chief towns on its banks include OXFORD (where the river is called the Isis), READING, WINDSOR and Windsor Castle, RICHMOND UPON THAMES, KINGSTON UPON THAMES, and below London, GREENWICH, GRAVESEND, and TILBURY.

THAMUGADI. See TIMGAD.

THAMUGADIS. See TIMGAD.

THANA [Tana] (India) Town in W Maharashtra state, 21 mi NNE of Bombay, at the mouth of the Thana River, W India. A major Indian port in the 13th century, it was here in April 1321 that several Franciscan missionaries from Italy, including Thomas of Tolentino, James of Padua, and Peter of Siena, were killed by the Muslims in the city. It was an early settlement of the Portuguese before they were expelled by the MARATHAS in 1737.

THANESAR (India) Town in E Punjab, 21 mi NNW of Karnal, NW India. It was the capital of Harsha, the fourth king of Thanesar, who conquered an evanescent empire in northern India at the beginning of the seventh century AD. Thanesar was razed by Mahmud of GHAZNI in 1014.

THANET. See MARGATE.

THANET, ISLE OF (England) Former island, now an area in the corner of NE Kent. It is the site of two third-century Roman forts guarding the channel that once made the Isle of Thanet a true island. The island was said to be the landing place of the Anglo-Saxon invader Hengist c.450 AD. The mission sent by Pope Gregory the Great to Britain first touched shore here in 597 under the leadership of Augustine of CANTERBURY. Later it was the victim of the Danish Viking raiders, who first wintered in England here in 850, marking the beginning of their conquest. In the later Middle Ages it was in the jurisdiction of the CINQUE PORTS.

THANJAVUR [former: Tanjore] (India) City in Tamil Nadu state, in the Cauvery delta, 190 mi SSE of Madras, SE India. The capital of the CHOLA dynasty in the 10th and 11th centuries, it was an independent state under VIJAYANAGARA in the 16th century and was taken by the Marathas in 1674. It passed to the British in 1855, and it was here that the Protestant missionaries did their earliest work in India. See also MARATHA CONFEDERACY.

THAPSACUS [biblical: Tiphsah; modern: Dibse] (Syria) Ancient city on the EUPHRATES RIVER, 60 mi ESE of Aleppo, in Aleppo province, N central Syria. In antiquity it was the site of a ford used by conquering armies, including that of Alexander the Great. It is mentioned in the Bible in 1 Kings 4:24.

THAPSUS (Tunisia) Ancient town and port of North Africa, 100 mi SE of Carthage, SE of Sousse, E Tunisia.

During the conflict between Julius Caesar and the Roman Senate, Thapsus was the last fortress of Pompey's party and was invested by Caesar. On Feb. 6, 46 BC Quintus Metellus Scipio and a Numidian contingent under Juba I were defeated while trying to lift the siege. The Pompeians suffered enormous losses, and after the battle Caesar's control of Roman Africa was assured.

THASOS [Greek: Thásos] (Greece) Island in the N AEGEAN SEA, NE Greece. In antiquity it was known for its gold mines, which were worked by the Phoenicians. Colonized and fortified by the Greeks from 681 to 628 BC, it came under the control of PERSIA, then of ATHENS in the fifth century BC. It was seized by the Crusaders in 1204, then passed to the OTTOMAN EMPIRE in 1455. It remained part of Turkey until 1913, when it came under Greece after the Balkan Wars. See also PHOENICIA.

THATO. See TATTA.

THATON (Burma) Town in Tenasserim division, 35 mi NNW of Moulmein, Lower Burma. Established in 534 BC, it was once the capital of the Mon Kingdom, although its political power waned after the founding of PEGU. Until the 11th century, when it was conquered by Burma under the leadership of Anawratha, it was a famous center of Buddhism.

THATTA. See TATTA.

THAUMACI. See DOMOKOS.

THEBAE. See THEBES, Egypt.

THEBEN. See DEVIN.

THEBES [ancient: Diospolis, Diospolis Magna, Thebae; biblical: No] (Egypt) Ancient city of Upper Egypt, on the NILE RIVER, S of Qena, in modern Qena governorate. The great temple complexes of LUXOR and KARNAK now occupy parts of its site. Although it was settled very early, not much is known about the city until c.2135 BC, when the Theban family established the Eleventh Dynasty. Thebes gained importance as the site of the royal residence and as the center of worship of the god Amon. It reached its apex during the empire or New Kingdom (c.1580–1090 BC), when it was a storehouse of the wealth of defeated nations. Its power waned as the empire declined, and it was razed by the Assyrians in 661 BC. It was destroyed by the Romans in 29 BC; only a few villages remained by 20 BC. The surviving tombs, including Tutankhamen's, are considered to be some of the world's most magnificent, and Thebes has been the site of very important archaeological discoveries.

THEBES [Greek: Thívai] (Greece) City in Boeotia, 33 mi NNW of Athens, central Greece. The chief city of ancient BOEOTIA, it was identified in legend with King Cadmus who traditionally founded it in 1313 BC, and with Oedipus, and was the locale of many Greek tragedies. A Mycenaean palace has been identified beneath the modern town. It entered into a power struggle with ATHENS at the end of the sixth century BC. From 480 to 479 it sided with PERSIA against Athens but was defeated. Initially a supporter of SPARTA in the Peloponnesian War, it later joined a confederation against Sparta and defeated the Spartans at LEUCTRA in 371 BC, briefly gaining the hegemony of Greece. Thebes was defeated by Philip II of Macedon at CHAERONEA in 338 BC, and the city was destroyed by Alexander the Great in 336 BC. Although rebuilt in 316 BC by Cassander, Thebes never regained its former importance. It was destroyed by Sulla in 86 BC. Rebuilt, it was sacked in 248 and 396 AD by the Goths.

In the Byzantine period Thebes was the capital of Byzantine Hellas. It was taken by the Bulgars in 1040, and in 1146 fell to the forces of George of Antioch, of Norman Sicily. From here the Normans introduced silk production into Sicily, and with a loss of its market the city declined. It fell to Boniface II of Montferrat in 1205 during the Fourth Crusade and became capital of the duchy of Athens under Otto de la Roche. It withered completely under the Ottoman Turks.

THÉLINÉ. See ARLES.

THEODORAPOLIS. See GIURGIU.

THEODOSIA. See FEODOSIYA.

THEOTMALLI. See DETMOLD.

THERA [Thíra] [*ancient:* **Calliste;** *former:* **Santorin;** *Italian:* **Santorini**] (Greece) Volcanic island in the S CYCLADES, in the Aegean Sea, on the N side of the Sea of Crete, SE Greece. Traditionally believed to have been settled by the Phoenicians, it was later occupied by Laconians and in 631 BC sent colonists to North Africa to found CYRENE. Ruins of the Hellenistic city of Thera have been unearthed on the eastern coast of the island.

Archaeological evidence suggests that an eruption here and ensuing tidal wave in 1500 BC destroyed the coast and center of CRETE, causing the decline of KNOSSOS and the Minoan civilization of the Aegean. It may also have given rise to the legend of lost Atlantis. The Minoan town of Akrotiri, with houses and superb wall paintings, preserved under tons of volcanic ash from the eruption, has recently been excavated here.

THERESIENSTADT. See TEREZIN.

THERMA. See THESSALONÍKI.

THERMAE HIMERENSES. See TERMINI IMERESE.

THERMON [*ancient:* **Thermum;** *former:* **Kephalovryson**] (Greece) Village in Acarnania department, 19 mi NE of Missolonghi, on the E shore of Lake Trichonis, W central Greece. It was the political and religious seat of the Aetolian League and was destroyed in 218 BC by Philip V of MACEDON. Ruins of the ancient temple of Apollo can be seen to this day. See also AETOLIA.

THERMOPÍLAE. See THERMOPYLAE.

THERMOPYLAE [*Greek:* **Thermopílae**] (Greece) Pass in E central Greece, Euboea region, 9 mi SE of Lamía, between the cliffs of Mt Oeta and the Malic Gulf. A route for invaders coming from the north, this pass has been the scene of many battles. During the Persian Wars, in 480 BC, Sparta and her allies with a force of 7,500 men under King Leonidas fought heroically but were defeated here by the overwhelming Persian force of 300,000 under King Xerxes I, who won the day only by outflanking the pass after the Greeks had been betrayed by treachery. The remaining 300 Spartans under Leonidas fought to the last two men.

In 279 the Gauls under Brennus were held up by the Greeks here, and Antiochus III of Syria was defeated here in 191 BC by the Romans under Acilios Glabrio. Alaric took the pass unopposed in 395 AD. Justinian fortified it in the sixth century. During World War II the German army was delayed here from April 20 to 25, 1941 by an ANZAC rearguard action. Since 1955 a new memorial to Leonidas and the 300 Spartans has stood here. The grave mound of the Greek dead still stands on the opposite side of the road.

THERMUM. See THERMON.

THÉROUANNE (France) Village in Pas-de-Calais department, S of St. Omer, N France. Once the site of a fortress that was captured by the English in 1380 and 1513, it was sacked in 1553 by the Emperor Charles V.

THESPIAE [*Greek:* **Thespiai**] (Greece) Ancient city of S central BOEOTIA, SW of Thebes, near Mt Helicon, central Greece. Settled in Neolithic and Mycenaean times, it was an enemy of Thebes, and its soldiers fought against the Persians at THERMOPYLAE and PLATAEA in 480 BC. It was destroyed by Thebes in 371 BC but was rebuilt and became an important town of Boeotia under the ROMAN EMPIRE. Its temple held the Eros of Praxiteles, one of the ancient world's best-known statues. The statue was taken to Rome by Caligula, restored to Thespiae, and snatched again by Nero. The town was devoted to the Nine Muses and, according to legend, was associated with King Thespius who sought to match all 50 of his daughters with Hercules.

THESPIAI. See THESPIAE.

THESPROTIA (Greece) Department of NW Greece and region of ancient EPIRUS, N of the Ambracian Gulf, on the W coast of Greece. The Thesprotians were the earliest settlers of EPIRUS, and their famous oracle at DODONA was one of the oldest in Greece.

THESSALÍA. See THESSALY.

THESSALONICA. See THESSALONÍKI.

THESSALONIKE. See THESSALONÍKI.

THESSALONÍKI [Salonica, Saloniki, Thessalonike] [*ancient:* **Therma, Thessalonica**] (Greece) City, port, and capital of Thessaloníki department, in MACEDONIA, on the Gulf of Thessaloníki, on the W side of the CHALCIDICE peninsula, N Greece. Established by Cassander of Macedon c.315 BC, it was made the capital of the Roman province of Macedon in 146 BC and prospered thereafter. It was to the Thessalonians that St. Paul addressed two epistles, when the city became an early Christian diocese. Its importance was second only to Constantinople under the BYZANTINE EMPIRE. The Emperor Theodosius I was excommunicated in 390 AD by St. Ambrose of Milan for slaughtering the mutinous population of Thessaloníki.

It became the largest fief of the Latin Empire of

The famous Vale of Tempe in Thessaly, between mounts Olympus and Ossa. Only a part of modern Greece since 1881, mountainous Thessaly has always been a place apart.

CONSTANTINOPLE, founded in 1204 by the leaders of the Fourth Crusade. Taken by the Ottoman Sultan Murad I in 1387, it remained under Turkish rule until 1912, during the Balkan Wars, when it was seized by Greece. Kemal Atatürk, founder of modern TURKEY, was born here; and in the beginning of the 20th century the city was the seat of the Young Turk movement. During World War I the Allies landed here at the start of the Thessaloníki campaigns in 1915. The pro-Allied government of Greece was established here in 1916 by Eleutherios Venizelos. During World War II it was severely damaged, and its large Jewish population was exterminated by the German occupation force. Many fine Byzantine churches survive. See also OTTOMAN EMPIRE.

THESSALY [*Greek:* **Thessalía**] (Greece) Region of N central Greece, S of Macedonia, between Epirus and the Aegean Sea. Largely hemmed in by mountains, including the Pindus Mts on the west, it was the site of prehistoric civilizations and was settled by Thessalians before 1000 BC. Its chief cities—LARISSA, CRANNON, and PHERAE—were ruled as oligarchies and exercised considerable power in the sixth century BC thanks to their control of the Amphictyonic League. Thessaly declined but was united again under Jason, the tyrant of Pherae, in 374 BC. Conquered by Philip II of MACEDON in 344 BC, it was included in the Roman province of Macedon in 148 BC. During the Middle Ages Thessaly had a large Rumanian population, and the region was part of the OTTOMAN EMPIRE from 1355 to 1881. See also MACEDONIA.

THETFORD (England) Town in Norfolk, 27 mi SW of Norwich. In the center of the ancient region of Breckland, it has the ruins of a Cluniac priory, a Benedictine nunnery, and a large medieval castle mound. Its local school was noted in the *Anglo-Saxon Chronicle* under the year 631 and was reestablished in 1567.

THEVESTE. See TEBESSA.

THIAKI. See ITHACA.

THIEL. See TIEL.

THIELT. See TIELT.

THIEPVAL (France) Village in Somme department, just N of Albert, N France. It was the site of several battles in September 1916 and August 1918 during World War I.

THINGVALLA. See KARLSTAD.

THINGVELLIR [*Icelandic:* **Þingvellir**] (Iceland) Historic site and national park, on the N shore of Thingvallavatn, 30 mi NE of Reykjavík, SW Iceland. Situated on a lava plain, it was the meeting place of the Icelandic parliament, or *Althing*, from 930 to 1798 AD. The Republic of Iceland was proclaimed here on June 17, 1944.

THINIS. See THIS.

THIONVILLE [*German:* **Diedenhofen**] (France) Town in Moselle department, on the Moselle River, 16 mi N of Metz, in LORRAINE, NE France. One of the towns preferred by Charlemagne, it was here the emperor wrote the Testament of Thionville in 806 AD, which divided his kingdom among his heirs. Once part of the HOLY ROMAN EMPIRE, the town was seized from Spain by Louis II of Bourbon, the Great Condé, in 1643. The Germans captured it in 1870 and retained it until 1919.

THÍRA. See THERA.

THIRHALA. See TRÍKALA.

THIS [Thinis] (Egypt) Ancient city of central Egypt, near the Nile River and modern Girga, in Sawhāj governorate. The home of Menes, first king of ancient Egypt c.3200 BC, it became the capital of the First and Second Thinite dynasties.

THÍVAI. See THEBES, Greece.

THO. See MÉRIDA, Mexico.

THOMAR. See TOMAR.

THON BURI [Dhonburi] (Thailand) City within metropolitan BANGKOK, on the Chao Phraya River, central Thailand. It was the national capital of Siam from 1767 to 1782 and is the site of the temple of Wat Arun.

THORENBURG. See TURDA.

THORN. See TORUŃ.

THORNEY (England) Town in Cambridgeshire, 6 mi ENE of Peterborough, in the Isle of Ely. Fighting took place here in the late 11th century between the Norman Duke William the Conqueror and Hereward the Wake, called the "last of the Anglo-Saxons."

THOUARS [*ancient:* **Toarcium**] (France) Town in Deux-Sèvres department, 49 mi N of Niort, W France. Pepin the Short captured the town in 754 AD. In the 11th century it became a viscountship. The feudal lords of Thouars remained loyal to the English throughout the Hundred Years War, but the town finally passed to France in 1476. During the 16th-century Wars of Religion it was a Protestant center. See also FRANKISH EMPIRE.

THOUNE. See THUN.

THRACE [*ancient:* **Thracia**; *Greek:* **Thráki**] (Bulgaria, Greece, Turkey) Region of SE Europe, in the SE tip of the Balkan peninsula, consisting of NE Greece, S Bulgaria, and European Turkey. Its chief towns are ISTANBUL, EDIRNE, and GALLIPOLI. It has been a constantly shifting region throughout history. The Thracians originally held land as far west as the Adriatic Sea, but the Illyrians forced them to move eastward c.1300 BC. They lost further western territories in the fifth century BC to MACEDON. During the Classical period Thrace failed to absorb Greek culture and its inhabitants were considered by the Greeks to be barbarians, especially by the Greeks of Byzantium, later CONSTANTINOPLE. Thrace was exploited by the Greeks for its gold and silver, and it became a vassal of PERSIA from c.510 to 479 BC. The region was united under Sitalces, fought with ATHENS in the Peloponnesian War, but in the fourth century BC passed under Lysimachus and Macedon. A province under ROME, Thrace was a constant battleground following the barbarian invasions of the third century AD, notably at Adrianople, now EDIRNE, in 378 AD. It passed to the Ottoman Turks in 1453 and was the scene of fighting between Bulgaria and Turkey in the Balkan Wars. After World War I Thrace was divided between Greece, Turkey, and Bulgaria along frontiers that, although still disputed, remain in force today. See also OTTOMAN EMPIRE.

THRACIA. See THRACE.

THRÁKI. See THRACE.

THREE RIVERS. See TROIS-RIVIÈRES.

THRINACRIA. See SICILY.

THROTMANNI. See DORTMUND.

THUGGA [*modern:* **Dougga**] (Tunisia) Ancient city SW of CARTHAGE, 68 mi SW of Tunis, N Tunisia. An important Punic city, it is famous, however, as the best-preserved Roman city of Tunisia, with temples, arches, a theater, a circus, and an aqueduct dating from the ROMAN EMPIRE.

THUINAM. See CHRISTCHURCH, England.

THULE (Greenland) Town in Thule district, NW Greenland, NW of Cape York. Founded in 1910 by the Danish explorer Knud Rasmussen, it derives its name from ancient and medieval concepts of the furthest unknown north, *Ultima Thule*. It, in turn, gives its name to a form of early Eskimo culture. The site of a U.S. military base in World War II, it is now the most important U.S. defense area in Greenland.

THULE. See DUNDAS, Greenland.

THUN [*French:* **Thoune**] (Switzerland) City in Bern canton, on the Aare River, 15 mi SSE of Bern, on the Lake of Thun, central Switzerland. The principal city of the Bernese Oberland, it was founded in the 12th century and was part of the kingdom of BURGUNDY until 1190, when it came under to the dukes of ZÄHRINGEN. It passed to the counts of Kyburg in 1218 and to the city-state of BERN in 1384.

THUNDER BAY [*former:* **Fort William, Port Arthur**] (Canada) City in SW ONTARIO, on the NW shore of LAKE SUPERIOR. A fur-trading post was built here in 1679, and in 1717 the French erected a fort, then known as Fort Kaministikwia. They later abandoned it. The fur-trading North West Company made the site its western headquarters in 1801 and renamed it Fort William. Port Arthur, a military post, was built in the same area in 1866. Both grew into cities and in 1970 were combined as Thunder Bay. The city is one of Canada's major ports.

THURGAU [*French:* **Thurgovie**] (Switzerland) Canton of NE Switzerland, S of the Lake of Constance, with its capital at FRAUENFELD. Inhabited since prehistoric times, it appeared first as a political unit in the eighth century AD. It belonged to the dukes of ZÄHRINGEN and the counts of Kyburg before passing to the Hapsburgs in 1264. Captured by the confederated Swiss states in 1460, it became a canton of the Helvetic Republic in 1798.

THURGOVIE. See THURGAU.

THURIA. See THURII.

THURII [**Thuria, Thurium**] (Italy) Ancient city of MAGNA GRAECIA, near the site of SYBARIS, in Lucania, on the Gulf of Taranto, Cosenza province, Calabria region, S Italy. Established in 443 BC by the Athenian statesman Pericles to replace SYBARIS, destroyed by CROTONE, it later allied itself with ROME and was consequently pillaged by Hannibal in 204 BC during the Second Punic War. Although restored by Rome, it never regained its former importance.

THÜRINGEN. See THURINGIA.

THURINGIA [*German:* **Thüringen**] (East Germany) Region of SW East Germany, around the Thuringian Forest, between the Werra River to the W and the Weisse Elster to the E, with its capital at WEIMAR. Vanquished by the Huns in the fifth century AD, the Thuringians were later briefly independent c.500 AD with a kingdom stretching from the HARZ MOUNTAINS to the DANUBE RIVER. Defeated by the Franks in 531 at Burgscheidungen, the Thuringian kingdom came under the rule of the Frankish dukes and was converted to Christianity in the eighth century. A Magyar invasion of Thuringia was stopped at Riade in 933 by Henry I. In the 11th century the landgraves of Thuringia became princes of the HOLY ROMAN EMPIRE, and following a dynastic dispute the succession passed to the house of Wettin in 1265. Thuringia, often associated with SAXONY, was divided into smaller states in the 15th century and was only reunited in 1920 as a *land*, or state, of the Weimar Republic. It was a center of the Lutheran Reformation in the 16th century.

THURIUM. See THURII.

THURLES [*Gaelic:* **Dúrla Éila**] (Irish Republic) Town in County Tipperary, 24 mi NNW of Clonmel, S central Ireland. Richard de Clare, second earl of Pembroke, known also as Richard Strongbow, was overthrown here in 1174 by Donal O'Brien and Roderick O'Connor. The Roman Catholic archbishop of CASHEL has his seat at Thurles.

THURSO (Scotland) Port in Caithness, Highland region, at the mouth of the Thurso River, 114 mi NNW of Aberdeen. The northernmost town of mainland United Kingdom, it was the seat of Norse power in Scotland until the Norse were defeated at LARGS in 1262. It became a free city in 1633.

THYATIRA. See AKHISAR.

TIAHUANACO [**Tiahuanacu**] (Bolivia) Prehistoric site in La Paz department, near the town of Tiahuanaco, near the SE end of LAKE TITICACA, W Bolivia. The site of an important pre-Columbian ruin, it has remains dating from 200 BC, including statues, monoliths, pillars, carvings, and the remains of the temple of the Sun. The culture of Tiahuanaco preceeded the Aymara and Inca civilizations and prospered for 200 years. See also INCA EMPIRE.

TIAHUANACU. See TIAHUANACO.

TIARET [**Tāhart, Tiharet**] [*ancient:* **Tingartia;** *modern:* **Tagdempt**] (Algeria) City and capital of Tiaret department, 110 mi E of Oran, in the N Atlas Mts, NW Algeria. Inhabited since Roman times, it became the capital of western Algeria during the Byzantine period and was the home of a Muslim dynasty in the later Middle Ages. It passed to the Turks in the 16th century, was taken by FRANCE in 1843, and was entirely rebuilt as a modern city. See also OTTOMAN EMPIRE.

TIBERIAS [*Arabic:* **Tabariya, Tubariya;** *Hebrew:* **Teverya**] (Israel) Town, spa, and port on the SEA OF GALILEE, Northern district, 30 mi E of Haifa, NE Israel. One of the four holy cities of Judaism, it was established by Herod Antipas c.20 AD, and following the destruction of JERUSALEM in 70 AD became a center of Jewish learning in the second century. It was the Roman capital of GALILEE. The Sanhedrin, or priestly council, met in the town, which fell to the Arabs in 637 and was taken by the Crusaders in the 11th century. Captured by Saladin in 1187, it became part of the OTTOMAN EMPIRE after 1517 and was again a center of Jewish scholarship in the 18th century. On April 18, 1948 it was the first Arab-Jewish city to be captured by the Israeli defense forces. See also JUDAEA, SAFAD.

TIBERIOPOLIS. See STRUMICA.

TIBERIS. See TIBER RIVER.

TIBER RIVER [*ancient:* **Tiberis;** *Italian:* **Tevere**] (Italy) River of central Italy, 250 mi long, rising in the Etruscan Apennines and flowing S through Tuscany, Umbria, and N Latium, then SW through the city of ROME to the Tyrrhenian Sea. Subject to severe flooding until modern times, it was used in the fifth century BC for shipping grain. During the Punic Wars in the third century BC the Romans built a naval base at OSTIA on the lower Tiber that was greatly improved during the ROMAN EMPIRE, but the port was eventually rendered unusable by silting. In the 1970's silting still prevented ships from passing beyond Rome.

TIBET [*Chinese:* **Si-tsang;** *Tibetan:* **Bodyul**] (China) Autonomous region in SW China, bordered on the S by Burma, India, Bhutan, Sikkim, and Nepal. Its capital is at LHASA. It is mostly a very high plateau, averaging 16,000 feet, surrounded by mountain ranges. In the Western view, Tibet has always been a land of mystery. Its capital, Lhasa, has long been known as the Forbidden City. It is also known for its emphasis on Lamaism, under which at one time as many as one sixth of the country's males were monks.

Tibet's early history is obscure until it emerged in the

seventh century AD as an independent kingdom. China established relations with Tibet during the T'ang dynasty (618–906). From an early association with Mahayana Buddhism there developed in Tibet in the eighth century a form of Buddhism known as Lamaism. The country came under Mongol influence in the 13th century; and in 1270 Kublai Khan, the Mongol emperor and founder of the Yüan dynasty of China, was converted to Lamaism. The abbot who converted him founded the Sakya dynasty in Tibet, which lasted from 1270 to 1340, and he became the first priest-king. This dynasty was corrupt and led to the rise of a reform movement known as the Yellow Hat Sect. Its influence spread so that in 1641 a Mongol prince gave both temporal and spiritual control to a grand lama, who became known as the Dalai Lama. Spiritual control, however, soon passed to another abbot, the Panchen Lama.

A valley in remote Tibet, famous for its lamaseries. Brutally subjugated by China in the 1950's, the Tibetans now receive better treatment under the new Chinese regime.

The Manchu dynasty replaced the Mongols in Tibet in 1720, and Chinese suzerainty became largely nominal. In the 18th century the British, from bases in INDIA, tried to establish relations with Tibet, but an invasion by the Gurkhas from NEPAL in 1788 and their war with Tibet in 1792 put an end to this effort. Tibet continued to isolate itself in the 19th century, but in mid-century KASHMIR seized the Ladakh region, and in 1890 the British took SIKKIM. In 1893 they finally obtained a trading post in the country, but, dissatisfied with their treatment, they sent a military expedition in 1904 that forced a treaty on the Dalai Lama and opened Tibet to Western trade. When the Manchu dynasty of China fell, Tibet in 1912 asserted its independence. After the 13th Dalai Lama died in 1933, however, Tibet gradually again came within China's orbit.

A dispute over the succession of the Panchen Lama led to a Chinese invasion of Tibet in October 1950. In May 1951 Tibet became, by agreement, a national autonomous region of China. Under communism, land reforms were introduced, and the powers of the monastic orders were reduced. These moves were unpopular, and a revolt broke out in 1959. The Dalai Lama fled to India, and the Chinese put down the rebellion brutally. Afterward they seized land and forced thousands of monks to seek work by nearly emptying the lamaseries. In 1962 China attacked India along the Tibetan border, claiming land that had been awarded to India in 1914. Later the Chinese withdrew, except in part of Ladakh. The Panchen Lama was deposed in 1964 and replaced by a secular Tibetan leader. In 1965 the Chinese Tibetan Autonomous Region was officially established.

TIBUR. See TIVOLI.

TICINO [*ancient:* **Ticinus**] (Italy, Switzerland) River rising on the slopes of Saint Gotthard and flowing through TICINO canton, S Switzerland, through Lake Maggiore to the PO RIVER, 4 mi SSE of Pavia, N Italy. During the Second Punic War, in 218 BC, the Carthaginians under Hannibal defeated the Romans under Publius Cornelius Scipio here. See also CARTHAGE, ROME.

TICINO [*French* and *German:* **Tessin**] (Switzerland) Canton of S Switzerland, in the Lepontine Alps, S of Uri canton. BELLINZONA is its capital. Under the ROMAN EMPIRE it was part of Transpadane GAUL. Its later history followed that of LOMBARDY until the 15th and 16th centuries, when it was taken from the duchy of MILAN by the Swiss Confederation. Until 1798 it was ruled by URI and SCHWYZ cantons, and in 1803 it became a canton of the Helvetic Republic.

TICINUM. See PAVIA.

TICINUS. See TICINO.

TICONDEROGA [*former:* **Fort Carillon**] (United States) Village in NE NEW YORK State, between Lake George and Lake Champlain, 85 mi NNE of Albany. Settled in the 17th century on the main portage route between Lakes George and Champlain, the fort here was the site of several battles in the French and Indian War. The French under Gen. Louis de Montcalm succeeded in defending Fort Carillon against Gen. James Abercromby in 1758, but it was captured the following year by the British under Maj. Gen. Jeffrey Amherst and was renamed Fort Ticonderoga. During the American Revolution it was captured by the Green Mountain Boys under Ethan Allen on May 10, 1775 but was abandoned without a shot to Gen. John Burgoyne and the British during the Saratoga campaign. The old fort was reconstructed and made into a museum in 1909. See also SARATOGA SPRINGS.

TIDDIM (Burma) Town in Chin Special Division, W Upper Burma, 40 mi WNW of Kalewa and E of the

Manipur River. Tiddim was the base of the Japanese forces in the campaign against India, from 1943 to 1945 during World War II.

TIDORE [*Indonesian:* **Pulau Tidore**] (Indonesia) Island in the MOLUCCA Islands group, 1 mi S of Ternate Island, Indonesia. Once the seat of an ancient and powerful sultanate, it was held by the Portuguese from 1521 to 1605. The Spanish, arriving in 1606, helped the island to resist the sultan of TERNATE and the Dutch but were driven out by the Dutch in 1654. During World War II Tidore was occupied by JAPAN from 1942 to 1945.

TIEL [*former:* **Thiel**] (Netherlands) Town in Gelderland province, 21 mi WSW of Arnhem, central Holland, on the RHINE RIVER. Founded in 1200, it was a port, trading center, and member of the HANSEATIC LEAGUE during the Middle Ages.

TIELT [*former:* **Thielt**] (Belgium) Town in West Flanders province, 9 mi ENE of Roulers, W Belgium. It was the site of the German headquarters on the FLANDERS front in the early phase of World War I.

TIEMBLO, EL (Spain) Town in Ávila province, 20 mi SE of Ávila, central Spain. To the south of the town are the ruins of the Hieronymite monastery where, in 1468, a pact was signed naming Isabella the heir to the throne of CASTILE. Also nearby are the prehistoric sculptures known as the Toros de Guisando.

T'IEN-CHING. See TIENTSIN.

TIENEN. See TIRLEMONT.

TIENTSIN [**T'ien-Ching**] (China) City and major international port within, though independent of, Hopei province, 80 mi SE of Peking, on the Hai River at its confluence with the GRAND CANAL, NE China. Strategically located on the overland route to MANCHURIA, it has frequently been a military target since becoming important in the late 18th century. In 1860 it became a treaty port and developed rapidly. The massacre of French by an angry Chinese mob on June 21, 1870 nearly precipitated war and the end of the cooperative policy between the Chinese and the treaty powers. Following the Boxer Rebellion in 1900 the city was placed under international control until 1907. It was returned to China in 1946 and is today the country's third-largest city.

TIERRA DEL FUEGO (Argentina, Chile) Archipelago at the S extremity of South America, S of the Strait of Magellan, divided between the Argentinian Territory of Tierra del Fuego and the Chilean province of Magallanes. Discovered by Ferdinand Magellan in 1520, it was named "Land of Fire" by Magellan, who observed the signal fires of the inhabitants burning on the mountain peaks at night. It was surveyed only in the early 19th century and was rapidly populated following the discovery of gold in the 1880's. Its aboriginal peoples gradually succumbed to disease. Many accounts of the fierceness of the land and its people survive from the early explorers and users of the strait.

TIFLIS. See TBILISI.

TIGARA. See HOPE, POINT.

TIGHINA. See BENDERY.

TIGIN. See BENDERY.

TIGRANOCERTA. See SIIRT.

TIGRIS RIVER [*Arabic:* **Shatt Dijla;** *biblical:* **Hiddekil**] (Iraq, Turkey) River of SW Asia, rising in the Taurus Mts, E Turkey and flowing SE through Iraq to join the EUPHRATES RIVER, to form the Shatt al Arab, emptying into the Persian Gulf. It is 1,180 miles long and is subject to sudden and violent flooding. Along with the Euphrates it formed the basis of the Fertile Crescent. The land between the two rivers, *Mesopotamia* in Greek, was an early center of civilization. In antiquity, when some of the great cities of MESOPOTAMIA were built on its banks, including ASHUR, NINEVEH, CTESIPHON, and SELEUCIA, it was important for transportation and was surrounded by irrigation systems. Today the improvement of rail and road facilities has caused its importance as an artery to decline. See also BAGHDAD, BASRA, MOSUL.

TIHARET. See TIARET.

TIHOO. See MÉRIDA, Mexico.

TI-HUA. See URUMCHI.

TIHWA. See URUMCHI.

TIKAL (Guatemala) Ancient Mayan city, in NW PETÉN department, NE of Petén Itza, N Guatemala. The biggest and perhaps the most ancient of the Mayan cities, it comprises nine sets of plazas and courts built on hills above the swampland, with bridges and causeways connecting the sets. It was an important ceremonial center between the first century AD and 300 and reached its height from 300 to 900, during the Classic period, when it began to decline and was all but abandoned.

TIKHVIN (USSR) City in Russian SFSR, 115 mi ESE of Leningrad, central European USSR. Inhabited since the end of the 14th century, it developed as a trading center. In 1611 it was temporarily occupied by the Swedes. The Germans captured it in 1941 during World War II. The composer Nikolai Rimsky-Korsakov was born here in 1844.

TIKRĪT [**Tekrit**] (Iraq) Town on the TIGRIS RIVER, 100 mi NNW of Baghdad, N central Iraq. It was the birthplace of Saladin, a Kurd and the Ayyubid sultan of EGYPT (1138–92). It was taken from the Turks during World War I on Nov. 6, 1917.

TILBURY (England) Port in Essex, on the THAMES RIVER, 22 mi E of London. Originally a fort built by Henry VIII, it was the site of a review of royal troops in 1588 by Elizabeth I, when the Spanish Armada threatened England. It is famous for its docks built between 1884 and 1886, which are now the main container center for the Port of LONDON.

TILLY [**Tilly-sur-Seulles**] (France) Village in Calvados department, NORMANDY, 7 mi SSE of Bayeux, NW France. During World War II it was recaptured from the Germans by Allied troops between June 7 and 11, 1944.

TILLY-SUR-SEULLES. See TILLY.

TILSIT. See SOVETSK.

TIMBUKTU [Tombouctou] (Mali) City in central Mali, near the Niger River. An old center of Islamic culture, it was important because of its position on the trans-Saharan caravan route. Established in the 11th century as a seasonal camp by Tuaregs, it became part of the MALI EMPIRE by the 14th century and was a major trading center of the western SUDAN. Famed for its gold trade, it came under the SONGHAI EMPIRE in the 15th and 16th centuries and was a Muslim educational center of great renown. In 1593 it was sacked by Moroccan invaders, an attack from which it never recovered. The French captured it in 1894. In the 20th century it became a symbol for the remote corners of the world. See also SAHARA DESERT.

TIMGAD [*ancient:* **Thamugadi, Thamugadis**] (Algeria) Archaeological site, Roman city, in Batna department, ESE of Batna, NE Algeria. The site of one of the best-preserved and most extensive Roman ruins in Africa, it has been called the Pompeii of North Africa. The city was founded by Emperor Trajan in 100 AD as a veteran's colony and was destroyed by Berbers in the seventh century. It was uncovered by excavations in 1881.

TIMIŞOARA [*ancient:* **Castrum Temesiensis;** *Hungarian:* **Temesvár**] (Rumania) City and capital of Timiş district, on the Beja canal, in the BANAT region, 28 mi NE of Belgrade, Yugoslavia, in W Rumania. The chief city of the former *banat* of Temesvár or Timişoara, it was an ancient Roman settlement and was razed by the Tatars in the 13th century. It was under the OTTOMAN EMPIRE from 1552 until 1716, when it was captured by AUSTRIA. Formally declared a part of Austria by the Treaty of Passarowitz in 1718, it was colonized by Swabian Germans. During the revolution of 1848 it withstood a 107-day long siege by Hungarian revolutionaries. It was assigned to Rumania in 1920.

TIMOR (Indonesia) Island in the S Malay Archipelago, between the Savu and Timor seas. The largest of the Lesser Sunda Islands, it was politically divided between Portuguese Timor to the east and Indonesian Timor to the west. Indonesian Timor, with the adjacent islands, formed the province of East Nusa Tenggara. The Portuguese began to trade with Timor in 1520, and the Dutch arrived in 1613. The island was divided by treaty between the Netherlands and PORTUGAL in 1860 and 1914 along the present boundaries. In 1950 western Timor became part of Indonesia, while the east remained a Portuguese colony. In 1976 the latter was seized in a civil war and also became part of Indonesia. Indonesian atrocities in suppressing the subsequent East Timor revolt gained worldwide attention and reportedly continued into the 1980's.

TINCHEBRAI [Tinchebray] (France) Town in NW Orne department, 9 mi SE of Vire, NW France. On Sept. 28, 1106 Henry I of ENGLAND defeated his brother Robert II of NORMANDY here and thus gained control of all Normandy.

TINCHEBRAY. See TINCHEBRAI.

TINGARTIA. See TIARET.

TINGIS. See TANGIER.

TINGVALLA. See KARLSTAD.

TINIAN (United States) Island in the MARIANA ISLANDS group, part of the U.S. Trust Territory of the Pacific Islands, in the W Pacific Ocean, 100 mi N of Guam. Under Japanese administration before World War II, the island was taken by U.S. troops in 1944. The United States built here what were then the longest runways in the world. The planes that dropped the atom bomb on HIROSHIMA and NAGASAKI were launched from Tinian in August 1945.

TINICUM ISLAND (United States) Small island in the DELAWARE RIVER, SW of Philadelphia, SE PENNSYLVANIA. It held the first Swedish settlement in Pennsylvania and was the capital of NEW SWEDEN from 1643 to 1655.

TINTAGEL HEAD (England) Cape on the coast of Cornwall, 35 mi NW of Plymouth. It is the site of the ruined Tintagel Castle, built on the site of a Celtic monastery in the 12th century. It is believed to be the birthplace of King Arthur.

TINTERN ABBEY (Wales) Ruin in Gwent, 15 mi ENE of Newport. A famous ecclesiastical ruin celebrated by the poet William Wordsworth, in a poem by the same name, the abbey was founded for Cistercians in 1131 by Walter de Clare but was not completed until the 14th century. It was dissolved in 1537.

TIOBRAID ÁRANN. See TIPPERARY.

TIPASA [*former:* **Tipaza**] (Algeria) Village in Alger department, on the Mediterranean Sea, 37 mi WSW of Algiers, N central Algeria. Of Punic origin, the settlement became a Roman colony in the first century AD. There are ancient remains. See also CARTHAGE.

TIPAZA. See TIPASA.

TIPHSAH. See THAPSACUS.

TIPITAPA (Nicaragua) Town in Managua department, 14 mi ENE of Managua, on the Tipitapa River, SW Nicaragua. In 1927 a peace pact was signed here between the United States and the leader of the Nicaraguan Liberal revolution, Moncada.

TIPPECANOE, BATTLE OF (United States) River in N INDIANA, rising in Tippecanoe Lake and flowing 166 mi S to the Wabash River. On Nov. 7, 1811 at the Indian capital of Prophetstown, now called Battle Ground, on the Tippecanoe River, a U.S. expeditionary force under Gen. William Henry Harrison defeated the Shawnee Indian forces under Tecumseh's brother Laulewasikau, often called the Prophet. It is said the Prophet sat on a rock working Indian magic throughout the battle. Although losses on both sides were about equal, the battle is generally considered to have been a U.S. victory, and the event contributed to establishing Harrison's reputation before his campaign for the presidency in 1840.

TIPPERARY [*Gaelic:* **Tiobraid Árann**] (Irish Republic) Town in County Tipperary, 21 mi WNW of Clonmel. The town developed around a castle built by King John when he was lord of Ireland and was burned by the O'Briens in 1339. During the 19th century it was a center of the Land League unrest.

TIPPERMUIR (Scotland) Battlefield in Tayside region, near Perth. James Graham, fifth earl of Montrose, defeated the Covenanters under the earl of Wemyss here on Sept. 1, 1644.

TIRAH (Pakistan) Mountainous region in Northwest Frontier Province, WSW of the Khyber Pass and Peshawar, on the Afghan border, Pakistan. Inhabited mostly by Afridi and Orakzai Pathan tribes, it was the scene of a holy war in 1897/98 when the Afridi rebelled against the British, capturing posts in the KHYBER PASS and threatening PESHAWAR. The uprising was put down by British and Indian troops.

TIRANA. See TIRANË.

TIRANË [former: **Teheran**; Italian: **Tirana**] (Albania) City and capital of Albania and of Tiranë district, on the Ishm River, 18 mi E of Durrës, central Albania. Founded by the Turkish general Sulayman Pasha in the early 17th century, it developed for the most part after 1920, when it was chosen as the capital of Albania. The Communist Peoples' Republic was proclaimed here on Jan. 11, 1946, and the city was subsequently expanded with aid from the Soviet Union and China. It is the industrial and cultural center of Albania.

TIRANO (Italy) Town in Sondrio province, in N LOMBARDY region, 15 mi E of Sondrio, near the Swiss border, N Italy. The church of the Madonna di Tirano, built in 1503, is a pilgrimage center. Tirano was the site of a massacre of Protestants on July 11, 1620.

TIRASPOL (USSR) City in Moldavian SSR, on the DNIESTER RIVER, 55 mi NW of Odessa, SW European USSR. It was established in 1795 as a Russian fortress at the location of a Moldavian settlement. It became the capital of the MOLDAVIAN AUTONOMOUS REPUBLIC in 1924 and remained so until 1940. See also MOLDAVIA.

TÎRGOVIŞTE [**Târgovişte**] (Rumania) Town and capital of Dîmboviţa district, in WALACHIA, 45 mi NW of Bucharest, on the Ialomiţa River, S central Rumania. The capital of Walachia from 1383 to 1698, it was razed by the Turks in 1737. It has a 15th-century monastery and a 16th-century cathedral.

TÎRGU-JIU [**Târgu-Jiu, Turgu-Jiu**] (Rumania) Town and capital of Gorj district, on the Jiu River, 50 mi NNW of Craiova, SW Rumania. Bitter fighting took place in the valley of the Jiu during both world wars, particularly in 1916.

TÎRGU-MUREŞ [**Osorhei, Târgu-Mureş**] [German: **Neumarkt**; Greek: **Agropolis**; Hungarian: **Maros Vásárhely**] (Rumania) City and capital of Mures district, 50 mi ESE of Cluj, in TRANSYLVANIA, N central Rumania. An old market town first described in the 14th century, it had 30 guilds in the 15th century. The proclamation of Francis II Rakoczy as ruling prince of HUNGARY took place here in 1704. The city remained part of Hungary until 1918, when it was ceded to Rumania, and became part of Hungary again from 1940 to 1945.

TÎRGU-NEAMŢ [**Târgul-Neamţ, Târgu-Neamţu**] (Rumania) Town in Neamt district, in MOLDAVIA, 60 mi WNW of Iaşi, NE Rumania. Founded by the Teutonic knights in the 13th century, it was for a long time an important cultural center. The Neamţ monastery west of the town was founded by Stephen the Great in 1497.

TÍRINS. See TIRYNS.

TIRLEMONT [Flemish: **Tienen**] (Belgium) Town in BRABANT province, 11 mi ESE of Louvain, central Belgium. Repeatedly pillaged and besieged during the Middle Ages, Tirlemont was the scene of the closing actions of the Belgian war of independence in 1831.

TIRNOVO [**Tărnovo, Trnova, Trnovo, Tŭrnovo, Veliko Tŭrnovo**] (Bulgaria) City and capital of Veliko Tŭrnovo province, 55 mi ESE of Pleven, on almost vertical slopes over the Yantra River, N Bulgaria. Settled in prehistoric times, it was the site of a Roman fortress and was the capital of the Second Bulgarian Empire from 1185 to 1396. During this period it was a splendidly embellished town but was sacked and burned by the Turks in 1393. It remained part of the OTTOMAN EMPIRE until 1877, during which time it was a cultural and educational center. In 1879 the first Bulgarian constitution was drafted and passed here, and the independent kingdom of Bulgaria was proclaimed here in 1908. The city was destroyed in 1911 by an earthquake but was restored in the 1970's as a national monument.

TIROL. See TYROL.

TIROLO. See TYROL.

TIRUCHCHIRAPPALLI [**Tiruchirapalli, Trichinopoly**] (India) City in central Tamil Nadu, on the Cauvery River, 200 mi SSW of Madras, S India. An important regional capital between the seventh and 17th centuries AD, it was often the scene of fighting from the 17th to 19th centuries among the Muslims, Marathas, British, and French. Today it is an important commercial, religious, and educational center.

TIRUCHIRAPPALI. See TIRUCHCHIRAPPALLI.

TIRUKKALIKKUNRAM [**Pakshitirtham**] (India) Town in E Tamil Nadu, 35 mi SSW of Madras, SE India. A Shivaite and Vishnuite pilgrimage center, it is nine miles west of MAHABALIPURAM, where there are famous rock-cut temples.

TIRUVANANTAPURAM. See TRIVANDRUM.

TIRUVANNAMALAI (India) City in E central Tamil Nadu, 50 mi S of Vellore, SE India. To the northwest of the city is an isolated peak that is the site of a large Shivaite temple. Of strategic importance in the 18th century, the peak was the retreat of the 20th-century religious recluse Sri Ramana Maharshi.

TIRYNS [modern: **Tírins**] (Greece) Prehistoric city and major archaeological site in Argolis, 3 mi N of Nauplia, in the NE PELOPONNESUS, S Greece. Thought to be the home of the original Greek-speaking people, it is prominent in Greek legend and is connected with Perseus and Hercules. It was inhabited from the third millennium BC and was a magnificent city from c.1600 BC to c.1100 BC. It developed into a center of Mycenaean culture but was destroyed by ARGOS *c*.470 BC. The city's ruins, including massive fortifications, have provided valuable information on pre-Homeric life in Greece. An interesting feature here are the narrow passageways formed within the massive bastion walls, roofed not by arches, but by progressively corbeled stone courses. See also MYCENAE.

TIRZAH [*modern:* **Tell el-Far'a**] (Israel) Ancient town of CANAAN, 7 mi NE of Nablus, in Israeli-occupied Jordan. Frequently mentioned in the Bible, it was the capital of the northern kingdom of ISRAEL from *c*.910 to 887 BC. Noted for its beauty, it was captured by Joshua as related in Joshua 12:24 and was the home of Jeroboam (as related in I Kings 14:17). Excavations have revealed habitation here from the fourth millennium BC to the ninth century BC, when it was abandoned. It then became briefly the Israelite capital until it was moved to SAMARIA. See also PALESTINE.

TISSA. See TISSAMAHARAMA.

TISSAMAHARAMA [**Tissa**] [*ancient:* **Magama, Mahagama**] (Sri Lanka) Village in Southern province, 16 mi NE of Hambantota, S Sri Lanka. The location of one of the old ruined cities of Ceylon, it became the capital of the Singhalese kingdom in the third century BC. It is a Buddhist pilgrimage center, and there are extensive Buddhist ruins.

TITCHFIELD (England) Village in Hampshire, 8 mi NW of Portsmouth. Charles I of England was arrested here in 1647 by the Parliamentarians. It is the site of a 15th-century church containing Anglo-Saxon remains, and of the ruins of 13th-century Titchfield Abbey.

TITIA. See ATIENZA.

TITICACA, LAKE [*Spanish:* **Lago Titicaca**] (Bolivia, Peru) Lake in the ANDES MOUNTAINS, on the border of S Peru and W Bolivia. The largest freshwater lake in South America, at 12,500 feet it is the highest large lake in the world. It was a seat of pre-Incan Indian civilization. TIAHUANACO is near the south shore of the lake.

TITOGRAD [*ancient:* **Birsinium;** *former:* **Podgorica,Podgoritsa, Ribnica**] (Yugoslavia) City and capital of MONTENEGRO, 120 mi WNW of Skopje, S Yugoslavia. A caravan stop called Birsinium in Roman times, it was a feudal capital in the early Middle Ages, when it was called Ribnica. The capital of SERBIA in the 11th century, it fell to the Turks in 1474 and was only restored to Montenegro in 1878. Occupied in both world wars, it was almost completely destroyed in World War II. In 1946 it was renamed in honor of Marshal Josip Tito. See also OTTOMAN EMPIRE.

TITOVO UŽICE [*former:* **Užice**] (Yugoslavia) Town in W SERBIA, 70 mi SSW of Belgrade, central Yugoslavia. Strategically important in the Middle Ages, it was the headquarters of the Yugoslav partisan army and the center of the Free Republic of Užice during World War II. It was renamed in honor of Marshal Josip Tito in 1946.

TITOV VELES [*former:* **Veles;** *Turkish:* **Köprülü**] (Yugoslavia) Town in MACEDONIA, 26 mi SSE of Skopje, S Yugoslavia. First mentioned as early as 216

BC, it was occupied by the Romans and has Roman and medieval remains.

TITTMONING (West Germany) Town in BAVARIA, 15 mi NNE of Traunstein, S West Germany. It is the site of the former castle of the archbishops of SALZBURG dating from the 15th to 17th centuries. The medieval walls of the town have been partly preserved.

TITUSVILLE (United States) City in NW PENNSYLVANIA, 14 mi N of Oil City, on Oil Creek. Founded in 1796 by Jonathan Titus, it was the site of the drilling of the first successful oil well in the United States on Aug. 27, 1859, which started Pennsylvania's oil boom. It was also the location of the nation's first oil refinery. The last refinery here was closed in 1950.

TIUMEN. See TYUMEN.

TIVERTON (England) Town in Devon, 12 mi N of Exeter. Mentioned in the Norman *Domesday Book* of 1086, it was given by Henry I to the Redvers family in the 12th century. It has a 12th-century castle.

TIVOLI [*ancient:* **Tibur**] (Italy) Town in Roma province, Latium region, 16 mi ENE of Rome, on the Aniene River, central Italy. Strategically positioned on an outcropping atop a natural route east from ROME, it has been occupied since prehistoric times. Once an independent member of the Latin League, it was conquered by Rome in the fourth century BC and became a prosperous summer resort under the late Republic and early Empire. Its Roman remains are among the most impressive of antiquity and include the elaborate ruined Hadrian's villa nearby and the circular Temple of Vesta. The gardens of the Villa d'Este here are magnificent examples of Renaissance landscape architecture.

TIXTLA [**Tixtla de Guerrero**] (Mexico) City in Guerrero state, 5 mi NE of Chilpancingo, SW Mexico. In 1811 Spanish Royalists were defeated here by Mexican patriots under Morelos y Pavón. The revolutionary leader Vicente Guerrero was born in the city.

TIXTLA DE GUERRERO. See TIXTLA.

TJILATJAP [**Chilachap**] (Indonesia) Port on the S coast of JAVA, in Central Java province, 175 mi SE of Jakarta, Indonesia. In World War II, during the last stages of the Battle of the JAVA SEA in February 1942, it was used as a base for the Allied fleet.

TLACOLULA [**Tlacolula de Matamoros**] (Mexico) City in Oaxaca state, 10 mi SE of Oaxaca, S Mexico. The site of an Indian town established in 1250, it was settled by the Spanish in 1560 and has a 16th-century church.

TLACOLULA DE MATAMOROS. See TLACOLULA.

TLACOTALPAN (Mexico) City in Veracruz state, 32 mi WNW of San Andrés Tuxtla, SE Mexico. An old Indian settlement, it was the scene of a battle in 1847 during the Mexican War in which U.S. forces were defeated.

TLALNEPANTLA [**Tlalnepantla de Galeana**] (Mexico) Town in México state, 8 mi NNW of Mexico City, central Mexico. An ancient city, it was established by Otomi Indians and was later seized by the Aztecs. There are remarkable Aztec pyramids nearby. See also AZTEC EMPIRE.

TLALNEPANTLA DE GALEANA. See TLALNE-PANTLA.

TLALPAM. See TLALPÁN.

TLALPÁN [Tlalpam] [*former:* **San Agustín de las Cuevas**] (Mexico) Town in Federal District, 12 mi S of Mexico City, central Mexico. Founded by the Spanish, it was the residence of some of the early Spanish viceroys and was the capital of México state from 1827 to 1830. The ruins of a pre-Columbian town are nearby, as is the site of the San Cuicuilco Pyramid, which is thought to be the oldest man-made structure in North America, dating from between 8000 and 7000 BC.

TLASCALA. See TLAXCALA.

TLAXCALA [Tlascala, Tlaxcala de Xicohténcatl] (Mexico) Town and capital of Tlaxcala state, in the mountains between Veracruz and Mexico City, central Mexico. Originally inhabited by Tlascalan Indians, who were enemies of the Aztecs in TENOCHTITLÁN, the town was conquered by Hernando Cortés in 1519. The Indians then aided the Spanish in their attack on Montezuma and the Aztecs. The first Christian church in the Americas, the church of San Fernando, was established here in 1521 by Cortés. See also AZTEC EMPIRE.

TLAXCALA DE XICOHTÉNCATL. See TLAX-CALA.

TLEMCEN [Tlemsen] [*ancient:* **Pomaria;** *former:* **Agadir**] (Algeria) City and capital of Tlemcen department, 75 mi SW of Oran, NW Algeria, near the Moroccan border. It was known as Pomaria when settled by the Romans and as Agadir when inhabited by the Berbers. It was important in the 13th century AD as an Islamic religious and cultural center, situated at the focal point of many North African trade routes. From the 13th to 15th centuries it was the capital of a Muslim Berber dynasty. In 1559 it fell to Algerian Turks and passed to FRANCE in 1842. It was the headquarters of the Nationalist leader Ahmed Ben Bella in 1962.

TLEMSEN. See TLEMCEN.

TLUMACH [*Polish:* **Tłumacz**] (USSR) City in the UKRAINE, on the DNIESTER RIVER, 14 mi ESE of Stanislav, W European USSR. The site of an old palace, it passed from POLAND to AUSTRIA in 1772, was returned to Poland in 1919, and was ceded to the USSR in 1945.

TŁUMACZ. See TLUMACH.

TOAMASINA. See TAMATAVE.

TOARCIUM. See THOUARS.

TOBAGO. See TRINIDAD AND TOBAGO.

TOBERMORY. See MULL.

TOBOLSK (USSR) City and port at the confluence of the Irtysh and Tobol rivers, 300 mi NW of Omsk, in NW Russian SFSR, W Siberian USSR. Founded by Cossacks in 1587, it was one of the first towns in Russian SIBERIA. Under the czars political prisoners were often sent here, and the deposed Czar Nicholas II and his family were brought here in 1917 before their execution at Ekatcrinburg, now SVERDLOVSK.

TOBRUCH. See TOBRUK.

TOBRUK [*ancient:* **Antipyrgos;** *Arabic:* **Tubruq;** *Italian:* **Tobruch**] (Libya) City and port in Derna governorate, on the Mediterranean Sea, 220 mi E of Benghazi, NE Libya. In antiquity it was the site of a Greek agricultural colony and a Roman fortress protecting the frontier of CYRENAICA. Taken by the Italians in 1911, it was used as a military base, and in World War II it was of vital strategic importance as the only natural harbor in Libya. It changed hands several times, during 1941/42, finally falling to the British on Nov. 30, 1942 after the el-Alamein offensive. It was the residence of Libya's former King Idris. See ALAMEIN, EL.

TOCRA [*ancient:* **Arsinoë, Tauchira, Teuchira**] (Libya) Town in Benghazi province, near the Mediterranean Sea, 40 mi NE of Benghazi, N Libya. It was an important Greek colony in antiquity and later was settled by the Romans. From 1941 to 1942, during World War II, it was the scene of fighting between the British and Axis forces.

TODI [*ancient:* **Tuder**] (Italy) Town in Perugia province, UMBRIA region, on the Tiber River, 24 mi S of Perugia, central Italy. An ancient Etruscan fortress, it has extensive Etruscan and Roman ruins that include an amphitheater, theater, and forum. Its medieval walls also remain. It is the site of the church of Santa Maria della Consolazione built between 1508 and 1524 by Caprarola, Barocci, and da Vita. Influenced by the classical ideas of Bramante, this central-plan, domed church is a masterpiece of the Renaissance and looks forward to the central plan of St. Peter's in Rome.

TOGGENBURG (Switzerland) District of NE Switzerland, in ST. GALL canton, in the upper valley of the Thur. Its chief town is Wattwil. Following the death of the last count of Toggenburg in 1436, the district was claimed by ZURICH. In the ensuing civil war, Zurich was opposed and defeated by the rest of the Swiss Confederation. The land passed to the abbot of St. Gall in 1468, and in 1712 disputes between the abbot and the Protestant community led to the War of the Toggenburg between the Catholic and Protestant cantons. The Protestants were victorious, and the Toggenburg became part of St. Gall in 1803.

TOGO [*former:* **French Togo**] Republic in West Africa, on the Bight of Benin, between Benin and Ghana. Its capital is LOMÉ. Togo was granted independence by the French on April 27, 1960. It maintains close links with FRANCE and receives considerable economic aid from her. The government was overturned by coups in 1963 and 1967. Relations with Ghana became strained in 1966 when the Ghanaians wanted to merge with Togo. See also TOGOLAND.

TOGOLAND Former territory of the coast of West Africa, bordering on the Gulf of Guinea and now comprising Togo and part of Ghana. The peoples of Togoland furnished many captives for the slave traders of neighboring ASHANTI and Dahomey, modern BENIN, during the 17th and 18th centuries. German missionaries entered the region in 1840, and German commercial interests quickly became established. In 1885 a German protectorate in Togoland was acknowledged at the Berlin conference, which parceled out the continent to European colonial powers. German rule lasted until 1914, when French and British forces occupied the territory.

In 1919 Togoland was partitioned under a League of Nations directive to form two mandates. French Togoland encompassed the coast and adjoining lands; while British Togoland, a smaller portion of the northern region, was administered by Great Britain along with its GOLD COAST colony. Movements to reunite the two territories were never able to gain a consensus, and in 1956 British Togoland voted to merge with the Gold Coast territory, which was about to become the nation of GHANA. French TOGO became an autonomous republic in the French Community the same year and achieved independence in 1960.

TOKAIDO ROAD (Japan) Ancient highway, the Eastern Sea Route connecting TOKYO (Edo) with KYOTO, approx. 275 mi WSW, on Honshū. It ran along the Pacific coast a large part of the way, and the district formed by the provinces along the route was also called Tokaido. The route is now followed by a modern highway and by two rail lines, one of them for high-speed trains and called the New Tokaido Line. Circa 1835 Utagawa Hiroshige, the celebrated artist of the Ukiyo-e, or pictures of the floating world, school, did a series of 55 woodblock prints he called *Tokaido Gojusantsugi*, or Fifty-Three Stations on the Tokaido. They depict people en route or at the relay stations that controlled traffic and where travelers could refresh themselves at teahouses. The series made Hiroshige famous.

TOKAR (Sudan) Town in Kassala province, 40 mi SSE of Port Sudan, near the Red Sea, E Sudan. During the Mahdi Wars two battles were fought here in 1844.

TOKELAU ISLANDS [*former:* **Union Islands**] (New Zealand) Island group in the South Pacific, N of American Samoa, 2,400 mi SW of Hawaii. It is a territory of New Zealand. Discovered by the English navigator John Byron in 1765, the islands were the target of slave traders from 1850 to 1870. In 1877 the British declared a protectorate over the islands to stop the slave trade, and in 1916 the islands were included in the Gilbert and Ellice Islands colony, now KIRIBATI. They were transferred to New Zealand in 1925 and incorporated with New Zealand in 1948.

TOKIO. See TOKYO.

A Tokyo street in 1904. It is hard to recognize in this placid oriental town the glittering modern metropolis of some 9 million people we know today.

TOKYO [Tokio] [*former:* **Edo, Eddo, Yeddo**] (Japan) City on E central HONSHŪ Island, at the head of Tokyo Bay, capital of the country. Stone Age tribes lived on the site, but the present city was established as the village of Edo in the 12th century AD, and a local warlord built a fort here. Ota Dokan erected a castle in 1456/57 and governed the region under the shogun, the feudal military ruler who held the real power in Japan rather than the emperor. In 1590 this castle came into the possession of Ieyasu Tokugawa, founder of the line of shoguns who ruled Japan for nearly three centuries. After he formally took the shogunate in 1603, Edo, in effect, became the capital of Japan, although the imperial capital continued to be KYOTO.

The town's new prominence caused it to grow and become both a commercial and cultural center. By the time the Emperor Meiji came to the throne in 1867 the Tokugawa shogunate had little strength left, and on April 11, 1868 the last shogun surrendered Edo Castle to imperial troops. The emperor renamed the city Tokyo and made it his capital. Tokyo then became the heart of the Westernizing movement that turned Japan into a powerful, modern nation within one generation. In 1923 the city was badly damaged by an earthquake and fire that killed more than 150,000 people. Afterward the city was rebuilt with wider streets.

Tokyo was again half destroyed in World War II by U.S. bombing attacks, and after the defeat of Japan it was the headquarters of U.S. occupation forces. Rebuilt once more, Tokyo today is one of the largest cities in the world, the heart of the bustling Japanese economy. The Ginza has a worldwide reputation as a shopping and entertainment center. Tokyo also has noted landmarks, such as the Hie Shrine, the Korakuen, a 17th-century landscape garden, and a number of temples.

TOLBIACUM [*modern:* **Zülpich**] (West Germany) Town in North Rhine-Westphalia, approx 20 mi SW of Cologne. Clovis I, king of the Franks, defeated the Alamanni here in 496 AD in the Battle of Tolbiac, thus blocking a westward push by the Germanic people living in Gaul and extending Frankish influence over most of them. While fighting the battle, Clovis is said to have vowed to become a Christian if victorious. He was subsequently baptized by the bishop of RHEIMS with perhaps as many as 3,000 of his followers.

TOLBUKHIN [*former:* **Dobrič, Dobrich;** *Turkish:* **Bazardzhik**] (Bulgaria) Town in Tolbukhin province, 26 mi N of Varna, NE Bulgaria. An old market town, it was under Turkish control from the 15th century until 1878 and was part of RUMANIA from 1913 to 1914. During World War II it was captured from the Germans in 1944 by the Russian general Fyodor I. Tolbukhin, and the town received his name. See also OTTOMAN EMPIRE.

TOLEDO [*ancient:* **Toletum**] (Spain) City and capital of Toledo province, in New Castile, on the Tagus River, 42 mi SSW of Madrid, S central Spain. Culturally and historically Toledo is one of Spain's most valuable cities and dates back to pre-Roman times. It was conquered by ROME in 193 BC and became the capital of Carpentia. It was an early archiepiscopal see, and its archbish-

ops are today the primates of Spain. It flourished in the sixth century AD as the capital of the VISIGOTHIC KINGDOM, and several important church councils were held here. Under the Moors from 712 to 1085, it was the seat of an emir until 1031, and was then the capital of an independent kingdom. From the 11th to the 15th century it was a center of Moorish, Spanish, and Jewish cultures, was a center of translation and philosophical research, and was noted for its tolerance toward aliens. Steel sword blades made in Toledo were famous throughout the world. In the 15th century it was replaced by VALLADOLID as the residence of the kings of CASTILE but in the 16th century became the spiritual center of Spanish Catholicism and the seat of the Inquisition. The painter El Greco settled in Toledo c.1575. In 1936, during the Spanish civil war, the Insurgents defended the Alcázar (fortified palace) in one of the most dramatic episodes of the war. The architectural wealth of Toledo is such that the whole urban area has been declared a national monument. The Gothic cathedral is one of the finest in Spain.

Toledo's Moorish Alcántara bridge, and the Alcázar, restored after the terrible siege of 1936. Memorialized in El Greco's famous painting, Toledo is Spain's most historic city.

TOLEDO [*former:* **Fort Industry, Port Lawrence**] (United States) City and port of entry on the Maumee River and the SW tip of LAKE ERIE, NW OHIO, 55 mi SSW of Detroit. Fort Industry was built here in 1794 after the Battle of FALLEN TIMBERS. The city was settled in 1817 as Port Lawrence, and joined with nearby Vistula in 1833 to become Toledo. An Ohio-MICHIGAN border dispute resulted in the Toledo War in 1835/36, which ended when a decision was made in favor of Ohio. Toledo developed rapidly in the 1830's and 1840's as communications improved and with the discovery of gas and oil in 1844. Today it is a principal Great Lakes port and industrial center.

TOLENTINO [*ancient:* **Tolentinum**] (Italy) Town in Macerata province, in the Marches region, central Italy, 12 mi WSW of Macerata. In 1797 Pope Pius VI signed a humiliating treaty with Napoleon I here, surrendering much territory of the PAPAL STATES and many works of art. Toward the end of the Napoleonic Wars, on May 2, 1815, Murat was defeated near here by AUSTRIA and thus lost the throne of NAPLES. The town is known widely for St. Nicholas of Tolentino, who died here in 1305.

TOLENTINUM. See TOLENTINO.

TOLETUM. See TOLEDO.

TOLLAN. See TULA, Mexico.

TOLOSA. See TOULOUSE.

TOLPUDDLE (England) Village in Dorset, 18 mi W of Bournemouth. The village was the setting in 1834 of the affair of the Tolpuddle Martyrs. In 1833 six agricultural workers led by George and James Loveless (Lovelace) organized a branch of the Friendly Society of Agricultural Laborers. The Whig government, unduly alarmed by trade-union activity and economic discontent, arrested the six on a trumped-up charge that they had illegally administered oaths. They were sentenced in March 1834 to be transported to Australia for seven years. Popular reaction against this action made heroes of the men and led to demonstrations, especially in LONDON. Finally, in March 1836 the sentences were remitted. One of the men returned to Tolpuddle; the rest emigrated to Canada.

TOMAR [*former:* **Thomar**] (Portugal) City in Ribatejo province, 29 mi NNE of Santarém, central Portugal. Famous for the convent-castle of the Knights Templars, it was fortified against the Moors in the 12th century and was the seat of the Knightly Order of Christ from the 14th to 16th centuries. Philip II of SPAIN was proclaimed king of Portugal here in 1581.

TOMBOUCTOU. See TIMBUKTU.

TOMBSTONE (United States) City in SE ARIZONA, Cochise county, 20 mi NNW of Bisbee. Following the discovery of silver here in 1877, it became one of the richest towns of the Southwest, attracting many outlaws, who gave the city a reputation for lawlessness.

TOMI. See CONSTANTA.

TOMIS. See CONSTANTA.

TOMSK (USSR) City and port on the Tom River, in central Russian SFSR, 1,800 mi E of Moscow, W central Siberian USSR. Founded by Czar Boris Godunov in 1604 as a fort, it was an important trading center in SIBERIA until superseded by NOVOSIBIRSK. The first university in Siberia was founded here in 1885.

TOMS RIVER (United States) Resort in E NEW JERSEY, 22 mi SSW of Asbury Park, on an inlet of Barnegat Bay. Inhabited before 1727, it was the scene of guerrilla fighting during the American Revolution and was burned by the British in 1782.

TONALE PASS (Italy) Pass in the Rhaetian Alps, 3 mi E of Ponte di Legno, on the border of Lombardy and Trentino-Alto Adige regions, N Italy. It was once on the Austro-Italian border and was the scene of fighting between the Austrians and the Italians in World War I.

TONGA [**Friendly Islands, Tonga Islands**] [*Tongan:* **Pule 'Anga Tonga**] Island kingdom in the S Pacific Ocean, 2,000 mi SE of Sydney, Australia. Its capital is Nukualofa. The only independent kingdom remaining in the South Pacific, it consists of more than 150 islands. By 1643 all the islands had been discovered by the Dutch, and they were visited in 1773 and 1777 by Capt. James Cook. The 19th-century civil wars in Tonga were followed by the accession of King George Tupou I, who unified the islands and gave them a constitution. Tonga became a British protectorate in 1900 and was granted full independence on June 4, 1970.

TONGA ISLANDS. See TONGA.

TONGEREN [*ancient:* **Aduatica Tungrorum;** *French:* **Tongres**] (Belgium) City in Limburg province, 11 mi NNW of Liège, NE Belgium. It is the oldest city in Belgium and was important in Roman times as the capital of the Germanic Tungri tribe. In 54 BC it was the center of a revolt against ROME. It was sacked many times: in the fourth century AD by the Salic Franks, in 451 by Attila, in 881 by the Normans, in 1212 by the duke of BRABANT, and by the French in 1677.

TONGKING. See TONKIN.

TONGRES. See TONGEREN.

TONKIN [**Tongking, Tonking**] [*Vietnamese:* **Bac-Phan**] (Vietnam) Region of N Vietnam, centered on the Red River Delta and forming the largest part of N Vietnam. Its major towns are HANOI, HAIPHONG, and Nam Dinh. Conquered by the Chinese in 111 BC, it was held by CHINA until 939 AD, when it became independent. By 1471 Tonkin had acquired CHAMPA and became part of the empire of Vietnam in 1802. It was made a French protectorate in 1884 and was the main center of anti-French fighting after World War II.

TONKING. See TONKIN.

TONKIN, GULF OF (China, Vietnam) The NW arm of the South China Sea, off N Vietnam and S China. The gulf was the scene of an alleged attack on U.S. naval forces by North Vietnamese gunboats in August 1964. This led the U.S. Congress to adopt the Gulf of Tonkin Resolution that stepped up U.S. involvement in the Vietnam War. In 1972 the U.S. Army mined the entrance to North Vietnamese ports on the gulf. See also UNITED STATES.

TÖNNING (West Germany) Town in Schleswig-Holstein, 12 mi SW of Husum, near the North Sea, N West Germany. First described in 1186, it was a fortress from 1644 to 1714. Until 1900 it was a center of the cattle-export trade with England. See also SCHLESWIG-HOLSTEIN.

TØNSBERG (Norway) Town and port in Vestfold county, at the head of Tønsbergfjorden, 45 mi S of Oslo, SE Norway. Thought to be the oldest town in Norway, it was established c.870 AD and became an important trading center. Destroyed by fire in 1536, it later developed into a major shipping and whaling center in the 18th and 19th centuries.

TONTIO. See GORI.

T'O-PA WEI, KINGDOM OF. See TA-T'UNG.

TOPEKA (United States) City and capital of KANSAS, 55 mi W of Kansas City, on the Kansas River. A ferry was established here on the OREGON TRAIL in 1842, and the city was founded in 1854 by antislavery settlers. In 1855 the short-lived Free State Constitution was framed here. Topeka became the state capital in 1861 and is now the site of the world-famous Menninger Clinic.

TOPOLA (Yugoslavia) Village in central SERBIA, 40 mi S of Belgrade, central Yugoslavia. In 1804 it was the site of the Serbian insurrection and was the residence of the Serbian patriot Karageorge. A white marble church nearby contains the tombs of Karageorge and of kings Alexander I and Peter I.

TORBAY [Torquay] (England) Resort district in Devon, on the ENGLISH CHANNEL, 19 mi S of Exeter, incorporating Torquay, Paignton, and Brixham. It is the site of the ruins of Tor Abbey, dating from the 12th century, and of the Spanish Barn, which is said to have been the refuge of survivors of the Armada. Paleolithic remains have been uncovered in nearby KENT'S CAVERN.

TORDA. See TURDA.

TORDESILLAS (Spain) Village in Valladolid province, on the Duero River, 18 mi SW of Valladolid, in León, N Spain. Queen Joanna the Mad resided here from 1509 to 1555. The Treaty of Tordesillas, signed here on June 7, 1494, enabled Spain and PORTUGAL to divide the non-Christian world into two spheres of influence. By the terms of the treaty, amending a papal grant of 1493, the boundary between their respective discoveries in the New World was moved to the west, thereby allowing Portugal to claim the eastern part of BRAZIL.

TORGAU (East Germany) City and port on the ELBE RIVER, SE of Dessau, in Leipzig district, S central East Germany. At a strategic crossover point on the Elbe, it was often the home of the electors of SAXONY after 1456. In 1526 a league of Protestant princes formed the Torgenauer Bund here against the Roman Catholic princes. Martin Luther was active in Torgau at that time, and the city became the site of the first Protestant church in 1543. On Nov. 3, 1760, during the Seven Years War, the Austrians were defeated near Torgau by Frederick II of PRUSSIA. The first contact between advance delegations of the U.S. and Soviet armies was made here on April 27, 1945 toward the end of World War II.

TORINO. See TURIN.

TORNEÅ. See TORNIO.

TORNIO [Swedish: Torneå] (Finland) City in Lapi county, on a small island in the Tornio River, near the Gulf of Bothnia, 15 mi NW of Kemi, NW Finland. Originally part of SWEDEN, it was ceded to Finland in

1809. It was an important transit point during World Wars I and II for refugees, the wounded, and prisoners of war.

TORO (Spain) Town in Zamora province, on the Duero River, 35 mi W of Valladolid, NW central Spain. The seat of the Spanish parliament in 1371, 1442, and 1505, it was the site of a battle in 1476 between the forces of Ferdinand and Isabella of ARAGON and the Portuguese under Charles V. The defeat of Portugal secured the throne of CASTILE for Isabella.

TORONTO [former: York] (Canada) City, port, and capital of ONTARIO, on the NW end of LAKE ONTARIO. An early fur-trading post, it was the site of the French-built Fort Rouillé from 1749 to 1759. In 1787 it was purchased from the Indians by the British. Founded in 1793, as York, it was made the capital of Upper Canada in 1797. The city was attacked twice by the Americans during the War of 1812. It changed its name to Toronto in 1834 and was capital of Canada from 1849 to 1851 and from 1855 to 1859. Today it is Canada's second-largest city and the banking and stock-exchange center of Canada.

TOROPETS (USSR) City in Russian SFSR, 40 mi ENE of Velikiye Luki, central European USSR. Formerly the capital of a principality, it passed to LITHUANIA in the 14th century and to MOSCOW in the 15th century. It is the site of a teachers' college founded in 1167.

TOROS DAĞLARI. See TAURUS MOUNTAINS.

TORQUAY. See TORBAY.

TORRES VEDRAS (Portugal) Town in Lisboa district, 26 mi N of Lisbon, in Estremadura, W central Portugal. Captured by Alfonso I from the Moors in 1147, it was an important fortress and royal residence in the Middle Ages. During the Peninsular campaign of the Napoleonic Wars it was the site of the famous lines built by the duke of Wellington to defend Lisbon against the French.

TORRIJOS (Spain) Town in Toledo province, 16 mi WNW of Toledo, in New Castile, S Spain. An ancient town, it is the site of the palace of the counts of Altamira. Parts of the old walls and fortifications are still standing.

TORTOISE ISLANDS. See GALAPAGOS ISLANDS.

TORTONA [ancient: Dertona] (Italy) Town in Alessandria province, PIEDMONT region, 12 mi E of Alessandria, N Italy. Settled by Ligurians, it was made a Roman colony in 148 BC and was a Guelph fortress during the Middle Ages. It was razed by Frederick I Barbarossa in 1155 and was taken by the Visconti in 1347. After the Battle of MARENGO the town's citadel was dismantled by Napoleon in 1801.

TORTOSA [ancient: Colonia Julia Augusta Dertosa, Dertosa] (Spain) City in Tarragona province, on the Ebro River, 40 mi SW of Tarragona, in Catalonia, NE Spain. An ancient Iberian town, it passed to the Romans in 218 BC and fell to the Moors in the eighth century AD. Under Moorish rule, it was a frontier town of the caliphate of CÓRDOVA and was for some time the capital of a small Moorish kingdom. It was captured by Count Raymond Berenger IV of Barcelona in 1148. It was badly damaged in fighting toward the end of the Spanish civil war in 1939.

TORTOSA, Syria. See TARTUS.

TORTUGA ISLAND [*French:* Île de la Tortue] (Haiti) Island off the N coast of Haiti, opposite Port-de-Paix. It was settled in 1629 by European privateers, who became known as the Brethren of the Coast and who preyed on Spanish ships in the CARIBBEAN SEA. The island was controlled by English, French, and Spanish until passing to France in 1697.

TORTUGAS. See DRY TORTUGAS.

TORUŃ [*German:* Thorn] (Poland) City and port on the VISTULA RIVER, in Bydgoszcz province, 110 mi NW of Warsaw, N central Poland. Founded by Teutonic Knights in 1231, it was a prosperous member of the HANSEATIC LEAGUE from the 14th to 16th centuries in spite of its being contested by Poland and the Teutonic Knights. In 1454 it was burned by the knights for recognizing the Polish crown. By the Second Peace of Toruń in 1466 Poland gained the city and large Prussian territories. In the 17th century its population was as large as that of Warsaw, though it was reduced by the Swedish invasions. In 1724 a religious riot at Toruń forced RUSSIA and Poland to safeguard the rights of religious minorities in Poland. The city was part of PRUSSIA from 1793 to 1919. The astronomer Nicholas Copernicus was born here in 1473.

TORZHOK (USSR) City in Russian SFSR, 35 mi WNW of Kalinin, central European USSR. Settled in 1130, it was sacked by the Mongols in 1238 and came under MOSCOW in 1478. It has the ruins of old underground fortifications. See MONGOL EMPIRES.

TOSA (Japan) Former province, now in Kochi prefecture, S SHIKOKU Island. It was the seat of the Tosa clan, one of Japan's great feudal landholders, known as the daimyo. The Tosa were one of the *tozama*, or "outside lords," who were excluded from the government because they opposed the Tokugawa shogunate, the military power that ruled Japan for more than 250 years. In 1867 the Tosa and three other *tozama* led a revolt against the shogunate that returned power to the emperor in the Meiji Restoration of the following year. The Tosa clan was represented in the new government by Taisuke Itagaki. With the other *tozama* he voluntarily surrendered all feudal privileges in 1869. Itagaki and others advocated war with KOREA in 1873, and when they were overruled Itagaki resigned. He later founded Japan's first political party.

TOSCANA. See TUSCANY.

TOSCANELLA. See TUSCANIA.

TOSHIMOE. See KASATKA.

TOTNES (England) Town in Devon, 20 mi SSW of Exeter. It was an important town in Anglo-Saxon times and is mentioned in the *Domesday Book* of 1086. It was chartered in 1205 and has the remains of a medieval castle.

TOTOWA (United States) City in NE NEW JERSEY, 3 mi W of Paterson. Patriots camped here during the American Revolution, and George Washington made his headquarters in the nearby Theunis Dey Mansion.

TOUL [*ancient:* Tullum] (France) Town in Meurthe-et-Moselle department, on the MOSELLE RIVER, 13 mi WSW of Nancy, NE France. Once the capital of the Leuci tribe within the Belgic Confederation, it was important under the Romans. A bishopric from the fourth century AD until 1801, it was part of the Trois-Évêchés (Three Bishoprics) territory during the Middle Ages and was important in the defense of France's eastern frontier in the early modern period. Fortified by Vauban in 1700, it was severely damaged in the Franco-Prussian War and in World War II.

TOULON [*ancient:* Telo Martius] (France) City and port in Var department, 30 mi ESE of Marseilles, on the Mediterranean Sea, in Provence, SE France. France's principal naval center, it was the site of a Roman naval station. Fortified by Vauban in the 17th century, it was the locus of many important naval battles. During the French Revolutionary Wars the Royalists gave up the city to the British in 1793, but it was retaken the same year by the young Napoleon. After 1815 it became the seat of French naval power. During World War II a large part of the French fleet was scuttled at Toulon in 1942 to prevent its being captured by the Germans.

TOULOUSE [*ancient:* Tolosa] (France) City and capital of Haute-Garonne department, on the Garonne River, 133 mi SE of Bordeaux, in Languedoc, S France. Once the stronghold of the Volcae Tectosages, it was taken by ROME in 106 BC and later by the Visigoths, who made the city their capital from 419 to 507 AD. In the eighth century it was the capital of the kingdom of AQUITAINE and became a center of artistic and literary activity for LANGUEDOC in medieval Europe. In 1159 it was the scene of confrontation between Henry II of England, who sought to extend his rule over Languedoc, and his feudal lord, Louis VII of France, who rushed to the city just in time to prevent its capture. The county of Toulouse was destroyed in the early 13th century by the northern French lords under Simon de Montfort during the Albigensian Crusade in an attempt to quell the Albigensian Cathar heresy. It was finally joined to the French crown through escheat in the reign of Philip III (1270–85).

Its parliament, founded in 1420, exercised authority over Languedoc until the French Revolution. The last battle of the Peninsular campaign of the Napoleonic Wars was fought here on April 10, 1814 when the British under the duke of Wellington defeated the French under Marshal Nicolas Soult. Today the city is one of the great cultural and commercial centers of France. The great cluniac cathedral of St. Sernin here was begun at the end of the 11th century. See also ALBI, VISIGOTHIC KINGDOM.

TOUNGOO [*former:* Ketumadi] (Burma) Town in Pegu division, on the Sittang River, 150 mi N of Rangoon, NE Lower Burma. Founded by King Minkyinyo in 1510, until 1540 it was the capital of the Toungoo kingdom, one of the three chief states of Burma. It was occupied by the Japanese from March 1942 to April 1945 during World War II.

TOURAINE (France) Region and former province in W central France, roughly corresponding to the present department of Indre-et-Loire. TOURS is the region's capital. Called the Garden of France because of its fertility, it was originally inhabited by the Gallic Turones tribe. Contested by the counts of BLOIS and of ANJOU in the 10th century, it finally passed to Anjou in 1044. Annexed by France in the early 13th century, it was King Charles VII's main base during the Hundred Years War. The splendor of Touraine during the Renaissance can be seen in the magnificent châteaux that still stand today. The region declined in importance when the court moved to VERSAILLES after 1700 and following the emigration of the Huguenot silk weavers.

TOURANE. See DA NANG.

TOURCOING (France) Town in Nord department, on the Belgian border, in FLANDERS, 8 mi NE of Lille, NE France. With ROUBAIX it forms one of the most important textile centers of France and has been noted for its textiles since the 15th century. It was granted a trade fair license by the Emperor Maximilian of AUSTRIA in 1491. It became part of France under King Louis XIV in 1668. During the French Revolutionary Wars the French defeated the British and Austrians here on May 18, 1794. It was seriously damaged in World War I.

TOURNAI [Tournay] [*ancient:* **Turnacum;** *Flemish:* **Doornik**] (Belgium) City in Hainaut province, on the SCHELDE RIVER, 45 mi SW of Brussels, SW Belgium. One of the oldest cities in Belgium, it was famous in the Middle Ages for its tapestries and copperware. In Roman times it was the fortified capital of a province, and in the fifth century AD it was captured by the Salic Franks. The Frankish King Clovis was born here *c.*465, and the city became a Merovingian capital. Part of France from 1188, it retained a large degree of independence but fell to Henry VIII of ENGLAND in 1513. It was attached to the NETHERLANDS in 1521 and was a center of Calvinism from 1543, but it was captured by

Alessandro Farnese for SPAIN in 1581. It later passed to the French and the Hapsburgs and was severely damaged in World War I. See also FRANKISH EMPIRE, HAINAUT.

TOURNAY. See TOURNAI.

TOURS [*ancient:* **Caesarodunum, Turoni**] (France) City and capital of Indre-et-Loire department and of TOURAINE, 129 mi SW of Paris, on the LOIRE RIVER, W central France. An old Gallo-Roman town, it was an early medieval center of learning, especially under Gregory of Tours and Alcuin. The Moorish invasion of Europe was halted by Charles Martel, master of the Frankish Kingdom, at the Battle of Tours fought nearby in 732 AD. Tours was the residence of many French kings, including Louis XI, who held his states general here. During the Franco-Prussian War in 1870/71, the city was the headquarters of the government of national defense and was again briefly the seat of the French government in June 1940 during World War II. The novelist Honoré de Balzac was born here in 1799. See also FRANKISH EMPIRE.

TOWCESTER (England) Town in Northamptonshire, 9 mi SSW of Northampton. Situated on WATLING STREET, it was the site of a Roman camp and was important in Anglo-Saxon times.

TOWER OF LONDON. See LONDON.

TOWTON (England) Village in North Yorkshire, 10 mi SW of York. The biggest and bloodiest battle of the Wars of the Roses was fought here on March 29, 1461 when the Yorkists defeated the Lancastrians, securing the throne for Edward IV.

TOYAMA (Japan) City, port, and capital of Toyama prefecture, E central HONSHŪ, 110 mi N of Nagoya, on Tokyo Bay. Now a center of the patent medicine industry, from the 16th century it was a major seat of the daimyos, or territorial barons, under the Tokugawa shogunate.

TRABZON. See TREBIZOND.

TRACHEA. See SELEUCIA TRACHEOTIS.

TRAFALGAR, BATTLE OF (Spain) Battle fought

A lovely painting of ancient Tours in 1797. The Loire River, famous for its châteaux, runs through the city. At the left is the magnificent cathedral of St. Gatien.

off Cape Trafalgar, on the SW coast of Spain, SE of CÁDIZ. The British won a famous naval victory here on Oct. 21, 1805 during the Napoleonic Wars. Their fleet under Adm. Horatio Nelson defeated the combined French and Spanish fleets under Adm. Pierre de Villeneuve, thus destroying France's sea power and making a French invasion of ENGLAND impossible. Nelson was killed in the battle aboard his flagship H.M.S. *Victory*, which is now a naval museum.

TRAGURIUM. See TROGIR.

TRAJANI PORTUS. See CIVITAVECCHIA.

TRAJECTUM AD RHENUM. See UTRECHT.

TRÄLABORG. See TRELLEBORG.

TRALEE (Irish Republic) Port and county town of County Kerry, at the head of Tralee Bay, 55 mi SW of Limerick, SW Irish Republic. It was the seat of the earls of DESMOND in the 14th and 15th centuries and has the remains of a Dominican abbey dating from the late Middle Ages.

TRALLES. See AYDIN.

TRANCOSO (Portugal) Town in Guarda district, N central Portugal, 16 mi NNW of Guarda. In 1385 it was the scene of a Portuguese victory over the Spanish. Its medieval ramparts are still standing.

TRANI [*ancient:* **Turenum**] (Italy) Town and port on the Adriatic Sea, in Bari province, APULIA region, 8 mi ESE of Barletta, S Italy. Originally a Roman town, it prospered under the Norman and Hohenstaufen Swabian kings of SICILY because of its trade with the Middle East. The *Ordinamenta maris*, written here in 1063, is thought to be the first maritime code of the Mediterranean Sea. The town has an 11th-century Romanesque-Apulian cathedral dedicated to St. Peregrinus, who died here.

TRANQUEBAR (India) Town in Tamil Nadu state, 50 mi NE of Tanjore, S India. Once an important port, it was settled by the Danes in 1616 and was captured by the British in 1801. Returned to the Danes in 1814, it was finally purchased by the British in 1845.

TRANSCAUCASIA. See TRANSCAUCASIAN SFSR.

TRANSCAUCASIAN FEDERATION. See TRANSCAUCASIAN SFSR.

TRANSCAUCASIAN SFSR [Transcaucasia, Transcaucasian Federation] (USSR) Former federated union that included the modern republics of ARMENIA, GEORGIA, and AZERBAIJAN, S European USSR. Its capital was TBILISI. Formed after the Russian Revolution on Sept. 20, 1917, it was the scene of fighting in 1919/20 as Turkish nationalists fought with Bolsheviks for control of the area. It became part of the Soviet Union on July 6, 1923 and was split into its modern republics in December 1936.

TRANSILVANIA. See TRANSYLVANIA.

TRANSJORDAN. See JORDAN.

TRANSJUBA. See JUBALAND.

TRANSKEI (South Africa) Bantu territory within South Africa, in the extreme E part of Cape Province, on the Indian Ocean. UMTATA is its largest city. The largest of South Africa's Bantu "national units," it was inhabited by Nguni tribesmen in the 19th century and was used as a base for cattle raids on Cape Colony, which resulted in the Sixth and Seventh Kaffir Wars of 1834/35 and 1846/47. It was joined to CAPE PROVINCE in 1865 and by parliamentary acts of 1959 and 1963 became the first nominally self-governing territory of South Africa. The president of South Africa retains the right to veto any decision of the Transkei government. No government other than that of South Africa has ever recognized the legitimacy of any of these "homelands."

TRANSOXIANA [Sogdiana] [*Arabic:* **Ma Wara An-Nahr**] (USSR) Ancient region of TURKISTAN, E of the Oxus River and W of the Jaxartes River, corresponding roughly to the modern Uzbek SSR and part of S Kazakh SSR, in Central Asian USSR. Conquered by Alexander the Great in 329 BC, it was traversed by the SILK ROAD and became a great center of Muslim civilization in the Middle Ages. Ruled by the Mongols from the 13th to 15th centuries, it was the seat of the Timurid Empire in the 15th century. At this time its cities, BUKHARA and SAMARKAND, were known throughout the world. It came under RUSSIA in the 19th century. See also MONGOL EMPIRES.

TRANSPADANE REPUBLIC (Italy) Republic provisionally organized by Napoleon in N Italy, N of the Po River, around Milan, Bergamo, Brescia, and Cremona. Created in 1796, it was incorporated into the CISALPINE REPUBLIC in 1797.

TRANSVAAL [*former:* **South African Republic**] (South Africa) Province of NE South Africa, between the Limpopo River and the Vaal River, W of Mozambique and Swaziland. Its capital is PRETORIA. Originally inhabited by Bantu-speaking Africans, it was settled by Boers in the 1830's. Under the Sand River Convention of 1852 Great Britain recognized the Boers' claims to the land beyond the Vaal River, and in 1857 the South African Republic was inaugurated. By 1877 the republic had gone bankrupt and was annexed by GREAT BRITAIN.

The Boers rebelled in 1880, forcing the British to grant them internal self-government. In 1886 large gold deposits were found at WITWATERSRAND, which was to become the richest goldfield in the world, and many foreigners entered the Transvaal, causing friction with the Boers, who denied them political rights. This led to the South African or Boer War in 1899 and Great Britain's annexation of the Transvaal in 1900. By the Treaty of VEREENIGING in 1902, the Transvaal became a crown colony of the BRITISH EMPIRE; and in 1910, under Louis Botha and Jan Smuts, it became a founding province of the Union of South Africa. It is still a major gold producer.

TRANSYLVANIA, Kentucky. See BOONESBORO.

TRANSYLVANIA [*German:* **Siebenbürgen**; *Hungarian:* **Erdély**; *Rumanian:* **Ardeal, Transilvania**] (Rumania) Region and province of central Rumania. Its chief city is CLUJ. Originally the center of the Dacian kingdom, it became part of the Roman province of

DACIA in 107 AD and from the ninth century was occupied by barbarian tribes, including the Saxons, Vlachs, and Szeklers. In 1003 it came under the Hungarian crown, and it attracted German Saxon settlers in the 12th and 13th centuries. The region developed into a distinctive autonomous unit, becoming independent in 1526 following the Turks' defeat of the Hungarians at MOHÁCS. Under the OTTOMAN EMPIRE it was an autonomous principality of international importance, safeguarding Hungarian liberties against the Hapsburgs and upholding Protestantism in eastern Europe. In 1687 it passed under the Hapsburgs and became a scene of ethnic conflict as the Magyar population pressed for union with HUNGARY. This was granted in 1867. Following the defeat of AUSTRIA-HUNGARY in World War I, the Rumanians of Transylvania demanded union with Rumania, which was granted by the Treaty of Trianon in 1920.

TRANSYLVANIAN ALPS [Southern Carpathians] [*Rumanian:* **Carpaţii Meridionali**] (Rumania) Mountain range extending 225 mi E across Rumania from the Danube River at the Iron Gate. The southern branch of the CARPATHIAN MOUNTAINS, the range is famous as a hunting ground and has coal, iron, and lignite deposits. It is the legendary home of the vampire Count Dracula.

TRAPANI [*ancient:* **Drepanum**] (Italy) City, port, and capital of Trapani province, on the W coast of SICILY, 48 mi SW of Palermo. A major Carthaginian naval base, it fell to ROME during the First Punic War after the Battle of the Aegates in 241 BC. It prospered during the Middle Ages and later was damaged by Allied bombs in World War II. See also EGADI ISLANDS, CARTHAGE.

TRAPESUS. See TREBIZOND.

TRAPPES (France) Town in Seine-et-Oise department, 6 mi WSW of Versailles, N central France. Nearby is the ruined abbey of Port-Royal-des-Champs, which was the headquarters of the Jansenists in the 17th century. Founded in 1204, it was razed in 1710 and was the center of a strict reform movement within Roman Catholicism that sought to counter the influence of Calvinism with its own brand of strict asceticism in behavior and sexual mores. Though eventually disbanded, the members of Port Royal had a profound influence, especially in Ireland and in Italy, where they were pioneers of the Enlightenment. They fought against the Inquisition and absolutism but were opposed by the Jesuits. Blaise Pascal was among their disciples.

TRASIMENE, LAKE [Lake of Perugia] [*ancient:* **Trasimenus**; *Italian:* **Trasimeno**] (Italy) Lake in Perugia province, Umbria region, W of Perugia, central Italy. The largest lake of the Italian peninsula, it was the scene of a battle in the Second Punic War in 217 BC, in which the Carthaginians under Hannibal inflicted a bloody defeat on the Romans under the consul Gaius Flaminius on the lake's north shore. Flaminius was killed in the battle. See also CARTHAGE, ROME.

TRASIMENO. See TRASIMENE, LAKE.
TRASIMENUS. See TRASIMENE, LAKE.

TRAU. See TROGIR.

TRAVANCORE (India) Former state, now part of Kerala state in SW India, on the Arabian Sea. In the 11th century the region was under the rule of the CHOLA Empire and from 1534 to 1565 was held by the Vijayanagara Kingdom. An English settlement in the area was made at ANJENGO in 1684. A local prince, Martanda Varma, unified Travancore and made it independent in the mid-18th century. He allied his kingdom with the British to oppose Haidar Ali, ruler of MYSORE to the north. In 1789 Haidar Ali's son and successor, Tippoo Sahib, invaded Travancore but was defeated in 1792. In the early 19th century there were revolts against British domination, but they were put down. According to tradition, St. Thomas, one of the twelve Disciples, came to Travancore in the first century AD as a missionary.

TRAVENDAL (West Germany) Village in Schleswig-Holstein, 15 mi W of Lübeck, N West Germany. Charles XII of SWEDEN forced DENMARK to make peace under the terms of a treaty signed here on Aug. 18, 1700.

TRAVNIK (Yugoslavia) Town in Bosnia and Herzegovina, 45 mi NW of Sarajevo, W central Yugoslavia. The capital of BOSNIA from 1686 to 1850, it is the site of Roman remains and has a Turkish citadel.

TREBBIA [*ancient:* **Trebia**] (Italy) River of Emilia-Romagna, N Italy, rising in the Ligurian Apennines, NE of Genoa and flowing 70 mi NNE to the Po River, just W of Piacenza. Two battles were fought on its banks: the first near BOBBIO during the Second Punic War in 218 BC, when the Carthaginians under Hannibal heavily defeated the Romans under Scipio Africanus and Tiberius Sempronius Longus. The second was fought during the French Revolutionary Wars from June 17 to 19, 1799 when a Russo-Austrian army under Marshal Alexander Suvorov defeated the French under Marshal Jacques-Etienne Macdonald. Bobbio was a major monastic center in the early Middle Ages. See also CARTHAGE, ROME.

TREBIA. See TREBBIA.

TREBIZOND [Trabzon] [*ancient:* **Trapesus**] (Turkey) City, port, and capital of Trabzon province, on the BLACK SEA, 12 mi NW of Erzurum, NE Turkey. Founded in the eighth century BC by Greeks from SINOPE, it was at the end of a trade route from PERSIA followed by Xenophon of the *Anabasis*. It was conquered by Mithridates VI in the first century BC and later became part of the ROMAN EMPIRE. It reached its pinnacle following the creation by the Comneni in 1204 of the empire of Trebizond, of which it was the capital, after the Crusaders had seized CONSTANTINOPLE. Under Alexius II in the 14th century it became a major trading center, famous for its great wealth and artistic activity. It was annexed by the OTTOMAN EMPIRE in 1461 and in modern times was included in the short-lived state of ARMENIA in 1920.

TREBIZOND, EMPIRE OF (Turkey) Greek empire of N Anatolia, originally comprising the entire S coastal region of the BLACK SEA, but eventually reduced to include only the E part of this region around TREBI-ZOND. The empire was founded, following the Crusaders' overthrow of the BYZANTINE EMPIRE in 1204, by the Comnenus family, the former imperial dynasty. Reduced in size by the encroachments of NICAEA in the west and by the Seljuk capture of SINOPE, it enjoyed great prosperity following the Mongol invasion, as it lay on their commercial routes from Asia Minor to the Far East and from Russia to the Middle East. The height of its splendor was reached under Alexius II from 1297 to 1330, when the empire was a great cultural and artistic center and the last outpost of Hellenistic-Byzantine civilization. As Mongol power declined after 1320, the empire was weakened by troubles from within and without. It was annexed in 1461 by the OTTOMAN EMPIRE after David Comnenus, the last emperor of Trebizond, had promoted an alliance of non-Ottoman Asian states against Sultan Muhammad II. See also MONGOL EMPIRES.

TREBLINKA (Poland) Village in Warszawa province, 5 mi S of Malkinia, E central Poland. During World War II it was the site of one of the most notorious Nazi extermination camps.

TŘEBOŇ [*German:* **Wittingau**] (Czechoslovakia) Town in Southern Bohemia region, 13 mi ENE of Budweis, Czechoslovakia. Situated among numerous man-made lakes, it has been the site of a famous freshwater fishing industry since the Middle Ages. In 1660 the town passed to the Schwarzenbergs, a powerful Austrian noble family.

TREFALDWYN. See MONTGOMERY, Wales.

TRELLEBORG, Denmark. See SLAGELSE.

TRELLEBORG [*former:* **Trälaborg**] (Sweden) Town and port in Malmöhus county, on the Baltic Sea, 17 mi SSE of Malmö, S Sweden. An important fishing and commercial center in the Middle Ages, it declined after being plundered during the war of 1563 to 1570 and after a devastating fire in 1617. As the southernmost town in Sweden, it became important in modern times as a ferry port and during both world wars was a focal point in the transportation of the sick and the wounded and in the exchange of prisoners of war.

TREMEZZO (Italy) Village and port on Lake Como, in Como province, Lombardy region, 14 mi NNE of Como, N Italy. Benito Mussolini and several other important fascist leaders were executed on April 28, 1945 in the nearby hamlet of Giulino di Messegra.

TREMONIA. See DORTMUND.

TRENGGANU [Terengganu] (Malaysia) Former vassal state, now a state of Malaysia, in the central MALAY PENINSULA, on the South China Sea. Once subject to the SRIVIJAYA Kingdom of SUMATRA, Trengganu passed to the control of JAVA in the 14th century. It remained a vassal state of the various powers that dominated the Malay Peninsula, the rulers paying tribute to SIAM after 1776. By a treaty in 1909 between Siam and Great Britain, Trengganu became a protectorate of the latter. It was one of the four Unfederated Malay States until 1948, when it became part of the Federation of Malaya. In 1957 it became part of the independent Federation of Malaysia.

TRENT [*German:* **Trient**; *Italian:* **Trento**; *Latin:* **Tridentum**] (Italy) City and capital of Trento province and of Trentino-Alto Adige region, on the Adige River, 106 mi ENE of Milan, N Italy. Possibly founded in the fourth century BC, it was a Roman military base and in the sixth century AD was the seat of a Lombard duchy. It was a Frankish march, or borderland, in the eighth century; its bishops held considerable lands by the 11th century. Trent was ruled by prince-bishops until 1802, when it became part of the TYROL. The Roman Catholic Council of Trent from 1545 to 1563 established the basic doctrines and practices of the Catholic Reformation and the Counter-Reformation and formed the basis of modern Roman Catholicism until the Second Vatican Council in 1962. Trent was returned to Italy by the Treaty of Saint-Germain in 1919 after World War I.

TRENTINO-ALTO ADIGE [*former:* **Venezia Tridentina**] (Italy) Region of N Italy, S of Austria, comprising the provinces of Trento and Bolzano. TRENT is the region's capital. The region is 40 percent German-speaking and was divided between the episcopal principalities of Trent and BRESSANONE from the 11th century until 1802. Included in the TYROL as part of AUSTRIA in 1815, it passed to Italy by the Treaty of Saint-Germain in 1919. The fascists initiated a vigorous program of Italianization of the region, which met with fierce opposition. In 1938 Hitler and Mussolini agreed to plan the forced migration of much of the German-speaking population to Germany or elsewhere in Italy. The plan was unsuccessful, and in 1947, after World War II, both German and Italian became official languages with the granting of increased autonomy to the region. A further treaty in 1971 promised more autonomy for BOLZANO province.

TRENTO. See TRENT.

TRENTON [*former:* **The Falls, Stacy's Mills**] (United States) City and capital of NEW JERSEY, at the head of navigation on the DELAWARE RIVER, 28 mi NE of Philadelphia. Settled by Quakers in 1679, it was the scene of two actions during the American Revolution. The first took place on Dec. 26, 1776 when the Hessian garrison was defeated after a surprise attack led by Gen. George Washington. The second occurred on Jan. 2, 1777 when the British under Gen. Charles Cornwallis drove out the Americans. Trenton served as the U.S. capital in 1784 and 1799 and became the state capital in 1790.

TRESCO. See SCILLY ISLANDS.

TRES TABERNAE. See SAVERNE.

TRES ZAPOTES (Mexico) Mesoamerican archaeological site in E Veracruz state, S of Alvarado, E Mexico. In 1939 a massive sculpted stone head and inscribed monuments, dating from a pre-Mayan culture of *c.*300 BC, were unearthed here. The finds were the first evidence of the Indian Olmec culture, the earliest in CENTRAL AMERICA.

TREVES. See TRIER.

TREVISO [*ancient:* **Tarvisium**] (Italy) City and capital of Treviso province, Veneto region, 17 mi NW of Venice, NE Italy. A Celtic and Roman town, it was the site of an important mint during Charlemagne's time. As capital of the march of Trevigiana, it became a cultural center in the 13th century. It was loyal to VENICE from 1339 until the Napoleonic era and was under AUSTRIA from 1815 to 1866.

TRÉVOUX (France) Town in Ain department, on the SAÔNE RIVER, 13 mi NNW of Lyons, E France. The capital of the principality of DOMBES from the 11th to 16th centuries, it was known for its Jesuit press, which between 1801 and 1830 published a newspaper and a dictionary.

TRIADITSA. See SOFIA.

TRICCA. See TRÍKALA.

TRICHINOPOLY. See TIRUCHCHIRAPPALLI.

TRIDENTUM. See TRENT.

TRIENT. See TRENT.

TRIER [*ancient:* **Augusta Treverorum;** *English:* **Treves;** *French:* **Trèves**] (West Germany) City in Rhineland-Palatinate, on the MOSELLE RIVER, 58 mi SW of Koblenz, W West Germany. One of Germany's oldest cities, it was founded by Emperor Augustus *c.*15 BC and later became the capital of the Roman province of Belgica. As the capital of the prefecture of GAUL in the third century AD, it was a major commercial city, especially in the wine trade. In the fourth century it was often the residence of the Western Roman emperors and was an episcopal see. It was created an archiepiscopal see in the ninth century; its archbishops were powerful temporal princes, ranked second among the spiritual electors of the HOLY ROMAN EMPIRE. From 1473 to 1797 a commercial and cultural center with a university, it passed to PRUSSIA in 1815 and was occupied by the French in World War I. Damaged in World War II, it still has Roman monuments and other important buildings, including a brick Roman basilica built in the fourth century AD and used for imperial audiences, an amphitheater, the Porta Nigra, a massive city gate, and its cathedral, built on the plan of the original Double Cathedral of 325. The city retains much of its original Roman plan. Karl Marx was born in Trier in 1818.

TRIEST. See TRIESTE.

TRIESTE [*ancient:* **Tergeste;** *German:* **Triest;** *Slovene and Serbo-Croatian:* **Trst**] (Italy) City, port, and capital of Trieste province and of Friuli-Venezia Giulia region, on the Gulf of Trieste, approx. 70 mi E of Venice, NE Italy. The site of an ancient settlement, it became a Roman colony in the second century BC and was made a free commune in the 12th century AD. After a long struggle with its rival, VENICE, it put itself under the protection of the duke of AUSTRIA in 1382 and prospered as Austria's only port and as a maritime outlet for central Europe. It passed to Italy after World War I and was claimed by YUGOSLAVIA after World War II. As a compromise, the Free Territory of Trieste was created in 1947. This arrangement proved to be unworkable, and the territory was partitioned in 1954

between Italy and Yugoslavia, with the former taking Trieste itself.

The Grand Canal of Trieste, the major port of the Adriatic Sea. An Italian city and once an Austrian port, Trieste has been on the border of Yugoslavia since 1954.

TRÍKALA [**Tríkkala**] [*ancient:* **Tricca, Trikke;** *Turkish:* **Thirhala**] (Greece) City and capital of Tríkala department, in THESSALY, 35 mi W of Larissa, Greece. The legendary home of the god Asclepius in antiquity, it figures in Homer's *Iliad*. Its sanctuary was said to be the oldest in Greece. It was a stronghold under the BYZANTINE EMPIRE, which built a fort on the Frourion on a Hellenistic site. The Normans captured the city in 1081 AD, after which it became a noted 12th-century trading center and was Thessaly's most important town for several centuries. It was the seat of the pasha of Thessaly under the rule of the OTTOMAN EMPIRE and was ceded to Greece in 1881.

TRÍKKALA. See TRÍKALA.

TRIKKE. See TRÍKALA.

TRIM [*Gaelic:* **Baile Átha Truim**] (Irish Republic) County town of County Meath, on the BOYNE RIVER, 25 mi NW of Dublin. It was an important town in the Middle Ages. Its ruined 12th-century castle was the seat of several Irish parliaments until the 15th century.

TRIMONTIUM. See PLOVDIV.

TRINACRIA. See SICILY.

TRINCOMALEE [**Trinkomali**] (Sri Lanka) Town, port, and capital of Eastern province, on the Bay of Bengal, 110 mi SE of Jaffna, NE Sri Lanka. The site of one of the world's finest natural harbors, it was originally settled by Indian Tamils who built the temple of a Thousand Columns here. During the colonial era the town changed hands many times between the Portuguese, Dutch, French, and British. The British finally gained control in 1795, and it became Great Britain's main base in the Far East after the fall of SINGAPORE in World War II. The British surrendered the harbor to Sri Lanka in 1957.

TRINIDAD. See TRINIDAD AND TOBAGO.

TRINIDAD AND TOBAGO Independent state in the WEST INDIES, off the NE coast of Venezuela. Its capital is PORT OF SPAIN. Both islands were discovered by Christopher Columbus in 1498. Tobago, settled by the English in 1616, changed hands frequently but was retained by GREAT BRITAIN after 1814. Trinidad was settled by Spanish in 1577 and in 1802 passed to Great Britain under the terms of the Treaty of Amiens. The two islands were joined politically as a British colony in 1888. From 1958 to 1962 they were part of the short-lived West Indies Federation and became independent in 1962.

TRINKOMALI. See TRINCOMALEE.

TRIPOLI [Tarabulus] [*ancient:* **Tripolis;** *Arabic:* **Tarabulus esh Sham**] (Lebanon) City, port, and capital of North Lebanon governorate, on the Mediterranean Sea, 43 mi NNE of Beirut, NW Lebanon. Founded *c.*700 BC, it was not mentioned until Persian times when it was the capital of the Phoenician federation of TYRE, SIDON, and Aradus (now ARWAD). It prospered under the SELEUCID and ROMAN Empires and was later captured by Arabs and Crusaders. Sacked by the MAMLUK sultan of Egypt in 1289, it was rebuilt, came under the OTTOMAN EMPIRE until 1918, and became part of Lebanon in 1920. Today Tripoli is a major port and the second city of Lebanon.

TRIPOLI [*ancient:* **Oea;** *Arabic:* **Tarabalus al-Gharb**] (Libya) City, port, and capital of Libya and of Tripoli district, on the Mediterranean Sea, 400 mi W of Benghazi. Founded by Phoenicians from TYRE in the seventh century BC, it was the chief city of the region of TRIPOLITANIA and was seized by the Romans in the first century BC. Occupied by Vandals in the fifth century and Arabs in the late seventh century AD, it came under the OTTOMAN EMPIRE in 1551 and was the home of the Karamanli dynasty from 1711 to 1835. It was an important base of the Barbary pirates, a fact which prompted the Tripolitan War with the UNITED STATES from 1801 to 1805. After passing to ITALY in 1911, it became the capital of the Italian colony of Libya. During World War II it was captured by the British in 1943. Today it is Libya's largest city and chief port. See also BARBARY STATES, PHOENICIA.

TRIPOLIS [Tripolitsa, Tripolitza] [*former:* **Droboglitza**] (Greece) Town and capital of Arcadia department, in the central Peloponnesus, S Greece. Founded in the 14th century as the seat of the Turkish pashas of Morea, or the PELOPONNESUS, it flourished until the Greek war of independence when it was captured by Greek patriots and then burned by Ibrahim Pasha of Egypt during the Ottoman retreat of 1828.

TRIPOLIS, Lebanon. See TRIPOLI, Lebanon.

TRIPOLIS, Libya. See TRIPOLITANIA.

TRIPOLITANA. See TRIPOLITANIA.

TRIPOLITANIA [*ancient:* **Tripolis, Tripolitana;** *Arabic:* **Tarabalus**] (Libya) Former region of W Libya, bordering the Mediterranean Sea. Its chief city is TRIPOLI. Its original inhabitants were probably Berbers. In the seventh century BC coastal colonies were established by the Phoenicians at LEPTIS MAGNA, Oea (Tripoli), and SABRATA, in the colony of Tripolis. The region fell to NUMIDIA in 146 BC and to ROME in 46 BC, under which it eventually became the province of Tripolitana. Occupied by Vandals in the fifth century AD, it was retaken by the Byzantines in the sixth century, and fell to the Arabs in the late seventh century. It came under the OTTOMAN EMPIRE in 1553 and was a stronghold of Barbary pirates. The region was entirely under Italian control by 1912 and in 1939 was incorporated into the kingdom of ITALY. In 1951 Tripolitania became a province of the independent federal kingdom of Libya but ceased to exist as a political unit in 1963 when Libya became a unified state. See also BARBARY STATES, PHOENICIA.

TRIPOLITSA. See TRIPOLIS.

TRIPOLITZA. See TRIPOLIS.

TRIPURA [*former:* **Hill Tippera**] (India) State of NE India, bordered on the N, W, and S by BANGLADESH. Its capital is Agartala. Annexed by the MOGUL EMPIRE in 1733, it was ruled by the British in the 19th century. It became part of India in 1949 and was made a state in 1972.

TRISTAN DA CUNHA (Great Britain) Group of four volcanic islands, in the S Atlantic Ocean, midway between South America and South Africa. They are a dependency of the British colony of ST. HELENA. They were discovered by the Portuguese in 1506. The first settlers arrived from St. Helena in the 19th century, and the islands were annexed by Great Britain in 1816. After a volcanic eruption in 1961, the population of some 200 was evacuated to GREAT BRITAIN, where they were studied by linguists because of their unusual 19th-century speech. Most of the islanders returned home in 1963. Only one of the islands, Tristan da Cunha, is inhabited.

TRIVANDRUM [*ancient:* **Tiruvanantapuram**] (India) City, port, and capital of Kerala state, 140 mi SW of Madurai, on the Arabian Sea, SW India. In 1745 it was made the capital of the former kingdom of TRAVANCORE.

TRNOVA. See TIRNOVO.

TRNOVO. See TIRNOVO.

TROAD, THE. See TROAS.

TROAS [The Troad] (Turkey) Ancient region on the NW coast of Asia Minor, around TROY and on the Hellespont (DARDANELLES), NW Turkey. An ancient site of Aegean civilization, and of many archaeological finds, it was the setting of the events of Homer's epic *Iliad.*

TROBRIAND ISLANDS (Papua New Guinea) Island group off SE NEW GUINEA, in the Solomon Sea. There are 22 islands, of which Kiriwina is the largest. In World War II Kiriwina was occupied in July 1943 by U.S. and Australian troops and made into an air base. The Trobriands became part of Papua New Guinea when the state became independent in September 1975. Bronislaw Malinowski, the Polish-born British anthropologist, first gained renown with his studies of the indigenous people of the islands, carried out between 1914 and 1918.

TROE. See TROY.

TROGIR [*ancient:* **Tragurium;** *German:* **Trau**] (Yugoslavia) Town and port in DALMATIA, on the island of Ciovo, in the Adriatic Sea, near Split, W Yugoslavia. Colonized by Greeks from SYRACUSE *c.*385 BC, it was ruled successively by Byzantines, Croatians, Normans, Venetians, and Bosnians. It became part of Yugoslavia in 1920. It has one of the most beautiful cathedrals in Dalmatia and important shipbuilding yards.

TROIA. See TROY.

TROINA (Italy) Town in Enna province, central SICILY, 24 mi NE of Enna, on the W slope of Mt Etna, S Italy. Heavy fighting took place here from July 29 to Aug. 5, 1943 between the Germans and the Allies during World War II.

TROIS-RIVIÈRES [Three Rivers] (Canada) City and port on the ST. LAWRENCE RIVER, at its confluence with the St. Maurice River, 75 mi NE of Montreal, in S Quebec province. Founded by Samuel Sieur de Champlain in 1634, it is one of the oldest communities in Canada. It was an important French trading post and an early industrial center. Today it is one of the world's largest producers of newsprint.

TROJA. See TROY.

TROMSØ (Norway) Town, port, and capital of Troms county, on Tromsøy Island, 95 mi NNE of Narvik, off the NW coast of Norway. Dating from the 13th century AD, it was a major Arctic trading port by the end of the 19th century. During World War II it was briefly the seat of the Norwegian government. The German battleship *Tirpitz* was sunk by the British near Tromsø on Nov. 12, 1944 during World War II.

TRONDHEIM [Nidaros] [*former:* **Trondhjem**] (Norway) City, port, and capital of Sør-Trøndelag county, on the Trondheimsfjord, 250 mi N of Oslo, central Norway. Founded by Olaf I Trygvesson of Norway in 997 AD, it was the political and religious capital of medieval Norway but declined after the forced introduction of the Reformation in 1537. It regained economic importance in the 19th century. Haakon VII was crowned as the first king of an independent Norway in Trondheim Cathedral in 1906. It fell to GERMANY in World War II on April 9, 1940 and became an important German naval base, frequently bombed by the Allies. It was the center of the Norwegian resistance.

TRONDHJEM. See TRONDHEIM.

TROPPAU. See OPAVA.

TROTSKOYE. See GATCHINA.

TROY [Ilion, Ilios] [*Greek:* **Troe, Troia;** *Latin:* Il-

ium, Troja] (Turkey) Ancient city of NW Anatolia, in modern Canakkale province, 4 mi from the S mouth of the DARDANELLES, at a mound called Hissarlik, NW Turkey. One of the most important archaeological sites of the ancient world, the locality was occupied from Neolithic times by nine successive settlements of varying sizes. Strategically situated at the junction of routes between Europe and Asia, it was a flourishing cultural center in the third and second millennia BC but was abandoned from 1100 to 700 BC, when it was reoccupied by Greek settlers. The city fell into obscurity following the founding of CONSTANTINOPLE in 324 AD.

In Greek legend and in Homer's *Iliad* and *Odyssey*, Troy was the object of the Trojan War between the Greeks and the Trojans, which lasted ten years and resulted in the fall of Troy by the famous ruse of the wooden Trojan Horse. This legendary conflict forms the basis of the epics of Homer and is probably based on a real war fought between the early Greeks or Mycenaeans, and the people of TROAS *c.*1200 BC. The legend of Troy and its refugees also formed the basis of the legend surrounding the foundation of ROME. Vergil's *Aeneid* recounts the story of how Aeneas led a group of survivors across the Mediterranean to Latium and secured the Trojan line there. The medieval French considered themselves the descendants of the Trojans.

Long considered mere legend, the site of Troy was rediscovered and first excavated by Heinrich Schliemann between 1871 and 1890 and has been extensively reexcavated since. The seventh city has been identified as the Troy of Homer. See also MYCENAE.

TROY (United States) City in E NEW YORK State, on the HUDSON RIVER, 8 mi NE of Albany, near the ERIE CANAL. Laid out in 1786, it was an industrial city from 1812 to 1920 and an early center of the steel industry. Samuel Wilson of Troy, said to be America's original Uncle Sam, filled large contracts for U.S. Army beef here during the War of 1812.

TROYES [*ancient:* **Augustobona Tricassium**] (France) City and capital of Aube department and of Champagne region, on the SEINE RIVER, 92 mi SE of Paris, NE France. Settled in pre-Roman times, it was converted to Christianity in the third century AD and under Bishop St. Loup repulsed Attila the Hun in the fifth century. It become the capital of CHAMPAGNE in the 11th century and developed into an important commercial center. During the Hundred Years War the Treaty of Troyes was signed here on May 21, 1420. It secured a temporary peace by arranging the marriage of Catherine of France, the daughter of Charles VI of France, to Henry V of ENGLAND. Henry thus became Charles' heir.

TRST. See TRIESTE.

TRUCIAL COAST. See UNITED ARAB EMIRATES.

TRUCIAL OMAN. See UNITED ARAB EMIRATES.

TRUCIAL SHAYKDOMS. See UNITED ARAB EMIRATES.

TRUCIAL STATES. See UNITED ARAB EMIRATES.

TRUJILLO (Honduras) City, port, and capital of Colón department, 58 mi NE of TEGUCIGALPA, NE

Honduras. It was founded in 1525, and was the first capital of the Spanish colonial province of Honduras. It prospered in the early 17th century until it was destroyed by Dutch pirates in 1643. The city was resettled by Galicians in 1787.

TRUJILLO (Peru) City in NW Peru, approx. 9 mi inland from the Pacific Ocean. Today a busy industrial and commercial center, it played an important part in the early 19th-century struggle of Latin American countries for independence from Spain. The city declared its own independence in 1820 and was the provisional capital of Peru in 1825, while Simón Bolívar, known as the Liberator for his major part in the rebellions of the time, used it as his headquarters. Trujillo processes food products and manufactures leather goods and textiles. Part of the wall built in 1617 to protect the town against English pirates can be seen, while nearby are the remains of CHAN CHAN, the capital city of the Chimu, a pre-Incan civilization.

TRUK ISLANDS [*former:* **Hogoleu**] (United States) Cluster of 11 volcanic islands in the CAROLINE ISLANDS, W Pacific Ocean, administered as part of the United States Trust Territory of the Pacific Islands. Visited in the 19th century, the islands were purchased by GERMANY from SPAIN in 1899. They were annexed by the Japanese in 1914 and were heavily fortified for use in World War II. They were bombed by U.S. forces in 1944/45.

TRURO [*former:* **Cobequid**] (Canada) Town in central NOVA SCOTIA, 50 mi NNE of Halifax, on an arm of the Minas Basin. One of the principal settlements of ACADIA, it was destroyed and its inhabitants were expelled in 1755 by the British. It was resettled by New Englanders and Northern Irish in 1759.

TSARGRAD. See ISTANBUL.

TSARIGRAD. See ISTANBUL.

TSARITSYN. See VOLGOGRAD.

TSARSKOYE SELO. See PUSHKIN.

TSELINOGRAD [*former:* **Akmolinsk**] (USSR) City of Central Asian USSR, in Kazakh SSR, on the Ishim River, 120 mi NW of Karaganda. It was founded as a Russian military station in 1824. Its importance was increased by the Soviet Virgin and Idle Lands Campaign of the 1950's. See also RUSSIA.

TSERNAGORA. See MONTENEGRO.

TSESIS. See CESIS.

TSIENFOTUNG. See TUN-HUANG, China.

TSINAN [**Chinan**] (China) City and capital of Shantung province, 225 mi S of Peking, NE China. An ancient walled city, it was a provincial center in the 12th century and became the capital of the province under the Ming dynasty. In September 1948 it was taken by the communists with the loss of 75,000 Nationalist troops.

TSINGHAI [**Ch'ing-Hai, Koko Nor**] (China) Province of W central China, E of Tibet and Sinkiang Uighur, in the Tibetan Highlands. Its capital is HSINING. Once part of TIBET, it was controlled by the Mongol overlords of China in the 14th century and came under the Ch'ing dynasty in 1724. It became a province of China in 1928 and was settled by people attracted to the mineral extraction industries of the area.

TSINGTAO [**Ch'ing-Tao**] [*German:* **Tsingtau**] (China) City and port on the Yellow Sea, in SE Shantung province, 345 mi SE of Peking, E China. Leased to Germany in 1898, it was the administrative seat of Kiaochow territory and was held by JAPAN from 1914 to 1922. From 1945 to 1949 when it was surrendered to the communists, it was the U.S. naval headquarters of the western Pacific Ocean.

TSINGTAU. See TSINGTAO.

TSINGYUAN. See PAO-TING.

TSINKIANG. See CH'ÜAN-CHOU.

TSIPORI. See ZIPPORI.

TSUN-I [**Zun-I**] (China) City in N Kweichow province, 75 mi N of Kweiyang, China. The seat of a county since the T'ang dynasty, it was the scene of a revolt led by Yang Ying-Lung from 1597 to 1599. In 1935 the Central Political Bureau of the Chinese Communist Party held a conference here at which Mao Tse-tung established his authority in the party.

TSUSHIMA (Japan) Archipelago in the Korea Strait, between Japan and KOREA, in Nagasaki prefecture, Japan. In mythology Tsushima is believed to be one of the original islands of Japan. Its position makes it a good stepping stone between Japan and Korea, and in its early history it was continually raided by Japanese and Korean pirates, while also helping to transmit the culture of CHINA through Korea to Japan. It was a fief of the Sō family from the 12th century until 1868. In 1274 and 1281 its population was massacred by Mongols during their attempts to invade Japan. See also MONGOL EMPIRES.

TSUSHIMA STRAIT (Japan) Channel between TSUSHIMA Island and NW KYŪSHŪ, Japan, forming the SE part of the Korea Strait. During the Russo-Japanese War, on May 27/28, 1905, the Russian Baltic fleet under Adm. Rozhdestvenski suffered a crippling defeat here at the hands of the Japanese under Count Togo. The Russians lost most of their ships and were forced to sue for peace. Naval radio was used for the first time in this battle, which is also called the Battle of the Sea of Japan.

TUAMOTU ISLANDS. See FRENCH POLYNESIA.

TUBAC. See NOGALES, Arizona.

TUBARIYA. See TIBERIAS.

TUBARTIS. See MISRATAH.

TÜBINGEN [*former:* **Castra Alamannorum**] (West Germany) City in Baden-Württemberg, on the Neckar River, 17 mi S of Stuttgart, SW West Germany. Chartered *c.*1200 AD, it was purchased in 1342 by the counts of WÜRTTEMBERG. In the mid-15th century it became the second capital of Württemberg. Its university, established in 1477, is one of the most noted in Germany. Philosopher George Hegel and poet Frederick Hölderlin were both students at the Protestant theological seminary here.

TUBRUQ. See TOBRUK.

TUBUAI ISLANDS. See FRENCH POLYNESIA.

TUCSON (United States) City in SE ARIZONA, 103 mi SE of Phoenix, on the Santa Cruz River. Settled in the late 17th century by the Spanish, it was founded as a walled presidio in 1776 and was a military border station of NEW SPAIN, MEXICO, and later of the United States. The territorial capital from 1867 to 1877, it expanded following the arrival of the Southern Pacific Railroad in 1880. It is a popular tourist resort today.

TUCUMÁN. See SAN MIGUEL DE TUCUMÁN.

TUDELA [*ancient:* **Tutela**] (Spain) Town in Navarra province, on the Ebro River, 52 mi S of Pamplona, N Spain. It prospered under the Moors, who captured it in 716, and was reconquered by Alfonso I of ARAGON in 1115. Later it became an important city of the kingdom of NAVARRE and a noted fortress. During the Penninsular campaign of the Napoleonic Wars the Battle of the EBRO, a major French victory, was fought nearby in 1808. The town remained under French occupation until 1813.

TUDER. See TODI.

TUGHLAKABAD (India) Ancient city of N India, in Delhi territory, 4 mi E of the site of old DELHI. It was built *c.*1320 by Ghiyasud-din Tughlak, the founder of the Tughlak dynasty, which ruled the Delhi Sultanate from 1320 to 1413.

TUKAROI (India) Village in West Bengal, between Jalesar and Midnapore, NE India. On March 3, 1575 the army of the Mogul Emperor Akbar shattered the army of Da'ud Khan, the Afghan sultan of BENGAL. The conquest of Bengal was achieved the following year. See also MOGUL EMPIRE.

TULA [**Tula de Allende**] (Mexico) Town and important archaeological site, in Hidalgo state, 45 mi N of Mexico City, central Mexico. Scholars believe Tula to be the site of the ancient Toltec capital Tollán, which was important from 900 to 1200 AD and which had a population numbering tens of thousands. Many ruins of the city remain, including a temple pyramid, a palace, and sculptured columns.

TULA [*former:* **Taydula**] (USSR) City in W Russian SFSR, on the Upa River, 110 mi S of Moscow, N central European USSR. First described in 1146, it was part of the RYAZAN principality. In the 16th century it became a major stronghold of the grand duchy of MOSCOW. In the 17th century it was a great metallurgical center and was the site of Russia's first arms factory, built by Peter the Great in 1712. During World War II it underwent heavy attack as the southern bastion of Moscow's defense line. Writer Leo Tolstoy lived here and is buried nearby.

TULA DE ALLENDE. See TULA, Mexico.

TULLAHOMA (United States) City in S central TENNESSEE, 25 mi ENE of Fayetteville. Founded as a railroad work camp *c.*1850, it fell to the union during the Civil War in July 1863, before the CHATTANOOGA campaign. After World War II it became the location of the vast Arnold Engineering and Development Center, which serves NASA and the U.S. armed forces.

TULLE (France) Town and capital of Corrèze department, 47 mi SSE of Limoges, S central France. Founded in the seventh century AD, it was twice captured by the English during the Hundred Years War and was retaken by Charles V of France in 1370. See also ENGLAND.

TULLUM. See TOUL.

TULSA (United States) City and inland port on the Arkansas River, 15 mi NE of Sapulpa, NE OKLAHOMA. A major center of the petroleum industry, it houses the plants and offices of over 800 oil companies. Once inhabited by the Creek Indians, it was incorporated in 1898 and boomed after oil was discovered nearby in 1901. Since 1971 it has been connected with the Gulf of Mexico by the McClellan-Kerr Waterway.

T'U-LU-FAN. See TURFAN.

TULUM. See QUINTANA ROO, Mexico.

TUMBES [**Tumbez**] (Peru) Town and capital of Tumbes department and province, 645 mi NW of Lima, on the Pacific coastal plain, NW Peru. In 1532 Francisco Pizarro landed near here at the start of his conquest of Peru. See also INCA EMPIRE, SPAIN.

TUMBEZ. See TUMBES.

TUMIBAMBA. See CUENCA, Ecuador.

TUMLUK. See TAMLŪK.

TUNES. See TUNIS.

TUNGCHOW. See TA-LI.

TUNGSHA. See PRATAS ISLAND.

TUN-HUANG [**Tunhwang**] (China) Town in NW Kansu province of central China. It is of importance and interest both because of its location on the ancient SILK ROAD and because of the Caves of the Thousand Buddhas at nearby Tsienfotung. The oasis at Tun-huang was an early hub of transportation routes, being the first trading town reached by foreign merchants entering China from the West. Here also the westward road divided into two parts, the South Road that led to INDIA and the North Road to TURKISTAN. Ancient ROME and China exchanged goods and ideas over the road, silk being shipped west, while wool, gold, and silver traveled east. Over the Silk Road Buddhist monks brought Buddhism to China circa the first century AD; while Nestorian Christians, Taoists, and Zoroastrians also used it.

Buddhist monks first established communities among the Caves of the Thousand Buddhas in 366. Many frescoes were painted in these caves between the fifth and 13th centuries. They show Greco-Roman, Indian, and Iranian influences. Later the caves were sealed up, and it was not until 1900 that a Hungarian-British archaeologist, Sir Aurel Stein, reopened them, revealing not only paintings and drawings but nearly 15,000 manuscripts. Among these was the *Diamond Sutra*, an important monument of Sanskrit literature, which is reputed to be the first printed book, produced in 868 AD. Today a new highway and a railroad run north of Tun-huang.

TUNHWANG. See TUN-HUANG.

TUNIS [*ancient:* **Tunes;** *Arabic:* **Tūnus**] (Tunisia) City and capital of Tunisia and of Tunis et Banlieue governorate, on the North African coast and the Lake of Tunis. Its port is at Halq al-Wadi. It is possibly of pre-Carthaginian origin. The ruins of CARTHAGE itself lie to the northeast and have been excavated.

Under the rule of the Hafsid dynasty from the 13th to 16th centuries AD, Tunis became the capital of Tunisia and a major city of the Muslim world. It was captured by the Turks under Barbarossa in 1534 and later came under Spanish rule twice in the 16th century. The Turkish governors of Tunis were virtually autonomous after 1591, and the city flourished as a trading center and pirate base. Occupied by the French in 1881, it was the headquarters for the last stand of the Axis forces in North Africa during World War II and fell on May 7, 1943. It has notable mosques. See also BARBARY STATES, FRANCE, OTTOMAN EMPIRE.

TUNISIA [*former:* **Ifriqiya;** *French:* **Tunisie**] A nation of North Africa, bounded by the Mediterranean Sea, Algeria, and Libya. PHOENICIA established colonies along the North African coast of modern Tunisia *c.*1200 BC. CARTHAGE was founded in the eighth century BC and became the leading maritime power in the western Mediterranean Sea until the Punic Wars ended with its destruction by ROME in 146 BC. The victorious Romans founded the Province of AFRICA, and their capital at TUNIS became the center of an ambitious program of development aimed both at cities and agriculture.

Vandals occupied Tunisia in 439 AD, but it was recaptured by the BYZANTINE EMPIRE in 533/34. The province was drained by this struggle and was unable to repel the Islamic wave that swept over North Africa in the seventh century. Tunis fell in 647, and by 703 the entire country was under Muslim rule and was renamed *Ifriqiya,* the Arabic word for Africa. An inland capital at KAIROUAN became the center of a dynamic Arab state in the ninth century, which conquered SICILY. In 972 a Tunisian-based Fatimid dynasty conquered EGYPT and moved to newly founded CAIRO. From the 12th to 16th centuries Tunisia prospered, though Normans from Sicily briefly took most of its ports in the 12th century. Tunisia came under Moroccan influence in 1159 when it was incorporated into the ALMOHAD Caliphate.

Regaining its independence after the Almohad rule collapsed, Tunisia prospered under the Hafsid dynasty until the 16th century, when it became a possession of the OTTOMAN EMPIRE. Tunisia became famous as a BARBARY STATE sponsoring Mediterranean piracy. In the 19th century Tunisia's path closely paralleled Egypt's, as ambitious beys (rulers) tried to modernize it.

In 1864 the country went bankrupt, and a commission formed by Great Britain, France, and Italy took financial control. In 1878 Great Britain gave FRANCE a free hand in Tunisia in exchange for French agreement to its occupation of CYPRUS. France quickly established a protectorate, installed a colonial bureaucracy, and began massive development.

In the early 20th century nationalism began to stir in Tunisia. During the 1930's Habib Bourguiba became the leading spokesman for independence and was imprisoned several times by French authorities. Tunisia was controlled by Germany during World War II until 1943, when Free French rule was restored. With the end of the war the nationalists renewed their pressure for independence, but France refused to negotiate. In 1952 Tunisia erupted into violence, and by 1954 France was ready to relinquish its hold. Independence was achieved on June 1, 1956 with Bourguiba in charge of forming a government under the nominal leadership of the bey. In 1957 Tunisia was declared a republic, and Bourguiba was elected president.

The country pursued a moderate political course, maintaining fairly close ties with France and the United States and rejecting the Arab militancy promoted by Egypt's President Gamal Abdel Nasser. It maintained relations with the United States during the Arab-Israeli war of 1967, but it condemned Egypt for its peace treaty with Israel in 1979. Tunis became the headquarters of the Arab League following Egypt's expulsion from that group in the same year. See also ABBASID CALIPHATE, ARABIAN PENINSULA.

TUNISIE. See TUNISIA.

TUNJA [*former:* **Hunza**] (Colombia) Town and capital of Boyacá department, 85 mi NE of Bogotá, central Colombia. It was founded in 1539, and it proclaimed itself independent from SPAIN in 1811. In 1819 the town served as Simón Bolívar's base before his victory over the Spanish at BOYACÁ. It has many colonial buildings.

TUNNA-CEASTER. See CAISTOR.

TŪNUS. See TUNIS.

TUPELO (United States) City in NE MISSISSIPPI, 57 mi NNW of Columbus. It was founded in 1859 and was the site of a Civil War battle fought on July 14, 1864 when Gen. A.J. Smith and the Union forces defeated Gen. Nathan Forrest and the Confederates. The site is now a national historic battlefield.

TURBA. See TERUEL.

TURCKHEIM [*German:* **Türkheim**] (France) Village in Haut-Rhin department, near Colmar, NE France. During the wars of Louis XIV of France the French under the viscount of Turenne defeated the imperial forces of the Austrian Hapsburgs here on Jan. 5, 1675. Turenne was killed in June at BADEN.

TURDA [*ancient:* **Dierna, Potaissa;** *German:* **Thorenburg;** *Hungarian:* **Torda**] (Rumania) Town in Cluj district, TRANSYLVANIA, 15 mi SE of Cluj, NW central Rumania. Originally a Dacian settlement, it became a Roman camp and later a Roman colony. The Romans worked the nearby salt mines. During the Middle Ages it was the meeting place of the Transylvanian diet.

TURENUM. See TRANI.

TURFAN [**T'u-lu-fan**] (China) Town in E central Sinkiang Uighur, 90 mi SE of Urumchi, W China. It is the main town of the T'u-lu-fan Depression, which from 200 to 400 AD was the center of a prosperous civilization of mixed Persian and Indian cultures. From the ninth to 13th centuries it was ruled by the Uighurs, who had their capital at Turfan.

TURGU-JIU. See TÎRGU-JIU.

TURIN [*ancient:* **Augusta Taurinorum, Julia Taurinorum, Taurasia;** *Italian:* **Torino**] (Italy) City and capital of Torino province and PIEDMONT region, on the PO RIVER, 78 mi NW of Genoa, NW Italy. Once the chief Roman town of the western Po valley, it later became a Lombard duchy and a Frankish county. It became the capital of the house of Savoy in the late 11th century and eventually became the capital of the duchy. It was ruled by the French from 1506 to 1562 but was granted to Duke Emmanuel Philibert in 1559 by the Treaty of Cateau-Cambrésis. The city was the object of siege in 1639/40 and during the War of the Spanish Succession. The latter ended in the defeat of the French by Eugene of Savoy in 1706. It was the capital of the kingdom of SARDINIA between 1720 and 1861 and the capital of the new kingdom of Italy from 1861 to 1864.

Badly bombed during World War II because of its industries, it is still a major industrial center today. The cathedral of San Giovanni houses the Shroud of Turin, which is believed to have been used to wrap the body of Jesus after his crucifixion. The royal palace and archaeological museum here are also noteworthy.

TURKESTAN. See TURKISTAN.

TURKEY [*Turkish:* **Türkiye**] Nation of SW Asia occupying most of ASIA MINOR, which constitutes approx. 97 percent of its territory, as well as E THRACE in SE Europe. It includes parts of ARMENIA and KURDISTAN. ANKARA is the capital. As a nation Turkey came into existence following the collapse of the OTTOMAN EMPIRE after its defeat in World War I. By the Treaty of Sèvres in 1920 the Allies set up a small Turkish state in the northern part of Asia Minor. The reigning sultan, Muhammad VI, accepted the treaty, but Turkish nationalists known as the Young Turks refused it. Under Mustafa Kemal, later known as Kemal Atatürk, they organized resistance, set up a government at Ankara, and fought the Allies. A treaty with the USSR in 1921 led to the restoration of the KARS and ARDAHAN regions, while a Greek offensive against the nationalists was routed in 1922. The nationalists declared the sultan deposed on Nov. 1, 1922.

A new agreement, the Treaty of Lausanne of 1923, recognized Turkey with its present boundaries, except for the *sanjak* of ALEXANDRETTA, a province now in southern Turkey, which was transferred to Turkey in 1939. In October 1923 Turkey officially became a republic, and Kemal became its first president, a position he held until his death in 1938. He westernized Turkey, abolishing the caliphate in 1924, granting suffrage to women in 1934, ending polygamy and the wearing of the traditional fez, adopting new civil and criminal law codes, and substituting the Latin alphabet for the Arabic. CONSTANTINOPLE was officially renamed ISTANBUL in 1930.

In 1934 Turkey joined Greece, Rumania, and Yugoslavia in the Balkan Entente and in 1937 the Saadabad

Pact with Afghanistan, Iran, and Iraq. The Montreux Convention of 1936 allowed Turkey to control and fortify the DARDANELLES, which had not been permitted under the Treaty of Lausanne. Kemal was succeeded as president by Ismet Inönü, who tried to keep Turkey neutral in World War II, but it finally joined the Allies in February 1945. Relations with the USSR deteriorated in 1945, and in 1947 Turkey began to receive aid from the United States under the Truman Doctrine, aimed at "containing" communism. Turkey became a member of the North Atlantic Treaty Organization (NATO) in 1952 and helped create the Central Treaty Organization in 1955.

In the mid-1950's a dispute with GREECE arose over the island of CYPRUS. Turkey supported the demands of the Turkish minority there for partition of the island. After Cyprus became independent in 1960 there was fighting between Greeks and Turks, and in 1974 Turkey invaded the island to protect the Turkish Cypriots. Since the late 1950's there has been much political unrest in Turkey, with government suppression of dissidents, and numerous changes of rulers. General Kenan Evren led a military takeover of the government in September 1980 and in 1981 abolished the two leading political parties amid widespread repression.

The harbor of Antalya, an ancient city of Turkey's southern coast, founded in the second century BC. Above it rises a splendid medieval Seljuk minaret made of brick.

TÜRKHEIM. See TURCKHEIM.

TURKISTAN [**Turkestan**] (Afghanistan, China, USSR) Region in central Asia, bounded on the N by Siberia; on the E by the Gobi Desert; on the S by Afghanistan, India, Iran, and Tibet; and on the W by the Caspian Sea. Western Turkistan is the Soviet part, in Soviet Central Asia; eastern Turkistan is the SINKIANG Uigur Autonomous Region of China; the southern part is now an area of northeastern Afghanistan. Turkistan was so named to indicate that it was inhabited by Turkic-speaking peoples, but many are not. Because of its location, since antiquity Turkistan has been one of the most important land links between East and West. Over its expanse have traveled traders, conquerors, missionaries, and migrating peoples. It is also the site of some of the oldest cities in the world, particularly BUKHARA, MERV, SAMARKAND, and TASHKENT. One branch of the SILK ROAD between China and the West traversed the region.

By c.500 BC the Persian Empire had brought most of Turkistan under its rule. Alexander the Great of the MACEDONIAN EMPIRE marched through Turkistan in 328 BC when he conquered PERSIA. After Alexander's death, control of Turkistan was taken by Seleucus, one of his generals, and later, in the middle of the second century, the region was divided between the kingdoms of PARTHIA in the west and BACTRIA in the east. The former expanded later at Bactria's expense. In the meantime, the Chinese Empire was conquering eastern Turkistan, but in the third century AD it lost it to the Sassanid dynasty of Persia. China regained control in the seventh century, with Persia ruling most of the rest of Turkistan. In the eighth century an Arab invasion ended Persian rule and brought Islam with it, first under the Umayyad caliphate, and then under the ABBASID CALIPHATE. When both the Arabs and the Chinese regimes weakened, a number of states arose in Turkistan, the most important being KHOREZM, while the UIGURS invaded eastern Turkistan from MONGOLIA. Although it was conquered by the Seljuk Turks in their 11th-century invasion, Khorezm regained its independence with the final defeat of the Seljuks in 1157.

Khorezm's ruled ended again in 1221 when Genghis Khan, the Mongol emperor, invaded it, and in 1260 one of his sons became ruler of Turkistan as head of the Jagatai Khanate. A century later, in 1369, another Mongol emperor, Tamerlane, conquered the region. For another century following his death in 1405, his successors, the Timurids, controlled much of Turkistan, after which there was a long period of struggle involving the khanates of Bukhara, KHIVA, and KOKAND, as well as various nomadic peoples. Russian power entered the region, and in the late 17th and early 18th centuries China lost some of eastern Turkistan. RUSSIA invaded Kokand in 1865, and Bukhara and Khiva were forced to accept Russian protection in 1868. By agreement in 1859 Russia gave up its claim to Afghan Turkistan. After having changed hands a number of times, eastern Turkistan became the Chinese province of Sinkiang in 1881. Since the Russian Revolution of 1917 Turkistan has been governed by the Soviets, with several changes of administrative boundaries and names. Nevertheless, Turkistan retains a certain cultural and ethnic distinctiveness to this day. See also MONGOL EMPIRES, SELEUCID EMPIRE.

TÜRKIYE. See TURKEY.

TURKMANCHAI. See AZERBAIJAN SSR.

TURKMENISTAN. See TURKMEN SSR.

TURKMEN SSR [Turkmenistan] (USSR) Constituent republic of central Asian USSR, N of Afghanistan and Iran. Its capital is ASHKHABAD. The region passed under many rulers in its early history, including the Achaemenid Persians, the Arabs in the eighth century AD, Seljuk Turks in the 11th, Genghis Khan and Tamerlane in the 13th and 14th centuries, and the Uzbeks. Russian military conquest began in 1869 and was completed in 1881, after which the region was included in the former Transcaspian region. During the Russian Revolution fighting broke out between the Bolsheviks and the Transcaspian provincial government, resulting in the fall of Ashkhabad to the Red Army in July 1919. Turkmenistan then became a constituent republic of the Soviet Union in 1925.

TURKS AND CAICOS ISLANDS (Great Britain) British colony in the WEST INDIES, SE of the Bahamas and N of Hispaniola, consisting of over 30 islands and cays, of which six are inhabited. Discovered in 1512 by the Spanish explorer Ponce de León, the islands were uninhabited until 1678 when some Bermudians arrived to set up a salt-panning operation. The first permanent settlement was c.1780. The islands were a dependency of JAMAICA from 1874 to 1959 and became a crown colony in 1962, with a new constitution in 1969. Salt is the main export, and the population is mostly of black African descent. Grand Turk, on the island of the same name, is the capital.

TURKU [*Swedish:* **Åbo**] (Finland) City, port, and capital of Turku and Pori province, on the Baltic Sea, 100 mi WNW of Helsinki, SW Finland. Said to be the cradle of Finnish culture, it is the oldest city in Finland and in 1220 AD became the seat of the first bishop of Finland. It was the capital of Finland until 1812. By the Treaty of Åbo signed here in 1743, part of southeastern Finland was ceded to SWEDEN. Although almost completely destroyed by fire in 1827, the city is today Finland's largest port. It has a bilingual population.

TURNACUM. See TOURNAI.

TŬRNOVO. See TIRNOVO.

TURNU-SEVERIN [*ancient:* **Drobeta**] (Rumania) City, port, and capital of Mehedinţi district, in WALACHIA, on the DANUBE RIVER, near the Iron Gate, SW Rumania. The oldest Roman settlement in Rumania, it was the site of a bridge over the Danube built for Emperor Trajan. It declined until 1833, when it was reinhabited by refugees from Cerneţi and grew rapidly under the Rumanian People's Republic. It has large shipyards.

TURONI. See TOURS.

TURRIS HANNIBALIS. See MAHDIA.

TURRIS LIBISONIS. See PORTO TORRES.

TUS. See MASHHAD.

TUSBUN. See CTESIPHON.

TUSCALOOSA (United States) City in W ALABAMA, 50 mi SW of Birmingham. Founded in 1816, on the site of an Indian village, it was the state capital from 1826 to 1846 and was partly burned during the Civil War.

TUSCANA. See TUSCANIA.

TUSCANIA [*ancient:* **Tuscana;** *former:* **Toscanella**] (Italy) Town in Viterbo province, LATIUM region, W of Viterbo, central Italy. It was a flourishing Etruscan town in the third century BC. In 1971 Tuscania was badly damaged by an earthquake. Etruscan tombs have been found nearby.

TUSCANY [*Italian:* **Toscana**] (Italy) Region of central Italy, on the Tyrrhenian Sea. Its capital is FLORENCE. Corresponding to the larger part of ancient ETRURIA, it was conquered by the Romans in the mid-fourth century BC. It became a Lombard duchy, with its capital at LUCCA, from the sixth to the eighth centuries AD and an important Frankish march and province of the HOLY ROMAN EMPIRE from the eighth to 12th centuries. The last Frankish ruler, Countess Matilda of Tuscany, heavily influenced later Italian history by leaving all her lands to the papacy. In the 11th and 12th centuries most of Tuscany's cities became free communes; and PISA, Lucca, SIENA, AREZZO, and Florence were powerful republics. Tuscany was an important center of the wool production and cloth trade, and its merchants, bankers, and financiers were active throughout Europe. Ruled by Robert of Naples in the 14th century, Tuscany was the scene of intense fighting between Guelphs and Ghibellines in the late Middle Ages, and by the 15th century had passed under the control of Florence, whose history it then shared. In 1569 the region became a grand duchy under the famous Medici family of Florence, after the Spanish conquest of Italy. It passed to Francis of Lorraine in 1737. During the Napoleonic period Tuscany became part of the kingdom of Etruria from 1801 to 1807, but again became a grand duchy in 1814, after the fall of Napoleon. In 1861 it was united with the new kingdom of Italy. Tuscany's contribution to the arts of the Renaissance was outstanding. Its Romanesque style of architecture was distinctive, and the Tuscan school of painting first gave impetus to the European-wide painting style of the 14th century. The Tuscan dialect, through Dante, Petrarch, Boccaccio, and others, became the language of all Italy.

TUSCULUM (Italy) Ancient Italic city, 15 mi S of Rome, in Roma province, LATIUM region, central Italy. A Latin settlement in rivalry with ROME during the early Iron Age, it became subject to Rome in the early fifth century BC and was a popular resort of wealthy Romans from the first century BC until the fourth century AD. Among its residents were Pliny the Younger, Cicero, and the emperors Nero and Titus. Cicero wrote his *Tusculan Disputations* here. It was an early medieval stronghold until the Romans destroyed it in 1190 AD. According to legend it was established by Telegonus, the son of Ulysses. Ruins of the 2,000-ft high city, including a rock-cut theater and many surrounding villas, may be seen today.

TUSKEGEE (United States) City in SE ALABAMA, approx. 35 mi E of Montgomery. Settled before 1763, it is the home of the Tuskegee Institute, one of the first important educational institutions for blacks. The school was founded in 1881 by Booker T. Washington, the black educator, as the Tuskegee Normal and Industrial Institute. George Washington Carver, the black agricultural chemist who is remembered for the many uses he found for peanuts and other vegetables, had his laboratory here. In 1960 the U.S. Supreme Court declared void a 1957 Alabama law that would have excluded blacks from the city by changing the city's boundaries.

TUTELA. See TUDELA.

TUTICORIN (India) Town and port in S Tamil Nadu, 75 mi S of Madurai, on the Gulf of Mannar, S India. It developed into a prosperous Portuguese colony in the 16th century, was taken by the Dutch in 1658, and passed to the British in 1825. Although its importance waned with the growth of MADRAS, it is today TAMIL NADU's second port.

TUTUB. See KHAFAJE.

TUVA ASSR [**Tuvinian ASSR**] [*former:* **Tannu Tuva, Uriankhai**] (USSR) Administrative division of Russian SFSR, on the Mongolian border, S Siberian USSR. Its capital is Kyzyl. Once ruled by the Mongols, Tannu Tuva was part of Outer MONGOLIA in the Chinese Empire from 1757 to 1911. Separatist movements within the country were encouraged by the czarist regime in RUSSIA, which took control of the area in 1914. In 1921 the Tannu Tuva People's Republic became independent, but it was annexed in 1944 by the USSR and made an autonomous oblast of the Russian SFSR. It became an autonomous republic in 1961. See also CHINA, MONGOL EMPIRES.

TUVALU [*former:* **Ellice Islands**] Nation in the W Pacific Ocean, S of the equator and E of the Solomon Islands. Tuvalu is an island nation, consisting of the nine coral atolls of the Ellice Islands, sometimes called the Lagoon Islands. People from SAMOA invaded the islands in the 16th century, and Polynesians replaced the Melanesian inhabitants. The island group as a whole was discovered in 1764 by John Byron of Great Britain. One of the islands, Nanumea, was probably discovered in 1781; and Fanafuti, the main island, was reached in 1819. GREAT BRITAIN declared a protectorate over the islands in 1892 and in 1915 made them part of the Gilbert and Ellice Islands Colony.

In April 1943, during World War II, U.S. Marines occupied Fanafuti and established a military base, as they did on Nanumea in September. The people of the islands voted to separate from the Gilberts, now KIRIBATI, in 1974, and the separation took place on Jan. 1, 1976. On Oct. 1, 1978 the Ellice Islands became independent as Tuvalu, a special member of the British Commonwealth. Sovereignty over four of the islands is in dispute between Great Britain and the UNITED STATES. Copra is the main export.

TUVINIAN ASSR. See TUVA ASSR.

TUXTEPEC [**San Juan Bautista Tuxtepec**] (Mexico) Town in NE Oaxaca state, 80 mi NNE of Oaxaca. The Plan of Tuxtepec of January 1876 was a declaration opposing the politics of President Lerdo de Tejada of Mexico.

TUXTLA. See SAN ANDRÉS TUXTLA.

TÚY (Spain) Town on the Miño River, in Pontevedra province, Galicia, 30 mi S of Pontevedra, NW Spain. It was the capital of King Witiza of the VISIGOTHIC KINGDOM in the early eighth century AD. It was important in the wars between PORTUGAL and CASTILE and was seized by Portugal in 1388 and 1397.

TVER. See KALININ.

TWEED RIVER (England, Scotland) River rising in the Borders region of Scotland and in its lower course forming part of the border between Scotland and England. It is 97 miles long and enters the North Sea at BERWICK UPON TWEED, Northumberland, which changed hands many times before becoming English in 1482. On the Tweed also are COLDSTREAM, which gave its name to one of Great Britain's most famous military units; MELROSE, with the ruins of an abbey founded in 1136; Peebles, which has ruins of a 13th-century church and a castle; and Abbotsford, home of author Sir Walter Scott from 1812 to 1832. Scott wrote of the area in his books.

TWO SICILIES, KINGDOM OF THE (Italy) Former kingdom, consisting of the kingdom of NAPLES, including southern Italy, and the kingdom of SICILY, the island of Sicily in the Mediterranean Sea adjacent to the mainland. The name was first used in the Middle Ages. In 1442, when Alfonso V of ARAGON reunited the two kingdoms, which had been separated in 1282, he named himself King of the Two Sicilies. The kingdoms were separated under his successors, but from 1504 to 1713, when SPAIN ruled both regions, the name was used once more. Again in 1759, when a branch of the Spanish Bourbons had acquired power in both regions, the term was revived. Finally, in 1816 Ferdinand IV of Naples merged the two kingdoms and named himself Ferdinand I of the Two Sicilies. This arrangement lasted until 1860, when both Sicily and Naples were captured by Italian nationalist forces under Giuseppe Garibaldi; and in 1861 the Two Sicilies became part of the united kingdom of Italy.

TYANA (Turkey) Ancient city of SW CAPPADOCIA, on the N slopes of the Taurus Mts, 15 mi SSW of Niğde, in Niğde province, S central Turkey. A powerful fortress and important commercial center by the fifth century BC, it became part of the ROMAN EMPIRE in 272 AD. The Greek philosopher Apollonius was born here in the first century AD, and it was an early Christian bishopric, surviving into the early Middle Ages. There are extensive ruins.

TYNE AND WEAR (England) Metropolitan county formed in 1974 from parts of Northumberland and Durham. The admin. hq. is SOUTH SHIELDS.

TYNEMOUTH (England) Port in Tyne and Wear, on the Tyne River, 9 mi E of Newcastle upon Tyne. A highly industrialized town, it began to grow in the 14th century. It has the remains of a seventh-century priory founded by King Edwin of NORTHUMBRIA on the site.

TYNGSTOWN. See MANCHESTER, New Hampshire.

TYR. See TYRE.

TYRAS. See BELGOROD-DNESTROVSKY, DNIESTER RIVER.

TYRE [*ancient:* **Tyrus**; *Arabic:* **Es Sur, Sur**; *French:* **Sour, Tyr**; *Hebrew:* **Zor**] (Lebanon) Ancient city of PHOENICIA, S of Sidon on the Mediterranean Sea, in S Lebanon. A prosperous city by 1400 BC, it may have been a colony of nearby SIDON. By 1100 it had gained maritime supremacy and had established colonies in Spain, North Africa, and elsewhere, including CARTHAGE, founded in the eighth century. As overlord of the Phoenician cities from the 11th century until 573 BC, Tyre was famous for its industries, which included the production of silken garments and the purple Tyrian dye. It was King Hiram of Tyre who helped Solomon of ISRAEL build his temple. Tyre was often under foreign rule, including that of PERSIA, but also successfully held off attacks from ASSYRIA and Babylon. In the sixth century BC it successfully withstood a 13-year siege by Nebuchadnezzar of BABYLON but had to yield to Alexander the Great of the MACEDONIAN EMPIRE in 332 after another arduous siege.

Originally built on two islands, Tyre now stands on a peninsula formed by the silting up of a mole built by Alexander out to the city. Ruled by the SELEUCID EMPIRE, it was subjected to ROME in 64 BC and was an early convert to Christianity during the ROMAN EMPIRE. It was occupied by the Arabs in the seventh century AD, and in 1124 was taken by the Crusaders, under whom it became the chief city of the LATIN KINGDOM OF JERUSALEM. After its destruction by the Muslims in 1291, it never recovered. The remains of the city today date chiefly from the Crusader period.

TYROL [**Tirol**] [*Italian:* **Tirolo**] (Austria) Federal state of W Austria, between BAVARIA and the TRENTINO-ALTO ADIGE region, N Italy. Its capital is INNSBRUCK. The South Tyrol is now part of ITALY. A mountainous region, it has a strategic position guarding both sides of the BRENNER PASS. Once inhabited by Rhaetic tribes, it fell to ROME in 15 BC and was conquered by Teutonic tribes at the end of the ROMAN EMPIRE and by the Franks. From the 11th to the 19th centuries, large areas of the South Tyrol were ruled by the bishops of TRENT and of Brixen.

The North Tyrol passed to the Hapsburgs in 1363, and both regions were united under Austria in 1801. Napoleon passed the Tyrol to Bavaria in 1805, but in 1809 Andreas Hofer led the Tyrolians against both the French and Bavarians. The area was returned to Austria in 1815 but was divided again by the Treaty of Saint-Germain, which gave the southern part to Italy. Under Benito Mussolini's regime the German-speaking South Tyrol was subjected to a rigorous program of Italianization. Today the rights of the German-speaking inhabitants of the South Tyrol are guaranteed by the Italian constitution. See also BRESSANONE, FRANCE, FRANKISH EMPIRE.

TYRONE (Northern Ireland) Ancient region and former county of Northern Ireland, most of which has been divided into the districts of Cookstown, Dungannon, Omagh, and Strabane. It is sometimes loosely referred to as ULSTER. Prehistoric megalithic tombs, called court tombs, are to be found here, as are the

The Alpine town of Lech, in the Austrian Tyrol. The ancient German-speaking territory of Tyrol is now divided between Austria and Italy but is essentially a single enclave.

remains of timber-built rectangular houses belonging to the tomb builders.

From the fifth to the 16th century Tyrone was ruled by the O'Neills (O'Nialls, O'Neals). An earldom of Tyrone was created in 1542 by Henry VIII of ENGLAND.

Hugh O'Neill, the third earl of Tyrone, rose against the English in 1596 and in 1601 was defeated by Royalist forces under Lord Mountjoy, who established fortifications here and started colonizing Tyrone with Protestant Scots, Welsh, and English. The earl fled from the English in 1607, and his estates passed to the crown. They were divided and granted out by the king.

Tyrone suffered again when Cromwell continued the process of colonization as commander-in-chief and lord lieutenant of Ireland in 1649. In 1688/89 James II occupied Tyrone and badly damaged its capital, Omagh. The long-term effect of the colonization process was that Tyrone and the north of IRELAND became predominantly Protestant and allied emotionally and economically with the English, while the southern part remained predominantly Catholic and vigorously supported independence. Under the Government of Ireland Act (or Home Rule Act) of 1920, six of the nine original political subdivisions of Tyrone became Northern Ireland, an administrative unit of the UNITED KINGDOM.

TYROS. See BAHRAIN.

TYRUS. See TYRE.

TYTHIA. See ATIENZA.

TYUMEN [Tiumen] (USSR) City and port on the Tura River, in Russian SFSR, 190 mi E of Sverdlovsk, on the Trans-Siberian Railroad, SW Siberian USSR. Founded in 1585 by Yermak, a Russian Cossack leader, it is the oldest city in SIBERIA. It was once important in trade with China.

TZEFIYA. See SAFED.

TZIA. See KEOS.

U

UA BHFAILGHE. See OFFALY.

UAL UAL. See WAL WAL.

UBAID. See AL-UBAYYID.

UBANGI-SHARI [*French:* **Oubangi-Chari;** *1910–1920:* **Oubangi-Chari-Tchad, Ubangi-Shari-Chad**] (Central African Republic) Former French territory in what is now the Central African Republic. Defined as a French colony *c.*1895–99 after the first French explorations here *c.*1890, it was incorporated with CHAD in FRENCH EQUATORIAL AFRICA in 1910. It was given the status of overseas territory with representation in the French parliament in 1946 and became the Central African Republic in 1958.

UBANGI-SHARI-CHAD. See UBANGI SHARI.

UBE (Japan) Seaport city, 18 mi E of Shimonoseki. Coal was mined here as early as the late 17th century. When undersea mining was introduced in 1868 the city became a prosperous industrial center. It has declined since World War II along with coal mining in Japan.

UBEDA [**Úbeda**] (Spain) City, 22 mi NE of Jaén. An Iberian city, it was occupied by Arabs in the seventh century AD and captured in 1234 by Ferdinand III of CASTILE. Famous for its historic architecture, it has Renaissance churches, mansions, and a hospital.

ÜBERLINGEN (West Germany) City, 7 mi N of Constance. Once an imperial city, it has a 14th-century church and a 15th-century town hall.

UCAYALI (Peru) River beginning at the confluence of the Apurímac and Urubamba rivers in central Peru and flowing N to unite with the Marañón river to form the main head of the AMAZON. The Franciscan monk Illescas discovered it in 1641. It was first mapped in 1700.

UCCLE. See UKKEL.

UCH [**Uch-i-Sharif, Uch Sharif**] (Pakistan) Town, 39 mi WSW of Bahawalpur. In medieval times it was a Muslim center of learning.

UCH-I-SHARIF. See UCH.

UCH SHARIF. See UCH.

UCLÉS (Spain) Town 40, mi W of Cuenca. Here in 1108 the Moors defeated the Seven Counts of resurgent Spain. Its noted fortified monastery was founded by the Santiago Order and later became a Jesuit college.

UDAIPUR [**Odeypore, Oodeypore, Udaypur**] [*former:* **Mewar**] (India) City and former state in RAJASTHAN; the city is 210 mi SW of Jaipur. The state was founded *c.* the eighth century AD with its capital at CHITOR. Its dynasty of warrior princes persistently resisted Muslim invasion. Weakened by wars with the Marathas, it came under British control in 1818. The city, founded *c.*560, became the capital in 1568. In its beautiful island palace Mogul Shah Jehan, who ruled from 1628 to 1658, hid during his revolt against his father, Jahangir. It has numerous temples and its old fortifications. See also MARATHA CONFEDERACY, MOGUL EMPIRE.

UDAYAPUR (India) Village, 29 mi NNE of Bhilsa. It has a temple of the 11th century with fine carvings and Muslim ruins with inscriptions.

UDAYPUR. See UDAIPUR.

UDDEVALLA [*ancient:* **Odensvold**] (Sweden) Town near the coast, 45 mi N of Göteborg. A site of pagan sacrifice, founded in 1498, it suffered serious damage in the Danish-Swedish wars of the 17th-18th centuries.

UDINE [*ancient:* **Utina**] (Italy) City and province. The province, belonging to Friuli-Venezia Giulia, borders on AUSTRIA, YUGOSLAVIA, and the Adriatic. The city is 65 mi NE of VENICE. Capital of the patriarchs of AQUILEIA from 1238 to 1751, the city was taken by Venice in 1420, ceded to Austria in 1797 by the Treaty of CAMPO FORMIO, and included in Italy in 1866. The Italian army had headquarters here from 1915 to 1917 during World War I. It has a 14th-century cathedral, the early castle of the Venetian governors, rebuilt in 1517, now a museum, a 15th-century town hall, and a 16th-century loggia and fountain. The 16th-century archepiscopal palace has frescoes by Tiepolo.

UDINSK. See ULAN-UDE.

UDINSKOYE. See ULAN-UDE.

UDMURT AUTONOMOUS SOVIET SOCIALIST REPUBLIC [*former:* **Votskaya ASSR**] (USSR) Autonomous republic in the E Russian SFSR. The region was inhabited from Neolithic times by the Finno-Ugrian Udmurts, who were ruled by the Bulgar State in the eighth century AD. It came under the khanate of KAZAN in the 13th and 16th centuries and under RUSSIA in 1552. It became an autonomous oblast in 1920.

UDNY (Scotland) Village in Grampian region, 14 mi NNW of Aberdeen. Its castle is built on the remains of a very early fortress.

UDO (Japan) Village 10 mi S of the provincial capital Miyazaki on SE HONSHŪ. A national shrine here is dedicated to the father of Jimmu, the first emperor of Japan.

UEDA [**Uyeda**] (Japan) City, 18 mi SSE of Nagano. A castle town from the 17th century, it developed in the late 19th century into a center of the silk industry. Its professional school declined in the 1950's.

UELE [**Welle**] (Zaire) River that rises in N Zaire and flows W to unite with the Bomu, forming the Ubangi, at the border of Zaire and the CENTRAL AFRICAN REPUBLIC. The Ubangi's main headstream, it was discovered by Georg Schweinfurth in 1870.

UFA (USSR) Capital of the Bashkir ASSR in the Russian SFSR 250 mi NE of Kuibyshev. Established by Moscow as a fortress in 1574 and then as a colony in 1586, it developed as a trading center on the route to SIBERIA. The cultural center of the Bashkirs, it has a noted early cathedral, several professional colleges, and museums of art, regional history, and the Revolution.

UFFENHEIM (West Germany) Town, 9 mi WNW of Windsheim, which is 15 mi NNW of Ansbach. Chartered c.1350, it has remains of medieval fortifications.

UGANDA Landlocked country of East Africa bordered by Sudan on the N, and clockwise by Kenya, Tanzania, Rwanda, and Zaire. Uganda's early history is only vaguely known, but it appears that a Bantu civilization ruled by Cweźi kings was overthrown by northern Luo Nilotic invaders c.1500 AD. The Luo became assimilated into the Bantu culture and founded the major Ugandan kingdoms of Ankole, BUGANDA, and Bunyoro. Buganda quickly ousted Bunyoro as the dominant state and built up a substantial governmental bureaucracy. In the late 19th century European interests in Uganda were dominated by a fierce struggle between existing Muslim interests, and Catholic and Protestant missionaries. A series of massacres and three-cornered religious wars was ended by 1893 when the British Imperial East Africa Company sent a military force to take control. That same year GREAT BRITAIN assumed control from the company and by 1901 had made Ankole, Bunyoro, and Buganda British protectorates.

In 1901 LAKE VICTORIA was reached by the Kenya-Uganda railway, and the country was opened up to commercial development. Cotton was introduced and quickly made the colony self-supporting. Much of Uganda's land was taken by European settlers, but in the aftermath of the Great Depression of the 1930's African farmers regained control of much of the productive cropland. Coffee became the most important crop, and Buganda prospered as its major supplier.

After World War II Great Britain began to deal with the question of Ugandan nationalism. Buganda pressed for independence from the rest of Uganda, making the formation of a new country difficult. In 1962 independence was finally achieved by Uganda, with Buganda retaining semi-autonomous privileges. In 1966 Prime Minister Milton Obote, the leader of the nationalist movement who became the new president, imposed a new constitution repealing Buganda's status. His troops quickly overcame Bugandan resistance.

In 1971 Obote was overthrown by the army, led by Gen. Idi Amin. Amin assumed dictatorial powers and mercilessly initiated an erratic reign of terror that by 1977 had resulted in an estimated 300,000 deaths. In 1978 President Nyerere of TANZANIA invaded Uganda with the general sympathy of most of Africa. LIBYA alone supported Amin, and he fled there in 1979 when KAMPALA, the capital, fell to Tanzanian troops. Uganda's government was restored to civilian opponents of Amin's regime. In 1980 a military coup overthrew the second civilian government to hold office in a single year. The country remains devastated, the countryside depopulated, its agriculture, economic life, urban centers, and infrastructure in a shambles.

UGARIT (Syria) Archaeological site located at modern Ras Shamra just N of LATAKIA. An ancient city inhabited from the Neolithic period of the fifth millennium BC, it was an important commercial center with ties to MESOPOTAMIA. It was highly civilized by the fourth millennium BC. It reached its height in the 15th and 14th centuries BC, when it produced sophisticated art works. It declined in the 12th century BC. Its cuneiform tablets have revealed much about Canaanite poetry and religion. See also CANAAN.

UGERNUM. See BEAUCAIRE.

UGIJAR (Spain) City, 24 mi SSE of Guadix. An uprising of the Moriscos began here in 1568. It was suppressed after a bitter struggle by Philip II with the support of John of Austria.

UGLICH (USSR) City in the Russian SFSR 55 mi W of Yaroslavl. Dating from 1148 and the capital of a principality in 1218, it came under MOSCOW's control in 1364. It was supposedly the scene of the murder in 1591 of Ivan the Terrible's son, Dmitri, in a 15th-century castle that is now a museum. The city has a 14th-century monastery and a 15th-century cathedral.

UHERSKE HRADISTE [*Czech:* **Uherskè Hradĭstĕ;** *German:* **Ungarisch-Hradisch**] (Czechoslovakia) Town 14 mi SW of Gottwaldov, which is 48 mi ENE of Brno. Founded in 1257, it has a 17th-century abbey and an early town hall. Its new town hall has notable frescoes.

UHERSKY OSTROH [*Czech:* **Uherský Ostroh;** *German:* **Ungarisch-Ostra**] (Czechoslovakia) Town, 20 mi SW of Gottwaldov, which is 48 mi ENE of Brno. It has an early fort, built against the incursions of the Magyars, and is the cultural center of a region rich in folk traditions.

UÍGE [**Uíje**] (Angola) Battle site, 150 mi NE of LUANDA. Here in the 17th century occurred the Battle of Ambuila, in which the Portuguese defeated the emperor of the KONGO.

UIGHUR. See UIGUR EMPIRE.

UIGUR EMPIRE [**Uighur**] (China) Ancient empire on the W borders of China, in the Sinkiang area. The Uigurs, a seminomadic people of central Asia who speak a Turkic language, first entered history in the seventh century AD at the time of the T'ang Empire in China, when they displaced the Turks in central Asia. When the T'ang withdrew from central Asia in the second half of the eighth century, the Uigurs invaded and occupied MONGOLIA but in 840 were driven into SINKIANG by the KIRGIZ. Here they founded an empire that survived for nearly half a century until it was destroyed by the invading Mongols. Some 4 million Uigurs still live in Sinkiang. See also MONGOL EMPIRES.

UÍJE. See UÍGE.

UIJONGBU [*Japanese:* **Giseifu;** *Korean:* **Ŭijǒngbu**] (South Korea) Town, 12 mi NNE of Seoul. The cabinet office was located here for a time during the Yi dynasty of 1392 to 1910.

UITENHAGE (South Africa) Town, 17 mi NW of Port Elizabeth. Jacob A. Uitenhage, commissioner general of the Dutch CAPE COLONY, founded it in 1804. It has municipal buildings dating from 1815, 1882, and 1898.

UJDA. See OUJDA.

UJELANG [*former:* **Providence Island**] (United States) Atoll in Kwajalein district of the Ralik Chain and 430 miles WNW of Kwajalein, U.S. Trust Territory of the Pacific Islands. U.S. forces took it in 1944 during World War II. In 1947 the U.S. government moved Bikini natives here from Kongerik and moved them away to Kili in 1949.

UJI (Japan) Town 10 mi S of Kyōto. It has an 11th-century monastery with a famous central hall.

UJIJI (Tanzania) Town, 4 mi S of Kigoma. Here on October 28, 1871, Stanley found Livingstone.

UJI-YAMADA. See ISE.

UJJAIN (India) City approx. 200 mi E of Ahmadabad. Inhabited as early as the second millennium BC, it was capital of the Aryan kingdom of AVANTI of the sixth to fourth centuries BC. It was a center of Sanskrit learning and a great city that became very holy to Hindus. It was a central city of MALWA from c.120 to 395 AD. The legendary ruler Vikramaditya ruled here c.400. Destroyed by the Muslims in the 13th century, it was retaken by the Sindhias and made their capital in the 15th century. It declined in the early 19th century. It has many notable buildings both Hindu and Muslim, including a revered 13th-century temple, now in ruins, an 11th-century cave temple, and an 18th-century observatory.

UJUNG PANDANG. See MAKASAR, Indonesia..

ÚJVIDÉK. See NOVI SAD.

UKEREWE. See VICTORIA, LAKE.

UKHRUL (India) Town, approx. 38 mi NNE of Imphal near the border of Burma. The Japanese made it their base in their invasion of India in 1944 during World War II. The British captured it in July 1944.

UKKEL [**Uccle**] (Belgium) Suburb S of BRUSSELS. Originally a town dating from the 12th century, it is the site of the Belgian royal observatory.

UKRAINA. See UKRAINE.

UKRAINE [*Russian:* **Ukraina**] (USSR) Region in European Russia, now included in the Ukrainian Soviet Socialist Republic of the USSR. For centuries a pathway from Central Asia to Europe for numerous peoples, it is now inhabited generally by Slavic Ukrainians. It extends W from the Carpathian Mts to the Sea of Azov in the E and 500 mi N from the Crimean peninsula. It is bounded by Rumania, Hungary, and Czechoslovakia in the W, and Poland to the NW. The ancient city of KIEV is its capital.

It was settled in the Paleolithic Age c.8500 BC; the Pontic Tardenosian culture was followed c.2750 BC by various Neolithic cultures involving early Caucasians and Finns. The Thracian-Cimmerians arrived in the Ukraine c.1850 BC and the Cimmerians proper, who were known to Homer, c.1300 BC. Arriving c.670 BC, the Scythians were displaced by the Sarmatians c.200 BC. In early Christian times the Ukraine was invaded by waves of Alans, Ostrogoths, and Huns, the latter arriving c.375 AD. Between the fourth and seventh centuries an alliance of tribes emerged that represented a definite Slavic strain, but they were soon submerged under the Avar Khanate from c.560 to 600, which was followed by the KHAZAR EMPIRE from further east c.650. The Magyars followed in 737.

It was only with the founding of the great principality of Kiev in the ninth century that the common strain in Ukrainians, Belorussians, and Russians become manifest in a single culture. Established by a Viking Varangian dynasty originating in SCANDINAVIA, the state of Kiev achieved its zenith under Yaroslav the Great (1019–54), adopting Eastern Orthodox Christianity and becoming a powerful political and cultural center. With Yaroslav's death the principality broke up into smaller units that had disparate histories, following the incursions of the Patzinaks c.1050, of the Cumans c.1070, and by the Mongol invasion of 1221/22.

By the mid-14th century the expansion of the principality of LITHUANIA east and south began to free the Ukraine from domination by the Mongol khanate of the GOLDEN HORDE and allowed it to flourish. A loose union of the Polish and Lithuanian dynasties by 1400 brought new influences into the Ukraine by 1430. This culminated with the formal political union of POLAND with Lithuania and subsequent Polish hegemony in the Ukraine. Western feudal and manorial institutions brought serfdom to the peasants of the Ukraine and Catholic Polish harassment of the Ukrainian Orthodox Church. The harsh rule of the Poles caused many Ukrainians to flee to the east and south where they acquired the name "Cossacks" or "Kozaks," meaning outlaws or adventurers. They were organized as a courageous, militant group, initially opposed to Polish rule.

In 1648 the hetman Bohdan Chmielnicki led the Cossacks in a successful rebellion against Poland. However, the Cossacks' strength was inadequate to retain total independence. With the Treaty of Pereyaslav in 1654, Chmielnicki tried to reach an accommodation that acknowledged Moscow's authority but assured the independence of the Ukraine. However, MOSCOW continued its pressure. In 1658 the Ukrainians turned to the Republic of Poland once more, signing a treaty of protection designed to avoid Russian rule. Instead, Poland and RUSSIA went to war, and with the Treaty of ANDRUSOVO in 1667 the Ukraine was divided between the two. In the reign of Peter the Great the Cossack Hetman Ivan Mazepa, ruler of a much-diminished Cossack state and desirous of freeing the Ukraine from Russian control, allied with Charles XII of SWEDEN against Peter in the Great Northern War. The Cossacks were defeated with the Swedes at POLTAVA in 1709, and Mazepa was slain. Fifty-five years later, in 1764, Empress Catherine II compelled the last Ukrainian Cossack hetman to step down. The partitions of Poland in 1772, 1793, and 1795 led to the unification of the Ukraine under Russian hegemony. The 19th century brought mineral and industrial development as well as a surge of nationalist sentiment.

In 1917, with the onset of the Russian Revolution, the Ukraine proclaimed its independence and founded an independent government. But by January 1919 the Red Army had invaded the region. A four-way war followed between the White and Red Armies, the independence-minded forces of the Ukraine, and Poland. The Red Army was the victor, and in 1922 the Ukraine became a component republic of the Soviet Union. Ukrainian nationalism was assuaged by Lenin, but Stalin ruthlessly forced the collectivization of agriculture while ordering the entire Ukrainian grain production exported, causing mass starvation of the Ukrainian people. As a result, in World War II the Nazi invasion and occupation was initially received enthusiastically by numerous Ukrainians as a desirable alternative to Stalin's reign of terror. When they became aware of Hitler's disdain for all things Slavic, however, many joined the underground resistance. Following World War II, and particularly since the 1960's, Ukrainians have assumed a more active role in the Soviet government—especially with the accession to power of Leonid I. Brezhnev, the late leader of the USSR, who was born in the Ukraine. See also BELORUSSIA, MONGOL EMPIRES, SARMATIA, SCYTHIA.

UKRAINIAN SOVIET SOCIALIST REPUBLIC. See UKRAINE.

ULAANBAATAR. See ULAN BATOR.

ULAN BATOR [Ulaanbaatar, Ulaan Baatar] [*Chinese:* **K'u-lun;** *former:* **Da Khure, Urga**] (Mongolian People's Republic) City approx. 720 mi W of Peking, CHINA, capital of the Mongolian People's Republic. The seasonal home of Mongolian princes, it was founded as a monastery in 1649 and for two centuries was the residence of the high priest of Tibetan Buddhism. It became commercially important as a trading center between RUSSIA and China in the 18th century. Here in 1911 autonomous MONGOLIA was declared a state. There was an army headquarters of Russian counter-revolutionaries here in 1921, when the Soviets occupied it. It has its original monastery buildings and a library with ancient Oriental manuscripts.

ULAN-UDE [*1766–83:* **Udinsk, Udinskoye;** *1783–1934:* **Verkhne-Udinsk**] (USSR) Capital of the Buryat ASSR in the Russian SFSR, 70 mi SE of Lake Baikal and 2,750 mi ESE of Moscow. Cossacks founded it as a wintering camp in 1649. It was a fortress from 1689. Later used as a place of exile, by 1775 it had developed into a city. From then on it prospered increasingly, first as a trading center on the tea route to CHINA and on other routes, then with the discovery of gold in the 1840's, and later with the arrival of the Trans-Siberian railroad in 1900. It was made capital of the FAR EASTERN REPUBLIC in 1920, which was first declared here, and then capital of the BURYAT ASSR in 1923.

ULASUTAI. See ULIASTAY.

ULCINJ [*ancient:* **Olcinium;** *Italian:* **Dulcigno**] (Yugoslavia) Seaport, 35 mi S of Titograd. It was taken by the Romans *c.*165 BC. Later a medieval pirate fortress, it was held by VENICE from 1421 to 1571, when the Turks captured it and held it until 1878. It has a ruined castle.

ULEABORG. See OULU.

ULEAI. See WOLEAI.

ULHĀSNAGAR (India) Town, approx. 25 mi NE of Bombay. In 1947 it became the site of a camp for refugees from West Pakistan.

ULIANOVSK. See ULYANOVSK.

ULIARUS INSULA. See OLÉRON.

ULIASSUTAI. See ULIASTAY.

ULIASTAY [Dzhibkhalantu, Jobhalanta, Ulasutai, Uliassutai, Ulyassatay] (Mongolian People's Republic) Town, approx. 460 mi W of Ulan Bator. Site of a Chinese fortress built in 1765, it developed from that time as an administrative center of MONGOLIA.

ULITHI [Mackenzie Island, Urushi] (United States) Atoll group, 108 mi ENE of Yap, U.S. Trust Territory of the Pacific Islands. First discovered in 1791, it was included in the Japanese mandate in 1920 and heavily fortified. The United States captured it in 1944 during World War II and used it as a naval base.

ULLSWATER (England) Lake, 5 mi SW of Penrith, in Cumbria. A picturesque lake in the famous LAKE DISTRICT, it is bordered on the west by Gowbarrow, a national park since 1910. It was the supposed inspiration of William Wordsworth's poem *Daffodils.*

ULM [Ulm-an-der-Donau] (West Germany) City, 45 mi SE of Stuttgart, on the DANUBE RIVER. A royal domain in 854, it was chartered in 1027. It became an imperial city in 1155. The city was a powerful and thriving trading and textile manufacturing center in the 14th and 15th centuries. Accepting Protestantism in 1530, it joined the Schmalkaldic League in the Reformation. It declined as the result of GERMANY's religious wars in the 16th and 17th centuries. It passed to BAVARIA in 1503 and to WÜRTTEMBERG in 1810. Here between September 25 and October 30, 1805, Napoleon fought and won a major battle against AUSTRIA. Albert Einstein was born here in 1879. The city has a great Gothic cathedral from the 14th century, a 14th-century town hall, a 16th-century corn exchange, and other historic buildings.

ULM-AN-DER-DONAU. See ULM.

ULPIANUM. See KYUSTENDIL.

ULPIA PAUTANIA. See KYUSTENDIL.

ULPIA TRAIANA. See SARMIZEGETUSA.

ULRICEHAMN [*before 1741:* **Bogesund]** (Sweden) City, 30 mi W of Jönköping. Founded in the 14th century and chartered in 1604, it has a 17th-century church and an 18th-century town hall.

ULSTER (Northern Ireland) Province of Northern Ireland, formerly consisting of nine counties (now divided into 26 districts). Six of them were in Northern Ireland, which is often called Ulster: Antrim, Armagh, Down, Fermanagh, Londonderry, and Tyrone. The other three are in the Republic of Ireland: Cavan, Donegal, and Monaghan. BELFAST, the largest city in Ulster, is the capital of Northern Ireland. Niall of the Nine Hostages, who died c.405 AD, was the founder of the O'Neill family, which exercised great power in Ulster for centuries. His son Eoghan, with the aid of a younger brother, Connall, conquered northwestern Ulster c.400 and founded the kingdom of Aileach, or Tyrconnell. In 1177 the Anglo-Norman John de Courci conquered Ulster, and in 1205 King John of ENGLAND made Hugh de Lacy earl of Ulster, the first title of English creation in IRELAND. Hugh O'Neill was created earl of TYRONE in 1585 and in 1593 became the head of the O'Neill clan. He was the most powerful nobleman in Ulster, but after losing a struggle with the English his power declined.

In County Antrim are Ballymena near where, according to tradition, St. Patrick worked as a herdsman, and CARRICKFERGUS, off whose shores John Paul Jones, the American naval hero, won a battle in 1778. In County Armagh is the city of ARMAGH, the ecclesiastical capital of Ireland since the fifth century. CAVAN, the county town of Cavan County, was burned in 1690 by supporters of William of Orange. County DONEGAL is

Ulm's magnificent 14th-century cathedral, which escaped damage in World War II. In the Middle Ages Ulm was one of the most powerful cities in the Holy Roman Empire.

the site of a castle that was the stronghold of the O'Donnell clan. In County Down is DOWNPATRICK, a longtime center of religious pilgrimage. ENNISKILLEN in County Fermanagh is famous for its Belleek Ware pottery. County Londonderry, originally Derry, was renamed after the O'Neill family estates were confiscated in 1609 and granted to the city companies of London. The city of LONDONDERRY grew up around an abbey built in 546. The county town of County Tyrone is Omagh.

In Gaelic literature Ulster is the setting for the Ulster Cycle, which deals with popular heroes who lived in the first century BC. The chief hero is Cuchulain who, the story says, stood at a ford on the boundary of Ulster and single-handedly fought off the armies of the rest of Ireland. On the north coast of County Antrim is a headland called the Giant's Causeway, consisting of thousands of columns of basalt, forming three platforms. According to legend the causeway was built so that giants could travel across it to SCOTLAND. A ship of the Spanish Armada was wrecked nearby in 1588.

ULTIMA THULE. See ICELAND.

ULTRAJECTUM. See UTRECHT.

ULÚA (Honduras) River rising in the Sierra de Gujiquiro and flowing approx. 200 mi N to the Gulf of Honduras, 15 mi ENE of Puerto Cortés. Its valley was the center of the Chorotega civilization, an Indian culture contemporaneous with the Mayan. This civilization was eradicated by the Spanish. No extensive remains survive.

ULUNDI (South Africa) Battle site, 115 mi NNE of Durban. Former capital of ZULULAND, it was the site of the final victory of the British under Lord Chelmsford over the Zulus under Cetewayo on July 4, 1879.

ULVERSTON (England) Town in Cumbria, 55 mi N of Liverpool. Documented in 1086, it was granted a market in 1280. George Fox, 17th-century founder of the Quakers, lived in Swarthmoor Hall here. It has a 12th-century church. The meetinghouse has a 15th-century Bible.

ULYANOVSK [Ulianovsk] [*former:* **Simbirsk**] (USSR) City, 48 mi ESE of Moscow. It was founded by MOSCOW in 1648 as a frontier fort. Developing as a trading center, it was attacked by rebel Cossacks in 1670. The city was chartered in 1796. The novelist Ivan Goncharov and Alexander Kerensky were born here. V.I. Lenin was born to the Ulyanov family here in 1870, and the town's name was changed in his honor.

ULYASSATAY. See ULIASTAY.

UMAL. See SANA.

UMAN (USSR) City in the Ukrainian SSR, 125 mi SW of Kiev. Dating from the Middle Ages, it was a stronghold protecting POLAND against the Crimean Tatars and a seat of Polish nobility until 1834. An uprising here in 1768 of Ukrainians and Cossacks resulted in the death of 18,000 Poles and Jews. It passed to RUSSIA in 1793 and was held by GERMANY in World War II from 1941 to 1943. See UKRAINE.

UMANAK [Umanaq] (Greenland) Settlement on a small island in Umanak Fjord. A hunting and fishing post, it was founded in 1763.

UMANAQ. See UMANAK.

UMARKOT (Pakistan) Town in the SW Thar Desert, 175 mi ENE of Karachi. A Rajput fort in medieval times, it was the place of exile of Humayun the Mogul from c.1540 to 1544. It was the birthplace of Akbar in 1542. See MOGUL EMPIRE.

UMBRIA (Italy) Region in the Apennines, bounded by TUSCANY on the NW, LATIUM on the SW and the MARCHES to the E. Inhabited c.600 BC by Umbrians and Etruscans, it was subdued by ROME c.300 BC. At the end of the Roman Empire it fell to the Goths, the Lombard duchy of SPOLETO, and then to the BYZANTINE EMPIRE. Local rule of city states prevailed here from the 12th to the mid-16th century, when the PAPAL STATES conquered the region. FRANCE held it from 1795 to 1800 and from 1808 to 1814. Revolts broke out in 1831, 1848, and 1859. It joined the kingdom of SARDINIA in 1860, and Italy in 1861. It has Roman and Etruscan remains, and its towns abound in great architecture and art of the Middle Ages and Renaissance. See also: ASSISI, GUBBIO, ORVIETO, PERUGIA, TODI.

UMEÅ (Sweden) Seaport 320 mi NNE of Stockholm. It was incorporated in 1622 by Gustavus II Adolphus. The town was burned by RUSSIA in 1720 and occupied by it in 1809. Almost entirely rebuilt after a fire in 1888, it has historic museums and a university.

UMMA [Tell Jokha] (Iraq) Ancient city, 50 mi NNW of Nasiriya, near ancient ERECH. It was a flourishing Sumerian city in the third millennium BC.

UMM AL-QAIWAIN [Umm Al-Qaywayn] (United Arab Emirates) Sheikdom in E Arabia on the Persian Gulf. Controlled by Persian Gulf pirates in the early 19th century, it was forced by Great Britain to sign the General Treaty of Peace in 1820. From then on it was a British protectorate until it was incorporated as a founding member of the United Arab Emirates in 1971.

UMM AL-QAYWAYN. See UMM AL-QAIWAIN.

UMM DURMĀN. See OMDURMAN.

UMM KAIS. See GADARA.

UMM QAYS. See GADARA.

UMNAK (United States) Island in the ALEUTIAN ISLANDS of ALASKA 5 mi W of Unalaska. When army and air bases were built here in World War II, the native sheepherders were removed, and their sheep stocks died out. New herds were introduced in 1944.

UMTALI [former: Fort Umtali] (Zimbabwe) Town, 130 mi ESE of Harare. Founded in 1890 by white settlers, its site was moved several times. It prospered after the coming of the Salisbury-Beira railroad in 1899.

UMTATA (South Africa) Town, 114 mi NNE of East London. Founded as a military post in 1860, it became capital of the Transkei, an African "homeland," in 1963. It has an Anglican cathedral.

UMUAHIA (Nigeria) Former province in Imo State. Its capital, of the same name, is 26 mi NNE of Aba.

Thirty-three miles east-southeast of Umuahia town is Abo Chuku, site of the supreme oracle of the Ibo people.

UMURBROGOL MOUNTAIN. See BLOODY NOSE RIDGE.

UMVUMA (Zimbabwe) Town, 140 mi ENE of Bulawayo. Founded in 1902, it was the site of the highly productive Falcon copper mine, which brought it prosperity from 1912 to 1924.

UNALASKA (United States) Island and city in the Fox Island group of the ALEUTIAN ISLANDS in ALASKA. Discovered by Bering in 1741, in 1759 the island became the site of the earliest Russian settlement in the Aleutian Islands. In 1762 they brutally repressed an Aleutian uprising here.

UNCHAHRA [Unchehra] (India) Town, 14 mi S of Satna, which is 90 mi SW of Allahabad. Before 1720 it was the capital of the princely state of NAGOD.

UNCHEHRA. See UNCHAHRA.

UNCI. See ALMERIA.

UNGA (United States) Village on SE Unga Island in the Shumagin Islands in ALASKA. The Russians made it an otter-fishing base. Gold was extensively mined here c.1900.

UNGARAN [Oengaran] (Indonesia) Town, 10 mi S of Semarang in JAVA. It is the site of a fort built in 1786.

UNGARISCH-HRADISCH. See UHERSKE HRADISTE.

UNGARISCH-OSTRA. See UHERSKY OSTROH.

UNGARN. See HUNGARY.

UNGAVA [former: New Quebec] (Canada) Region in northern QUEBEC E of the HUDSON BAY and N of the Eastmain River. Originally controlled by the Hudson's Bay Company, it was included in the NORTHWEST TERRITORIES in 1869. Its eastern portion was included in NEWFOUNDLAND in 1927.

UNGGI [Unggi-Dong] [Japanese: Yuki] (North Korea) Seaport, 10 mi NNE of Najin. North Korea's northernmost port, it was occupied by JAPAN from 1910 to 1945 and taken by the Soviets on Aug. 12, 1945.

UNGGI-DONG. See UNGGI.

UNGJIN. See KONGJU.

UNGUJA UKUU (Tanzania) Village, 17 mi SSE of Zanzibar town. The ancient capital of ZANZIBAR, it was destroyed in the 16th and 17th centuries by Portuguese and Arabs.

UNGVÁR. See UZHGOROD.

UNIÃO. See UNIÃO DOS PALMARES.

UNIÃO DOS PALMARES [former: União] (Brazil) City, 40 mi NW of MACEIÓ. It was founded in the 16th century and was the scene of a quickly suppressed slave rebellion in 1650.

UNION [former: Connecticut Farms] (United States) Township, 5 mi NW of Elizabeth, NEW JERSEY. Settled by colonists from CONNECTICUT in 1749, it was the scene of a battle in 1780 during the Revolutionary

War. It has restored 18th-century buildings and a residence, dating from 1762, of New Jersey's first governor, William Livingston.

UNION [*Originally:* **Unionville**] (United States) City, 25 mi SE of Spartanburg, SOUTH CAROLINA. Founded in 1791, it became the site of South Carolina's government for a time after COLUMBIA was burned in the Civil War. Its Union Church was built in 1765. Nearby Rose Hill State Park is the former estate of Governor William H. Gist.

UNION CITY (United States) City, 33 mi NNE of Dyersburg, TENNESSEE. Scene of three Civil War battles from 1862 to 1863, it has a Civil War cemetery and memorials.

UNION, FORT. See FORT UNION, Montana.

UNION, FORT. See FORT UNION, New Mexico.

UNION HALL [Unionhall] [*Gaelic:* **Bréantráigh**] (Irish Republic) Town, 5 miles E of Skibbereen, County Cork. Dean Jonathan Swift, who stayed here in 1723, wrote a poem celebrating it.

UNION ISLANDS. See TOKELAU ISLANDS.

UNION MILLS (United States) Village, 35 mi NW of Baltimore, MARYLAND. It has a flour mill dating from 1796 and still in operation.

UNION OF BURMA. See BURMA.

UNION OF RAJASTHAN. See RAJASTHAN.

UNION OF SOUTH AFRICA. See SOUTH AFRICA, REPUBLIC OF.

UNION OF SOVIET SOCIALIST REPUBLICS [Soviet Union, USSR] [*former:* Russia] Nation extending from eastern Europe E across Siberia to the Pacific Ocean. In the N it borders on the Arctic Ocean and in the S on China, and on southwestern Asian countries. The USSR, successor to the Russian Empire, is the world's largest nation in area and is third in population. It consists of 15 constituent soviet socialist republics: the Armenian, Azerbaijan, Belorussian, Estonian, Georgian, Kazakh, Kirgiz, Latvian, Lithuanian, Moldavian, Russian Soviet Federated, Tadzhik, Turkmen, Ukrainian, and Uzbek.

After the abdication of Czar Nicholas II and the creation of the Provisional Government under Alexander Kerensky in March 1917, the Bolsheviks, the most powerful group among Russian communists, seized power from the democratic regime on Nov. 7, 1917 and established the first Marxist government in the world. In January 1918 the popularly elected Constituent Assembly was abolished. Vladimir I. Lenin, now leader of the renamed Communist Party, became virtual dictator of the former Russian Empire until his death in 1924. Moscow once again became the capital, replacing Petrograd, or St. Petersburg (LENINGRAD).

The new rulers, often called the Bolsheviks or Reds, inherited a country devastated by World War I, from which they had withdrawn their armies on Dec. 5, 1917. Civil war soon broke out when anti-Bolsheviks, or Whites, formed a loose and never very effective alliance. The Whites were aided by forces from the UNITED STATES, GREAT BRITAIN, FRANCE, and JA-

PAN. The civil war lasted from 1918 to 1920, much of it being fought in SIBERIA and it ended with the defeat of the Whites amidst more devastation. The period of the war also saw the purges of the Red Terror, and the creation of the Red Army under Leon Trotsky. A further result was a dire famine in 1921. By the Treaty of BREST-LITOVSK of 1918 between the Central Powers and the Soviets, the latter recognized the independence of the UKRAINE, GEORGIA, FINLAND, and the Baltic states. When Germany lost the war in 1918, however, the treaty was declared void. War with POLAND in 1920 resulted in some of the Ukraine and BELORUSSIA being taken by Poland. In 1919 the new Bolshevik government founded the Comintern to provide leadership for international communism.

Between 1919 and 1921 the new rulers also imposed a state of "war communism" on the nation, taking control of its entire economy. This step was not successful, and the economy continued to falter. In March 1921 Lenin introduced his New Economic Policy to increase production and quiet general unrest. The policy allowed some capitalist enterprise in order to encourage small farmers and businessmen to accumulate wealth.

In 1922 the Union of Soviet Socialist Republics (USSR) was formally established. Up to this time, Soviet territory had consisted of the RUSSIAN SOVIET FEDERATED SOCIALIST REPUBLIC, a vast territory in eastern Europe and northern Asia, but in that year the RSFSR was united with the Ukraine, Belorussia, and TRANSCAUCASIA to form the new USSR. This made the nation coextensive with the former empire, except for the loss in the war of Finland, ESTONIA, LATVIA, LITHUANIA, BESSARABIA, and Poland. The union eventually encompassed 15 republics in a federation granting some local autonomy to its 50 nationalities, speaking over 100 languages. The Slavic, Russian, and imperial traditions, however, soon came to predominate everywhere. By the Treaty of RAPALLO in 1922, Germany became the first nation to give full recognition to the Soviet government. Other European nations delayed until 1924, and after that they did their best to "quarantine" the USSR to prevent the spread of communism.

After Lenin's death a struggle for power between Leon Trotsky and Joseph V. Stalin resulted in the triumph of the latter through his manipulation of the Communist Party structure. Stalin launched the First Five Year Plan in 1928, intended to centralize economic and social life by organizing the economy from the top and to industrialize the USSR as rapidly as possible. The plan, ruthlessly enforced, included the use of forced labor in mines and mills. Thousands of political dissidents were sent to concentration camps. In 1929 Stalin imposed a collective farm system, nationalizing private farms and combining them into larger units. By February 1930 half the small farms had been collectivized, but the policy was only partly successful in terms of increasing agricultural output, while thousands of peasants starved and many more thousands of landowners were "liquidated." Between 1936 and 1938 Stalin carried out a series of brutal purge trials of alleged dissidents, including many of the top leaders who were his rivals. These were executed or imprisoned.

THE GROWTH OF RUSSIA, 1904-1955

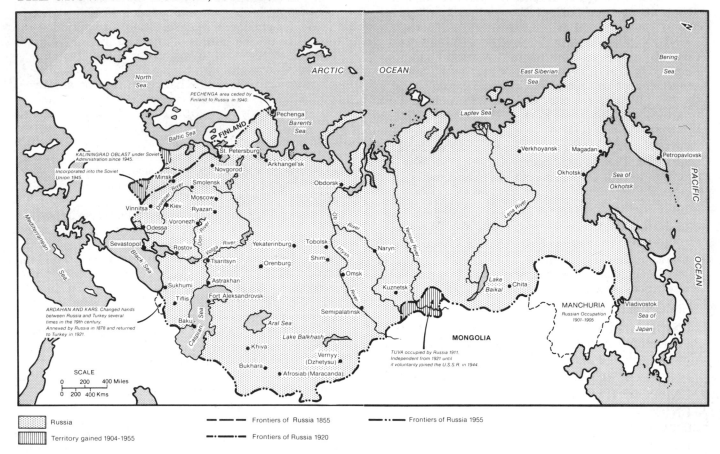

Russia	------- Frontiers of Russia 1855
Territory gained 1904-1955	-----··- Frontiers of Russia 1920
	-·-··- Frontiers of Russia 1955

In August 1939 the USSR and Germany signed a nonaggression pact that left Hitler free to invade Poland the next month, bringing on World War II. On September 17 Russia occupied eastern Poland. On June 22, 1941, however, Hitler turned on his ally and without warning invaded the USSR. By Sept. 16, 1942 German troops had reached Stalingrad, now VOLGOGRAD, their farthest eastern penetration, but were turned back after a brutal winter siege. Even more bitter was the siege of Leningrad from September 1941 to January 1944, also in the end unsuccessful, in which some 1 million people died and the city was extensively damaged. Altogether the USSR suffered some 20 million military and civilian casualties in World War II, but with massive aid from the West and a remarkable internal mobilization it recovered from initial disasters to advance all the way to BERLIN by April 1945.

In the meantime, the Soviets had invaded Finland in 1939 and after a struggle forced it in 1940 to cede some territory. By the POTSDAM Conference of July 1945 the USSR, United States, and Great Britain agreed on spheres of influence in Europe along the lines already determined by their advancing armies. The USSR was granted virtual control of Eastern Europe and some expansion of its own territories, retaining that part of eastern Poland taken in 1939, as well as parts of eastern PRUSSIA taken from Germany. It also annexed the

Baltic states of Lithuania, Latvia, and Estonia, which became Soviet republics. In the east, in the final days of the war, the USSR declared war on Japan and annexed the southern portion of SAKHALIN Island.

Differences between the USSR and its wartime allies, however, soon brought on the Cold War that lasted into the early 1960's. The differences were ideological in part but also involved the power politics of influence and status all over the world. By developing its own nuclear armaments soon after those of the United States, the USSR took the place already won in World War II as one of the two superpowers of the world. It brought Eastern Europe more firmly within its orbit and in 1948 tried unsuccessfully to deny the Allies access to their sectors of occupied Berlin, already deep within communist territory. The Warsaw Treaty Organization, consisting of the USSR and seven satellite nations, was formed in 1955 to offset the North Atlantic Treaty Organization (NATO). When a revolt in HUNGARY threatened the communist government there in 1956, the Soviets intervened militarily to put it down.

After Stalin's death in 1953 a struggle for power within the leadership of the Communist Party ended with the emergence in 1958 of Nikita S. Khrushchev as head of both party and state. Although Khrushchev professed to stand for "peaceful coexistence," 1962 brought on a short-lived crisis with the United States when the Soviets began to build missile bases in CUBA, a satellite nation. The crisis was resolved through quiet diplomacy between Khrushchev and U.S. President John F. Kennedy. In 1964 there were armed border classes with CHINA over boundary lines that have since escalated into a continuing confrontation between the two countries. On Oct. 4, 1957 the Soviet Union became the first nation to put an artificial satellite, the *Sputnik*, into orbit, and on April 8, 1961 it launched the first manned orbital space flight. Khrushchev fell from power in 1964, largely because of renewed shortages in agricultural production.

Leonid I. Brezhnev rose to the top of the communist hierarchy in October 1964. His rule brought a measure of withdrawal from the harsher aspects of the Stalin days and, beginning in 1972, a measure also of detente in relations with the United States and the West, especially with regard to the nuclear arms race and trade. Nevertheless, the Soviet grip on its satellites and its interventionist policies did not change. This was exemplified in the Soviet suppression by force of a liberal regime in CZECHOSLOVAKIA in 1968, the invasion and occupation of AFGHANISTAN in December 1979, and its successful repression of the unrest and calls for reform in Poland beginning in 1980. The 1980's have also seen renewed political and economic tensions with the West and a new arms race with the United States. On Brezhnev's death in November 1982, he was succeeded as effective ruler of the USSR by Yuri V. Andropov.

The Soviet economy, although plagued by industrial inefficiency and food shortages—admittedly caused by overcentralization from Moscow—has grown to be the world's second-largest, after that of the United States. Although comprising only 5 percent of the population, the Communist Party still holds all effective economic and political power.

UNION PASS (United States) Mountain pass in the Wind River Range in W WYOMING. In 1807 John Colter, a member of Lewis and Clark's expedition, passed through here.

UNIONTOWN (United States) Battle site, 40 mi SSE of Pittsburgh, PENNSYLVANIA. Near here, at FORT NECESSITY, founded in 1754, the English under Maj. George Washington were defeated by the French and Indians on July 3, 1754.

UNIONVILLE. See UNION.

UNITED ARAB EMIRATES [*former:* **Trucial Coast, Trucial Oman, Trucial Shaykdoms, Trucial States**] Federation of seven states on the E ARABIAN PENINSULA, from Qatar to the Gulf of Oman, including as members ABU DHABI, Ajman, Dubai, Fujairah, Ras al-Khaimah, SHARJAH, and UMM AL-QAIWAN. Before its truce with Great Britain in 1820, the coast was famous for piracy. Other pacts with Great Britain followed in 1839, 1853, and 1892. After World War II it gained internal autonomy. The independent federation was formed in 1971. It has been an important source of oil since the early 1960's.

UNITED ARAB REPUBLIC [*Arabic:* **Al-'Arabīyah Al-Muttahahidah, Al-Jumhurīyah**] Former union of EGYPT, SYRIA, and YEMEN proclaimed in 1958 with Gamal Abdel Nasser as president. A move toward uniting the Arab world, it ended when Syria withdrew in 1961.

UNITED COLONIES OF NEW ENGLAND (United States) Confederation consisting of PLYMOUTH, NEW HAVEN, MASSACHUSETTS, and CONNECTICUT. It lasted from 1643 to 1684 and was the first attempt at confederation in America. Its main purposes were defense and the resolution of boundary questions.

UNITED DECCAN STATE (India) Former confederacy formed on August 26, 1947 by the union of Aundh, Bhor, Kurundwad, Miraj, Phaltan, Ramdurg, and Sangli. See DECCAN.

UNITED KINGDOM Known properly as the United Kingdom of Great Britain and Northern Ireland, it is the largest national unit of the British Isles and comprises ENGLAND, WALES, SCOTLAND, the ISLE OF MAN, the CHANNEL ISLANDS, and NORTHERN IRELAND. Known as the United Kingdom of Great Britain and Ireland from 1801, it emerged in its present form in 1920 after the creation of the Irish Free State. The legislative center of the United Kingdom is the Westminster Parliament in LONDON. See also GREAT BRITAIN, IRELAND.

UNITED KINGDOM OF GREAT BRITAIN AND IRELAND. See GREAT BRITAIN, UNITED KINGDOM.

UNITED PROVINCES, India. See UTTAR PRADESH.

UNITED PROVINCES (Netherlands) Formed in 1579 by the Treaty of Utrecht, which joined together the seven Protestant provinces of FRIESLAND, GELDERLAND, GRONINGEN, HOLLAND, OVERIJSSEL, UTRECHT, and ZEELAND. This event marked the separation of the NETHERLANDS from the SPANISH NETHERLANDS, which remained in Hapsburg hands. Although the United Provinces declared independence in 1581, the state was not recognized by the major European powers until the Treaty of Westphalia in 1648.

UNITED PROVINCES OF AGRA AND OUDH. See UTTAR PRADESH.

UNITED PROVINCES OF CENTRAL AMERICA Former confederation, established in Guatemala City at the instigation of Manuel José Arce in 1821. It lasted until 1838 and included GUATEMALA, SAN SALVADOR, COSTA RICA, NICARAGUA, and HONDURAS.

UNITED STATES OF AMERICA [**United States**] Nation whose main territory consists of North America S of Canada and N of Mexico. It also includes the state of Alaska in the NW corner of North America, the state of Hawaii, consisting of Pacific islands approx. 3,000 mi SW of San Francisco, the Commonwealth of Puerto Rico, and the American Virgin Islands in the West Indies, and until 1999 the Panama Canal Zone. Pacific islands under direct U.S. control include American Samoa, Guam, Midway, and Wake. Pacific islands held under U.N. trusteeship include the Marianas, in part, the Carolines, and the Marshalls.

In the 15th century, when Europeans first arrived in North America, it was already inhabited by American Indians whose ancestors had come across the Bering Strait from SIBERIA some time before 30,000 BC. Although there were only a few million Indians in the area that became the United States, their impact on the early European explorers and settlers was immediate and lasting, as is attested by the large number of Indian names on the land today. The primitive Indian cultures of North America were also strongly affected by the encroaching Europeans: for example the buffalo-hunting culture of the Great Plains developed only after the western Indians had acquired the horse from the Spanish.

From the earliest period of European settlement to the final defeat of the Indians in the 1890's, the story was always much the same. The Indians were at first often friendly and even helpful, but then as the settlers multiplied and encroached on their lands there were wars, usually very bitter, with atrocities on both sides—the Pequot War in CONNECTICUT in 1637, King Philip's War in NEW ENGLAND in 1675/76, the bloody uprising of the Pueblo Indians of NEW MEXICO against the

Spanish in 1680, known as the Pueblo Revolt, Pontiac's Rebellion in the Northwest in 1763, the Indian forays on both sides during the American Revolution, the conquest of the NORTHWEST TERRITORY at FALLEN TIMBERS in 1794 and TIPPECANOE in 1811, and then, as the Indians were driven westward, the final protracted Indian Wars on the Great Plains, culminating in 1878. The Indians fought bravely, but in the end were defeated, and those who did not die in battle were decimated by the diseases and the liquor of the settlers or were forcibly moved west, as were the Five Civilized Tribes of GEORGIA and NORTH CAROLINA. The battle of WOUNDED KNEE in 1890 is generally considered the last of the long sequence of wars. After this the remaining Indians were moved onto reservations and reduced to the status of a second-class minority, as they still are considered by many today.

Exploration of the present continental United States began in 1498 and was carried on mainly by Spanish, French, and English explorers. SPAIN made the first settlement in the area at ST. AUGUSTINE, Florida, in 1565; while the first permanent settlement by ENGLAND was at JAMESTOWN, Virginia, in 1607. By 1733

UNITED STATES IN 1820

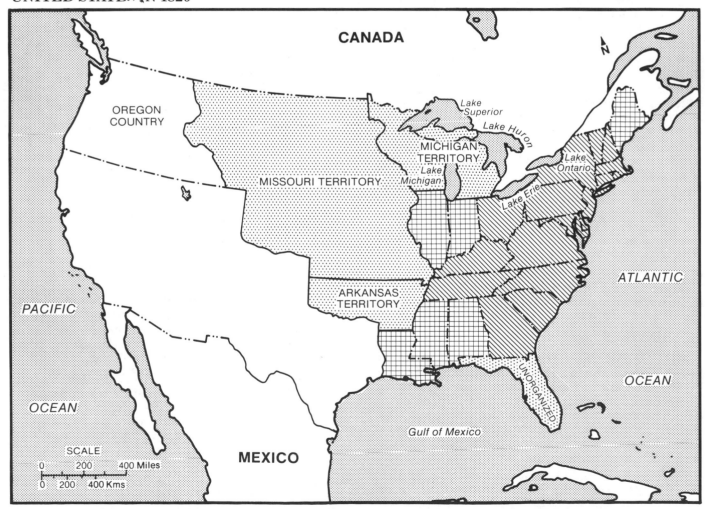

Areas Granted Statehood prior to 1812

Areas Granted Statehood after 1912

Territories

UNITED STATES IN 1860

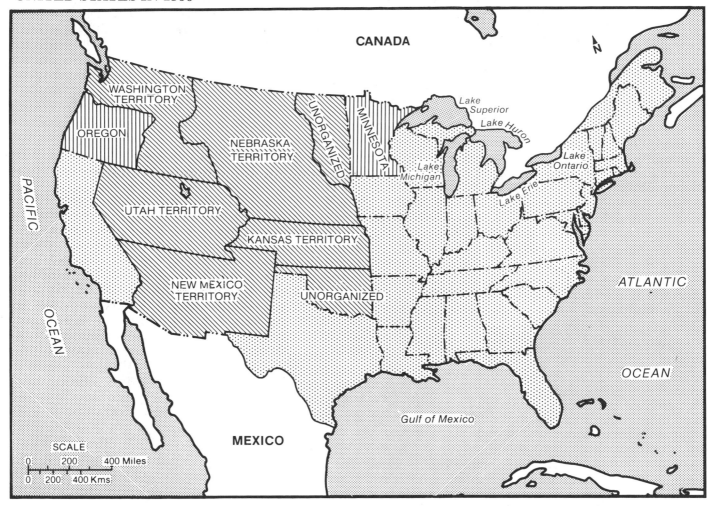

 Areas Granted Statehood prior to 1858 ||||||| Areas Granted Statehood in 1858 and 1859

///// Territories

there were 13 British colonies along the Atlantic seaboard. Agriculture, mostly by small yeoman farmers, was the main occupation; while black slave labor was used, particularly on the larger southern plantations. After FRANCE was driven out of eastern North America in 1763 at the end of the French and Indian War, the colonists saw less need for British protection and forcefully resisted both taxes levied by the British for imperial defense and their mercantilist system of discouraging colonial industry in favor of importing raw materials to the mother country.

The conflict, fed by abuses of royal prerogatives and powers, became armed rebellion in the American Revolution. The first hostilities took place in 1775, and the colonies declared their independence on July 4, 1776. They achieved independence, however, only in 1783 when the British admitted defeat, relinquishing to the United States their rule over almost all the land east of the MISSISSIPPI RIVER and south of Canada. The weak Articles of Confederation of 1781 were replaced by the present Constitution in 1789, establishing a federal republic with a strong central government. The docu-

ment was ratified by the new states between 1787 and 1790. George Washington, commander of the Continental Army during the Revolution, was named the first president.

The early republic pursued its agricultural life along the coast, but in 1803, through the LOUISIANA PURCHASE, President Thomas Jefferson acquired a large region west of the Mississippi from France. The War of 1812 began ostensibly because of British interference with American shipping, but it was strongly opposed in New England and among commercial interests. After victories and defeats on both sides, the war ended in 1815 with no changes in boundaries or other matters. There followed an era of growth as industry, chiefly water-powered, developed and settlers spread westward. Growing sectional differences over slavery, political autonomy, and differing economies between North and South were temporarily resolved by the Missouri Compromise of 1820. The election of President Andrew Jackson, a Democrat, in 1828 opened a period of the "common man," coupled with a new spirit of nationalism expressed in the term "Manifest Destiny." In 1846 an agreement with GREAT BRITAIN settled the boundaries of the OREGON COUNTRY, and in 1845 TEXAS was annexed. The latter led to the Mexican War of 1848 by which the United States acquired the rest of its continental territory, except for the GADSDEN PURCHASE of 1853 and the purchase of ALASKA from RUSSIA in 1867.

The Compromise of 1850 again averted a crisis over slavery, but the Kansas-Nebraska Act of 1854 weakened the previous compromises and, as northern abolitionists became more assertive, intensified the North-South conflict. The election of Abraham Lincoln, a Republican, in 1860 triggered the secession of 11 slave-holding southern states. The Civil War followed, from 1861 to 1865, a bloody and bitter struggle that was eventually won by the North. Though the nation was reunited and slavery abolished, the scars of the ensuing Reconstruction period left the South desperate and impoverished and many issues of local and civil rights unresolved. The Gilded Age that followed was marked by corruption and vulgar displays of wealth, but at the same time by unprecedented industrial growth and the development of new capitalist institutions. At the end of the century the western frontier was finally closed, and the country saw a new wave of immigration from Europe. The last decades of the 19th century also saw rapid urban growth, the organizing of labor to obtain decent work and living conditions, and of the farmers to protect themselves from rapacious railroads and banks. The complex, urbanized industrial society we have today had its roots in this period.

The Spanish-American War of 1898 resulted in the acquisition of PUERTO RICO, the PHILIPPINE Islands, and GUAM. That year, also, the Hawaiian Islands were annexed. The Panama Canal Zone was secured in 1903 and the PANAMA CANAL built, from 1904 to 1914, to link the Atlantic and Pacific Oceans by water. In the early years of the 20th century, when the Republican Theodore Roosevelt was president, the Progressive and Populist movements brought about much-needed government reforms, a pure food act, and laws to conserve natural resources, as well as to regulate the corporate, financial, and industrial institutions of the country. Under Roosevelt the United States began for the first time to demonstrate its strength and importance as a world power.

Elected president in 1912, Woodrow Wilson, in a bow to the spirit of reform, proclaimed the New Freedom and in 1913 sponsored the establishment of the Federal Reserve System to regulate the nation's finances. Winning reelection in 1916 on a pledge to keep the United States out of World War I, then raging in Europe, he stressed U.S. neutrality in Big Power conflicts. Nevertheless, he was forced to bring the nation into the war in April 1917, U.S. troops contributing to the final victory over GERMANY in 1918. At the VERSAILLES Peace Conference that followed, Wilson was the acknowledged world leader, but when he brought the treaty home, the Senate refused to approve U.S. membership in his own creation, the League of Nations. A period of hectic prosperity in the 1920's led, in October 1929, to the famous stock market crash, which had been preceded by business and farm failures. The country

was plunged into the Great Depression, the worst economic collapse in the nation's history. The election of Franklin D. Roosevelt, a Democrat, in 1932 ushered in the liberal New Deal period, during which the Securities and Exchange Commission was established, the Social Security Administration set up, and a host of industrial, financial, business, farm, and social laws enacted in an attempt to make the federal government a catalyst for recovery.

In World War II the nation was at first again officially neutral, but soon began giving aid to the Allies, especially to beleaguered Great Britain. A sudden attack by JAPAN on the U.S. base at PEARL HARBOR in HAWAII on Dec. 7, 1941, however, thrust the country into war with both Japan and the Axis alliance of Germany and ITALY. After Germany surrendered on May 7, 1945, the United States dropped the first atomic bombs on HIROSHIMA and NAGASAKI in Japan, forcing that country into surrender on August 14. During 1945 the United States played a leading role in the creation of the United Nations, and between 1947 and 1952 operated the Marshall Plan, giving large amounts of aid to help rebuild the shattered nations of western Europe. As a result of the war, the United States and the USSR became the world's two first superpowers, and the confrontation between them led to the Cold War struggle for ideological, political, and economic supremacy throughout the world. One result was the creation of the North Atlantic Treaty Organization (NATO) in 1949, which was countered in 1955 by the setting up of a Russian-dominated similar grouping, the Warsaw Pact Treaty Organization.

The Korean War from 1950 to 1953 began when North Korean forces invaded the U.S.-protected South KOREA. After a back-and-forth struggle that also involved U.N. and Chinese forces, the war ended with the reinstatement of the previous boundary. In the United States, as a result of the Korean War, the continued Cold War, and the acquisition of atomic weapons by the USSR, the McCarthy era set in, a period of intense anticommunist feeling, of increased defense consciousness, purges of leftists and liberals, and the blacklisting of media and industrial figures. During the presidency of Dwight D. Eisenhower, a Republican, from 1953 to 1961, economic conditions improved while the country once more reached a consensus in public policy. The administration's outlook was international, though tinged with the strong anticommunism of the country as a whole. The launching of the first satellite into space in 1958 by the USSR shocked the country and led to U.S. competition in sciences and technology, producing the first intercontinental missiles and space flights by both countries.

In 1954 the Supreme Court, in an epic decision, declared segregation in public schools on the basis of race unconstitutional, resulting in the ensuing years of much civil strife, especially in the South, and other civil rights issues were fought out at the same time. The 1960's saw a period of great social unrest, mobility, and conflict, especially on the student campuses, with the nuclear threat overshadowing all. When it was discovered in the fall of 1962 that the Soviets were placing missiles in

CUBA, the United States and the USSR came close to nuclear war, but with careful diplomacy the Soviets were persuaded to remove the missiles. After the assassination of president John F. Kennedy in November 1963, President Lyndon B. Johnson announced the Great Society program, which resulted in strong civil rights legislation and antipoverty measures that set government goals for the decade.

While the Great Society was growing at home, the United States gradually became involved in war in VIETNAM, with support troops and advisers first sent east in 1961. As the war escalated, so did U.S. participation in the actual fighting. By the time the war ended in early 1973, with a cease-fire and withdrawal of U.S. forces, the United States had not achieved its goal of containing communism and supporting the South Vietnamese regime. At home there had been much unrest. Hundreds of thousands had mobilized to demand an end to the war, while concern over the civil rights issue and the continuing lack of economic opportunity for blacks sometimes led to violent and destructive riots in many cities during the 1960's. At the same time, and largely among the young, the counterculture, dedicated to alternative life-styles and communal living, had a brief flowering. Meanwhile, in striking contrast, two U.S. astronauts in July 1969 became the first humans to set foot on the moon.

In February 1972 President Richard M. Nixon made a surprise visit to CHINA, with which the United States had had no relations for nearly a quarter of a century since the communist takeover, thus demonstrating the effectiveness of a new policy of practical detente. That year, however, also saw the beginning of the infamous Watergate Affair. Because the president had tried to cover up the illegal activities of some of his White House aides and was implicated in other illegalities, he was forced to resign his office on Aug. 9, 1974. The aftermath of the 1960's, of the Vietnam War, and the revelation of corruption in high places shook the American people, while at the same time the economy began to falter. Growing inflation was aggravated in late 1973 when the petroleum-producing nations in the OPEC organization temporarily cut off the supply of oil to the United States and the West. The "energy crisis" became a seemingly permanent problem, as did unemployment and inflation.

Two decades of conflict and crisis were reflected in the ambivalent administration of President Jimmy Carter. Although the Senate ratified treaties with PANAMA, giving that nation possession of the PANAMA CANAL by the end of the century, many saw this as a collapse of U.S. firmness in foreign relations. The Senate refused to act on a strategic arms limitation with the USSR, but on the other hand full diplomatic relations with China were resumed in December 1978. In December 1979, Islamic militants seized the U.S. embassy in TEHERAN, Iran, and held the personnel hostage until January 1981. Carter's Republican successor, President Ronald Reagan, succeeded in getting through Congress in 1981 his program of very large federal budget reductions, particularly in the social programs of his Democratic predecessors, as well as

sizable cuts in the income tax. At the same time he pressed for greatly increased military expenditures. In 1982, as a nationwide recession deepened and unemployment approached Great Depression levels, Reagan's economic policies came under strong attack from liberals as well as working-class people, while conservatives continued to press for the new economic policies and a revived anticommunist crusade. The results of mid-term elections held in November 1982 forced the Reagan administration to readjust many of its goals. Nevertheless by 1983 recovery appeared to be in sight.

UNNA (West Germany) City, 10 mi E of Dortmund. Established by Charlemagne, but first mentioned only in 1032, it received its charter in 1290. The city declined after the Thirty Years War of 1618 to 1648. It revived in 1798 when it acquired the first steam pump engine in western Germany. It has a 14th-century church and town hall and 13th-century walls.

UNST (Scotland) Island in the SHETLAND ISLANDS NNE of Scotland. It has many remains of the Picts and Norsemen.

UNSTRUT (East Germany) River rising near Dingelstadt and flowing approx. 115 mi E through central GERMANY. Immediately following the Battle of LEIPZIG in October 1813, Napoleon was defeated in the Battle of the Unstrut by the Allies as he was retreating to the west.

UNTER DEN LINDEN (East Germany) Avenue, now in East BERLIN, starting from the Brandenburg Gate. Formerly lined with linden trees, it was the location of many palaces and museums, including the Imperial Palace of 1538, razed in 1951. It was the center of BERLIN's social and cultural activity before World War II.

UNTERSBERG (Austria, Germany) Mountain peak in the Salzburg Alps, 5 mi SSW of SALZBURG. According to legend it is the resting place of Charlemagne, who waits here to succor GERMANY in its time of greatest need.

UNTERWALD. See UNTERWALDEN.

UNTERWALDEN [*French:* **Unterwald**] (Switzerland) Canton in central Switzerland, consisting of the half-cantons Obwalden and Nidwalden. Ruled by the Hapsburgs from 1173, in 1291 it joined with URI and SCHWYZ in a confederation that formed the basis of the later Swiss Confederation.

UPARKOT (India) Archaeological site on the E side of JUNAGADH town. It is an ancient rock-cut citadel of Hindu kings.

UPERNAVIK [**Upernivik**] (Greenland) This Eskimo settlement was founded in 1772 on an islet in Baffin Bay. On nearby Kingigtok Island a stone with 14th-century runes was discovered.

UPERNIVIK. See UPERNAVIK.

UPLAND. See CHESTER, Pennsylvania.

UPOLU (Western Samoa) Island, approx. 38 mi W by N of Tutuila Island. Robert Louis Stevenson's home is located here. See SAMOA.

UPPER AUSTRIA [*former:* **Upper Danube, Oberdonau;** *German:* **Oberösterreich**] (Austria) State and former duchy between LOWER AUSTRIA and WEST GERMANY. Part of the Roman colony of NORICUM and later in BAVARIA and STYRIA, it became an Austrian duchy in 1156. It was invaded by the Turks in the 16th century. The area was the scene of many battles in the Thirty Years War of 1616 to 1648 and in the Napoleonic Wars.

UPPER CANADA (Canada) Former province corresponding to the S part of modern ONTARIO. It became a province in 1791 and was settled by English Loyalist refugees from the American Revolution. From 1841 to 1867 it was named Canada West under the Act of Union.

UPPER DANUBE. See UPPER AUSTRIA.

UPPER HESSE [*German:* **Oberhessen**] (West Germany) Former province surrounded by HESSE-NASSAU. It was abolished in 1945.

UPPER PERU (Bolivia) Former region, approximately the same as modern Bolivia. It was included in the viceroyalty of PERU from 1559 to 1776 and in the viceroyalty of LA PLATA from 1776 to 1825, when it became the state of Bolivia. Its capital city was Chuquisaca, modern SUCRE.

UPPER SANDUSKY (United States) Town, 17 mi NNW of Marion, OHIO. Founded in 1843, it is the site of the Wyandot National Museum, which contains artifacts of Indians and pioneers.

UPPER VOLTA Small landlocked country lying in the sub-Saharan region of Africa, directly N of Ghana and S of the great bend in the NIGER RIVER in Mali. Upper Volta is an agricultural country occupying the region of the medieval Mossi Empire. French colonialists seized the region in 1896 and ruled it until 1960, when independence was achieved. Under its first leader, Maurice Yaméogo, Upper Volta approached total bankruptcy and disorganization. A military group led by Col. Sangoulé Lamizana took control in 1966, and Upper Volta slowly began to improve its infrastructure systems and agriculture with aid from France, the rest of the Common Market, and the World Bank. In the early 1970's the great drought of the sub-Saharan SAHEL region brought starvation and death to many thousands in the northern part of the country. Military rule ended in 1978, and Lamizana was elected president.

UPPINGHAM (England) Town in Leicestershire, 18 mi E of Leicester. Its well-known public school was founded in 1584. It has a 14th-century church and notable 16th-century houses.

UPPLAND (Sweden) Province in E Sweden bounded by the Gulf of Bothnia and the Baltic Sea on the E and by the provinces of Sodennanland on the S, Västmanland on the W, and Gästrikland on the N. Inhabited since the Stone Age and active in trade with areas to the south by 2000 BC, it became the early center of the pagan kingdom of Svea, or Sweden (9th century AD), uniting nearby states, with its capital at UPPSALA. It was weakened by religious conflicts after the arrival of Christianity, but recovered to become the seat of the church and government.

UPPSALA [Upsala] (Sweden) City, 40 mi NNW of Stockholm, in UPPLAND. Near the sixth-century capital of pagan Sweden, it was founded as the archiepiscopal see in 1164 and became the coronation site of Sweden's kings. Its university, founded in 1477, is one of the greatest in the world. Its 13th- to 15th-century cathedral has tombs of Gustavus I, Linnaeus, and Swedenborg. The city also has a medieval episcopal palace, now a museum, a 16th-century castle, and the great university library with many early holdings.

UPSALA. See UPPSALA.

UR [*Arabic:* **Mugheir, Mukayyar, Muqaiyir, Muqayyar, Tall al Muqayir;** *biblical:* **Ur of the Chaldees**] (Iraq) Ancient city 11 mi SW of An Nasiriya. A city as early as the fourth millennium BC and long a great commercial center, its first ruling dynasty of c.3200 to 2600 BC attained a high level of civilization. At the beginning of its third dynasty, of c.2300 to 2200 BC, its great ziggurat was built by the ruler Ur-Nammu. Abraham may have lived here c.2000 BC and migrated from here to CANAAN. Ur was destroyed by the Elamites, by BABYLON, and by others. Its fortunes varied before its restoration by Nebuchadnezzar in the sixth century BC, after which it soon declined. It was deserted and unknown until its excavation in the early 20th century.

URACH (West Germany) Town, 8 mi E of Reutlingen in Baden-Württemberg. Founded in the 12th century and chartered c.1260, it has a 15th-century castle and church. Nearby is the ruined stronghold of Hohenurach.

Typical compound of the Gurunsi tribe in Upper Volta. In this poverty-stricken country, now slowly improving its economy, the natives still live largely by subsistence farming.

URAGA (Japan) Port, 5 mi S of Yokosuka. Here in 1846 the first U.S. emissaries to Japan under Commodore Biddle landed and were repulsed. This led to Commodore Perry's expedition of 1853.

URAL INDUSTRIAL REGION (USSR) Important region including CHELYABINSK, SVERDLOVSK, Kurgan, ORENBURG, and PERM oblasts and the UDMURT SSR. It developed especially during World War II when industries were moved here from the European SSR to evade German depredations.

URAL MOUNTAINS [*Russian:* **Uralsky Khnebet**] (USSR) Mountain range extending approx. 1,640 mi from the Kara Sea to W Kirgiz in the KAZAKH SSR. They are Russia's single greatest mineral resource. The first Russian penetration was by fur hunters from NOVGOROD in the 12th century. Colonization spread rapidly in the 16th century. A military expedition in 1581 was the first Russian penetration beyond the range. Mining and metallurgy flourished here under Peter the Great in the 17th century, but the region did not again become industrially productive until the 1930's.

URAL RIVER (USSR) River originating in the Ural Mts and flowing N to S through the SW central Soviet Union. It is of historic importance as a water route for migration, invasion, and commerce.

URALSK [**Ural'sk**] [*former:* **Yaitski Gorodok, Yaitsky Gorodok**] (USSR) Town, 230 mi E of Saratov. Founded in 1613 by rebellious Ural Cossacks, it became their headquarters and an important trading point between RUSSIA and Kazakhstan. It declined in the 20th century. There is a museum of Cossack artifacts in its old cathedral. See KAZAKH SSR.

URALSKY KHNEBET. See URAL MOUNTAINS.

URARTU [**Van**] [*biblical:* **Ararat**] (Turkey) Former kingdom in Van province around Lake VAN and N of ancient ASSYRIA. Its origins date from *c.*1270 BC. It reached its height in the eighth century BC when it controlled a large part of northern SYRIA. Plagued throughout its history by recurring attacks by the Assyrians, it finally fell *c.*610 BC to the Medes and Scythians. Its civilization was advanced, using a cuneiform script and sophisticated metalworking and masonry techniques.

URA-TYUBE (USSR) Town in the NW Tadzhik SSR, 40 mi WSW of Leninabad. Possibly inhabited as early as the sixth century AD, it is one of the most ancient towns in the region, known by its current name since the 15th century. The Russians took it in 1866. It has a 15th-century mosque.

URBANA (United States) Town adjoining Champaign, Illinois, 47 mi ENE of Decatur, ILLINOIS. Settled in 1824 and incorporated in 1833, it was the site in 1854 of a speech given by Lincoln against the Kansas-Nebraska Bill.

URBINO [*Latin:* **Urbinum Hortense, Urbinum Metaurense**] (Italy) City, 19 mi SW of Pesaro. It was the home of Umbrians, Etruscans, Celts, and Gauls before ROME took it in the third century BC. The city was held by the church in the ninth century AD. In the 12th century it passed to the Montefeltro family, under whose rule it became a center of Renaissance culture in the 15th century. It declined somewhat under the succeeding family of Della Rovere, who ruled it from 1508 to 1631. It passed to the PAPAL STATES in 1626 and to Italy in 1860. The painter Raphael was born here in 1483. It has an old town center with 17th- and 18th-century buildings, the 15th-century ducal palace, now a national art museum, the cathedral, rebuilt in 1789, and a 14th-century church.

The 15th-century cathedral and ducal palace of picturesque Urbino, Italy. A great Renaissance center, it was the birthplace of the painter Raphael, whose family home survives here.

URBINUM HORTENSE. See URBINO.

URBINUM METAURENSE. See URBINO.

URBISAGLIA. See URBS SALVIA.

URBS SALVIA [*Italian:* **Urbisaglia**] (Italy) Ancient town, 8 mi SSW of Macerata. Ruins of the ancient Roman theater and amphitheater are near the modern town.

URBS VETUS. See ORVIETO.

UREWERA (New Zealand) District on E central North Island, bounded by Lake Waikaremoana on the S, the Waimana and Waioka rivers on the E, and the Rangitaiki River on the W. The first Europeans visited it in 1841. In 1896 it was made a reserve to prevent any further white settlement.

URFA [*ancient:* **Arrhoe, Edessa, Orrhoe**] (Turkey) City in SE Turkey, 75 mi E of Gaziantep. It was first known as Arrhoe or Orrhoe in the fourth century BC, and was renamed Edessa by Seleucis I, king of SYRIA, who conquered much of Asia Minor c.300 BC. Edessa was the capital of the kingdom of OSROENE, which in the second century BC won independence from the SELEUCID EMPIRE. The city came under Roman rule in the second century AD. Here in 260 Shapur I, king of PERSIA, defeated and captured the Roman Emperor Valerian, marking a turning point in power relations between Persia and the ROMAN EMPIRE. In the third century AD Edessa was an early center of Christianity where Bardesanes, Syrian philosopher and poet, founded a Gnostic sect.

The Arabs captured the city in 639 and held it until members of the First Crusade under Baldwin I took it in 1097. The Crusader County of Edessa, nominally under the LATIN KINGDOM OF JERUSALEM, was established, but the city fell again to the Muslims in 1144 and to the OTTOMAN EMPIRE in 1637, when the name was changed to Urfa. In the late 19th century, under the rule of the Turkish Sultan Abd al-Hamid, called the Great Assassin, there were several massacres of Armenian Christians here. Arabic tradition cites the city as the birthplace of Abraham, the founder of Judaism. See also ARMENIA.

URGA. See ULAN BATOR.

URGEL. See URGEL, SEO DE.

URGEL, SEO DE [Urgel] (Spain) Town, 10 mi SSW of ANDORRA. Since 840 AD its bishop has been joint prince of Andorra along with the president of France. It has an 11th-century Romanesque cathedral.

URGENCH (USSR) Ancient city on the site of modern Kunya-Urgench, 85 mi NW of modern Urgench, the capital of Khorezm oblast in the TURKMEN SSR. It was a thriving trading center from the 10th to 13th centuries and became capital of the khanate of KHOREZM in the 12th century. Destroyed by Mongols in the 13th century, it was finally abandoned in the 16th century. Excavations have revealed remains of an 11th-century mosque, tombs, shops, and a 14th-century gate portal.

URI (Switzerland) Early canton in central Switzerland. Given to the convent at ZURICH in 853 AD, its privileges were granted by the Holy Roman emperor in the 13th century. In 1291, with Unterwalden and Schwyz, it formed the nucleus of the Swiss federation. Rejecting the Reformation in the 16th century, it joined the Catholic Sonderbund in 1845. The William Tell legend is set here.

URIANKHAI. See TUVA ASSR.

URITSK [former: Ligovo] (USSR) City, 8 mi SW of LENINGRAD. The Germans held it as an advance position during their long siege of Leningrad from 1941 to 1944 during World War II.

URMIA. See REZAIYEH.

UR OF THE CHALDEES. See UR.

URONARTI [Arabic: Bezira al Melik, Jazurat al-Malik] (Sudan) Island in the NILE RIVER 37 mi SW of old Wadi Halfa. It has a ruined fortress of the Egyptian Middle Kingdom of c.2100 to 1700 BC.

URSO. See OSUNA.

URUAPAN [Uruapan del Progreso] (Mexico) City, 60 mi SW of Morelia. Founded in 1540 as a center of the Tarascan Indians, it is now an Indian crafts and tourist center with a colonial atmosphere and pleasant parks.

URUAPAN DEL PROGRESO. See URUAPAN.

URUBAMBA (Peru) River that rises in the ANDES and flows approx. 45 mi NNW before joining the Apurímac and becoming the Ucayali. It rises as the Vilcanota, the river sacred to the Incas. The ancient Inca city of MACHU PICCHU is above its gorge. See also CUZCO, INCA EMPIRE.

URUGUAY [earlier: Banda Oriental] Nation in E central South America, with the Atlantic Ocean to the E, Brazil to the N, and Argentina to the S and W. Its colonial name, Banda Oriental, "eastern shore," referred to the alluvial plain in the SE on the banks of the Rio de la Plata.

Before Europeans arrived the region was inhabited by the Charrúa Indians, who were eventually absorbed after strong resistance. The first explorer was Amerigo Vespucci, in Portuguese service, who discovered the Rio de LA PLATA in 1502. Following him in the same area came Juan Diaz de Solís of Spain in 1516 and Sebastian Cabot, in Spanish service, in 1526. SPAIN made its first settlement at Soriano in 1624; and PORTUGAL founded COLONIA in 1680, but this was short-lived. The Portuguese also built a fort on the site of present MONTEVIDEO in 1717, but the Spanish drove them out in 1724, and from then until independence Spain controlled the region. Uruguay became part of the viceroyalty of Rio de la Plata in 1776.

The move for independence that began in 1810 under the leadership of José Gervasio Artigas was part of the Argentinian revolt. The revolt failed at first, Spanish rule was restored, and in 1820 BRAZIL occupied Montevideo and annexed it. In 1825 a group of patriots called the Thirty Three Immortals, led by Juan Antonio Lavalleja, declared Uruguay independent. ARGENTINA and Brazil both claimed sovereignty over the country, but after Brazil was defeated at the Battle of ITUZAINGÓ by the other two nations, a treaty in 1828 recognized Uruguay's independence.

Fructuoso Rivera became the first president and later revolted against his successor, Manuel Oribe, in 1836. Out of this struggle rose two permanent factions: Rivera's Colorados, Reds, and Oribe's Blancos, Whites. Civil War followed, and Montevideo was besieged from 1843 to 1851 before Oribe was defeated. Demanding compensation for civil-war damages, Brazil invaded Uruguay in 1864, aided by the Colorados. But when the dictator of PARAGUAY, Francisco Solano López, came to the assistance of the Blancos, Brazil, Argentina, and Uruguay united against him and defeated him in 1870 in the War of the Triple Alliance.

An era of frequent revolutions followed until Batlle y Ordóñez became president in 1903. His regime was marked by stability and social legislation. In 1951 Uruguay adopted an executive council system in place of the presidency. This plan did not work well, and by 1958 the Colorados, after having been in power for 93 years, were overpowered by the Blancos. The 1960's were marked by economic decline and the rise of terrorist groups, and by 1965 the nation was bankrupt. The following year the presidency was restored, and the Colorado candidate was elected. In February 1973 President Juan Maria Bordaberry agreed to let the military control the government, and they have continued to do so since then. Meanwhile, the urban guerrilla Tupamaros were brought under control. In 1977 the military rulers promised free elections in 1981 but in 1980 cancelled the plans. The government has been charged with violating human rights, especially those of political prisoners. It is now planning elections for 1984.

Montevideo is the capital and largest city; others include SALTO, PAYSANDÚ, and LAS PIEDRAS.

URUK. See ERECH.

URUMCHI [Di-Hua, Ti-Hua, Tihwa] [*Chinese:*** Wu-lu-mu-chi, Wu-lu-mu-ch'i]** (China) City and capital of Sinkiang Uighur. Under Chinese influence as early as the second century BC, it was controlled by China in the seventh and eighth centuries AD and again in the 18th century. In the 19th century it grew into a great city of central Asia, which Russia and Britain tried to influence toward the end of the Chinese empire in 1911. See also SINKIANG.

URUMIYEH. See REZAIYEH.

URUNDI. See BURUNDI.

URUSHI. See ULITHI.

UŞAK [Ushak] (Turkey) Town, 55 mi W of Afyonkarahisar. Nearby is the ruined city of Flaviopolis. Uşak was the scene of bitter fighting in the Turkish War of Independence.

USAMBARA (Tanzania) Highlands, approx. 70 mi long and 30 mi wide, in the NE Tanga region. Circa 1900 they were one of the earliest areas settled by European farmers in East Africa.

UŚCILUG. See USTILUG.

USEDOM [*Polish:*** Uznam]** (Poland, East Germany) Island off the coast of NE East Germany. Taken by Gustavus Adolphus in 1630, it passed to SWEDEN in 1648 and to PRUSSIA in 1720. PEENEMÜNDE, Germany's chief missile research and testing base in World War II, was located here. The town of the same name has a Gothic gate and church.

USHA (Israel) Ancient city, 7 mi E of Haifa. It was briefly capital of PALESTINE and seat of the Sanhedrin after the destruction of the Second Temple. In 1936 a modern settlement was established here.

USHAK. See UŞAK.

USHANT. See ÎLE D'OUESSANT.

USK (Wales) Town and river in Gwent county. The town is 9 mi NNE of Newport on the river that rises in S central Wales and flows E and S to the sea just below Newport. It was the site of a Celtic settlement upon which the Romans built a fort. A Norman castle built here in the 12th century was partially destroyed c.1400. Usk has the castle ruins, a palace, and a 12th- to 15th-century church. The river is associated with the Arthurian legends.

ÜSKÜB. See SKOPJE.

USKUDAMA. See EDIRNE.

ÜSKÜDAR [*ancient:*** Chrysopolis; ***former:*** Scutari]** (Turkey) City across the BOSPORUS from ISTANBUL. Part of ancient CHALCEDON, it was the gateway to CONSTANTINOPLE. It reached its height under the OTTOMAN EMPIRE, which ruled it from the 14th century. Florence Nightingale's work in the hospital here was famous in the Crimean War in 1854 to 1856. It has a great 16th-century mosque and a cemetery for 8,000 British soldiers.

ÜSKÜP. See SKOPJE.

USPALLATA (Argentina) City, 45 mi ENE of Uspallata Pass. José de San Martin's army camped here during the wars of independence. Scientist Charles Darwin visited it in 1835.

USPALLATA PASS [Bermejo Pass, La Cumbre] (Argentina, Chile) Mountain pass between MENDOZA, Argentina and SANTIAGO, Chile. Part of the army of José de San Martin marched through here in 1817 during the Chilean war for independence to fight the Spanish Royalists. The statue of Christ of the Andes was erected here in 1904 as a symbol of peace between Argentina and Chile.

USPENSKOYE. See BOLGAR.

USSR. See UNION OF SOVIET SOCIALIST REPUBLICS.

USSURI [Usuri] [*Mandarin:*** Wu-Shu-li, Wu-su-li]** (USSR, China) River forming the boundary between W Primorski Krai (USSR) and NE China N of Vladivostok. Since 1964 clashes between the USSR and China have occurred along it.

UST DVINSK. See DAUGAGRIVA.

ÚSTÍ. See ÚSTÍ NAD LABEM.

USTICA (Italy) Island in the Tyrrhenian Sea, 40 mi NNW of Palermo. Inhabited since ancient times, it was taken by the Saracens in the Middle Ages. The prey of pirates thereafter, it was abandoned until the late 18th century.

USTILUG [*Polish:*** Uścilug]** (USSR) City, 7 mi W of Vladimir-Volynski. Founded as early as the 12th century, it was the site of Polish Wladislaw II Jagiello's defeat of the Lithuanians and Tatars in 1431. In 1795 RUSSIA obtained it. POLAND held it again from 1921 to 1945.

ÚSTÍ NAD LABEM [Ústí] [*German:*** Aussig]** (Czechoslovakia) City, 45 mi NNW of Prague. The site was inhabited in the 10th century and the city founded in the 13th. It has medieval and Renaissance churches, a medieval castle, and a museum.

UST-IZHORA [Ust'-Izhora] (USSR) Battle site in the Russian SFSR, 13 miles SE of Leningrad. Here in 1240 Alexander Nevski defeated the Swedes.

UST-KAMENOGORSK [*former:*** Zashchita]** (USSR) Town in the E Kazakh SSR, 100 mi E of Semipalatinsk. It was founded in 1720 as a military base on the Russian frontier. Trade with China and Mongolia helped it grow. After the Revolution it became an important center of metallurgy.

UST ZEISK. See BLAGOVESHCHENSK.

USUKI (Japan) Town, approx. 12 mi SE of Oita. It was an early town that traded with the Portuguese. It has famous Buddhist cliff carvings dating from the ninth to the 12th centuries, when it was a temple site.

USUMBURA. See BUJUMBURA.

USURI. See USSURI.

UTAH (United States) State, in the ROCKY MOUNTAINS, in the western part of the country. Utah was admitted to the Union in 1896 as the 45th state. Its name comes from that of an Indian tribe, usually spelled Ute.

People inhabited the area c.9000 BC, while in Capitol Reef and Hovenweep National Monuments can be seen cliff dwellings built in the 11th to 14th centuries AD by ancestors of the present Pueblo Indians. The first Europeans here may have been Francisco Vásquez de Coronado's party in 1540; but it was 1776 before Europeans permanently reached Utah. At that time two missionaries from SPAIN opened the Old Spanish Trail between SANTA FE, New Mexico, and Utah Lake. A treaty of 1819 between the United States and Spain recognized the region as Spanish. Nevertheless, as American mountain men came after furs, the GREAT SALT LAKE was discovered, the honor probably belonging to James Bridger in 1825. A fur trader from Canada, Peter Skene Ogden, also reached here, but by 1830 there were few furs left.

In 1841 California-bound pioneers first crossed the Great Salt Lake Desert, but it was several years later before Miles Goodyear set up a trading post, Fort Buenaventura, at present OGDEN. Permanent settlement began in 1847 with the arrival of the first group of Mormons, members of the Church of Jesus Christ of Latter Day Saints. They were escaping persecution in the East and Midwest and were led by Brigham Young, a remarkably able administrator. SALT LAKE CITY was laid out, and a cooperative community of industrious people began building, irrigating land, and increasing in numbers. Even so, they had a difficult time contending with an arid climate, grasshoppers, Indian enmity, and the hostility of fellow whites, due in large part to Mormon polygamy.

In 1848 the region became part of the United States as a result of the Mexican War. The Mormons wished to call their new home Deseret (honeybee); but Utah Territory, an area larger than the present state, was the name Congress gave to it in 1850. The Mormons also had trouble with the Federal government because of their polygamy, and their petitions for statehood were therefore denied. Young was appointed governor, however. Angered because land was taken from them, the Ute Indians rose in the Walker War of 1853/54 and the Black Hawk War of 1865 to 1868. In 1857 some 140 emigrants bound for CALIFORNIA were massacred at MOUNTAIN MEADOWS by Paiute Indians, accompanied by some whites, and there were charges that the Mor-

mons had incited the attack. The U.S. government declared the Mormons to be in rebellion, Young was removed as governor, and troops were dispatched. Although known as the Utah War, the conflict was settled without bloodshed.

In 1862, 1882, and 1887 Congress passed laws forbidding polygamy; and the government enforced these laws by seizing Mormon Church property and infringing on individual rights. In 1890 the Mormon Church advised its members to abandon polygamy. Meanwhile the completion of the first transcontinental railroad boosted Utah's population as the east and west sections of the railroad were joined at PROMONTORY POINT near Ogden in 1869. Non-Mormons entered the state, but the church still remains the dominant power today. World War II and the prosperity of the 1950's caused rapid industrial growth and a trend toward urbanization. Hydroelectric power has been an economic stimulant since the 1950's. Utah has voted Republican in presidential elections four consecutive times since 1968. Salt Lake City is the capital and largest city; other major cities are Ogden and PROVO.

The famous Mormon Temple in Salt Lake City, Utah, still under construction in 1886. The Temple choir has broadcast for years from its acoustically remarkable interior.

UTAH BEACH (France) Battle site near CARENTAN. It was the code name for one of the landing sites on the NORMANDY coast during the Allied invasion of France on D-Day, June 6, 1944, toward the end of World War II.

UTE PASS (United States) Pass near Pike's Peak in COLORADO. In the late 19th century gold miners heading for Cripple Creek and Leadville used it frequently.

UTICA (Tunisia) Ancient city, 15 mi NW of ancient CARTHAGE and 18 mi N of modern Tunis. Founded by Phoenicians c. the eighth century BC, it sided with Carthage against ROME in the first two Punic Wars. In the Third Punic War it joined with Rome. After Carthage's defeat, *c.*145 BC, it became capital of the Roman province of AFRICA. Cato the Younger committed suicide here after his defeat by Caesar in 46 BC. An episcopal see in the third century AD, it was taken by the Vandals in 439 and by the Byzantines in 534. The Arabs destroyed it *c.*700. Eighth-century cemeteries and Roman residences, an amphitheater, baths, and fortifications have been excavated.

UTICA (United States) City, approx. 50 mi W of Syracuse, NEW YORK State. Site of a British fort in 1758, the town did not emerge until after the fort's destruction by Tories and Indians in 1776 during the Revolution. It became a prosperous industrial center with the completion of the ERIE CANAL in 1825. The first Woolworth store opened here in 1879.

UTINA. See UDINE.

UTRECHT [*ancient:* **Trajectum ad Rhenum, Ultrajectum**] (Netherlands) City, 20 mi SSE of Amsterdam. Settled by Romans as early as 48 AD, it was made a bishop's see in 696. German emperors often lived here. Chartered in 1122, it was ruled by bishops until 1527 and was an important ecclesiastical, cultural, and commercial city, only surpassed by Amsterdam in the 15th century. It was the home of Adrian VI, the only Dutch pope. The Union of Utrecht, forming the UNITED PROVINCES against SPAIN, was signed here in 1579. The Peace of Utrecht, ending the War of Spanish Succession in 1713 was also signed here. Held by the French from 1795 to 1813, it was the residence of Louis Bonaparte, king of HOLLAND. It has many 11th- to 15th-century churches, a university founded in 1636, many museums, and other historic buildings.

UTRECHT, UNION OF. See NETHERLANDS.

UTRERA [*ancient:* **Utricula**] (Spain) Town, 19 mi SSE of Seville. A site of prehistoric occupation and Roman settlement, it was an episcopal see in the ninth century AD. It fell to the Moors, was retaken temporarily by CASTILE in the 13th century, and made Christian again in 1340. A medieval outlaws' retreat, it was destroyed and rebuilt in 1368 and again from 1808 to 1814. It has a Moorish character, with old mansions and a Moorish castle, and has two Gothic churches.

UTRICULA. See UTRERA.

UTSUNOMIYA [**Utunomiya**] (Japan) City, 60 mi N of Tokyo. Originating around a castle in the 11th century, it became a trading post in the Tokugawa period from 1603 to 1867 and a government center in 1884. It has the oldest Buddhist carvings in Japan in a ninth-century temple. Much 19th-century architecture is preserved here.

UTTAR PRADESH [*former:* **United Provinces,**

The old center of Utrecht, Netherlands, a city of many canals and splendid old buildings that date from its period as a leading commercial metropolis in the Middle Ages.

United Provinces of Agra and Oudh] (India) The country's most populous state, located in the N central region, bordering on Nepal and Tibet. LUCKNOW is its capital, with DELHI to the W and PATNA to the E. An important region in early Indian history, it was the setting for the two great Hindu epics, the *Ramayana* and the *Mahabharata.* Uttar Pradesh bore witness to the rise of Buddhism under Asoka's empire and was ruled by the Guptas and Harsha before the Mogul Empire's conquest in the 16th century, when AGRA became the principal city.

The arrival of GREAT BRITAIN in the region in the second half of the 18th century brought a rapid extension of British sovereignty from 1798 to 1833. In 1835 Uttar Pradesh became part of the North-West Provinces, which were joined by OUDH in 1856. Under a single administration from 1877, the region was again adjusted to form the United Provinces of Agra and Oudh.

Under a single governor from 1921, Uttar Pradesh achieved autonomous government with a two-chamber legislature in 1937, and with the achievement of Indian independence in 1947, it was made a state of India. In 1950 the state was further enlarged with the merging of the United Provinces and the smaller, former royal states of Benares, Rampur, and TEHRI. See also GUPTA, MAURYA and MOGUL EMPIRES.

UTTI (Finland) Battle site in Kymi province, 4 mi E of the provincial capital, Kyuvala. Gustavus III of SWEDEN defeated the Russians here in 1789.

UTUNOMIYA. See UTSUNOMIYA.

UUSIKAUPUNKI [*Swedish:* **Nystad**] (Finland) City, 35 mi W of Turku. Founded in 1617, it was the scene in 1721 of the signing of the Treaty of Nystad ending the Great Northern War, by which RUSSIA gained SWEDEN's valuable Baltic territories. It has a 17th-century church.

UVA (Sri Lanka) Province in the SE. It was included in the kingdom of KANDY before the English invaded it in the early 19th century. It revolted against British control in 1817 and was made a British province in 1886.

UVALDE [*former:* **Encina**] (United States) City, approx. 80 mi WSW of San Antonio, TEXAS. First settled in 1853, it was the home and first seat of political power of John N. Garner, vice-president of the United States from 1933 to 1941.

UWAJIMA (Japan) Town, 45 mi SSW of Matsuyama, the capital of Ehima prefecture. Dating from the 16th century at the latest, it has the remains of an ancient castle and a famous shrine.

UXANTIS. See ÎLE D'OUESSANT.

UXBRIDGE (England) Ancient market town, now in the borough of Hillingdon, outer LONDON, in the W. Situated on the Colne River, it was the place where a group of Parliamentarians fruitlessly negotiated with Charles I at the Treaty House in 1645.

UXELLODUNUM. See ISSOUDUN.

UXMAL (Mexico) Ancient city, approx. 50 mi S of Mérida, Yucatán. A great Mayan city with magnificent ruins, it flourished from *c.*600 to *c.*900 AD when many great stone buildings and sculptures were erected in a monumental, classic style. Building ceased *c.*1000 AD, but it remained an active city and political center until *c.*1450, when it was abandoned.

UYEDA. See UEDA.

UYUNI (Bolivia) Town, 191 mi S of Oruro. Founded in 1890 and settled by Slavs and Syrians, it grew rapidly as a mining terminus.

UZBEKISTAN. See UZBEK SOVIET SOCIALIST REPUBLIC.

UZBEK SOVIET SOCIALIST REPUBLIC [Uzbekistan] [*Persian:* **Sogdiana**] (USSR) Region and constituent republic bounded by the Kazakh SSR on the N and E, the Kirgiz and Tadzhik SSRs on the E, and the Turkmen SSR and Afghanistan on the S. An early center of civilization, it was taken by Alexander the Great in the fourth century BC. Inhabited by nomadic peoples, it became Islamicized when Arabs conquered it in the eighth century AD. It was later ruled by Seljuk Turks. It fell to Genghis Khan in the 13th century and Tamerlane in the 14th century. The latter established his capital at SAMARKAND. The Uzbeks, descendants of the GOLDEN HORDE, who invaded in the 16th century, had a short-lived empire that soon became divided into the khanates of KHIVA, BUKHARA, and KOKAND. The great cities on the main routes to China, Persia, India, and Europe—Samarkand, Bukhara, and TASHKENT—were rich and highly civilized trading centers for centuries. The Russians took the area in the 1860's and 1870's, allowing native rule to continue in Khiva and Bukhara. In 1917 the Uzbeks attempted to establish a democratic autonomous government, but by 1924 the various former states were joined into the Uzbek SSR. See also KHOREZM.

UZERCHE (France) Ancient town, 15 mi NW of Tulle. It was originally a Roman settlement. The town has some 15th- and 16th-century houses.

UZÈS (France) Town, approx. 15 mi N of Nîmes. An episcopal see from the fifth to 18th centuries, it has a ducal castle dating from the 12th to 14th centuries and a 17th-century cathedral.

UZHGOROD [*Hungarian:* **Ungvár**; *Slovak:* **Užhorod**] (USSR) City in the Ukrainian SSR, 165 mi ENE of Budapest. Long an important strategic site, it was inhabited by Slavs in the eighth and ninth centuries and was part of Kievan RUSSIA in the 10th and 11th centuries. At the end of the 11th century it was conquered by Hungarians. It was absorbed by AUSTRIA-HUNGARY in 1867. In the late 19th century it became a center of Ukrainian nationalism. It passed to CZECHOSLOVAKIA in 1919, HUNGARY in 1938, and the USSR in 1945. It has a medieval fortress, a 16th-century palace, and an 18th-century church. See also UKRAINE.

UŽHOROD. See UZHGOROD.

UŽICE. See TITOVO UŽICE.

UZNAM. See USEDOM.

V

VAAL KRANTZ [Vaalkrantz] (South Africa) Village in W NATAL, just SW of LADYSMITH. On Feb. 5, 1900, during the Boer War, the Boers defeated the British here.

VAAL RIVER (South Africa) River of the NE, rising in the SE TRANSVAAL and flowing into the Orange River, N CAPE PROVINCE. Crossed by the Boers during the Great Trek in 1835/36, today it forms the main part of the Transvaal-ORANGE FREE STATE border. The river has yielded millions of dollars worth of diamonds.

VAASA [*former:* Nikolainkaupunki, Nikolaistad; *Swedish:* Vasa] (Finland) City, port, and capital of Vaasa province, on the Gulf of Bothnia, 220 mi NW of Helsinki. Founded in 1606, it was rebuilt near the sea after a fire in 1852. During the civil war of 1918 it was the capital of White Finland.

VÁC [*ancient:* Vacs, Vacz; *German:* Waitzen] (Hungary) City on the DANUBE RIVER, 20 mi N of Budapest. Known to the Romans, it became a bishopric under St. Stephen, the "apostolic king," in 1008. It has an 18th-century cathedral and episcopal palace.

VACCA. See BEJA, Tunisia.

VACS. See VÁC.

VACZ. See VÁC.

VADSTENA (Sweden) Town in Östergötland county, on Lake Vättern, 25 mi W of Linköping. First mentioned in the early 14th century, it is the site of the convent of St. Bridget, founded *c.*1370, which was the most important medieval cloister in Sweden. The town has many other historic buildings.

VADUZ (Liechtenstein) Town and capital of Liechtenstein, on the Upper RHINE RIVER, 50 mi SE of ZURICH. Severely damaged in 1499 during a war between the Swiss and the HOLY ROMAN EMPIRE, it was rebuilt in the 16th century and passed to the Liechtenstein family in 1712. The town is dominated by its fine medieval castle.

VAGA. See BEJA, Tunisia.

VAGARSHAPAT. See ECHMIADZIN.

VAILIMA (Samoa) Estate on Upolu Island, 4 mi S of Apia. The estate was the home of Robert Louis Stevenson, the Scottish author, from 1888 until his death six years later. His last works were written here.

VAISALI [Basarh] [*Pali:* Vesali] (India) Ancient city of the NE, on the Gandar River, NE of Patna, in Bihar state. The ancient capital of the Licchavi republic, it is connected with both the Buddhist and Jain religions and was visited often by the Buddha himself. The second Buddhist council was held here *c.*485 BC, after the Buddha's death, to lay down rules for the faith.

VAISON-LA-ROMAINE [*ancient:* Vasio] (France) Town in Vaucluse department, 26 mi NNE of Avignon. Originally an important town of the Vocontii tribe, it was occupied by the Romans and was possibly the birthplace of the historian Tacitus *c.*65 AD. It was the site of a bishopric from the third century until 1791. There are extensive Roman remains.

VALAAM [*Finnish:* Valamo] (USSR) Island group in LAKE LADOGA, NE of Leningrad, in Russian SFSR. The island of Valaam in the group is the site of a famous Russian monastery dating at least from the 12th century. The islands were within FINLAND until 1940.

VALAIS [*ancient:* Valais Poenina; *former:*Vallais; *German:* Wallis] (Switzerland) Canton on the Italian border, with its capital at SION. Inhabited since prehistoric times, it was occupied by ROME under Julius Caesar in 57 BC. It was granted to the bishop of Sion in 999 AD and remained Roman Catholic during the Reformation. After the French Revolution it became a canton of the Helvetic Republic but was incorporated into a department of FRANCE by Napoleon in 1810. It finally joined the Swiss Confederation in 1815.

VALAIS POENINA. See VALAIS.

VALAMO. See VALAAM.

VALCOUR ISLAND (United States) Island in LAKE CHAMPLAIN, 5 mi SE of Plattsburgh, E NEW YORK State. Two naval battles were fought off the island's coast; the first during the American Revolution on Oct. 11, 1776, when the British defeated the Americans. The second was fought on Sept. 11, 1814 when the Americans under Thomas Macdonough defeated the British.

VALDEZ (United States) City and port on Prince William Sound, 370 mi S of Fairbanks, S ALASKA. Named by the Spanish in 1790, it was established in 1898 as the debarkation point for prospectors bound for the YUKON gold fields. During World War II it was a military base and was devastated by an earthquake in 1964. It is the most northerly port in North America that is open all year. Today it is an important port for Alaska's oil industry and the southern terminus of the Trans-Alaska pipeline from Prudhoe Bay in the north.

VALDIVIA (Chile) City and capital of Valdivia province, on the Valdivia River, 460 mi SSW of Santiago. Founded in 1552 by Pedro de Valdivia, it was strategically important in the struggle against the Araucanian Indians. It was a Royalist center during the war of liberation. It only developed economically when settled by Germans in the mid-19th century.

VALENCE [*ancient:* Valentia, Ventia] (France)

City and capital of Drôme department, on the RHÔNE RIVER, 62 mi S of Lyons. Originally the capital of the Gallic Segalauni, it became an important town of the Roman province of Viennensis Prima. A bishopric from the fourth century AD, it was the capital of the medieval duchy of Valentinois. The town saw the arrival of many cardinals fleeing from rioting in CARPENTRAS during a conclave held in 1314 to elect a new pope. In the 15th century it became the site of a famous university. Its prosperity declined after the revocation of the Edict of NANTES.

VALENCIA, Ireland. See VALENTIA.

VALENCIA [*ancient:* **Valentia;** *former:* **Valencia del Cid**] (Spain) City and capital of Valencia province, 188 mi ESE of Madrid, near the Mediterranean Sea. First mentioned in the second century BC, it was a prosperous Roman colony and under the Moors from the eighth to 13th centuries was twice the seat of an independent state. The city's conquest from the Moors and rule by Rodrigo Díaz de Bivar, known as The Cid, from 1094 until his defeat by the ALMORAVIDES forms the basis of the *Poem of the Cid.* United with CASTILE in 1479, the city became a cultural center and in 1474 was the site of the first Spanish printing press. As a Loyalist center in 1936/37, during the civil war, it suffered severe damage.

VALENCIA (Spain) Region of E Spain, comprising the modern provinces of Alicante, Castellón de la Plana, and Valencia. It was originally inhabited by Iberians as early as 1600 BC and by the Urnfield Celts between c.670 BC and 560 BC. The region was later colonized by Greek and Carthaginian traders by c.500 BC until its conquest by Rome from c.220 BC to c.190 BC. It fell to the Visigoths in the fifth century AD and passed to the Moors in the eighth century. Created an independent emirate in 1022, it prospered due to the development of irrigation techniques by the Moors. Parts of the region along the coast were taken by Christians c.1100 AD. In 1238 it passed under James I of ARAGON. It declined following the expulsion of the Moors in 1609.

VALENCIA (Venezuela) City and capital of Carabobo state, 80 mi W of Caracas. Founded in 1555, it was briefly the national capital in 1812 and in 1830, when it was the site of a convention that proclaimed Venezuela's secession from GRAN COLOMBIA. Today it is a major industrial center.

VALENCIA DEL CID. See VALENCIA, Spain.

VALENCIENNES (France) Town in Nord department, on the Escaut River, 29 mi SE of Lille. First mentioned in 693 AD, it passed to the counts of HAINAUT in 1047 and became famous for its lacemaking in the 15th century. It was ceded to France in 1678 by the Treaty of NIJMEGEN. It was the birthplace of the historian Jean Froissart c.1335 and of the painter Jean Watteau in 1684.

VALENTIA, France. See VALENCE.

VALENTIA [**Valencia**] [*Gaelic:* **Dairbhre**] (Irish Republic) Island off the SW coast, in County Kerry. Named by Spanish traders, it is famous as the eastern terminus of the first permanent transatlantic cable, laid by the *Great Eastern* steamship in 1866. The cable linked Europe with Trinity Bay, NEWFOUNDLAND.

VALENTIA, Spain. See VALENCIA.

VALENTINOIS, DUCHY OF. See VALENCE.

VALE OF KASHMIR. See KASHMIR.

VALERIAN WAY [*ancient:* **Via Valeria**] (Italy) Ancient Roman road running across Italy from TIVOLI, in Roma province, Latium region, to PESCARA, in the Abruzzi region, where it turns N along the ADRIATIC SEA. One of the chief Roman roads to cross the Apennines, it was probably conceived by M. Valerius Messalla in 154 BC.

VALÉRIEN, MONT (France) Small hill, 6 mi W of PARIS and close to Suresne on the W, which took an important part in the Franco-Prussian War of 1870/71. A fort was built here between 1841 and 1843 which became a vital defensive position during the siege of Paris.

VALETTA. See VALLETTA.

VALLADOLID, Mexico. See MORELIA.

VALLADOLID (Spain) City and capital of Valladolid province, 100 mi NW of Madrid. Captured from the Moors in the 10th century, it virtually replaced TOLEDO as the chief residence of the kings of CASTILE in the 15th century. Ferdinand of ARAGON and Isabella of Castile were married here in 1469, and Columbus died here in 1506. The city declined when Philip II made MADRID the capital of Spain in 1561. It suffered during the Peninsular campaign of the Napoleonic Wars and was occupied by the Insurgents at the start of the Civil War of 1936 to 1939.

VALLADOLID LA NUEVA. See COMAYAGUA.

VALLAIS. See VALAIS.

VALLE D'AOSTA (Italy) Autonomous region bordering on FRANCE and SWITZERLAND, with its capital at AOSTA. Inhabited originally by the Salassi, it became part of the ROMAN EMPIRE under Augustus. In the 11th century it came under SAVOY and was made an autonomous region of Italy in 1948. The Grand and Petite ST. BERNARD and Mont Blanc routes all enter Italy in Valle d'Aosta and converge at Aosta before heading south to Piedmont.

VALLEDUPAR (Colombia) Town and capital of César department, 80 mi SSW of Ríohacha. Founded in 1550, it flourished during the colonial era but suffered damage during the civil wars of the 19th century.

VALLEJO (United States) City in W CALIFORNIA, on San Pablo Bay, 20 mi N of Oakland. Named after the Mexican General Mariano Vallejo, who explored the region in 1830, it was the state capital for two brief periods in 1852 and 1853.

VALLETTA [**Valetta**] (Malta) City, port, and capital of Malta, on the NE coast of the island. Strategically located between two harbors, it was built in 1565 after the Great Siege of Malta by the Turks. It became the capital in 1570. The city was annexed by GREAT BRITAIN in 1814 at the Treaty of Paris as a base for its fleet

The port of Valparaiso in Chile, depicted in 1850. In earlier centuries its fine harbor was often raided by Dutch and English pirates, including Sir Francis Drake.

in the Mediterranean Sea. During World War II it was the headquarters of the British Mediterranean Fleet and consequently suffered severely from bombing.

VALLEY FORGE (United States) Valley in SE PENNSYLVANIA, 20 mi NW of Philadelphia, on the Schuylkill River. During the American Revolution George Washington established the main camp of the Continental Army here in December 1777. Despite the terrible privations of the winter and many desertions, the army left the camp as an efficient fighting force in June 1778. The French General Lafayette and the Prussian General Steuben were with the troops and helped train them.

VALLOMBROSA (Italy) Village in Firenze province, TUSCANY region, 25 mi E of Florence. A Benedictine monastery was founded here in 1040 by St. John Gualberto and became the first house of the Vallombrosan Order, a strict reform group. Pillaged by the troops of Charles V in 1529 and by those of Napoleon in 1808, the monastery was dissolved in 1866 following the Risorgimento. It was restored in 1963. The present structure dates from the 17th century with some 16th-century elements.

VALMY (France) Village in Marne department, 6 mi W of SAINTE MENEHOULD, in the ARGONNE. The first major engagement of the French Revolutionary Wars was fought here on Sept. 20, 1792 when the French

under Generals Dumouriez and F.C. Kellermann, later the duke of Valmy, skirmished with an Austro-Prussian force under the duke of Brunswick. Although indecisive, the incident revealed the superiority of the French artillery.

VALOIS [*ancient:* **Pagus Vadensis**] (France) Ancient region in the N, comprising the modern departments of Oise and Aisne. Inhabited originally by the Suessiones, it became a county under the Merovingian and early Carolingian kings and was annexed to the French crown in 1214 by King Philip Augustus. Philip of Valois became king of France in 1328, and his descendants ruled after him until 1589.

VALONA. See VLORË.

VALPARAISO [*Spanish:* **Valparáiso**] (Chile) City and capital of Valparaiso department, on a bay of the Pacific Ocean, 75 mi WNW of Santiago. Founded in 1536 by Juan de Saavedra, it was occupied by Sir Francis Drake in 1578 and by Sir John Hawkins in 1595. It was bombarded by SPAIN in 1866. The city has suffered many earthquakes, of which the most severe was in 1906 when nearly all the city was destroyed.

VALTELLINA (Italy) Valley of the upper Adda River, in the ALPS, stretching from Lake Como to the Stelvio Pass, in Sondrio province, LOMBARDY region. Of great strategic value, it was captured from MILAN by the Grisons (GRAUBÜNDEN) in 1512 and was the scene of bitter fighting between Catholics and Protestants during the Thirty Years War from 1618 to 1648. The Grisons regained control of the valley by the Peace of Milan in 1639, and it remained in their hands until incorporated into the CISALPINE REPUBLIC in 1797. It became part of Italy in 1859.

VALVA. See CORFINIUM.

VAN (Turkey) Town and capital of Van province, on Lake Van, 150 mi SE of Erzurum. From the ninth to the seventh centuries BC it was the capital of the kingdom of URARTU, and it was occupied thereafter successively by Medes, Achaemenid Persians, and the kings of PONTUS. It was the center of a powerful Armenian kingdom by the first century AD. It fell to the Seljuk Turks in 1071 following the Battle of MANZIKERT here, a disastrous defeat for the BYZANTINE EMPIRE. It became part of the OTTOMAN EMPIRE in 1543. During World War I it was occupied by RUSSIA from 1915 to 1917. See also ARMENIA, PERSIA.

VAN. See URARTU.

VANCOUVER [former: **Granville**] (Canada) City and port on an inlet of the Strait of Georgia, 12 mi W of Port Moody, SW BRITISH COLUMBIA. The site of a small settlement by 1865, it was incorporated as a city in 1886 but suffered a severe fire that same year. The city's recovery was accelerated by the completion of the Canadian Pacific Railway in 1887 and by the opening of the PANAMA CANAL in 1914, which facilitated trade with Europe. Today it is the largest city in western Canada and a major Canadian port.

VANCOUVER [former: **Fort Vancouver**] (United States) City in SW WASHINGTON, on the COLUMBIA RIVER, 8 mi N of Portland. Established by the Hudson's Bay Company in 1824, it is the oldest permanent settlement in the Pacific Northwest. Until 1846, when it became part of the United States, it was the company's headquarters for all operations west of the Continental Divide. It was fortified by the U.S. Army in 1849.

VANCOUVER ISLAND (Canada) Island in the Pacific Ocean, off SW BRITISH COLUMBIA. Captain Cook was the first European to land on the island in 1778, and the area was chartered in 1792 by Capt. George Vancouver. In 1849 it became a British crown colony, and was made part of British Columbia in 1866. It is the largest island off the west coast of North America.

VANDALIA (United States) City in S central ILLINOIS, 30 mi N of Centralia. Laid out in 1819, it was the state capital from 1820 to 1839. Abraham Lincoln received his license to practice law here.

VAN DIEMAN'S LAND. See TASMANIA.

VANNES [ancient: **Civitas Venetorum, Dariorigum**; Breton: **Gwened**] (France) Town and capital of Morbihan department, BRITTANY, 67 mi WNW of Nantes. The ancient capital of the Veneti, it led the Armorican League in their unsuccessful campaign against Julius Caesar. It was the capital of Brittany from the ninth to the 16th century, when it was united with France. Nearby are many prehistoric megalithic monuments.

VANUATA. See NEW HEBRIDES.

VAPINCUM. See GAP.

VARANASI [former: **Banaras, Benares**; Hindi: **Kasi**] (India) City in SE Uttar Pradesh, 70 mi E of Allahabad, on the GANGES RIVER. Believed to be one of the oldest cities in India, it probably dates from the 13th century BC, and was the first Aryan settlement in the middle Ganges Valley. By the late second millennium BC it had become a center of Aryan philosophy and religion. It changed hands several times until falling to the Muslims in 1033 AD, and it suffered great destruction under the Mogul Emperor Aurangzeb (1618-1707). When the MOGUL EMPIRE declined, Hindu rule was reestablished. Today it is the most holy city of the Hindus. There are about 1,500 temples, palaces, and shrines here. It is also holy to Buddhists and to Jains.

VARDARES. See VARDAR RIVER.

VARDAR RIVER [Greek: **Vardares**; Latin: **Axius**] (Greece, Yugoslavia) River 240 mi long, that rises in the Sar Planina, S Yugoslavia and flows through Skopje and NE Greece to the AEGEAN SEA, near THESSALONÍKI. The route of the river was used during World War II by German forces in the conquest of Yugoslavia and subsequent invasion of Greece.

VARDKESAVAN. See ECHMIADZIN.

VARENNES [**Varennes-En-Argonne**] (France) Town in Meuse department, 40 mi WNW of Verdun. After their flight from PARIS, during the French Revolution, Louis XVI and Marie Antoinette were arrested here on June 21, 1791 while attempting to escape over the border.

VARENNES-EN-ARGONNE. See VARENNES.

VARESE (Italy) City and capital of Varese province, LOMBARDY region, 30 mi NW of Milan. It has a museum housing archaeological relics from prehistoric times to the Roman and Gallic periods. The gardens of the 18th-century Palazzo Comunale, former palace of the last dukes of ESTE, are among the most beautiful in Italy. Nearby is a church founded in the fourth century by St. Ambrose.

VARIA CAPELLA. See FALKIRK.

VARKANA. See GORGAN.

VARNA [ancient: **Odessus**, former: **Stalin**] (Bulgaria) City, port, and capital of Varna province, on the BLACK SEA, 230 mi ENE of Sofia. Founded by Greeks in 580 BC, it became part of the ROMAN EMPIRE in the first century AD. It was taken from the BYZANTINE EMPIRE by the Bulgars c.680 and retaken c.970. Captured by the Turks from the Bulgarian Empire in 1391, it became an active port and was the scene of a battle in 1444 when the Turks under Murad II decisively defeated the Crusaders under Ladislaus III of POLAND and HUNGARY, thus enabling the Turks to sweep up toward Central Europe. It was the chief Anglo-French naval base during the Crimean War from 1854 to 1856 and was ceded to Bulgaria in 1878.

VASA. See VAASA.

VASAI. See BASSEIN.

VASCONGADAS. See BASQUE PROVINCES.

VASCONIA. See GASCONY.

VASILKOV (USSR) Town in NW Ukraine, 19 mi S of Kiev. Founded in 988 AD, it was destroyed by the Mongols in the 13th century and passed to RUSSIA in 1686. In 1825 it was the center of an uprising of the Decembrist revolutionaries. See also UKRAINE.

VASIO. See VAISON-LA-ROMAINE.

VASLUI (Rumania) City and capital of Vaslui county, 35 mi S of Iaşi. A battle was fought nearby in 1475 at Racova in which Stephen the Great of MOLDAVIA defeated a massively superior Turkish army.

VÄSTERÅS [*Swedish:* **Västra Aros**] (Sweden) City and capital of Västmanland county, 60 mi W of Stockholm, on Lake Mälaren. Founded in 1100 AD, it was one of the great medieval cities of Sweden. The scene of 11 important diets, it was here that Gustavus Vasa formally introduced the Reformation into Sweden in 1527 by creating a Lutheran state church. The throne of Sweden was made hereditary here by the diet of 1544.

VASTO [*ancient:* **Histonium**] (Italy) Town in Chieti province, ABRUZZI region, on the Adriatic Sea, 32 mi ESE of Chieti. Originally a town of the Frentani, it became a flourishing Roman town lying on a SE extension of the FLAMINIAN WAY. Its medieval walls still stand.

VÄSTRA AROS. See VÄSTERAS.

VASVÁR [*German:* **Eisenburg**] (Hungary) Town in Vas county, 15 mi SE of Szombathely. Following the defeat of the Turks at the battle of SZENTGOTTHÁRD, a 20-year truce was signed here with the Holy Roman Emperor Leopold I on Aug. 10, 1664. See HOLY ROMAN EMPIRE, OTTOMAN EMPIRE.

VATAPIPURA. See BADAMI.

VATI. See BATUMI.

VATICAN CITY [State of Vatican City] [*Italian:* **Stato della Città del Vaticano**] Papal state, independent since 1929, situated within the city of ROME. Here, on the site of the Ager Vaticanus, the Emperor Caligula (37–41 AD) began a circus that was completed by Emperor Nero (54–68). According to tradition, St. Peter was martyred near the Circus of Nero, *c.*65, and an oratory was constructed on the site by Pope Anacletus II *c.*155. In *c.*325 Pope Sylvester I persuaded Emperor Constantine I to erect a basilica to St. Peter on the hill. Charlemagne was crowned Roman Emperor in this basilica in 800. In the 15th century the old basilica began to be replaced, a section at a time, by the present church, St. Peter's Basilica, which was completed in 1626 according to plans by Raphael, Bramante, Michelangelo, and others. In 1656 Bernini completed the famous piazza with the colonnade that now forms the gateway to Vatican City.

Behind St. Peter's Basilica are the Sistine Chapel, with its famous frescoes by Perugino, Pinturicchio, Boticelli, and others, and the ceiling and *Last Judgement* by Michelangelo. In the papal palace are the stanze and loggia of Raphael and the Borgia apartments. Also in the Vatican City are the Vatican Library, one of the most important in the world, with its collection of manuscripts and printed books, and the Vatican Museums with their collections of Egyptian, Etruscan, Greek and Roman, early Christian, Renaissance, and Baroque arts.

The Vatican City proper does not include the area of the Vatican once part of the medieval Borgo, or Leonine City, which was surrounded by the Leonine wall built by Pope Leo IV in 850 against the Saracens; nor does it include the Castel Sant'Angelo, built as the Mausoleum of Hadrian in 135 AD and long a papal fortress. The Castel was most famously used during the sack of Rome under Emperor Charles V in 1527, and it was where Benvenuto Cellini and others were imprisoned. Until 1377, when the papacy returned to Rome from AVIGNON, the Lateran Palace in Rome was the official residence of the pope. The cathedral of St. John Lateran in Rome remains the official seat of the pope as bishop of Rome.

Since the Lateran Treaty *(La Conciliazione)* on Feb. 11, 1929, negotiated between Pope Pius XI and Benito Mussolini, Vatican City has enjoyed full extraterritoriality. This extends not only to the Vatican Hill but also to other buildings in and around Rome, including the Lateran Cathedral and Palace, the basilica of Sta. Maria Maggiore of the fourth and fifth century, the basilica of San Paolo fuori le Mura, down the Tiber, first built in the fourth century and rebuilt in 1854, the Renaissance Cancelleria Palace, and others, including the papal villa at Castel Gandolfo. The Swiss Guard, formed in 1506, is still the official peacekeeping force of Vatican City. See also PAPAL STATES.

VATLNA. See VETULONIA.

VATLUNA. See VETULONIA.

VAUD [*German:* **Waadt**] (Switzerland) Canton in the W with its capital at LAUSANNE. Inhabited since prehistoric times, it was the home of the Helvetii, originally subdued by Julius Caesar. The area later came under the ROMAN EMPIRE. It was part of Transjurane BURGUNDY from 888 to 1032 and in 1536 passed to the Bernese, who forcibly imposed the Reformation. The region revolted against BERN in 1798 and joined the Helvetic Republic as the canton of Léman. It became part of the Swiss Confederation in 1803.

VAUXHALL (England) District of the LONDON borough of Lambeth. Its public gardens, laid out in 1661, were frequented by royalty and by such people as Samuel Pepys (1633–1703) and William Makepeace Thackeray (1811–63). Although fashionable throughout the 18th and early 19th centuries, the gardens were closed in 1859.

VÄXJÖ [Vexio, Wexiö] (Sweden) Town in Kronoberg county, 60 mi WNW of Kalmar, on Lake Växjö. Founded, according to tradition, in the 11th century by the English missionary, St. Siegfrid, Växjö became a bishopric *c.*1170. It is now modern in appearance, having been burned down in 1843 and rebuilt.

VECKALACKS. See HAMINA.

VECTIS. See WIGHT, ISLE OF.

VEDAGARBHA. See BUXAR.

VEEDERSBURG. See AMSTERDAM, New York.

VEGA REAL. See LA VEGA.

VEGLIA. See KRK.

VEII [*Italian:* **Veio**] (Italy) Ancient city of ETRURIA, 10 mi NW of Rome. Originally a collection of villages in the ninth century BC, it became one of the most important cities of the Etruscan League, dominating ROME in the seventh and sixth centuries BC. It fell to the Romans c.395 BC after a ten-year siege and was destroyed. Julius Caesar founded a colony here that became a municipium under Augustus. Though the town had declined by the second century AD, it was an important religious center until the third century. Excavations on the deserted site have revealed the oldest known Etruscan frescoes. Many finds are now in Rome.

VEIO. See VEII.

VELATHRI. See VOLTERRA.

VELBERT (West Germany) City in North Rhine-Westphalia, 8 mi S of Essen, in the RUHR Valley. First mentioned in 875 AD, it is today the center of the West German lock-making industry. Locks have been manufactured here since the 16th century.

VELCH. See VULCI.

VELDIDENA. See INNSBRUCK.

VELES. See TITOV VELES.

VELESTER. See VELLETRI.

VÉLEZ-MÁLAGA (Spain) Town in Málaga province, ANDALUSIA, on the Mediterranean Sea, 16 mi ENE of Málaga. Captured from the Moors by Ferdinand V in 1487, it is the site of a church that, according to tradition, was founded by St. Peter.

VELIA. See ELEA.

VELIKIYE LUKI (USSR) City in Russian SFSR, 85 mi NNE of Vitebsk. Originally under the control of NOVGOROD, it was sacked by LITHUANIA in 1198 and passed to MOSCOW in 1448. It was completely destroyed by SWEDEN in 1611 but was rebuilt in 1619. It was the scene of heavy fighting during World War II.

VELIKIY-NOVGOROD. See NOVGOROD.

VELIKO TŬRNOVO. See TIRNOVO.

VELIKY USTYUG (USSR) City and port on the Sukhona River, in NW Russian SFSR, 35 mi SSW of Kotlas. Dating at least from the 13th century, it is one of the oldest settlements of European Russia. In the 16th century it was an important trading center on the route between MOSCOW and ARKHANGELSK.

VELITRAE. See VELLETRI.

VELLA GULF (Solomon Islands) Part of the W Pacific Ocean, off the Solomon Islands, SE of Vella Lavella Island. During World War II, on Aug. 6, 1943, U.S. forces won a naval victory over the Japanese here, thus following up their earlier victories at Kula Gulf.

VELLETRI [*ancient:* **Velitrae**, *Volscian:* **Velester**] (Italy) Town in Roma province, LATIUM region, 20 mi SE of Rome. Originally a town of the Volsci, it was of strategic importance because it controlled the valley between the Alban and Volscian mountains. It was sacked by the Romans in 338 BC. It was the seat of the gens Octavia, the ancestors of Emperor Augustus. The town was an independent city-state from the 11th century to 1549, when it fell to the PAPAL STATES. During World War II it fell to U.S. forces on June 2, 1944 after severe fighting.

VELLORE [*Tamil:* **Velluru**] (India) Town in Tamil Nadu, 75 mi WSW of Madras, on the Palar River. It is the site of an old and important fortress built around a Dravidian temple. It was captured by the Marathas in 1676 and occupied by the British in 1760, at the end of the CARNATIC wars. It successfully resisted a siege by Haidar Ali from 1780 to 1782. After 1799, when Haidar Ali's son, Tipu Sahib the sultan of MYSORE, was killed at SERINGAPATAM, Tipu's sons lived in Vellore. In 1806 Indian troops here mutinied and briefly held the fort. The sultan's sons were then transferred to Calcutta.

VELLURU. See VELLORE.

VELOBRIGA. See VIANA DO CASTELO.

VELSEN (Netherlands) City in North Holland province, 13 mi WNW of Amsterdam. Velsen's port of IJmuiden was a German torpedo-boat base during World War II and suffered severe damage from Allied bombing.

VELSUNA. See ORVIETO.

VEN [**Hveen, Hven**] (Sweden) Island in the Øresund, off the SW coast. It was the home of the 16th-century Danish astronomer Tycho Brahe. Here he built a remarkable observatory.

VENDÉE (France) Department of W France, in POITOU, on the Bay of Biscay with its capital at LA ROCHE-SUR-YON. Created a department at the time of the French Revolution, it gave its name to the Wars of the Vendée from 1793 to 1832. In the first war the peasants, incensed by the anticlericalism of the revolution, launched an unsuccessful counterrevolutionary campaign. There were later, smaller, uprisings in 1799, 1815, and 1832.

VENDÔME [*ancient:* **Vindocinum**] (France) Town in Loir-et-Cher department, on the Loir River, 22 mi NW of Blois. Originally a Gallic oppidum or fort, it was a prosperous town in the Middle Ages and became a duchy in 1515. It became part of France under Henry IV in 1589.

VENDYEN. See CESIS.

VENEDIG. See VENICE.

VENETIA [*Italian:* **Veneto, Venezia Euganea**] (Italy) Region of NE Italy, bordering on the Gulf of Venice on the E, Austria on the N, Lombardy to the W, and Emilia Romagna to the S. The historic region is now divided between Veneto, Trentino-Alto Adige, and Friuli-Venezia Giulia regions. Its name comes from the Veneti, a people of ancient Italy. They settled here c.1000 BC and came under Roman rule in the second century BC. In the next century Venetia was joined with ISTRIA as a province, with AQUILEIA as the capital. In the mid-fifth century AD the Huns ravaged Venetia, and it was approximately 500 years before the towns of the area again attained major importance.

VERONA and PADUA especially grew strong and the Veronese League held sway in the 12th century. By c.1420 VENICE had overcome them and ruled most of the region. The modern Veneto region roughly coincides with Venetian possessions at this time.

In 1797 the Treaty of Campo Formio between FRANCE and AUSTRIA gave Venetia to the latter, but in 1805 the Treaty of Pressburg between Napoleon I and Francis II of Austria made it part of the Napoleonic kingdom of Italy. It was once more given to Austria in 1814, which held it until 1866, when it became part of the newly unified kingdom of Italy. Following World War II the eastern province of UDINE was combined with part of VENEZIA GIULIA to form the region of Friuli-Venezia Giulia.

VENETO [Venetia] (Italy) Region of NE Italy, with its capital at VENICE. It stretches from Lago di GARDA on the W to the Gulf of Venice on the E. The ADIGE and PIAVE rivers flow through it, and the PO RIVER forms part of its southern border. Settled by the Veneti c.1000 BC, it came under Roman rule in the second century BC and was ravaged by Attila the Hun in the mid-fifth century AD. In the 10th century the towns of the region began to acquire importance, and by the 15th century most of the Veneto was under Venice. It passed to AUSTRIA in 1797 and was ceded to Italy in 1866.

VENEZIA. See VENICE.

VENEZIA EUGANEA. See VENETIA.

VENEZIA GIULIA (Italy) Former region on the Adriatic Sea, in NE Italy, formed after World War I from some of the land ceded by AUSTRIA to Italy in 1919. Fiume, now RIJEKA, Yugoslavia, became part of Venezia Giulia in 1922 when Italian fascists seized it, ending its status as a free port. Venezia Giulia also included eastern FRIULI, TRIESTE, ISTRIA, and part of CARNIOLA. At the end of World War II most of the region was ceded to YUGOSLAVIA by Italy. The part of Venezia Giulia that stayed Italian was joined with UDINE province to form a new region, Friuli-Venezia Giulia. Trieste, created a free territory in 1947, was divided between Italy and Yugoslavia in 1954, and the Italian section was put in the new region.

VENEZIA TRIDENTINA. See TRENTINO-ALTO ADIGE.

Lush Indian country in eastern Venezuela, meticulously rendered in a painting from 1641. Venezuela is rich in natural resources; its principal product is now oil. It is a leading oil-exporting nation.

VENEZUELA Republic in N South America on the CARIBBEAN SEA, with Brazil to the S, Colombia to the W, and Guyana to the E. People of the Saladero culture lived along the ORINOCO RIVER c.1000 BC, and the Barrancas dwelt in the area approximately 100 years later. By 1500 AD an agricultural population inhabited the Lake Valencia region. Early European explorers met the Carib Indians, ferocious warriors from whose name the word "cannibal" is derived and after which the sea is named. On his third expedition, in 1498, Christopher Columbus sailed across the mouth of the Orinoco River and knew from the strength and freshness of the current that he had reached a continent, not another island. The following year both Alonso de Ojeda and Amerigo Vespucci sailed for SPAIN along the northern coast of South America. Coming upon an island where the Indians built homes on stilts over water, Vespucci named the area *Venezuela*—Little Venice. Juan de la Cosa also explored the coast in 1504.

Missionaries attempted the first settlements in 1510 but were driven out by the Indians. Another missionary, Bartolomé de Las Casas, founded CUMANÁ in 1520. It was destroyed by Indians in 1522 but resettled the next year. CORO was established in 1527. From 1528 to 1546 the region was a commercial concession of a German banking family, the Welsers from AUGSBURG, who were creditors to Charles V, Holy Roman emperor and king of Spain. In payment he gave them practical sovereignty over Venezuela. Led by Nikolaus Federmann, the Germans explored the interior, enslaved Indians, and sought unsuccessfully to find gold. Spanish government over the region was established in 1549. In 1717 and again from 1739 Venezuela, along with present ECUADOR, COLOMBIA, and PANAMA, made up the viceroyalty of NEW GRANADA. The Guipúzcoa Company, given a monopoly of commerce on the Venezuelan coast in 1728, expanded the production of cacao, coffee, and cotton.

Revolt against Spanish rule began in 1810, and independence was declared in 1811. However, the struggle, led by Simón Bolívar, went on for some years, and independence was not assured until victory at CARABOBO on June 24, 1821. Bolívar became president of GRAN COLOMBIA, which included Ecuador, Colombia, and Panama, as well as Venezuela. In 1830 Venezuela seceded from the union, and José Antonio Paez became its first president. José Tadeo Monagas, who became president in 1847, ended slavery; while Antonio Guzmán Blanco, a "benevolent" despot, dominated the country from 1870 to 1888. The long-standing Venezuela Boundary Dispute marked Joaquin Crespo's presidency. The dispute concerned the border between Venezuela and British Guiana, and the UNITED STATES became involved because it felt GREAT BRITAIN was violating the Monroe Doctrine. In December 1895 President Grover Cleveland threatened war if Great Britain did not agree to arbitration, which it then did. In 1899 a U.S. commission set a border favorable to Great Britain. The controversy is still going on, with modern GUYANA.

The regime of Cipriano Castro (1901–08) was involved in the Venezuela Claims. When the country was unable to pay debts owed to Great Britain, GERMANY, and ITALY, in 1902 those nations sent warships that blockaded and shelled Venezuelan seaports. Again the United States felt the Monroe Doctrine was involved, but the European nations disclaimed territorial ambitions. A peaceful solution was reached in 1904. From 1908 to 1935 Venezuela was under the thumb of a tyrannical dictator, Juan Vicente Gómez. Since then power has shifted between democratic and dictatorial regimes. In 1947 Rómulo Gallegos became the first president elected by direct popular vote, but his rule was short-lived. In November 1960 Venezuela was one of the founding members of the Organization of Petroleum Exporting Countries, and is now one of the largest oil-exporting nations. On Jan. 1, 1976 President Carlos Andrés Perez nationalized all foreign-owned oil companies. Since 1978 President Luis Herrera Campins has headed a moderate government and in 1981 began the country's sixth five-year economic plan.

CARACAS is the capital and largest city; next largest are MARACAIBO and BARQUISIMETO.

VENGI. See ELURU.

VENICE [*German:* **Venedig**; *Italian:* **Venezia**; *Latin:* **Venetia**] (Italy) City and former republic in NE Italy, in Venezia province, Veneto region, 162 mi E of Milan, built on 118 small islands in the Lagoon of Venice, at the N end of the Adriatic Sea. There are approximately 150 canals between the islands, crossed by some 400 bridges. The main traffic route in the city is the Grand Canal. Once one of the most powerful city-states in Europe, Venice long ago lost its military and commercial glory, but it continues to be one of the world's great cities for its unique plan, its watery way of life, and its many cultural treasures.

With ISTRIA, Venice was a Roman province in the fifth century AD. According to tradition, after the Huns invaded northern Italy in 452, refugees from AQUILEIA and other towns fled south and settled the islands that now make up the city. Nominally part of the BYZANTINE EMPIRE until c.650, in 697 these island villagers and fishers joined forces under a leader called the *doge*, dialect for *duce* or "duke." By the ninth century they had formed the city, the location of which prevented its conquest by the Carolingian Empire and encouraged the handling of trade between the Byzantine East and the interior of Italy and northern Europe. By the 11th century Venice possessed Istria and most of northern DALMATIA, the regions on the northeastern side of the ADRIATIC SEA. These areas swayed between Venice, the revived Byzantine Empire, and the Slavs until taken by the kingdom of HUNGARY in 1108. By the 12th century Venice had gained favorable trading privileges with the Byzantines and controlled trade in the LEVANT.

Near the end of the 12th century there rose to power the Dandolo family, which produced four doges and other leaders. One of them, Enrico, encouraged the members of the Fourth Crusade, of 1201 to 1204, to pay Venice for supplying passage to the Holy Land by helping attack ZARA and other towns and islands along the Dalmatian coast and by finally taking CONSTANTI-

NOPLE, capital of the Byzantine Empire. It was sacked by the Crusaders in 1204 and its empire dismembered. In the course of this nefarious bargain, ultimately condemned by the pope, Venice also acquired trade monopolies in the Byzantine capital and throughout the old empire, and control of CRETE and ports in the PELOPONNESUS. Venice was, with GENOA and PISA, a major shipper and supplier to the Latin Crusader states in the East from the 11th to 14th centuries and grew rich carrying spices, cloth, luxury goods, and pilgrims across the Mediterranean. Its pilgrim routes were especially well used and carried thousands between the Levant and Venice every year.

Nominally a republic, Venice took on the forms of a rigid oligarchy much sooner than other major Italian city-states. It was governed through most of the Middle Ages by the Great Council, or assembly of the great merchants. In 1297 membership in the council was made hereditary and restricted to a small number of families. In 1310, after a plot to establish a despotism was destroyed, the Great Council formed the ruling Council of Ten, which became an absolute governing body, eliminating its enemies through secret denunciations and purges. Nevertheless, this oligarchy retained many of the councils, courts, and other institutions of a republic and managed to merge the business interests of its citizens with those of the state. The city itself owned the merchant and war fleets, and its wealthy capitalists formed its administrative and military corps. Among the city's main activities was the maintenance of the Arsenal, the great military depot and shipbuilding center, still in use. It employed thousands of workers and had established a full-blown capitalist enterprise by 1300, setting wages, working hours, and production quotas and establishing a complete specialization of labor and management positions. Venice was so aware of the importance of its control of the seas that the doges annually celebrated a symbolic marriage with the Adriatic.

For many years Genoa was Venice's chief rival, and several naval battles were fought in 1379 and 1380 off the city of CHIOGGIA, at the south end of the Lagoon of Venice. The city's power peaked in the 15th century, controlling over 12 islands in the eastern Mediterranean and annexing CYPRUS in 1489. Its domination of East-West trade made it enormously wealthy. This position began to decline somewhat after 1453, the year in which the OTTOMAN EMPIRE captured Constantinople and cut off much of Venice's trade with the Levant. A half century later the discovery of the New World and the establishment of Atlantic routes to the East began to shift trade from the Mediterranean to the West; nevertheless Venice's trade routes via ALEXANDRIA and the Levant continued to prosper, with occasional interruptions, into the 17th century.

By the late 14th century the mainland around Venice, the *terra firma*, began to come under the city's control and eventually included large areas to the north and west of the city, now in the regions of the VENETO, and Trentino-Alto Adige, and Friuli-Venezia Giulia. These brought the republic into the emerging balance of power politics of the Italian peninsula. Throughout the Renaissance Venice formed or broke alliances with one or more of the major powers, including MILAN, FLORENCE, the PAPAL STATES, and NAPLES. This balance was finally recognized by the Peace of LODI in 1455. In the Italian Wars of 1494 to 1559 this balance came to an end, and Venice was forced to challenge both the HOLY ROMAN EMPIRE and the papacy, which with France, Spain, and England formed the League of Cambrai in 1508. The city-state could not match these new nations, and in 1509 the French defeated Venice at AGNADELLO and occupied much of its territory.

By the 15th century the Venetian nobility had begun to turn from trade and banking and was establishing large agricultural estates on the *terra firma*. These later supported the magnificent building projects of the Veneto, the most famous of which are Palladio's villas around Venice and VICENZA. On Oct. 7, 1571, however, the city reasserted its prestige when its ships led a Christian fleet in a crushing defeat of the Ottoman Empire off LEPANTO, Greece. Nevertheless, the Turks captured Cyprus that year, took Crete in 1669, and despite Venetian conquest of the Peloponnesus in 1699, this too fell to the Turks in 1718.

Despite Venice's commercial and political exhaustion from its long struggle with the Turks, it remained a center of European culture and fashion into the 18th century and was the only republic to survive in Italy. Although Venice tried to stay neutral between AUSTRIA and Napoleonic FRANCE, the Treaty of Campo Formio made by those nations in 1797 gave Istria, Dalmatia, and a good deal of Venetia to Austria; the IONIAN ISLANDS to France; and other Venetian lands to the newly created CISALPINE REPUBLIC. In 1848 a revolt drove out the Austrians, but Austria besieged and captured the city in 1849. Venice became part of the new, united kingdom of Italy in 1866.

Culturally Venice was a major force during the Renaissance and the early modern periods, and as a free republic stayed immune from the pressures of the Roman, Protestant, and national inquisitions and censors. It offered a haven to scholars, writers, scientists, and thinkers of all types. The University of PADUA, ruled by Venice, is famous for the freedom it gave to scientists and thinkers like Galileo. The city itself was the home of such painters as the Bellinis, Giorgione, Titian, Tintoretto, Tiepolo, and Canaletto; of architects like Jacopo Sansovino, Palladio, and the Lombardo family; and of the pioneer printers Nicolas Jenson and Aldo and Paolo Manutius. Its great families included the Dandolo, Contarini, Foscari, and the Tiepolo. Venice was one of the first states to establish a diplomatic service, with representatives permanently stationed in foreign lands; it named two merchants to represent it in London as early as 1496. Today the city faces new perils as it slowly sinks into the Adriatic in the face of official inability to implement plans to save it.

Venice's most famous landmark is the Byzantine basilica of St. Mark, whose symbol of the winged lion and book became Venice's emblem and remains a testimony of its former power from Verona to Crete. Here is also the Piazza of San Marco, with its famous bell tower and medieval Doge's Palace, one of the most perfect urban spaces in the world. Here is also the Bridge of Sighs, where those awaiting execution took their final steps, and the Rialto Bridge over the Grand Canal, erected between 1588 and 1591. Here too are Palladio's masterpieces, the churches of the Redentore and San Giorgio Maggiore; and many palaces, including the Ca' d'Oro and the Ca' Foscari, both on the Grand Canal. The city also boasts numerous museums, churches, and many smaller squares, or *campi*, one of the finest examples of urban planning in the West. The city has been the subject of writers from Shakespeare to Casanova to Thomas Mann and of painters from Bellini to Turner.

Among its famous citizens are Marco Polo, the famous traveler to the court of Kublai Khan in CHINA; the geographer Marino Sanudo; the humanist Pietro Bembo; the church reformer Gasparo Contarini; the explorers John and Sebastian Cabot; writers Paolo Sarpi and Carlo Goldoni; several popes; the composers Giovanni Gabrieli and Antonio Vivaldi; and Lorenzo da Ponte, Mozart's librettist.

VENLO [Venloo] (Netherlands) Commune in Limburg province, on the MEUSE RIVER, 15 mi NNE of Roermond. Chartered in 1343, it joined the HANSEATIC LEAGUE in 1364 and was a medieval fortress and trading center. It suffered severe damage in World War II.

VENLOO. See VENLO.

VENOSA [*ancient:* **Venusia**] (Italy) Town in Potenza province, Basilicata region, 22 mi N of Potenza. Originally a Lucanian settlement, it passed to the Romans in 291 BC after the Samnite War and became an important garrison town, strategically situated on the APPIAN WAY. The poet Horace was born here *c.*65 BC; and the 11th-century Norman soldier of fortune, Robert Guiscard, is buried in the town's abbey. Manfred, the last of the Hohenstaufen kings of Naples and Sicily, was born here in 1232. See also LUCANIA.

VENTA BELGARUM. See WINCHESTER, England.

VENTA ICENORUM. See CAISTOR ST. EDMUNDS.

VENTA SILURUM. See CAERWENT.

VENTIA. See VALENCE.

VENTIMIGLIA [*ancient:* **Albium Intemelium;** *French:* **Vintimille**] (Italy) Town and port on the Ligurian Sea, in Imperia province, Liguria region, 18 mi ENE of Nice. The seat of a county from the 10th century, it later came under GENOA. It is the site of the ruins of the ancient town of Albium Intemelium, which was the capital of the Intemelii and later became a Roman municipium.

VENTNOR (England) Town on the S coast of the ISLE OF WIGHT, 15 mi SSW of Portsmouth. Originally a small fishing village, it became a fashionable health resort during the 19th century. The writer Charles Dickens lived nearby at Bonchurch.

VENTSPILS [*German:* **Vindau, Windau**] (USSR) City and port on the Baltic Sea, in the Latvian SSR, 100 mi WNW of Riga. Occupied by Wends in the 10th century, it grew up around a castle founded in 1290 by the Livonian Order. In the 17th century, under Jacob, duke of KURLAND, it was an important port engaged in

trade with the WEST INDIES and West Africa. It suffered during the Swedish-Polish Wars but again enjoyed considerable prosperity in the 20th century when it was linked by rail to MOSCOW. See also LATVIA.

VENTURA [San Buenaventura] (United States) City and port on the Pacific Ocean, 62 mi WNW of Los Angeles, SW CALIFORNIA. Founded by Father Junípero Serra in 1782, it grew up around a Franciscan mission for Chumash Indians. It is now a center of electronic and missile research.

VENUSIA. See VENOSA.

VERACRUZ [Veracruz Llave] [*former:* **Villa Rica de Vera Cruz**] (Mexico) City and port in Veracruz state, on the Gulf of Mexico, 263 mi E of Mexico City. Hernando Cortez landed near the site of Veracruz in 1519. The first Spanish city in Mexico, it became the chief port for Spanish fleets traveling between Mexico and CADIZ. It suffered frequent pirate attacks and was fortified in the 17th century. In 1821 a fort in the harbor was the site of the last stand by SPAIN in Mexico. Captured by the French in 1838 and 1861, it fell to the UNITED STATES under Gen. Winfield Scott in 1847 during the Mexican War. It was again occupied by the United States between April and November 1914.

VERACRUZ (Mexico) State of E central Mexico, with its capital at JALAPA de Enriquez. The center of pre-Columbian civilizations, it was the home of the Olmecs and various tribes of the Remojadas culture. Hernando Cortez made the first Spanish landing on the coast of Veracruz in 1519 leading to the conquest of the AZTEC EMPIRE. Veracruz became a state in 1824.

VERACRUZ LLAVE. See VERACRUZ.

VERAGUA (Panama) Region in the W part of the Isthmus of Panama. It was discovered and named by Christopher Columbus in 1502. In 1537 Columbus's son Luis was given the title of Duke of Veragua by Charles I of SPAIN, grandson of Ferdinand and Isabella.

VERBANO. See MAGGIORE, LAGO.

VERBANUS LACUS. See MAGGIORE, LAGO.

VERCELLAE. See VERCELLI.

VERCELLI [*ancient:* **Vercellae**] (Italy) Town and capital of Vercelli province, in PIEDMONT region, 39 mi WSW of Milan. Originally the capital of the Libici tribe, it later became a Roman municipium. At the nearby Campi Raudii Hannibal won his first victory on Roman soil in 218 BC during the Second Punic War. In 101 BC the Cimbri were defeated here by Marius and Catullus. An independent republic during the Middle Ages, it came under MILAN in 1335 and passed to SAVOY in 1427. The library of the cathedral contains the 10th-century Anglo-Saxon manuscript, the *Codex Vercellensis*.

VERDE, CAPE [Cape Vert] (Senegal) Peninsula on the W coast of Senegal, extending into the Atlantic Ocean. The most westerly point of the African continent, it was discovered by PORTUGAL in 1445 and became of strategic importance for trade with BRAZIL and Europe. DAKAR, the capital of Senegal, is on the southern coast of the peninsula.

VERDEN [Verden an der Aller] (West Germany) City in Lower Saxony, on the Aller River, 57 mi SW of Hamburg. It became a bishopric c.800. In 1648, as a duchy, it was ceded to SWEDEN. It became part of PRUSSIA in 1866.

VERDEN AN DER ALLER. See VERDEN.

VERDUN [Verdun-sur-Meuse] [*ancient:* **Verodunum**] (France) City in Meuse department, LORRAINE, 40 mi W of Metz. A prosperous center in Roman times, it was the scene of the Treaty of Verdun in 843 AD, which partitioned the empire of Charlemagne. In 1552, together with METZ and TOUL, it was seized from the HOLY ROMAN EMPIRE by Henry II of France. Because of its strategic importance on the route to PARIS from the east, it was fortified by Marshal Vauban during the reign of Louis XIV. By 1871 it was the center of defense against PRUSSIA and later became the site of the longest battle of World War I, when the Germans launched a massive offensive against the city on Feb. 21, 1916. Pressure on Verdun was only relieved when the British attacked along the SOMME RIVER in July 1916. There were more than 700,000 casualties, and the city was almost completely destroyed. It was rebuilt, and today the town and the military cemeteries are a national monument. See also FRANKISH EMPIRE.

VERDUN-SUR-MEUSE. See VERDUN.

VEREENIGING (South Africa) Town in S TRANSVAAL, on the Vaal River, 33 mi S of Johannesburg. The Treaty of Vereeniging, which ended the Boer War and by which the SOUTH AFRICAN REPUBLIC and the ORANGE FREE STATE lost their independence, was negotiated here. The treaty itself was signed in PRETORIA on May 31, 1902. Today the city is one of the main industrial centers of South Africa.

VERGENNES (United States) City on Otter Creek, near Lake Champlain, 21 mi S of Burlington, W VERMONT. During the War of 1812 the U.S. ships that defended LAKE CHAMPLAIN and the border with CANADA were constructed here.

VERIA. See VEROIA.

VERKHNE-UDINSK. See ULAN-UDE.

VERKHOYANSK (USSR) Town in N central Yakutsk ASSR, in Russian SFSR, 385 mi NNE of Yakutsk. Founded in 1638, it was a place of political exile until 1917. It is famous as the coldest place in the inhabited world. A temperature of -90° F (-68° C) was recorded here in 1892.

VERMANDOIS (France) Ancient district of E PICARDY, included in the modern departments of Aisne, Somme, and Oise. The region became an earldom under Charlemagne in the ninth century, and its rulers came to hold immense power. It was annexed by the French crown c.1200 but was ceded to BURGUNDY in 1435. It finally became part of France under Louis XI in 1477.

VERMILIONVILLE. See LAFAYETTE.

VERMONT (United States) The farthest NW of the NEW ENGLAND states, it lies between New Hampshire on the E and New York State on the W. The Connecticut River forms its E boundary. The Green Mountains, running N and S, are its dominant geographical feature.

The French explorer Samuel Sieur de Champlain was the first European to enter the area, journeying south in 1609 with a Huron Indian war party to the lake that bears his name. FRANCE, however, made no settlement until 1666 when Fort Ste. Anne was built on Isle La Motte in LAKE CHAMPLAIN. They later withdrew from this and other settlements, and the region was abandoned by Europeans for many years. In 1724 the British established Fort Dummer on the site of BRATTLEBORO to protect settlers to the south against the Indians.

After Benning Wentworth became the royal governor of NEW HAMPSHIRE in 1741, he claimed that the colony's land ran west to within 20 miles of the HUDSON RIVER. NEW YORK, however, claimed its territory continued east to the Connecticut River. Thus both claimed Vermont. Wentworth made the New Hampshire Grants, the first in 1749 being to a group for a township called Bennington in his honor. The village of BENNINGTON was founded in 1761. In 1764 the British government ruled in favor of New York, but a little later the Green Mountain Boys organized, and in 1777—to the accompaniment of some violence—they declared independence. Their leader was Ethan Allen. After abortive negotiations with CANADA about a possible union, most Vermonters supported the 13 colonies in the American Revolution. The constitution of free Vermont was the first in America to provide for universal male suffrage. It was also in 1777 that a Dr. Thomas Young suggested the name "Vermont," taking over and modifying a French term for the area. The only engagement of the Revolution fought in Vermont took place near Bennington in August, 1777, when the Green Mountain Boys and others defeated a British force taking part in the SARATOGA Campaign.

Vermont remained independent until New York gave up its claim in 1790. The next year Vermont was admitted to the Union as the 14th state, the first after the original 13. Population increased, and the state prospered. Vermonters disliked the Embargo Act of 1807 and the War of 1812 because they hindered trade with Canada. There was considerable smuggling. The state also opposed the Mexican War because it was seen as benefiting the slave interests, and during the Civil War no state was stronger in support of the Union. In 1864 a group of Confederates, who had entered neutral Canada, held up two banks in ST. ALBANS, in northwestern Vermont. Then in 1870 a group of Fenians, fighting for the independence of IRELAND, sought to aid their cause by using Vermont as a base from which to invade Canada.

Vermont began as an agricultural state, but most of its farm products could not compete with those of the American West when it was opened to agriculture, and population declined. Vermonters took to sheep raising and then to dairy farming, which was more profitable. The state was strongly Republican for many years, being one of only two states (MAINE was the other) to vote Republican in the 1936 presidential election. In the late 1950's and 1960's there was a turn toward the Democratic Party, but the people of the state remain inherently conservative. In recent years Vermont has become not only a popular vacation area but also has attracted both retired and younger people who seek to lead a more "natural" life. MONTPELIER has been the capital since 1805; BURLINGTON is the largest city; others are BARRE and RUTLAND.

VERNEUIL (France) Town in Eure department, 25 mi SW of Evreux. In 1424, during the Hundred Years War, the English under the duke of Bedford defeated the French and the Scots here. Its castle has a cylindrical keep built in 1120 by Henry I of England.

VERNOLENINSK. See NIKOLAYEV.

VERNON (France) Town in Eure department, on the SEINE RIVER, 17 mi ENE of Evreux. Joined to the French crown under Philip Augustus in 1198, it was held by the English from 1419 to 1449. The first estates of NORMANDY were held here in 1452.

VERNYI. See ALMA-ATA.

VERODUNUM. See VERDUN.

VEROIA [Veria, Verria, Verroia] [*ancient:* **Berea, Beroea**] [*Turkish:* **Karaferieh**] (Greece) Town, capital of Imathiá department, MACEDONIA, 40 mi WSW of Thessaloníki. Known as early as the fifth century BC, it was the first city of Macedonia to submit to ROME after the Battle of Pydna in 168 BC. It is mentioned in Acts 17:10 as a place where Paul and Silas preached. The city was one of the two capitals of Macedonia under the Emperor Diocletian in the fourth century. It was taken by the Bulgars in the 10th century and by the Serbs in the 14th. The town was a fortress under the OTTOMAN EMPIRE.

VERONA (Italy) City and capital of Verona province, VENETO region, 92 mi E of Milan, on the Adige River. Strategically located on the route to and from central Europe through the BRENNER PASS, it has always been of commercial and military importance. It was originally inhabited by the Euganeans. Captured by ROME in 89 BC, it later became the chief residence of Theodoric the Goth, who defeated Odoacer here in 489 AD. It became an independent republic in 1104 and in 1164 joined the Veronese League, which fought against Frederick I, Barbarossa, Holy Roman emperor. It reached the height of its power in the 14th century when it was ruled by the Ghibelline della Scala family, which was called in to end party strife. Ruled by VENICE from 1405 to 1796, it passed back and forth between the rule of AUSTRIA and FRANCE until 1814, when it was given to Austria. It became part of the kingdom of Italy in 1866. During World War II it was damaged by Allied bombs. It was a great center of the Italian Renaissance, producing the architects Giocondo and Sanmichele and the artists Pisanello and Paolo Veronese. It has a large Roman amphitheater. The Roman poet Catullus (87–47 BC) and the architect Vitruvius (first century BC) were born here. Dante spent some of his exile from FLORENCE here and is commemorated by a statue in the Piazza dei Signori, a fine assemblage of Northern Italian Romanesque and Gothic buildings. Other historic sites include the Torre dei Lamberti, the Piazza delle Erbe on the outline of the old Roman forum, the 12th-century Palazzo della Ragione, the 12th-century Duomo and the 14th-century castle. Also here are the tombs of the della Scala and the 13th-century House of Juliet, whose legendary affair with Romeo took place here.

VERRIA. See VEROIA.

VERROIA. See VEROIA.

VERSAILLES (France) City and capital of Yvelines department, 11 mi WSW of PARIS. Originally the site of a hunting lodge for French kings, it is famous for the palace built here in the 17th century by Louis Le Vau and Jules Mansart for Louis XIV. As the residence of the royal court its elaborate and expensive ceremonial bankrupted the nobility and tied them to the crown. It was the capital of France from 1682 to 1789. Versailles itself and its opulence were a symbol of the hated *Ancien Régime.* Here in May 1789 the French Estates-General met as summoned by the king but soon reconstituted themselves into The National Assembly. Shut out by the king, in June the assembly moved to the tennis court and swore the Tennis Court Oath to draft a constitution, thus starting the French Revolution. After the Franco-Prussian War, Versailles was the scene of the proclamation of the GERMAN EMPIRE and of the Third French Republic in 1871. It has been the scene of the signing of several important treaties, including the Treaty of Versailles of 1919 that ended World War I and set up the League of Nations. It is also important as the site of two treaties, between the United States and France, and France and Great Britain, signed in 1782 and 1783, both recognizing U.S. independence.

VERSECZ. See VRŠAC.

VERULAMIUM [*modern:* **Saint Albans**] (England) Ancient city of Roman Britain, now ST. ALBANS, 23 mi NNW of London, in the modern county of Hertfordshire. Originally the capital of the Catuvellauni, it was made a municipium following the Roman conquest of Britain. It was destroyed by Queen Boudicca (Boadicea) *c.*60 AD but prospered again under the Roman Governor Agricola. Verulamium was renamed after a Roman soldier, St. Alban, who was martyred here *c.*305 AD. There are extensive Roman remains.

VERVINS (France) Town in Aisne department, 32 mi NE of Laon. The Treaty of Vervins, signed here on May 2, 1598 by Philip II of SPAIN and Henry IV of France, ended the French Wars of Religion of 1562 to 1592. Philip's agreement to withdraw his troops from France deprived the Catholic League of Spanish support.

VESALI. See VAISALI.

VESCERA. See BISKRA.

VESONTIO. See BESANÇON.

VESOUL [*ancient:* **Vesulium, Vesulum**] (France) Town and capital of Haute-Saône department, 58 mi ENE of Dijon. Of ancient origin, it was later the capital of the bailiwick of Amont. Overrun by Germans in 1369, it was ravaged by plague in 1586. In 1678 it became part of France. It was named capital of the department in 1790.

The fishing village of Vestmannaeyjar on an island off Iceland's coast. Quite incredibly, the town was raided and burned in 1627 by Algerian pirates, who enslaved 250 people.

VESTERBYGD (Greenland) One of two ancient Norse settlements on the SW coast of Greenland made in the 11th century. The other was Osterbygd. They were extinct by the early 15th century, but archeological traces remain.

VESTMANNAEYJAR (Iceland) Town on Heimaey Island in the Westman Islands off the S coast. One of the oldest settlements in Iceland, it was raided throughout the 15th century by the English and was attacked by Algerian pirates in 1627. It suffered from nearby volcanic eruptions in 1963 and 1973.

VESTSPITSBERGEN. See SPITSBERGEN.

VESULIUM. See VESOUL.

VESULUM. See VESOUL.

VESUNA. See PÉRIGUEUX.

VESUVIO. See VESUVIUS.

VESUVIUS [*Italian:* **Vesuvio**] (Italy) Volcano in Napoli province, CAMPANIA region, 8 mi ESE of NAPLES, near the Bay of Naples. The only active volcano on the mainland of Europe, its most famous eruption was on Aug. 24/25, 79 AD, when POMPEII, HERCULANEUM and STABIAE were buried under mud and ashes. Since then there have been almost 50 eruptions, the most recent in 1944.

VETULONIA [*Etruscan:* **Vatlna, Vatluna**] (Italy) Ancient city of ETRURIA, in modern Grosseto province, Tuscany region, 10 mi NW of Grosseto. Occupied in the Late Bronze Age, the city was a member of the Etruscan League but was unimportant in Roman times. Many Villanovan and Etruscan tombs have been excavated in the area.

VEURNE [*French:* **Furnes**] (Belgium) Municipality in West Flanders province, 6 mi WSW of Nieuport. Founded by Baldwin I of FLANDERS *c.*870, it became an important town of the SPANISH NETHERLANDS and was often besieged during the 17th century. In World War I it was the chief city of unoccupied Belgium.

VEVEY [*ancient:* **Vibiscum, Viviscus;** *German:* **Vivis**] (Switzerland) Town in VAUD canton, on LAKE GENEVA, 11 mi ESE of Lausanne. Originally a Roman settlement, it was a prosperous trading center during the Middle Ages and has many fine medieval buildings.

VEXIN (France) Ancient district in the N between the Seine and Oise rivers. The region was divided in 911 AD between Rollo of NORMANDY and the royal domain of France by the Treaty of Saint-Clair-sur-Epte. The whole area passed under the French crown in 1196 when Richard I, the Lion-Hearted, of ENGLAND ceded the northern section to Philip Augustus in 1196.

VEXIO. See VÄXJÖ.

VÉZELAY (France) Village in Yonne department, 10 mi WSW of Avallon. It is the site of a famous Benedictine abbey built here in the ninth century, which became an important pilgrimage center. The Second Crusade was preached here in 1146 by St. Bernard. The abbey declined after the 13th century. The 17th-century military architect Marshal Vauban is buried nearby. The 12th-century abbey church of Sainte-Madeleine here is a monument of Romanesque art and architecture. Gislebertus, the sculptor of many of the works here, is one of the earliest identified European artists.

VIA AEMILIA. See AEMILIAN WAY.

VIA APPIA. See APPIAN WAY.

VIA AURELIA. See AURELIAN WAY.

VIA CASSIA. See CASSIAN WAY.

VIADUA. See ODER RIVER.

VIA EGNATIA. See EGNATIAN WAY.

VIA FLAMINIA. See FLAMINIAN WAY.

VIA LATINA. See LATIN WAY.

VIANA DO CASTELO [*ancient:* **Velobriga**] (Portugal) Town, port, and capital of Viana do Castelo district, Minho province, near the Atlantic Ocean, N of Oporto. Dating from Roman times, it was an important port during the Middle Ages and traded with VENICE and GENOA. Much later it became a base for Atlantic codfishing fleets.

VIA OSTIENSIS. See OSTIAN WAY.

VIAPORI. See SUOMENLINNA.

VIAREGGIO (Italy) Town in Lucca province, TUSCANY region, on the Ligurian Sea, 13 mi WNW of Lucca. It is a modern resort town almost exclusively devoted to tourism. The English poet Percy Bysshe Shelley was cremated here in 1822 after his death by drowning near LA SPEZIA. The Italian operatic composer, Giacomo Puccini, is buried here.

VIA SALARIA. See SALARIAN WAY.

VIATKA. See KIROV.

VIA VALERIA. See VALERIAN WAY.

VIBISCUM. See VEVEY.

VIBORG (Denmark) City and capital of Viborg county, in N central JUTLAND, 37 mi NW of Århus. Originally a pagan religious center, it later became an early capital of Jutland and in 1065 an episcopal see. The first Danish coins were struck here in the 11th century. The largest town in Jutland from the 15th to 17th centuries, it declined with the growing importance of COPENHAGEN.

VIBORG, USSR. See VYBORG.

VIBO VALENTIA [*ancient:* **Hipponium;** *former:* **Monteleone di Calabria**] (Italy) Town in Catanzaro province, CALABRIA region, near the Tyrrhenian Sea, 30 mi SW of Catanzaro. A Greek colony founded by ancient Locri nearby, it was taken by Carthage in 379 BC and was occupied by the Bruttii in 356 BC. Later it was a flourishing Roman colony. It was destroyed by the Arabs in the ninth century AD. The remains of the ancient city walls represent the finest early Greek architecture in Calabria. There is a castle built by Frederick II.

VICENTIA. See VICENZA.

VICENZA [*ancient:* **Vicentia, Vicetia**] (Italy) City and capital of Vicenza province, 40 mi W of Venice, in Veneto region. Originally a Gallic settlement, it was later a Roman city and was destroyed during the barbarian invasions. In 1164 it joined the Veronese League against Frederick I Barbarossa. It was ruled by the della Scala of Verona from 1314 to 1404, when it was annexed by VENICE. The city passed to AUSTRIA in 1813 and was united to the kingdom of Italy in 1866. The famous architect, Andrea Palladio, was born here in 1508, and the city and its environs are the site of many of his most important buildings.

VICETIA. See VICENZA.

VICHEGDA. See VYCHEGDA RIVER.

VICHY [*ancient:* **Vicus Calidus**] (France) Town in Allier department, on the Allier River, in the AUVERGNE, 227 mi SSE of Paris. Dating from Roman times, it became famous as a spa in the 17th century and was frequently visited by the royal families of Europe. During World War II, after the Franco-German armistice of 1940, it was the seat of the collaborationist government of Marshal Henri-Philippe Pétain. Toward the end of the war the Vichy government withdrew to SIGMARINGEN in Germany where it finally collapsed in 1945.

VICKSBURG (United States) City and port on the MISSISSIPPI RIVER, 140 mi N of New Orleans, W MISSISSIPPI. It was the site of a French fort in 1718, and of the Spanish Fort Nogales in 1791. Part of the United States by 1798, it was incorporated in 1825. It became an important shipping point and was the commercial center of a cotton-growing region. During the Civil War it was a vital Confederate stronghold and was the major objective of Union forces during Grant's Vicksburg campaign. It finally fell on July 4, 1863, thus leaving the Mississippi River open to the Union and splitting the Confederacy in two.

VICTORIA, Brazil. See VITÓRIA.

VICTORIA [*former:* **Fort Camosun, Fort Victoria**] (Canada) City and capital of BRITISH COLUMBIA, on SE VANCOUVER ISLAND, 70 mi S of Vancouver. One of the oldest settlements of British Columbia, it was founded in 1843 as a fur-trading headquarters and became capital of the colony of Vancouver Island in 1851. It became the capital of British Columbia in 1871 and was the province's commercial center until eclipsed by the rise of Vancouver c.1900.

VICTORIA (United States) City in S TEXAS, on the Guadalupe River, 100 mi SE of San Antonio. Founded in 1824, it played an active part in the Texas Revolution and was incorporated as a city in the REPUBLIC OF TEXAS in 1839. Today it is an important oil and gas center.

VICTORIACUM. See VITORIA, Spain.

VICTORIA FALLS [*Zambian:* **Mosi-Oa-Tunya;** *translated:* **The Smoke That Thunders**] (Zambia, Zimbabwe) Waterfall on the ZAMBESI RIVER, near LIVINGSTONE, now Maramba, on the border of Zimbabwe and Zambia. Approximately one mile wide and 400 ft high, this waterfall is more remarkable than NIAGARA FALLS. It was first seen by a European in November 1855 by the Scottish explorer David Livingstone and became a popular tourist site when it was joined to BULAWAYO by railway in 1905.

VICTORIA, LAKE [**Victoria Nyanza**] [*Arabic:* **Ukerewe**] (Kenya, Tanzania, Uganda) Lake of E central Africa, on the borders of Uganda, Tanzania, and Kenya. The largest lake in Africa, it is also the second-largest freshwater lake in the world. Discovered by J.H. Speke in 1858, it was thoroughly explored in 1875 by H. M. Stanley and is accepted as the main source of the NILE RIVER. The completion of the Owen Falls Dam in 1954 transformed the lake into a reservoir and provided for the generation of electricity for the surrounding area.

VICTORIA LAND [**South Victoria Land**] (Antarctica) Region of E Antarctica, S of New Zealand, on the Ross Sea. Discovered by Sir James Clark Ross's expedition of 1839 to 1843, the area was more fully explored by the Douglas Mawson expedition of 1911 to 1914.

VICTORIA NYANZA. See VICTORIA, LAKE.

VICTORIA STATE (Australia) State of SE Australia, on the Indian Ocean, with its capital at MELBOURNE. Settled originally by sheep ranchers from TASMANIA in the 1830's, it became part of NEW SOUTH WALES in 1836. In 1851 it was made a separate British colony, and its population expanded rapidly after the discovery of gold around BALLARAT. It became a state of the Commonwealth of Australia in 1901.

VICUS CALIDUS. See VICHY.

VICUS ELBII. See VITERBO.

VICUS JULII. See AIRE.

VIDIN [**Bdin**] [*ancient:* **Bononia, Dunonia**] (Bulgaria) City, port, and capital of Vidin province, on the DANUBE RIVER, 65 mi NW of Vratsa. Built on the site of a Celtic settlement of the third century BC, it became the site of the large Roman fortress of Bononia in the first century AD. It was the capital of an independent kingdom under Ivan Sratsimir in the 14th century but was captured by the Turks in 1396. It was the capital of an autonomous district under Pasha Osman Pazvantoğlu from 1794 to 1807.

VIDISA. See BHILSA.

VIDISHA. See BHILSA.

VIENNA [*ancient:* **Vindobona;** *German:* **Wien**] (Austria) Capital city of the Republic of Austria, it is situated near the border with Hungary, on the DANUBE RIVER. Formerly a capital of the HOLY ROMAN EMPIRE and of the AUSTRO-HUNGARIAN EMPIRE, it has a rich cultural tradition. Its situation near the center of Europe gives it a distinctly cosmopolitan atmosphere, and its population includes Germans, Slavs, Italians, and Hungarians, reminding the visitor of the city's imperial past.

Originally a Celtic settlement, Vienna became the important Roman military settlement of Vindobona and was the home of the emperor Marcus Aurelius in the second century AD. With the collapse of the ROMAN EMPIRE in the late fourth century, Vienna was overrun by barbarian invaders and was destroyed by Attila in the fifth century.

By 800 Vienna was again important as a border fortress of the Ostmark of the FRANKISH EMPIRE, but it was occupied by the Magyars in 907, then passed to the Babenbergs in 976. In 1156 Henry Jasomirgott made Vienna capital of the duchy of Austria, and the city started to develop as a commercial center. It was occupied by Ottocar II of BOHEMIA from 1251 to 1276, and in 1282 it became the chief residence of the house of Hapsburg. Made capital of the Holy Roman Empire in 1438, it was occupied by Matthias Corvinus of HUNGARY from 1485 to 1490, during which period the capital of Austria was moved to WIENER NEUSTADT.

Vienna was unsuccessfully besieged by the Turks in 1529 and in 1683, and the population was ravaged by plague in 1679. During the 18th century Vienna emerged as one of the great cultural centers of Europe. Much building was carried out, and the city was the home of Mozart, Beethoven, Haydn, and Schubert.

During the Napoleonic Wars Vienna was occupied by the French in 1805 and 1809, and between 1814 and 1815 it was the scene of the Congress of Vienna, which reorganized postwar Europe. Vienna was one of the centers of the 1848 uprisings. The liberal rebellion in the city was only suppressed by military force under

An early view of Victoria on Vancouver Island, capital of British Columbia. Named after Great Britain's famous queen in 1852, it is still very British in appearance and feeling.

Prince Alfred Windischgrätz. Toward the end of the 19th century Vienna's intellectual status was again enhanced by the work of Sigmund Freud, Gustav Mahler, Johannes Brahms, and Richard Strauss.

After the defeat of the Austro-Hungarian Empire and Germany in World War I the economic life of the city declined as Vienna was cut off politically from the old territories of the empire. Despite this, Vienna was the first city in the world to initiate a housing program for workers. The Nazi annexation of Austria in 1938 was signaled by Hitler's entry into Vienna, and during World War II a large portion of the city's Jewish population was exterminated. Vienna was liberated by the Russians in 1945 and remained under Allied control until 1955. Now rebuilt after the ravages of the war, the city remains a major center of international diplomacy.

VIENNA, France. See VIENNE.

VIENNE (France) Department of W central France, in POITOU; its capital is POITIERS. Strategically situated on the SW approaches to PARIS, it has been the scene of many battles in French history. In 732 Charles Martel defeated the Saracens at the first Battle of Poitiers between Poitiers and TOURS, and in 1356 the English under Edward the Black Prince defeated the French in the second Battle of Poitiers. During the Hundred Years War the region changed hands many times. It was annexed to the French crown after the war.

VIENNE [*ancient:* **Vienna**] (France) Town in Isère department, on the RHÔNE RIVER, 17 mi S of Lyons. Originally the capital of the Celtic Allobroges tribe, it fell to the Romans in 121 BC and grew to be one of the chief cities of Roman GAUL under Augustus and Tiberius. It was the capital of BURGUNDY from 413 to 534 and from 879 to 933, becoming part of the HOLY ROMAN EMPIRE in 882. A council held here abolished the Knights Templars in 1312. One of the earliest archiepiscopal sees, it suffered severely during the Wars of Religion and never fully recovered.

VIENNENSIS PRIMA. See VALENCE.

VIENTIANE (Laos) City and administrative capital of Laos, 130 mi SE of Luang Prabang, on the MEKONG RIVER. The capital of the kingdom of Vientiane from 1707, it declined after falling to SIAM in 1827. It became capital of the French protectorate of Laos in 1899 and was governed by the French until 1954.

VIERWALDSTÄTTER SEE. See LUCERNE, LAKE.

VIETNAM, SOCIALIST REPUBLIC OF [Viet Nam] Nation of SE Asia. A narrow, elongated midsection links the N and S parts of this country that extends for 1,000 miles down the E coast of INDOCHINA. The geographical spread of the country has led to recurring power struggles between its northern and southern regions.

Vietnamese history is legendary before 208 BC, when a renegade Chinese general founded the kingdom of Nam Viet, covering much of south China and as far south as present DA NANG. In 111 BC CHINA reconquered Nam Viet and renamed it Giao Chi and later

Giao Chau. In the south, FUNAN and CHAMPA were founded in the first and second centuries AD. Funan was conquered by the Khmers from Cambodia, now KAMPUCHEA, in the eighth century. Champa retained its independence but constantly clashed with its northern neighbor, Vietnam.

From 111 BC to 939 AD Vietnam, then the northern part of the current nation, was ruled by China. The downfall of the powerful T'ang dynasty of China in 907 led to the end of Chinese rule. The Chinese were decisively defeated in 939, and an independent state was formed. The country was unstable until the accession of the Ly dynasty from 1004 to 1225. The Ly rulers called the country Dai Viet, rejecting the Chinese name of ANNAM, and set up a centralized agricultural state. Dai Viet prospered, but constant attacks by Champa and Cambodia harassed the country. The Tran dynasty, from 1225 to 1400, continued the policies of the Ly and preserved the nation's sovereignty in the face of continued Champa pressure and a renewed Chinese threat from Kublai Khan. In 1257, 1284, and 1287 enormous invasions by the MONGOL EMPIRE were repulsed.

The Tran dynasty was ousted in 1400, and rule passed to a new dynasty, the Le. Vietnam prospered, and a growing population made territorial expansion desirable. Champa was conquered and absorbed in 1471, and the MEKONG RIVER delta region was wrested from the declining Cambodian Khmers by 1757, stretching Vietnam's length to 1,000 miles. During this time the country twice underwent civil wars, pitting rulers of the south and north against each other, and Vietnam was effectively divided until a civil war lasting from 1772 to 1802 reunited the country under Emperor Gia Long. Military assistance from FRANCE was instrumental in Gia Long's assumption of power, and he retained many French advisers in his court. His successor was violently anti-Western and persecuted Christian missionaries and their converts, killing several and setting the stage for French military intervention. In 1857, Napoleon III decided that the time was right for Vietnam's conquest. After initial reverses, the French army and fleet overcame resistance, and by 1867 France was the undisputed master of the southern part of the country, which they called COCHIN CHINA; they referred to the center and north as Annam. Attempts to conquer Annam in 1873 failed, and it took ten years to mount a successful invasion. After the bombardment of HUE in 1883, TONKIN and Annam became French colonial possessions. In 1887 Vietnam was included with Cambodia in France's Indochinese Union.

The early years of French rule in Vietnam were marked by rebellion, but with the arrival of governor-general Paul Douner in 1897 firm control was established, and what became known as French Indochina was run with the sole aim of profitable exploitation. Nationalist sentiment remained strong in Vietnam, and consistent though poorly organized acts of resistance and terror harried the French. In 1930 the Indochinese Communist Party took the forefront of resistance under the leadership of Ho Chi Minh. During World War II the VICHY French ran Vietnam as a Japanese possession, but Ho Chi Minh formed an effective fighting opposition known as the Viet Minh. After the surrender of JAPAN, Ho proclaimed Vietnamese independence. The French rejected this and recaptured the south. The First Indochinese War, from 1946 to 1954, lasted until the French were beaten at DIEN BIEN PHU and agreed, in a conference at GENEVA, to the temporary partition of the country at the 17th parallel into a communist north and anticommunist south. With aid from the UNITED STATES South Vietnam built up a huge military and police apparatus to cope with continuing communist pressure. Starting in 1965, 3,500 U.S. troops entered into direct combat against the communists. By 1968, more than 510,000 U.S. soldiers were fighting against North Vietnam and the guerrilla Vietcong. Tremendous bombing and devastation against both military and civilian targets by the United States were fruitless and met with increased and eventually successful opposition from the U.S. public. From 1970 to 1973 negotiations brought about the withdrawal of all U.S. troops. In 1975 the South Vietnamese government in SAIGON fell, and the country became reunified under communist rule. Since then the country has been attempting a slow reconstruction and has continued to meet with hostility in China, the United States, and southeast Asia, especially since its military intervention in KAMPUCHEA in 1978, which continues with the aid of the USSR, a long ally of communist Vietnam.

VIGEVANO (Italy) Town in Pavia province, LOMBARDY region, on the Ticino River, 18 mi NW of Pavia. An old silk-manufacturing town, it was the site of a hunting villa of the Sforza family of MILAN during the Renaissance. It has a 16th-century cathedral.

VIGO (Spain) City and port on an inlet of the Atlantic Ocean, in Pontevedra province, GALICIA, 100 mi N of Oporto. Its fine natural harbor was attacked by Sir Francis Drake in 1585 and 1589. A Franco-Spanish fleet carrying gold from the New World was destroyed by the British and Dutch in 1702 in the Bay of Vigo. Vigo was captured by the British in 1719. For many years it was a fortress guarding the coast, and it remains an important shipping port.

VIIPURI. See VYBORG.

VIJAYANAGARA [*modern:* **Hampi**] (India) Ancient city on the Tungabhadra River, 30 mi WNW of Bellary, SW Andhra Pradesh. Established in 1336, it was the capital of the Hindu empire of Vijayanagara from the 14th century until 1565, when it was sacked and the empire destroyed following the Muslims' victory over the Hindus at TALIKOTA. At its peak, under Krishnadeva Raya from 1509 to 1529, it was a vast and flourishing city that traded with many European and Asian countries. Extensive ruins can be seen today on the site of the modern town of Hampi.

VIJAYAPURA. See BIJAPUR.

VIJAYAWADA [*former:* **Bezwada**] (India) City in Andhra Pradesh, near the Krishna River delta, 150 mi ESE of Hyderabad. An ancient religious center, it has Dravidian cave temples of the seventh century AD. Cuttings in hills nearby are thought to mark the site of a Buddhist monastery.

VIKEN. See BOHUSLAN.

VIKRAMAPURA. See DACCA.

VILA DO CONDE (Portugal) Town in Pôrto district, 16 mi NW of Oporto, on the Rio Ave. Dating from Roman times, it was chartered by King Manuel I in 1500 and was an important Atlantic port throughout the 15th and 16th centuries.

VILA RICA. See OURO PRÊTO.

VILCACONGA (Peru) Mountain pass and battle site in the Cordillera Oriental range of the Andes Mts, in S Peru, approx. 60 mi W of Cuzco. Here Hernando de Soto, leading a detachment of 60 of Francisco Pizarro's Spanish cavalry toward CUZCO was ambushed by Peruvian Indians in late October 1533, during the conquest of the INCA EMPIRE. The first day of the battle was a draw, but during the night Diego de Almagro, another of Pizarro's officers, arrived with reinforcements, and the next morning the Indians withdrew.

VILJANDI [**Vilyandi, Wiljandi**] [*German:* **Fellin**] (USSR) Town in S ESTONIAN SSR, approx. 42 mi E of Pärnu. One of the oldest towns in Estonia, it was a member of the HANSEATIC LEAGUE. It was founded in the 13th century by the Livonian Knights, who conquered the region and continued to threaten LITHUANIA and NOVGOROD into the 14th century. With the dissolution of the Livonian Knights the town passed to POLAND in 1561 and to SWEDEN in 1629. RUSSIA captured it in 1710. In 1920 it was made part of independent Estonia, until the country fell to the USSR in 1940. The ruined castle of a Livonian grand master survives.

VILLA AMERICANA. See AMERICANA.

VILLA ARIA. See MARZABOTTO.

VILLACH [*Slovenian:* **Beljak**] (Austria) City in CARINTHIA, on the Drava River, 22 mi W of Klagenfurt. An important Roman settlement, it was part of the bishopric of BAMBERG from 1007 to 1759, when it passed to Austria. It was an important trading center during the Middle Ages.

VILLA CLARA. See SANTA CLARA, Cuba.

VILLA DE LA VEGA. See SPANISH TOWN.

VILLA DE SAN FRANCISCO DE QUITO. See QUITO.

VILLA HERMOSA DE LA ASUNCIÓN. See AREQUIPA.

VILLA NUEVA. See SAN JOSÉ, Costa Rica.

VILLA REAL. See CIUDAD REAL.

VILLA RICA DE VERA CRUZ. See VERACRUZ.

VILLARROBLEDO (Spain) City in Albacete province, 42 mi WNW of Albacete. Founded in the 13th century, it was the site of a battle during the First Carlist War, on Sept. 20, 1836, in which the troops of Queen Christina defeated Carlists under Miguel Gómez.

VILLA SANJURJO. See AL-HOCEIMA.

VILLA SCAFHUSUN. See SCHAFFHAUSEN.

VILLEFRANCHE. See VILLEFRANCHE-SUR-SAÔNE.

VILLEFRANCHE-DE-ROUERGUE (France) Town in Aveyron department, 26 mi W of Rodez. Founded c.1250 by Alphonse of TOULOUSE, it flourished during the early 14th century but fell to the English under Edward the Black Prince during the Hundred Years War. It was later the first town in GUIENNE to rise against the English.

VILLEFRANCHE-SUR-SAÔNE [Villefranche] (France) Town in Rhône department, on the Morgon River, 21 mi NW of Lyons. Founded in 1212 by Guichard IV, count of Beaujeu, it became the capital of BEAUJOLAIS in the 14th century and was annexed to the French crown in 1531. It is situated in what is now one of the great wine-growing areas of France.

VILLE-MARIE DE MONTRÉAL. See MONTREAL.

VILLENA (Spain) City in Alicante province, 26 mi NW of Alicante. Dating from Roman times, it was included in the Moorish kingdom of VALENCIA and was captured by Christian forces in the 13th century.

VILLERS-COTTERÊTS (France) Town in Aisne department, 14 mi SW of Soissons. A nearby forest was the scene of the opening action of a large Allied offensive against the Germans that began on July 18, 1918 during World War I. The town was the birthplace in 1802 of Alexandre Dumas *père*, French novelist and playwright.

VILLINGEN (West Germany) City in Baden-Württemberg, on the edge of the BLACK FOREST, 49 mi E of Freiburg. It was granted market rights in 999 by Otto III. Its center was laid out in 1120 and still stands today.

VILLMANSTRAND. See LAPPEENRANTA.

VILNA. See VILNIUS.

VILNIUS [*German:* **Wilna**; *Polish:* **Wilno**; *Russian:* **Vilna, Vilno**] (USSR) City and capital of the Lithuanian SSR, on the Neris River, 240 mi NE of Warsaw. Situated between Eastern and Western Europe, it bears the characteristics of many cultures and religions. Founded in the 10th century, it became the capital of LITHUANIA in 1323 but was destroyed by the Teutonic Knights in 1377. From the 16th to the 18th century the city suffered many misfortunes including plagues, fires, and occupation by foreign powers. In 1795 it became part of RUSSIA after the Partition of POLAND. It again fell into Polish hands from 1920 to 1939. The city's large Jewish population, which had made it a leading Jewish center of eastern Europe since the 16th century, was completely exterminated during the German occupation of World War II.

VILNO. See VILNIUS.

VILYANDI. See VILJANDI.

VIMINAL HILL. See ROME, SEVEN HILLS.

VIMY RIDGE (France) Ridge in Pas-de-Calais department, NE of Arras. During World War I the ridge was a major German defensive position. Its capture by Canadians from April 9 to 12, 1917 safeguarded ARRAS and AMIENS during the German offensive of March 1918.

VINCENNES (France) Suburb E of PARIS, in Val-de-Marne department. A royal residence since the 12th century, it is the site of a famous 14th-century château in which Henry V of England died in 1422. In the 17th and 18th centuries the château was a state prison that held Henry of Navarre, the Grand Condé, and the duke of Beaufort. The conservative orator, the Comte de Mirabeau, was held here during the French Revolution.

VINCENNES (United States) City in SW INDIANA, on the Wabash River, 57 mi S of Terre Haute. The oldest town in Indiana, it was settled in 1702 and became the most important center of the Northwest Frontier. It was ceded by the French to the British in 1763 but remained virtually self-governing until the American Revolution. From 1800 to 1813 it was the capital of Indiana Territory.

VINDAU. See VENTSPILS.

VINDELICIA [Raetia Secunda] (West Germany) Ancient province of the ROMAN EMPIRE, comprising the modern West German states of Bavaria and Baden-Württemberg, S of the DANUBE RIVER. Originally inhabited by the Vindelici, the region was conquered by ROME in 15 BC and was administered with RAETIA. See also AUGSBURG.

VINDOCINUM. See VENDÔME.

VINDONISSA. See WINDISCH.

VINEGAR HILL (Irish Republic) Hill in County Wexford, E of Enniscorthy. Irish rebels, the United Irishmen, were defeated here by Gen. Lake on June 21, 1798, resulting in the Act of Union between IRELAND and GREAT BRITAIN that created the United Kingdom.

VINELAND. See VINLAND.

VINH CAM RANH. See CAMRANH BAY.

VINLAND [Vineland, Wineland] (Canada, United States) Coastal area of North America; its exact location is believed by experts to be somewhere between VIRGINIA, E United States, and NEWFOUNDLAND, E Canada. This coastal region was visited c.1000 AD by the Norse explorer, Leif Ericsson, who discovered a fertile land where grapes grew. The account of the landing in the Norse *Vineland Saga* is vague, but if, as is believed, this land was North America, it is Ericsson rather than Columbus who should be credited with the discovery of the New World. The name is due to many wild grape vines, still present in the region.

VINNITSA (USSR) City on the Southern Bug River, 130 mi SW of Kiev, in the UKRAINE. Founded in the 14th century, it passed to POLAND in 1569 and became part of RUSSIA in 1793 after the second partition of Poland. During World War II it was under German occupation from 1941 to 1944.

VINOVIA. See BINCHESTER.

VINTIMILLE. See VENTIMIGLIA.

VIONVILLE. See MARS-LA-TOUR.

VIRDEN (United States) City in SW central ILLINOIS, 23 mi SSW of Springfield. Laid out in 1852, it was the scene of a miners' riot on Oct. 12, 1898 in which at least 10 people were killed. The incident helped awareness, and improvement, of miners' conditions.

VIRE (France) Town in Calvados department, on the VIRE RIVER, 32 mi SW of Caen. It grew up around a castle built by Henry I of ENGLAND during the 12th century and became an important stronghold. The nearby valley of Vau-de-Vire was the home of Oliver Basselin, whose 15th-century drinking songs gave rise to the term "vaudeville." During World War II the town was occupied by the Allies in July 1944 after the landings in NORMANDY.

VIRE RIVER (France) River of the NW; it flows through VIRE and SAINT-LÔ to the Bay of the SEINE RIVER near Isigny, in NORMANDY. During the Allied invasion of Normandy in World War II in June 1944, the river's estuary marked the dividing line between the OMAHA BEACH and UTAH BEACH landing sites.

VIRGILIO [*ancient:* **Andes,** *former:* **Pietola**] (Italy) Town in Mantova province, LOMBARDY region, 3 mi S of Mantua. The famous Latin poet, Vergil, author of the *Aeneid*, was born here in 70 BC.

VIRGINIA (United States) Northernmost of the southern states, it was the 10th of the 13 colonies to ratify the Constitution, in June 1788. Virginia is on the Atlantic Ocean and its borders touch Maryland, West Virginia, Kentucky, Tennessee, and North Carolina.

Virginia was named for Queen Elizabeth I, called the Virgin Queen, and the name when first used applied to all of North America not held by FRANCE or SPAIN. In 1606 James I gave a charter to the London Company, later known as the Virginia Company. The company sent out an expedition in 1607 that in May founded JAMESTOWN on a peninsula in the JAMES RIVER, the first permanent English settlement in America. It fared poorly; and by 1610, despite the leadership of John Smith, more than half the colonists were dead.

The colony's prospects improved when the demand for tobacco, first cultivated in 1612, grew. The governor, Sir George Yeardley, convened the first legislative assembly in America at Jamestown in 1619. That same year a Dutch ship brought the first blacks, most of whom were indentured servants, and toward the end of the century slavery became a characteristic feature of the economy. A group of Indian tribes, the Powhatan Confederacy, made a surprise attack on the colony in 1622 and killed a third of the settlers before being defeated.

In 1660 the first of the British Navigation Acts, which restricted the way trade could be carried on, put an end to a prosperous era. The resulting economic slowdown and the refusal of the governor to campaign against the frontier Indians lay behind Bacon's Rebellion of 1675/76, led by Nathaniel Bacon. After he died in 1676 his followers were cruelly suppressed. Farming and commerce prospered in the 18th century, and settlement expanded into the SHENANDOAH VALLEY in 1726. During the American Revolution the British burned NORFOLK in 1776 and three years later invaded and took PORTSMOUTH and SUFFOLK. The final battle of the Revolution was fought at YORKTOWN, where Gen. Cornwallis surrendered to Gen. George Washington on

Alexandria, Virginia, now really part of surburban Washington, D.C., but still a typical Virginian town with its red brick houses, as shown in this 19th-century print.

Oct. 19, 1781. Of the first five U.S. presidents, four were Virginians, as were seven of the first twelve.

In the 19th century Virginia's worn-out soil could not compete with fresher lands south and west, but some plantation owners bred slaves for profit. In spite of a slave insurrection led by Nat Turner in 1831, the state came near to abolishing slavery, and in the contentious period of the 1840's and 1850's, Virginians acted as mediators between both sides of the slavery question. In the end, Virginia reluctantly voted secession in April 1861, and RICHMOND became the capital of the CONFEDERATE STATES OF AMERICA. Virginia was the main battleground of the war: the first Battle of BULL RUN in July 1861; the Seven Days Battles of the PENINSULA campaign of April to July 1862; the second Battle of Bull Run of August 1862; FREDERICKSBURG in December 1862; CHANCELLORSVILLE in May 1863; the WILDERNESS Campaign of May to June 1864; the siege of PETERSBURG; and the surrender of Lee at APPOMATTOX COURTHOUSE on April 9, 1865, were all fought in the state. During the war West Virginia became a separate state in support of the Union.

Following the war, Radical Republicans controlled the state government for a time, and after the 14th and 15th amendments were ratified, Virginia was readmitted to the Union in January 1870. The war and the end of slavery brought hard times before the economy improved. In the late 19th century rural discontent was expressed through the Populist Party. The state was long strongly Democratic, and its government and business sectors were more forward-looking than in most southern states. Nevertheless, there was a furor over school integration, and by the mid-1960's only token integration had taken place. The state is strongly conservative and Republican today.

Richmond has been the capital since 1779; Norfolk is the largest city; WILLIAMSBURG was the colonial capital; other cities are NEWPORT NEWS, Portsmouth, and ROANOKE. Virginia has many historical sites, including Mt. Vernon, Washington's home; Monticello, Jefferson's home near CHARLOTTESVILLE and Arlington, on the site of Robert E. Lee's home.

VIRGINIA BEACH (United States) City in SE VIRGINIA on the Atlantic Coast. It was created in 1963 by merging the town of this name and Princess Anne County to create a unit 302 sq mi in area. The city starts at the North Carolina line and runs north approximately 28 mi to the mouth of CHESAPEAKE BAY. It is a historic area with military installations and is a popular vacation resort. A memorial at CAPE HENRY marks the approximate spot where the JAMESTOWN settlers landed on April 26, 1607. The Cape Henry Lighthouse dates to 1791. The oldest brick residence in the United States, built here in 1636, has been restored.

VIRGINIA CITY (United States) Town in SW MONTANA, 55 mi SE of Butte. Founded in 1863 after gold was discovered in nearby Alder Gulch, it grew into a city of 90,000 people, almost all men, in approximately three months. It was filled with gambling houses and dance halls. An eyewitness said every third cabin was a saloon. Lawlessness was the order of the day until a vigilante group wiped out the notorious Plummer gang. The rush, however, was short-lived, and the town declined. Virginia City was the first town in Montana to be incorporated, in 1864, and from 1865 to 1875 it was the territorial capital. There is a museum with mementoes of the gold-rush era.

VIRGINIA CITY (United States) Village in W NEVADA, 16 mi SSE of Reno. The discovery of the Comstock Lode, a gold and silver strike in 1857, claimed in 1859 by H. T. Comstock, turned the surrounding area into a region of fabulous wealth. Until 1886 the mines yielded half the silver output of the United States. As the supplies of ore began to dwindle in the 1880's, Virginia City became a ghost town. It is now a tourist center.

VIRGINIA MILITARY DISTRICT. See OHIO.

VIRGIN ISLANDS Group of approximately 100 islands, the westernmost part of the Lesser Antilles, in the WEST INDIES, E of Puerto Rico, divided politically between the UNITED STATES and GREAT BRITAIN. The U.S. islands are an organized, unincorporated territory; and the British islands are a crown colony. The islands were discovered and named by Christopher Columbus in 1493. The chief U.S. islands are ST. CROIX, ST. THOMAS, and ST. JOHN. St. Thomas was claimed by DENMARK in 1666 and settled in 1672. The Danes claimed St. John in 1683 and in 1733 purchased St. Croix from FRANCE, which had held it since 1651. In 1754 the islands became a royal colony as the Danish West Indies. Concerned about the defense of the PANAMA CANAL in the midst of World War I, the United States purchased the islands from Denmark in 1917 for $25 million. The official name is the Virgin Islands of the United States. St. Croix is the largest and most populous; St. Thomas is second in size but the most important commercially. On St. John is Virgin Islands National Park, established in 1956, in which are Carib Indian relics and remains of Danish sugar plantations. Tourism is important. The capital is CHARLOTTE AMALIE on St. Thomas.

Of the 30-odd British Virgin Islands, 16 are inhabited. The most important ones are Anegada, Tortola, and Virgin Gorda. The islands were acquired from the Dutch in 1666. Tourism is important here, too. The capital is Road Town on Tortola.

VIRICONIUM. See WROXETER.

VIRUNGA MOUNTAINS [Mfumbiro, Mufumbiro] (Rwanda, Uganda, Zaire) Volcanic mountain range of E central Africa, in E Zaire, SW Uganda, and N Rwanda. This group of eight cones over 10,000 ft high was first sighted by J. H. Speke in 1861 during his search for the source of the NILE RIVER. They were put on the map by Franz Stuhlmann in 1891.

VIS [*Greek:* Issa; *Italian:* Lissa] (Yugoslavia) Island in the Adriatic Sea, off the coast of DALMATIA, 33 mi SSW of Split. It was the site of a Greek colony founded in 390 BC by Dionysius the Elder of SYRACUSE, Sicily. During the Roman Civil War of 49 to 45 BC, it came under the rule of ROME. In the Middle Ages it came successively under the BYZANTINE EMPIRE, CROATIA, and VENICE. During the Napoleonic Wars it was held by FRANCE until GREAT BRITAIN won a naval victory over a Franco-Venetian fleet off its coast on March 13, 1811. The first battle fought by modern ironclad steam fleets was fought off Vis between ITALY and AUSTRIA on July 20, 1866 during the Austro-Prussian War. The Italians were defeated. Ceded to Yugoslavia in 1918, Vis became the headquarters of the Yugoslav partisans during World War II.

VISAYAN ISLANDS [Bisayas] (Philippines) An island group in the Visayan Sea in the central Philippines, including Bohol, Cebu, Leyte, Masbate, Negros, Panay, Samar, and others. The group is bounded on the N by LUZON, on the E by the Pacific Ocean, on the S by MINDANAO, and on the W by MINDORO and the SULU SEA. LEYTE was discovered in March 1521 by the Spanish explorer Magellan. The town of PANAY on Panay island is the second-oldest in the Philippines. The Visayan Sea was the scene of much naval and land fighting in the latter part of World War II. Japanese forces occupied most of the islands until the invasion by U.S. forces on Oct. 20, 1944 and the defeat of the Japanese fleet in LEYTE GULF on October 25/26, 1944.

VISBY [*German:* **Wisby**] (Sweden) City, port, and capital of Gotland county, on the W coast of GOTLAND Island. The site of a Stone Age settlement and a religious center, it was an important trading center by the end of the Stone Age. From the 10th to the 14th century AD it was a major commercial center of northern Europe and a member of the HANSEATIC LEAGUE. It declined after falling to the Swedes in 1280. Several times under different rulers, it finally became part of Sweden in 1645. It did not regain its commercial importance until the 19th century.

VISÉ [Wezet] (Belgium) Town in Liège province, on the Meuse River, NE of Liège. The first battle of World War I was fought here on Aug. 4, 1914, a day after GERMANY declared war on FRANCE.

VISEU [Vizeu] (Portugal) Town and capital of Viseu district and Beira Alta province, 41 mi NE of Coimbra. Founded by the Romans, it came under the Moors in 893 AD and was captured by Ferdinand I of CASTILE in 1058. The earthworks of the Roman military camp of Vacca are nearby.

VISHAKHAPATNAM [Vizagapatam] (India) City and port on the Bay of Bengal, 310 mi ENE of Hyderabad, NE Andhra Pradesh. An English station was established here in 1683. It later became the site of major shipyards from which the first Indian-built steamer was launched in 1948. It has the only sheltered harbor on the COROMANDEL COAST.

VISHNUPUR. See BISHNUPUR.

VISIGOTHIC KINGDOM One of two kingdoms that evolved after the exodus of large numbers of Goths, the Gotar people, from S SWEDEN to the region N of the BLACK SEA in the late second-early third centuries AD. In the late third and early fourth centuries they separated into two groups—the Ostrogoths (East Goths) occupying the UKRAINE, and the Visigoths (West Goths) settling in DACIA, now part of HUNGARY and RUMANIA, at the eastern boundaries of the ROMAN EMPIRE. Threatened from the east by the Huns, the Visigoths began making inroads into the Roman province of PANNONIA and were of concern to Emperor Constantine I. Under Athanaric they ravaged THRACE in 364 AD and took part in a revolt led by Procopius. The Romans under Emperor Valens retaliated and defeated them in 369 AD. Under continuing threat from the Huns, they fled deeper into the Roman Empire, suffering attacks by the Romans as they moved. Ultimately, however, they defeated the Romans at ADRIANOPLE in 378 AD, NW of Constantinople, killing Valens. By 395, after a peace had been negotiated with Rome, Alaric emerged as the strong leader of the Visigoths and served as a Roman general of his people under Emperor Theodosius. With the execution of the vandal leader Stilicho in 408, Alaric moved against Rome and eventually controlled the Italian peninsula. He sacked Rome itself in 410 AD. On his death, however, leadership passed to Ataulf, who initiated a move first to southern GAUL and then to northern SPAIN.

In Gaul the Visigoths invaded and took control of AQUITAINE, with TOULOUSE as their capital, reaching the acme of their power under Euric (466–84). They went on to conquer all of Spain and controlled a vast domain, extending into Gaul, until the Franks under Clovis defeated Alaric II at the battle of VOUILLÉ in Gaul in 507. Following this defeat, the Visigoths moved the seat of their government to TOLEDO in Spain, where they were besieged by both Basques and Franks, with occasional Byzantine inroads from the south. In the late 6th century however, Leovigild and Recared emerged as strong, wise kings, and the Visigothic kingdom regained its vitality. The Visigoths were the first Germanic people converted to Christianity by Ulfilas in Dacia in the fourth century, but their Arianism alienated them from the Catholic Romans. Recared's conversion to Catholicism from Arianism in the sixth century encouraged the mixing of the Romano-Hispanic with the Visigoth populations in Spain. The next step toward homogeneity came in 654 when King Recceswith ordered the establishment of a common law for both Visigothic and Roman subjects, who until then had been living under different sets of laws.

The Catholic Church in Toledo began to appear the stronger governing element as the Visigoth royal authority weakened to the point of civil war. However, it was the Moors under the leadership of Tarik Ibn Ziyad who destroyed the Visigothic Kingdom. The defeat of Roderick, the last Visigothic king, in 711 AD, in the vicinity of MEDINA SIDONIA, ushered in many centuries of Moorish hegemony in Spain.

VISLA. See VISTULA RIVER.

VISTULA RIVER [*German:* **Weichsel;** *Polish:* **Wisla;** *Russian:* **Visla**] (Poland) River rising on the N slope of the CARPATHIAN MTS, it flows through Poland to the Baltic Sea at Gdańsk. Approximately 675 miles long, it is navigable for most of its course and has always been a major Polish trade route. It is connected to the ODER and DNIEPER rivers by canal.

VITEBSK (USSR) City in NE Belorussian SSR, on

The papal palace at Viterbo, north of Rome, built in the 13th century when Viterbo was a papal stronghold and a favorite residence of the popes.

the Western Dvina River, 140 mi NE of Minsk. First mentioned in 1021, it passed to LITHUANIA in 1320 and to POLAND in the 16th century. It finally passed to RUSSIA in 1772. It suffered severe damage during the Great Northern War, from 1700 to 1721, during the Napoleonic Wars in 1812, and during World War II. See also BELORUSSIA.

VITERBO [*ancient:* **Vicus Elbii**] (Italy) City and capital of Viterbo province, LATIUM region, 42 mi NNW of Rome. Originally inhabited by Etruscans, it was captured by the Romans c.310 BC. In the 11th century it was given to the papacy by Countess Matilda of TUSCANY. In 1145 Pope Eugenius III fled here for safety, and from 1257 it was the residence of several popes. Five popes were elected here. It declined in importance when the papacy moved to AVIGNON in 1309. Most of the city was destroyed during World War II, but it has recovered.

VITÓRIA [*former:* **Victoria**] (Brazil) City, port, and capital of Espírito Santo state, on an island in the Bay of Espírito Santo, 250 mi NE of Rio de Janeiro. Founded by Vasco Fernandes Coutinho in 1535, it was strategically placed to repel Indian attacks. Throughout the 16th and 17th centuries it also successfully resisted French, English, and Dutch attacks.

VITORIA [*medieval:* **Victoriacum**] (Spain) City and capital of Álava province, in the BASQUE PROVINCES, 32 mi SSE of Bilbao. Founded by the Visigoths in 581 AD to commemorate the victory of King Leovigild over the Basques, it was fortified by Sancho VI of NAVARRE after his defeat of the Moors in 1181. The decisive battle of the Peninsular campaign of the Napoleonic Wars was fought here on June 21, 1813, when the Allies under the duke of Wellington defeated the French under Joseph Bonaparte. See also VISIGOTHIC KINGDOM.

VITRÉ (France) Town in Ille-et-Vilaine department, 22 mi E of Rennes. It became a center for the French Huguenots in the Reformation while ruled by the Rieux and Coligny families. A Protestant church was established here, which was suppressed after the revocation of the Edict of NANTES in 1685.

VITRIACUM. See VITRY-SUR-SEINE.

VITRY-EN-PERTHOIS. See VITRY-LE-FRANÇOIS.

VITRY-LE-FRANÇOIS (France) Town in Marne department, on the MARNE RIVER, 20 mi SE of Châlons. It was built in 1545 by Francis I to replace the old town of Vitry-en-Perthois, which had been destroyed in 1544 by Charles V. Gen. Joseph Joffre had his headquarters here at the start of World War I, and the town changed hands several times during the Battle of the Marne. It was almost totally destroyed during World War II.

VITRY-SUR-SEINE [*ancient:* **Vitriacum**] (France) Suburb of S PARIS, in Val-de-Marne department, on the SEINE RIVER. A village in Roman times, it later became the site of much property owned by Parisian religious establishments. Many country houses were built here after the French Revolution.

VITTORIA VENETO (Italy) Town in Treviso province, 23 mi N of Treviso, in Veneto region. One of the last battles of World War I was fought here between Oct. 24 and Nov. 3, 1918, in which the troops of AUSTRIA were decisively defeated by the Italians. This led to the Austrian surrender and the signing of an armistice at the Villa Giusti near PADUA on Nov. 3, 1918.

VITTORIOSA [Birgu] (Malta) Town on the Grand Harbor opposite VALLETTA. With COSPICUA and Senglea it was one of the Three Cities of Malta and was of considerable importance during the Middle Ages. In 1530 it became the first residence of the Knights of St. John on Malta and was their refuge during the Turks' Great Siege of Malta in 1565. It was replaced as the knights' capital by Valletta in 1570. See also OTTOMAN EMPIRE.

VITUDURUM. See WINTERTHUR.

VIVARAIS (France) Ancient district, mostly in the modern department of Ardèche. Part of the kingdom of ARLES in the early Middle Ages, it was held by the counts of TOULOUSE but passed to the French crown in 1229 following the Albigensian Crusade.

VIVIERS (France) Town in Ardèche department, on the RHÔNE RIVER, SSE of Privas. It was the ancient capital of VIVARAIS and has a cathedral with six Gobelin tapestries.

VIVIS. See VEVEY.

VIVISCUS. See VEVEY.

VIZAGAPATAM. See VISHAKHAPATNAM.

VIZCAYA [Biscay, Biscaya] (Spain) Province within the BASQUE PROVINCES, on the Bay of Biscay. Inhabited since ancient times by the fiercely independent Basques, it was only nominally subject to the Romans, Visigoths, and Franks, and resisted the Moors. Included in the kingdom of NAVARRE, which united all the Basques in the 11th century, it passed to CASTILE in 1370. It lost its special privileges after the Carlist Wars of 1834 to 1876. The province is a center of Basque nationalism and has continually been the scene of activity aimed against the central government.

VIZEU. See VISEU.

VIZIANAGRAM (India) City in Andhra Pradesh, 410 mi NNE of Madras. Founded in 1712, it was the headquarters of the rajas of Vizianagram, who were important in the 18th century. Their fort, built in 1714, is in the vicinity.

VIZILLE (France) Town in Isère department, S of Grenoble. Originally the site of a Roman military post, it was here that the estates of DAUPHINÉ convened on July 21, 1788 to make a protest that presaged the French Revolution. The meeting, which took place in a tennis court, occurred a year before the National Assembly took the Tennis Court Oath at VERSAILLES.

VLAANDEREN. See FLANDERS.

VLAARDINGEN, Indonesia. See MAKASAR.

VLAARDINGEN (Netherlands) Municipality and port in South Holland province, 6 mi W of Rotterdam. An early Dutch naval victory was won nearby in 1037 when Dirk IV defeated Emperor Henry III. In 1351 the Bavarian line of Holland was secured when Count William V won several victories nearby. Today it is the third-largest seaport in Holland.

VLADIKAVKAZ. See ORDZHONIKIDZE.

VLADIMIR (USSR) City in Russian SFSR, on the Klyazma River, 110 mi E of Moscow. One of Russia's oldest towns, it was founded in the 12th century by Vladimir II of KIEV and became the center of a princedom and a trading town. It recovered quickly after being devastated by Tatar invasions in 1238 and 1293 and was the center of the Russian Orthodox Church between 1300 and 1328. See also GORKI.

VLADIMIR, DUCHY OF. See UKRAINE, VLADIMIR-VOLYNSKI.

VLADIMIR IN VOLHYNIA. See LODOMERIA.

VLADIMIR-VOLYNSKI [*Polish:* **Włodzimierz**] (USSR) City in the Ukraine, 45 mi WNW of Lutsk, on the Lug River. Founded in the 10th century, it is one of the oldest settlements in the UKRAINE and was an important trade center from the 10th to the 13th century. The capital of the grand duchy of Vladimir, it later became the capital of the Galich-Volhynian duchy in 1300. It passed to POLAND in 1347. After changing hands many times, it finally passed to RUSSIA in 1795. See also GALICIA, VOLHYNIA.

VLADIVOSTOK (USSR) City and port on a bay of the Sea of Japan, in Russian SFSR, 380 mi SSW of Khabarovsk. Founded as a military post in 1860, it was an important base for colonization by RUSSIA in the Far East. The Trans-Siberian Railroad linked it with Europe in 1903. Following the fall of PORT ARTHUR to JAPAN in 1905, it became Russia's most important naval base on the Pacific coast. In World War I it was an Allied supply base. After the Russian Revolution of 1917 the Allies, mostly Japan, continued to occupy it until 1922. In World War II it was again a major Allied supply base. In November 1974 U.S. President Gerald Ford and Soviet Premier Leonid Brezhnev met here to begin negotiations on the Strategic Arms Limitation Talks (SALT) to limit the arms race.

VLISSINGEN [*English:* **Flushing**] (Netherlands) Seaport on the S coast of WALCHEREN Island, at the mouth of the SCHELDE estuary, SW Netherlands, approx. 40 mi NW of Antwerp. In 1572 Vlissingen was one of the first Dutch towns to rebel against SPAIN. During World War II Vlissingen was the objective of the Allied Walcheren expedition of October to November 1944 to clear the Schelde estuary for access to ANTWERP. Vlissingen was the birthplace in 1607 of Michel de Ruyter, admiral and naval hero of the Dutch wars of 1652–1676, and of the poet Jacobus Bellarmy in 1757.

VLONA. See VLORË.

VLONË. See VLORË.

VLORA. See VLORË.

VLORË [Vlona, Vlonë, Vlora] [*former:* **Avlona;** *Greek:* **Aulon;** *Italian:* **Valona**] (Albania) City, port, and capital of Vlorë province, on an inlet of the Adriatic Sea, 62 mi SSW of Tiranë. Important in classical antiquity, it also played a major role in wars between Normans and Byzantines of the 11th and 12th centuries. In 1464 it came under the OTTOMAN EMPIRE. On Nov. 28, 1912 it was the scene of the proclamation of the independence of Albania by Ismail Bey Vlora. It was occupied by ITALY in both world wars.

VLOTSLAVSK. See WŁOCŁAWEK.

VLTAVA RIVER [*German:* **Moldau**] (Czechoslovakia) Rising in the Bohemian Forest of SW Czechoslovakia, flowing first SE and then N, the Vltava is approximately 270 mi long and is the longest river in the country. It joins the ELBE RIVER at Melnik. It flows past PRAGUE, the capital of the country, and Ceské Budejovice, an important transportation center founded in the 13th century. The 19th-century Czech composer Bedrich Smetana devoted one section of his 1879 symphonic poem, *My Fatherland*, to the Vltava.

VODENA. See EDESSA.

VOGESEN. See VOSGES MOUNTAINS.

VOGESUS. See VOSGES MOUNTAINS.

VOGHERA (Italy) Town in Pavia province, LOMBARDY region, 15 mi SSW of Pavia. Probably the site of the Roman colony of Iria, it was fortified by the Visconti family of MILAN in the 14th century.

VOIOTIA. See BOEOTIA.

VOIVODINA. See VOJVODINA.

VOJVODINA [Voivodina, Voyvodina] (Yugoslavia) Autonomous province of N SERBIA. Its chief city is NOVI SAD. Originally part of HUNGARY and CROATIA, the region was conquered by the Turks in the 16th century but was restored to Hungary in 1699. It became a refuge for Serbians and Croatians fleeing the OTTOMAN EMPIRE and was ceded to Yugoslavia in 1920 by the Treaty of Trianon. It is the country's richest agricultural region.

VOLATERRAE. See VOLTERRA.

VOLCANO ISLANDS [*Japanese:* **Iwo Retto, Kazan-Retto**] (Japan) Group of three islands in the W Pacific Ocean, S of Bonin Island. Settled by fishermen and sulfur miners in 1887, the islands were claimed by Japan in 1891. The group's largest island, IWO JIMA, was made the site of a Japanese air base and fell to the UNITED STATES in 1945 after a bloody battle during World War II. It remained under U.S. administration until it was returned to Japan in 1968.

VOLGA-BALTIC WATERWAY [*former:* **Mariinsk Waterway**] (USSR) River and canal system linking the VOLGA RIVER with the BALTIC SEA. The waterway, which follows the ancient Baltic-Volga trade route, was

begun in 1709 to connect St. Petersburg, now LENINGRAD, with the Russian interior. The major canals along its course were built in the 1930's and modernized in the 1960's. The system is approximately 700 miles long.

VOLGA-DON CANAL (USSR) Canal in Russian SFSR, linking the VOLGA RIVER with the DON RIVER, near Volgograd. Projects to link the Don and Volga rivers go back to the 17th century, when Peter the Great started to construct a canal in the area. Work on the modern canal began in earnest only after World War II and was completed in July 1952. It is of vital importance to Soviet trade.

VOLGA GERMAN AUTONOMOUS SOVIET SOCIALIST REPUBLIC [German Volga Republic] (USSR) Former autonomous republic, on the VOLGA RIVER, with its capital at ENGELS, Russian SFSR. The area was settled by 27,000 Germans under decrees of Catherine II in 1760 and 1761. Although it enjoyed special privileges initially, the region had lost all autonomy by 1870 but was organized as an autonomous republic in 1924. It was abolished finally in September 1941.

VOLGA RIVER [*ancient:* **Oarus, Rha;** *Finnish:* **Rau;** *Tatar:* **Atel, Etil, Itil**] (USSR) River of central and E European USSR, rising in the Valdai Hills, in N Kalinin Oblast, and flowing 2,293 mi to the Caspian Sea near Astrakhan. The longest river in Europe, it has played an extremely important part in the history of RUSSIA as a trade route and as the main transport route for colonization in the East. Muscovite trading centers had been established on the river by the 12th century at Nizhny Novogorod, now GORKI; Tver, now KALININ; UGLICH; and YAROSLAV. After the Tatar invasions of the 13th century, it replaced the DNIEPER RIVER as the main trade route between Muscovy and Central Asia. The importance of the river as a trade artery increased in the 16th century when Ivan the Terrible conquered its whole course and established fortress towns on its banks.

VOLGOGRAD [*former:* **Stalingrad, Tsaritsyn**] (USSR) City, port, and capital of Volgograd oblast, on the VOLGA RIVER, 580 mi SE of Moscow in Russian SFSR. Founded as a fort by Russians in 1589, it was captured by Cossack rebels in 1670 and 1774. It became of vital importance because of its position on the route between the Volga and DON rivers and was reached by railways in the 19th century. During the Russian Revolution, in 1918, it was held by Bolsheviks under Stalin, for whom it was renamed in 1925. In September 1942, during World War II, the city was subjected to a massive offensive by Axis forces under Gen. Friedrich von Paulus. The Germans failed to capture the whole city, and in November 1942 the Soviets under Marshal Grigori Zhukov counterattacked, encircling the besieging enemy and winning a battle that was to prove a major turning point in the war. In the Stalingrad campaign the Germans alone lost more than 300,000 men, and the Axis forces were never again able to return to the offensive against the Soviets. The city regained its former name in 1961, in Krushchev's de-Stalinization period.

VOLGOGRAD OBLAST [*former:* **Stalingrad Oblast**] (USSR) Subdivision of the Russian SFSR, on the lower VOLGA RIVER. Its capital is VOLGOGRAD. Occupied by Bulgars in the fifth century AD, it passed to the KHAZARS in the 10th century. In the 13th and 14th centuries it formed part of the empire of the Tatar GOLDEN HORDE. In the 17th and 18th centuries it was the scene of continuous fighting between Russians and Volga tribesmen, and in 1773 of E. Pugachev's Cossack rebellion. It suffered severe famine in 1921 after the Russian Revolution.

VOLGSK. See VOLSK.

VOLHYNIA [*Polish:* **Wołyń;** *Russian:* **Volyn, Volynia**] (USSR) Region of NW Ukraine, around the headstreams of the Pripyat and Western Bug rivers. One of the oldest Slavic settlements in Europe, from 981 it was divided between the Russian duchies of VLADIMIR and Galich, and *c.*1390 was shared between POLAND and LITHUANIA. In 1795 it again passed to RUSSIA, though Poland acquired part of the region by the Treaty of RIGA in 1921. The Polish section was ceded to the Soviet Union in 1939. See also GALICIA, UKRAINE.

VOLKHOV RIVER (USSR) River of NW central European USSR. It rises in Lake Ilmen and flows NNE to LAKE LADOGA, Russian SFSR. In early times it was an important Russian trade route, forming part of the waterway system linking the BALTIC SEA and CONSTANTINOPLE. It was linked to the Neva River by canal in the 18th century. The Soviet Union's first hydroelectric station was built on the river at Volkhov in 1926.

VOLNEY. See FULTON, Missouri.

VOLOGDA (USSR) City in N central Russian SFSR, on the Vologda River, 110 mi N of Yaroslavl. Founded in 1147 by NOVGOROD traders, it became important early as a commercial center. In the 14th century it was the object of a struggle between Novgorod and MOSCOW. It passed to Moscow in 1478. It continued to be of commercial importance until the 18th century, when it was eclipsed by St. Petersburg, now LENINGRAD, but it recovered in the 19th century with the development of the railways and the timber industry.

VOLOS [*Greek:* **Bolos, Vólos;** *Turkish:* **Gholos**] (Greece) City, port, and capital of Magnesia department, on the Gulf of Vólos, 100 mi NNW of Athens, E THESSALY. Standing near the site of ancient IOLCUS, it is in a region full of remains dating from Neolithic times. The legendary Jason and the Argonauts are said to have sailed from either Iolcus or Pegasae, lying just to the south. During the Greek War of Independence the Greeks of Zagora tried in vain to take the city from the Turks in 1827. It became part of Greece in 1881. In 1955 it suffered a severe earthquake.

VOLSINII (Italy) Ancient town of ETRURIA. It has been sited at ORVIETO, Terni province, Umbria region. A powerful member of the Etruscan League, it was apparently the richest of the 12 cities of Etruria. The Volsinienses were defeated by ROME in 294 BC, and their city was sacked in 280 BC. A new city was built later on the site of today's BOLSENA.

VOLSK [*former:* **Malykovka, Volgsk**] (USSR) City and port in Russian SFSR, on the VOLGA RIVER, 70 mi NE of Saratov. Originally a small settlement, it became a town in 1780 and is today an important river port.

VOLTA RIVER (Ghana) River formed in central Ghana by the confluence of the Black Volta and White Volta rivers, it flows SE and S to the Gulf of Guinea at Ada. Discovered by the Portuguese in the 15th century, it has become the most important river in Ghana. Its dam, forming Lake Volta and completed in 1966, has proved vital to the country's economic development.

VOLTERRA [*Etruscan:* **Velathri;** *Latin:* **Volaterrae**] (Italy) Town in Pisa province, TUSCANY, 29 mi SE of Pisa. A member of the Etruscan League, it fell to Rome in the third century BC. It supported ROME during the Second Punic War and Marius in the Civil War but fell to Sulla after a lengthy siege. It was the capital of the Lombard kings for some time during the early Middle Ages. After falling to Florence in 1361, its fortunes followed those of FLORENCE. It has many Etruscan remains, including a gateway and walls. The town also contains a 12th- and 13th-century cathedral and a museum of Etruscan antiquities.

VOLTURNO RIVER (Italy) River rising in the Apennine Mts in MOLISE region and flowing through CAMPANIA to the Tyrrhenian Sea. It has always been of strategic importance because it crosses the roads linking NAPLES and ROME. On Oct. 1, 1860 Garibaldi defeated the Neapolitan army on its banks. After the fall of Naples in World War II it was a German defense line and was crossed by the Allies after severe fighting between Oct. 12 and 14, 1943. CAPUA is the most important city along its course.

VOLUBILIS [*later:* **Oulili**] (Morocco) Ancient city of North Africa, 19 mi N of Meknes. A flourishing center of late Hellenistic culture in the first century BC and the first century AD, it became a Roman municipium *c.*45 AD and was the chief inland city of the Roman province of MAURETANIA Tingitana. After 788 it was the capital of the Arab Idrisid dynasty. There are extensive Roman ruins here, especially of the town walls.

VOLYN. See VOLHYNIA.

VOLYNIA. See VOLHYNIA.

VORARLBERG (Austria) Province on the Swiss border, with its capital at BREGENZ. Inhabited since Neolithic times, it was conquered by the Romans in 15 BC and was included in the province of RAETIA. In the sixth century AD it became part of the Frankish kingdom and belonged to the counts of Montfort during the later Middle Ages. It gradually came under Hapsburg rule between the 14th and 16th century, and it became a distinct province of Austria in 1918.

VORDINGBORG (Denmark) City in Storstrøms county, on the Masnedsund, in SE Sjaelland, 50 mi SSW of Copenhagen. First settled around a castle in the 12th century, it became a favorite meeting place of the national assembly. In 1241 Denmark's oldest national statute was published here.

VORONEZH (USSR) City in Russian SFSR, on the Voronezh River, 165 mi NE of Kharkov. Built as a fortress in 1586, it became a shipbuilding center and was used by Peter the Great to assemble a fleet for his campaigns to capture the Turkish fortress of AZOV in 1695/96. Commercially and culturally important since the 1830's, it was almost destroyed during the German occupation of World War II in the six months after July 1942. It has since been rebuilt.

VOROSHILOVGRAD [*former:* **Lugansk**] (USSR) City in UKRAINE, 100 mi N of Rostov-on-Don. The oldest center of the Donets Basin, it was founded in 1795 around a state iron foundry that used the abundant surrounding coal. Industrialization accelerated its development in the 1920's. It is named after the Bolshevik leader, Marshal Voroshilov.

VOROSHILOVSK. See STAVROPOL.

VORSKLA RIVER (USSR) River of W European USSR, it rises in Kursk oblast and flows S to the DNIEPER RIVER, above Dnepropetrovsk, in the Ukraine. On Aug. 12, 1399 the Tatar GOLDEN HORDE under Edigü won a decisive victory here over the Lithuanian ruler Vytautas the Great (1350–1430). As a result Vytautas lost all hope of subjugating the Golden Horde and turned west to break the power of the German Teutonic Knights over LITHUANIA. In June 1709 Peter the Great's army routed the forces of Charles XII of SWEDEN in a decisive battle at POLTAVA, on the river's banks.

VOSEGUS. See VOSGES MOUNTAINS.

VOSGES MOUNTAINS [*ancient:* **Vogesus, Vosegus;** *German:* **Vogesen**] (France) Mountain range in E France. From the Belfort Gap, between the Vosges Mts and the JURA MTS, the range runs generally north, approx. 120 mi, parallel to the RHINE RIVER. The Moselle, Meurthe, and Sarre rivers rise here. PLOMBIÈRES-les-Bains is a popular spa, its springs used since Roman times. The spa was the scene of a meeting in 1858 between Napoleon III of France and Sardinian Premier Camillo Cavour, at which it was agreed that France would receive NICE and SAVOY for helping to expel the Austrians from Italy. BELFORT, in the Belfort Gap, has been a military stronghold since the 17th century, because its site dominates the routes between France, Germany, and Switzerland. In World War I U.S. troops were stationed on this front. In World War II German troops seized Belfort in June 1940, and it was retaken by French and U.S. troops during August and September 1944.

VOTKINSK [*former:* **Votkinski Zovod**] (USSR) Town in Udmurt Autonomous SSR, Russian SFSR, 30 mi NE of Izhevsk. Founded in 1759, it was pillaged by the Cossack Pugachev in 1774 in the rebellion against Catherine II. The composer Peter I. Tchaikovsky was born here in 1840. His home is preserved as a museum.

VOTKINSKI ZOVOD. See VOTKINSK.

VOTSKAYA ASSR. See UDMURT AUTONOMOUS SOVIET SOCIALIST REPUBLIC.

VOUILLÉ (France) Village in W central France, 10 mi WNW of Poitiers. It was probably the site of a battle in 507 AD between the forces of Alaric II, the Visigothic king of Spain and southern Gaul from *c.*485 to 507, and Clovis I, the Frankish king and founder of the Merovingian Dynasty, who ruled from 481 to 511. Clovis was a champion of orthodox Christianity, but Alaric was an adherent of Arianism, which was considered a Christian heresy. Alaric was defeated and lost nearly all the Visigoth lands north of the Pyrenees, while the victory of Clovis added AQUITAINE to the domain of the Merovingians. Some opinion holds that the battle was fought 20 miles south at Voulon. See also FRANKISH EMPIRE, VISIGOTHIC KINGDOM.

VOYVODINA. See VOJVODINA.

VRACA. See VRATSA.

VRATSA [**Vraca**] (Bulgaria) City and capital of Vratsa province, 35 mi NNE of Sofia. Under the OTTOMAN EMPIRE from the 15th to 19th centuries it was an administrative and commercial center that traded with FRANCE, ITALY, EGYPT, and ISTANBUL. It declined when Bulgaria became independent in 1878.

VRH-BOSNA. See SARAJEVO.

VRIESLAND. See FRIESLAND.

VRINDAVAN. See BRINDABAN.

VRŠAC [*German:* **Werschetz;** *Hungarian:* **Versecz**] (Yugoslavia) City in SERBIA, 45 mi NW of Belgrade. During the Revolution of 1848/49 the Serbs were defeated here by the Hungarians in 1848. The following year the Hungarians were themselves defeated here by the Austrians. Vršac again came under Hungarian control in 1941 after the German invasion of World War II.

VRYBURG (South Africa) Town in CAPE PROVINCE, 125 mi N of KIMBERLEY. From 1882 to 1885 it was the capital of the former Boer republic of STELLALAND. During the Boer War it was occupied by the Boers between 1899 and 1902.

VRYHEID (South Africa) Town in NW NATAL, 140 mi N of Durban. It was the chief town of a district that was ceded by the Zulus to the Boers in 1884. The district was declared a republic but became part of the TRANSVAAL in 1888 and of Natal in 1902.

VULCI [*Etruscan:* **Velch**] (Italy) Ancient city of ETRURIA, in Viterbo province, Latium region, 10 mi NW of Tarquinia. The largest of the 12 cities of Etruria, it flourished between the sixth and fourth century BC due to its trade. It was overcome by the Roman Coruncanius in 280 BC together with VOLSINII. Vulci is famous for its extensive Etruscan cemeteries and important frescoes.

VYATKA. See KIROV.

VYAZMA (USSR) City in Russian SFSR, 125 mi WSW of Moscow. It was a trading town in the 11th century. From the 15th to 17th centuries it was held, in turn, by LITHUANIA, RUSSIA, and POLAND. The city was finally ceded to Russia in 1634. During World War II it was occupied by the Germans between 1941 and 1943.

VYBORG [*Finnish:* **Viipuri;** *Swedish:* **Viborg**] (USSR) City and port on the Gulf of Finland, 70 mi NW of Leningrad, in Russian SFSR. Founded by the Swedes as a fortress town in 1293, it later became a member of the HANSEATIC LEAGUE. Captured by Peter the Great of Russia in 1710, in 1812 it was incorporated into FINLAND, which at that time was under Russian sovereignty. Prior to the Russian Revolution it was an important transit point for revolutionaries going into RUSSIA. Included in Finland in 1918, it was finally ceded to the USSR in 1947 after occupation by Finns and Germans in World War II from August 1941 to June 1944.

VYCHEGDA RIVER [**Vichegda**] (USSR) River of NE European USSR, it rises in the URAL MOUNTAINS and flows W through the Russian SFSR to the Northern Dyina River at Kotlas. During the 16th century the river was an important water route to SIBERIA.

VYERNYI. See ALMA-ATA.

VYSHNI VOLOCHEK (USSR) Town in Russian SFSR, 70 mi NW of Kalinin. It was important in the 18th and 19th centuries since it lay on the Vyshnevo-Lotsk canal system, built by Peter the Great between 1703 and 1709 to link the Volga River with the Neva River and the BALTIC SEA.

W

WAADT. See VAUD.

WABASH (United States) City on the Wabash River, 64 mi SE of South Bend, INDIANA. A mill was constructed here in 1820 for the Miami Indians. White settlers entered the area in the following decade; Wabash was settled c.1835. It is reputed to be the first city in the world to have had municipal electric street lighting.

WABASH RIVER (United States) River, 475 mi long, rising in W Ohio, flowing SW across INDIANA to form the S Illinois state line, and joining the OHIO RIVER in SW Indiana. In the 18th century it was widely used by French fur traders traveling between Canada and New Orleans. Early in the 19th century it became an important east-west trade route used by steamers and flatboats until the arrival of the railroad in the middle of the century.

WACO (United States) Industrial city on the Brazos River, 94 mi SW of Dallas, E central TEXAS. Settled in 1849 on the site of former Hueco Indian villages, it was a cotton plantation and cattle-ranching center prior to the Civil War. A suspension bridge erected in 1870 and its first railroad connection, constructed here in 1871, revived Waco's economy after the war.

WADAI [Ouadaï] (Chad) Former Muslim sultanate in E Chad. Established in the 16th century, it became powerful as a slave-trading state as late as the 19th century, when it was strongly influenced by a Sufi order, the Sanusi. The French displaced the sultanate during the decade prior to World War I.

WĀDĪ AL-HIJĀRAH. See GUADALAJARA, Spain.

WĀDĪ-ASH. See GUADIX.

WADI HALFA [Halfa] (Sudan) Port on Lake Nubia, Northern Province, N Sudan. It was founded in the 19th century on the site of an ancient Egyptian city that archaeologists tried to rescue in the 1960's before it was flooded by waters of the recently constructed ASWAN High Dam.

WAGADU. See GHANA EMPIRE.

WAGADUGU. See OUAGADOUGOU.

WAGRAM (Austria) Village 11 mi NE of Vienna, NE Austria. Napoleon won a particularly bloody victory here over Archduke Charles Louis and his Austrian forces on July 5 and 6, 1809 during the Napoleonic Wars.

WAHLSTATT. See LEGNICKIE POLE.

WAIMEA (United States) Village on the SW coast of Kauai Island, HAWAII. British explorer, Captain James Cook, landed at Waimea Bay in January 1778. Later, the first missionaries to work the Hawaiian Islands settled here. A Russian trading fort of the early 19th century lies in ruins nearby.

WAITZEN. See VAC.

WAKAYAMA (Japan) Seaport on the Inland Sea, S HONSHŪ, 35 mi SW of ŌSAKA, an old Tokugawa capital. Its impressive castle, built by Hideyoshi in 1585, has been reconstructed since its destruction in World War II.

WAKDE (Indonesia) Island off the NE coast of IRIAN BARAT. A Japanese airfield, established here during World War II, was captured by Allied forces on May 21, 1944.

WAKEFIELD (England) City on the Calder River, South Yorkshire, 8 mi SSE of Leeds. Dating to Anglo-Saxon times, it has been a center of the wool industry since the 14th century. Richard Plantagenet, third duke of York, was defeated and slain here in 1460 by a force of Lancastrians during the Wars of the Roses. The Towneley, or Wakefield, Mysteries, one of the cycles of English miracle plays, were initially performed here c.1450.

WAKE ISLAND (United States) U.S. military base and island, between Guam and Hawaii, central Pacific. The island was discovered by the Spanish in the 16th century and visited in 1796 by the British captain William Wake. It was annexed by the United States in 1898. It became a civil base in 1935, then a military base in 1939 before it fell on Dec. 23, 1941 to a Japanese raid that was initiated on December 7. It was bombed many times during World War II before it was recaptured on Sept. 4, 1945 by U.S. troops.

WALACHIA [Wallachia] (Rumania) Former small kingdom between the Transylvanian Alps and the DANUBE RIVER, which with MOLDAVIA to the N comprises modern Rumania. Bordered by Bulgaria on the S, the Danube River and Yugoslavia on the W, it includes the oil-rich region of PLOIEŞTI and the industrial sector around BUCHAREST, the capital, which make it the country's most technologically developed and affluent region. Walachia's agricultural productivity has earned it the title of Rumania's bread basket. Once part of the ancient Roman province of DACIA, the modern descendants sustain the strong Latin heritage of their Romance language despite inroads by numerous foreign elements through invasion, occupation, and migration.

As a nominal part of the BYZANTINE EMPIRE from the sixth to the 11th centuries, it was invaded and occupied by Avars, Bulgars, and Magyars. By the 10th century part of Walachia was held by the kingdom of

HUNGARY but in the 12th century was ravaged first by the Cumans and then by the Mongols in 1240. During the Mongol occupation and under the principality of GALICIA its native inhabitants retreated to mountain hideouts until the MONGOL EMPIRE withdrew. Then c.1290 the Walachian leader Radu Negru, or Rudolf the Black, founded the principality of Walachia.

Under Mircea the Great (1368–1418) Walachia suffered two major defeats by the Turks in 1389 and 1396, and was forced to pay tribute to the sultan, although it continued to be self-governing under Turkish authority. These defeats began a long period of Turkish suzerainty that, with brief interruptions, continued until the Crimean War in 1854. As the OTTOMAN EMPIRE fell into decadence, it turned to Greek Phanariots to administer its possessions, which they did ruthlessly until the Greeks themselves rebelled against the Turks in 1822.

Walachia was invaded by RUSSIA early in the Crimean War in 1853, but Russia then withdrew in a diplomatic trade to gain Austrian neutrality. Walachia and Moldavia, known then as the Danubian Principalities, passed to AUSTRIA, under whose authority they remained until the end of the Crimean War. Although the Congress of Paris ended the war in 1856 and placed them under Turkish authority, that authority was nominal. In 1859 Alexander John Cuza was named prince of Walachia and Moldavia, and the history of modern Rumania began.

WALATA. See MALI EMPIRE.

WAŁBRZYCH [*German:* **Waldenburg**] (Poland) City on the Bóbr River, 40 mi SW of Wrocław, SILESIA. Dating from at least the 15th century, it became an important coal-mining center during the industrial revolution. Bombed and almost destroyed during World War II, it was transferred from Germany to Poland in 1945 at the Potsdam Conference.

WALCHEREN (Netherlands) Island in the North Sea, just off the SW coast, W of Bregen. In 1809 during the Napoleonic Wars the earl of Chatham staged an ill-fated campaign here to capture Antwerp. The British took Walcheren during World War II in November 1944 on their drive toward Antwerp, but they badly damaged the island when they bombed its North Sea dikes to force out the occupying German troops.

WALDECK (West Germany) Former German principality and republic, in modern HESSE. A medieval county of the HOLY ROMAN EMPIRE, it was united to Pyrmont and in 1712 raised to a principality. It passed to PRUSSIA in 1867, became a semi-independent republic in 1918, and was incorporated into Hesse following World War II.

WALDENBURG. See WAŁBRZYCH.

WALDEN POND (United States) Pond, near CONCORD, NE MASSACHUSETTS. Henry David Thoreau made his home on its banks from 1845 to 1847 in a cabin he built himself. That experience was recorded in *Walden,* a series of essays published in 1854.

WALES [*Welsh:* **Cimru, Cymru**] Country of Great Britain, it forms a peninsula to the west of ENGLAND into the Irish Sea. It has been politically united with England since 1282 but has maintained a sense of its own national culture. The Welsh language still survives among much of the population, and the Welsh Nationalist Party is represented in the British parliament. The capital, CARDIFF, is situated in the south of the country, which is one of Great Britain's major industrial centers.

Inhabited originally by Celts, Wales was never fully subdued by the Romans. After the Anglo-Saxon invasion of Britain in the fifth century AD, Wales became the chief stronghold of the Celts and Britons. Continually engaged in border wars with Anglo-Saxon kingdoms, under Cadwallon the Welsh attempted to recover northern England from them, but they were defeated at the battle of CHESTER c.615 AD.

From the seventh century Wales was ruled by numerous petty princes, but the Welsh united in the ninth century in a successful effort to repulse Danish incursions. The great prince, Gruffydd ap Llewelyn, the first prince of Wales, united the country again in the 11th century and waged war on England. After the Norman conquest of England in 1066, however, increased pressure was put on Wales by the Norman kings, who placed powerful barons along the Welsh Marches. However, Wales retained her independence for a further two centuries and in the 12th century was still a flourishing cultural center.

Finally in 1282, with the defeat of Llewelyn ap Gruffydd, the country fell to Edward I of England; and Wales ceased to exist as an independent political unit in 1284. As a move to appease the Welsh, Edward I made his son Prince of Wales in 1301, a title that has since been held by all male heirs to the English and British throne.

With English rule Wales disintegrated under the harsh dominance of the barons. In the early 15th century the Welsh revolted under Owen Glendower, who had gained supremacy in Wales by 1404. His rebellion was later crushed, but by the act of Union of 1536 Wales was granted representation in the English parliament. A century earlier Owen Tudor, of Welsh ancestry, had married Catherine, the widow of Henry V, and was thus the grandfather of Henry VII.

The industrial revolution of the 19th century exploited the mineral resources of the country so that by the end of the century south Wales was the largest coal-exporting region in the world. Since then, however, the country has been plagued by unemployment and poverty due to agricultural and social displacement.

WALLACHIA. See WALACHIA.

WALLA WALLA (United States) City, approx. 160 mi SW of Spokane, SE WASHINGTON. A fort was erected here in 1818 as a fur-trading post. Pioneers began arriving here in the 1830's. In 1858 the United States built Fort Walla Walla here along the wagon train route known as the OREGON TRAIL. Four years later the settlement around the fort was incorporated as a town.

WALLIS. See VALAIS.

WALLIS ISLANDS [*French:* **Îles Wallis**] (France)

Archipelago in the SW Pacific Ocean, W of SAMOA. Discovered by the British explorer Samuel Wallis in 1767, the islands were taken by the French in 1842 as part of NEW CALEDONIA. In 1887 they became part of the French protectorate of the Wallis and Futuna Islands, and formally became a French territory in 1961.

WALLONIA [*French:* **Wallonie**] (Belgium) Country of the Walloons, named from the Teutonic word meaning foreign and a term usually used in reference to Belgium's French-speaking provinces. These include HAINAUT, LIÈGE, LUXEMBOURG, NAMUR, and a portion of BRABANT. The ancestors of the Walloons were Gallic Belgi with a strong Roman influence. The Walloon dialect constitutes a clear division of the Romance languages and has a healthy literary tradition dating from the Middle Ages. The strong nationalist sentiment in 19th-century Europe stimulated the development of a forceful movement for the revival of Walloon literature.

WALLONIE. See WALLONIA.

WALLSEND (England) Town in Tyne and Wear, on the Tyne River, 3 mi NE of Newcastle upon Tyne. An old Roman military post, it received its name from its position at the E end of HADRIAN'S WALL.

WALPI (United States) A Hopi Indian pueblo, NE of Flagstaff, NE ARIZONA. Founded early in the 18th century as a refuge for Pueblo Indians in revolt against the Spanish, Walpi is now a major tourist attraction.

WALSALL (England) Town in West Midlands, 8 mi NW of Birmingham. A royal residence in the 11th century, it was chartered in 1589. It continues to hold fairs that began in the Middle Ages. It is the location of a 15th-century church and of several schools established by Queen Mary in 1554.

WALSINGHAM (England) Village in NORFOLK, 26 mi NW of Norwich. It was the site of the famous medieval Walsingham, the major English shrine of the Virgin Mary. In the early 16th century it was England's most popular pilgrimage center.

WALTHAM (United States) City on the Charles River, NW suburb of Boston, NE MASSACHUSETTS. Settled in 1636, it was separated from WATERTOWN in 1738. Several industrial innovations were developed here, including the nation's first paper mill in 1788. Theodore Lyman, noted naturalist and congressman from 1882 to 1885, was born here in 1833. His home still stands.

WALTHAM ABBEY. See WALTHAM HOLY CROSS.

WALTHAM FOREST (England) Borough of Outer LONDON, in the N. Located here is Water House, the former residence of the Victorian poet, artist, and humanitarian William Morris. A hunting lodge of Queen Elizabeth I is preserved here as a museum.

WALTHAM HOLY CROSS [**Waltham Abbey**] (England) Village in Essex, 14 mi NNE of London. A famous Norman Abbey was built here in the 11th century. It housed a bit of the true cross, said to have been found in Somerset. Remains of the great nave, now a parish church, and of the abbey survive. The

Anglo-Saxon King Harold, who founded the abbey and was killed at the battle of Hastings in 1066, is buried here. A simple stone behind the abbey ruins, inscribed "Harold, King of the English," marks the spot.

WALVIS BAY (Namibia) Port and territory on the Atlantic Ocean, 710 mi N of Cape Town. Long under British protection, Walvis Bay was incorporated as an exclave into South Africa in 1922. Namibia's only deep-water port, it is still under the sovereignty of SOUTH AFRICA.

WAL WAL [**Ual Ual**] (Ethiopia) Village approx. 80 mi from the border of Somalia. On Oct. 3, 1935 Mussolini's Italy began war on Ethiopia following the League of Nations' inability to quell hostilities between the two countries. Hostilities had erupted on Dec. 5, 1934 at Wal Wal, a watering hole in OGADEN province, which at the time was at the juncture of Ethiopia, British Somaliland, and Italian Somaliland and which was held by Italian troops.

WANA (Pakistan) Village near the border of Afghanistan, 85 mi NW of Dera Ismail Khan, in the tribal lands of WAZIRISTAN, NORTH-WEST FRONTIER PROVINCE. Then part of India, it was occupied in 1894 by the British during the Waziristan expedition. Wana was turned over to native troops, but was reoccupied in 1922, following the three-year Mahsud revolt known as the Third Afghan War.

WAN-CH'UAN. See KALGAN.

WANDEWASH. See WANDIWASH.

WANDIWASH [**Wandewash**] (India) Town, 60 mi SW of Madras, Tamil Nadu. Several battles occurred here during the Seven Years War. French General Lally was defeated here on Jan. 22, 1760. A crucial blow to French ambitions to empire in India was thus dealt by the British under Sir Eyre Coote.

WANDSWORTH (England) Borough of Inner LONDON, on the Thames River, in the SW. It was a center of an 18th-century textile industry operated by Huguenot refugees who had fled the effects of the revocation of the Edict of Nantes in 1685. Within its area is PUTNEY HEATH, once a notorious refuge for highwaymen.

WANGANUI (New Zealand) Port on SW North Island, near the mouth of the Wanganui River. Founded in 1842, until 1870 it saw repeated hostilities between Maori tribes and British settlers.

WAN-HSIEN (China) Port on the YANGTZE RIVER, 165 mi E of Chungking, E Szechwan province. An old Chinese town, situated where the Yangtze River narrows, it was the home of Li Po, the great Chinese poet of the eighth century. A temple built in his honor stands here. During the early 20th century the port was opened to trade with the West.

WAN-T'ING [**Wanting**] (China) Town on the Shweli River, W Yunnan. On the famous BURMA ROAD, Wan-T'ing is a border village of Yunnan province and BURMA. During World War II, it was occupied by Japanese troops invading from Burma. Chinese and American forces liberated the town in January 1945.

WARANGAL (India) City in Andhra Pradesh state,

86 mi NE of Hyderabad. It was the 12th-century capital of the kingdom of the Telúgu, or ANDHRA, a Hindu state of Dravidian-speaking people.

WARBURG (West Germany) Town in North Rhine-Westphalia. Here in 1760 Frederick II the Great's general Ferdinand, duke of Brunswick, won a notable victory over Chevalier du Muy, Louis XV's commander. The battle forced the French to retreat and signaled the end of the Seven Years War in western Europe.

WARDASTALLA. See GUASTALLA.

WAREHAM (England) Town, former port, on the ISLE OF PURBECK, 10 mi W of Bournemouth, Dorset. A pre-Saxon settlement, Wareham still displays British earthworks. The site is strategically located on the Frome River. A castle was built here before 1086. Wareham itself was an important port of medieval England. The castle changed hands several times during the wars of the 13th and 14th centuries. It was taken in 1644 by Cromwell's forces. Edward the Martyr was assassinated at nearby Corfe Castle, and his coffin rests in St. Mary, a Saxon and Norman church here.

WARGLA. See OUARGLA.

WARKWORTH (England) Town in Northumberland, 26 mi N of Newcastle upon Tyne. For four centuries a Norman stronghold, Warkworth was dominated by Warkworth Castle, which was begun c.1140 by Henry, son of David I of Scotland. Warkworth's church of St. Laurence has a tower from c.1200. In the vicinity there are ruins of a Benedictine monastery dating from the 13th century.

WARMIA. See ERMELAND.

WARM SPRINGS (United States) Resort in W GEORGIA. The healing waters from Pine Mountain were known by the Indians. In 1830 a health resort was established at Warm Springs. Warm Springs Foundation, created to help polio victims, was founded in 1927 by Franklin D. Roosevelt, who died here in 1945.

WARQLA. See OUARGLA.

WARREN, New York State. See HAVERSTRAW.

WARREN (United States) City, 125 mi NE of Pittsburgh, NW PENNSYLVANIA. A Seneca Indian village on this site was burned by Colonel Daniel Brodhead in 1781 to punish the Indians who had followed Tory Joseph Brant during the Revolutionary War.

WARREN (United States) Resort on NARRAGANSETT BAY, 10 mi SE of Providence, E RHODE ISLAND. Founded in the early 1630's, it was originally claimed by both Massachusetts and Rhode Island colonies, but became part of Rhode Island in 1746. Brown University was founded here in 1764 as Rhode Island College. Lafayette established his headquarters here during the Revolutionary War. The town was burned by British troops in 1778. It thrived for many years as a whaling center.

WARRINGTON (England) Town in Cheshire, on the Mersey River, 14 mi E of Liverpool. An ancient British site, Warrington was on the Roman road to CHESTER.

It was a notable Royalist stronghold from 1642 to 1648 and endured siege and occupation during the Civil War. The Primitive Methodists initiated their religious sect here, and Joseph Priestley taught at Warrington's school for religious dissenters from 1757 to 1783.

WARSAW [*German:* **Warschau;** *Polish:* **Warszawa**] (Poland) City in central Poland, capital of the country, on the VISTULA RIVER. Although there were settlements on the site by the 11th century AD, the city developed after the duke of Masovia built a castle here in the 13th century. Warsaw became the capital of the duchy of MASOVIA in 1413 and in 1596 replaced CRACOW as Poland's capital. It was an important trading center in this period and also enjoyed a reputation for its cultural life. During the reign of Stanislaus II (1764–95), Warsaw was the home of the cultural movement called the Polish Enlightenment. Nevertheless, from the mid-17th to the 20th century Warsaw, with Poland itself, fell into the hands of numerous conquerors: SWEDEN in 1655/56 and 1702; RUSSIA in 1792 and 1794; PRUSSIA in 1795; and FRANCE in 1806 during Napoleon's invasion of Russia.

The following year the city became the capital of the grand duchy of Warsaw and in 1812 was the site of the official reestablishment of the Polish nation, which lasted only until 1813, when the Russians again captured the city. Warsaw was the headquarters of uprisings against the Russians in 1830 and 1863, but both revolts were unsuccessful. During World War I German troops subdued the city in 1915, but in November 1918 Polish troops liberated it, and it once more became the capital. The Russo-Polish War in 1920 was decided by the successful defense of Warsaw.

Warsaw's greatest trial came in World War II. Once again GERMANY occupied the city, from 1939 to 1945. The Nazis created a Jewish ghetto in which there was a desperate uprising in February 1943. Using the utmost force they crushed the ghetto defenders and murdered thousands of those who survived the battle. From August to October 1944 the Polish underground resistance fought German troops for control while the Soviet Army waited outside the city, ignoring pleas for help. In the end the Germans won, drove out the inhabitants and virtually destroyed the city; but, as the Soviets hoped, they were too weakened to hold it.

Freed in January 1945, Warsaw has been rebuilt, and much of the old city reconstructed in its original style. One of Europe's most historic cities, Warsaw is now a political, industrial, transportation, and cultural center of a communist nation dominated by the USSR. It has been a center of the postwar strikes and riots of workers in 1956, 1970, and most lately, in the 1980's.

WARSCHAU. See WARSAW.

WARSZAWA. See WARSAW.

WARWICK (England) Admin. hq. of WARWICKSHIRE, on the Avon River, 20 mi SE of Birmingham. The famous Norman Warwick Castle, much of it built in the 14th century on the site of a 10th-century fortress, still stands here on a cliff above the river. The earldom of Warwick was created c.1090 by William II, Rufus. It has been held by a number of the most famous families of England, including the Beauchamps, Nevilles, Dudleys, and Grevilles.

WARWICK (United States) City on NARRAGANSETT BAY, 10 mi S of Providence, central RHODE ISLAND. Founded in 1642 by Samuel Gorton, leader of the Gortonites, a sect of quaking dissenters, in 1647 it became one of the Providence Plantations. Severely damaged in 1676 in King Philip's War, in 1772 it was the scene of the patriots' destruction of the royal cutter *Gaspee* during the disputes over Britain's taxation policies. It was a textile center in the 19th century, and is now a center of a resort area. The Revolutionary War hero, Nathanael Greene, was born here in 1742.

WARWICKSHIRE (England) County of central England. The Romans invaded the area in the first century AD and occupied it until the fifth century. It contains the sites of several Norman castles: KENILWORTH, Maxstoke, and WARWICK. The ruins of Merevale and Stoneleigh abbeys also are here. William Shakespeare was born and spent much of his life in STRATFORD-UPON-AVON in southeastern Warwickshire.

WASATCH MOUNTAINS (United States) A range in the ROCKY MOUNTAINS, extending from SE IDAHO to central UTAH. Known from at least the beginning of the 18th century, in 1847 they were crossed by Brigham Young and his company of Mormons who settled in SALT LAKE CITY. The Pony Express, followed by several railroad lines, crossed the range in the second half of the 19th century.

WASCONIA. See GASCONY.

WASHINGTON (United States) City coextensive with the DISTRICT OF COLUMBIA, on the E coast, between Maryland and Virginia. It is the capital of the country. Beginning as a new town on the banks of the POTOMAC RIVER, during nearly two centuries the city had grown with the nation and today has all the trappings of an imperial city, the seat of government of a superpower. Its broad avenues and world-famous museums mingle with numerous government buildings.

Its swampy, humid site was selected by President George Washington, and a plan was made by Pierre Charles L'Enfant, a French engineer, although not much of this was used for many years. Construction of the White House, the president's residence, began in 1792 and of the Capitol building the following year. The government moved to Washington in 1800, John Adams being the first president to occupy the White House and Thomas Jefferson the first president inaugurated here, in 1801. During the War of 1812 the British captured Washington in 1814 and burned most of the public buildings, including the White House and the Capitol. The city was rebuilt but grew very slowly, and by the middle of the 19th century it was still a muddy, provincial town, although between 1851 and 1865 the Capitol was much enlarged. Several times during the Civil War the Confederacy threatened to capture the city. In 1901 L'Enfant's plan was revived, and the city was developed along his lines, which provided for a gridiron of streets with avenues cutting diagonally across them, creating parks and circles.

With the growth of the nation in the 20th century, Washington has become the focal point of much mass protest. In the 1930's the encampments of the Bonus Marchers, unemployed World War I veterans, threatened the capital and were dispersed only by military force. The assassination of Martin Luther King, Jr. in May 1968 brought six days of burning and looting in the city's black areas. The city was the scene of mass protests throughout the late 1960's against the VIETNAM War and for the Civil Rights and women's movements. In 1974 Congress passed legislation to allow the city and the District to elect its own mayor. World War I, the Great Depression, World War II, and the position of leadership thrust on the United States in the postwar years have stimulated the bureaucratic expansion of the federal government and therefore the expansion of Washington in size and importance. As a result, although much of the population changes with successive elections, it has become the center of a thriving metropolitan region that attracts not only innumerable tourists who visit monuments and historic sites, but also labor union and trade association headquarters, lobbyists, law firms, other businesses, and of course, the large international diplomatic and commercial communities.

WASHINGTON (United States) City, 25 mi SW of Pittsburgh, SW PENNSYLVANIA. It was settled in 1769. David Bradford, leader of the Whiskey Rebellion in 1794, used his home here as a secret meeting place. The house is still preserved, as is that of Dr. Francis Le Moyne, the noted 19th century abolitionist. Washington and Jefferson College was established here in 1780.

WASHINGTON COURT HOUSE. See FAYETTEVILLE, Arkansas.

WASHINGTON CROSSING (United States) Two state parks, one in NEW JERSEY and one in PENNSYLVANIA, on opposite sides of the DELAWARE RIVER, approx. 8 mi NNW of TRENTON, New Jersey. They were established to mark the crossing of the ice-filled river by George Washington and his Continental Army on Christmas night, 1776. The next day the force attacked and defeated the British at Trenton.

WASHINGTON, FORT. See FORT WASHINGTON.

WASHINGTON ISLAND, Kiribati. See LINE ISLANDS.

WASHINGTON ISLAND (United States) Island in NW LAKE MICHIGAN, NE WISCONSIN, S of Green Bay. It was reached in the 17th century by two Frenchmen, the fur trader Pierre Esprit Radisson in 1657 and the explorer Sieur de La Salle in 1679.

WASHINGTON ISLANDS. See MARQUESAS ISLANDS.

WASHINGTON-ON-THE-BRAZOS (United States) Town in S central TEXAS, on the Brazos River. Settled in 1821, on March 2, 1836 this town was the site of the convention that drafted Texas's declaration of independence from Mexico. On March 17 a constitution was drawn and a candidate for president, Samuel Houston, was selected. He was elected in September.

Washington-on-the-Brazos served as the capital of the REPUBLIC OF TEXAS in 1842.

WASHITA RIVER (United States) River, 500 mi long, rising in NW TEXAS, flowing SE across OKLAHOMA. On Nov. 23, 1868 Gen. George Custer decisively defeated a band of Cheyenne Indians at the Battle of Washita near Cheyenne, Oklahoma.

WATAUGA (United States) River, approx. 60 mi long, rising in NW NORTH CAROLINA and flowing NW through TENNESSEE to join the Holston River. The Watauga pioneer settlements, established from 1769 in the river's valley in eastern Tennessee, spawned much of the migration into western Tennessee and beyond.

WATAUGA RIVER VALLEY (United States) Area in NE TENNESSEE along the Watauga River. The river, which is approx. 75 mi long, rises in northwestern North Carolina and flows northwest into the south fork of the Holston River southeast of KINGSPORT, Tennessee. The first settlers were from Virginia, crossing the mountains through Boone's Gap in 1769. They were followed about two years later by settlers from North Carolina who had participated in the abortive Regulator Movement. In 1772 these settlers, meeting at Elizabethton, united as the Watauga Association for protection against the Indians. They were joined by other settlements on the Watauga River and on the Nolichucky.

In 1775 the settlers organized Washington District, but the next year they asked North Carolina to take them over, which it did, creating Washington County. After North Carolina ceded its western lands to the United States, the Watauga Valley residents and other inhabitants of eastern Tennessee formed the State of FRANKLIN in 1784. Congress, however, refused to recognize the state, and in 1796 the region became part of the new state of Tennessee. The Sycamore Shoals Monument honors these historic events, a treaty of 1775 with the Indians, and the men from here who fought in the battle of KINGS MOUNTAIN.

WATERBURY (United States) City at the confluence of the NAUGATUCK and Mad Rivers, 23 mi SW of Hartford, central CONNECTICUT. The city was settled in 1651. Its brass industry has flourished since the first years of the 19th century. Waterbury was known as the capital of American clock and watch manufacture throughout the 19th century. It was especially noted for the "dollar" watches of the period.

WATERFORD (Irish Republic) Port on the Suir River in county WATERFORD. It was founded as a fort by the Vikings in the ninth century AD. King John granted its first charter in 1205; a later charter was revoked in 1618 when its government leaders refused to take the English oath of supremacy. It was the only town in IRELAND to hold out against Cromwell, but in 1650 it fell to the Parliamentary general, Henry Ireton. An 11th-century fort and the ruins of 13th-century Franciscan and Dominican priories are located here.

WATERFORD (Irish Republic) County in MUNSTER province. Often hostile to English rule, it was crushed in the late 16th century by British forces called in to put down the Desmond rebellion. One of the main rebel leaders, Gerald, 15th earl of Desmond, was finally captured and executed in 1583.

WATERLOO (Belgium) Town in BRABANT province, approx. 12 mi S of Brussels. The Battle of Waterloo was lost here by Napoleon on June 18, 1815, bringing an end to the Napoleonic Wars. Napoleon, whose chief military tactic, surprise, had enabled him to defeat armies of superior strength, was outmaneuvered and outnumbered by Wellington, in command of a combined British and Dutch force. Blücher's Prussian reinforcements dealt Napoleon's army its final blow. Napoleon was permanently exiled to ST. HELENA following the defeat.

WATERLOO (United States) Village in W central NEW YORK State, 15 mi W of Auburn. It was settled in the 1790's following the defeat of Seneca Indians and British, by General John Sullivan. It became a center of the women's suffrage movement in the 19th century.

WATERTOWN (United States) Town on the Charles River, suburb W of Boston, NE MASSACHUSETTS. Settled in 1630, it is the site of one of the nation's oldest grist mills dating from 1634. The Provincial Congress convened here in the spring of 1775. The Perkins Institute for the Blind, established in Boston in 1829, has been located here since 1912.

WATERTOWN (United States) Town, 45 mi W of Milwaukee, SE WISCONSIN. It was founded in 1836. Carl Schurz, U.S. ambassador to Spain, Civil War general, and later senator from Missouri, lived here for about 10 years from 1856. In 1856 his wife founded the country's first kindergarten here.

WATERVLIET (United States) City on the HUDSON RIVER 6 mi N of Albany, E NEW YORK State. It was settled as early as 1640. Dutch colonists came here in 1735. The first American Shaker community was founded here in 1776 by Ann Lee. The Schuyler Home of 1666 is located here.

WATLING. See SAN SALVADOR, Bahamas.

WATLINGS ISLAND. See SAN SALVADOR, Bahamas.

WATLING STREET (England) Ancient Roman road extending NW from LONDON to WROXETER, intersecting the FOSSE WAY near Leicester. It divided the ninth-century kingdom of MERCIA between Danish Mercia in the DANELAW to the northeast, and Anglo-Saxon Mercia. An extension from London to DOVER is often called Watling Street.

WATTIGNIES [Wattignies-La-Victoire] (France) Village in Nord department. A French revolutionary force commanded by Jean Baptiste Jourdan defeated the Austrians under Friedrich Josias Coburg, prince of Saxe-Coburg, in a battle fought here on Oct. 15 and 16, 1793.

WATTIGNIES-LA-VICTOIRE. See WATTIGNIES.

WATTS (United States) Suburb of LOS ANGELES, SW CALIFORNIA. Violent racial riots occurred here in 1965.

WATTWIL. See TOGGENBURG, Switzerland.

WAU (Papua New Guinea) Community in E New Guinea Island, 32 mi SW of Salamaua. It was settled in the 1920's as a center for the surrounding gold fields. The area was taken by Japanese forces early in World War II. Australian and American forces liberated it early in 1943.

WAUKEGAN [*former:* **Little Fort**] (United States) City on Lake Michigan, 40 mi N of Chicago, NE Illinois. A French trading post, before the Treaty of Paris that ended the French and Indian War in 1763, it was settled as Little Fort in 1835, and took its present name *c.*1850.

WAUSAU (United States) Industrial city on the Wisconsin River, 84 mi NW of Green Bay, central Wisconsin. Founded in the early 1840's and incorporated in 1872, it was a center of Wisconsin's thriving logging industry in the 19th century.

WAUWASET. See Brandywine Creek.

WAVRE (Belgium) City of Brabant province, 14 mi SE of Brussels. The French general, Marquis Emmanuel de Grouchy, held the field here against the Prussian general Blücher on June 18, 1815, the day of the nearby Battle of Waterloo. Grouchy failed to come to Napoleon's help; the Prussians arrived at Waterloo instead, turning the tide against the French there.

WAWA (Philippines) Village in Rizal province, Luzon, near Manila. The Wawa Dam, a Japanese military stronghold during World War II, was captured by U.S. forces on May 28, 1945.

WAYNESBORO (United States) City, 96 mi NE of Roanoke, N central Virginia. Settled in the mid-1730's, it was the site of the Civil War battle of Waynesboro. Here on March 2, 1865 Union troops led by Gen. George Custer routed and almost destroyed a much smaller Confederate force under Gen. Jubal Early.

WAZAN. See Wazzan.

WAZIRISTAN [Wana] (Pakistan) Region of Pakistan, SW North-West Frontier Province. It effectively resisted British influence throughout the 19th century. Waziristan was incorporated into Pakistan in 1947. From 1919 to 1922 it was the scene of the Third Afghan War (see Wana). An independence movement, encouraged by Afghanistan, has been at work in Waziristan recently.

WAZZAN [Wazan] [*French:* **Ouezzane**] (Morocco) City, 60 mi NW of Fès. The center of a significant Muslim sect established around the tomb of Idrisi Sharif, who lived here in 1727, it is regarded as a sacred city.

WEALD, THE (England) Agricultural district of Kent, Surrey, and Sussex counties, between the North Downs and South Downs. Once a densely forested area, most of its timber was harvested to power a thriving iron-smelting and gun manufacturing industry located here in the 18th century.

WEBSTER (United States) Resort town, 15 mi S of Worcester, on Lake Webster, central Massachusetts. The lake was once a popular Indian fishing spot. The town was settled *c.*1715 and was separated from Dudley and Oxford when it was incorporated in 1832. Cotton was first milled here in 1811. It throve as a textile center in the 19th century, largely through the efforts of Samuel Slater, pioneer New England textile manufacturer.

WEDMORE (England) Village in Somerset, 19 mi NE of Taunton. Alfred the Great of Wessex and the Danish King Guthrum of East Anglia signed a treaty here after the battle of Edington in 878. The treaty limited the holdings of the Danes to an area north of Watling Street. The region thereafter became known as the Danelaw.

WEEHAWKEN (United States) Township on the Hudson River, opposite New York City, NE New Jersey. The Highwood Estate, located here, is on the site where Aaron Burr killed Alexander Hamilton in a duel on July 11, 1804.

WEENEN (South Africa) Town in central Natal, 85 mi NW of Durban. Boer Voortrekkers were massacred here in 1838 by a band of Zulus. The town, founded in the same year, was the second settlement in Natal.

WEHLAU [*since 1945:* **Znamensk**] (USSR) Town on the S bank of the Pregolya River at the mouth of the Lava River. By a treaty concluded here in 1657 with Brandenburg, Poland gave up the duchy of Prussia.

WEI [*Chinese:* **Wei-He**] (China) River, approx. 535 mi long, rising in SE Kansu and flowing E across Kansu and Shensi provinces to the Yellow River (Huang-Ho) at Tun-Huang, N central China. Its valley saw the beginnings of some of the earliest Chinese civilizations, including that of the Chou people, who migrated from the Wei valley and established the Chou dynasty *c.*1025 BC. It lasted until 256 BC, the longest dynasty in Chinese history.

WEICHSEL. See Vistula River.

WEI-HAI. See Wei-Hai-Wei.

WEI-HAI-WEI [**Wei-Hai, Weihaiwei**] (China) Seaport on the Strait of Po Hai, NE Shantung province, NE China. The Japanese defeated the Chinese Navy offshore here in 1895, during the first Sino-Japanese War. The Japanese occupied the town from 1895 to 1898. From 1898 to 1930 it was leased to the British, who developed the area into a major port and naval base. During World War II it was occupied by the Japanese again.

WEI-HE. See Wei.

WEIMAR (East Germany) City on the Ilm River, 54 mi SW of Leipzig, Erfurt district. Established as early as the 10th century, it was chartered in 1348 and served as the capital first of the duchy from 1547 and then, after 1815, of the grand duchy of Saxe-Weimar to 1918. The so-called Weimar Republic of Germany was set up here in 1919, lasting until 1933. It was bombed and taken by U.S. troops in 1945. The city flourished in the 18th and 19th centuries as the cultural center of Germany. Bach, Goethe, Schiller, and Nietzsche lived and worked here. During World War II the infamous Buchenwald concentration camp was located nearby.

WEIMAR REPUBLIC. See Germany.

WEINSBERG (West Germany) Town near Heilbronn, Baden-Württemberg. The Hohenstaufen German king, Conrad III, defeated the Saxon forces of Count Guelph VI in a battle fought here in 1140 during a civil war over the royal succession. From 1331 to 1440 Weinsberg, a free imperial city, was a member of the league of Swabian cities. In 1440 it was captured by the nobles and sold to the PALATINATE, which deprived it of its traditional liberties.

WEISSENBURG. See WISSEMBOURG.

WEISSENFELS (East Germany) City on the Saale River, HALLE district. Known from at least the mid-12th century, from 1656 to 1746 it was the capital of Saxe-Weissenfels, a small duchy belonging to the Electorate of SAXONY. In 1815, after the Napoleonic Wars, it passed to PRUSSIA.

WEISSER BERG. See WHITE MOUNTAIN.

WELLE. See UELE.

WELLINGBOROUGH (England) Town in Northamptonshire, on the Nene River, 10 mi ENE of Northampton. An old trading and commercial center, it was also the site of healing springs, from which its name derives. It has a 16th-century grammar school.

WELLINGTON (New Zealand) Capital city of New Zealand, S North Island on Port Nicholson or Wellington harbor. The city was founded in 1840, the first settlement of New Zealand colonists. In 1865 it replaced AUCKLAND as the national capital.

WELLS (England) City in SOMERSET, 17 mi S of Bristol. Dating from the early eighth century, in the 10th century it was an important trading center of WESSEX. The town became a bishopric in 909 and was chartered in 1201. A 12th-century cathedral is adorned with a large collection of 13th-century sculptured figures. The moat and walls of a 14th-century palace remain next to the cathedral. There is also a 15th-century church here.

WELS [*ancient:* **Ovilava**] (Austria) City on the Traun River, Upper Austria, 26 mi SW of Linz. Inhabited since prehistoric times, it was a Roman town and a medieval military post. In 1519 the Holy Roman emperor, Maximilian I, died here in the imperial palace. The city was heavily bombed in World War II.

WELWYN GARDEN CITY (England) Residential town in Hertfordshire, 20 mi N of London. It is a pioneer garden city, a specially planned community that combines decentralized industrialization with a rural atmosphere. It was founded in 1920 by the originator of the movement, Sir Ebenezer Howard. After World War II, it was developed to relieve London's overpopulation. See also LETCHWORTH.

WEMYSS (Scotland) Town on the Firth of Forth, E Scotland. Mary, Queen of Scots, first met her second husband, the earl of Darnley, at Wemyss Castle in 1565.

WEN-CHOU. See WENCHOW.

WENCHOW [**Wen-Chou**] [*former:* **Yungkia**] (China) Port in SE Chekiang province, on the Wu River, approx. 160 mi S of Hangchow. It dates to the fourth century AD. A former treaty port opened to foreign trade in 1876, it was occupied by Japanese troops during World War II. The port has many ancient buildings.

WENDEN. See CESIS.

WERNIGERODE (East Germany) City in MAGDEBURG district, 30 mi SE of Brunswick. It was founded in the ninth century AD. In the 13th century it joined the HANSEATIC LEAGUE. A former residence of the Stolberg-Wernigerode counts and the chief city of the county of Stolberg-Wernigerode, it passed to PRUSSIA in 1714. It has a restored medieval castle and a 15th-century town hall.

WERSCHETZ. See VRŠAC.

WESEL (West Germany) Port at the confluence of the RHINE and Lippe Rivers, 49 mi SW of Münster, North Rhine-Westphalia. Dating from as early as the eighth century, in the 13th century it fell under the control of the counts of KLEVE and, in 1666, of the elector of BRANDENBURG. It flourished as a cultural and commercial center in the late Middle Ages, and joined the HANSEATIC LEAGUE in 1407. The site of many historical military maneuvers, it was occupied by French troops from 1808 to 1814 during the Napoleonic Wars. It was almost totally destroyed in heavy fighting during World War II when Allied forces crossed the Rhine here on March 24, 1945.

WESSEX (England) Saxon kingdom of Britain, roughly included in the modern counties of Berkshire, Dorset, Somerset, Hampshire, and Wiltshire. Firmly established by the time Ceawlin began his reign in 560 AD, it surpassed NORTHUMBRIA and MERCIA during the reigns of Caedwalla (685–88) and Ine (688–726). Under Alfred the Great (871–99) it successfully resisted the invasion of the Danes. By the early 10th century it had taken control of most of modern England. From that point its history became that of England.

WESTBORO. See WESTBOROUGH.

WESTBOROUGH [**Westboro**] (United States) Town and suburb E of Worcester, on the Assabet River, central MASSACHUSETTS. Incorporated in 1717, it was the birthplace in 1765 of Eli Whitney, inventor of the cotton gin and innovator of mass production methods. The Whitney birthplace has been preserved.

WEST BRANCH. See IOWA.

WESTCHESTER COUNTY (United States) County in NEW YORK State, N of NEW YORK CITY, E of the Hudson River, S of Putnam County, and W of Connecticut. The area was part of the Dutch province of NEW NETHERLAND until the English seized the province in 1664. Settlement had begun under the Dutch regime, and on Nov. 1, 1683 Westchester became one of the first 12 counties formed in the province of New York. The Dutch and British made large grants of land, such as Van Cortlandt Manor of 86,000 acres and Phillipsburg Manor. By the time of the American Revolution nearly all parts of the county had some settlers. On July 9, 1776 the New York provincial council, meeting in WHITE PLAINS, ratified the Declaration of Independence. However, on October 28 Washington's Continental Army was defeated by the British at the battle of White Plains. During the war the county was the scene of skirmishing and pillaging by both Patriots and Tories. In a famous spy case, British Major John André was captured in Westchester on Sept. 23, 1780 and executed.

The 19th century saw the influx of Irish and Italians who between 1837 and 1842 built the CROTON Dam and Aqueduct, New York City's water supply system, and went on to become the upper middle and professional class of the county. As railroad lines spread and, later, with the arrival of the automobile, Westchester became a bedroom community for people who commuted to New York City to work. The move to the suburbs intensified after World War II, but many large corporations also moved to Westchester, providing jobs nearer home. The nation's first parkway, Bronx River Parkway, was constructed here beginning in 1916. Westchester takes it name from the city of CHESTER, England. Among its interesting historic towns are:MAMARONECK, MT. VERNON, NewROCHELLE, OSSINING, PORT CHESTER, RYE, SCARSDALE, TARRYTOWN, White Plains, and YONKERS.

WEST COLUMBIA (United States) City, 19 mi NE of Bay City, SE TEXAS. In 1836 it served temporarily as the capital of the newly formed REPUBLIC OF TEXAS.

WESTERLY [*former:* **Misquamicut**] (United States) Town on the Pawcatuck River, 27 mi SW of Newport, S RHODE ISLAND. First settled in 1648, and again by colonists from Newport, it was disputed by Connecticut and Rhode Island until 1728. Since the early 19th century it has been a textile center and a popular resort.

WESTERN AUSTRALIA (Australia) State in W Australia. First visited by the Dutch explorer, Dirck Hartog, in 1616, it was settled in 1826 with the establishment of a penal colony at Albany. The free Swan River Settlement was founded at PERTH-FREMANTLE three years later. The state was mainly a penal colony of NEW SOUTH WALES, from which it was separated in 1890, before the discovery of gold at COOLGARDIE and KALGOORLIE in the 1880's. It became a state of the Commonwealth of Australia in 1901.

WESTERN BUG. See BUG.

WESTERN ISLANDS. See HEBRIDES, THE.

WESTERN ISLES (Scotland) Island area that includes the Outer HEBRIDES. The admin. hq. is Stornoway.

WESTERN PROVINCE [*former:* **Barotseland**] (Zambia) Province of W Zambia, S central Africa. The Barotse ruled this area from the early 19th century until they were displaced by the Kalolo or Makalolo warriors from LESOTHO in 1838. Their rule was reestablished in 1864. They gave the British trading rights here toward the end of the century. It became a province of the British protectorate of NORTHERN RHODESIA in 1911, and part of the newly formed independent republic of Zambia in 1964.

WESTERN RESERVE [**Connecticut Reserve**] (United States) Tract of land in NE OHIO, now forming more than 10 counties. It was settled during the 1790's by Connecticut immigrants; it had been retained by CONNECTICUT when it ceded its NORTHWEST TERRITORY holdings to the U.S. government in 1786. In 1796 CLEVELAND became its first permanent settlement. It was ceded to Ohio as Trumbull county in 1800.

WESTERN SAHARA. See MAURITANIA, MOROCCO, SPANISH SAHARA.

WESTERN SAMOA Island nation in the Pacific Ocean, halfway between Hawaii and Sydney, Australia. The Independent State of Western Samoa comprises those of the Samoa Islands W of 171° W. The islands to the east comprise AMERICAN SAMOA. The two largest islands of Western Samoa are Savai'i and UPOLU. Under an agreement made in 1899 by GERMANY, Great Britain, and the United States, what is now Western Samoa became German territory. In World War I NEW ZEALAND took the islands in 1914 and received a League of Nations mandate to administer them in 1921. In 1946 Western Samoa became a United Nations trusteeship, administered by New Zealand. New Zealand's rule was unpopular with both the European and the Polynesian inhabitants, however. After a plebiscite conducted by the United Nations in 1961, Western Samoa became an independent constitutional monarchy on Jan. 1, 1962 and is a member of the Commonwealth of Nations. Apia, on Opolu, is the capital and the nation's only port and city. Robert Louis Stevenson, the popular Scottish author, spent his last years on Upolu, dying in 1894. He is buried here.

WESTERN UKRAINIA (USSR) Territory in W Ukrainian SSR. A short-lived republic in the former Austrian crownland of GALICIA was formed here from 1918 to 1919. In 1919 it was ceded to Poland after the defeat of the Central Powers in World War I. It was almost immediately occupied by Bolshevik troops, who reunited it to the rest of the UKRAINE. It was part of the Ukrainian Soviet Socialist Republic when the latter was formed in 1922.

WESTFALAHI. See WESTPHALIA.

WESTFALEN. See WESTPHALIA.

WESTFIELD (United States) Town and suburb of NEW YORK CITY, NE NEW JERSEY. Settled by the Dutch in 1700, it was separated from ELIZABETH in 1794. During the Revolutionary War it became a center of frequent skirmishes between British troops, who held New York City, and the Americans who held most of New Jersey.

WEST FRISIAN ISLANDS. See FRISIAN ISLANDS.

WEST GERMANY. See FEDERAL REPUBLIC OF GERMANY.

WEST GLAMORGAN (Wales) County in the S, on the Bristol Channel. Created from part of the former county of Glamorganshire, it is important for its metal-processing. Its admin. hq. is SWANSEA.

WEST HANOVER. See MORRISTOWN.

WEST HARTFORD (United States) Town and suburb of HARTFORD, N CONNECTICUT. Founded in 1679, it was incorporated in 1854. It is the birthplace of Noah Webster (1758–1843), the famous American lexicographer. The American School for the Deaf was founded here in 1817 by Thomas Hopkins Gallaudet.

WEST HAVERSTRAW (United States) Village on the HUDSON RIVER, 34 mi N of New York City, SE NEW YORK State. American Gen. Benedict Arnold and British Maj. John André conspired in 1780 at the Treason House, located in the village, to deliver WEST POINT to the British during the American Revolution.

WEST INDIES Archipelago extending in an arc from SE North America to N South America, from Florida to Venezuela. The islands separate the Gulf of Mexico and the CARIBBEAN SEA on the west and south from the Atlantic Ocean. It was in the West Indies that Europeans first made permanent contact with and settlement of the New World during their voyages seeking the Far East and its wealth. From here expeditions were launched that conquered parts of North and South America.

The first land reached by Columbus was SAN SALVADOR Island on Oct. 12, 1492. The Spanish gained a head start in taking possession of many islands, but they were soon followed by the British, French, Dutch, and, later, by the Danes. The first native Indian people found by these explorers were the peaceful Arawak Indians and the fierce Caribs. Almost the entire Indian population fell victim to disease, war, and slavery and was replaced by black slaves imported from Africa to work the rich plantations that soon developed. The blacks became the most numerous race in the West Indies.

Until the 20th century the West Indies remained an area of imperialistic competition by European nations. As a result of the Spanish-American War of 1898, and of its growing power in general, the UNITED STATES became the most influential nation in the area, with the most pressing strategic interest in it. Most of the islands have become independent since World War II, but many of them are unstable politically and troubled economically.

Among the islands and states of the West Indies are ANTIGUA, ARUBA, BAHAMAS, BARBADOS, BIMINIS, CAYMANS, CUBA, CURAÇAO, DOMINICA, DOMINICAN REPUBLIC, ELEUTHERA, GRENADA, GUADELOUPE, HAITI, HISPANIOLA, JAMAICA, MARGARITA, Maria Galante, MARTINIQUE, MONTSERRAT, NETHERLANDS ANTILLES, New Providence, PUERTO RICO, SABA, ST. EUSTATIUS, ST. KITTS-NEVIS, ST. LUCIA, ST. MARTIN, ST. VINCENT AND THE GRENADINES, TORTUGA, TRINIDAD-TOBAGO, TURKS AND CAICOS and the VIRGIN ISLANDS.

WEST IRIAN. See IRIAN BARAT.

WEST JERSEY. See NEW JERSEY.

WESTKAPELLE (Netherlands) Town in Zeeland province, on WALCHEREN Island, SW Netherlands. During World War II it was liberated in November 1944 by Allied troops, leading to the capture of Walcheren Island on November 8, 1944 and thus opening the SCHELDE estuary and sea lanes to Antwerp, Belgium, which had been liberated in September.

WEST LAFAYETTE. See TIPPECANOE, Indiana.

WESTMARK. See SAARLAND.

WESTMINSTER [City of Westminster] [*Latin:* Westmonasterium] (England) National government center, borough of Inner LONDON, in the W, on the THAMES RIVER. Buckingham Palace, the royal residence, is located here, as is Westminster Abbey, first established in the 10th century, and one of England's major national shrines. Government offices include Downing Street and WHITEHALL. A public school was founded here in the 14th century and chartered in 1560 by Queen Elizabeth. Westminster Palace, an early royal residence, served as the meeting place of Parliament since the 14th century. It burned down in 1834. The new Parliament buildings replaced it in 1852.

WESTMONASTERIUM. See WESTMINSTER.

WESTMORLAND (England) Former county, now incorporated in Cumbria. In the 14th century Flemish immigrants began a woolens industry here, especially in KENDAL, that is still operating. William Wordsworth, the eminent English poet, lived and worked here from 1799 to 1850, and is now buried at GRASMERE. See also LAKE DISTRICT.

WEST NEW GUINEA. See IRIAN BARAT.

WESTON-SUPER-MARE (England) Seaside resort and port in Avon, on the Bristol Channel at the mouth of the SEVERN RIVER, 18 mi SW of Bristol. Incorporated in 1932, it is the site of a hillside fort that dates to the Iron Age.

WEST ORANGE (United States) Town and suburb of both NEWARK, to the SE, and of NEW YORK CITY, to the E, NE NEW JERSEY. It was founded in 1862 when it was set off from Orange. Glenwood, the home of Thomas Edison from 1887 to 1931, is located in Llewellyn Park. It is now a national shrine.

WESTPHALIA [*ancient:* **Westfalahi;** *German:* **Westfalen**] (West Germany) Meaning "western plain," originally Westphalia was a duchy founded in the 12th century following the imperial censure of Duke Henry the Lion of SAXONY, who was deprived of his lands. Its capital was MÜNSTER, where the Peace of Westphalia was concluded October 24, 1648. Prussian inroads into Westphalia began with the BRANDENBURG acquisition of territories in the 17th century, but domination came only after the Congress of Vienna in 1815. Prior to this, at the conclusion of the peace of TILSIT in 1807, Napoleon had created a much enlarged kingdom of Westphalia, which he presented to his brother, Jerome. Its capital was KASSEL. Following the battle of LEIPZIG in October 1813, the Russians invaded Westphalia, forced King Jerome Bonaparte to flee, and reestablished the earlier province. With the Congress of Vienna in 1815 the kingdom of PRUSSIA acquired the whole of Westphalia, which remained a Prussian province until 1945. Westphalia became part of the state of North Rhine-Westphalia in 1946.

WEST POINT (United States) U.S. military post, and U.S. Military Academy headquarters, on the HUDSON RIVER, approx. 50 mi N of New York City, SE

NEW YORK. Taken by the Continental Army in 1778, it was used as a fort to protect the Hudson River valley during the Revolutionary War. An iron chain extended from this point to Constitution Island as a deterrent to British naval advances along the Hudson. Benedict Arnold's plot to surrender West Point to the British was exposed in 1780 when British Maj. André was captured. The military academy was established here by Congress in 1802. See also WEST HAVERSTRAW.

WESTPORT [*former:* **Saugatuck**] (United States) Town on the LONG ISLAND SOUND and the Saugatuck River, SW CONNECTICUT. Settled in 1645, it was a favorite hiding place for smugglers throughout the colonial era. Attacked twice by Tory forces during the Revolutionary War, it was William Tryon's base for his Tory raid on DANBURY in 1777.

WESTPORT, BATTLE OF. See INDEPENDENCE, Missouri.

WESTPREUSSEN. See WEST PRUSSIA.

WEST PRUSSIA [*German:* **Westpreussen**] Former province of PRUSSIA, on the Baltic Coast of NE Germany. A part of east Pomerania as early as the 13th century, it was ceded to Prussia during the Polish partitions in 1772 and 1793. It was reorganized and assigned to POLAND in 1919 after World War I by the terms of the Treaty of Versailles. Occupied by the Germans during World War II, the region was again assigned to Poland in 1945, this time by the Potsdam Conference. See also GDAŃSK and POLISH CORRIDOR.

WEST ROXBURY (United States) Former town in E MASSACHUSETTS. It was incorporated into BOSTON in 1874. A utopian community operated here at Brook Farm from 1841 to 1847. Founded by the Unitarian minister, George Ripley, its communal life was based on the philosophical principles of transcendentalism. A fire destroyed part of the main building in 1846, and the community succumbed to financial plight soon after.

WEST SPRINGFIELD (United States) Town and suburb of Springfield, on the Connecticut River, SW MASSACHUSETTS. It was settled in 1654. Farmers, who believed that state-issued paper money would save them from foreclosure, initiated Shays's Rebellion here in 1786.

WEST VIRGINIA (United States) State located in the E central region, bounded on the N by Pennsylvania and by Ohio across the Ohio River, on the S and W by Kentucky, and on the E by Virginia. It was admitted to the Union in 1863 as the 35th state. Called the Mountain State, it is hilly and rugged and lies almost entirely in the Allegheny plateau.

The Indian Mound Builders were the earliest known inhabitants. The Grave Creek Mound at MOUNDSVILLE is one of the largest in the country. When European explorers and fur traders first came here in the 1670's, the land was sparsely inhabited, and it became a common hunting and battle ground for settlers and Indians. Cut off by mountains from the rest of VIRGINIA, of which it was then a part, the area of West Virginia grew more slowly than the colonies of the seaboard. Germans and Scotch-Irish from PENNSYLVANIA were the first settlers; the former made a settlement at Mecklenburg, now Shepherdstown, in the eastern panhandle *c.*1730.

Concerned about penetration of the Ohio Valley by FRANCE, in 1749 the British granted a large tract of land west of the ALLEGHENY MTS to the Ohio Company, which promoted land settlement. The French and Indian War ended in 1763 with the British victorious in North America. During the war there were so many Indian massacres in the area that most settlers fled the region, but they quickly returned when the British took FORT DUQUESNE, now PITTSBURGH, Pennsylvania, in 1758 and thus regained control of the Ohio Valley. To avoid Indian uprisings, Great Britain forbade settlement west of the Alleghenies after 1763; but colonists ignored the prohibition, causing widespread Indian attacks. The Indians were subdued in October 1774 in Lord Dunmore's War.

During the American Revolution the region was invaded three times by British troops and their Indian allies, but George Rogers Clark's victories in the Old Northwest removed this threat. The region benefited by the LOUISIANA PURCHASE of 1803, which increased traffic on the OHIO RIVER as the entire MISSISSIPPI RIVER trading system became controlled by the United States. Further benefit in the form of western migration came in 1818 when the NATIONAL ROAD reached WHEELING from CUMBERLAND, Maryland.

The early 19th century saw the beginning of conflict between small farmers, with almost no slaveholdings, and the eastern Virginia planters, large slave owners. Constitutional changes in 1830 and 1851 put some reforms into effect, but the East remained in control. In October 1859, the abolitionist John Brown led a small band that seized the Federal arsenal at HARPERS FERRY. U.S. Marines captured them and, after a trial, Brown was hanged on Dec. 2, 1859 at CHARLES TOWN.

The people strongly opposed secession in 1861. A convention met in June, declared Virginia's secession null and void, and set up its own government. Two years later Congress recognized this government as a separate state of West Virginia.

In the summer of 1861, during the Civil War, the Union won a number of battles in the state, notably at PHILIPPI and RICH MOUNTAIN. In September Gen. R.E. Lee's Confederate forces were defeated at CHEAT MOUNTAIN. Later there was also fighting in the eastern panhandle, and Harpers Ferry changed hands several times.

After the war the Radical Republicans gained control; but the Democrats regained power in a few years. In the late 19th century, large scale industrialization began; the chemical industry entered the state; and all industry expanded throughout the first half of the 20th century. Both wars created enormous demands for the state's coal and steel and further helped industrial growth. The extensive coal fields throughout the state were exploited; and steel mills reached south into the northern panhandle from Pittsburgh.

West Virginian coal fields have been the scene of much union organizing for decent wages and safety standards. This has led to many strikes, especially in

1912 to 1913 and 1920 to 1921. The Great Depression of the 1930's was especially hard on the miners; but the New Deal of President Franklin Roosevelt supported union organization, and the miners' union became powerful. However, in the 1950's the coal industry weakened, and mechanization cost many jobs, resulting in Federal aid to attract new industry in the 1960's. In the 1970's the Congress initiated steps to control strip mining throughout the region.

CHARLESTON is the capital of West Virginia, and HUNTINGTON the largest city; PARKERSBURG and Wheeling are also important cities.

WESTWALL. See SIEGFRIED LINE.

WETHERSFIELD (United States) Town on the Connecticut River, a suburb S of HARTFORD, N CONNECTICUT. Founded in the winter of 1634 by settlers from Massachusetts, it was the first permanent white settlement in the state. The town was incorporated three years later. The Wethersfield Massacre of 1637 led to the Pequot Indian War. A flourishing commercial center during the colonial era, it was one of the first ports to conduct trade with the WEST INDIES. There are many colonial homes located here, including those of Silas Deane and Joseph Webb, the latter the scene of a secret meeting in 1781 between George Washington and Comte de Rochambeau to discuss the upcoming Yorktown Campaign.

WETTINGEN (Switzerland) City of the AARGAU canton, approx. 10 mi NW of Zurich. A Cistercian abbey containing the tomb of the Holy Roman Emperor Albert I (1298–1308) was established here in 1227.

WETZLAR (West Germany) City on the LAHN RIVER, HESSE, 30 mi N of Frankfurt am Main. A free imperial city from the 12th century to the Napoleonic Wars, it contained the HOLY ROMAN EMPIRE's supreme court from 1693 to 1806. Wetzlar became part of PRUSSIA in 1815 after Napoleon's final defeat. Johann Wolfgang von Goethe (1749–1832) was a lawyer here in the early 1770's when he met the young woman whom he immortalized as Lotte in *The Sorrows of Young Werther* of 1774, his first popular book.

WEWAK (Papua New Guinea) Port on the N central coast of NE NEW GUINEA. A Japanese military base and airfield during World War II, it was attacked on Aug. 17, 1943 by Allied planes. It was captured by the Australians on May 10, 1945.

WEWOKA (United States) City, 65 mi SE of Oklahoma City, central OKLAHOMA. Once inhabited by resettled Creek and Seminole Indians, the site was settled by whites in 1866. The city still serves as the capital of the Seminole Nation, consisting of about 3000 members.

WEXFORD (Irish Republic) Seaport of COUNTY WEXFORD. An early naval stronghold of the Danes, later settled by the Anglo-Normans, it was captured, after fierce opposition, by Oliver Cromwell's army in 1649 during the English Civil War.

WEXFORD (Irish Republic) County in LEINSTER province, SE Ireland. Once inhabited by the Danes, it was the center of several Irish rebellions, particularly that by the United Irishmen in 1798 led by Theobald Wolfe Tone (1763–98). The famous American Kennedy family has ancestral roots in the county.

WEXIÖ. See VÄXJÖ.

WEYMOUTH (United States) Town, suburb SE of Boston, E MASSACHUSETTS. Settled in 1622, it is the birthplace of former first lady Abigail Adams (1744–1818). The old Indian Town Path located here dates from the 17th century.

WEYMOUTH AND MELCOMBE REGIS (England) Port and resort in Dorset, on the ENGLISH CHANNEL, 28 mi WSW of Bournemouth. A thriving medieval port, it was incorporated as an amalgamated borough in the 16th century by Queen Elizabeth. It was bombed repeatedly during World War II and was a base for the invasion of Normandy in 1944.

WEZET. See VISÉ.

WHAMPOA. See HUANG-PU.

WHEELING (United States) City on the OHIO RIVER, 61 mi SW of Pittsburgh, Pennsylvania, NW WEST VIRGINIA. Settled in 1769, it was originally known especially for its stockade built in 1774 as Fort Fincastle. In 1776 this was renamed Fort Henry after the greatly admired patriot Patrick Henry. It protected the area against Indian raids and withstood an assault of British and Indian forces in 1782 in one of the last actions of the Revolutionary War. From 1818 Wheeling developed as the western terminus of the NATIONAL ROAD. A center of Union sentiment during the Civil War, it was the site of the conventions in 1861 and 1862 that developed the state constitution. It became West Virginia's first capital in 1863.

WHITBY [*former:* **Streonshalh**] (England) Port on the Esk River and the North Sea, 16 mi NW of Scarborough, North Yorkshire. An abbey founded here in 657 AD by St. Hilda was destroyed by the Danes in 867 but was revived by the Benedictines in 1078. The abbey is now in ruins. At the Synod of Whitby in 663, King Oswy of NORTHUMBRIA decided to associate the English church with Roman, rather than Celtic, practices, especially in the determination of Easter, thus keeping England in the mainstream of western Christian development. Caedmon, the poet, was a monk here.

WHITEHALL (England) Road in the Inner LONDON borough of WESTMINSTER. It contains many government buildings. Its name is therefore often used synonymously for that of the British government. It was the site of Whitehall Palace, dating from the 13th century, rebuilt in the 16th and 17th centuries. Part of it is still used for official functions.

WHITEHAVEN (England) Town on the Solway Firth, in Cumbria, 35 mi SW of CARLISLE. John Paul Jones attacked the town in 1778 in a raid on the British coast during the American Revolution.

WHITE HILL. See WHITE MOUNTAIN.

WHITEHORSE (Canada) Capital of YUKON TERRITORY, on the Yukon River, 90 mi N of Skagway, Alaska. Founded in 1898, it throve during the KLONDIKE gold rush of 1897/98. It replaced DAWSON in 1955 as the capital of the Yukon.

WHITE HORSE, VALE OF THE (England) Valley of the Ock River, in Oxfordshire. Many ancient earthworks are located here. The principal town of the valley is Wantage, where Alfred the Great was born. The valley's name comes from the figure of a galloping horse on White Horse Hill, shaped in prehistoric times by cutting away the turf to expose the chalk. By tradition only, it is said to commemorate Alfred's victory at Ashdown in 871.

WHITEMARSH (United States) Village on the Wissahickon Creek, 14 mi N of Philadelphia, SE PENNSYLVANIA. The Continental Army, led by Gen. George Washington, encamped here in 1777 during the battle of GERMANTOWN in the Revolutionary War.

WHITE MOUNTAIN [White Hill] [*Czech:* **Bílá Hora;** *German:* **Weisser Berg**] (Czechoslovakia) Hill just W of PRAGUE. A battle fought here on Nov. 8, 1620 between Frederick V, king of Bohemia, and Ferdinand II, Holy Roman emperor, opened the Thirty Years War. Frederick's Protestant troops, commanded by Christian of Anhalt, were decisively defeated by the Roman Catholic forces of Maximillian I of Bavaria, an ally of the emperor. Frederick was deposed shortly thereafter and was known as the "Winter King" because of his short reign. BOHEMIA thus lost its independence for 300 years, and Europe was plunged into a new struggle between Protestant and Catholic interests.

WHITE NILE. See NILE RIVER.

WHITE PASS (United States) Mountain pass in the Coast Mountains, N of SKAGWAY, on the border of British Columbia in Canada, and SE ALASKA. It was used as an alternate route during the KLONDIKE gold rush, replacing the CHILKOOT PASS.

WHITE PLAINS (United States) City, 25 mi N of New York City, SE NEW YORK State. It was settled in 1683 by a group of Puritans. During the Revolutionary War the indecisive battle of White Plains was fought here on Oct. 28, 1776 between British forces commanded by Gen. William Howe and Americans led by Gen. George Washington. The British captured a commanding position, the Americans withdrew to the north, and Howe recalled his troops to New York City.

WHITE RUSSIA. See BELORUSSIA.

WHITE SANDS (United States) Uninhabited desert region, SE of the San Andres Mountains, S NEW MEXICO. The U.S. military operates a missile range here near the Holloman Air Force Base. On July 16, 1945 it was the testing site of the first atomic bomb.

WHITE'S FORT. See KNOXVILLE.

WHITE SULPHUR SPRINGS (United States) City near the border of Virginia, SE WEST VIRGINIA. Settled in 1750, it became known as a resort during the 19th century, when the U.S. president Martin Van Buren (1782–1862) visited the hot springs. The Old White Hotel, built in 1854, housed interned German and Japanese diplomats during World War II.

WHITHORN (Scotland) Town in Dumfries and Galloway region, 40 mi SW of Dumfries. According to tradition, the oldest stone church in Scotland, the *Candida casa* dating from 397 AD, was built here by St. Ninian. The ruins of a 12th-century priory built on the site of Ninian's church remain.

WHITSTABLE (England) Resort on the North Sea, 50 mi E of London, in Kent. It was once a port for pilgrims traveling to CANTERBURY.

WHYDAH. See OUIDAH.

WIAK. See BIAK.

WICHITA (United States) City on the Arkansas River, 177 mi SW of Kansas City, S central KANSAS. Settled during the Civil War by Indians and traders, it became a trading center on the CHISHOLM TRAIL. It developed into a major cow town in the 1870's following the arrival of the railroad. It has prospered since oil was discovered in the area during World War I. It was a major aircraft manufacturer during World War II.

WICHITA FALLS (United States) City on the Wichita River, 105 mi NW of Fort Worth, N TEXAS. Known early to Spanish explorers, it was founded as a city in 1876 and developed rapidly as a cow town after the railroad arrived in 1882. It boomed when oil was discovered in the area in 1919.

WICKLOW (Irish Republic) Port on the Irish Sea, in County WICKLOW. Said to have been founded by St. Mantan, it was the site of a Franciscan priory. It has notable ruins of a medieval castle.

WICKLOW (Irish Republic) County in LEINSTER province. A church was established here in the Vale of GLENDALOUGH in the sixth century AD. It still has extensive monastic ruins. The county withstood English control for many years, but became a shire in 1606. See also WICKLOW.

WIDA. See OUIDAH.

WIENER NEUSTADT (Austria) City on the Kerbach River, Lower Austria, 24 mi SW of Vienna. Founded in 1194, it flourished in the late Middle Ages when it was the residence of several Austrian kings. Emperor Maximilian I (1459–1519) was born here and is buried in the city's cathedral. Here in 1609 Emperor Rudolf II was forced to grant equal rights to the Bohemian Protestants. These were not recognized by Emperor Matthias in 1618. His refusal caused a revolt that was the immediate cause of the Thirty Years War.

WIENERWALD (Austria) Mountainous region of the Eastern Alps, Lower Austria, S of the Danube River, near VIENNA. A beautiful and famous resort area, it has inspired works by Strauss, Beethoven, and others. A medieval Augustinian monastery is located here in the town of KLOSTERNEUBURG. The Lainzer Tiergarten is a former royal hunting ground.

WIERINGERMEER (Netherlands) NW region of former ZUIDER ZEE, a modern polder. Reclaimed from the sea in the 1930's, it was flooded by German troops on April 18, 1945, but it was reclaimed again a year later.

WIESBADEN [*ancient:* **Aquae Mattiacorum**] (West

Germany) Capital of HESSE, on the RHINE RIVER, 20 mi W of Frankfurt am Main. A Celtic settlement dating from the third century BC, it was fortified in 12 BC by the Romans, who developed its thermal springs into a spa. It had passed to NASSAU in 1281 AD and was its capital from 1806 to 1866. It came under PRUSSIA in 1866, was bombed during World War II, and became the capital of Hesse in 1945. The ruins of a Roman wall of the fourth century AD, a city castle of 1837 to 1841 and the Kurhaus of 1905 to 1907 are all located here.

The Kurhaus in the attractive spa of Wiesbaden, high in the Hessian hills of West Germany. It has been known for its hot springs since Roman times.

WIFFLISBURG. See AVENCHES.

WIGAN (England) Town in Manchester, on the Douglas River, connected by canal with LIVERPOOL, 18 mi W of Manchester. An old medieval barony, Wigan changed hands several times in the Civil War. The Royalists suffered a major defeat here on Aug. 25, 1651. It has been a coal-mining, bell-founding, and pottery center since the 14th century and an iron manufacturing center since the 19th century.

WIGHT, ISLE OF [*ancient:* **Vectis**] (England) Island county, off the S coast of England. Its admin. hq., NEWPORT, is 13 mi SW of Portsmouth. Seized by the Romans in 43 AD, it was joined to WESSEX in 661, and was Christianized soon after. In the 10th century it was a seat of Danish power. Charles I found brief refuge here in 1647/48 in Carisbrooke Castle, whose ruins may still be seen. Queen Victoria often retreated to the Osborne House here, where she died in 1901. Perhaps the Isle of Wight's most famous resident was Alfred Lord Tennyson, poet laureate of Great Britain, who lived from 1853 until his death in 1892 at Farringford, an estate near Freshwater.

WIGTOWNSHIRE (Scotland) Former maritime county, now incorporated in Dumfries and Galloway region. Lake dwellings, hill forts, and stone circles indicate Pictish habitation of great antiquity.

WIJK BIJ DUURSTEDE. See DORESTAD.

WILDERNESS (United States) Region S of the Rapidan River, N VIRGINIA. Union forces under Gen. Ulysses S. Grant and Confederate troops under Gen. Robert E. Lee met for the first time here during the Wilderness campaign of May to June 1864. Although indecisive, the campaign included some of the bloodiest combat of the Civil War. Grant lost 55,000 men and Lee 39,000. The heaviest losses of the whole war were recorded at COLD HARBOR, where Grant lost 6,000 men in one hour.

WILDERNESS ROAD (United States) Old pioneer road, beginning in W VIRGINIA and winding SW into KENTUCKY and then NW to the OHIO RIVER. Originally scouted by Daniel Boone in 1775, it soon became a major route of the westward migration. By the 1840's it was abandoned as the NATIONAL or CUMBERLAND ROAD gained popularity.

WILHELMSHAVEN (West Germany) Port on the Jade Bay of the North Sea, Lower Saxony, 45 mi NW of Bremen. It was purchased by PRUSSIA from the grand duchy of Oldenburg in 1853. A naval base was established here in 1869. As such it figured prominently during both world wars, and was heavily bombed during World War II.

WILJANDI. See VILJANDI.

WILKES-BARRE (United States) City on the SUSQUEHANNA RIVER, approx. 100 mi NW of Philadelphia, E PENNSYLVANIA. It was founded in 1769 and was burned by the British and their allies during the Revolutionary War and again by rival settlers in 1784. It was also damaged greatly by a flood in 1972.

WILKES LAND (Antarctica) Region of Antarctica extending along the Indian Ocean. Discovered in 1839 by the American Charles Wilkes, it was claimed in 1908 by Great Britain, and in the 1930's by Australia.

WILLAMETTE RIVER (United States) River in NW OREGON, 190 mi long, flowing N from Lane County to the COLUMBIA RIVER near Portland. Located at the western end of the OREGON TRAIL, it was the goal of many settlers. The Hudson's Bay Company had established a trading post at OREGON CITY on its banks in 1829, but the river valley was developed most rapidly by the California gold rush of 1848. A hydroelectric plant established at Willamette Falls in 1889 was the first to transmit electricity to another community.

WILLAMETTE VALLEY. See OREGON COUNTRY.

WILLEMSTAD (Netherlands) Capital of NETHERLANDS ANTILLES, a port on Sint Ana Bay, SW CURAÇAO island. Settled by the Spanish in 1527, it was captured by the Dutch in 1634. Peter Stuyvesant developed it into a center for the slave trade. Today it is a major oil-refining center.

WILLIAM HENRY, FORT. See FORT WILLIAM HENRY.

WILLIAMSBURG (United States) City, between Richmond and Newport News, SE VIRGINIA. Settled in 1632 it was known as Middle Plantation when it replaced Jamestown in 1699 as the capital of Virginia. In 1722 it became the first city in the colony to be incorporated. In the 18th century it was the political and cultural center of the colony. The capital was moved in 1780 to RICHMOND. The colony's first theater in 1716, printing press in 1730, and newspaper, *Virginia Gazette* in 1736, were established here. The College of William and Mary, located here since 1693, is the nation's second-oldest college. The battle of Richmond was fought here on May 5, 1862 during the Civil War. Beginning in 1926, John D. Rockefeller, Jr. funded the city's restoration. The Colonial Williamsburg Foundation maintains one of the nation's finest reconstructions of colonial life in its 170-acre site. There are over 500 colonial buildings here, restored or rebuilt, including the Governor's palace and the old capitol.

WILLIAMSPORT (United States) City on the SUSQUEHANNA RIVER, 70 mi N of Harrisburg, central PENNSYLVANIA. Settled in 1772, it suffered several Indian massacres during the colonial era. In the mid-19th century it throve as a lumbering center until that resource was depleted. The Little League baseball World Series is held here.

WILLIAMSPORT. See MONONGAHELA.

WILLIAMSTOWN (United States) Town on the Hoosic River, 19 mi N of Pittsfield, W MASSACHUSETTS. Founded in 1750, it is the site of Williams College. The college, chartered as a free school in 1785, includes the Van Rensselaer Manor, the Hopkins observatory, the first in the nation, founded in 1838, and the Chapin Library of Rare Books.

WILLISTON (United States) City on the MISSOURI RIVER, 160 mi NW of Bismarck, W NORTH DAKOTA. Chief Sitting Bull, the Sioux who led a resistance against the forced settlement of Indians on government reservations, was captured at nearby Fort Buford. Fort Union here was the first trading post of the region. Williston was incorporated as a town in 1880 and as a city in 1904.

WILLSBORO (United States) Village, S of Plattsburg, NE NEW YORK State. It was settled in 1765. The British general, John Burgoyne, stationed his troops here in 1777 during the American Revolution.

WILL'S CREEK. See CUMBERLAND, Maryland.

WILMETTE (United States) Village and suburb N of Chicago, on LAKE MICHIGAN, NE ILLINOIS. Founded in 1869, it is noted today especially for the great temple of the Bahai faith, built here as its national headquarters.

WILMINGTON (United States) City on the DELAWARE AND Christina Rivers, 25 mi SW of Philadelphia, Pennsylvania, N DELAWARE. In 1638 Fort Christina was established here by a group of Swedes led by the Dutchman, Peter Minuit. The capital of NEW SWEDEN until 1643, it was captured by the Dutch in 1655 and by the British in 1664. George Washington failed to stop the British march on Philadelphia in the Revolutionary War battle of BRANDYWINE, fought just outside the city on Sept. 11, 1777. E.I. Du Pont built powder mills on the Brandywine here in 1802. The city was incorporated in 1832. Old Swedes Church from 1698, the Hendrickson House, and the Old Town Hall of 1798 are all here.

WILMINGTON (United States) Port on Cape Fear River, 135 mi SE of Raleigh, SE NORTH CAROLINA. Settled in 1732 and incorporated in 1866, it was the first town to stage a Stamp Act riot in 1765/66. It was occupied in 1781 during the Revolutionary War by Gen. Cornwallis. A port for Confederate blockade runners during the Civil War, it was captured by Union forces following the fall of FORT FISHER on Jan. 15, 1865. It was a shipbuilding center in World War II. The old Cornwallis and Confederate army headquarters are both located here.

WILNA. See VILNIUS.

WILNO (USSR) Former department of POLAND, now part of USSR. Lithuanians, Poles, and Russians have fought over it since the 14th century. It has long been disputed territory, especially since World War I. It was ceded to Poland in 1922, and a portion of it was given to LITHUANIA in 1939. See also VILNIUS.

WILSON'S CREEK (United States) Stream near Springfield in SW MISSOURI. Confederate Gen. Sterling Price defeated Union troops and killed their general, Nathaniel Lyon, in a battle fought here on Aug. 10, 1861 during the Civil War.

WILTON (England) Town in Wiltshire, 3 mi E of Salisbury. It was an ancient capital of WESSEX and the residence of its kings. Alfred the Great fought a battle here against the Danes in 871 AD. Historic Wilton House is nearby. The town is famous for its carpets.

WILTS. See WILTSHIRE.

WILTSHIRE [Wilts] (England) County in SW England. Prehistoric monuments are located at STONEHENGE, AVEBURY, and SILBURY HILL. OLD SARUM was the site of a bishopric until the 13th century, when the city was moved to SALISBURY, site of a famous 13th-century cathedral. The capital of the Saxon kingdom of Wessex was at WILTON. The admin. hq. of Wiltshire is at Trowbridge.

WILTWYCK. See KINGSTON, New York.

WIMBLEDON, England. See MERTON.

WINCHELSEA (England) Village in East Sussex, 8 mi NE of Hastings. It was one of the CINQUE PORTS since the 12th century, and was raided by the French in the Hundred Years War. The village contains the ruins of a church dedicated to Thomas à Becket.

WINCHELSEA, Papua New Guinea. See BUKA.

WINCHESTER [*ancient:* **Venta Belgarum**] (England) City in HAMPSHIRE, 61 mi SW of London. The capital of the kingdom of WESSEX, Winchester is the burial site of many Saxon and Danish kings, including Alfred the Great and Canute. According to tradition, the Round Table of King Arthur is preserved in a

Norman castle here. William the Conqueror was crowned here, as well as in London, in 1066. Winchester is an episcopal seat, and its bishops played an important role in English history. It has a magnificent 11th–14th-century cathedral. The town itself was the intellectual center of England until London gained ascendancy later in the Middle Ages. Winchester College, established in the late 14th century, is the oldest public school in England.

WINCHESTER (United States) City, 20 mi E of Muncie, E INDIANA. Settled c.1820, it contains Fudge Mounds, an Indian archaeological site.

WINCHESTER (United States) City in the SHENANDOAH VALLEY, 72 mi W of Washington, DC, N VIRGINIA. The city was first settled in 1732. In 1748 George Washington, who began his career as a surveyor here, used Winchester as his headquarters during the French and Indian Wars. After the defeat of Gen. Edward Braddock by the French and Indians on July 9, 1755, Washington established Fort Loudon near here. During the Civil War Winchester changed hands several times and was badly damaged by major engagements between Gen. Nathaniel Banks, the Union commander, and Gen. Thomas (Stonewall) Jackson, the Confederate commander, on May 26, 1862; between Union Gen. Robert Milroy and Confederate Gen. Richard Ewell on June 14 and 15, 1863; and between Gen. Philip Sheridan, in command of Union forces attacking up the Shenandoah Valley, and Gen. Jubal Early, Confederate commander stationed at Winchester, on September 19, 1864. Winchester was the birthplace of explorer and aviator, Admiral Richard E. Byrd (1888–1957), and of author Willa Cather (1876–1947).

WINDAU. See VENTSPILS.

WINDHOEK [Windhuk] (Namibia) Capital city in central SW Africa. Taken from the Namas Hottentots by the Germans in 1855, it became the capital of the German colony of South-West Africa in 1892. South African troops captured it during World War I. It is now an important commercial and shipping center, the largest city of Namibia.

WINDHUK. See WINDHOEK.

WINDISCH [*Latin:* **Vindonissa**] (Switzerland) Town on the Reuss River, AARGAU canton, N Switzerland. It was an old Helvetian settlement and then a Roman military post. In 1308 Holy Roman Emperor Albert I was assassinated at the nearby site where the famous Königsfelden monastery was established two years later. A large Roman amphitheater has been excavated here.

WIND RIVER RANGE (United States) Range of the ROCKY MOUNTAINS, W central WYOMING. There are several important passes over this range, particularly SOUTH PASS on the OREGON TRAIL, leading to the basin of the COLORADO RIVER, to the GREAT SALT LAKE, and to the headwaters of the Snake River.

WINDSOR [*former:* **Pisiquid**] (Canada) Town of central NOVA SCOTIA, on the Avon River, 37 mi NW of Halifax. Settled by French Acadians in 1703, it was formally founded as Pisiquid in 1710. In 1750 it was taken by the British, who built Fort Edward here. King's College, the oldest English college in the country, was established here in 1789 but was removed to Halifax in 1923.

WINDSOR (Canada) Port on the Detroit River opposite DETROIT, Michigan, SE ONTARIO. The French began to settle here shortly after the founding of Detroit in 1701. It received an influx of Tory immigrants after the Revolutionary War and was held by U.S. troops during the War of 1812.

WINDSOR [*officially:* **New Windsor**] (England) Town on the THAMES RIVER, 20 mi W of London, Berkshire. A Roman settlement, the town grew up around Windsor Castle, a royal residence since the time of William the Conqueror, who established it. The castle contains a round tower built by Henry II. There is also a royal mausoleum in the park where Queen Victoria and Prince Albert are buried. Several English kings, including Henry VIII and Charles I, are buried in St. George's Chapel, begun by Edward IV and considered one of the most magnificent churches of England. Roman remains have been discovered at Windsor.

WINDSOR [*former:* **New Dorchester**] (United States) Town and suburb N of Hartford, at the confluence of the Farmington River and the Connecticut River, N CONNECTICUT. Settled first as a trading post by Pilgrims from Plymouth Colony and later by residents from Dorchester, Massachusetts, it was known as New Dorchester until 1637. Windsor, the first white settlement in Connecticut, is the state's oldest town.

WINDSOR (United States) Village on the Connecticut River, 13 mi N of Springfield, E VERMONT. Chartered by the governor of New Hampshire in 1761, it was settled in 1764. The formation of the new state of Vermont resulted from conventions held here in 1777. Windsor was the state's unofficial capital until 1805. The Old Constitution House, where the state's constitution was adopted on July 9, 1777, is here, as well as the nation's oldest prison house, built in 1808.

WINDSOR LOCKS (United States) Town on the Connecticut River, 12 mi N of Hartford, N CONNECTICUT. Settled in 1663, it was separated from WINDSOR when it was incorporated in 1854. Windsor Locks has been a trading and shipping center for Connecticut's tobacco industry since early colonial days. In 1828 a canal with locks was built here to bypass rapids in the Connecticut River.

WINDWARD ISLANDS. See WEST INDIES.

WINDWARD PASSAGE Channel between E CUBA and NW HISPANIOLA, 55 mi wide. On the route from the United States to the PANAMA CANAL, it has been protected by the U.S. military since 1903. See also GUANTANAMO BAY.

WINELAND. See VINLAND.

WINNEBA (Ghana) Port on the Gulf of Guinea, approx. 35 mi SW of Accra, S Ghana, West Africa. A British fort built here in 1663 became the center of a prosperous trade in gold. It declined as a commercial

Fort Garry on the Red River in 1869, a few years before Winnipeg, now a large city and capital of Manitoba, began to grow up around it.

center when a harbor was opened at Tema in 1961.

WINNESHIEK. See FREEPORT.

WINNETKA (United States) Town, 19 mi N of Chicago, on LAKE MICHIGAN, NE ILLINOIS. Founded in 1854, it became known for an innovative educational program. Called the Winnetka Plan, this was based on principles enunciated by John Dewey and developed by C.W. Washburne, the superintendent of the Winnetka public schools. The program centers on individualized instruction with pupils advancing at their own pace.

WINNIPEG (Canada) Commercial and transportation center, city and capital of MANITOBA, at the confluence of the Assiniboine and Red Rivers. The French built a fur-trading post here in 1738. The Hudson's Bay Company established another post here early in the 19th century, and soon after Lord Selkirk established a Scottish colony at the site. The North West Company, which had already established trade here, competed with the new settlers. The two companies merged in 1821 and established Fort Gibraltar, renamed Fort Garry in 1835, on the Red River. In 1873 the town was incorporated as Winnipeg.

WINSTON-SALEM (United States) City in the Piedmont, 93 mi NW of Raleigh, N central NORTH CAROLINA. Salem was founded in 1766 and Winston in 1849. The two towns merged in 1913. Salem was settled by Moravians from nearby Bethabara. Numerous original Moravian buildings exist today as part of the restoration of Old Salem. Winston-Salem, in the heart of the state's tobacco lands, is the world's largest producer of tobacco products.

WINTER PARK (United States) Resort city, 5 mi NE of Orlando, central FLORIDA. Founded in 1858, it contains Florida's oldest institution of higher education, Rollins College, founded in 1885.

WINTERTHUR [*Latin:* **Vitudurum**] (Switzerland) City of Zurich canton, 12 mi NE of Zurich. Originally the Roman settlement of Vitudurum, in 1180 it became part of the domains of the counts of Kyburg. In 1264 it was inherited by the Hapsburgs. It became a free imperial city in 1415; in 1467 it was sold to the Swiss Confederation, becoming part of Zurich canton.

WIRRAL (England) Area in Cheshire and Merseyside, on a peninsula between the Dee and Mersey estuaries. An old royal forest, it became noted as a haven for outlaws. Emma Lyon, later Lady Hamilton, was born, *c.*1765, in Wirral, at Heswall parish.

WIRTEMBERG. See WÜRTTEMBERG.

WISBY. See VISBY.

WISCONSIN (United States) State, in the N central region, with Minnesota and Iowa to the W, Illinois to the S, on both LAKE MICHIGAN to the E and LAKE SUPERIOR to the N. Wisconsin was admitted to the Union in 1848 as the 30th state. Its name is a modification of the French interpretation of the Ojibway Indian name for the Wisconsin River, *Wees-kon-san* (a gathering of waters).

Since the Great Lakes provide easy passage to this region, French fur traders from CANADA were early explorers. Jean Nicolet reached the site of GREEN BAY in 1634, seeking furs and the NORTHWEST PASSAGE. Others included Père Marquette and Louis Jolliet, who discovered the upper MISSISSIPPI RIVER, Louis Hennepin, and Robert de La Salle. In 1678 the Sieur Duluth claimed the upper Mississippi region for FRANCE. Nicolas Perrot helped make Green Bay a center for the fur trade in 1667, and this became Wisconsin's first permanent settlement in 1701.

At the end of the French and Indian War, in 1763, France was forced to cede all of New France to GREAT

BRITAIN; but in 1783, at the end of the American Revolution, the region became part of the United States and was governed after 1787 under the Northwest Ordinance. However, the British refused to leave some posts until 1794. During the War of 1812 Great Britain won control again, but the United States recovered the land by the treaty ending the war. The first large influx of settlers came in the 1820's as a result of a boom in lead mining in the southwestern part of the state. After the opening of the ERIE CANAL in New York State in 1825 provided a connection from the Great Lakes to the HUDSON RIVER, still more settlers arrived. The Army built forts to protect the settlers against Indians and to secure the area against the British at Green Bay and PRAIRIE DU CHIEN in 1816, and PORTAGE in 1828. Nevertheless, there was trouble with the Indians, leading to the Black Hawk War; its last battle, which almost wiped out the Sac and Fox tribes was fought in Wisconsin at the BAD AXE River in 1832.

Wisconsin became a separate territory in 1836. Its first state constitution in 1848 was liberal in suffrage and in the protection of debt-laden farmers. Immigration increased, especially from GERMANY, after the abortive revolution of 1848. Many Irish, Scandinavians, Russians, and Poles also came. Antislavery sentiment was strong: the Free Soil party gained support in 1848; and Wisconsin men helped to organize the new Republican Party. The Civil War and its aftermath caused a boom; growth through the 1860's was rapid, particularly in meat packing and brewing. The pine forests of the north were exploited ruthlessly in the 1870's, but conservation measures later restored them. The late 19th century here was prosperous for the most part; and so the Granger Movement had less impact on Wisconsin farmers than on those elsewhere. Laws were passed, nevertheless, to regulate the railroads, and a practical kind of socialism came into favor, especially in MILWAUKEE.

The Progressive movement was strong in Wisconsin in the early 20th century, resulting in such reforms as a direct primary law and the pure food acts. The 1920's were prosperous on the whole. In the 1924 presidential race the Progressive Party carried the state for Robert M. LaFollette, a native son. It was the only state to do so. Wisconsin pioneered with an old age pension act in 1925 and an unemployment insurance law in 1931. The Great Depression of the 1930's struck hard, but World War II and peace in the 1950's restored prosperity.

MADISON is the capital and the main site of the University of Wisconsin; Milwaukee is the largest city; and Green Bay, OSHKOSH, and RACINE are important centers.

WISLA. See VISTULA RIVER.

WISMAR (East Germany) Port on Wismar Bay, 64 mi NE of Hamburg, Rostock district. It flourished during the Middle Ages as a wealthy member of the HANSEATIC LEAGUE and as the seat of the princes of MECKLENBURG from 1256–1306. It was given to Sweden in 1648 by the Treaty of Westphalia and to Mecklenburg-Schwerin in 1803. It was badly damaged during World War II before being taken by British troops on May 4, 1945.

WISSAHICKON CREEK (United States) Stream in SE PENNSYLVANIA, flowing SE to meet the SCHUYLKILL RIVER in Philadelphia. A colonial paper mill established here in 1690 was the first in America.

WISSEMBOURG [Weissenburg] (France) Town, approx. 40 mi NE of Strasbourg, Bas-Rhin department. A monastery was established here by Dagobert II in the seventh century AD. Otfried von Weissenburg, German monk and poet, retold the gospel stories in Old High German verse here during the ninth century. The first battle of the Franco-Prussian War was fought here between Gen. Helmuth von Moltke and Marshall MacMahon on Aug. 4, 1870. The French were driven from the field.

WITTEN (West Germany) City on the RUHR RIVER, 9 mi SW of Dortmund, North Rhine-Westphalia. First mentioned in the 13th century and chartered in 1825, it was formerly part of WESTPHALIA province. A steel-manufacturing center and part of the Ruhr industrial complex, it was frequently bombed and nearly destroyed during World War II.

WITTENBERG (East Germany) City on the ELBE RIVER, 42 mi NE of Leipzig, Halle district. It was the capital of the duchy of SAXE-WITTENBERG from 1273 to 1422, but it declined after DRESDEN replaced it in 1547 as the Saxon capital. It was turned over to PRUSSIA in 1815 after the Napoleonic Wars. The university was the center of Luther's activities and of the Protestant Reformation, which began here with Luther's nailing of the 95 Theses to the Shlosskirche door in 1517. The first Lutheran Bible was printed here in 1534. A 16th-century town hall, the Schlosskirche, and many landmarks of the Reformation are located in the city.

WITTINGAU. See TŘEBOŇ.

WITTSTOCK (East Germany) Town, 58 mi NW of Berlin. During the Thirty Years War Swedish and Scottish troops commanded by Field Marshall Johan Banér defeated the Saxon and Imperial army led by Count Melchior von Hatzfeldt here on Oct. 4, 1636. The victory gave new hope to Protestant, northern Germany in its struggle against the Hapsburgs.

WITU (Kenya) Former sultanate on the SE coast. A German protectorate from 1885, it was ceded to England five years later and became a part of the East Africa Protectorate formed by the British in 1895.

WITWATERSRAND [The Rand] (South Africa) Region in S TRANSVAAL. Gold was first discovered here in 1886. The Rand gold-mining center produces about one third of the world's supply.

WŁOCŁAWEK [Russian: Vlotslavsk] (Poland) Port on the VISTULA RIVER, 87 mi NW of Warsaw, Bydgoszcz province. Founded in the 12th century, it flourished in the Middle Ages. It was sacked by the Teutonic Knights in the 14th century. It passed to Russia in 1815 after the Napoleonic Wars, and was retaken by Poland in World War I. It was occupied by the Germans during World War II.

WŁODZIMIERZ. See VLADIMIR-VOLYNSKI.

WOBURN (England) Village, 12 mi NW of Luton, in Bedfordshire. A Cistercian priory established in 1145 once stood where Woburn Abbey, the residence of the dukes of Bedford, was built in the 18th century.

WOBURN (United States) City and suburb NW of Boston, NE MASSACHUSETTS. Settled in 1640, it was the birthplace of the noted British loyalist and physicist Benjamin Thompson, who in 1791 was given the imperial title of Count Rumford.

WOEFUL DANE BOTTOM. See MINCHINHAMPTON.

WOEVRE (France) Plateau E of VERDUN. This region is famous for the battles fought during World War I, especially in 1914 and 1918.

WOLEAI [Uleai] (United States) Small atoll in the W CAROLINE ISLANDS, about halfway between Truk and Palau Islands, W Pacific Ocean, United States Trust Territory of the Pacific Islands. Held by Japanese forces during World War II, it was the object of an American raid on March 31, 1944 that sank several Japanese ships.

WOLFENBÜTTEL (West Germany) City on the Oker River, near BRUNSWICK, E West Germany. It developed around an 11th-century castle, which became a seat of the Guelphs in the 13th and 14th centuries. It was the residence of the dukes of Brunswick-Wolfenbüttel from 1432 to 1753. Its famous ducal library, founded in the 17th century, employed as librarians both Gottfried Wilhelm von Leibniz, the philosopher and mathematician, and Gotthold Ephraim Lessing, the playwright and critic. The house in which Lessing wrote *Nathan the Wise* still stands.

WOLFVILLE (Canada) Town on the Minas Basin, 15 mi NW of Windsor, W NOVA SCOTIA. Longfellow's *Evangeline* recounts the tale of the British deportations of the peaceful Acadians who were once settled here and in nearby GRAND PRÉ.

WOLIN [*German:*** Wollin]** (Poland) Island in the Baltic Sea, off the NW coast of Szczecin province. The town of Wolin dates from the ninth century. It was the possible site of the Slavic military and trading post of Julin c.1075. Before it was destroyed by the Danes near the end of the century, it was said to have been the largest town of northern Europe. The island was turned over to Sweden in 1648, to Prussia in 1720, and to Poland in 1945.

WOLLIN. See WOLIN.

WOLVERHAMPTON (England) Town in West Midlands, 12 mi NW of Birmingham. It became an ecclesiastical holding in 1204, passed to Northumberland in 1553, but was returned to the Church soon after. Incorporated in 1848, it contains the 13th-century St. Peter's Church and a Reformation era grammar school. The town is an industrial center in the historic BLACK COUNTRY area.

WOŁYŃ. See VOLHYNIA.

WŎNSAN [*Japanese:*** Genzan]** (North Korea) Port and capital of Kangwŏn province, on the Sea of Japan. A former treaty port, it was opened to foreign trade in 1883. It was a Japanese naval base in World War II, and was heavily bombed during the Korean War.

WOODBRIDGE (United States) Industrial city, 14 mi S of Newark, central NEW JERSEY. Settled and incorporated in 1664 by Puritans from New England, it was the site of the state's first printing press in 1751.

WOODBURY (United States) City, 8 mi S of Camden, SW NEW JERSEY. Settled c.1665 by Quakers, it was a frequent battleground during the Revolutionary War. In 1777 British General Charles Cornwallis briefly established his headquarters at the Cooper House, which still stands. Also in the city is a Friends Meeting House of 1716, a colonial hotel of 1720, and the historic John Lawrence House of 1765.

WOODHENGE. See DURRINGTON.

WOODLARK [Murua] (Papua New Guinea) Island in the Solomon Sea, NE of NEW GUINEA. It was the site of considerable gold-mining operations for several years before World War II. Allied troops were unopposed when they landed here June 30, 1943 and established a base.

WOODS HOLE (United States) Village and seaport, 16 mi SE of New Bedford, on CAPE COD, SE MASSACHUSETTS. Once a thriving whaling town and shipbuilding center, it now houses the Woods Hole Oceanographic Institution, which operates a research laboratory aboard the *Atlantis*.

WOODSTOCK (Canada) Town on the ST. JOHN RIVER, 48 mi NW of Fredericton, W NEW BRUNSWICK. It was founded during the American Revolution by exiled Tories who came to be known as United Empire Loyalists.

WOODSTOCK (England) Town in OXFORDSHIRE, 8 mi NW of Oxford. There was a royal hunting lodge here in the Anglo-Saxon era; on the site there stood a castle in which Edward the Black Prince, noted warrior and eldest son of Edward III, was born in 1330. In the mid-16th century, Mary I imprisoned her half-sister, the future Elizabeth I, here.

Today Woodstock is chiefly noted as the location of Blenheim Palace, the seat of the dukes of Marlborough. The estate was granted to John Churchill, who was created the first duke of Marlborough in 1702 by Queen Anne to honor him for his victories in the War of the Spanish Succession between 1701 and 1714. It is named Blenheim Park for his greatest victory, against the French at BLENHEIM, Bavaria on Aug. 13, 1704. The enormous palace, much of which is now open to the public, was designed by a foremost architect, Sir John Vanbrugh, and built between 1705 and 1724. It is an outstanding example of English baroque style. The superb park was designed by Lancelot "Capability" Brown, the most famous landscape architect of his time. Sir Winston Churchill, a descendant of the first duke and Britain's indomitable leader in World War II, was born in the palace in 1874.

WOODSTOCK, United States. See ANNISTON.

WOOLWICH (England) Former metropolitan borough of LONDON, now divided into the present boroughs of Newham and GREENWICH. Settled since Roman times and noted in Domesday Book, Woolwich was the main naval base of England from the 16th to the 19th centuries. In 1515 King Henry VIII here launched the *Harry Grâce de Dieu*, famous for its size of 1000 tons.

WOOMERA [Woomera-Maralinga] (Australia) Town in SE central SOUTH AUSTRALIA State, 100 mi NW of Port Augusta. A missile-testing base was established here in 1945. In 1967 Australia launched its first earth satellite from here.

WOOMERA-MARALINGA. See WOOMERA.

WORCESTER (England) City in Hereford and Worcester, on the SEVERN RIVER, 25 mi SW of Birmingham. Worcester has been an ecclesiastical center since the founding of a Saxon bishopric near here c.680. In the 11th century St. Wulfstan began the Norman cathedral, most of which now dates from the 14th century. Near here was fought the final battle of the English Civil War, when the Parliamentarian army of Cromwell decisively routed the Scottish troops of Charles II on Sept. 3, 1651, forcing the king to flee in disguise. The young king, in hiding for six weeks, finally managed to escape to the European Continent.

WORCESTER (United States) Industrial city on the Blackstone River, 40 mi W of Boston, central MASSACHUSETTS. Settlements begun in 1673 were abandoned when faced with hostile Indians. Worcester was permanently settled in 1713 and was incorporated in 1722. It flourished as an early industrial center following the completion in 1828 of the Blackstone Canal. The scene of riots during Shays's Rebellion in 1786 and the slavery controversy in 1854, it also provided the setting for the first woman's suffrage national convention in 1850. It was severely damaged by a tornado in 1953, and by floods in 1955. The College of Holy Cross was founded here in 1843. The illustrious Unitarian clergyman, Edward Everett Hale, was pastor here from 1842 to 1856.

WORMATIA. See WORMS.

WORMS [*ancient:* Borbetomagus; *Latin:* **Augusta Vangionum, Civitas Vangionum, Wormatia**] (West Germany) City of Rhineland-Palatinate state situated on the RHINE RIVER 10 mi NNW of Mannheim. Fortified by the Romans in 14 BC, it was destroyed by the Huns in 436 AD. Reconstructed in 486 AD by Clovis I, it became capital of the first kingdom of BURGUNDY. It came to prominence as the site of the Concordat of Worms in 1122 settling the issue of investiture. Nearly fifty years earlier, in 1076 during the Investiture Conflict, an episcopal synod here had deposed Pope Gregory VII.

A free imperial city from the early 13th century, it joined the Rhenish Confederation in 1255 and was the site of many imperial diets, the most famous of which was held in 1521, convened by Charles V to hear the defense of Martin Luther. When Luther refused to recant his teachings, the Edict of Worms of May 25, 1521 proclaimed him an outlaw.

Razed by Louis XIV and the French in 1689, the city suffered the same fate in 1792 at the hands of Napoleon. It was ceded to FRANCE by the Peace of Lunéville in 1801. The Congress of Vienna passed it to Hesse-Darmstadt in 1815. Following World War I, it was again occupied from 1918 to 1930 by the French. After suffering severe damage in World War II, it was occupied by the Allies May 20, 1945. Now generally restored, it is the site of a notable cathedral of the 11th to 14th centuries.

WORSTEAD (England) Village in Norfolk, 13 mi NNE of Norwich. A woolens industry was begun here by Flemish immigrants who founded the village in the 12th century. A medieval church is located here.

WÖRTH (France) Town in Bas-Rhin department. Crown Prince Frederick William of Prussia led his troops to a victory over the French forces of Marshal MacMahon in a battle fought here on Aug. 6, 1870 during the Franco-Prussian War. The battle is sometimes named after the nearby hamlet of Fröschwiller.

WORTHING (England) Resort in West Sussex, on the ENGLISH CHANNEL, 47 mi SW of London. Many prehistoric and Roman ruins have been unearthed here, including a complete Roman bath complex.

WORTH ISLAND. See HOWLAND ISLAND.

WOTHO (United States) Small atoll in the N central portion of the Ralik Chain, W MARSHALL ISLANDS, W Pacific Ocean, United States Trust Territory of the Pacific Islands. It was taken by U.S. forces in March 1944 during World War II.

WOTJE (United States) Small island in the central portion of the Ratak Chain, E MARSHALL ISLANDS, W Pacific Ocean, United States Trust Territory of the Pacific Islands. It was bombed, but not taken, by U.S. forces during World War II.

WOUNDED KNEE (United States) Creek rising in SW SOUTH DAKOTA and flowing NW to join the White River. Here in the Badlands of South Dakota on Dec. 29, 1890 the U.S. Army massacred hundreds of Sioux men, women, and children who had been captured the day before in the last major American Indian war.

WRANGEL ISLAND [Wrangell Island] [*Russian:* **Ostrov Vrangelya**] (USSR) Island in the Arctic Ocean, approx. 90 mi N of the Siberian coast, NE USSR. Russian explorer Baron Ferdinand Petrovitch von Wrangel searched for it in 1823; but the American whaler, Thomas Long, discovered it in 1867. It was first settled by Russia in 1911. In 1933 the Soviet ship *Chelyuskin* was stranded here, and the survivors were marooned for some time on the island.

WRANGELL (United States) Town on N Wrangell Island, SE ALASKA. The Russians built a fort here in the mid-19th century to prevent the Hudson's Bay Company from trading in the area. The United States took possession in 1867 with the purchase of Alaska and operated a military post here for a decade. In the 1890's it became a supply station for gold miners heading for the YUKON.

WROCŁAW [*German:* **Breslau**] (Poland) City of Wrocław province, on the ODER RIVER, approx. 190 mi

SW of Warsaw. An episcopal see since *c.* 1000, in 1163 it became the capital of SILESIA. After being sacked and destroyed by the Tatars in 1241, it was refounded by the Germans. Located on a strategic crossing of the Oder River, Wrocław was a thriving member of the HANSEATIC LEAGUE in the 14th and 15th centuries. In 1335 it became part of BOHEMIA, and in 1526, when Bohemia was subdued by imperial forces under the Hapsburgs, it was absorbed by AUSTRIA. It finally became a territory of PRUSSIA in 1742. During the Napoleonic Wars it was occupied by the French. It was badly damaged by the Russians during a siege in 1945 in World War II that lasted four months. It was assigned to Poland in 1945.

WROXETER [*Latin:* **Viriconium**] (England) Village on the SEVERN RIVER, 5 mi SE of Shrewsbury, Salop. Extensive Roman remains unearthed here include a town hall, market, forum and baths. The village was founded on the site of the Roman city.

WU. See KIANGSU.

WU-CH'ANG [**Wuchang**] (China) City and capital of Hupeh province, on the YANGTZE RIVER, part of WU-HAN in SE Hupeh province, 425 mi W of Shanghai. The oldest of the Wuhan Han cities, it was founded by the Han dynasty of 206 BC to 220 AD. The Chinese Republic was established after the Manchus were overthrown during the Revolution of 1911 that began here with an uprising on October 10. It was occupied by Japanese troops in the 1930's and throughout World War II.

WU-CHOU (China) Port at the confluence of the Hsi and Kuei Rivers, 115 mi W of Canton, E Kwangsi Chuang Autonomous Region, S China. A Manchu political center, it became a treaty port in 1897. A U.S. Air Force base during World War II, it was destroyed on Sept. 22, 1944 by U.S. forces in the face of advancing Japanese troops.

WU-HAN [**Wuhan**] (China) Industrial and commercial center, city of HUPEH Province, at the joining of the Yangtze and Han Rivers, 425 mi W of Shanghai. It is a conglomeration of the former cities of HANKOW, HAN-YANG, and WU-CH'ANG. The Han cities, as they were called, were consolidated in 1950.

WUHSIEN. See SUCHOU.

WU-HU [**Wuhu, Wu-Na-Mu**] (China) Commercial center, city, and port on the YANGTZE RIVER, 50 mi SW of Nanking, E Anhwei, E China. A former treaty port, it was opened to foreign trade in 1877. There are several notable temples here, foremost being the one dedicated to the great T'ang dynasty poet, Li Po (*c.*700–762 AD), who was drowned in the nearby Yangtze River.

WU-LU-MU-CHI. See URUMCHI.

WU-NA-MU. See WU-HU.

WÜRTEMBERG. See WÜRTTEMBERG.

WÜRTTEMBERG [*former:* **Wirtemberg, Würtemberg**] (West Germany) German state and former kingdom in the SW, bordering on Bavaria and Switzerland. A portion of the state of Baden-Württemberg since 1952, its modern capital, STUTTGART, continues its traditional role.

An early settlement of the Celts, it was later conquered and inhabited by the Suevi, the Romans, and the Alamanni, who were themselves conquered by Clovis and the Franks in 496 AD. It remained Frankish for 400 years before its southern portion became part of the duchy of SWABIA. The portion north of Stuttgart became part of FRANCONIA. By the late Middle Ages the counts of Württemberg enjoyed a direct relation with the HOLY ROMAN EMPIRE. The original lands, secured by the 11th century, were centered on ESSLINGEN. Expanding in the late 14th century, Württemberg acquired the principality of MONTBÉLIARD in FRANCE, plus several properties in ALSACE. By 1495 it had achieved ducal status under the spirited leadership of Eberhard V.

In 1519, the Swabian League, fearing the increased power of Württemberg's flamboyant Duke Ulrich, expelled him and in 1520 sold the duchy to Emperor Charles V. The resulting conflict over Ulrich's holding brought a political and religious division between Ulrich's Lutheran allies and the Catholic Hapsburg forces. This division of religious allegiance continues to the present day.

WÜRZBURG (West Germany) City on the MAIN RIVER, BAVARIA, 60 mi SE of Frankfurt am Main. A bishopric since 742 AD, it was ruled for centuries by FRANCONIA. In the 10th century, following the dissolution of the duchy of Franconia, the bishopric developed

Würzburg in Bavaria, its magnificent old buildings restored after World War II bombing. In the 18th century it was a wealthy cultural center under its prince-bishops.

considerable influence within the HOLY ROMAN EM-PIRE. The bishops gained princely status and turned the city into a lavish seat of power during the 17th and 18th centuries. Würzburg was secularized in 1801 and was turned over to Bavaria in 1815 after the Napoleonic Wars. Wilhelm Roentgen discovered X-rays at the university here in 1895. A center of Nazi influence, the city was almost completely destroyed in a fire-bomb raid during World War II. Nearly all the historic buildings were heavily damaged. Most have been restored, however. An especially fine example of a medieval fortress is the Marienberg castle here, the residence of the bishops from the 13th to the 18th centuries.

WU-SHU-LI. See USSURI.

WU-SU-LI. See USSURI.

WU-T'AI SHAN [Wu Tai Shan] (China) Mountain in NE SHANSI and NW HOPEH. One of the four Buddhist sacred mountains in China, it was the object of great pilgrimages. It is dotted with temples, monastic houses, and lamaseries, dating from the first century AD on.

WYANDOTTE. See KANSAS CITY, Kansas.

WYE RIVER (Wales) River, 130 mi long, rising in Dyfed and flowing SE into the SEVERN RIVER, 2 mi S of Chepstow, in Gwent. The ruins of the 12th-century Cistercian house of Tintern Abbey are located on its banks just north of Chepstow. They inspired William Wordsworth's famous poem of the same name.

WYOMING (United States) State in the NW region. Montana is to the N, the Dakotas and Nebraska to the E, Colorado and Utah to the S, and Idaho to the W. It was admitted to the Union as the 44th state in 1890. Its name is an Indian word meaning "large meadows," originally applied to a valley in Pennsylvania, but given to it by Congress in 1868 when Wyoming Territory was created.

The Crow Indians inhabited the eastern part of the area but were driven into the mountains by the Sioux as they themselves were being pushed west. At various times portions of the state were claimed by SPAIN, FRANCE, and GREAT BRITAIN. The United States acquired part of it by the LOUISIANA PURCHASE of 1803; other sections by an 1819 treaty with Spain, by a cession from the Republic of TEXAS in 1836; still more from Texas after it became a state in 1845, and as a result of the Mexican War; and finally by the 1846 treaty with Great Britain concerning the OREGON COUNTRY. French trappers may have been here from the middle to the late 18th century, but the first authentic account of the region came from John Colter, who, after trapping here, returned to ST. LOUIS in 1810 with stories of geysers, canyons, and other wonders in what

Buffalo Bill's Irma Hotel, named for his daughter, in Cody, Wyoming in 1908. William F. Cody, or Buffalo Bill, the Western scout and showman, founded the town in 1901.

later became YELLOWSTONE NATIONAL PARK.

In 1811 a fur-trading party on the way to found ASTORIA, Ore. went through Teton Pass; and the next year a returning member of the party used SOUTH PASS, largely following what became the OREGON TRAIL. William H. Ashley led four fur-trading expeditions into Wyoming, and other mountain men soon roamed the land. In 1832 Capt. B.L.E. de Bonneville took the first wagons through South Pass. The first permanent trading post was established in 1834 as Fort William, later FORT LARAMIE. The explorer John C. Frémont reached here in 1842, and FORT BRIDGER was built in 1843. By the 1840's the Oregon Trail was becoming heavily traveled, and Pony Express riders could be seen on the trails in 1860 and 1861. They disappeared after the telegraph came through in 1861. By the early 1870's Indian attacks forced stagecoaches to use the OVERLAND TRAIL farther south.

Gold found at South Pass brought the first sizable number of settlers, and a little later the discovery of coal in southwestern Wyoming also increased the sparse population. The arrival of the Union Pacific Railroad in 1868 was a further stimulus. The next year, the territory of Wyoming became the first state or territory to allow women to vote. By the late 1870's the Indians' power was broken, the Arapaho and Shoshone being placed on a reservation. The Wyoming Stock Growers' Association was formed in 1873 to punish cattle rustling and to make the interests of the cattlemen paramount. For almost twenty years it controlled the government and rendered vigilante justice. The cattlemen used violence against the sheepmen and tried to prevent farmers from fencing their lands.

Wyoming adopted a liberal state constitution with provisions for the secret ballot. A fierce political battle ended in 1915 with the Progressives winning and setting up a state utilities commission. In 1924 Wyoming became the first state to elect a woman governor. The state has a great deal of oil, and its Teapot Dome field figured in the scandals of the Harding administration in the 1920's. In the Great Depression of the 1930's the state benefited from New Deal soil-conservation programs, but a four-year drought in the 1950's was damaging. Offsetting such problems has been a boom in minerals, oil, and gas, especially since the energy crisis of the early 1970's.

CHEYENNE is the capital and largest city; other cities are CASPER, LARAMIE, and ROCK SPRINGS.

WYOMING VALLEY (United States) Valley, approx. 20 mi long, along the SUSQUEHANNA RIVER, E PENNSYLVANIA. Connecticut and Pennsylvania contested control of the valley throughout the second half of the 18th century. Two Pennamite Wars, of 1769 to 1771 and of 1784, were fought over the issue. During the Revolutionary War a Tory-Indian army led by Sir John Johnson, John Butler, leader of Butler's Rangers, and Joseph Brant, brutally raided the Connecticut settlers of the valley. They tortured and massacred those settlers who had fled for protection to old Forty Fort. Pennsylvania finally secured its claim in 1799.

WYTSCHAETE (Belgium) Village in W Flanders province, S of Ieper, or Ypres. Several battles were fought near here in World War I, including one phase of the battle of MESSINES Ridge on June 7, 1917 as British troops pushed to recapture the ridge.

X

XALAPA. See JALAPA.

XANTEN (West Germany) Town on the left bank of the RHINE RIVER, formerly in the Prussian RHINE PROVINCE, now in North Rhine-Westphalia, 7 mi W of Wesel. Xanten is mentioned in the *Nibelungenlied* as the birthplace of the legendary folk hero, Siegfried. A Treaty of Xanten, signed here in 1614, resolved a long dispute over the inheritance of the elector of BRANDEN-BURG. Xanten's famed Gothic St. Victor Church was badly damaged in heavy fighting here in World War II.

XANTHE. See XANTHI.

XANTHI [Xanthe] [*Bulgarian:* **Skatchia;** *Greek:* **Xánthi;** *Turkish:* **Eskije**] (Turkey) Town and capital of Xánthi prefecture, THRACE, on the E bank of the Nestos River, 30 mi W of Komotiné. It has the remains of a medieval Byzantine citadel, and on the plains to the south are the ruins of an ancient Greek town.

XANTHUS [*Turkish:* **Günük**] (Turkey) Ancient city of LYCIA, in SE Muğla province. Its ruins are situated 5 mi from the mouth of the Xanthus River, now the Koca, on the Mediterranean. The city flourished from the seventh century BC until Byzantine times, when its harbor silted up. It was twice besieged and devastated, once by the armies of PERSIA in 546 BC and by those of ROME under Marcus Junius Brutus in 42 BC. The excavated ruins include a Roman theater, walls, an agora, and many Lycian rock-cut tombs. The fine Classical sculptures from the latter, especially friezes from the Harpy Tomb and the entire Nereid tomb, were removed to the British Museum.

XATIVA. See JATIVA.

XAUEN. See CHECHAOUÉN.

XERES. See JEREZ DE LA FRONTERA.

XOCHIMILCO (Mexico) Town of the Federal district, 10 mi S of MEXICO CITY, on the W shore of Lake Xochimilco. It is the site of the famous *chinampas* or floating gardens. The original Aztec *chinampas* were of mud piled on rafts, which were then floated on the lake until the roots of plants anchored them to the bottom. Eventually they formed new land interspersed with canals.

XOÏS (Egypt) A capital city of ancient Egypt, in the NILE RIVER delta, 20 mi NW of Busiris. In the 17th century BC it was the capital of the Fourteenth, or Xoite, dynasty.

Y

YACHOW-FU (China) City of Szechwan, on the banks of the Ya River. First mentioned during the Chou dynasty (1122–255 BC), it is situated at the E end of the tea and tobacco trade route to TIBET and of the cotton trade route west to YUNNAN. Its city wall, two miles in circumference, is pierced by four gates.

YAFA. See JAFFA.

YAFO. See JAFFA.

YAITSKI GORODOK. See URALSK.

YAITSKY GORODOK. See URALSK.

YAKIMA (United States) Town of WASHINGTON State, in the Yakima Valley, 140 mi SE of Seattle. It is named after the confederation of 14 Indian tribes living on the nearby Yakima reservation.

YAKUTSK (USSR) Town and capital of YAKUTSK AUTONOMOUS SOVIET SOCIALIST REPUBLIC, on a branch of the Lena River, 1,165 mi NE of Irkutsk. It was founded in 1632. Five wooden towers of the old Russian fort remain. The town is also the site of a cathedral.

YAKUTSK AUTONOMOUS SOVIET SOCIALIST REPUBLIC [Yakut] (USSR) One of the largest socialist republics, in NE SIBERIA. It was first settled by the Yakut around the Lena River between the 13th and 15th centuries. A Russian fort was established here in 1632, and Russian colonization then began. Many Yakut, who speak a Turkic language with Mongolian admixture, have been converted to Christianity, but shamanism is still practiced. Gold mines in the region were first worked in 1850.

YALO. See AIJALON.

YALTA [*Arabic:* **Galita, Jalita**] (USSR) Port of the Ukraine, at the S tip of the Crimean peninsula, on the BLACK SEA, 32 mi S of Simferopol. A favorite Russian winter and summer resort, it was the site of the Yalta Conference of the Big Three between President Franklin D. Roosevelt of the United States, Prime Minister Winston Churchill of Great Britain, and Premier Joseph Stalin of the USSR from February 3 to 11, 1945, toward the end of World War II. Meeting at the nearby estate of Livadia, the leaders issued a statement on February 11 in which they agreed on plans for a San Francisco Conference to form the United Nations, for the occupation of Germany, and for setting up a new Polish government. They also reaffirmed the Atlantic Charter. The Soviets, however, failed to uphold the agreements of the conference. Yalta is also the site of a palace of the former czars and was occupied by GERMANY from 1941 to 1944.

YALU RIVER (China, North Korea) River rising in the Chang pai Shan or Long White Mts of MANCHURIA, and forming most of the boundary between Manchuria and North KOREA, eventually flowing into the Yellow Sea. In 1894 the Yalu was the scene of a naval battle on Sept. 17 around HAI-YANG ISLAND, near its mouth, in which the Chinese were defeated by the Japanese. Then on May 1, 1904 the Russians were defeated near the river in the first land battle of the Russo-Japanese War. In recent times it was important during the Korean War when the Chinese troops entered the war by crossing the river on October 25, 1950. U.N. forces reached the river 27 days later.

YAM. See KINGISEPP.

YAMA. See KINGISEPP.

YAMAGUCHI (Japan) City and capital of Yamaguchi prefecture, in SE HONSHŪ. The stronghold of the Ouchi family from the 14th to 16th centuries, it was one of the more important cities of medieval Japan, and also was prominent during the Restoration or Meiji period, from 1862 to 1868. A great castle city, it is also the site of many Buddhist temples. In 1550 a mission was established here by the Jesuit Francis Xavier.

YAMATO (Japan) Former province in W central HONSHŪ, now part of Nara prefecture. In Japanese legend it was the area where the Japanese imperial clan originally settled and where in 660 BC Jimmu Tenno first ruled. In early centuries the Japanese people were called "people of Yamato." Yamato was, in fact, the heartland of ancient Japan.

YAMAZAKI. See KANAZAWA.

YAMBOL [Jambol] [*ancient:* **Dampolis, Hyampolis;** *Turkish:* **Yanboli**] (Bulgaria) Town in the SE, on the Tundzha River, 45 mi E of Stara Zagora. It was first mentioned in the 11th century when, under Byzantine rule, it was known as Dampolis or Hyampolis. It was the residence of Turkish beys from the 15th to 18th centuries. Several Turkish mosques, an 18th-century church, and the remains of old fortifications remain. See also BYZANTINE EMPIRE.

YAMBURG. See KINGISEPP.

YAM-HA-MELAH. See DEAD SEA.

YANAM. See YANAON.

YANAON [Yanam] (India) Former French settlement near the mouth of the Godavari River, approx. 300 mi NE of Madras. Founded c.1750, it endured the various changes of fortune of French history in southern India. In British hands, it was restored to FRANCE in 1817 after the Napoleonic Wars and became part of India in modern times.

YANBOLI. See YAMBOL.

YANDABU. See ARAKAN, ASSAM.

YANG-CHOU [Yangchow, Yang-Chow Fu] [*former:* **Kiang-tu**] (China) City of Kiangsu, in the E, on the GRAND CANAL, 15 mi N of Chen-Chiang. Its old walled city, early known as a wealthy literary and cultural center, served as the capital of China under the Sui dynasty (589–618 AD). It was governed by the Venetian traveler Marco Polo from 1282 to 1285 by appointment from Emperor Kublai Khan. A center of Nestorian Christianity, in 1868 it was the scene of a serious religious uprising when Hudson Taylor, founder of the China Inland Mission, opened a station here. Later it became a Protestant missionary center. From early times it has been known for its storytellers, who still perform. It is the site of numerous historic buildings and former palaces.

YANGCHOW. See YANG-CHOU.

YANG-CHOW FU. See YANG-CHOU.

YANG-KU. See T'AI-YÜAN.

YANGTZE [Yangtze-Kiang] [*Chinese:* **Ch'ang Chiang (Long River)**] (China) River, 3,100 mi long, rising in the Kunlun Mts of TIBET at an altitude of 16,000 ft, flowing E, SE, and S to Yunnan, then NE across Szechuan province, and finally E to the Yellow Sea. Known as the Kinsha in its upper reaches, it is the principal east-west transport and trade route in China and is of enormous economic, social, political, and military importance. It passes through one of the world's most populated regions. Numerous temples and pagodas crown prominent hills along its gorges.

YANGTZE-KIANG. See YANGTZE.

YANI. See DZHAMBUL.

YANKTON [*Sioux:* **Ihanktonwan, "End Village"**] (United States) City of SOUTH DAKOTA, on the MISSOURI RIVER, 60 mi NW of Sioux City, Iowa. It began as a trading post in 1858 after the conclusion of a treaty with the Yankton tribe of Sioux Indians. In 1861 it was named capital of the Dakota Territory, which included North and South Dakota and all the land west to the Rockies. It held this position until c.1885. In 1862 it was the scene of an Indian uprising. The old capitol building still stands.

YANNINA. See IOÁNNINA.

YAOUNDÉ (Cameroon) Capital city, in the SW central region of Cameroon, Africa. Founded in 1888 by German traders as a base for tapping the ivory trade, it became the capital in 1922 and is the transport and commercial center for the area. Occupied by Belgian troops in World War I, it was capital of French Cameroon after that war, except for the years 1940 to 1946.

YAP ISLANDS (United States) Island group, part of the CAROLINE ISLANDS, in the U.S. Trust Territory of the Pacific Islands, in the W Pacific Ocean, 1,000 mi E of the central Philippines and 2,000 mi S of Yokohama. Consisting of four large and 10 small islands, they were first discovered and controlled by SPAIN, were seized by GERMANY in 1885, and were finally sold to Germany

in 1899. Japan held them under a mandate from 1920. They became internationally important in 1905 as a cable station between the United States, the Netherlands Indies (INDONESIA), and JAPAN, and are still the principal cable station of the Pacific. A Japanese naval and air base in World War II, they were bombed by U.S. forces in 1944/45. After the war they were placed under U.S. control as a trusteeship of the United Nations. The islands are known for their stone disks, used as money by the Micronesian natives. Ancient stone platforms are part of numerous remains of the early inhabitants. See also PACIFIC ISLANDS, U.S. TRUST TERRITORY OF THE.

YARKAND [Yarkend] [*Chinese:* **So-ch'e**] (China) An oasis town, the largest in the Tarim Basin, in SW Sinkiang Uighur, on the Yarkand River, at the edge of the Takla Makan desert, 100 mi SE of Kashgar. An old town with many mosques, it was on the important SILK ROAD between China and Europe, was visited by Marco Polo, the Venetian traveler, in 1271 and 1275, and today is still an important trade link between Sinkiang and INDIA and the USSR.

YARKEND. See YARKAND.

YARMOUTH [*former:* **Cap Fourchu**] (Canada) City of SW NOVA SCOTIA, on the Atlantic Ocean, approx. 140 mi SW of Halifax. Named Cap Fourchu by Samuel Sieur de Champlain on his visit in 1604, it became a French fishing settlement. In 1759 settlers from YARMOUTH, Massachusetts, renamed it Yarmouth, and in 1761 it was formally founded with a larger group of settlers arriving from SANDWICH, Massachusetts. Its population further increased with the arrival in 1767 of Acadians from the GRAND PRÉ district and in 1785 of United Empire Loyalists, or Colonial American Tories.

YARMOUTH [Great Yarmouth] (England) Town of NORFOLK, on the NORTH SEA, at the mouth of the Yare River, 18 mi E of Norwich. A very old fishing village, with herring a speciality then as now, it is also today a seaside resort. Although the town was heavily bombed in World War II, its church of St. Nicholas, dating from 1101, and the 14th-century Tolhouse survive. The latter is one of the oldest such buildings in Great Britain. It still retains it Rows, a series of exceedingly narrow lanes, some only as wide as 29 inches.

YARMOUTH (England) Small port on the ISLE OF WIGHT, 14 mi SSW of Southampton. Now a resort, it is the site of a castle built by Henry VIII.

YARMOUTH (United States) Resort town of Barnstable county in SE MASSACHUSETTS. Settled c.1640, it is a picturesque place with many well-preserved old houses, particularly the Thacher House, which dates from 1680. Yarmouth port is a designated historic district.

YARMUK (Jordan) River in the NW, flowing W into the Jordan River just S of the SEA OF GALILEE. In biblical times it separated BASHAN on the north from GILEAD to the south.

YAROSLAV. See JAROSŁAW.

YAROSLAVL (USSR) Industrial city and capital of

Yaroslavl oblast, on the VOLGA RIVER, approx. 160 mi NE of Moscow. Founded in 1010 by Yaroslav the Wise of Kievan RUSSIA, in 1218 it became capital of the independent Yaroslavl principality, which was taken over by MOSCOW in 1463. Burned by the Tatars in 1238 and 1332, in the 16th and 17th centuries it was an important commercial center on the Moscow-Archangelsk route to the Middle East. From March to July of 1612, during the Time of Troubles, it served briefly as the Russian capital. Russia's first modern ships were built here in 1564, her first cloth factory was opened here in 1722. By the 18th century Yaroslavl had become a major Russian manufacturing city, specializing in textiles.

YARROW [Yarrow Water] (Scotland) River in Borders region, 30 mi SSE of Edinburgh, flowing into the Ettrick River and thence into the Tweed. Wordsworth celebrated its beauty in his verse. Melrose Abbey's ruins are on its lower courses; Dryburgh Abbey is further down.

YARROW WATER. See YARROW.

YASNAYA POLYANA (USSR) Village of Tula oblast, approx. 13 mi S of Tula. The village was the birthplace, residence, and burial place of Count Leo Tolstoi. His home here has been made a national shrine, the Tolstoi Museum. Looted and destroyed by the Germans in World War II, it has been restored since 1946.

YASODHARAPURA. See ANGKOR.

YASSY. See IAŞI.

YATHRIB. See MEDINA.

YAWATA [Kitakyūshū] (Japan) Industrial city on the coast of N KYŪSHŪ, a center of heavy industry. It was the target of the first air strike by American B-29 bombers on June 15, 1944, during World War II. In the 1960's Yawata was joined with four other towns to form the major industrial center of Kitakyūshū.

YAZD [Yezd] (Iran) City of Esfahan province, 170 mi SE of Esfahan, on the main highway from Teheran and Qom to Kermān. Dating from the fifth century AD, it has the largest Zoroastrian community in Iran and was an important Zoroastrian center in Sassanid times. Conquered by the Arabs in 642, it was a large and flourishing city by the 13th century, when Marco Polo visited it. Annexed to PERSIA by Shah Ismail in the 16th century, it is the site of several fine medieval mosques, especially the 13th to 15th century Great Mosque. Its narrow winding streets and medieval walls make it most picturesque. The Zoroastrians erected a modern fire temple here in 1942.

YAZOO (United States) Navigable river of W central MISSISSIPPI, flowing SW into the Mississippi River above Vicksburg. It gave its name to the Yazoo Fraud, a deal involving 35 million acres of land, which were sold for $500,000 by an act of the state of Georgia on January 7, 1795. Shareholders of the four land companies involved were later found to include members of the Georgia state legislature.

YAZOO CITY (United States) City and county seat of Yazoo county, in W central MISSISSIPPI. During the Civil War the ironclad ram C.S.S. *Arkansas* was built in the Confederate navy yard here. In 1864 Union troops occupied the town and burned many of its buildings.

Y BARRI. See BARRY.

YBELIN. See JAMNIA.

YEB. See ELEPHANTINE.

YEDDO. See TOKYO.

YEKATERINBURG. See SVERDLOVSK.

YEKATERINENSHTADT. See MARKS.

YEKATERINODAR. See KRASNODAR.

YEKATERINOSLAV. See DNEPROPETROVSK.

YELABUGA [Elabuga] (USSR) Town in the N Tatar ASSR, in the Russian SFSR, a port on the Kama River, approx. 100 mi E of Kazan. The town was chartered in 1780. In 1858 a remarkable burial mound was discovered three miles from the town, on the river, containing burial goods from the Stone, Bronze, and Iron ages.

YELETS (USSR) City of Lipetsk oblast, in Russian SFSR, on the Sosna River, a tributary of the Don, approx. 100 mi E of Orel. First mentioned in 1146, it was a frontier fortress protecting the duchy of RYAZAN from Polovtsian Cuman attacks. Destroyed by the Mongols in 1239 and 1305, it was captured by Tamerlane in 1395. Raided and severely plundered by the Tatars in the 15th century, it was even abandoned for a time. Its modern prosperity dates from the 17th century, and it has been famous for lace-making since the 19th century. In World War II it was taken by the Germans in 1941 and 1942.

YELGAVA. See JELGAVA.

YELISAVETPOL. See KIROVABAD.

YELIZAVETGRAD. See KIROVOGRAD.

YELLOW. See HUANG HO RIVER.

YELLOW BANKS. See OWENSBORO.

YELLOWKNIFE (Canada) Town in SW NORTHWEST TERRITORIES, and its capital, on the north shore of the GREAT SLAVE LAKE. It was founded in 1935 after the discovery of gold here. When another mine was discovered in 1944, the townsite was moved. The capital of the Northwest Territories since 1967, it is the transportation, business, and government center for a vast region.

YELLOWSTONE NATIONAL PARK AND YELLOWSTONE RIVER (United States) The park, covering nearly 2.25 million acres, is mostly in NW WYOMING, with small areas in MONTANA and IDAHO. It is one of the world's most fascinating geological regions, with hot springs, geysers, vents, hot-mud pots, lava formations, and petrified forests. Best known is the geyser Old Faithful, which erupts regularly almost once an hour. The Yellowstone River, 671 miles long, rises in northwestern Wyoming and flows north through the park, including Yellowstone Lake, then east and northeast into the Missouri River near the North Dakota line. In the park it also flows through the Grand Canyon of the Yellowstone, 1,200 feet deep. The park takes its

Tourists today would hardly recognize the United States's first and largest park, the Yellowstone, in this old photograph of 1903. It is one of the world's largest nature preserves.

name from the river, which in turn is a translation of the French *Roche Jaune*, so called for a yellow rock near the mouth of the river. John Colter, one of the mountain men, trappers and hunters who explored much of the American West, was probably the first man of European ancestry to see the region that is now the park, in 1807. That same year, Colter and Manuel Lisa, an Indian trapper, established the first trading post on the river at the mouth of the Bighorn River in what is now southern Montana.

The Yellowstone River was first explored the previous year by William Clark of the Lewis and Clark Expedition, which since 1803 had been traversing the LOUISIANA PURCHASE. He went down some of the river on his way back from the Pacific Coast. It was not until the 1870's, however, that any scientific study of the Yellowstone area was made. This was primarily the work of Ferdinand V. Hayden, a soldier and paleontologist, who spent 12 years from 1867 surveying the West. His work, when it became known, was largely responsible for the creation of Yellowstone National Park in 1872. It was the first such park and is the largest in the United States.

YEMEN [Peoples Democratic Republic of Yemen] [*former:* **Southern Yemen**] Republic in the S ARABIAN PENINSULA, bounded by Saudi Arabia to the N, Oman to the E, the Gulf of Aden to the S, and the YEMEN Arab Republic to the W. Formed in 1967, its capital is ADEN, with an administrative capital at Madinat ash

Sha'b. The area became a British protectorate on April 1, 1937 following treaties signed with the surrounding states. Aden joined the Federation of SOUTH ARABIA on Jan. 18, 1963 and was granted independence as Southern Yemen on Nov. 30, 1967. It was given its present name in 1970.

In 1972, after fighting and clashes between the two Yemens, an agreement was signed that ended the fighting and called for a merger of the two nations. However, the merger has not been effected, and Salim Robea Ali, chairman of the Presidential Council since 1969, who favored union, was ousted and executed in 1978. His successor, Abdul Fattah Ismail, opposed the union. A close ally of the Soviet Union and its interests in the Middle East, he resigned in 1980. Yemen has since become more conciliatory toward Saudi Arabia and other conservative Arab states.

YEMEN [Yemen Arab Republic] Republic in the SW ARABIAN PENINSULA, bounded by Saudi Arabia to the N, Yemen (formerly Southern Yemen) to the E, and the Red Sea to the W. Its capital is SANA. Once the seat of an ancient Minaean kingdom, it was conquered by EGYPT *c.*1600 BC and was subsequently invaded by both the Romans and the Ethiopians. Converted to Islam in 628 AD, it was then ruled by a caliphate. Under Turkish control in the 16th century, it became nearly independent until Mehmet Ali of Egypt established control in 1819. In the aftermath of severe revolts, its autonomy was guaranteed by the OTTOMAN

EMPIRE in 1913. Following World War I, it again became independent and in 1934 reached a boundary agreement with GREAT BRITAIN. The monarchy was overthrown in 1962, and from 1962 to 1969 civil war raged between royalist and republican forces. A series of military leaders have ruled the country since then. Col. Ali Abdulla Saleh was named president in 1978.

Ancient Sana, one of the world's oldest cities, now the capital of the Arab Republic of Yemen. A center of Islamic studies, Sana is southern Arabia's largest city.

YEMEN ARAB REPUBLIC. See YEMEN.

YEN (China) A feudal state in earliest China, in the extreme NE. It was part of the China of the Chou dynasty (1028–221 BC), the succeeding dynasty to the Shang, the first authenticated dynasty of ancient China. There are documents that also record it in the first to sixth centuries AD, under the Latter Han and Wei dynasties.

YEN-AN [Fushih, Yenan] (China) Town of N Shensi province, in the NE central region, on the S bank of a tributary of the Yellow River. It was the headquarters after 1938 for the Communist Eighth Route Army in the war against the Japanese. The communists controlled approximately 1.5 million people in parts of SHENSI, KANSU, and NINGSIA-HUI. During the Chinese civil war following World War II, Yen-an continued as the communist capital, was captured by the Nationalists March 19, 1947 and was reoccupied by the communists in April, 1948, remaining their capital until

their capture of Peiping (PEKING) in January 1949. It is famed as the terminus of the long march of the communists under Mao Tse-tung. The former homes of the leaders are preserved, and a museum honors Mao and the years of the Communist Party's presence here. Now a place of pilgrimage, a nine-story pagoda built during the Sung dynasty (960–1279 AD) has been made a monument to the revolution.

YENANGYAUNG (Burma) Town of the Magwe division, Upper Burma, on the IRRAWADDY RIVER, 130 mi SW of Mandalay. During World War II it was destroyed by the British when they abandoned it on April 17, 1942. It was retaken on April 16, 1945 and is presently the site of the largest and most important oil field in Burma.

YENI-PAZA. See NOVI PAZAR.

YENISEI [Enisei, Yenisey] (USSR) Chief river of SIBERIA, formed by a confluence of the Bolshoi Yenisei and the Maly Yenisei. Flowing through country inhabited since antiquity, the region is dotted with burial mounds, rock inscriptions, and the smelting furnaces of successive generations of inhabitants. The river was first visited by the Cossacks in 1618.

YENISEY. See YENISEI.

YEN-T'AI. See CHEFOO.

YEOVIL (England) Town of Somerset, on the Yeo River, 36 mi S of Bristol. Part of the private domains of the Anglo-Saxon kings before the Norman Conquest, since 1565 it has been well known for the manufacture of gloves. Notable buildings include the late 14th-century Perpendicular Gothic church of St. John, the "Lantern of the West," and numerous old houses.

YERBA BUENA. See SAN FRANCISCO.

YEREVAN [Erevan, Erivan] (USSR) Capital city of Armenian SSR, in the W region, on the Razdan River, 110 mi S of Tbilisi. On the site of the ancient fortress of Yerbuni, which existed in the eighth century BC, it has been part of the Armenian kingdom since the sixth century AD and was the capital of ARMENIA under Persian rule. Thereafter under a succession of rulers, it was historically and strategically important as the crossroads of the caravan routes between Transcaucasia and India. After the fall of Tamerlane's empire in the 15th century, it alternated between Persian and Turkish rule but became the chief city of East Armenia in 1440. A caravan trading point and frontier fort in the 17th century, it was the capital of the Yerevan khanate of PERSIA in 1725. In 1827 it was finally taken by RUSSIA. It was the center of the short-lived but courageous independent state of Armenia from 1918 to 1920, when it was made the capital of the new Armenian SSR. The ruins of a 16th-century Turkish fortress are of interest.

YERUSHALAYIM. See JERUSALEM.

YESILKÖY [Italian: San Stefano] (Turkey) Village of Istanbul province, on the Sea of Marmara, approx. 7 mi W of Istanbul. After the end of the last Russo-Turkish War a treaty was signed here on Mar. 3, 1878 between RUSSIA and the OTTOMAN EMPIRE, which was greatly in Russia's favor. It vastly enlarged Russian-protected BULGARIA, making it a principality; provided for independent RUMANIA, MONTENEGRO, and SERBIA, all formerly under Ottoman control; and gave part of ARMENIA to Russia. It also granted Russia a large indemnity. The Treaty of San Stefano so greatly enlarged Russian influence in eastern Europe that at the BERLIN Congress of 1878 the alarmed great powers modified its terms.

YESKI-ZAGRA. See STARA ZAGORA.

YEU, ÎLE D' (France) Island off the coast of Vendée department, in the BAY OF BISCAY. Marshal Pétain, the leader of the French Vichy government in World War II, was imprisoned here in November 1945 after the liberation of France and his trial for treason.

YEVELCHESTER. See ILCHESTER.

YEVPATORIYA [Eupatoria, Evpatoria] [ancient: Kerkinitida] (USSR) Town and port of the Crimean oblast, in the Ukraine, approx. 45 mi NW of Simferopol. Located on the site of the ancient Greek colony of Kerkinitida, founded in the sixth century BC, it was captured in the first century BC by the Pontian King Mitridat Evpator, after whom it is named. Under many different rulers, it came under Turko-Tatar control in the 13th century AD. Conquered and made a vassal state of Turkey in 1478, in 1783 it was annexed by RUSSIA along with the rest of the CRIMEA. During the Crimean War of 1854 to 1856 it was the landing place for the Allied armies in September 1854 and was occupied by British, French, and Turkish troops. Historic buildings include a 16th-century mosque and the ruins of a 15th-century Tatar fortress.

YEZD. See YAZD.

YEZO. See HOKKAIDO.

YIBNA. See JAMNIA.

YIN-CH'UAN [Yinchwan] (China) Capital city of Ningsia Hui Autonomous Region, on the HUANG HO, or Yellow River, in the fertile Ningsia plain. It was visited by Marco Polo in the 13th century.

YINCHWAN. See YIN-CH'UAN.

YING-K'OU [Yingkow] (China) City of S Liaoning province, on the Liao River, near its mouth on the Po Hai, Manchuria. Because of its superior location it succeeded inland Newchwang as a trading port by a treaty of 1858 and was the only Manchurian open port until 1907. In the 20th century it has lost trade to Dairen (TA'LIEN) and Tan-tung.

YINGKOW. See YING-K'OU.

YITHION. See GYTHIUM.

YNGAVI. See INGAVI.

YNYS BYR. See CALDY ISLAND.

YO-CHOW FU (China) Prefectural city in Hu-nan province, E of the outlet of Tung t'ing Lake. Opened to foreign trade in 1899, it is situated in a district that was the ancient home of the aboriginal San Miao tribes. The present city dates from 1371. Surrounded by high walls,

it was attacked by rebels of the Taiping Rebellion in 1853.

YOKKAICHI (Japan) Port city of Mie prefecture, in W HONSHŪ, on Ise Bay. A manufacturing city, it was bombed by U.S. forces in 1945, toward the end of World War II.

YOKOHAMA (Japan) Port and the country's third-largest city, in Kanagawa prefecture, SE HONSHŪ, on the W shore of Tokyo Bay, 18 mi S of Tokyo. A major port of TOKYO and an industrial center, it was a small fishing village when visited by U.S. Commodore Perry in 1854. After 1859 it was the site of a foreign settlement whose extraterritorial rights were abolished in 1899. Although it was heavily bombed and damaged during World War II, numerous Shinto shrines, temples, churches, parks, and gardens have survived, notably Nogeyama Park.

YOKOSUKA (Japan) City of Kanagawa prefecture, in SE HONSHU on Tokyo Bay, 12 mi S of Yokohama. It is a base for the U.S. Navy and the Japanese Maritime Self-Defense Force. A simple fishing village before 1865, it became a naval base in 1884 and through World War II served as both an important naval base and a shipyard. It has been rebuilt after being largely destroyed by U.S. bombing in 1945. The city is the site of the tomb of William Adams, the first Englishman to visit Japan.

YOLA (Nigeria) Port city, in the E, on the upper Benue River, near the Cameroon border. Founded in 1841 as the capital of a Muslim Fulani state, it was captured by the British in 1901 and incorporated into British Nigeria. See also ADAMAWA, FULANI EMPIRE.

YONKERS (United States) City of Westchester County, in SE NEW YORK State on the HUDSON RIVER, just N of New York City. Included in a purchase from the Indians made by the Dutch West India Company in 1639, it was part of a grant made in 1646 to the *Jonkheer* (young nobleman) Van der Donck, hence its name, and was part of Philipse Manor after 1672. It was fought over by both sides during the American Revolution. It is the site of the 17th-century Philipse Manor, built by Frederick Philipse.

YORBA LINDA (United States) City in SW CALIFORNIA, 25 mi SE of Los Angeles. It was the birthplace of former president Richard M. Nixon in 1913.

YORK, Canada. See TORONTO.

YORK [*Danish:* Jorvik; *Latin:* Eboracum, Eburacum] (England) City of NORTH YORKSHIRE, situated at the confluence of the Foss and Ouse rivers, 20 mi ENE of Leeds. Originally a settlement of the Celtic Brigantes, under the Romans it became the principal military base for the north, lying at the center of a network of roads, military forts, and camps south of HADRIAN'S WALL.

Founded as a legionary fortress in 71 AD, it became a flourishing city but never lost its importance as a military center, with its great *principia*, or headquarters, the remains of which have now been partly revealed under the present York Minster. The emperor Septimius Severus died here in 211 AD, and Constantine the Great was proclaimed emperor by his troops and his

Yokohama, a principal port for Tokyo, in an old photograph showing both modern street lamps and decorative traditional Japanese lanterns. Yokohama developed as an entrepôt for Western trade.

father here in 306 AD. In Anglo-Saxon times it was an important center of the flourishing kingdom of NORTHUMBRIA. With the consecration of St. Paulinus in the seventh century as the first archbishop of York, it became and has remained the ecclesiastical center of the north. Paulinus baptized King Edwin of Northumbria here on Easter Day in 627 in a small wooden church built over the site of the *principia*, where York Minster now stands.

By the eighth century York had become one of the outstanding cultural and educational centers of Europe. Alcuin, principal adviser to Charlemagne, was born here. York was also a trading town, with connections with Frisia in particular, and under the Danish Viking settlers in the ninth and 10th centuries it continued to display intensive industrial and commercial activity, chiefly with SCANDINAVIA. A recent excavation at Coppergate has revealed the remains of the shops and workshops of the Danes. In the later Middle Ages York was a center of the wool trade and the meeting place for several parliaments. In the 15th and 16th centuries it was famous for its cycle of 48 mystery plays. York's massive Gothic Minster, or cathedral, was founded in 1291 and there are extensive remains of the town walls, guildhall, Merchant and Adventurers Hall, Roman, Anglo-Saxon, and later medieval fortifications. The Shambles, a section of medieval buildings and butcher shops here, has given its generic name to any awkward or disorderly area or building. There is also a transport museum and the ruins of St. Mary's Abbey.

YORK [*former:* **Gorgeana**] (United States) Township of MAINE, 45 mi SW of Portland. Chartered in 1641/42 by Sir Ferdinando Gorges as a city named Gorgeana, in 1692 it was the scene of an Indian attack in which most of the inhabitants were killed and their houses burned. The York village county jail, dating from 1653/54, still stands.

YORK (United States) City and county seat of York county, PENNSYLVANIA, 23 mi S of Harrisburg, in the Pennsylvania Dutch country. Historically it served as capital of the American colonies during the British occupation of PHILADELPHIA in 1777/78. During the Civil War it was occupied briefly in June 1863 by Gen. Jubal Early and his Confederate soldiers during the GETTYSBURG campaign. It is the site of several notable colonial houses.

YORK, CAPE (Denmark) Cape of GREENLAND, in N Baffin Bay, W of Melville Bay. It is the site of the discovery by the explorer Robert E. Peary of the large iron Cape York meteorites, the largest of which, weighing approximately 100 tons, was brought to the American Museum of Natural History in New York City. A monument to Peary was erected at Cape York in 1932.

YORK FACTORY (Canada) Fur-trading post at the mouth of the Hayes River, on HUDSON BAY, in NE

MANITOBA. The name was used for several late 17th-century trading posts in a region that shifted between ENGLAND and FRANCE during their struggle to control the fur trade. The British finally won after the Peace of Utrecht in 1713. The present post, built between 1788 and 1793, was a principal warehouse for the Hudson's Bay Company until it was closed in 1957.

YORKSHIRE (England) Formerly the largest county of England. Since 1974 it has been divided into North Yorkshire, West Yorkshire, South Yorkshire, Humberside, and parts of Cleveland. It evolved from the Anglo-Saxon kingdom of DEIRA, first known in the sixth century under the kingship of Ella, who was succeeded by his son Edwin. Edwin's defeat at Hatfield in 633 began a series of struggles between MERCIA and NORTHUMBRIA for supremacy over Deira. Conquered by the Danes c.875, it became part of the DANELAW until it was retaken by the kings of WESSEX in 954, when Eric Broadaxe was driven from York. In 1013 the area, with the rest of England, again came under Scandinavian control when Sweyn conquered England and joined it to DENMARK. In the crucial year of 1066 the descendants of Sweyn and Cnut attempted to reconquer England when Edward the Confessor died but were defeated, and Harold Hardrada killed, at STAMFORD BRIDGE in Yorkshire. Harold of England, the victor, then marched south, only to be defeated by William the Conqueror at HASTINGS, thus turning England's history toward NORMANDY and the continent rather than toward SCANDINAVIA.

In later years several assaults on Yorkshire by the Scots ended in failure, and in the Battle of BOROUGHBRIDGE in 1322 the rebel English barons were defeated by the forces of Edward II of England. In 1400

Scene in the Pennine Mountains in western Yorkshire. The stone walls, so typical of this hilly country down into Derbyshire, would remind any New Englander of his home.

Richard II was murdered in Pontrefact Castle in Yorkshire, which as a shire had been a strong supporter of Henry Bolingbroke (King Henry IV) against the king. In 1405 Archbishop Scrope of York and Earl Marshal Thomas Mowbray joined the revolt against Henry IV, leading the rebels to battle at Skipton Moor. After their defeat by the earl of Westmorland they were beheaded under the walls of York. Yorkshire was also the base for the Yorkists during the Wars of the Roses of 1455 to 1485, the dukes of York holding the shire almost as a personal possession since the 14th century.

During the Middle Ages Yorkshire, especially the Dales, was a favored area for the large sheep industry, which led directly to dominance in the wool trade, for which England became internationally famous. During the Industrial Revolution of the 18th and 19th centuries Yorkshire continued to hold an important place in the wool and fabric industries.

YORKSHIRE, NORTH (England) Largest county, which includes the Cleveland Hills and York Moors. The admin. hq. is Northallerton. See YORKSHIRE.

YORKSHIRE, SOUTH (England) Industrial county with admin. hq. at Sheffield. See YORKSHIRE.

YORKSHIRE, WEST (England) Industrial county famous for its coalfields and textile industry. The admin. hq. is Wakefield. See YORKSHIRE.

YORKTOWN (United States) Town on the York River, in VIRGINIA, 62 mi SE of Richmond. In 1781 Lord Cornwallis surrendered to Gen. George Washington here in the final British defeat by the Americans and their French allies in the American Revolution. In 1862, during the Civil War, Confederate forces were besieged here by Union forces under Gen. McClellan and were finally forced to retreat to RICHMOND. Notable buildings include Grace Church of 1697 and the Moore House of c.1725 where the Cornwallis surrender was effected.

YORUBALAND (Nigeria) Region of West Africa inhabited by the Yorubas since c.1000 AD. During the 18th century they were engaged in constant warfare with neighboring Dahomey (now BENIN), capturing Kana, the sacred city of the kings of Dahomey, in 1738. From 1747 until the time of King Gezo in 1818 Dahomey paid tribute to the Yorubas. In 1825 they pushed south to found a colony at LAGOS but from 1830 to 1835 were overrun by Fulan invaders, who forced the breakup of the empire. The coming of the British brought more fighting but eventually the British subdued the region. See also OYO, SOKOTO.

YOUGHAL (Irish Republic) Port and market town of county Cork, on the W side of Blackwater estuary, 26 mi E of Cork. Settled by Norsemen in the ninth century, it was incorporated by King John of ENGLAND in 1209. In 1224 the first Franciscan monastery in Ireland was founded here. During the English Civil War the town sided with the Parliamentarians and in 1649 became Cromwell's headquarters. Notable buildings include the collegiate church of St. Mary from the 11th century; fragments of a Dominican friary dating from 1269; and Myrtle Grove, the former home of Sir Walter

Raleigh, who was mayor of the town in 1588/89 and is said to have cultivated the first potato imported from the New World here. The Clock Gate dates from 1771.

YOUNGSTOWN (United States) City in OHIO, on the Mahoning River, 60 mi SE of Cleveland. It is one of the great steel-producing centers of the world, ranking fourth in the United States. It is named for John Young, a native of Peterborough, New Hampshire, who in 1796 bought the tract of land on which the city now stands from the Connecticut Land Company.

YPIRANGA [Ipiranga] (Brazil) Plain of São Paulo state, near the city of São Paulo. On Sept. 7, 1822 the regent, Dom Pedro, here proclaimed the independence of Brazil from PORTUGAL while on his way to São Paulo. The next month he was declared constitutional emperor of Brazil.

YPRES [Ieper] (Belgium) City of West FLANDERS, 35 mi SW of Ostend. In 1300 it reached its height as a center of the textile industry, ranking with BRUGES and GHENT and being one of the largest European cities of that period. Its townsmen, often at odds with the feudal aristocracy, also maintained their independence against France, Burgundy, and the Hapsburgs. In World War I three major battles were fought here: the first was the latest in a series in the Race for the Sea, fought in November 1914, in which the British stopped the Germans but lost half their force; the second was on April 22, 1915 in which the Germans used gas for the first time, launching a massive but unsuccessful assault; and the third, known as PASSCHENDAELE, began on July 31 and continued until November 1917. The British sought to break the German line but, slowed by mud and rain, they lost 300,000 lives. In World War II Ypres was again a battlefield.

YPSILANTI (United States) City of Washtenaw county, MICHIGAN, on the Huron River, 30 mi SW of Detroit. It was founded in 1825 on the site of an Indian village and French trading post dating from 1809 to c.1820. The city was named in honor of Demetrius Ypsilanti, the Greek patriot.

YSABEL. See SANTA ISABEL.

YSLETA. See TEXAS.

YSTAD (Sweden) Port, city, and resort of Malmöhus county, on the Baltic Sea. Here in 1799 Gustavus IV issued his declaration of war against Napoleon I of FRANCE. A despotic ruler, Gustavus later involved Sweden in war with RUSSIA from 1806 to 1809 and was deposed in 1809.

YUCATÁN (Mexico) State in the SE occupying most of the N YUCATÁN PENINSULA. It was named a state when Mexico gained her independence in 1821 and has remained such to the present, except for a period of secession from 1839 to 1843. There are many ruins dating from the late MAYA EMPIRE. Yucatán was the scene of serious Indian revolts in 1847 and 1910.

YUCATÁN PENINSULA (Mexico) Peninsula forming the SE extremity of the republic, including the states of CAMPECHE and YUCATÁN and the territory of QUINTANA ROO. It was a seat of Mayan civilization; its pre-Columbian history dates from the Maya Classic period (c.100 BC–630 AD) into the period of Toltec domination (1200–1450). Its present inhabitants, called Yuatecos, are descendants of the original Maya Indians. Francisco Hernández de Córdoba spearheaded the Spanish conquest of the region in 1517, and by 1542 Francisco de Montejo the Younger had established Spanish rule over half the peninsula and had enslaved some of the Indians. In 1847 and 1910 the Indians' revolts won them land from their Mexican landlords; and the governors Salvador Alvarado and Felipe Carillo introduced numerous reforms in the early 20th century. There are notable Mayan ruins at CHICHEN-ITZA, UXMAL and Tulum. See also MAYA EMPIRE.

YUCHANG. See NAN-CH'ANG.

YÜEH. See SHAO-HSING.

YUGOSLAVIA [Jugoslavia] [*former:* **Kingdom of the Serbs, Croats, and Slovenes;** *official:* **Federal Republic of Yugoslavia**] Nation in SE Europe, mostly in the BALKANS and with the Adriatic Sea And Italy on the W, Austria and Hungary to the N, Rumania and Bulgaria on the E, and Albania and Greece on the S. It is a federation of six people's republics: SERBIA, CROATIA, MACEDONIA, SLOVENIA, MONTENEGRO, and BOSNIA AND HERZEGOVINA. All except the last named are formed mostly on ethnic lines and historic division. Primarily, Yugoslavia is a Slavic nation, the Serbs, Croats, Slovenes, Macedonians, and Montenegrins accounting for most of the population. Prior to World War I only Serbia, including the present Macedonia, and Montenegro were independent. The others were under Austro-Hungarian control.

Yugoslavia came into existence as the Kingdom of the Serbs, Croats and Slovenes in December 1918, after the defeat of AUSTRIA-HUNGARY in World War I, with Peter I of Serbia as king. The name was changed in 1929. In 1920/21 Yugoslavia formed the Little Entente with CZECHOSLOVAKIA and RUMANIA to oppose attempts by HUNGARY and BULGARIA to get treaty boundaries revised. At this time Yugoslavia had close ties with FRANCE. There were internal problems with ethnic groups, especially the Croats, demanding more autonomy. As a result King Alexander made himself dictator in 1929. In March 1941 during World War II, the government, now under regent Prince Paul, joined in alliance with Nazi GERMANY. This unpopular move resulted in the immediate overthrow of the government, but in April Germany and her allies invaded the country and conquered it in a week.

Resistance groups formed and fought the invaders energetically. By the end of the war, Tito (Josip Broz), a Marxist, emerged as the most popular and successful leader. He became premier in March 1945, and by 1946 Yugoslavia was under communist rule. Nationalization of industries began, but most farming had been left in private hands. Yugoslavia was a member of the Cominform, formed by the USSR in 1947, along with other communist nations, to exchange information. In 1948 Yugoslavia was expelled because Tito refused to accept the hegemony of the USSR. Since then Yugoslavia has gone its own way, becoming the most liberal and decentralized communist nation of Europe and a leader among the nonaligned Third World nations. Relations with the USSR have improved. Marshal Tito continued to rule until his death on May 4, 1980.

Since Tito's death the nation has been ruled by a rotating presidency giving equal representation to the constituent republics, according to constitutional changes ratified in 1974. Since 1981 Albanian separatists in the south have gained widespread support in repeated clashes with the central government.

A monastery near Novi Pazar in the typical mountainous countryside of Serbia. Now a leading constituent republic in Yugoslavia, Serbia was a proudly independent principality for many centuries.

YU-HO. See GRAND CANAL.

YUKI. See UNGGI.

YUKON TERRITORY (Canada) A governmental division of the Dominion of Canada, in the northwestern part of the country. The land was first sighted by Europeans during the expedition of Sir John Franklin of 1825 to 1827, which explored the Arctic coastline. The region was entered overland in 1834 when John McLeod of the Hudson's Bay Company arrived. The company owned a vast area of Canada as a result of a grant made by Charles II of England in 1670. In the 1840's John Bell and Robert Campbell, company employees, built trading posts in the Yukon. Campbell established the first at Frances Lake in 1843; and in 1848 he built Fort Selkirk, which was destroyed by Chilcat Indians in 1852.

In 1870 the Dominion took over the company's lands, and the Yukon became part of the NORTHWEST TERRITORIES. The discovery of gold in 1896 in the KLONDIKE area caused an influx of nearly 30,000 fortune hunters in 1897/98. As a result, the Yukon was made a separate territory in 1898. A dispute over the southwest boundary with ALASKA was settled by arbitration in 1903. During World War II the ALASKA HIGHWAY across the Yukon was built for strategic purposes in just nine months by U.S. and Canadian troops.

YUMA (United States) Trading center of SW ARIZONA, on the COLORADO RIVER, opposite the old Fort Yuma. Laid out in 1854, it became a gold-mining center and early river port. It was named Yuma after the Yuma Indian tribe. The first railroad in Arizona crossed the Colorado River at Yuma in 1877.

YÜ-MEN [Lao-Chün-Miao, Yümen] (China) City of NW Kansu province, on the old SILK ROAD to SINKIANG. It is named for an ancient gateway in the Great Wall, which is nearby. It is now a leading oil center.

YUNGAY (Peru) City of Ancash department, in the NW, W of Mt Huascarán. On January 20, 1839 a battle was fought here in which an army from CHILE, led by Manuel Bulnes, defeated a confederation of BOLIVIA and Peru.

YUNGKIA. See WENCHOW.

YUNG-NING. See NANNING.

YÜN-HO. See GRAND CANAL.

YUN-NAN (China) Province in the SW, bordered on the W by Burma and Tibet, and on the S by Vietnam. Its name means Cloudy South. Its capital is K'UN-MING. Long an independent state because of its isolation, it was subdued by Kublai Khan in the 13th century and was completely conquered by China in 1382. In the 19th century it was the principal center of the great Panthay or Muslim Rebellion, which lasted from 1855 to 1873 and was followed by a barbaric repression. Part of the province's southern section was seized by the Japanese in 1942, during World War II.

YUN-NAN FU (China) Capital city of YUN-NAN province, approx. 500 mi NNW of Haiphong, Tongking. The large Muslim population here spurred the Muslim Rebellion in 1855.

YURYEV. See TARTU.

YUSOVKA. See DONETSK.

YVERDON [Yverdun] [ancient: **Eburodunum**; German: **Iferten**] (Switzerland) Town of VAUD canton, in the W, 18 mi N of Lausanne, at the S end of the Lake of Neuchâtel. Heinrich Pestalozzi, the educator, held his experimental classes in the 13th-century castle here from 1805 to 1825. Notable structures include the castle, an old spa with Roman ruins, and an 18th-century church.

YVERDUN. See YVERDON.

YVETOT (France) Town of Seine-Maritime department, 20 mi NW of Rouen. A small monarchy in the 15th and 16th centuries, its lords bore the title of king and were the subject of one of Béranger's most famous songs, *Le Roi d'Yvetot* of 1813. In 1592 Henry IV defeated the troops of the Catholic League here during the Wars of Religion.

YZABAL. See IZABAL, LAKE.

Z

ZAACHILA [*former:* **Teozapotlán**] (Mexico) Town 7 mi S of Oaxaca. Once a capital of the powerful Zapotec people, it has pre-Columbian ruins.

ZAANDAM (Netherlands) Town in North Holland province, on the Zaan river, near Amsterdam. Peter the Great of RUSSIA lived and studied shipbuilding here in 1697, when the town was a center of that industry. The hut he stayed in is still preserved.

ZABERN. See SAVERNE.

ZABĪD [**Zebid**] (Yemen) Medieval dynastic center in Hodeida province, on the bank of the Zabīd, approx. 10 mi from the Red Sea coast, Yemen Arab Republic. The Ziyadi dynasty ruled from here over large parts of SW Arabia after its founding by Muhammed ibn Zayid in 820 AD, during the Muslim conquest. A religious center of Sunni Islam, here also was the capital of the brilliant Rasulid dynasty from *c.*1230 AD, which claimed dominion far beyond Yemen.

ZABŌL. See SEISTAN.

ZACATECAS (Mexico) Province and capital city on the great central plateau of Mexico. The area was a refuge for Indians defeated in the Mixtón War of 1541, an Indian revolt put down by the Spanish under the governor, Cristóbal de Oñate, with great difficulty. Until the 19th century, the mines discovered here in 1548 yielded one-fifth of the world's silver. The city, founded in 1848, was a center of struggle in the Mexican wars and revolutions throughout the 19th and 20th centuries.

ZACATECOLUCA (El Salvador) City in La Paz department, S central El Salvador. It was the birthplace of José Simenón Cañas, who fought for and secured the emancipation of slaves in Central America by 1825.

ZACYNTHUS [**Zakynthos**] [*Italian:* **Zante;** *Modern Greek:* **Zákinthos**] (Greece) Ancient and modern town and island, one of the IONIAN ISLANDS, in the Ionian Sea, off the NW coast of the Peloponnesus, 8 mi S of Cephalonia. According to Greek legend, it was settled by Zacynthus, son of the Arcadian chief Dardanus. Homer knew the island by its present name. Thucydides says it was colonized by Achaeans from the PELOPONNESUS. It was captured and often used as a military base by ATHENS, ROME, the Norman kings of SICILY, and successive Italian rulers. It was finally held by VENICE from 1484 to 1797. It was then held by FRANCE, RUSSIA, and GREAT BRITAIN and was ceded to Greece in 1864.

ZADAR [*Italian:* **Zara,** *Latin:* **Iadera, Jadera**] (Yugoslavia) Port on the Dalmatian coast, 70 mi NW of Split, until the late 19th century the most heavily fortified town on the ADRIATIC SEA. Founded by Illyrians in the fourth century BC, it was made a Roman colony in 100 BC. Under Byzantine protection, this natural harbor city was a cultural and artistic center until 1001 AD, after which it changed hands many times. It was besieged and taken by a Latin Crusader army in 1202, at the instigation of VENICE and against the will of Pope Innocent III. This was the first planned attack by Crusaders on a Christian city; they subsequently went on to capture CONSTANTINOPLE. Zadar was the capital of DALMATIA from 1815 to 1918. There are several Roman monuments and a forum, medieval churches, and palaces. See also BYZANTINE EMPIRE, ILLYRIA, ROME.

ZAFĀR [*biblical:* **Sephar;** *Classical:* **Sapphar, Saphar**] (Yemen) Archaeological site SW of Yarim, Yemen Arab Republic. According to both Arab historians and geographers and Greek and Roman authors, it was one of the most important and celebrated towns in southern Arabia. Much of the peninsula was ruled from this capital by the Himyarites from *c.*115 BC to *c.*525 AD. See also ARABIAN PENINSULA.

ZAGAN. See SAGAN.

ZAGORSK [**Sergiev, Sergievo, Sergievski Posad, Sergiyev, Sergiyevo, Sergiyevski Posad**] (USSR) Town, 44 mi NNE of Moscow. It grew around the Troitsko (Trinity) Sergiyevskaya monastery, once the most sacred spot in middle RUSSIA. Famous for its manufacture of icons, it was held in even greater veneration than the churches and relics of the KREMLIN. The Uspensky cathedral, within the monastery walls, was erected in 1585 and is close to the graves of the czar Boris Godunov (d.1605) and his family. When the Poles invaded Russia in the early 17th century, the monastery organized national resistance, and in 1608/09 withstood a 16-month siege. In 1685 it provided refuge for Peter the Great during the revolt of the Streltzi.

ZÁGRÁB. See ZAGREB.

ZAGRABIA. See ZAGREB.

ZAGREB [*ancient:* **Zagrabia;** *German:* **Agram;** *Hungarian:* **Zágráb**] (Yugoslavia) Capital of Croatia, on the Sava River. Originally a suburb of the ancient Roman town of Andautonia, it was first documented in 1093 when a bishopric was established here. Two medieval settlements continued as rival entities until 1557, when nearby Gradec merged with Zagreb. Overrun by the Mongols in 1242, by the 13th century Zagreb became the chief city of CROATIA and of SLAVONIA, then provinces of HUNGARY. The surrounding region escaped both Turkish domination and later attempted Germanization by AUSTRIA.

The city became capital of an independent Croatia in 1867. In the 19th century it was a center of the Yugoslav nationalist movement. In 1918 the Croatian Diet, meeting here, severed all links with Austria-Hungary and proclaimed Croatia, Slavonia, and DALMATIA an independent state. Soon after these states united with SERBIA, SLOVENIA, and MONTENEGRO to form the nucleus of Yugoslavia. Between World Wars I and II Zagreb was a center for Croatian nationalists who opposed the Serbian tendencies toward centralization. During World War II, in 1941, the Axis powers made it the capital of a puppet government, which collapsed shortly after Germany surrendered in 1945. The University of Zagreb was founded in 1669. For centuries a cultural center, the city has several museums and many buildings surviving from the Middle Ages.

Cathedral of the Assumption in the old center of Zagreb, capital of Croatia. Unlike most of Yugoslavia, this area was never Turkish-held, and was long under Hungarian and Austrian rule.

ZAGROS (Iran) Mountains extending NW to SE from the Sīrvān River to Shīrāz. They formed the ancient boundary between ASSYRIA and MEDIA. They are inhabited by various nomadic groups, some of whom, especially the Kurds, are now sedentary. Iran's great oilfields lie along the western foothills of the central Zagros. See also KURDISTAN.

ZAHEDAN. See ZAHIDAN.

ZAHIDAN [Zahedan] (Iran) Ancient city, 12 mi ESE of Zabōl. It was once capital of SEISTAN. Its ruins date from its destruction by Tamerlane in 1383. The modern town of Zahidan, located 115 miles south of Zabul, was named after it in the 1930's.

ZÄHRINGEN (West Germany) A ruined castle, near Freiburg im Breisgau, 80 mi SW of Stuttgart. It was the ancestral stronghold of the house of Zähringen, an important dynasty throughout the history of southwestern Germany.

ZAIRE [*former:* **Belgian Congo, Congo, Congo Free State**] An inland country of south-central Africa with a narrow access to the Atlantic Ocean along the north bank of the CONGO RIVER estuary.

After the former colony of the BELGIAN CONGO was granted independence in 1960, a fragile coalition emerged from national elections that hoped to rule the country. In less than a week the new nation's stability was shattered as a mutiny by Congolese soldiers against Belgian officers spread and led to widespread attacks on Belgian nationals. The civil service disintegrated as its Belgian administration fled, and chaos reigned. In response to the widening turmoil, BELGIUM airlifted troops in to restore order. Taking advantage of the governmental breakdown, Moise Tshombe declared the mineral-rich Katanga, now SHABA, region an independent state.

The fledgling Congolese government appealed to the United Nations to resist Belgium's reoccupation, and an international peacekeeping force of Africans replaced the Belgian troops. Katanga, the key to the country's wealth, was ignored by the United Nations, and direct Belgian aid helped consolidate its secession. By 1961 three rival governments were fighting for control of the country: Col. Joseph Mobutu had seized power in LEOPOLDVILLE; Tshombe was in control of Katanga; and Patrice Lumumba's followers were centered in STANLEYVILLE. Lumumba was mysteriously killed while held prisoner in Katanga, and the resulting world outrage led to a strong U.N. stand against all foreign aid to the Katanga rebels. The secession was finally broken by U.N. forces in 1963, but rebellion and fighting continued to rock the countryside.

Stability was finally achieved in 1966 when Gen. Mobutu seized power and wiped out a greatly weakened rebel movement, while establishing a strong central control with himself as president. Mobutu's government retained Western ties while it nationalized the country's major economic resources. In 1971 the Congo was renamed Zaire, and Mobutu led a movement to replace European influence with native Zairean custom and usage wherever possible. Zaire opposed the successful Soviet-backed faction in the ANGOLA civil war of 1975/76, and in 1977 an invasion of former Katanga rebels was mounted from Angola. Mobutu defeated this attack with the help of 1,500 Moroccan troops flown in by France. In 1978 a second invasion was repulsed with the direct military assistance of France, Belgium, and the United States, which perceived a Soviet- and Cuban-sponsored threat. See also CABINDA.

ZAÏRE RIVER. See CONGO RIVER.

ZÁKINTHOS. See ZACYNTHUS.

ZAKOPANE (Poland) Resort city in the Tatra Mts, 52 mi S of Cracow. First settled in the 16th century it became part of Poland when purchased by the Polish patriot Wladyslaw Zamoyski from a Berlin businessman in 1889.

ZAKRO (Greece) Archaeological site, approx. 6 mi ESE of Iráklion on the E end of the island of CRETE. It was the site of a Minoan palace of the same period (c.1700–1450 BC) as the palace at KNOSSOS and others in Crete. All except Knossos were destroyed by invaders c.1450 BC.

ZAKYNTHOS. See ZACYNTHUS.

ZAKZAK. See ZARIA.

ZALACA. See ZALAKA.

ZALAKA [Salaca, Zalaca, Zallaka] [*Arabic:* Al-Zallāqah; *Spanish:* Sacralias] (Spain) Ancient town, N of Badajoz city, in Badajoz province, 52 mi SW of Cáceres, near the Portuguese border. It was the site of an important battle on Oct. 23, 1086 in which Yusuf ibn-Tashfin of the ALMORAVIDS defeated the Christian Alfonso VI of LEÓN and CASTILE.

ZALAMEA DE LA SERENA (Spain) Town, 40 mi E of Almendralejo. It has a splendid parochial church whose steeple is a relic of an arch built by Trajan; a Moorish castle; and the house supposedly lived in by the mayor of Zalamea, immortalized in Calderón's play.

ZALLAKA. See ZALAKA.

ZAMA (Tunisia) Ancient battle site, SE of El Kef, which is approx. 100 mi SW of Tunis. According to the Roman historian Nepos, the forces of ROME led by Scipio Africanus defeated those of CARTHAGE led by Hannibal here in 202 BC. This was the decisive battle of the Second Punic War.

ZAMBESI. See ZAMBEZI RIVER.

ZAMBEZE. See ZAMBEZI RIVER.

ZAMBEZI RIVER [Zambesi] *Portuguese:* Zambeze] (Africa) Rising in NW Zambia, it flows S across E Angola and W Zambia to the border of Botswana, forms the boundary between Zambia and Zimbabwe, crosses Mozambique and empties into the Mozambique Channel of the Indian Ocean. One of Africa's greatest rivers, its origin was unknown until the 19th century. The Arabs used it as a trading artery into Africa from the 10th century on. The Portuguese came on it in the 16th century, seeking to develop trade in ivory, gold, and slaves. The explorer David Livingstone (1813–73) made the first accurate charts of it in the 1850's. In 1959 the construction of the Kariba Dam made necessary the resettlement of 51,000 Tongan agriculturalists.

ZAMBIA Nation in S Africa, with Angola to the W, Zaire to the N, Tanzania, Malawi, and Mozambique to the E, and Zimbabwe to the S. Landlocked Zambia is the former British colony of NORTHERN RHODESIA. Independence was attained in 1964, and under the

Lusaka, modern capital of Zambia, a black African country ruled since 1964 by President Kenneth Kaunda. He is determined to free it from the economic dominance of its neighboring South Africa.

leadership of Kenneth Kaunda the country moved toward a socialized economy, attempting to bring the benefits of the nation's enormous foreign-held copper reserves to the subsistence farmers making up the great bulk of the population. In 1967 Zambia accepted a Chinese offer to build a rail line linking it with the Indian Ocean port of DAR ES SALAAM. In 1969 the copper mines were nationalized.

Zambia's relations with its southern neighbor, white-dominated RHODESIA, now ZIMBABWE, were stormy. In 1973 the border was closed, and Zambia became a safe haven and supplier for Zimbabwe guerrilla fighters. In 1976 the great Tanzan railway was opened, but it soon became a target for retaliatory strikes by Rhodesian military forces raiding guerrilla bases and was often cut. Kaunda moved to strengthen Zambia's military establishment, and the nation's economy was badly weakened. In 1979 the capital of LUSAKA hosted a meeting by British Commonwealth heads of state, which approved a plan for elections in Zimbabwe-Rhodesia leading to African majority rule.

Freed of the Rhodesian threat, Zambia in 1980 moved with eight other southern African nations to establish an economic alliance free of the dominance of SOUTH AFRICA. Zambia also spent more than $80 million buying Soviet weapons for its army.

ZAMBOANGA [City of Zamboanga] (Philippines) City in Zamboanga del Sur province, on the SW tip of MINDANAO Island, 600 mi S of Manila. Fort San Pedro, now a national monument, was founded here in 1635 by Christian settlers and was a center for expeditions against the Moros in the south under both Spanish and U.S. regimes. In World War II the city was a Japanese defense headquarters. It was taken by U.S. troops on March 10, 1945.

ZAMORA (Spain) Ancient city in Zamora province, in León, 129 mi NW of Madrid. Resisting Moorish attack in a famous siege in 939 AD, it was also strategically important in the early period of the *Reconquista*, the Christian reconquest of Spain. The city was besieged, without success, by Sancho II, son of Ferdinand I of CASTILE, in 1065, though the famous Cid Rodriguez Diaz de Vivar, El Cid, was among his warriors. A treaty negotiated here in 1143 secured the de jure independence of PORTUGAL and papal protection for the succession of its ruling dynasty.

ZAMOŚĆ [*Russian:* **Zamoste, Zamostye**] (Poland) Town, 48 mi SE of Lublin, on the Wieprz River. Jan Zamojski, a chancellor of Poland whose family influenced the nation's history and politics for 400 years, founded the town in 1579. His estate here lay on the trade route between the BLACK SEA and northern and western Europe. The college that he also founded here made Zamość a cultural and scientific center for hundreds of years.

The town's design was conceived and executed by Bernardo Morando of Padua in 1578 and is still a fine example of urban planning. Notable sites are the town hall of the early 17th century and Morando's collegiate church of St. Thomas, one of the finest Renaissance churches in Poland.

ZAMOSTE. See ZAMOŚĆ.

ZAMOSTYE. See ZAMOŚĆ.

ZAMUA (Iraq) Ancient kingdom in the ZAGROS Mts, 60 mi E of Kirkuk, near the Iranian border. It was conquered by the brilliant king Tiglath-Pileser II of ASSYRIA (ruled 745–727 BC) during his creation of the last Assyrian Empire. It was once a prosperous area, which had been conquered and reconquered several times during the ups and downs of the empire.

ZANCLE. See MESSINA.

ZANESVILLE (United States) Capital of Muskingum county, OHIO, on the Muskingum River, 50 mi E of Columbus. It was founded in 1797 by Ebenezer Zane, surveyor of Zane's Trace, the gateway to the NORTHWEST TERRITORY, on land awarded him by Congress for his clearing of the road west. It was the state capital from 1810 to 1812 and benefited from its location on the NATIONAL ROAD. The novelist Zane Grey, a descendant of Ebenezer Zane, was born here.

ZANTE. See ZACYNTHUS.

ZANZIBAR (Tanzania) Town and region consisting of the coral islands of Zanzibar and Tumbatu, in the Indian Ocean, off East Africa. The first traders—from Arabia, the Persian Gulf region of Iran, especially SHIRAZ, and from western INDIA—probably arrived as early as the first century AD, landing at a sheltered harbor, now the site of modern Zanzibar. From the 11th and 12th centuries, Persian Gulf traders settled and intermarried with the groups of original African peoples, from which two hereditary rulers of mixed descent eventually emerged.

The first European visitor was the Portuguese Vasco da Gama in 1499. By 1503 the Portuguese controlled Zanzibar and most of the East African coast. In 1698, however, they were ousted from the whole area by Arabs from OMAN. One of these, Sultan Sayyid Said (1804–56), recognizing the trade potential of East Africa, permanently moved his court to Zanzibar town in 1841, forcing the inhabitants to migrate east or work on the clove plantations. Zanzibar became the center of the ivory and slave trades, as Said also controlled much of the East African coast. Caravans to the interior were organized by Omanis, and trade was largely financed by Indian residents, often as agents for BOMBAY firms.

British influence began in 1841, with a representative advising the sultan, and increased until 1890, when Great Britain gained a protectorate over the region by a treaty with Germany, dividing large areas of Africa between the two nations. Under British rule the Arabs were favored above all other groups, and the sultanate, though largely nominal, was maintained.

Zanzibar became independent in 1963, and the head of state and prime minister were both Arabs. In 1964 the Arab government was overthrown by a leftist black African revolt, and a republic was declared. The sultan was exiled, the land nationalized, and the two mainly Arab parties banned. The Revolutionary Council and the black African Afro-Shirazi Party wielded sole power. Many Arabs and Indians subsequently left the country. Zanzibar and TANGANYIKA agreed to merge in 1964, and the resulting republic was named TANZANIA.

ZAPADNYY BUG. See BUG.

ZAPOROZHYE [*former:* **Aleksandrovsk**] (USSR) City and region on the left bank of the DNIEPER RIVER, 45 mi S of Dnepropetrovsk, opposite the island of Khortitsa. Headquarters of the Zaporozhye Cossacks, the first Ukrainian Cossacks, from the 16th to 18th centuries, it was the rallying point for the Ukrainians' struggle against oppression. When Poland could not defend the UKRAINE against Tatar raids in the late 16th century, the Ukrainian Cossacks arose as its defenders. In the 17th century they formed an independent state, in 1654 they were persuaded to transfer allegiance to RUSSIA but were troublesome to the Russians up to the 19th century. The Zaporozhye Cossack headquarters were destroyed by orders of Catherine II in 1775.

ZAPOTLÁN. See CIUDAD GUZMÁN.

ZAPOTLÁN EL GRANDE. See CIUDAD GUZMÁN.

ZARA. See ZADAR.

ZARAGOZA. See SARAGOSSA.

ZAREK. See BREMBERG.

ZAREPHATH [*modern:* **As-Sarafand, Sarafand**] (Lebanon) Town of ancient PHOENICIA, on the coast, approx. 33 mi S of Beirut, between Sidon and Tyre. It was formerly under the control of SIDON. The village of Sarafand lies on the site.

ZARIA [*former:* **Zakzak, Zazzau, Zegzeg, Zozo**] (Nigeria) Kingdom, emirate, and modern province with its capital city in Kaduna State, approx. 87 mi W of Kano. Founded *c.*1000 AD, it was one of the seven Hausa states. It captured slaves and was a trading center for salt from the Sahara. Islam was introduced *c.*1455. The kingdom was conquered by Mohammed Askia the Great *c.*1510, as recorded by Leo Africanus. In 1734 it became a tributary of the BORNU Kingdom, then became an emirate of the caliphate of the FULANI Moslems at SOKOTO in 1835. Zaria was conquered by the British in 1901. See also HAUSALAND.

ZARIASPA. See BACTRIA.

ZARQA [**Zerka**] (Jordan) River, approx. 100 mi long, rising in the hills W of Amman, flowing generally N then W to the JORDAN RIVER, approx. 25 mi N of the Dead Sea. Indentified with the biblical Jabbok, on whose south bank Jacob wrestled with the angel, it was in GILEAD in ancient PALESTINE and formed the northern boundary of the Amorites.

ŻARY. See SORAU.

ZASHCHITA. See UST-KAMENOGORSK.

ZÁTEC [*German:* **Saaz**] (Czechoslovakia) Town on the Ohře River, approx. 45 mi WNW of Prague. It was founded in the 11th century and was captured and burned by the Swedes in 1639, during the Thirty Years War.

ZAWI CHEMI-SHANIDAR (Iraq) Archaeological site on the Great Zab River, NW of Rawāndūz, in the ZAGROS Mts, 80 mi ENE of Mosul. The site typifies the first settlements on the borders of MESOPOTAMIA, dating from *c.*9000 BC. It shows the earliest evidence for the slow transition to sedentary life, agriculture, and the domestication of animals that was the Neolithic way of life. Evidence of domesticated sheep and mills for grinding either wild or cultivated grain have been found. Nearby is the SHANIDAR cave with similar evidences in the uppermost levels.

ZAZZAU. See ZARIA.

ZBARAZ. See ZBARAZH.

ZBARAZH [*Polish:* **Zbaraz**] (USSR) Town in the Ukraine, just NE of Ternopol, formerly in POLAND. It was central in the 17th century wars between Poland and RUSSIA for the possession of the UKRAINE.

ZBOROV. See ZBOROW.

ZBOROW [**Zborov**] (USSR) Battle site, on the Strypa River, 22 mi WNW of Ternopol. A battle fought here in 1649 was followed by a compromise pact that temporarily ended a rebellion of the ZAPOROZHYE Cossacks under Hetman Bogdan Chmielnicki against POLAND under King John II Casimir.

ZBRUCH RIVER [*Polish:* **Zbrucz**] (USSR) It rises N of Volochisk and flows 120 mi S to the Dniester River NW of Khotin. It formed the frontier between AUSTRIA-HUNGARY and RUSSIA prior to World War I and the border between POLAND and the USSR from 1921 to 1939.

ZBRUCZ. See ZBRUCH RIVER.

ZEA. See KEOS.

ZEBID. See ZABĪD.

ZEBRAK (Czechoslovakia) Village, 27 mi SW of Prague. It has a historical museum and, just NNW, remains of the 12th-century Zebrak Castle and the Tocnik Castle of the 14th century, both associated with Wenceslaus IV.

ZEEBRUGGE (Belgium) Port of the city of BRUGES. Developed *c.*1900 to replace the silted-in port of Bruges, to which it is connected by a six-mile canal, it was occupied by the Germans during World War I in 1914. On April 22/23, 1918 the British under Adm. Sir Roger J.B. Keyes carried out the daring Zeebrugge Raid, during which they partially blocked the harbor by destroying installations and sinking three ships. See also FLANDERS.

ZEELAND (Netherlands) Province consisting of a strip of the mainland between FLANDERS and the Western SCHELDE and six former islands. United with Holland by the time of its inheritance by the Counts of HAINAULT in 1299, it resisted the Spanish under Alva and Requesens from 1572 to 1576 during the Revolt of the Netherlands. It was united with the rest of the country during the reign of Stadholder William III (1672–1702). It is notable for the continuing struggle of its inhabitants against the sea. After the flood of 1953, in which more than 1,800 people were killed, the Dutch government created the Delta Plan to dam the sea channels.

ZEFAT. See SAFAD.

ŻEGÁN. See SAGAN.

ZEGZEG. See ZARIA.

ZEILA (Somalia) Town on the Gulf of Aden, approx. 20 mi S of Djibouti. The most important Arab settlement on the Somali coast from c.800 to 1900 AD, it was the center for trade between the Christian kingdom of ETHIOPIA and Muslim Arabia. It was coveted by European colonial powers in the 19th century, but was eclipsed by the railroad built from DJIBOUTI to ADDIS ABABA. See also ARABIAN PENINSULA.

ZEITZ (East Germany) City on the Weisse Elster River, 21 mi SSW of Leipzig. In 968 it became the seat of a bishopric that was in 1028 removed to NAUMBURG. It passed to SAXONY in 1564 and became the capital of the dukes of Saxe-Zeitz from 1563 to 1718. Notable buildings include a 13th-century castle-church incorporating 10th-century remains, a town hall built between 1502 and 1509, and a 17th-century castle with a chapel containing the tomb of the 16th-century scientist and humanist Georg Agricola.

ZELA [*Turkish:* **Zile**] (Turkey) Ancient city of Pontus in Tokat province, on a tributary of the Yesil Irmak River. In 67 BC Mithridates VI of PONTUS defeated Triarius of ROME here; in 47 BC Pharnaces, Mithridates's son, was defeated here by Julius Caesar, who then sent the famous dispatch, *Veni, vidi, vici* (I came, I saw, I conquered.)

ZELAZOWA WOLA [*Polish:* **Żelazowa Wola**] (Poland) Village 30 mi W of Warsaw. It was the birthplace in 1810 of Frédéric Chopin, the composer. There is a Chopin museum in the village.

ZELL (West Germany) Town on the MOSELLE RIVER, in the Hunsrück Hills, S of Koblenz. Chartered in 1222, it served as a residence of the electors of TRIER; their palace of 1542 is now a hotel. See also HOLY ROMAN EMPIRE.

ZELLE. See CELLE.

ŽEMAITIJA. See SAMOGITIA.

ZEMLYA FRANTSA IOSIFA. See FRANZ JOSEF LAND.

ZENSHU. See CHONJU.

ZENTSUJI (Japan) Town on NE SHIKOKU Island. It is well known for its large eighth-century Buddhist temple. Zentsuji was the birthplace of Kobo Daishi, founder of the Shingon sect of Buddhism. In World War II it housed a camp for U.S. prisoners of war.

ZERBST (East Germany) City, 11 mi NW of Dessau. Empress Catherine II of Russia spent her youth here. It was the capital of the duchy of Anhalt-Zerbst from 1603 to 1793. The Old City was destroyed by heavy bombings in World War II. See also ANHALT.

ZERKA. See ZARQA.

ZERTA. See SENTA.

ZETLAND. See SHETLANDS.

ZEUGMA [*modern:* **Bâlkîs**] (Turkey) Ancient town in present Turkey, approx. 45 mi WSW of Urfa. Two settlements were established here by Seleucus I, king of SYRIA, who died in 280 BC. The one on the right bank of the EUPHRATES RIVER was called Seleuceia, while the one on the left, Apamea, was on the site of the Til-Barsib mentioned in old Assyrian inscriptions.

The towns were connected by a bridge of boats and came to be known together as *Zeugma*, the Greek word for junction. The town became an important military post. Under PARTHIA, which overthrew the SELEUCID EMPIRE c 250 BC, it prospered by its location on a main east-west trade route. Later Zeugma was in the ROMAN EMPIRE, and legions were permanently stationed in the region by Vespasian, emperor from 69 to 79 AD. Justinian I, ruler of the BYZANTINE EMPIRE from 527 to 565, fortified the town against the Sassanid dynasty of PERSIA, but in 639 Zeugma was captured by the Muslim Arabs.

ZEVEN (West Germany) Town, 24 mi NE of Bremen. In 1757, during the Seven Years War, the English duke of Cumberland here concluded the Convention of Kloster-Zeven (Closter-Seven), abandoning HANOVER to the French. It has the Romanesque church of a former Benedictine monastery, founded in 1141.

ZHANG-JIA-KOU. See KALGAN.

ZHDANOV. See MARIUPOL.

ZHICHA. See ZIÇA.

ZHIGATSE. See JIH-K'A-TSE.

ZHIKATSE. See JIH-K'A-TSE.

ZHITOMIR (USSR) City on the Teterev River, 85 mi W of Kiev. Believed to date from the ninth century AD, it was located on the trade route from SCANDINAVIA to CONSTANTINOPLE and was an important trading center up to the time of the Russian October Revolution in 1917. Destroyed by the Tatars in 1240, it passed from KIEV to LITHUANIA in 1320 and to POLAND in 1569. Sacked by the Cossacks in 1648, it was returned to RUSSIA with the Second Partition of Poland in 1793. Occupied by Axis forces in 1941, it was retaken by the Soviets in 1943, during World War II.

ZHLOBIN (USSR) Town, on the right bank of the DNIEPER RIVER, approx. 75 mi S of Mogilev. In World War II, during the Soviet counterattack against the German invasion, the town was bitterly fought over and was finally retaken by the Soviets in June 1944.

ZHMERINKA (USSR) Town, 20 mi S of Vinnitsa, in the UKRAINE. As a railroad junction and communications center, it was fought over by both Germans and Soviets in the Soviet counterattacks of 1944 against the German invasion. The Soviets finally captured it on March 30, 1944.

ZHOB (Pakistan) River, the direct route between the NORTH-WEST FRONTIER and Quetta. Less than 100 miles N of QUETTA are a number of sites in the river valley that have yielded evidence of very early settlement on the frontier of south Asia, where the Neolithic Revolution is dated to after 4000 BC.

ZIA. See KEOS.

ZIBIA. See ZIWIYE.

ZIÇA [**Zhicha**] (Yugoslavia) Monastery, 3 mi SW of Rankovicevo. Founded around c.1205, it was the coronation church of the medieval kings of SERBIA and the first seat of its archbishops.

ZICHRON YA'AKOV. See NETANYA, Israel.

ZIDON. See SIDON.

ZIDZHA. See DZHIDA.

ZIELONA GÓRA [*German:* **Grünberg, Grünberg in Schlesien**] (Poland) City, 50 mi SE of Frankfurt-an-der-Oder. It prospered as a textile center after Flemish weavers settled here in the 13th century, and it became prominent on the trade route from BERLIN to Upper SILESIA, reaching its height of prosperity in the 15th century. Birthplace of the painter Tadeusz Konicz in 1733, its notable buildings include a 13th-century church and a 14th-century town hall with a 15th-century tower.

ZILE. See ZELA.

ZIMBABWE [*former:* **Rhodesia, Southern Rhodesia**] Nation of S Africa, formerly the British colony of Rhodesia. It is bordered on the N by Zambia, on the E by Mozambique, on the S by South Africa, and on the W by Botswana. Its capital is HARARE. White minority-dominated RHODESIA reluctantly permitted black participation in national elections for the first time in 1979, hoping to end 15 years of guerrilla conflict and international condemnation and isolation. Bishop Abel Muzorewa, a moderate black leader, became the first prime minister of the newly independent nation of Zimbabwe-Rhodesia. Warfare continued, however, carried on by radical guerrilla leaders who felt they had been denied representation in the electoral process.

Fighting ceased when Muzorewa consented to turn over rule to Great Britain pending the results of an open, British-supervised, national election in 1980. The Zimbabwe African National Unity Party of Robert Mugabe was voted in, and on April 18, 1980 the Republic of Zimbabwe was born, named for GREAT ZIMBABWE. Both Great Britain and the United States immediately offered aid to the new nation. While thousands of the white minority settlers left, relocating largely in SOUTH AFRICA, many remained in the newly-integrated nation. Zimbabwe is trying to reestablish a strong economy while reconciling its remaining white inhabitants with its blacks, after long years of bitter and bloody conflict.

Since independence political rivalry between former independence movements have reemerged. In January 1982 Prime Minister Robert Mugabe removed his former ally Joshua Nkomo from the government on the discovery of arms caches on Nkomo's Patriot Front properties. Since then Mugabe's government has moved against both Nkomo's supporters and those of former Rhodesian prime minister Ian Smith. In early 1983 the government began a massive crackdown on dissidents, the political opposition, and bases of possible armed rebellions.

ZIMBABWE-RHODESIA. See RHODESIA.

ZIMBIR. See SIPPAR.

ZINDER [**Sinder**] (Niger) Town, approx. 65 mi N of the Nigerian border and 620 mi NE of Lagos. It was originally on an old trans-Saharan caravan route that connected northern NIGERIA with the African coast as early as the 11th century AD. A walled town, it was the capital of the Muslim state controlled by BORNU from the 16th to the mid-19th century. It was then occupied by the French in 1899, and was capital of FRENCH WEST AFRICA until 1926.

ZINNIK. See SOIGNIES.

ZINOVIEVSK. See KIROVOGRAD.

ZION [**Sion**] (Israel) Hill in the city of JERUSALEM. It was defined in the Bible as the City of David. The name originally referred to the Jebusite fortress conquered by David on the southeastern hill of Jerusalem and now being excavated, but has become symbolic of Jerusalem itself, the Promised Land, of Israel's hope of returning to PALESTINE, and hence, of Zionism. Among Christians it has long been a symbol of the Heavenly Jerusalem, of heaven.

ZION (United States) City in ILLINOIS, on LAKE MICHIGAN, 5 mi N of Waukegan. Founded in 1901 by John Alexander Dowie of the Christian Catholic Church, it was a communal society with a theocratic government that lasted until 1935. Notable buildings include the Zion Hotel of 1902, one of the nation's largest all-frame buildings with a 367-foot frontage.

ZION CANYON (United States) Archaeological site, in Zion National Park, in SW UTAH. It was first named by Mormon settlers who discovered it in the 1850's. Its walls contain numerous fossils and evidence of prehistoric cave dwellers.

ZIPPORI [**Tsipori**] [*ancient:* **Sepphoris**] (Israel) Village in N Israel, approx. 3 mi NNW of Nazareth. An important town in antiquity when it was in a Roman province, it was later, after the fall of JERUSALEM in 70 AD, the seat of the Sanhedrin, the Jewish religious and legal court. In the first century AD Zippori was the chief city of GALILEE and a rival of TIBERIAS. During the Crusades it was held for a time in the 12th century by the Knights Templar.

ZITÁCUARO [**Heroica Zitácuaro**] (Mexico) City, 60 mi SE of Morelia. It was one of the earliest centers of the Mexican War of Independence from 1810 on. The Junta of Zitácuaro was the independence movement's first governing organ. Zitácuaro saw fighting between French and Mexicans in 1864 and was burned in 1865.

ZITTAU [*Old Slavic:* **Sitowir**] (East Germany) City on the left bank of the Neisse River, 45 mi ESE of Dresden. Originating as a Slavic settlement, it was chartered in 1255 and joined the Lusatian League in 1346. It fell to SAXONY in 1635. It was an important medieval textile center. See also LUSATIA.

ZITUNI. See LAMIA.

ZIWIYE [*ancient:* **Zibia**] (Iran) Archaeological site in Azerbāijān province, near Saqqez. A collection of gold, silver, and ivory objects found here in 1946, supposedly by a shepherd boy, is important for the study of early Median art. Dating to the late eighth and the seventh century BC, it is believed by some scholars to be part of the dowry of Assyrian King Esarhaddon's daughter on her marriage to the Scythian King Parpatua. Various West Asiatic influences are apparent: Assyrian, Urartian, Scythian, Mannaean, and even Syrian. See also ASSYRIA, MEDIA, SCYTHIA.

ZNAIM. See ZNOJMO.

ZNAMENSK. See WEHLAU.

ZNOJMO [*German:* **Znaim**] (Czechoslovakia) City on the Dyje River, 35 mi SW of Brno. Founded in the 11th century, it was a stronghold of the Přemyslide princes until the 13th century, and was chartered in 1226. Designated an historic monument, it has a 13th-century Romanesque castle chapel with fine frescoes, a 14th-century Gothic church, and a 15th-century town hall with a tower. It was the site of an armistice signed after Napoleon's victory at WAGRAM over AUSTRIAN forces under Archduke Charles in 1809.

ZOAN. See TANIS.

ZOAR [**Bela**] (Israel) Biblical town probably now submerged in the S end of the DEAD SEA. According to the Bible, it was the only one of the Cities of the Plain to escape destruction. Here Lot and his daughters took refuge. See also GOMMORAH, SODOM.

ZOAR (United States) Village in OHIO, on the Tuscarawas River, N of Dover. It was founded in 1817 by Protestant Separatists from southern Germany on land obtained with assistance from the PHILADELPHIA Quakers. A communistic economic system and a strict moral and religious life was established. The society declined after 1853 when its founder, Joseph Michael Bimeler, died. It was closed down in 1898.

ZOMBA (Malawi) Town in the Shire Highlands, approx. 70 mi S of Lake Nyasa. It was the capital of Malawi until 1966, when it was replaced by Lilongwe on Malawi's becoming a republic. It was founded by European planters *c.*1880.

ZOPPOT. See SOPOT.

ZOR. See TYRE.

ZORNDORF [*modern:* **Sarbinowo**] (Poland) Village in Zielona Góra province, formerly in Prussia. It was the site of a battle on Aug. 25, 1758, during the Seven Years' War when the Prussians under Frederick the Great defeated the Russians under Count William of Fermor. See also PRUSSIA, RUSSIA.

ZOUG. See ZUG.

ZOZO. See ZARIA.

ZUARA. See ZUWARĀH.

ZUG [*French:* **Zoug**] (Switzerland) City on the Lake of Zug, 15 mi S of Zurich. First mentioned in 1242 as a possession of the counts of Kyburg and purchased by the Hapsburg family in 1273, the city still retains a strong medieval flavor. Zug first joined the Swiss Confederation in 1353 and again in 1364, reverting to Hapsburg control in between. It finally threw off Hapsburg domination in 1386 after joining the League of Swabian cities. During the Reformation Zug remained Catholic and joined the Golden, or Boromean, League in 1586. Notable buildings here include the late Gothic church of St. Oswald built between 1478 and 1545, the clock tower of 1480, and the town hall of 1505. See also SEMPACH.

ZUID AFRIKAANSCHE REPUBLIEK. See SOUTH AFRICAN REPUBLIC.

ZUIDER ZEE [**Zuyder Zee**] [*ancient:* **Flevo Lacus**] (Netherlands) A former large, landlocked inlet off the NORTH SEA, on the N coast of the Netherlands. The Sea washed into it only during floods. Once again it is landlocked by a dike, partly drained, and is divided into the IJsselmeer and the Waddenzee. As early as the 16th century plans were made to enclose the southern part of the sea. After the last break in 1916, a vast drainage project was begun, and a dam was completed in 1932, making the Dutch coastline shorter and easier to protect and providing for an increasing number of polders, or areas of drained land.

ZUIDHOLLAND. See SOUTH HOLLAND.

ZUIDVEEN. See ZUTPHEN.

ZULA (Ethiopia) Port town, on the Gulf of Zula. The ruins of ancient ADULIS, a major Axumite port, are nearby. Zula became an Italian protectorate in 1888 and part of ERITREA in 1890. See also AXUM, ITALY.

ZULIA (Venezuela) State in NW Venezuela, and one of the richest oil-producing regions in the world, between the Sierra de Perija of the Andes Mts to the W, the Gulf of Venezuela on the N, and Lake Maracaibo to the E. The entire economy of Venezuela was changed with the development of the oil wells after World War II. MARACAIBO is its major city.

ZÜLPICH. See TOLBIACUM.

ZULULAND (South Africa) Region bounded by the Indian Ocean on the E, Mozambique on the N, and Swaziland on the W. It has been the home of the Zulus since the 17th century, who in the early 19th century subjugated all the tribes in what is now NATAL with an army of 40,000 under their chief, Chaka. After his successor, Dingaan, ambushed and killed approximately 500 Boer settlers in 1838, the Boer forces of Andries Pretorius killed almost 3,000 Zulus in revenge at the Battle of BLOOD RIVER. When the British took over Natal in 1843, the Zulu chief Cetewayo ignored a British ultimatum, and the result was war in 1878, which the British finally won in July 1879. Zulu rebellions continued, but the British annexed Zululand to Natal in 1897.

ZUNGARIA. See DZUNGARIA.

ZUN-I, China. See TSUN-I.

ZUÑI (United States) Pueblo in NW NEW MEXICO, on the Zuñi Indian Reservation, approx. 32 mi S of Gallup. Home of Pueblo Indians of the Zuñi linguistic family, it is one of seven villages, the seven cities of CIBOLA, that were attacked in 1540 by Francisco Vásquez de Coronado, who believed them to contain vast stores of gold. The Pueblo Indians abandoned the villages during their unsuccessful Pueblo Revolt against the Spanish in 1680, after which all the Zuñi were crammed into just one pueblo. They retain a strong commitment to their ancient customs and religion.

ZURICH [*German:* **Zürich**] (Switzerland) Famous city on the lake of Zurich, 60 mi NE of Bern. Occupied in the Neolithic period by lake dwellers, it was later settled by the Gallic Helvetii. After the fifth century AD it passed successively to the Alemanni, the Franks, and to the German Stem duchy of SWABIA. A free imperial city after 1218, it joined the Swiss Confederation in 1351. When it claimed the TOGGENBURG, a region in the Thur valley, a ruinous war with the rest of the Swiss Confederation resulted between 1436 and 1450. In the 16th century, under the influence of Ulrich Zwingli, Zurich became a leading power of the Swiss Reformation, provoking civil war, which was ended by the Roman Catholic victory at KAPPEL in 1531. Scene of two battles of the French Revolutionary Wars in 1799, it became a cultural and artistic center in the 18th and 19th centuries. A treaty ending the Franco-Italian War was concluded here in 1859, and a convention here in 1959 laid down the provisions for an independent CYPRUS. James Joyce is buried here. Notable buildings include the Romanesque Grossmünster of the 11th to 13th centuries, where Zwingli preached, and the Fraumünster of the 12th and 15th centuries.

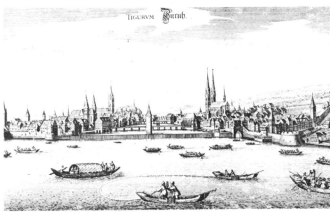

Zurich in the 16th century when, with Geneva, it was a leader in the Swiss Reformation. Zurich was often embroiled in the past with its neighbors in religious and territorial wars.

ZUTFEN. See ZUTPHEN.

ZUTPHEN [Zutfen] [*former:* **Zuidveen**] (Netherlands) City in E Netherlands, on the IJssel River. Chartered in 1191, it was an important stronghold of the Spanish during the 16th-century Dutch struggle for independence. Sir Philip Sidney was wounded and died here in 1586 while serving with his uncle, the earl of Leicester, during the campaign to take the town from SPAIN. The Dutch captured it in 1591 under Maurice of Nassau. FRANCE held it in 1672/73 and again from 1795 to 1813. It was occupied by GERMANY during World War II. Noteworthy buildings include a 12th-century Gothic church, 14th- and 15th-century fortifications, and the Grote Kerk of the 13th to 15th centuries. Gerard of Zutphen, a leader of the Devotio Moderna reform movement and the Brethren of the Common Life, was born here.

ZUWARAH [Zuara] [*Portuguese:* **Punta dar Zoyara**] (Libya) Port, 65 mi W of Tripoli. It was first mentioned in a Portuguese sailing manual of 1375. As the terminus of the now-defunct railway from TRIPOLI, it was the western outpost of Italian control of Libya from 1912 to 1943.

ZUYDER ZEE. See ZUIDER ZEE.

ZVENIGOROD (USSR) City, 30 mi W of Moscow. Chartered in 1328, it has the remains of an 11th- to 14th-century fortress and Uspenski Cathedral of 1393, with its frescoes. Advanced German units reached it in 1941 in their MOSCOW campaign during World War II.

ZVORNIK [Turkish: Izvornik] (Yugoslavia) Town on the Drina River, 23 mi ESE of Tuzla. It was the seat of the Greek Orthodox metropolitan under Turkish rule. The town has an 11-span stone bridge of the 16th century and the ruins of a medieval fortress.

ZWEIBRÜCKEN [French: Deuxponts; medieval: Bipontium] (West Germany) City and duchy, 5 mi WSW of Mannheim. Chartered in 1352, it passed to the Bavarian house of Wittelsbach in 1385 and became capital of the independent duchy of Pfalz-Zweibrücken in 1410. Its early editions of Greek and Roman classics are well known to scholars. It became part of BAVARIA when the elector and first king of Bavaria united all the Wittelsbach holdings. FRANCE controlled it from 1797 to 1814/15. Notable buildings include a Gothic church of 1493 and a castle of 1720 to 1725. See also RHINELAND PALATINATE.

ZWELLENDAM. See SWELLENDAM.

ZWICKAU (East Germany) City, on the Mulde River, 42 mi S of Leipzig. Slavic in origin, it was first mentioned in 1118 as a trading center and was chartered in 1212. It developed into a free imperial city in the 12th century until it passed to the margraves of MEISSEN in 1323. It became the center of the Anabaptist movement of Thomas Münzer between 1520 and 1523. It was often plundered during the Thirty Years War of 1618 to 1648. The composer Robert Schumann was born here in 1810; a Schumann museum was opened in 1956.

ZWOLLE (Netherlands) Town and capital of Overijssel province, 18 mi N of Deventer. Chartered in 1230, as a member of the HANSEATIC LEAGUE it was a strategic stronghold until its ramparts were destroyed in 1674 during the Dutch wars. Notable buildings include two churches and the town hall, all 15th century. It was a center of the Devotio Moderna reform movement of the Brethren of the Common Life. In nearby Agnietenberg is the 14th-century monastery where Thomas à Kempis, author of the *Imitation of Christ*, lived from 1407 to 1471.

CREDITS

The author wishes to thank these publishers and individuals for permission to reprint the following photographs:

Ajanta, India   The Illustrated London News Library.

Avar, Yugoslavia   *Jugoslawien*, Otto Siegner. Copyright © 1968 by Verlag Ludwig Simon.

Brazil
Manaus
Salvador   *Brazil*, Fulvio Roiter. Copyright © 1969 by Atlantis Verlag. English language translation Copyright © 1971 by Thames and Hudson. Reprinted by permission of Viking Penguin, Inc.

Belfast, Ireland   *Patriot Graves: Resistance in Ireland*, Michael O'Sullivan. Follett Publishing Company.

Brooklyn Bridge, New York   The Metropolitan Museum of Art. The Edward W.C. Arnold Collection of New York Prints, Maps and Pictures. Bequest of E.W.C. Arnold. 1954.

Caernarvon, Wales   Jarrold Colour Publications, Norwich.

Caithness, Scotland   *Land of the Scots*, Nigel Godwin Tranter. Photograph by L.S. Paterson. Hodder & Stoughton.

Ctesiphon, Iraq   The Illustrated London News Picture Library.

Dead Sea, Israel   *Jesus Lived Here*, Bruin and Giegel. Harrap Limited, London.

Faiyûm, Egypt   "Ibshawai, Faiyum, Egypt 1959." Copyright © 1969. The Paul Strand Foundation, as published in *Living Egypt* by Paul Strand, Aperture, 1969.

France
Aigues-Mortes
Albi
Lyons
Mont-St.-Michel   *France*, Martin Hurlimann. Copyright © 1951, 1957 by Atlantis Verlag. Copyright © 1968 by Thames and Hudson. Reprinted by permission of Viking Penguin, Inc.

Frankfurt, Germany   *Germany*, Martin Hurlimann. Copyright © 1961 by Thames and Hudson. Reprinted by permission of Viking Penguin, Inc.

French Guiana   The Illustrated London News Picture Library.

Gaspé, Canada   Notman Photographic Archives.

Ghana   Werner Forman Archive.

Hazor, Israel   © Prof. Yigael Yadin. The Rothschild Expedition at Hazor.

London Bridge, England   Engraving by Nicholas Visscher, 1616.

Mecca, Saudi Arabia   Aramco.

Mesa Verde, Colorado   National Park Service.

Montenegro, Yugoslavia   *Jugoslawien*, Otto Siegner. Copyright © 1968 by Verlag Ludwig Simon.

Montreal, Quebec   Notman Photographic Archives.

New Zealand   K. and J. Bigwood, Photographers.

Orkney Islands, Scotland   Photograph by Edwin Smith.

Passau, Germany   *The Federal Republic of Germany*. Copyright © 1970 by Verlag Ludwig Simon. Reproduced with the permission of Charles Scribner's Sons.

Peshawar, Pakistan   The Illustrated London News Picture Library.

Ronda, Spain   Photograph by Arrielli.

Rostov-Veliky, Russia   Dieter Blum.

Saumur, France   Paul Almasy, Photojournaliste.

Trieste, Italy   Jos. Jeiter. *Italy*, Otto Siegner, ed., with the permission of Charles Scribner's Sons. Copyright © 1970, Verlag Ludwig Simon.

Urbino, Italy   Jos. Jeiter. *Italy*, Otto Siegner, ed., with the permission of Charles Scribner's Sons. Copyright © 1970, Verlag Ludwig Simon.

Utah   Collection of Rell G. Francis. Copyright © 1979 by the University of Nebraska Press.

Victoria, British Columbia   Notman Photographic Archives/McCord Museum.

Weisbaden, Germany   "The Pumphouse, Wiesbaden," *The Federal Republic of Germany*, Otto Siegner. Copyright © 1970 by Verlag Ludwig Simon. Reproduced with the permission of Charles Scribner's Sons.

Yugoslavia
Bosnia
Pula
Sarajevo
Serbia
Zagreb   *Yugoslavia*, Sir Fitzroy Maclean. Copyright © 1969 by Thames and Hudson. Reprinted by permission of Viking Penguin, Inc.